Third Edition

FINANCIAL ACCOUNTING

The Impact on Decision Makers

Two Industry Leaders. One Superior Teaching Tool.
Infinite Learning Possibilities.

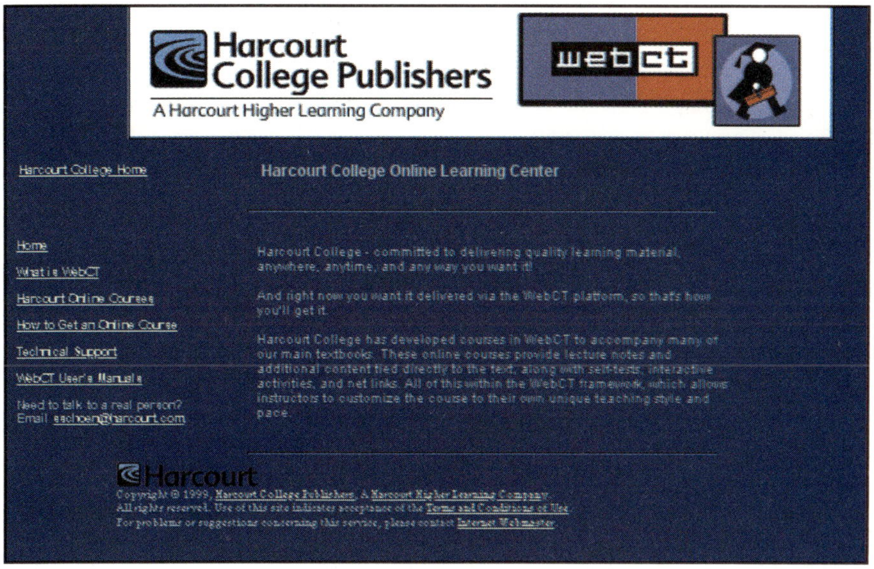

Whether you want to supplement your classroom with customizable online content or deliver your class totally at a distance, Harcourt accommodates all your distance learning needs. Harcourt, a leader in providing lifelong learning solutions, in partnership with WebCT, a leading platform in electronic learning, brings you and your students the industry's most robust online courses.

WebCT facilitates the creation of sophisticated Web-based educational environments. It provides a set of course design tools to help you manage course content, a set of communication tools to facilitate online classroom collaboration, and a set of administrative tools for tracking and managing your students' progress.

Via the WebCT platform, Harcourt offers the following program choices:

1. **WebCT Testing Service.** If testing is all you want, we will upload the computerized test bank into a course with no publisher content. If you like, we will even host it for you on our server.
2. **Free access to a blank WebCT template.** With a qualified adoption, Harcourt will host a course (without any Harcourt content) for you to input your original materials and use in your classroom.
3. **Customized course creation.** Harcourt will create an online course from your original content, your school's content, Harcourt's content, or any combination of these. Contact your local Harcourt representative for more details.

Harcourt WebCT Manuals
If you adopt a Harcourt Online Course, your students will receive Harcourt's Guide to the World Wide Web and WebCT packaged with the textbook.

(ISBN 0-03-045503-0)

To view a demo of any of our online courses, go to **webct.harcourtcollege.com.**

Third Edition

FINANCIAL ACCOUNTING

The Impact on Decision Makers

GARY A. PORTER
The University of Montana

CURTIS L. NORTON
Northern Illinois University

Harcourt College Publishers

Fort Worth Philadelphia San Diego New York Orlando Austin
San Antonio Toronto Montreal London Sydney Tokyo

Publisher Mike Roche
Acquisitions Editor Bill Schoof
Market Strategist Charles Watson
Developmental Editor Craig Avery
Project Editor Jim Patterson
Art Director April Eubanks
Production Manager Lois West

Cover Design: Bill Brammer

ISBN: 0-03-033696-1
Library of Congress Catalog Card Number: 00-100122

Address for Domestic Orders
Harcourt, Inc., 6277 Sea Harbor Drive, Orlando, FL 32887-6777
800-782-4479

Address for International Orders
International Customer Service
Harcourt, Inc., 6277 Sea Harbor Drive, Orlando, FL 32887-6777
407-345-3800
(fax) 407-345-4060
(e-mail) hbintl@harcourt.com

Address for Editorial Correspondence
Harcourt College Publishers, 301 Commerce Street, Suite 3700, Fort Worth, TX 76102

Web Site Address
http://www.harcourtcollege.com

Printed in the United States of America

0 1 2 3 4 5 6 7 8 9 048 9 8 7 6 5 4 3 2

Harcourt College Publishers

To those who really "count":
Melissa
Kathy, Amy, Andrew

The Harcourt Series in Accounting

PRINCIPLES OF ACCOUNTING
INTEGRATED FINANCIAL/MANAGERIAL
Cunningham, Nikolai, and Bazley
ACCOUNTING: Information for Business Decisions

TECHNOLOGY COMPONENTS
Guided Exploration, LLC
Interactive Decision Cases for Financial Accounting

Bell, Kirby, and Gantt
Guide to Understanding and Using Annual Reports
Second Edition

Davis
OMAR (Online Multimedia Accounting Review): The Accounting Cycle

COMMUNICATION
McKay and Rosa
The Accountant's Guide to Professional Communication: Writing and Speaking the Language of Business

FINANCIAL
Hanson and Hamre
Financial Accounting
Eighth Edition

Porter and Norton
Financial Accounting: The Impact on Decision Makers
Third Edition

Porter and Norton
Financial Accounting: The Impact on Decision Makers
Alternate Second Edition

Stickney and Weil
Financial Accounting: An Introduction to Concepts, Methods, and Uses
Ninth Edition

Knechel
The Monopoly Game Practice Set

MANAGERIAL
Jackson and Sawyers
Managerial Accounting: A Focus on Decision Making

Maher, Stickney, and Weil
Managerial Accounting: An Introduction to Concepts, Methods, and Uses
Seventh Edition

INTERMEDIATE
Williams, Stanga, and Holder
Intermediate Accounting
Fifth Edition
1998 Update

ADVANCED
Pahler and Mori
Advanced Accounting: Concepts and Practice
Seventh Edition

FINANCIAL STATEMENT ANALYSIS
Stickney and Brown
Financial Reporting and Statement Analysis: A Strategic Perspective
Fourth Edition

AUDITING
Guy, Alderman, and Winters
Auditing
Fifth Edition

Rittenberg and Schwieger
Auditing: Concepts for a Changing Environment
Third Edition

THEORY
Bloom and Elgers
Foundations of Accounting Theory and Policy: A Reader

Bloom and Elgers
Issues in Accounting Policy: A Reader

GOVERNMENTAL AND NOT-FOR-PROFIT
Douglas
Governmental and Nonprofit Accounting: Theory and Practice
Second Edition

REFERENCE
Bailey
Miller GAAS Guide
College Edition

Williams
Miller GAAP Guide
College Edition

Students: Turn Directly to Page xxiii to Learn How to Get the Most From This Book

To the Instructor

Welcome to the Third Edition!

Every instructor we've ever met would prefer something tangible in hand to read and examine when considering a new approach for students or when comparing current teaching material. That's the purpose of this Preface to the Third Edition: to share our vision of the financial accounting course—which has been refined in our successful earlier editions—in a way that embodies the best combination of innovations in this new edition, as honestly and effectively as we can.

Just as accounting education has changed, and continues to change for most of us as instructors, students are also changing in how they learn. With the Third Edition, once again we hold true to our original vision of teaching financial accounting for both users and preparers of financial information—but with a revision focused on greater accessibility by the variety of students we teach.

Because there *are* so many new features and ideas embodied in the Third Edition—and because of our intensified commitment to students and their learning needs—we have organized this introductory material a little differently, as you'll soon see. By directing students to their own introduction, we believe they can get started in the course just that much more efficiently. Naturally you'll want to turn to the Student section on page xxiii when you've finished exploring here.

A Balanced Approach to a Financial Statement User Orientation

When we developed our book in its first two editions, we found that most instructors wanted the best of both worlds: the streamlined topics and the special focus and features for teaching the use of financial accounting information to make decisions, as well as rock-solid coverage and materials for teaching the language and preparation of financial statements from transactions. By striking the right balance with the best combination of topical coverage and pedagogical features for both these valid approaches, we created the most successful new vehicle for teaching financial accounting in twenty years.

As the basis for that success, we created a book and package that was flexible enough so that instructors who wanted elements of both user and preparer approaches could combine topics and features to match their individual vision of the course. Our success has been a byproduct of that commitment to all instructors who teach using elements of both the user and the preparer approach.

"The improvements made to this text are very good."
Sheila Ammons,
Austin Community College

Even More Flexibility in the Third Edition

For the Third Edition, we've increased our *flexibility* in the book and the support materials, as you'll soon see:

- This edition contains *financial information* of public companies that is organized and highlighted to focus efficiently on both what is important about those companies and what is vital for beginning students. At the same time, we continue to include important *procedural material* needed by accounting majors. Similarly, the support materials make access to online financial information easier for study and analysis, while we also introduce a new, highly interactive online minicourse in the accounting cycle to supplement the text's coverage.

- For the first two editions, we shrink-wrapped the full annual report of Ben & Jerry's Homemade, Inc. with every copy of our text. We quickly became known as "the Ben & Jerry's book" for our inclusion of its annual report. This approach had several advantages: It was fun for students, but more importantly it included all the features to which we believed they should be exposed. Instructors and students alike responded favorably to Ben & Jerry's. Indeed, a single annual report has served until now, when instructors have told us they want to further expand their students' awareness of actual annual reports.
- So for the Third Edition we offer Ben & Jerry's Homemade, Inc., and Gateway, Inc., along with supporting features within each chapter. *The complete 1998 annual reports for both these companies are reprinted in the entirety at the back of the book.* We chose to add Gateway because it is a high-technology company that students can identify with and has financial statements that can be read and understood by beginning accounting students.

Many instructors ask for the latest financial information as a means to keeping students as current as possible and to keep motivation high throughout the course. To meet this need, we will provide updates of the book's features that refer to Ben & Jerry's and Gateway, along with access to the latest-year annual reports, online through our WebCT course. (This WebCT course is available to adopters for use with this book.) Further, adopters will benefit from regular updates via our Web site's Resources page, where news, features, and links to late-breaking information about these two key companies will be found.

With these two guiding elements—a flexible balance and a new annual report update program—we've added a new emphasis on evolving student needs that, we believe, will keep the Third Edition of *Financial Accounting: The Impact on Decision Makers* on target with the needs of your students in their first accounting course.

NEW "GETTING STARTED" MODULE: A ROAD MAP FOR STUDENTS

"['Getting Started'] presents a good framework for introducing financial accounting."
Gail Cook, University of Wisconsin, Parkside

Students and instructors alike have said that getting started in financial accounting can be difficult. So for the Third Edition we've made the start of the course a priority. One key to getting started is our "To the Student" introduction, starting on page xxiii. Another key is the module that opens the book before Chapter 1.

For the Third Edition, we provide you and your students with a road map to the financial accounting course in the form of an introductory module, **"Getting Started in Business."** It is designed to help students orient themselves to the business world—from how two partners started a business, to the importance of decision-making, to the forms businesses take and the activities of a business entity.

"These topics are important and may get ignored if [they were part of] . . . Chapter 1. This is a good way to start the first class. If students have not yet bought the text, this material can still be discussed."
Sheila Ammons, Austin Community College

A major focus of this revision is making the book even more student-friendly—and getting students off on the right foot in the course is the most friendly thing we can do for them. After checking out "To the Student," and "Getting Started in Business," students are better prepared to focus on the core introductory topics which we've streamlined in Chapters 1 and 2.

ORGANIZATION, PEDAGOGY, AND PACKAGE DESIGNED FOR *ENHANCED LEARNING*

For the Third Edition, we remain committed to four principles that have been instrumental to the success of the first two editions:

- An emphasis on *pedagogy and student appeal that accommodates most learning styles.*
- A focus on *financial statements.*
- A focus on *actual public companies.*
- A *decision-making* emphasis.

Students learn and understand in a variety of ways, so we have provided a variety of features, including a number of **NEW** features, to help them along the way. The first of these student-oriented features is our book's revised organization and topical changes, which are designed to improve students' ability to focus on what's important.

Organization and Topical Changes to *Enhance Learning*

First, combined with "Getting Started," for the Third Edition Chapters 1 and 2 provide a true "first gear" for the course.

Chapter 1, "Accounting as a Form of Communication," has been revised and streamlined to <u>highlight the key introductory issues</u>:

"This is a good way to start the process of learning accounting."
Sheila Ammons,
Austin Community College

- We moved the first section on the startup of Ben & Jerry's to the "Getting Started in Business" module.
- To start students off right, we reflect the purchase of Ben & Jerry's by Unilever in the chapter-opening vignette and in the Internet research case.
- We provide a **NEW** Exhibit 1-1 on typical questions of users of financial information.
- We revised the text's introduction of the balance sheet to better focus on the relationship of the balance sheet to the accounting equation.
- We annotate and highlight the balance sheet of Ben & Jerry's to focus on this accounting equation relationship.
- We include a **NEW** Exhibit 1-3 on the accounting equation and the balance sheet.
- We add **NEW** brief examples of typical balance sheet items.
- We annotate the income statement to provide students with simple summaries of the two line items introduced in Chapter 1—sales and cost of sales.
- We removed the statement of stockholders' equity and refer students to the shrink-wrapped annual report or the online versions of this statement.
- We moved the introduction to the statement of cash flows, and the statement itself, to Chapter 2.
- We revised the conceptual framework for greater understanding.
- We simplified the introduction of the standard-setting organizations and included this material in Learning Objective 3.

Chapter 2, "Financial Statements and the Annual Report," has been shortened and streamlined to make it <u>more accessible to beginning accounting students</u>.

"I was impressed by the readability of the chapters. There seems to be a strong effort to get the language at a level that students who have never really thought about what businesses do can relate to. The examples relating to common experiences and specifically to student experiences go a long way to help in this regard."
Gail Cook, University of Wisconsin, Parkside

- Rather than show financial statements for both a hypothetical and a real-world company in each section as in the past, the chapter progresses from enhanced, more graphic coverage of the hypothetical (i.e. "textbook") company statements to example real-world statements using Gateway, Inc.
- We have simplified the language of the objectives of financial reporting.
- We have simplified the explanations of the qualitative characteristics.
- We have focused on introducing the objectives and qualitative characteristics so as to better place them in the context of the use of financial statements.
- We have simplified Exhibit 2-1, "The Application of Financial Reporting Objectives," for better use as a study aid.
- We no longer introduce the details of different depreciation methods in this chapter.
- We have revised Exhibit 2-3 on the operating cycle to be more graphic and to introduce the length of the operating cycle into the exhibit to reinforce the importance of that concept.
- We have annotated the Dixon balance sheet to summarize long-term vs. current assets and liabilities and to aid its use as a study reference.

- We have eliminated several ratios from this introductory chapter, as their coverage in Chapter 2 duplicated coverage elsewhere in the book.
- We have annotated and highlighted Exhibits 2-5 and 2-6 on the income statement for the hypothetical company to better focus on the differences between the single-step and the multi-step formats and as a study reference for the multiple-step concept.
- We have annotated and highlighted Exhibit 2-8 on the hypothetical company's statement of cash flows, to aid study of the three types of activities shown on the statement.
- For simplicity, we have changed the method illustrated on this cash flows statement to the direct method.
- We have minimally annotated Gateway's income statement and balance sheet to show the line items that would be used for simple ratio analysis.
- To avoid adding a level of complication, we have replaced the use of an actual public company in the review problem with a generic company, Grizzly, Inc.

Changes to other chapters are equally exciting for instructors and students. Here are just some of those revisions:

Chapter 5, "Merchandise Accounting and Internal Control," continues to serve as an introduction to inventory accounting in Chapter 6. A new Exhibit 5-4 more graphically illustrates the cost of goods sold model, and a sample of the privacy and security policy for The Gap from its website has been added in the internal control section of the chapter.

Chapter 6, "Inventories and Cost of Goods Sold," has been revised to focus attention on the fundamental differences in inventory costing methods. Inventory errors have been moved to later in the chapter, and a consignments example has been removed from the errors section as a move toward streamlining.

Chapter 7, "Cash, Investments, and Receivables," has been revised to incorporate the material on investments previously covered in Chapter 13. The more complex and seldom-used material on business combinations, consolidated financial statements, and foreign currency has been eliminated from the book.

Chapter 8, "Operating Assets: Property, Plant, and Equipment, Natural Resources, and Intangibles," has been updated with new financial statements for all companies and has also been updated for new FASB developments concerning goodwill and the amortization of intangible assets. The AOL/Time Warner merger is introduced.

Chapter 9, "Current Liabilities, Contingent Liabilities, and the Time Value of Money," has been updated with new financial statements for all companies. It continues to cover current liabilities, contingent liabilities and the time value of money concepts for those instructors who wish to provide that background material. The appendix concerning payroll accounting has been retained because students find it applicable to their daily work lives.

Chapter 10, "Long-Term Liabilities," now utilizes the real-world statements of both Coca-Cola and PepsiCo to allow instructors to compare two companies within the same industry. The section on analysis of long-term liabilities has been moved toward the end of the chapter. Finally, the chapter has been simplified by moving the more advanced topics of deferred tax and pensions to an appendix.

Chapter 11, "Stockholders' Equity," now utilizes the financial statements from Delta Air Lines and other companies from the airline industry. A section has been added to stress the role of retained earnings as a link between the income statement and balance sheet, and a new exhibit illustrates this important concept graphically. We have eliminated Chapter 12 and moved sections on the statement of stockholders' equity and comprehensive income to Chapter 11.

Chapters 12 and 13 from the Second Edition have been eliminated. Sections on the statement of stockholders' equity and comprehensive income have been moved from the old Chapter 12 to Chapter 11 in the Third Edition. The sections on investments in the old Chapter 13 have been moved to Chapter 7 as noted above.

Previous Chapters 14 and 15 now become 12 and 13 respectively, for a book shortened to 13 chapters plus the "Getting Started in Business" module.

PEDAGOGY DESIGNED TO *ENHANCE LEARNING*

We place greater emphasis in the Third Edition on making learning financial accounting enjoyable, relevant, and interesting. New features combine with successful approaches used in previous editions to accommodate the variety of learning and instructional styles emerging across the country.

- ***Study Links*** at the beginning of each chapter give the student an integrated perspective on the material. They review the previous chapter, introduce the current chapter, and look forward to applications for the following chapter.

  NEW: Key topics in the *current chapter* are highlighted with underlining as a time saver and study aid.

- ***Learning Objectives*** are stated at the beginning of each chapter and keyed in the margin and used throughout the book and package as a study aid.

Study Links

A Look at This Chapter

We begin the study of accounting by considering what accounting is and who uses the information it provides. We will see that accounting is an important form of communication and that financial statements are the medium that accountants use to communicate with those who in some way have an interest in the financial affairs of a company.

This is the part of the Study Link that focuses on the current chapter. Look at the Chapter 2 opener on page 44 to see how the previous, current, and next chapters are linked.

LEARNING OBJECTIVES — **AT START OF CHAPTER**

After studying this chapter, you should be able to:

LO 1 Identify the primary users of accounting information and their needs. (p. 4)

LO 2 Explain the purpose of each of the financial statements and the relationships among them and prepare a set of simple statements. (p. 6)

LO 3 Identify and explain the primary assumptions made in preparing financial statements. (p. 12)

LO 4 Describe the various roles of accountants in organizations. (p. 15)

NEW: Page references have been added to the initial listing for easier use.

BESIDE CHAPTER SECTION

LO 1 Identify the primary users of accounting information and their needs.

Multi-Concept Exercises — **IN HOMEWORK ASSIGNMENTS**

LO 1,2 **Exercise 1-12** Users of Accounting Information and the Financial Statements

Listed below are a number of users of accounting information and examples of questions they need answered before making decisions. Fill in each blank to indicate whether the user is most likely to find the answer by looking at the income statement (IS), the balance sheet (BS), or the statement of retained earnings (RE).

- **NEW! *Marginal Glosses*** help students identify and grasp terminology better by locating definitions of boldfaced key terms where first used. (These terms and their definitions are later tested in the Key Terms Quiz at the end of the chapter.)
- **NEW! *Study Tips*** in the margin focus students on key concepts in a section.
- **NEW! *Two-Minute Review*** boxes at the ends of selected sections invite students to pause, think, and review concepts just learned before continuing on:

OPERATING CYCLE

The period of time between the purchase of inventory and the collection of any receivable from the sale of that inventory.

Study Tip

The operating cycle of a business is the basis for deciding which assets are current and which ones are noncurrent.

Two-Minute Review

1. *Give at least three examples of current assets.*
2. *Give the three common categories of noncurrent assets.*

Answers:

1. *Cash, accounts receivable, inventory, short-term investments, and prepaid expenses.*
2. *Investments, property, plant and equipment, and intangibles.*

- ***From Concept to Practice*** boxes in the margins invite students to apply what they have learned in the text and class to financial statements of the chapter-opening companies, Ben & Jerry's, and Gateway.

From Concept **TO PRACTICE 8.3**

REFER TO GATEWAY'S CASH FLOW STATEMENT What amount did the company spend on capital expenditures during 1998?

- **NEW!** ***Warmup Exercises with Suggested Solutions*** give students a preview of assignments to come. These simple exercises, like the Two-Minute Reviews and Key Terms Quizzes, help students move from reading the text to doing the end-of-chapter assignments. Warmup Exercises precede the Review Problem and Solution in each chapter.

Warmup Exercises

LO 2 **Warmup Exercise 1-3** Ben & Jerry's and the Accounting Equation
Place Ben & Jerry's total assets, total liabilities, and total owners' equity in the form of the accounting equation.

Key to the Solution
Recall Exhibit 1-2. You will have to separate the liabilities and the stockholders' equity since they are not subtotaled for you.

Solutions to Warmup Exercises

Warmup Exercise 1-3 Ben & Jerry's and the Accounting Equation

Assets	=	Liabilities	+	Owners' Equity
$149,501		$58,593	+	$90,908

Solutions to Warmup Exercises appear following the Review Problem

- ***Review Problem with Suggested Solutions.*** At the end of every chapter is a review problem and a suggested solution to test students' understanding of some of the major ideas presented in the chapter. (For example, see page 71)

Financial Statement Focus Using *Public Companies*

Through the first two editions, our hallmark has been the use of actual financial statements as examples throughout the book. For the Third Edition we are remaining true to this principle with significant improvements.

- Our chapter-opening vignettes, called "Focus on Financial Results," have been updated and rewritten using many **NEW** companies. They focus on a key aspect of the company and the financial information it presents that relates to the chapter.
    - To view a sample and see how students may use these vignettes effectively, turn to "To the Student," page xxiii.
    - To review the focus of each vignette, see the Table of Contents. In the margin we have included the key issue discussed by the vignette and illustrated in a related financial statement.
- **NEW Business Strategy** boxes, one per chapter, generally focus on a competitor to the chapter-opening company and a key business strategy that is reflected in its financial statements. This is part of one Business Strategy box:

Instructor's can use these strategy boxes as additional research topics for homework assignments.

Business Strategy

Dell Computers, like Gateway, is in the business of selling computers directly to consumers and to business and government organizations. It makes each machine to order and, like Gateway, carries a very small inventory at any one time. Dell also shares with Gateway a strategy of growth, seeking to enlarge its market share against such established giants as Compaq and IBM. However, focusing only on growth led Dell to two missteps in the mid-1990s. First, the firm expanded its

- **All real-world financial statements have been updated in the text to the latest possible 1998 or 1999 annual report year.** Many have been further highlighted or annotated to focus attention on the specific line item or section being discussed.
- Because many instructors prefer to use the latest financial statements available, we are putting renewed emphasis on **accessing the latest annual report information online. NEW:** The **URLs** of real companies cited are now listed in the margins, and in the chapter openers.

www.benjerry.com
www.gateway.com
www.hoovers.com

- An updated **Internet Research Case** is again included at the back of each chapter.

INTERNET RESEARCH CASE

Case 2-8 Gateway

You can probably do this from your everyday knowledge, but this is good practice in researching a company using the internet. Find a WWW site or a source of information that will list the competitors to Gateway. Choose the top two competitors and answer the following questions:

1. Looking at their balance sheets, what are their total current assets and their total current liabilities? From these numbers, calculate each company's working capital and current ratio. How do they compare to these ratios for Gateway, shown on page 65?
2. From their income statements, calculate their profit margins for the latest year available. How do they compare to those of Gateway, which you were asked to calculate in the From Concept to Practice box on page 67?

Optional Research: From the financial information available on their WWW sites, what other comparisons can you make about these companies? Based on your research, are the companies themselves comparable, in such areas as size, products, assets, liabilities, net income? If not, explain five ways in which they differ. Is the financial information itself comparable for the three companies? Explain.

Fill in your source for industry information:
www.____________.com

Gateway and its main competitors:
www.gateway.com
www.____________.com
www.____________.com

"The Web page references are great additions to the text . . . The material flows well, and a lot is covered in an efficient manner."
Paquita Friday,
University of Notre Dame

- Actual WWW graphics of financial information for selected companies are used throughout. The text's WWW site is enhanced for better research capabilities.
- **Financial information from more public companies** has been included in the end-of-chapter material.

FEATURES THAT SUPPORT OUR *DECISION-MAKING* EMPHASIS

Practice in decision making using financial information has been an important principle in past editions. For the Third Edition, we have strengthened the use of financial information to make business and personal financial decisions.

- **Accounting for Your Decisions** boxes in each chapter place the student in a role-playing situation as a user of financial statements, as a decision-maker, and as a future businessperson.
- **Focus on Users** boxes are **NEW** interviews with young businesspersons who use financial information in their everyday decision making. **NEW:** Now included in *every* chapter.
- **Making Financial Decisions cases** and **Accounting and Ethics cases** at the end of the chapter provide additional end-of-chapter support for decision-making using financial information.

- **Internet Research Cases** give the perspective of an actual user or company, provide engaging questions, place the students in a role-playing situation, and give them directions to specific Internet resources for decision-oriented projects.
- **NEW Video Cases** at the end of each of the four parts of the textbook are based on **NEW videos** that focus on financial accounting and business decision-making in four public companies: Tweeter Home Entertainment Inc.; Stride-Rite Inc.; Uno Restaurant Corp., and Lycos.

About our Use of Icons **Icons** are like signposts helping students identify their way along the route. For the Third Edition, we include icons for selected functions.

Decision Making opportunities in the text (Accounting for Your Decisions boxes) and end-of-chapter material are identified with this icon.

Internet resources are identified by a general Internet icon. Specific Web addresses are provided in the margins with this notation: www.harcourtcollege.com.

Problems that may be solved or their solution aided by the Windows **general ledger** program accompanying the text are identified with this icon.

Problems that are supported by the **spreadsheet** problem support tool accompanying the text are identified with this icon.

SUPPLEMENTS FOR THE INSTRUCTOR

A number of ancillary items are available for the instructor's use:

- **NEW! Instructor's Resource CD**: Includes the Solutions Manual, Instructor's Manual, Test Bank in Word, Lectures in PowerPoint, Spreadsheet Problem Support (instructor version), and General Ledger Problem Solver (instructor version).
- **Solutions Manual** by the text authors, with Donna Hetzel (Western Michigan University) and Kathy Horton (College of DuPage). Solutions are included for every Question, Exercise, Problem, and Case in the text with the exception of the Internet Research Cases. (Solutions and suggested answers to the internet research cases are on the book's website.)
- **Test Bank** by Rita Kingery (University of Delaware). We have made a special effort to assure that test items are well correlated with the end-of-chapter assignments. This test bank is also available in a **Computerized Test Bank** from ExaMaster.
- **Instructor's Manual** by Sheila Ammons (Austin Community College, Northridge) and Susan Looney (Mohave Community College, Kingsland) contains chapter outlines, projects and activities, and a bibliography of readings. Numerous activities throughout are keyed to public companies; their URLs are included to facilitate further research.
- **Teaching and Solutions Transparencies** consist of 100 exhibits from the text and other lecture aids, along with acetates of exercises, problems, and solutions in the text.
- **Web site.** Company research, downloads of instructor and student supplements, and a whole range of activities for students can be found at www.harcourtcollege.com/accounting/porter3e. Included is Getting Started, an online supplement for Financial Accounting organized by topic that contains resources, review questions, including company profiles with financial information. (For a preview, see the front endpapers.)

www.harcourtcollege.com/accounting/porter3e

- **NEW WebCT course administration tools** for two student WebCT courses to accompany the textbook:
  - **WebCourse** The WebCourse to accompany the Third Edition, by Sarah Brown (University of North Alabama), allows instructors to develop and manage their course using tools and resources provided by the publisher as well as their own teaching materials. Examples include a conferencing system, online chat, student progress tracking, group project organization, grade maintenance and distribution, access control, navigation tools, auto-graded quizzes, e-mail, course calendar, and syllabus generator.
  - **OMAR: Online Multimedia Accounting Review** OMAR, by Charles Davis (Baylor University), is our new highly graphical and interactive computer-based tutorial

short course on the concepts and mechanics of the accounting cycle. It may be used in conjunction with Chapters 3 and 4 of Porter/Norton if the instructor believes that additional review and drill-and-practice in accounting cycle procedures is needed for his or her students. Built on a WebCT platform, OMAR is available as an e-commerce product. Access is also available via a personal information number (PIN) found within a custom student guide to OMAR and WebCT sold to students through the bookstore.

Basic administration of OMAR is simple and uncomplicated—instructors can track student progress through the frequent lesson exercises and module-ending mastery exams, viewing percent completed, time to complete, and which test items were completed.

A little about WebCT. WebCT is a software tool that facilitates the creation of sophisticated World Wide Web-based educational environments by non-technical users. Using web browsers as the interface, WebCT can be used to create entire on-line courses, or to simply publish materials that supplement existing courses. For more information about WebCT, and to see current Harcourt courses using WebCT, go to Harcourt College Online Learning Center at www.webct.harcourtcollege.com, or to www.webct.com

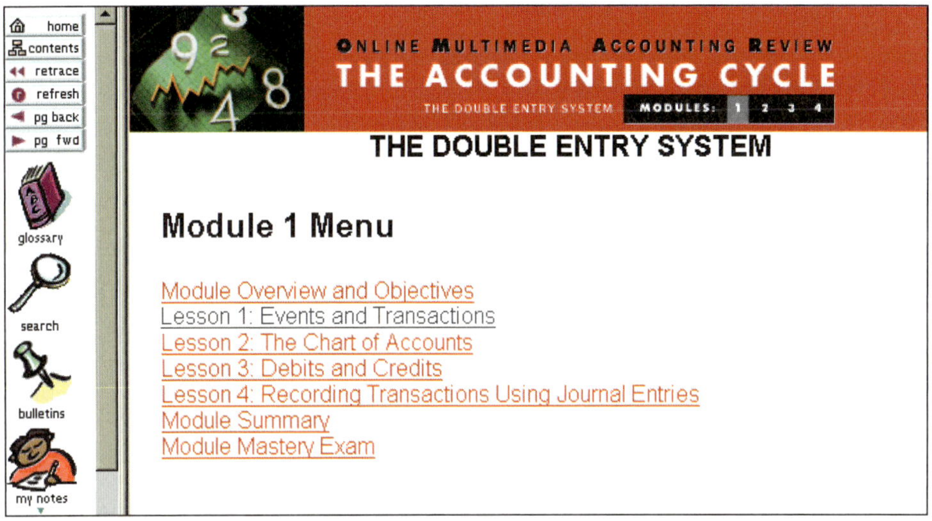

A little about OMAR. OMAR has four modules covering the concepts and procedures of the accounting cycle:

- The Double Entry System
- The Accounting Cycle—Part 1
- Accrual Accounting
- The Accounting Cycle—Part 2

Lessons in each module contain interactive activities, quizzes, graphics, and animations. Each module ends with a grade-reported one-time mastery exam.

- **NEW Video segments,** tied to a new Video Case at the end of each of the four parts of the textbook, focus on financial information and management issues for four public companies, Tweeter Home Entertainment, Stride-Rite, Uno's Restaurant Corp., and Lycos.

Availability of all instructor ancillaries, including the Solutions Manual, is restricted to instructors only under their pre-designated ISBNs. Instructors desiring to make any instructor ancillaries available to their students must contact their local Harcourt representative or the Harcourt College Publishers Marketing Department for special arrangement exceptions.

For Student Supplements
see "To the Student" on page xxiii following Meet the Authors

A NEW MANAGERIAL TITLE TO PAIR WITH *FINANCIAL ACCOUNTING*

Harcourt's **NEW Managerial Accounting book** by Jackson/Sawyers uses a 4-step **decision-making model** throughout the discussion and end-of-chapter material. It contains extensive coverage of contemporary topics such as ABC, ABM, the value chain, just-in-time and balanced scorecard methods. It also contains a unique chapter (13) on the development of **knowledge management** and the integration of accounting information throughout the whole organization's information systems.

Acknowledgments

In preparing for the Third Edition, we have conducted considerable research into evolving preferences nationwide. Through two rounds of telephone surveys, focus groups, and reviews, we have taken to heart the advice of over 150 instructors. That level of commitment to our fellow instructors has once again allowed us to remain on target with the demands of the ever-changing financial accounting course.

Among these many instructors, we are especially grateful to the following for their recommendations and comments, whether concerning the book and the financial accounting course at their school, for their detailed reviews of the Second Edition, or for their analysis of chapters in the Third Edition.

Sheila Ammons, Austin Community College
Sarah Brown, University of Northern Alabama
Ronnie Burrows, University of Dayton
David N. Champagne, Antelope Valley College
Gail Cook, University of Wisconsin, Parkside
Susan Coomer Galbreath, Tennessee Tech University
Betty Driver, Murray State University
Paquita Y. Friday, University of Notre Dame
Hubert Gill, University of North Florida
Jeanne Hamilton, Cypress College
Christopher Jones, George Washington University
Greg Krippel, Coastal Carolina University
James Kurtenbach, Iowa State University
Tom Lee, Winona State University
Gina Lord, Santa Rosa Junior College
Don Loster, University of California, Santa Barbara
Spencer Martin, University of Rhode Island
Muroki Mwaura, William Paterson University
Jane Park, California State University, Los Angeles
Kathy Petroni, Michigan State University
Robert Rouse, College of Charleston
Donna Rudderow, Franklin University
Judith Sage, University of Southern Colorado
David P. Weiner, University of San Francisco
Michael Williams, Century College

We also would like to thank the following individuals who have helped by their work on the supplements: Sheila Ammons, Sarah Brown, Charles Davis, Sandy Devona, Jerry Funk, Leo Gabriel, Elise Gantt, Coby Harmon, Donna Hetzel, Kathy Horton, Rita Kingery, Floyd Kirby, Susan Looney, Mark McCarthy, Mary Nisbet, Angela Sandberg, Doug Schneider, and Barbara Reider. A special thanks goes to Barbara Reider and Beth Woods, CPA, for help in solutions and test item checking. We are grateful to the work of Katherine Xenophon-Rybowiak for her work on the solutions manual.

We are indebted to Karen Hill and Jen Frazier for their work on the project.

Reviewers and Focus Group Participants for the First Edition:

Diana Adcox, University of North Florida
Saul Ahiaria, SUNY at Buffalo
Mike Akers, Marquette University
Marcia Anderson, University of Cincinnati

David Angelovich, San Francisco State University
Alana Baier, Marquette University
Amelia A. Baldwin-Morgan, Eastern Michigan University
Bobbe M. Barnes, University of Colorado at Denver
Maj. Curt Barry, U.S. Military Academy
Peter Battell, University of Vermont
Paul Bayes, East Tennessee State University
Mark Bettner, Bucknell University
Frank Biegbeder, Rancho Santiago Community College
Francis Bird, University of Richmond
Karen Bird, University of Michigan
Eddy Birrer, Gonzaga University
Michelle Bissonnette, California State University—Fresno
John Blahnik, Lorain County Community College
Ed Bresnahan, American River College
Sarah Brown, University of North Alabama
Philip Buchanan, George Washington University
Rosie Bukics, Lafayette College
Carolyn Callahan, University of Notre Dame
Linda Campbell, University of Toledo
Jim Cashell, Miami University
Charles Caufield, Loyola University Chicago
Gyan Chandra, Miami University
Mayer Chapman, California State University at Long Beach
Alan Cherry, Loyola Marymount University
Mike Claire, College of San Mateo
David C. Coffee, Western Carolina University
David Collins, Eastern Kentucky University
Judith Cook, Grossmont College
John C. Corless, California State University—Sacramento
Dean Crawford, University of Toledo
Shirley J. Daniel, University of Hawaii at Manoa
Alan Davis, Community College of Philadelphia
Henry H. Davis, Eastern Illinois University
Lyle E. Dehning, Metropolitan State College—Denver
Patricia Doherty, Boston University
Margaret Douglas, University of Arkansas
Kathy Dunne, Rider College
Kenneth Elvik, Iowa State University
Anette Estrada, Grand Valley State University
Ed Etter, Syracuse University
Alan Falcon, Loyola Marymount University
Charles Fazzi, Robert Morris College
Anita Feller, University of Illinois
Howard Felt, Temple University
David Fetyko, Kent State University
Richard File, University of Nebraska—Omaha
Ed Finkhauser, University of Utah
Jeannie M. Folk, College of DuPage
J. Patrick Forrest, Western Michigan University
Patrick Fort, University of Alaska—Fairbanks
Diana Franz, University of Toledo
Tom Frecka, University of Notre Dame
Gary Freeman, University of Tulsa
Veronique Frucot, Rutgers University—Camden
Joe Gallo, Cuyahoga Community College
Michelle Gannon, Western Connecticut State University
Will Garland, Coastal Carolina University
John Gartska, Loyola Marymount University
Roger Gee, San Diego Mesa College
Cynthia Van Gelderen, Aquinas College
Linda Genduso, Nova University
Don E. Giacomino, Marquette University
Claudia Gilbertston, Anoka Ramsey Community College
Lorraine Glascock, University of Alabama
Larry Godwin, University of Montana
Lynn Grace, Edison Community College
Marilyn Greenstein, Lehigh University
Paul Griffin, University of California—Davis
Leon Hanouille, Syracuse University
Joseph Hargadon, Widener University
Robert Hartwig, Worcester State College
Jean Hatcher, University of South Carolina at Sumner
Donna Sue Hetzel, Western Michigan University
Thomas F. Hilgeman, St. Louis Community College—Meramec
Robert E. Holtfreter, Ft. Hays State University
Kathy Horton, University of Illinois, Chicago
Bruce Ikawa, Loyola Marymount University
Danny Ivancevich, University of Nevada—Las Vegas
Janet Jackson, Wichita State University
Sharon Jackson, Auburn University at Montgomery
Randy Johnston, Pennsylvania State University
William Jones, Seton Hall University
Naida Kaen, University of New Hampshire
Manu Kai'ama, University of Hawaii at Manoa
Jane Kapral, Clark University
Marcia Kertz, San Jose State University
Jean Killey, Midlands Technical College
Ronald King, Washington University
William Kinsella, Loyola Marymount University
Jay LaGregs, Tyler Junior College
Michael Lagrone, Clemson University
Lucille E. Lammers, Illinois State University
Ellen Landgraf, Loyola University Chicago
Horace Landry, Syracuse University
Kristine Lawyer, North Carolina State University
Terry Lease, Loyola Marymount University
Susan Lightle, Wright State University
Tom Linsmeier, University of Iowa
Chao-Shin Liu, University of Notre Dame
Bruce Lubich, Syracuse University
Catherine Lumbattis, Southern Illinois University
Patsy Lund, Lakewood Community College
Raymond D. MacFee, Jr., University of Colorado
David Malone, University of Idaho
Janice Mardon, Green River Community College
Mary D. Maury, St. John's University
Al Maypers, University of North Texas
John C. McCabe, Ball State University
Nancy McClure, Lock Haven University
Margaret McCrory, Marist College
Christine McKeag, University of Evansville

Thomas D. McLaughlin, Monmouth College
Laura McNally, Black Hills State College
Mallory McWilliams, San Jose State University
E. James Meddaugh, Ohio University
Cynthia Miller, GM Institute
William Mister, Colorado State University
Tami Mittelstaedt, University of Notre Dame
Perry Moore, David Lipscomb University
Barbara Morris, Angelo State University
Mike Morris, University of Notre Dame
Theodore D. Morrison, Valparaiso University
Howard E. Mount, Seattle Pacific University
Rafael Munoz, University of Notre Dame
Mary J. Nisbet, University of California—Santa Barbara
Curtis L. Norton, Northern Illinois University
Priscilla O'Clock, Xavier University
Phil Olds, Virginia Commonwealth University
Michael O'Neill, Gannon University
Janet O'tousa, University of Notre Dame
Rimona Palas, William Paterson College of New Jersey
Beau Parent, Tulane University
Paul Parkison, Ball State University
Sue Pattillo, University of Notre Dame
Ron Pawliczek, Boston College
Donna Philbrick, Portland State University
Gary A. Porter, Loyola University Chicago
Harry V. Poynter, Central Missouri State University
Joseph Ragan, St. Joseph's University
Mitchell Raiborn, Bradley University
Ann Riley, American University
Mary Rolfes, Mankato State University
Leo A. Ruggle, Mankato State University
Victoria Rymer, University of Maryland
George Sanderson, Moorhead State University
Karen Saurlander, University of Toledo
Warren Schlesinger, Ithaca College
Edward S. Schwan, Susquehanna University
Don Schwartz, National University
Richard Scott, University of Virginia
Richard Sherman, St. Joseph's University
Ray Slager, Calvin College
Amy Spielbauer, St. Norbert College
Charles Stanley, Baylor University
Catherine Staples, Virginia Commonwealth University
Anita Stellenwerf, Ramapo College
Stephen Strange, Indiana University at Kokomo
Linda Sugarman, University of Akron
Kathy Sullivan, George Washington University
Jeanie Sumner, Pacific Lutheran University
Judy Swingen, Rochester Institute of Technology
Tim Tancy, University of Notre Dame
Bente Villadsen, Washington University
Alan K. Vogel, Cuyahoga Community College—Western
Vicki Vorell, Cuyahoga Community College—Western
Phil Walter, Bellevue Community College
Ann Watkins, Louisiana State University
Judy Wenzel, Gustavus Adolphus College
Charles Werner, Loyola University Chicago
Michael Werner, University of Miami
Paul Wertheim, Pepperdine University
Shari Wescott, Houston Baptist University
T. Sterling Wetzel, Oklahoma State University
Steven D. White, Western Kentucky University
Samuel Wild, Loyola Marymount University
Jack Wilkerson, Wake Forest University
Lyle Wimmergren, Worcester Polytechnic Institute
Carol Wolk, University of Tennessee
Steve Wong, San Jose City College
Robert Zahary, California State University at Los Angeles
Thomas L. Zeller, Loyola University Chicago

Survey Respondents, Focus Group Participants, and Reviewers for the Second Edition:

Ray Bainbridge, Lehigh University
Angela Bell, Jacksonville University
Dorcas Berg, Wingate University
Bruce Bolick, University of Mary Hardin Baylor
Frank Bouchlers, North Carolina State University
Thomas Brady, University of Dayton
Bob Brill, St. Bonaventure University
Sarah Brown, University of North Alabama
David Brunn, Carthage College
Gary Bulmash, American University
Bryan Burks, Harding University
Judith Cadle, Tarleton State University
John E. Coleman, University of Massachusetts at Boston
Judith Cook, Grossmont Community College
Rosalind Cranor, Virginia Polytechnic Institute
Carrie Cristea, Augustana College, South Dakota
Fred Current, Furman University
Jim Davis, Clemson University
Les Dlabay, Lake Forest College
Jaime Doran, Muhlenberg College
Patricia Douglas, Loyola Marymount University
Alan Doyle, Pima Community College East
Alan Drebin, Northwestern University
Dean Edmiston, Emporia State University
Joan Friedman, Illinois Wesleyan University
Leo Gabriel, Bethel College
Sharon Garvin, Wayne State College
Art Goldman, University of Kentucky
Lorraine Glasscock, University of North Alabama
Bud Granger, Mankato State University
Jack Grinnell, University of Vermont
Bonnie Hairrell, Birmingham Southern
Al Hannan, College of Notre Dame
Suzanne Hartley, Franklin University

Donna Hetzel, Western Michigan University
Nathan Hindi, Shippensburgh University of Pennsylvania
Betty Horn, Southern Connecticut State University
Fred Ihrke, Winona State University
Sharon Jackson, Auburn University, Montgomery
Stanley Jenne, University of Montana
Patricia Johnson, Canisius College
Becky Jones, Baylor University
Mary Keim, California State University—Bakersfield
Anne Marie Keinath, Indiana University Northwest
Don Kellogg, Rock Valley College
Robert Kelly, Corning Community College
Rita Kingery, University of Delaware
Paul Kleichman, University of Richmond
George Klersey, Birmingham Southern College
Charles Konkol, University of Wisconsin—Milwaukee
Frank Korman, Mountain View College
Lynn Koshiyama, University of Alaska
Bobby Kuhlmann, Chaffey College
James Kurtenbach, Iowa State University
Jay LaGregs, Tyler Junior College
Laurie Larson, Valencia Community College
Tom Lee, Winona State University
Chao Liu, Tarleton State University
Alan Lord, Bowling Green State University
Gina Lord, Santa Rosa Junior College
Bruce Lubich, American University
George Macklin, Susquehanna University
Jim Martin, University of Montevallo
Laurie McWhorter, University of Kentucky
Paul Mihalek, University of Hartford
Charles Milliner, Glendale Community College
Marcia Niles, University of Idaho
Mary Ellen O'Grady, Ramapo College
Bruce Oliver, Rochester Institute of Technology
Daniel O'Mara, Quinnipiac College
John Osborn, California State University—Fresno
Prakash Pai, Kent State University
Paul Parkison, Ball State University
Victor Pastena, SUNY Buffalo
Charles A. Pauley, Gannon University
Chris Pew, Galivan College
Al Rainford, Greenfield Community College
John Rhode, University of San Francisco
Keith Richardson, Indiana State University
Joseph Rue, Syracuse University
Marilyn Sagrillo, University of Wisconsin—Green Bay
Rick Samuelson, San Diego State University
Gail Sanderson, Lebanon Valley College
Richard Sathe, University of St. Thomas
Karen Sedatole, Stephen F. Austin
John Sherman, University of Texas, Dallas
Richard Silkoff, Quinnipiac College
Ron Singer, University of Wisconsin—Parkside
David Smith, Metropolitan State University
David Smith, University of Dayton
Jill Smith, Idaho State University
Kim Sorenson, Eastern Oregon State University
Jens Stephan, University of Cincinnati
Donna Street, James Madison University
David Strupeck, Indiana University NW
Larry Tartaglino, Cabrillo College
Martha Turner, Bowling Green State University
Karen Walton, John Carroll University
Dewey Ward, Michigan State University
Michael Welker, Drexel University
Jane Wells, University of Kentucky
Jennifer Wells, University of San Francisco
Paul Wertheim, Pepperdine University
Jill Whitley, Sioux Falls College
Jane Wiese, Valencia Community College
David Willis, Illinois Wesleyan University
Betty Wolterman, St. John's University, MN
Steven Wong, San Jose City College
Gail Wright, Bryant College

Gary A. Porter
Curtis L. Norton

Meet the Authors

Gary A. Porter, CPA, is Professor and Chair of the Department of Accounting and Finance at the University of Montana. He earned Ph.D. and M.B.A. degrees from the University of Colorado and his B.S.B.A. from Drake University. He has published in the *Journal of Accounting Education*, *Journal of Accounting, Auditing & Finance*, and *Journal of Accountancy*, among others and has conducted numerous workshops on the subject of introductory accounting education.

Dr. Porter's professional activities include experience as a staff accountant with Deloitte & Touche in Denver, a participant in KPMG Peat Marwick Foundation's Faculty Development program and as a leader in numerous bank training programs. He has won an Excellence in Teaching award from the University of Colorado and an Outstanding Professor Award from San Diego State University.

He served on the Illinois CPA Society's Innovations in Accounting Education Grants Committee, the steering committee of the midwest region of the American Accounting Association, and the board of directors of the Chicago chapter of the Financial Executives Institute. Dr. Porter is also a member of the Montana Society of Certified Public Accountants. At the University of Montana, Dr. Porter was recently selected as Beta Alpha Psi's Outstanding Undergraduate Accounting Professor. He also received university-wide recognition from Mortar Board for his teaching excellence.

Curtis L. Norton is Deloitte & Touche Professor of Accountancy at Northern Illinois University. He earned his Ph.D. from Arizona State University, his M.B.A. from the University of South Dakota, and his B.S. from Jamestown College, North Dakota. His extensive list of publications includes articles in *Accounting Horizons*, *The Journal of Accounting Education*, *Journal of Accountancy*, *Journal of Corporate Accounting*, *Journal of the American Taxation Association*, *Real Estate Review*, *The Accounting Review*, *CPA Journal*, and many others. In 1988–89, Dr. Norton received the University Excellence in Teaching Award, the highest university-wide teaching recognition at NIU. He is also a consultant and has conducted training programs for governmental authorities, banks, utilities, and other entities.

Dr. Norton is a member of the American Accounting Association and a member and officer of the Financial Executives Institute.

To the Student

Now that you've enrolled in Financial Accounting, and have bought your books and assigned supplements, you probably have more questions than answers:

- How can I get the most out of the book and its features?
- How can study aids help me be more successful in the course?

For many, Financial Accounting will be your first course in business. "So what is business, anyway?" you may ask. The strategies in this section, and the *Getting Started in Business* module that follows next before Chapter 1, will start you out on the right foot in the course.

Features to Help You Learn

We're dedicated to getting you out of the gate fast in Financial Accounting. In "To the Instructor," we've described and shown images of these features. Here we give you an overview of how you might use them.

Apart from reading the chapter, you can use the study aids in every part of the book:

1. ***Get a feel for the chapter—turn to the chapter-opening spread.*** Financial accounting is about companies, how they operate and how their managers think. So we've provided you with an actual company in each chapter as a study example—complete with a profile, a sample financial statement, some questions that will help put the company in context, and their Web address.

FOCUS ON FINANCIAL RESULTS

- Chapter-opening introduction illustrates a key financial issue related to the chapter.

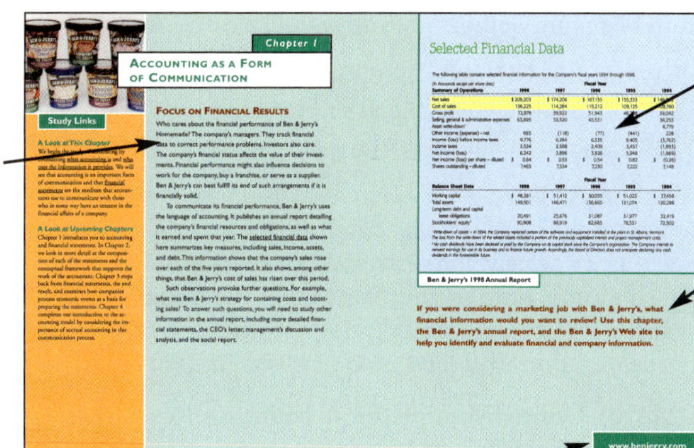

- A financial statement or excerpt from the company's annual report.
- Thought-provoking questions relates the company back to the chapter.
- The company's Web site.

These companies will be referred to in the chapter, so use the opener as a model of your growing understand of how this company—and all companies—perform.

A Business Strategy box later in the chapter can help you better understand the company, its strategies for success, and its competitors. It's background that may help you if your instructor assigns homework to research the company.

2. ***Organize your study using the Learning Objectives.*** They are keyed to sections in the text, to the homework assignments, and to the Study Guide. Look them over first, then use them to organize your study.

3. ***Refer back to the key terms and definitions in the margins.*** Terminology is important in accounting, so these definitions will help you retain the important concepts. Some students use them as visual references for sections or concepts to reread. Later, a **Key Terms Quiz** at the back of the chapter will help you fix terms in your mind.

Study Tip

Use the Study Links at the left of the opening spread to see, chapter-by-chapter, where you are in the course.

Study Tip

To see some sample Learning Objectives and how they will appear, turn back to page xi.

KEY TERM

An important concept or term that is boldfaced in text, appears with its definition in the margin, and is used in the Key Terms Quiz at the back of the chapter.

Study Tip

To see a sample Two-Minute Review, turn back to page xi.

Study Tip

To see a sample Warmup Exercise, turn back to page xii.

4. ***Make sure to check out the Study Tips in the margins.*** These brief aids are designed to help by focusing on making connections between what you've read before and the current topic, or stating a point in a different way.
5. ***Use the Two-Minute Reviews in the middle of each chapter to help keep you on track.*** These quick reviews have the answers underneath, but going through the process will help you understand the concepts you've just read about in the section.
6. ***Prepare for the homework assignments using Warmup Exercises.*** These exercises at the end of the chapter, with answers following, focus on helping you learn to format and prepare homework assignments.

The *Getting Started in Business* Module: How Can It Help?

"Getting Started in Business," following next after the table of contents, will help you answer these questions before you start Chapter 1:

- What is business?
- Could I start a successful business?
- What are the forms that businesses take?
- What are some of the activities that businesses engage in?

Use this module to get a head start on understanding how accounting fits into the business scheme.

Student Supplements Are There to Help

www.harcourtcollege.com/store/

Your instructor may not require all of these ancillaries, but it's still good to know that Harcourt publishes them if you need a little help. You can obtain these ancillaries online from Harcourt College Store at *www.harcourtcollege.com/store/.*

NEW Student CD You'll be up and running with your homework assignments the ***Student CD.*** Containing a General Ledger program for solving selected end-of-chapter homework; **NEW** spreadsheet homework problem support.

www.harcourtcollege.com/accounting/porter3e

Web Site An extensive book web-site is provided for performing **research on each public company** mentioned in the text. **Online quizzing and testing** is available for each chapter. There are also many non-text-specific **activities and resources** that are useful for accounting students, such as the Getting Started tour with resources, review questions, company profiles by topic. Play a stock market game, learn to select stocks, and conduct company research all at *www.harcourtcollege.com/accounting/porter3e.* (For a preview, see the front endpapers.)

A sample page from OMAR

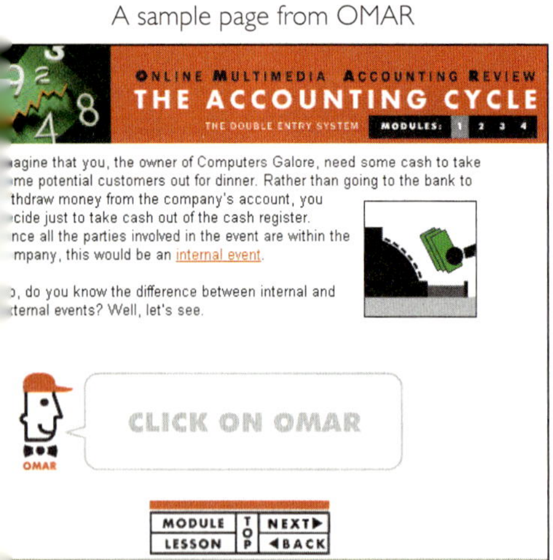

Easy navigation, plenty of activities, links to key terms, and audio commentary are some of the features that make **OMAR** a great way to study the basic concepts and skills of accounting—the accounting cycle.

OMAR—Online Multimedia Accounting Review OMAR is a graphical, interactive web-based minicourse that helps you to master the concepts and skills of basic accounting procedures. This four-module course gets you started by identifying events in a company's operations. And, using activities and animation, you'll be preparing financial statements by the end of Module 4. You can take the course and the quizzes again and again to master the material. Your instructor may assign you to take the one-time test for a grade. See the demo of OMAR at http://webct.harcourtcollege.com/public/omardemo. OMAR may be purchased online at www.harcourtcollege.com/store/ and is also available with a custom Student Manual through the bookstore. See your instructor for details.

WebCourse Your instructor has the option of using the course management web tools available with this book. If so, here is a preview of what's in store for you.

- **Course Notes** will help guide you through the textbook.
- **Online Quizzing and Testing** supports the text and extends the chapter homework.
- **Glossary**—You'll be able to review terminology online along with other online resources found here.
- **Syllabus**—Your instructor's syllabus is online, on one site with the other course materials.

- **Web activities**—Porter/Norton already includes a number of opportunities to use the web, especially for the Internet Research Case at the end of the chapter. These are separate activities to keep you up-to-date with the financials of public companies.
- **Discussion Questions**—Your instructor may use this feature to keep classes interesting and lively.
- **Group projects**—Again, your instructor can choose to assign several of these projects to deepen your learning.

Guide to Understanding and Using Annual Reports, by Angela Sandberg, Floyd W. Kirby, and Elise M. Gantt (all of Jacksonville State University). This popular booklet, revised and enhanced for the Third Edition, is a step-by step guide to understanding and using any annual report your instructor may assign.

Study Guide, by Mary Nisbet and Coby Harmon (both of the University of California, Santa Barbara). Use the Study Guide to review the chapter's main focus, key concepts, key terms, and brush up your homework and test-taking skills (including solutions).

Procedural Review, by Douglas Schneider and Mark McCarthy (both of East Carolina University). This supplement provide you with more opportunity to practice the accounting procedures covered in the book. Arranged by Learning Objective for each chapter, the Procedural Review can be an invaluable tool if you need more help in building your skills.

Working Papers by Diana Tanner (University of North Florida). Why use notebook paper for your homework when you can save time by simply entering the answers in the format preferred by your instructor? This handy book provides all the forms you'll need when your instructor asks you to manually prepare the homework assignments at the back of each chapter.

Tamije Garden Supply, Inc., a Corporate Practice Set by Leon Hanouille (Syracuse University) and Jerry Funk (Brazosport College, Business Branch Office, Inc.) This booklet with general ledger program CD allows you to sharpen your accounting cycle skills. Can be starting any time after Chapter 3 of the textbook and completed any time after Chapter 9.

Also available to enhance your business education

Interactive Decision Cases for Financial Accounting by Guided Exploration LLC With this CD, you gain hands-on practice in making accounting and business decisions while you learn and practice key financial accounting skills applied to today's business. Each of the 8 cases uses data from public companies like Whirlpool, Kmart, Dell, Seagrams, and Apple.

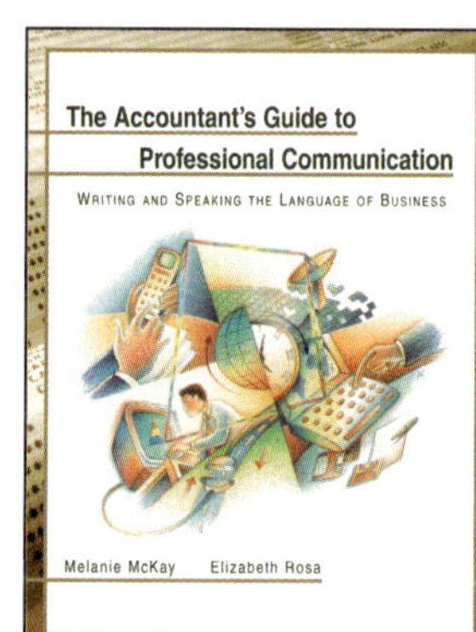

The Accountant's Guide to Professional Communication: Writing and Speaking the Language of Business by Melanie McKay (Loyola University of New Orleans) and Elizabeth Rosa (Allentown College of St. Francis de Sales). This supplement can help you write and speak more effectively in this course, and throughout your business education. From written communication to oral presentations and visual aids, this guide includes actual examples from the careers of accounting professionals. One chapter even helps you get a job in the accounting field.

Now turn to the opening module, *Getting Started in Business!*

Brief Contents

Contents

Ben & Jerry's / Unilever
Boosting sales and containing costs; Ben & Jerry's sale to Unilever.

Each chapter contains the following material: Warmup Exercises, Solutions to Warmup Exercises, Review Problem, Solution to Review Problem, Chapter Highlights, Key Terms Quiz, Alternate Terms, Questions, Exercises, Problems, Cases, Solutions to Key Terms Quiz

Gateway Inc.
A doubling of cash and equivalents, and an increase in property, plant, and equipment.

K2
Increasing net sales with a diversity of products.

McDonald's
Maintaining growth in revenue will require global strategies.

The Gap
Managing for success in retail: doubling of net sales in two years, and a decrease in cost of goods sold.

Circuit City
Managing inventory using in-store Build-to-Order stations. Inventory is half of total assets.

PepsiCo
Effect of business and brand changes on accounts and notes receivable, as well as cash and equivalents and short-term investments.

Time Warner / AOL
Merger with AOL. Tangible and intangible operating assets, and "originating brands as engines of growth."

JCPenney
Improving profitability means managing accounts payable and other current liabilities.

Coca-Cola
Investing heavily in worldwide marketing and infrastructure means incurring long-term debt.

Delta Air Lines
Strategies for building shareholder value as a key goal at Delta.

e-business

IBM
With record revenues, and with healthy investments in three key areas, substantial cash is left over for shareholders and stock buybacks.

Wrigley
With record net earnings, paying dividends is a tradeoff against greater investments in key markets.

Getting Started in Business

Learning Objectives

After studying this module, you should be able to:

LO 1 Explain why financial information is important in making decisions. (p. GS1)

LO 2 Understand what business is about. (p. GS2)

LO 3 Distinguish among the forms of organization. (p. GS3)

LO 4 Describe the various types of business activity. (p. GS5)

LO 1 Explain why financial information is important in making decisions.

Pick your favorite company. Maybe it is The Gap, because you buy all of your clothes there. Or maybe it is The Tribune Company because they own your favorite team, the Chicago Cubs. Or is it Gateway because you like their commercials? At any rate, have you ever wondered how the company got started? Here is the abbreviated story of the birth of a well-known ice cream company:

> Ben & Jerry's, Vermont's Finest All Natural Ice Cream & Frozen Yogurt, was founded in 1978 in a renovated gas station in Burlington, Vermont by childhood friends Ben Cohen and Jerry Greenfield with a $12,000 investment ($4,000 of which was borrowed). With the help of an old-fashioned rock salt ice cream maker and a then-$5 correspondence course in ice cream making from Penn State under their belt, they soon became popular for their funky, chunky, flavors, made from fresh Vermont milk and cream. A year later they were delivering Ben & Jerry's ice cream to grocery stores and restaurants.

Ben & Jerry's: The Need to Make Financial Decisions

From these humble beginnings, Ben & Jerry's made tremendous strides in its first 20 years. Sales in 1998 exceeded $209 million. Numerous reasons account for the company's phenomenal success. From its beginning, the company has taken an extremely active role in promoting social responsibility. It has some of the most far-reaching and liberal employment policies in U.S. business. However, any company owes a major part of its success to its ability to make *financial decisions*. Initially, Ben Cohen and Jerry Greenfield made the decision to invest $8,000 of their own money and borrow $4,000 to start their ice cream–making business. Would *you* have been willing to risk your savings to start a new business? Would you have been willing to sign a note agreeing to repay a loan in the future? Both of these were financial decisions the two had to make.

In 1980, after two years in business, Ben and Jerry decided to rent space in an old mill and to begin packing ice cream in pints. Once again, they were faced with a financial decision: could they make enough money from selling pints of ice cream to pay the rent? More decisions, each one involving higher stakes, faced the young entrepreneurs during the 1980s. In 1984 Ben and Jerry decided to sell stock to the public for the first time (staying loyal to their adopted state, the stock was available only to Vermonters.) What prompted them to make this financial decision? On the basis of record sales of $4 million in 1984, they realized that their current production facilities were inadequate to handle the increased

From two guys making ice cream came today's Ben & Jerry's Homemade, Inc. Growing their business required skills in making and selling ice cream, in expanding their operation with new equipment and resources, and in working with managers and professionals who could understand the financial side of the business.

volume. They needed money to build a new plant. The sale of stock that year netted the company about $700,000. The company made an even larger decision that same year, however: it borrowed more than $2 million. At that point, major financial decisions about the company were being made not only by the original owners but also by outsiders. Given the opportunity back then, would you have bought stock in this company? Would you have been willing to lend money to it that year, as many people and organizations did?

In 1985 the company borrowed more money and sold stock to people outside Vermont for the first time. It was the first year the stock of Ben & Jerry's was traded on an organized stock exchange. Then came more decisions for Ben & Jerry's and those who lent money to the company and bought stock in it. Construction on the new manufacturing plant and company headquarters began in 1985 and was completed the following year. Was it a wise decision to sell stock and borrow money to build the new facility? Sales in 1986 were double those of the prior year, reaching almost $20 million. By 1992 the company was so successful that it began construction on its *third* manufacturing plant. At the end of 1995, Ben & Jerry's had spent approximately $38.2 million in building and equipping the new plant.

The most recent chapter in the Ben & Jerry's success story began to unfold in 2000. For a number of years, various companies have viewed Ben & Jerry's with envy and some have even made attempts to buy the ice cream maker. Finally on April 12, 2000, Unilever, a Dutch-based conglomerate, and Ben & Jerry's announced that Unilever would buy the company for approximately $326 million. Once again, financial information about Ben & Jerry's was crucial to a decision to make this announcement: in this case whether to invest a significant amount of money in another company.

All of us use financial information in making decisions. For example, when you were deciding whether to enroll at your present school, you needed information on the tuition and room-and-board costs at the different schools you were considering. When a stockbroker decides whether to recommend to a client the purchase of stock in a company, the broker needs information on the company's profits and whether it pays dividends. When trying to decide whether to lend money to a company, a banker must consider the company's current debts.

In this book, we explore how accounting can help all of us in making informed financial decisions. Before we turn to the role played by accounting in decision making, we need to explore business in more detail. What *is* business? What forms of organization carry on business activity? In what types of business activity do those organizations engage?

What Is Business?

LO 2 Understand what business is about.

Business
All the activities necessary to provide the members of an economic system with goods and services.

Just as Ben & Jerry's got its start in a renovated gas station, your study of accounting has to start somewhere. All disciplines have a foundation on which they rest. For accounting, that foundation is business.

Broadly defined, **business** consists of all the activities necessary to provide the members of an economic system with goods and services. Certain business activities focus on the providing of goods or products, such as ice cream, automobiles, and computers. Some of these companies produce or manufacture the products. Others are involved in the distribution of the goods, either as wholesalers (who sell to retail outlets) or retailers (who sell to consumers). Other business activities by their nature are service oriented. Corporate giants such as Citicorp, Walt Disney, Time Warner and United Airlines remind us of the prominence of service activities in the world today. The relatively recent phenomenon of various "service providers," such as health-care organizations and internet companies, are a testimony to the growing importance of the service sector in the U.S. economy.

To appreciate the kinds of business enterprises in our economy, consider the various types of companies that have a stake in the delivery of a pint of ice cream to the grocery store. First, Ben & Jerry's must contract with a *supplier* of milk. The company buys much of its milk from a local company, St. Albans Cooperative Creamery. As a *manufacturer* or *producer,* Ben & Jerry's takes the milk and other various raw materials, such as sugar and chocolate, and transforms them into a finished product. At this stage, a *distributor* or *wholesaler* gets

EXHIBIT GS-1 Types of Businesses

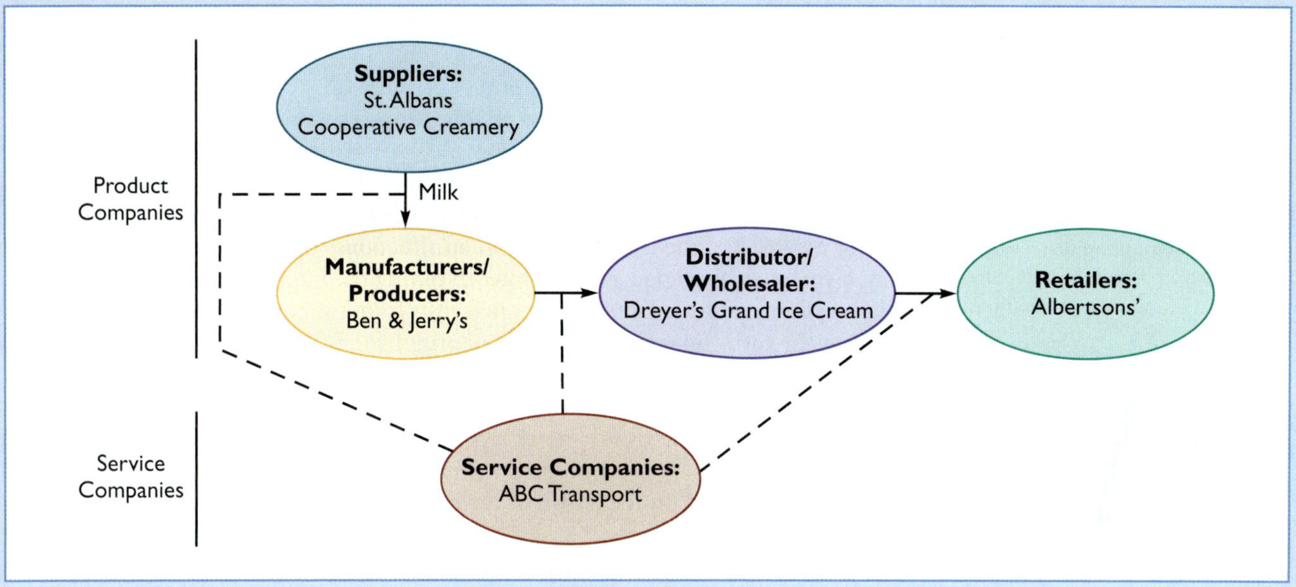

involved. For example, Ben & Jerry's sells a considerable amount of its ice cream to Dreyer's Grand Ice Cream. Dreyer's, in turn, sells the products to many different *retailers,* such as Albertsons and Safeway. Although maybe less obvious, any number of *service* companies are involved in the process. For example, various trucking companies transport the milk to Ben & Jerry's for production, and others move the ice cream along to Dreyer's. Still others get it to supermarkets and other retail outlets. Exhibit GS-1 summarizes the process.

FORMS OF ORGANIZATION

LO 3 Distinguish among the forms of organization.

There are many different types of organizations in our society. One convenient way to categorize the myriad types is to distinguish between those that are organized to earn money and those that exist for some other purpose. Although the lines can become blurred *business entities* generally are organized to earn a profit, whereas *nonbusiness entities* generally exist to serve various segments of society. Both types are summarized in Exhibit GS-2.

EXHIBIT GS-2 Forms of Organization

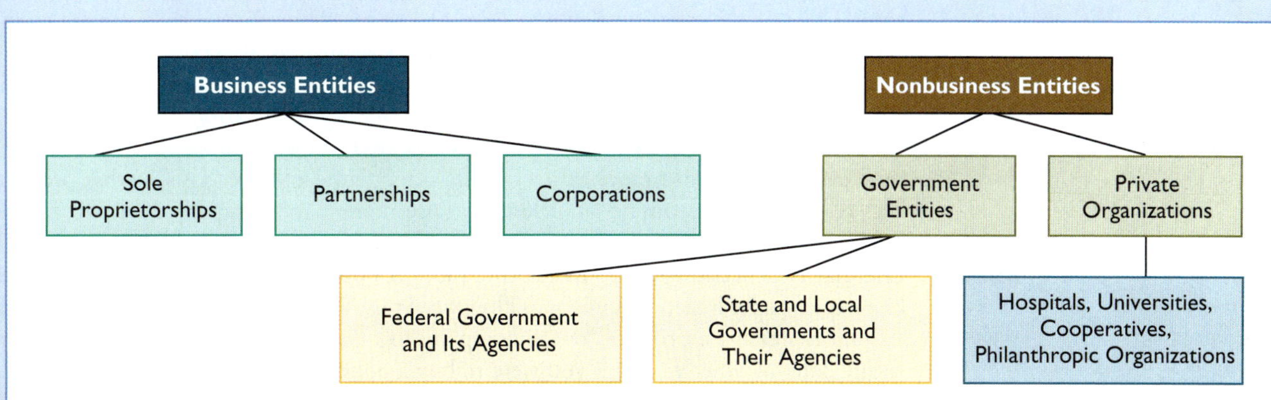

BUSINESS ENTITIES

BUSINESS ENTITY
An organization operated to earn a profit.

Business entities are organized to earn a profit. Legally, a profit-oriented company is one of three types: sole proprietorships, partnerships, and corporations.

SOLE PROPRIETORSHIP
Form of organization with a single owner.

ECONOMIC ENTITY CONCEPT
The assumption that a single, identifiable unit must be accounted for in all situations.

Sole Proprietorships

This form of organizaion is characterized by a single owner. Many small businesses are organized as **sole proprietorships.** Very often the business is owned and operated by the same person. Because of the close relationship between the owner and the business, the affairs of the two must be kept separate. This is one example in accounting of the **economic entity concept,** which requires that a single, identifiable unit of organization be accounted for in all situations. For example, assume that Bernie Berg owns a neighborhood grocery store. In paying the monthly bills, such as utilities and supplies, Bernie must separate his personal costs from the costs associated with the grocery business. In turn, financial statements prepared for the business must not intermingle Bernie's personal affairs with the affairs of the company.

Unlike the distinction made for accounting purposes between an individual's personal and business affairs, the IRS does not recognize the separate existance of a proprietorship from its owner. That is, a sole proprietorship is not a taxable entity; any profits earned by the business are taxed on the return of the individual.

PARTNERSHIP
A business owned by two or more individuals; organizational form often used by accounting firms and law firms.

Partnerships

A **partnership** is a business owned by two or more individuals. Ben & Jerry's began as a partnership. When the two partners started selling ice cream, they needed some sort of agreement as to how much each would contribute to the business and how they would divide any profits. In many small partnerships, the agreement is often just an oral understanding between the partners. In large businesses, the partnership agreement is formalized in a written document.

Although Ben & Jerry's involved just two owners, some partnerships have thousands of partners. Public accounting firms, law firms, and other types of service companies are often organized as partnerships. Like a sole proprietorship, a partnership is not a taxable entity. The individual partners pay taxes on their proportionate shares of the profits of the business.

CORPORATION
A form of entity organized under the laws of a particular state; ownership evidenced by shares of stock.

SHARE OF STOCK
A certificate that acts as ownership in a corporation.

Corporations

Although sole proprietorships and partnerships dominate in sheer number, corporations control an overwhelming majority of the private resources in this country. A **corporation** is an entity organized under the laws of a particular state. Each of the 50 states is empowered to regulate the creation and operation of businesses organized as corporations in it.

To start a corporation, one must file articles of incorporation with the state. If the articles are approved by the state, a corporate charter is issued, and the corporation can begin to issue stock. A **share of stock** is a certificate that acts as evidence of ownership in a corporation. Although not always the case, stocks of many corporations are traded on organized stock exchanges, such as the New York and American Stock Exchanges.

What are the advantages of running a business as a corporation rather than a partnership? This was the question Ben and Jerry had to ask themselves. The company enjoyed early success in the market, and to capitalize on that success, it needed to grow. To grow meant that it would need a larger production facility, more equipment, and a larger staff. All of these things cost money. Where would the money come from?

BOND
A certificate that represents a corporation's promise to repay a certain amount of money and interest in the future.

One of the primary advantages of the corporate form of organization is the ability to raise large amounts of money in a relatively brief period of time. This is what prompted Ben & Jerry's to "go public" in 1984. To raise money, the company sold two different types of securities: stocks and bonds. As stated earlier, a share of stock is simply a certificate that evidences ownership in a corporation. A **bond** is similar in that it is a certificate or piece of paper issued to someone. However, it is different from a share of stock in that a bond represents a promise by the company to repay a certain amount of money at a future date. In other words, if you were to buy a bond from Ben & Jerry's, you would be lending it money. Interest on the bond is usually paid semiannually. We will have more to say about stocks and bonds when we discuss financing activities later.

The ease of transfer of ownership in a corporation is another advantage of this form of organization. If you hold shares of stock in a corporation whose stock is actively traded and you decide that you want out, you simply call your broker and put in an order to sell. Another distinct advantage is the limited liability of the stockholder. Generally speaking, a stockholder is liable only for the amount contributed to the business. That is, if a company goes out of business, the most the stockholder stands to lose is the amount invested. On the other hand, both proprietors and general partners usually can be held personally liable for the debts of the business.

Nonbusiness Entities

Most **nonbusiness entities** are organized for a purpose other than to earn a profit. They exist to serve the needs of various segments of society. For example, a hospital is organized to provide health care to its patients. A municipal government is operated for the benefit of its citizens. A local school district exists to meet the educational needs of the youth in the community.

Nonbusiness entity Organization operated for some purpose other than to earn a profit.

All these entities are distinguished by the lack of an identifiable owner. The lack of an identifiable owner and of the profit motive changes to some extent the type of accounting used by nonbusiness entities. This type, called *fund accounting,* is discussed in advanced accounting courses. Regardless of the lack of a profit motive in nonbusiness entities, there is still a demand for the information provided by an accounting system. For example, a local government needs detailed cost breakdowns in order to levy taxes. A hospital may want to borrow money and will need financial statements to present to the prospective lender.

Organizations and Social Responsibility

Although nonbusiness entities are organized specifically to serve members of society, U.S. business entities also have become more sensitive to their broader social responsibilities. Because they touch the lives of so many members of society, most large corporations recognize the societal aspects of their overall mission. For example, Ben & Jerry's statement of mission consists of three parts: a product mission, a social mission, and an economic mission. Its social mission is as follows:

> To operate the company in a way that actively recognizes the central role that business plays in the structure of society by initiating innovative ways to improve the quality of life of a broad community: local, national, & international.

Ben & Jerry's has done more than just pay lip service to its social mission. Each year it donates 7.5% of its pretax earnings to a foundation that in turn awards monies to charities (an initiative that Unilever intends to continue). In fact, many of the organizations that these charitable contributions support are highlighted in the 1998 annual report. Although not unique, Ben & Jerry's annual report is certainly unusual, in that it contains both a social performance report and a letter from the "social auditor" to the board of directors and the stakeholders. Included in the report are a number of interesting exhibits to highlight the company's progress in its quest to fulfill its social mission.

Most other large corporations have established programs to meet their social responsibilities. Some companies focus their efforts on local charities while others donate to national or international causes. Certainly all of the companies showcased in the chapter openers of this book have programs in place to meet their objectives in the area of corporate giving.

The Nature of Business Activity

LO 4 Describe the various types of business activity.

Because corporations dominate business activity in the United States, in this book we will focus on this form of organization. Corporations engage in a multitude of different types of activities. It is possible to categorize all of them into one of three types, however: financing, investing, and operating.

Financing Activities

All businesses must start with financing. Simply put, money is needed to start a business. Ben and Jerry needed $12,000 to start their business. They came up with $8,000 of their own funds and borrowed the other $4,000. As described earlier, the company found itself in need of additional financing in 1984 when it started construction on the new manufacturing plant. At that point, it obtained approximately $2 million from the sale of bonds and another $700,000 from the sale of stock to citizens of Vermont. In 1985 the company continued to look for sources of financing. For the first time, it issued stock to investors outside the state of Vermont and raised more than $5 million. The company borrowed approximately $15 million in each of the years 1993 and 1994 on a long-term basis.

Liability
An obligation of a business.

As you will see throughout this book, accounting has its own unique terminology. In fact, accounting is often referred to as *the language of business.* The discussion of financing activities brings up two important accounting terms: liabilities and capital stock. A **liability** is an obligation of a business; it can take many different forms. When a company borrows money at a bank, the liability is called a *note payable* When a company sells bonds, the obligation is termed *bonds payable.* Amounts owed to the government for taxes are called *taxes payable.* Ben & Jerry's happens to buy the milk it needs to produce ice cream from the St. Albans Cooperative Creamery. Assume that St. Albans gives the company 30 days to pay for purchases. During this 30-day period, Ben & Jerry's has an obligation called *accounts payable.*

Capital stock
A category on the balance sheet to indicate the owners' contributions to a corporation.

Stockholder
One of the owners of a corporation. Also called a *shareholder.*

Creditor
Someone to whom a company or person has a debt.

Capital stock is the term used by accountants to indicate the dollar amount of stock sold to the public. Capital stock differs from liabilities in one very important respect. Those who buy stock in a corporation are not lending money to the business, as are those who buy bonds in the company or make a loan in some other form to the company. Someone who buys stock in a company is called a **stockholder,** and that person is providing a *permanent* form of financing to the business. In other words, there is not a due date at which time the stockholder will be repaid. Normally, the only way for a stockholder to get back his or her original investment from buying stock is to sell it to someone else. Occasionally, a corporation buys back the stock of one of its stockholders. Someone who buys bonds in a company or in some other way makes a loan to it is called a **creditor.** A creditor does *not* provide a permanent form of financing to the business. That is, the creditor expects repayment of the amount loaned and, in many instances, payment of interest for the use of the money as well.

Investing Activities

There is a natural progression in a business from financing activities to investing activities. That is, once funds are generated from creditors and stockholders, money is available to invest. Ben & Jerry's used the cash obtained from selling stock and bonds to build its manufacturing plant and to add to its equipment, in particular its storage freezer.

Asset
A future economic benefit.

An **asset** is a future economic benefit to a business. For example, cash is an asset to a company. Ben & Jerry's buildings are assets to it, as are its storage freezers and its other equipment. At any point in time, Ben & Jerry's has a supply of ice cream awaiting sale, as well as supplies of raw materials such as milk and other ingredients to be used in the production of ice cream. The finished products and the raw materials are called *inventory* and are another valuable asset of a company.

inventories + plant + equipment are tangible assets.

patent - is an asset because it provides future economic benefits.

An asset represents the right to receive some sort of benefit in the future. The point is that not all assets are tangible in nature, as are inventories and plant and equipment. For example, assume that Ben & Jerry's sells ice cream to one of its distributors and allows this customer to pay for its purchase at the end of 30 days. At the time of the sale, Ben & Jerry's doesn't have cash yet, but it has another valuable asset. The right to collect the amount due from the customer in 30 days is an asset called an *account receivable.* As a second example, assume that a company acquires from an inventor a patent that will allow the company the exclusive right to manufacture a certain product. The right to the future economic benefits from the patent is an asset. In summary, an asset is a valuable resource to the company that controls it.

At this point, you should notice the inherent tie between assets and liabilities. How does a company satisfy its liabilities, that is, its obligations? Although there are some exceptions, most liabilities are settled by transferring assets. The asset most often used to settle a liability is cash.

Operating Activities

Once funds are obtained from financing and investments are made in productive assets, a business is ready to begin operations. Every business is organized with a purpose in mind. The purpose of some businesses is to sell a *product.* Ben and Jerry organized their company to sell ice cream. Other companies provide *services.* Service-oriented businesses are becoming an increasingly important sector of the U.S. economy. Some of the largest corporations in this country, such as banks and airlines, sell services rather than products. Some companies sell both products and services.

Accountants have a name for the sale of products and services. **Revenue** is the inflow of assets resulting from the sale of products and services. When a company makes a cash sale, the asset it receives is cash. When a sale is made on credit, the asset received is an account receivable. For now, you should understand that revenue represents the dollar amount of sales of products and services for a specific period of time.

REVENUE
Inflow of assets resulting from the sale of goods and services.

-when a sale is made on credit, the asset received is accounts receivable.
-when a company makes a cash sale, they receive cash as their asset.

We have thus far identified one important operating activity: the sale of products and services. However, costs must be incurred to operate a business. Employees must be paid salaries and wages. Suppliers must be paid for purchases of inventory, and the utility company has to be paid for heat and electricity. The government must be paid the taxes owed it. All of these are examples of important operating activities of a business. As you might expect by now, accountants use a specific name for the costs incurred in operating a business. An **expense** is the outflow of assets resulting from the sale of goods and services.

EXPENSE
Outflow of assets resulting from the sale of goods and services.

> examples of operating activities.

Exhibit GS-3 summarizes the three types of activities conducted by a business. Our discussion and the exhibit present a simplification of business activity, but actual businesses are in a constant state of motion with many different financing, investing, and operating activities going on at any one time. The model as portrayed in Exhibit GS-3 should be

EXHIBIT GS-3 A Model of Business Activities

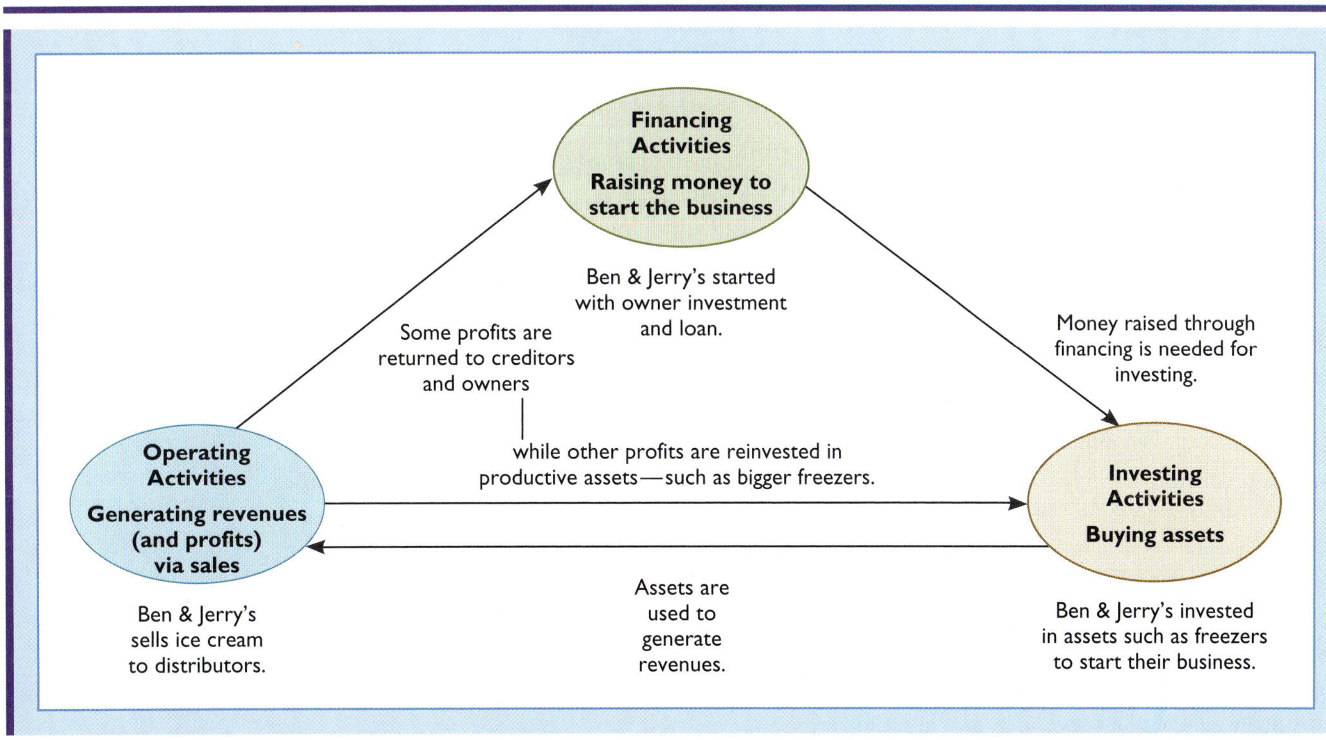

helpful as you begin the study of accounting, however. To summarize, a company obtains money from various types of financing activities, uses the money raised to invest in productive assets, and then provides goods and services to its customers.

Starting the Study of Accounting

The purpose of this module was to introduce you to business and help you to understand why it is the foundation on which accounting is based. Now that you have a basic understanding of what business is, the types of organizations that engage in business, and the various activities they conduct, you are ready to begin the study of accounting itself.

This module introduced you to business and decision making by telling a brief story of how Ben & Jerry's got started. You will learn more about the company and its relationship to Unilever in Chapter 1. Beginning in Chapter 2, another new feature company will start off each chapter as a way of introducing the material in that chapter.

If you do not own stock in one of these companies, how can you get access to its financial statements and other information about it? One way is by calling or writing to the company's investor relations department. A much more efficient and timely approach to gathering this information, however, is to use the Internet. Nearly all major corporations, as well as many smaller ones, now post financial statements and other information on their Web sites. To help in your search, each chapter contains the URLs of the companies discussed there.

Key Terms Quiz

Note to the student: We conclude each chapter with a quiz on the key terms, which are in bold where they appear in the chapter. We have included a quiz for the numerous important terms introduced in this getting started module.

Read each definition below and then write the number of that definition in the blank beside the appropriate term it defines. The first one has been done for you. The solution appears at the end of this module. When reviewing terminology, come back to your completed key terms quiz. Study tip: Also check the glossary in the margin or at the end of the book.

___ Business
___ Sole proprietorship
___ Partnership
___ Share of stock
___ Nonbusiness entity
___ Capital stock
___ Creditor
___ Revenue
___ Business entity
___ Economic entity concept
___ Corporation
___ Bond
___ Liability
___ Stockholder
_1_ Asset
___ Expense

1. **A future economic benefit.**
2. A business owned by two or more individuals; organization form often used by accounting firms and law firms.
3. An inflow of assets resulting from the sale of goods and services.
4. A form of entity organized under the laws of a particular state; ownership evidenced by shares of stock.
5. Organization operated for some purpose other than to earn a profit.
6. An outflow of assets resulting from the sale of goods and services.
7. An obligation of a business.
8. A certificate that acts as ownership in a corporation.
9. A certificate that represents a corporation's promise to repay a certain amount of money and interest in the future.
10. One of the owners of a corporation.
11. Someone to whom a company or person has a debt.
12. The assumption that a single, identifiable unit must be accounted for in all situations.
13. Form of organization with a single owner.
14. A category on the balance sheet to indicate the owners' contributions to a corporation.
15. All the activities necessary to provide the members of an economic system with goods and services.
16. Organization operated to earn a profit.

Questions

1. What is business about? What do all businesses have in common?
2. What is an asset? Give three examples.
3. What is a liability? How does the definition of *liability* relate to the definition of *asset*?
4. Business entities are organized as one of three distinct forms. What are these three forms?
5. What are the three distinct types of bus companies engage? Assume you start yoı bicycles in the summer and skiis in the wı... of at least one of each of the three types of business a. which you would engage.

Solutions to Key Terms Quiz

15 Business (p. GS2)	16 Business entity (p. GS4)
13 Sole proprietorship (p. GS4)	12 Economic entity concept (p. GS4)
2 Partnership (p. GS4)	4 corporation (p. GS4)
8 Share of stock (p. GS4)	9 Bond (p. GS4)
5 Nonbusiness entity (p. GS5)	7 Liability (p. GS6)
14 Capital stock (p. GS6)	10 Stockholder (p. GS6)
11 Creditor (p. GS6)	1 Asset (p. GS6)
3 Revenue (p. GS7)	6 Expense (p. GS7)

Third Edition

Financial Accounting

The Impact on Decision Makers

Part I

The Accounting Model

A Word to Students about this Course

Knowing accounting is just smart for everyone in today's job market. Thus this book is not just for accounting majors—it's for anyone who wants to learn how to read and understand financial information. You'll manipulate numbers in this course. But at every turn, this book and its study aids—not to mention your instructor—will walk you through the details. You'll write some memorandums backing up your calculations, pitting your analytical skills against real financial statements and problems. And you'll have the chance to put yourself in different business roles. **In fact, this book will help you think, talk, and write skillfully about accounting information.**

Chapter 1
Accounting as a Form of Communication

Chapter 2
Financial Statements and the Annual Report

Chapter 3
Processing Accounting Information

Chapter 4
Income Measurement and Accrual Accounting

Appendix 4A
Accounting Tools: Work Sheets

Chapter 1

Accounting as a Form of Communication

Study Links

A Look at This Chapter

We begin the study of accounting by considering what accounting is and who uses the information it provides. We will see that accounting is an important form of communication and that financial statements are the medium that accountants use to communicate with those who in some way have an interest in the financial affairs of a company.

A Look at Upcoming Chapters

Chapter 1 introduces you to accounting and financial statements. In Chapter 2, we look in more detail at the composition of each of the statements and the conceptual framework that supports the work of the accountant. Chapter 3 steps back from financial statements, the end result, and examines how companies process economic events as a basis for preparing the statements. Chapter 4 completes our introduction to the accounting model by considering the importance of accrual accounting in this communication process.

Focus on Financial Results

Who cares about the financial performance of Ben & Jerry's Homemade? Since its founding over 20 years ago, the company's managers, investors, employees, franchisees, and suppliers have all had a vested interest in the financial health of the company with the wild ice cream flavors.

On April 12, 2000, it was announced that UNILEVER, the Anglo-Dutch consumer-product conglomerate, and Ben & Jerry's had reached an agreement in which Unilever would pay approximately $326 million to acquire Ben & Jerry's. According to the announcement, which appeared on Ben & Jerry's Web site and subsequently in the financial news, each shareholder was entitled to receive $43.60 for every share owned.

To communicate its financial performance, Ben & Jerry's uses the language of accounting. The selected financial data shown here summarizes key measures, including sales, income, assets, and debt. This information shows that the company's sales rose over each of the five years reported. This growth pattern was presumably a factor in Unilever's decision to announce a purchase of the company. During its first 20 years, the Vermont-based Ben & Jerry's focused most of its attention on selling ice cream in the U.S. Unilever—already the world's largest ice cream maker through such brands as Breyer's and Good Humor—saw an acquisition of Ben & Jerry's as a way to expand globally into the superpremium ice cream market.

What will be the future of Ben & Jerry's? While its financial performance can only be conjectured, it can be assumed that Ben & Jerry's will continue its high-profile social causes. For example, according to news reports, Unilever will contribute a percentage of Ben & Jerry's pretax profits to charity and it will continue to buy milk from Vermont dairy farmers.

Selected Financial Data

Cost also ro[...] during th[...]

Company sales rose from 1994 to 1998.

The following table contains selected financial information for the Company's fiscal years 1994 through 1998.

(In thousands except per share data) **Summary of Operations**	**Fiscal Year** 1998	1997	1996	1995	1994
Net sales	$ 209,203	$ 174,206	$ 167,155	$ 155,333	$ 148,802
Cost of sales	136,225	114,284	115,212	109,125	109,760
Gross profit	72,978	59,922	51,943	46,208	39,042
Selling, general & administrative expenses	63,895	53,520	45,531	36,362	36,253
Asset write-down[1]					6,779
Other income (expense) – net	693	(118)	(77)	(441)	228
Income (loss) before income taxes	9,776	6,284	6,335	9,405	(3,762)
Income taxes	3,534	2,388	2,409	3,457	(1,893)
Net income (loss)	6,242	3,896	3,926	5,948	(1,869)
Net income (loss) per share – diluted	$ 0.84	$ 0.53	$ 0.54	$ 0.82	$ (0.26)
Shares outstanding – diluted	7,463	7,334	7,230	7,222	7,148

Balance Sheet Data	**Fiscal Year** 1998	1997	1996	1995	1994
Working capital	$ 48,381	$ 51,412	$ 50,055	$ 51,023	$ 37,456
Total assets	149,501	146,471	136,665	131,074	120,296
Long-term debt and capital lease obligations	20,491	25,676	31,087	31,977	32,419
Stockholders' equity[2]	90,908	86,919	82,685	78,531	72,502

[1] Write-down of assets – In 1994, the Company replaced certain of the software and equipment installed at the plant in St. Albans, Vermont. The loss from the write-down of the related assets included a portion of the previously capitalized interest and project management costs.

[2] No cash dividends have been declared or paid by the Company on its capital stock since the Company's organization. The Company intends to reinvest earnings for use in its business and to finance future growth. Accordingly, the Board of Directors does not anticipate declaring any cash dividends in the foreseeable future.

Ben & Jerry's 1998 Annual Report

If you were considering a marketing job with Ben & Jerry's, how would your decision be affected by such an announcement? Have the company's sales continued to rise? If so, at a slower or faster pace than in the previous five years? Use this chapter and the succeeding ones to help you better understand the financial performance of Ben & Jerry's.

www.benjerry.com

G Objectives

his chapter, you should be able to:

the primary users of accounting infor-mation and their needs. (p. 6)

LO 2 Explain the purpose of each of the financial statements and the relationships among them and prepare a set of simple statements. (p. 8)

LO 3 Identify and explain the primary assumptions made in preparing financial statements. (p. 14)

LO 4 Describe the various roles of accountants in organizations. (p. 16)

What Is Accounting?

Accounting
The process of identifying, measuring, and communicating economic information to various users.

Many people have preconceived notions about what accounting is. They think of it as a highly procedural activity practiced by people who are "good in math." This notion of accounting is very narrow and focuses only on the record-keeping or bookkeeping aspects of the discipline. Accounting is in fact much broader than this in its scope. Specifically, **accounting** is "the process of identifying, measuring, and communicating economic information to permit informed judgments and decisions by users of the information.[1]

Each of the three activities in this definition—*identifying, measuring,* and *communicating*—requires the judgment of a trained professional. We will return later in this chapter to acccounting as a profession and the various roles of accountants in our society. Note that the definition refers to the users of economic information and the decisions they make. Who *are* the users of accounting information? We turn now to this important question.

Users of Accounting Information and Their Needs

LO 1 Identify the primary users of accounting information and their needs.

who are the users in accounting?

It is helpful to categorize users of accounting information on the basis of their relationship to the organization. Internal users, primarily the managers of a company, are involved in the daily affairs of the business. All other groups are external users.

Internal Users

Management accounting
The branch of accounting concerned with providing management with information to facilitate planning and control.

The management of a company is in a position to obtain financial information in a way that best suits its needs. For example, if a production manager at Ben & Jerry's needs to know how much it costs to produce a pint of Chubby Hubby ice cream, this information exists in the accounting system and can be reported. If a department supervisor wants to find out if monthly expenditures are more or less than the budgeted amount, a report can be generated to provide the answer. **Management accounting** is the branch of accounting concerned with providing internal users (management) with information to facilitate planning and control. The ability to produce management accounting reports is limited only by the extent of the data available and the cost involved in generating the relevant information.

External Users

External users, those not involved directly in the operations of a business, need information that differs from that needed by internal users. In addition, the ability of external users to obtain the information is more limited. Without the day-to-day contact with the

[1]American Accounting Association, *A Statement of Basic Accounting Theory* (Evanston, Ill.: American Accounting Association, 1966), p. 1.

affairs of the business, outsiders must rely on the information presented to them by the management of the company.

Certain external users, such as the Internal Revenue Service, require that information be presented in a very specific manner, and they have the authority of the law to ensure that they get the required information. Stockholders, bondholders, and other creditors must rely on *financial statements* for their information.[2] **Financial accounting** is the branch of accounting concerned with communication with outsiders through financial statements.

FINANCIAL ACCOUNTING The branch of accounting concerned with the preparation of financial statements for outsider use.

Stockholders and Potential Stockholders Both existing and potential stockholders need financial information about a business. If you currently own stock in a company, you need information that will aid in your decision either to continue to hold the stock or to sell it. If you are considering buying stock in a company, you need financial information that will help in choosing among competing alternative investments. What has been the recent performance of the company in the stock market? What were its profits for the most recent year? How do these profits compare with those of the prior year? How much did the company pay in dividends? One source for much of this information is the company's financial statements.

BUSINESS STRATEGY

Satisfying the Customer vs. Satisfying the Shareholders

Ben & Jerry's, like any other company, works hard to boost the sales of its products and lower the costs of making those products. One of the primary costs for an ice cream producer like Ben & Jerry's is for milk. Faced with rising dairy prices, Ben & Jerry's made the decision for 1998 to pass on a portion of those dairy costs to consumers in the form of higher prices for its products.

Companies often have the choice of paying more for materials and maintaining the same prices—or raising prices to allow the consumer to pay some or all of the higher costs. Either way, the company management is taking a calculated risk. To simplify the issue, if they absorb the costs, they may be eroding their own profits in order to hold on to their customers; if they pass on the costs, they may be maintaining their profits—until customers decide to buy a less expensive brand of ice cream and sales begin to fall.

Ben & Jerry's, in the Management's Discussion and Analysis section of its 1998 annual report, says that there is no guarantee that it will continue to raise its prices to offset further rises in costs. In effect, Ben & Jerry's is warning its shareholders and investors, "Gross profit may fall if we choose to keep prices in line." (Gross profit is the third line on the summary of operations, right under cost of sales.)

You'll learn more about the relationship between sales, costs, and profits later in the book.

Bondholders, Bankers, and Other Creditors Before buying a bond in a company (remember you are lending money to the company), you need to feel comfortable that the company will be able to pay you the amount owed at maturity and the periodic interest payments. Financial statements can help you to decide whether to purchase a bond. Similarly, before lending money, a bank needs information that will help it to determine the company's ability to repay both the amount of the loan and interest. Therefore, a set of financial statements is a key ingredient in a loan proposal.

Government Agencies Numerous government agencies have information needs specified by law. For example, the Internal Revenue Service (IRS) is empowered to collect a

www.irs.gov

[2]Technically, stockholders are insiders because they own stock in the business. In most large corporations, however, it is not practical for stockholders to be involved in the daily affairs of the business. Thus, they are better categorized here as external users because they normally rely on general-purpose financial statements, as do creditors.

EXHIBIT 1-1 Users of Accounting Information

Categories of Users	Examples of Users	Common Decision	Relevant Question
Internal	Management	Should we introduce a new flavor of ice cream?	What will be the cost to produce a pint of this new flavor?
External	Stockholder	Should I buy shares of Ben & Jerry's stock?	How much did the company earn last year?
	Banker	Should I lend money to Ben & Jerry's?	What existing debts or liabilities does the company have?
	Employee	Should I ask for a raise?	How much is the company earning in sales, and how much is it paying out in salaries and wages? Is it paying out too much in compensation compared to its sales?
	Supplier	Should I allow Ben & Jerry's to buy milk from me and pay me later?	What is the current amount of the company's accounts payable?

www.sec.gov

tax on income from both individuals and corporations. Every year a company prepares a tax return to report to the IRS the amount of income it earned. Another government agency, the Securities and Exchange Commission (SEC), was created in the aftermath of the Great Depression. This regulatory agency sets the rules under which financial statements must be prepared for corporations that sell their stock to the public on organized stock exchanges. Similar to the IRS, the SEC prescribes the manner in which financial information is presented to it. Companies operating in specialized industries submit financial reports to other regulatory agencies, such as the Interstate Commerce Commission and the Federal Trade Commission.

Other External Users Many other individuals and groups rely on financial information given to them by businesses. A supplier of raw material needs to know the credit-worthiness of a company before selling it a product on credit. To promote its industry, a trade association must gather financial information on the various companies in the industry. Other important users are stockbrokers and financial analysts. They use financial reports in advising their clients on investment decisions. In reaching their decisions, all of these users rely to a large extent on accounting information provided by management. Exhibit 1-1 summarizes the various users of financial information and the types of decisions they must make.

FINANCIAL STATEMENTS: HOW ACCOUNTANTS COMMUNICATE

LO 2 Explain the purpose of each of the financial statements and the relationships among them and prepare a set of simple statements.

The primary focus of this book is financial accounting. This branch of accounting is concerned with informing management and outsiders about a company through financial statements. We turn our attention now to the composition of three of the major statements: the balance sheet, the income statement, and the statement of retained earnings.[3]

THE ACCOUNTING EQUATION AND THE BALANCE SHEET

The *accounting equation* is the foundation for the entire accounting system:

Assets = Liabilities + Owners' Equity

[3]The fourth major financial statement is the statement of cash flows. This important statement will be introduced in Chapter 2.

The left side of the accounting equation refers to the *assets* of the company. Those items that are valuable economic resources and will provide future benefit to it should appear on the left side of the equation. The right side of the equation indicates who provided, or has a claim to, those assets. Some of the assets were provided by creditors, and they have a claim to them. For example, if a company has a delivery truck, the dealer that provided the truck to the company has a claim to the assets until the dealer is paid. The delivery truck would appear on the left side of the equation as an asset to the company; the company's *liability* to the dealer would appear on the right side of the equation. Other assets are provided by the owners of the business. Their claim to these assets is represented by the portion of the right side of the equation called **owners' equity.**

The term *stockholders' equity* is used to refer to the owners' equity of a corporation. **Stockholders' equity** is the mathematical difference between a corporation's assets and its obligations or liabilities. That is, after the amounts owed to bondholders, banks, suppliers, and other creditors are subtracted from the assets, the amount remaining is the stockholders' equity, the amount of interest or claim that the owners have on the assets of the business.

Stockholders' equity arises in two distinct ways. First, it is created when a company issues stock to an investor. As we noted earlier, capital stock reflects ownership in a corporation in the form of a certificate. It represents the amounts contributed by the owners to the company. Second, as owners of shares in a corporation, stockholders have a claim on the assets of a business when it is profitable. **Retained earnings** represents the owners' claims to the company's assets that result from its earnings that have not been paid out in dividends. It is the earnings accumulated or retained by the company.

The **balance sheet** (sometimes called the *statement of financial position*) is the financial statement that summarizes the assets, liabilities, and owners' equity of a company. It is a "snapshot" of the business at a certain date. A balance sheet can be prepared on any day of the year, although it is most commonly prepared on the last day of a month, quarter, or year. At any point in time, the balance sheet must be "in balance." That is, assets must equal liabilities and owners' equity.

Balance sheets for Ben & Jerry's at the end of two recent years are shown in Exhibit 1-2. As the exhibit makes clear, there are the three main sections of the balance sheet corresponding to the three elements of the accounting equation: Assets, Liabilities, and Stockholders' Equity.

In the following table, note some of the main types of items that appear on the balance sheet:

1. Cash and Cash Equivalents: Includes cash on hand as well as cash in various checking and savings accounts
2. Trade Accounts Receivable: Arises from selling ice cream to distributors and allowing them to pay later
3. Inventories: Refers to the ice cream and related products that the company sells
4. Property, Plant, and Equipment: Includes buildings, production lines, and storage freezers
5. Accounts Payable and Accrued Expenses: Arises from buying supplies and other items and being allowed to pay later
6. Retained Earnings: Amount of income earned over life of the company (Ben & Jerry's has never paid dividends)

Exhibit 1-3 summarizes the relationship between the accounting equation and the items that appear on a balance sheet.

THE INCOME STATEMENT

An **income statement,** or statement of income, as it is sometimes called, summarizes the revenues and expenses of a company for a period of time. Comparative income

Study Tip

The accounting equation and the financial statements are at the heart of this course. Memorize the accounting equation, and make sure you study this introduction to how the financial statements should look, how to read them, and what they say about a company.

OWNERS' EQUITY
The owners' claim on the assets of an entity.

STOCKHOLDERS' EQUITY
The owners' equity in a corporation.

RETAINED EARNINGS
The part of owners' equity that represents the income earned less dividends paid over the life of an entity.

BALANCE SHEET
The financial statement that summarizes the assets, liabilities, and owners' equity at a specific point in time.

www.benjerry.com

Companies like Ben & Jerry's have responded to the call by consumers as well as users of financial information to provide company information online. This is a portion of Ben & Jerry's financial information page at its Web site.

INCOME STATEMENT
A statement that summarizes revenues and expenses.

EXHIBIT 1-2 Ben & Jerry's Balance Sheets

Consolidated Balance Sheets

(In thousands except share amounts)

	Assets	A = L + SE	December 26, 1998	December 27, 1997
	Current assets:	A		
1	Cash and cash equivalents		$ 25,111	$ 47,318
	Short-term investments		22,118	481
2	Trade accounts receivable (less allowance of $979 in 1998 and $1,066 in 1997 for doubtful accounts)		11,338	12,710
3	Inventories		13,090	11,122
	Deferred income taxes		7,547	6,071
	Prepaid expenses and other current assets		3,105	2,378
	Total current assets		82,309	80,080
4	Property, plant and equipment, net		63,451	62,724
	Investments		303	1,061
	Other assets		3,438	2,606
			$ 149,501	$ 146,471
	Liabilities and Stockholders' Equity	=		
	Current liabilities:	L		
5	Accounts payable and accrued expenses		$ 28,662	$ 23,266
	Current portion of long-term debt and obligations under capital leases		5,266	5,402
	Total current liabilities		33,928	28,668
	Long-term debt and obligations under capital leases		20,491	25,676
	Deferred income taxes		4,174	5,208
		+		
	Stockholders' equity:	SE		
	$1.20 noncumulative Class A preferred stock – par value $1.00 per share, redeemable at $12.00 per share; 900 shares authorized, issued and outstanding; aggregated preference on liquidation – $9,000		1	1
	Class A common stock – $.033 par value; authorized 20,000,000 shares; issued: 6,592,392 at December 26, 1998 and 6,494,835 at December 27, 1997		218	214
	Class B common stock – $.033 par value; authorized 3,000,000 shares; issued: 824,480 at December 26, 1998 and 866,235 at December 27, 1997		27	29
	Additional paid-in-capital		50,556	49,681
6	Retained earnings		45,328	39,086
	Accumulated other comprehensive loss		(151)	(129)
	Treasury stock, at cost: 291,032 Class A and 1,092 Class B shares at December 26, 1998 and 124,532 Class A and 1,092 Class B shares at December 27, 1997		(5,071)	(1,963)
	Total stockholders' equity		90,908	86,919
			$ 149,501	$ 146,471

See notes to consolidated financial statements.

EXHIBIT 1-3 The Relationship between the Accounting Equation and the Balance Sheet

Assets	=	Liabilities	+	Owners' Equity
Economic resources Examples: • Cash • Accounts receivable • Inventory		**Creditors' claims to the assets** Examples: • Accounts payable • Notes payable		**Owners' claims to the assets** Examples: • Capital stock • Retained earnings

Exhibit 1-3 refers to Owners' Equity while Exhibit 1-2 refers to Stockholders' Equity. Remember, both are correct! "Owners' equity" is the general term by which we refer to ownership. "Stockholders' equity" refers only to ownership of a corporation by shareholders.

statements for Ben & Jerry's for three recent years are shown in Exhibit 1-4. Note that Ben & Jerry's uses the title *statements of operations* as an alternative to *income statements.* Unlike the balance sheet, an income statement is a *flow* statement. That is, it summarizes the flow of revenues and expenses for the year. As was the case for the balance sheet, you are not expected at this point to understand fully all of the complexities involved in preparing an income statement. However, note the two largest items on the income statement: Net Sales and Cost of Sales. For now, it is sufficient to understand that Net Sales is Ben & Jerry's primary source of revenue and Cost of Sales is its most significant expense.

From Concept **TO PRACTICE 1.1**

READING GATEWAY'S INCOME STATEMENT Now that you've seen Ben & Jerry's income statement, turn to the end of the book to Gateway's income statement. Note the large amount of Cost of Sales—$5,921,651—on Gateway's 1998 income statement (consolidated income statement). What types of costs would fall into the Cost of Sales category for Gateway?

THE STATEMENT OF RETAINED EARNINGS

As discussed earlier, Retained Earnings represents the accumulated earnings of a corporation less the amount paid in dividends to stockholders. **Dividends** are distributions of the net income or profits of a business to its stockholders. Not all businesses pay cash dividends. Ben & Jerry's rationale for not paying dividends to stockholders is stated in its annual report:

> No cash dividends have been declared or paid by the Company on its capital stock since the company's organization. *The Company intends to reinvest earnings for use in its business and to finance future growth* [emphasis added]. Accordingly, the Board of Directors does not anticipate declaring any cash dividends in the foreseeable future.

DIVIDENDS
A distribution of the net income of a business to its owners.

A **statement of retained earnings** explains the change in retained earnings during the period. The basic format for the statement is as follows:

STATEMENT OF RETAINED EARNINGS
The statement that summarizes the income earned and dividends paid over the life of a business.

Beginning balance	$xxx,xxx
Add: Net income for the period	xxx,xxx
Deduct: Dividends for the period	xxx,xxx
Ending balance	$xxx,xxx

Revenues minus expenses, or net income, is an increase in retained earnings, and dividends are a decrease in the balance. Why are dividends shown on a statement of retained earnings instead of on an income statement? Dividends are not an expense and thus are *not a component of* net income, as are expenses. Instead, they are a *distribution of* the income of the business to its stockholders.

EXHIBIT 1-4 Ben & Jerry's Income Statements

Consolidated Statements of Operations

(In thousands except share amounts)

	December 26, 1998	Fiscal Year Ended December 27, 1997	December 28, 1996
Net sales	$ 209,203	$ 174,206	$ 167,155
Cost of sales	136,225	114,284	115,212
Gross profit	72,978	59,922	51,943
Selling, general and administrative expenses	63,895	53,520	45,531
Other income (expense):			
Interest income	2,248	1,938	1,676
Interest expense	(1,888)	(1,992)	(1,996)
Other income (expense), net	333	(64)	243
	693	(118)	(77)
Income before income taxes	9,776	6,284	6,335
Income taxes	3,534	2,388	2,409
Net income	$ 6,242	$ 3,896	$ 3,926
Shares used to compute net income per common share			
Basic	7,197	7,247	7,189
Diluted	7,463	7,334	7,230
Net income per common share			
Basic	$ 0.87	$ 0.54	$ 0.55
Diluted	$ 0.84	$ 0.53	$ 0.54

See notes to consolidated financial statements.

Ben & Jerry's primary source of revenue

Ben & Jerry's most significant expense

Recall that stockholders' equity consists of two parts: capital stock and retained earnings. In lieu of a separate statement of retained earnings, many corporations prepare a comprehensive statement to explain the changes both in the various capital stock accounts and in retained earnings during the period. Ben & Jerry's, for example, presents the more comprehensive statement of stockholders' equity. (It is not shown here, but you will find it in the printed annual report or online with Ben & Jerry's other financial statements.) Because Ben & Jerry's does not pay dividends, the only activity reported in the Retained Earnings column of its statement of stockholders' equity is net income.

ACCOUNTING FOR YOUR DECISIONS

You Are a Potential Stockholder

You are deciding whether to invest in a company's stock. Which financial statement would you want to see, and which areas would you be most interested in?

ANS: All of them. The balance sheet will show the relative size of the assets and liabilities, and the stockholders' equity section should state how many shares of stock have been sold (outstanding shares) and how many more are available (authorized but not yet issued). The income statement's net sales, gross profit, operating income, and net income are important, not only for the most current year but also for previous years to determine trends. The statement of retained earnings will report if dividends were paid and, if so, the amount.

EXHIBIT 1-5 Relationships among Financial Statements: Ben & Jerry's Example

INCOME STATEMENT FOR 1998

Revenues	$ xxx
Less: Expenses	xxx
Net income	**$ 6,242**

1

STATEMENT OF RETAINED EARNINGS FOR 1998

Beginning balance, retained earnings	$ 39,086
Add: Net income	**6,242**
Deduct: Cash dividends	0
Ending balance, retained earnings	**$ 45,328**

2

BALANCE SHEETS

	END OF	
	1997	**1998**
Total assets	$ xxx	$ xxx
Liabilities	$ xxx	$ xxx
Capital stock	xxx	xxx
Retained earnings	39,086	**45,328**
Total liabilities and stockholders' equity	$ xxx	$ xxx

RELATIONSHIPS AMONG BEN & JERRY'S FINANCIAL STATEMENTS

Because the statements of a company such as Ben & Jerry's are complex, it may not be easy at this point to see the important links among them. The relationships among the statements are summarized for you in Exhibit 1-5. Recall that in its annual report, Ben & Jerry's does not present a separate statement of retained earnings. The information for the statement of retained earnings in Exhibit 1-5 appears as one of the columns in Ben & Jerry's statement of stockholders' equity. Two important relationships are seen by examining the exhibit (NOTE: Here and throughout the book, the numbers that follow correspond to the highlighted numbers in the exhibit; numbers in this exhibit are stated in thousands of dollars):

1 The 1998 income statement reports net income of $6,242. Net income increases retained earnings, as reported on the statement of retained earnings.

2 The ending balance of $45,328 in retained earnings, as reported on the statement of retained earnings for 1998, is transferred to the balance sheet at the end of 1998.

Two-Minute Review

1. *State the accounting equation, and indicate what each term means.*
2. *What are the three financial statements presented in this chapter?*
3. *How do amounts in the three statements interrelate?*

Answers on next page.

Answers:

1. Assets = Liabilities + Owners' Equity
Assets are economic resources. Liabilities are creditors' claims against assets. Owners' Equity is owners' claims against assets. See Exhibit 1-3.

2. The three financial statements are the balance sheet, the income statement, and the statement of retained earnings.

3. Net income on the income statement increases retained earnings on the statement of retained earnings. The ending balance in retained earnings is transferred to the balance sheet. See Exhibit 1-5.

THE CONCEPTUAL FRAMEWORK: FOUNDATION FOR FINANCIAL STATEMENTS

LO 3 Identify and explain the primary assumptions made in preparing financial statements.

Study Tip

The concepts in this section underlie everything you will learn throughout the course. You'll encounter them later in the context of specific topics.

Many people perceive the work of an accountant as being routine. In reality, accounting is anything but routine and requires a great deal of judgment on the part of the accountant. The record-keeping aspect of accounting—what we normally think of as bookkeeping—is the routine part of the accountant's work and only a small part of it. Most of the job deals with communicating relevant information to financial statement users.

The accounting profession has developed a *conceptual framework for accounting* that aids accountants in their role as interpreters and communicators of relevant information. The purpose of the framework is to act as a foundation for the specific principles and standards needed by the profession. An important part of the conceptual framework is a set of assumptions accountants make in preparing financial statements. We will briefly consider these assumptions, returning to a more detailed discussion of them in later chapters.

The *economic entity concept* was introduced in "Getting Started" when we first discussed different types of business entities. This assumption requires that an identifiable, specific entity be the subject of a set of financial statements. For example, even though Ben Cohen and Jerry Greenfield are stockholders and therefore own part of Ben & Jerry's, their personal affairs must be kept separate from the business affairs. When we look at a balance sheet for the ice cream business, we need assurance that it shows the financial position of that entity only and does not intermingle the personal assets and liabilities of Ben, Jerry, or any of the other stockholders.

COST PRINCIPLE
Assets recorded at the cost to acquire them.

The **cost principle** requires that accountants record assets at the cost paid to acquire them and continue to show this amount on all balance sheets until the company disposes of them. With a few exceptions, companies do not carry assets at their market value (how much they could sell the asset for today) but at original cost. Accountants use the term *historical cost* to refer to the original cost of an asset. Why not show an asset such as land at market value? The *subjectivity* inherent in determining market values supports the practice of carrying assets at their historical cost. The cost of an asset is verifiable by an independent observer and is much more *objective* than market value.

GOING CONCERN
The assumption that an entity is not in the process of liquidation and that it will continue indefinitely.

Accountants assume that the entity being accounted for is a **going concern.** That is, they assume that Ben & Jerry's is not in the process of liquidation and that it will continue indefinitely into the future. Another important reason for using historical cost rather than market value to report assets is the going concern assumption. If we assume that a business is *not* a going concern, then we assume that it is in the process of liquidation. If this is the case, market value might be more relevant than cost as a basis for recognizing the assets. But if we are able to assume that a business will continue indefinitely, cost can be more easily justified as a basis for valuation. The **monetary unit** used in preparing the statements of Ben & Jerry's was the dollar. The reason for using the dollar as the monetary unit is that it is the recognized medium of exchange in the United States. It provides a convenient yardstick to measure the position and earnings of the business. As a yardstick, however, the dollar, like the currencies of all other countries, is subject to instability. We are all well aware that a dollar will not buy as much today as it did 10 years ago.

MONETARY UNIT
The yardstick used to measure amounts in financial statements; the dollar in the United States.

Inflation is evidenced by a general rise in the level of prices in an economy. Its effect on the measuring unit used in preparing financial statements is an important concern to the accounting profession. Although accountants have experimented with financial statements adjusted for the changing value of the measuring unit, the financial statements now prepared by corporations are prepared under the assumption that the monetary unit is relatively stable. At various times in the past, this has been a reasonable assumption and at other times not so reasonable.

Under the **time period** assumption, accountants assume that it is possible to prepare an income statement that accurately reflects net income or earnings for a specific time period. In the case of Ben & Jerry's, this time period was one year. It is somewhat artificial to measure the earnings of a business for a period of time indicated on a calendar, whether it be a month, a quarter, or a year. Of course, the most accurate point in time to measure the earnings of a business would be at the end of its life. Accountants prepare periodic statements, however, because the users of the statements demand information about the entity on a regular basis.

TIME PERIOD
Artificial segment on the calendar, used as the basis for preparing financial statements.

Financial statements prepared by accountants must conform to **generally accepted accounting principles (GAAP).** This term refers to the various methods, rules, practices, and other procedures that have evolved over time in response to the need for some form of regulation over the preparation of financial statements. As changes have taken place in the business environment over time, GAAP have developed in response to these changes.

GENERALLY ACCEPTED ACCOUNTING PRINCIPLES (GAAP)
The various methods, rules, practices, and other procedures that have evolved over time in response to the need to regulate the preparation of financial statements.

ACCOUNTING AS A SOCIAL SCIENCE

Accounting is a service activity. As we have seen, its purpose is to provide financial information to decision makers. Thus, accounting is a *social* science. Accounting principles are much different from the rules that govern the *physical* sciences. For example, it is a rule of nature that an object dropped from your hand will eventually hit the ground rather than be suspended in air. There are no rules comparable to this in accounting. The principles that govern financial reporting are not governed by nature but instead develop in response to changing business conditions. For example, consider the lease of an office building. Leasing has developed in response to the need to have access to valuable assets, such as office space, without spending the large sum necessary to buy the asset. As leasing has increased in popularity, it has been left to the accounting profession to develop guidelines, some of which are quite complex, to be followed in accounting for leases. Those guidelines are now part of GAAP.

Two-Minute Review

1. Name the four concepts (other than the economic entity concept) in the conceptual framework presented in this section.

2. Give a brief example of each concept.

3. What is "GAAP"?

Answers:

1. Cost principle, going concern, monetary unit, and time period assumption.

2. Under the cost principle, we record assets at their cost rather than at market value. Example: Ben & Jerry's would record a new ice cream freezer at its purchase price. Under going concern, we assume that the company will continue existing indefinitely. Example: Ben & Jerry's will continue to operate rather than begin liquidating its assets. The monetary unit, such as the dollar, is the company's recognized medium of exchange. Example: Ben & Jerry's uses the dollar as the monetary unit. The time period assumption imposes, for reporting purposes, an arbitrary time period (such as a year) that is shorter than the company's life span. Example: Ben & Jerry's income statement is for the fiscal year ended December 26, 1998.

3. GAAP is the methods, rules, practices, and other procedures that have evolved to govern the preparation of financial statements.

Is this company a going concern?
One firm goes out of business; another thrives in the same location. The difference may lie in making the best decisions possible based on high-quality financial information.

Who Determines the Rules of the Game?

Securities and Exchange Commission (SEC) The federal agency with ultimate authority to determine the rules in preparing statements for companies whose stock is sold to the public.

www.sec.gov

Financial Accounting Standards Board (FASB) The group in the private sector with authority to set accounting standards.

www.fasb.org

American Institute of Certified Public Accountants (AICPA) The professional organization for certified public accountants.

www.aicpa.org

International Accounting Standards Committee (IASC) The organization formed to develop worldwide accounting standards.

www.iasc.org.uk

Who determines the rules to be followed in preparing an income statement or a balance sheet? No one group is totally responsible for setting the standards or principles to be followed in preparing financial statements. The process is a joint effort among the following groups.

The federal government, through the **Securities and Exchange Commission (SEC),** has the ultimate authority to determine the rules for preparing financial statements by companies whose securities are sold to the general public. However, for the most part the SEC has allowed the accounting profession to establish its own rules.

The **Financial Accounting Standards Board (FASB)** sets these accounting standards in the United States. A small independent group with a large staff, the board has issued more than 130 financial accounting standards, and six statements of financial accounting concepts, since its creation in the early 1970s. These standards deal with a variety of financial reporting issues, such as the proper accounting for lease arrangements and pension plans, and the concepts are used to guide the board in setting accounting standards.

The **American Institute of Certified Public Accountants (AICPA)** is the professional organization of certified public accountants. It advises the FASB, but actually sets the auditing standards to be followed by public accounting firms.

Finally, if you are considering buying stock in Porsche, the German-based car manufacturer, you'll want to be sure that the rules Porsche followed in preparing the statements are similar to those the FASB requires for U.S. companies. Unfortunately, accounting standards can differ considerably from one country to another. The **International Accounting Standards Committee (IASC)** was formed in 1973 to develop worldwide accounting standards. More than 100 organizations from 80 different countries, including the FASB in this country, participate in the IASC's efforts to develop international reporting standards. Although the group has made considerable progress, compliance with the standards of the IASC is strictly voluntary, and much work remains to be done in developing international accounting standards.

The Accounting Profession

LO 4 Describe the various roles of accountants in organizations.

Accountants play many different roles in society. Understanding the various roles will help you to appreciate more fully the importance of accounting in organizations.

Employment by Private Business

Many accountants work for business entities. Regardless of the types of activities companies engage in, accountants perform a number of important functions for them. A partial organization chart for a corporation is shown in Exhibit 1-6. The chart indicates that three individuals report directly to the chief financial officer: the controller, the treasurer, and the director of internal auditing.

Controller The chief accounting officer for a company.

The **controller** is the chief accounting officer for a company and typically has responsibility for the overall operation of the accounting system. Accountants working for the controller record the company's activities and prepare periodic financial statements. In this organization, the payroll function is assigned to the controller's office, as is responsibility for the preparation of budgets.

Treasurer The officer responsible in an organization for the safeguarding and efficient use of a company's liquid assets.

The **treasurer** of an organization is typically responsible for the safeguarding, as well as the efficient use, of the company's liquid resources, such as cash. Note that the director of the tax department in this corporation reports to the treasurer. Accountants in the tax department are responsible for both preparing the company's tax returns and planning transactions in such a way that the company pays the least amount of taxes possible within the laws of the Internal Revenue Code.

EXHIBIT 1-6 Partial Organization Chart

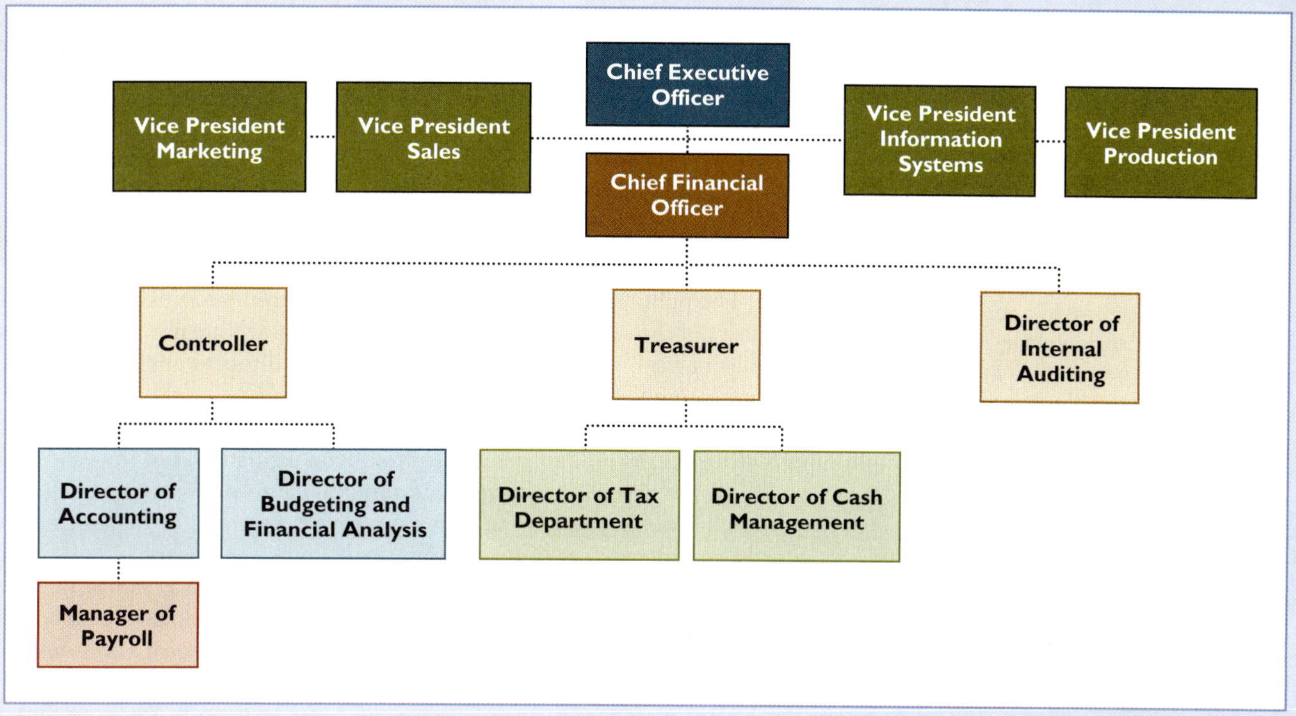

This partial organization chart does not show details of the other departments in the company—such as marketing, sales, production, and so on. That does not mean they are unimportant to the flow of accounting information. In fact, accounting information for internal decision making forms a complex system of reporting, responsibility, and control collectively known as management accounting.

Internal auditing is the department responsible in a company for the review and appraisal of accounting and administrative controls. The department must determine whether the company's assets are properly accounted for and protected from losses. Recommendations are made periodically to management for improvements in the various controls.

INTERNAL AUDITING
The department responsible in a company for the review and appraisal of its accounting and administrative controls.

EMPLOYMENT BY NONBUSINESS ENTITIES

Nonbusiness organizations, such as hospitals, universities, and various branches of the government, have as much need for accountants as do companies organized to earn a profit. Although the profit motive is not paramount to nonbusiness entities, all organizations must have financial information to operate efficiently. A county government needs detailed cost information in determining the taxes to levy on its constituents. A university must pay close attention to its various operating costs in setting the annual tuition rates. Accountants working for nonbusiness entities perform most of the same tasks as their counterparts in the business sector. In fact, many of the job titles in business entities, such as controller and treasurer, are also used by nonbusiness entities.

EMPLOYMENT IN PUBLIC ACCOUNTING

Public accounting firms provide valuable services in much the same way as do law firms or architectural firms. They provide a professional service for their clients in return for a fee. The usual services provided by public accounting firms include auditing and tax and management consulting services.

AUDITING
The process of examining the financial statements and the underlying records of a company in order to render an opinion as to whether the statements are fairly represented.

AUDITORS' REPORT
The opinion rendered by a public accounting firm concerning the fairness of the presentation of the financial statements.

From Concept **TO PRACTICE 1.2**

READING BEN & JERRY'S AUDITORS' REPORT Note the date at the bottom of the report. Why do you think it takes one month after the end of the year to issue this report?

www.ey.com

Auditing Services The auditing services rendered by public accountants are similar in certain respects to the work performed by internal auditors. However, there are key differences between the two types of auditing. Internal auditors are more concerned with the efficient operation of the various segments of the business, and therefore, the work they do is often called *operational auditing*. On the other hand, the primary objective of the external auditor or public accountant, is to assure stockholders and other users that the statements are fairly presented. In this respect, **auditing** is the process of examining the financial statements and the underlying records of a company in order to render an opinion as to whether the statements are fairly presented.

As we discussed earlier, the financial statements are prepared by the company's accountants. The external auditor performs various tests and procedures to be able to render his or her opinion. The public accountant has a responsibility to the company's stockholders and any other users of the statements. Because most stockholders are not actively involved in the daily affairs of the business, they must rely on the auditors to ensure that management is fairly presenting the financial statements of the business.

Note that the **auditors' report** is an *opinion*, not a statement of fact. For example, one important procedure performed by the auditor to obtain assurance as to the validity of a company's inventory is to observe the year-end physical count of inventory by the company's employees. However, this is done on a sample basis. It would be too costly for the auditors to make an independent count of every single item of inventory.

The auditors' report on the financial statements for Ben & Jerry's is shown in Exhibit 1-7. Note first that the report is directed to the company's stockholders and board of directors. The company is audited by Ernst & Young, a large international accounting firm. Public accounting firms range in size from those with a single owner to others, such as Ernst & Young, that have thousands of partners. The opinion given by Ernst & Young on the company's financial statements is the *standard auditors' report*. The first paragraph indicates that the firm has examined the company's balance sheet and the related statements of income, stockholders' equity, and cash flows. Note that the second paragraph of the report indicates that evidence supporting the amounts and disclosures in the statements was examined on a *test* basis. The third paragraph states the firm's *opinion* that the financial statements are fairly presented in conformity with GAAP. (We have highlighted these paragraphs for clarity.)

Tax Services In addition to auditing, public accounting firms provide a variety of tax services. Firms often prepare the tax returns for the companies they audit. They also usually work throughout the year with management to plan acquisitions and other transactions to take full advantage of the tax laws. For example, if tax rates are scheduled to decline next year, a public accounting firm would advise its client to accelerate certain expenditures this year as much as possible to receive a higher tax deduction than would be possible by waiting until next year.

Management Consulting Services By working closely with management to provide auditing and tax services, a public accounting firm becomes very familiar with various aspects of a company's business. This vantage point allows the firm to provide expert advice to the company to improve its operations. The management consulting services rendered by public accounting firms to their clients take a variety of forms. For example, the firm might advise the company on the design and installation of a computer system to fill its needs. The services provided in this area have grown dramatically to include such diverse activities as advice on selection of a new plant site or an investment opportunity.

ACCOUNTANTS IN EDUCATION

Some accountants choose a career in education. As the demand for accountants in business entities, nonbusiness organizations, and public accounting has increased, so has the need for qualified professors to teach this discipline. Accounting programs range from two years of study at community colleges to doctoral programs at some universities. All these programs

EXHIBIT 1-7 Ben & Jerry's Auditors' Report

Auditor's report

Report of Ernst & Young LLP, Independent Auditors

The Board of Directors and Stockholders
Ben & Jerry's Homemade, Inc.

We have audited the accompanying consolidated balance sheets of Ben & Jerry's Homemade, Inc. as of December 26, 1998 and December 27, 1997, and the related consolidated statements of operations, stockholders' equity, and cash flows for each of the three years in the period ended December 26, 1998. These financial statements are the responsibility of the Company's management. Our responsibility is to express an opinion on these financial statements based on our audits.

We conducted our audits in accordance with generally accepted auditing standards. Those standards require that we plan and perform the audit to obtain reasonable assurance about whether the financial statements are free of material misstatement. An audit includes examining, on a test basis, evidence supporting the amounts and disclosures in the financial statements. An audit also includes assessing the accounting principles used and significant estimates made by management, as well as evaluating the overall financial statement presentation. We believe that our audits provide a reasonable basis for our opinion.

In our opinion, the consolidated financial statements referred to above present fairly, in all material respects, the consolidated financial position of Ben & Jerry's Homemade, Inc. at December 26, 1998 and December 27, 1997 and the consolidated results of its operations and its cash flows for each of the three years in the period ended December 26, 1998, in conformity with generally accepted accounting principles.

Ernst + Young LLP

Boston, Massachusetts
January 22, 1999, except for Note 17,
as to which the date is February 26, 1999

Standard Auditor's Report

First Paragraph says that the auditor has examined the statements.

Second Paragraph indicates that evidence was gathered on a test basis.

Third Paragraph states the auditor's opinion.

Exhibit 1-8 Salaries in the Accounting Profession

Position	Salary Range	
Public Accounting		
Staff Auditors (1–3 years' experience)	$27,000–$36,000	$
Managers	$54,000–$85,750	$$
Partners	$130,000+	$$$
Industry		
Staff Accountants (1–3 years' experience)	$26,250–$36,250	$
Corporate Controllers	$46,000–$136,000	$$–$$$
Chief Financial Officers	$61,000–$300,000	$$–$$$$
Government (entry-level)		
Federal	$26,300 average	$
State/Local	$25,000 average	$

Accounting graduates start here.

American Accounting Association The professional organization for accounting educators.

www.aaa-edu.org

require the services of knowledgeable instructors. In addition to their teaching duties, many accounting educators are actively involved in research. The **American Accounting Association** is a professional organization of accounting educators and others interested in the future of the profession. The group advances its ideas through its many committees and the publication of a number of journals.

Accounting as a Career

As you can see, a number of different career paths in accounting are possible. The stereotypical view of the accountant as a "numbers person and not a people person" is a seriously outdated notion. Various specialties are now emerging, including tax accounting, environmental accounting, forensic accounting, software development, and accounting in the entertainment and telecommunications industries. Some of these opportunities exist in both the business and the nonbusiness sectors. For example, forensic accounting has become an exciting career field as both corporations and various agencies of the federal government, such as the FBI, concern themselves with fraud and white-collar crime.

As in any profession, salaries in accounting vary considerably depending on numerous factors, including educational background and other credentials, number of years of experience, and size of the employer. For example, most employers pay a premium for candidates with a master's degree and professional certification, such as the CPA. Exhibit 1-8 indicates salaries for various positions within the accounting field.[4]

Accounting for Your Decisions

You Are a Student

As a student, you decide to go into the accounting profession. However, you are not sure which area to focus on: private, nonbusiness, public, or education. What information would you seek to help you make this decision?

ANS: You may want to consider the following (not necessarily in this order): (1) both starting and potential increases in salaries; (2) education requirements; (3) advancement opportunities; (4) fringe benefits; and (5) challenging work.

[4] The information in this section regarding career opportunities and salaries was drawn primarily from the AICPA's Web site (http://www.aicpa.org). In addition, the AICPA publishes *Room Zoom,* an innovative and entertaining CD-ROM product.

Lynn Homburg, a general sales manager for a promotional marketing company in New York, has relied on accounting principles since the day she entered the work force.

FOCUS ON USERS

Name: Lynn Homburg
Education: B.S., Miami University (Oxford, Ohio)
College Major: Marketing
Occupation: General Sales Manager, Boise Marketing Services, Inc., New York
Age: 30

Using Financial Data to Make Career Decisions

Most people are faced with tough financial decisions at one point or another during their lives. Understanding the principles of accounting and putting them to work, both in professional and personal situations, can make these decisions easier to manage. Lynn Homburg, a general sales manager for a promotional marketing company in New York, has relied on accounting principles since the day she entered the work force. But, she has made use of these same principles since college, when her quality of life depended on her ability to budget.

In college, Lynn wanted to take advantage of her school's program to study abroad. Because of the expense involved, she decided that she needed to start bringing in more money. She took two part-time jobs during the year leading up to the summer trip, both of which helped her to finance the program. After college, Lynn took the idea of financial management a step further. She initiated a monthly budgeting system based on her income, accounting for everything from rent to magazine subscriptions. She immediately started to notice the positive effects of this regimen. As she says, "I was aware of my tendency to overextend myself financially, so I knew that the only way for me to reach my financial goals was to know where my money was going each month. By implementing this system, I've been able to live the Manhattan lifestyle I want and to invest in my future." Lynn's budget has also helped her to make periodic spending decisions. As she explains, "I knew I wanted to take a long vacation to Spain. Figuring out the costs of this and then plugging them into my overall budget made me realize that getting a ski house with my friends that winter wouldn't make sense."

Personal decisions such as these mirror the decisions Lynn faces in her professional life today. She says, "As a sales manager, it is my responsibility to ensure that my team is meeting our sales and profit goals. By closely following these numbers, I am able to figure out what the team needs to be doing to reach those goals: Do we need to do a sales blitz to generate more sales, increase our profit margin by 5 percent on each sale, or scale back on entertainment expenses? It's very similar to the questions I ask with regard to my own finances: Do I need to increase my income, put more into investments, or cut my expenses?"

ACCOUNTANTS AND ETHICAL JUDGMENTS

Remember the primary goal of accounting: to provide useful information to aid in the decision-making process. As we discussed, the work of the accountant in providing useful information is anything but routine and requires the accountant to make subjective judgments about what information to present and how to present it. The latitude given accountants in this respect is one of the major reasons accounting is a profession and its members are considered professionals. Along with this designation as a professional, however, comes a serious responsibility. As we noted, financial statements are prepared for external parties who must rely on these statements to provide information on which to base important decisions.

At the end of each chapter are cases titled "Accounting and Ethics: What Would You Do?" The cases require you to evaluate difficult issues and make a decision. Judgment is needed in deciding which accounting method to select or how to report a certain item in the statements. As you are faced with these decisions, keep in mind the trust placed in the accountant by various financial statement users. This is central to reaching an ethical decision.

A Final Note about Ben & Jerry's and Gateway

As you have seen in this chapter, accounting is a practical discipline. Financial statements of real companies, including Ben & Jerry's and Gateway, are used throughout the remainder of the book to help you learn more about this practical discipline. For example, some of the From Concept to Practice sidebars in future chapters will require you to return to the financial statements of these two companies, as will some of the cases at the end of the chapters. Because no two sets of financial statements look the same, however, you will be introduced to the financial statements of many other real companies as well. Use this opportunity to learn more not only about accounting but also about each of these companies.

Warmup Exercises

Study Tip

Use these exercises to get accustomed to the assignments that follow.

LO 2 Warmup Exercise 1-1 Your Assets and Liabilities

Consider your own situation in terms of assets and liabilities.

Required

1. Name three of your financial assets.
2. Name three of your financial liabilities.

Key to the Solution

Recall Exhibit 1-3 for definitions of assets and liabilities.

LO 2 Warmup Exercise 1-2 Ben & Jerry's Assets and Liabilities

www.benjerry.com

Think about Ben & Jerry's business in balance sheet terms.

Required

1. Name three of Ben & Jerry's assets.
2. Name three of Ben & Jerry's liabilities.

Key to the Solution

Recall Exhibit 1-2 if you need to see Ben & Jerry's balance sheet. Also consult the list on page 9.

LO 2 Warmup Exercise 1-3 Ben & Jerry's and the Accounting Equation

www.benjerry.com

Place Ben & Jerry's total assets, total liabilities, and total owners' equity in the form of the accounting equation.

Key to the Solution

Recall Exhibit 1-2. You will have to separate the liabilities and the stockholders' equity since they are not subtotaled for you.

Solutions to Warmup Exercises

Warmup Exercise 1-1 Your Assets and Liabilities

1. Possible personal financial assets might include: checking accounts, savings accounts, certificates of deposit, money market accounts, stocks, bonds and mutual funds.
2. Possible personal financial liabilities might include: student loans, car loans, home mortgage and amounts borrowed from relatives.

Warmup Exercise 1-2 Ben & Jerry's Assets and Liabilities

1. Ben & Jerry's assets are: Cash and cash equivalents, Short-term investments, Trade accounts receivable, Inventories, Deferred income taxes, Prepaid expenses and other current assets, Property, plant and equipment, Investments and Other assets.
2. Ben & Jerry's liabilities are: Accounts payable and accrued expenses, Current portion of long-term debt and obligations under capital leases, Long-term debt and obligations under capital leases and Deferred income taxes.

Warmup Exercise 1-3 Ben & Jerry's and the Accounting Equation

Assets	=	Liabilities	+	Owners' Equity
$149,501		$58,593	+	$90,908

Review Problem

Greenway Corporation is organized on June 1, 2001. The company will provide lawn-care and tree-trimming services on a contract basis. Following is an alphabetical list of the items that should appear on its income statement for the first month and on its balance sheet at the end of the first month (you will need to determine on *which* statement each should appear).

Accounts payable	$ 800
Accounts receivable	500
Building	2,000
Capital stock	5,000
Cash	3,300
Gas, utilities, and other expenses	300
Land	4,000
Lawn-care revenue	1,500
Notes payable	6,000
Retained earnings (beginning balance)	–0–
Salaries and wages expense	900
Tools	800
Tree-trimming revenue	500
Truck	2,000

Study Tip

Note to the student: At the end of each chapter is a problem to test your understanding of some of the major ideas presented in the chapter. Try to solve the problem before turning to the solution that follows it.

Required

1. Prepare an income statement for the month of June.
2. Prepare a balance sheet at June 30, 2001. *Note:* You will need to determine the balance in Retained Earnings at the end of the month.
3. The financial statements you have just prepared are helpful, but in many ways they are a starting point. Assuming this is your business, what additional questions do they raise that you need to consider?

Solution to Review Problem

1.

GREENWAY CORPORATION
INCOME STATEMENT
FOR THE MONTH ENDED JUNE 30, 2001

Revenues:		
Lawn care	$1,500	
Tree trimming	500	$2,000
Expenses:		
Salaries and wages	$ 900	
Gas, utilities, and other expenses	300	1,200
Net income		$ 800

2.

GREENWAY CORPORATION
BALANCE SHEET
AT JUNE 30, 2001

Assets		**Liabilities and Owners' Equity**	
Cash	$ 3,300	Accounts payable	$ 800
Accounts receivable	500	Notes payable	6,000
Truck	2,000	Capital stock	5,000
Tools	800	Retained earnings	800
Building	2,000		
Land	4,000		
Total Assets	$12,600	Total Liabilities and Owners' Equity	$12,600

3. Following are examples of questions that the financial statements raise:
   - During June, 75% of the revenue was from lawn care and the other 25% from trimming trees. Will this relationship hold in future months?
   - Are the expenses representative of those that will be incurred in the future? Will any other expenses arise, such as advertising and income taxes?
   - When can we expect to collect the accounts receivable? Is there a chance that not all will be collected?
   - How soon will the accounts payable need to be paid?
   - What is the interest rate on the note payable? When is interest paid? When is the note itself due?

CHAPTER HIGHLIGHTS

1. **LO 1** Both individuals external to a business and those involved in the internal management of the company use accounting information. External users include present and potential stockholders, bankers and other creditors, government agencies, suppliers, trade associations, labor unions, and other interested groups.
2. **LO 2** The accounting equation is the basis for the entire accounting system: **Assets = Liabilities + Owners' Equity.** Assets are valuable economic resources. Liabilities are the claims of outsiders to the assets of a business. Owners' equity is the residual interest that remains after deducting liabilities from assets.
3. **LO 2** A balance sheet summarizes the financial position of a company at a *specific point in time.* An income statement reports on its revenues and expenses for a *period of time.* A statement of retained earnings explains the changes in retained earnings *during a particular period.*
4. **LO 3** A number of assumptions are made in preparing financial statements. Accounting is not an exact science, and judgment must be used in deciding what to report on financial statements and how to report the information. Generally accepted accounting principles (GAAP) have evolved over time and are based on a conceptual framework. The *Securities and Exchange Commission* in the public sector and the *Financial Accounting Standards Board* in the private sector have the most responsibility for developing GAAP at the present time.
5. **LO 4** Accountants are employed by business entities, nonbusiness entities, public accounting firms, and educational institutions. Public accounting firms provide audit services for their clients, as well as tax and management consulting services.

KEY TERMS QUIZ

Read each definition below and then write the number of that definition in the blank beside the appropriate term it defines. The solution appears at the end of the chapter.

pg. 6 4 **Accounting**
pg. 6 9 **Management accounting**
pg. 8 5 **Financial accounting**
pg. 9 6 **Owners' equity**
pg. 9 3 **Stockholders' equity**
pg. 9 8 **Retained earnings**

7 Balance sheet
1 Income statement
10 Dividends
2 Statement of retained earnings
12 Cost principle
16 Going concern
18 Monetary unit
21 Time period
11 Generally accepted accounting principles (GAAP)
13 Securities and Exchange Commission (SEC)
17 Financial Accounting Standards Board (FASB)
19 American Institute of Certified Public Accountants (AICPA)
24 International Accounting Standards Committee (IASC)
22 Controller
15 Treasurer
20 Internal auditing
23 Auditing
25 Auditors' report
14 American Accounting Association

1. A statement that summarizes revenues and expenses for a period of time.
2. The statement that summarizes the income earned and dividends paid over the life of a business.
3. The owners' equity of a corporation.
4. The process of identifying, measuring, and communicating economic information to various users.
5. The branch of accounting concerned with communication with outsiders through financial statements.
6. The owners' claim to the assets of an entity.
7. The financial statement that summarizes the assets, liabilities, and owners' equity at a specific point in time.
8. The part of owners' equity that represents the income earned less dividends paid over the life of an entity.
9. The branch of accounting concerned with providing management with information to facilitate the planning and control functions.
10. A distribution of the net income of a business to its stockholders.
11. The various methods, rules, practices, and other procedures that have evolved over time in response to the need to regulate the preparation of financial statements.
12. Assets recorded and reported at the cost paid to acquire them.
13. The federal agency with ultimate authority to determine the rules in preparing statements for companies whose stock is sold to the public.
14. The professional organization for accounting educators.
15. The officer of an organization who is responsible for the safeguarding and efficient use of the company's liquid assets.
16. The assumption that an entity is not in the process of liquidation and that it will continue indefinitely.
17. The group in the private sector with authority to set accounting standards.
18. The yardstick used to measure amounts in financial statements; the dollar in the United States.
19. The professional organization for certified public accountants.
20. The department in a company responsible for the review and appraisal of a company's accounting and administrative controls.
21. A length of time on the calendar used as the basis for preparing financial statements.
22. The chief accounting officer for a company.
23. The process of examining the financial statements and the underlying records of a company in order to render an opinion as to whether the statements are fairly presented.
24. The organization formed to develop worldwide accounting standards.
25. The opinion rendered by a public accounting firm concerning the fairness of the presentation of the financial statements.

Alternate Terms

Auditors' report Report of independent accountants

Balance sheet Statement of financial position

Cost principle Original cost; historical cost

Creditor Lender

Income statement Statement of income

Net income Profits or earnings

Stockholder Shareholder

Questions

1. What is accounting? Define it in terms understandable to someone without a business background.
2. How do financial accounting and management accounting differ?
3. What are five different groups of users of accounting information? Briefly describe the types of decisions each group must make.
4. How does owners' equity fit in to the accounting equation?

5. What are the two distinct elements of owners' equity in a corporation? Define each element.
6. What is the purpose of a balance sheet?
7. How should a balance sheet be dated: as of a particular day or for a particular period of time? Explain your answer.
8. What does the term *cost principle* mean?
9. What is the purpose of an income statement?
10. How should an income statement be dated: as of a particular day or for a particular period of time? Explain your answer.
11. Rogers Corporation starts the year with a Retained Earnings balance of $55,000. Net income for the year is $27,000. The ending balance in Retained Earnings is $70,000. What was the amount of dividends for the year?
12. How do the duties of the controller of a corporation typically differ from those of the treasurer?
13. What are the three basic types of services performed by public accounting firms?
14. How would you evaluate the following statement: "The auditors are in the best position to evaluate a company because they have prepared the financial statements"?
15. What is the relationship between the cost principle and the going concern assumption?
16. Why does inflation present a challenge to the accountant? Relate your answer to the monetary unit assumption.
17. What is meant by the phrase *generally accepted accounting principles?*
18. What role has the Securities and Exchange Commission played in setting accounting standards? Contrast its role with that played by the Financial Accounting Standards Board.

EXERCISES

LO 1 Exercise 1-1 Users of Accounting Information and Their Needs

Listed below are a number of the important users of accounting information. Below the list are descriptions of a major need of each of these various users. Fill in the blank with the one user group that is most likely to have the need described to the right of the blank.

Company management	**Banker**
Stockholder	**Supplier**
Securities and Exchange Commission	**Labor union**
Internal Revenue Service	

User Group	Needs Information About
________	1. The profitability of each division in the company
________	2. The prospects for future dividend payments
________	3. The profitability of the company since the last contract with the work force was signed
________	4. The financial status of a company issuing securities to the public for the first time
________	5. The prospects that a company will be able to meet its interest payments on time
________	6. The prospects that a company will be able to pay for its purchases on time
________	7. The profitability of the company based on the tax code

LO 2 Exercise 1-2 The Accounting Equation

For each of the following independent cases, fill in the blank with the appropriate dollar amount.

	Assets	=	Liabilities	+	Owners' Equity
Case 1	$125,000		$ 75,000		$______
Case 2	400,000		______		100,000
Case 3	______		320,000		95,000

LO 2 Exercise 1-3 The Accounting Equation

Ginger Enterprises began the year with total assets of $500,000 and total liabilities of $250,000. Using this information and the accounting equation, answer each of the following independent questions.

Required

1. What was the amount of Ginger's owners' equity at the beginning of the year?
2. If Ginger's total assets increased by $100,000 and its total liabilities increased by $77,000 during the year, what was the amount of Ginger's owners' equity at the end of the year?
3. If Ginger's total liabilities increased by $33,000 and its owners' equity decreased by $58,000 during the year, what was the amount of its total assets at the end of the year?
4. If Ginger's total assets doubled to $1,000,000 and its owners' equity remained the same during the year, what was the amount of its total liabilities at the end of the year?

LO 2 **Exercise 1-4** The Accounting Equation

Using the accounting equation, answer each of the following independent questions.

1. Burlin Company starts the year with $100,000 in assets and $80,000 in liabilities. Net income for the year is $25,000, and no dividends are paid. How much is owners' equity at the end of the year?
2. Chapman Inc. doubles the amount of its assets from the beginning to the end of the year. Liabilities at the end of the year amount to $40,000, and owners' equity is $20,000. What is the amount of Chapman's assets at the beginning of the year?
3. During the year, the liabilities of Dixon Enterprises triple in amount. Assets at the beginning of the year amount to $30,000, and owners' equity is $10,000. What is the amount of liabilities at the end of the year?

LO 2 **Exercise 1-5** Changes in Owners' Equity

The following amounts are available from the records of Coaches and Carriages Inc. at the end of the years indicated:

December 31	Total Assets	Total Liabilities
1999	$ 25,000	$ 12,000
2000	79,000	67,000
2001	184,000	137,000

Required

1. Compute the changes in Coaches and Carriages' owners' equity during 2000 and 2001.
2. Compute the amount of Coaches and Carriages' net income (or loss) for 2000 assuming that no dividends were paid during the year.
3. Compute the amount of Coaches and Carriages' net income (or loss) for 2001 assuming that dividends paid during the year amounted to $10,000.

LO 2 **Exercise 1-6** The Accounting Equation

For each of the following independent cases, fill in the blank with the appropriate dollar amount.

SPREADSHEET

	Case 1	Case 2	Case 3	Case 4
Total assets, end of period	$40,000	$_____	$75,000	$50,000
Total liabilities, end of period	_____	15,000	25,000	10,000
Capital stock, end of period	10,000	5,000	20,000	15,000
Retained earnings, beginning of period	15,000	8,000	10,000	20,000
Net income for the period	8,000	7,000	_____	9,000
Dividends for the period	2,000	1,000	3,000	_____

LO 2 **Exercise 1-7** Classification of Financial Statement Items

Classify each of the following items according to (1) whether it belongs on the income statement (IS) or balance sheet (BS) and (2) whether it is a revenue (R), expense (E), asset (A), liability (L), or owners' equity (OE) item.

Item	Appears on the	Classified As
Example: Cash	BS	A
1. Salaries expense	IS	E
2. Equipment	BS	A
3. Accounts payable	BS	L
4. Membership fees earned	IS	R
5. Capital stock	BS	OE
6. Accounts receivable	BS	A
7. Buildings	BS	A
8. Advertising expense	IS	E
9. Retained earnings	BS	OE

LO 2 **Exercise 1-8** Net Income (or Loss) and Retained Earnings

The following information is available from the records of Prestige Landscape Design Inc. at the end of the 2001 calendar year:

Accounts payable	$ 5,000	Office equipment	$ 7,500
Accounts receivable	4,000	Rent expense	6,500
Capital stock	8,000	Retained earnings, beginning of year	8,500
Cash	13,000	Salary and wage expense	12,000
Dividends paid during the year	3,000	Supplies	500
Landscaping revenues	25,000		

Required

Use the information above to answer the following questions:

1. What was Prestige's net income for the year ended December 31, 2001?
2. What is Prestige's retained earnings balance at the end of the year?
3. What is the total amount of Prestige's assets at the end of the year?
4. What is the total amount of Prestige's liabilities at the end of the year?
5. How much owners' equity does Prestige have at the end of the year?
6. What is Prestige's accounting equation at December 31, 2001?

LO 2 **Exercise 1-9** Statement of Retained Earnings

Ace Corporation has been in business for many years. Retained earnings on January 1, 2001 is $235,800. The following information is available for the first two months of 2001:

	January	February
Revenues	$83,000	$96,000
Expenses	89,000	82,000
Dividends paid	–0–	5,000

Required

Prepare a statement of retained earnings for the month ended February 28, 2001.

LO 3 **Exercise 1-10** Accounting Principles and Assumptions

The following basic accounting principles and assumptions were discussed in the chapter:

Economic entity **Going concern**
Monetary unit **Time period**
Cost principle

Fill in each of the blanks with the accounting principle or assumption that is relevant to the situation described.

_______________ 1. Genesis Corporation is now in its 30th year of business. The founder of the company is planning to retire at the end of the year and turn the business over to his daughter.

_______________ 2. Nordic Company purchased a 20-acre parcel of property on which to build a new factory. The company recorded the property on the records at the amount of cash given to acquire it.

_______________ 3. Jim Bailey enters into an agreement to operate a new law firm in partnership with a friend. Each partner will make an initial cash investment of $10,000. Jim opens a checking account in the name of the partnership and transfers $10,000 from his personal account into the new account.

_______________ 4. Multinational Corp. has a division in Japan. Prior to preparing the financial statements for the company and all its foreign divisions, Multinational translates the financial statements of its Japanese division from yen to U.S. dollars.

_______________ 5. Camden Company has always prepared financial statements annually, with a year-end of June 30. Because the company is going to sell its stock to the public for the first time, quarterly financial reports will also be required by the Securities and Exchange Commission.

LO 3 Exercise 1-11 Organizations and Accounting

Match each of the organizations listed below with the statement that most adequately describes the role of the group.

Securities and Exchange Commission
International Accounting Standards Committee
Financial Accounting Standards Board
American Institute of Certified Public Accountants
American Accounting Association

Securities and exchange 1. Federal agency with ultimate authority to determine rules used in preparing financial statements for companies whose stock is sold to the public

Financial Accounting Standards / Amer. Acct. Assoc. 2. Professional organization for accounting educators

_______________ 3. Group in the private sector with authority to set accounting standards

Amer. Inst. of CPA 4. Professional organization for certified public accountants

Int'l Acct. Standards 5. Organization formed to develop worldwide accounting standards

Multi-Concept Exercises

LO 1, 2 Exercise 1-12 Users of Accounting Information and the Financial Statements

Listed below are a number of users of accounting information and examples of questions they need answered before making decisions. Fill in each blank to indicate whether the user is most likely to find the answer by looking at the income statement (IS), the balance sheet (BS), or the statement of retained earnings (RE).

User	Question	Financial Statement
Stockholder	How did this year's sales compare to last year's?	_______________
Banker	How much debt does the company already have on its books?	_______________
Supplier	How much does the company currently owe to its suppliers?	_______________
Stockholder	How much did the company pay in dividends this past year?	_______________
Advertising account manager	How much did the company spend this past year to generate sales?	_______________
Banker	What collateral or security can the company provide to ensure that any loan I make will be repaid?	_______________

Pg-8 top?

LO 2, 3 Exercise 1-13 Ben & Jerry's Inventories

Refer to Ben & Jerry's balance sheet reproduced in the chapter.

Required

What was the amount of Inventories at December 26, 1998? What monetary unit is this amount based on? Given the relatively brief time that ice cream would remain in inventory, do you think the stability of the monetary unit is a concern? Explain your answer.

LO 1, 4 Exercise 1-14 Roles of Accountants

One day on campus, you overhear two nonbusiness majors discussing the reasons each did not major in accounting. "Accountants are bean counters. They just sit in a room and play with the books all day. They do not have people skills, but I suppose it really doesn't matter because no one ever looks at the statements they prepare," said the first student. The second student replied, "Oh, they are very intelligent, though, because they must know all about the tax laws, and that's too complicated for me."

Required

Comment on the students' perceptions of the roles of accountants in society. Do you agree that no one ever looks at the statements they prepare? If not, identify who the primary users are.

PROBLEMS

LO 1 Problem 1-1 You Won the Lottery

You have won a lottery! You will receive $200,000, after taxes, each year for the next five years.

Required

Describe the process you will go through in determining how to invest your winnings. Consider at least two options and make a choice. You may consider the stock of a certain company, bonds, real estate investments, bank deposits, and so on. Be specific. What information did you need to make a final decision? How was your decision affected by the fact that you will receive the winnings over a five-year period rather than in one lump sum? Would you prefer one payment? Explain.

LO 1 Problem 1-2 Users of Accounting Information and Their Needs

Havre Company would like to buy a building and equipment to produce a new product line. Some information about Havre is more useful to some people involved in the project than to others.

Required

Complete the following chart by identifying the information listed on the right with the user's need to know the information. Identify the information as

a. *need* to know;

b. *helpful* to know; or

c. *not necessary* to know.

User of the Information			
Management	**Stockholders**	**Banker**	**Information**
______	______	______	**1.** Amount of current debt, repayment schedule, and interest rate
______	______	______	**2.** Fair market value of the building
______	______	______	**3.** Condition of the roof and heating and cooling, electrical, and plumbing systems
______	______	______	**4.** Total cost of the building, improvements, and equipment to set up production
______	______	______	**5.** Expected sales from the new product, variable production costs, related selling costs

LO 2 Problem 1-3 Balance Sheet

The following items are available from records of Freescia Corporation at the end of the 2001 calendar year:

Accounts payable	$12,550
Accounts receivable	23,920
Advertising expense	2,100
Buildings	85,000
Capital stock	25,000
Cash	4,220
Notes payable	50,000
Office equipment	12,000
Retained earnings, end of year	37,590
Salary and wage expense	8,230
Sales revenue	14,220

Required

Prepare a balance sheet. *Hint:* Not all the items listed should appear on a balance sheet. For each of these items, indicate where it should appear.

LO 2 Problem 1-4 Corrected Balance Sheet

Dave is the president of Avon Consulting Inc. Avon began business on January 1, 2001. The company's controller is out of the country on business. Dave needs a copy of the company's balance sheet for a meeting tomorrow and asked his secretary to obtain the required information from the company's records. She presented Dave with the following balance sheet. He asks you to review it for accuracy.

AVON CONSULTING INC.
BALANCE SHEET
FOR THE YEAR ENDED DECEMBER 31, 2001

Assets		Liabilities and Owners' Equity	
Accounts payable	$13,000	Accounts receivable	$16,000
Cash	21,000	Capital stock	20,000
Cash dividends paid	16,000	Net income for 2001	72,000
Furniture and equipment	43,000	Supplies	9,000

Required

1. Prepare a corrected balance sheet.
2. Draft a memo explaining the major differences between the balance sheet Dave's secretary prepared and the one you prepared.

LO 2 Problem 1-5 Income Statement, Statement of Retained Earnings, and Balance Sheet

SPREADSHEET

Shown below, in alphabetical order, is a list of the various items that regularly appear on the financial statements of Maple Park Theatres Corp. The amounts shown for balance sheet items are balances as of September 30, 2001 (with the exception of Retained Earnings, which is the balance on September 1, 2001), and the amounts shown for income statement items are balances for the month ended September 30, 2001:

Accounts payable	$17,600
Accounts receivable	6,410
Advertising expense	14,500
Buildings	60,000
Capital stock	50,000
Cash	15,230
Concessions revenue	60,300
Cost of concessions sold	23,450
Dividends paid during the month	8,400
Furniture and fixtures	34,000
Land	26,000
Notes payable	20,000
Projection equipment	25,000

Rent expense—movies	50,600
Retained earnings	73,780
Salaries and wages expense	46,490
Ticket sales	95,100
Water, gas, and electricity	6,700

Required

1. Prepare an income statement for the month ended September 30, 2001.
2. Prepare a statement of retained earnings for the month ended September 30, 2001.
3. Prepare a balance sheet at September 30, 2001.
4. You have $1,000 to invest. On the basis of the statements you prepared, would you use it to buy stock in Maple Park? What other information would you want before making a final decision?

LO 2 Problem 1-6 Income Statement and Balance Sheet

Green Bay Corporation began business in July 2001 as a commercial fishing operation and passenger service between islands. Shares of stock were issued to the owners in exchange for cash. Boats were purchased by making a down payment in cash and signing a note payable for the balance. Fish are sold to local restaurants on open account, and customers are given 15 days to pay their account. Cash fares are collected for all passenger traffic. Rent for the dock facilities is paid at the beginning of each month. Salaries and wages are paid at the end of the month. The following amounts are from the records of Green Bay Corporation at the end of its first month of operations:

Accounts receivable	$18,500
Boats	80,000
Capital stock	40,000
Cash	7,730
Dividends	5,400
Fishing revenue	21,300
Notes payable	60,000
Passenger service revenue	12,560
Rent expense	4,000
Retained earnings	???
Salary and wage expense	18,230

Required

1. Prepare an income statement for the month ended July 31, 2001.
2. Prepare a balance sheet at July 31, 2001.
3. What information would you need about Notes Payable to assess fully Green Bay's long-term viability? Explain your answer.

LO 2 Problem 1-7 Corrected Financial Statements

Hometown Cleaners Inc. operates a small dry-cleaning business. The company has always maintained a complete and accurate set of records. Unfortunately, the company's accountant left in a dispute with the president and took the 2001 financial statements with him. The balance sheet and the income statement shown below were prepared by the company's president.

HOMETOWN CLEANERS INC.
INCOME STATEMENT
FOR THE YEAR ENDED DECEMBER 31, 2001

Revenues:		
Accounts receivable	$15,200	
Cleaning revenue—cash sales	32,500	$47,700
Expenses:		
Dividends	$ 4,000	
Accounts payable	4,500	
Utilities	12,200	
Salaries and wages	17,100	37,800
Net income		$ 9,900

HOMETOWN CLEANERS INC.
BALANCE SHEET
DECEMBER 31, 2001

Assets		**Liabilities and Owners' Equity**	
Cash	$ 7,400	Cleaning revenue—	
Building and equipment	80,000	credit sales	$26,200
Less: Notes payable	(50,000)	Capital stock	20,000
Land	40,000	Net income	9,900
		Retained earnings	21,300
		Total liabilities and	
Total assets	$77,400	owners' equity	$77,400

The president is very disappointed with the net income for the year because it has averaged $25,000 over the last 10 years. She has asked for your help in determining whether the reported net income accurately reflects the profitability of the company and whether the balance sheet is prepared correctly.

Required

1. Prepare a corrected income statement for the year ended December 31, 2001.
2. Prepare a statement of retained earnings for the year ended December 31, 2001. (The actual balance of retained earnings on January 1, 2001, was $42,700. Note that the December 31, 2001, balance shown above is incorrect. The president simply "plugged" this amount in to make the balance sheet balance.)
3. Prepare a corrected balance sheet at December 31, 2001.
4. Draft a memo to the president explaining the major differences between the income statement she prepared and the one you prepared.

LO 2 **Problem 1-8** Statement of Retained Earnings for the Walt Disney Company

The Walt Disney Company reported the following amounts in various statements included in its 1998 annual report (all amounts are stated in millions of dollars):

www.disney.com

Net income for 1998	$ 1,850
Dividends declared and paid in 1998	412
Retained earnings, September 30, 1997	9,543
Retained earnings, September 30, 1998	10,981

Required

1. Prepare a statement of retained earnings for Walt Disney for the year ended September 30, 1998.
2. Walt Disney does not actually present a statement of retained earnings in its annual report. Instead, it presents a broader statement of stockholders' equity. Describe the information that would be included on this statement and that is not included on a statement of retained earnings.

LO 4 **Problem 1-9** Role of the Accountant in Various Organizations

The following positions in various entities require a knowledge of accounting practices:

1. Chief financial officer for the subsidiary of a large company
2. Tax adviser to a consolidated group of entities
3. Independent computer consultant
4. Financial planner in a bank
5. Real estate broker in an independent office
6. Production planner in a manufacturing facility
7. Quality control adviser
8. Superintendent of a school district
9. Manager of one store in a retail clothing chain
10. Salesperson for a company that offers subcontract services to hospitals, such as food service and maintenance

Required

For each position listed above, identify the entity in which it occurs as business or nonbusiness and describe the kind of accounting knowledge (such as financial, managerial, taxes, not-for-profit) required by each position.

www.pathfinder.com/corp/

LO 1 Problem 1-10 Information Needs and Setting Accounting Standards

The Financial Accounting Standards Board recently released a new statement that requires companies to supplement their consolidated financial statements with disclosures about segments of their businesses. To comply with this standard, Time Warner's 1998 annual report provides various disclosures for the five segments in which it operates: Cable Systems, Cable Networks, Publishing, Entertainment, and Music.

Required

Which users of accounting information do you think the Financial Accounting Standards Board had in mind when it set this standard? What types of disclosures do you think these users would find helpful?

Multi-Concept Problem

LO 2, 3 Problem 1-11 Primary Assumptions Made in Preparing Financial Statements

Joe Hale opened a machine repair business in leased retail space, paying the first month's rent of $300 and a $1,000 security deposit with a check on his personal account. He took the tools and equipment, worth about $7,500, from his garage to the shop. He also bought some more equipment to get started. The new equipment had a list price of $5,000, but Joe was able to purchase it on sale at Sears for only $4,200. He charged the new equipment on his personal Sears charge card. Joe's first customer paid $400 for services rendered, so Joe opened a checking account for the company. He completed a second job, but the customer has not paid Joe the $2,500 for his work. At the end of the first month, Joe prepared the following balance sheet and income statement.

JOE'S MACHINE REPAIR SHOP
BALANCE SHEET
JULY 31, 2001

Cash	$ 400		
Tools	5,000	Equity	$5,400
Total	$5,400	Total	$5,400

JOE'S MACHINE REPAIR SHOP
INCOME STATEMENT
FOR MONTH ENDED JULY 31, 2001

Sales		$2,900
Rent	$ 300	
Tools	4,200	4,500
Loss		($1,600)

Joe believes that he should show a greater profit next month because he won't have large expenses for items such as tools.

Required

Identify the assumptions that Joe has violated and explain how each event should have been handled. Prepare a corrected balance sheet and income statement.

Alternate Problems

LO 1 Problem 1-1A What to Do with a Million Dollars

You have inherited $1 million!

Required

Describe the process you will go through in determining how to invest your inheritance. Consider at least two options and choose one. You may consider the stock of a certain company, bonds, real estate investments, bank deposits, and so on. Be specific. What information did you need to make a final decision? Where did you find the information you needed? What additional information will you need to consider if you want to make a change in your investment?

LO 1 Problem 1-2A Users of Accounting Information and Their Needs

Billings Inc. would like to buy a franchise to provide a specialized service. Some information about Billings is more useful to some people involved in the project than to others.

Required

Complete the following chart by identifying the information listed on the left with the user's need to know the information. Identify the information as

a. *need* to know;

b. *helpful* to know; or

c. *not necessary* to know.

Information	User of the Information: Manager	Stockholders	Franchisor
1. Expected revenue from the new service.	_____	_____	_____
2. Cost of the franchise fee and recurring fees to be paid to the franchisor.	_____	_____	_____
3. Cash available to Billings, the franchisee, to operate the business after the franchise is purchased.	_____	_____	_____
4. Expected overhead costs of the service outlet.	_____	_____	_____
5. Billings' required return on its investment.	_____	_____	_____

LO 2 Problem 1-3A Balance Sheet

The following items are available from the records of Victor Corporation at the end of its fiscal year ended July 31, 2001:

Accounts payable	$16,900
Accounts receivable	5,700
Buildings	35,000
Butter and cheese inventory	12,100
Capital stock	25,000
Cash	21,800
Computerized mixers	25,800
Delivery expense	4,600
Notes payable	50,000
Office equipment	12,000
Retained earnings, end of year	26,300
Salary and wage expense	8,230
Sales revenue	14,220
Tools	5,800

Required

Prepare a balance sheet. *Hint:* Not all the items listed should appear on a balance sheet. For each of these items, indicate where it should appear.

LO 2 Problem 1-4A Corrected Balance Sheet

Pete is the president of Island Enterprises. Island Enterprises began business on January 1, 2001. The company's controller is out of the country on business. Pete needs a copy of the company's balance sheet for a meeting tomorrow and asked his secretary to obtain the required information from the company's records. She presented Pete with the following balance sheet. He asks you to review it for accuracy.

ISLAND ENTERPRISES
BALANCE SHEET
FOR THE YEAR ENDED DECEMBER 31, 2001

Assets		**Liabilities and Owners' Equity**	
Accounts payable	$ 29,600	Accounts receivable	$ 23,200
Cash	14,750	Capital stock	100,000
Cash dividends paid	16,000	Net income for 2001	113,850
Building and equipment	177,300	Supplies	12,200

Required

1. Prepare a corrected balance sheet.
2. Draft a memo explaining the major differences between the balance sheet Pete's secretary prepared and the one you prepared.

LO 2 Problem 1-5A Income Statement, Statement of Retained Earnings, and Balance Sheet
Shown below, in alphabetical order, is a list of the various items that regularly appear on the financial statements of Sterns Audio Book Rental Corp. The amounts shown for balance sheet items are balances as of December 31, 2001 (with the exception of retained earnings, which is the balance on January 1, 2001), and the amounts shown for income statement items are balances for the year ended December 31, 2001:

Accounts payable	$ 4,500
Accounts receivable	300
Advertising expense	14,500
Audio tape inventory	70,000
Capital stock	50,000
Cash	2,490
Display fixtures	45,000
Dividends paid during the year	12,000
Notes payable	10,000
Rental revenue	125,900
Rent paid on building	60,000
Retained earnings	35,390
Salaries and wages expense	17,900
Water, gas, and electricity	3,600

Required

1. Prepare an income statement for the year ended December 31, 2001.
2. Prepare a statement of retained earnings for the year ended December 31, 2001.
3. Prepare a balance sheet at December 31, 2001.
4. You have $1,000 to invest. On the basis of the statements you prepared, would you use it to buy stock in this company? What other information would you want before making a final decision?

LO 2 Problem 1-6A Income Statement and Balance Sheet
Fort Worth Corporation began business in January 2001 as a commercial carpet cleaning and drying service. Shares of stock were issued to the owners in exchange for cash. Equipment was purchased by making a down payment in cash and signing a note payable for the balance. Services are performed for local restaurants and office buildings on open account, and customers are given 15 days to pay their account. Rent for office and storage facilities is paid at the beginning of each month. Salaries and wages are paid at the end of the month. The following amounts are from the records of Fort Worth Corporation at the end of its first month of operations:

Accounts receivable	$24,750
Capital stock	80,000
Cash	51,650
Cleaning revenue	45,900
Dividends	5,500

Equipment	62,000
Notes payable	30,000
Rent expense	3,600
Retained earnings	???
Salary and wage expense	8,400

Required

1. Prepare an income statement for the month ended January 31, 2001.
2. Prepare a balance sheet at January 31, 2001.
3. What information would you need about Notes Payable to fully assess Fort Worth's long-term viability? Explain your answer.

LO 2 **Problem 1-7A** Corrected Financial Statements

Heidi's Bakery Inc. operates a small pastry business. The company has always maintained a complete and accurate set of records. Unfortunately, the company's accountant left in a dispute with the president and took the 2001 financial statements with her. The balance sheet and the income statement shown below were prepared by the company's president.

HEIDI'S BAKERY INC.
INCOME STATEMENT
FOR THE YEAR ENDED DECEMBER 31, 2001

Revenues:		
Accounts receivable	$15,500	
Pastry revenue—cash sales	23,700	$39,200
Expenses:		
Dividends	$ 5,600	
Accounts payable	6,800	
Utilities	9,500	
Salaries and wages	18,200	40,100
Net loss		$ (900)

HEIDI'S BAKERY INC.
BALANCE SHEET
DECEMBER 31, 2001

Assets		**Liabilities and Owners' Equity**	
Cash	$ 3,700	Pastry revenue—credit sales	$22,100
Building and equipment	60,000	Capital stock	30,000
Less: Notes payable	(40,000)	Net loss	(900)
Land	50,000	Retained earnings	22,500
Total assets	$73,700	Total liabilities and owners' equity	$73,700

The president is very disappointed with the net loss for the year because net income has averaged $21,000 over the last 10 years. He has asked for your help in determining whether the reported net loss accurately reflects the profitability of the company and whether the balance sheet is prepared correctly.

Required

1. Prepare a corrected income statement for the year ended December 31, 2001.
2. Prepare a statement of retained earnings for the year ended December 31, 2001. (The actual amount of Retained Earnings on January 1, 2001, was $39,900. The December 31, 2001, balance shown above is incorrect. The president simply "plugged" this amount in to make the balance sheet balance.)
3. Prepare a corrected balance sheet at December 31, 2001.
4. Draft a memo to the president explaining the major differences between the income statement he prepared and the one you prepared.

LO 2 **Problem 1-8A** Statement of Retained Earnings for Brunswick Corporation

www.brunswickcorp.com

Brunswick Corporation reported the following amounts in various statements included in its 1998 annual report (all amounts are stated in millions of dollars):

Net earnings for 1998	$ 186.3
Cash dividends declared and paid in 1998	49.0
Retained earnings, December 31, 1997	1,052.2
Retained earnings, December 31, 1998	1,189.5

Required

1. Prepare a statement of retained earnings for Brunswick for the year ended December 31, 1998.
2. Brunswick does not actually present a statement of retained earnings in its annual report. Instead, it presents a broader statement of shareholders' (stockholders') equity. Describe the information that would be included on this statement and that is not included on a statement of retained earnings.

LO 4 **Problem 1-9A** Role of the Accountant in Various Organizations

The following positions in various entities require a knowledge of accounting practices:

______ 1. Chief financial officer for the subsidiary of a large company
______ 2. Tax adviser to a consolidated group of entities
______ 3. Accounts receivable computer analyst
______ 4. Financial planner in a bank
______ 5. Budget analyst in a real estate office
______ 6. Production planner in a manufacturing facility
______ 7. Quality control adviser
______ 8. Manager of the team conducting an audit on a state lottery
______ 9. Assistant superintendent of a school district
______ 10. Manager of one store in a retail clothing chain
______ 11. Controller in a company that offers subcontract services to hospitals, such as food service and maintenance
______ 12. Staff accountant in a large audit firm

Required

For each position listed above, fill in the blank to classify the position as one of the general categories of accountants listed below.

Financial accountant
Managerial accountant
Tax accountant
Accountant for not-for-profit organization
Auditor
Not an accounting position

LO 1 **Problem 1-10A** Information Needs and Setting Accounting Standards

www.marriott.com

The Financial Accounting Standards Board recently released a new statement that requires companies to supplement their consolidated financial statements with disclosures about segments of their businesses. To comply with this standard, Marriott International's 1998 annual report provides various disclosures for the three segments in which it operates: Lodging, Senior Living Services, and Distribution Services (a wholesale food-distribution business).

Required

Which users of accounting information do you think the Financial Accounting Standards Board had in mind when it set this standard? What types of disclosures do you think these users would find helpful?

Alternate Multi-Concept Problem

LO 2, 3 Problem 1-11A Primary Assumptions Made in Preparing Financial Statements
Millie Abrams opened a ceramic studio in leased retail space, paying the first month's rent of $300 and a $1,000 security deposit with a check on her personal account. She took molds and paint, worth about $7,500, from her home to the studio. She also bought a new firing kiln to start the business. The new kiln had a list price of $5,000, but Millie was able to trade in her old kiln, worth $500 at the time of trade, on the new kiln, and therefore she paid only $4,500 cash. She wrote a check on her personal checking account. Millie's first customers paid a total of $1,400 to attend classes for the next two months. She opened a checking account in the company's name with the $1,400. She has conducted classes for one month and has sold for $3,000 unfinished ceramic pieces called *greenware.* Greenware sales are all cash. Millie incurred $1,000 of personal cost in making the greenware. At the end of the first month, Millie prepared the following balance sheet and income statement.

MILLIE'S CERAMIC STUDIO
BALANCE SHEET
JULY 31, 2001

Cash	$1,400		
Kiln	5,000	Equity	$6,400
Total	$6,400	Total	$6,400

MILLIE'S CERAMIC STUDIO
INCOME STATEMENT
FOR THE MONTH ENDED JULY 31, 2001

Sales		$4,400
Rent	$300	
Supplies	600	900
Income		$3,500

Millie needs to earn at least $3,000 each month for the business to be worth her time. She is pleased with the results.

Required

Identify the assumptions that Millie has violated and explain how each event should have been handled. Prepare a corrected balance sheet and income statement.

CASES

Reading and Interpreting Financial Statements

LO 1, 2 Case 1-1 An Annual Report as Ready Reference
Refer to the Gateway annual report, and identify where each of the following users of accounting information would first look to answer their respective questions about Gateway:

www.gateway.com

1. Investors: How much did the company earn for each share of stock I own? How much of those earnings did I receive, and how much was reinvested in the company?
2. Potential investors: What amount of earnings can I expect to see from Gateway in the near future?
3. Bankers and creditors: Should I extend the short-term borrowing limit to Gateway? Do they have sufficient cash or cash-like assets to repay short-term loans?
4. IRS: How much does Gateway owe for taxes?
5. Employees: How much money did the president and vice presidents earn? Should I ask for a raise?

LO 2 Case 1-2 Reading and Interpreting Ben & Jerry's Financial Statements
Refer to the financial statements for Ben & Jerry's reproduced in the chapter and answer the following questions:

1. What was the company's net income for 1998?
2. State Ben & Jerry's financial position on December 26, 1998, in terms of the accounting equation.
3. Explain the reason for the change in retained earnings from a balance of $39,086,000 on December 27, 1997, to a balance of $45,328,000 on December 26, 1998. Also, what amount of dividends did the company pay in 1998?

Making Financial Decisions

LO 1 Case 1-3 An Investment Opportunity

You have saved enough money to pay for your college tuition for the next three years when a high school friend comes to you with a deal. He is an artist who has spent most of the past two years drawing on the walls of old buildings. The buildings are about to be demolished and your friend thinks you should buy the walls before the buildings are demolished and open a gallery featuring his work. Of course, you are levelheaded and would normally say "No!" Recently, however, your friend has been featured on several local radio and television shows and is talking to some national networks about doing a feature on a well-known news show. To set up the gallery would take all your savings, but your friend feels that you will be able to sell his artwork for 10 times the cost of your investment. What kinds of information about the business do you need before deciding to invest all your savings? What kind of profit split would you suggest to your friend if you decide to open the gallery?

LO 2 Case 1-4 Preparation of Projected Statements for a New Business

Upon graduation from MegaState University, you and your roommate decide to start your respective careers in accounting and salmon fishing in Remote, Alaska. Your career as a CPA in Remote is going well, as is your roommate's job as a commercial fisher. After one year in Remote, he approaches you with a business opportunity.

> As we are well aware, the video rental business has yet to reach Remote, and the nearest rental facility is 250 miles away. We each put up our first year's savings of $5,000 and file for articles of incorporation with the state of Alaska to do business as Remote Video World. In return for our investment of $5,000, we will each receive equal shares of capital stock in the corporation. Then we go to the Corner National Bank and apply for a $10,000 loan. We take the total cash of $20,000 we have now raised and buy 2,000 videos at $10 each from a mail-order supplier. We rent the movies for $3 per title and sell monthly memberships for $25, allowing a member to check out an unlimited number of movies during the month. Individual rentals would be a cash-and-carry business, but we would give customers until the 10th of the following month to pay for a monthly membership. My most conservative estimate is that during the first month alone, we will rent 800 movies and sell 200 memberships. As I see it, we will have only two expenses. First, we will hire two high school students to run the store for 30 hours each per week and pay them $5 per hour. Second, the landlord of a vacant store in town will rent us space in the building for $1,000 per month.

Required

1. Prepare a projected income statement for the first month of operations.
2. Prepare a balance sheet as it would appear at the end of the first month of operations.
3. Assume that the bank is willing to make the $10,000 loan. Would you be willing to join your roommate in this business? Explain your response. Also, indicate any information other than what he has provided that you would like to have before making a final decision.

Accounting and Ethics: What Would You Do?

LO 1, 2 Case 1-5 Identification of Errors in Financial Statements and Preparation of Revised Statements

Lakeside Slammers Inc. is a minor-league baseball organization that has just completed its first season. You and three other investors organized the corporation; each put up $10,000 in cash for shares of capital stock. Because you live out of state, you have not been actively involved in the daily affairs of the club. However, you are thrilled to receive a dividend check for $10,000 at the end of the season—an amount equal to your original investment! Included with the check are the following financial statements, along with supporting explanations.

LAKESIDE SLAMMERS INC.
INCOME STATEMENT
FOR THE YEAR ENDED DECEMBER 31, 2001

Revenues:		
Single-game ticket revenue	$420,000	
Season-ticket revenue	140,000	
Concessions revenue	280,000	
Advertising revenue	100,000	$940,000
Expenses:		
Cost of concessions sold	$110,000	
Salary expense—players	225,000	
Salary and wage expense—staff	150,000	
Rent expense	210,000	695,000
Net Income		$245,000

LAKESIDE SLAMMERS INC.
STATEMENT OF RETAINED EARNINGS
FOR THE YEAR ENDED DECEMBER 31, 2001

Beginning balance, January 1, 2001	$ –0–
Add: Net income for 2001	245,000
Deduct: Cash dividends paid in 2001	(40,000)
Ending balance, December 31, 2001	$205,000

LAKESIDE SLAMMERS INC.
BALANCE SHEET
AT DECEMBER 31, 2001

Assets		**Liabilities and Owners' Equity**	
Cash	$ 5,000	Notes payable	$ 50,000
Accounts receivable		Capital stock	40,000
Season tickets	140,000	Additional owners' capital	80,000
Advertisers	100,000	Parent club's equity	125,000
Auxiliary assets	80,000	Retained earnings	205,000
Equipment	50,000		
Player contracts	125,000	Total liabilities and	
Total assets	$500,000	owners' equity	$500,000

Additional information:

a. Single-game tickets sold for $4 per game. The team averaged 1,500 fans per game. With 70 home games × $4 per game × 1,500 fans, single-game ticket revenue amounted to $420,000.

b. No season tickets were sold during the first season. During the last three months of 2001, however, an aggressive sales campaign resulted in the sale of 500 season tickets for the 2002 season. Therefore, the controller (who is also one of the owners) chose to record an Account Receivable—Season Tickets and corresponding revenue for 500 tickets × $4 per game × 70 games, or $140,000.

c. Advertising revenue of $100,000 resulted from the sale of the 40 signs on the outfield wall at $2,500 each for the season. However, none of the advertisers have paid their bills yet (thus, an account receivable of $100,000 on the balance sheet) because the contract with Lakeside required them to pay only if the team averaged 2,000 fans per game during the 2001 season. The controller believes that the advertisers will be sympathetic to the difficulties of starting a new franchise and be willing to overlook the slight deficiency in the attendance requirement.

d. Lakeside has a working agreement with one of the major-league franchises. The minor-league team is required to pay $5,000 *every* year to the major-league team for each of the 25 players on its roster. The controller believes that each of the players is certainly an asset to the organization and has therefore recorded $5,000 × 25, or $125,000, as an asset called Player Contracts. The item on the right side of the balance sheet entitled Parent Club's Equity is the amount owed to the major league team by February 1, 2002, as payment for the players for the 2001 season.

e. In addition to the cost described in **d,** Lakeside directly pays each of its 25 players a $9,000 salary for the season. This amount—$225,000—has already been paid for the 2001 season and is reported on the income statement.

f. The items on the balance sheet entitled Auxiliary Assets on the left side and Additional Owners' Capital on the right side represent the value of the controller's personal residence. She has a mortgage with the bank for the full value of the house.

g. The $50,000 note payable resulted from a loan that was taken out at the beginning of the year to finance the purchase of bats, balls, uniforms, lawn mowers, and other miscellaneous supplies needed to operate the team (equipment is reported as an asset for the same amount). The loan, with interest, is due on April 15, 2002. Even though the team had a very successful first year, Lakeside is a little short of cash at the end of 2001 and has therefore asked the bank for a three-month extension of the loan. The controller reasons, "By the due date of April 15, 2002, the cash due from the new season ticket holders will be available, things will be cleared up with the advertisers, and the loan can be easily repaid."

Required

1. Identify any errors that you think the controller has made in preparing the financial statements.
2. On the basis of your answer in **1,** prepare a revised income statement, statement of retained earnings, and balance sheet.
3. On the basis of your revised financial statements, identify any ethical dilemma you now face. Do you have a responsibility to share these revisions with the other three owners? What is your responsibility to the bank?

INTERNET RESEARCH CASE

www.benjerry.com
www.unilever.com

www.sec.com

Case 1-6 Ben & Jerry's (Unilever)

Imagine brown sugar ice cream with roasted pecans. Add chunks of pecan pieces and a pecan-caramel swirl, and you have Ben & Jerry's Southern Pecan Pie ice cream. This is just one of the many ice cream products the company has developed to attract customers. Every purchase of a Ben & Jerry's product influences the company's sales, cost of sales, net income, and other financial aspects.

On April 12, 2000, Unilever announced that it was purchasing Ben & Jerry's. The results of this announcement would be that the purchase would eliminate Ben & Jerry's as a separate public company, and its financial results become part of Unilever's. But as a public company for its 1999 fiscal year, Ben & Jerry's reporting of 1999 results to the Securities and Exchange Commission (SEC) are a matter of record, and you can compare its 1998 annual report with the 1999 numbers in its Form 10-K using EDGAR Online, a database of SEC filings at its Web site.

To track the results of the deal, access Ben & Jerry's Web site, Unilever's Web site, business news pages, and EDGAR Online. Then answer the following questions.

1. Locate Ben & Jerry's net sales and cost of sales in its 1999 statement of income. How do these numbers compare with the amounts for these items in the Selected Financial Data for 1998 in the opening vignette shown at the start of the chapter?
2. From Ben & Jerry's 1999 income statement, what is its gross profit? How has this amount changed from 1998? What may have caused this change?
3. Access business news sites to find out what announcements have been made by both companies.
4. How well is Ben & Jerry's performing? Where did you find this information?

Solutions to Key Terms Quiz

__4__ Accounting (p. 6)
__9__ Management accounting (p. 6)
__5__ Financial accounting (p. 7)
__6__ Owners' equity (p. 9)
__3__ Stockholders' equity (p. 9)
__8__ Retained earnings (p. 9)
__7__ Balance sheet (p. 9)
__1__ Income statement (p. 9)
__10__ Dividends (p. 11)
__2__ Statement of retained earnings (p. 11)
__12__ Cost principle (p. 14)
__16__ Going concern (p. 14)
__18__ Monetary unit (p. 14)
__21__ Time period (p. 15)
__11__ Generally accepted accounting principles (GAAP) (p. 15)
__13__ Securities and Exchange Commission (SEC) (p. 16)
__17__ Financial Accounting Standards Board (FASB) (p. 16)
__19__ American Institute of Certified Public Accountants (AICPA) (p. 16)
__24__ International Accounting Standards Committee (IASC) (p. 16)
__22__ Controller (p. 16)
__15__ Treasurer (p. 16)
__20__ Internal auditing (p. 17)
__23__ Auditing (p. 18)
__25__ Auditors' report (p. 18)
__14__ American Accounting Association (p. 20)

Chapter 2

Financial Statements and the Annual Report

Study Links

A Look at the Previous Chapter

Chapter 1 introduced the role of accounting in our society. We explored how investors, creditors, and others use accounting and the outputs of an accounting system—financial statements—in making informed decisions.

A Look at This Chapter

In this chapter, we take a closer look at the financial statements, as well as the other elements that make up an annual report. In the first part of the chapter, we explore the underlying conceptual framework of accounting. Every discipline has a set of interrelated concepts, principles, and conventions that guide daily practice. In the second part of the chapter, we will see how the concepts introduced in the first part of the chapter are used in the development of financial statements.

A Look at Upcoming Chapters

Chapter 2 focuses on the end result by examining the outputs of an accounting system, the financial statements. We will take a step back in Chapters 3 and 4, to consider how economic events are processed in an accounting system and are then summarized in the financial statements.

Focus on Financial Results

Gateway, the computer manufacturer and retailer, had a banner year in 1998, setting company records for sales and market share. Some important strategic moves accompanied these financial gains. The company moved its headquarters to San Diego and expanded its offices to Irvine, California. A large new manufacturing center in Salt Lake City was opened in 1998, and new information technology headquarters opened in Lakewood, Colorado, along with phone centers in Colorado Springs and Rio Rancho, New Mexico. The company introduced new products, including notebook and networking hardware and customer support software and services. It also hired 10 new top-level executives. Quick response to competitors and continual change are critical in this fast-paced industry.

All these changes cost money, but Gateway sees it as money well spent. Investments in the future make sense to this successful and growing firm. In fact, Gateway's 1998 annual report says the company is already starting to see the results of the changes.

According to John Todd, senior vice president and chief financial officer, "A company has three kinds of resources—human, technology, and financial." Gateway's 1998 balance sheet highlights the big changes in the firm's financial resources. Its holdings of cash and cash equivalents almost doubled, and property, plant, and equipment also increased considerably. Are these the financial results you would expect from a firm committed to improving all three kinds of resources?

Note to students: Gateway chooses to report the current year to the right side of the prior year. Most companies report the current year on the left side.

CONSOLIDATED BALANCE SHEETS

December 31, 1997 and 1998

(in thousands, except per share amounts)

	1997	1998
ASSETS		
Current assets:		
Cash and cash equivalents	$ 593,601	$ 1,169,810
Marketable securities	38,648	158,657
Accounts receivable, net	510,679	558,851
Inventory	249,224	167,924
Other	152,531	172,944
Total current assets	1,544,683	2,228,186
Property, plant and equipment, net	376,467	530,988
Intangibles, net	82,590	65,944
Other assets	35,531	65,262
	$ 2,039,271	$ 2,890,380
LIABILITIES AND STOCKHOLDERS' EQUITY		
Current liabilities:		
Notes payable and current maturities of long-term obligations	$ 13,969	$ 11,415
Accounts payable	488,717	718,071
Accrued liabilities	271,250	415,265
Accrued royalties	159,418	167,873
Other current liabilities	70,552	117,050
Total current liabilities	1,003,906	1,429,674
Long-term obligations, net of current maturities	7,240	3,360
Warranty and other liabilities	98,081	112,971
Total liabilities	1,109,227	1,546,005
Commitments and Contingencies (Notes 3 and 4)		
Stockholders' equity:		
Preferred stock, $.01 par value, 5,000 shares authorized; none issued and outstanding	—	—
Class A common stock, nonvoting, $.01 par value, 1,000 shares authorized; none issued and outstanding	—	—
Common stock, $.01 par value, 220,000 shares authorized; 154,128 shares and 156,569 shares issued and outstanding, respectively	1,541	1,566
Additional paid-in capital	299,483	365,986
Retained earnings	634,509	980,908
Accumulated other comprehensive loss	(5,489)	(4,085)
Total stockholders' equity	930,044	1,344,375
	$ 2,039,271	$ 2,890,380

Cash and cash equivalents nearly doubled from 1997 to 1998.

Property, plant, and equipment increased considerably as company growth occurred.

The accompanying notes are an integral part of the consolidated financial statements.

Gateway 1998 Annual Report

If you were thinking of buying shares of Gateway stock, what questions about Gateway's future plans would you want answered? Use this chapter, Gateway's annual report, and its Web site to help you identify and evaluate information about the company's financial performance and the management's plans for use of the firm's resources.

www.gateway.com

Learning Objectives

After studying this chapter, you should be able to:

- **LO 1** Describe the objectives of financial reporting. (p. 46)
- **LO 2** Describe the qualitative characteristics of accounting information. (p. 47)
- **LO 3** Explain the concept and purpose of a classified balance sheet and prepare the statement. (p. 53)
- **LO 4** Use a classified balance sheet to analyze a company's financial position. (p. 58)
- **LO 5** Explain the difference between a single-step and a multiple-step income statement and prepare each type of income statement. (p. 60)
- **LO 6** Use a multiple-step income statement to analyze a company's operations. (p. 62)
- **LO 7** Identify the components of the statement of retained earnings and prepare the statement. (p. 62)
- **LO 8** Identify the components of the statement of cash flows and prepare the statement. (p. 63)
- **LO 9** Read and use the financial statements and other elements in the annual report of a publicly held company. (p. 64)

Why Does Accounting Information Need to Be Useful? Objectives of Financial Reporting

LO 1 Describe the objectives of financial reporting.

The users of financial information are the main reason financial statements are prepared. After all, it is the investors, creditors, and other groups and individuals outside and inside the company who must make economic decisions based on these statements. Therefore, as we learned in Chapter 1, financial statements must be based on agreed-upon assumptions like time-period, going concern, and other generally accepted accounting principles.

Moreover, when the accountants for companies like Ben & Jerry's and Gateway prepare their financial statements, they must keep in mind financial reporting objectives, which are focused on providing the most understandable and useful information possible. Financial reporting has one overall objective and a set of related objectives, all of them concerned with how the information may be most useful to the readers.

The Primary Objective: Provide Information for Decision Making

The primary objective of financial reporting is *to provide economic information to permit users of the information to make informed decisions.* Users include both the management of a company (internal users) and others not involved in the daily operations of the business (external users). Without access to the detailed records of the business and without the benefit of daily involvement in the affairs of the company, external users make their decisions based on *financial statements* prepared by management. According to the Financial Accounting Standards Board (FASB), "Financial reporting should provide information that is useful to present and potential investors and creditors and other users in making rational investment, credit, and similar decisions".[1]

We see from this statement how closely the objective of financial reporting is tied to decision making. *The purpose of financial reporting is to help the users reach their decisions in an informed manner.*

[1] *Statement of Financial Accounting Concepts [SFAC] No. 1,* "Objectives of Financial Reporting by Business Enterprises" (Stamford, Conn.: Financial Accounting Standards Board, November 1978), par. 34.

Secondary Objective: Reflect Prospective Cash Receipts to Investors and Creditors

Present stockholders must decide whether to hold their stock in a company or sell it. For potential stockholders, the decision is whether to buy the stock in the first place. Bankers, suppliers, and other types of creditors must decide whether to lend money to a company. In making their decisions, all these groups rely partially on the information provided in financial statements. (Other sources of information are sometimes as important, or more important, in reaching a decision. For example, the most recent income statement may report the highest profits in the history of a company. However, a potential investor may choose not to buy stock in a company if the *Wall Street Journal* or *Business Week* reports that a strike is likely to shut down operations for an indeterminable period of time.)

www.wsj.com
www.businessweek.com

If you buy stock in a company, your primary concern is the *future cash to be received from the investment.* First, how much, if anything, will you periodically receive in *cash dividends?* Second, how much cash will you receive from the *sale of the stock?* The interests of a creditor, such as a banker, are similar. The banker is concerned with receiving the original amount of money lent and the interest on the loan. In summary, another objective of financial reporting is to "provide information to help present and potential investors and creditors and other users in assessing the amounts, timing, and uncertainty of prospective cash receipts from dividends or interest and the proceeds from the sale, redemption, or maturity of securities or loans".[2]

Secondary Objective: Reflect Prospective Cash Flows to the Enterprise

As an investor your ultimate concern is not the company's cash flows—how much comes in and goes out in the course of doing business—but the cash you receive from your investment. But since your investment depends to some extent on the company's business skills in managing its cash flows, another objective of accounting is to provide information that will allow users to make decisions about the cash flows of a company. (We will discuss cash flows briefly later in the chapter and will return to them in Chapter 12.)

Secondary Objective: Reflect the Enterprise's Resources and Claims to Its Resources

The FASB emphasizes the roles of the balance sheet and the income statement in providing useful information. These financial statements should reflect what *resources* (or assets) the company or enterprise has, what *claims to these resources* (liabilities and stockholders' equity) there are, and the effects of transactions and events that change these resources and claims.[3] Thus, another objective of financial reporting is to show the effect of transactions on the entity's "accounting equation."

Exhibit 2-1 summarizes the objectives of financial reporting as they pertain to someone considering whether to buy stock in Gateway. The exhibit should help you to understand how something as abstract as a set of financial reporting objectives can be applied to a decision-making situation.

What Makes Accounting Information Useful? Qualitative Characteristics

LO 2 Describe the qualitative characteristics of accounting information.

Since accounting information must be useful for decision making, what makes this information useful? This section focuses on the qualities that accountants strive for in

[2] *SFAC No. 1,* par. 37.
[3] *SFAC No. 1,* par. 40.

EXHIBIT 2-1 The Application of Financial Reporting Objectives

Financial Reporting Objective	Potential Investor's Questions
1. The primary objective: Provide information for decision making.	"Based on the financial information, should I buy shares of stock in Gateway?"
2. Secondary objective: Reflect prospective cash receipts to investors and creditors.	"How much cash will I receive in dividends each year and from the sale of the stock of Gateway in the future?"
3. Secondary objective: Reflect prospective cash flows to an enterprise.	"After paying its suppliers and employees, and meeting all of its obligations, how much cash will Gateway take in during the time I own the stock?"
4. Secondary objective: Reflect resources and claims to resources.	"How much has Gateway invested in new plant and equipment?"

their financial reporting and on some of the challenges they face in making reporting judgments. It also reveals what users of financial information expect from financial statements.

Quantitative considerations, such as tuition costs, certainly were a concern when you chose your current school. In addition, your decision required you to make subjective judgments about the *qualitative* characteristics you were looking for in a college. Similarly, there are certain qualities that make accounting information useful.

Characteristics:

UNDERSTANDABILITY

UNDERSTANDABILITY The quality of accounting information that makes it comprehensible to those willing to spend the necessary time.

For anything to be useful, it must be understandable. Usefulness and understandability go hand in hand. However, **understandability** of financial information varies considerably, depending on the background of the user. For example, should financial statements be prepared so that they are understandable by anyone with a college education? Or should it be assumed that all readers of financial statements have completed at least one accounting course? Is a background in business necessary for a good understanding of financial reports, regardless of one's formal training? As you might expect, there are no simple answers to these questions. However, the FASB believes that financial information should be comprehensible to *those who are willing to spend the time to understand it:* "Financial information is a tool and, like most tools, cannot be of much direct help to those who are unable or unwilling to use it or who misuse it. Its use can be learned, however, and financial reporting should provide information that can be used by all—nonprofessionals as well as professionals—who are willing to learn to use it properly."[4]

RELEVANCE

RELEVANCE The capacity of information to make a difference in a decision.

Understandability alone is certainly not enough to render information useful. To be useful, information must be relevant. **Relevance** is the capacity of information to make a difference in a decision.[5] For example, assume that you are a banker evaluating the financial statements of a company that has come to you for a loan. All of the financial statements point to a strong and profitable company. However, today's newspaper revealed that the company has been named in a multimillion-dollar lawsuit. Undoubtedly, this information would be relevant to your talks with the company, and disclosure of the lawsuit in the financial statements would make them even more relevant to your lending decision.

[4] *SFAC No. 1,* par. 36.

[5] *Statement of Financial Accounting Concepts [SFAC] No. 2,* "Qualitative Characteristics of Accounting Information" (Stamford, Conn.: Financial Accounting Standards Board, May 1980), par. 47.

Accounting for Your Decisions

You Are the Stockholder

ABC Technology produces a highly technical product used in the computer industry. You are a stockholder and are currently in the process of reading this year's annual report. You find that you can't understand the report because it contains so much accounting jargon. But the annual report contains a 1-800 number for shareholder inquiries. You call the number and complain about the annual report, but the corporate spokesman politely tells you that "that's the way people talk in accounting." Is your complaint valid?

ANS: One of the purposes of an annual report is to interest potential stockholders in the company. A small percentage of those potential investors are professional money managers who are familiar with the accounting terminology. However, most readers are individual investors who probably don't have a sophisticated accounting background. It is true that the report must assume a minimum level of formal education; accountants expect those who read the report to take the time to understand it. Technicalities aside, however, it is important to write an annual report for as broad an audience as possible.

Reliability

What makes accounting information reliable? According to the FASB, "Accounting information is reliable to the extent that users can depend on it to represent the economic conditions or events that it purports to represent."[6]

Reliability has three basic characteristics:

Reliability The quality that makes accounting information dependable in representing the events that it purports to represent.

- *Verifiability* Information is verifiable when we can make sure that it is free from error—for example, by looking up the cost paid for an asset in a contract or an invoice.

Business Strategy

Dell Computers, like Gateway, is in the business of selling computers directly to consumers and to business and government organizations. It makes each machine to order and, like Gateway, carries a very small inventory at any one time. Dell also shares with Gateway a strategy of growth, seeking to enlarge its market share against such established giants as Compaq and IBM. However, focusing only on growth led Dell to two missteps in the mid-1990s. First, the firm expanded its product line with notebook computers that fell short of its quality standards, and second, Dell began selling its computers through retail outlets such as CompUSA, Wal-Mart, and Staples.

The flawed notebook computers were quickly withdrawn from the market, and within a year the firm also took itself out of the retail business, which had increased sales at first but which ultimately led to a net loss due to the high cost of protecting dealers from price changes.

Dell is now refocusing on its real strength: selling directly to large and small customers who know what they need and want. As Chairman Michael Dell tells it today: "The real benefit in exiting retail was not just the profit and loss, but the internal clarification. Everybody began to understand the strategy of Dell."

Source: Lawrence M. Fisher, "Inside Dell Computer Corporation: Managing Working Capital," *Strategy and Business* 10 (first quarter 1998): 68–75.

www.dell.com

[6] *SFAC No. 2,* par. 62.

- *Representational faithfulness* Information is representationally faithful when it corresponds to an actual event—such as when the purchase of land corresponds to a transaction in the company's records.
- *Neutrality* Information is neutral when it is not slanted to portray a company's position in a better or worse light than the actual circumstances would dictate—such as when the probable losses from a major lawsuit are disclosed accurately in the notes to the financial statements, with all its potential effects on the company, rather than minimized as a very remote possible loss.

Comparability and Consistency

Comparability
For accounting information, the quality that allows a user to analyze two or more companies and look for similarities and differences.

Depreciation
The process of allocating the cost of a long-term tangible asset over its useful life.

Comparability allows comparisons to be made *between or among companies.* Generally accepted accounting principles (GAAP) allow a certain amount of freedom in choosing among competing alternative treatments for certain transactions.

For example, under GAAP, companies may choose from a number of methods of accounting for the depreciation of certain long-term assets. **Depreciation** is the *process of allocating* the cost of a long-term tangible asset, such as a building or equipment, over its useful life. Each method may affect the value of the assets differently. (We discuss depreciation in Chapter 8.) How does this freedom of choice affect the ability of investors to make comparisons between companies?

Assume you were considering buying stock in one of three companies. As their annual reports indicate, two of the companies use what is called the "accelerated" depreciation method, and the other company uses what is called the "straight-line" depreciation method. (We'll learn about these methods in a later chapter.) Does this lack of a common depreciation method make it impossible for you to compare the performance of the three companies?

Obviously, comparisons among the companies would be easier and more meaningful if all three used the same depreciation method. However, comparisons are not impossible just because companies use different methods. Certainly, the more alike—that is, uniform—statements are in terms of the principles used to prepare them, the more comparable they will be. However, the profession allows a certain freedom of choice in selecting from among alternative generally accepted accounting principles.

To render statements of companies using different methods more meaningful, *disclosure* assumes a very important role. For example, as we will see later in this chapter, the first footnote in the annual report of a publicly traded company is the disclosure of its accounting policies. The reader of this footnote for each of the three companies is made aware that the companies do not use the same depreciation method. Disclosure of accounting policies allows the reader to make some sort of subjective adjustment to the statements of one or more of the companies and thus to compensate for the different depreciation method being used.

Consistency
For accounting information, the quality that allows a user to compare two or more accounting periods for a single company.

Consistency is closely related to the concept of comparability. Both involve the relationship between two numbers. *However, whereas financial statements are comparable when they can be compared between one company and another, statements are* consistent *when they can be compared within a single company from one accounting period to the next.*

Occasionally, companies decide to change from one accounting method to another. Will it be possible to compare a company's earnings in a period in which it switches methods with its earnings in prior years if the methods differ? Like the different methods used by different companies, changes in accounting methods from one period to the next do not make comparisons impossible, only more difficult. When a company makes an accounting change, accounting standards require various disclosures to help the reader evaluate the impact of the change.

Companies still produce printed annual reports as a way to summarize the past year's business activities, discuss the firm's performance, preview upcoming products and business trends, and give investors and other users of financial information a format for analyzing the financial information. But most companies also provide annual report information—along with news reports and current information—at the *Investor Relations* page on their Web site. You can search for Gateway's at www.gateway.com.

MATERIALITY

For accounting information to be useful, it must be relevant to a decision. The concept of **materiality** is closely related to relevance and deals with the size of an error in accounting information. The issue is whether the error is large enough to affect the judgment of someone relying on the information. Consider the following example. A company pays cash for two separate purchases: one for a $5 pencil sharpener and the other for a $50,000 computer. Theoretically, each expenditure results in the acquisition of an asset that should be depreciated over its useful life. However, what if the company decides to account for the $5 as an expense of the period rather than treat it in the theoretically correct manner by depreciating it over the life of the pencil sharpener? *Will this error in any way affect the judgment of someone relying on the financial statements?* Because such a slight error will *not* affect any decisions, minor expenditures of this nature are considered *immaterial* and are accounted for as an expense of the period.

MATERIALITY
The magnitude of an accounting information omission or misstatement that will affect the judgment of someone relying on the information.

The *threshold* for determining materiality will vary from one company to the next, depending to a large extent on the size of the company. Many companies establish policies that *any* expenditure under a certain dollar amount should be accounted for as an expense of the period. The threshold might be $50 for the corner grocery store but $1,000 for a large corporation. Finally, in some instances the amount of a transaction may be immaterial by company standards but may still be considered significant by financial statement users. For example, a transaction involving either illegal or unethical behavior by a company officer would be of concern, regardless of the dollar amounts involved.

CONSERVATISM

The concept of **conservatism** is a holdover from earlier days when the primary financial statement was the balance sheet and the primary user of this statement was the banker. It was customary to deliberately understate assets in the balance sheet because this resulted in an even larger margin of safety that the assets being provided as collateral for a loan were sufficient.

CONSERVATISM
The practice of using the least optimistic estimate when two estimates of amounts are about equally likely.

EXHIBIT 2-2 Qualitative Characteristics of Accounting Information

SITUATION A bank is trying to decide whether to extend a $1 million loan to Russell Corporation. Russell presents the bank with its most recent balance sheet, showing its financial position on a historical cost basis. Each quality of the information is summarized in the form of a question.

Quality	Question
Understandability	Can the information be used by those willing to learn to use it properly?
Relevance	Would the information be useful in deciding whether or not to loan money to Russell?
Reliability	
Verifiability	Can the information be verified? Is the information free from error?
Representational faithfulness	Is there agreement between the information and the events represented?
Neutrality	Is the information slanted in any way to present the company more favorably than is warranted?
Comparability	Are the methods used in assigning amounts to assets the same as those used by other companies?
Consistency	Are the methods used in assigning amounts to assets the same as those used in prior years?
Materiality	Will a specific error in any way affect the judgment of someone relying on the financial statements?
Conservatism	If there is any uncertainty about any of the amounts assigned to items in the balance sheet, are they recognized using the least optimistic estimate?

Today the balance sheet is not the only financial statement, and deliberate understatement of assets is no longer considered desirable. The practice of conservatism is reserved for those situations in which there is *uncertainty* about how to account for a particular item or transaction: "Thus, if two estimates of amounts to be received or paid in the future are about equally likely, conservatism dictates using the less optimistic estimate; however, if two amounts are not equally likely, conservatism does not necessarily dictate using the more pessimistic amount rather than the more likely one."[7]

Various accounting rules are based on the concept of conservatism. For example, inventory held for resale is reported on the balance sheet at *the lower-of-cost-or-market value.* This rule requires a company to compare the cost of its inventory with the market price, or current cost to replace that inventory, and report the lower of the two amounts on the balance sheet at the end of the year. In Chapter 6 we will more fully explore the lower-of-cost-or-market rule as it pertains to inventory.

Exhibit 2-2 summarizes the qualities that make accounting information useful as these characteristics pertain to a banker's decision regarding whether to lend money to a company.

FINANCIAL REPORTING: AN INTERNATIONAL PERSPECTIVE

In Chapter 1 we introduced the International Accounting Standards Committee (IASC) and its efforts to improve the development of accounting standards around the world. Interestingly, four of the most influential members of this group, representing the standard-setting bodies in the United States, the United Kingdom, Canada, and Australia, agree on

[7] *SFAC No. 2,* par. 95.

the primary objective of financial reporting. All recognize that the primary objective is to provide information useful in making economic decisions.

The standard-setting body in the United Kingdom distinguishes between qualitative characteristics that relate to *content* of the information presented and those that relate to *presentation.* Similar to the FASB, this group recognizes relevance and reliability as the primary characteristics related to content. Comparability and understandability are the primary qualities related to the presentation of the information.

The concept of conservatism is also recognized in other countries. For example, both the IASC and the standard-setting body in the United Kingdom list "prudence" among their qualitative characteristics. Prudence requires the use of caution in making the various estimates required in accounting. Like the U.S. standard-setting body, these groups recognize that prudence does not justify the deliberate understatement of assets or revenues or the deliberate overstatement of liabilities or expenses.

The Classified Balance Sheet

LO 3 Explain the concept and purpose of a classified balance sheet and prepare the statement.

Now that we have learned about the conceptual framework of accounting, we turn to the outputs of the system: the financial statements. First, we will consider the significance of a *classified balance sheet.* We will then examine the *income statement,* the *statement of retained earnings,* and the *statement of cash flows.* The chapter concludes with a brief look at the financial statements of a real company, Gateway, and at the other elements in an annual report.

What Are the Parts of the Balance Sheet? Understanding the Operating Cycle

In the first part of this chapter, we stressed the importance of *cash flow.* For a company that sells a product, the **operating cycle** begins when cash is invested in inventory and ends when cash is collected by the enterprise from its customers.

Operating cycle The period of time between the purchase of inventory and the collection of any receivable from the sale of the inventory.

Assume that on August 1 a retailer, Laptop Computer Sales, buys a computer for $5,000 from the manufacturer, BIM Corp. At this point, Laptop has merely substituted one asset, cash, for another, inventory. On August 20, 20 days after buying the computer, Laptop sells it to an accounting firm, Arthur & Company, for $6,000. Under the purchase agreement, Arthur will pay for the computer within the next 30 days. At this point, both the form of the asset and the amount have changed. The form of the asset held by Laptop has changed from inventory to accounts receivable. Also, because the inventory has been sold for $1,000 more than its cost of $5,000, the size of the asset held, the account receivable, is now $6,000. Finally, on September 20, Arthur pays $6,000 to Laptop, and the operating cycle is complete. As we will explore more fully in later chapters, Laptop has earned $1,000, the difference between what it sold the computer for and what it initially paid for the computer. The cycle starts again when Laptop buys another computer for resale.

Laptop's operating cycle is summarized in Exhibit 2-3. The length of the company's operating cycle was 50 days. The operating cycle consisted of two distinct parts. From the time Laptop purchased the inventory, 20 days elapsed before it sold the computer. Another 30 days passed before the account receivable was collected. The length of the operating cycle depends to a large extent on the nature of a company's business. For example, in our illustration, the manufacturer of the computer, BIM Corp., received cash immediately from Laptop and did not have to wait to collect a receivable. However, additional time is added to the operating cycle of BIM Corp. to *manufacture* the computer.

Study Tip

The operating cycle of a business is the basis for deciding which assets are current and which are noncurrent. When you look at a company's balance sheet, be sure you understand the length of its operating cycle so you are clear about how it classifies its assets.

The operating cycle of the accounting firm in our example, Arthur & Company, differs from that of either the manufacturer or the retailer. Arthur sells a service rather

EXHIBIT 2-3 The Operating Cycle for a Retailer

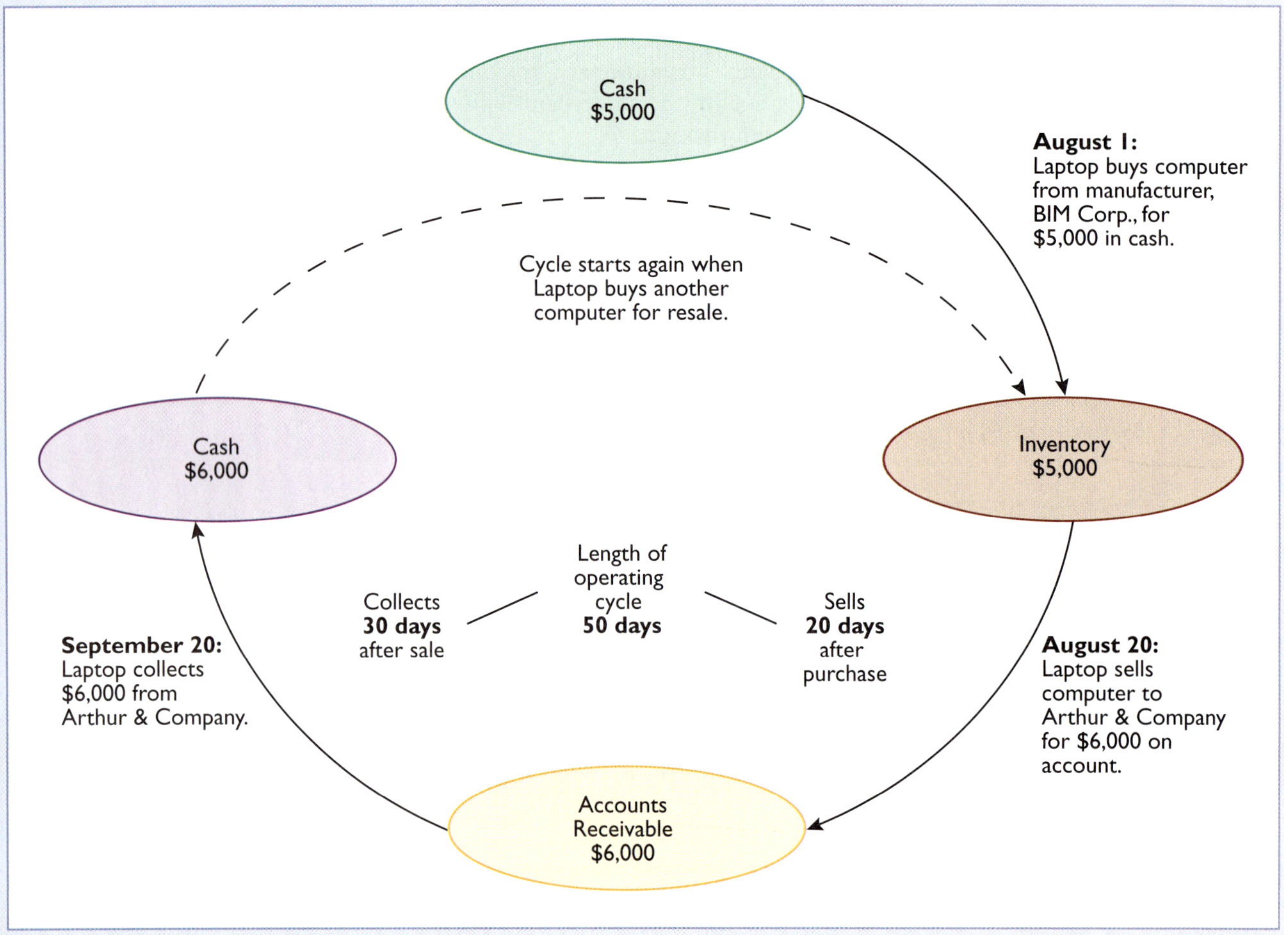

than a product. Its operating cycle is determined by two factors: the length of time involved in providing a service to the client and the amount of time required to collect any account receivable.

A classified balance sheet for a hypothetical company, Dixon Sporting Goods Inc., is shown in Exhibit 2-4. You will want to refer to it as you learn about the different categories on a classified balance sheet. (The bulleted numbers below refer to Exhibit 2-4.)

CURRENT ASSETS 1

CURRENT ASSET
An asset that is expected to be realized in cash or sold or consumed during the operating cycle or within one year if the cycle is shorter than one year.

The basic distinction on a classified balance sheet is between current and noncurrent items. **Current assets** are "cash and other assets that are reasonably expected to be realized in cash or sold or consumed during the normal operating cycle of a business or within one year if the operating cycle is shorter than one year."[8]

Most businesses have an operating cycle shorter than one year. The operating cycle for Laptop Computer Sales in our illustration was 50 days. Therefore cash, accounts receivable, and inventory are classified as current assets because they *are* cash, will be *realized* in (converted to) cash (accounts receivable), or will be *sold* (inventory) within one year.

[8]Accounting Principles Board, *Statement of the Accounting Principles Board, No. 4,* "Basic Concepts and Accounting Principles Underlying Financial Statements of Business Enterprises" (New York: American Institute of Certified Public Accountants, 1970), par. 198.

EXHIBIT 2-4 Balance Sheet for Dixon Sporting Goods

1. These assets are realizable, sold, or consumed in one year or operating cycle.
2. These assets will not be realizable, sold, or consumed within one year or operating cycle.
3. These are liabilities that will be satisfied within one year or operating cycle.
4. These are liabilities that will not be satisfied within one year or operating cycle.
5. These are owners' claims on assets.

DIXON SPORTING GOODS INC.
BALANCE SHEET
AT DECEMBER 31, 2001

ASSETS			
Current assets			
Cash		$ 5,000	
Marketable securities		11,000	
Accounts receivable		23,000	
Merchandise inventory		73,500	
Prepaid insurance		4,800	
Store supplies		700	
Total current assets			$118,000
Investments			
Land held for future office site			150,000
Property, plant, and equipment			
Land		100,000	
Buildings	$150,000		
Less: Accumulated depreciation	60,000	90,000	
Store furniture and fixtures	$ 42,000		
Less: Accumulated depreciation	12,600	29,400	
Total property, plant, and equipment			219,400
Intangible assets			
Franchise agreement			55,000
Total assets			$542,400
LIABILITIES			
Current liabilities			
Accounts payable		$ 15,700	
Salaries and wages payable		9,500	
Income taxes payable		7,200	
Interest payable		2,500	
Bank loan payable		25,000	
Total current liabilities			$ 59,900
Long-term debt			
Notes payable, due December 31, 2011			120,000
Total liabilities			$179,900
STOCKHOLDERS' EQUITY			
Contributed capital			
Capital stock, $10 par, 5,000 shares issued and outstanding		$ 50,000	
Paid-in capital in excess of par value		25,000	
Total contributed capital		$ 75,000	
Retained earnings		287,500	
Total stockholders' equity			362,500
Total liabilities and stockholders' equity			$542,400

Can you think of a situation in which a company's operating cycle is longer than one year? A construction company is a good example. A construction company essentially builds an item of inventory, such as an office building, to a customer's specifications. The entire process, including constructing the building and collecting the sales amount from the customer, may take three years to complete. According to our earlier definition, because the inventory will be sold and the account receivable will be collected within the operating cycle, they will still qualify as current assets.

In addition to cash, accounts receivable, and inventory, the two other most common types of current assets are marketable securities and prepaid expenses. Excess cash is often invested in the stocks and bonds of other companies, as well as in various government instruments. If the investments are made for the short term, they are classified as current and are typically called either *short-term investments* or *marketable securities.* (Alternatively, some investments are made for the purpose of exercising influence over another company and thus are made for the long term. These investments are classified as noncurrent assets.) Various prepayments, such as office supplies, rent, and insurance, are classified as *prepaid expenses* and thus are current assets. These assets qualify as current because they will usually be *consumed* within one year.

Compare the length of the operating cycle of a builder of an office building (or of communications equipment for the Internet) to that of a computer retailer. From the time a construction project "launches" to cash collection may be years, not weeks or months.

NONCURRENT ASSETS 2

Any assets that do not meet the definition of a current asset are classified as *long-term* or *noncurrent assets.* Three common categories of long-term assets are: investments; property, plant, and equipment; and intangibles.

Investments Recall, from the discussion of current assets, that stocks and bonds expected to be sold within the next year are classified as current assets. Securities that are *not* expected to be sold within the next year are classified as *investments.* In many cases, the investment is in the common stock of another company. Sometimes companies invest in another company either to exercise some influence or actually to control the operation of the other company. Other types of assets classified as investments are land held for future use and buildings and equipment not currently used in operations. Finally, a special fund held for the retirement of debt or for the construction of new facilities is also classified as an investment.

Property, Plant, and Equipment This category consists of the various *tangible, productive assets* used in the operation of a business. Land, buildings, equipment, machinery, furniture and fixtures, trucks, and tools are all examples of assets held for use in the *operation* of a business rather than for *resale.* The distinction between inventory and equipment, for example, depends on the company's *intent* in acquiring the asset. For example, IBM classifies a computer system as inventory because its intent in manufacturing the asset is to offer it for resale. However, this same computer in the hands of a law firm would be classified as equipment because its intent in buying the asset from IBM is to use it in the long-term operation of the business.

www.ibm.com

The relative size of property, plant, and equipment depends largely on a company's business. Consider US West, a telecommunications company with over $18 billion in total assets at the end of 1998. Over 80% of the total assets was invested in property, plant, and equipment. On the other hand, property and equipment represented less than 7% of the total assets of Microsoft, the highly successful software company. Regardless of the relative size of property, plant, and equipment, all assets in this category are subject to depreciation, with the exception of land. A separate accumulated depreciation account is used to account for the depreciation recorded on each of these assets over its life.

www.uswest.com

www.microsoft.com

Intangibles Intangible assets are similar to property, plant, and equipment in that they provide benefits to the firm over the long term. The distinction, however, is in the *form* of the asset. *Intangible assets lack physical substance.* Trademarks, copyrights, franchise rights, patents, and goodwill are examples of intangible assets. The cost principle governs the accounting for intangibles, just as it does for tangible assets. For example, the amount paid to an inventor for the patent rights to a new project is recorded as an intangible asset. Similarly, the amount paid to purchase a franchise for a fast-food restaurant for the exclusive right to operate in a certain geographic area is recorded as an intangible asset. Like tangible assets, intangibles are written off to expense over their useful lives. *Depreciation* is the name given to the process of writing off tangible assets; the same process for intangible assets is called *amortization.* Depreciation and amortization are both explained more fully in Chapter 8.

Two-Minute Review

1. *Give at least three examples of current assets.*
2. *Give the three common categories of noncurrent assets.*

Answers:

1. *Cash, accounts receivable, inventory, short-term investments, and prepaid expenses.*
2. *Investments, property, plant, and equipment, and intangibles.*

ACCOUNTING FOR YOUR DECISIONS

You Are a Student

Identify any assets you currently have, and then categorize them as either current or noncurrent.

ANS: Among your current assets would be cash and any investments you expect to sell in the near future. Your car would be a noncurrent asset.

CURRENT LIABILITIES 3

The definition of a current liability is closely tied to that of a current asset. A **current liability** is an obligation that will be satisfied within the next operating cycle or within one year, if the cycle is shorter than one year. For example, the classification of a note payable on the balance sheet depends on its maturity date. If the note will be paid within the next year, it is classified as current; otherwise, it is classified as a long-term liability. On the other hand, accounts payable, wages payable, and income taxes payable are all short-term or current liabilities.

CURRENT LIABILITY
An obligation that will be satisfied within the next operating cycle or within one year if the cycle is shorter than one year.

Most liabilities, such as those for purchases of merchandise on credit, are satisfied by the payment of cash. However, certain liabilities are eliminated from the balance sheet when the company performs services. For example, the liability Subscriptions Received in Advance, which would appear on the balance sheet of a magazine publisher, is satisfied not by the payment of any cash but by the delivery of the magazine to the customers. Finally, it is possible to satisfy one liability by substituting another in its place. For example, a supplier might ask a customer to sign a written promissory note to replace an existing account payable if the customer is unable to pay at the present time.

LONG-TERM LIABILITIES 4

Any obligation that will not be paid or otherwise satisfied within the next year or the operating cycle, whichever is longer, is classified as a long-term liability, or long-term debt. Notes payable and bonds payable, both promises to pay money in the future, are two common forms of long-term debt. Some bonds have a life as long as 25 or 30 years.

STOCKHOLDERS' EQUITY 5

Recall that stockholders' equity represents the owners' claims on the assets of the business. These claims arise from two sources: *contributed capital* and *earned capital.* Contributed capital appears on the balance sheet in the form of capital stock, and earned capital takes the form of retained earnings. *Capital stock* indicates the owners' investment in the business. *Retained earnings* represents the accumulated earnings, or net income, of the business since its inception less all dividends paid during that time.

Most companies have a single class of capital stock called *common stock.* This is the most basic form of ownership in a business. All other claims against the company, such as those of *creditors* and *preferred stockholders,* take priority. *Preferred stock* is a form of capital stock that, as the name implies, carries with it certain preferences. For example, the company must pay dividends on preferred stock before it makes any distribution of dividends on common stock. In the event of liquidation, preferred stockholders have priority over common stockholders in the distribution of the entity's assets.

Capital stock may appear as two separate items on the balance sheet: *Par Value* and *Paid-in Capital in Excess of Par Value.* The total of these two items tells us the amount that has been paid by the owners for the stock. We will take a closer look at these items in Chapter 11.

USING A CLASSIFIED BALANCE SHEET

LO 4 Use a classified balance sheet to analyze a company's financial position.

As we have now seen, a classified balance sheet separates both assets and liabilities into those that are current and those that are noncurrent. This distinction is very useful in any analysis of a company's financial position.

WORKING CAPITAL

LIQUIDITY
The ability of a company to pay its debts as they come due.

WORKING CAPITAL
Current assets minus current liabilities.

Investors, bankers, and other interested readers use the balance sheet to evaluate the liquidity of a business. **Liquidity** is a relative term and deals with the ability of a company to pay its debts as they come due. As you might expect, bankers and other creditors are particularly interested in the liquidity of businesses to which they have lent money. A comparison of current assets and current liabilities is a starting point in evaluating the ability of a company to meet its obligations. **Working capital** is the difference between current assets and current liabilities at a point in time. Referring back to Exhibit 2-4, we see that the working capital for Dixon Sporting Goods on December 31, 2001, is as follows:

WORKING CAPITAL

FORMULA	FOR DIXON SPORTING GOODS
Current Assets − Current Liabilities	$118,000 − $59,900 = $58,100

The management of working capital is an important task for any business. A company must continually strive for a *balance* in managing its working capital. For example, too little working capital—or in the extreme, negative working capital—may signal the inability to pay creditors on a timely basis. However, an overabundance of working capital could indicate that the company is not investing enough of its available funds in productive resources, such as new machinery and equipment.

CURRENT RATIO

CURRENT RATIO
Current assets divided by current liabilities.

Because it is an absolute dollar amount, working capital is limited in its informational value. For example, $1 million may be an inadequate amount of working capital for a large corporation but far too much for a smaller company. In addition, a certain dollar amount of working capital may have been adequate for a company earlier in its life but is inadequate now. However, a related measure of liquidity, the **current ratio,** allows us to *compare* the liquidity of companies of different sizes and of a single company over time. The ratio is computed by dividing current assets by current liabilities. Dixon Sporting goods has a current ratio of just under 2 to 1:

CURRENT RATIO

FORMULA	FOR DIXON SPORTING GOODS
$\frac{\text{Current Assets}}{\text{Current Liabilities}}$	$\frac{\$118{,}000}{\$59{,}900} = 1.97 \text{ to } 1$

Some analysts use a rule of thumb of 2 to 1 for the current ratio as a sign of short-term financial health. However, as is always the case, rules of thumb can be dangerous. Historically, companies in certain industries have operated quite efficiently with a current ratio of less than 2 to 1, whereas a ratio much higher than this is necessary to survive in other industries. Consider Tommy Hilfiger Corp., the popular clothing company. At the end of the fiscal year 1998, it had a current ratio of 4.74 to 1. On the other hand, companies in the telephone communication business routinely have current ratios well under 1 to 1. Sprint's current ratio at the end of 1998 was only .80 to 1.

www.tommy.com

www.sprint.com

Unfortunately, neither the amount of working capital nor the current ratio tells us anything about the *composition* of current assets and current liabilities. For example, assume two companies both have total current assets equal to $100,000. Company A has cash of $10,000, accounts receivable of $50,000, and inventory of $40,000. Company B also has cash of $10,000 but accounts receivable of $20,000 and inventory of $70,000. All other things being equal, Company A is more liquid than Company B because more of its total current assets are in receivables than inventory. Receivables are only one step away from being cash, whereas inventory must be sold and then the receivable collected. Note that Dixon's inventory of $73,500 makes up a large portion of its total current assets of $118,000. An examination of the *relative* size of the various current assets for a company may reveal certain strengths and weaknesses not evident in the current ratio.

In addition to the composition of the current assets, the *frequency* with which they are "turned over" is important. For instance, how long does it take to sell an item of inventory? How long is required to collect an account receivable? Many companies could not exist with the current ratio of .52 reported by the McDonald's Corporation at the end of 1998. However, think about the nature of the fast-food business. The frequency of its sales and thus the numerous operating cycles within a single year mean that it can operate with a much lower current ratio than a manufacturing company, for example.

www.mcdonalds.com

The Income Statement

The income statement is used to summarize the results of operations of an entity for a *period of time.* At a minimum, all companies prepare income statements at least once a year. Companies that must report to the Securities and Exchange Commission prepare financial statements, including an income statement, every three months. Monthly income statements are usually prepared for internal use by management.

www.sec.gov

What Appears on the Income Statement?

From an accounting perspective, it is important to understand what transactions of an entity should appear on the income statement. In general, the income statement reports the excess of *revenue over expense,* that is, the *net income,* or in the event of an excess of *expense over revenue,* the *net loss* of the period. As a reference to the "bottom line" on an income statement, it is common to use the terms *profits* or *earnings* as synonyms for *net income.*

As discussed in Chapter 1, *revenue* is the inflow of assets resulting from the sale of products and services. It represents the dollar amount of sales of products and services for a period of time. An *expense* is the outflow of assets resulting from the sale of goods and services for a period of time. The cost of products sold, wages and salaries, and taxes are all examples of expenses.

Certain special types of revenues, called *gains,* are sometimes reported on the income statement, as are certain special types of expenses, called *losses.* For example, assume that Sanders Company holds a parcel of land for a future building site. The company paid $50,000 for the land 10 years ago. The state pays Sanders $60,000 for the property to use in a new highway project. Sanders has a special type of revenue from the condemnation of its property. It will recognize a *gain* of $10,000: the excess of the cash received from the state, $60,000, over the cost of the land, $50,000.

FORMAT OF THE INCOME STATEMENT

LO 5 Explain the difference between a single-step and a multiple-step income statement and prepare each type of income statement.

Different formats are used by corporations to present their results. The major choice a company makes is whether to prepare the income statement in a single-step or a multiple-step form. Both forms are generally accepted. According to the AICPA's annual survey of 600 companies, more than twice as many use the multiple-step form than the single-step form. Next, we'll explain the differences between the two forms and their variations.

SINGLE-STEP INCOME STATEMENT An income statement in which all expenses are added together and subtracted from all revenues.

Single-Step Format for the Income Statement

In a **single-step income statement,** all expenses and losses are added together and then are deducted *in a single step* from all revenues and gains to arrive at net income. A single-step format for the income statement of Dixon Sporting Goods is presented in Exhibit 2-5. The primary advantage of the single-step form is its simplicity. No attempt is made to classify either revenues or expenses or to associate any of the expenses with any of the revenues.

MULTIPLE-STEP INCOME STATEMENT An income statement that shows classifications of revenues and expenses as well as important subtotals.

GROSS PROFIT Sales less cost of goods sold.

Multiple-Step Format for the Income Statement

The purpose of the **multiple-step income statement** is to subdivide the income statement into specific sections and provide the reader with important subtotals. This format is illustrated for Dixon Sporting Goods in Exhibit 2-6.

The multiple-step income statement for Dixon indicates three important subtotals. First, **1** cost of goods sold is deducted from sales to arrive at **gross profit:**

Gross profit = Sales − Cost of goods sold

Sales	$357,500
Cost of goods sold	218,300
Gross profit	$139,200

Cost of goods sold, as the name implies, is the cost of the units of inventory sold during the year. It is logical to associate cost of goods sold with the sales revenue for the year because the latter represents the *selling price* of the inventory sold during the period.

EXHIBIT 2-5 Income Statement (Single-Step Format) for Dixon Sporting Goods Inc.

DIXON SPORTING GOODS INC.
INCOME STATEMENT (SINGLE-STEP FORMAT)
FOR THE YEAR ENDED DECEMBER 31, 2001

Revenues		
Sales	$357,500	
Interest	1,500	
Total revenues		$359,000
Expenses		
Cost of goods sold	$218,300	
Depreciation on store furniture and fixtures	4,200	
Advertising	13,750	
Salaries and wages for sales staff	22,000	
Depreciation on buildings and amortization of trademark	6,000	
Salaries and wages for office staff	15,000	
Insurance	3,600	
Supplies	1,050	
Interest	16,900	
Income taxes	17,200	
Total expenses		318,000
Net income		$ 41,000

In a **single-step** income statement, expenses are deducted from revenues in one step.

EXHIBIT 2-6 Income Statement (Multiple-Step Format) for Dixon Sporting Goods

In a **multiple-step** income statement:

1. Sales and the **costs** of sales are compared.

Expenses of the business are detailed.

Isolating expenses and revenues by type is useful in analyzing a business.

2. Operating income is highlighted.

3. 4. "Nonoperating" revenues and expenses are included here.

DIXON SPORTING GOODS INC.
INCOME STATEMENT (MULTIPLE-STEP FORMAT)
FOR THE YEAR ENDED DECEMBER 31, 2001

Sales		$357,500	
Cost of goods sold		218,300	
Gross profit			$139,200
Operating expenses			
Selling expenses			
Depreciation on store furniture and fixtures	$ 4,200		
Advertising	13,750		
Salaries and wages	22,000		
Total selling expenses		$ 39,950	
General and administrative expenses			
Depreciation on buildings and amortization of trademark	$ 6,000		
Salaries and wages	15,000		
Insurance	3,600		
Supplies	1,050		
Total general and administrative expenses		25,650	
Total operating expenses			65,600
Income from operations			$ 73,600
Other revenues and expenses			
Interest revenue		$ 1,500	
Interest expense		16,900	
Excess of other expenses over other revenue			15,400
Income before taxes			$ 58,200
Income tax expense			17,200
Net income			$ 41,000

The second important subtotal on Dixon's income statement is 2 *income from operations* of $73,600. This is found by subtracting *total operating expenses* of $65,600 from the gross profit of $139,200. Operating expenses are further subdivided between *selling expenses* and *general and administrative expenses.* For example, note that two depreciation amounts are included in operating expenses. Depreciation on store furniture and fixtures is classified as a selling expense because the store is where sales take place. On the other hand, we will assume that the buildings are offices for the administrative staff and thus depreciation on the buildings is classified as a general and administrative expense.

The third important subtotal on the income statement is 3 *income before taxes* of $58,200. Interest revenue and interest expense, neither of which is an operating item, are included in *other revenues and expenses.* The excess of interest expense of $16,900 over interest revenue of $1,500, which equals $15,400, is subtracted from income from operations to arrive at income before taxes. Finally, 4 *income tax expense* of $17,200 is deducted to arrive at *net income* of $41,000.

Two-Minute Review

1. Give at least two examples of items that would appear on a multiple-step income statement but not a single-step statement.

2. Classify each of the following expenses as either selling or general and administrative: advertising, depreciation on office building, salespersons' commissions and office salaries.

Answers on next page.

Answers:

1. *Gross profit, income from operations and income before taxes.*
2. *Advertising: selling*
   Depreciation on office building: general and administrative
   Salespersons' commissions: selling
   Office salaries: general and administrative

USING A MULTIPLE-STEP INCOME STATEMENT

LO 6 Use a multiple-step income statement to analyze a company's operations.

An important advantage of the multiple-step income statement is that it provides additional information to the reader. Although all the amounts needed to calculate certain ratios are available on a single-step statement, such calculations are easier to figure with a multiple-step statement. For example, the deduction of cost of goods sold from sales to arrive at gross profit, or *gross margin* as it is sometimes called, allows us to quickly calculate the **gross profit ratio.** The ratio of Dixon's gross profit to its sales, rounded to the nearest percent, is as follows:

GROSS PROFIT RATIO Gross profit divided by sales.

GROSS PROFIT RATIO

FORMULA	FOR DIXON SPORTING GOODS
$\frac{\text{Gross Profit}}{\text{Sales}}$	$\frac{\$139{,}200}{\$357{,}500} = 39\%$

The gross profit ratio tells us that after paying for the product, for every dollar of sales, 39¢ is available to cover other expenses and earn a profit. The complement of the gross profit ratio is the ratio of cost of goods sold to sales. For Dixon, this ratio is 1 − .39 = .61, or 61%. For every dollar of sales, Dixon spends $.61 on the cost of the product.

An important use of the income statement is to evaluate the *profitability* of a business. For example, a company's **profit margin** is the ratio of its net income to its sales. Some analysts refer to a company's profit margin as its *return on sales.* Dixon's profit margin is as follows:

PROFIT MARGIN Net income divided by sales.

PROFIT MARGIN

FORMULA	FOR DIXON SPORTING GOODS
$\frac{\text{Net Income}}{\text{Sales}}$	$\frac{\$41{,}000}{\$357{,}500} = 11\%$

For every dollar of sales, Dixon has $.11 in net income.

Two important factors should be kept in mind in evaluating any financial statement ratio. First, how does this year's ratio differ from ratios of prior years? For example, a decrease in the profit margin may indicate that the company is having trouble this year controlling certain costs. Second, how does the ratio compare with industry norms? For example, in some industries the profit margin is considerably lower than in many others, such as in mass merchandising (Wal-Mart's profit margin was only 3.2% for the year ended January 31, 1999). It is always helpful to compare key ratios, such as the profit margin, with an industry average or with the same ratio for a close competitor of the company.

From Concept **TO PRACTICE 2.1**

READING BEN & JERRY'S INCOME STATEMENT Which income statement format does Ben & Jerry's use: single-step or multiple-step? Calculate Ben & Jerry's 1998 and 1997 gross profit ratio. Explain what happened from 1997 to 1998.

www.walmart.com

THE STATEMENT OF RETAINED EARNINGS

LO 7 Identify the components of the statement of retained earnings and prepare the statement.

The purpose of a statement of stockholders' equity is to explain the changes in the components of owners' equity during the period. Retained earnings and capital stock are the two primary components of stockholders' equity. If there are no changes during the period in a company's capital stock, it may choose to present a statement of retained earnings instead

EXHIBIT 2-7 Statement of Retained Earnings for Dixon Sporting Goods Inc.

DIXON SPORTING GOODS INC.
STATEMENT OF RETAINED EARNINGS
FOR THE YEAR ENDED DECEMBER 31, 2001

Retained earnings, January 1, 2001	$271,500
Add: Net income for 2001	41,000
	$312,500
Less: Dividends declared and paid in 2001	(25,000)
Retained earnings, December 31, 2001	$287,500

of a statement of stockholders' equity.[9] A statement of retained earnings for Dixon Sporting Goods is shown in Exhibit 2-7.

The statement of retained earnings provides an important link between the income statement and the balance sheet. Dixon's net income of $41,000, as detailed on the income statement, is an *addition* to retained earnings. Note that the dividends declared and paid of $25,000 do not appear on the income statement because they are a payout, or *distribution,* of net income to stockholders rather than one of the expenses deducted to arrive at net income. Accordingly, they appear as a direct deduction on the statement of retained earnings. The beginning balance in retained earnings is carried forward from last year's statement of retained earnings.

THE STATEMENT OF CASH FLOWS

LO 8 Identify the components of the statement of cash flows and prepare the statement.

All publicly held corporations are required to present a statement of cash flows in their annual reports. The purpose of the statement is to summarize the cash flow effects of a company's operating, investing, and financing activities for the period.

THE CASH FLOW STATEMENT FOR DIXON SPORTING GOODS

The statement for Dixon Sporting Goods is shown in Exhibit 2-8. The statement consists of three categories: operating activities, investing activities, and financing activities. Each of these three categories can result in a net inflow of cash or a net outflow of cash.

Dixon's *operating activities* generated $56,100 of cash during the period. Operating activities **1** concern the purchase and sale of a product, in this case the acquisition of sporting goods from distributors and the subsequent sale of those goods. As we can readily see, Dixon had one major source of cash, the collection from its customers of $362,500. Similarly, Dixon's largest use of cash was the $217,200 it paid for inventory. In Chapter 12, we will discuss the statement of cash flows in detail and the preparation of this section of the statement.

Financing and investing activities were described in "Getting Started." *Investing activities* **2** involve the acquisition and sale of long-term assets, such as long-term investments, property, plant, and equipment, and intangible assets. *Financing activities* **3** result from the issuance and repayment, or retirement, of long-term liabilities and capital stock. The one investing activity on Dixon's statement of cash flows, the purchase of land for a future office site, required the use of cash and thus is shown as a net outflow of $150,000. Dixon

[9]According to the AICPA's annual survey, most corporations (almost 85%) present a statement of stockholders' equity. A separate statement of retained earnings, or a combined statement of income and retained earnings, is used by a small minority of companies.

EXHIBIT 2-8 Statement of Cash Flows for Dixon Sporting Goods Inc.

DIXON SPORTING GOODS INC.
STATEMENT OF CASH FLOWS
FOR THE YEAR ENDED DECEMBER 31, 2001

CASH FLOWS FROM OPERATING ACTIVITIES		
Cash collected from customers	$362,500	
Cash collected in interest	1,500	
Total cash collections		$364,000
Cash payments for:		
Inventory	$217,200	
Insurance	4,800	
Store supplies	850	
Salaries and wages	38,500	
Income taxes	15,900	
Interest	16,900	
Advertising	13,750	
Total cash payments		307,900
Net cash provided by operating activities		$ 56,100
CASH FLOWS FROM INVESTING ACTIVITIES		
Purchase of land for future office site		(150,000)
CASH FLOWS FROM FINANCING ACTIVITIES		
Dividends declared and paid	$ (25,000)	
Proceeds from issuance of long-term note	120,000	
Net cash provided by financing activities		95,000
Net increase in cash		$ 1,100
Cash at beginning of year		3,900
Cash at end of year		$ 5,000

1 Operating activities involve the purchase and sale of products or services.

2 Investing activities involve the acquisition and sale of long-term assets.

3 Financing activities involve the issuance and repayment of long-term liabilities and stock.

had two financing activities: dividends of $25,000 required the use of cash, and the issuance of a long-term note generated cash of $120,000. The balance in cash on the bottom of the statement of $5,000 must agree with the balance for this item as shown on the balance sheet in Exhibit 2-4.

THE FINANCIAL STATEMENTS FOR GATEWAY

LO 9 Read and use the financial statements and other elements in the annual report of a publicly held company.

The financial statements for our hypothetical company, Dixon Sporting Goods Inc., introduced the major categories on each of the statements. We now turn to the financial statements of an actual company, Gateway. These statements are more complex and require additional analysis and a better understanding of accounting to fully appreciate them. However, we will concentrate on certain elements of the statements. At this stage in your study, look for the similarities rather than the differences between these statements and those of Dixon.

www.gateway.com

Gateway was founded by Ted Waitt in 1985 in an empty farmhouse near Sioux City, Iowa. What began as a mail-order business has grown to the point that sales in 1998 reached nearly $7.5 billion. Early on, Gateway adopted a cow as its mascot and began to ship all its products in boxes that looked like the markings on a Holstein cow.[10]

[10] *International Directory of Company Histories*, vol. 10 (St. James Press, 1995), p. 308.

As we will see later, the notes to a set of financial statements give the reader a variety of information about a company. Like the statements of many other companies, Gateway's financials include a note that describes its business:

> Gateway 2000, Inc. (the "Company") is a direct marketer of personal computers ("PCs") and PC-related products. The Company develops, manufactures, markets and supports a broad line of desktop and portable PCs, digital media (convergence) PCs, servers, workstations, and PC-related products used by individuals, families, businesses, government agencies and educational institutions.[11]

Gateway's Balance Sheet

The balance sheets for Gateway at the end of each of two years are shown in Exhibit 2-9. Like most other companies, Gateway chose an accounting or fiscal year that corresponds to the calendar, that is, beginning on January 1 and ending on December 31. However, some companies choose a fiscal year that ends at a point when sales are at their lowest in the annual cycle. For example, Wal-Mart ends its fiscal year on January 31, after the busy holiday season.

www.walmart.com

Gateway releases what are called *consolidated financial statements,* which reflect the position and results of all operations that are controlled by a single entity. Like most other large corporations, Gateway owns other companies. Often these companies are legally separate and are called *subsidiaries.* How a company accounts for its investment in a subsidiary is covered in advanced accounting courses.

Gateway presents comparative balance sheets to indicate its financial position at the end of each of the last two years. As a minimum standard, the Securities and Exchange Commission requires that the annual report include balance sheets as of the two most recent years and income statements for each of the three most recent years. Note that all amounts on the balance sheet are stated in thousands of dollars. This type of rounding is a common practice in the financial statements of large corporations and is justified under the materiality concept. Knowing the exact dollar amount of each asset would not change a decision made by an investor.

The presentation of comparative balance sheets allows the reader to make comparisons between years. For example, Gateway's *working capital* increased significantly during 1998:

WORKING CAPITAL

	December 31, 1997	December 31, 1998
Current Assets – Current Liabilities	\$1,544,683 – \$1,003,906 = \$540,777	\$2,228,186 – \$1,429,674 = \$798,512

Gateway's *current ratio* at each of the two dates follows:

CURRENT RATIO

	December 31, 1997	December 31, 1998
Current Assets / Current Liabilities	\$1,544,683 / \$1,003,906 = 1.54 to 1	\$2,228,186 / \$1,429,674 = 1.56 to 1

Although both the amount of working capital and the current ratio increased between 1997 and 1998, the increase in the current ratio was relatively minor. The largest change in the current assets was the increase in cash and cash equivalents, from approximately \$594 million to \$1,170 million.

On the liability side of its balance sheet, Gateway lists two noncurrent liabilities: long-term obligations, net of current maturities, and warranty and other liabilities. Given the nature of the products it sells (PCs), Gateway provides its customers with warranties. (As we will see in Chapter 9, warranties often create a liability for companies. Long-term obligations will be discussed more fully in Chapter 10.)

[11] *Gateway 1998 Annual Report,* p. 29.

EXHIBIT 2-9 Comparative Balance Sheets for Gateway

CONSOLIDATED BALANCE SHEETS
December 31, 1997 and 1998
(in thousands, except per share amounts)

	1997	1998
ASSETS		
Current assets:		
Cash and cash equivalents	$ 593,601	$ 1,169,810
Marketable securities	38,648	158,657
Accounts receivable, net	510,679	558,851
Inventory	249,224	167,924
Other	152,531	172,944
Total current assets	1,544,683	2,228,186
Property, plant and equipment, net	376,467	530,988
Intangibles, net	82,590	65,944
Other assets	35,531	65,262
	$ 2,039,271	$ 2,890,380
LIABILITIES AND STOCKHOLDERS' EQUITY		
Current liabilities:		
Notes payable and current maturities of long-term obligations	$ 13,969	$ 11,415
Accounts payable	488,717	718,071
Accrued liabilities	271,250	415,265
Accrued royalties	159,418	167,873
Other current liabilities	70,552	117,050
Total current liabilities	1,003,906	1,429,674
Long-term obligations, net of current maturities	7,240	3,360
Warranty and other liabilities	98,081	112,971
Total liabilities	1,109,227	1,546,005
Commitments and Contingencies (Notes 3 and 4)		
Stockholders' equity:		
Preferred stock, $.01 par value, 5,000 shares authorized; none issued and outstanding	—	—
Class A common stock, nonvoting, $.01 par value, 1,000 shares authorized; none issued and outstanding	—	—
Common stock, $.01 par value, 220,000 shares authorized; 154,128 shares and 156,569 shares issued and outstanding, respectively	1,541	1,566
Additional paid-in capital	299,483	365,986
Retained earnings	634,509	980,908
Accumulated other comprehensive loss	(5,489)	(4,085)
Total stockholders' equity	930,044	1,344,375
	$ 2,039,271	$ 2,890,380

The accompanying notes are an integral part of the consolidated financial statements.

Use these to find:
- Working capital
- Current ratio

GATEWAY'S INCOME STATEMENT

We have examined two basic formats for the income statement: the single-step format and the multiple-step format. In practice, numerous variations on these two basic formats exist, depending to a large extent on the nature of a company's business. For example, the multiple-step form, with its presentation of gross profit, is not used by service businesses

EXHIBIT 2-10 Consolidated Income Statements for Gateway

CONSOLIDATED INCOME STATEMENTS
For the years ended December 31, 1996, 1997 and 1998
(in thousands, except per share amounts)

	1996	1997	1998
Net sales	$ 5,035,228	$ 6,293,680	$ 7,467,925
Cost of goods sold	4,099,073	5,217,239	5,921,651
Gross profit	936,155	1,076,441	1,546,274
Selling, general and administrative expenses	580,061	786,168	1,052,047
Nonrecurring expenses	–	113,842	–
Operating income	356,094	176,431	494,227
Other income, net	26,622	27,189	47,021
Income before income taxes	382,716	203,620	541,248
Provision for income taxes	132,037	93,823	194,849
Net income	$ 250,679	$ 109,797	$ 346,399
Net income per share:			
Basic	$ 1.64	$ .71	$ 2.23
Diluted	$ 1.60	$ .70	$ 2.18
Weighted average shares outstanding:			
Basic	152,745	153,840	155,542
Diluted	156,237	156,201	158,929

The accompanying notes are an integral part of the consolidated financial statements.

Use these to find:
• Gross profit ratio

because they do not sell a product. (Remember that gross profit is sales less cost of goods sold.) As we will see for Gateway, the form of the income statement is a reflection of a company's operations.

Multiple-step income statements for Gateway for a three-year period are presented in Exhibit 2-10. Note the significant increase in Gateway's *gross profit ratio* from 1997 to 1998:

GROSS PROFIT RATIO

	1997	1998
$\frac{\text{Gross Profit}}{\text{Net Sales}}$	$\frac{\$1,076,441}{\$6,293,680} = 17\%$	$\frac{\$1,546,274}{\$7,467,925} = 21\%$

Both Gateway's management and its stockholders should be pleased with this improvement in the gross profit ratio. It is a clear sign that the company has successfully increased its sales while controlling the costs to make its products. Also, note the inclusion of net income per share information at the bottom of the statement. The per share information helps users of the statement in various ways and is discussed in more detail in Chapter 13.

From Concept **TO PRACTICE 2.2**

READING GATEWAY'S INCOME STATEMENT Compute Gateway's profit margin for the past two years. Did it go up or down from the prior year to the current year?

OTHER ELEMENTS OF AN ANNUAL REPORT

No two annual reports look the same. The appearance of an annual report depends not only on the size of a company but also on the budget devoted to the preparation of the report. Some companies publish "bare-bones" annual reports, whereas others issue a glossy

EXHIBIT 2-11 Report of Independent Accountants for Gateway

Report of Independent Accountants

To the Stockholders and Board of Directors of Gateway 2000, Inc.

In our opinion, the accompanying consolidated balance sheets and the related consolidated statements of income, cash flows and changes in stockholders' equity and comprehensive income presents fairly, in all material respects, the consolidated financial position of Gateway 2000, Inc. at December 31, 1997 and 1998, and the consolidated results of its operations and its cash flows for each of the three years in the period ended December 31, 1998, in conformity with generally accepted accounting principles. These financial statements are the responsibility of the Company's management; our responsibility is to express an opinion on these financial statements based on our audits. We conducted our audits of these statements in accordance with generally accepted auditing standards which require that we plan and perform the audit to obtain reasonable assurance about whether the financial statements are free of material misstatement. An audit includes examining, on a test basis, evidence supporting amounts and disclosures in the financial statements, assessing the accounting principles used and significant estimates made by management, and evaluating the overall financial statement presentation. We believe that our audits provide a reasonable basis for the opinion expressed above.

PricewaterhouseCoopers LLP

San Diego, California
January 21, 1999

www.starbucks.com
www.walmart.com

report complete with pictures of company products and employees. In recent years, many companies, as a cost-cutting measure, have scaled back the amount spent on the annual report. The creativity in annual reports varies as well. Starbuck's 1998 annual report included a coupon good for a 12-ounce beverage at any of its stores. The 1998 Wal-Mart annual report was designed to give the appearance of a magazine, complete with feature articles and an ad for Sam's Club.

Privately held companies tend to distribute only financial statements, without the additional information normally included in the annual reports of public companies. For the annual reports of public companies, however, certain basic elements are considered standard. A letter to the stockholders from either the president or the chairman of the board of directors appears in the first few pages of most annual reports. A section describing the company's products and markets is usually included. At the heart of any annual report is the financial report or review, which consists of the financial statements accompanied by footnotes to explain various items on the statements. We will now consider these other elements as presented in the 1998 annual report of Gateway.

Report of Independent Accountants As you see in Exhibit 2-11, Gateway is audited by PricewaterhouseCoopers LLP, one of the largest international accounting firms. Two key phrases should be noted in the first sentence of the independent accountants' report: *in our opinion* and *presents fairly.* The report indicates that responsibility for the statements rests with Gateway and that the auditors' job is to *express an opinion* on the statements, based on certain tests. It would be impossible for an auditing firm to spend the time or money to retrace and verify every single transaction entered into during the year by Gateway. Instead, the auditing firm performs various tests of the accounting records to be able to assure itself that the statements are free of *material misstatement.* Auditors do not "certify" the total accuracy of a set of financial statements but render an opinion as to the reasonableness of those statements. Finally, note that this format for the auditors' report differs from the one for Ben & Jerry's presented in Chapter 1. However, both formats contain the same basic information.

The Ethical Responsibility of Management and the Auditors The management of a company and its auditors share a common purpose: to protect the interests of stockholders. In large corporations, the stockholders are normally removed from the daily affairs of the business. The need for a professional management team to run the business is a practical

> "I was familiar with the basic elements of the [annual] report, but the line-by-line specifics were foreign to me."
> –Matthew Butler

FOCUS ON USERS

Name: Matthew Butler
Education: B.A., University of Virginia
College Majors: Economics; Psychology
Occupation: Financial advisor in retail sales at a large investment firm
Age: 27

Using Financial Statements Becomes Second Nature

Annual reports reveal a company's financial health. For this reason, all kinds of professionals use reports and their financial statements as a guide in making business decisions or in helping others make investment decisions.

Matthew Butler, a financial advisor for a large brokerage firm in Washington, D.C., has learned along the way how important the financial statements are in the business world. "I knew what an annual report was to the extent that I knew that every year a company sends a formal accounting of its financial status to shareholders. I was familiar with the basic elements of the report, but the line-by-line specifics were foreign to me," Matthew says. "Then, when I went to get licensed as a financial advisor, I was required to pass a group of financial exams, including the Series 7. Studying for and acing this exam taught me everything I would ever want to know about financial statements and how to interpret them. Now, I use them every day without even thinking about it."

As a financial advisor, Matthew's job is to provide potential investors with opinions about stocks and the companies behind them. "The first thing I do when a client asks me about a particular stock is look at the numbers. On the income statement, I look at the net income and revenues to find out how much the company is making and at the costs to see how much it is spending. From there, I go to the 'earnings per share'—net income divided by the total number of shares outstanding—and to the 'price/earnings ratio'—which is the current price of the stock divided by earnings per share. These calculations are huge in my business. They're the most important numbers I can provide my clients."

By looking at corporate financial statements day to day and doing what is called "fundamental analysis" for his clients, Matthew now has the experience to render, in an instant, an opinion on the financial health of a company. As he says, "It's what I do for a living."

necessity, as is the need for a periodic audit of the company's records. Because stockholders cannot run the business themselves, they need assurances that the business is being operated effectively and efficiently and that the financial statements presented by management are a fair representation of the company's operations and financial position. The management and the auditors have a very important ethical responsibility to their constituents, the stockholders of the company.

Management Discussion and Analysis Preceding the financial statements is a section of Gateway's annual report titled "Management's Discussion and Analysis of Financial Condition and Results of Operations." This report gives management the opportunity to discuss the financial statements and provide the stockholders with explanations for certain amounts reported in the statements. For example, management explains the increase in sales as follows:

> *Sales.* Gateway added over $1.1 billion in sales in 1998 compared to 1997, achieving annual sales of $7.47 billion. This represents an increase of 19% over 1997. Sales to the consumer segment represented 53% of total sales while business segment sales were 47% of total sales. Sales were driven by continued strong unit growth of 37% in 1998 compared to unit growth of 35% in 1997. The Company's unit growth outpaced the worldwide market in 1998 by approximately three times the market growth rate, leading to continued gains in market share.[12]

[12] *Gateway 1998 Annual Report,* p. 20.

3) **Notes to Consolidated Financial Statements** The sentence "The accompanying notes are an integral part of the consolidated financial statements" appears at the bottom of each of Gateway's four financial statements. These comments, or *footnotes,* as they are commonly called, are necessary to satisfy the need for *full disclosure* of all the facts relevant to a company's results and financial position. The first footnote in all annual reports is a summary of *significant accounting policies.* A company's policies for valuing inventories, depreciating assets, and recognizing revenue are among the important items contained in this footnote. For example, Gateway describes its policy for depreciating assets as follows: "Depreciation is provided using straight-line and accelerated methods over the assets' estimated useful lives, ranging from four to forty years."[13] In addition to the summary of significant accounting policies, other footnotes discuss such topics as income taxes and retirement savings plans.

footnotes

This completes our discussion of the makeup of the annual report. By now you should appreciate the flexibility that companies have in assembling the report, aside from the need to follow generally accepted accounting principles in preparing the statements. The accounting standards followed in preparing the statements, as well as the appearance of the annual report itself, differ in other countries. As has been noted elsewhere, although many corporations operate internationally, accounting principles are far from being standardized.

WARMUP EXERCISES

LO 4, 6 Warmup Exercise 2-1 Identifying Ratios
State the equation for each of the following ratios:

1. Current ratio
2. Gross profit ratio
3. Profit margin

Key to the Solution
Review the various ratios as discussed in the chapter.

LO 4, 6 Warmup Exercise 2-2 Calculating Ratios
Bridger reported net income of $150,000, sales of $1,000,000 and cost of goods sold of $800,000.

Required

Compute each of the following ratios for Bridger:

1. Gross profit ratio
2. Profit margin

Key to the Solution
Recall the equation for each of these ratios as presented in the chapter.

LO 4 Warmup Exercise 2-3 Determining Liquidity
Big has current assets of $500,000 and current liabilities of $400,000. Small reports current assets of $80,000 and current liabilities of $20,000.

Required

Which company is more liquid? Why?

Key to the Solution
Calculate the current ratio for each company and compare them.

[13] *Gateway 1998 Annual Report,* p. 29.

Solutions to Warmup Exercises

Warmup Exercise 2-1

1. $\text{Current ratio} = \dfrac{\text{Current Assets}}{\text{Current Liabilities}}$

2. $\text{Gross profit ratio} = \dfrac{\text{Gross Profit}}{\text{Sales}}$

3. $\text{Profit margin} = \dfrac{\text{Net income}}{\text{Sales}}$

Warmup Exercise 2-2

1. $\dfrac{\$1{,}000{,}000 - \$800{,}000}{\$1{,}000{,}000} = \dfrac{\$200{,}000}{\$1{,}000{,}000} = \underline{\underline{20\%}}$

2. $\dfrac{\$150{,}000}{\$1{,}000{,}000} = \underline{\underline{15\%}}$

Warmup Exercise 2-3

Small Company appears on the surface to be more liquid. Its current ratio of $80,000/$20,000 or 4 to 1 is significantly higher than Big's current ratio of $500,000/$400,000 or 1.25 to 1.

The following review problem will give you the opportunity to apply what you have learned by preparing both an income statement and a balance sheet.

Review Problem

Shown below, in alphabetical order, are items taken from the records of Grizzly Inc., a chain of outdoor recreational stores in the Northwest. Use the items to prepare two statements. First, prepare an income statement for the year ended December 31, 2001. The income statement should be in multiple-step form. Second, prepare a classified balance sheet at December 31, 2001. All amounts are in thousands of dollars.

Accounts payable	$ 6,500
Accounts receivable	8,200
Accumulated depreciation—buildings	25,000
Accumulated depreciation—furniture and fixtures	15,000
Advertising expense	3,100
Buildings	80,000
Capital stock, $1 par, 10,000 shares issued and outstanding	10,000
Cash	2,400
Commissions expense	8,600
Cost of goods sold	110,000
Depreciation on buildings	2,500
Depreciation on furniture and fixtures	1,200
Furniture and fixtures	68,000
Income taxes payable	2,200
Income tax expense	13,000
Insurance expense	2,000
Interest expense	12,000
Interest payable	1,000
Interest revenue	2,000
Land	100,000
Long-term notes payable, due December 31, 2009	120,000
Merchandise inventories	6,000

Office supplies	900
Paid-in capital in excess of par value	40,000
Prepaid rent	3,000
Rent expense for salespersons' autos	9,000
Retained earnings	48,800
Salaries and wages for office staff	11,000
Sales revenue	190,000

Solution to Review Problem

1. Multiple-step income statement:

GRIZZLY INC.
INCOME STATEMENT
FOR THE YEAR ENDED DECEMBER 31, 2001
(IN THOUSANDS OF DOLLARS)

Sales revenue		$190,000	
Cost of goods sold		110,000	
Gross profit			$ 80,000
Operating expenses:			
Selling expenses:			
Advertising	$ 3,100		
Depreciation on furniture and fixtures	1,200		
Rent for salespersons' autos	9,000		
Commissions	8,600		
Total selling expenses		$ 21,900	
General and administrative expenses:			
Depreciation on buildings	$ 2,500		
Insurance	2,000		
Salaries and wages for office staff	11,000		
Total general and administrative expenses		15,500	
Total operating expenses			37,400
Income from operations			$ 42,600
Other revenues and expenses:			
Interest revenue		$ 2,000	
Interest expense		12,000	
Excess of other expenses over other revenue			10,000
Income before taxes			$ 32,600
Income tax expense			13,000
Net income			$ 19,600

2. Classified Balance Sheet:

GRIZZLY INC.
BALANCE SHEET
AT DECEMBER 31, 2001
(IN THOUSANDS OF DOLLARS)

Assets

Current assets:		
Cash	$ 2,400	
Accounts receivable	8,200	
Merchandise inventories	6,000	
Office supplies	900	
Prepaid rent	3,000	
Total current assets		$ 20,500

Property, plant, and equipment:			
Land		$100,000	
Buildings	$ 80,000		
Less: Accumulated depreciation	25,000	55,000	
Furniture and fixtures	$ 68,000		
Less: Accumulated depreciation	15,000	53,000	
Total property, plant, and equipment			208,000
Total assets			$228,500
Liabilities			
Current liabilities:			
Accounts payable		$ 6,500	
Income taxes payable		2,200	
Interest payable		1,000	
Total current liabilities			$ 9,700
Long-term notes payable, due December 31, 2009			120,000
Total liabilities			$129,700
Stockholders' Equity			
Contributed capital:			
Capital stock, $1 par, 10,000 shares issued and outstanding		$ 10,000	
Paid-in capital in excess of par value		40,000	
Total contributed capital		$ 50,000	
Retained earnings		48,800	
Total stockholders' equity			98,800
Total liabilities and stockholders' equity			$228,500

Chapter Highlights

1. **LO 1** The primary objective of financial reporting is to provide information that is useful in making investment, credit, and similar decisions.
2. **LO 1** Investors and creditors are ultimately interested in their own prospective cash receipts from dividends or interest and the proceeds from the sale, redemption, or maturity of securities or loans. Because these expected cash flows are related to the expected cash flows to the company, its cash flows are of interest to investors and creditors. The entity's economic resources, claims to them, and the effects of transactions that change resources and claims to those resources are also of interest.
3. **LO 2** Financial information should be understandable to those who are willing to spend the time to understand it. To be useful, the information should be relevant and reliable. Relevant information has the capacity to make a difference in a decision. Reliable information can be depended on to represent the economic events that it purports to represent.
4. **LO 2** *Comparability* is the quality that allows for comparisons to be made between two or more companies, whereas *consistency* is the quality that allows for comparisons to be made within a single company from one period to the next. These two qualities of useful accounting information are aided by full disclosure—in the footnotes to the financial statements—of all relevant information.
5. **LO 3** The operating cycle depends to a large extent on the nature of a company's business. For a retailer, it encompasses the period of time from the investment of cash in inventory to the collection of any account receivable from sale of the product. The operating cycle for a manufacturer is expanded to include the period of time required to convert raw materials into finished products.
6. **LO 3** Current assets will be realized in cash or sold or consumed during the operating cycle or within one year if the cycle is shorter than one year. Because most businesses have numerous operating cycles within a year, the cutoff for classification as a current asset is usually one year. Cash, accounts receivable, inventory, and prepaid expenses are all examples of current assets.
7. **LO 3** The definition of *current liability* is related to that of *current asset.* A current liability is an obligation that will be satisfied within the operating cycle or within one year if the cycle is shorter than one year. Many liabilities are satisfied by making a cash payment. However, some obligations are settled by rendering a service.
8. **LO 4** A classified balance sheet is helpful in evaluating the liquidity of a business. Working capital, the difference between current assets and current liabilities, indicates the buffer of protection for creditors. The current ratio, current assets divided by current liabilities, provides the reader with a relative measure of liquidity.
9. **LO 5, 6** All expenses are added together and subtracted from all revenues in a single-step income statement. The multiple-step income statement provides the reader with classifications of revenues and expenses as well as with important subtotals. Cost of goods sold is subtracted from sales revenue on a multiple-step

statement, with the result reported as gross profit. Profitability analysis includes such measures as the gross profit ratio (the ratio of gross profit to sales) and the profit margin (the ratio of net income to sales).

10. **LO 7, 8** If there are no changes in the capital stock accounts, some companies present a statement of retained earnings or a combined statement of income and retained earnings in lieu of a statement of stockholders' equity. The statement of cash flows summarizes the operating, investing, and financing activities of an entity for the period.

11. **LO 9** No two annual reports are the same. However, certain basic elements are included in most of them. In addition to the financial statements, annual reports include, among other items, the independent accountants' report, management's discussion of the amounts appearing in the statements, and footnotes to the statements.

KEY TERMS QUIZ

Read each definition below and then write the number of that definition in the blank beside the appropriate term it defines. The solution appears at the end of the chapter.

p. 48 __6__ Understandability
p. 48 __3__ Relevance
p. 49 __9__ Reliability
p. 50 __14__ Comparability
p. 50 __19__ Depreciation
p. 50 __17__ Consistency
p. 51 __2__ Materiality
p. 51 __5__ Conservatism
p. 53 __11__ Operating cycle
p. 54 __15__ Current asset
p. 57 __10__ Current liability
p. 58 __16__ Liquidity
p. 58 __12__ Working capital
p. 58 __8__ Current ratio
p. 60 __1__ Single-step income statement
p. 60 __4__ Multiple-step income statement
p. 60 __18__ Gross profit
p. 62 __7__ Gross profit ratio
p. 62 __13__ Profit margin

1. An income statement in which all expenses are added together and subtracted from all revenues.
2. The magnitude of an omission or misstatement in accounting information that will affect the judgment of someone relying on the information.
3. The capacity of information to make a difference in a decision.
4. An income statement that provides the reader with classifications of revenues and expenses as well as with important subtotals.
5. The practice of using the least optimistic estimate when two estimates of amounts are about equally likely.
6. The quality of accounting information that makes it comprehensible to those willing to spend the necessary time.
7. Gross profit divided by sales.
8. Current assets divided by current liabilities.
9. The quality of accounting information that makes it dependable in representing the events that it purports to represent.
10. An obligation that will be satisfied within the next operating cycle or within one year if the cycle is shorter than one year.
11. The period of time between the purchase of inventory and the collection of any receivable from the sale of the inventory.
12. Current assets minus current liabilities.
13. Net income divided by sales.
14. The quality of accounting information that allows a user to analyze two or more companies and look for similarities and differences.
15. An asset that is expected to be realized in cash or sold or consumed during the operating cycle or within one year if the cycle is shorter than one year.
16. The ability of a company to pay its debts as they come due.
17. The quality of accounting information that allows a user to compare two or more accounting periods for a single company.
18. Sales less cost of goods sold.
19. The allocation of the cost of a tangible, long-term asset over its useful life.

ALTERNATE TERMS

Balance sheet Statement of financial position or condition
Capital stock Contributed capital
Cost of goods sold Cost of sales
Gross profit Gross margin
Income statement Statement of income
Income tax expense Provision for income taxes
Long-term assets Noncurrent assets
Long-term liability Long-term debt
Net income Profits or earnings
Report of independent accountants Auditors' report
Retained earnings Earned capital
Stockholders' Equity Shareholders' equity

Questions

1. How would you evaluate the following statement: "The cash flows to a company are irrelevant to an investor; all the investor cares about is the potential for receiving dividends on the investment"?
2. A key characteristic of useful financial information is understandability. How does this qualitative characteristic relate to the background of the user of the information? pg. 48
3. What does *relevance* mean with regard to the use of accounting information? pg. 48
4. What is the qualitative characteristic of comparability, and why is it important in preparing financial statements? pg. 50
5. What is the difference between comparability and consistency as they relate to the use of accounting information? pg. 50
6. How does the concept of materiality relate to the size of a company? pg. 51
7. How does the operating cycle of a retailer differ from that of a service company? pg. 53
8. How does the concept of the operating cycle relate to the definition of a current asset? pg. 53 + 54
9. What are two examples of the way a company's intent in using an asset affects classification of the asset on the balance sheet?
10. How would you evaluate the following statement: "A note payable with an original maturity of five years will be classified on the balance sheet as a long-term liability until it matures"?
11. How do the two basic forms of owners' equity items for a corporation—capital stock and retained earnings—differ?
12. What are the limitations of working capital as a measure of the liquidity of a business as opposed to the current ratio?
13. What is meant by a company's capital structure?
14. What is the major weakness of the single-step form for the income statement? pg. 60
15. Why might a company's gross profit ratio increase from one year to the next but its profit margin ratio decrease?
16. How does a statement of retained earnings act as a link between an income statement and a balance sheet?
17. In auditing the financial statements of a company, does a certified public accountant *certify* that the statements are totally accurate and without errors of any size or variety? no, pg. 68 bottom
18. What is the first footnote in the annual report of all publicly held companies, and what is its purpose? pg. 70 top

Exercises

LO 2 Exercise 2-1 Characteristics of Useful Accounting Information

Fill in the blank with the qualitative characteristic for each of the following descriptions:

Reliability 1. Information that users can depend on to represent the events that it purports to represent

Relevance 2. Information that has the capacity to make a difference in a decision

Faithful Representation 3. Information that is valid, that indicates an agreement between the underlying data and the events represented

Consistency 4. Information that allows for comparisons to be made from one accounting period to the next

Verifiability 5. Information that is free from error

Understandability 6. Information that is meaningful to those who are willing to learn to use it properly

neutrality 7. Information that is not slanted to portray a company's position any better or worse than the circumstances warrant

Comparability 8. Information that allows for comparisons to be made between or among companies

LO 3 Exercise 2-2 Classification of Assets and Liabilities

Indicate the appropriate classification of each of the following as a current asset (CA), noncurrent asset (NCA), current liability (CL), or long-term liability (LTL):

CA 1. Inventory

CL 2. Accounts payable

CA 3. Cash

NCA 4. Patents

CL 5. Notes payable, due in six months

CL 6. Taxes payable

CA 7. Prepaid rent (for the next nine months)

NCL 8. Bonds payable, due in 10 years

NCA 9. Machinery

LO 5 Exercise 2-3 Selling Expenses and General and Administrative Expenses

Operating expenses are subdivided between selling expenses and general and administrative expenses when a multiple-step income statement is prepared. From the following list, identify each item as a selling expense (S) or general and administrative expense (G&A):

_____ 1. Advertising expense
_____ 2. Depreciation expense—store furniture and fixtures
_____ 3. Office rent expense
_____ 4. Office salaries expense
_____ 5. Store rent expense
_____ 6. Store salaries expense
_____ 7. Insurance expense
_____ 8. Supplies expense
_____ 9. Utilities expense

LO 5 Exercise 2-4 Missing Income Statement Amounts

For each of the following independent cases, fill in the blank with the appropriate dollar amount:

	Sara's Coffee Shop	**Amy's Deli**	**Jane's Bagels**
Net sales	$35,000	$ _____	$78,000
Cost of goods sold	_____	45,000	_____
Gross profit	7,000	18,000	_____
Selling expenses	3,000	_____	9,000
General and administrative expenses	1,500	2,800	_____
Total operating expenses	_____	8,800	13,600
Net income	$ 2,500	$ 9,200	$25,400

LO 6 Exercise 2-5 Income Statement Ratios

The 2001 income statement of Holly Enterprises shows net income of $45,000, comprising net sales of $134,800, cost of goods sold of $53,920, selling expenses of $18,310, general and administrative expenses of $16,990, and interest expense of $580. Holly's stockholders' equity was $280,000 at the beginning of the year and $320,000 at the end of the year. The company has 20,000 shares of stock outstanding at December 31, 2001.

Required

Compute Holly's (1) gross profit ratio and (2) profit margin. What other information would you need to be able to comment on whether these ratios are favorable?

LO 7 Exercise 2-6 Statement of Retained Earnings

Landon Corporation was organized on January 2, 1999, with the investment of $100,000 by each of its two stockholders. Net income for its first year of business was $85,200. Net income increased during 2000 to $125,320 and to $145,480 during 2001. Landon paid $20,000 in dividends to each of the two stockholders in each of the three years.

Required

Prepare a statement of retained earnings for the year ended December 31, 2001.

LO 8 Exercise 2-7 Components of the Statement of Cash Flows

From the following list, identify each item as operating (O), investing (I), financing (F), or not on the statement of cash flows (N):

_____ 1. Paid for supplies
_____ 2. Collected cash from customers
_____ 3. Purchased land (held for resale)
_____ 4. Purchased land (for construction of new building)
_____ 5. Paid dividend
_____ 6. Issued stock
_____ 7. Purchased computers (for use in the business)
_____ 8. Sold old equipment

LO 9 Exercise 2-8 Basic Elements of Financial Statements

Most financial reports contain the following list of basic elements. For each element, identify the person(s) who prepared the element and describe the information a user would expect to find in each element. Some information is verifiable; other information is subjectively chosen by management. Comment on the verifiability of information in each element.

1. Letter from the president
2. Product/markets of company
3. Financial statements
4. Notes to financial statements
5. Independent accountants' report

Multi-Concept Exercises

LO 3, 5, 7 Exercise 2-9 Financial Statement Classification

Potential stockholders and lenders are interested in a company's financial statements. For the list below, identify the statement—balance sheet (BS), income statement (IS), retained earnings statement (RE)—on which each item would appear.

______ **1.** Accounts payable
______ **2.** Accounts receivable
______ **3.** Advertising expense
______ **4.** Bad debt expense
______ **5.** Bonds payable
______ **6.** Buildings
______ **7.** Cash
______ **8.** Common stock
______ **9.** Deferred income taxes
______ **10.** Depreciation expense
______ **11.** Dividends
______ **12.** Land held for future expansion
______ **13.** Loss on the sale of equipment
______ **14.** Office supplies
______ **15.** Organizational costs
______ **16.** Patent amortization expense
______ **17.** Retained earnings
______ **18.** Sales
______ **19.** Unearned revenue
______ **20.** Utilities expense

LO 5, 6 Exercise 2-10 Single- and Multiple-Step Income Statement

Some headings and/or items are used on either the single-step or the multiple-step income statement. Some are used on both. For the list below, indicate the following: single-step (S), multiple-step (M), both formats (B), or not used on either income statement (N).

______ **1.** Sales
______ **2.** Cost of goods sold
______ **3.** Selling expenses
______ **4.** Total revenues
______ **5.** Utilities expense
______ **6.** Administrative expense
______ **7.** Net loss
______ **8.** Supplies on hand
______ **9.** Accumulated depreciation
______ **10.** Gross profit

LO 5, 6 Exercise 2-11 Multiple-Step Income Statement

Gaynor Corporation's partial income statement follows:

Sales	$1,200,000
Cost of sales	450,000
Selling expenses	60,800
General and administrative expenses	75,000

Required

Determine the gross profit ratio and profit margin. Would you consider investing in Gaynor Corporation? Explain your answer.

PROBLEMS

LO 2 Problem 2-1 Materiality

Joseph Knapp, a newly hired accountant, wanted to impress his boss, so he stayed late one night to analyze the office supplies expense. He determined the cost by month, for the past 12 months, of each of the following: computer paper, copy paper, fax paper, pencils and pens, note pads, postage, stationery, and miscellaneous items.

1. What did Joseph think his boss would learn from this information? What action might be taken as a result of knowing it?
2. Would this information be more relevant if Joseph worked for a hardware store or for a real estate company? Discuss.

LO 2 Problem 2-2 Costs and Expenses

The following costs are incurred by a retailer:

1. Display fixtures in a retail store
2. Advertising - Expense
3. Merchandise for sale
4. Incorporation (i.e., legal costs, stock issue costs)
5. Cost of a franchise - Asset
6. Office supplies
7. Wages in a restaurant
8. Computer software
9. Computer hardware Asset

Required

For each of these costs, explain whether all of the cost or only a portion of the cost would appear as an expense on the income statement for the period in which the cost was incurred. If not all of the cost would appear on the income statement for that period, explain why not.

LO 3 Problem 2-3 Classified Balance Sheet

The following balance sheet items, listed in alphabetical order, are available from the records of Ruth Corporation at December 31, 2001:

Accounts payable	$ 18,255
Accounts receivable	23,450
Accumulated depreciation—automobiles	22,500
Accumulated depreciation—buildings	40,000
Automobiles	112,500
Bonds payable, due December 31, 2005	160,000
Buildings	200,000
Capital stock, $10 par value	150,000
Cash	13,230
Income taxes payable	6,200
Interest payable	1,500
Inventory	45,730
Land	250,000
Long-term investments	85,000
Notes payable, due June 30, 2002	10,000
Office supplies	2,340
Paid-in capital in excess of par value	50,000
Patents	40,000
Prepaid rent	1,500
Retained earnings	311,095
Salaries and wages payable	4,200

Required

1. Prepare in good form a classified balance sheet as of December 31, 2001.
2. Compute Ruth's current ratio.
3. On the basis of your answer to requirement **2,** does Ruth appear to be *liquid?* What other information do you need to fully answer this question?

LO 4 **Problem 2-4** Financial Statement Ratios

The following items, in alphabetical order, are available from the records of Walker Corporation as of December 31, 2001 and 2000:

	December 31, 2001	December 31, 2000
Accounts payable	$ 8,400	$ 5,200
Accounts receivable	13,230	19,570
Cash	10,200	9,450
Cleaning supplies	450	700
Interest payable	–0–	1,200
Inventory	24,600	26,200
Marketable securities	6,250	5,020
Note payable, due in six months	–0–	12,000
Prepaid rent	3,600	4,800
Taxes payable	1,450	1,230
Wages payable	1,200	1,600

Required

1. Calculate the following, as of December 31, 2001, and December 31, 2000:
   a. Working capital
   b. Current ratio
2. On the basis of your answers to **1,** comment on the relative liquidity of the company at the beginning and the end of the year. As part of your answer, explain the change in the company's liquidity from the beginning to the end of 2001.

LO 4 **Problem 2-5** Working Capital and Current Ratio

The balance sheet of Stevenson Inc. includes the following items:

Cash	$ 23,000
Accounts receivable	13,000
Inventory	45,000
Prepaid insurance	800
Land	80,000
Accounts payable	54,900
Salaries payable	1,200
Capital stock	100,000
Retained earnings	5,700

Required

1. Determine the current ratio and working capital.
2. Beyond the information provided in your answers to **1,** what does the composition of the current assets tell you about Stevenson's liquidity?
3. What other information do you need to fully assess Stevenson's liquidity?

LO 5 **Problem 2-6** Single-Step Income Statement

The following income statement items, arranged in alphabetical order, are taken from the records of Shaw Corporation for the year ended December 31, 2001:

Advertising expense	$ 1,500
Commissions expense	2,415
Cost of goods sold	29,200
Depreciation expense—office building	2,900
Income tax expense	1,540
Insurance expense—salesperson's auto	2,250
Interest expense	1,400
Interest revenue	1,340
Rent revenue	6,700
Salaries and wages expense—office	12,560
Sales revenue	48,300
Supplies expense—office	890

Required

1. Prepare a single-step income statement for the year ended December 31, 2001.
2. What weaknesses do you see in this form for the income statement?

LO 5 **Problem 2-7** Multiple-Step Income Statement

Refer to the list of income statement items in Problem 2-6. Assume that Shaw Corporation classifies all operating expenses into two categories: (1) selling and (2) general and administrative.

1. Prepare a multiple-step income statement fo the year ended December 31, 2001.
2. Compute Shaw's gross profit percentage.
3. What does this percentage tell you about Shaw's markup on its products?

LO 6 **Problem 2-8** Albertsons' Gross Profit Ratio

www.albertsons.com

Albertsons Inc. is a large, retail food and drug chain, with nearly 1,000 stores throughout the western, midwestern, and southern states. The following items appeared in the company's 1998 annual report (all amounts are in thousands of dollars):

	52 Weeks January 28, 1999	52 Weeks January 29, 1998	52 Weeks January 30, 1997
Sales	$16,005,115	$14,689,511	$13,776,678
Cost of sales	11,622,026	10,807,687	10,211,348

Required

1. Note that Albertsons' fiscal year ends toward the end of January (actually, on the Thursday nearest to January 31 each year). Why do you think this particular company would choose this time, rather than December 31, to end its accounting year?
2. Compute Albertsons' gross profit and its gross profit ratio for each of the three years.
3. Comment on the *change* in the gross profit ratio over the three-year period. What possible explanations are there for the change?

LO 8 **Problem 2-9** Statement of Cash Flows

Colorado Corporation was organized on January 1, 2001, with the investment of $250,000 in cash by its stockholders. The company immediately purchased an office building for $300,000, paying $210,000 in cash and signing a three-year promissory note for the balance. Colorado signed a five-year, $60,000 promissory note at a local bank during 2001 and received cash in the same amount. During its first year, Colorado collected $93,970 from its customers. It paid $65,600 for inventory, $20,400 in salaries and wages, and another $3,100 in taxes. Colorado paid $5,600 in cash dividends.

1. Prepare a statement of cash flows for the year ended December 31, 2001.
2. What does this statement tell you that an income statement does not?

LO 9 **Problem 2-10** Basic Elements of Financial Reports

Comparative income statements for Grammar Inc. are presented on the following page.

	2001	2000
Sales	$1,000,000	$500,000
Cost of sales	500,000	300,000
Gross margin	$ 500,000	$200,000
Operating expenses	120,000	100,000
Operating income	$ 380,000	$100,000
Loss on sale of subsidiary	(400,000)	—
Net income	$ (20,000)	$100,000

Required

The president and management believe that the company performed better in 2001 than it did in 2000. Write the president's letter to be included in the 2001 annual report. Explain why the company is financially sound and why shareholders should not be alarmed by the $20,000 loss in a year when sales have doubled.

Multi-Concept Problems

LO 2, 4 Problem 2-11 Comparing Coca-Cola and PepsiCo

The following current items, listed in alphabetical order, are taken from the consolidated balance sheets of Coca-Cola and PepsiCo as of December 31, 1998, and December 26, 1998, respectively (all amounts are in millions of dollars):

www.cocacola.com
www.pepsico.com

SPREADSHEET

Coca-Cola

Accounts payable and accrued expenses	$3,141
Accrued income taxes	1,037
Cash and cash equivalents	1,648
Current maturities of long-term debt	3
Inventories	890
Loans and notes payable	4,459
Marketable securities	159
Prepaid expenses and other assets	2,017
Trade accounts receivable, less allowance of $10	1,666

PepsiCo

Accounts and notes receivable, less allowance of $127	$2,453
Accounts payable and other current liabilities	3,870
Cash and cash equivalents	311
Income taxes payable	123
Inventories	1,016
Prepaid expenses, deferred income taxes, and other current assets	499
Short-term borrowings	3,921
Short-term investments, at cost	83

Required

1. Compute working capital and the current ratio for both companies.
2. On the basis of your answers to **1** above, which company appears to be more liquid?
3. As you know, other factors affect a company's liquidity in addition to its working capital and current ratio. Comment on the *composition* of each company's current assets and how this composition affects its liquidity.

LO 2, 5 Problem 2-12 Comparability and Consistency in Income Statements

The following income statements were provided by Gleeson Company, a retailer:

2001 Income Statement	
Sales	$1,700,000
Cost of sales	520,000
Gross profit	$1,180,000
Selling expense	702,000
Administrative expense	95,000
Total selling and administrative expense	$ 797,000
Net income	$ 383,000

2000 Income Statement	
Sales	$1,500,000
Cost of sales	450,000
Sales salaries	398,000
Advertising	175,000
Office supplies	54,000
Depreciation—building	40,000
Delivery expense	20,000
Total expenses	$1,137,000
Net income	$ 363,000

Required

1. Identify each income statement as either single-step or multiple-step format.
2. Convert the 2000 income statement to the same format as the 2001 income statement.

LO 3, 5, 7 Problem 2-13 Classified Balance Sheet, Multiple-Step Income Statement, and Statement of Retained Earnings for Kellogg's

www.kelloggs.com

Shown below, in alphabetical order, are items taken from Kellogg's 1998 consolidated financial statements:

SPREADSHEET

	(in millions)
Accounts payable	$ 386.9
Accounts receivable, less allowance of $12.9	693.0
Accumulated other comprehensive income (reduction of owners' equity listed after treasury stock)	(292.4)
Capital in excess of par value	105.0
Cash and cash equivalents	136.4
Cash dividends	375.3
Common stock	103.8
Cost of goods sold	3,282.6
Current maturities of long-term debt	1.1
Income taxes (expense)	279.9
Interest expense	119.5
Inventories	451.4
Long-term debt	1,614.5
Net sales	6,762.1
Non-recurring charges (operating expense)	70.5
Notes payable (current liability)	620.4
Other assets (long-term assets)	666.2
Other current assets	215.7
Other current liabilities	710.1
Other income (expense), net	6.9
Other liabilities (long-term liabilities)	828.7
Property, net	2,888.8
Retained earnings, beginning of year	1,240.4
Selling and administrative expense	2,513.9
Treasury stock (reduction of owners' equity listed after retained earnings)	(394.3)

(NOTE: The descriptions in parentheses are not part of the items but have been added to provide you with hints as you complete this problem.)

Required

1. Prepare a multiple-step income statement for Kellogg's for the year ended December 31, 1998.
2. Prepare a statement of retained earnings for Kellogg's for the year ended December 31, 1998.
3. Prepare a classified balance sheet for Kellogg's at December 31, 1998.

LO 4, 6 **Problem 2-14** Using Kellogg's Classified Balance Sheet and Multiple-Step Income Statement

(Note: Consider completing this problem after Problem 2-13 to ensure that you have the various items on the financial statements properly classified.)

www.kelloggs.com

Refer to the information set forth in Problem 2-13.

Required

1. Compute Kellogg's working capital and its current ratio at December 31, 1998.
2. Does Kellogg's appear to be liquid? What other factors need to be considered in answering this question?
3. Compute Kellogg's gross profit ratio and its profit margin for 1998.
4. As a Kellogg's stockholder, would you be satisfied with the company's gross profit ratio and its profit margin? What other factors need to be considered in answering this question?

LO 1, 4, 8 **Problem 2-15** Cash Flow

Franklin Co., a specialty retailer, has a history of paying quarterly dividends of $.50 per share. Management is trying to determine whether the company will have adequate cash on December 31, 2001, to pay a dividend if one is declared by the board of directors. The following additional information is available:

- All sales are on account, and accounts receivable are collected one month after the sale. Sales volume has been increasing 5% each month.
- All purchases of merchandise are on account, and accounts payable are paid one month after the purchase. Cost of sales is 40% of the sales price. Inventory levels are maintained at $75,000.
- Operating expenses in addition to the mortgage are paid in cash. They amount to $3,000 per month and are paid as they are incurred.

FRANKLIN CO.
BALANCE SHEET
SEPTEMBER 30, 2001

Cash	$ 5,000	Accounts payable	$ 5,000
Accounts receivable	12,500	Mortgage note†	150,000
Inventory	75,000	Common stock—$1 par	50,000
Note receivable*	10,000	Retained earnings	66,500
Building/Land	169,000	Total liabilities	
Total assets	$271,500	and stockholders' equity	$271,500

*Note receivable represents a one-year, 5% interest-bearing note, due November 1, 2001.

†Mortgage note is a 30-year, 7% note due in monthly installments of $1,200.

Required

Determine the cash that Franklin will have available to pay a dividend on December 31, 2001. Round all amounts to the nearest dollar. What can Franklin's management do to increase the cash available? Should management recommend that the board of directors declare a dividend?

ALTERNATE PROBLEMS

LO 2 **Problem 2-1A** Materiality

Jane Erving, a newly hired accountant, wanted to impress her boss, so she stayed late one night to analyze the long-distance calls by area code and time of day placed. She determined the monthly cost, for the past 12 months, by hour and area code called.

Required

1. What did Jane think her boss would learn from this information? What action might be taken as a result of knowing it?
2. Would this information be more relevant if Jane worked for a hardware store or for a real estate company? Discuss.

LO 2 Problem 2-2A Costs and Expenses

The following costs are incurred by a retailer:

1. Point-of-sale systems in a retail store
2. An ad in the yellow pages
3. An inventory-control computer software system
4. Shipping merchandise for resale to chain outlets

For each of these costs, explain whether all of the cost or only a portion of the cost would appear as an expense on the income statement for the period in which the cost is incurred. If not all of the cost would appear on the income statement for that period, explain why not.

LO 3 Problem 2-3A Classified Balance Sheet

The following balance sheet items, listed in alphabetical order, are available from the records of Singer Company at December 31, 2001:

Accounts payable	$ 34,280
Accounts receivable	26,700
Accumulated depreciation—buildings	40,000
Accumulated depreciation—equipment	12,500
Bonds payable, due December 31, 2007	250,000
Buildings	150,000
Capital stock, $1 par value	200,000
Cash	60,790
Equipment	84,500
Income taxes payable	7,500
Interest payable	2,200
Land	250,000
Marketable securities	15,000
Merchandise inventory	112,900
Notes payable, due April 15, 2002	6,500
Office supplies	400
Paid-in capital in excess of par value	75,000
Patents	45,000
Prepaid rent	3,600
Retained earnings	113,510
Salaries payable	7,400

Required

1. Prepare a classified balance sheet as of December 31, 2001.
2. Compute Singer's current ratio.
3. On the basis of your answer to **2,** does Singer appear to be *liquid?* What other information do you need to fully answer this question?

LO 4 Problem 2-4A Financial Statement Ratios

The following items, in alphabetical order, are available from the records of Quinn Corporation as of December 31, 2001 and 2000:

	December 31, 2001	December 31, 2000
Accounts payable	$10,500	$ 6,500
Accounts receivable	16,500	26,000
Cash	12,750	11,800
Interest receivable	200	–0–
Note receivable, due 12/31/2003	12,000	12,000
Office supplies	900	1,100
Prepaid insurance	400	250
Salaries payable	1,800	800
Taxes payable	10,000	5,800

Required

1. Calculate the following, as of December 31, 2001, and December 31, 2000:
   a. Working capital
   b. Current ratio
2. On the basis of your answers to **1**, comment on the relative liquidity of the company at the beginning and the end of the year. As part of your answer, explain the change in the company's liquidity from the beginning to the end of 2001.

LO 4 **Problem 2-5A** Working Capital and Current Ratio

The balance sheet of Kapinski Inc. includes the following items:

Cash	$ 23,000
Accounts receivable	43,000
Inventory	75,000
Prepaid insurance	2,800
Land	80,000
Accounts payable	84,900
Salaries payable	3,200
Capital stock	100,000
Retained earnings	35,700

Required

1. Determine the current ratio and working capital.
2. Kapinski appears to have a positive current ratio and a large net working capital. Why would it have trouble paying bills as they come due?
3. Suggest three things that Kapinski can do to help pay its bills on time.

LO 5 **Problem 2-6A** Single-Step Income Statement

The following income statement items, arranged in alphabetical order, are taken from the records of Corbin Enterprises, a software sales firm, for the year ended December 31, 2001:

Advertising expense	$ 9,000
Cost of goods sold	150,000
Depreciation expense—computer	4,500
Dividend revenue	2,700
Income tax expense	30,700
Interest expense	1,900
Rent expense—office	26,400
Rent expense—salesperson's car	18,000
Sales revenue	350,000
Supplies expense—office	1,300
Utilities expense	6,750
Wages expense—office	45,600

Required

1. Prepare a single-step income statement for the year ended December 31, 2001.
2. What weaknesses do you see in this form for the income statement?

LO 5 **Problem 2-7A** Multiple-Step Income Statement

Refer to the list of income statement items in Problem 2-6A. Assume that Corbin Enterprises classifies all operating expenses into two categories: (1) selling and (2) general and administrative.

Required

1. Prepare a multiple-step income statement for the year ended December 31, 2001.
2. Compute Corbin's gross profit percentage.
3. What does this percentage tell you about Corbin's markup on its products?

LO 6 **Problem 2-8A** Saks Gross Profit Ratio

www.saksincorporated.com

Saks Incorporated is a national retailer operating department stores under various names, with the most recognizable being Saks Fifth Avenue. The following items appeared in the company's 1998 annual report (all amounts are in thousands of dollars):

	Year Ended		
	January 30, 1999	**January 31, 1998**	**February 1, 1997**
Net sales	$6,219,893	$5,726,346	$4,926,862
Cost of sales	4,093,467	3,731,293	3,208,989

Required

1. Note that Saks' fiscal year ends toward the end of January (actually, on the Saturday closest to January 31 each year). Why do you think this particular company would choose this time to end its accounting year rather than December 31?
2. Compute Saks' gross profit and its gross profit ratio for each of the three years.
3. Comment on any *change* in the gross profit ratio over the three-year period. What possible explanations are there for the change?

LO 8 **Problem 2-9A** Statement of Cash Flows

Wisconsin Corporation was organized on January 1, 2001, with the investment of $400,000 in cash by its stockholders. The company immediately purchased a manufacturing facility for $300,000, paying $150,000 in cash and signing a five-year promissory note for the balance. Wisconsin signed another five-year note at the bank for $50,000 during 2001 and received cash for the same amount. During its first year, Wisconsin collected $310,000 from its customers. It paid $185,000 for inventory, $30,100 in salaries and wages, and another $40,000 in taxes. Wisconsin paid $4,000 in cash dividends.

Required

1. Prepare a statement of cash flows for the year ended December 31, 2001.
2. What does this statement tell you that an income statement does not?

LO 9 **Problem 2-10A** Basic Elements of Financial Reports

Comparative income statements for Thesaurus Inc. are presented below:

	2001	**2000**
Sales	$1,000,000	$500,000
Cost of sales	500,000	300,000
Gross margin	$ 500,000	$200,000
Operating expenses	120,000	100,000
Operating income	$ 380,000	$100,000
Gain on the sale of subsidiary	—	400,000
Net income	$ 380,000	$500,000

Required

The president and management believe that the company performed better in 2001 than it did in 2000. Write the president's letter to be included in the 2001 annual report. Explain why the company is financially sound and why shareholders should not be alarmed by the reduction in income in a year when sales have doubled.

Alternate Multi-Concept Problems

LO 2, 4 **Problem 2-11A** Comparing Compaq and Dell

www.compaq.com
www.dell.com

The following current items, listed in alphabetical order, are taken from the consolidated balance sheets of Compaq Computer Corporation and Dell Computer Corporation as of December 31, 1998, and February 1, 1998, respectively (all amounts are in millions of dollars):

Compaq	
Accounts payable	$4,237
Accounts receivable, less allowance of $318	6,998
Accrued restructuring costs	1,110

Cash and cash equivalents	4,091
Deferred income taxes (asset)	1,602
Income taxes payable	282
Inventories	2,005
Other current assets	471
Other current liabilities	5,104

Dell

Accounts payable	$1,643
Accounts receivable, net	1,486
Accrued and other (liabilities)	1,054
Cash	320
Inventories	233
Marketable securities	1,524
Other (assets)	349

(NOTE: the descriptions in parentheses are not part of the items but have been added to provide you with assistance as you complete this problem.)

Required

1. Compute working capital and the current ratio for both companies.
2. On the basis of your answers to **1** above, which company appears to be more liquid?
3. As you know, other factors affect a company's liquidity in addition to its working capital and current ratio. Comment on the *composition* of each company's current assets and how this composition affects its liquidity.

LO 2, 5 **Problem 2-12A** Comparability and Consistency in Income Statements

The following income statements were provided by Chisholm Company, a wholesale food distributor:

	2001	2000
Sales	$1,700,000	$1,500,000
Cost of sales	612,000	450,000
Sales salaries	427,000	398,000
Delivery expense	180,000	175,000
Office supplies	55,000	54,000
Depreciation—truck	40,000	40,000
Computer line expense	23,000	20,000
Total expenses	$1,337,000	$1,137,000
Net income	$ 363,000	$ 363,000

Required

1. Identify each income statement as either single-step or multiple-step format.
2. Restate each item in the income statements as a percentage of sales. Why did net income remain unchanged when sales increased in 2001?

LO 3, 5, 7 **Problem 2-13A** Classified Balance Sheet, Multiple-Step Income Statement, and Statement of Retained Earnings for Walgreen's

Shown below, in alphabetical order, are items taken from Walgreen's 1998 consolidated financial statements. Walgreen Co. has a fiscal year ending August 31.

www.walgreens.com

	(in millions)
Accounts receivable, net	$ 373
Accrued expenses and other liabilities (current liability)	618
Cash and cash equivalents	144
Cash dividends declared	124
Common stock	78
Cost of sales	11,140

Cumulative effect of accounting change for system development costs (last item, deduction on income statement before net income)	26
Deferred income taxes (long-term liabilities)	89
Gain on sale of long-term care pharmacies (other income)	37
Income taxes (current liability)	55
Income tax provision (expense)	340
Interest expense	1
Interest income	6
Inventories	2,027
Net sales	15,307
Other current assets	79
Other non-current assets	135
Other non-current liabilities	384
Paid-in capital	118
Property and equipment, net	2,144
Retained earnings, beginning of year	2,266
Selling, occupancy, and administration (expense)	3,332
Trade accounts payable	907

(NOTE: the descriptions in parentheses are not part of the items but have been added to provide you with hints as you complete this problem.)

Required

1. Prepare a multiple-step income statement for Walgreen's for the year ended August 31, 1998.
2. Prepare a statement of retained earnings for Walgreen's for the year ended August 31, 1998.
3. Prepare a classified balance sheet for Walgreen's at August 31, 1998.

LO 4, 6 **Problem 2-14A** Using Walgreen's Classified Balance Sheet and Multiple-Step Income Statement

www.walgreens.com

(**Note:** Consider completing this problem after Problem 2-13A to ensure that you have the various items on the financial statements properly classified.)

Refer to the information set forth in Problem 2-13A.

Required

1. Compute Walgreen's working capital and its current ratio at August 31, 1998.
2. Does Walgreen's appear to be liquid? What other factors need to be considered in answering this question?
3. Compute Walgreen's gross profit ratio and its profit margin for the year ended August 31, 1998.
4. As a Walgreen's stockholder, would you be satisfied with the company's gross profit ratio and its profit margin? What other factors need to be considered in answering this question?

LO 1, 4, 8 **Problem 2-15A** Cash Flow

Roosevelt Inc., a consulting service, has a history of paying annual dividends of $1 per share. Management is trying to determine whether the company will have adequate cash on December 31, 2001, to pay a dividend if one is declared by the board of directors. The following additional information is available:

- All sales are on account, and accounts receivable are collected one month after the sale. Sales volume has been decreasing 5% each month.
- Operating expenses are paid in cash in the month incurred. Average monthly expenses are $10,000 (excluding the biweekly payroll).
- Biweekly payroll is $4,500, and it will be paid December 15 and December 31.
- Unearned revenue is expected to be earned in December. This amount was taken into consideration in the expected sales volume.

ROOSEVELT INC.
BALANCE SHEET
DECEMBER 1, 2001

Cash	$ 15,000	Unearned Revenue	$ 2,000
Accounts receivable	40,000	Note payable*	30,000
Computer equipment	120,000	Common stock—$2 par	50,000
		Retained earnings	$ 93,000
		Total liabilities and	
Total assets	$175,000	stockholder's equity	$175,000

*The note payable plus 3% interest for six months is due January 15, 2002.

Required

Determine the cash that Roosevelt will have available to pay a dividend on December 31, 2001. Round all amounts to the nearest dollar. Should management recommend that the board of directors declare a dividend?

CASES

Reading and Interpreting Financial Statements

LO 3 Case 2-1 Boeing's Operating Cycle

In Boeing's annual report, footnote 1, "Summary of Significant Accounting Policies," includes the following explanation of Boeing's Inventories:

www.boeing.com

> *Inventories*
> Inventoried costs on commercial aircraft programs and long-term contracts include direct engineering, production and tooling costs, and applicable overhead, not in excess of estimated realizable value. In accordance with industry practice, inventoried costs include amounts relating to programs and contracts with long production cycles, a portion of which is not expected to be realized within one year. Commercial spare parts and general stock materials are stated at average cost not in excess of realizable cost.[14]

Required

1. Based on the note above, describe Boeing's inventory. That is, what types of items would you expect to find in the inventory of this type of company?
2. Why would Boeing expect that a portion of its inventoried costs would *not* be realized within one year?
3. Based on your answer to **2** above, should Boeing classify its inventories as current or as non-current assets? Explain your answer.

LO 4 Case 2-2 Ben & Jerry's Current Assets and Current Liabilities

Refer to Ben & Jerry's balance sheets as of December 26, 1998 and December 27, 1997.

www.benjerry.com

Required

1. Compute Ben & Jerry's working capital as of each of the two balance sheet dates. Also, compute the change in working capital from the end of 1997 to the end of 1998.
2. Compute Ben & Jerry's current ratio as of each of the two balance sheet dates. Compute the percentage change in the ratio from the end of 1997 to the end of 1998.
3. Assume that you are a dairy farmer and are considering whether to sell milk to Ben & Jerry's in return for their promise to pay any amounts owed within sixty days. On the basis of your answers to **1** and **2** above, what would your decision be? Justify your decision.

LO 3, 4 Case 2-3 Interpreting Gateway's Liabilities

Refer to Gateway's balance sheet as of December 31, 1998.

www.gateway.com

[14] *Boeing Company 1998 Annual Report,* p. 59.

Required

1. The first current liability Gateway reports is titled "Notes payable and current maturities of long-term obligations." Explain *why* a long-term obligation would be classified as a current liability.
2. Directly below the current liabilities is an account titled "Long-term obligations, net of current maturities." Explain the meaning of this account, specifically what Gateway means by the phrase *net.*
3. The last liability reported on the balance sheet is titled "Warranty and other liabilities." Explain why warranties result in the recognition of a liability to Gateway.

Making Financial Decisions

LO 8 **Case 2-4** Analysis of Cash Flow for a Small Business

Charles, a financial consultant, has been self-employed for two years. His list of clients has grown, and he is earning a reputation as a shrewd investor. Charles rents a small office, uses the pool secretarial services, and has purchased a car that he is depreciating over three years. The following income statements cover Charles's first two years of business:

	Year I	Year 2
Commissions revenue	$ 25,000	$65,000
Rent	12,000	12,000
Secretarial services	3,000	9,000
Car expenses, gas, insurance	6,000	6,500
Depreciation	15,000	15,000
Net income	$(11,000)	$22,500

Charles believes that he should earn more than $11,500 for working very hard for two years. He is thinking about going to work for an investment firm where he can earn $40,000 per year. What would you advise Charles to do?

LO 9 **Case 2-5** Factors Involved in an Investment Decision

As an investor, you are considering purchasing stock in a fast-food restaurant chain. The annual reports of several companies are available for comparison.

Required

Prepare an outline of the steps you would follow to make your comparison. Start by listing the first section that you would read in the financial reports. What would you expect to find there, and why did you choose that section to read first? Continue with the other sections of the financial report.

Many fast-food chains are owned by large conglomerates. What limitation does this create in your comparison? How would you solve it?

Accounting and Ethics: What Would You Do?

LO 2 **Case 2-6** The Expenditure Approval Process

Roberto is the plant superintendent of a small manufacturing company that is owned by a large corporation. The corporation has a policy that any expenditure over $1,000 must be approved by the chief financial officer in the corporate headquarters. The approval process takes a minimum of three weeks. Roberto would like to order a new labeling machine that is expected to reduce costs and pay for itself in six months. The machine costs $2,200, but Roberto can buy the sales rep's demo for $1,800. Roberto has asked the sales rep to send two separate bills for $900 each.

What would you do if you were the sales rep? Do you agree or disagree with Roberto's actions? What do you think about the corporate policy?

LO 4, 6 **Case 2-7** Barbara Applies For a Loan

Barbara Bites, owner of Bites of Bagels, a drive-through bagel shop, would like to expand her business from its current one location to a chain of bagel shops. Sales in the bagel shop have been increasing an average of 8% each quarter. Profits have been increasing accordingly. Barbara is conservative in spending and a very hard worker. She has an appointment with a banker to apply for a loan to expand the business. To prepare for the appointment, she instructs you, as the chief financial officer and payroll clerk, to copy the quarterly income statements for the past two years but not to include a balance sheet. Barbara already has a substantial loan from another bank. In fact, she has very little of her own money invested in the business.

What should you do? Do you think the banker will lend Barbara more money?

Internet Research Case

Case 2-8 Gateway

You can probably do this from your everyday knowledge, but this is good practice in researching a company using the internet. Find a WWW site or a source of information that will list the competitors to Gateway. Choose the top two competitors and answer the following questions:

1. Looking at their balance sheets, what are their total current assets and their total current liabilities? From these numbers, calculate each company's working capital and current ratio. How do they compare to these ratios for Gateway, shown on page 65?
2. From their income statements, calculate their profit margins for the latest year available. How do they compare to those of Gateway, which you were asked to calculate in the From Concept to Practice box on page 67?

Optional Research: From the financial information available on their WWW sites, what other comparisons can you make about these companies? Based on your research, are the companies themselves comparable, in such areas as size, products, assets, liabilities, net income? If not, explain five ways in which they differ. Is the financial information itself comparable for the three companies? Explain.

Fill in your source for industry information:

www.__________.com

Gateway and its main competitors:

www.gateway.com

www.__________.com

www.__________.com

Solution to Key Terms Quiz

6 Understandability (p. 48)
3 Relevance (p. 48)
9 Reliability (p. 49)
14 Comparability (p. 50)
19 Depreciation (p. 50)
17 Consistency (p. 50)
2 Materiality (p. 51)
5 Conservatism (p. 51)
11 Operating cycle (p. 53)
15 Current asset (p. 54)
10 Current liability (p. 57)
16 Liquidity (p. 58)
12 Working capital (p. 58)
8 Current ratio (p. 58)
1 Single-step income statement (p. 60)
4 Multiple-step income statement (p. 60)
18 Gross profit (p. 60)
7 Gross profit ratio (p. 62)
13 Profit margin (p. 62)

Chapter 3

Processing Accounting Information

Study Links

A Look at Previous Chapters

Up to this point, we have focused our attention on the role of accounting in decision making and the way accountants use financial statements to communicate useful information to the various users of the statements.

A Look at This Chapter

In this chapter, we consider how accounting information is processed. We begin by considering the *inputs* to an accounting system, that is, the transactions entered into by a business. We look at how transactions are analyzed, and then we turn to a number of accounting tools and procedures designed to facilitate the preparation of the *outputs* of the system, the financial statements. Ledger accounts, journal entries, and trial balances are tools that allow a company to process vast amounts of data efficiently.

A Look at Upcoming Chapters

Chapter 4 concludes our overview of the accounting model. We will examine the accrual basis of accounting and its effect on the measurement of income. Adjusting entries, which are the focus of the accrual basis, will be discussed in detail in Chapter 4, along with the other steps in the accounting cycle.

Focus on Financial Results

When snowboarding became a full-medal sport at the 1998 Winter Olympics, two companies took note. One was Ride Inc., a successful young manufacturer of snowboards and related equipment. The other was K2, a leading designer, manufacturer, and marketer of brand-name sporting goods. K2 purchased Ride in 1999.

K2 is a company that wants to grow, and it measures growth in terms of sales. It markets a broad range of sports products, including K2 and Olin Alpine skis; K2 snowboards, boots, and bindings; K2 in-line skates and bikes; Stearns sports equipment; Shakespeare fishing tackle; and Dana Design backpacks. Diversity helps K2 survive the ups and downs of its market.

Sales are sometimes negatively affected by weather, changing consumer tastes and interests, retailers' shifting inventory strategies, and K2's own inability to deliver products on time. Sales can be buoyed by the birth of new products, crossovers into related product categories, and increase in K2's market share, which its purchase of Ride accomplished. K2 hopes to use all these strategies—product innovation, line expansion, and growth of market share—to fulfill its goal of enhancing shareholder value through sales. In addition, part of the company's strategy involves growing earnings by reducing costs. K2 has various cost initiatives which include the relocation of certain operations to lower cost areas and improvements in sourcing.

STATEMENTS OF CONSOLIDATED INCOME

K2 concentrates on growing sales

To raise net income, K2 will focus on reducing costs

K2 Inc. Year ended December 31	1998	1997	1996
	(In thousands, except per share figures)		
Net sales	$574,510	$559,030	$513,170
Cost of products sold	418,950	391,860	360,029
Gross profit	155,560	167,170	153,141
Selling expenses	87,389	79,832	67,324
General and administrative expenses	39,030	38,303	38,490
Research and development expenses	12,391	11,979	9,317
Operating income	16,750	37,056	38,010
Interest expense	12,163	10,560	9,294
Other income, net	(236)	(619)	(1,476)
Income from continuing operations before provision for income taxes	4,823	27,115	30,192
Provision for income taxes	955	7,815	9,105
Income from continuing operations	3,868	19,300	21,087
Discontinued operations, net of taxes	975	2,600	4,130
Net Income	$ 4,843	$ 21,900	$ 25,217
Basic earnings per share:			
Continuing operations	$ .23	$ 1.17	$ 1.27
Discontinued operations	.06	.15	.25
Net income	$ .29	$ 1.32	$ 1.52
Diluted earnings per share:			
Continuing operations	$ .23	$ 1.15	$ 1.26
Discontinued operations	.06	.16	.25
Net income	$ .29	$ 1.31	$ 1.51
Basic shares outstanding	16,554	16,541	16,574
Diluted shares outstanding	16,637	16,713	16,734

See notes to consolidated financial statements

K2's 1998 Annual Report

K2's income statement, pictured here, tells a story of the need for growth and a decrease in costs. As you study the accounting process introduced in this chapter, consider how the accounting system would help you process information for K2. How would you record sales figures, the purchase of Ride, or the effects of your cost-cutting campaign?

www.K2sports.com

Learning Objectives

After studying this chapter, you should be able to:

- **LO 1** Explain the difference between an external and an internal event. (p. 94)
- **LO 2** Explain the role of source documents in an accounting system. (p. 94)
- **LO 3** Analyze the effects of transactions on the accounting equation. (p. 95)
- **LO 4** Define the concept of a general ledger and understand the use of the T account as a method for analyzing transactions. (p. 102)
- **LO 5** Explain the rules of debits and credits. (p. 103)
- **LO 6** Explain the purposes of a journal and the posting process. (p. 108)
- **LO 7** Explain the purpose of a trial balance. (p. 111)

Economic Events: The Basis for Recording Transactions

LO 1 Explain the difference between an external and an internal event.

Event A happening of consequence to an entity.

Many different types of economic events affect an entity during the year. A sale is made to a customer. Inventory is purchased from a supplier. A loan is taken out at the bank. A fire destroys a warehouse. A new contract is signed with the union. In short, "An **event** is a happening of consequence to an entity."[1]

External and Internal Events

External event An event involving interaction between an entity and its environment.

Internal event An event occurring entirely within an entity.

Transaction Any event that is recognized in a set of financial statements.

Two types of events affect an entity: internal and external. An **external event** "involves interaction between the entity and its environment."[2] For example, the *purchase* of raw material from a supplier is an external event, as is the *sale* of inventory to a customer. An **internal event** occurs entirely within the entity. The *transfer* of raw material into production is an internal event, as is the use of a piece of equipment. We will use the term **transaction** to refer to any event, external or internal, that is recognized in a set of financial statements.[3]

What is necessary to recognize an event in the records? Are all economic events recognized as transactions by the accountant? The answers to these questions involve the concept of *measurement.* An event must be measured to be recognized. Certain events are relatively easy to measure: the payroll for the week, the amount of inventory destroyed by an earthquake, or the sales for the day. Not all events that affect an entity can be measured *reliably,* however. For example, how does a manufacturer of breakfast cereal measure the effect of a drought on the price of wheat? A company hires a new chief executive. How can it reliably measure the value of the new officer to the company? There is no definitive answer to the measurement problem in accounting. It is a continuing challenge to the accounting profession and something we will return to throughout the text.

From Concept **to PRACTICE 3.1**

Reading K2's Financial Statements K2 Inc. purchases materials to use in making snowboards. Is this an internal or an external event? The company subsequently uses the materials in the production process. Is this an internal or an external event?

The Role of Source Documents in Recording Transactions

LO 2 Explain the role of source documents in an accounting system.

Source document A piece of paper that is used as evidence to record a transaction.

The first step in the recording process is *identification.* A business needs a systematic method for recognizing events as transactions. A **source document** provides the evidence needed in an accounting system to record a transaction. Source documents take many different forms. An invoice received from a supplier is the source document for a purchase of inventory on credit. A cash register tape is the source document used by a retailer to recognize a cash sale.

[1] *Statement of Financial Accounting Concepts (SFAC) No. 3,* "Elements of Financial Statements of Business Enterprises" (Stamford, Conn.: Financial Accounting Standards Board, 1982), par. 65.

[2] *SFAC No. 3.*

[3] Technically, a *transaction* is defined by the Financial Accounting Standards Board as a special kind of external event in which the entity exchanges something of value with an outsider. Because the term *transaction* is used in practice to refer to any event that is recognized in the statements, we will use this broader definition.

Source documents like these receipts are records that document transactions that the business engages in. Shown here are an employee's travel expense receipts, which will be turned in to the company for reimbursement. Other source documents may be contracts, lease agreements, invoices, delivery vouchers, check stubs, and deposit slips.

The payroll department sends the accountant the time cards for the week as the necessary documentation to record wages.

Not all recognizable events are supported by a standard source document. For certain events, some form of documentation must be generated. For example, no standard source document exists to recognize the financial consequences from a fire or the settlement of a lawsuit. Documentation is just as important for these types of events as it is for standard, recurring transactions.

Analyzing the Effects of Transactions on the Accounting Equation

LO 3 Analyze the effects of transactions on the accounting equation.

Economic events are the basis for recording transactions in an accounting system. For every transaction, it is essential to analyze its effect on the accounting equation:

Assets = Liabilities + Owners' Equity

We will now consider a series of events and their recognition as transactions for a hypothetical corporation, Glengarry Health Club. The transactions are for the month of January 2001, the first month of operations for the new business.

(1) *Issuance of capital stock.* The company is started when Mary-Jo Kovach and Irene McGuinness file articles of incorporation with the state to obtain a charter. Each invests $50,000 in the business. In return, each receives 5,000 shares of capital stock. Thus, at this point, each of them owns 50 percent of the outstanding stock of the company and has a claim to 50 percent of its assets. The effect of this transaction on the accounting equation is to increase both assets and owners' equity:

	Assets					=	Liabilities		+	Owners' Equity	
TRANSACTION NUMBER	**CASH**	**ACCOUNTS RECEIVABLE**	**EQUIPMENT**	**BUILDING**	**LAND**		**ACCOUNTS PAYABLE**	**NOTES PAYABLE**		**CAPITAL STOCK**	**RETAINED EARNINGS**
1	$100,000									$100,000	
Totals			$100,000							$100,000	

As you see, each side of the accounting equation increases by $100,000. Cash is increased, and because the owners contributed this amount, their claim to the assets is increased in the form of Capital Stock.

(2) *Acquisition of property in exchange for a note.* The company buys a piece of property for $200,000. The seller agrees to accept a five-year promissory note. The note is given by the health club to the seller and is a written promise to repay the principal amount of the loan at the end of five years. To the company, the promissory note is a liability. The property consists of land valued at $50,000 and a newly constructed building valued at $150,000. The effect of this transaction on the accounting equation is to increase both assets and liabilities by $200,000:

	Assets					=	Liabilities		+	Owners' Equity	
TRANSACTION NUMBER	CASH	ACCOUNTS RECEIVABLE	EQUIPMENT	BUILDING	LAND		ACCOUNTS PAYABLE	NOTES PAYABLE		CAPITAL STOCK	RETAINED EARNINGS
Bal.	$100,000									$100,000	
2				$150,000	$50,000			$200,000			
Bal.	$100,000			$150,000	$50,000			$200,000		$100,000	
Totals			$300,000					$300,000			

(3) *Acquisition of equipment on an open account.* Mary-Jo and Irene contact an equipment supplier and buy $20,000 of exercise equipment: treadmills, barbells, and stationary bicycles. The supplier agrees to accept payment in full in 30 days. The health club has acquired an asset and at the same time incurred a liability:

	Assets					=	Liabilities		+	Owners' Equity	
TRANSACTION NUMBER	CASH	ACCOUNTS RECEIVABLE	EQUIPMENT	BUILDING	LAND		ACCOUNTS PAYABLE	NOTES PAYABLE		CAPITAL STOCK	RETAINED EARNINGS
Bal.	$100,000			$150,000	$50,000			$200,000		$100,000	
3			$20,000				$20,000				
Bal.	$100,000		$20,000	$150,000	$50,000		$20,000	$200,000		$100,000	
Totals			$320,000					$320,000			

(4) *Sale of monthly memberships on account.* The owners open their doors for business. During January, they sell 300 monthly club memberships for $50 each, or a total of $15,000. The members have until the 10th of the following month to pay. Glengarry does not have cash from the new members but instead has a promise from each member to pay cash in the future. The promise from a customer to pay an amount owed is an asset called an *account receivable.* The other side of this transaction is an increase in the owners' equity (specifically, Retained Earnings) in the business. In other words, the assets have increased by $15,000 without any increase in a liability or decrease in another asset. The increase in owners' equity indicates that the owners' residual interest in the assets of the business has increased by this amount. More specifically, an inflow of assets resulting from the sale of goods and services by a business is called *revenue.* The change in the accounting equation follows:

	Assets					=	Liabilities		+	Owners' Equity	
TRANSACTION NUMBER	CASH	ACCOUNTS RECEIVABLE	EQUIPMENT	BUILDING	LAND		ACCOUNTS PAYABLE	NOTES PAYABLE		CAPITAL STOCK	RETAINED EARNINGS
Bal.	$100,000		$20,000	$150,000	$50,000		$20,000	$200,000		$100,000	
4		$15,000									$15,000
Bal.	$100,000	$15,000	$20,000	$150,000	$50,000		$20,000	$200,000		$100,000	$15,000
Totals			$335,000					$335,000			

(5) *Sale of court time for cash.* In addition to memberships, Glengarry sells court time. Court fees are paid at the time of use and amount to $5,000 for the first month:

	Assets					= Liabilities		+ Owners' Equity	
TRANSACTION NUMBER	CASH	ACCOUNTS RECEIVABLE	EQUIPMENT	BUILDING	LAND	ACCOUNTS PAYABLE	NOTES PAYABLE	CAPITAL STOCK	RETAINED EARNINGS
Bal.	$100,000	$15,000	$20,000	$150,000	$50,000	$20,000	$200,000	$100,000	$15,000
5	5,000								5,000
Bal.	$105,000	$15,000	$20,000	$150,000	$50,000	$20,000	$200,000	$100,000	$20,000
Totals			$340,000					$340,000	

The only difference between this transaction and **(4)** is that cash is received rather than a promise to pay at a later date. Both transactions result in an increase in an asset and an increase in the owners' claim to the assets. In both cases, there is an inflow of assets, in the form of either Accounts Receivable or Cash. Thus, in both cases, the company has earned revenue.

(6) *Payment of wages and salaries.* The wages and salaries for the first month amount to $10,000. The payment of this amount results in a decrease in Cash and a decrease in the owners' claim on the assets, that is, a decrease in Retained Earnings. More specifically, an outflow of assets resulting from the sale of goods or services is called an *expense.* The effect of this transaction is to decrease both sides of the accounting equation:

	Assets					= Liabilities		+ Owners' Equity	
TRANSACTION NUMBER	CASH	ACCOUNTS RECEIVABLE	EQUIPMENT	BUILDING	LAND	ACCOUNTS PAYABLE	NOTES PAYABLE	CAPITAL STOCK	RETAINED EARNINGS
Bal.	$105,000	$15,000	$20,000	$150,000	$50,000	$20,000	$200,000	$100,000	$20,000
6	− 10,000								−10,000
Bal.	$ 95,000	$15,000	$20,000	$150,000	$50,000	$20,000	$200,000	$100,000	$10,000
Totals			$330,000					$330,000	

(7) *Payment of utilities.* The cost of utilities for the first month is $3,000. Glengarry pays this amount in cash. Both the utilities and the salaries and wages are expenses, and they have the same effect on the accounting equation. Cash is decreased, accompanied by a corresponding decrease in the owners' claim on the assets of the business:

	Assets					= Liabilities		+ Owners' Equity	
TRANSACTION NUMBER	CASH	ACCOUNTS RECEIVABLE	EQUIPMENT	BUILDING	LAND	ACCOUNTS PAYABLE	NOTES PAYABLE	CAPITAL STOCK	RETAINED EARNINGS
Bal.	$95,000	$15,000	$20,000	$150,000	$50,000	$20,000	$200,000	$100,000	$10,000
7	− 3,000								− 3,000
Bal.	$92,000	$15,000	$20,000	$150,000	$50,000	$20,000	$200,000	$100,000	$ 7,000
Totals			$327,000					$327,000	

(8) *Collection of accounts receivable.* Even though the January monthly memberships are not due until the 10th of the following month, some of the members pay their bills by the end of January. The amount received from members in payment of their accounts is $4,000. The effect of the collection of an open account is to increase Cash and decrease Accounts Receivable:

	Assets					= Liabilities		+ Owners' Equity	
TRANSACTION NUMBER	CASH	ACCOUNTS RECEIVABLE	EQUIPMENT	BUILDING	LAND	ACCOUNTS PAYABLE	NOTES PAYABLE	CAPITAL STOCK	RETAINED EARNINGS
Bal.	$92,000	$15,000	$20,000	$150,000	$50,000	$20,000	$200,000	$100,000	$7,000
8	4,000	− 4,000							
Bal.	$96,000	$11,000	$20,000	$150,000	$50,000	$20,000	$200,000	$100,000	$7,000
Totals			$327,000					$327,000	

This is the first transaction we have seen that affects only one side of the accounting equation. In fact, the company simply traded assets: Accounts Receivable for Cash. Thus, note that the totals for the accounting equation remain at $327,000. Also note that Retained Earnings is not affected by this transaction because revenue was recognized earlier, in **(4),** when Accounts Receivable was increased.

(9) *Payment of dividends.* At the end of the month, Mary-Jo and Irene, acting on behalf of Glengarry Health Club, decide to pay a dividend of $1,000 on the shares of stock owned by each of them, or $2,000 in total. The effect of this dividend is to decrease both Cash and Retained Earnings. That is, the company is returning cash to the owners, based on the profitable operations of the business for the first month. The transaction not only reduces Cash but also decreases the owners' claims on the assets of the company. Dividends are not an expense but rather a direct reduction of Retained Earnings. The effect on the accounting equation follows:

	Assets					=	Liabilities		+	Owners' Equity	
TRANSACTION NUMBER	**CASH**	**ACCOUNTS RECEIVABLE**	**EQUIPMENT**	**BUILDING**	**LAND**		**ACCOUNTS PAYABLE**	**NOTES PAYABLE**		**CAPITAL STOCK**	**RETAINED EARNINGS**
Bal.	$96,000	$11,000	$20,000	$150,000	$50,000		$20,000	$200,000		$100,000	$7,000
9	− 2,000										−2,000
Bal.	$94,000	$11,000	$20,000	$150,000	$50,000		$20,000	$200,000		$100,000	$5,000
Totals			$325,000						$325,000		

The Cost Principle An important principle governs the accounting for both the exercise equipment in **(3)** and the building and land in **(2).** The *cost principle* requires that we record an asset at the cost to acquire it and continue to show this amount on all balance sheets until we dispose of the asset. With a few exceptions, an asset is not carried at its market value but at its original cost. Why not show the land on future balance sheets at its market value? Although this might seem more appropriate in certain instances, the *subjectivity* inherent in determining market values is a major reason behind the practice of carrying assets at their historical cost. The cost of an asset can be verified by an independent observer and is much more *objective* than market value.

Companies engage in transactions in many ways. The shoe company from whom this woman is ordering supports sales transactions over the phone using a credit card number. A sales representative may be inputting the card number and the order information into an order database. The company links its order-processing system and other business systems to this customer input.

Two-Minute Review

Assume that on February 1 Glengarry buys additional exercise equipment for $10,000 in cash.

1. Indicate which two accounts are affected and the increase or decrease in each.

2. What will be the total dollar amount of each of the two sides of the accounting equation after this transaction is recorded?

Answers:

1. Equipment will increase by $10,000, and Cash will decrease by $10,000.

2. $325,000 (the effect of the transaction is to increase and decrease assets by the same amount).

BALANCE SHEET AND INCOME STATEMENT FOR THE HEALTH CLUB

To summarize, Exhibit 3-1 indicates the effect of each transaction on the accounting equation, specifically the individual items increased or decreased by each transaction. Note the *dual* effect of each transaction. At least two items were involved in each transaction. For example, the initial investment by the owners resulted in an increase in an asset and an increase in Capital Stock. The payment of the utility bill caused a decrease in an asset and a decrease in Retained Earnings.

You can now see the central idea behind the accounting equation: Even though individual transactions may change the amount and composition of the assets and liabilities, the

EXHIBIT 3-1 Glengarry Health Club Transactions for the Month of January

	ASSETS					= LIABILITIES		+ OWNERS' EQUITY	
TRANS. NO.	CASH	ACCOUNTS RECEIVABLE	EQUIPMENT	BUILDING	LAND	ACCOUNTS PAYABLE	NOTES PAYABLE	CAPITAL STOCK	RETAINED EARNINGS
1	$100,000							$100,000	
2				$150,000	$50,000		$200,000		
Bal.	$100,000			$150,000	$50,000		$200,000	$100,000	
3			$20,000			$20,000			
Bal.	$100,000		$20,000	$150,000	$50,000	$20,000	$200,000	$100,000	
4		$15,000							$15,000
Bal.	$100,000	$15,000	$20,000	$150,000	$50,000	$20,000	$200,000	$100,000	$15,000
5	5,000								5,000
Bal.	$105,000	$15,000	$20,000	$150,000	$50,000	$20,000	$200,000	$100,000	$20,000
6	− 10,000								−10,000
Bal.	$ 95,000	$15,000	$20,000	$150,000	$50,000	$20,000	$200,000	$100,000	$10,000
7	− 3,000								− 3,000
Bal.	$ 92,000	$15,000	$20,000	$150,000	$50,000	$20,000	$200,000	$100,000	$ 7,000
8	4,000	− 4,000							
Bal.	$ 96,000	$11,000	$20,000	$150,000	$50,000	$20,000	$200,000	$100,000	$ 7,000
9	− 2,000								− 2,000
Bal.	$ 94,000	$11,000	$20,000	$150,000	$50,000	$20,000	$200,000	$100,000	$ 5,000

Total assets: $325,000

Total liabilities and owners' equity: $325,000

equation must always balance *for* each transaction, and the *balance sheet* must balance *after* each transaction.

A balance sheet for Glengarry Health Club appears in Exhibit 3-2. All of the information needed to prepare this statement is available in Exhibit 3-1. The balances at the bottom of this exhibit are entered on the balance sheet, with assets on the left side and liabilities and owners' equity on the right side.

An income statement for Glengarry is shown in Exhibit 3-3. An income statement summarizes the revenues and expenses of a company for a period of time. In our example, the statement is for the month of January, as indicated on the third line of the heading of the statement. Glengarry earned revenues from two sources: (1) memberships and (2) court fees. Two types of expenses were incurred: (1) salaries and wages and (2) utilities.

EXHIBIT 3-2 Balance Sheet for Glengarry Health Club

GLENGARRY HEALTH CLUB
BALANCE SHEET
JANUARY 31, 2001

Assets		**Liabilities and Owners' Equity**	
Cash	$ 94,000	Accounts payable	$ 20,000
Accounts receivable	11,000	Notes payable	200,000
Equipment	20,000	Capital stock	100,000
Building	150,000	Retained earnings	5,000
Land	50,000		
Total assets	$325,000	Total liabilities and owners' equity	$325,000

EXHIBIT 3-3 Income Statement for Glengarry Health Club

GLENGARRY HEALTH CLUB
INCOME STATEMENT
FOR THE MONTH ENDED JANUARY 31, 2001

Revenues:		
Memberships	$15,000	
Court fees	5,000	$20,000
Expenses:		
Salaries and wages	10,000	
Utilities	3,000	13,000
Net income		$ 7,000

The difference between the total revenues of $20,000 and the total expenses of $13,000 is the net income for the month of $7,000. Finally, remember that dividends appear on a statement of retained earnings rather than on the income statement. They are a *distribution* of net income of the period, not a *determinant* of net income as are expenses.

We have seen how transactions are analyzed and how they affect the accounting equation and ultimately the financial statements. While the approach we took in analyzing the nine transactions of the Glengarry Health Club was manageable, can you imagine using this type of analysis for a company with *thousands* of transactions in any one month? We now turn our attention to various *tools* used by the accountant to process a large volume of transactions effectively and efficiently.

BUSINESS STRATEGY

K2 and Ride, mentioned in the opening pages of this chapter, are not the only companies to join forces in the growing snowboarding market. In 1992 two friends, Erik Anderson and Jeff Sand, began what proved to be two years of night and weekend work developing a new, step-in snowboard binding—without inconvenient straps and plastic frames. Along the way they discovered they needed to design a boot to fit the new binding. The results, a revolutionary device they named the Autolock and a boot line called Flexible, were the first products of their new company, Switch Manufacturing.

Racing to market against giant competitors like K2 and Ride, then separate firms, and others like Burton, Airwalk, and Salomon, the two partners decided to license their boot and binding system to boot manufacturers. By 1996, Switch had licensed its technology to seven established boot manufacturers, one of whom was Vans Inc.

www.vans.com

What made licensing its new technology so critical for Switch in its early days was the need to compensate for being a small player in a large market. To be successful, Autolock had to become an industry standard, and it could do that only with the support of established boot manufacturers.

Anderson and Sand's licensing strategy was so successful that in 1998 Vans, which had long been making boots to fit the Autolock binding, purchased Switch. And the partnering process continued: in March 1999, Switch and Vans announced the signing of a three-year agreement with Nike, one of the world's most powerful brands. Nike has agreed to use the Switch system as its exclusive step-in binding system for the new line of snowboard boots for the winter 2000/2001 season. It would seem that Autolock is here to stay.

SOURCES: "Nike and Switch Announce Partnership," *Snowboarding-Online.com,* March 13, 1999, accessed at www.snowboarding-online.com/news/99/92.html; and Christopher Caggiano, "Kings of the Hill," *Inc.,* August 1, 1996.

THE ACCOUNT: THE BASIC UNIT FOR RECORDING TRANSACTIONS

An **account** is the record used to accumulate monetary amounts for each asset, liability, and component of owners' equity, such as Capital Stock, Retained Earnings, and Dividends. It is the basic recording unit for each element in the financial statements. Each revenue and expense has its own account. In the Glengarry Health Club example, nine accounts were used: Cash, Accounts Receivable, Equipment, Building, Land, Accounts Payable, Notes Payable, Capital Stock, and Retained Earnings. (Recall that revenues, expenses, and dividends were recorded directly in the Retained Earnings account. Later in the chapter we will see that normally each revenue and expense is recorded in a separate account.) In the real world, a company might have hundreds, or even thousands, of individual accounts.

No two entities have exactly the same set of accounts. To a certain extent, the accounts used by a company depend on its business. For example, a manufacturer normally has three inventory accounts: Raw Materials, Work in Process, and Finished Goods. A retailer uses just one account for inventory, a Merchandise Inventory account. A service business has no need for an inventory account.

ACCOUNT
Record used to accumulate amounts for each individual asset, liability, revenue, expense, and component of owners' equity.

From Concept **TO PRACTICE 3.2**

READING BEN & JERRY'S BALANCE SHEET AND FOOTNOTES How many liability accounts does the company report on its balance sheet? How are these liability accounts broken down in the accompanying notes?

CHART OF ACCOUNTS

Companies need a way to organize the large number of accounts they use to record transactions. A **chart of accounts** is a numerical list of all of the accounts an entity uses. The numbering system is a convenient way to identify accounts. For example, all asset accounts might be numbered from 100 to 199, liability accounts from 200 to 299, equity accounts from 300 to 399, revenues from 400 to 499, and expenses from 500 to 599. A chart of accounts for a hypothetical company, Widescreen Theaters Corporation, is shown in Exhibit 3-4. Note the division of account numbers within each of the financial statement categories. For example, within the asset category, the various cash accounts are numbered from 100 to 109, receivables from 110 to 119, and so forth. Not all of the numbers are currently assigned. For example, only three of the available nine numbers are currently utilized for cash accounts. This allows the company to add accounts as the need arises.

CHART OF ACCOUNTS
A numerical list of all the accounts used by a company.

EXHIBIT 3-4 Chart of Accounts for a Theater

100–199:	ASSETS
100–109:	Cash
101:	Cash, Checking, Second National Bank
102:	Cash, Savings, Third State Bank
103:	Cash, Change, or Petty Cash Fund (coin and currency)
110–119:	Receivables
111:	Accounts Receivable
112:	Due from Employees
113:	Notes Receivable
120–129:	Prepaid Assets
121:	Cleaning Supplies
122:	Prepaid Insurance
130–139:	Property, Plant, and Equipment
131:	Land
132:	Theater Buildings
133:	Projection Equipment
134:	Furniture and Fixtures

(continued)

EXHIBIT 3-4 Chart of Accounts for a Theater *(continued)*

200–299:	LIABILITIES
200–209:	Short-Term Liabilities
201:	Accounts Payable
202:	Wages and Salaries Payable
203:	Taxes Payable
203.1:	Income Taxes Payable
203.2:	Sales Taxes Payable
203.3:	Unemployment Taxes Payable
204:	Short-Term Notes Payable
204.1:	Six-Month Note Payable to First State Bank
210–219:	Long-Term Liabilities
211:	Bonds Payable, due in 2013
300–399:	STOCKHOLDERS' EQUITY
301:	Preferred Stock
302:	Common Stock
303:	Retained Earnings
400–499:	REVENUES
401:	Tickets
402:	Video Rentals
403:	Concessions
404:	Interest
500–599:	EXPENSES
500–509:	Rentals
501:	Films
502:	Videos
510–519:	Concessions
511:	Candy
512:	Soda
513:	Popcorn
520–529:	Wages and Salaries
521:	Hourly Employees
522:	Salaries
530–539:	Utilities
531:	Heat
532:	Electric
533:	Water
540–549:	Advertising
541:	Newspaper
542:	Radio
550–559:	Taxes
551:	Income Taxes
552:	Unemployment Taxes

THE GENERAL LEDGER

LO 4 Define the concept of a general ledger and understand the use of the T account as a method for analyzing transactions

GENERAL LEDGER
A book, file, hard drive, or other device containing all the accounts.

Companies store their accounts in different ways, depending on their accounting system. In a manual system, a separate card or sheet is used to record the activity in each account. A **general ledger** is simply the file or book that contains the accounts.[4] For example, the general ledger for Widescreen Theaters Corporation might consist of a file of cards in a cabinet, with a card for each of the accounts listed in the chart of accounts.

[4]In addition to a general ledger, many companies maintain subsidiary ledgers. For example, an accounts receivable subsidiary ledger contains a separate account for each customer. The use of a subsidiary ledger for Accounts Receivable is discussed further in Chapter 7.

In today's business world, most companies have an automated accounting system. The computer is ideally suited for the job of processing vast amounts of data rapidly. *All of the tools discussed in this chapter are as applicable to computerized systems as they are to manual systems. It is merely the appearance of the tools that differs between manual and computerized systems.* For example, the ledger in an automated system might be contained on a computer file server rather than stored in a file cabinet. Throughout the book, we will use a manual system to explain the various tools, such as ledger accounts. The reason is that it is easier to illustrate and visualize the tools in a manual system. However, all of the ideas apply just as well to a computerized system of accounting.

The Double-Entry System

The origin of the double-entry system of accounting can be traced to Venice, Italy, in 1494. In that year, Fra Luca Pacioli, a Franciscan monk, wrote a mathematical treatise. Included in his book was the concept of debits and credits that is still used almost universally today.

The T Account

The form for a general ledger account will be illustrated later in the chapter. However, the form of account often used to analyze transactions is called the *T account,* so named because it resembles the capital letter T. The name of the account appears across the horizontal line. One side is used to record increases and the other side decreases, but as you will see, the same side is not used for increases for every account. As a matter of convention, the *left* side of an *asset* account is used to record *increases* and the *right* side to record *decreases.* To illustrate a T account, we will look at the Cash account for Glengarry Health Club. The transactions recorded in the account can be traced to Exhibit 3-1.

CASH

debit INCREASES		credit DECREASES	
Investment by owners	100,000	Wages and salaries	10,000
Court fees collected	5,000	Utilities	3,000
Accounts collected	4,000	Dividends	2,000
	109,000		15,000
Bal.	94,000		

The amounts $109,000 and $15,000 are called *footings.* They represent the totals of the amounts on each side of the account. Neither these amounts nor the balance of $94,000 represents transactions. They are simply shown to indicate the totals and the balance in the account.

Debits and Credits

LO 5 Explain the rules of debits and credits.

Rather than refer to the left or right side of an account, accountants use specific labels for each side. The *left* side of any account is the **debit** side, and the *right* side of any account is the **credit** side. We will also use the terms *debit* and *credit* as verbs. If we *debit* the Cash account, we enter an amount on the left side. Similarly, if we want to enter an amount on the right side of an account, we *credit* the account. To *charge* an account has the same meaning as to *debit* it. No such synonym exists for the act of crediting an account.

Debit
An entry on the left side of an account.

Credit
An entry on the right side of an account.

Note that *debit* and *credit* are *locational* terms. They simply refer to the left or right side of a T account. They do *not* represent increases or decreases. As we will see, when one type of account is increased (for example, the Cash account), the increase is on the left or *debit* side. When certain other types of accounts are increased, however, the entry will be on the right or *credit* side.

Study Tip

Once you know the rule to increase an asset with a debit, the rules for the other increases and decreases follow logically. For example, because a liability is the opposite of an asset, it is increased with a credit. And it follows logically that it would be decreased with a debit.

As you would expect from your understanding of the accounting equation, the conventions for using T accounts for assets and liabilities are opposite. Assets are future economic benefits, and liabilities are obligations to transfer economic benefits in the future. If an asset is *increased* with a *debit,* how do you think a liability would be increased? *Because assets and liabilities are opposites, if an asset is increased with a debit, a liability is increased with a credit.* Thus, the right side, or credit side, of a liability account is used to record an increase. Like liabilities, owners' equity accounts are on the opposite side of the accounting equation as are assets. *Thus, like a liability, an owners' equity account is increased with a credit.* We can summarize the logic of debits and credits, increases and decreases, and the accounting equation in the following way:

ASSETS		=	LIABILITIES		+	OWNERS' EQUITY	
Debits	Credits		Debits	Credits		Debits	Credits
Increases	Decreases		Decreases	Increases		Decreases	Increases
+	−		−	+		−	+

Note again that debits and credits are location-oriented. Debits are always on the left side of an account and credits on the right side.

ACCOUNTING FOR YOUR DECISIONS

You Are a Student

A classmate comes to you with a question about the bank statement she has received. Why does the bank credit her account when she makes a deposit to her account, but accounting rules state that cash is increased with a debit?

ANS: The bank is looking at customer deposits from its perspective and not the customers'. Checking account deposits represent liabilities to the bank, such as "Deposits Payable." Thus, when customers make deposits, the bank has increased its liability to those customers, with a credit to its "Deposits Payable."

DEBITS AND CREDITS FOR REVENUES, EXPENSES, AND DIVIDENDS

In our Glengarry Health Club example, revenues were an increase in Retained Earnings. The sale of memberships was not only an increase in the asset Accounts Receivable but also an increase in the owners' equity account Retained Earnings. The transaction resulted in an increase in the owners' claim on the assets of the business. Rather than being recorded directly in Retained Earnings, however, each revenue item is maintained in a separate account. The following logic is used to arrive at the rules for increasing and decreasing revenues:[5]

1. Retained Earnings is increased with a credit.
2. Revenue is an increase in Retained Earnings.
3. Revenue is increased with a credit.
4. Because revenue is increased with a credit, it is decreased with a debit.

The same logic is applied to the rules for increasing and decreasing expense accounts:

1. Retained Earnings is decreased with a debit.
2. Expense is a decrease in Retained Earnings.

[5]We normally think of both revenues and expenses as being only increased, not decreased. Because we will need to decrease them as part of the closing procedure, it is important to know how to reduce these accounts as well as increase them.

3. Expense is increased with a debit.
4. Because expense is increased with a debit, it is decreased with a credit.

Recall that dividends reduce cash. But they also reduce the owners' claim on the assets of the business. Earlier we recognized this decrease in the owners' claim as a reduction of Retained Earnings. As we do for revenue and expense accounts, we will use a separate Dividends account:

1. Retained Earnings is decreased with a debit.
2. Dividends are a decrease in Retained Earnings.
3. Dividends are increased with a debit.
4. Because dividends are increased with a debit, they are decreased with a credit.

Summary of the Rules for Increasing and Decreasing Accounts

The rules for increasing and decreasing the various types of accounts are summarized as follows:

Type of Account	Debit	Credit
Asset	Increase	Decrease
Liability	Decrease	Increase
Owners' Equity	Decrease	Increase
Revenue	Decrease	Increase
Expense	Increase	Decrease
Dividends	Increase	Decrease

Normal Account Balances

Each account has a "normal" balance. For example, assets normally have debit balances. Would it be possible for an asset such as Cash to have a credit balance? Assume that a company has a checking account with a bank. A credit balance in the account would indicate that the decreases in the account, from checks written and other bank charges, were more than the deposits into the account. If this were the case, however, the company would no longer have an asset, Cash, but instead would have a liability to the bank. The normal balances for the accounts we have looked at are as follows:

Type of Account	Normal Balance
Asset	Debit
Liability	Credit
Owners' Equity	Credit
Revenue	Credit
Expense	Debit
Dividends	Debit

Debits Aren't Bad, and Credits Aren't Good

Students often approach their first encounter with debits and credits with preconceived notions. The use of the terms *debit* and *credit* in everyday language leads to many of these notions. "Joe is a real credit to his team." "Nancy should be credited with saving Mary's career." These both appear to be very positive statements. You must resist the temptation to associate the term *credit* with something good or positive and the term *debit* with something bad or negative. *In accounting, debit means one thing: an entry made on the left side of an account. A credit means an entry made on the right side of an account.*

Debits and Credits Applied to Transactions

Recall the first transaction recorded by Glengarry Health Club earlier in the chapter: the owners invested $100,000 cash in the business. The transaction resulted in an increase in the Cash account and an increase in the Capital Stock account. Applying the rules of debits and credits, we would *debit* the Cash account for $100,000 and *credit* the Capital Stock account for the same amount:[6]

CASH	
(1) 100,000	

CAPITAL STOCK	
	100,000 (1)

Double-entry system
A system of accounting in which every transaction is recorded with equal debits and credits and the accounting equation is kept in balance.

You now can see why we refer to the **double-entry system** of accounting. Every transaction is recorded so that the equality of debits and credits is maintained, and in the process, the accounting equation is kept in balance. *Every transaction is entered in at least two accounts on opposite sides of T accounts. Our first transaction resulted in an increase in an asset account and an increase in an owners' equity account. For every transaction, the debit side must equal the credit side. The debit of $100,000 to the Cash account equals the credit of $100,000 to the Capital Stock account.* It naturally follows that if the debit side must equal the credit side for every transaction, at any point in time the total of all debits recorded must equal the total of all credits recorded. Thus, the fundamental accounting equation remains in balance.

Transactions for Glengarry Health Club

Three distinct steps are involved in recording a transaction in the accounts.

1. First, we *analyze* the transaction. That is, we decide what accounts are increased or decreased and by how much.
2. Second, we *recall* the rules of debits and credits as they apply to the transaction we are analyzing.
3. Finally, we *record* the transaction using the rules of debits and credits.

We return to the transactions of the health club. We have already explained the logic for the debit to the Cash account and the credit to the Capital Stock account for the initial investment by the owners. We will now analyze the remaining eight transactions for the month. Refer to Exhibit 3-1 for a summary of the transactions.

(2) A building and land are exchanged for a promissory note.

(a) *Analyze:* Two asset accounts are increased: Building and Land. The liability account Notes Payable is also increased.

(b) *Recall the rules of debits and credits:* An asset is increased with a debit, and a liability is increased with a credit.

(c) *Record the transaction:*

BUILDING	
(2) 150,000	

NOTES PAYABLE	
	200,000 (2)

LAND	
(2) 50,000	

(3) Exercise equipment is purchased from a supplier on open account. The purchase price is $20,000.

A +
L+

(a) *Analyze:* An asset account, Equipment, is increased. A liability account, Accounts Payable, is also increased. Thus, the transaction is identical to the last transaction in that an asset or assets are increased and a liability is increased.

(b) *Recall the rules of debits and credits:* An asset is increased with a debit, and a liability is increased with a credit.

(c) *Record the transaction:*

[6] We will use the numbers of each transaction, as they were labeled earlier in the chapter, to identify the transactions. In practice, a formal ledger account is used, and transactions are entered according to their date.

EQUIPMENT	
(3) **20,000**	

ACCOUNTS PAYABLE	
	20,000 (3)

(4) Three hundred club memberships are sold for $50 each. The members have until the 10th of the following month to pay.

(a) *Analyze:* The asset account Accounts Receivable is increased by $15,000. This amount is an asset because the company has the right to collect it in the future. The owners' claim to the assets is increased by the same amount. Recall, however, that we do not record these claims—revenues—directly in an owners' equity account but instead use a separate revenue account. We will call the account Membership Revenue.

(b) *Recall the rules of debits and credits:* An asset is increased with a debit. Owners' equity is increased with a credit. Because revenue is an increase in owners' equity, it is increased with a credit.

(c) *Record the transaction:*

ACCOUNTS RECEIVABLE	
(4) 15,000	

MEMBERSHIP REVENUE	
	15,000 (4)

(5) Court fees are paid at the time of use and amount to $5,000 for the first month.

(a) *Analyze:* The asset account Cash is increased by $5,000. The owners' claim to the assets is increased by the same amount. The account used to record the increase in the owners' claim is Court Fee Revenue.

(b) *Recall the rules of debits and credits:* An asset is increased with a debit. Owners' equity is increased with a credit. Because revenue is an increase in owners' equity, it is increased with a credit.

(c) *Record the transaction:*

CASH	
(1) 100,000	
(5) 5,000	

COURT FEE REVENUE	
	5,000 (5)

(6) Wages and salaries amount to $10,000, and they are paid in cash.

(a) *Analyze:* The asset account, Cash, is decreased by $10,000. At the same time, the owners' claim to the assets is decreased by this amount. However, rather than record a decrease directly to Retained Earnings, we set up an expense account, Wage and Salary Expense.

(b) *Recall the rules of debits and credits:* An asset is decreased with a credit. Owners' equity is decreased with a debit. Because expense is a decrease in owners' equity, it is increased with a debit.

(c) *Record the transaction:*

CASH	
(1) 100,000	**10,000 (6)**
(5) 5,000	

WAGE AND SALARY EXPENSE	
(6) 10,000	

(7) The utility bill of $3,000 for the first month is paid in cash.

(a) *Analyze:* The asset account Cash is decreased by $3,000. At the same time, the owners' claim to the assets is decreased by this amount. However, rather than record a decrease directly to Retained Earnings, we set up an expense account, Utility Expense.

(b) *Recall the rules of debits and credits:* An asset is decreased with a credit. Owners' equity is decreased with a debit. Because expense is a decrease in owners' equity, it is increased with a debit.

(c) *Record the transaction:*

CASH	
(1) 100,000	10,000 (6)
(5) 5,000	**3,000 (7)**

UTILITY EXPENSE	
(7) 3,000	

(8) Cash of $4,000 is collected from members for their January dues.

(a) *Analyze:* Cash is increased by the amount collected from the members. Another asset, Accounts Receivable, is decreased by the same amount. Glengarry has simply traded one asset for another.

(b) *Recall the rules of debits and credits:* An asset is increased with a debit and decreased with a credit. Thus, one asset is debited, and another is credited.

(c) *Record the transaction:*

CASH

(1)	100,000	10,000	(6)
(5)	5,000	3,000	(7)
(8)	**4,000**		

ACCOUNTS RECEIVABLE

(4)	15,000	**4,000**	**(8)**

(9) Dividends of $2,000 are distributed to the owners.

(a) *Analyze:* The asset account Cash is decreased by $2,000. At the same time, the owners' claim to the assets is decreased by this amount. Earlier in the chapter, we decreased Retained Earnings for dividends paid to the owners. Now we will use a separate account, Dividends, to record these distributions.

(b) *Recall the rules of debits and credits:* An asset is decreased with a credit. Retained earnings is decreased with a debit. Because dividends are a decrease in retained earnings, they are increased with a debit.

(c) *Record the transaction:*

CASH

(1)	100,000	10,000	(6)
(5)	5,000	3,000	(7)
(8)	4,000	**2,000**	**(9)**

DIVIDENDS

(9)	**2,000**		

Two-Minute Review

1. Assume Glengarry pays the supplier the amount owed on open account. Record this transaction in the appropriate T accounts.

2. Assume Glengarry collects the remaining amount owed by members for dues. Record this transaction in the appropriate T accounts.

Answers:

1.

CASH

Debit	Credit
	20,000

ACCOUNTS PAYABLE

Debit	Credit
20,000	

2.

CASH

Debit	Credit
11,000	

ACCOUNTS RECEIVABLE

Debit	Credit
	11,000

THE JOURNAL: THE FIRM'S CHRONOLOGICAL RECORD OF TRANSACTIONS

LO 6 Explain the purposes of a journal and the posting process.

JOURNAL
A chronological record of transactions, also known as the book of original entry.

POSTING
The process of transferring amounts from a journal to the ledger accounts.

Each of the nine transactions was entered directly in the ledger accounts. By looking at the Cash account, we see that it increased by $5,000 in transaction **(5).** But what was the other side of this transaction? That is, what account was credited? To have a record of *each entry,* transactions are recorded first in a journal. A **journal** is a chronological record of transactions entered into by a business. Because a journal lists transactions in the order in which they took place, it is called the *book of original entry.* Transactions are recorded first in a journal and then are posted to the ledger accounts. **Posting** is the process of transferring a journal entry to the ledger accounts:

Note that posting does not result in any change in the amounts recorded. It is simply a process of re-sorting the transactions from a chronological order to a topical arrangement.

A journal entry is recorded for each transaction. **Journalizing** is the process of recording entries in a journal. A standard format is normally used for recording journal entries. Consider the original investment by the owners of Glengarry Health Club. The format of the journal entry is as follows:

JOURNALIZING The act of recording journal entries.

			DEBIT	CREDIT
Jan.	xx	Cash	100,000	
		Capital Stock		100,000
		To record the issuance of 10,000 shares of stock for cash.		

Each journal entry contains a date with columns for the amounts debited and credited. Accounts credited are indented to distinguish them from accounts debited. A brief explanation normally appears on the line below the entry.

Transactions are normally recorded in a **general journal.** Specialized journals may be used to record repetitive transactions. For example, a cash receipts journal may be used to record all transactions in which cash is received. Special journals accomplish the same purpose as a general journal, but they save time in recording similar transactions. In this chapter, we will use a general journal to record all transactions.

GENERAL JOURNAL The journal used in place of a specialized journal.

An excerpt from Glengarry Health Club's general journal appears in the top portion of Exhibit 3-5. One column needs further explanation. *Post. Ref.* is an abbreviation for *Posting Reference.* As part of the posting process explained below, the debit and credit amounts are posted to the appropriate accounts, and this column is filled in with the number assigned to the account.

From Concept **TO PRACTICE 3.3**

READING GATEWAY'S FINANCIAL STATEMENTS Refer to Gateway's income statement and its balance sheet. Using the appropriate accounts from these statements, prepare the journal entry Gateway would record if it sold a computer for $2,000 and gave the customer 30 days to pay.

Journal entries and ledger accounts are both *tools* used by the accountant. The end result, a set of financial statements, is the most important part of the process. Journalizing provides us with a chronological record of each transaction. So why not just prepare financial statements directly from the journal entries? Isn't it just extra work to *post* the entries to the ledger accounts? In our simple example of Glengarry Health Club, it would be possible to prepare the statements directly from the journal entries. In real-world situations, however, the number of transactions in any given period is so large that it would be virtually impossible, if not terribly inefficient, to bypass the accounts. Accounts provide us with a convenient summary of the activity, as well as the balance, for a specific financial statement item.

The posting process for Glengarry Health Club is illustrated in Exhibit 3-5 for the health club's fifth transaction, in which cash is collected for court fees. Rather than a T-account format for the general ledger accounts, the *running balance form* is illustrated. A separate column indicates the balance in the ledger account after each transaction. The use of the explanation column in a ledger account is optional. Because an explanation of the entry in the account can be found by referring to the journal, this column is often left blank.

Note the cross-referencing between the journal and the ledger. As amounts are entered in the ledger accounts, the Posting Reference column is filled in with the page number of the journal. At the same time, the Posting Reference column of the journal is filled in with the appropriate account number (for example, GJ1 to indicate page 1 from general journal).

The frequency of posting differs among companies, partly based on the degree to which their accounting system is automated. For example, in some computerized systems, amounts are posted to the ledger accounts at the time an entry is recorded in the journal. In a manual system, posting is normally done periodically, for example, daily, weekly, or monthly. Regardless of when performed, the posting process changes nothing. It simply reorganizes the transactions by account.

EXHIBIT 3-5 Posting from the Journal to the Ledger

General Journal — Page No. 1

Date		Account Titles and Explanation	Post. Ref.	Debit	Credit
2001 Jan.	XX	Accounts Receivable	5	15000	
		Membership Revenue	40		15000
		Sold 300 memberships at $50 each.			
	XX	Cash	1	5000	
		Court Fee Revenue	44		5000
		Collected court fees.			

General Ledger

Cash — Account No. 1

Date		Explanation	Post. Ref.	Debit	Credit	Balance
2001 Jan.	XX		GJ1	100000		100000
	XX		GJ1	5000		105000

Court Fee Revenue — Account No. 44

Date		Explanation	Post. Ref.	Debit	Credit	Balance
2001 Jan.	XX		GJ1		5000	5000

ACCOUNTING FOR YOUR DECISIONS

You Are the Manager

You are the community relations manager for a company. You need to determine whether the company is spending its money wisely in promoting its image in the local community.

1. What types of accounts would you examine? Give examples of the possible names for some of these accounts.
2. Would a general journal or a general ledger be more useful to you in making your determination? Explain your answer.

ANS: 1. Among the possible accounts that you want to examine are Entertainment, Travel, Promotions, Advertising, and Miscellaneous, in addition to any accounts that might contain expenditures related to community relations.

2. You may want to examine the general ledger for each of the accounts listed in part 1. The ledger contains a record for each of the accounts and the activity in them during the period.

If the accounts are always kept up to date, the data we need for analysis will always be there when those critical decisions come up.

FOCUS ON USERS

This New Company Relies Heavily on Its Account-Processing System

As the owner of a start-up company in its second year of business, Mark Gleason knows how important it is to keep good accounting records from the time the first transaction takes place. Without an accountant for the first few weeks of operation, it was up to Mark to initiate a processing system for his new business. "It's amazing how fast even a small business's accounting can get complicated. In the very early days, it was just a matter of keeping a checkbook ledger, but after a couple of months, we wanted to know how we were doing in terms of our budget. I remember in the beginning, before we computerized, I sorted expenses into about a dozen file folders. A year later, we've got well over a hundred expense accounts that are recorded electronically on a regular and systematic basis."

There are many reasons to keep tight controls on the way accounting information is processed in a working business, whether it be new or old, big or small. For Mark, whose company launched a national magazine, the benefits of meticulous recordkeeping are obvious. As he says, "It ensures that we pay bills on time, which is critical to maintaining good relationships. It forces us to keep track of expenses, rein them in if necessary, and plan future cash flow." But probably the most valuable result of a good processing system is having a quantifiable basis for analysis. Mark explains, "When a strategic decision needs to be made, it helps to be able to look at the financial history—at what happened in a similar situation—and see how much money came in, what kind of pressure was put on cash flow, and what the tax impact was." If the accounts are always kept up to date, the data we need for analysis will always be there when those critical decisions come up.

Name: Mark Gleason Jr.
Education: B.A., Georgetown University; M.S., Medill School of Journalism
College Major: American Studies
Occupation: President and Publisher, West Egg Communications LLC
Age: 34

THE TRIAL BALANCE

LO 7 Explain the purpose of a trial balance.

Accountants use one other tool to facilitate the preparation of a set of financial statements. A **trial balance** is a list of each account and its balance at a specific point in time. The trial balance is *not* a financial statement but merely a convenient device to prove the equality of the debit and credit balances in the accounts. It can be as informal as an adding-machine tape with the account titles penciled in next to the debit and credit amounts. A trial balance for Glengarry Health Club as of January 31, 2001, is shown in Exhibit 3-6. The balance in each account was determined by adding the increases and subtracting the decreases for the account for the transactions detailed earlier.

TRIAL BALANCE
A list of each account and its balance; used to prove equality of debits and credits.

Certain types of errors are detectable from a trial balance. For example, if the balance of an account is incorrectly computed, the total of the debits and credits in the trial balance will not equal. If a debit is posted to an account as a credit, or vice versa, the trial balance will be out of balance. The omission of part of a journal entry in the posting process will also be detected by the preparation of a trial balance.

Do not attribute more significance to a trial balance, however, than is warranted. It does provide a convenient summary of account balances for preparing financial statements. It also assures us that the balances of all the debit accounts equal the balances of all the credit accounts. But an equality of debits and credits does not necessarily mean that the *correct* accounts were debited and credited in an entry. For example, the entry to record the purchase of land by signing a promissory note *should* result in a debit to Land and a credit to Notes Payable. If the accountant incorrectly debited Cash instead of Land, the trial balance would still show an equality of debits and credits. A trial balance can be prepared at any time; it is usually prepared before the release of a set of financial statements.

Study Tip

Remember from p. 105 that every account has a normal balance, either debit or credit. Note the normal balances for each account on this trial balance.

see pg 99 to get these #'s

EXHIBIT 3-6 Trial Balance for Glengarry Health Club

GLENGARRY HEALTH CLUB
TRIAL BALANCE
AT JANUARY 31, 2001

Account Title	Debits	Credits
Cash	$ 94,000	
Accounts Receivable	11,000	
Building	150,000	
Land	50,000	
Equipment	20,000	
Accounts Payable		$ 20,000
Notes Payable		200,000
Capital Stock		100,000
Membership Revenue		15,000
Court Fee Revenue		5,000
Wage and Salary Expense	10,000	
Utility Expense	3,000	
Dividends	2,000	
Totals	$340,000	$340,000

ACCOUNTING FOR YOUR DECISIONS

You Are the Stockholder

You own 100 shares of stock in General Motors. Every year you receive GM's annual report, which includes a chairman's letter, a description of new models, a financial section, and footnotes to financial statements. Nowhere in the report do you see a general ledger or a trial balance. Is General Motors hiding something?

ANS: GM's balance sheet, income statement, and statement of cash flows are derived from the company's journal entries, general ledgers, trial balances, and so on. These documents are the building blocks of the final statements. There could literally be millions of transactions during the year—which even the most diehard accounting fan would tire of reading.

WARMUP EXERCISES

LO 3, 5 Warmup Exercise 3-1 Your Debits and Credits

Assume that you borrow $1,000 from your roommate by signing an agreement to repay the amount borrowed in six months.

Required

1. What is the effect of this transaction on your own accounting equation?
2. Prepare the journal entry to record this transaction in your own records.

Key to the Solution

Recall Exhibit 3-1 for the effects of transactions on the accounting equation, and refer to the summary of the rules for increasing and decreasing accounts on p. 105.

LO 3, 5 Warmup Exercise 3-2 A Bank's Debits and Credits

The Third State Bank loans a customer $5,000 in exchange for a promissory note.

Required

1. What is the effect of this transaction on the bank's accounting equation?
2. Prepare the journal entry to record this transaction in the bank's records.

Key to the Solution

Recall Exhibit 3-1 for the effects of the transaction on the accounting equation, and refer to the summary of the rules for increasing and decreasing accounts on p. 105.

LO 3, 5 Warmup Exercise 3-3 Debits and Credits for Ben & Jerry's

Assume Ben & Jerry's goes to its bank and borrows $10,000 by signing a promissory note. The next day the company uses the money to buy an ice cream freezer.

Required

1. What is the effect of each of these two transactions on Ben & Jerry's accounting equation?
2. Prepare the journal entries to record both transactions in Ben & Jerry's records.

Key to the Solution

Recall Exhibit 3-1 for the effects of transactions on the accounting equation, and refer to the summary of the rules for increasing and decreasing accounts on p. 105.

Solutions to Warmup Exercises

Warmup Exercise 3-1

1. If you borrow $1,000 from your roommate, assets in the form of cash, increase $1,000, and liabilities in the form of a note payable, increase $1,000.
2. Journal entry:

Cash	1,000	
Notes Payable		1,000

Warmup Exercise 3-2

1. If a bank loans a customer $5,000, the bank's assets, in the form of a note receivable, increase $5,000, and its assets, in the form of cash, decrease $5,000.
2. Journal entry:

Notes Receivable	5,000	
Cash		5,000

Warmup Exercise 3-3

1. If Ben & Jerry's borrows $10,000 from its bank, assets, in the form of cash, increase $10,000, and liabilities, in the form of a note payable, increase $10,000. If the company uses the money to buy a freezer, assets, in the form of equipment, increase $10,000, and assets, in the form of cash, decrease $10,000.
2. Journal entries:

Cash	10,000	
Notes Payable		10,000
Equipment	10,000	
Cash		10,000

Review Problem

The following transactions are entered into by Sparkle Car Wash during its first month of operations:

a. Articles of incorporation are filed with the state, and 20,000 shares of capital stock are issued. Cash of $40,000 is received from the new owners for the shares.

b. A five-year promissory note is signed at the local bank. The cash received from the loan is $120,000.

c. An existing car wash is purchased for $150,000 in cash. The values assigned to the land, building, and equipment are $25,000, $75,000, and $50,000, respectively.

d. Cleaning supplies are purchased on account for $2,500 from a distributor. All of the supplies are used in the first month.

e. During the first month, $1,500 is paid to the distributor for the cleaning supplies. The remaining $1,000 will be paid next month.

f. Gross receipts from car washes during the first month of operations amount to $7,000.

g. Wages and salaries paid in the first month amount to $2,000.

h. The utility bill of $800 for the month is paid.

i. A total of $1,000 in dividends is paid to the owners.

Required

1. Prepare a table to summarize the preceding transactions as they affect the accounting equation. Use the format in Exhibit 3-1. Identify each transaction by letter.
2. Prepare an income statement for the month.
3. Prepare a balance sheet at the end of the month.

Solution to Review Problem

1.

SPARKLE CAR WASH
TRANSACTIONS FOR THE MONTH

	Assets				=	Liabilities + Owners' Equity			
TRANS.	**CASH**	**LAND**	**BUILDING**	**EQUIPMENT**		**ACCOUNTS PAYABLE**	**NOTES PAYABLE**	**CAPITAL STOCK**	**RETAINED EARNINGS**
a.	$ 40,000							$40,000	
b.	120,000						$120,000		
Bal.	$160,000						$120,000	$40,000	
c.	−150,000	$25,000	$75,000	$50,000					
Bal.	$ 10,000	$25,000	$75,000	$50,000			$120,000	$40,000	
d.						$2,500			$−2,500
Bal.	$ 10,000	$25,000	$75,000	$50,000		$2,500	$120,000	$40,000	$−2,500
e.	−1,500					−1,500			
Bal.	$ 8,500	$25,000	$75,000	$50,000		$1,000	$120,000	$40,000	$−2,500
f.	7,000								7,000
Bal.	$ 15,500	$25,000	$75,000	$50,000		$1,000	$120,000	$40,000	$ 4,500
g.	−2,000								−2,000
Bal.	$ 13,500	$25,000	$75,000	$50,000		$1,000	$120,000	$40,000	$ 2,500
h.	−800								−800
Bal.	$ 12,700	$25,000	$75,000	$50,000		$1,000	$120,000	$40,000	$ 1,700
i.	−1,000								−1,000
Bal.	$ 11,700	$25,000	$75,000	$50,000		$1,000	$120,000	$40,000	$ 700

Total Assets: $161,700

Total Liabilities and Owners' Equity: $161,700

2.

SPARKLE CAR WASH
INCOME STATEMENT
FOR THE MONTH ENDED XX/XX/XX

Car wash revenue		$7,000
Expenses:		
Supplies	$2,500	
Wages and salaries	2,000	
Utilities	800	5,300
Net income		$1,700

3.

SPARKLE CAR WASH
BALANCE SHEET
XX/XX/XX

Assets		**Liabilities and Owners' Equity**	
Cash	$ 11,700	Accounts payable	$ 1,000
Land	25,000	Notes payable	120,000
Building	75,000	Capital stock	40,000
Equipment	50,000	Retained earnings	700
		Total Liabilities	
Total Assets	$161,700	and Owners' Equity	$161,700

Chapter Highlights

1. **LO 1** Both internal and external events affect an entity. External events, such as the purchase of materials, involve the entity and its environment. Internal events, such as the placement of the materials into production, do not involve an outside entity. For any event to be recorded, it must be measurable.
2. **LO 2** Source documents are used as the basis for recording events as transactions. For certain repetitive transactions, a standard source document is used, such as a time card to document the payroll for the week. For other nonrepetitive transactions, a source document has to be generated for the specific event.
3. **LO 3** Economic events are the basis for recording transactions. These transactions result in changes in the company's financial position. Transactions change the amount of individual items on the balance sheet, but the statement must balance after each transaction is recorded.
4. **LO 4** A separate account is used for each identifiable asset, liability, revenue, expense, and component of owners' equity. No standard set of accounts exists, and the types of accounts used depend to a certain extent on the nature of a company's business. A chart of accounts is a numerical list of all the accounts used by an entity. The general ledger in a manual system might consist of a set of cards, one for each account, in a file cabinet. In a computerized system, a magnetic tape or diskette might be used to store the accounts.
5. **LO 4** Accountants use T accounts as the basic form of analysis of transactions. The left side of an account is used for debits, and the right side is for credits. Transactions are recorded in the ledger in more formal accounts than the typical T account.
6. **LO 5** By convention, the left side of an asset account is used to record increases. Thus, an asset account is increased with a debit. Because liabilities are on the opposite side of the accounting equation, they are increased with a credit. Similarly, owners' equity accounts are increased with a credit. Because revenue is an increase in owners' equity, it is increased with a credit. Thus, an expense, as well as a dividend, is increased with a debit. According to the double-entry system, there are two sides to every transaction. For each transaction, the debit or debits must equal the credit or credits.
7. **LO 6** Transactions are not recorded directly in the accounts but are recorded initially in a journal. A separate entry is recorded in the journal for each transaction. The account(s) debited appears first in the entry, with the account(s) credited listed next and indented. Separate columns for debits and credits are used to indicate the amounts for each. A general journal is used in lieu of any specialized journals.
8. **LO 6** Amounts appearing in journal entries are posted to the ledger accounts. Posting can be done either at the time the entry is recorded or periodically. The Post. Ref. column in a journal indicates the account number to which the amount is posted, and a similar column in the account acts as a convenient reference back to the particular page number in the journal.
9. **LO 7** A trial balance proves the equality of the debits and credits in the accounts. If only one side of a transaction is posted to the accounts, the trial balance will not balance. Other types of errors are detectable from the process of preparing a trial balance. It cannot, however, detect all errors. A trial balance could be in balance even though the wrong asset account is debited in an entry.

Key Terms Quiz

Read each definition below, and then write the number of the definition in the blank beside the appropriate term it defines. The solution appears at the end of the chapter.

pg. 94 3 Event
pg 94 10 External event
pg. 94 5 Internal event
pg 94 14 Transaction
pg 94 6 Source document
pg. 101 11 Account

pg. 101 1 Chart of accounts
p. 102 12 General ledger
p. 103 8 Debit
p. 103 4 Credit
p. 106 16 Double-entry system
p. 108 13 Journal

pg.108 9 Posting
pg.109 7 Journalizing
pg.109 15 General journal
pg.111 2 Trial balance

1. A numerical list of all the accounts used by a company.
2. A list of each account and its balance at a specific point in time; used to prove the equality of debits and credits.
3. A happening of consequence to an entity.
4. An entry on the right side of an account.
5. An event occurring entirely within an entity.
6. A piece of paper, such as a sales invoice, that is used as the evidence to record a transaction.
7. The act of recording journal entries.
8. An entry on the left side of an account.
9. The process of transferring amounts from a journal to the appropriate ledger accounts.
10. An event involving interaction between an entity and its environment.
11. The record used to accumulate monetary amounts for each individual asset, liability, revenue, expense, and component of owners' equity.
12. A book, file, hard drive, or other device containing all of a company's accounts.
13. A chronological record of transactions, also known as the *book of original entry.*
14. Any event, external or internal, that is recognized in a set of financial statements.
15. The journal used in place of a specialized journal.
16. A system of accounting in which every transaction is recorded with equal debits and credits and the accounting equation is kept in balance.

ALTERNATE TERMS

Credit side of an account Right side of an account

Debit an account Charge an account

Debit side of an account Left side of an account

General ledger Set of accounts

Journal Book of original entry

Journalize an entry Record an entry

Posting an account Transferring an amount from the journal to the ledger

QUESTIONS

1. What are the two types of events that affect an entity? Describe each.
2. What is the significance of source documents to the recording process? Give two examples of source documents.
3. What are four different forms of cash?
4. How does an account receivable differ from a note receivable?
5. What is meant by the statement "One company's account receivable is another company's account payable"?
6. What do accountants mean when they refer to the "double-entry system" of accounting?
7. Owners' equity represents the claim of the owners on the assets of the business. What is the distinction relative to the owners' claim between the Capital Stock account and the Retained Earnings account?
8. If an asset account is increased with a debit, what is the logic for increasing a liability account with a credit?
9. A friend comes to you with the following plight: "I'm confused. An asset is something positive, and it is increased with a debit. However, an expense is something negative, and it is also increased with a debit. I don't get it." How can you straighten your friend out?
10. The payment of dividends reduces cash. If the Cash account is reduced with a credit, why is the Dividends account debited when dividends are paid?
11. If Cash is increased with a debit, why does the bank credit your account when you make a deposit?
12. Your friend presents the following criticism of the accounting system: "Accounting involves so much duplication of effort. First, entries are recorded in a journal, and then the same information is recorded in a ledger. No wonder accountants work such long hours!" Do you agree with this criticism?
13. How does the T account differ from the running balance form for an account? How are they similar?
14. What is the benefit of using a cross-referencing system between a ledger and a journal?
15. How often should a company post entries from the journal to the ledger?
16. What is the purpose of a trial balance?

Exercises

LO 1 Exercise 3-1 Types of Events

For each of the following events, identify whether it is an external event that would be recorded as a transaction (E), an internal event that would be recorded as a transaction (I), or not recorded (NR):

E 1. A supplier of a company's raw material is paid an amount owed on account.
E 2. A customer pays its open account.
NR 3. A new chief executive officer is hired.
E 4. The biweekly payroll is paid.
I 5. Raw materials are entered into production.
NR 6. A new advertising agency is hired to develop a series of newspaper ads for the company.
E 7. The advertising bill for the first month is paid.
I 8. The accountant determines the federal income taxes owed based on the income earned during the period.

LO 2 Exercise 3-2 Source Documents Matched with Transactions

Following are a list of source documents and a list of transactions. Indicate by letter next to each transaction the source document that would serve as evidence for the recording of the transaction.

Source Documents

a. Purchase invoice
b. Sales invoice
c. Cash register tape
d. Time cards
e. Promissory note
f. Stock certificates
g. Monthly statement from utility company
h. No standard source document would normally be available

Transactions

g 1. Utilities expense for the month is recorded.
h 2. A cash settlement is received from a pending lawsuit.
f 3. Owners contribute cash to start a new corporation.
d 4. The biweekly payroll is paid.
c 5. Cash sales for the day are recorded.
a 6. Equipment is acquired on a 30-day open account.
b 7. A sale is made on open account.
e 8. A building is acquired by signing an agreement to repay a stated amount plus interest in six months.

LO 3 Exercise 3-3 The Effect of Transactions on the Accounting Equation

For each of the following transactions, indicate whether it increases (I), decreases (D), or has no effect (NE) on the total dollar amount of each of the elements of the accounting equation.

Transactions	**Assets**	=	**Liabilities**	+	**Owners' Equity**
Example: Common stock is issued in exchange for cash.	I		NE		I
1. Equipment is purchased for cash.	NE	=	NE	+	NE
2. Sales are made on account.	I	=	NE	+	I
3. Cash sales are made.	I	=	NE	+	I
4. An account payable is paid off.	D	=	D	+	NE
5. Cash is collected on an account receivable.	NE	=	NE	+	NE

Transactions	Assets = Liabilities + Owners' Equity
6. Buildings are purchased in exchange for a three-year note payable.	I = I + NE
7. Advertising bill for the month is paid.	D = NE + D
8. Dividends are paid to stockholders.	D = NE + D
9. Land is acquired by issuing shares of stock to the owner of the land.	I = NE + I

LO 3 Exercise 3-4 Types of Transactions

As you found out in reading the chapter, there are three elements to the accounting equation: assets, liabilities, and owners' equity. You also learned that every transaction affects at least two of these elements. Although other possibilities exist, five types of transactions are described below. For *each* of these five types, write out descriptions of at least *two* transactions that illustrate these types of transactions.

Type of Transaction	Assets =	Liabilities +	Owners' Equity
1.	Increase	Increase	
2.	Increase		Increase
3.	Decrease	Decrease	
4.	Decrease		Decrease
5.	Increase Decrease		

LO 4 Exercise 3-5 Balance Sheet Accounts and Their Use

Choose from the following list of account titles the one that most accurately fits the description of that account or is an example of that account. An account title may be used more than once or not at all.

Cash	**Accounts Receivable**	**Notes Receivable**
Prepaid Asset	**Land**	**Buildings**
Investments	**Accounts Payable**	**Notes Payable**
Taxes Payable	**Retained Earnings**	**Common Stock**
Preferred Stock		

Notes payable	1. A written obligation to repay a fixed amount, with interest, at some time in the future
Investments	2. Twenty acres of land held for speculation
Acct's. receivable	3. An amount owed by a customer
Taxes pay.	4. Corporate income taxes owed to the federal government
Preferred stock	5. Ownership in a company that allows the owner to receive dividends before common shareholders receive any distributions
Land	6. Five acres of land used as the site for a factory
Acct's pay.	7. Amounts owed on an open account to a supplier of raw materials, due in 90 days
Cash	8. A checking account at the bank
Buildings	9. A warehouse used to store merchandise
R.E.	10. Claims by the owners on the undistributed net income of a business
Prepaid Asses	11. Rent paid on an office building in advance of use of the facility

LO 5 Exercise 3-6 Normal Account Balances

Each account has a normal balance. For the following list of accounts, indicate whether the normal balance of each is a debit or a credit.

Account	Normal Balance
1. Cash	Dr
2. Prepaid Insurance	Dr
3. Retained Earnings	Cr

4. Bonds Payable ______
5. Investments ______
6. Capital Stock ______
7. Advertising Fees Earned ______
8. Wages and Salaries Expense ______
9. Wages and Salaries Payable ______
10. Office Supplies ______
11. Dividends ______

LO 5 Exercise 3-7 Debits and Credits

The new bookkeeper for Darby Corporation is getting ready to mail the daily cash receipts to the bank for deposit. Because his previous job was at a bank, he is aware that the bank "credits" your account for all deposits and "debits" your account for all checks written. Therefore, he makes the following entry before sending the daily receipts to the bank:

June 5	Accounts Receivable	10,000	
	Sales Revenue	2,450	
	Cash		12,450
	To record cash received on June 5: $10,000 collections on account and $2,450 in cash sales.		

Required

Explain why this entry is wrong, and prepare the correct journal entry. Why does the bank refer to cash received from a customer as a *credit* to that customer's account?

LO 7 Exercise 3-8 Trial Balance

The following list of accounts was taken from the general ledger of Spencer Corporation on December 31, 2001. The bookkeeper thought it would be helpful if the accounts were arranged in alphabetical order. Each account contains the balance normal for that type of account (for example, Cash normally has a debit balance). Prepare a trial balance as of this date, with the accounts arranged in the following order: (1) assets, (2) liabilities, (3) owners' equity, (4) revenues, (5) expenses, and (6) dividends.

Account	Balance
Accounts Payable	$ 7,650
Accounts Receivable	5,325
Automobiles	9,200
Buildings	150,000
Capital Stock	100,000
Cash	10,500
Commissions Expense	2,600
Commissions Revenue	12,750
Dividends	2,000
Equipment	85,000
Heat, Light, and Water Expense	1,400
Income Tax Expense	1,700
Income Taxes Payable	2,500
Interest Revenue	1,300
Land	50,000
Notes Payable	90,000
Office Salaries Expense	6,000
Office Supplies	500
Retained Earnings	110,025

Multi-Concept Exercises

LO 3, 4, 5 Exercise 3-9 Journal Entries Recorded Directly in T Accounts

Record each transaction shown below directly in T accounts, using the numbers preceding the transactions to identify them in the accounts. Each account involved needs a separate T account.

1. Received contribution of $6,500 from each of the three principal owners of the We-Go Delivery Service in exchange for shares of stock.
2. Purchased office supplies for cash of $130.
3. Purchased a van for $15,000 on an open account. The company has 25 days to pay for the van.
4. Provided delivery services to residential customers for cash of $125.
5. Billed a local business $200 for delivery services. The customer is to pay the bill within 15 days.
6. Paid the amount due on the van.
7. Received the amount due from the local business billed in transaction **(5)** above.

LO 4, 7 **Exercise 3-10** Trial Balance

Refer to the transactions recorded directly in T accounts for the We-Go Delivery Service in Exercise 3-9. Assume that the transactions all took place during December 2001. Prepare a trial balance at December 31, 2001.

LO 3, 4, 5 **Exercise 3-11** Determining an Ending Account Balance

Jessie's Bead Shop was organized on June 1, 2001. The company received a contribution of $1,000 from each of the two principal owners. During the month, Jessie's Bead Shop had cash sales of $1,400, had sales on account of $450, received $250 from customers in payment of their accounts, purchased supplies on account for $600 and equipment on account for $1,350, received a utility bill for $250 which will not be paid until July, and paid the full amount due on the equipment. Use a T account to determine the company's Cash balance on June 30, 2001.

LO 3, 4, 5 **Exercise 3-12** Reconstructing a Beginning Account Balance

During the month, services performed for customers on account amounted to $7,500, and collections from customers in payment of their accounts totaled $6,000. At the end of the month, the Accounts Receivable account had a balance of $2,500. What was the Accounts Receivable balance at the beginning of the month?

LO 3, 5, 6 **Exercise 3-13** Journal Entries

Prepare the journal entry to record each of the following independent transactions (use the number of the transaction in lieu of a date for identification purposes):

1. Sales on account of $1,530
2. Purchases of supplies on account for $1,365
3. Cash sales of $750
4. Purchase of equipment for cash of $4,240
5. Issuance of a promissory note for $2,500
6. Collections on account for $890
7. Sale of capital stock in exchange for a parcel of land; the land is appraised at $50,000
8. Payment of $4,000 in salaries and wages
9. Payment of open account in the amount of $500

LO 3, 5, 6 **Exercise 3-14** Journal Entries

Following is a list of transactions entered into during the first month of operations of Gardener Corporation, a new landscape service. Prepare in journal form the entry to record each transaction.

April 1: Articles of incorporation are filed with the state, and 100,000 shares of common stock are issued for $100,000 in cash.

April 4: A six-month promissory note is signed at the bank. Interest at 9% per annum will be repaid in six months along with the principal amount of the loan of $50,000.

April 8: Land and a storage shed are acquired for a lump sum of $80,000. On the basis of an appraisal, 25% of the value is assigned to the land and the remainder to the building.

April 10: Mowing equipment is purchased from a supplier at a total cost of $25,000. A down payment of $10,000 is made, with the remainder due by the end of the month.

April 18: Customers are billed for services provided during the first half of the month. The total amount billed of $5,500 is due within 10 days.

April 27: The remaining balance due on the mowing equipment is paid to the supplier.

April 28: The total amount of $5,500 due from customers is received.

April 30: Customers are billed for services provided during the second half of the month. The total amount billed is $9,850.

April 30: Salaries and wages of $4,650 for the month of April are paid.

LO 5, 6 Exercise 3-15 The Process of Posting Journal Entries to General Ledger Accounts
On June 1, Campbell Corporation purchased 10 acres of land in exchange for a promissory note in the amount of $50,000. Using the formats shown in Exhibit 3-5, prepare the journal entry to record this transaction in a general journal, and post it to the appropriate general ledger accounts. The entry will be recorded on page 7 of the general journal. Use whatever account numbers you would like in the general ledger. Assume that none of the accounts to be debited or credited currently contain a balance.

If at a later date you wanted to review this transaction, would you examine the general ledger or the general journal? Explain your answer.

PROBLEMS

LO 1 Problem 3-1 Events to be Recorded in Accounts
The following events take place at Dillon's Drive-In:

1. Food is ordered from vendors, who will deliver the food within the week.
2. Vendors deliver food on account, payment due in 30 days.
3. Employees take frozen food from the freezers and prepare it for customers.
4. Food is served to customers, and sales are rung up on the cash register; sales will be totaled at the end of the day.
5. Trash is taken to dumpsters, and the floors are cleaned.
6. Cash registers are cleared at the end of the day.
7. Cash is deposited in the bank night depository.
8. Employees are paid weekly paychecks.
9. Vendors noted in item **2** are paid for the food delivered.

Required

Identify each event as internal (I) or external (E), and indicate whether each event would be recorded in the *accounts* of the company. For each event that is to be recorded, identify the names of at least two accounts that would be affected.

LO 3 Problem 3-2 Transaction Analysis and Financial Statements

GENERAL LEDGER

Just Rolling Along Inc. was organized on May 1, 2001, by two college students who recognized an opportunity to make money while spending their days at a beach along Lake Michigan. The two entrepreneurs plan to rent bicycles and in-line skates to weekend visitors to the lakefront. The following transactions occurred during the first month of operations:

May 1: Received contribution of $9,000 from each of the two principal owners of the new business in exchange for shares of stock.

May 1: Purchased 10 bicycles for $300 each on an open account. The company has 30 days to pay for the bicycles.

May 5: Registered as a vendor with the city and paid the $15 monthly fee.

May 9: Purchased 20 pairs of in-line skates at $125 per pair, 20 helmets at $50 each, and 20 sets of protective gear (knee and elbow pads and wrist guards) at $45 per set for cash.

May 10: Purchased $100 in miscellaneous supplies on account. The company has 30 days to pay for the supplies.

May 15: Paid $125 bill from local radio station for advertising for the last two weeks of May.

May 17: Customers rented in-line skates and bicycles for cash of $1,800.

May 24: Billed the local park district $1,200 for in-line skating lessons provided to neighborhood kids. The park district is to pay one-half of the bill within 5 working days and the rest within 30 days.

May 29: Received 50% of the amount billed to the park district.

May 30: Customers rented in-line skates and bicycles for cash of $3,000.

May 30: Paid wages of $160 to a friend who helped out over the weekend.

May 31: Paid the balance due on the bicycles.

Required

1. Prepare a table to summarize the preceding transactions as they affect the accounting equation. Use the format in Exhibit 3-1. Identify each transaction with the date.
2. Prepare an income statement for the month ended May 31, 2001.
3. Prepare a classified balance sheet at May 31, 2001.
4. Why do you think the two college students decided to incorporate their business rather than operate it as a partnership?

LO 3 Problem 3-3 Transaction Analysis and Financial Statements

Expert Consulting Services Inc. was organized on March 1, 2001, by two former college roommates. The corporation will provide computer consulting services to small businesses. The following transactions occurred during the first month of operations:

March 2: Received contributions of $20,000 from each of the two principal owners of the new business in exchange for shares of stock.

March 7: Signed a two-year promissory note at the bank and received cash of $15,000. Interest, along with the $15,000, will be repaid at the end of the two years.

March 12: Purchased $700 in miscellaneous supplies on account. The company has 30 days to pay for the supplies.

March 19: Billed a client $4,000 for services rendered by Expert in helping to install a new computer system. The client is to pay 25% of the bill upon its receipt and the remaining balance within 30 days.

March 20: Paid $1,300 bill from the local newspaper for advertising for the month of March.

March 22: Received 25% of the amount billed the client on March 19.

March 26: Received cash of $2,800 for services provided in assisting a client in selecting software for its computer.

March 29: Purchased a computer system for $8,000 in cash.

March 30: Paid $3,300 of salaries and wages for March.

March 31: Received and paid $1,400 in gas, electric, and water bills.

Required

1. Prepare a table to summarize the preceding transactions as they affect the accounting equation. Use the format in Exhibit 3-1. Identify each transaction with the date.
2. Prepare an income statement for the month ended March 31, 2001.
3. Prepare a classified balance sheet at March 31, 2001.
4. From reading the balance sheet you prepared in part **3,** what events would you expect to take place in April? Explain your answer.

LO 3 Problem 3-4 Transactions Reconstructed from Financial Statements

The following financial statements are available for Elm Corporation for its first month of operations:

ELM CORPORATION
INCOME STATEMENT
FOR THE MONTH ENDED JUNE 30, 2001

Service revenue		$93,600
Expenses:		
Rent	$ 9,000	
Salaries and wages	27,900	
Utilities	13,800	50,700
Net income		$42,900

ELM CORPORATION
BALANCE SHEET
JUNE 30, 2001

Assets		Liabilities and Owners' Equity	
Cash	$ 22,800	Accounts payable	$ 18,000
Accounts receivable	21,600	Notes payable	90,000
Equipment	18,000		
Building	90,000	Capital stock	30,000
Land	24,000	Retained earnings	38,400
Total	$176,400	Total	$176,400

Required

Using the format illustrated in Exhibit 3-1, prepare a table to summarize the transactions entered into by Elm Corporation during its first month of business. State any assumptions you believe are necessary in reconstructing the transactions.

Multi-Concept Problems

LO 1, 2 Problem 3-5 Identification of Events with Source Documents

Many events are linked to a source document. The following is a list of events that occurred in an entity:

a. Paid a one-year insurance policy.

b. Paid employee payroll.

c. Sold merchandise to a customer on account.

d. Identified supplies in the storeroom destroyed by fire.

e. Received payment of bills from customers.

f. Purchased land for future expansion.

g. Calculated taxes due.

h. Entered into a car lease agreement and paid the tax, title, and license.

Required

For each item **a** through **h,** indicate whether the event should or should not be recorded in the entity's accounts. For each item that should be recorded in the entity's books:

1. Identify one or more source documents that are generated from the event.
2. Identify which source document would be used to record an event when it produces more than one source document.
3. For each document, identify the information that is most useful in recording the event in the accounts.

LO 3, 5 Problem 3-6 Accounts Used to Record Transactions

A list of accounts, with an identifying number for each, is shown below. Following the list of accounts is a series of transactions entered into by a company during its first year of operations.

Required

For each transaction, indicate the account or accounts that should be debited and credited.

1. Cash
2. Accounts Receivable
3. Office Supplies
4. Buildings
5. Automobiles
6. Land
7. Accounts Payable
8. Income Tax Payable
9. Notes Payable
10. Capital Stock
11. Retained Earnings
12. Service Revenue
13. Wage and Salary Expense
14. Selling Expense
15. Utilities Expense
16. Income Tax Expense

Transactions	Accounts Debited	Accounts Credited
Example: Purchased land and building in exchange for a three-year promissory note.	4, 6	9
a. Issued capital stock for cash.	______	______
b. Purchased 10 automobiles; paid part in cash and signed a 60-day note for the balance.	______	______
c. Purchased land in exchange for a note due in six months.	______	______
d. Purchased office supplies; agreed to pay total bill by the 10th of the following month.	______	______
e. Billed clients for services performed during the month, and gave them until the 15th of the following month to pay.	______	______
f. Received cash on account from clients for services rendered to them in past months.	______	______
g. Paid employees salaries and wages earned during the month.	______	______
h. Paid newspaper for company ads appearing during the month.	______	______
i. Received monthly gas and electric bill from the utility company; payment is due anytime within the first 10 days of the following month.	______	______
j. Computed amount of taxes due based on the income of the period; amount will be paid in the following month.	______	______

GENERAL LEDGER

LO 3, 4, 5 Problem 3-7 Transaction Analysis and Journal Entries Recorded Directly in T Accounts

Four brothers organized Beverly Entertainment Enterprises on October 1, 2001. The following transactions occurred during the first month of operations:

October 1: Received contribution of $10,000 from each of the four principal owners of the new business in exchange for shares of stock.

October 2: Purchased the Arcada Theater for $125,000. The seller agreed to accept a down payment of $12,500 and a seven-year promissory note for the balance. The Arcada property consists of land valued at $35,000 and a building valued at $90,000.

October 3: Purchased new seats for the theater at a cost of $5,000, paying $2,500 down and agreeing to pay the remainder in 60 days.

October 12: Purchased candy, popcorn, cups, and napkins for $3,700 on an open account. The company has 30 days to pay for the concession supplies.

October 13: Sold tickets for the opening-night movie for cash of $1,800, and took in $2,400 at the concession stand.

October 17: Rented out the theater to a local community group for $1,500. The community group is to pay one-half of the bill within 5 working days and has 30 days to pay the remainder.

October 23: Received 50% of the amount billed to the community group.

October 24: Sold movie tickets for cash of $2,000, and took in $2,800 at the concession stand.

October 26: The four brothers, acting on behalf of Beverly Entertainment, paid a dividend of $750 on the shares of stock owned by each of them, or $3,000 in total.

October 27: Paid $500 for utilities.

October 30: Paid wages and salaries of $2,400 total to the ushers, the projectionist, concession stand workers, and the maintenance crew.

October 31: Sold movie tickets for cash of $1,800, and took in $2,500 at the concession stand.

Required

1. Prepare a table to summarize the preceding transactions as they affect the accounting equation. Use the format in Exhibit 3-1. Identify each transaction with a date.
2. Record each transaction directly in T accounts, using the dates preceding the transactions to identify them in the accounts. Each account involved in the problem needs a separate T account.

LO 4, 7 **Problem 3-8** Trial Balance and Financial Statements
Refer to the table for Beverly Entertainment Enterprises in part **1** of Problem 3-7.

Required

1. Prepare a trial balance at October 31, 2001.
2. Prepare an income statement for the month ended October 31, 2001.
3. Prepare a statement of retained earnings for the month ended October 31, 2001.
4. Prepare a classified balance sheet at October 31, 2001.

LO 3, 5, 6 **Problem 3-9** Journal Entries

Atkins Advertising Agency began business on January 2, 2001. Listed below are the transactions entered into by Atkins during its first month of operations.

a. Acquired its articles of incorporation from the state, and issued 100,000 shares of capital stock in exchange for $200,000 in cash.
b. Purchased an office building for $150,000 in cash. The building is valued at $110,000, and the remainder of the value is assigned to the land.
c. Signed a three-year promissory note at the bank for $125,000.
d. Purchased office equipment at a cost of $50,000, paying $10,000 down and agreeing to pay the remainder in 10 days.
e. Paid wages and salaries of $13,000 for the first half of the month. Office employees are paid twice a month.
f. Paid the balance due on the office equipment.
g. Sold $24,000 of advertising during the first month. Customers have until the 15th of the following month to pay their bills.
h. Paid wages and salaries of $15,000 for the second half of the month.
i. Recorded $3,500 in commissions earned by the salespeople during the month. They will be paid on the fifth of the following month.

Required

Prepare in journal form the entry to record each transaction.

LO 3, 4, 5 **Problem 3-10** Journal Entries Recorded Directly in T Accounts
Refer to the transactions for Atkins Advertising Agency in Problem 3-9.

Required

1. Record each transaction directly in T accounts, using the letters preceding the transactions to identify them in the accounts. Each account involved in the problem needs a separate T account.
2. Prepare a trial balance at January 31, 2001.

LO 3, 5, 7 **Problem 3-11** The Detection of Errors in a Trial Balance and Preparation of a Corrected Trial Balance
Malcolm Inc. was incorporated on January 1, 2001, with the issuance of capital stock in return for $90,000 of cash contributed by the owners. The only other transaction entered into prior to beginning operations was the issuance of a $75,300 note payable in exchange for building and equipment. The following trial balance was prepared at the end of the first month by the bookkeeper for Malcolm Inc.

MALCOLM INC.
TRIAL BALANCE
JANUARY 31, 2001

Account Titles	Debits	Credits
Cash	$ 9,980	
Accounts Receivable	8,640	
Land	80,000	
Building	50,000	
Equipment	23,500	

Account Titles	Debits	Credits
Notes Payable		$ 75,300
Capital Stock		90,000
Service Revenue		50,340
Wage and Salary Expense	$ 23,700	
Advertising Expense	4,600	
Utilities Expense	8,420	
Dividends		5,000
Totals	$208,840	$220,640

Required

1. Identify the *two* errors in the trial balance. Ignore depreciation expense and interest expense.
2. Prepare a corrected trial balance.

LO 3, 5, 6, 7 Problem 3-12 Journal Entries, Trial Balance, and Financial Statements

Blue Jay Delivery Service is incorporated on January 2, 2001, and enters into the following transactions during its first month of operations:

January 2: Filed articles of incorporation with the state, and issued 100,000 shares of capital stock. Cash of $100,000 is received from the new owners for the shares.

January 3 Purchased a warehouse and land for $80,000 in cash. An appraiser values the land at $20,000 and the warehouse at $60,000.

January 4: Signed a three-year promissory note at the Third State Bank in the amount of $50,000.

January 6: Purchased five new delivery trucks for a total of $45,000 in cash.

January 31: Performed services on account that amounted to $15,900 during the month. Cash amounting to $7,490 was received from customers on account during the month.

January 31: Established an open account at a local service station at the beginning of the month. Purchases of gas and oil during January amounted to $3,230. Blue Jay has until the 10th of the following month to pay its bill.

Required

1. Prepare journal entries on the books of Blue Jay to record the transactions entered into during the month.
2. Prepare a trial balance at January 31, 2001.
3. Prepare an income statement for the month ended January 31, 2001.
4. Prepare a classified balance sheet at January 31, 2001.
5. Assume that you are considering buying stock in this company. Beginning with the transaction to record the purchase of the property on January 3, list any additional information you would like to have about each of the transactions during the remainder of the month.

LO 3, 5, 6, 7 Problem 3-13 Journal Entries, Trial Balance, and Financial Statements

Neveranerror Inc. was organized on June 2, 2001, by a group of accountants to provide accounting and tax services to small businesses. The following transactions occurred during the first month of business:

June 2: Received contributions of $10,000 from each of the three owners of the business in exchange for shares of stock.

June 5: Purchased a computer system for $12,000. The agreement with the vendor requires a down payment of $2,500 with the balance due in 60 days.

June 8: Signed a two-year promissory note at the bank and received cash of $20,000.

June 15: Billed $12,350 to clients for the first half of June. Clients are billed twice a month for services performed during the month, and the bills are payable within 10 days.

June 17: Paid a $900 bill from the local newspaper for advertising for the month of June.

June 23: Received the amounts billed to clients for services performed during the first half of the month.

June 28: Received and paid gas, electric, and water bills. The total amount is $2,700.

June 29: Received the landlord's bill for $2,200 for rent on the office space that Neveranerror leases. The bill is payable by the 10th of the following month.

June 30: Paid salaries and wages for June. The total amount is $5,670.

June 30: Billed $18,400 to clients for the second half of June.

June 30: Declared and paid dividends in the amount of $6,000.

Required

1. Prepare journal entries on the books of Neveranerror Inc. to record the transactions entered into during the month. Ignore depreciation expense and interest expense.
2. Prepare a trial balance at June 30, 2001.
3. Prepare the following financial statements:
   a. Income statement for the month ended June 30, 2001.
   b. Statement of retained earnings for the month ended June 30, 2001.
   c. Classified balance sheet at June 30, 2001.
4. Assume that you have just graduated from college and have been approached to join this company as an accountant. From your reading of the financial statements for the first month, would you consider joining the company? Explain your answer. Limit your answer to financial considerations only.

ALTERNATE PROBLEMS

LO 1 **Problem 3-1A** Events to Be Recorded in Accounts

The following events take place at Anaconda Accountants Inc.:

1. Supplies are ordered from vendors, who will deliver the supplies within the week.
2. Vendors deliver supplies on account, payment due in 30 days.
3. New computer system is ordered.
4. Old computer system is sold for cash.
5. Services are rendered to customers on account. The invoices are mailed and due in 30 days.
6. Cash received from customer payments is deposited in the bank night depository.
7. Employees are paid weekly paychecks.
8. Vendors noted in item **2** are paid for the supplies delivered.

Required

Identify each event as internal (I) or external (E), and indicate whether each event would be recorded in the *accounts* of the company. For each event that is to be recorded, identify the names of at least two accounts that would be affected.

LO 3 **Problem 3-2A** Transaction Analysis and Financial Statements

Beachway Enterprises was organized on June 1, 2001, by two college students who recognized an opportunity to make money while spending their days at a beach in Florida. The two entrepreneurs plan to rent beach umbrellas. The following transactions occurred during the first month of operations:

June 1: Received contribution of $2,000 from each of the two principal owners of the new business in exchange for shares of stock.

June 1: Purchased 25 beach umbrellas for $250 each on account. The company has 30 days to pay for the beach umbrellas.

June 5: Registered as a vendor with the city and paid the $35 monthly fee.

June 10: Purchased $50 in miscellaneous supplies on an open account. The company has 30 days to pay for the supplies.

June 15: Paid $70 bill from a local radio station for advertising for the last two weeks of June.

June 17: Customers rented beach umbrellas for cash of $1,000.

June 24: Billed a local hotel $2,000 for beach umbrellas provided for use during a convention being held at the hotel. The hotel is to pay one-half of the bill in 5 days and the rest within 30 days.

June 29: Received 50% of the amount billed to the hotel.

June 30: Customers rented beach umbrellas for cash of $1,500.

June 30: Paid wages of $90 to a friend who helped out over the weekend.

June 30: Paid the balance due on the beach umbrellas.

Required

1. Prepare a table to summarize the preceding transactions as they affect the accounting equation. Use the format in Exhibit 3-1. Identify each transaction with a date.
2. Prepare an income statement for the month ended June 30, 2001.
3. Prepare a classified balance sheet at June 30, 2001.

LO 3 Problem 3-3A Transaction Analysis and Financial Statements

Dynamic Services Inc. was organized on March 1, 2001, by two former college roommates. The corporation will provide computer tax services to small businesses. The following transactions occurred during the first month of operations:

March 2: Received contributions of $10,000 from each of the two principal owners in exchange for shares of stock.

March 7: Signed a two-year promissory note at the bank and received cash of $7,500. Interest, along with the $7,500, will be repaid at the end of the two years.

March 12: Purchased miscellaneous supplies on account for $350, payment due in 30 days.

March 19: Billed a client $2,000 for tax-preparation services. According to an agreement between the two companies, the client is to pay 25% of the bill upon its receipt and the remaining balance within 30 days.

March 20: Paid a $650 bill from the local newspaper for advertising for the month of March.

March 22: Received 25% of the amount billed the client on March 19.

March 26: Received cash of $1,400 for services provided in assisting a client in preparing its tax return.

March 29: Purchased a computer system for $4,000 in cash.

March 30: Paid $1,650 in salaries and wages for March.

March 31: Received and paid $700 of gas, electric, and water bills.

Required

1. Prepare a table to summarize the preceding transactions as they affect the accounting equation. Use the format in Exhibit 3-1. Identify each transaction with the date.
2. Prepare an income statement for the month ended March 31, 2001.
3. Prepare a classified balance sheet at March 31, 2001.
4. From reading the balance sheet you prepared in part **3**, what events would you expect to take place in April? Explain your answer.

LO 3 Problem 3-4A Transactions Reconstructed from Financial Statements

The following financial statements are available for Oak Corporation for its first month of operations:

OAK CORPORATION
INCOME STATEMENT
FOR THE MONTH ENDED JULY 31, 2001

Service revenue		$75,400
Expenses:		
Rent	$ 6,000	
Salaries and wages	24,600	
Utilities	12,700	43,300
Net income		$32,100

OAK CORPORATION
BALANCE SHEET
JULY 31, 2001

Assets		Liabilities and Owners' Equity	
Cash	$ 13,700	Wages payable	$ 6,000
Accounts receivable	25,700	Notes payable	50,000
Equipment	32,000	Unearned service revenue	4,500
Furniture	14,700	Capital stock	30,000
Land	24,000	Retained earnings	19,600
Total	$110,100	Total	$110,100

Required

Describe as many transactions as you can that were entered into by Oak Corporation during the first month of business.

Alternate Multi-Concept Problems

LO 1, 2 Problem 3-5A Identification of Events with Source Documents

Many events are linked to a source document. The following is a list of events that occurred in an entity:

a. Paid a security deposit and six months' rent on a building.

b. Hired three employees and agreed to pay them $400 per week.

c. Sold merchandise to a customer for cash.

d. Reported a fire that destroyed a billboard that is on the entity's property and is owned and maintained by another entity.

e. Received payment of bills from customers.

f. Purchased stock in another entity to gain some control over it.

g. Signed a note at the bank and received cash.

h. Contracted with a cleaning service to maintain the interior of the building in good repair. No money is paid at this time.

Required

For each item **a** through **h,** indicate whether the event should or should not be recorded in the entity's accounts. For each item that should be recorded in the entity's books:

1. Identify one or more source documents that are generated from the event.
2. Identify which source document would be used to record an event when it produces more than one source document.
3. For each document, identify the information that is most useful in recording the event in the accounts.

LO 3, 5 Problem 3-6A Accounts Used to Record Transactions

A list of accounts, with an identifying number for each, is shown below. Following the list of accounts is a series of transactions entered into by a company during its first year of operations.

Required

For each transaction, indicate the account or accounts that should be debited and credited.

1. Cash
2. Accounts Receivable
3. Prepaid Insurance
4. Office Supplies
5. Automobiles
6. Land
7. Accounts Payable
8. Income Tax Payable
9. Notes Payable
10. Capital Stock
11. Retained Earnings
12. Service Revenue
13. Wage and Salary Expense
14. Utilities Expense
15. Income Tax Expense

Transactions	Accounts Debited	Accounts Credited
Example: Purchased office supplies for cash.	4	1
a. Issued capital stock for cash.	______	______
b. Purchased an automobile and signed a 60-day note for the total amount.	______	______
c. Acquired land in exchange for capital stock.	______	______
d. Received cash from clients for services performed during the month.	______	______
e. Paid employees salaries and wages earned during the month.	______	______
f. Purchased flyers and signs from a printer, payment due in 10 days.	______	______
g. Paid for the flyers and signs purchased in part **f.**	______	______
h. Received monthly telephone bill; payment is due within 10 days of receipt.	______	______
i. Paid for a six-month liability insurance policy.	______	______
j. Paid monthly telephone bill.	______	______
k. Computed amount of taxes due based on the income of the period and paid the amount.	______	______

LO 3, 4, 5 Problem 3-7A Transaction Analysis and Journal Entries Recorded Directly in T Accounts

Three friends organized Rapid City Roller Rink on October 1, 2001. The following transactions occurred during the first month of operations:

October 1: Received contribution of $22,000 from each of the three principal owners of the new business in exchange for shares of stock.

October 2: Purchased land valued at $15,000 and a building valued at $75,000. The seller agreed to accept a down payment of $9,000 and a five-year promissory note for the balance.

October 3: Purchased new tables and chairs for the lounge at the roller rink at a cost of $25,000, paying $5,000 down and agreeing to pay for the remainder in 60 days.

October 9: Purchased 100 pairs of roller skates for cash at $35 per pair.

October 12: Purchased food and drinks for $2,500 on an open account. The company has 30 days to pay for the concession supplies.

October 13: Sold tickets for cash of $400 and took in $750 at the concession stand.

October 17: Rented out the roller rink to a local community group for $750. The community group is to pay one-half of the bill within 5 working days and has 30 days to pay the remainder.

October 23: Received 50% of the amount billed to the community group.

October 24: Sold tickets for cash of $500, and took in $1,200 at the concession stand.

October 26: The three friends, acting on behalf of Rapid City Roller Rink, paid a dividend of $250 on the shares of stock owned by each of them, or $750 in total.

October 27: Paid $1,275 for utilities.

October 30: Paid wages and salaries of $2,250.

October 31: Sold tickets for cash of $700, and took in $1,300 at the concession stand.

Required

1. Prepare a table to summarize the preceding transactions as they affect the accounting equation. Use the format in Exhibit 3-1. Identify each transaction with a date.
2. Record each transaction directly in T accounts, using the dates preceding the transactions to identify them in the accounts. Each account involved in the problem needs a separate T account.

LO 4, 7 **Problem 3-8A** Trial Balance and Financial Statements

Refer to the table for Rapid City Roller Rink in part **1** of Problem 3-7A.

Required

1. Prepare a trial balance at October 31, 2001.
2. Prepare an income statement for the month ended October 31, 2001.
3. Prepare a statement of retained earnings for the month ended October 31, 2001.
4. Prepare a classified balance sheet at October 31, 2001.

LO 3, 5, 6 **Problem 3-9A** Journal Entries

Castle Consulting Agency began business in February 2001. Listed below are the transactions entered into by Castle during its first month of operations.

a. Acquired articles of incorporation from the state, and issued 10,000 shares of capital stock in exchange for $150,000 in cash.

b. Paid monthly rent of $400.

c. Signed a five-year promissory note for $100,000 at the bank.

d. Received $5,000 cash from a customer for services to be performed over the next two months.

e. Purchased software to be used on future jobs. The software costs $950 and is expected to be used on five to eight jobs over the next two years.

f. Billed customers $12,500 for work performed during the month.

g. Paid office personnel $3,000 for the month of February.

h. Received a utility bill of $100. The total amount is due in 30 days.

Required

Prepare in journal form the entry to record each transaction.

LO 3, 4, 5 **Problem 3-10A** Journal Entries Recorded Directly in T Accounts

Refer to the transactions for Castle Consulting Agency in Problem 3-9A.

Required

1. Record each transaction directly in T accounts, using the letters preceding the transactions to identify them in the accounts. Each account involved in the problem needs a separate T account.
2. Prepare a trial balance at February 28, 2001.

LO 3, 4, 5, 7 **Problem 3-11A** Entries Prepared from a Trial Balance and Proof of the Cash Balance

Russell Company was incorporated on January 1, 2001, with the issuance of capital stock in return for $120,000 of cash contributed by the owners. The only other transaction entered into prior to beginning operations was the issuance of a $50,000 note payable in exchange for equipment and fixtures. The following trial balance was prepared at the end of the first month by the bookkeeper for Russell Company:

RUSSELL COMPANY
TRIAL BALANCE
JANUARY 31, 2001

Account Titles	Debits	Credits
Cash	$???	
Accounts Receivable	30,500	
Equipment and Fixtures	50,000	
Wages Payable		$ 10,000
Notes Payable		50,000
Capital Stock		120,000
Service Revenue		60,500
Wage and Salary Expense	24,600	
Advertising Expense	12,500	
Rent Expense	5,200	

Required

1. Determine the balance in the Cash account.
2. Identify all of the transactions that affected the Cash account during the month. Use a T account to prove what the balance in Cash would be after all transactions are recorded.

GENERAL LEDGER

LO 3, 5, 6 Problem 3-12A Journal Entries

Overnight Delivery Inc. is incorporated on January 2, 2001, and enters into the following transactions during its second month of operations:

February 2: Paid $400 for wages earned by employees for the week ending January 31.

February 3: Paid $3,230 for gas and oil billed on an open account in January.

February 4: Declared and paid $2,000 cash dividends to stockholders.

February 15: Received $8,000 cash from customer accounts.

February 26: Provided $16,800 of services on account during the month.

February 27: Received a $3,400 bill from the local service station for gas and oil used during February.

Required

1. Prepare journal entries on the books of Overnight to record the transactions entered into during February.
2. For the transactions on February 2, 3, 4, and 27, indicate whether the amount is an expense of operating in the month of January or February or is not an expense in either month.

GENERAL LEDGER

LO 3, 5, 6 Problem 3-13A Journal Entries and a Balance Sheet

Krittersbegone Inc. was organized on July 1, 2001, by a group of technicians to provide termite inspections and treatment to homeowners and small businesses. The following transactions occurred during the first month of business:

July 2: Received contributions of $3,000 from each of the six owners in exchange for shares of stock.

July 3: Paid $1,000 rent for the month of July.

July 5: Purchased flashlights, tools, spray equipment, and ladders for $18,000, with a down payment of $5,000 and the balance due in 30 days.

July 17: Paid a $200 bill for the distribution of door-to-door advertising.

July 28: Paid August rent and July utilities to the landlord in the amounts of $1,000 and $450, respectively.

July 30: Received $8,000 in cash from homeowners for services performed during the month. In addition, billed $7,500 to other customers for services performed during the month. Billings are due in 30 days.

July 30: Paid commissions of $9,500 to the technicians for July.

July 31: Received $600 from a business client to perform services over the next two months.

Required

1. Prepare journal entries on the books of Krittersbegone to record the transactions entered into during the month. Ignore depreciation expense.
2. Prepare a classified balance sheet dated July 31, 2001. From the balance sheet, what cash inflow and what cash outflow can you predict in the month of August? Who would be interested in the cash flow information and why?

Cases

Reading and Interpreting Financial Statements

LO 3, 5, 6 Case 3-1 Reading and Interpreting Ben & Jerry's Statement of Cash Flows

Refer to Ben & Jerry's statement of cash flows for the year ended December 26, 1998.

Required

1. What amount did the company spend on additions to property, plant, and equipment during 1998? Prepare the journal entry to record these additions, assuming cash was paid.
2. What amount did the company receive from issuing common stock during 1998? Prepare the journal entry to record the issuance of stock. Do not be concerned at this point with the distinction between par value and additional paid-in capital on the balance sheet. This distinction will be explored in Chapter 11.

LO 4 Case 3-2 Reading and Interpreting Gateway's Balance Sheet and Footnotes

Refer to Gateway's balance sheet as of December 31, 1998 and Footnote 10 titled "Selected Balance Sheet Information."

Required

1. Using Exhibit 3-4 from the chapter as an example, prepare the asset section of a chart of accounts for Gateway. Do not go beyond the major categories of assets on your chart.
2. For the Property, plant, and equipment section of your chart of accounts, extend it to the next level to include the various types of these assets.
3. Which type of assets is the most significant among Gateway's property, plant, and equipment? What is the dollar amount of this asset at December 31, 1998? What does this dollar amount represent, that is, what attribute is being measured?

LO 1, 3, 5, 6 Case 3-3 Reading and Interpreting Delta's Balance Sheet

www.delta-air.com

The following item appears in the current liabilities section of Delta Airlines' balance sheet at June 30, 1998.

Air traffic liability	$1,667 million

In addition, one of Delta's footnotes states: "Passenger ticket sales are recorded as air traffic liability in the Company's Consolidated Balance Sheets. Passenger and Cargo revenues are recognized when the transportation is provided, reducing the air traffic liability, as applicable."

Required

1. What economic event caused Delta to incur this liability? Was it an external or an internal event?
2. Describe the effect on the accounting equation from the transaction to record the air traffic liability.
3. Assume that one customer purchases a $500 ticket in advance. Prepare the journal entry on Delta's books to record this transaction.
4. What economic event will cause Delta to reduce its air traffic liability? Is this an external or an internal event?

Making Financial Decisions

LO 2, 3 Case 3-4 Cash Flow Versus Net Income

Shelia Young started a real estate business in December of last year. After approval by the state for a charter to incorporate, she issued 1,000 shares of stock to herself and deposited $20,000 in a bank account under the name Young Properties. Because business was "booming," she spent all of her time during the first month selling properties rather than keeping financial records.

At the end of January, Shelia comes to you with the following plight:

> I put $20,000 in to start this business last month. My January 31 bank statement shows a balance of $17,000. After all of my efforts, it appears as if I'm "in the hole" already! On the other hand, that seems impossible—we sold five properties for clients during the month.

The total sales value of these properties was $600,000, and I receive a commission of 5% on each sale. Granted, one of the five sellers still owes me an $8,000 commission on the sale, but the other four have been collected in full. Three of the sales, totaling $400,000, were actually made by my assistants. I pay them 4% of the sales value of a property. Sure, I have a few office expenses for my car, utilities, and a secretary, but that's about it. How can I have possibly lost $3,000 this month?

You agree to help Shelia figure out how she really did this month. The bank statement is helpful. The total deposits during the month amount to $22,000. Shelia explains that this amount represents the commissions on the four sales collected so far. The canceled checks reveal the following expenditures:

Check No.	Payee—Memo at Bottom of Check	Amount
101	Stevens Office Supply	$ 2,000
102	Why Walk, Let's Talk Motor Co.—new car	3,000
103	City of Westbrook—heat and lights	500
104	Alice Hill—secretary	2,200
105	Ace Property Management—office rent for month	1,200
106	Jerry Hayes (sales assistant)	10,000
107	Joan Harper (sales assistant)	6,000
108	Don's Fillitup - gas and oil for car	100

According to Shelia, the $2,000 check to Stevens Office Supply represents the down payment on a word processor and a copier for the office. The remaining balance is $3,000 and it must be paid to Stevens by February 15. Similarly, the $3,000 check is the down payment on a car for the business. A $12,000 note was given to the car dealer and is due along with interest in one year.

1. Prepare an income statement for the month of January for Young Properties.
2. Prepare a statement of cash flows for the month of January for Young Properties.
3. Draft a memorandum to Shelia Young explaining as simply and as clearly as possible why she *did* in fact have a profitable first month in business but experienced a decrease in her cash account. Support your explanation with any necessary figures.
4. The down payments on the car and the office equipment are reflected on the statement of cash flows. They are assets that will benefit the business for a number of years. Do you think that *any* of the cost associated with the acquisition of these assets should be recognized in some way on the income statement? Explain your answer.

LO 3, 5, 6, 7 Case 3-5 Loan Request

Simon Fraser started a landscaping and lawn-care business in April 2001 by investing $20,000 cash in the business in exchange for capital stock. Because his business is in the Midwest, the season begins in April and concludes in September. He prepared the following trial balance (with accounts in alphabetical order) at the end of the first season in business.

FRASER LANDSCAPING
TRIAL BALANCE
SEPTEMBER 30, 2001

	Debits	Credits
Accounts Payable		$13,000
Accounts Receivable	$23,000	
Capital Stock		20,000
Cash	1,200	
Gas and Oil Expense	15,700	
Insurance Expense	2,500	
Landscaping Revenue		33,400
Lawn Care Revenue		24,000
Mowing Equipment	5,000	
Rent Expense	6,000	
Salaries Expense	22,000	
Truck	15,000	
Totals	$90,400	$90,400

Simon is pleased with his first year in business. "I paid myself a salary of $22,000 during the year and still have $1,200 in the bank. Sure, I have a few bills outstanding, but my accounts receivable will more than cover those." In fact, Simon is so happy with the first year, that he has come to you in your role as a lending officer at the local bank to ask for a $20,000 loan to allow him to add another truck and mowing equipment for the second season.

Required

1. From your reading of the trial balance, what does it appear to you that Simon did with the $20,000 in cash he originally contributed to the business? Reconstruct the journal entry to record the transaction you think took place.
2. Prepare an income statement for the six months ended September 30, 2001.
3. The mowing equipment and truck are assets that will benefit the business for a number of years. Do you think that any of the costs associated with the purchase of these assets should have been recognized as expenses in the first year? How would this have affected the income statement?
4. Prepare a classified balance sheet as of September 30, 2001. As a banker, what two items on the balance sheet concern you the most? Explain your answer.
5. As a banker, would you loan Simon $20,000 to expand his business during the second year? Draft a memo to respond to Simon's request for the loan, indicating whether you will make the loan.

Accounting and Ethics: What Would You Do?

LO 3, 5, 6 Case 3-6 Delay in the Posting of a Journal Entry

As assistant controller for a small consulting firm, you are responsible for recording and posting the daily cash receipts and disbursements to the ledger accounts. After you have posted the entries, your boss, the controller, prepares a trial balance and the financial statements. You make the following entries on June 30, 2001:

2001			
June 30	Cash	1,430	
	Accounts Receivable	1,950	
	Service Revenue		3,380
	To record daily cash receipts.		
June 30	Advertising Expense	12,500	
	Utilities Expense	22,600	
	Rent Expense	24,000	
	Salary and Wage Expense	17,400	
	Cash		76,500
	To record daily cash disbursements.		

The daily cash disbursements are much larger on June 30 than any other day because many of the company's major bills are paid on the last day of the month. After you have recorded these two transactions and *before* you have posted them to the ledger accounts, your boss comes to you with the following request:

> As you are aware, the first half of the year has been a tough one for the consulting industry and for our business in particular. With first-half bonuses based on net income, I am concerned whether you or I will get any bonus this time around. However, I have a suggestion that should allow us to receive something for our hard work and at the same time will not hurt anyone. Go ahead and post the June 30 cash receipts to the ledger but don't bother to post that day's cash disbursements. Even though the treasurer writes the checks on the last day of the month and you normally journalize the transaction on the same day, it is pretty silly to bother posting the entry to the ledger, since it takes at least a week for the checks to clear the bank.

Required

1. Explain *why* the controller's request will result in an increase in net income.
2. Do you agree with the controller that the omission of the entry on June 30 "will not hurt anyone"? If not, be explicit as to why you don't agree. Whom could it hurt?
3. What would you do? Whom should you talk to about this issue?

LO 5, 6 Case 3-7 Debits and Credits

You are controller for an architectural firm whose accounting year ends on December 31. As part of the management team, you receive a year-end bonus directly related to the firm's earnings for the year. One of your duties is to review the journal entries recorded by the bookkeepers. A new bookkeeper prepared the following journal entry:

Dec. 3	Cash	10,000	
	Service revenue		10,000
	To record deposit from client.		

You notice that the explanation for the journal entry refers to the amount as a deposit, and the bookkeeper explains to you that the firm plans to provide the services to the client in March of the following year.

1. Did the bookkeeper prepare the correct journal entry to account for the client's deposit? Explain your answer.
2. What would you do as controller for the firm? Do you have a responsibility to do anything to correct the books?

INTERNET RESEARCH CASE

Case 3-8 K2 Inc.

www.finance.yahoo.com
www.hoovers.com
www.k2sports.com

Although K2 Inc. does not currently post its financial statements or annual report on its Web site, you can research the company in a number of ways to answer the following questions. Use the URLs in the margin to learn more about the company, and go to K2's home page to get product, company history, and related information.

1. Investigate K2 Inc. as though you were interested in the company as a whole—its lines of products, its divisions, its means of distribution.
   - (a) How are K2 products distributed?
   - (b) How many lines of products does K2 have?
   - (c) See K2's history page. What aspects of its recent history are emphasized there? What does that tell you about the financial focus of the company?
2. Investigate K2 Inc. from its available financial information.
   - (a) What is K2's stock symbol and where is it traded?
   - (b) K2's 1998 annual report indicates that one of management's goals is to "lower . . . the cost of products and maintain . . . tight controls on expenses. . . ." From looking at information from your World Wide Web research, where would these cost reductions come from?

SOLUTION TO KEY TERMS QUIZ

__3__ Event (p. 94)
__10__ External event (p. 94)
__5__ Internal event (p. 94)
__14__ Transaction (p. 94)
__6__ Source document (p. 94)
__11__ Account (p. 101)
__1__ Chart of accounts (p. 101)
__12__ General ledger (p. 102)
__8__ Debit (p. 103)
__4__ Credit (p. 103)
__16__ Double-entry system (p. 106)
__13__ Journal (p. 108)
__9__ Posting (p. 108)
__7__ Journalizing (p. 109)
__15__ General journal (p. 109)
__2__ Trial Balance (p. 111)

Chapter 4

Income Measurement and Accrual Accounting

Study Links

A Look at Previous Chapters

We focused our attention in Chapter 3 on how accounting information is processed. Debits and credits, journal entries, accounts, and trial balances were introduced as convenient tools to aid in the preparation of periodic financial statements.

A Look at This Chapter

We begin this chapter by considering the roles of recognition and measurement in the process of preparing financial statements. We explore in detail the accrual basis of accounting and its effect on the measurement of income. The recognition of revenues and expenses in an accrual system is examined, and we look at the role of adjusting entries in this process. In the appendix to this chapter, we see how the accountant uses work sheets to prepare financial statements.

A Look at Upcoming Chapters

Chapter 4 completes our overview of the accounting model. In the next section, we will examine accounting for the various types of assets. We begin by looking at accounting by merchandise companies in Chapter 5.

Focus on Financial Results

McDonald's operates nearly 25,000 restaurants in 115 countries and has more than 40 percent market share of the U.S. fast-food business. Its remarkable performance continues a pattern of growth that CEO Jack M. Greenberg refers to as McDonald's "unique heritage—a history of success and innovation."

The consolidated statement of income excerpted here shows that tradition continuing. Total revenues increased in each of the three years. Two kinds of revenue are shown—sales by company-operated restaurants and revenues from franchised and affiliated restaurants, whose operators pay McDonald's a fee plus a share of their income for the right to operate as part of the chain. Thus, only a portion of the franchisees' revenue appears in the second line of the income statement, whereas all the revenue of company-operated restaurants appears in the first line.

How will revenue growth be sustained? McDonald's 1998 annual report lists five global strategies for maintaining growth, among them to "reinvent the category in which we compete and develop other business and growth opportunities."

Consolidated Statement of Income

(In millions, except per share data) Years ended December 31,	**1998**	1997	1996
Revenues			
Sales by Company-operated restaurants	**$ 8,894.9**	$ 8,136.5	$ 7,570.7
Revenues from franchised and affiliated restaurants	**3,526.5**	3,272.3	3,115.8
Total revenues	**12,421.4**	11,408.8	10,686.5
Operating costs and expenses			
Company-operated restaurants			
Food and packaging	**2,997.4**	2,772.6	2,546.6
Payroll and employee benefits	**2,220.3**	2,025.1	1,909.8
Occupancy and other operating expenses	**2,043.9**	1,851.9	1,706.8
	7,261.6	6,649.6	6,163.2
Franchised restaurants—occupancy expenses	**678.0**	613.9	570.1
Selling, general and administrative expenses	**1,458.5**	1,450.5	1,366.4
Made For You costs	**161.6**		
Special charges	**160.0**		72.0
Other operating (income) expense	**(60.2)**	(113.5)	(117.8)
Total operating costs and expenses	**9,659.5**	8,600.5	8,053.9
Operating income	**2,761.9**	2,808.3	2,632.6
Interest expense—net of capitalized interest of $17.9, $22.7 and $22.2	**413.8**	364.4	342.5
Nonoperating (income) expense	**40.7**	36.6	39.1
Income before provision for income taxes	**2,307.4**	2,407.3	2,251.0
Provision for income taxes	**757.3**	764.8	678.4
Net income	**$ 1,550.1**	$ 1,642.5	$ 1,572.6
Net income per common share	**$ 1.14**	$ 1.17	$ 1.11
Net income per common share—diluted	**1.10**	1.15	1.08
Dividends per common share	**$ .18**	$ .16	$ .15
Weighted-average shares	**1,365.3**	1,378.7	1,396.4
Weighted-average shares—diluted	**1,405.7**	1,410.2	1,433.3

Maintaining growth in revenues will require global strategies.

The accompanying Financial Comments are an integral part of the consolidated financial statements.

McDonald's 1998 Annual Report

How long can McDonald's continue to surpass its past performance, and how will its two types of revenue affect profits? Will it matter that 80 percent of its restaurants are franchises? As you study this chapter, you'll understand the effect of the timing of revenues and expenses and their impact on reported profits.

www.mcdonalds.com

Learning Objectives

After studying this chapter, you should be able to:

LO 1 Explain the significance of recognition and measurement in the preparation and use of financial statements. (p. 140)

LO 2 Explain the differences between the cash and accrual bases of accounting. (p. 142)

LO 3 Describe the revenue recognition principle and explain its application in various situations. (p. 146)

LO 4 Describe the matching principle and the various methods for recognizing expenses. (p. 148)

LO 5 Identify the four major types of adjusting entries and prepare them for a variety of situations. (p. 150)

LO 6 Explain the steps in the accounting cycle and the significance of each step. (p. 163)

LO 7 Explain why and how closing entries are made at the end of an accounting period. (p. 164)

LO 8 Understand how to use a work sheet as a basis for preparing financial statements (Appendix 4A). (p. 171)

Recognition and Measurement in Financial Statements

LO 1 Explain the significance of recognition and measurement in the preparation and use of financial statements.

Accounting is a communication process. To successfully communicate information to the users of financial statements, accountants and managers must answer two questions:

1. What economic events should be communicated, or *recognized,* in the statements?
2. How should the effects of these events be *measured* in the statements?

The dual concepts of recognition and measurement are crucial to the success of accounting as a form of communication.

Recognition

Recognition The process of recording an item in the financial statements as an asset, liability, revenue, expense, or the like.

"**Recognition** is the process of formally recording or incorporating an item into the financial statements of an entity as an asset, liability, revenue, expense, or the like. Recognition includes depiction of an item in both words and numbers, with the amount included in the totals of the financial statements."[1] We see in this definition the central idea behind general-purpose financial statements. They are a form of communication between the entity and external users. Stockholders, bankers, and other creditors have limited access to relevant information about a company. They depend on the periodic financial statements issued by management to provide the necessary information to make their decisions. Acting on behalf of management, accountants have a moral and ethical responsibility to provide users with financial information that will be useful in making their decisions. The process by which the accountant depicts, or describes, the effects of economic events on the entity is called *recognition.*

The items, such as assets, liabilities, revenues, and expenses, depicted in financial statements are *representations.* Simply stated, the accountant cannot show a stockholder or other user the company's assets, such as cash and buildings. What the user sees in a set of financial statements is a depiction of the real thing. That is, the accountant describes, with words and numbers, the various items in a set of financial statements. The system is imperfect at best and, for that reason, is always in the process of change. As society and the business environment have become more complex, the accounting profession has striven for ways to improve financial statements as a means of communicating with statement users.

[1] *Statement of Financial Accounting Concepts No. 5,* "Recognition and Measurement in Financial Statements of Business Enterprises" (Stamford, Conn.: Financial Accounting Standards Board, December 1984), par. 6.

MEASUREMENT

Accountants depict a financial statement item in both words and *numbers.* The accountant must *quantify* the effects of economic events on the entity. It is not enough to decide that an event is important and thus warrants recognition in the financial statements. To be able to recognize it, the statement preparer must measure the financial effects of the event on the company.

Measurement of an item in financial statements requires that two choices be made. First, the accountant must decide on the *attribute* to be measured. Second, a scale of measurement, or *unit of measure,* must be chosen.

The Attribute to Be Measured Assume that a company holds a parcel of real estate as an investment. What attribute—that is, *characteristic*—of the property should be used to measure and thus recognize it as an asset on the balance sheet? The cost of the asset at the time it is acquired is the most logical choice. *Cost* is the amount of cash, or its equivalent, paid to acquire the asset. But how do we report the property on a balance sheet a year from now?

- The simplest approach is to show the property on the balance sheet at its original cost, thus the designation **historical cost.** The use of historical cost is not only simple but also *verifiable.* Assume that two accountants are asked to independently measure the cost of the asset. After examining the sales contract for the land, they should arrive at the same amount.
- An alternative to historical cost as the attribute to be measured is **current value.** Current value is the amount of cash, or its equivalent, that could be received currently from the sale of the asset. For the company's piece of property, current value is the *estimated* selling price of the land, reduced by any commissions or other fees involved in making the sale. But the amount is only an estimate, not an actual amount. If the company has not yet sold the property, how can we know for certain its selling price? We have to compare it to similar properties that *have* sold recently.

HISTORICAL COST
The amount paid for an asset and used as a basis for recognizing it on the balance sheet and carrying it on later balance sheets.

CURRENT VALUE
The amount of cash, or its equivalent, that could be received by selling an asset currently.

The choice between current value and historical cost as the attribute to be measured is a good example of the trade-off between *relevance* and *reliability.* As indicated earlier, historical cost is verifiable and is thus to a large extent a reliable measure. But is it as relevant to the needs of the decision makers as current value? Put yourself in the position of a banker trying to decide whether to lend money to the company. In evaluating the company's assets as collateral for the loan, is it more relevant to your decision to know what the firm paid for a piece of land 20 years ago or what it could be sold for today? But what *could* the property be sold for today? Two accountants might not necessarily arrive at the same current value for the land. Whereas value or selling price may be more relevant to your decision on the loan, the reliability of this amount is often questionable.

Because of its objective nature, historical cost is the attribute used to measure many of the assets recognized on the balance sheet. However, certain other attributes, such as current value, have increased in popularity in recent years. In other chapters of the book, we will discuss some of the alternatives to historical cost.

The Unit of Measure Regardless of the attribute of an item to be measured, it is still necessary to choose a yardstick or unit of measure. The yardstick we currently use is units of money. *Money* is something accepted as a medium of exchange or as a means of payment. The unit of money in the United States is the dollar. In Japan the medium of exchange is the yen, and in Great Britain it is the pound.

The use of the dollar as a unit of measure for financial transactions is widely accepted. The *stability* of the dollar as a yardstick is subject to considerable debate, however. Consider an example. You are thinking about buying a certain parcel of land. As part of your decision process, you measure the dimensions of the property and determine that the lot is 80 feet wide and 120 feet deep. Thus, the unit of measure used to determine the lot's size is the square foot. The company that owns the land offers to sell it for $10,000. Although the offer sounds attractive, you decide against the purchase today.

You return in one year to take a second look at the lot. You measure the lot again and, not surprisingly, find the width to still be 80 feet and the depth 120 feet. The owner is still

What events have economic consequences to a business? The destructive effects of a warehouse fire, for example, will result in losses to buildings and other business assets. These losses will surely be reflected in the next year's financial statements of the affected companies—possibly in the income statement, as a downturn in revenues due to lost sales. What other financial statements would be affected by a big fire?

EXHIBIT 4-1 Recognition and Measurement in Financial Statements

ECONOMIC EVENTS	are	RECOGNIZED with	MEASURED with
Such as: **Purchase of supplies** **Sale of products** **Payment of wages** **Warehouse fire** **Many other events**	→	*Words:* Cash Land *Numbers:* $3 million $13,927	*Attribute:* Historical cost *Unit of Measure:* The dollar

willing to sell the lot for $10,000. This may appear to be the same price as last year. But the *purchasing power* of the unit of measure, the dollar, may very possibly have changed since last year. Even though the foot is a stable measuring unit, the dollar often is not. A *decline* in the purchasing power of the dollar is evidenced by a continuing *rise* in the general level of prices in an economy. For example, rather than paying $10,000 last year to buy the lot, you could have spent the $10,000 on other goods or services. However, a year later, the same $10,000 may very well not buy the same amount of goods and services.

Inflation, or a rise in the general level of prices in the economy, results in a decrease in purchasing power. In the past, the accounting profession has experimented with financial statements adjusted for the changing value of the dollar. As inflation has declined in recent years in the United States, the debate over the use of the dollar as a stable measuring unit has somewhat subsided.[2] It is still important to recognize the inherent weakness in the use of a measuring unit that is subject to change, however.

SUMMARY OF RECOGNITION AND MEASUREMENT IN FINANCIAL STATEMENTS

The purpose of financial statements is to communicate various types of economic information about a company. The job of the accountant is to decide which information should be recognized in the financial statements and how the effects of that information on the entity should be measured. Exhibit 4-1 summarizes the role of recognition and measurement in the preparation of financial statements.

THE ACCRUAL BASIS OF ACCOUNTING

LO 2 Explain the differences between the cash and accrual bases of accounting.

The accrual basis of accounting is the foundation for the measurement of income in our modern system of accounting. The best way to understand the accrual basis is to compare it with the simpler cash approach.

COMPARING THE CASH AND ACCRUAL BASES OF ACCOUNTING

The cash and accrual bases of accounting differ with respect to the *timing* of the recognition of revenues and expenses. For example, assume that on July 24, Barbara White, a salesperson for Spiffy House Painters, contracts with a homeowner to repaint a house for $1,000. A large

[2]The rate of inflation in some countries, most noticeably those in South America, has far exceeded the rate in the United States. Companies operating in some of these countries with hyperinflationary economies are required to make adjustments to their statements.

crew comes in and paints the house the next day, July 25. The customer has 30 days from the day of completion of the job to pay and does, in fact, pay Spiffy on August 25. *When* should Spiffy recognize the $1,000 as revenue? As soon as the contract is signed on July 24? Or on July 25, when the work is done? Or on August 25, when the customer pays the bill?

In an income statement prepared on the **cash basis,** revenues are recognized when cash is *received.* Thus, on a cash basis, the $1,000 would not be recognized as revenue until the cash is collected, on August 25. On an **accrual basis,** revenue is recognized when it is *earned.* On this basis, the $1,000 would be recognized as revenue on July 25, when the house is painted. This is the point at which the revenue is earned.

CASH BASIS
A system of accounting in which revenues are recognized when cash is received and expenses when cash is paid.

ACCRUAL BASIS
A system of accounting in which revenues are recognized when earned and expenses when incurred.

Recall from Chapter 3 the journal entry to recognize revenue before cash is received. Although cash has not yet been received, another account, Accounts Receivable, is recognized as an asset. This asset represents the right to receive cash in the future. The entry on completion of the job is as follows:

July 25	Accounts Receivable	1,000	
	Service Revenue		1,000
	To recognize revenue from house painting.		

Recall from Chapter 3 that the accounting equation must balance after each transaction is recorded. Throughout the remainder of the book, each time we record a journal entry, we illustrate the effect of the entry on the equation. The effect of the preceding entry on the equation is as follows:

Assets	=	Liabilities	+	Owners' Equity
+1,000				+1,000

At the time cash is collected, accounts receivable is reduced and cash is increased:

Aug. 25	Cash	1,000	
	Accounts Receivable		1,000
	To record cash received from house painting.		

Assets	=	Liabilities	+	Owners' Equity
+1,000				
−1,000				

Assume that Barbara White is paid a 10% commission for all contracts and is paid on the 15th of the month following the month a house is painted. Thus, for this job, she will receive a $100 commission check on August 15. When should Spiffy recognize her commission of $100 as an expense? On July 24, when White gets the homeowner to sign a contract? When the work is completed, on July 25? Or on August 15, when she receives the commission check? Again, on a cash basis, commission expense would be recognized on August 15, when cash is *paid* to the salesperson. But on an accrual basis, expenses are recognized when they are *incurred.* In our example, the commission expense is incurred when the house is painted, on July 25.

Exhibit 4-2 summarizes the essential differences between recognition of revenues and expenses on a cash basis and recognition on an accrual basis.

EXHIBIT 4-2 Comparing the Cash and Accrual Bases of Accounting

	Cash Basis	Accrual Basis
Revenue is recognized	**When Received**	**When Earned**
Expense is recognized	**When Paid**	**When Incurred**

www.mcdonalds.com

Business Strategy

McDonald's has experienced rapid and continuous growth. Its global sales (that is, sales revenues earned by the corporation as well as those earned by the franchise owners) reached $36 billion in 1998, the same year in which its stock delivered investors a total return of 62 percent and its share of the U.S. hamburger market reached its highest level of the decade. The company's vision is "to be the world's best quick service restaurant experience," and it works hard to make that vision a reality. The key is not just to offer food and service that meet customers' needs and corporate quality standards but also to dominate the market, both at home and abroad, through the sheer number of outlets.

Despite having typically opened 300 to 400 restaurants a year in the United States, McDonald's management now believes it could have opened even more in those early days when the competition in the fast-food business was not as strong. Perhaps some of today's Burger Kings or Wendy's could have been McDonald's stores that could have contributed to revenue and growth.

With the benefit of hindsight, McDonald's has applied its U.S. experience to its rapidly growing international business, which in 1998 consisted of more than 12,000 restaurants in 114 countries. CEO Jack Greenberg notes that 50,000 people tried to get into the new McDonald's in Belarus, and the line for the drive-through window when McDonald's opened in Kuwait was reported to be 7 miles long.

In spite of occasional resistance to U.S. brands in some parts of Europe, it appears that McDonald's strategy of expanding deep and fast will continue to bring in the profits its many shareholders have long enjoyed.

Source: McDonald's 1998 annual report.

What the Income Statement and the Statement of Cash Flows Reveal

Most business entities, other than the very smallest, use the accrual basis of accounting. Thus, the income statement reflects the accrual basis. Revenues are recognized when they are earned and expenses when they are incurred. At the same time, however, stockholders and creditors are also interested in information concerning the cash flows of an entity. The purpose of a statement of cash flows is to provide this information. Keep in mind that even though we present a statement of cash flows in a complete set of financial statements, the accrual basis is used for recording transactions and for preparing a balance sheet and an income statement.

Recall the example of Glengarry Health Club in Chapter 3. The club earned revenue from two sources, memberships and court fees. Both of these forms of revenue were recognized on the income statement presented in that chapter and are reproduced in the top portion of Exhibit 4-3. Recall, however, that members have 30 days to pay and that, at the end of the first month of operation, only $4,000 of the membership fees of $15,000 had been collected.

Now consider the statement of cash flows for the first month of operation, partially reproduced in the bottom portion of Exhibit 4-3. Because we want to compare the income statement to the statement of cash flows, only the Operating Activities section of the statement is shown. (The Investing and Financing Activities sections have been omitted from the statement.) Why is net income for the month a *positive* $7,000 but cash from operating activities a *negative* $4,000? Of the membership revenue of $15,000 reflected on the income statement, only $4,000 was collected in cash. Glengarry has accounts receivable for the other $11,000. Thus, cash from operating activities, as reflected on a statement of cash flows, is $11,000 *less* than net income of $7,000, or a negative $4,000.

Each of these two financial statements serves a useful purpose. The income statement reflects the revenues actually earned by the business, regardless of whether cash has been collected. The statement of cash flows tells the reader about the actual cash inflows during a period of time. The need for the information provided by both statements is summarized by the Financial Accounting Standards Board as follows:

EXHIBIT 4-3 Comparing the Income Statement and the Statement of Cash Flows

Membership revenue is $15,000 but only $4,000 was collected in cash. This $11,000 difference explains why net income is different from cash used by operating activities

Net income and cash used by operating activities differ by $11,000

The **income statement** for Glengarry Health Club shows the following:

Revenues:		
Memberships	$15,000	
Court fees	5,000	$ 20,000
Expenses:		
Salaries and wages	$10,000	
Utilities	3,000	(13,000)
Net income		$ 7,000

A **partial statement of cash flows** for Glengarry Health Club shows the following:

Cash received from membership fees	$ 4,000	
Cash received from court fees	5,000	$ 9,000
Cash paid for:		
Salaries and wages	$10,000	
Utilities	3,000	(13,000)
Cash used by operating activities		$ (4,000)

Statements of cash flows commonly show a great deal about an entity's current cash receipts and payments, but a cash flow statement provides an incomplete basis for assessing prospects for future cash flows because it cannot show interperiod relationships. Many current cash receipts, especially from operations, stem from activities of earlier periods, and many current cash payments are intended or expected to result in future, not current, cash receipts. Statements of earnings and comprehensive income, especially if used in conjunction with statements of financial position, usually provide a better basis for assessing future cash flow prospects of an entity than do cash flow statements alone.[3]

Accrual Accounting and Time Periods

The *time period* assumption was introduced in Chapter 1. We assume that it is possible to prepare an income statement that fairly reflects the earnings of a business for a specific period of time, such as a month or a year. It is somewhat artificial to divide the operations of a business into periods of time as indicated on a calendar. The conflict arises because earning income is a *process* that takes place *over a period of time* rather than *at any one point in time.*

Consider an alternative to our present system of reporting on the operations of a business on a periodic basis. A new business begins operations with an investment of $50,000. The business operates for 10 years, during which time no records are kept other than a checkbook for the cash on deposit at the bank. At the end of the 10 years, the owners decide to go their separate ways and convert all of their assets to cash. They split among them the balance of $80,000 in the bank account. What is the profit of the business for the 10-year period? The answer is $30,000, the difference between the original cash of $50,000 contributed and the cash of $80,000 available at liquidation.

The point of this simple example is that we could be very precise and accurate in our measurement of the income of a business if it were not necessary to artificially divide operations according to a calendar. Stockholders, bankers, and other interested parties cannot wait until a business liquidates to make decisions, however. They need information on a periodic basis. Thus, the justification for the accrual basis of accounting lies in the needs of financial statement users for periodic information on the financial position as well as the profitability of the entity.

[3] *SFAC No. 5,* par. 24c.

The Revenue Recognition Principle

LO 3 Describe the revenue recognition principle and explain its application in various situations.

Revenues Inflows of assets or settlements of liabilities from delivering or producing goods, rendering services, or conducting other activities.

Revenue recognition principle Revenues are recognized in the income statement when they are realized, or realizable, and earned.

"**Revenues** are inflows or other enhancements of assets of an entity or settlements of its liabilities (or a combination of both) from delivering or producing goods, rendering services, or other activities that constitute the entity's ongoing major or central operations."[4] Two points should be noted about this formal definition of revenues. First, an asset is not always involved when revenue is recognized. The recognition of revenue may result from the settlement of a liability rather than from the acquisition of an asset. Second, entities generate revenue in different ways: some companies produce goods, others distribute or deliver the goods to users, and still others provide some type of service.

On the accrual basis, revenues are recognized when earned. However, the **revenue recognition principle** involves two factors. Revenues are recognized in the income statement when they are both *realized* and *earned.*[5] Revenues are *realized* when goods or services are exchanged for cash or claims to cash.

Accounting for Your Decisions

You Are the Marketing Manager

The end of the year is fast approaching, and your department has not sold its quota of computers. As you understand the company's accounting policies, revenues are recorded when computers are ordered and shipped to customers. You know that if your department does not make its quota, then your job could be in jeopardy. So you get an idea. You call up some friends and tell them to order computers that they don't really need yet. In return, you'll get them a great price on the machines. Besides, if they don't want the computers, they can send them back in January and get a full refund. Meanwhile, you'll make your quota. Do you think there is anything wrong with this idea?

ANS: Yes, there is something wrong with the idea. For one thing, it is very poor business judgment to push products on customers if you believe they will be returned. Although many customers will say no to your idea, others will go along to get a lower price, only to later regret buying something they don't need. And if the computers are indeed returned in January, then the company's auditors will be obliged to indicate that the company has not followed generally accepted accounting principles, because the intent of the transaction was merely to boost sales in the current year. This shortcut is not only unethical but in violation of the revenue recognition principle.

Other Applications of the Revenue Recognition Principle

At what point are revenues realized and earned by an entity? As a practical rule, revenue is usually recognized at the time of sale. This is normally interpreted to mean at the time of delivery of the product or service to the customer. However, consider the following examples in which it is necessary either to modify or to interpret the meaning of the revenue recognition principle.

Percentage-of-completion method The method used by contractors to recognize revenue before the completion of a long-term contract.

Long-Term Contracts The **percentage-of-completion method** allows a contractor to recognize revenue over the life of a project rather than at its completion. For long-term contracts in which the sales price is fixed by contract and in which the realization of revenue depends only on production, such as constructing the bridge or the dam (in the box on page 147), the method is a reasonable alternative to deferring the recognition of revenue until the project is completed. The following excerpt from the 1998 annual

[4]*Statement of Financial Accounting Concepts No. 6,* "Elements of Financial Statements" (Stamford, Conn.: Financial Accounting Standards Board, December 1985), par. 78.

[5]An alternative is to recognize revenues when they are *realizable* and earned. *Realizable* has a slightly different meaning, which will be explained later when we look at commodities.

Accounting for Your Decisions

You Are the Stockholder

Assume that a construction company starts two projects during the year. One is a $5 million contract for a bridge. The other is a $4 million contract for a dam. Based on actual costs incurred to date and estimates of costs yet to be incurred, the contractor estimates that at the end of the year the bridge is 20% complete and the dam is 50% complete. Which would be more informative to you as a stockholder of the construction company: (1) an end-of-the-year report that indicates no revenue because no contracts are finished yet or (2) an end-of-the-year report that indicates revenue of $1 million on the bridge (20% of $5 million) and $2 million on the dam (50% of $4 million), both based on the extent of completion?

ANS: As a stockholder, you need information on a timely basis to evaluate your various investments. The percentage-of-completion method will allow you to assess the profitability of your investment in the construction company on a regular basis rather than only at the point when projects are completed.

report of Morrison Knudsen Corporation is an example of how revenue is recognized by most companies in the construction industry:

www.mk.com

> Revenue is generally recognized on a percentage-of-completion method. Completion is generally measured for engineering and construction costs based on the proportion of costs incurred to total estimated contract costs. For certain long-term contracts involving mining, environmental and hazardous substance remediation, completion is measured on estimated physical completion or units of production.

Franchises Over the last 30 years, franchising has achieved enormous popularity as a way to conduct business. It has been especially prevalent in retail sales, including the fast-food (McDonald's), motel (Holiday Inn), and car rental (Hertz) businesses. Typically, the franchisor grants the exclusive right to sell a product or service in a specific geographic area to the franchisee. As discussed in the chapter opener, a franchisor such as McDonald's generates revenues from one or both of two sources: (1) from the sale of the franchise and related services, such as help in selecting a site and hiring employees and (2) from continuing fees based on performance, for example, a fixed percentage of sales by the franchisee.

From Concept **to PRACTICE 4.1**

Reading McDonald's Income Statement Refer to McDonald's comparative income statements for 1998, 1997, and 1996 in the chapter opener. What percentage of total revenues was derived from franchised restaurants? Has this percentage changed over the three-year period?

At what point should the revenue from the sale of a franchise be recognized? An FASB standard allows a franchisor to recognize initial franchise fees as revenue only when it has made "substantial performance" of its obligations and when collection of the fee is reasonably assured.[6] An excerpt from the 1998 annual report of Ben & Jerry's Homemade Inc. indicates how one company recognizes the initial franchise fee as revenue:

www.benjerry.com

> *Revenue Recognition*
> The Company recognizes franchise fees as income for individual stores when services required by the franchise agreement have been substantially performed and the store opens for business. Franchise fees relating to area franchise agreements are recognized in proportion to the number of stores for which the required services have been substantially performed. Franchise fees recognized as income and included in net sales were approximately $708,000, $553,000, and $301,000 in 1998, 1997, and 1996, respectively.

Commodities Corn, wheat, gold, silver, and other agricultural and mining products trade on the open market at established prices. Readily convertible assets such as these are interchangeable and can be sold at a quoted price in an active market that can absorb the quantity being sold without significantly affecting the price.[7] Earlier we mentioned that to

[6] *Statement of Financial Accounting Standards No. 45,* "Accounting for Franchise Fee Revenue" (Stamford, Conn.: Financial Accounting Standards Board, December 1981), par. 5.

[7] *SFAC No. 5,* par. 83a.

be recognized, revenues must be realized. An acceptable alternative is to recognize revenues when they are realizable. Revenues are *realizable* when assets received or held are readily convertible to known amounts of cash or claims to cash.

Assume that a company mines gold. Revenues are realizable by the company at the time the product is mined because each ounce of gold is interchangeable with another ounce of gold and the commodities market can absorb all of the gold the company sells without having an effect on the price. This is one of the few instances in which it is considered acceptable to recognize revenue *prior* to the point of sale. The exception is justified because the important event in the revenue-generation process is the *production* of the gold, not the sale of it. The **production method** of recognizing revenue is used for precious metals, as well as certain agricultural products and marketable securities.

PRODUCTION METHOD The method in which revenue is recognized when a commodity is produced rather than when it is sold.

Installment Sales Various consumer items, such as automobiles, appliances, and even vacation properties, are sold on an installment basis. A down payment is followed by a series of monthly payments over a period of years. Default on the payments and repossession of the item by the seller are more common in these types of sales than with most other arrangements. For this reason, it is considered acceptable, in limited circumstances, to defer the recognition of revenue on an installment sale until cash is actually collected. The **installment method,** which is essentially a cash basis of accounting, is acceptable only when the seller has no reasonable basis for estimating the degree of collectibility. Note that the production and installment methods are at opposite ends of the spectrum. Under the production method, revenue is recognized *before* a sale takes place; with the installment method, revenue is recognized *after* the sale.

INSTALLMENT METHOD The method in which revenue is recognized at the time cash is collected.

Rent and Interest In some cases, revenue is earned *continuously* over time. In these cases, a product or service is not delivered at a specific point in time; instead, the earnings process takes place with the passage of time. Rent and interest are two examples. Interest is the cost associated with the use of someone else's money. When should a bank recognize the interest earned from granting a 90-day loan? Even though the interest may not be received until the loan itself is repaid, interest is earned every day the loan is outstanding. Later in the chapter, we will look at the process for recognizing interest earned but not yet received. The same procedure is used to recognize revenue from rent that is earned but uncollected.

Long-term contracts, franchises, commodities, installment sales, rent, and interest are not the only situations in which the revenue recognition principle must be interpreted. The intent in examining these particular examples was to help you think about the variety of ways in which businesses generate revenue and about the need to apply judgment in deciding when to recognize revenue. These examples should help you to realize the subjective nature of the work of an accountant and to understand that the discipline is not as precise as it may sometimes seem.

EXPENSE RECOGNITION AND THE MATCHING PRINCIPLE

LO 4 Describe the matching principle and the various methods for recognizing expenses.

Companies incur a variety of costs. A new office building is constructed. Inventory is purchased. Employees perform services. The electric meter is read. In each of these situations, the company incurs a cost, regardless of when it pays cash. Conceptually, *any time a cost is incurred, an asset is acquired.* However, according to the definition in Chapter 1, an asset represents a future economic benefit. An asset ceases being an asset and becomes an expense when the economic benefits from having incurred the cost have expired. Assets are unexpired costs, and expenses are expired costs.

At what point do costs expire and become expenses? The expense recognition principle requires that we recognize expenses in different ways, depending on the nature of the cost. The ideal approach to recognizing expenses is to match them with revenues. Under the **matching principle,** the accountant attempts to associate revenues of a period with the costs necessary to generate those revenues. For certain types of expenses, a direct form of matching is possible; for others, it is necessary to associate costs with a particular period.

MATCHING PRINCIPLE The association of revenue of a period with all of the costs necessary to generate that revenue.

The classic example of direct matching is cost of goods sold expense with sales revenue. Cost of goods sold is the cost of the inventory associated with a particular sale. A cost is incurred and an asset is recorded when the inventory is purchased. The asset, inventory, becomes an expense when it is sold. Another example of a cost that can be matched directly with revenue is commissions. The commission paid to a salesperson can be matched directly with the sale.

An indirect form of matching is used to recognize the benefits associated with certain types of costs, most noticeably long-term assets, such as buildings and equipment. These costs benefit many periods, but usually it is not possible to match them directly with a specific sale of a product. Instead, they are matched with the periods during which they will provide benefits. For example, an office building may be useful to a company for 30 years. *Depreciation* is the process of allocating the cost of a tangible long-term asset to its useful life. Depreciation Expense is the account used to recognize this type of expense.

The benefits associated with the incurrence of certain other costs are treated in accounting as expiring simultaneously with their acquisition. The justification for this treatment is that no future benefits from the incurrence of the cost are discernible. This is true of most selling and administrative costs. For example, the costs of heat and light in a building benefit only the current period and therefore are recognized as expenses as soon as the costs are incurred. Likewise, income taxes incurred during the period do not benefit any period other than the current period and are thus written off as an expense in the period incurred.

The relationships among costs, assets, and expenses are depicted in Exhibit 4-4 using three examples. First, costs incurred for purchases of merchandise result in an asset, Merchandise Inventory, and are eventually matched with revenue at the time the product is sold. Second, costs incurred for office space result in an asset, Office Building, which is recognized as Depreciation Expense over the useful life of the building. Third, the cost of heating and lighting benefits only the current period and is thus recognized immediately as Utilities Expense.

According to the FASB, **expenses** are "outflows or other using up of assets or incurrences of liabilities (or a combination of both) from delivering or producing goods,

EXPENSES
Outflows of assets or incurrences of liabilities resulting from delivering goods, rendering services, or carrying out other activities.

EXHIBIT 4-4 Relationships among Costs, Assets, and Expenses

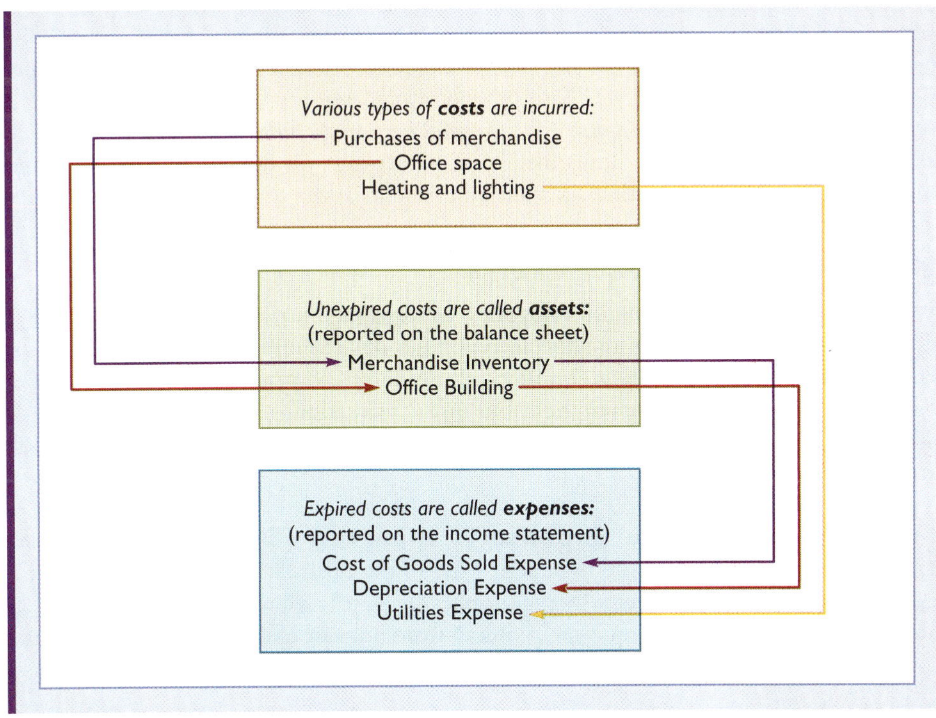

rendering services, or carrying out other activities that constitute the entity's ongoing major or central operations."[8] The key point to note about expenses is that they come about in two different ways: from the use of an asset or from the recognition of a liability. For example, when a retailer sells a product, the asset sacrificed is Inventory. Cost of Goods Sold is the expense account that is debited when the Inventory account is credited. As we will see in the next section, the incurrence of an expense may also result in a liability.

Two-Minute Review

1. Explain the difference between the attribute to be measured and the unit of measure.

2. Give at least three examples of situations in which revenues are recognized other than at the time of sale.

3. Explain the different ways in which expenses are matched with revenues.

Answers:

1. Accountants must decide whether to use historical cost or another attribute or characteristic of an asset, such as its current value, to measure it. Regardless of the attribute measured, it is necessary to choose a yardstick, or unit of measure. In this country, accountants use the dollar to measure assets and other financial statement items.

2. The percentage-of-completion method, the production method, and the installment method are all alternatives to recognizing revenue at the point of sale. Also, franchisors normally recognize revenue when they have made substantial performance of their obligations.

3. For certain costs, such as cost of goods sold, it is possible to directly match the expense with revenue generated. For other costs, such as depreciation, an indirect form of matching is necessary in which expenses are allocated to the periods benefited, rather than matched with specific revenues. Finally, the benefits associated with the incurrence of certain costs, such as utilities, expire immediately and therefore expense is recognized as soon as the cost is incurred.

Accrual Accounting and Adjusting Entries

LO 5 Identify the four major types of adjusting entries and prepare them for a variety of situations.

Adjusting entries
Journal entries made at the end of a period by a company using the accrual basis of accounting.

The accrual basis of accounting necessitates a number of adjusting entries at the end of a period. **Adjusting entries** are the journal entries the accountant makes at the end of a period for a company on the accrual basis of accounting. *Adjusting entries are not needed if a cash basis is used. It is the very nature of the accrual basis that results in the need for adjusting entries.* The frequency of the adjustment process depends on how often financial statements are prepared. Most businesses make adjustments at the end of each month.

Types of Adjusting Entries

Why are there four basic types, or categories, of adjusting entries? The answer lies in the distinction between the cash and the accrual bases of accounting. On an accrual basis, *revenue* can be earned either *before* or *after* cash is received. *Expenses* can be incurred either *before* or *after* cash is paid. Each of these four distinct situations requires a different type of adjustment at the end of the period. We will consider each of the four categories and look at some examples of each.

(1) Cash Paid before Expense Is Incurred (Deferred Expense)

Assets are often acquired before their actual use in the business. Insurance policies typically are prepaid, as often is rent. Office supplies are purchased in advance of their use, as are all types of property and equipment. Recall from our earlier discussion that unexpired

[8] *SFAC No. 6*, par. 80.

costs are assets. As the costs expire and the benefits are used up, the asset must be written off and replaced with an expense.

Assume that on September 1 a company prepays $2,400 in rent on its office space for the next 12 months. The entry to record the prepayment follows:

Sept. 1	Prepaid Rent	2,400	
	Cash		2,400
	To prepay the rent on office space for 12 months.		

Assets	=	Liabilities	+	Owners' Equity
+2,400				
−2,400				

An asset account, Prepaid Rent, is recorded because the company will receive benefits over the next 12 months. Because the rent is for a 12-month period, $200 of benefits from the asset expires at the end of each month. The adjusting entry at the end of September to record this expiration accomplishes two purposes: (1) it recognizes the reduction in the asset Prepaid Rent, and (2) it recognizes the expense associated with using up the benefits for one month. From the last chapter you should recall that an asset is decreased with a credit and that an expense is increased with a debit, as follows:

Sept. 30	Rent Expense	200	
	Prepaid Rent		200
	To recognize $200 of rent expense for the month.		

Assets	=	Liabilities	+	Owners' Equity
−200				−200

T accounts are an invaluable aid in understanding adjusting entries. They allow us to focus on the transactions and balances that will be included in the more formal general ledger accounts. The T accounts for Prepaid Rent and Rent Expense appear as follows after posting the original entry on September 1 and the adjusting entry on September 30:

PREPAID RENT

	Debit	Credit	
9/1	2,400		
		200	9/30
Bal.	2,200		

RENT EXPENSE

	Debit	Credit
9/30	200	

The balance in Prepaid Rent represents the unexpired benefits from the prepayment of rent for the remaining 11 months: $200 × 11 = $2,200. The Rent Expense account reflects the expiration of benefits during the month of September.

As discussed earlier in the chapter, depreciation is the process of allocating the cost of a long-term tangible asset over its estimated useful life. The accountant does not attempt to measure the decline in *value* of the asset but simply tries to allocate its cost over its useful life. Thus, the adjustment for depreciation is similar to the one we made for rent expense. Assume that on January 1 a company buys a delivery truck, for which it pays $21,000. The entry to record the purchase is as follows:

Jan. 1	Delivery Truck	21,000	
	Cash		21,000
	To record purchase of delivery truck for cash.		

Assets	=	Liabilities	+	Owners' Equity
+21,000				
−21,000				

Two estimates must be made in depreciating the delivery truck: (1) the useful life of the asset and (2) the salvage value of the truck at the end of its useful life. Estimated salvage value is the amount a company expects to be able to receive when it sells an asset at the end of its estimated useful life. Assume a five-year estimated life for the truck and an estimated salvage value of $3,000 at the end of that time. Thus, the *depreciable cost* of the truck is $21,000 − $3,000, or $18,000. In a later chapter, we will consider alternative

From Concept **TO PRACTICE 4.2**

READING BEN & JERRY'S BALANCE SHEET Refer to the balance sheet in Ben & Jerry's annual report. How does Ben & Jerry's classify prepaid expenses? What types of prepaid expenses would you expect the company to have?

Accounting for Your Decisions

You Are the Store Manager

You are responsible for managing a new running shoe store. The landlord requires a security deposit as well as prepayment of the first year's rent. The security deposit is refundable at the end of the first year. After the first year, rent is payable on a monthly basis. After three months in business, the owner asks you for an income statement. How should the security deposit and the prepayment of the first year's rent be recognized on this income statement?

ANS: The security deposit will not affect the income statement. It is an asset that will be converted to cash at the end of the first year, assuming that you are entitled to a full refund. One-fourth of the prepayment of the first year's rent should be recognized as an expense on the income statement for the first three months.

STRAIGHT-LINE METHOD The assignment of an equal amount of depreciation to each period.

CONTRA ACCOUNT An account with a balance that is opposite that of a related account.

methods for allocating the depreciable cost over the useful life of an asset. For now, we will use the simplest approach, called the **straight-line method,** which assigns an equal amount of depreciation to each period. The monthly depreciation is found by dividing the depreciable cost of $18,000 over the estimated useful life of 60 months, which equals $300 per month.

The adjustment to recognize depreciation is conceptually the same as the adjustment to write off Prepaid Rent. That is, the asset account is reduced, and an expense is recognized. However, accountants normally use a contra account to reduce the total amount of long-term tangible assets by the amount of depreciation. A **contra account** has a balance that is the opposite of the balance in its related account. For example, Accumulated Depreciation is used to record the decrease in a long-term asset for depreciation, and thus it carries a credit balance. An *increase* in Accumulated Depreciation is recorded with a *credit* because we want to *decrease* the amount of assets and assets are *decreased* by a *credit.* The entry to record depreciation at the end of January is as follows:

Jan. 31	Depreciation Expense	300	
	Accumulated Depreciation		300
	To record depreciation on delivery truck.		

Assets	=	Liabilities	+	Owners' Equity
−300				−300

Why do companies use a contra account for depreciation rather than simply reducing the long-term asset directly? If the asset account were reduced each time depreciation is recorded, its original cost would not be readily determinable from the accounting records. Businesses need to know the original cost of each asset, for various reasons. One of the most important of these reasons is the need to know historical cost for computation of depreciation for tax purposes.

The T accounts for Delivery Truck, Accumulated Depreciation, and Depreciation Expense show the following balances at the end of the first month:

DELIVERY TRUCK

Debit		Credit	
1/1	21,000		

ACCUMULATED DEPRECIATION

Debit		Credit	
		300	1/31

DEPRECIATION EXPENSE

Debit		Credit	
1/31	300		

Study Tip

Think of the Accumulated Depreciation account as simply an extension of the related asset account, in this case the truck. Therefore, although the truck account is not directly reduced for depreciation, a credit to its companion account, Accumulated Depreciation, has the effect of reducing the asset.

On a balance sheet prepared on January 31, the contra account is shown as a reduction in the carrying value of the truck:

Delivery Truck	$21,000	
Less: Accumulated Depreciation	300	$20,700

(2) Cash Received before Revenue Is Earned (Deferred Revenue)

You can benefit greatly in your study of accounting by recognizing its *symmetry.* By this we mean that one company's asset is another company's liability. In the earlier example involving the rental of office space, a second company, the landlord, received the cash paid by the first company, the tenant. At the time cash is received, the landlord has a liability because it has taken cash from the tenant but has not yet performed the service to earn the revenue. The revenue will be earned with the passage of time. This is the entry on the books of the landlord on September 1:

Sept. 1	Cash	2,400	
	Rent Collected in Advance		2,400
	To record receipt of rent on office space for 12 months.		

Assets	=	Liabilities	+	Owners' Equity
+2,400		+2,400		

The account Rent Collected in Advance is a liability. The landlord is obligated to provide the tenant uninterrupted use of the office facilities for the next 12 months. With the passage of time, the liability is satisfied as the tenant is provided the use of the space. The adjusting entry at the end of each month accomplishes two purposes: it recognizes (1) the reduction in the liability and (2) the revenue earned each month as the tenant occupies the space. Recall that we decrease a liability with a debit and increase revenue with a credit:

Sept. 30	Rent Collected in Advance	200	
	Rent Revenue		200
	To recognize rent earned for the month.		

Assets	=	Liabilities	+	Owners' Equity
		−200		+200

The balance in Rent Collected in Advance reflects the remaining liability, and the balance in the Rent Revenue account indicates the amount earned for the month:

RENT COLLECTED IN ADVANCE

		2,400	9/1
9/30	200		
		2,200	Bal.

RENT REVENUE

		200	9/30

In another example, many magazine subscriptions require the customer to pay in advance. For example, you pay $12 for a one-year subscription to your favorite magazine, and the publisher in turn sends you 12 monthly issues. At the time you send money to the publisher, it incurs a liability. It has taken your money but has not yet done anything to earn it. The publisher has an obligation either to provide you with the magazine over the next 12 months or to refund your $12.

A gift certificate like this is a good example of a deferred revenue. Amazon.com has received the $75 in payment for the certificate, but because it must wait for the recipient of the gift to pick out a book, it considers the obligation to deliver the book in the future a liability.

www.timewarner.com

At what point should the publisher recognize revenue from magazine sales? The publisher receives cash at the time the subscription is sold. The revenue has not been *earned* until the company publishes the magazine and mails it to you, however. Thus, a publisher usually recognizes revenue at the time of delivery. An excerpt from the 1998 annual report of Time Warner Inc. (the media conglomerate and publisher of such popular magazines as *Time, People,* and *Sports Illustrated*) reflects this policy:

> The unearned portion of paid magazine subscriptions is deferred until magazines are delivered to subscribers. Upon each delivery, a proportionate share of the gross subscription price is included in revenues.

Assume that on March 1 Time Warner sells 500 one-year subscriptions to a monthly magazine at a price of $12 each. The entry to record the receipt of cash from the 500 subscribers is as follows:

Mar. 1	Cash	6,000	
	Subscriptions Collected in Advance		6,000
	To record receipt of cash from sale of 500 one-year subscriptions at $12 each.		

Assets	=	Liabilities	+	Owners' Equity
+6,000		+6,000		

Assuming that each of the subscriptions starts with the March issue of the magazine, Time Warner accountants would make the following entry at the end of the month:

Mar. 31	Subscriptions Collected in Advance	500	
	Subscription Revenue		500
	To recognize subscriptions earned for the month.		

Assets	=	Liabilities	+	Owners' Equity
		−500		+500

The Subscriptions Collected in Advance and Subscription Revenue accounts appear as follows after posting the two entries:

SUBSCR. COLLECTED IN ADVANCE

		6,000	3/1
3/31	500		
		5,500	Bal.

SUBSCRIPTION REVENUE

		500	3/31

Accounting for Your Decisions

You Are the Banker

A new midwestern publisher comes to you for a loan. Through an aggressive ad campaign, the company sold a phenomenal number of subscriptions to a new sports magazine in its first six months and needs additional money to go national. The first issue of the magazine is due out next month. The publisher presents you an income statement for its first six months and you notice that it includes all of the revenue from the initial subscriptions sold in the Midwest. What concerns do you have?

ANS: First, the accounting treatment for the magazine revenue is improper. Because the magazine has not yet been delivered to the customer, the subscriptions have not yet been earned, and therefore no revenue should be recognized. As a banker, you should be sufficiently concerned that a potential customer would present improper financial statements, and you should deny the loan on that basis alone. That does not even take into account the fact that the company has yet to establish a sufficient track record to warrant the credit risk.

As you know by now, accounting terminology differs among companies. The account title Subscriptions Collected in Advance is only one of any number of possible titles for the liability related to subscriptions. For example, this same account on Time Warner's balance sheet is called Unearned Portion of Paid Subscriptions.

(3) Expense Incurred before Cash Is Paid (Accrued Liability) This situation is just the opposite of (1). That is, cash is paid *after* an expense is actually incurred rather than *before* its incurrence, as was the case in (1). Many normal operating costs, such as payroll and utilities, fit this situation. The utility bill is received at the end of the month, but the company has 10 days to pay it. Or consider the biweekly payroll for Jones Corporation. The company pays a total of $28,000 in wages on every other Friday. Assume that the last payday was Friday, May 31. The next two paydays will be Friday, June 14, and Friday, June 28. The journal entry will be the same on each of these paydays:

June 14	Wages Expense	28,000	
(and	Cash		28,000
June 28)	To pay the biweekly payroll.		

Assets	=	Liabilities	+	Owners' Equity
−28,000				−28,000

On a balance sheet prepared as of June 30, a liability must be recognized. Even though the next payment is not until July 12, Jones *owes* employees wages for the last two days of June and must recognize an expense for the wages earned by employees for these two days. We will assume that the company operates seven days a week and that the daily cost is 1/14th of the biweekly amount of $28,000, or $2,000. In addition to recognizing a liability on June 30, Jones must adjust the records to reflect an expense associated with the cost of wages for the last two days of the month:

June 30	Wages Expense	4,000	
	Wages Payable		4,000
	To record wages for last two days of the month.		

Assets	=	Liabilities	+	Owners' Equity
		+4,000		−4,000

What entry will be made on the next payday, July 12? Jones will need to eliminate the liability of $4,000 for the last two days of wages recorded on June 30 because the amount has now been paid. An additional $24,000 of expense has been incurred for the $2,000 cost per day associated with the first 12 days in July. Finally, cash is reduced for $28,000, which represents the biweekly payroll. The entry recorded is:

July 12	Wages Payable	4,000	
	Wages Expense	24,000	
	Cash		28,000
	To pay the biweekly payroll.		

Assets	=	Liabilities	+	Owners' Equity
−28,000		−4,000		−24,000

The following time line illustrates the amount of expense incurred in each of the two months, June and July, for the biweekly payroll:

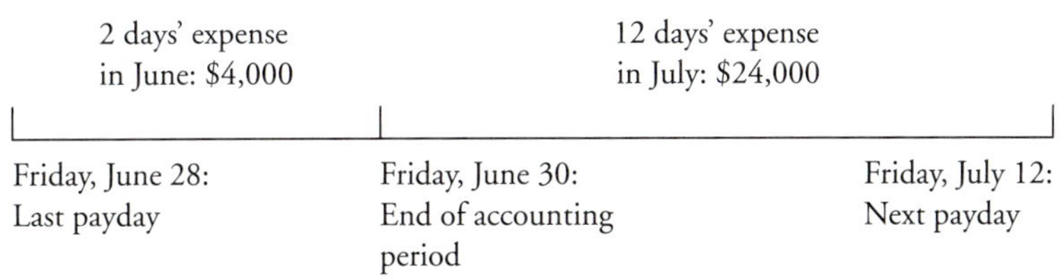

Another typical expense incurred before the payment of cash is interest. In many cases, the interest on a short-term loan is repaid with the amount of the loan, called the *principal,*

on the maturity date. For example, Granger Company takes out a 9%, 90-day, $20,000 loan with its bank on March 1. The principal and interest will be repaid on May 30. The entry on Granger's books on March 1 follows:

Mar. 1	Cash	20,000	
	Notes Payable		20,000
	To record issuance of 9%, 90-day, $20,000 note.		

Assets	=	Liabilities	+	Owners' Equity
+20,000		+20,000		

The basic formula for computing interest follows:

$$I = P \times R \times T,$$

where I = the dollar amount of interest

P = the principal amount of the loan

R = the annual rate of interest as a percentage

T = time in years (often stated as a fraction of a year).

The total interest on Granger's loan is as follows:

$$\$20{,}000 \times .09 \times 3/12 = \underline{\underline{\$450}}$$

Therefore, the amount of interest that must be recognized as expense at the end of March is one-third of $450 because one month of a total of three has passed. Alternatively, the formula for finding the total interest on the loan can be modified to compute the interest for one month:[9]

$$\$20{,}000 \times .09 \times 1/12 = \underline{\underline{\$150}}$$

The adjusting entry for the month of March is as follows:

Mar. 31	Interest Expense	150	
	Interest Payable		150
	To record interest for one month on a 9%, $20,000 loan.		

Assets	=	Liabilities	+	Owners' Equity
		+150		−150

The same adjusting entry is also made at the end of April:

Apr. 30	Interest Expense	150	
	Interest Payable		150
	To record interest for one month on a 9%, $20,000 loan.		

Assets	=	Liabilities	+	Owners' Equity
		+150		−150

The entry on Granger's books on May 30 when it repays the principal and interest is as follows:

May 30	Interest Payable	300	
	Interest Expense	150	
	Notes Payable	20,000	
	Cash		20,450
	To record payment of a 9%, 90-day, $20,000 loan with interest.		

Assets	=	Liabilities	+	Owners' Equity
−20,450		−20,300		−150

[9]In practice, interest is calculated on the basis of days rather than months. For example, the interest for March would be $20,000 × .09 × 30/365, or $147.95, to reflect 30 days in the month out of a total of 365 days in the year. The reason the number of days in March is 30 rather than 31 is because in computing interest, businesses normally count the day a note matures but not the day it is signed. To simplify the calculations, we will use months, even though the result is slightly inaccurate.

The reduction in Interest Payable eliminates the liability recorded at the end of March and April. The recognition of $150 in Interest Expense is the cost associated with the month of May.[10] The reduction in Cash represents the $20,000 of principal and the total interest of $450 for three months.

(4) Revenue Earned before Cash Is Received (Accrued Asset)

Revenue is sometimes earned before the receipt of cash. Rent and interest are both earned with the passage of time and require an adjustment if cash has not yet been received. For example, assume that Grand Management Company rents warehouse space to a number of tenants. Most of its contracts call for prepayment of rent for six months at a time. Its agreement with one tenant, however, allows the tenant to pay Grand $2,500 in monthly rent anytime within the first 10 days of the following month. The adjusting entry on Grand's books at the end of April, the first month of the agreement, is as follows:

Apr. 30	Rent Receivable	2,500	
	Rent Revenue		2,500
	To record rent earned for the month of April.		

Assets	=	Liabilities	+	Owners' Equity
+2,500				+2,500

When the tenant pays its rent on May 7, the effect on Grand's books is as follows:

May 7	Cash	2,500	
	Rent Receivable		2,500
	To record rent collected for the month of April.		

Assets	=	Liabilities	+	Owners' Equity
+2,500				
−2,500				

Although we used the example of rent to illustrate this category, the membership revenue of Glengarry Health Club in Chapter 3 also could be used as an example. Whenever a company records revenue before cash is received, some type of receivable is increased and revenue is also increased. In that chapter, the health club earned membership revenue even though members had until the following month to pay their dues.

Accruals and Deferrals

One of the challenges in learning accounting concepts is to gain an understanding of the terminology. Part of the difficulty stems from the alternative terms used by different accountants to mean the same thing. For example, the asset created when insurance is paid for in advance is termed a *prepaid asset* by some and a *prepaid expense* by others. Someone else might refer to it as a *deferred expense.*

We will use the term **deferral** to refer to a situation in which cash has been either paid or received but the expense or revenue has been deferred to a later time. A **deferred expense** indicates that cash has been paid but the recognition of expense has been deferred. Because a deferred expense represents a *future benefit* to a company, it is an *asset.* An alternative name for deferred expense is *prepaid expense.* Prepaid insurance and office supplies are deferred expenses. An adjusting entry is made periodically to record the portion of the deferred expense that has expired. A **deferred revenue** means that cash has been received but the recognition of any revenue has been deferred until a later time. Because a deferred revenue represents an *obligation* to a company, it is a *liability.* An alternative name for deferred revenue is *unearned revenue.* Rent collected in advance is deferred revenue. The periodic adjusting entry recognizes the portion of the deferred revenue that is earned in that period.

In this chapter, we have discussed in detail the accrual basis of accounting, which involves recognizing changes in resources and obligations as they occur, not simply when

[10] This assumes that Granger did not make a separate entry prior to this to recognize interest expense for the month of May. If a separate entry had been made, a debit of $450 would be made to Interest Payable.

From Concept TO PRACTICE 4.3

Reading Gateway's Balance Sheet Refer to the balance sheet in Gateway's annual report. How does Gateway classify accrued liabilities? By how much did they go up or down from 1997 to 1998? What types of accrued liabilities would you expect the company to have?

Study Tip

Now that we have seen examples of all four types of adjusting entries, think about a key difference between deferrals (the first two categories) and accruals (the last two categories). When we make adjusting entries involving deferrals, we must consider any existing balance in a deferred account. Conversely, there is no existing account when making an accrual.

Deferral
Cash has either been paid or received, but expense or revenue has not yet been recognized.

Deferred expense
An asset resulting from the payment of cash before the incurrence of expense.

Deferred revenue
A liability resulting from the receipt of cash before the recognition of revenue.

ACCRUAL
Cash has not yet been paid or received, but expense has been incurred or revenue earned.

ACCRUED LIABILITY
A liability resulting from the recognition of an expense before the payment of cash.

ACCRUED ASSET
An asset resulting from the recognition of a revenue before the receipt of cash.

cash changes hands. More specifically, we will use the term **accrual** to refer to a situation in which no cash has been paid or received yet but it is necessary to recognize, or accrue, an expense or a revenue. An **accrued liability** is recognized at the end of the period in cases in which an expense has been incurred but cash has not yet been paid. Wages payable and interest payable are examples of accrued liabilities. An **accrued asset** is recorded when revenue has been earned but cash has not yet been collected. Rent receivable is an accrued asset.

SUMMARY OF ADJUSTING ENTRIES

The four types of adjusting entries are summarized in Exhibit 4-5. Common examples of each are shown, along with the structure of the entries associated with the four categories. Finally, the following generalizations should help you in gaining a better understanding of adjusting entries and how they are used:

1. An adjusting entry is an internal transaction. It does not involve another entity.
2. Because it is an internal transaction, an adjusting entry *never* involves an increase or decrease in Cash.
3. At least one balance sheet account and one income statement account are involved in an adjusting entry. It is the nature of the adjustment process that an asset or liability account is adjusted with a corresponding change in either a revenue or an expense account.

Two-Minute Review

Assume a company wants to prepare financial statements at the end of its first month of operations. Each of the following transactions were recorded on the company's books on the first day of the month.

1. Purchased a 24-month insurance policy for $3,600.

2. Collected $4,800 from a tenant for office space that the tenant has rented for the next 12 months.

3. Took out a 6%, 180-day, $10,000 loan at the bank.

Prepare the necessary adjusting journal entries at the end of the month.

EXHIBIT 4-5 Accruals and Deferrals

Type	Situation	Examples	Entry during Period	Entry at End of Period
Deferred expense	Cash paid before expense is incurred	Insurance policy Supplies Rent Buildings, equipment	Asset Cash	Expense Asset
Deferred revenue	Cash received before revenue is earned	Deposits, rent Subscriptions Gift certificates	Cash Liability	Liability Revenue
Accrued liability	Expense incurred before cash is paid	Salaries, wages Interest Taxes Rent	No Entry	Expense Liability
Accrued asset	Revenue earned before cash is received	Interest Rent	No Entry	Asset Revenue

Answers:

1. Insurance Expense	*150*	
Prepaid Insurance		*150*
To recognize $150 of insurance expense for the month.		

Assets	=	*Liabilities*	+	*Owners' Equity*
−150				*−150*

2. Rent Collected in Advance	*400*	
Rent Revenue		*400*
To recognize $400 of rent earned for the month.		

Assets	=	*Liabilities*	+	*Owners' Equity*
		−400		*+400*

3. Interest Expense	*50*	
Interest Payable		*50*
To record interest for one month on a 6%, $10,000 loan.		

Assets	=	*Liabilities*	+	*Owners' Equity*
		+50		*−50*

Comprehensive Example of Adjusting Entries

We will now consider a comprehensive example involving the transactions for the first month of operations and the end-of-period adjusting entries for a hypothetical business, Duffy Transit Company. The trial balance in Exhibit 4-6 was prepared after posting to the accounts the transactions entered into during the first month of business. As discussed in Chapter 3, a trial balance can be prepared at any point in time. Because the trial balance is prepared *before* taking into account adjusting entries, it is called an *unadjusted* trial balance. This is the first month of operations for Duffy. Thus, the Retained Earnings account does not yet appear on the trial balance. After the first month, this account will have a balance and will appear on subsequent trial balances.

Exhibit 4-6 Unadjusted Trial Balance

DUFFY TRANSIT COMPANY
UNADJUSTED TRIAL BALANCE
JANUARY 31

	Debit	Credit
Cash	$ 50,000	
Prepaid Insurance	48,000	
Land	20,000	
Buildings—Garage	160,000	
Equipment—Buses	300,000	
Discount Tickets Sold in Advance		$ 25,000
Notes Payable		150,000
Capital Stock		400,000
Daily Ticket Revenue		30,000
Gas, Oil, and Maintenance Expense	12,000	
Wage and Salary Expense	10,000	
Dividends	5,000	
Totals	$605,000	$605,000

Duffy wants to prepare a balance sheet at the end of January and an income statement for its first month of operations. Use of the accrual basis necessitates a number of adjusting entries to update certain asset and liability accounts and to recognize the correct amounts for the various revenues and expenses.

Using a Trial Balance to Prepare Adjusting Entries

A trial balance is an important tool to use in preparing adjusting entries. The deferred expenses on Duffy's trial balance, such as Prepaid Insurance, must be reduced with a corresponding increase in expense. Similarly, any deferred revenues, such as Discount Tickets Sold in Advance, must be adjusted and a corresponding amount of revenue recognized. In addition, any accrued assets, such as Rent Receivable, and accrued liabilities, such as Interest Payable, which do not currently appear on the trial balance, must be recognized.

Adjusting Entries at the End of January

At the beginning of January, Duffy issued an 18-month, 12%, $150,000 promissory note for cash. Although interest will not be repaid until the loan's maturity date, Duffy must accrue interest for the first month. The calculation of interest for one month is $150,000 × .12 × 1/12. The adjusting entry is as follows:

(a)	Interest Expense	1,500	
	Interest Payable		1,500
	To record interest for one month on 12%, $150,000 promissory note.		

Assets	=	Liabilities	+	Owners' Equity
		+1,500		−1,500

The wages and salaries on the trial balance were paid in cash. At the end of the month, Duffy owes employees an additional $2,800 in salaries and wages:

(b)	Wage and Salary Expense	2,800	
	Wages and Salaries Payable		2,800
	To record wages and salaries owed.		

Assets	=	Liabilities	+	Owners' Equity
		+2,800		−2,800

At the beginning of January, Duffy acquired a garage to house the buses at a cost of $160,000. Land is not subject to depreciation. The cost of the land acquired in connection with the purchase of the building will remain on the books until the property is sold. The garage has an estimated useful life of 20 years and an estimated salvage value of $16,000 at the end of its life. The monthly depreciation is found by dividing the depreciable cost of $144,000 by the useful life of 240 months:

$$\frac{\$160{,}000 - \$16{,}000}{20 \text{ years} \times 12 \text{ months}} = \frac{\$144{,}000}{240 \text{ months}} = \underline{\underline{\$600}} \text{ per month}$$

The entry to record the depreciation on the garage for January for a full month is as follows:

(c)	Depreciation Expense—Garage	600	
	Accumulated Depreciation—Garage		600
	To record depreciation for the month.		

Assets	=	Liabilities	+	Owners' Equity
−600				−600

Duffy purchased 10 buses for $30,000 each at the beginning of January. The buses have an estimated useful life of five years, at which time the company plans to sell them for $6,000 each. The monthly depreciation on the 10 buses is

$$10 \times \frac{\$30{,}000 - \$6{,}000}{5 \text{ years} \times 12 \text{ months}} = 10 \times \frac{\$24{,}000}{60 \text{ months}} = \underline{\underline{\$4{,}000}} \text{ per month.}$$

The entry to recognize the depreciation on the buses for the first month is as follows:

(d) Depreciation Expense—Buses	4,000	
Accumulated Depreciation—Buses		4,000
To record depreciation for the month.		

Assets	=	Liabilities	+	Owners' Equity
−4,000				−4,000

Prepaid Insurance on the trial balance represents an insurance policy purchased for $48,000 on January 1. The policy provides property and liability protection for a 24-month period. The adjusting entry to allocate the cost to expense for the first month is as follows:

(e) Insurance Expense	2,000	
Prepaid Insurance		2,000
To record expiration of insurance benefits.		

Assets	=	Liabilities	+	Owners' Equity
−2,000				−2,000

In addition to selling tickets on the bus, Duffy sells discount tickets at the terminal. The tickets are good for a ride anytime within 12 months of purchase. Thus, as these tickets are sold, Duffy debits Cash and credits a liability account, Discount Tickets Sold in Advance. The sale of $25,000 worth of these tickets was recorded during January and is thus reflected on the trial balance. At the end of the first month, Duffy counts the number of tickets that have been redeemed. Because $20,400 worth of tickets has been turned in, this is the amount by which the company reduces its liability and recognizes revenue for the month:

(f) Discount Tickets Sold in Advance	20,400	
Discount Ticket Revenue		20,400
To record redemption of discount tickets.		

Assets	=	Liabilities	+	Owners' Equity
		−20,400		+20,400

Duffy does not need all of the space in its garage and rents a section of it to another company for $2,500 per month. The tenant has until the 10th day of the following month to pay its rent. The adjusting entry on Duffy's books on the last day of the month is as follows:

(g) Rent Receivable	2,500	
Rent Revenue		2,500
To record rent earned but not yet received.		

Assets	=	Liabilities	+	Owners' Equity
+2,500				+2,500

Corporations pay estimated taxes on a quarterly basis. Because Duffy is preparing an income statement for the month of January, it must estimate its taxes for the month. We will assume a corporate tax rate of 34% on income before tax. The computation of Income Tax Expense is as follows (the amounts shown for the revenues and expenses reflect the effect of the adjusting entries):

Revenues:		
Daily Ticket Revenue	$30,000	
Discount Ticket Revenue	20,400	
Rent Revenue	2,500	$52,900
Expenses:		
Gas, Oil, and Maintenance Expense	$12,000	
Wage and Salary Expense	12,800	
Depreciation Expense	4,600	

Insurance Expense	$ 2,000	
Interest Expense	1,500	$32,900
Net Income before Tax		$20,000
Times the Corporate Tax Rate		× .34
Income Tax Expense		$ 6,800

Based on this estimate of taxes, the final adjusting entry recorded on Duffy's books for the month is

(h) Income Tax Expense	6,800	
Income Tax Payable		6,800
To record estimated income taxes for the month.		

Assets	=	Liabilities	+	Owners' Equity
		+6,800		−6,800

An *adjusted* trial balance, shown in Exhibit 4-7, indicates the equality of debits and credits after the adjusting entries have been recorded. Note the addition of a number of new accounts that did not appear on the unadjusted trial balance in Exhibit 4-6. The new trial balance includes the accounts that were added when adjusting entries were recorded.

EXHIBIT 4-7 Adjusted Trial Balance

DUFFY TRANSIT COMPANY
UNADJUSTED TRIAL BALANCE
JANUARY 31

	Debit	Credit
Cash	$ 50,000	
Prepaid Insurance	46,000	
Land	20,000	
Buildings—Garage	160,000	
Accumulated Depreciation—Garage		$ 600
Equipment—Buses	300,000	
Accumulated Depreciation—Buses		4,000
Gas, Oil, and Maintenance Expense	12,000	
Wage and Salary Expense	12,800	
Dividends	5,000	
Discount Tickets Sold in Advance		4,600
Notes Payable		150,000
Capital Stock		400,000
Daily Ticket Revenue		30,000
Rent Receivable	2,500	
Interest Expense	1,500	
Income Tax Expense	6,800	
Depreciation Expense—Garage	600	
Depreciation Expense—Buses	4,000	
Insurance Expense	2,000	
Interest Payable		1,500
Wages and Salaries Payable		2,800
Income Tax Payable		6,800
Discount Ticket Revenue		20,400
Rent Revenue		2,500
Totals	$623,200	$623,200

Ethical Considerations for a Company on the Accrual Basis

As you have seen, the accrual basis requires the recognition of revenues when earned and expenses when incurred, regardless of when cash is received or paid. It was also noted earlier that adjusting entries are *internal* transactions in that they do not involve an exchange with an outside entity. Because adjustments do not involve another company, accountants may at times feel pressure from others within the organization to either speed or delay the recognition of certain adjustments.

Consider the following two examples for a construction company that is concerned about its "bottom line," that is, its net income. A number of jobs are in progress, but because of inclement weather, none of them are very far along. Management asks the accountant to recognize 50% of the revenue from a job in progress even though by the most liberal estimates it is only 25% complete. Further, the accountant has been asked to delay the recognition of various short-term accrued liabilities (and, of course, the accompanying expenses) until the beginning of the new year.

The "correct" response of the accountant to each of these requests may seem obvious: only 25% of the revenue on the one job should be recognized, and all accrued liabilities should be expensed at year-end. The pressures of the daily work environment make these decisions difficult for the accountant, however. The accountant must always remember that his or her primary responsibility in preparing financial statements is to accurately portray the affairs of the company to the various outside users. Bankers, stockholders, and others rely on the accountant to serve their best interests.

The Accounting Cycle

LO 6 Explain the steps in the accounting cycle and the significance of each step.

We have focused our attention in this chapter on accrual accounting and the adjusting entries it necessitates. Adjusting entries are one key component in the **accounting cycle.** The accountant for a business follows a series of steps each period. The objective is always the same: *collect the necessary information to prepare a set of financial statements.* Together, these steps make up the accounting cycle. The name comes from the fact that the steps are repeated each period.

ACCOUNTING CYCLE
A series of steps performed each period and culminating with the preparation of a set of financial statements.

The steps in the accounting cycle are shown in Exhibit 4-8. Note that step 1 involves not only *collecting* information but also *analyzing* it. Transaction analysis is probably the most challenging of all the steps in the accounting cycle. It requires the ability to think logically about an event and its effect on the financial position of the entity. Once the transaction is analyzed, it is recorded in the journal, as indicated by the second step in the exhibit. The first two steps in the cycle take place continuously.

Journal entries are posted to the accounts on a periodic basis. The frequency of posting to the accounts depends on two factors: the type of accounting system used by a company and the volume of transactions. In a manual system, entries might be posted daily, weekly, or even monthly, depending on the amount of activity. The larger the number of transactions a company records, the more often it posts. In an automated accounting system, posting is likely done automatically by the computer each time a transaction is recorded.

The Use of a Work Sheet

Step 4 in Exhibit 4-8 calls for the preparation of a work sheet. The end of an accounting period is a busy time. In addition to recording daily recurring transactions, the accountant must record adjusting entries as the basis for preparing financial statements. The time available to prepare the statements is usually very limited. The use of a **work sheet** allows the accountant to gather and organize the information required to adjust the accounts without actually recording and posting the adjusting entries to the accounts. Actually recording adjusting entries and posting them to the accounts can be done after the financial statements are prepared. *A work sheet itself is not a financial statement.*

WORK SHEET
A device used at the end of the period to gather the information needed to prepare financial statements without actually recording and posting adjusting entries.

EXHIBIT 4-8 Steps in the Accounting Cycle

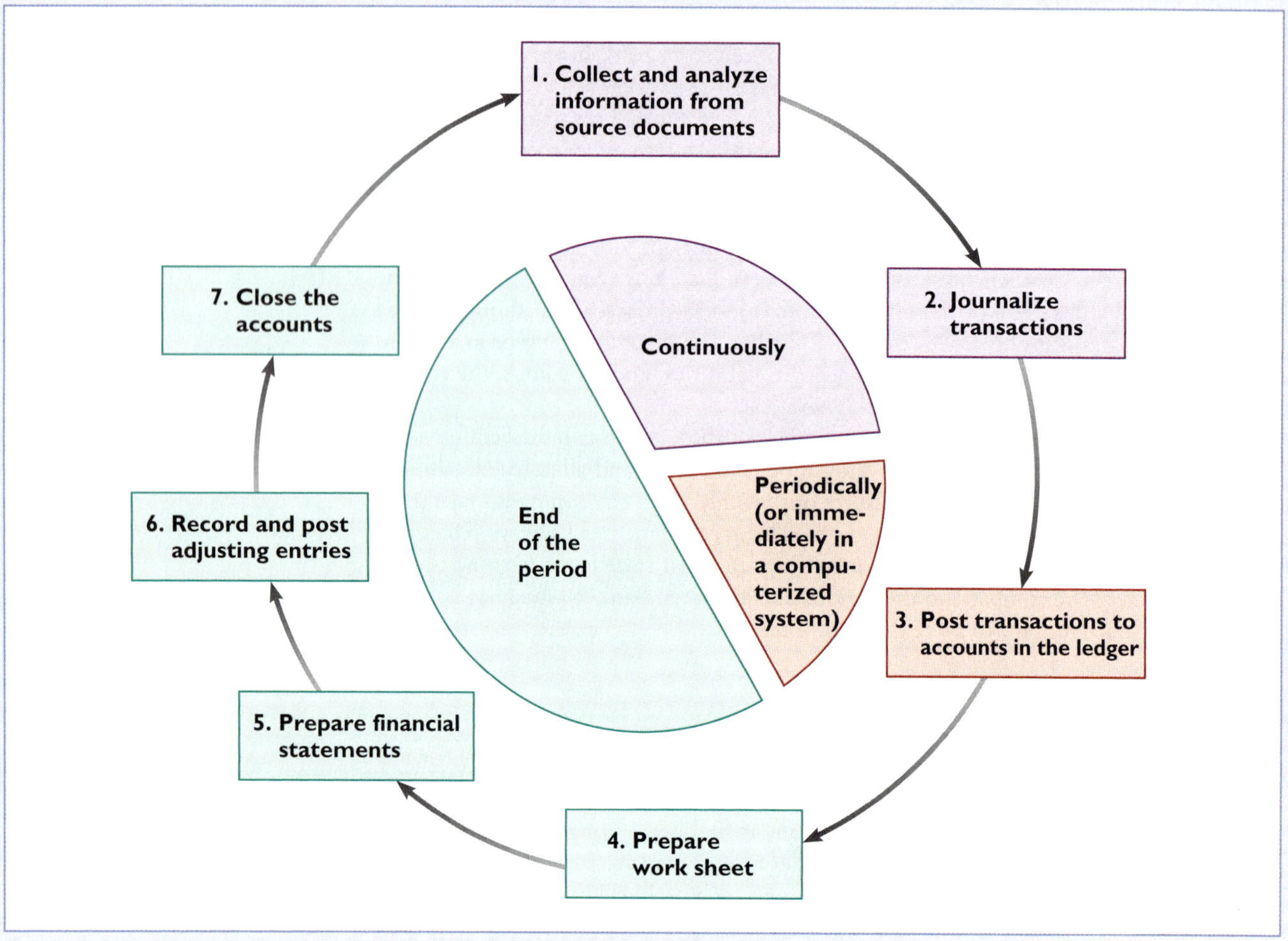

Instead, it is a useful device to *organize* the information needed to prepare the financial statements at the end of the period.

It is not essential that a work sheet be used before preparing financial statements. If it is not used, step 6, recording and posting adjusting entries, comes before step 5, preparing the financial statements. Appendix 4A illustrates how a work sheet is used to facilitate the preparation of financial statements.

THE CLOSING PROCESS

LO 7 Explain why and how closing entries are made at the end of an accounting period.

REAL ACCOUNTS The name given to balance sheet accounts because they are permanent and are not closed at the end of the period.

Two types of accounts appear on an adjusted trial balance. Balance sheet accounts are called **real accounts** because they are permanent in nature. For this reason, they are never closed. The balance in each of these accounts is carried over from one period to the next. In contrast, revenue, expense, and dividend accounts are *temporary* or **nominal accounts.** The balances in the income statement accounts and the Dividends account are *not* carried forward from one accounting period to the next. For this reason, these accounts are closed at the end of the period.

Closing entries serve two important purposes: (1) to return the balances in all temporary or nominal accounts to zero to start the next accounting period and (2) to transfer the net income (or net loss) and the dividends of the period to the Retained Earnings account.

An account with a debit balance is closed by crediting the account for the amount of the balance. An account with a credit balance is closed by debiting the account for the amount of the balance. Thus, revenue accounts are debited in the closing process. Expense accounts are credited to close them. In this way, the balance of each income statement account is restored to zero to start the next accounting period.

Various approaches are used to accomplish the same two purposes: restore the temporary accounts to zero and update the Retained Earnings account. We will use a holding account called Income Summary to facilitate the closing process. A single entry is made to close all of the revenue accounts. The total amount debited to the revenue accounts is credited to Income Summary. Similarly, a single entry is made to close all of the expense accounts, and the offsetting debit is made to Income Summary. This account acts as a temporary storage account. After closing the revenue and expense accounts, Income Summary has a *credit* balance *if revenues exceed expenses.* Finally, the credit balance in Income Summary is itself closed by debiting the account and crediting Retained Earnings for the same amount. The net result of the process is that all of the revenues less expenses, that is, net income, have been transferred to Retained Earnings.

The Dividends account is closed directly to Retained Earnings. Because dividends are *not* an expense, the Dividends account is not closed first to the Income Summary account, as are expense accounts. A credit is made to close the Dividends account with an offsetting debit to Retained Earnings.

NOMINAL ACCOUNTS
The name given to revenue, expense, and dividend accounts because they are temporary and are closed at the end of the period.

CLOSING ENTRIES
Journal entries made at the end of the period to return the balance in all nominal accounts to zero and transfer the net income or loss and the dividends to Retained Earnings.

The closing process for Duffy Transit Company is illustrated with the use of T accounts in Exhibit 4-9. Rather than show each individual revenue and expense account, a single revenue account and a single expense account are used in the exhibit to illustrate the flow in the closing process.

The first closing entry results in a zero balance in each of the three revenue accounts, and the total of the three amounts, $52,900, which represents all of the revenue of the period, is transferred to the Income Summary account. The second entry closes each of the seven expense accounts and transfers the total expenses of $39,700 as a debit to the Income Summary account. At this point, the Income Summary account has a credit balance of $13,200, which represents the net income of the period. The third entry closes this temporary holding account and transfers the net income to the Retained Earnings account. Finally, the fourth entry closes the Dividends account and transfers the $5,000 to the debit side of the Retained Earnings account. The Retained Earnings account is now updated to its correct ending balance of $8,200.

EXHIBIT 4-9 The Closing Process

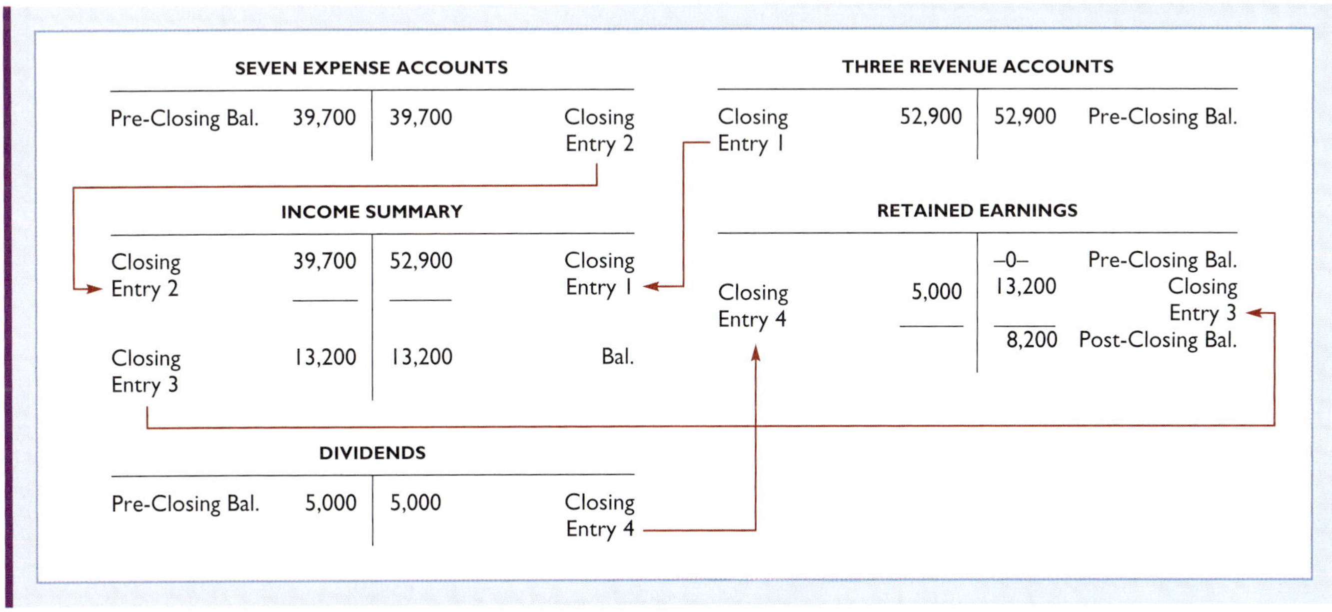

The four closing entries in journal form are shown in Exhibit 4-10. Note that each individual revenue and expense account is closed. Keep in mind that the Post. Ref. column will be filled in with the appropriate account numbers when the entries are posted to the ledger accounts.

INTERIM FINANCIAL STATEMENTS

INTERIM STATEMENTS
Financial statements prepared monthly, quarterly, or at other intervals less than a year in duration.

We mentioned earlier in this chapter that certain steps in the accounting cycle are sometimes carried out only once a year rather than each month as in our example. For ease of illustration, we assumed a monthly accounting cycle. Many companies adjust and close the accounts only once a year, however. They use a work sheet more frequently than this as the basis for preparing interim statements. Statements prepared monthly, quarterly, or at other intervals less than a year in duration are called **interim statements.** Many companies prepare monthly financial statements for their own internal use. Similarly, corporations whose shares are publicly traded on one of the stock exchanges are required to file quarterly financial statements with the Securities and Exchange Commission.

Suppose that a company prepares monthly financial statements for internal use and completes the accounting cycle in its entirety only once a year. In this case, a work sheet is prepared each month as the basis for interim financial statements. Formal adjusting and closing entries are prepared only at the end of each year. The adjusting entries that appear on the monthly work sheet are not posted to the accounts. They are entered on the work sheet simply as a basis for preparing the monthly financial statements.

EXHIBIT 4-10 Closing Entries Recorded in the Journal

DATE		ACCOUNT TITLES AND EXPLANATION	POST. REF.	DEBIT	CREDIT
Jan.	31	Daily Ticket Revenue		30,000	
		Discount Ticket Revenue		20,400	
		Rent Revenue		2,500	
		Income Summary			52,900
		To close revenue accounts to Income Summary.			
	31	Income Summary		39,700	
		Gas, Oil, and Maintenance Expense			12,000
		Wage and Salary Expense			12,800
		Interest Expense			1,500
		Depreciation Expense—Garage			600
		Depreciation Expense—Buses			4,000
		Insurance Expense			2,000
		Income Tax Expense			6,800
		To close expense accounts to Income Summary.			
	31	Income Summary		13,200	
		Retained Earnings			13,200
		To close Income Summary to Retained Earnings.			
	31	Retained Earnings		5,000	
		Dividends			5,000
		To close Dividends account to Retained Earnings.			

Focus on Users

Name: Michael Clarke
Education: B.A., Manchester University, UK
College Majors: Economics; Social Studies
Occupation: Business Analysis Manager, The Coca-Cola Company, Atlanta
Age: 44

This Manager Analyzes His Company's Financial Statements to Support Strategic Decisions

The relationship between revenue and expenses is fundamental to the analysis of any company's performance. For Michael Clarke, Business Analysis Manager for Coca-Cola in Atlanta, the balance between the two is an important measure of Coke's profitability, which is tracked by paying close attention to what happens on the income statement throughout the year. As Michael explains: "We break down the income statements for different pieces of the business so that we can analyze which areas are contributing to operating income and which are generating losses or below target income. Based on these analyses, we can make decisions about product pricing, investment opportunities, and cost controls."

Not surprisingly, Michael also relies on the matching principle to make judgments about the economic efficiency of each of Coke's expenditures. "Tracking which expenses are associated with which revenues for our different products or promotions allows us to measure their relative success and profitability." For example, Coke decides whether to continue or cease a promotion program depending on the income it brings in. "We identify our various costs of research, development, and execution for the specific program and match those against the incremental revenues generated during the promotional period. Using this information and depending on the results, we might decide to execute similar promotions on a more widespread or national basis." This kind of comparative analysis allows Michael and his colleagues at Coke to "focus on the good stuff" and continue to create value for their customers.

Warmup Exercises

LO 5 Warmup Exercise 4-1 Prepaid Insurance

ABC Corp. purchases a 24-month fire insurance policy on January 1, 2001, for $5,400.

Required

Prepare the necessary adjusting journal entry on January 31, 2001.

Key to the Solution

Determine what proportion and therefore what dollar amount of the policy has expired after one month.

LO 5 Warmup Exercise 4-2 Depreciation

DEF Corp. purchased a new car for one of its salespeople on March 1, 2001, for $25,000. The estimated useful life of the car is four years with an estimated salvage value of $1,000.

Required

Prepare the necessary adjusting journal entry on March 31, 2001.

Key to the Solution

Determine what dollar amount of the cost of the car should be depreciated and then how much should be depreciated each month.

LO 5 Warmup Exercise 4-3 Interest on a Note

On April 1, 2001, GHI Corp. took out a 12%, 120-day, $10,000 loan at its bank.

Required

Prepare the necessary adjusting journal entry on April 30, 2001.

Key to the Solution

Determine the monthly interest cost on a loan that accrues interest at the rate of 12% per year.

Solutions to Warmup Exercises

Warmup Exercise 4-1

Jan. 31	Insurance Expense	225	
	Prepaid Insurance		225
	To recognize $225 of insurance expense for the month.		

Assets	=	Liabilities	+	Owners' Equity
−225				−225

Warmup Exercise 4-2

Mar. 31	Depreciation Expense	500	
	Accumulated Depreciation		500
	To recognize depreciation on car.		

Assets	=	Liabilities	+	Owners' Equity
−500				−500

Warmup Exercise 4-3

April 30	Interest Expense	100	
	Interest Payable		100
	To record interest for one month on a 12%, $10,000 loan.		

Assets	=	Liabilities	+	Owners' Equity
−100				−100

Review Problem

The trial balance of Northern Airlines at January 31 is shown below. It was prepared after posting the recurring transactions for the month of January, but it does not reflect any month-end adjustments.

NORTHERN AIRLINES
UNADJUSTED TRIAL BALANCE
JANUARY 31

Cash	$ 75,000	
Parts Inventory	45,000	
Land	80,000	
Buildings—Hangars	250,000	
Accumulated Depreciation—Hangars		$ 24,000
Equipment—Aircraft	650,000	
Accumulated Depreciation—Aircraft		120,000
Tickets Sold in Advance		85,000
Capital Stock		500,000
Retained Earnings		368,000
Ticket Revenue		52,000
Maintenance Expense	19,000	
Wage and Salary Expense	30,000	
Totals	$1,149,000	$1,149,000

The following additional information is available:

a. Airplane parts needed for repairs and maintenance are purchased regularly, and the amounts paid are added to the asset account Parts Inventory. At the end of each month, the inventory is counted. At the end of January, the amount of parts on hand is $36,100. *Hint:* What adjusting entry is needed to reduce the asset account to its proper carrying value? Any expense involved should be included in Maintenance Expense.

b. The estimated useful life of the hangar is 20 years with an estimated salvage value of $10,000 at the end of its life. The original cost of the hangar was $250,000.

c. The estimated useful life of the aircraft is 10 years with an estimated salvage value of $50,000. The original cost of the aircraft was $650,000.

d. As tickets are sold in advance, the amounts are added to Cash and to the liability account Tickets Sold in Advance. A count of the redeemed tickets reveals that $47,000 worth of tickets were used during January.

e. Wages and salaries owed to employees, but unpaid, at the end of January total $7,600.

f. Northern rents excess hangar space to other companies. The amount owed to Northern but unpaid at the end of January is $2,500.

g. Assume a corporate income tax rate of 34%.

Required

1. Set up T accounts for each of the accounts listed on the trial balance. Set up any other T accounts that will be needed to prepare adjusting entries.
2. Post the month-end adjusting entries directly to the T accounts; do not take the time to put the entries in journal format first. Use the letters **(a)** through **(g)** from the additional information to identify each entry.
3. Prepare a trial balance to prove the equality of debits and credits after posting the adjusting entries.

SOLUTION TO REVIEW PROBLEM

1. and **2.**:

CASH

Bal.	75,000		

PARTS INVENTORY

Bal.	45,000		
		8,900	(a)
Bal.	36,100		

LAND

Bal.	80,000		

TICKETS SOLD IN ADVANCE

		85,000	Bal.
(d)	47,000		
		38,000	Bal.

BUILDINGS—HANGARS

Bal.	250,000		

EQUIPMENT—AIRCRAFT

Bal.	650,000		

ACCUMULATED DEPRECIATION—HANGARS

		24,000	Bal.
		1,000	(b)
		25,000	Bal.

ACCUMULATED DEPRECIATION—AIRCRAFT

		120,000	Bal.
		5,000	(c)
		125,000	Bal.

CAPITAL STOCK

		500,000	Bal.

RETAINED EARNINGS

		368,000	Bal.

MAINTENANCE EXPENSE		
Bal.	19,000	
(a)	8,900	
Bal.	27,900	

TICKET REVENUE		
	52,000	Bal.
	47,000	(d)
	99,000	Bal.

WAGE AND SALARY EXPENSE		
Bal.	30,000	
(e)	7,600	
Bal.	37,600	

WAGES AND SALARIES PAYABLE		
	7,600	(e)

RENT RECEIVABLE		
(f)	2,500	

RENT REVENUE		
	2,500	(f)

INCOME TAX EXPENSE		
(g)	10,200	

INCOME TAXES PAYABLE		
	10,200	(g)

DEPRECIATION EXPENSE—HANGARS		
(b)	1,000	

DEPRECIATION EXPENSE—AIRCRAFT		
(c)	5,000	

3.

NORTHERN AIRLINES
ADJUSTED TRIAL BALANCE
JANUARY 31

Cash	$ 75,000	
Parts Inventory	36,100	
Land	80,000	
Buildings—Hangars	250,000	
Accumulated Depreciation—Hangars		$ 25,000
Equipment—Aircraft	650,000	
Accumulated Depreciation—Aircraft		125,000
Tickets Sold in Advance		38,000
Capital Stock		500,000
Retained Earnings		368,000
Ticket Revenue		99,000
Maintenance Expense	27,900	
Wage and Salary Expense	37,600	
Depreciation Expense—Hangars	1,000	
Depreciation Expense—Aircraft	5,000	
Rent Receivable	2,500	
Rent Revenue		2,500
Wages and Salaries Payable		7,600
Income Tax Expense	10,200	
Income Taxes Payable		10,200
Totals	$1,175,300	$1,175,300

APPENDIX 4A

ACCOUNTING TOOLS: WORK SHEETS

Work sheets were introduced in the chapter as useful tools to aid the accountant. In this appendix we present a detailed discussion of these.

WORK SHEETS

LO 8 Understand how to use a work sheet as a basis for preparing financial statements.

A work sheet is used to organize the information needed to prepare financial statements without recording and posting formal adjusting entries. There is no one single format for a work sheet. We will illustrate a 10-column work sheet by using the information in the chapter for the Duffy Transit Company example. The format for a 10-column work sheet appears in Exhibit 4-11. We will concentrate on the *steps* to complete the work sheet, which has already been completed.

STEP 1: THE UNADJUSTED TRIAL BALANCE COLUMNS

The starting point for the work sheet is the first two columns, which must be filled in with the appropriate amounts from the unadjusted trial balance of Duffy Transit Company as shown in Exhibit 4-6. The trial balance is labeled *unadjusted* because it does not reflect the adjusting entries at the end of the period.

At this point, only the accounts used during the period are entered on the work sheet. Any accounts that are used for the first time during the period because of the adjusting entries will be added in the next step. All but the first two columns of the work sheet should be ignored at this time. Three accounts are included on the work sheet even though they do not have a balance: (1) Accumulated Depreciation—Garage, (2) Accumulated Depreciation—Buses, and (3) Retained Earnings. After this first month of operations, these accounts will always have a balance and will appear on an unadjusted trial balance.

STEP 2: THE ADJUSTING ENTRIES COLUMNS

The third and fourth columns of the work sheet have been completed in Exhibit 4-11. Rather than take the time now to prepare adjusting entries and post them to their respective accounts, the accountant makes the entries in these two columns of the work sheet. Formal entries can be made after the financial statements have been prepared. The addition of these two columns to the work sheet requires that we add the accounts used for the first time in the period because of the adjustment process. Letters are typically used on a work sheet to identify the adjusting entries and are therefore used here. In practice, the work sheet can be many pages long, and the use of identifying letters makes it easier to locate and match the debit and credit sides of each adjusting entry.

The two columns are totaled to ensure the equality of debits and credits for the adjusting entries. Keep in mind that the entries made in these two columns of the work sheet are *not* the actual adjusting entries; those will be recorded in the journal at a later time, after the financial statements have been prepared.

STEP 3: THE ADJUSTED TRIAL BALANCE COLUMNS

Columns 5 and 6 of the work sheet represent an adjusted trial balance. The amounts entered in these two columns are found by adding or subtracting any debits or credits in the adjusting entries columns to or from the unadjusted balances. For example, Cash is not

EXHIBIT 4-11 The Work Sheet

DUFFY TRANSIT COMPANY
WORK SHEET
FOR THE MONTH ENDED JANUARY 31

Account Titles	Unadjusted Trial Balance		Adjusting Entries		Adjusted Trial Balance		Income Statement		Balance Sheet	
	Debit	Credit	Debit	Credit	Debit	Credit	Debit	Credit	Debit	Credit
Cash	50,000				50,000				50,000	
Prepaid Insurance	48,000			(e) 2,000	46,000				46,000	
Land	20,000				20,000				20,000	
Buildings—Garage	160,000				160,000				160,000	
Accumulated Depreciation—Garage		–0–		(c) 600		600				600
Equipment—Buses	300,000				300,000				300,000	
Accumulated Depreciation—Buses		–0–		(d) 4,000		4,000				4,000
Discount Tickets Sold in Advance		25,000	(f) 20,400			4,600				4,600
Notes Payable		150,000				150,000				150,000
Capital Stock		400,000				400,000				400,000
Retained Earnings		–0–				–0–				–0–
Daily Ticket Revenue		30,000				30,000		30,000		
Gas, Oil, and Maintenance Expense	12,000				12,000		12,000			
Wage and Salary Expense	10,000		(b) 2,800		12,800		12,800			
Dividends	5,000				5,000				5,000	
	605,000	605,000								
Interest Expense			(a) 1,500		1,500		1,500			
Depreciation Expense—Garage			(c) 600		600		600			
Depreciation Expense—Buses			(d) 4,000		4,000		4,000			
Insurance Expense			(e) 2,000		2,000		2,000			
Discount Ticket Revenue				(f) 20,400		20,400		20,400		
Rent Receivable			(g) 2,500		2,500				2,500	
Rent Revenue				(g) 2,500		2,500		2,500		
Interest Payable				(a) 1,500		1,500				1,500
Wages and Salaries Payable				(b) 2,800		2,800				2,800
Income Tax Expense			(h) 6,800		6,800		6,800			
Income Tax Payable				(h) 6,800		6,800				6,800
			40,600	40,600	623,200	623,200	39,700	52,900	583,500	570,300
Net Income							13,200			13,200
							52,900	52,900	583,500	583,500

adjusted, and thus the $50,000 unadjusted amount is carried over to the Debit column of the adjusted trial balance. The $2,000 credit adjustment to Prepaid Insurance is subtracted from the unadjusted debit balance of $48,000, resulting in a debit balance of $46,000 on the adjusted trial balance. Finally, note the equality of the debits and credits on the new trial balance, $623,200.

Step 4: The Income Statement Columns

An adjusted trial balance is the basis for preparing the financial statements. The purpose of the last four columns of the work sheet is to separate the accounts into those that will appear on the income statement and those that will appear on the balance sheet. The income statement columns will be completed next.

The three revenue accounts appear in the credit column, and the seven expense accounts appear in the debit column. These amounts are simply carried over, or extended, from the adjusted trial balance. Because Duffy's revenues exceed its expenses, the total of the credit column, $52,900, exceeds the total of the debit column, $39,700. The difference between the two columns, the net income of the period of $13,200, is entered in the debit column. One purpose for showing the net income in this column is to balance the two columns. In addition, the entry in the debit column will be matched with an entry in the balance sheet credit column to represent the transfer of net income to retained earnings. If revenues were *less* than expenses, the *net loss* would be entered in the income statement *credit* column.

Step 5: The Balance Sheet Columns

Why do the income statement columns appear *before* the balance sheet columns on the work sheet? The income statement is in fact a *subset* of the balance sheet, and information from the income statement columns flows into the balance sheet columns. Recall that net income causes an increase in the owners' claim to the assets, that is, an increase in owners' equity, through the Retained Earnings account and, thus, is entered in the balance sheet credit column of the work sheet. In Exhibit 4-11, the amount of *net income,* $13,200, is carried over from the debit column of the income statement to the credit column of the balance sheet. If a company experiences a *net loss* for the period, the amount of the loss is entered in the credit column of the income statement and in the debit column of the balance sheet.

You will note that the Retained Earnings account has a zero balance in the last column of the work sheet, because this is the first month of operations for Duffy Transit Company. On future work sheets, the account will reflect the balance from the *end* of the *previous* month. Dividends appear in the debit column, and net income appears in the credit column. Thus, the ending balance of Retained Earnings can be found by taking its beginning balance, adding the net income of the period, and deducting the dividends. The completed work sheet provides all the necessary information to prepare an income statement, a statement of retained earnings, and a balance sheet.

Appendix Review Problem

Note to the Student: The following problem is based on the information for the Northern Airlines review problem at the end of this chapter. Try to prepare the work sheet without referring to the adjusting entries you prepared in solving that problem.

Required

Refer to the unadjusted trial balance and the additional information for Northern Airlines as presented previously. Prepare a 10-column work sheet for the month of January.

SOLUTION TO REVIEW PROBLEM

NORTHERN AIRLINES
WORK SHEET
FOR THE MONTH ENDED JANUARY 31

Account Titles	Unadjusted Trial Balance Debit	Unadjusted Trial Balance Credit	Adjusting Entries Debit	Adjusting Entries Credit	Adjusted Trial Balance Debit	Adjusted Trial Balance Credit	Income Statement Debit	Income Statement Credit	Balance Sheet Debit	Balance Sheet Credit
Cash	75,000				75,000				75,000	
Parts Inventory	45,000			(a) 8,900	36,100				36,100	
Land	80,000				80,000				80,000	
Buildings—Hangars	250,000				250,000				250,000	
Accumulated Depreciation—Hangars		24,000		(b) 1,000		25,000				25,000
Equipment—Aircraft	650,000				650,000				650,000	
Accumulated Depreciation—Aircraft		120,000		(c) 5,000		125,000				125,000
Tickets Sold in Advance		85,000	(d) 47,000			38,000				38,000
Capital Stock		500,000				500,000				500,000
Retained Earnings		368,000				368,000				368,000
Ticket Revenue		52,000		(d) 47,000		99,000		99,000		
Maintenance Expense	19,000		(a) 8,900		27,900		27,900			
Wage and Salary Expense	30,000		(e) 7,600		37,600		37,600			
	1,149,000	1,149,000								
Depreciation Expense—Hangars			(b) 1,000		1,000		1,000			
Depreciation Expense—Aircraft			(c) 5,000		5,000		5,000			
Rent Receivable			(f) 2,500		2,500				2,500	
Income Tax Expense			(g) 10,200		10,200		10,200			
Wages and Salaries Payable				(e) 7,600		7,600				7,600
Rent Revenue				(f) 2,500		2,500		2,500		
Income Taxes Payable				(g) 10,200		10,200				10,200
			82,200	82,200	1,175,300	1,175,300	81,700	101,500	1,093,600	1,073,800
Net Income							19,800			19,800
							101,500	101,500	1,093,600	1,093,600

CHAPTER HIGHLIGHTS

1. **LO 1** The success of accounting as a form of communication depends on two concepts: recognition and measurement. The items depicted in financial statements are representations. The accountant cannot show the reader an asset but instead depicts it with words and numbers.
2. **LO 1** Measurement in accounting requires choosing an attribute and a unit of measure. Historical cost is the attribute used for many of the assets included in financial statements. One alternative to historical cost is current value. The dollar as a unit of measure is subject to instability, depending on the level of inflation.
3. **LO 2** Under the accrual basis of accounting, revenues are recognized when earned and expenses when incurred. The income statement is prepared on an accrual basis, and the statement of cash flows complements it by providing valuable information about the operating, financing, and investing cash flows of a business.
4. **LO 3** According to the revenue recognition principle, revenues are recognized when they are realized or realizable and earned. On a practical basis, revenue is normally recognized at the time a product or service is delivered to the customer. Certain types of sales arrangements, such as long-term contracts and franchises, present special problems in applying the principle.
5. **LO 4** The matching principle attempts to associate with the revenue of the period all costs necessary to generate that revenue. A direct form of matching is possible for certain types of costs, such as cost of goods sold and commissions. Costs, such as depreciation, are recognized as expenses on an indirect basis. Depreciation is the allocation of the cost of a tangible, long-term asset over its useful life. The benefits from most selling and administrative expenses expire immediately and are recognized as expenses in the period the costs are incurred.
6. **LO 5** The accrual basis necessitates adjusting entries at the end of a period. The four types of adjusting entries result from differences between the recognition of revenues and expenses on an accrual basis and the receipt or payment of cash.
7. **LO 5** Cash paid before expense is incurred results in a deferred expense, which is recognized as an asset on the balance sheet. The adjusting entry reduces the asset and recognizes a corresponding amount of expense. Cash received before revenue is earned requires the recognition of a liability, a deferred revenue. The adjusting entry reduces the liability and recognizes a corresponding amount of revenue.
8. **LO 5** If cash is paid after an expense is incurred, an adjusting entry is needed to recognize the accrued liability and the related expense. Similarly, if cash is received after the revenue is earned, the adjusting entry recognizes the accrued asset and the corresponding revenue. The liability or asset is eliminated in a later period when cash is either paid or received.
9. **LO 5** Adjusting entries are prepared by reference to a trial balance and certain additional information. A trial balance prepared after posting the adjustments to the accounts ensures the equality of debits and credits in the ledger.
10. **LO 6** Steps in the accounting cycle are carried out each period as a basis for the preparation of financial statements. Some of the steps, such as journalizing transactions, are performed continuously, while others, such as recording adjusting entries, are performed only at the end of the period.
11. **LO 7** After adjusting entries are recorded and posted to the accounts, closing entries are made. They have two important purposes: (1) to return the balances in all revenue, expense, and dividend accounts to zero to start the following accounting period and (2) to transfer the net income (or net loss) and the dividends of the period to the Retained Earnings account.
12. **LO 7** A revenue account is closed by debiting it for the credit balance in the account and crediting Income Summary. An expense account is closed by crediting it and debiting Income Summary. If revenues exceed expenses, Income Summary will have a credit balance at this point, representing the net income of the period. Income Summary is closed by debiting it and crediting Retained Earnings. Finally, the Dividends account is closed with a credit and a corresponding debit to Retained Earnings.
13. **LO 8** A work sheet is not itself a financial statement. It is a useful device for organizing the necessary information to prepare financial statements without going through the formal process of recording and posting adjusting entries. The format for a 10-column work sheet includes two columns each (debits and credits) for the unadjusted trial balance, the adjustments, the adjusted trial balance, the income statement, and the balance sheet. (Appendix 4A)

KEY TERMS QUIZ

Read each definition below and then write the number of the definition in the blank beside the appropriate term it defines. The solution appears at the end of the chapter.

___ Recognition
___ Current value
___ Accrual basis
___ Revenue recognition principle
___ Production method
___ Matching principle
___ Adjusting entries
___ Contra account
___ Deferred expense
___ Accrual
___ Accrued asset
___ Work sheet
___ Nominal accounts
___ Interim statements
___ Historical cost
___ Cash basis
___ Revenues
___ Percentage-of-completion method

___ Installment method
___ Expenses
___ Straight-line method
___ Deferral
___ Deferred revenue
___ Accrued liability
___ Accounting cycle
___ Real accounts
___ Closing entries

1. A device used at the end of the period to gather the information needed to prepare financial statements without actually recording and posting adjusting entries.
2. Inflows or other enhancements of assets or settlements of liabilities from delivering or producing goods, rendering services, or other activities.
3. The method in which revenue is recognized when a commodity is produced rather than when it is sold.
4. Journal entries made at the end of a period by a company using the accrual basis of accounting.
5. Journal entries made at the end of the period to return the balance in all nominal accounts to zero and transfer the net income or loss and the dividends of the period to Retained Earnings.
6. The method used by contractors to recognize revenue before the completion of a long-term contract.
7. A liability resulting from the receipt of cash before the recognition of revenue.
8. The method in which revenue is recognized at the time cash is collected; used for various types of consumer items, such as automobiles and appliances.
9. The name given to balance sheet accounts because they are permanent and are not closed at the end of the period.
10. An asset resulting from the recognition of a revenue before the receipt of cash.
11. The amount of cash, or its equivalent, that could be received by selling an asset currently.
12. The assignment of an equal amount of depreciation to each period.
13. Cash has either been paid or received, but expense or revenue has not yet been recognized.
14. A system of accounting in which revenues are recognized when earned and expenses when incurred.
15. Cash has not yet been paid or received, but expense has been incurred or revenue earned.
16. Financial statements prepared monthly, quarterly, or at other intervals less than a year in duration.
17. Revenues are recognized in the income statement when they are realized, or realizable, and earned.
18. The process of recording an item in the financial statements as an asset, liability, revenue, expense, or the like.
19. An asset resulting from the payment of cash before the incurrence of expense.
20. The name given to revenue, expense, and dividend accounts because they are temporary and are closed at the end of the period.
21. A system of accounting in which revenues are recognized when cash is received and expenses when cash is paid.
22. A liability resulting from the recognition of an expense before the payment of cash.
23. The association of revenue of a period with all of the costs necessary to generate that revenue.
24. An account with a balance that is opposite that of a related account.
25. The amount that is paid for an asset and that is used as a basis for recognizing it on the balance sheet and carrying it on later balance sheets.
26. Outflows or other using up of assets or incurrences of liabilities resulting from delivering goods, rendering services, or carrying out other activities.
27. A series of steps performed each period and culminating with the preparation of a set of financial statements.

ALTERNATE TERMS

Historical cost Original cost

Asset Unexpired cost

Deferred expense Prepaid expense, prepaid asset

Deferred revenue Unearned revenue

Expense Expired cost

Nominal account Temporary account

Real account Permanent account

QUESTIONS

1. What is meant by the following statement? "The items depicted in financial statements are merely *representations* of the real thing."
2. What is the meaning of the following statement? "The choice between historical cost and current value is a good example of the trade-off in accounting between relevance and reliability."
3. A realtor earns a 10% commission on the sale of a $150,000 home. The realtor lists the home on June 5, the sale occurs on June 12, and the seller pays the realtor the $15,000 commission on July 8. When should the realtor recognize revenue from the sale, assuming (a) the cash basis of accounting and (b) the accrual basis of accounting?

4. What does the following statement mean? "If I want to assess the cash flow prospects for a company down the road, I look at the company's most recent statement of cash flows. An income statement prepared under the accrual basis of accounting is useless for this purpose."

5. What is the relationship between the time period assumption and accrual accounting?

6. Is it necessary for an asset to be acquired when revenue is recognized? Explain your answer.

7. What is the justification for recognizing revenue on a long-term contract by the percentage-of-completion method?

8. Illinois Fried Chicken sells franchises granting the franchisee in a specific geographic area the exclusive right to use the company name and sell chicken using its secret recipe. An initial franchise fee of $50,000 is charged by Illinois, along with a continuing fee of 3% of sales. The initial fee is for Illinois' assistance in selecting a site and training personnel. When should Illinois recognize the $50,000 as revenue?

9. When should a publisher of magazines recognize revenue?

10. What is the justification for recognizing revenue in certain industries at the time the product is *produced* rather than when it is *sold?*

11. A friend says to you: "I just don't get it. Assets cost money. Expenses reduce income. There must be some relationship among *assets, costs,* and *expenses*—I'm just not sure what it is!" What is the relationship? Can you give an example of it?

12. What is the meaning of *depreciation* to the accountant?

13. What are the four basic types of adjusting entries? Give an example of each.

14. What are the rules of debit and credit as they apply to the contra asset account Accumulated Depreciation?

15. Which of the following steps in the accounting cycle requires the most thought and judgment by the accountant: (a) preparing a trial balance, (b) posting adjusting and closing entries, or (c) analyzing and recording transactions? Explain your answer.

16. What is the difference between a real account and a nominal account?

17. What two purposes are served in making closing entries?

18. Why is the Dividends account closed directly to Retained Earnings rather than to the Income Summary account?

19. Assuming the use of a work sheet, are the formal adjusting entries recorded and posted to the accounts before or after the financial statements are prepared? Explain your answer. Would your answer change if a work sheet is not prepared? (Appendix 4A)

20. Some companies use an eight-column work sheet rather than the ten-column format illustrated in the chapter. Which two columns would you think are not used in the eight-column format? Why could these two columns be eliminated? (Appendix 4A)

21. Why do the income statement columns appear before the balance sheet columns on a work sheet? (Appendix 4A)

22. Does the Retained Earnings account that appears in the balance sheet credit column of a work sheet reflect the beginning or the ending balance in the account? Explain your answer. (Appendix 4A)

23. One asset account will always be carried over from the unadjusted trial balance columns of a work sheet to the balance sheet columns of the work sheet without any adjustment. What account is this? (Appendix 4A)

EXERCISES

LO 3 Exercise 4-1 Revenue Recognition

The highway department contracted with a private company to collect tolls and maintain facilities on a turnpike. Users of the turnpike can pay cash as they approach the toll booth, or they can purchase a pass. The pass is equipped with an electronic sensor that subtracts the toll fee from the pass balance as the motorist slowly approaches a special toll booth. The passes are issued in $10 increments. Refunds are available to motorists who do not use the pass balance, but these are issued very infrequently. Last year $3,000,000 was collected at the traditional toll booths, $2,000,000 of passes were issued, and $1,700,000 of passes were used at the special toll booth. How much should the company recognize as revenue for the year? Explain how the revenue recognition rule should be applied in this case.

LO 4 Exercise 4-2 The Matching Principle

Three methods of matching costs with revenue were described in the chapter: (a) directly match a specific form of revenue with a cost incurred in generating that revenue, (b) indirectly match a cost with the periods during which it will provide benefits or revenue, and (c) immediately recognize a cost incurred as an expense because no future benefits are expected. For each of the following costs, indicate how it is normally recognized as expense by indicating either *a, b,* or *c.* If you think there is more than one possible answer for any of the situations, explain why.

1. New office copier
2. Monthly bill from the utility company for electricity
3. Office supplies
4. Biweekly payroll for office employees
5. Commissions earned by salespeople
6. Interest incurred on a six-month loan from the bank

7. Cost of inventory sold during the current period
8. Taxes owed on income earned during current period
9. Cost of three-year insurance policy

LO 5 Exercise 4-3 Accruals and Deferrals

For the following situations, indicate whether each involves a deferred expense (DE), a deferred revenue (DR), an accrued liability (AL), or an accrued asset (AA).

Example: DE Office supplies purchased in advance of their use.

_______ 1. Wages earned by employees but not yet paid
_______ 2. Cash collected from subscriptions in advance of publishing a magazine
_______ 3. Interest earned on a customer loan for which principal and interest have not yet been collected
_______ 4. One year's premium on life insurance policy paid in advance
_______ 5. Office building purchased for cash
_______ 6. Rent collected in advance from a tenant
_______ 7. State income taxes owed at the end of the year
_______ 8. Rent owed by a tenant but not yet collected

LO 5 Exercise 4-4 Office Supplies

Somerville Corp. purchases office supplies once a month and prepares monthly financial statements. The asset account Office Supplies on Hand has a balance of $1,450 on May 1. Purchases of supplies during May amount to $1,100. Supplies on hand at May 31 amount to $920. Prepare the necessary adjusting entry on Somerville's books on May 31. What would be the effect on net income for May if this entry is *not* recorded?

LO 5 Exercise 4-5 Prepaid Rent—Quarterly Adjustments

On September 1, Northhampton Industries signed a six-month lease, effective September 1, for office space. Northhampton agreed to prepay the rent and mailed a check for $12,000 to the landlord on September 1. Assume that Northhampton prepares adjusting entries only four times a year, on March 31, June 30, September 30, and December 31.

Required

1. Compute the rental cost for each full month.
2. Prepare the journal entry to record the payment of rent on September 1.
3. Prepare the adjusting entry on September 30.
4. Assume that the accountant prepares the adjusting entry on September 30 but forgets to record an adjusting entry on December 31. Will net income for the year be understated or overstated? By what amount?

LO 5 Exercise 4-6 Depreciation

On July 1, 2001, Red Gate Farm buys a combine for $100,000 in cash. Assume that the combine is expected to have a seven-year life and an estimated salvage value of $16,000 at the end of that time.

Required

1. Prepare the journal entry to record the purchase of the combine on July 1, 2001.
2. Compute the depreciable cost of the combine.
3. Using the straight-line method, compute the monthly depreciation.
4. Prepare the adjusting entry to record depreciation at the end of July 2001.
5. Compute the combine's carrying value that will be shown on Red Gate's balance sheet prepared on December 31, 2001.

LO 5 Exercise 4-7 Prepaid Insurance—Annual Adjustments

On April 1, 2001, Briggs Corp. purchases a 24-month property insurance policy for $72,000. The policy is effective immediately. Assume that Briggs prepares adjusting entries only once a year, on December 31.

Required

1. Compute the monthly cost of the insurance policy.
2. Prepare the journal entry to record the purchase of the policy on April 1, 2001.
3. Prepare the adjusting entry on December 31, 2001.
4. Assume that the accountant forgets to record an adjusting entry on December 31, 2001. Will net income for the year ended December 31, 2001, be understated or overstated? Explain your answer.

LO 5 **Exercise 4-8** Subscriptions

Country Living publishes a monthly magazine for which a 12-month subscription costs $30. All subscriptions require payment of the full $30 in advance. On August 1, 2001, the balance in the Subscriptions Received in Advance account was $40,500. During the month of August, the company sold 900 yearly subscriptions. After the adjusting entry at the end of August, the balance in the Subscriptions Received in Advance account is $60,000.

Required

1. Prepare the journal entry to record the sale of the 900 yearly subscriptions during the month of August.
2. Prepare the adjusting journal entry on August 31.
3. Assume that the accountant made the correct entry during August to record the sale of the 900 subscriptions but forgot to make the adjusting entry on August 31. Would net income for August be overstated or understated? Explain your answer.

LO 5 **Exercise 4-9** Customer Deposits

Wolfe & Wolfe collected $9,000 from a customer on April 1 and agreed to provide legal services during the next three months. Wolfe & Wolfe expects to provide an equal amount of services each month.

Required

1. Prepare the journal entry for the receipt of the customer deposit on April 1.
2. Prepare the adjusting entry on April 30.
3. What would be the effect on net income for April if the entry in **(2)** is not recorded?

LO 5 **Exercise 4-10** Wages Payable

Denton Corporation employs 50 workers in its plant. Each employee is paid $10 per hour and works seven hours per day, Monday through Friday. Employees are paid every Friday. The last payday was Friday, October 20.

Required

1. Compute the dollar amount of the weekly payroll.
2. Prepare the journal entry on Friday, October 27, for the payment of the weekly payroll.
3. Denton prepares monthly financial statements. Prepare the adjusting journal entry on Tuesday, October 31, the last day of the month.
4. Prepare the journal entry on Friday, November 3, for the payment of the weekly payroll.
5. Would net income for the month of October be understated or overstated if Denton doesn't bother with an adjusting entry on October 31? Explain your answer.

LO 5 **Exercise 4-11** Interest Payable

Billings Company takes out a 12%, 90-day, $100,000 loan with First National Bank on March 1, 2001.

Required

1. Prepare the journal entry on March 1, 2001.
2. Prepare the adjusting entries for the months of March and April 2001.
3. Prepare the entry on May 30, 2001, when Billings repays the principal and interest to First National.

LO 5 Exercise 4-12 Property Taxes Payable—Annual Adjustments

Lexington Builders owns property in Kaneland County. Lexington's 2000 property taxes amounted to $50,000. Kaneland County will send out the 2001 property tax bills to property owners during April 2002. Taxes must be paid by June 1, 2002. Assume that Lexington prepares adjusting entries only once a year, on December 31, and that property taxes for 2001 are expected to increase by 5% over those for 2000.

Required

1. Prepare the adjusting entry required to record the property taxes payable on December 31, 2001.
2. Prepare the journal entry to record the payment of the 2001 property taxes on June 1, 2002.

LO 5 Exercise 4-13 Interest Receivable

On June 1, 2001, MicroTel Enterprises lends $60,000 to MaxiDriver Inc. The loan will be repaid in 60 days with interest at 10%.

Required

1. Prepare the journal entry on MicroTel's books on June 1, 2001.
2. Prepare the adjusting entry on MicroTel's books on June 30, 2001.
3. Prepare the entry on MicroTel's books on July 31, 2001, when MaxiDriver repays the principal and interest.

LO 5 Exercise 4-14 Unbilled Accounts Receivable

Mike and Cary repair computers for small local businesses. Heavy thunderstorms during the last week of June resulted in a record number of service calls. Eager to review the results of operations for the month of June, Mike prepared an income statement and was puzzled by the lower-than-expected amount of revenues. Cary explained that he had not yet billed the company's customers for $40,000 of work performed during the last week of the month.

Required

1. Should revenue be recorded when services are performed or when customers are billed? Explain your answer.
2. Prepare the adjusting entry required on June 30.

LO 5 Exercise 4-15 The Effect of Ignoring Adjusting Entries on Net Income

For each of the following independent situations, determine whether the effect of ignoring the required adjusting entry will result in an understatement (U), an overstatement (O), or no effect (NE) on net income for the period.

Situation	Effect on Net Income
Example: Taxes owed but not yet paid are ignored.	O
1. A company fails to record depreciation on equipment.	______
2. Sales made during the last week of the period are not recorded.	______
3. A company neglects to record the expired portion of a prepaid insurance policy (its cost was originally debited to an asset account).	______
4. Interest due but not yet paid on a long-term note payable is ignored.	______
5. Commissions earned by salespeople but not payable until the 10th of the following month are ignored.	______
6. A landlord receives cash on the date a lease is signed for the rent for the first six months and credits Unearned Rent Revenue. The landlord fails to make any adjustment at the end of the first month.	______

LO 5 Exercise 4-16 The Effect of Adjusting Entries on the Accounting Equation

Determine whether recording each of the following adjusting entries will increase (I), decrease (D), or have no effect (NE) on each of the three elements of the accounting equation.

	Assets	=	Liabilities	+	Owners' Equity
Example: Wages earned during the period but not yet paid are accrued.	NE		I		D
1. Prepaid insurance is reduced for the portion of the policy that has expired during the period.	______		______		______
2. Interest incurred during the period but not yet paid is accrued.	______		______		______
3. Depreciation for the period is recorded.	______		______		______
4. Revenue is recorded for the earned portion of a liability for amounts collected in advance from customers.	______		______		______
5. Rent revenue is recorded for amounts owed by a tenant but not yet paid.	______		______		______
6. Income taxes owed but not yet paid are accrued.	______		______		______

LO 5 Exercise 4-17 Reconstruction of Adjusting Entries from Unadjusted and Adjusted Trial Balances

Following are the unadjusted and adjusted trial balances for Power Corp. on May 31, 2001:

	Unadjusted Trial Balance		Adjusted Trial Balance	
	Debit	**Credit**	**Debit**	**Credit**
Cash	$ 3,160		$ 3,160	
Accounts Receivable	7,300		9,650	
Supplies on Hand	400		160	
Prepaid Rent	2,400		2,200	
Equipment	9,000		9,000	
Accumulated Depreciation		$ 2,800		$ 3,200
Accounts Payable		2,600		2,600
Capital Stock		5,000		5,000
Retained Earnings		8,990		8,990
Service Revenue		6,170		8,520
Promotions Expense	2,050		2,050	
Wage Expense	1,250		2,350	
Wages Payable				1,100
Supplies Expense			240	
Depreciation Expense			400	
Rent Expense			200	
Totals	$25,560	$25,560	$29,410	$29,410

Required

1. Reconstruct the adjusting entries that were made on Power's books at the end of May.
2. By how much would Power's net income for May have been overstated or understated (indicate which) if these adjusting entries had not been recorded?

LO 6 Exercise 4-18 The Accounting Cycle

The steps in the accounting cycle are listed below in random order. Fill in the blank next to each step to indicate its *order* in the cycle. The first step in the cycle is filled in as an example.

Order	Procedure
______	Prepare a work sheet.
______	Close the accounts.

1 Collect and analyze information from source documents.
___ Prepare financial statements.
___ Post transactions to accounts in the ledger.
___ Record and post adjusting entries.
___ Journalize daily transactions.

LO 6 Exercise 4-19 Trial Balance

The following account titles, arranged in alphabetical order, are from the records of Hadley Realty Corporation. The balance in each account is the normal balance for that account. The balances are as of December 31, after adjusting entries have been made. Prepare an adjusted trial balance, listing the accounts in the following order: (1) assets, (2) liabilities, (3) owners' equity accounts, including dividends, (4) revenues, and (5) expenses.

Accounts Payable	$12,300
Accounts Receivable	21,230
Accumulated Depreciation—Automobiles	12,000
Accumulated Depreciation—Buildings	15,000
Automobiles	48,000
Buildings	60,000
Capital Stock	25,000
Cash	2,460
Commissions Earned	17,420
Commissions Expense	2,300
Dividends Declared and Paid	1,500
Insurance Expense	300
Interest Expense	200
Interest Payable	200
Land	40,000
Notes Payable	20,000
Office Supplies	1,680
Office Supplies Expense	5,320
Prepaid Insurance	1,200
Rent Expense	2,400
Retained Earnings	85,445
Wages and Salaries Expense	1,245
Wages and Salaries Payable	470

LO 7 Exercise 4-20 Closing Entries

At the end of the year, the adjusted trial balance for Devonshire Corporation contains the following amounts for the income statement accounts (the balance in each account is the normal balance for that type of account).

Account	Balance
Advertising Fees Earned	$58,500
Interest Revenue	2,700
Wage and Salary Expense	14,300
Utilities Expense	12,500
Insurance Expense	7,300
Depreciation Expense	16,250
Interest Expense	2,600
Income Tax Expense	3,300
Dividends	2,000

Required

1. Prepare all necessary journal entries to close Devonshire Corporation's accounts at the end of the year.
2. Assume that the accountant for Devonshire forgets to record the closing entries. What will be the effect on net income for the *following* year? Explain your answer.

LO 7 Exercise 4-21 Preparation of a Statement of Retained Earnings from Closing Entries

Fisher Corporation reported a Retained Earnings balance of $125,780 on January 1, 2001. Fisher Corporation made the following three closing entries on December 31, 2001 (the entry to transfer net income to Retained Earnings has been intentionally left out). Prepare a statement of retained earnings for Fisher for the year.

Dec.	31	Service Revenue	65,400	
		Interest Revenue	20,270	
		Income Summary		85,670
Dec.	31	Income Summary	62,345	
		Salary and Wage Expense		23,450
		Rent Expense		20,120
		Interest Expense		4,500
		Utilities Expense		10,900
		Insurance Expense		3,375
Dec.	31	Retained Earnings	6,400	
		Dividends		6,400

LO 7 Exercise 4-22 Reconstruction of Closing Entries

The T accounts shown below summarize entries made to selected general ledger accounts of Cooper & Company. Certain entries, dated December 31, are closing entries. Prepare the closing entries that were made on December 31.

MAINTENANCE REVENUE

12/31	90,000	64,000	12/1 bal.
		13,000	12/15
		13,000	12/30

WAGES EXPENSE

12/1 bal.	11,000	12,000	12/31
12/15	500		
12/30	500		

SUPPLIES EXPENSE

12/1 bal.	2,500	2,750	12/31
12/31	250		

RETAINED EARNINGS

12/31	5,000	45,600	12/1 bal.
		75,250	12/31

DIVIDENDS

12/1 bal.	5,000	5,000	12/31

INCOME SUMMARY

12/31	14,750	90,000	12/31
12/31	75,250		

LO 7 Exercise 4-23 Closing Entries for Ben & Jerry's

www.benjerry.com

The following accounts appear on Ben & Jerry's 1998 income statement. The accounts are listed in alphabetical order, and the balance in each account is the normal balance for that account. Prepare closing entries for Ben & Jerry's for 1998.

Cost of Sales	$136,225,000
Income Tax Expense	3,534,000
Interest Expense	1,888,000
Interest Income	2,248,000
Net Sales	209,203,000
Other Income	333,000
Selling, General, and Administrative Expenses	63,895,000

LO 7 Exercise 4-24 Closing Entries

Royston Realty reported the following accounts on its income statement:

Commissions Earned	$54,000
Real Estate Board Fees Paid	5,000
Computer Line Charge	864
Depreciation on Computer	450
Car Expenses	2,200
Travel and Entertainment	4,500

Insurance Expired	$ 780
Advertising Expense	1,460
Office Supplies Used	940

Required

1. Prepare the necessary entries to close the temporary accounts.
2. Explain why the closing entries are necessary and when they should be recorded.

LO 8 Exercise 4-25 The Difference between a Financial Statement and a Work Sheet (Appendix 4A)

The balance sheet columns of the work sheet for Jones Corporation show total debits and total credits of $255,000 each. Dividends for the period are $3,000. Accumulated depreciation is $14,000 at the end of the period. Compute the amount that should appear on the balance sheet (i.e., the formal financial statement) for *total assets.* How do you explain the difference between this amount and the amount that appears as the total debits and total credits on the work sheet?

LO 8 Exercise 4-26 Ten-Column Work Sheet (Appendix 4A)

Indicate whether amounts in each of the following accounts should be carried over from the adjusted trial balance columns of the work sheet to the income statement (IS) columns or to the balance sheet (BS) columns. Also indicate whether the account normally has a debit (D) balance or a credit (C) balance.

BS-D **Example:** Cash

_____ **1.** Accumulated Depreciation—Trucks
_____ **2.** Subscriptions Sold in Advance
_____ **3.** Accounts Receivable
_____ **4.** Dividends
_____ **5.** Capital Stock
_____ **6.** Prepaid Insurance
_____ **7.** Depreciation Expense—Trucks
_____ **8.** Office Supplies
_____ **9.** Office Supplies Expense
_____ **10.** Subscription Revenue
_____ **11.** Interest Receivable
_____ **12.** Interest Revenue
_____ **13.** Interest Expense
_____ **14.** Interest Payable
_____ **15.** Retained Earnings

Multi-Concept Exercises

LO 1, 2, 3 Exercise 4-27 Revenue Recognition, Cash and Accrual Basis

Hathaway Health Club sold three-year memberships at a reduced rate during its opening promotion. It sold 1,000 three-year, nonrefundable memberships for $366 each. The club expects to sell 100 additional three-year memberships for $900 each over each of the next two years. Membership fees are paid when clients sign up. The club's bookkeeper has prepared the following income statement for the first year of business and projected income statements for Years 2 and 3.

Cash-basis income statements:

	Year 1	Year 2	Year 3
Sales	$366,000	$90,000	$90,000
Equipment*	100,000	–0–	–0–
Salaries and Wages	50,000	50,000	50,000
Advertising	5,000	5,000	5,000
Rent and Utilities	36,000	36,000	36,000
Income (Loss)	$175,000	$ (1,000)	$ (1,000)

*Equipment was purchased at the beginning of Year 1 for $100,000 and is expected to last for three years and then to be worth $1,000.

Required

1. Convert the income statements for each of the three years to the accrual basis.
2. Describe how the revenue recognition principle applies. Do you believe that the cash-basis or the accrual-basis income statements are more useful to management? to investors? Why?

LO 1, 2, 3 **Exercise 4-28** The Effect of the Percentage-of-Completion Method on Financial Statements

Fox Valley Inc. is building a bridge. During the first year of the three-year project, Fox Valley incurred construction costs of $1.2 million. The company expects to spend an additional $600,000 in each of the next two years of the project. The state has agreed to pay Fox Valley $4 million for the bridge, $2 million in the first year and $2 million on completion. The company would like to use the percentage-of-completion method to report revenue and income.

Required

1. Complete the following table, comparing the percentage-of-completion method with the cash basis. Use the percentage of costs incurred to date to estimated total costs to determine the percentage of completion.

	Income Recognized Under	
Year	**Percentage of Completion**	**Cash Basis**
1		
2		
3		
Total		

2. Explain how the revenue recognition principle applies to the percentage-of-completion method.

LO 4, 5 **Exercise 4-29** Depreciation Expense

During 2001, Carter Company acquired three assets with the following costs, estimated useful lives, and estimated salvage values:

Date	**Asset**	**Cost**	**Estimated Useful Life**	**Estimated Salvage Value**
March 28	Truck	$ 18,000	5 years	$ 3,000
June 22	Computer	55,000	10 years	5,000
October 3	Building	250,000	30 years	10,000

The company uses the straight-line method to depreciate all assets and computes depreciation to the nearest month. For example, the computer system will be depreciated for six months in 2001.

Required

1. Compute the depreciation expense that Carter will record on each of the three assets for 2001.
2. Comment on the following statement: "Accountants could save time and money by simply expensing the cost of long-term assets when they are purchased. In addition, this would be more accurate because depreciation requires estimates of useful life and salvage value."

LO 4, 5 **Exercise 4-30** Accrual of Interest on a Loan

On July 1, 2001, Paxson Corporation takes out a 12%, two-month, $50,000 loan at Friendly National Bank. Principal and interest are to be repaid on August 31.

Required

1. Prepare the journal entries for July 1 to record the borrowing, for July 31 to record the accrual of interest, and for August 31 to record repayment of the principal and interest.
2. Evaluate the following statement: "It would be much easier not to bother with an adjusting entry on July 31 and simply record interest expense on August 31 when the loan is repaid."

PROBLEMS

LO 3 Problem 4-1 The Revenue Recognition Principle

Each of the following paragraphs describes a situation involving revenue recognition.

a. ABC Realty receives a 6% commission for every house it sells. It lists a house for a client on April 3 at a selling price of $150,000. ABC receives an offer from a buyer on April 28 to purchase the house at the asking price. The realtor's client accepts the offer on May 1. ABC will receive its 6% commission at a closing scheduled for May 16.

b. Chicken King is a fast-food franchisor on the West Coast. It charges all franchisees $10,000 to open an outlet in a designated city. In return for this fee, the franchisee receives the exclusive right to operate in the area, as well as assistance from Chicken King in selecting a site. On January 5, Chicken King signs an agreement with a franchisee and receives a down payment of $4,000, with the balance of $6,000 due in three months. On March 13, Chicken King meets with the new franchisee, and the two parties agree on a suitable site for the business. On April 5, the franchisee pays Chicken King the remaining $6,000.

c. Refer to part **b.** In addition to the initial fee, Chicken King charges a continuing fee equal to 2% of the franchisee's sales each month. Each month's fee is payable by the 10th of the following month. The franchisee opens for business on June 1. On July 3, Chicken King receives a report from the franchisee indicating its sales for the month of June amount to $60,000. On July 8, Chicken King receives its 2% fee for June sales.

d. Goldstar Mining Corporation mines and sells gold and other precious commodities on the open market. During August, the company mines 50 ounces of gold. The market price throughout August is $300 per ounce. The 50 ounces are eventually sold on the open market on September 5 for $310 per ounce.

e. Whatadeal Inc. sells used cars. Because of the uncertainties involved in collecting from customers, Whatadeal uses the installment basis of accounting. On December 2, Whatadeal sells a car for $10,000 with a 25% down payment and the balance due in 60 days. The company's accounting year ends on December 31. Whatadeal receives the balance of $7,500 on February 1.

Required

For each situation, indicate when revenue should be recognized, as well as the dollar amount. Give a brief explanation for each answer.

LO 5 Problem 4-2 Adjusting Entries

Water Corporation prepares monthly financial statements and therefore adjusts its accounts at the end of every month. The following information is available for March 2001:

a. Water Corporation takes out a 90-day, 8%, $15,000 note on March 1, 2001, with interest and principal to be paid at maturity.

b. The asset account Office Supplies on Hand has a balance of $1,280 on March 1, 2001. During March, Water adds $750 to the account for the purchases of the period. A count of the supplies on hand at the end of March indicates a balance of $1,370.

c. The company purchased office equipment last year for $62,600. The equipment has an estimated useful life of six years and an estimated salvage value of $5,000.

d. The company's plant operates seven days per week with a daily payroll of $950. Wage earners are paid every Sunday. The last day of the month is Saturday, March 31.

e. The company rented an idle warehouse to a neighboring business on February 1, 2001, at a rate of $2,500 per month. On this date, Water Corporation credited Rent Collected in Advance for six months' rent received in advance.

f. On March 1, 2001, Water Corporation credited a liability account, Customer Deposits, for $4,800. This sum represents an amount that a customer paid in advance and that will be earned evenly by Water over a four-month period.

g. Based on its income for the month, Water Corporation estimates that federal income taxes for March amount to $3,900.

Required

For each of the preceding situations, prepare in general journal form the appropriate adjusting entry to be recorded on March 31, 2001.

LO 5 Problem 4-3 Effects of Adjusting Entries on the Accounting Equation
Refer to the information provided for Water Corporation in Problem 4-2.

Required

1. Prepare a table to summarize the required adjusting entries as they affect the accounting equation. Use the format in Exhibit 3-1. Identify each adjustment by letter.
2. Assume that Water reports income of $23,000 before any of the adjusting entries. What net income will Water report for March?

LO 5 Problem 4-4 Adjusting Entries—Annual Adjustments
Palmer Industries prepares annual financial statements and adjusts its accounts only at the end of the year. The following information is available for the year ended December 31, 2001:

a. Palmer purchased computer equipment two years ago for $15,000. The equipment has an estimated useful life of five years and an estimated salvage value of $250.
b. The Office Supplies account had a balance of $3,600 on January 1, 2001. During 2001, Palmer added $17,600 to the account for purchases of office supplies during the year. A count of the supplies on hand at the end of December 2001 indicates a balance of $1,850.
c. On August 1, 2001, Palmer credited a liability account, Customer Deposits, for $24,000. This sum represents an amount that a customer paid in advance and that will be earned evenly by Palmer over a six-month period.
d. Palmer rented some office space on November 1, 2001, at a rate of $2,700 per month. On that date, Palmer debited Prepaid Rent for three months' rent paid in advance.
e. Palmer took out a 120-day, 9%, $200,000 note on November 1, 2001, with interest and principal to be paid at maturity.
f. Palmer operates five days per week with an average daily payroll of $500. Palmer pays its employees every Friday. December 31, 2001, is a Monday.

Required

1. For each of the preceding situations, prepare in general journal form the appropriate adjusting entry to be recorded on December 31, 2001.
2. Assume that Palmer's accountant forgets to record the adjusting entries on December 31, 2001. Will net income for the year be understated or overstated? By what amount? (Ignore the effect of income taxes.)

LO 5 Problem 4-5 Recurring and Adjusting Entries
The following are Butler Realty Corporation's accounts, identified by number. The company has been in the real estate business for 10 years and prepares financial statements monthly. Following the list of accounts is a series of transactions entered into by Butler. For each transaction, enter the number(s) of the account(s) to be debited and credited.

Accounts

1. Cash	**11.** Notes Payable
2. Accounts Receivable	**12.** Capital Stock, $10 par
3. Prepaid Rent	**13.** Paid-in Capital in Excess of Par
4. Office Supplies	**14.** Commissions Revenue
5. Automobiles	**15.** Office Supply Expense
6. Accumulated Depreciation	**16.** Rent Expense
7. Land	**17.** Salaries and Wages Expense
8. Accounts Payable	**18.** Depreciation Expense
9. Salaries and Wages Payable	**19.** Interest Expense
10. Income Tax Payable	**20.** Income Tax Expense

Transaction	Debit	Credit
a. **Example:** Issued additional shares of stock to owners at amount in excess of par.	1	12, 13
b. Purchased automobiles for cash.	______	______

Transaction	Debit	Credit
c. Purchased land; made cash down payment and signed a promissory note for the balance.	______	______
d. Paid cash to landlord for rent for next 12 months.	______	______
e. Purchased office supplies on account.	______	______
f. Collected cash for commissions from clients for the properties sold during the month.	______	______
g. Collected cash for commissions from clients for the properties sold in the prior month.	______	______
h. During the month, sold properties for which cash for commissions will be collected from clients next month.	______	______
i. Paid for office supplies purchased on account in an earlier month.	______	______
j. Recorded an adjustment to recognize wages and salaries incurred but not yet paid.	______	______
k. Recorded an adjustment for office supplies used during the month.	______	______
l. Recorded an adjusting entry for the portion of prepaid rent that expired during the month.	______	______
m. Made required month-end payment on note taken out in **(c)**; payment is part principal and part interest.	______	______
n. Recorded adjusting entry for monthly depreciation on the autos.	______	______
o. Recorded adjusting entry for income taxes.	______	______

LO 5 **Problem 4-6** Use of Account Balances as a Basis for Adjusting Entries—Annual Adjustments

The following account balances are taken from the records of Chauncey Company at December 31, 2001. The Prepaid Insurance account represents the cost of a three-year policy purchased on August 1, 2001. The Rent Collected in Advance account represents the cash received from a tenant on June 1, 2001, for 12 months' rent, beginning on that date. The Note Receivable represents a nine-month promissory note received from a customer on September 1, 2001. Principal and interest at an annual rate of 9% will be received on June 1, 2002.

Prepaid Insurance	$ 7,200 debit	
Rent Collected in Advance		$6,000 credit
Note Receivable	50,000 debit	

Required

1. Prepare the three necessary adjusting entries on the books of Chauncey on December 31, 2001. Assume that Chauncey prepares adjusting entries only once a year, on December 31.
2. Assume that adjusting entries are made at the end of each month rather than only at the end of the year. What would be the balance in Prepaid Insurance *before* the December adjusting entry is made? Explain your answer.

GENERAL LEDGER

LO 5 **Problem 4-7** Use of a Trial Balance as a Basis for Adjusting Entries

Bob Reynolds operates a real estate business. A trial balance on April 30, 2001, *before* recording any adjusting entries, appears as follows:

REYNOLDS REALTY COMPANY
UNADJUSTED TRIAL BALANCE
APRIL 30, 2001

	Debit	Credit
Cash	$15,700	
Prepaid Insurance	450	
Office Supplies	250	

Office Equipment	$50,000	
Accumulated Depreciation—Office Equipment		$ 5,000
Automobile	12,000	
Accumulated Depreciation—Automobile		1,400
Accounts Payable		6,500
Unearned Commissions		9,500
Notes Payable		2,000
Capital Stock		10,000
Retained Earnings		40,000
Dividends	2,500	
Commissions Earned		17,650
Utility Expense	2,300	
Salaries Expense	7,400	
Advertising Expense	1,450	
Totals	$92,050	$92,050

Other Data

a. The monthly insurance cost is $50.

b. Office supplies on hand on April 30, 2001, amount to $180.

c. The office equipment was purchased on April 1, 2000. On that date, it had an estimated useful life of 10 years.

d. On September 1, 2000, the automobile was purchased; it had an estimated useful life of five years.

e. A deposit is received in advance of providing any services for first-time customers. Amounts received in advance are recorded initially in the account Unearned Commissions. Based on services provided to these first-time customers, the balance in this account at the end of April should be $5,000.

f. Repeat customers are allowed to pay for services one month after the date of the sale of their property. Services rendered during the month but not yet collected or billed to these customers amount to $1,500.

g. Interest owed on the note payable but not yet paid amounts to $20.

h. Salaries owed to employees but unpaid at the end of the month amount to $2,500.

Required

1. Prepare in general journal form the necessary adjusting entries at April 30, 2001. Label the entries **a** through **h** to correspond to the other data.
2. Note that the unadjusted trial balance reports a credit balance in Accumulated Depreciation—Office Equipment of $5,000. Explain *why* the account contains a balance of $5,000 on April 30, 2001.

LO 5 **Problem 4-8** Effects of Adjusting Entries on the Accounting Equation

Refer to the information provided for Reynolds Realty Company in Problem 4-7.

Required

1. Prepare a table to summarize the required adjusting entries as they affect the accounting equation. Use the format in Exhibit 3-1. Identify each adjustment by letter.
2. Compute the net increase or decrease in net income for the month from the recognition of the adjusting entries you prepared in part **1.** (Ignore income taxes.)

LO 5 **Problem 4-9** Reconstruction of Adjusting Entries from Account Balances

Taggart Corp. records adjusting entries each month before preparing monthly financial statements. The following selected account balances are taken from its trial balances on June 30, 2001. The "unadjusted" columns set forth the general ledger balances before the adjusting entries were posted. The "adjusted" columns reflect the month-end adjusting entries.

Account Title	Unadjusted Debit	Unadjusted Credit	Adjusted Debit	Adjusted Credit
Prepaid Insurance	$3,600		$3,450	
Equipment	9,600		9,600	
Accumulated Depreciation		$1,280		$1,360
Notes Payable		9,600		9,600
Interest Payable		2,304		2,448

Required

1. The company purchased a 36-month insurance policy on June 1, 2000. Reconstruct the adjusting journal entry for insurance on June 30, 2001.
2. What was the original cost of the insurance policy? Explain your answer.
3. The equipment was purchased on February 1, 2000, for $9,600. Taggart uses straight-line depreciation and estimates that the equipment will have no salvage value. Reconstruct the adjusting journal entry for depreciation on June 30, 2001.
4. What is the equipment's estimated useful life in months? Explain your answer.
5. Taggart signed a two-year note payable on February 1, 2000, for the purchase of the equipment. Interest on the note accrues on a monthly basis and will be paid at maturity along with the principal amount of $9,600. Reconstruct the adjusting journal entry for interest on June 30, 2001.
6. What is the *monthly* interest rate on the loan? Explain your answer.

LO 5 Problem 4-10 Use of a Trial Balance to Record Adjusting Entries in T Accounts

Four Star Video has been in the video rental business for five years. An unadjusted trial balance at May 31, 2001, follows.

FOUR STAR VIDEO
UNADJUSTED TRIAL BALANCE
MAY 31, 2001

	Debit	Credit
Cash	$ 4,000	
Prepaid Rent	6,600	
Video Inventory	25,600	
Display Stands	8,900	
Accumulated Depreciation		$ 5,180
Accounts Payable		3,260
Customer Subscriptions		4,450
Capital Stock		5,000
Retained Earnings		22,170
Rental Revenue		9,200
Wage and Salary Expense	2,320	
Utility Expense	1,240	
Advertising Expense	600	
Totals	$49,260	$49,260

The following additional information is available:

a. Four Star rents a store in a shopping mall and prepays the annual rent of $7,200 on April 1 of each year.

b. The asset account Video Inventory represents the cost of videos purchased from suppliers. When a new title is purchased from a supplier, its cost is debited to this account. When a title has served its useful life and can no longer be rented (even at a reduced price), it is removed from the inventory in the store. Based on the monthly count, the cost of titles on hand at the end of May is $23,140.

c. The display stands have an estimated useful life of five years and an estimated salvage value of $500.

d. Wages and salaries owed to employees but unpaid at the end of May amount to $1,450.

e. In addition to individual rentals, Four Star operates a popular discount subscription program. Customers pay an annual fee of $120 for an unlimited number of rentals. Based on the $10 per month earned on each of these subscriptions, the amount earned for the month of May is $2,440.

f. Four Star accrues income taxes using an estimated tax rate equal to 30% of the income for the month.

Required

1. Set up T accounts for each of the accounts listed in the trial balance. Based on the additional information given, set up any other T accounts that will be needed to prepare adjusting entries.
2. Post the month-end adjusting entries directly to the T accounts but do not bother to put the entries in journal format first. Use the letters **a** through **f** from the additional information to identify the entries.
3. Prepare a trial balance to prove the equality of debits and credits after posting the adjusting entries.
4. On the basis of the information you have, does Four Star appear to be a profitable business? Explain your answer.

LO 5 Problem 4-11 Effects of Adjusting Entries on the Accounting Equation

Refer to the information provided for Four Star Video in Problem 4-10.

Required

Prepare a table to summarize the required adjusting entries as they affect the accounting equation. Use the format in Exhibit 3-1. Identify each adjustment by letter.

Multi-Concept Problems

LO 2, 3 Problem 4-12 Cash and Accrual Income Statements for a Manufacturer

Drysdale Company was established to manufacture components for the auto industry. The components are shipped the same day they are produced. The following events took place during the first year of operations.

a. Issued common stock for a $50,000 cash investment.

b. Purchased delivery truck at the beginning of the year at a cost of $10,000 cash. The truck is expected to last five years and will be worthless at the end of that time.

c. Manufactured and sold 500,000 components the first year. The costs incurred to manufacture the components are (1) $1,000 monthly rent on a facility that included utilities and insurance, (2) $400,000 of raw materials purchased on account ($100,000 is still unpaid as of year-end, but all materials were used in manufacturing), and (3) $190,000 paid in salaries and wages to employees and supervisors.

d. Paid $100,000 to sales and office staff for salaries and wages.

e. Sold all components on account for $2 each. As of year-end, $150,000 is due from customers.

Required

1. How much revenue will Drysdale recognize under the cash basis and under the accrual basis?
2. Describe how Drysdale should apply the matching principle to recognize expenses.
3. Prepare an income statement under the accrual basis. Ignore income taxes.

LO 3, 4 Problem 4-13 Revenue Recognition on Installment Sales and Commodities

John Deare, an Illinois corn farmer, retired in South Carolina. While retired, he volunteered his time at the Small Business Administration office. One day, Frances Hirise, a condominium builder, came in with a question about the amount of sales she should recognize on her income statement. She had constructed a complex of 200 units. Half of the units sell for $50,000 each, and the other half sell for $60,000. The developer agreed to finance the sale of all units, and by the end of the year, 40 units at $50,000 and 30 units at $60,000 had been sold. Each buyer made a down payment of 10% cash and agreed to pay the remainder in equal annual payments plus interest on the unpaid balance over the next nine years. No payments have been received other than the down payments. John advised Frances that she should recognize sales of $11 million (100 × $50,000) + (100 × $60,000).

Required

Do you agree with John? Why did he suggest this amount? What amount of revenue would you suggest that Frances recognize in the current and subsequent years as a result of these sales? When should the costs to build the condos (lumber, labor, etc.) be recognized as expenses?

LO 3, 4, 7 Problem 4-14 Revenue and Expense Recognition and Closing Entries

Two years ago, Darlene Darby opened a delivery service. Darby reports the following accounts on her income statement:

Sales	$69,000
Advertising expense	3,500
Salaries expense	39,000
Rent expense	10,000

These amounts represent two years of revenue and expenses. Darby has asked you how she can tell how much of the income is from the first year of business and how much is from the second year. She provides the following additional data:

a. Sales in the second year were double those of the first year.

b. Advertising expense is for a $500 opening promotion and weekly ads in the newspaper.

c. Salaries represent one employee for the first nine months and then two employees for the remainder of the time. Each is paid the same salary. No raises have been granted.

d. Rent has not changed since the business opened.

Required

1. Prepare income statements for Years 1 and 2.
2. Prepare the closing entries for each year. Prepare a short explanation for Darby about the purpose of closing temporary accounts.

LO 5, 6, 8 Problem 4-15 Ten-Column Work Sheet (Appendix 4A)

The following unadjusted trial balance is available for Ace Consulting Inc. on June 30, 2001.

ACE CONSULTING INC.
UNADJUSTED TRIAL BALANCE
JUNE 30, 2001

Cash	$ 6,320	
Accounts Receivable	14,600	
Supplies on Hand	800	
Prepaid Rent	4,800	
Furniture and Fixtures	18,000	
Accumulated Depreciation		$ 5,625
Accounts Payable		5,200
Capital Stock		10,000
Retained Earnings		17,955
Consulting Revenue		12,340
Utility Expense	4,100	
Wage and Salary Expense	2,500	
Totals	$51,120	$51,120

Required

1. Enter the unadjusted trial balance in the first two columns of a 10-column work sheet.
2. Enter the necessary adjustments in the appropriate columns of the work sheet for each of the following:
   a. Wages and salaries earned by employees at the end of June but not yet paid amount to $2,380.
   b. Supplies on hand at the end of June amount to $550.
   c. Depreciation on furniture and fixtures for June is $375.

d. Ace prepays the rent on its office space on June 1 of each year. The rent amounts to $400 per month.

e. Consulting services rendered and billed for which cash has not yet been received amount to $4,600.

3. Complete the remaining columns of the work sheet.

LO 5, 6, 8 Problem 4-16 Monthly Transactions, 10-Column Work Sheet, and Financial Statements (Appendix 4A)

GENERAL LEDGER

Moonlight Bay Inn is incorporated on January 2, 2001, by its three owners, each of whom contributes $20,000 in cash in exchange for shares of stock in the business. In addition to the sale of stock, the following transactions are entered into during the month of January:

January 2: A Victorian inn is purchased for $50,000 in cash. An appraisal performed on this date indicates that the land is worth $15,000 and the remaining balance of the purchase price is attributable to the house. The owners estimate that the house will have an estimated useful life of 25 years and an estimated salvage value of $5,000.

January 3: A two-year, 12%, $30,000 promissory note was signed at the Second State Bank. Interest and principal will be repaid on the maturity date of January 3, 2003.

January 4: New furniture for the inn is purchased at a cost of $15,000 in cash. The furniture has an estimated useful life of 10 years and no salvage value.

January 5: A 24-month property insurance policy is purchased for $6,000 in cash.

January 6: An advertisement for the inn is placed in the local newspaper. Moonlight Bay pays $450 cash for the ad, which will run in the paper throughout January.

January 7: Cleaning supplies are purchased on account for $950. The bill is payable within 30 days.

January 15: Wages of $4,230 for the first half of the month are paid in cash.

January 16: A guest mails the business $980 in cash as a deposit for a room to be rented for two weeks. The guest plans to stay at the inn during the last week of January and the first week of February.

January 31: Cash receipts from rentals of rooms for the month amount to $8,300.

January 31: Cash receipts from operation of the restaurant for the month amount to $6,600.

January 31: Each stockholder is paid $200 in cash dividends.

Required

1. Prepare journal entries to record each of the preceding transactions.

2. Post each of the journal entries to T accounts.

3. Place the balance in each of the T accounts in the unadjusted trial balance columns of a 10-column work sheet.

4. Enter the appropriate adjustments in the next two columns of the work sheet for each of the following:

a. Depreciation of the house

b. Depreciation of the furniture

c. Interest on the promissory note

d. Recognition of the expired portion of the insurance

e. Recognition of the earned portion of the guest's deposit

f. Wages earned during the second half of January amount to $5,120 and will be paid on February 3.

g. Cleaning supplies on hand on January 31 amount to $230.

h. A gas and electric bill that is received from the city amounts to $740 and is payable by February 5.

i. Income taxes are to be accrued at a rate of 30% of income before taxes.

5. Complete the remaining columns of the work sheet.

6. Prepare in good form the following financial statements:
   a. Income statement for the month ended January 31, 2001
   b. Statement of retained earnings for the month ended January 31, 2001
   c. Balance sheet at January 31, 2001
7. Assume that you are the loan officer at Second State Bank (refer to the transaction on January 3). What are your reactions to Moonlight's first month of operations? Are you comfortable with the loan you made?

ALTERNATE PROBLEMS

LO 3 Problem 4-1A The Revenue Recognition Principle

Each of the following paragraphs describes a situation involving revenue recognition.

a. Zee Zitter Inc. paints and decorates office buildings. On September 30, 2001, it received $5,750 for work to be completed over the next six months.

b. Tan Us is a tanning salon franchisor in the Midwest. It charges all franchisees a fee of $2,500 to open a salon and an ongoing fee equal to 5% of all revenue during the first five years. The $2,500 is for training and accounting systems to be used in each salon. During January 2001, Tan Us signed an agreement with five individuals to open salons over the next three months.

c. On June 1, 2001, Dan Diver Bridge Building Inc. entered into a contract with the county to renovate an old covered bridge. The county gives Dan an advance of $500,000 and agrees to pay Dan $75,000 each month for 20 months, at which time the project should be completed.

d. Joe Cropper, a wheat grower, harvested the current year's crop and delivered it to the elevator for storage on October 1, 2001, until it is sold to one of several foreign countries. The expected sales value of the wheat is $450,000.

e. Shop-n-Here, a convenience store chain, constructed a strip shopping center next to one of its stores. The spaces are being sold to individuals who will open auto parts and repair facilities. One person is planning to open a brake-repair shop, another will set up a transmission-repair shop, a third will do 10-minute oil changes, and so on. The store spaces sell for $25,000 each. There are six spaces, four of which are sold in May of 2001.

Required

For each of the preceding situations, indicate when in 2001 revenue should be recognized, as well as the dollar amount. Give a brief explanation for each answer.

LO 5 Problem 4-2A Adjusting Entries

Flood Relief Inc. prepares monthly financial statements and therefore adjusts its accounts at the end of every month. The following information is available for June 2001:

a. Flood received a $10,000, 4%, two-year note receivable from a customer for services rendered. The principal and interest are due on June 1, 2003. Flood expects to be able to collect the note and interest in full at that time.

b. Office supplies totaling $5,600 were purchased during the month. The asset account Supplies is debited whenever a purchase is made. A count in the storeroom on June 30, 2001, indicated that supplies on hand amount to $507. The supplies on hand at the beginning of the month total $475.

c. The company purchased machines last year for $170,000. The machines are expected to be used for four years and have an estimated salvage value of $2,000.

d. On June 1, the company paid $4,650 for rent for June, July, and August. The asset Prepaid Rent was debited; it did not have a balance on June 1.

e. The company operates seven days per week with a weekly payroll of $7,000. Wage earners are paid every Sunday. The last day of the month is Saturday, June 30.

f. Based on its income for the month, Flood estimates that federal income taxes for June amount to $2,900.

Required

For each of the preceding situations, prepare in general journal form the appropriate adjusting entry to be recorded on June 30, 2001.

LO 5 Problem 4-3A Effects of Adjusting Entries on the Accounting Equation

Refer to the information provided for Flood Relief Inc. in Problem 4-2A.

Required

1. Prepare a table to summarize the required adjusting entries as they affect the accounting equation. Use the format in Exhibit 3-1. Identify each adjustment by letter.
2. Assume that Flood Relief reports income of $35,000 before any of the adjusting entries. What net income will Flood Relief report for June?

LO 5 Problem 4-4A Adjusting Entries—Annual Adjustments

GENERAL LEDGER

Ogonquit Enterprises prepares annual financial statements and adjusts its accounts only at the end of the year. The following information is available for the year ended December 31, 2001:

a. Ogonquit purchased office furniture last year for $25,000. The furniture has an estimated useful life of seven years and an estimated salvage value of $4,000.

b. The Supplies account had a balance of $1,200 on January 1, 2001. During 2001, Ogonquit added $12,900 to the account for purchases of supplies during the year. A count of the supplies on hand at the end of December 2001 indicates a balance of $900.

c. On July 1, 2001, Ogonquit credited a liability account, Customer Deposits, for $8,800. This sum represents an amount that a customer paid in advance and that will be earned evenly by Ogonquit over an eight-month period.

d. Ogonquit rented some warehouse space on September 1, 2001, at a rate of $4,000 per month. On that date, Ogonquit debited Prepaid Rent for six months' rent paid in advance.

e. Ogonquit took out a 90-day, 6%, $30,000 note on November 1, 2001, with interest and principal to be paid at maturity.

f. Ogonquit operates five days per week with an average weekly payroll of $4,150. Ogonquit pays its employees every Friday. December 31, 2001, is a Monday.

Required

1. For each of the preceding situations, prepare in general journal form the appropriate adjusting entry to be recorded on December 31, 2001.
2. Assume that Ogonquit's accountant forgets to record the adjusting entries on December 31, 2001. Will net income for the year be understated or overstated? By what amount? (Ignore the effect of income taxes.)

LO 5 Problem 4-5A Recurring and Adjusting Entries

The following are the accounts of Dominique Inc., an interior decorator. The company has been in the decorating business for 10 years and prepares quarterly financial statements. Following the list of accounts is a series of transactions entered into by Dominique. For each transaction, enter the number(s) of the account(s) to be debited and credited.

Accounts

1. Cash	**11.** Capital Stock, $1 par
2. Accounts Receivable	**12.** Paid-in Capital in Excess of Par
3. Prepaid Rent	**13.** Consulting Revenue
4. Office Supplies	**14.** Office Supply Expense
5. Office Equipment	**15.** Rent Expense
6. Accumulated Depreciation	**16.** Salaries and Wages Expense
7. Accounts Payable	**17.** Depreciation Expense
8. Salaries and Wages Payable	**18.** Interest Expense
9. Income Tax Payable	**19.** Income Tax Expense
10. Interim Financing Notes Payable	

Transaction	Debit	Credit
a. **Example:** Issued additional shares of stock to owners; shares issued at greater than par.	1	11, 12
b. Purchased office equipment for cash.		
c. Collected open accounts receivable from customer.		
d. Purchased office supplies on account.		
e. Paid office rent for the next six months.		
f. Paid interest on an interim financing note.		
g. Paid salaries and wages.		
h. Purchased office equipment; made a down payment in cash and signed an interim financing note.		
i. Provided services on account.		
j. Recorded depreciation on equipment.		
k. Recorded income taxes due next month.		
l. Recorded the used office supplies.		
m. Recorded the used portion of prepaid rent.		

LO 5 **Problem 4-6A** Use of Account Balances as a Basis for Adjusting Entries—Annual Adjustments

The following account balances are taken from the records of Laugherty Inc. at December 31, 2001. The Supplies account represents the cost of supplies on hand at the beginning of the year plus all purchases. A physical count on December 31, 2001, shows only $1,520 of supplies on hand. The Unearned Revenue account represents the cash received from a customer on May 1, 2001, for 12 months of service, beginning on that date. The Note Payable represents a six-month promissory note signed with a supplier on September 1, 2001. Principal and interest at an annual rate of 10% will be paid on March 1, 2002.

Supplies	$5,790 debit	
Unearned Revenue		$ 1,800 credit
Note Payable		60,000 credit

Required

1. Prepare the three necessary adjusting entries on the books of Laugherty on December 31, 2001. Assume that Laugherty prepares adjusting entries only once a year, on December 31.
2. Assume that adjusting entries are made at the end of each month rather than only at the end of the year. What would be the balance in Unearned Revenue *before* the December adjusting entry is made? Explain your answer.

GENERAL LEDGER

LO 5 **Problem 4-7A** Use of a Trial Balance as a Basis for Adjusting Entries

Lori Matlock operates a graphic arts business. A trial balance on June 30, 2001, *before* recording any adjusting entries, appears as follows:

MATLOCK GRAPHIC ARTS STUDIO
UNADJUSTED TRIAL BALANCE
JUNE 30, 2001

	Debit	Credit
Cash	$ 7,000	
Prepaid Rent	18,000	
Supplies	15,210	
Office Equipment	46,120	
Accumulated Depreciation—Equipment		$ 4,000
Accounts Payable		1,800
Notes Payable		2,000
Capital Stock		50,000
Retained Earnings		24,350

Dividends	$ 8,400	
Revenue		$ 46,850
Utility Expense	2,850	
Salaries Expense	19,420	
Advertising Expense	12,000	
Totals	$129,000	$129,000

Other Data

a. The monthly rent cost is $600.

b. Supplies on hand on June 30, 2001, amount to $1,290.

c. The office equipment was purchased on June 1, 2000. On that date, it had an estimated useful life of 10 years and a salvage value of $6,120.

d. Interest owed on the note payable but not yet paid amounts to $50.

e. Salaries of $620 are owed to employees but unpaid at the end of the month.

Required

1. Prepare in general journal form the necessary adjusting entries at June 30, 2001. Label the entries a through e to correspond to the other data.
2. Note that the unadjusted trial balance reports a credit balance in Accumulated Depreciation—Equipment of $4,000. Explain *why* the account contains a balance of $4,000 on June 30, 2001.

LO 5 Problem 4-8A Effects of Adjusting Entries on the Accounting Equation

Refer to the information provided for Matlock Graphic Arts Studio in Problem 4-7A.

Required

1. Prepare a table to summarize the required adjusting entries as they affect the accounting equation. Use the format in Exhibit 3-1. Identify each adjustment by letter.
2. Compute the net increase or decrease in net income for the month from the recognition of the adjusting entries you prepared in part 1 (ignore income taxes).

LO 5 Problem 4-9A Reconstruction of Adjusting Entries from Account Balances

Zola Corporation records adjusting entries each month before preparing monthly financial statements. The following selected account balances are taken from its trial balances on June 30, 2001. The "unadjusted" columns set forth the general ledger balances before the adjusting entries were posted. The "adjusted" columns reflect the month-end adjusting entries.

	Unadjusted		Adjusted	
Account Title	**Debit**	**Credit**	**Debit**	**Credit**
Prepaid Rent	$4,000		$3,000	
Equipment	9,600		9,600	
Accumulated Depreciation		$ 800		$ 900
Notes Payable		9,600		9,600
Interest Payable		768		864

Required

1. The company paid for a six-month lease on April 1, 2001. Reconstruct the adjusting journal entry for rent on June 30, 2001.
2. What amount was prepaid on April 1, 2001? Explain your answer.
3. The equipment was purchased on September 30, 2000, for $9,600. Zola uses straight-line depreciation and estimates that the equipment will have no salvage value. Reconstruct the adjusting journal entry for depreciation on June 30, 2001.
4. What is the equipment's estimated useful life in months? Explain your answer.
5. Zola signed a two-year note on September 30, 2000, for the purchase of the equipment. Interest on the note accrues on a monthly basis and will be paid at maturity along with the principal amount of $9,600. Reconstruct the adjusting journal entry for interest expense on June 30, 2001.
6. What is the *monthly* interest rate on the loan? Explain your answer.

LO 5 Problem 4-10A Use of a Trial Balance to Record Adjusting Entries in T Accounts
Lewis and Associates has been in the termite inspection and treatment business for five years. An unadjusted trial balance at June 30, 2001, follows:

LEWIS AND ASSOCIATES
UNADJUSTED TRIAL BALANCE
JUNE 30, 2001

	Debit	Credit
Cash	$ 6,200	
Accounts Receivable	10,400	
Prepaid Rent	4,400	
Chemical Inventory	9,400	
Equipment	18,200	
Accumulated Depreciation		$ 1,050
Accounts Payable		1,180
Capital Stock		5,000
Retained Earnings		25,370
Treatment Revenue		40,600
Wages and Salary Expense	22,500	
Utility Expense	1,240	
Advertising Expense	860	
Totals	$73,200	$73,200

The following additional information is available:

a. Lewis rents a warehouse with office space and prepays the annual rent of $4,800 on May 1 of each year.

b. The asset account Equipment represents the cost of treatment equipment, which has an estimated useful life of 10 years and an estimated salvage value of $200.

c. Chemical inventory on hand equals $1,300.

d. Wages and salaries owed to employees but unpaid at the end of the month amount to $1,080.

e. Lewis accrues income taxes using an estimated tax rate equal to 30% of the income for the month.

Required

1. Set up T accounts for each of the accounts listed in the trial balance. Based on the additional information given, set up any other T accounts that will be needed to prepare adjusting entries.
2. Post the month-end adjusting entries directly to the T accounts but do not bother to put the entries in journal format first. Use the letters **a** through **e** from the additional information to identify the entries.
3. Prepare a trial balance to prove the equality of debits and credits after posting the adjusting entries.
4. On the basis of the information you have, does Lewis appear to be a profitable business? Explain your answer.

LO 5 Problem 4-11A Effects of Adjusting Entries on the Accounting Equation
Refer to the information provided for Lewis and Associates in Problem 4-10A.

Required

Prepare a table to summarize the required adjusting entries as they affect the accounting equation. Use the format in Exhibit 3-1. Identify each adjustment by letter.

Alternate Multi-Concept Problems

LO 2, 3 Problem 4-12A Cash and Accrual Income Statements for a Manufacturer
Marie's Catering makes sandwiches for vending machines. The sandwiches are delivered to the vendor on the same day that they are made. The following events took place during the first year of operations.

a. On the first day of the year, issued common stock for a $20,000 cash investment and a $10,000 investment of equipment. The equipment is expected to last 10 years and will be worthless at the end of that time.

b. Purchased a delivery truck at the beginning of the year at a cost of $14,000 cash. The truck is expected to last five years and will be worthless at the end of that time.

c. Made and sold 50,000 sandwiches during the first year of operations. The costs incurred to make the sandwiches are (1) $800 monthly rent on a facility that included utilities and insurance, (2) $25,000 of meat, cheese, bread, and condiments (all food was purchased on account, and $4,000 is still unpaid at year-end even though all of the food has been used), and (3) $35,000 paid in salaries and wages to employees and supervisors.

d. Paid $12,000 for part-time office staff salaries.

e. Sold all sandwiches on account for $2 each. As of year-end, $25,000 is still due from the vendors.

Required

1. How much revenue will Marie's Catering recognize under the cash basis and under the accrual basis?
2. Explain how accountants apply the revenue recognition principle to Marie's small business. What conditions would allow Marie's to use the cash method to recognize revenue?
3. Prepare an income statement according to the accrual method. Ignore income taxes.

LO 3, 4 **Problem 4-13A** Revenue Recognition on the Percentage-of-Completion and Commodities Methods

Judy Darling owns a diamond mine in South Africa. While vacationing on an island in the Caribbean, she discussed with Marty Jones a recent dig that yielded $1.5 million of raw diamonds. The product is stored with an agent until a buyer is located. The agent expects it to take about two and a half years to sell all of the diamonds. Judy's company spent $1 million to extract the diamonds in 2001.

Marty's company constructs airplane runways and hangars. He is in the process of building a runway for the island and expects to incur the following costs over the next two and one-half years:

2001	$400,000
2002	500,000
2003	100,000

Local residents and the government have already paid Marty $1 million in 2001 and will pay another $500,000 when the project is completed in 2003.

Required

Explain the difference between revenue and cash flow for Judy and Marty. How much revenue will each recognize in 2001, 2002, and 2003?

LO 3, 4, 7 **Problem 4-14A** Revenue and Expense Recognition and Closing Entries

Two years ago, Sue Stern opened an audio book rental shop. Sue reports the following accounts on her income statement:

Sales	$84,000
Advertising expense	10,500
Salaries expense	12,000
Depreciation on tapes	5,000
Rent expense	18,000

These amounts represent two years of revenue and expenses. Sue has asked you how she can tell how much of the income is from the first year and how much is from the second year of business. She provides the following additional data:

a. Sales in the second year are triple those of the first year.

b. Advertising expense is for a $1,500 opening promotion and weekly ads in the newspaper.

c. Salaries represent one employee who was hired eight months ago. No raises have been granted.

d. Rent has not changed since the shop opened.

Required

1. Prepare income statements for Years 1 and 2.
2. Prepare the closing entries for each year. Prepare a short explanation for Sue about the purpose of closing temporary accounts.

GENERAL LEDGER

SPREADSHEET

LO 5, 7, 8 Problem 4-15A Ten-Column Work Sheet and Closing Entries (Appendix 4A)
The unadjusted trial balance for Forever Green Landscaping on August 31, 2001, follows:

FOREVER GREEN LANDSCAPING
UNADJUSTED TRIAL BALANCE
AUGUST 31, 2001

Cash	$ 6,460	
Accounts Receivable	23,400	
Supplies on Hand	1,260	
Prepaid Insurance	3,675	
Equipment	28,800	
Accumulated Depreciation—Equipment		$ 9,200
Buildings	72,000	
Accumulated Depreciation—Buildings		16,800
Accounts Payable		10,500
Notes Payable		10,000
Capital Stock		40,000
Retained Earnings		42,100
Service Revenue		14,200
Advertising Expense	1,200	
Gasoline and Oil Expense	1,775	
Wage and Salary Expense	4,230	
Totals	$142,800	$142,800

Required

1. Enter the unadjusted trial balance in the first two columns of a 10-column work sheet.
2. Enter the necessary adjustments in the appropriate columns of the work sheet for each of the following:
   a. A count of the supplies on hand at the end of August reveals a balance of $730.
   b. The company paid $4,200 in cash on May 1, 2001, for a two-year insurance policy.
   c. The equipment has a four-year estimated useful life and no salvage value.
   d. The buildings have an estimated useful life of 30 years and no salvage value.
   e. The company leases space in its building to another company. The agreement requires the tenant to pay Forever Green $700 on the 10th of each month for the previous month's rent.
   f. Wages and salaries earned by employees at the end of August but not yet paid amount to $3,320.
   g. The company signed a six-month promissory note on August 1, 2001. Interest at an annual rate of 12% and the principal amount of $10,000 are due on February 1, 2002.
3. Complete the remaining columns of the work sheet.
4. Assume that Forever Green closes its books at the end of each month before preparing financial statements. Prepare the necessary closing entries at August 31, 2001.

GENERAL LEDGER

LO 5, 6, 8 Problem 4-16A Ten-Column Work Sheet and Financial Statements (Appendix 4A)
The following unadjusted trial balance is available for Tenfour Trucking Company on January 31, 2001:

TENFOUR TRUCKING COMPANY
UNADJUSTED TRIAL BALANCE
JANUARY 31, 2001

Cash	$ 27,340	
Accounts Receivable	41,500	
Prepaid Insurance	18,000	
Warehouse	40,000	
Accumulated Depreciation—Warehouse		$ 21,600
Truck Fleet	240,000	
Accumulated Depreciation—Truck Fleet		112,500

Land	$ 20,000	
Accounts Payable		$ 32,880
Notes Payable		50,000
Interest Payable		4,500
Customer Deposits		6,000
Capital Stock		100,000
Retained Earnings		40,470
Freight Revenue		165,670
Gas and Oil Expense	57,330	
Maintenance Expense	26,400	
Wage and Salary Expense	43,050	
Dividends	20,000	
Totals	$533,620	$533,620

Required

1. Enter the unadjusted trial balance in the first two columns of a 10-column work sheet.
2. Enter the necessary adjustments in the appropriate columns of the work sheet for each of the following:
   - **a.** Prepaid insurance represents the cost of a 24-month policy purchased on January 1, 2001.
   - **b.** The warehouse has an estimated useful life of 20 years and an estimated salvage value of $4,000.
   - **c.** The truck fleet has an estimated useful life of six years and an estimated salvage value of $15,000.
   - **d.** The promissory note was signed on January 1, 2000. Interest at an annual rate of 9% and the principal of $50,000 are due on December 31, 2001.
   - **e.** The customer deposits represent amounts paid in advance by new customers. A total of $4,500 of the balance in Customer Deposits was earned during January 2001.
   - **f.** Wages and salaries earned by employees at the end of January but not yet paid amount to $8,200.
   - **g.** Income taxes are accrued at a rate of 30% at the end of each month.
3. Complete the remaining columns of the work sheet.
4. Prepare in good form the following financial statements:
   - **a.** Income statement for the month ended January 31, 2001
   - **b.** Statement of retained earnings for the month ended January 31, 2001
   - **c.** Balance sheet at January 31, 2001
5. Compute Tenfour's current ratio. What does this ratio tell you about the company's liquidity?
6. Explain why it is not possible to compute a gross profit ratio for Tenfour. Describe a ratio that you believe would be a meaningful measure of profitability for a trucking company. Feel free to "invent" a ratio if you think it would be a meaningful measure of profitability.

CASES

Reading and Interpreting Financial Statements

LO 3 Case 4-1 Reading and Interpreting Ben & Jerry's Footnotes—Revenue Recognition

Refer to the excerpt on page 147 where Ben & Jerry's explains how it recognizes initial franchise fees as revenue. www.benjerry.com

Required

1. Is the way in which Ben & Jerry's recognizes franchise fees for individual stores as revenue in accordance with the revenue recognition principle? Explain your answer.
2. Explain the logic behind the method Ben & Jerry's uses to recognize as revenue franchise fees relating to area franchise agreements.
3. Refer to Ben & Jerry's financial statements. How important are franchise fees as a form of revenue for the company? Support your answer with any necessary computations.

LO 3 Case 4-2 Reading and Interpreting Gateway's Footnotes—Revenue Recognition

www.gateway.com

Refer to Gateway's first footnote, "Summary of Significant Accounting Policies," and specifically the section that discusses revenue recognition.

Required

1. At what point in time does Gateway recognize revenue?
2. Explain what Gateway means by "extended warranty programs."
3. Why would Gateway recognize the revenue from these programs over "the extended warranty period" rather than in the period a product is sold?

LO 3 Case 4-3 Reading and Interpreting Sears, Roebuck's Footnotes—Revenue Recognition

www.searsroebuck.com

The following excerpt is taken from Sears' 1998 annual report: "The Company sells extended service contracts with terms of coverage generally between 12 and 36 months. Revenue and incremental direct acquisition costs from the sale of these contracts are deferred and amortized over the lives of the contracts. Costs related to servicing the contracts are expensed as incurred."

Required

1. Why do retailers recognize the revenue over the life of the service contract even though cash is received at the time of the sale?
2. If a product is sold in Year 1 for $2,500, including a $180 service contract that will cover three years, how much revenue is recognized in Years 1, 2, and 3? (Assume a straight-line approach.) What corresponding account can you look for in the financial statements to determine the amount of service contract revenue that will be recognized in the future?

Making Financial Decisions

LO 2, 3, 4 Case 4-4 The Use of Net Income and Cash Flow to Evaluate a Company

After you have gained five years of experience with a large CPA firm, one of your clients, Duke Inc., asks you to take over as chief financial officer for the business. Duke advises its clients on the purchase of software products and assists them in installing the programs on their computer systems. Because the business is relatively new (it began servicing clients in January 2001), its accounting records are somewhat limited. In fact, the only statement available is an income statement for the first year:

DUKE INC.
STATEMENT OF INCOME
FOR THE YEAR ENDED DECEMBER 31, 2001

Revenues		$1,250,000
Expenses:		
Salaries and wages	$480,000	
Supplies	65,000	
Utilities	30,000	
Rent	120,000	
Depreciation	345,000	
Interest	138,000	
Total expenses		$1,178,000
Net income		$ 72,000

Based on its relatively modest profit margin of 5.76% (net income of $72,000 divided by revenues of $1,250,000), you are concerned about joining the new business. To alleviate your concerns, the president of the company is able to give you the following additional information:

a. Clients are given 90 days to pay their bills for consulting services provided by Duke. On December 31, 2001, $230,000 of the revenues is yet to be collected in cash.

b. Employees are paid on a monthly basis. Salaries and wages of $480,000 include the December payroll of $40,000, which will be paid on January 5, 2002.

c. The company purchased $100,000 of operating supplies when it began operations in January. The balance of supplies on hand at December 31 amounts to $35,000.

d. Office space is rented in a downtown high-rise building at a monthly rental of $10,000. When the company moved into the office in January, it prepaid its rent for the next 18 months, beginning January 1, 2001.

e. On January 1, 2001, Duke purchased its own computer system and related accessories at a cost of $1,725,000. The estimated useful life of the system is five years.

f. The computer system was purchased by signing a three-year, 8% note payable for $1,725,000 on the date of purchase. The principal amount of the note and interest for the three years are due on January 1, 2004.

Required

1. Based on the income statement and the additional information given, prepare a statement of cash flows for Duke for 2001. (*Hint:* Simply list all of the cash inflows and outflows that relate to operations.)
2. On the basis of the income statement given and the statement of cash flows prepared in part **1**, do you think it would be a wise decision on your part to join the company as its chief financial officer? Include in your response any additional questions that you believe are appropriate to ask before joining the company.

LO 4 **Case 4-5** Depreciation

Jenner Inc., a graphic arts studio, is considering the purchase of computer equipment and software for a total cost of $18,000. Jenner can pay for the equipment and software over three years at the rate of $6,000 per year. The equipment is expected to last 10 to 20 years, but because of changing technology, Jenner believes it may need to replace the system as soon as three to five years. A three-year lease of similar equipment and software is available for $6,000 per year. Jenner's accountant has asked you to recommend whether the company should purchase or lease the equipment and software and to suggest the length of the period over which to depreciate the software and equipment if the company makes the purchase.

Required

Ignoring the effect of taxes, would you recommend the purchase or the lease? Why? Referring to the definition of *depreciation,* what is the appropriate useful life to use for the equipment and software?

Accounting and Ethics: What Would You Do?

LO 2, 3, 4, 5 **Case 4-6** Revenue Recognition and the Matching Principle

Listum & Sellum Inc. is a medium-size midwestern real estate company. It was founded five years ago by its two principal stockholders, Willie Listum and Dewey Sellum. Willie is president of the company, and Dewey is vice-president of sales. Listum & Sellum has enjoyed tremendous growth since its inception by aggressively seeking out listings for residential real estate and paying a very generous commission to the selling agent.

The company receives a 6% commission for selling a client's property and gives two-thirds of this, or 4% of the selling price, to the selling agent. For example, if a house sells for $100,000, Listum & Sellum receives $6,000 and pays $4,000 of this to the selling agent. At the time of the sale, the company records a debit of $6,000 to Accounts Receivable and a credit of $6,000 to Sales Revenue. The accounts receivable is normally collected within 30 days. Also at the time of sale, the company debits $4,000 to Commissions Expense and credits Commissions Payable for the same amount. Sales agents are paid by the 15th of the month following the month of the sale. In addition to the commissions expense, Listum & Sellum's other two major expenses are advertising of listings in local newspapers and depreciation of the company fleet of Cadillacs (Dewey has always believed that all of the sales agents should drive Cadillacs). The newspaper ads are taken for one month, and the company has until the 10th of the following month to pay that month's bill. The automobiles are depreciated over four years (Dewey doesn't believe that any salesperson should drive a car that is more than four years old).

Due to a downturn in the economy in the Midwest, sales have been sluggish for the first 11 months of the current year, which ends on June 30. Willie is very disturbed by the slow sales this particular year because a large note payable to the local bank is due in July and the company plans to ask the bank to renew the note for another three years. Dewey seems less concerned by the unfortunate timing of the recession and has some suggestions as to how they can "paint the rosiest possible picture for the banker" when they go for the loan extension in July. In fact, he has some very specific recommendations for you as to how to account for transactions during June, the last month in the fiscal year.

You are the controller for Listum & Sellum and have been treated very well by Willie and Dewey since joining the company two years ago. In fact, Dewey insists that you personally drive the top-of-the-line Cadillac. Following are his suggestions:

> First, for any sales made in June, we can record the 6% commission revenue immediately but delay recording the 4% commission expense until July, when the sales agent is paid. We record the sales at the same time we always have, the sales agents get paid when they always have, the bank sees how profitable we have been, we get our loan, and everybody is happy!
>
> Second, since we won't be paying our advertising bills for the month of June until July 10, we can just wait until then to record the expense. The timing seems perfect, given that we are to meet with the bank for the loan extension on July 8.
>
> Third, since we will be depreciating the fleet of Caddys for the year ending June 30, how about just changing the estimated useful life on them to eight years instead of four years? We won't say anything to the sales agents; no need to rile them up about having to drive their cars for eight years. Anyhow, the change to eight years would just be for accounting purposes. In fact, we could even switch back to four years for accounting purposes next year. Likewise, the changes in recognizing commission expense and advertising expense don't need to be permanent either; these are just slight bookkeeping changes to help us get over the hump!

Required

1. Explain why each of the three proposed changes in accounting will result in an increase in net income for the year ending June 30.
2. Identify any concerns you have with each of the three proposed changes in accounting from the perspective of generally accepted accounting principles.
3. Identify any concerns you have with each of the three proposed changes in accounting from an ethical perspective.
4. What would you do? Draft your response to Willie and Dewey in the form of a business memo.

LO 4 **Case 4-7** Advice to a Potential Investor

Century Company was organized 15 months ago as a management consulting firm. At that time, the owners invested a total of $50,000 cash in exchange for stock. Century purchased equipment for $35,000 cash and supplies to be used in the business. The equipment is expected to last seven years with no salvage value. Supplies are purchased on account and paid for in the month after the purchase. Century normally has about $1,000 of supplies on hand. Its client base has increased so dramatically that the president and chief financial officer have approached an investor to provide additional cash for expansion. The balance sheet and income statement for the first year of business are presented below:

CENTURY COMPANY
BALANCE SHEET
DECEMBER 31, 2001

Assets		**Liabilities and Owners' Equity**	
Cash	$10,100	Accounts payable	$ 2,300
Accounts receivable	1,200	Common stock	50,000
Supplies	16,500	Retained earnings	10,500
Equipment	35,000		
Total	$62,800	Total	$62,800

CENTURY COMPANY
INCOME STATEMENT
FOR THE YEAR ENDED DECEMBER 31, 2001

Revenues		$82,500
Wages and salaries	$60,000	
Utilities	12,000	72,000
Net income		$10,500

Required

The investor has asked you to look at these financial statements and give an opinion about Century's future profitability. Are the statements prepared in accordance with generally accepted accounting principles? If not, explain why. Based on only these two statements, what would you advise? What additional information would you need in order to give an educated opinion?

INTERNET RESEARCH CASE

Case 4-8 McDonald's

McDonald's is the largest and best known fast-food supplier in the world, with worldwide (systemwide) sales of nearly $36 billion in 1998. Yet it claims to serve only 1% of the world's population. One of its strategic goals is to increase market share—currently at 40% of the US market.

Review the chapter-opening introduction to McDonald's and the Business Strategy box. Then go to McDonald's Web site, examine its most recent annual report, and research how this company can fulfill management's goals of ever greater market share, higher customer satisfaction, and increased profitability.

www.mcdonalds.com

1. McDonald's total revenues include all the revenues from company-operated restaurants and a portion of the revenues of franchisees' restaurants.

a. Looking at the latest year's income statement, what are McDonald's total revenues for the current year?

b. McDonald's also refers to total "systemwide" sales in the management section of its annual report. By looking at the current year's annual report, find its systemwide sales for the current year and indicate what that term refers to.

c. Why is total revenue reported in the income statement and systemwide revenue not reported there? That is, why can't McDonald's place systemwide sales on its income statement?

2. Look at McDonald's Web site and its latest annual report carefully. How is the company working to achieve its strategic goals mentioned above? In what financial statements and line items might you see these goals reflected?

SOLUTION TO KEY TERMS QUIZ

18 Recognition (p. 140)
11 Current value (p. 141)
14 Accrual basis (p. 143)
17 Revenue recognition principle (p. 146)
3 Production method (p. 148)
23 Matching principle (p. 148)
4 Adjusting entries (p. 150)
24 Contra account (p. 152)
19 Deferred expense (p. 157)
15 Accrual (p. 158)
10 Accrued asset (p. 158)
1 Work sheet (p. 163)
20 Nominal accounts (p. 165)
16 Interim statements (p. 166)
25 Historical cost (p. 141)
21 Cash basis (p. 143)
2 Revenues (p. 146)
6 Percentage-of-completion method (p. 146)
8 Installment method (p. 148)
26 Expenses (p. 149)
12 Straight-line method (p. 152)
13 Deferral (p. 157)
7 Deferred revenue (p. 157)
22 Accrued liability (p. 158)
27 Accounting cycle (p. 163)
9 Real accounts (p. 164)
5 Closing entries (p. 165)

Part I

INTEGRATIVE PROBLEM

Completing Financial Statements, Computing Ratios, Comparing Accrual vs. Cash Income, and Evaluating the Company's Cash Needs

SPREADSHEET

Mountain Home Health Inc. was formed in 1993 to provide home nursing services in the Great Smoky Mountains of Tennessee. When contacted by a client or referred by a physician, nurses visit with the patient and discuss needed services with the physician.

Mountain Home Health earns revenue from patient services. Most of the revenue comes from billing either insurance companies, the state of Tennessee, or the Medicare program. Amounts billed are recorded in the Billings Receivable account. Insurance companies, states, and the federal government do not fully fund all procedures. For example, the state of Tennessee pays an average 78% of billed amounts. Mountain Home Health has already removed the uncollectible amounts from the Billings Receivable account and reports it and Medical Services Revenue at the net amount. Services extended on Saturday, December 30, and Sunday, December 31, 2000, totaled $16,000, net of allowances for uncollectible amounts. The firm earns a minor portion of its total revenue directly from patients in the form of cash.

Employee salaries, medical supplies, depreciation, and gasoline are the major expenses. Employees are paid every Friday for work performed during the Saturday-to-Friday pay period. Salaries amount to $800 per day. In 2000, December 31 falls on a Sunday. Medical supplies (average use of $1,500 per week) are purchased periodically to support health care coverage. The inventory of supplies on hand on December 31 amounted to $8,653.

The firm owns five automobiles (all purchased at the same time) that average 50,000 miles per year and are replaced every 3 years. They typically have no residual value. The building has an expected life of 20 years with no residual value. Straight-line depreciation is used on all firm assets. Gasoline costs, which are a cash expenditure, average $375 per day. The firm purchases a 3-year, extended warranty contract to cover maintenance costs. The contract costs $9,000 (assume equal use each year).

On December 29, 2000, Mountain Home Health declared a dividend of $10,000, payable on January 15, 2001. The firm makes annual payments of principal and interest each June 30 on the mortgage. The interest rate on the mortgage is 6%.

The following unadjusted trial balance is available for Mountain Home Health on December 31, 2000.

MOUNTAIN HOME HEALTH
UNADJUSTED TRIAL BALANCE
DECEMBER 31, 2000

	Debit	Credit
Cash	$ 75,000	
Billings Receivable (net)	151,000	
Medical Supplies	73,000	
Extended Warranty	3,000	
Automobiles	90,000	
Accumulated Depreciation—Automobiles		$ 60,000
Building	200,000	
Accumulated Depreciation—Building		50,000
Accounts Payable		22,000
Dividend Payable		10,000
Mortgage Payable		100,000
Capital Stock		100,000
Additional Paid-in-Capital		50,000
Retained Earnings		99,900
Medical Services Revenue		550,000
Salary and Wages Expense	290,400	

Gasoline Expense	$ 137,500	
Utilities Expense	12,000	
Dividends	10,000	
	$1,041,900	$1,041,900

Required

1. Set up T accounts for each of the accounts listed on the trial balance. Based on the information provided, set up any other T accounts that will be needed to prepare adjusting entries.
2. Post the year-end adjusting entries directly to the T accounts, but do not bother to put the entries in journal format first.
3. Prepare a statement of income and a statement of retained earnings for Mountain Home Health for the year ended December 31, 2000.
4. Prepare a balance sheet for Mountain Home Health as of December 31, 2000.
5. Compute the following as of December 31, 2000: **a.** Working capital **b.** Current ratio
6. Which of the adjusting entries might cause a difference between cash and accrual based income?
7. Mary Francis, controller of Mountain Home, became concerned about the company's cash flow after talking to a local bank loan officer. The firm tries to maintain a 7-week supply of cash to meet the demands of payroll, medical supply purchases, and gasoline. Determine the amount of cash Mountain Home needs to meet the 7-week supply.

TWEETER HOME ENTERTAINMENT GROUP — VIDEO CASE I

Tweeter Home Entertainment Group (www.tweeter.com) is a leading retailer of mid- to high-end audio and video electronics products. Its stores feature an extensive selection of home and car audio systems and components, portable audio equipment, cellular phones, and home video products. Installation and repair services are offered. Tweeter also has a corporate sales division.

Tweeter opened its first store in Boston in 1972 and grew to 18 stores in New England over the next 20 years. By growing in new regional markets, Tweeter maintains 76 retail stores in the mid-Atlantic states, the Southeast, Texas, and California. It operates these stores under the Tweeter name, as well as Bryn Mawr Stereo & Video, HiFi Buys, Home Entertainment, and DOW Stereo/Video. The firm's future plans include adding stores in its current markets, as well as relocating some stores to more favorable sites. It employs nearly 1,600 people and went public in 1998.

Tweeter has a growth strategy for the Internet, too. In late 1999, the firm entered a joint venture with Cyberian Outpost to jointly market and sell consumer electronics over the Internet. Making an equity investment of $1 million in Cyberian's common stock, Tweeter chose to enter the world of e-commerce with a proven partner. Sandy Bloomberg, CEO and founder of Tweeter, and president and COO Jeffrey Stone both thought that this strategy would minimize the firm's risk, limit Tweeter's investment in Web infrastructure by allowing it to use Outpost.com's existing facilities, and provide a proven structure for customer fulfillment instead of building a system from scratch. Both partners in the venture, known as Tweeter.Outpost.com, plan to jointly market the new site, which is expected to start generating earnings in fiscal 2000.

Selling strategies have evolved to help manage the product mix, which includes generally higher-end items from over 50 vendors. Video products have yielded lower gross margin than audio products, although total sales of video have increased at faster rates than audio. To enhance the overall gross margin, Tweeter has adopted a "Sell Audio with Video" strategy. Purchasing strategies are important, too. Tweeter is a member of a national volume-buying group that often saves costs by getting additional vendor rebates and product discounts.

With the huge amount of information needed to manage the chain, Tweeter has developed a sophisticated management information system. It is automatically updated after every transaction, and information is accessible in real time to managers, sales associates, and buyers alike. Store managers and retail associates have access to real-time data on sales volume by category, and upper management and store managers can view sales volume, gross margin, and product mix on a per-store or per-sales-associate basis. Store managers are evaluated and compensated based on this information.

Like most retailers, Tweeter experiences seasonal variations in its business. A significant portion of total revenue and net income are realized during the first and fourth fiscal quarters, with most of the net income being realized in the first fiscal quarter. The biggest single influence on the firm's financial condition is the holiday shopping season, although the timing of new store openings, acquisitions, and unexpected changes in supplier prices or the competitive environment are also important.

Required

1. How do you think the joint venture with Cyberian Outpost will affect Tweeter's financial position? Where in its financial statements will the results be shown?
2. Describe the decision-making process at Tweeter as well as you can. What role does financial information seem to play? What role do you think information about the external or competitive environment plays?
3. Select one of Tweeter's long-term goals as identified in the video. Explain how you think the firm's managers can use financial information to determine how well Tweeter is reaching that goal.

Part II

Accounting for Assets

A Word to Students about Part II

In Part I you learned how companies communicate their activities and financial results to users of financial information. You also discovered new ways of thinking about events as transactions, and how these business transactions culminate in a company's financial statements. You learned specialized terminology, used the accounting equation, and began to understand the basis for making financial decisions.

Part II tells what happens when assets flow into the business. Chapter 5 introduces the effects of buying and selling merchandise on the financial statements, and the internal control necessary for keeping a business running smoothly. Chapter 6 expands on inventory issues and shows how inventory transactions affect the statement of cash flows. Chapter 7 covers the inflow of cash and receivables into the business and investments that a company makes. Chapter 8 recognizes that the business must invest its cash and receivables in operating assets.

Finally, you'll focus on how investors and other financial statement users evaluate companies with ratios and make decisions based on that information.

Chapter 5
Merchandise Accounting and Internal Control

Appendix 5A
Accounting Tools: Internal Control for a Merchandising Company

Chapter 6
Inventories and Cost of Goods Sold

Appendix 6A
Accounting Tools: Inventory Costing Methods with the Use of a Perceptual Inventory System

Chapter 7
Cash, Investments, and Receivables

Chapter 8
Operating Assets: Property, Plant, and Equipment, Natural Resources, and Intangibles

Chapter 5

Merchandise Accounting and Internal Control

Study Links

A Look at Previous Chapters

Chapter 4 completed our introduction to the accounting model. We examined the role of adjusting entries in an accrual accounting system.

A Look at This Chapter

In this chapter, we move beyond the basic accounting model to consider the accounting for the various elements of financial statements. We begin by looking at how merchandise companies—retailers and wholesalers—account for their inventory and the effects that buying and selling merchandise have on the income statement. The second part of the chapter introduces the concept of internal control and its applicability to merchandise inventory.

A Look at Upcoming Chapters

Chapter 6 continues the discussion begun in this chapter by focusing on valuation issues for inventory. In each of the remaining chapters in this part, we look at the accounting for other valuable assets of an entity.

Focus on Financial Results

With over 2,500 stores in the United States, Canada, France, Germany, Japan, and the United Kingdom, The Gap has become a global success story. This youth-oriented retailer of casual fashions encompasses three distinct brands—Gap, Banana Republic, and Old Navy. AOL showcases all three on its popular Internet shopping site, and Gap and Banana Republic have Web sites of their own. Gap Inc.'s revenues exceed $9 billion a year, and 1998 was the best overall year in the company's 30-year history.

As a retailer, Gap measures its success in terms of what it earns from buying and selling merchandise. Sales are a fundamental measure of that goal, and as you can see from its 1998 statement of earnings, pictured here, net sales almost doubled from two years ago. At the same time, cost of goods sold as a percentage of net sales steadily decreased. This measure indicates that Gap is successfully managing the difference between what it costs the firm to acquire goods and what it earns by selling them. By 1998, according to the company's annual report, only about 59 cents of every sales dollar went to cover cost of goods sold.

Consolidated Statements of Earnings

($000 except per share amounts)	Fifty-two Weeks Ended January 30, 1999	Percentage to Sales	Fifty-two Weeks Ended January 31, 1998	Percentage to Sales	Fifty-two Weeks Ended February 1, 1997	Percentage to Sales
Net sales	$9,054,462	100.0%	$6,507,825	100.0%	$5,284,381	100.0%
Costs and expenses						
Cost of goods sold and occupancy expenses	5,318,218	58.7	4,021,541	61.8	3,285,166	62.2
Operating expenses	2,403,365	26.5	1,635,017	25.1	1,270,138	24.0
Net interest expense (income)	13,617	0.2	(2,975)	0.0	(19,450)	(0.4)
Earnings before income taxes	1,319,262	14.6	854,242	13.1	748,527	14.2
Income taxes	494,723	5.5	320,341	4.9	295,668	5.6
Net earnings	$ 824,539	9.1%	$ 533,901	8.2%	$ 452,859	8.6%
Weighted-average number of shares–basic	576,041,373		594,269,963		625,719,947	
Weighted-average number of shares–diluted	602,916,255		615,301,137		640,900,830	
Earnings per share–basic	$1.43		$.90		$.72	
Earnings per share–diluted	1.37		.87		.71	

See Notes to Consolidated Financial Statements.

Cost of goods sold has decreased from 1996 to 1998 fiscal years.

Net sales of over $9 billion are almost double 1997's nearly $5.3 billion

Gap Inc.'s 1999 Annual Report

If you were a Gap manager, you would want the cost of goods sold percentage to keep decreasing and sales to continue to increase. How would the use of AOL and the company's own Web sites to market its products be likely to affect the GAP's sales and cost of goods sold and the relationship between them?

www.gap.com

Learning Objectives

After studying this chapter, you should be able to:

LO 1 Understand how wholesalers and retailers account for sales of merchandise. (p. 213)

LO 2 Explain the differences between periodic and perpetual inventory systems. (p. 218)

LO 3 Understand how wholesalers and retailers account for cost of goods sold. (p. 220)

LO 4 Explain the importance of internal control to a business. (p. 225)

LO 5 Describe the basic internal control procedures. (p. 228)

LO 6 Describe the various documents used in recording purchases of merchandise and their role in controlling cash disbursements (Appendix 5A). (p. 237)

The Income Statement for a Merchandiser

To this point, we have concentrated on the accounting for businesses that sell *services.* Banks, hotels, airlines, health clubs, real estate offices, law firms, and accounting firms are all examples of service companies. In this chapter we turn to accounting by merchandisers. Both retailers and wholesalers are merchandisers. They purchase inventory in finished form and hold it for resale. This is in contrast to manufacturers' inventory, which takes three different forms: raw materials, work in process, and finished goods. (Accounting for the three different forms of inventory for a manufacturer is more complex and is covered in a follow-up course to this one.) We focus in this chapter on accounting for merchandise, that is, inventory held by either a wholesaler or a retailer.

From Concept **to PRACTICE 5.1**

Reading Ben & Jerry's Annual Report Is Ben & Jerry's a merchandiser? What items in the annual report can you cite to support your answer?

www.gap.com
www.circuitcity.com

A *condensed* multiple-step income statement for Grizzly Hardware Stores is presented in Exhibit 5-1. First note the period covered by the statement: for the year ended December 31, 2001. Grizzly ends its fiscal year on December 31; however, many merchandisers end their *fiscal year* on a date other than December 31. Retailers often choose a date toward the end of January because the busy holiday shopping season is over and time can be devoted to closing the records and preparing financial statements. For example, The Gap Inc. ends its fiscal year on the Saturday closest to January 31, and Circuit City closes its books on February 28 each year.

We will concentrate on the first two items on Grizzly's statement: net sales and cost of goods sold. The major difference between this income statement and that for a service

Exhibit 5-1 Condensed Income Statement for a Merchandiser

* costs of good sold is shown on a merchandizers income statement, not on one for a service co.

GRIZZLY HARDWARE STORES
INCOME STATEMENT
FOR THE YEAR ENDED DECEMBER 31, 2001

Net sales	$100,000
Cost of goods sold	60,000
Gross margin	$ 40,000
Selling and administrative expenses	29,300
Net income before tax	$ 10,700
Income tax expense	4,280
Net income	$ 6,420

company is the inclusion of cost of goods sold. Because a service company does not sell a product, it does not report cost of goods sold. On the income statement of a merchandising company, cost of goods sold is deducted from net sales to arrive at gross margin or gross profit.

Gross margin as a percentage of net sales is a common analytical tool for merchandise companies. Analysts compare the gross margin percentages for various periods or for several companies and express concern if a company's gross margin is dropping. Every industry in the retail sector tracks its average gross margin ratio, average overhead cost per square foot, and average sales per square foot of retail space. Analysts can use these facts to see how one company is performing in comparison with others in the same industry. If analysts looked at The Gap's 10-year summary in its annual report, they would find that sales per square foot have increased from $389 in 1989 to $532 in 1998.

www.gap.com

Net Sales of Merchandise

LO 1 Understand how wholesalers and retailers account for sales of merchandise.

The first section of Grizzly's income statement is presented in Exhibit 5-2. Two deductions—for sales returns and allowances and sales discounts—are made from sales revenue to arrive at **net sales.** Sales revenue, or simply sales, as it is often called, is a *representation of the inflow of assets,* either cash or accounts receivable, from the sale of merchandise during the period:

Net sales
Sales revenue less sales returns and allowances and sales discounts.

- Sales revenue is also referred to as simply sales.
- Cash sales are recorded daily in a merchandising business.

- In a merchandising business, *cash sales* are recorded daily in the journal and are based on the total amount shown on the cash register tape. For example, suppose that the cash register tape in the paint department of Grizzly Hardware Stores shows sales on March 31, 2001, of $350. The transaction is recorded in the journal as follows:

Mar. 31	Cash	350	
	Sales Revenue		350
	To record daily cash receipts in paint department.		

The sales of paint inventory for a day.

Assets	=	Liabilities	+	Owners' Equity
+350				+350

- *Sales on credit* do not result in the immediate inflow of cash but in an increase in accounts receivable, a promise by the customer to pay cash at a later date. The entry to record a May 4 sale of tools on credit for $125 is recorded as follows:

May 4	Accounts Receivable	125	
	Sales Revenue		125
	To record sale on credit in tools department.		

To records a credit card sale

Assets	=	Liabilities	+	Owners' Equity
+125				+125

Exhibit 5-2 Net Sales Section of the Income Statement

GRIZZLY HARDWARE STORES
PARTIAL INCOME STATEMENT
FOR THE YEAR ENDED DECEMBER 31, 2001

Sales revenue	$103,500	
Less: Sales returns and allowances	2,000	
Sales discounts	1,500	
Net sales		$100,000

SALES RETURNS AND ALLOWANCES

www.nordstrom.com

The cornerstone of marketing is to satisfy the customer. Most companies have standard policies that allow the customer to *return* merchandise within a stipulated period of time. Nordstrom, the Seattle-based retailer, has a very liberal policy regarding returns. That policy has, in large measure, fueled its growth. A company's policy might be that a customer who is not completely satisfied can return the merchandise anytime within 30 days of purchase for a full refund. Alternatively, the customer may be given an *allowance* for spoiled or damaged merchandise—that is, the customer keeps the merchandise but receives a credit for a certain amount in the account balance. Typically, a single account, **Sales Returns and Allowances,** is used to account both for returns and for allowances. If the customer has already paid for the merchandise, either a cash refund is given or the credit amount is applied to future purchases.

SALES RETURNS AND ALLOWANCES
Contra-revenue account used to record both refunds to customers and reductions of their accounts.

The accounting for a return or allowance depends on whether the customer is given a cash refund or credit on an account. Assume that Grizzly's paint department gives a $25 cash refund on spoiled paint returned by a customer. The entry follows:

Study Tip

Recall Accumulated Depreciation, a contra account introduced in Chapter 4. It reduces a long-term asset. In other cases, such as this one involving sales, a contra account reduces an income statement account.

Apr. 25	Sales Returns and Allowances	25	
	Cash		25
	To record return of spoiled paint by customer for a cash refund.		

Assets	=	Liabilities	+	Owners' Equity
−25				−25

Sales Returns and Allowances is a *contra-revenue* account. A contra account has a balance opposite to its related account and is deducted from that account on the statement. Thus, the effect of the debit to this account is the same as if Sales Revenue had been reduced (debited) directly.

The purpose of this entry is to reduce the amount of previously recorded sales. So why didn't we simply reduce Sales Revenue for $25? The reason is that management needs to be able to *monitor* the amount of returns and allowances. If Sales Revenue is reduced for returns and at some point we need to determine the total dollars of returns for the period, we would need to add up all of the individual decreases to this account. A much more efficient method is to split the sales revenue into two accounts, one that includes only sales and another that includes only returns. In this way, the total amount of returns is readily available, and the decision-making process is more efficient and thus more effective.

Merchandisers stock and sell products that other companies manufacture. Whether they are retail shops like this one or wholesalers selling their merchandise to retail stores, merchandisers keep inventories of the different products they stock. Merchandisers must track these items and their cost as they are delivered to the store, as they leave the store as sold—and sometimes as they come back as returned merchandise.

The previous entry illustrates the accounting for a return of merchandise. The same account is normally used when a credit is given and the customer keeps the merchandise. Assume that on May 7 the customer that made the $125 purchase from Grizzly on May 4 notifies it that one of the purchased tools is defective. Grizzly agrees to reduce the customer's unpaid account by $10 because of the defect. The entry to record the allowance follows:

May 7	Sales Returns and Allowances	10	
	Accounts Receivable		10
	To record allowance given for defective merchandise.		

Assets	=	Liabilities	+	Owners' Equity
−10				−10

The Sales Returns and Allowances account gives management and stockholders an important piece of data: that merchandise is being returned or is not completely acceptable. It does not answer the following questions, however. Why is the merchandise being returned? Why are customers getting partial refunds? Is the merchandise shoddy? Are salespeople too aggressive? Should the store's liberal policy regarding returns be changed? Answers to these questions require management to look beyond the accounting data.

TRADE DISCOUNTS AND QUANTITY DISCOUNTS

TRADE DISCOUNT
Selling price reduction offered to a special class of customers.

Various types of discounts to the list price are given to customers. A **trade discount** is a selling price reduction offered to a special class of customers. For example, Grizzly's plumbing department might offer a special price to building contractors. The difference between normal selling price and this special price is called a *trade discount.* A **quantity discount** is sometimes offered to customers who are willing to buy in large quantities.

QUANTITY DISCOUNT
Reduction in selling price for buying a large number of units of a product.

Trade discounts and quantity discounts are not recorded in the accounts. Although a company might track the amount of these discounts for control purposes, the reason for ignoring the quantity and trade discounts in the accounting records is that the list price is not the actual selling price. The *net* amount is a more accurate reflection of the amount of a sale. For example, assume that Grizzly gives a 20% discount from the normal selling price to any single customer who buys between 10 and 25 kitchen sinks, and a 30% discount on purchases of more than 25 sinks. The list price for each unit is $200. The selling price and the related journal entry for a customer's purchase of 40 sinks on July 2 are as follows:

List price	$ 200
Less: 30% quantity discount	60
Selling price	140
× Number of sinks sold	× 40
Sales revenue	$5,600

July 2	Accounts Receivable	5,600	
	Sales Revenue		5,600
	To record sale of 40 kitchen sinks at list price less 30% quantity discount.		

Assets	=	Liabilities	+	Owners' Equity
+5,600				+5,600

Credit Terms and Sales Discounts

Most companies have a standard credit policy. Special notation is normally used to indicate a particular firm's policy for granting credit. For example, credit terms of *n/30* mean that the *net* amount of the selling price, that is, the amount determined after deducting any returns or allowances, is due within 30 days of the date of the invoice. *Net, 10 EOM* means that the net amount is due anytime within 10 days after the end of the month in which the sale took place.

Study Tip

To help you calculate amounts to enter in the end-of-chapter transactions, remember how to interpret these terms.

Another common element of the credit terms offered to customers is sales discounts, a reduction from the selling price given for early payment. For example, assume that Grizzly offers a building contractor credit terms of *1/10, n/30.* This means that the customer may deduct 1% from the selling price if the bill is paid within 10 days of the date of the invoice. Normally the discount period begins with the day *after* the invoice date. If the customer does not pay within the first 10 days, the full invoice amount is due within 30 days. Finally, note that the use of *n* for *net* in this notation is really a misnomer. Although the amount due is net of any returns and allowances, it is the *gross* amount that is due within 30 days. That is, no discount is given if the customer does not pay early.

How valuable to the customer is a 1% discount for payment within the first 10 days? Assume that a $1,000 sale is made. If the customer pays at the end of 10 days, the cash paid will be $990, rather than $1,000, a net savings of $10. The customer has saved $10 by paying 20 days earlier than required by the 30-day term. If we assume 360 days in a year, there are 360/20 or 18 periods of 20 days each in a year. Thus, a savings of $10 for 20 days is equivalent to a savings of $10 times 18, or $180 for the year. An annual return of $180/$990, or 18.2%, would be difficult to match with any other type of investment. In fact, a customer might want to consider borrowing the money to pay off the account early.

Some companies record sales *net* of any discounts for early payment; others record the *gross* amount of sales and then track sales discounts separately. Because the effect on the accounting equation does not differ between the two methods, we will concern ourselves only with the *gross method,* which assumes that customers will not necessarily take advantage of the discount offered for early payment. Sales discounts are rarely material, and companies do not normally disclose the method used on their financial statements.

-Record a credit card sale at the time of sale w/ terms.

Assume a sale on June 10 of $1,000 with credit terms of 2/10, net 30. The entry at the time of the sale is as follows:

June 10	Accounts Receivable	1,000	
	Sales Revenue		1,000
	To record sale on account, terms 2/10, net 30.		

Assets	=	Liabilities	+	Owners' Equity
+1,000				+1,000

If the customer pays after the discount period, the accountant simply makes an entry to record the receipt of $1,000 cash and the reduction of accounts receivable. However, assume the customer pays its account on June 20, within the discount period. The following entry would be made:

-customer pays account early to get discount.

June 20	Cash	980	
	Sales Discounts	20	
	Accounts Receivable		1,000
	To record collection on account.		

Assets	=	Liabilities	+	Owners' Equity
+ 980				−20
−1,000				

SALES DISCOUNTS
Contra-revenue account used to record discounts given customers for early payment of their accounts.

The **Sales Discounts** account is a *contra-revenue* account and thus reduces owners' equity, as shown in the accounting equation above. Also note in Exhibit 5-2 that sales discounts are deducted from sales on the income statement.

-Sales Returns + Allowances + Sales Discounts are both contra-revenue accounts.

BUSINESS STRATEGY

As it passed its fifth year of business, Old Navy was almost as big an operation as the Gap. It's estimated in the industry that by 2004, Old Navy will be bigger than Gap, babyGap, and GapKids combined. Is that what parent company Gap Inc. had in mind when it spun Old Navy off, almost out of thin air?

When Gap CEO Mickey Drexler read that a rival boasted he could create a successful cheap Gap knockoff, Drexler jumped at the chance to do it first. The company converted 48 Gap stores into "Gap Warehouses" that sold lower-priced items especially designed for the new concept. The stores were so successful that within a week, Gap management had decided to spin them off as a new chain with its own identify, and thus Old Navy was born.

With campy ads, piped-in pop music, industrial-style interior design, and innovative merchandising ideas, the chain soon took off. Growth was fast, thanks in part to the fact that the casual-clothing market had been saturated with lookalike products sold in utilitarian stores. "Everyone was taking themselves too seriously," according to Jenny Ming, Old Navy's first head of merchandising and now its president. Old Navy's goal was to make shopping fun again, and led by its mascot, Magic the Dog, it succeeded.

However, Gap relies on many of the same customers who've adopted Old Navy with such enthusiasm. Is the flight of these shoppers responsible in part for the recent shortfalls in sales that both Gap and GapKids have experienced? Nancy Ming doesn't think so. "If we really felt [Old Navy] is cannibalizing [Gap], why would we be opening stores down the street from Gap and in the same mall?" It's a good question. Time will tell whether the success of Old Navy has really dealt Gap a blow.

SOURCE: Carol Emert, "Old Navy's Model Plan: Reasonable Prices, Lively Stores, Offbeat Ads Fuel the Gap's Powerhouse Division," *San Francisco Chronicle*, October 20, 1999, p. C1.

The Cost of Goods Sold

The cost of goods sold section of the income statement for Grizzly is shown in Exhibit 5-3. We will soon turn to each line item in this section. First let us take a look at the basic model for cost of goods sold.

The Cost of Goods Sold Model

The recognition of cost of goods sold as an expense is an excellent example of the *matching principle.* Sales revenue represents the *inflow* of assets, in the form of cash and accounts receivable, from the sale of products during the period. Likewise, cost of goods sold represents the *outflow* of an asset, inventory, from the sale of those same products. The company needs to match the revenue of the period with one of the most important costs necessary to generate the revenue, the *cost* of the merchandise sold.

It may be helpful in understanding cost of goods sold to realize what it is *not. Cost of goods sold is not necessarily equal to the cost of purchases of merchandise during the period.* Except in the case of a new business, a merchandiser starts the year with a certain stock of inventory on hand, called *beginning inventory.* For Grizzly, beginning inventory is the dollar cost of merchandise on hand on January 1, 2001. During the year, Grizzly purchases merchandise. When the cost of goods purchased is added to beginning inventory, the result is **cost of goods available for sale.** Just as the merchandiser starts the period with an inventory of merchandise on hand, a certain amount of *ending inventory* is usually on hand at the end of the year. For Grizzly, this is its inventory on December 31, 2001.

Cost of goods available for sale
Beginning inventory plus cost of goods purchased.

As shown in Exhibit 5-4, think of cost of goods available for sale as a "pool" of costs to be distributed between what we sold and what we did not sell. If we subtract from the pool the cost of what we did *not* sell, the *ending inventory,* we will have the amount we *did* sell, the **cost of goods sold.** Cost of goods sold is simply the difference between the cost of goods available for sale and the ending inventory:

Cost of goods sold
Cost of goods available for sale minus ending inventory.

Beginning inventory	What is on hand to start the period
+ Purchases	What was acquired for resale during the period
= Cost of goods available for sale	The "pool" of costs to be distributed
− Ending inventory	What was not sold during the period and therefore is on hand to start the next period
= Cost of goods sold	What was sold during the period

Exhibit 5-3 Cost of Goods Sold Section of the Income Statement

GRIZZLY HARDWARE STORES
PARTIAL INCOME STATEMENT
FOR THE YEAR ENDED DECEMBER 31, 2001

Cost of goods sold:			
Inventory, January 1, 2001		$15,000	
Purchases	$65,000		
Less: Purchase returns and allowances	1,800		
Purchase discounts	3,700		
Net purchases	$59,500		
Add: Transportation-in	3,500		
Cost of goods purchased		63,000	
Costs of goods available for sale		$78,000	
Less: Inventory, December 31, 2001		18,000	
Cost of goods sold			$60,000

EXHIBIT 5-4 The Cost of Goods Sold Model

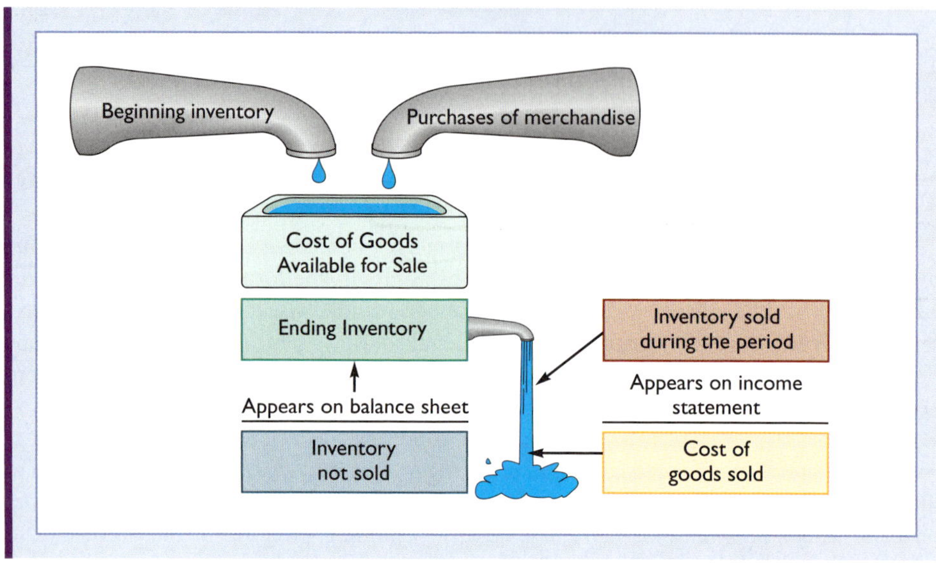

The cost of goods sold model for a merchandiser is illustrated in Exhibit 5-5. The amounts used for the illustration are taken from the cost of goods sold section of Grizzly's income statement as shown in Exhibit 5-3. Notice that ending inventory exceeds beginning inventory by $3,000. That means that the cost of goods purchased exceeds cost of goods sold by that same amount. Indeed, a key point for stockholders, bankers, and other users is whether inventory is building up, that is, whether a company is not selling as much inventory during the period as it is buying. A buildup may indicate that the company's products are becoming less desirable or that prices are becoming uncompetitive.

Inventory Systems: Perpetual and Periodic

LO 2 Explain the differences between periodic and perpetual inventory systems.

PERPETUAL SYSTEM System in which the inventory account is increased at the time of each purchase and decreased at the time of each sale.

PERIODIC SYSTEM System in which the Inventory account is updated only at the end of the period.

Before we look at the journal entries to account for cost of goods sold, it is necessary to understand the difference between the periodic and the perpetual inventory systems. All businesses use one of these two distinct approaches to account for inventory. With the **perpetual system,** the Inventory account is updated *perpetually,* or after each sale or purchase of merchandise. Conversely, with the **periodic system,** the Inventory account is updated only at the end of the *period.*

In a perpetual system, every time goods are purchased, the Inventory account is increased, with a corresponding increase in Accounts Payable for a credit purchase or a decrease in the Cash account for a cash purchase. In addition to recognizing the increases in Accounts Receivable or Cash and in Sales Revenue when goods are sold, the accountant also records an entry to recognize the *cost* of the goods sold and the decrease in the cost of inventory on hand:

Cost of Goods Sold	xxx	
Inventory		xxx
To record the sale of inventory under perpetual system.		

Assets	=	Liabilities	+	Owners' Equity
−xxx				−xxx

Thus, at any point during the period, the inventory account is up-to-date. It has been increased for the cost of purchases during the period and reduced for the cost of the sales.

Why don't all companies use the procedure we just described, the perpetual system? Depending on the volume of inventory transactions, that is, purchases and sales of merchandise, a perpetual system can be extremely costly to maintain. Historically, businesses that have a relatively small volume of sales at a high unit price have used perpetual systems. For example, dealers in automobiles, furniture, appliances, and jewelry normally

EXHIBIT 5-5 The Cost of Goods Sold Model: Example for a Merchandiser

Description	Item	Amount
Merchandise on hand to start the period	Beginning inventory	$15,000
Acquisitions of merchandise during the period	+ Cost of goods purchased	63,000
The pool of merchandise available for sale during the period	= Cost of goods available for sale	$78,000
Merchandise on hand at end of period	− Ending inventory	(18,000)
The expense recognized on the income statement	= Cost of goods sold	$60,000

A $3,000 excess of ending inventory over beginning inventory means the company bought $3,000 more than it sold ($63,000 bought versus $60,000 sold).

use a perpetual system. Each purchase of a unit of merchandise, such as an automobile, can be easily identified and an increase recorded in the Inventory account. When the auto is sold, the dealer can easily determine the cost of the particular car sold by looking at a perpetual inventory record.

Can you imagine, however, a similar system for a supermarket or a hardware store? Consider a checkout stand in a grocery store. Through the use of a cash register tape, the sales revenue for that particular stand is recorded at the end of the day. Because of the tremendous volume of sales of various items of inventory, from cans of vegetables to boxes of soap, it may not be feasible to record the cost of goods sold every time a sale takes place. This illustrates a key point in financial information: the cost of the information should never exceed its benefit. If a store manager had to stop and update the records each time a can of Campbell's soup was sold, the retailer's business would obviously be disrupted.

To a certain extent, the ability of mass merchandisers to maintain perpetual inventory records has improved with the advent of point-of-sale terminals. When a cashier runs a can of corn over the sensing glass at the checkout stand and the bar code is read, the company's computer receives a message that a can of corn has been sold. In some companies, however, updating the inventory record is in units only and is used as a means to determine when a product needs to be reordered. The company still relies on a periodic system to maintain the *dollar* amount of inventory. In the remainder of this chapter, we limit our discussion to the periodic system. We discuss the perpetual system in detail in Chapter 6.

From Concept **TO PRACTICE 5.2**

UNDERSTANDING GATEWAY'S INVENTORY SYSTEM Given the nature of its products, would you expect that Gateway uses a perpetual or a periodic inventory system? Explain your answer.

ACCOUNTING FOR YOUR DECISIONS

You Are the Entrepreneur

A year ago, you and your brother launched a running shoe company in your garage. You buy shoes from four of the major manufacturers and sell them over the phone. Your accountant suggests that you use a perpetual inventory system. Should you?

ANS: The periodic inventory system has the following advantages: The Inventory account is updated only once per year, not after every purchase; the inventory is physically counted on the last day of each period to determine ending inventory; and its cost is low. By operating out of your garage, you are focusing on keeping administrative costs down. A perpetual inventory system would be more costly and would not provide enough extra benefits at low volume. Your decision may change as your business grows, particularly if you began taking orders over the Internet.

Beginning and Ending Inventories in a Periodic System

In a periodic system, the Inventory account is *not* updated each time a sale or purchase is made. Throughout the year, the Inventory account contains the amount of merchandise on hand at the beginning of the year. The account is adjusted only at the end of the year. A company using the periodic system must physically *count* the units of inventory on hand at the end of the period. The number of units of each product is then multiplied by the cost per unit, to determine the dollar amount of ending inventory. Refer to Exhibit 5-3 for Grizzly Hardware Stores. The procedure just described was used to determine its ending inventory of $18,000. Because one period's ending inventory is the next period's beginning inventory, the beginning inventory of $15,000 was based on the count at the end of the prior year.

Periodic
disadv.
- Losses of merchadise due to theft, etc. will not be seen until end of yr.
- Hard to prepare interim financial statements.

In summary, the ending inventory in a periodic system is determined by counting the merchandise, not by looking at the Inventory account at the end of the period. The periodic system results in a trade-off. Use of the periodic system reduces record keeping but at the expense of a certain degree of control. Losses of merchandise due to theft, breakage, spoilage, or other reasons may go undetected in a periodic system because management may assume that all merchandise not on hand at the end of the year was sold. In a retail store, some of the merchandise may have been shoplifted rather than sold. In contrast, with a perpetual inventory system, a count of inventory at the end of the period serves as a *control device.* For example, if the Inventory account shows a balance of $45,000 at the end of the year but only $42,000 of merchandise is counted, management is able to investigate the discrepancy. No such control feature exists in a periodic system.

In addition to the loss of control, the use of a periodic system presents a dilemma when a company wants to prepare *interim* financial statements. Because most companies that use a periodic system find it cost-prohibitive to count the entire inventory more than once a year, they use estimation techniques to determine inventory for monthly or quarterly statements. (These techniques are discussed in Chapter 6.)

The Cost of Goods Purchased

LO 3 Understand how wholesalers and retailers account for cost of goods sold.

Transportation-in
Adjunct account used to record freight costs paid by the buyer.

The cost of goods purchased section of Grizzly's income statement is shown in Exhibit 5-6. The company purchased $65,000 of merchandise during the period. Two amounts are deducted from purchases to arrive at net purchases: purchase returns and allowances of $1,800 and purchase discounts of $3,700. The cost of $3,500 incurred by Grizzly to ship the goods to its place of business is called **transportation-in** and is added to net purchases of $59,500 to arrive at the cost of goods purchased of $63,000. Another name for transportation-in is *freight-in.*

Perpetual
Adv.
- searves as a control device, so they know when something has been shoplifted instead of waiting until the end of the yr.

Exhibit 5-6 Cost of Goods Purchased

GRIZZLY HARDWARE STORES
PARTIAL INCOME STATEMENT
FOR THE YEAR ENDED DECEMBER 31, 2001

Purchases	$65,000	
Less: Purchase returns and allowances	1,800	
Purchase discounts	3,700	
Net purchases	$59,500	
Add: Transportation-in	3,500	
Cost of goods purchased		$63,000

cost pd. by the buyer (Grizzly Hardware)

Purchases Assume that Grizzly buys merchandise on account from one of its wholesalers at a cost of $4,000. **Purchases** is the temporary account used in a periodic inventory system to record acquisitions of merchandise. The journal entry to record the purchase follows:

Feb. 8	Purchases	4,000	
	Accounts Payable		4,000
	To record the purchase of merchandise on account.		

Assets	=	Liabilities	+	Owners' Equity
		+4,000		−4,000

It is important to understand that Purchases is *not* an asset account. It is included in the income statement as an integral part of the calculation of cost of goods sold and is therefore shown as a reduction of owners' equity in the accounting equation. Because Purchases is a temporary account, it is closed at the end of the period.

PURCHASES
Account used in a periodic inventory system to record acquisitions of merchandise.

Purchase Returns and Allowances We discussed returns and allowances earlier in the chapter from the seller's point of view. From the standpoint of the buyer, purchase returns and allowances are reductions in the cost to purchase merchandise. Rather than record these reductions directly in the Purchases account, the accountant uses a separate account. The account, **Purchase Returns and Allowances**, is a *contra account* to Purchases. Because Purchases has a normal debit balance, the normal balance in Purchase Returns and Allowances is a credit balance. The use of a contra account allows management to monitor the amount of returns and allowances. For example, a large number of returns during the period relative to the amount purchased may signal that the purchasing department is not buying from reputable sources.

PURCHASE RETURNS AND ALLOWANCES
Contra-purchases account used in a periodic inventory system when a refund is received from a supplier or a reduction given in the balance owed to a supplier.

Suppose that Grizzly returns $850 of merchandise to a wholesaler for credit on its account. The return decreases both liabilities and purchases. Note that because a return reduces purchases, it actually *increases* net income and thus also increases owners' equity. The journal entry follows:

Sept. 6	Accounts Payable	850	
	Purchase Returns and Allowances		850
	To record the return of merchandise for credit to account.		

Assets	=	Liabilities	+	Owners' Equity
		−850		+850

The entry to record an allowance for merchandise retained rather than returned is the same as the entry for a return.

Study Tip

Earlier in the chapter we saw that the normal balance for the Sales Returns and Allowances account is a debit. Because sales and purchases are opposites, it stands to reason that the normal balance for Purchase Returns and Allowances is a credit.

ACCOUNTING FOR YOUR DECISIONS

You Are the President

You are the president of a mail-order computer business. Your company buys computers and related parts directly from manufacturers and sells them to consumers via direct mail. Recently, you have noticed an increase in the amount of purchase returns and allowances relative to the amount of purchases. What are some possible explanations for this increase?

ANS: Any number of explanations are possible. It is possible that the products are being damaged while in transit. Or it may be that the company has changed suppliers and the merchandise is not of the quality expected. Or it may be that the employees are becoming more demanding in what they accept than they used to be.

Purchase Discounts Discounts were discussed earlier in the chapter, from the seller's viewpoint. Merchandising companies often purchase inventory on terms that allow for a cash discount for early payment, such as 2/10, net 30. To the buyer, a cash discount is called a *purchase discount* and results in a reduction of the cost to purchase merchandise. The same two methods that are used to account for sales discounts are used to account for purchase discounts. Regardless of the method used, management must monitor the amount of purchase discounts taken as well as those opportunities missed by not taking advantage of the discounts for early payment. Because the effect on the accounting equation does not differ between the gross and the net methods, we will limit our discussion to the use of the *gross method.*

Assume a purchase of merchandise on March 13 for $500, with credit terms of 1/10, net 30. The entry at the time of the purchase is as follows:

Mar. 13	Purchases	500	
	Accounts Payable		500
	To record purchase on account, terms 1/10, net 30.		

Assets	=	Liabilities	+	Owners' Equity
		+500		−500

If the company does not pay within the discount period, the accountant simply makes an entry to record the payment of $500 cash and the reduction of accounts payable. However, assume the company does pay its account on March 23, within the discount period. The following entry would be made:

Mar. 23	Accounts Payable	500	
	Cash		495
	Purchase Discounts		5
	To record payment on account.		

Assets	=	Liabilities	+	Owners' Equity
−495		−500		+5

PURCHASE DISCOUNTS Contra-purchases account used to record reductions in purchase price for early payment to a supplier.

The **Purchase Discounts** account is contra to the Purchases account and thus increases owners' equity, as shown in the accounting equation above. Also note in Exhibit 5-6 that purchase discounts are deducted from purchases on the income statement. Finally, note that the effect on the income statement is the same as illustrated earlier for a purchase return: because purchases are reduced, net income is increased.

Shipping Terms and Transportation Costs The *cost principle* governs the recording of all assets. All costs necessary to prepare an asset for its intended use should be included in its cost. The cost of an item to a merchandising company is not necessarily limited to its invoice price. For example, any sales tax paid should be included in computing total cost. Any transportation costs incurred by the buyer should likewise be included in the cost of the merchandise.

FOB DESTINATION POINT Terms that require the seller to pay for the cost of shipping the merchandise to the buyer.

FOB SHIPPING POINT Terms that require the buyer to pay for the shipping costs.

The buyer does not always pay to ship the merchandise. This depends on the terms of shipment. Goods are normally shipped either **FOB destination point** or **FOB shipping point;** *FOB* stands for *free on board.* When merchandise is shipped FOB destination point, it is the responsibility of the seller to deliver the products to the buyer. Thus, the seller either delivers the product to the customer or pays a trucking firm, railroad, or other carrier to transport it. Alternatively, the agreement between the buyer and the seller may provide for the goods to be shipped FOB shipping point. In this case, the merchandise is the responsibility of the buyer as soon as it leaves the seller's premises. When the terms of shipment are FOB shipping point, the buyer incurs transportation costs.

Refer to Exhibit 5-6. Transportation-in represents the freight costs Grizzly paid for inbound merchandise. These costs are added to net purchases, as shown in the exhibit, and increase the cost of goods purchased. Assume that on delivery of a shipment of goods, Grizzly pays an invoice for $300 from the Rocky Mountain Railroad. The terms of shipment are FOB shipping point. The entry on the books of Grizzly follows:

May 10	Transportation-in	300	
	Cash		300
	To record the payment of freight costs.		

Assets	=	Liabilities	+	Owners' Equity
−300				−300

The total of net purchases and transportation-in is called the *cost of goods purchased.* Transportation-in will be closed at the end of the period. In summary, cost of goods purchased consists of the following:

Purchases
Less: Purchase returns and allowances
Purchase discounts
Equals: Net purchases
Add: Transportation-in
Equals: Cost of goods purchased

How should the *seller* account for the freight costs it pays when the goods are shipped FOB destination point? This cost, sometimes called *transportation-out,* is not an addition to the cost of purchases of the seller but is instead one of the costs necessary to *sell* the merchandise. Transportation-out is classified as a *selling expense* on the income statement.

Shipping Terms and Transfer of Title to Inventory Terms of shipment take on additional significance at the end of an accounting period. It is essential that a company establish a proper cutoff at year-end. For example, what if Grizzly purchases merchandise that is in transit at the end of the year? To whom does the inventory belong, Grizzly or the seller? The answer depends on the terms of shipment. If goods are shipped FOB destination point, they remain the legal property of the seller until they reach their destination. Alternatively, legal title to goods shipped FOB shipping point passes to the buyer as soon as the seller turns the goods over to the carrier.

The example in Exhibit 5-7 is intended to summarize our discussion about shipping terms and ownership of merchandise. The example involves a shipment of merchandise in transit at the end of the year. Horton, the seller of the goods, pays the transportation charges only if the terms are FOB destination point. Horton records a sale for goods in transit at year-end, however, only if the terms of shipment are FOB shipping point. If Horton does not record a sale, because the goods are shipped FOB destination point, the inventory appears on its December 31 balance sheet. Grizzly, the buyer, pays freight costs only if the goods are shipped FOB shipping point. Only in this situation does Grizzly record a purchase of the merchandise and include it as an asset on its December 31 balance sheet.

Accounting for Your Decisions

You Are the Manager

You manage the student bookstore. To get ready for the spring term, in December you order a large shipment of books from a publisher, with terms of FOB shipping point. On December 31, the books have not yet arrived. Should this shipment be included in the year-end inventory count even though it is not on hand to count? Assume a periodic inventory system.

ANS: Because the books were shipped FOB shipping point, they should be included in the year-end count even though they are not on hand to count. You should review the purchase invoice to determine the number of books ordered and the unit costs.

1) - Recording a purchase as a buyer under a periodic. Buying $3500 of inventory.

DR. Purchase 3,500
CR Accts pay. 3,500

perpetual

DR. Inventory 3,500
CR. Accts pay. 3,500

2) Periodic - Return of $500 for buyer

DR. CASH 500
CR. PURCHASE Return 500

periodic

3) Bought example tile at discount of 2/10, Net 30

we have a net 3,000
3,500 purchase - 500 return = 3,000 net.
- 2% is a $60 discount
- so we owe $2,940

DR. Accts pay $3,000
CR. CASH $60
CR. purchase discounts $2,940

* This discount decreases purchases

EXHIBIT 5-7 Shipping Terms and Transfer of Title to Inventory

FACTS On December 28, 2001, Horton Wholesale ships merchandise to Grizzly Hardware Stores. The trucking company delivers the merchandise to Grizzly on January 2, 2002. Grizzly's fiscal year-end is December 31.

		If Merchandise is Shipped FOB	
Company		**Destination Point**	**Shipping Point**
Horton	Pay freight costs?	Yes	No
(seller)	Record sale in 2001?	No	Yes
	Include inventory on balance sheet at December 31, 2001?	Yes	No
Grizzly	Pay freight costs?	No	Yes
(buyer)	Record purchase in 2001?	No	Yes
	Include inventory on balance sheet at December 31, 2001?	No	Yes

THE CLOSING PROCESS FOR A MERCHANDISER

The closing process serves two purposes. First, all income statement accounts are returned to a zero balance to start the next accounting period. Second, net income and dividends of the period are transferred to the Retained Earnings account. Many different procedural approaches may be used to close the accounts of a merchandising company. The following list indicates the normal balance in each of the accounts used in a periodic system and whether the account is closed with a debit or a credit:

Account	Normal Balance	Closed with a
Sales Revenue	Credit	Debit
Sales Returns and Allowances	Debit	Credit
Sales Discounts	Debit	Credit
Purchases	Debit	Credit
Purchase Returns and Allowances	Credit	Debit
Purchase Discounts	Credit	Debit
Transportation-in	Debit	Credit

Two-Minute Review

On April 13, 2001, Bitterroot Distributing sells merchandise to Darby Corp. for $1,000 with credit terms of 2/10, net 30. On April 19, Darby returns $150 of defective merchandise and receives a credit on account from Bitterroot. On April 23, Darby pays the amount due.

1. Prepare the necessary entries on Bitterroot's books from April 13 through April 23. Assume Bitterroot uses a periodic inventory system.

2. Prepare the necessary entries on Darby's books from April 13 through April 23. Assume Darby uses a periodic inventory system.

Answers:

1. April 13	*Accounts Receivable*	*1,000*	
	Sales Revenue		*1,000*
	To record sale on credit.		

Assets = Liabilities + Owners' Equity
+1,000 +1,000

April 19	*Sales Returns and Allowances*	*150*	
	Accounts Receivable		*150*
	To record return of defective merchandise for a credit on account.		

Assets	=	Liabilities	+	Owners' Equity
−150				−150

April 23	*Cash*	*833*	
	Sales Discounts	*17*	
	Accounts Receivable		*850*
	To record collection on account.		

Assets	=	Liabilities	+	Owners' Equity
+833				−17
−850				

2. April 13	*Purchases*	*1,000*	
	Accounts Payable		*1,000*
	To record the purchase of merchandise on account.		

Assets	=	Liabilities	+	Owners' Equity
		+1,000		−1,000

April 19	*Accounts Payable*	*150*	
	Purchase Returns and Allowances		*150*
	To record the return of merchandise for credit to account.		

Assets	=	Liabilities	+	Owners' Equity
		−150		+150

April 23	*Accounts Payable*	*850*	
	Cash		*833*
	Purchases Discounts		*17*
	To record payment on account.		

Assets	=	Liabilities	+	Owners' Equity
−833		−850		+17

AN INTRODUCTION TO INTERNAL CONTROL

LO 4 Explain the importance of internal control to a business.

An employee of a large auto parts warehouse routinely takes spare parts home for personal use. A payroll clerk writes and signs two checks for an employee and then splits the amount of the second check with the worker. Through human error, an invoice is paid for merchandise never received from the supplier. These cases sound quite different from one another, but they share one important characteristic. They all point to a deficiency in a company's internal control system. An **internal control system** consists of the policies and procedures necessary to ensure the safeguarding of an entity's assets, the reliability of its accounting records, and the accomplishment of its overall objectives.

INTERNAL CONTROL SYSTEM
Policies and procedures necessary to ensure the safeguarding of an entity's assets, the reliability of its accounting records, and the accomplishment of overall company objectives.

- Controls to make sure assets are protected & not used incorrectly (i.e. buying dinner for other than)
- ✓ to make sure accounting takes place

Three assets are especially critical to the operation of a merchandising company: cash, accounts receivable, and inventory. Activities related to these three assets compose the operating cycle of a business. Cash is used to buy inventory, the inventory is eventually sold, and assuming a sale on credit, the account receivable from the customer is collected. We turn now to the ways in which a company attempts to *control* the assets at its disposal. This section serves as an introduction to the important topic of internal control, which is explored further at appropriate points in the book. For example, controls to safeguard cash are discussed in Chapter 7.

Three important assets: Cash, acct's receiv., inventory

EXHIBIT 5-8 Report of Management—The Gap Inc.

Management's Report on Financial Information

Management is responsible for the integrity and consistency of all financial information presented in the Annual Report. The financial statements have been prepared in accordance with generally accepted accounting principles and necessarily include certain amounts based on Management's best estimates and judgments.

In fulfilling its responsibility for the reliability of financial information, Management has established and maintains accounting systems and procedures appropriately supported by internal accounting controls. Such controls include the selection and training of qualified personnel, an organizational structure providing for division of responsibility, communication of requirement for compliance with approved accounting control and business practices and a program of internal audit. The extent of the Company's system of internal accounting control recognizes that the cost should not exceed the benefits derived and that the evaluation of those factors requires estimates and judgments by Management. Although no system can ensure that all errors or irregularities have been eliminated, Management believes that the internal accounting controls in use provide reasonable assurance, at reasonable cost, that assets are safeguarded against loss from unauthorized use or disposition, that transactions are executed in accordance with Management's authorization and that the financial records are reliable for preparing financial statements and maintaining accountability for assets. The financial statements of the Company have been audited by Deloitte & Touche LLP, independent auditors whose report appears below.

The Audit and Finance Committee (the "Committee") of the Board of Directors is comprised solely of directors who are not officers or employees of the Company. The Committee is responsible for recommending to the Board of Directors the selection of independent auditors. It meets periodically with Management, the independent auditors and the internal auditors to assure that they are carrying out their responsibilities. The Committee also reviews and monitors the financial, accounting and auditing procedures of the Company in addition to reviewing the Company's financial reports. Deloitte & Touche LLP and the internal auditors have full and free access to the Committee, with and without Management's presence.

First Paragraph
Management's responsibility for the financial information

Second Paragraph
System of Internal controls

Third Paragraph
Role of the Audit and Finance Committee

THE REPORT OF MANAGEMENT: SHOWING RESPONSIBILITY FOR CONTROL

REPORT OF MANAGEMENT Written statement in the annual report indicating the responsibility of management for the financial statements.

INTERNAL AUDIT STAFF Department responsible for monitoring and evaluating the internal control system.

— independent accountants vs Internal auditors

Modern business is characterized by absentee ownership. In most large corporations, it is impossible for the owners—the stockholders—to be actively involved in the daily affairs of the business. Professional managers have the primary responsibility for the business's smooth operation. They are also responsible for the content of the financial statements.

Most annual reports now include a **report of management** to the stockholders. A typical management report, in this case for The Gap Inc., is shown in Exhibit 5-8. The first paragraph of the report clearly spells out management's responsibility for the financial information presented in the annual report. The second paragraph refers to the system of internal controls within the company. One of the features of The Gap's internal control system is the use of an **internal audit staff.** Most large corporations today have a full-time staff of internal auditors who have the responsibility for evaluating the entity's internal control system.

The primary concern of the independent public accountants, or external auditors, is whether the financial statements have been presented fairly. Internal auditors focus more on the efficiency with which the organization is run. They are responsible for periodically reviewing both accounting and administrative controls, which we discuss later in this chapter. The internal audit staff also helps to ensure that the company's policies and procedures are followed.

The second paragraph of the report states that the company's independent public accountants have audited the company's financial statements. The management of most corporations would consider it cost-prohibitive for the auditors to verify the millions of transactions recorded in a single year. Instead, the auditors rely to a certain degree on the system of internal control as assurance that transactions are properly recorded and reported. The degree of reliance that they are able to place on the company's internal controls is a significant factor in determining the extent of their testing. The stronger the system of internal control, the less testing is necessary. A weak system of internal control requires that the auditors extend their tests of the records.

The **board of directors** of a corporation usually consists of key officers of the corporation as well as a number of directors whom it does not directly employ. For example, The Gap's board of 11 directors consists of 4 insiders and 7 outsiders. The outsiders often include presidents and key executive officers of other corporations and sometimes business school faculty. The board of directors is elected by the stockholders.

As referred to in the third paragraph of Exhibit 5-8, the **audit committee** (or the Audit and Finance Committee for The Gap) of the board of directors provides direct contact between the stockholders and the independent accounting firm. Audit committees have assumed a much more active role since the passage of the **Foreign Corrupt Practices Act** in 1977. This legislation was passed in response to a growing concern over various types of improprieties by top management, such as kickbacks to politicians and bribes of foreign officials. The act includes a number of provisions intended to increase the accountability of management and the board of directors to stockholders. According to the act, management is responsible for keeping accurate records, and various provisions deal with the system of internal controls necessary to ensure the safeguarding of assets and the reliability of the financial statements. Audit committees have become much more involved in the oversight of the financial reporting system since the enactment of the act.

BOARD OF DIRECTORS
Group composed of key officers of a corporation and outside members responsible for general oversight of the affairs of the entity.

AUDIT COMMITTEE
Board of directors subset that acts as a direct contact between stockholders and the independent accounting firm.

FOREIGN CORRUPT PRACTICES ACT
Legislation intended to increase the accountability of management for accurate records and reliable financial statements.

ACCOUNTING SYSTEM
Methods and records used to accurately report an entity's transactions and to maintain accountability for its assets and liabilities.

From Concept **TO PRACTICE 5.3**

READING THE GAP'S MANAGEMENT REPORT Refer to the management's report for The Gap in Exhibit 5-8. What is the composition of its Audit and Finance Committee? Why do you think it is composed the way it is?

THE CONTROL ENVIRONMENT

The success of an internal control system begins with the competence of the people in charge of it. Management's operating style will have a determinable impact on the effectiveness of various policies. An autocratic style in which a few key officers tightly control operations will result in an environment different from that of a decentralized organization in which departments have more freedom to make decisions. Personnel policies and practices form another factor in the internal control of a business. An appropriate system for hiring competent employees and firing incompetent ones is crucial to an efficient operation. After all, no internal control system will work very well if employees who are dishonest or poorly trained are on the payroll. On the other hand, too few people doing too many tasks defeats the purpose of an internal control system. Finally, the effectiveness of internal control in a business is influenced by the board of directors, particularly its audit committee.

This woman is using the paper source document in her hand as a reference for entering data into the accounting system. From the standpoint of internal control, should she be the one who is ordering inventory, receiving it, and entering the information into the system? Is she authorized to make journal entries? If so, does her laptop have safeguards that prevent access by unauthorized personnel? These and other internal control procedures are part of the control environment within every company.

THE ACCOUNTING SYSTEM

An **accounting system** consists of all the methods and records used to accurately report an entity's transactions and to maintain accountability for its assets and liabilities. Regardless of the degree of computer automation, the use of a journal to record transactions is an integral part of all accounting systems. Refinements are sometimes made to the basic components of the system, depending on the company's needs. For example, most companies use specialized journals to record recurring transactions, such as sales of merchandise on credit.

An accounting system can be completely manual, fully computerized, or as is often the case, a mixture of the two. Internal controls are important to all businesses, regardless of the degree of automation of the accounting system. The system must be capable of handling both the volume and the complexity of transactions entered into by a business. Most businesses use computers because of the sheer volume of transactions. The computer is ideally suited to the task of processing large numbers of repetitive transactions efficiently and quickly.

The cost of computing has dropped so substantially that virtually every business can now afford a system. Today some computer software programs that are designed for home-based businesses cost under $100 and are meant to run on machines that cost less than $1,000. Inexpensive software programs that categorize expenses and print checks, produce financial statements, and analyze financial ratios are available.

INTERNAL CONTROL PROCEDURES

LO 5 Describe the basic internal control procedures.

ADMINISTRATIVE CONTROLS Procedures concerned with efficient operation of the business and adherence to managerial policies.

ACCOUNTING CONTROLS Procedures concerned with safeguarding the assets or the reliability of the financial statements.

Management establishes policies and procedures on a number of different levels to ensure that corporate objectives will be met. Some procedures are formalized in writing. Others may not be written but are just as important. Certain **administrative controls** within a company are more concerned with the efficient operation of the business and adherence to managerial policies than with the accurate reporting of financial information. For example, a company policy that requires all prospective employees to be interviewed by the personnel department is an administrative control. Other **accounting controls** primarily concern safeguarding assets and ensuring the reliability of the financial statements. We now turn to a discussion of some of the most important internal control procedures:

Proper authorizations
Segregation of duties
Independent verification
Safeguarding assets and records
Independent review and appraisal
The design and use of business documents

Proper Authorizations Management grants specific departments the authority to perform various activities. Along with the *authority* goes *responsibility.* Most large organizations give the authority to hire new employees to the personnel department. Management authorizes the purchasing department to order goods and services for the company and the credit department to establish specific policies for granting credit to customers. By specifically authorizing certain individuals to carry out specific tasks for the business, management is able to hold these same people responsible for the outcome of their actions.

The authorizations for some transactions are general in nature; others are specific. For example, a cashier authorizes the sale of a book in a bookstore by ringing up the transaction (a general authorization). It is likely, however, that the bookstore manager's approval is required before a book can be returned (a specific authorization).

Segregation of Duties What might happen if one employee is given the authority both to prepare checks and to sign them? What could happen if a single employee is allowed to order inventory and receive it from the shipper? Or what if the cashier at a checkout stand also records the daily receipts in the journal? If the employee in each of these situations is honest and never makes mistakes, nothing bad will happen. However, if the employee is dishonest or makes human errors, the company can experience losses. These situations all point to the need for the segregation of duties, which is one of the most fundamental of all internal control procedures. Without segregation of duties, an employee is able not only to perpetrate a fraud but also to conceal it. A good system of internal control requires that the *physical custody* of assets be separated from the *accounting* for those same assets.

Like most internal control principles, the concept of segregation of duties is an ideal that is not always completely attainable. For example, many smaller businesses simply do not have adequate personnel to achieve complete segregation of key functions. In certain instances, these businesses need to rely on the direct involvement of the owners in the business and on independent verification.

ACCOUNTING FOR YOUR DECISIONS

You Are the Chief Financial Officer

You have been hired by the owner of Mt. Rainier Broom Company to come in and replace the out-of-date accounting systems with a system that uses modern technology. The first thing you notice is that the company's bookkeeper, Mavis, is in charge of collecting receivables, recording payments, ordering and receiving inventory, and preparing and signing checks. When you suggest to her that she has too many duties, she gets angry and appeals to the owner. The owner backs up Mavis and tells you to focus entirely on new accounting technology. What should you do?

ANS: Ever so politely, you should inform the owner and Mavis in a three-way meeting that your suggestion that Mavis not do all the accounting functions is not meant as an insult but is simply good internal control. Even if Mavis is as honest as they come, there is a good chance that she will make errors, which could result in losses to the company. By having at least two people involved in a transaction, the chances are excellent that an error will be caught by one or the other.

Independent Verification Related to the principle of segregation of duties is the idea of independent verification. The work of one department should act as a check on the work of another. For example, the physical count of the inventory in a perpetual inventory system provides such a check. The accounting department maintains the general ledger card for inventory and updates it as sales and purchases are made. The physical count of the inventory by an independent department acts as a check on the work of the accounting department. As another example, consider a bank reconciliation as a control device. The reconciliation of a company's bank account with the bank statement by someone not responsible for either the physical custody of cash or the cash records acts as an independent check on the work of these parties. (We will take a closer look at the use of a bank reconciliation as a control device in Chapter 7.)

Safeguarding Assets and Records Adequate safeguards must be in place to protect assets and the accounting records from losses of various kinds. Cash registers, safes, and lockboxes are important safeguards for cash. Secured storage areas with limited access are essential for the safekeeping of inventory. Protection of the accounting records against misuse is equally important. For example, access to a computerized accounting record should be limited to those employees authorized to prepare journal entries. This can be done with the use of a personal identification number and a password to access the system.

Independent Review and Appraisal A well-designed system of internal control provides for periodic review and appraisal of the accounting system as well as the people operating it. The group primarily responsible for review and appraisal of the system is the internal audit staff. Internal auditors provide management with periodic reports on the effectiveness of the control system and the efficiency of operations.

The Design and Use of Business Documents *Business documents* are the crucial link between economic transactions entered into by an entity and the accounting record of these events. They are often called *source documents.* Some source documents are manual; others are computer-generated. The source document for the recognition of the expense of an employee's wages is the time card. The source documents for a sale include the sales order, the sales invoice, and the related shipping document. Business documents must be designed so that they capture all relevant information about an economic event. They are also designed to ensure that related transactions are properly classified.

Business documents themselves must be properly controlled. For example, a key feature for documents is a *sequential numbering system* just like you have for your personal checks. This system results in a complete accounting for all documents in the series and negates the

Name: Julie Weston
Education: B.A., Purdue University
College Major: Communications/Public Relations
Occupation: Design Operations Manager, John Wieland Homes & Neighborhoods, Atlanta
Age: 26

Focus on Users

Inventory Control Helps Avoid Upset Customers

"We run reports to check inventory weekly and monthly. If we don't have an accurate count, we may promise our customers items we can't deliver."
—Julie Weston

At J. W. Homes & Neighborhoods, a large residential builder in the Southeast, Julie Weston has been responsible for inventory control in the company's lighting division. The corporate income statement has been critical in Julie's management of inventory because it accounts for the cost of goods sold relative to sales, allowing her to make judgments about how to purchase and manage inventory going forward and to affect future profitability. She says: "To find our profits, we take our net sales minus cost of goods sold minus operating costs, which gives us our profit. If we were to look only at our net sales, we might outspend what our budget allows. We have to keep buying more finished goods to sell to homeowners to generate more profit." In addition to staying on top of the relationship between cost of goods sold and sales, being responsible for inventory control means constantly monitoring the level of inventories that are on hand for sale. As Julie explains: "We run reports to check inventory weekly and monthly. If we don't have an accurate count, we may promise our customers items we can't deliver. In the lighting division, our homeowners [customers] come in to select their lighting fixtures months before their homes go up. You can imagine how upset a customer would be if the closing of a house is delayed because of an inventory problem." This is just one example of how line items on the financial statements can affect corporate decision making and profitability.

opportunity for an employee to misdirect one. Another key feature of well-designed business documents is the use of *multiple copies.* The various departments involved in a particular activity, such as sales or purchasing, are kept informed of the status of outstanding orders through the use of copies of documents. Appendix 5A provides an example of the use of business documents for a merchandiser.

Limitations on Internal Control

Internal control is a relative term. No system of internal control is totally foolproof. An entity's size affects the degree of control that it can obtain. In general, large organizations are able to devote a substantial amount of resources to safeguarding assets and records

Internal control has taken on a whole new meaning now that transactions are occurring on the Web. Nearly every online retailer—Gap Inc. included—has developed privacy and security policies that are designed to ensure that the customer's information—including personal information as well as credit card information—is secure from unauthorized use or reuse.

because these companies have the assets to justify the cost. Because the installation and maintenance of controls can be costly, an internal audit staff is a luxury that many small businesses cannot afford. The mere segregation of duties can result in added costs if two employees must be involved in a task previously performed by only one.

Segregation of duties can be effective in preventing collusion, but no system of internal control can ensure that it will not happen. It does no good to have one employee count the cash at the end of the day and another to record it if the two act in concert to steal from the company. Rotation of duties can help to lessen the likelihood for problems of this sort. An employee is less likely to collude with someone to steal if the assignment is a temporary one. Another control feature, a system of authorizations, is meaningless if management continually overrides it. Management must believe in a system of internal control enough to support it.

Intentional acts to misappropriate company assets are not the only problem. All sorts of human errors can weaken a system of internal control. Misunderstood instructions, carelessness, fatigue, and distraction can all lead to errors. A well-designed system of internal control should result in the best-possible people being hired to perform the various tasks, but no one is perfect.

Two-Minute Review

1. Explain why an internal control system is important to the operation of a merchandising company.

2. Explain the difference between administrative controls and accounting controls.

3. Explain how the concept of segregation of duties involves an evaluation of costs versus benefits.

Answers:

1. An effective system of internal controls is critical to protecting a merchandiser's investment in three of its major assets: cash, accounts receivable, and inventory. Without an effective system, these assets are subject to misuse.

2. Administrative controls are concerned with the efficient operation of a business and adherence to managerial policies. Alternatively, accounting controls deal with safeguarding assets and ensuring the reliability of the financial statements.

3. Involving more than one employee in a specific function reduces the likelihood of theft or other misuse of company assets. However, all businesses must decide whether the benefit of segregation of duties outweighs the additional cost of involving more than one employee in a specific function such as the preparation and distribution of the payroll.

WARMUP EXERCISES

LO 1 Warmup Exercise 5-1 Net Sales

Victor Merchandising reported sales revenue, sales returns and allowances, and sales discounts of $57,000, $1500, and $900, respectively, in 2001.

Required

Prepare the net sales section of Victor's 2001 income statement.

Key to the Solution

Refer to Exhibit 5-2.

LO 3 Warmup Exercise 5-2 Cost of Goods Sold

The following amounts are taken from Redfield Inc.'s records (all amounts are for 2001):

Inventory, January 1	$14,200
Inventory, December 31	10,300
Purchases	87,500
Purchase Discounts	4,200
Purchase Returns and Allowances	1,800
Transportation-in	4,500

Required

Prepare the cost of goods sold section of Redfield's 2001 income statement.

Key to the Solution

Refer to Exhibit 5-3.

LO 5 Warmup Exercise 5-3 Internal Control

List the internal control procedures discussed in the text.

Key to the Solution

Refer to the section in the chapter that discusses internal control procedures.

SOLUTIONS TO WARMUP EXERCISES

Warmup Exercise 5-1

net sales section of income statement

VICTOR MERCHANDISING
PARTIAL INCOME STATEMENT
FOR THE YEAR ENDED DECEMBER 31, 2001

Sales revenue	$57,000	
Less: Sales returns and allowances	1,500	
Sales discounts	900	
Net sales		$54,600

Warmup Exercise 5-2

REDFIELD INC.
PARTIAL INCOME STATEMENT
FOR THE YEAR ENDED DECEMBER 31, 2001

Inventory, January 1, 2001		$ 14,200	
Purchases	$87,500		
Less: Purchase returns and allowances	1,800		
Purchase discounts	4,200		
Net purchases	$81,500		
Add: Transportation-in	4,500		
Cost of goods purchased		86,000	
Cost of goods available for sale		$100,200	
Less: Inventory, December 31, 2001		10,300	
Cost of goods sold			$ 89,900

Warmup Exercise 5-3

Internal control procedures

1. Proper authorizations
2. Segregation of duties
3. Independent verification
4. Safeguarding assets and records
5. Independent review and appraisal
6. Design and use of business documents

Review Problem

Mickey's Marts, which operates a chain of department stores, uses the periodic inventory system. The cost of inventory on hand at January 1 amounts to $12,000, and on January 31, it is $9,500. The following transactions are entered into by Mickey's during January:

a. Purchased merchandise on account from various vendors for $25,000. All merchandise is bought with terms of 1/10, net 30. All purchases are recorded initially at the gross amount.

b. Reduced the total amount owed to vendors by $20,000. This is *not* the amount paid but the amount before taking the 1% discount. All accounts are paid within 10 days of the date of the invoice.

c. Recognized purchase returns and allowances of $1,900 during the month.

d. Recognized total sales of $42,000 for the month, of which $28,000 is cash sales and the remainder is on account.

e. Made collections on account of $17,000 for the month.

f. Applied $3,200 of sales returns and allowances for the month to customers' account balances.

g. Paid the freight cost of $2,700 on *incoming* purchases of merchandise.

Required

1. Prepare the necessary journal entries to record each of the transactions **a** through **g.**
2. Prepare a *partial* income statement for the month of January. The last line on the partial statement should be gross margin.

Solution to Review Problem

1. Journal entries:

a. Purchases	25,000	
Accounts Payable		25,000
To record purchases on account.		

Assets	=	Liabilities	+	Owners' Equity
		+25,000		−25,000

b. Accounts Payable	20,000	
Purchase Discounts		200
Cash		19,800
To record payment of amounts owed on account, less 1% discount for early payment.		

Assets	=	Liabilities	+	Owners' Equity
−19,800		−20,000		+200

c. Accounts Payable	1,900	
Purchase Returns and Allowances		1,900
To record purchase returns and allowances for the month.		

Assets	=	Liabilities	+	Owners' Equity
		−1,900		+1,900

d. Cash	28,000	
Accounts Receivable	14,000	
Sales Revenue		42,000
To record sales for the month.		

Assets	=	Liabilities	+	Owners' Equity
+28,000				+42,000
+14,000				

e.	Cash	17,000	
	Accounts Receivable		17,000
	To record collections on account for the month.		

Assets	=	Liabilities	+	Owners' Equity
+17,000				
−17,000				

f.	Sales Returns and Allowances	3,200	
	Accounts Receivable		3,200
	To record sales returns and allowances for the month.		

Assets	=	Liabilities	+	Owners' Equity
−3,200				−3,200

g.	Transportation-in	2,700	
	Cash		2,700
	To record payment of freight bill on incoming merchandise.		

Assets	=	Liabilities	+	Owners' Equity
−2,700				−2,700

2. Partial income statement:

MICKEY'S MARTS
PARTIAL INCOME STATEMENT
FOR THE MONTH OF JANUARY

Sales revenue			$42,000
Less: Sales returns and allowances			3,200
Net sales			$38,800
Cost of goods sold:			
Inventory, January 1		$12,000	
Purchases	$25,000		
Less: Purchase discounts	200		
Purchase returns and allowances	1,900		
Net purchases	$22,900		
Add: Transportation-in	2,700		
Cost of goods purchased		25,600	
Cost of goods available for sale		37,600	
Less: Inventory, January 31		9,500	
Cost of goods sold			28,100
Gross margin			$10,700

APPENDIX 5A

ACCOUNTING TOOLS: INTERNAL CONTROL FOR A MERCHANDISING COMPANY

Specific internal controls are necessary to control cash receipts and cash disbursements in a merchandising company. In addition to the separation of the custodianship of cash from the recording of it in the accounts, two other fundamental principles apply to its control. First, all cash receipts should be deposited *intact* in the bank on a *daily* basis. *Intact* means that no disbursements should be made from the cash received from customers. The second basic principle is related to the first: all cash disbursements should be made by check. The use of sequentially numbered checks results in a clear record of all disbursements. The only exception to this rule is the use of a petty cash fund to make cash disbursements for minor expenditures such as postage stamps and repairs. (The use of such a fund is explained in Chapter 7.)

Control over Cash Receipts

Most merchandisers receive checks and currency from customers in two distinct ways: (1) cash received over the counter, that is, from cash sales and (2) cash received in the mail, that is, cash collections from credit sales. Each of these types of cash receipts poses its own particular control problems.

Cash Received over the Counter Several control mechanisms are used to handle these cash payments. First, cash registers allow the customer to see the display, which deters the salesclerk from ringing up a sale for less than the amount received from the customer and pocketing the difference. A locked-in cash register tape is another control feature. At various times during the day, an employee other than the clerk unlocks the register, removes the tape, and forwards it to the accounting department. At the end of the shift, the salesclerk remits the coin and currency from the register to a central cashier. Any difference between the amount of cash remitted to the cashier and the amount on the tape submitted to the accounting department is investigated.

Finally, prenumbered customer receipts, prepared in duplicate, are a useful control mechanism. The customer is given a copy, and the salesclerk retains another. The salesclerk is accountable for all numbers in a specific series of receipts and must be able to explain any differences between the amount of cash remitted to the cashier and the amount collected per the receipts.

Cash Received in the Mail Most customers send checks rather than currency through the mail. Any form of cash received in the mail from customers should be applied to their account balances. The customer wants assurance that the account is appropriately reduced for the amount of the payment. The company must be assured that all cash received is deposited in the bank and that the account receivable is reduced accordingly.

To achieve a reasonable degree of control, two employees should be present when the mail is opened.[1] The first employee opens the mail in the presence of the second employee, counts the money received, and prepares a control list of the amount received on that particular day. The list is often called a *prelist* and is prepared in triplicate. The second employee takes the original to the cashier along with the total cash received on that day. The cashier is the person who makes the bank deposit. One copy of the prelist is forwarded to the accounting department to be used as the basis for recording the increase in Cash and the decrease in Accounts Receivable. The other copy is retained by one of the two persons opening the mail. A comparison of the prelist to the bank deposit slip is a timely way to detect receipts that do not make it to the bank. Because the two employees acting in concert could circumvent the control process, rotation of duties is important.

Monthly customer statements act as an additional control device for customer payments received in the mail. Assume that the two employees responsible for opening the mail and remitting checks to the cashier decide to pocket a check received from a customer. Checks made payable to a company *can* be stolen and cashed. The customer provides the control element. Because the check is not remitted to the cashier, the accounting department will not be notified to reduce the customer's account for the payment. The monthly statement, however, should alert the customer to the problem. The amount the customer thought was owed will be smaller than the balance due on the statement. At this point, the customer should ask the company to investigate the discrepancy. As evidence of its payment on account, the customer will be able to point to a canceled check—which was cashed by the unscrupulous employees.

---

[1]In some companies this control procedure may be omitted because of the cost of having two employees present when the mail is opened.

EXHIBIT 5-9 Document Flow for the Purchasing Function

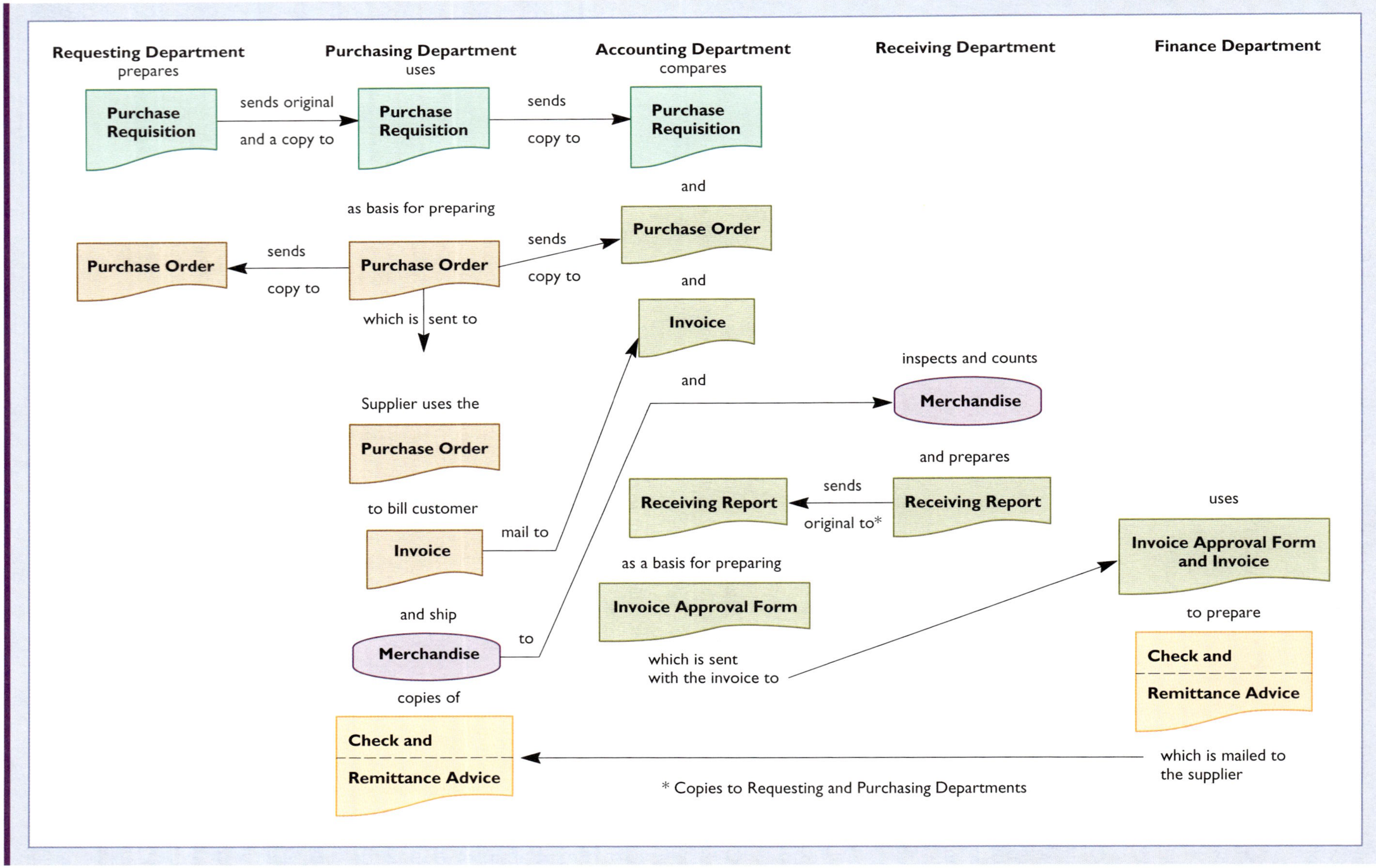

Finally, keep in mind that the use of customer statements as a control device will be effective only if the employees responsible for the custody of cash received through the mail, for record keeping, and for authorization of adjustments to customers' accounts are not allowed to prepare and mail statements to customers. Employees allowed to do so are in a position to alter customers' statements.

Cash Discrepancies Discrepancies occur occasionally due to theft by dishonest employees and to human error. For example, if a salesclerk either intentionally or unintentionally gives the wrong amount of change, the amount remitted to the cashier will not agree with the cash register tape. Any material differences should be investigated. Of particular significance are *recurring* differences between the amount remitted by any one cashier and the amount on the cash register tape.

The Role of Computerized Business Documents in Controlling Cash Disbursements

LO 6 Describe the various documents used in recording purchases of merchandise and their role in controlling cash disbursements.

A company makes cash payments for a variety of purposes: to purchase merchandise, supplies, plant, and equipment; to pay operating expenditures; and to cover payroll expenses, to name a few. We will concentrate on the disbursement of cash to purchase goods for resale, focusing particularly on the role of business documents in the process. Merchandising companies rely on a smooth and orderly inflow of quality goods for resale to customers. It is imperative that suppliers be paid on time so that they will continue to make goods available.

Business documents play a vital role in the purchasing function. The example that follows begins with a requisition for merchandise by the tool department of Grizzly Hardware Stores. The example continues through the receipt of the goods and the eventual payment to the supplier. The entire process is summarized in Exhibit 5-9. You will want to refer to this exhibit throughout the remainder of this appendix.

Purchase Requisition The tool department at Grizzly Hardware Stores weekly reviews its stock to determine whether any items need replenishing. On the basis of its needs, the supervisor of the tool department fills out the **purchase requisition form** shown in Exhibit 5-10. The form indicates the preferred supplier or vendor, A-1 Tool.

PURCHASE REQUISITION FORM Form a department uses to initiate a request to order merchandise.

The purchasing department has the responsibility for making the final decision on a vendor. Giving the purchasing department this responsibility means that it is held accountable for acquiring the goods at the lowest price, given certain standards for merchandise quality. Grizzly assigns a separate item number to each of the thousands of individual items of merchandise it stocks. Note that the requisition also indicates the vendor's number for each item. The unit of measure for each item is indicated in the quantity column. For example, "24 ST" means 24 sets, and "12 CD" means 12 cards. The original and a copy of the purchase requisition are sent to the purchasing department. The tool department keeps one copy for its records.

Purchase Order Like many other businesses, Grizzly uses a computerized purchasing system. Most companies either have purchased software or have developed software internally to perform such functions as purchasing, sales, and payroll. The software is capable not only of increasing the speed and accuracy of the process but also of generating the necessary documents.

PURCHASE ORDER Form sent by the purchasing department to the supplier.

A computer-generated **purchase order** is shown in Exhibit 5-11. Purchase orders are usually prenumbered; a company should periodically investigate any missing numbers. The purchasing department uses its copy of the purchase requisition as a basis for preparing the purchase order. An employee in the purchasing department keys in the relevant information from the purchase requisition and adds the unit cost for each item gathered from the vendor's price guide. The software program generates the purchase order as shown in Exhibit 5-11. You should trace all of the information for at least one of the three items ordered from the purchase requisition to the purchase order. The purchase order indicates the instructions for shipping, FOB destination point, and the terms for payment, 2/10, net 30.

EXHIBIT 5-10 Purchase Requisition

Grizzly Hardware Stores
676 Sentinel St.
Missoula, MT

PURCHASE REQUISITION

Date 5/28/01 **PR 75638**

Preferred vendor A-1 Tool Co.

Date needed by 6/5/01

The following items are requested for weekly dept. order

Item No.	**Quantity**	**Description/Vendor No.**
314627	24 ST	Hobby tool set/5265
323515	12 CD	Hobby blades 5 pk/7512
323682	6 ST	Screwdriver set 5/PC/1589

Requested by Joe Smith **Department** Tool department

The system generates the original purchase order and three copies. As indicated in Exhibit 5-9, the original is sent to the supplier after a supervisor in the purchasing department approves it. One copy is sent to the accounting department, where it will be matched with the original requisition. A second copy is sent to the tool department as confirmation that its request for the items has been attended to by the purchasing department. The purchasing department keeps the third copy for its records.

EXHIBIT 5-11 Computer-Generated Purchase Order

Grizzly Hardware Stores
676 Sentinel St.
Missoula, MT

PURCHASE ORDER

TO: PO 54296
A-1 Tool Co.
590 West St.
Milwaukee, WI

Date 5/30/01 Ship by Best Express Instructions FOB destination point
Terms 2/10, net 30 Date required 6/5/01

Item No.	Quantity	Description/Vendor No.	Unit price	Amount
314627	24 ST	Hobby tool set/5265	$28.59	$686.16
323515	12 CD	Hobby blades 5 pk/7512	.69	8.28
323682	6 ST	Screwdriver set 5/PC/1589	4.49	26.94
				$721.38

Approved by Mary Jones

A purchase order is not the basis for recording a purchase and a liability. Legally, the order is merely an offer by the company to purchase goods from the supplier. Technically, the receipt of goods from the supplier is the basis for the purchaser's recognition of a liability. As a matter of practice, however, most companies record the payable upon receipt of the invoice.

Invoice When A-1 Tool ships the merchandise, it also mails an invoice to Grizzly, requesting payment according to the agreed-upon terms, in this case 2/10, net 30. The **invoice** may be mailed separately or included with the shipment of merchandise. A-1 Tool, the seller, calls this document a *sales invoice;* it is the basis for recording a sale and an account receivable. Grizzly, the buyer, calls the same document a *purchase invoice,* which is the basis for recording a purchase and an account payable. The invoice that A-1 sent to Grizzly's accounting department is shown in Exhibit 5-12.

INVOICE
Form sent by the seller to the buyer as evidence of a sale.

Receiving Report The accounting department receives the invoice for the three items ordered. Within a few days before or after the receipt of the invoice, the merchandise arrives at Grizzly's warehouse. As soon as the items are unpacked, the receiving department inspects and counts them. The same software program that generated the purchase order also generates a receiving report, as shown in Exhibit 5-13.

Grizzly uses a **blind receiving report.** The column for the quantity received is left blank and is filled in by the receiving department. Rather than being able simply to indicate that the number ordered was received, an employee must count the items to determine that the number ordered is actually received. You should trace all of the relevant information for one of the three items ordered from the purchase order to the receiving report. The accounting system generates an original receiving report and three copies. The receiving department keeps one copy for its records and sends the original to the accounting department. One copy is sent to the purchasing department to be matched with the purchase order, and the other copy is sent to the tool department as verification that the items it originally requested have been received.

BLIND RECEIVING REPORT
Form used by the receiving department to account for the quantity and condition of merchandise received from a supplier.

EXHIBIT 5-12 Invoice

NO. 427953

A-1 Tool Co.
590 West St.
Milwaukee, WI

INVOICE

Sold to	Grizzly Hardware Stores	**Date**	6/2/01
	676 Sentinel St.	**Order No.**	54296
	Missoula, MT	**Shipped via**	Best Express
Ship to	Same	**Date shipped**	6/2/01
Terms	2/10, net 30	**Ship terms**	FOB destination

Quantity	**Description/No.**	**Price**	**Amount**
24 ST	Hobby tool set/5265	$28.59	$686.16
12 CD	Hobby blades 5 pk/7512	.69	8.28
6 ST	Screwdriver set 5 PC/1589	4.49	26.94
			$721.38

EXHIBIT 5-13 Computer-Generated Receiving Report

Grizzly Hardware Stores
676 Sentinel St.
Missoula, MT

Receiving Report

RR 23637

Purchase Order No. 54296	Date ordered 5/30/01
Vendor A-1 Tool Co.	Date required 6/5/01
Ship via Best Express	Instructions FOB Destination
Terms 2/10, net 30	

Quantity received	Our Item No.	Description/Item No.	Remarks
24 ST	314627	Hobby tool set/5265	Box damaged but merchandise ok
12 CD	323515	Hobby blades 5 pk/7512	
6 ST	323682	Screwdriver set 5/PC/1589	

Received by Bob Reed   Date 6/4/01

Invoice Approval Form At this point, Grizzly's accounting department has copies of the purchase requisition from the tool department, the purchase order from the purchasing department, the invoice from the supplier, and the receiving report from the warehouse. The accounting department uses an **invoice approval form** to document the accuracy of the information on each of these other forms. The invoice approval form for Grizzly Hardware is shown in Exhibit 5-14.

INVOICE APPROVAL FORM
Form the accounting department uses before making payment to document the accuracy of all the information about a purchase.

EXHIBIT 5-14 Invoice Approval Form

Grizzly Hardware Stores
676 Sentinel St.
Missoula, MT

Invoice Approval Form

	No.	Check
Purchase Requisition	PR 75638	✓
Purchase Order	PO 54296	✓
Receiving Report	RR 23637	✓

Invoice:

- **No.** 427953
- **Date** 6/2/01
- **Price** ✓
- **Extensions** ✓
- **Footings** ✓

Last Day to Pay for Discount 6/12/01

Approved for Payment by Alice Johnson

EXHIBIT 5-15 Check with Remittance Advice

3690

Grizzly Hardware Stores
676 Sentinel St.
Missoula, MT

June 12 19 01

PAY TO THE
ORDER OF A-1 Tool Co. $706.95

Seven hundred six and 95/100 DOLLARS

Second National Bank
Missoula, MT

3690 035932 9321

John B. Martin

Purchase Order No.	Invoice No.	Invoice Date	Description	Amount
PO 54296	427953	6/2/01	24 ST Hobby tool set	$686.16
			12 CD Hobby blades 5pk	8.28
			6 ST Screwdriver set 5PC	26.94
			Total	721.38
			Less: 2% discount	14.43
			Net remitted	706.95

The invoice is compared to the purchase requisition to ensure that the company is billed for goods that it requested. A comparison of the invoice with the purchase order ensures that the goods were in fact ordered. Finally, the receiving report is compared with the invoice to verify that all goods it is being billed for were received. An accounting department employee must also verify the mathematical accuracy of the amounts that appear on the invoice. The date the invoice must be paid to take advantage of the discount is noted so that the finance department will be sure to send the check by this date. At this point, the accounting department prepares the journal entry to increase Purchases and Accounts Payable. The invoice approval form and the invoice are then sent to the finance department. Some businesses call the invoice approval form a *voucher;* it is used for all expenditures, not just for purchases of merchandise. Finally, it is worth noting that some businesses do not use a separate invoice approval form but simply note approval directly on the invoice itself.

Check with Remittance Advice Grizzly's finance department is responsible for issuing checks. This results from the need to segregate custody of cash (the signed check) from record-keeping (the updating of the ledger). On receipt of the invoice approval form from the accounting department, a clerk in the finance department types a check with a remittance advice attached, as shown in Exhibit 5-15.[2]

Before the check is signed, the documents referred to on the invoice approval form are reviewed and canceled to prevent reuse. The clerk then forwards the check to one of the company officers authorized to sign checks. According to one of Grizzly's internal control policies, only the treasurer and the assistant treasurer are authorized to sign checks. Both officers must sign check amounts above a specified dollar limit. To maintain separation of duties, the finance department should mail the check. The remittance advice informs the supplier as to the nature of the payment and is torn off by the supplier before cashing the check.

[2]In some companies an employee in the accounting department prepares checks and sends them to the finance department for review and signature. Also, many companies use computer-generated checks, rather than manually typed ones.

CHAPTER HIGHLIGHTS

1. **LO 1** Merchandise is inventory purchased in finished form and held for resale. Both wholesalers and retailers sell merchandise. Sales revenue is a representation of the inflow of assets from the sale of merchandise during the period. Two deductions are made from sales revenue on the income statement. Sales returns and allowances and sales discounts are both subtracted from sales revenue to arrive at net sales.
2. **LO 2** A perpetual inventory system requires the updating of the Inventory account at the time of each purchase and each sale of merchandise. With the periodic system, the Inventory account is updated only at the end of the year. Separate accounts are used during the period to record purchases, purchase returns and allowances, purchase discounts, and transportation-in. The periodic system relies on a count of the inventory on the last day of the period to determine ending inventory.
3. **LO 3** Cost of goods sold is recognized as an expense under the matching principle. It represents the cost associated with the merchandise sold during the period and is matched with the revenue of the period.
4. **LO 3** The purchases of the period are reduced by purchase returns and allowances and by purchase discounts. Any freight costs paid to acquire the merchandise, called *transportation-in,* are added. The result, cost of goods purchased, is added to the beginning inventory to determine cost of goods available for sale. Cost of goods sold is found by deducting ending inventory from cost of goods available for sale.
5. **LO 3** *FOB destination point* means that the seller is responsible for the cost of delivering the merchandise to the buyer. Title to the goods does not transfer to the buyer until the buyer receives the merchandise from the carrier. *FOB shipping point* means that the buyer pays shipping costs. Title to the goods transfers to the buyer as soon as the seller turns them over to the carrier.
6. **LO 4** The purpose of an internal control system is to provide assurance that overall company objectives are met. Specifically, accounting controls are designed to safeguard the entity's assets and provide the company with reliable accounting records. Management has the primary responsibility for the reliability of the financial statements. Many companies employ a full-time internal audit staff to monitor and evaluate the internal control system.
7. **LO 5** Segregation of duties is the most fundamental of all internal control procedures. Possession of assets must be kept separate from the record-keeping function. Other important control procedures include a system of independent verifications, proper authorizations, adequate safeguards for assets and their records, independent review and appraisal of the accounting system, and the design and use of business documents.
8. **LO 5** Control over cash requires that all receipts be deposited intact on a daily basis and that all disbursements be made by check. Control procedures are important for cash received over the counter as well as for cash received in the mail. Any material discrepancies between the cash actually on hand and the amount that should be on hand need to be investigated.
9. **LO 6** Business documents play a vital role in various business activities such as the purchase of merchandise. The requesting department fills out a purchase requisition form and sends it to the purchasing department. The purchasing department uses the requisition to complete a purchase order, which it sends to the supplier. The supplier mails an invoice to the buyer's accounting department. The accounting department also gets a receiving report from the warehouse to indicate the quantity and condition of the goods delivered. The accounting department fills out an invoice approval form, which it sends with the invoice to the finance department, which uses them as the basis for preparing and sending a check to the supplier. (Appendix 5A)

KEY TERMS QUIZ

Because of the large number of terms introduced in this chapter, there are two key terms quizzes. Read each definition below and then write the number of the definition in the blank beside the appropriate term it defines. The solution appears at the end of the chapter.

Quiz 1: Merchandise Accounting

14 Net sales
4 Trade discount
7 Sales Discounts
15 Cost of goods sold
10 Periodic system
13 Purchases
12 Purchase Discounts
9 FOB shipping point
2 Sales Returns and Allowances
1 Quantity discount
11 Cost of goods available for sale
5 Perpetual system
3 Transportation-in
6 Purchase Returns and Allowances
8 FOB destination point

1. A reduction in selling price for buying a large number of units of a product.
2. The contra-revenue account used to record both refunds to customers and reductions of their accounts.
3. The adjunct account used to record freight costs paid by the buyer.
4. A selling price reduction offered to a special class of customers.

5. The system in which the Inventory account is increased at the time of each purchase of merchandise and decreased at the time of each sale.
6. The contra-purchases account used in a periodic inventory system when a refund is received from a supplier or a reduction given in the balance owed to the supplier.
7. The contra-revenue account used to record discounts given customers for early payment of their accounts.
8. Terms that require the seller to pay for the cost of shipping the merchandise to the buyer.
9. Terms that require the buyer to pay the shipping costs.
10. The system in which the Inventory account is updated only at the end of the period.
11. Beginning inventory plus cost of goods purchased.
12. The contra-purchases account used to record reductions in purchase price for early payment to the supplier.
13. The account used in a periodic inventory system to record acquisitions of merchandise.
14. Sales revenue less sales returns and allowances and sales discounts.
15. Cost of goods available for sale minus ending inventory.

Quiz 2: Internal Control

14 Internal control system
13 Internal audit staff
4 ~~8~~ Audit committee
3 ~~4~~ Accounting system
5 ~~3~~ Accounting controls
12 ~~5~~ Purchase order (Appendix 5A)
9 Blind receiving report (Appendix 5A)
8 Report of management
2 Board of directors
10 Foreign Corrupt Practices Act
11 Administrative controls
6 Purchase requisition form (Appendix 5A)
1 Invoice (Appendix 5A)
7 Invoice approval form (Appendix 5A)

1. The form sent by the seller to the buyer as evidence of a sale.
2. The group composed of key officers of a corporation and outside members responsible for the general oversight of the affairs of the entity.
3. The methods and records used to accurately report an entity's transactions and to maintain accountability for its assets and liabilities.
4. The board of directors subset that acts as a direct contact between the stockholders and the independent accounting firm.
5. Procedures concerned with safeguarding the assets or the reliability of the financial statements.
6. The form a department uses to initiate a request to order merchandise.
7. A form the accounting department uses before making payment to document the accuracy of all the information about a purchase.
8. A written statement in the annual report indicating the responsibility of management for the financial statements.
9. A form used by the receiving department to account for the quantity and condition of merchandise received from a supplier.
10. Legislation intended to increase the accountability of management for accurate records and reliable financial statements.
11. Procedures concerned with efficient operation of the business and adherence to managerial policies.
12. The form sent by the purchasing department to the supplier.
13. The department responsible for monitoring and evaluating the internal control system.
14. Policies and procedures necessary to ensure the safeguarding of an entity's assets, the reliability of its accounting records, and the accomplishment of overall company objectives.

Alternate Terms

Gross margin Gross profit
Invoice Purchase invoice, sales invoice
Invoice approval form Voucher
Merchandiser Wholesaler, retailer
Report of management Management's report
Sales revenue Sales
Transportation-in Freight-in

Questions

1. When a company gives a cash refund on returned merchandise, why doesn't it just reduce Sales Revenue instead of using a contra-revenue account? Ans: pg. 14
2. Why are trade discounts and quantity discounts not accorded accounting recognition? (The sale is simply recorded net of either of these types of discounts.)

3. What do credit terms of *3/20, n/60* mean? How valuable to the customer is the discount offered in these terms?

4. What is the difference between a periodic inventory system and a perpetual inventory system?

5. How have point-of-sale terminals improved the ability of mass merchandisers to use a perpetual inventory system?

6. In a periodic inventory system, what kind of account is Purchases? Is it an asset or an expense or neither?

7. Why are shipping terms, such as FOB shipping point or FOB destination point, important in deciding ownership of inventory at the end of the year?

8. How and why are transportation-in and transportation-out recorded differently?

9. How do the duties of an internal audit staff differ from those of the external auditors?

10. What is the typical composition of a board of directors of a publicly held corporation?

11. An order clerk fills out a purchase requisition for an expensive item of inventory and the receiving report when the merchandise arrives. The clerk takes the inventory home and then sends the invoice to the accounting department so that the supplier will be paid. What basic internal control procedure could have prevented this misuse of company assets?

12. What are some of the limitations on a company's effective system of internal control?

13. What two basic procedures are essential to an effective system of internal control over cash? (Appendix 5A)

14. How would you evaluate the following statement? "The only reason a company positions its cash register so that the customers can see the display is so that they feel comfortable they are being charged the correct amount for a purchase." (Appendix 5A)

15. Which document, a purchase order or an invoice, is the basis for recording a purchase and a corresponding liability? Explain your answer. (Appendix 5A)

16. What is a blind receiving report, and how does it act as a control device? (Appendix 5A)

17. What is the purpose in comparing a purchase invoice with a purchase order? in comparing a receiving report with a purchase invoice? (Appendix 5A)

EXERCISES

LO 1 Exercise 5-1 Journal Entries to Record Sales

Prepare the journal entries to record the following transactions on the books of Ace Corporation for March 3, 2001:

a. Sold merchandise on credit for $500 with terms of 2/10, net 30. Ace records all sales at the gross amount.

b. Recorded cash sales for the day of $1,250 from the cash register tape.

c. Granted a cash refund of $135 to a customer for spoiled merchandise returned.

d. Granted a customer a credit of $190 on its outstanding bill and allowed the customer to keep a defective product.

e. Applied cash of $2,300, received through the mail, to customers' accounts. All amounts received qualify for the discount for early payment.

LO 1 Exercise 5-2 Credit Terms

Ling Company sold merchandise on credit for $800 on September 10, 2001, to Letson Inc. For each of the following terms, indicate the last day Letson could take the discount, the amount Letson would pay if it took the discount, and the date full payment is due.

a. 2/10, n/30

b. 3/15, n/45

c. 1/7, n/21

d. 5/15, n/30

LO 1 Exercise 5-3 Journal Entries for Sales Discounts

Prepare the journal entries on the books of Rambler Corporation for the following transactions, using the gross method to record sales discounts (all sales on credit are made with terms of 2/10, net 30).

June 2: Sold merchandise on credit to Huskie Corp. for $1,200.

June 4: Sold merchandise on credit to Hawkeye Company for $2,000.

June 13: Collected cash from Hawkeye Company.

June 30: Collected cash from Huskie Corp.

LO 2 Exercise 5-4 Perpetual and Periodic Inventory Systems

Following is a partial list of account balances for two different merchandising companies. The amounts in the accounts represent the balances at the end of the year *before* any adjusting or closing entries are made.

Company A		**Company B**	
Sales revenue	$50,000	Sales revenue	$85,000
Sales discounts	3,000	Sales discounts	2,000
Merchandise inventory	12,000	Merchandise inventory	9,000
Cost of goods sold	38,000	Purchases	41,000
		Purchase discounts	4,000
		Purchases returns and allowances	1,000

Required

1. Identify which inventory system, perpetual or periodic, each of the two companies uses. Explain how you know which system each uses by looking at the types of accounts on their books.
2. How much inventory does Company A have on hand at the end of the year? What is its cost of goods sold for the year?
3. Explain why you cannot determine Company B's cost of goods sold for the year from the information available.

LO 2 Exercise 5-5 Perpetual and Periodic Inventory Systems

From the following list, identify whether the merchandisers described would most likely use a perpetual or periodic inventory system.

_______________ Appliance store
_______________ Car dealership
_______________ Drugstore
_______________ Furniture store
_______________ Grocery store
_______________ Hardware store
_______________ Jewelry store

How might changes in technology affect the ability of merchandisers to use perpetual inventory systems?

LO 3 Exercise 5-6 Missing Amounts in Cost of Goods Sold Model

For each of the following independent cases, fill in the missing amounts:

	Case 1	**Case 2**	**Case 3**
Beginning inventory	$ (a)	$2,350	$1,890
Purchases (gross)	6,230	5,720	(e)
Purchase returns and allowances	470	800	550
Purchase discounts	200	(c)	310
Transportation-in	150	500	420
Cost of goods available for sale	7,110	(d)	8,790
Ending inventory	(b)	1,750	1,200
Cost of goods sold	5,220	5,570	(f)

LO 3 Exercise 5-7 Journal Entries for Purchase Discounts

Prepare the journal entries on the books of Buckeye Corporation for the following transactions, using the gross method to record purchase discounts (all purchases on credit are made with terms of 1/10, net 30, and Buckeye uses the periodic system of inventory):

July 3: Purchased merchandise on credit from Wildcat Corp. for $3,500.
July 6: Purchased merchandise on credit from Cyclone Company for $7,000.
July 12: Paid amount owed to Wildcat Corp.
August 5: Paid amount owed to Cyclone Company.

LO 3 **Exercise 5-8** Journal Entries for Purchases—Periodic System

Prepare journal entries for the following transactions entered into by Wolverine Corporation. The company uses the periodic system and the gross method to record purchase discounts.

March 3:	Purchased merchandise from Spartan Corp. for $2,500 with terms of 2/10, net/30. Shipping costs of $250 were paid to Neverlate Transit Company.
March 7:	Purchased merchandise from Boilermaker Company for $1,400 with terms of net/30.
March 12:	Paid amount owed to Spartan Corp.
March 15:	Received a credit of $500 on defective merchandise purchased from Boilermaker Company. The merchandise was kept.
March 18:	Purchased merchandise from Gopher Corp. for $1,600 with terms of 2/10, net 30.
March 22:	Received a credit of $400 from Gopher Corp. for spoiled merchandise returned to them. This is the amount of credit exclusive of any discount.
April 6:	Paid amount owed to Boilermaker Company.
April 18:	Paid amount owed to Gopher Corp.

LO 3 **Exercise 5-9** Shipping Terms and Transfer of Title

On December 23, 2001, Miller Wholesalers ships merchandise to Michael Retailers with terms of FOB destination point. The merchandise arrives at Michael's warehouse on January 3, 2002.

Required

1. Identify who pays to ship the merchandise.
2. Determine whether the inventory should be included as an asset on Michael's December 31, 2001, balance sheet. Should the sale be included on Miller's 2001 income statement?
3. Explain how your answers to part **2** would have been different if the terms of shipment had been FOB shipping point.

LO 3 **Exercise 5-10** Transfer of Title to Inventory

From the following list, identify whether the transactions described should be recorded by Cameron Companies during December 2001 or January 2002.

Purchases of merchandise that are in transit from vendors to Cameron Companies on December 31, 2001:

______________ Shipped FOB shipping point

______________ Shipped FOB destination point

Sales of merchandise that are in transit to customers of Cameron Companies on December 31, 2001:

______________ Shipped FOB shipping point

______________ Shipped FOB destination point

LO 5 **Exercise 5-11** Internal Control

The university drama club is planning a raffle. The president overheard you talking about internal control to another accounting student, so she has asked you to set up some guidelines to "be sure" that all money collected for the raffle is accounted for by the club.

Required

1. Describe guidelines that the club should follow to achieve an acceptable level of internal control.
2. Comment on the president's request that she "be sure" all money is collected and recorded.

LO 5 **Exercise 5-12** Segregation of Duties

The following tasks are performed by three employees, each of whom is capable of performing all of them. Do not concern yourself with the time required to perform the tasks but with the need to provide for segregation of duties. Assign the duties by using a check mark to indicate which employee should perform each task. Remember that you may assign any one of the tasks to any of the employees.

Task	Employee		
	Mary	Sue	John
Prepare invoices			
Mail invoices			
Pick up mail from post office			
Open mail, separate checks			
List checks on deposit slip in triplicate			
Post payment to customer's account			
Deposit checks			
Prepare monthly schedule of accounts receivable			
Reconcile bank statements			

Multi-Concept Exercises

LO 1, 3 Exercise 5-13 Income Statement for a Merchandiser

Fill in the missing amounts in the following income statement for Carpenters Department Store Inc.:

Sales revenue		$125,600	
Less: Sales returns and allowances		(a) ?	
Net sales			$122,040
Cost of goods sold:			
Beginning inventory		23,400	
Purchases	(b) ?		
Less: Purchase discounts	1,300		
Net purchases	(c) ?		
Add: Transportation-in	6,550		
Cost of goods purchased		81,150	
Cost of goods available for sale		104,550	
Less: Ending inventory		(e) ?	
Cost of goods sold			(d) ?
Gross margin			38,600
Operating expenses			$ (f) ?
Income before tax			26,300
Income tax expense			10,300
Net income			$ (g) ?

LO 1, 3 Exercise 5-14 Partial Income Statement—Periodic System

LaPine Company has the following account balances as of December 31, 2001:

Purchase returns and allowances	$ 400
Inventory, January 1	4,000
Sales	80,000
Transportation-in	1,000
Sales returns and allowances	500
Purchase discounts	800
Inventory, December 31	3,800
Purchases	30,000
Sales discounts	1,200

Required

Prepare a partial income statement for LaPine Company for 2001 through gross margin. Calculate LaPine's gross margin (gross profit) ratio for 2001.

Problems

LO 1 Problem 5-1 Trade Discounts

Essex Inc. offers the following discounts to customers who purchase large quantities:

10% discount: 10–25 units

20% discount: >25 units

Mr. Essex, the president, would like to record all sales at the list price and record the discount as an expense.

Required

1. Explain to Mr. Essex why trade discounts do not enter into the accounting records.
2. Even though trade discounts do not enter into the accounting records, is it still important to have some record of these? Explain your answer.

LO 1 Problem 5-2 Calculation of Gross Margins for Wal-Mart and Kmart

www.walmart.com
www.bluelight.com

The following information was summarized from the consolidated statements of income of Wal-Mart Stores Inc. and Subsidiaries for the years ended January 31, 1999 and 1998, and the consolidated statements of operations of Kmart Corporation for the years ended January 27, 1999, and January 28, 1998 (for each company, years are labeled as 1998 and 1997 respectively):

	1998		1997	
(in Millions)	**Sales**	**Cost of Sales***	**Sales**	**Cost of Sales***
Wal-Mart	$137,634	$108,725	$117,958	$93,438
Kmart	$ 33,674	$ 26,319	$ 32,183	$25,152

*Described as "cost of sales, buying and occupancy" by Kmart Corporation.

Required

1. Calculate the gross margin (gross profit) ratios for Wal-Mart and Kmart for 1998 and 1997.
2. Which company appears to be performing better? What factors might cause the difference in the gross margin ratios of the two companies? What other information should you consider to determine how these companies are performing in this regard?

LO 5 Problem 5-3 Internal Control Procedures

You are opening a summer business, a chain of three drive-thru snow-cone stands. You have hired other college students to work and have purchased a cash register with locked-in tapes. You retain one key, and the other is available to the lead person on each shift.

Required

1. Write a list of the procedures for all employees to follow when ringing up sales and giving change.
2. Write a list of the procedures for the lead person to follow in closing out at the end of the day. Be as specific as you can so that employees will have few if any questions.
3. What is your main concern in the design of internal control for the snow cone stands? How did you address that concern? Be specific.

LO 6 Problem 5-4 The Design of Internal Control Documents (Appendix 5A)

Motel $49.99 has purchased a large warehouse to store all supplies used by housekeeping departments in the company's expanding chain of motels. In the past, each motel bought supplies from local distributors and paid for the supplies from cash receipts.

Required

1. Name some potential problems with the old system.
2. Design a purchase requisition form and a receiving report to be used by the housekeeping departments and the warehouse. Indicate how many copies of each form should be used and who should receive each copy.

Multi-Concept Problems

LO 1, 2, 3 Problem 5-5 Journal Entries for a Merchandiser

GENERAL LEDGER

The following transactions were entered into by North Coast Tires Inc. during the month of June:

June 2: Purchased 1,000 tires at a cost of $60 per tire. Terms of payment are 1/10, net 45.

June 4: Paid trucking firm $1,200 to ship the tires purchased on June 2.

June 5: Purchased 600 tires at a cost of $60 per tire. Terms of payment are 2/10, net 30.

June 6: Paid trucking firm $800 to ship the tires purchased on June 5.

June 7: Returned 150 of the tires purchased on June 2 because they were defective. Received a credit on open account from the seller.

June 11: Paid for tires purchased on June 2.

June 13: Sold 700 tires from those purchased on June 2. The selling price was $90 per tire. Terms are 1/10, net 30.

June 22: Received cash from sale of tires on June 13.

June 30: Paid for tires purchased on June 5.

Required

1. Prepare the journal entries to record these transactions on the books of North Coast Tires Inc. The company uses the gross method of recording purchase and sales discounts. North Coast uses a periodic inventory system.
2. Given the nature of its product, do you think it would be feasible for North Coast to use a perpetual inventory system? Why? If so, what advantages would accrue to the company by using a perpetual system?

LO 1, 2, 3 Problem 5-6 Journal Entries for a Merchandiser

DECISION MAKING

GENERAL LEDGER

Leisure Time Furniture Store entered into the following transactions in the month of April:

April 3: Purchased 50 lounge chairs at $150 each with terms 2/10, net 45. The chairs were shipped FOB destination.

April 7: Sold 6 chairs for $320 each, terms 2/10, net 30.

April 8: Purchased 20 patio umbrella tables for $120 each, FOB shipping point, terms 1/10, net 30.

April 9: Due to defects, returned 5 lounge chairs purchased on April 3. Received a credit memorandum, indicating that amount due has been reduced.

April 10: Paid the trucking firm $360 for delivery of the tables purchased on April 8.

April 13: Paid for the chairs purchased on April 3.

April 17: Received payment for the chairs sold on April 7.

April 20: Paid for the tables purchased on April 8.

Required

1. Prepare all journal entries needed to record these transactions for the furniture company. Leisure Time uses the gross method of recording purchase and sales discounts. The company uses a periodic inventory system.
2. Do you think Leisure Time should change to a perpetual inventory system, given the nature of its business? Why? What advantages would a company have using the perpetual system instead of the periodic system?

LO 1, 3 Problem 5-7 Trade and Cash Discounts

Billings Inc. publishes books and offers trade discounts to customers who purchase in large quantities: 30% for purchases of more than 50 units. It also offers credit terms of 2/10, net 30 to induce early payment. The list price of one book is $60. Columbus Company purchased 100 of these books on September 12. Payment was made on September 21.

Required

1. Prepare the journal entries on Billings' books to record the sale and the receipt of cash.
2. Prepare the journal entries on Columbus' books to record the purchase and the payment.

GENERAL LEDGER

LO 1, 3 **Problem 5-8** Journal Entries and Partial Income Statement for a Merchandiser

Weekend Wonders Inc. operates a chain of discount hardware stores. The company uses a periodic inventory system. Inventory on hand on June 1, 2001, amounts to $25,670; on June 30, 2001, it is $30,200. The company uses the gross method to record purchase and sales discounts. The following transactions take place during the month of June:

a. Purchased merchandise from suppliers at a cost of $80,000 with credit terms of 2/10, net 30.

b. Paid freight costs of $4,250 to the common carrier for merchandise purchased.

c. Returned defective merchandise to suppliers and received credits of $2,300, the amount of credit before taking into account any purchase discounts.

d. Realized $92,000 in sales for the month, of which $68,000 is on credit; the remainder was received in cash. The credit sales are made with terms of 2/10, net 45.

e. Gave sales returns and allowances on credit sales of $4,000 during the month.

f. Made cash payments of $62,000 to suppliers for earlier purchases on account. All amounts paid during the month are made within the discount period.

g. Received $56,000 in cash collections on account from customers. All amounts received during the month are within the discount period.

Required

1. Prepare the journal entries on the books of Weekend Wonders Inc. to record each transaction.
2. Prepare a partial income statement for the month of June. The last line on the statement should be gross margin.
3. Assume that Weekend Wonders decides as a matter of policy to forgo the discount for early payment on purchases (credit terms are 2/10, net 30). What return would Weekend Wonders need to earn on the money it invests by not paying early to justify this decision? Provide any necessary calculations to support your answer.

GENERAL LEDGER

LO 1, 2, 3 **Problem 5-9** Purchases and Sales of Merchandise, Cash Flows

Two Wheeler, a bike shop, opened for business on April 1. It uses a periodic inventory system and records purchases at gross. The following transactions occurred during the first month of business:

April 1: Purchased five units from Duhan Co. for $500 total, with terms 3/10, net 30, FOB destination.

April 10: Paid for the April 1 purchase.

April 15: Sold one unit for $200 cash.

April 18: Purchased 10 units from Clinton Inc. for $900 total, with terms 3/10, net/30, FOB destination.

April 25: Sold three units for $200 each, cash.

April 28: Paid for the April 18 purchase.

Required

1. Prepare the journal entries to record the April transactions.
2. Determine net income for the month of April. Two Wheeler incurred and paid $100 for rent and $50 for miscellaneous expenses during April. Ending inventory is $967 (ignore income taxes).
3. Assuming that the only transactions during April are given (including rent and miscellaneous expenses), compute net cash flow from operating activities.
4. Explain why cash outflow is so much larger than expenses on the income statement.

LO 1, 3 **Problem 5-10** The Gap's Sales, Cost of Goods Sold, and Gross Margin

www.gap.com

The consolidated balance sheets of The Gap Inc. included merchandise inventory in the amount of $1,056,444,000 as of January 30, 1999 (the end of fiscal year 1998) and $733,174,000 as of January 31, 1998 (the end of fiscal year 1997). Refer also to the The Gap's consolidated statements of earnings for fiscal 1998 and 1997, which are set forth in the opening vignette of this chapter.

Required

1. Unlike most other merchandisers, The Gap doesn't include accounts receivable on its balance sheet. Why doesn't The Gap's balance sheet include this account?
2. Prepare a summary journal entry for sales during the year ended January 30, 1999.
3. The Gap sets forth net sales but not gross sales on its income statement. What type(s) of deduction(s) would be made from gross sales to arrive at the amount of net sales reported? Why might the company decide not to report the amount(s) of the deduction(s) separately?
4. Reconstruct the cost of goods sold section of The Gap's 1998 income statement.
5. Calculate the gross margin (gross profit) ratios for The Gap for 1998, 1997, and 1996, and comment on the changes noted, if any. Is the company's performance improving? What factors might have caused the change in the gross margin ratio?

LO 4, 5 **Problem 5-11** Internal Control

At Morris Mart Inc. all sales are on account. Mary Morris-Manning is responsible for mailing invoices to customers, recording the amount billed, opening mail, and recording the payment. Mary is very devoted to the family business and never takes off more than one or two days for a long weekend. The customers know Mary and sometimes send personal notes with their payments. Another clerk handles all aspects of accounts payable. Mary's brother, who is president of Morris Mart, has hired an accountant to help with expansion.

Required

1. List some problems with the current accounts receivable system.
2. What suggestions would you make to improve internal control?
3. How would you explain to Mary that she personally is not the problem?

LO 1, 3 **Problem 5-12** Financial Statements

SPREADSHEET

A list of accounts for Maple Inc. at 12/31/01 follows:

Accounts Receivable	$ 2,359
Advertising Expense	4,510
Buildings and Equipment, Net	55,550
Capital Stock	50,000
Cash	590
Depreciation Expense	2,300
Dividends	6,000
Income Tax Expense	3,200
Income Tax Payable	3,200
Interest Receivable	100
Inventory:	
January 1, 2001	6,400
December 31, 2001	7,500
Land	20,000
Purchase Discounts	800
Purchases	40,200
Retained Earnings, January 1, 2001	32,550
Salaries Expense	25,600
Salaries Payable	650
Sales	84,364
Sales Returns	780
Transportation-in	375
Utilities Expense	3,600

Required

1. Determine cost of goods sold for 2001.
2. Determine net income for 2001.
3. Prepare a balance sheet dated December 31, 2001.

Alternate Problems

LO 1 **Problem 5-1A** Discounts

Whitefish Inc., a recording distributor, would like to offer discounts to customers who purchase large quantities. Whitefish is unsure about the terms to use and how to account for discounts extended to customers. The company also wants to consider a cash discount for early payment by customers. Whitefish expects sales of about $3 million this year. All sales are on account to about 100 different outlets located within 500 miles of the warehouse. Deliveries are made by Whitefish's own trucks and cost about $25 per 100 miles driven. A full truck will hold 1,000 units.

Required

1. Explain the difference between a quantity discount and a discount for early payment. How is each accounted for in the accounting records? What are the reasons to extend the different discounts to customers?
2. Set up a quantity discount plan and a sales discount plan for Whitefish to extend to customers. Be able to explain why you chose your bases for the discounts and the amount of discounts.

LO 1 **Problem 5-2A** Calculation of Gross Margins for Sears and JCPenney

www.sears.com
www.jcpenney.com

The following information was summarized from the 1998 and 1997 consolidated statements of income of Sears, Roebuck and Co. (for the years ended January 2, 1999, and January 3, 1998), and JCPenney Company, Inc. and Subsidiaries (for the years ended January 30, 1999, and January 31, 1998). For each company, years are labeled as 1998 and 1997).

	1998		1997	
(in Millions)	**Sales***	**Cost of Sales****	**Sales***	**Cost of Sales****
Sears	$36,704	$27,257	$36,371	$26,779
JCPenney	$29,656	$21,761	$29,618	$21,385

*Described as "merchandise sales and services" by Sears and "retail sales" by JCPenney.
**Described as "cost of sales, buying and occupancy" by Sears and "cost of goods sold" by JCPenney.

Required

1. Calculate the gross margin (gross profit) ratios for Sears and JCPenney for 1998 and 1997.
2. Which company appears to be performing better? What factors might cause the difference in the gross margin ratios of the two companies? What other information should you consider to determine how these companies are performing in this regard?

LO 5 **Problem 5-3A** Internal Control Procedures

The loan department in a bank is subject to regulation. Internal auditors work for the bank to ensure that the loan department complies with requirements. The internal auditors must verify that each car loan file has a note signed by the maker, verification of insurance, and a title issued by the state that names the bank as co-owner.

Required

1. Explain why the bank and the regulatory agency are concerned with these documents.
2. Describe the internal control procedures that should be in place to ensure that these documents are obtained and safeguarded.

LO 6 **Problem 5-4A** The Design of Internal Control Documents (Appendix 5A)

Tiger's Group is a newly formed company that produces and sells children's movies about an imaginary character. The movies are in such great demand that they are shipped to retail outlets as soon as they are produced. The company must pay a royalty to several actors for each movie that it sold to retail outlets.

Required

1. Describe some internal control features that should be in place to ensure that all royalties are paid to the actors.
2. Design the shipping form that Tiger's Group should use for the movies. Be sure to include authorizations and indicate the number of copies and the routing of the copies.

Alternate Multi-Concept Problems

LO 1, 3 Problem 5-5A Journal Entries for a Merchandiser

GENERAL LEDGER

The following transactions were entered into by Maxwell Inc. during the month of July:

July 2: Purchased 1,000 pounds of steak at a cost of $3 per pound. Terms of payment are 2/10, net 30.

July 4: Paid trucking firm $500 to ship the steak purchased on July 2.

July 5: Purchased 600 pounds of steak at a cost of $3 per pound. Terms of payment are 2/10, net 45.

July 6: Paid trucking firm $300 to ship the steak purchased on July 5.

July 7: Due to expired dates on some packages, returned 100 pounds of the steak purchased on July 2. Received a credit on open account from the seller.

July 11: Paid for steak purchased on July 2.

July 13: Sold 1,200 pounds of steak from those purchased on July 2 and July 5. The selling price was $7 per pound, cash.

July 30: Paid for steak purchased on July 5.

Required

1. Prepare the journal entries to record these transactions on the books of Maxwell Inc. The company uses the gross method of recording purchase discounts. Maxwell uses a periodic inventory system.
2. Maxwell assumes a $3 per pound cost of inventory when planning profit and setting prices. Is this accurate? Explain.

LO 1, 2, 3 Problem 5-6A Journal Entries for a Merchandiser

DECISION MAKING

GENERAL LEDGER

Deckside Furniture Store entered into the following transactions in the month of April:

April 3: Purchased 50 lounge chairs at $120 each with terms 2/10, net 45. The chairs were shipped FOB destination.

April 7: Sold 6 chairs for $256 each, terms 2/10, net 30.

April 8: Purchased 20 patio umbrella tables for $96 each, FOB shipping point, terms 1/10, net 30.

April 9: Due to defects, returned 5 lounge chairs purchased on April 3. Received a credit memorandum.

April 10: Paid the trucking firm $288 for delivery of the tables purchased on April 8.

April 13: Paid for the chairs purchased on April 3.

April 17: Received payment for the chairs sold on April 7.

April 20: Paid for the tables purchased on April 8.

Required

1. Prepare all journal entries needed to record these transactions for the furniture company. Deckside uses the gross method of recording purchase and sales discounts. The company uses a periodic inventory system.
2. Do you think Deckside should change to a perpetual inventory system, given the nature of their business? Why? What advantages would a company have using the perpetual system instead of the periodic system?

LO 1, 3 Problem 5-7A Trade and Cash Discounts

Kalispell Inc. publishes books and offers trade discounts to customers who purchase in large quantities: 20% for purchases of more than 50 units. It also offers credit terms of 2/10, net 30 to induce early payment. The list price of one book is $50. Glacier Company purchased 100 of these books on September 12. Payment was made on September 21.

Required

1. Prepare the journal entries on Kalispell's books to record the sale and the receipt of cash.
2. Prepare the journal entries on Glacier's books to record the purchase and the payment.

DECISION MAKING

GENERAL LEDGER

LO 1, 3 Problem 5-8A Journal Entries and Partial Income Statement for a Merchandiser

Toppsie Turn Inc. operates a chain of T-shirt stores. The company uses a periodic inventory system. Inventories on hand on June 1 and June 30, 2001, amount to $12,840. The company uses the gross method to record purchase discounts. The following transactions take place during the month of June:

a. Purchased merchandise from suppliers at a cost of $62,000 with credit terms of 2/10, net 30.

b. Paid freight cost of $3,400 to the common carrier for merchandise purchased.

c. Realized $124,000 of sales for the month, all of which are cash sales.

d. Paid for merchandise purchased during the month within the discount period.

e. Accepted $500 in returned merchandise during the month.

Required

1. Prepare the journal entries on the books of Toppsie Turn Inc. to record each transaction.
2. Determine the gross margin that Toppsie Turn would report on the income statement for the month of June.
3. Toppsie is thinking about extending credit to some of its major customers to encourage credit customers to pay quickly. Toppsie expects existing sales will increase by 10% and that, at the new sales level, 60% of sales will be credit sales. Should Toppsie extend credit terms of 2/10, net 30? Explain your answer.

GENERAL LEDGER

LO 1, 2, 3 Problem 5-9A Purchases and Sales of Merchandise, Cash Flows

Chestnut Corp., a ski shop, opened for business on October 1. It uses a periodic inventory system and the gross method to record purchase discounts. The following transactions occurred during the first month of business:

October 1: Purchased three units from Oshkosh Inc. for $249 total, terms 2/10, net 30, FOB destination.

October 10: Paid for the October 1 purchase.

October 15: Sold one unit for $200 cash.

October 18: Purchased 10 units from Wausau Company for $800 total, with terms 2/10, net/30, FOB destination.

October 25: Sold three units for $200 each, cash.

October 30: Paid for the October 18 purchase.

Required

1. Prepare the journal entries to record the October transactions.
2. Determine the number of units on hand on October 31.
3. If Chestnut started the month with $2,000, determine its balance in cash at the end of the month, assuming that these are the only transactions that occurred during October. Why has the cash balance decreased when the company reported net income?

LO 1, 3 Problem 5-10A Walgreen's Sales, Cost of Goods Sold, and Gross Margin

The following information was summarized from the consolidated balance sheets of Walgreen Co. and Subsidiaries as of August 31, 1999, and August 31, 1998, and the consolidated statements of income for the years ended August 31, 1999, and August 31, 1998.

(in millions)	1999	1998
Accounts receivable, net	$ 486.5	$ 373.2
Cost of sales	12,978.6	11,139.4
Inventories	2,462.6	2,026.9
Net sales	17,838.8	15,306.6

Required

1. Prepare summary journal entries related to the collection of accounts receivable and sales during 1999. Assume hypothetically that all of Walgreen's sales are on account.
2. Walgreen Co. sets forth net sales but not gross sales on its income statement. What type(s) of deduction(s) would be made from gross sales to arrive at the amount of net sales reported? Why might the company decide not to report the amount(s) of the deduction(s) separately?

3. Reconstruct the cost of goods sold section of Walgreen's 1999 income statement.
4. Calculate the gross margin (gross profit) ratios for Walgreen Co. for 1999 and 1998 and comment on the change noted, if any. Is the company's performance improving? What factors might have caused the change in the gross margin ratio?

LO 4, 5 **Problem 5-11A** Internal Control

Abbott Inc. is expanding and needs to hire more personnel in the accounting office. Barbara Barker, the chief accounting clerk, knew that her cousin Cheryl was looking for a job. Barbara and Cheryl are also roommates. Barbara offered Cheryl a job as her assistant. Barbara will be responsible for Cheryl's performance reviews and training.

Required

1. List some problems with the proposed personnel situations in the accounting department.
2. Explain why accountants are concerned with the hiring of personnel. What suggestions would you make to improve internal control at Abbott?
3. How would you explain to Barbara and Cheryl that they personally are not the problem?

LO 1, 3 **Problem 5-12A** Financial Statements

SPREADSHEET

A list of accounts for Lloyd Inc. at December 31, 2001, follows:

Accounts Receivable	$56,359
Advertising Expense	12,900
Capital Stock	50,000
Cash	22,340
Dividends	6,000
Income Tax Expense	1,450
Income Tax Payable	1,450
Inventory	
January 1, 2001	6,400
December 31, 2001	5,900
Purchase Discounts	1,237
Purchases	62,845
Retained Earnings, January 1, 2001	28,252
Salaries Payable	650
Sales	112,768
Sales Returns	1,008
Transportation-in	375
Utilities Expense	1,800
Wages and Salaries Expense	23,000
Wages Payable	120

Required

1. Determine cost of goods sold for 2001.
2. Determine net income for 2001.
3. Prepare a balance sheet dated December 31, 2001.

CASES

Reading and Interpreting Financial Statements

LO 1, 3 **Case 5-1** Reading and Interpreting Ben & Jerry's Financial Statements

Refer to the 1998 financial statements and footnotes included in Ben & Jerry's 1998 annual report. www.benjerry.com

Required

1. Determine net sales and cost of sales for 1998.
2. Is Ben & Jerry's a merchandiser, manufacturer, or service provider?

3. Refer to footnote 3 in the annual report. What components make up Ben & Jerry's inventory?
4. Note the statement in footnote 3: "The Company purchased certain ingredients from a company owned by the Company's Vice Chairperson and a member of the Board of Directors, which amounted to approximately $800,000 in 1997. Why do you think Ben & Jerry's makes this statement?

LO 1, 3 Case 5-2 Reading and Interpreting Gateway's Financial Statements

www.gateway.com

Refer to the 1998 financial statements and footnotes included in Gateway's annual report.

Required

1. Determine the amount of net sales and cost of goods sold for 1998.
2. Is Gateway a merchandiser, manufacturer, or service provider?
3. Compare and contrast the inventory for merchandisers and manufacturers (refer to footnote 10 in Gateway's annual report to assist you).

LO 4 Case 5-3 Reading and Interpreting Sears' Management Report

www.sears.com

Sears, Roebuck and Co.'s 1998 annual report includes a management's report. Included in the report is the following:

> Management maintains a system of internal controls that it believes provides reasonable assurance that, in all material respects, assets are maintained and accounted for in accordance with management's authorizations and transactions are recorded accurately in the books and records. The concept of reasonable assurance is based on the premise that the cost of internal controls should not exceed the benefits derived. To assure the effectiveness of the internal control system, the organizational structure provides for defined lines of responsibility and delegation of authority.

Required

1. Why did management include this report in the annual report?
2. What types of costs does Sears have in mind when it states that "the cost of internal controls should not exceed the benefits derived"?
3. Based on what you know about retail stores, and Sears stores in particular, list the kinds of accounting and system controls the company may have in place to safeguard assets.

Making Financial Decisions

LO 1, 3 Case 5-4 Gross Margin for a Merchandiser

Emblems For You sells specialty sweatshirts. The purchase price is $10 per unit, plus 10% tax and a shipping cost of 50¢ per unit. When the units arrive, they must be labeled, at an additional cost of 75¢ per unit. Emblems purchased, received, and labeled 1,500 units, of which 750 units were sold during the month for $20 each. The controller has prepared the following income statement:

Sales	$15,000
Cost of sales ($11 × 750)	8,250
Gross margin	$ 6,750
Shipping expense	750
Labeling expense	1,125
Net income	$ 4,875

Emblems is aware that a gross margin of 40% is standard for the industry. The marketing manager believes that Emblems should lower the price because the gross margin is higher than the industry average.

Required

1. Calculate Emblems' gross margin ratio.
2. Explain why you believe that Emblems should or should not lower its selling price.

LO 1, 3 Case 5-5 Pricing Decision

Caroline's Candy Corner sells gourmet chocolates. The company buys chocolates, in bulk, for \$5.00 per pound plus 5% sales tax. Credit terms are 2/10, net 25, and the company always pays promptly in order to take advantage of the discount. The chocolates are shipped to Caroline FOB shipping point. Shipping costs are \$.05 per pound. When the chocolates arrive at the shop, Caroline's Candy repackages them into one-pound boxes labeled with the store name. Boxes cost \$.70 each. The company pays its employees an hourly wage of \$5.25 plus a commission of \$.10 per pound.

DECISION MAKING

Required

1. What is the cost per one-pound box of chocolates?
2. What price must Caroline's Candy charge in order to have a 40% gross margin?
3. Do you believe this is a sufficient margin for this kind of business? What other costs might the company still incur?

LO 2 Case 5-6 Use of a Perpetual Inventory System

Darrell Keith is starting a new business. He would like to keep a tight control over it. Therefore, he wants to know *exactly* how much gross profit he earns on each unit he sells. Darrell has set up an elaborate numbering system to identify each item as it is purchased and then to match the item with a sales price. Each unit is assigned a number as follows:

DECISION MAKING

0000-000-00-000

a. The first four numbers represent the month and day an item was received.
b. The second set of numbers is the last three numbers of the purchase order that authorized the purchase of the item.
c. The third set of numbers is the two-number department code assigned to different types of products.
d. The last three numbers are a chronological code assigned to units as they are received during a given day.

Required

1. Write a short memo to Darrell explaining the benefits and costs involved in a perpetual inventory system in conjunction with his quest to know exactly how much he will earn on each unit.
2. Comment on Darrell's inventory system, assuming that he is selling (a) automobiles or (b) trees, shrubs, and plants.

Accounting and Ethics: What Would You Do?

LO 1 Case 5-7 Sales Returns and Allowances

You are the controller for a large chain of discount merchandise stores. You receive a memorandum from the sales manager for the midwestern region. He raises an issue regarding the proper treatment of sales returns. The manager urges you to discontinue the "silly practice" of recording Sales Returns and Allowances each time a customer returns a product. In the manager's mind, this is a waste of time and unduly complicates the financial statements. The manager recommends, "Things could be kept a lot simpler by just reducing Sales Revenue when a product is returned."

Required

1. What do you think the sales manager's *motivation* might be for writing you the memo? Is it that he believes the present practice is a waste of time and unduly complicates the financial statements?
2. Do you agree with the sales manager's recommendation? Explain why you agree or disagree.
3. Write a brief memo to the sales manager outlining your position on this matter.

LO 4, 5 Case 5-8 Cash Receipts in a Bookstore

You were recently hired by a large retail bookstore chain. Your training involved spending a week at the largest and most profitable store in the district. The store manager assigned the head cashier to train you on the cash register and closing procedures required by the company's home office. In the process, the head cashier instructed you to keep an envelope for cash over and short that would include cash or IOUs equal to the net amount of overages or shortages in the cash drawer. "It is impossible to balance exactly, so just put extra cash in this envelope and use the cash when you are short." You studied accounting for one semester in college and remembered your professor saying that "all deposits should be made intact, daily."

Required

Draft a memorandum to the store manager detailing any problems you see with the current system.

Internet Research Case

INTERNET

www.gap.com

Case 5-9 The Gap

The Gap, Inc. has over 2600 stores selling casual clothes worldwide, including its GapKids and babyGap stores and its Old Navy and Banana Republic stores. While its 1998 revenues were the best in its 30-year history, it will continue to face competition from other retail clothing, shoe, and accessory companies in the continually changing retail marketplace.

Go to The Gap's Web site, explore the site for company-related information, and view its most recent annual report.

1. For the most recent year available, what is The Gap's net sales? How does this compare to the previous year? What is shown for cost of goods sold and occupancy expenses? How does this compare to the previous year?
2. Based on the latest accounting year available, what percentage of net sales goes for cost of goods sold and occupancy expenses? How does this compare to the percentage calculated from the Focus on Financial Results chapter opening vignette? What does this tell you about how well The Gap is controlling its costs?
3. As a manager, how might changes in the gross profit percentage influence future actions? What actions might be taken by management to maximize the difference between net sales and cost of goods sold?
4. Find out from a source such as Hoovers.com or finance.yahoo.com what companies are in The Gap's industry segment. Conduct an online search for news articles that compare how well these companies are performing. Then compare the sales revenues and cost of goods sold for The Gap plus two of its competitors.
   - **a.** What are each company's sales revenues?
   - **b.** Over three years, how fast is each company growing in terms of revenues?
   - **c.** Compare each company's cost of goods sold as a percentage of sales.

Solutions to Key Terms Quiz

Quiz 1: Merchandise Accounting

__14__ Net sales (p. 213)
__4__ Trade discount (p. 214)
__7__ Sales Discounts (p. 216)
__15__ Cost of goods sold (p. 217)
__10__ Periodic system (p. 218)
__13__ Purchases (p. 221)
__12__ Purchase Discounts (p. 222)
__9__ FOB shipping point (p. 222)

__2__ Sales Returns and Allowances (p. 214)
__1__ Quantity discount (p. 215)
__11__ Cost of goods available for sale (p. 217)
__5__ Perpetual system (p. 218)
__3__ Transportation-in (p. 220)
__6__ Purchase Returns and Allowances (p. 221)
__8__ FOB destination point (p. 222)

Quiz 2: Internal Control

- __14__ Internal control system (p. 225)
- __13__ Internal audit staff (p. 226)
- __8__ Report of management (p. 226)
- __4__ Audit committee (p. 227)
- __3__ Accounting system (p. 227)
- __5__ Accounting controls (p. 228)
- __12__ Purchase order (Appendix 5A) (p. 237)
- __9__ Blind receiving report (Appendix 5A) (p. 239)
- __2__ Board of directors (p. 227)
- __10__ Foreign Corrupt Practices Act (p. 227)
- __11__ Administrative controls (p. 228)
- __6__ Purchase requisition form (Appendix 5A) (p. 237)
- __1__ Invoice (Appendix 5A) (p. 239)
- __7__ Invoice approval form (Appendix 5A) (p. 240)

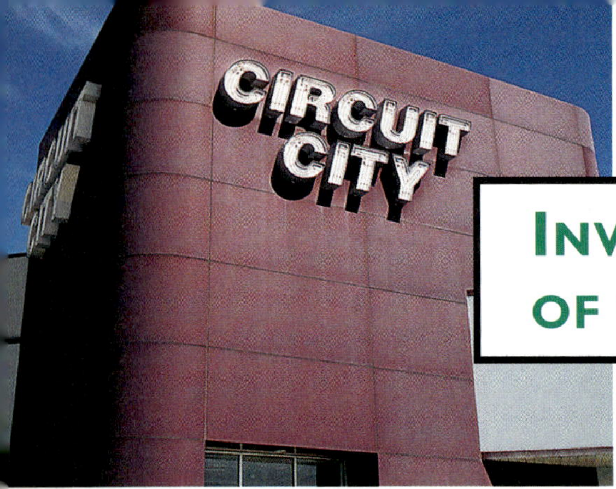

Chapter 6

Inventories and Cost of Goods Sold

Study Links

A Look at Previous Chapters

In Chapter 5, we introduced inventory for merchandisers and examined how they account for purchases and sales of their products. We saw that companies track their inventory using one of two systems, periodic or perpetual.

A Look at This Chapter

In this chapter, we continue our examination of inventory by considering inventory costing methods. Specific identification, FIFO, LIFO, and weighted average are choices available to a company in assigning a value to inventory on the balance sheet and in determining cost of goods sold on the income statement. Other inventory topics discussed in the chapter include the lower-of-cost-or-market rule and methods of estimating inventory.

A Look at Upcoming Chapters

Chapter 7 concludes our look at accounting for current assets. When a company makes a sale of inventory on credit, it records an account receivable. The collection of the receivable adds to the company's cash balance. Beyond the cash needed in day-to-day operations, management may decide to invest its excess cash. Chapter 7 looks at accounting issues for cash, receivables, and investments.

FIFO $10,250 Avail. for sale
unsold 7,250 — Sold 3,000
LIFO unsold 7,100 — sold 3,150

Focus on Financial Results

For the last few years the consumer electronics industry has sustained tremendous growth in a fiercely competitive environment. Circuit City remains a top retailer in the U.S. market. High-quality customer service and state-of-the-art merchandise have rewarded Circuit City with steady increases in net sales, which reached nearly $11 billion in 1999. (Circuit City also maintains a revolutionary used-car business known as CarMax.)

Sales volume is important for any merchandiser, but so is managing inventory effectively. Inventory is a major issue for Circuit City as it continues to grow; you can see from the accompanying partial balance sheets that merchandise represents about half the firm's total assets.

One innovation that should have an impact on Circuit City's inventory is its on-line ordering system. Computer Build-to-Order Stations™, added to all Circuit City stores in 1999, allow customers to use a touch-screen to design a computer that meets their specific needs from a broad range of available features. The system searches the configure-to-order capabilities of IBM, NEC, Hewlett Packard, and Compaq in real time so customers can compare available choices. Best of all, from an inventory standpoint, the products are delivered directly to the customer's home or sent to the store for customer pickup.

If the inventory you buy fluctuates everyday or week

5,000 10/8 → $1.00 → $5,000
<3,000> 10/9
5,000 10/10 → $1.05 → $5,250
7,000

i.e. $1.00/gal. = $5,000

Had 5,000 gallons on 10/8 sold 3,000 gallons on 10/9, 10/10 then received 5,000 more on 10/10. $1.05/gal ⇒ $5,250

CONSOLIDATED BALANCE SHEETS

(Amounts in thousands except share data)	At February 28 1999	1998
ASSETS		
CURRENT ASSETS:		
Cash and cash equivalents	**$ 265,880**	$ 116,612
Net accounts receivable [NOTE 12]	**574,316**	598,035
Inventory	**1,517,675**	1,410,545
Prepaid expenses and other current assets	**36,644**	21,157
TOTAL CURRENT ASSETS	**2,394,515**	2,146,349
Property and equipment, net [NOTES 4 AND 5]	**1,005,773**	1,048,434
Other assets	**44,978**	36,918
TOTAL ASSETS	**$3,445,266**	$3,231,701

Inventory is about half of Circuit City's total assets

CONSOLIDATED STATEMENTS OF EARNINGS

(Amounts in thousands except per share data)	1999	%	Years Ended February 28 1998	%	1997	%
NET SALES AND OPERATING REVENUES	**$10,804,447**	100.0	$8,870,797	100.0	$7,663,811	100.0
Cost of sales, buying and warehousing	**8,359,428**	77.4	6,827,133	77.0	5,902,711	77.0
GROSS PROFIT	**2,445,019**	22.6	2,043,664	23.0	1,761,100	23.0
Selling, general and administrative expenses [NOTE 11]	**2,186,177**	20.2	1,848,559	20.8	1,511,294	19.7
Interest expense [NOTE 5]	**28,319**	0.3	26,861	0.3	29,782	0.4
TOTAL EXPENSES	**2,214,496**	20.5	1,875,420	21.1	1,541,076	20.1
Earnings before income taxes	**230,523**	2.1	168,244	1.9	220,024	2.9
Provision for income taxes [NOTE 6]	**87,599**	0.8	63,933	0.7	83,610	1.1
NET EARNINGS	**$ 142,924**	1.3	$ 104,311	1.2	$ 136,414	1.8

Circuit City's 1999 annual report

How will the new system help Circuit City better manage its "inventory turns"—the number of times it turns over its merchandise each year? What will lower or higher inventory turns say about the company's effectiveness in choosing, pricing, and promoting its products? While studying this chapter, consider these questions and select the annual report items you need to estimate Circuit City's inventory turns each year.

www.circuitcity.com

Learning Objectives

After studying this chapter, you should be able to:

LO 1 Identify the forms of inventory held by different types of businesses and the types of costs incurred. (p. 262)

LO 2 Explain the relationship between the valuation of inventory and the measurement of income. (p. 263)

LO 3 Apply the inventory costing methods of specific identification, weighted average, FIFO, and LIFO using a periodic system. (p. 264)

LO 4 Analyze the effects of the different costing methods on inventory, net income, income taxes, and cash flow. (p. 269)

LO 5 Analyze the effects of an inventory error on various financial statement items. (p. 275)

LO 6 Apply the lower-of-cost-or-market rule to the valuation of inventory. (p. 278)

LO 7 Explain why and how the cost of inventory is estimated in certain situations. (p. 280)

LO 8 Analyze the management of inventory turnover. (p. 282)

LO 9 Explain the effects that inventory transactions have on the statement of cash flows. (p. 283)

LO 10 Explain the differences between a periodic and a perpetual inventory system (Appendix 6A). (p. 288)

LO 11 Apply the inventory costing methods using a perpetual system (Appendix 6A). (p. 289)

The Nature of Inventory

LO 1 Identify the forms of inventory held by different types of businesses and the types of costs incurred.

Inventory is an asset that is held for *resale* in the normal course of business. The distinction between inventory and an operating asset is the *intent* of the owner. For example, some of the computers that Circuit City owns are operating assets because they are used in various activities of the business such as the payroll and accounting functions. Many more of the computers Circuit City owns are inventory, however, because the company intends to sell them. This chapter is concerned with the proper valuation of inventory and the related effect on cost of goods sold.

It is important to distinguish between the *types* of inventory costs incurred and the *form* the inventory takes. Wholesalers and retailers incur a single type of cost, the *purchase price*, of the inventory they sell. On the balance sheet they use a single account for inventory, titled **Merchandise Inventory.** Wholesalers and retailers buy merchandise in finished form and offer it for resale without transforming the product in any way. Because they do not use factory buildings, assembly lines, or production equipment, merchandise companies have a relatively small dollar amount in operating assets and a large amount in inventory. For example, on its February 28, 1999, balance sheet, Circuit City reported inventory of approximately $1.5 billion and total assets of $3.4 billion. It is not unusual for inventories to account for half of the total assets of a merchandise company.

MERCHANDISE INVENTORY The account wholesalers and retailers use to report inventory held for resale.

The cost of inventory to a *merchandiser* is limited to the product's purchase price, which may include other costs we will mention soon. Conversely, three distinct *types* of costs are incurred by a *manufacturer:* direct materials, direct labor, and manufacturing overhead. Direct materials, also called **raw materials,** are the ingredients used in making a product. The costs of direct materials used in manufacturing an automobile include the costs of steel, glass, and rubber. Direct labor consists of the amounts paid to workers to manufacture the product. The $20 per hour paid to an assembly line worker is a primary ingredient in the cost to manufacture the automobile. Manufacturing overhead includes all other costs that are related to the manufacturing process but cannot be directly matched to specific units of output. Depreciation of a factory building and the salary of a supervisor are two examples of overhead costs. Accountants have developed various techniques to assign, or allocate, these manufacturing overhead costs to specific products.

RAW MATERIALS The inventory of a manufacturer before the addition of any direct labor or manufacturing overhead.

EXHIBIT 6-1 Relationships between Types of Businesses and Inventory Costs

Type of Business	Inventory	Costs Included in Inventory
Retailer/Wholesaler →	Merchandise inventory	Cost to purchase
Manufacturer →	Raw materials	Cost of materials before entered into production
	Work in process	Costs of direct materials used, direct labor, and overhead in unfinished items
	Finished goods	Cost of completed, but unsold, items

The inventory of a manufacturer consists of raw material, work in process, and finished goods. The electronic device being built here is part of a firm's work in process inventory. The direct materials probably consist of such items as the individual control knobs purchased from another manufacturer. When the manufacturing process is complete, the inventory of finished goods is ready for sale.

In addition to the three types of costs incurred in a production process, the inventory of a manufacturer takes three distinct *forms.* The three forms or stages in the development of inventory are raw materials, work in process, and finished goods. Direct materials or raw materials enter a production process in which they are transformed into a finished product by the addition of direct labor and manufacturing overhead. At any point in time, including the end of an accounting period, some of the materials have entered the process and some labor costs have been incurred but the product is not finished. The cost of unfinished products is appropriately called **work in process** or *work in progress.* Inventory that has completed the production process and is available for sale is called **finished goods.** Finished goods are the equivalent of merchandise inventory for a retailer or wholesaler in that both represent the inventory of goods held for sale. Many manufacturers disclose the dollar amounts of each of the three forms of inventory in their annual report. For example, Nike disclosed in its 1998 annual report the following amounts, stated in millions of dollars:

	Millions
Inventories:	
Finished goods	$1,303.8
Work in progress	34.7
Raw materials	58.1
	$1,396.6

Exhibit 6-1 summarizes the relationships between the types of costs incurred and the forms of inventory for different types of businesses.

WORK IN PROCESS
The cost of unfinished products in a manufacturing company.

FINISHED GOODS
A manufacturer's inventory that is complete and ready for sale.

www.nike.com

From Concept **TO PRACTICE 6.1**

READING GATEWAY'S FOOTNOTES
Footnote 10 in Gateway's 1998 annual report includes information about the composition of its inventory. How does Gateway categorize these elements of its inventory? What percentage of its total inventory at the end of 1998 is made up of finished goods?

INVENTORY VALUATION AND THE MEASUREMENT OF INCOME

Valuation is the major problem in accounting for inventories. Because of the additional complexities involved in valuing the inventory of a manufacturer, we will concentrate in this chapter on the valuation of *merchandise inventory.* (Accounting for the inventory costs incurred by a manufacturing firm is covered in detail in management accounting textbooks.)

One of the most fundamental concepts in accounting is the relationship between *asset valuation* and the *measurement of income.* Recall a point made in Chapter 4: assets are unexpired costs, and expenses are expired costs. Thus, the value assigned to an asset on the balance sheet determines the amount eventually recognized as an expense on the income statement. For example, the amount recorded as the cost of an item of plant and equipment will dictate the amount of depreciation expense recognized on the income statement

LO 2 Explain the relationship between the valuation of inventory and the measurement of income.

over the life of the asset. Similarly, the amount recorded as the cost of inventory determines the amount recognized as cost of goods sold on the income statement when the asset is sold. An error in assigning the proper amount to inventory on the balance sheet will affect the amount recognized as cost of goods sold on the income statement. The relationship between inventory as an asset and cost of goods sold can be understood by recalling the cost of goods sold section of the income statement. Assume the following example:

Beginning inventory	$ 500
Add: Purchases	1,200
Cost of goods available for sale	$1,700
Less: Ending inventory	(600)
Cost of goods sold	$1,100

The amount assigned to ending inventory is deducted from cost of goods available for sale to determine cost of goods sold. If the ending inventory amount is incorrect, cost of goods sold will be wrong, and thus the net income of the period will be in error as well. (We will look at inventory errors later in the chapter.)

Inventory Costs: What Should Be Included?

All assets, including inventory, are recorded initially at cost. Cost is defined as "the price paid or consideration given to acquire an asset. As applied to inventories, cost means in principle the sum of the applicable expenditures and charges directly or indirectly incurred in bringing an article to its existing condition and location."[1]

Note the reference to the existing *condition* and *location.* This means that certain costs may also be included in the "price paid." Here are examples:

- Any freight costs incurred by the buyer in shipping inventory to its place of business should be included in the cost of the inventory.
- The cost of insurance taken out during the time that inventory is in transit should be added to the cost of the inventory.
- The cost of storing inventory before the time it is ready to be sold should be included in cost.
- Various types of taxes paid, such as excise and sales taxes, are other examples of costs necessary to put the inventory into a position to be able to sell it.

It is often very difficult, however, to allocate many of these incidental costs among the various items of inventory purchased. For example, consider a $500 freight bill that a supermarket paid on a merchandise shipment that includes 100 different items of inventory. To address the practical difficulty in assigning this type of cost to the different products, many companies have a policy by which transportation costs are charged to expense of the period if they are immaterial in amount. Thus, shipments of merchandise are simply recorded at the net invoice price, that is, after taking any cash discounts for early payment. It is a practical solution to a difficult allocation problem. Once again, the company must apply the cost/benefit test to accounting information.

Inventory Costing Methods with a Periodic System

LO 3 Apply the inventory costing methods of specific identification, weighted average, FIFO, and LIFO using a periodic system.

To this point, we have assumed that the cost to purchase an item of inventory is constant. For most merchandisers, however, the unit cost of inventory changes frequently. Consider a simple example. Everett Company purchases merchandise twice during the first year of business. The dates, the number of units purchased, and the costs are as follows:

[1] *Accounting Research Bulletin No. 43,* "Inventory Pricing" (New York: American Institute of Certified Public Accountants, June 1953), ch. 4, statement 3.

Business Strategy

The days of expensive computer hardware appear to be over. As hardware manufacturers find themselves losing profits as prices fall, they are increasingly turning to other ways of generating revenue. One of the most popular is to offer customers generous rebates on hardware purchases in return for their commitment to a long-term contract for Internet service to be delivered by a specific provider.

Gateway and Compaq began bundling Internet service with their PCs in this way some time ago, but retailers, who are feeling the price squeeze even more, are just beginning to use the technique. Circuit City and its rival retailer Best Buy lead the way. Circuit City is offering new CompuServe customers a $400 rebate (in the form of store credit from CompuServe) on all desktop PCs in the store—which makes some of the cheaper systems practically free. The Emachines 333CS computer, for instance, sells for $475, but the actual cost to the customer will be zero after the $400 rebate from CompuServe and a $75 rebate from Emachines. The chain is also promoting rebates on printers and monitors, selling them as a package that comes to only $100 after mail-in rebates.

Of course, Circuit City hopes customers will use their rebate, which is stored in a Circuit City Merchandise Card good for 90 days, before they leave the store. "Certainly $400 will buy a veritable library of CDs and DVDs, but it will also cover quite a few of some of our newest cutting-edge products, such as digital cameras, camcorders, PC companions and even a personal computer," says President and CEO Alan McCollough.

SOURCES: Stephanie Miles, "Circuit City Joins Rush toward Free PCs," CNET News.com, June 30, 1999; "New Circuit City CompuServe Offer Enough to Fill Stockings without Care," Circuit City press release, December 9, 1999.

www.gateway.com
www.compaq.com
www.circuitcity.com

February 4	200 units purchased at $1.00 per unit	= $200
October 13	200 units purchased at $1.50 per unit	= $300

Everett sells 200 units during the first year. Individual sales of the units take place relatively evenly throughout the year. The question is: *which* 200 units did the company sell, the $1.00 units or the $1.50 units or some combination of each? Recall the earlier discussion of the relationship between asset valuation and income measurement. The question is important because the answer determines not only the value assigned to the 200 units of ending inventory *but also* the amount allocated to cost of goods sold for the 200 units sold.

One possible method of assigning amounts to ending inventory and cost of goods sold is to *specifically identify* which 200 units were sold and which 200 units are on hand. This method is feasible for a few types of businesses in which units can be identified by serial numbers, but it is totally impractical in most situations. As an alternative to specific identification, we could make an *assumption* as to which units were sold and which are on hand. Three different answers are possible:

1. 200 units sold at $1.00 each = $200 cost of goods sold
and 200 units on hand at $1.50 each = $300 ending inventory

or

2. 200 units sold at $1.50 each = $300 cost of goods sold
and 200 units on hand at $1.00 each = $200 ending inventory

or

3. 200 units sold at $1.25 each = $250 cost of goods sold
and 200 units on hand at $1.25 each = $250 ending inventory

The third alternative assumes an *average cost* for the 200 units on hand and the 200 units sold. The average cost is the cost of the two purchases of $200 and $300, or $500, divided by the 400 units available to sell, or $1.25 per unit.

If we are concerned with the actual *physical flow* of the units of inventory, all of the three methods illustrated may be incorrect. The only approach that will yield a "correct" answer in terms of the actual flow of *units* of inventory is the specific identification method. In the absence of a specific identification approach, it is impossible to say which particular units were *actually* sold. In fact, there may have been sales from each of the two purchases, that is, some of the $1.00 units may have been sold and some of the $1.50 units may have been sold. To solve the problem of assigning costs to identical units, accountants have developed inventory costing assumptions or methods. Each of these methods makes a specific *assumption* about the *flow of costs* rather than the physical flow of units. The only approach that uses the actual flow of the units in assigning costs is the specific identification method.

To take a closer look at specific identification as well as three alternative approaches to valuing inventory, we will use the following example:

	Units	Unit Cost	Total Cost
Beginning inventory			
January 1	500	$10	$ 5,000*
Purchases			
January 20	300	11	3,300
April 8	400	12	4,800
September 5	200	13	2,600
December 12	100	14	1,400
Total purchases	1,000 units		$12,100
Available for sale	1,500 units		$17,100
Units sold	900 units		?
Units in ending inventory	600 units		?

*Beginning inventory of $5,000 is carried over as the ending inventory from the prior period. It is highly unlikely that each of the four methods we will illustrate would result in the same dollar amount of inventory at any point in time. It is helpful when first learning the methods, however, to assume the same amount of beginning inventory.

The question marks indicate the dilemma. What portion of the cost of goods available for sale of $17,100 should be assigned to the 900 units sold? What portion should be assigned to the 600 units remaining in ending inventory? The purpose of an inventory costing method is to provide a reasonable answer to these two questions.

Specific Identification Method

SPECIFIC IDENTIFICATION METHOD
An inventory costing method that relies on matching unit costs with the actual units sold.

It is not always necessary to make an assumption about the flow of costs. In certain situations, it may be possible to specifically identify which units are sold and which units are on hand. A serial number on an automobile allows a dealer to identify a car on hand and thus its unit cost. An appliance dealer with 15 refrigerators on hand at the end of the year can identify the unit cost of each by matching a tag number with the purchase records. To illustrate the use of the **specific identification method** for our example, assume that the merchandiser is able to identify the specific units in the inventory at the end of the year and their costs as follows:

Units on Hand

Date Purchased	Units	Cost	Total Cost
January 20	100	$11	$1,100
April 8	300	12	3,600
September 5	200	13	2,600
Ending inventory	600		$7,300

One of two techniques can be used to find cost of goods sold. We can deduct ending inventory from the cost of goods available for sale:

Cost of goods available for sale		$17,100
Less:	Ending inventory	7,300
Equals:	Cost of goods sold	$ 9,800

Or we can calculate cost of goods sold independently by matching the units sold with their respective unit costs. By eliminating the units in ending inventory from the original acquisition schedule, the units sold and their costs are as follows:

Units Sold

Date Sold	Units	Cost	Total Cost
January 1	500	$10	$5,000
January 20	200	11	2,200
April 8	100	12	1,200
December 12	100	14	1,400
Cost of goods sold	900		$9,800

The practical difficulty in keeping track of individual items of inventory sold is not the only problem with the use of this method. The method also allows management to *manipulate income.* For example, assume that a company is not having a particularly good year. Management may be tempted to do whatever it can to boost net income. One way it can do this is by *selectively selling units with the lowest-possible unit cost.* By doing so, the company can keep cost of goods sold down and net income up. Because of the potential for manipulation with the specific identification method, coupled with the practical difficulty of applying it in most situations, it is not widely used.

WEIGHTED AVERAGE COST METHOD

The **weighted average cost method** is a relatively easy approach to costing inventory. It assigns the same unit cost to all units available for sale during the period. The weighted average cost is calculated as follows for our example:

WEIGHTED AVERAGE COST METHOD
An inventory costing method that assigns the same unit cost to all units available for sale during the period.

$$\frac{\text{Cost of Goods Available for Sale}}{\text{Units Available for Sale}} = \text{Weighted Average Cost}$$

$$\frac{\$17,100}{1,500} = \$11.40$$

Ending inventory is found by multiplying the weighted average unit cost by the number of units on hand:

$$\text{Weighted Average Cost} \times \text{Number of Units in Ending Inventory} = \text{Ending Inventory}$$

$$\$11.40 \times 600 = \$6,840$$

Cost of goods sold can be calculated in one of two ways:

Cost of goods available for sale		$17,100
Less:	Ending inventory	6,840
Equals:	Cost of goods sold	$10,260

or

$$\text{Weighted Average Cost} \times \text{Number of Units Sold} = \text{Cost of Goods Sold}$$

$$\$11.40 \times 900 = \$10,260$$

Note that the computation of the weighted average cost is based on the cost of *all* units available for sale during the period, not just the beginning inventory or purchases. Also note that the method is called the *weighted* average cost method. As the name indicates, each of the individual unit costs is multiplied by the number of units acquired at each price. The simple arithmetic average of the unit costs for the beginning inventory and the four purchases is ($10 + $11 + $12 + $13 + $14)/5 = $12. The weighted average cost is slightly less than $12 ($11.40), however, because more units were acquired at the lower prices than at the higher prices.

First-In, First-Out Method (FIFO)

FIFO method
An inventory costing method that assigns the most recent costs to ending inventory.

The **FIFO method** assumes that the first units in, or purchased, are the first units out, or sold. The first units sold during the period are assumed to come from the beginning inventory. After the beginning inventory is sold, the next units sold are assumed to come from the first purchase during the period and so forth. Thus, ending inventory consists of the most recent purchases of the period. In many businesses, this cost-flow assumption is a fairly accurate reflection of the *physical* flow of products. For example, to maintain a fresh stock of products, the physical flow in a grocery store is first-in, first-out.

To calculate *ending inventory,* we start with the *most recent* inventory acquired and work *backward:*

Units on Hand

Date Purchased	Units	Cost	Total Cost
December 12	100	$14	$1,400
September 5	200	13	2,600
April 8	300	12	3,600
Ending inventory	600		$7,600

Cost of goods sold can then be found:

Cost of goods available for sale		$17,100
Less:	Ending inventory	7,600
Equals:	Cost of goods sold	$ 9,500

Or, because the FIFO method assumes that the first units in are the first ones sold, cost of goods sold can be calculated by starting with the *beginning inventory* and working *forward:*

Units Sold

Date Purchased	Units	Cost	Total Cost
January 1	500	$10	$5,000
January 20	300	11	3,300
April 8	100	12	1,200
Units sold	900	Cost of goods sold	$9,500

Accounting for Your Decisions

You Are the Controller

Your company, Princeton Systems, is a manufacturer of components for personal computers. The company uses the FIFO method to account for its inventory. The CEO, a stickler for accuracy, asks you why you can't identify each unit of inventory and place a cost on it, instead of making an assumption that the first unit of inventory is the first sold when that is not necessarily the case.

ANS: The CEO is suggesting the specific identification method, which works best when there are fewer pieces of unique inventory, not thousands of units of identical pieces. Because the company makes thousands of identical components each year, it would be impractical to assign specific costs to each unit of inventory. The FIFO method, on the other hand, assumes that the first units in are the first units sold, an appropriate assumption under these circumstances.

Last-In, First-Out Method (LIFO)

The **LIFO method** assumes that the last units in, or purchased, are the first units out, or sold. The first units sold during the period are assumed to come from the latest purchase made during the period and so forth. Can you think of any businesses where the *physical* flow of products is last-in, first-out? Although this situation is not nearly so common as a first-in, first-out physical flow, a stockpiling operation, such as in a rock quarry, operates on this basis.

LIFO method
An inventory method that assigns the most recent costs to cost of goods sold.

To calculate *ending inventory* using LIFO, we start with the *beginning inventory* and work *forward:*

Units on Hand

Date Purchased	Units	Cost	Total Cost
Beginning inventory	500	$10	$5,000
January 20	100	11	1,100
Ending inventory	600		$6,100

Cost of goods sold can then be found:

Cost of goods available for sale		$17,100
Less:	Ending inventory	6,100
Equals:	Cost of goods sold	$11,000

Or, because the LIFO method assumes that the last units in are the first ones sold, *cost of goods sold* can be calculated by starting with the *most recent* inventory acquired and working *backward:*

Units Sold

Date Purchased	Units	Cost	Total Cost
December 12	100	$14	$ 1,400
September 5	200	13	2,600
April 8	400	12	4,800
January 20	200	11	2,200
Units sold	900	Cost of goods sold	$11,000

Study Tip

There may be cases, such as this illustration of LIFO, in which it is easier to determine ending inventory and then deduct it from cost of goods available for sale to find cost of goods sold. This approach is easier in this example because there are fewer layers in ending inventory than in cost of goods sold. In other cases, it may be quicker to determine cost of goods sold first and then plug ending inventory.

Selecting an Inventory Costing Method

LO 4 Analyze the effects of the different costing methods on inventory, net income, income taxes, and cash flow.

The mechanics of each of the inventory costing methods are straightforward. But how does a company decide on the best method to use to value its inventory? According to the accounting profession, *the primary determinant in selecting an inventory costing method should be the ability of the method to accurately reflect the net income of the period.* But how and why does a particular costing method accurately reflect the net income of the period? Because there is no easy answer to this question, a number of arguments have been raised by accountants to justify the use of one method over the others. We turn now to some of these arguments.

Costing Methods and Cash Flow

Comparative income statements for our example are presented in Exhibit 6-2. Note that with the use of the weighted average method, net income is between the amounts for FIFO and LIFO. Because the weighted average method normally yields results between the other two methods, we concentrate on the two extremes, LIFO and FIFO. The major advantage of using the weighted average method is its simplicity.

The original data for our example involved a situation in which prices were *rising* throughout the period: beginning inventory cost $10 per unit, and the last purchase during the year was at $14. With LIFO, the most recent costs are assigned to cost of

EXHIBIT 6-2 Income Statements for the Inventory Costing Methods

	Weighted Average	FIFO	LIFO
Sales revenue—$20 each	$18,000	$18,000	$18,000
Beginning inventory	5,000	5,000	5,000
Purchases	12,100	12,100	12,100
Cost of goods available for sale	$17,100	$17,100	$17,100
Ending inventory	**6,840**	**7,600**	**6,100**
Cost of goods sold	**$10,260**	**$ 9,500**	**$11,000**
Gross margin	**$ 7,740**	**$ 8,500**	**$ 7,000**
Operating expenses	2,000	2,000	2,000
Net income before tax	**$ 5,740**	**$ 6,500**	**$ 5,000**
Income tax expense (40%)	**2,296**	**2,600**	**2,000**
Net income	**$ 3,444**	**$ 3,900**	**$ 3,000**

NOTE: Figures that differ among the three methods are in bold.

goods sold; with FIFO, the older costs are assigned to expense. Thus, in a period of rising prices, the assignment of the *higher* prices to cost of goods sold under LIFO results in a *lower gross margin* under LIFO than under FIFO ($7,000 for LIFO and $8,500 for FIFO). Because operating expenses are not affected by the choice of inventory method, the lower gross margin under LIFO results in lower income before tax, which in turn leads to lower taxes. If we assume a 40% tax rate, income tax expense under LIFO is only $2,000, compared with $2,600 under FIFO, a savings of $600 in taxes. Another way to look at the taxes saved by using LIFO is to focus on the difference in the expense under each method:

LIFO cost of goods sold	$11,000
− FIFO cost of goods sold	9,500
Additional expense from use of LIFO	$ 1,500
× Tax rate	.40
Tax savings from the use of LIFO	$ 600

Study Tip

During a period of falling prices, all of the effects shown here would be just the opposite. For example, cost of goods sold would be lower under LIFO than under FIFO.

To summarize, *during a period of rising prices,* the two methods result in the following:

Item	LIFO	Relative To	FIFO
Cost of goods sold	Higher		Lower
Gross margin	Lower		Higher
Income before taxes	Lower		Higher
Taxes	Lower		Higher

In conclusion, lower taxes with the use of LIFO result in cash savings.

The tax savings available from the use of LIFO during a period of rising prices are largely responsible for its popularity. Keep in mind, however, that the cash saved from a lower tax bill with LIFO is only a temporary savings, or what is normally called a *tax deferral.* At some point in the life of the business, the inventory that is carried at the older, lower-priced amounts will be sold. This will result in a tax bill higher than that under FIFO. Yet even a tax deferral is beneficial; given the opportunity, it is better to pay less tax today and more in the future because today's tax savings can be invested.

Two-Minute Review

1. Which of the inventory methods will result in the least amount of income before taxes, assuming a period of rising prices?

2. What is the easiest way to calculate the tax savings from using one method versus another?

Answers:

1. LIFO

2. The easiest approach to calculating the tax savings is to multiply the tax rate times the difference in cost of goods sold between the two methods.

LIFO LIQUIDATION

Recall the assumption made about which costs remain in inventory when LIFO is used. The costs of the oldest units remain in inventory, and if prices are rising, the costs of these units will be lower than the costs of more recent purchases. Now assume that the company *sells more units than it buys during the period.* When a company using LIFO experiences a liquidation, some of the units assumed to be sold will come from the older layers, with a relatively low unit cost. This situation, called a **LIFO liquidation,** presents a dilemma for the company.

LIFO LIQUIDATION
The result of selling more units than are purchased during the period, which can have negative tax consequences if a company is using LIFO.

A partial or complete liquidation of the older, lower-priced units will result in a low cost of goods sold figure and a correspondingly high gross margin for the period. In turn, the company faces a large tax bill because of the relatively high gross margin. In fact, a liquidation causes the tax advantages of using LIFO to reverse on the company, which is faced with paying off some of the taxes that were deferred in earlier periods. Should a company facing this situation buy inventory at the end of the year to avoid the consequences of a liquidation? This is a difficult question to answer and depends on many factors, including the company's cash position. At the least, the accountant must be aware of the potential for a large tax bill if a liquidation occurs.

Of course, a LIFO liquidation also benefits—and may even distort—reported earnings if the liquidation is large enough. For this reason and the tax problem, many companies are reluctant to liquidate their LIFO inventory. The problem often festers, and companies find themselves with inventory costed at decade-old price levels.

THE LIFO CONFORMITY RULE

Would it be possible for a company to have the best of both worlds? That is, could it use FIFO to report its income to stockholders, thus maximizing the amount of net income reported to this group, and use LIFO to report to the IRS, minimizing its taxable income and the amount paid to the government? Unfortunately, the IRS says that if a company chooses LIFO for reporting cost of goods sold on its tax return, then it must also use LIFO on its books, that is, in preparing its income statement. This is called the **LIFO conformity rule.** Note that the rule applies only to the use of LIFO on the tax return. A company is free to use different methods in preparing its tax return and its income statement as long as the method used for the tax return is *not* LIFO.

LIFO CONFORMITY RULE
The IRS requirement that if LIFO is used on the tax return, it must also be used in reporting income to stockholders.

THE LIFO RESERVE: ESTIMATING LIFO'S EFFECT ON INCOME AND ON TAXES PAID FOR WHIRLPOOL

If a company decides to use LIFO, an investor can still determine how much more income the company would have reported had it used FIFO. In addition, he or she can approximate the tax savings or the additional taxes to the company from the use of LIFO. Consider the following footnote from the 1998 annual report for Whirlpool Corporation:

www.whirlpool.com

(4) Inventories

December 31 (millions of dollars)	1998	1997
Finished products	$ 960	$1,015
Work in process	54	69
Raw materials	279	304
Total FIFO cost	$1,293	$1,388
Less excess of FIFO cost over LIFO cost	193	218
	$1,100	$1,170

LIFO inventories represent approximately 23% and 24% of total inventories at December 31, 1998 and 1997.

Note that Whirlpool uses more than one inventory method and that at the end of 1998, LIFO inventories accounted for only 23% of the total inventory. It is not unusual for companies to use more than one method to value inventories. For now it is important to understand that Whirlpool reported $1,100,000,000 as its total inventory on the December 31, 1998, balance sheet.

The following steps explain the logic for using the information in the inventory footnote to estimate LIFO's effect on income and on taxes:

LIFO RESERVE
The excess of the value of a company's inventory stated at FIFO over the value stated at LIFO.

1. The excess of the value of a company's inventory stated at FIFO over the value stated at LIFO is called the **LIFO reserve.** The *cumulative* excess of the value of Whirlpool's inventory on a FIFO basis over the value on a LIFO basis is $193 million at the end of 1998.
2. Because Whirlpool reports inventory at a lower value on its balance sheet using LIFO, it will report a higher cost of goods sold amount on the income statement. Thus, the LIFO reserve not only represents the excess of the inventory balance on a FIFO basis over that on a LIFO basis but also *represents the cumulative amount by which cost of goods sold on a LIFO basis exceeds cost of goods sold on a FIFO basis.*
3. The decrease in Whirlpool's LIFO reserve in 1998 was $25 million ($218 million – $193 million). This means that the decrease in cost of goods sold for 1998 from using LIFO instead of FIFO was also this amount. Thus, income before tax for 1998 was $25 million higher because the company used LIFO.
4. If we assume a corporate tax rate of 35%, the additional taxes from using LIFO amounted to $25 million × .35, or $8.75 million.

COSTING METHODS AND INVENTORY PROFITS

FIFO, LIFO, and weighted average are all cost-based methods to value inventory. They vary in terms of which costs are assigned to inventory and which to cost of goods sold, but all three assign *historical costs* to inventory. In our previous example, the unit cost for inventory purchases gradually increased during the year from $10 for the beginning inventory to a high of $14 on the date of the last purchase.

REPLACEMENT COST
The current cost of a unit of inventory.

An alternative to assigning any of the historical costs incurred during the year to ending inventory and cost of goods sold would be to use **replacement cost** to value each of these. Assume that the cost to replace a unit of inventory at the end of the year is $15. Use of a replacement cost system results in the following:

Ending inventory	=	600 units	×	$15 per unit	=	$ 9,000
Cost of goods sold	=	900 units	×	$15 per unit	=	$13,500

INVENTORY PROFIT
The portion of the gross profit that results from holding inventory during a period of rising prices.

A replacement cost approach is not acceptable under the profession's current standards, but many believe that it provides more relevant information to users. Inventory must be replaced if a company is to remain in business. Many accountants argue that the use of historical cost in valuing inventory leads to what is called **inventory profit,** particularly if FIFO is used in a period of rising prices. For example, cost of goods sold in our illustration was only $9,500 on a FIFO basis, compared with $13,500 if the replacement cost of $15 per unit is used. The $4,000 difference between the two cost of goods sold figures is a profit from holding the inventory during a period of rising prices and is called *inventory profit.* To look at this another way, assume that the units are sold for $20 each. The following analysis reconciles the difference between gross margin on a FIFO basis and on a replacement cost basis:

Sales revenue—900 units × $20 =		$18,000
Cost of goods sold—FIFO basis		9,500
Gross margin—FIFO basis		$ 8,500
Cost of goods sold—replacement cost basis	$13,500	

Cost of goods sold—FIFO basis	9,500	
Profit from holding inventory during a period of inflation		4,000
Gross margin on a replacement cost basis		$ 4,500

Those who argue in favor of a replacement cost approach would report only $4,500 of gross margin. They believe that the additional $4,000 of profit reported on a FIFO basis is simply due to holding the inventory during a period of rising prices. According to this viewpoint, if the 900 units sold during the period are to be replaced, a necessity if the company is to continue operating, the use of replacement cost in calculating cost of goods sold results in a better measure of gross margin than if it is calculated using FIFO.

Given that our current standards require the use of historical costs rather than replacement costs, does any one of the costing methods result in a better approximation of replacement cost of goods sold than the others? Because LIFO assigns the cost of the most recent purchases to cost of goods sold, it most nearly approximates the results with a replacement cost system. The other side of the argument, however, is that whereas LIFO results in the best approximation of *replacement cost of goods sold* on the *income statement,* FIFO most nearly approximates replacement cost of the *inventory* on the *balance sheet.* A comparison of the amounts from our example verifies this:

	Ending Inventory	**Cost of Goods Sold**
Weighted average	$6,840	$10,260
FIFO	7,600	9,500
LIFO	6,100	11,000
Replacement cost	9,000	13,500

ACCOUNTING FOR YOUR DECISIONS

You Are a Student

The owner/manager of a dairy farm knows that you are an accounting student and has asked your advice about which inventory method to use to measure the cost of both the inventory and the cost of goods sold. Since the inventory of milk and milk byproducts spoils easily, does he have to use the FIFO inventory valuation method? Why or why not?

ANS: No, he does not have to use the FIFO method, just because his products are subject to spoilage. There is a difference between the actual physical flow of the product and the cost flow of that product. From a practical perspective, he would want to sell the milk and milk byproducts on a FIFO basis to minimize spoilage. However, he can keep track of the cost flows for inventory valuation and cost of goods sold purposes using the LIFO method or weighted average cost method.

CHANGING INVENTORY METHODS

The purpose of each of the inventory costing methods is to *match costs with revenues.* If a company believes that a different method will result in a better matching than that being provided by the method currently being used, it should change methods. A company must be able to justify a change in methods, however. Taking advantage of the tax breaks offered by LIFO is *not* a valid justification for a change in methods.

It is very important for a company to *disclose* any change in accounting principle, including a change in the method of costing inventory. For example, some companies justify a change from LIFO to FIFO on the basis of reduced prices, as illustrated by this excerpt from Fruit of the Loom's 1997 annual report:

www.fruit.com

If you counted your inventory + made a mistake, you income statement is effected.
- It will affect 2 yrs. on the inc. state.
ie.
count shows $2,000 in inventory
actual shows $20,000
C of GS will show up high the 1st yr., the you eventually have to make up for it. Too low the 2nd yr.

If the situation was reverse
+ counted 40,000
actual 20,000
C of GS will show up to low the 1st yr. + to high the second.

During the fourth quarter of 1997, the Company changed its method of determining the cost of inventories from the LIFO method to the FIFO method as it experienced reduced costs from offshore assembly operations and expects continuing cost reductions. The cost of inventories on a LIFO basis at December 31, 1997 was approximately equal to their replacement cost. Accordingly, the Company believes that the FIFO method will result in a better measurement of operating results. All previously reported results have been restated to reflect the retroactive application of this accounting change as required by generally accepted accounting principles. The accounting change increased the net loss for 1997 by $27,800,000, $.37 per share. Due principally to the effect of LIFO reserve liquidations, net earnings previously reported for 1996 were reduced by $4,600,000 or $.06 per share, and the net loss previously reported for 1995 increased by $500,000 or $.01 per share.

Popularity of the Costing Methods

From Concept to PRACTICE 6.2

Reading Ben & Jerry's Annual Report Which inventory method does Ben & Jerry's use? Where did you find this information? Do you think the company is justified in using the method it does?

An annual survey conducted by the AICPA indicates the relative popularity of the inventory costing methods. The inventory methods used by the 600 corporations in the survey are reported in Exhibit 6-3. Note that the number of companies each year totals more than 600. This happens because, as we saw for Whirlpool, many companies use more than one method to determine the total cost of inventory. The survey indicates the relatively equal popularity of LIFO and FIFO in practice. Rather than increasing in popularity, as it had during more inflationary times, the use of LIFO appears to have stabilized, as indicated in Exhibit 6-3.

Inventory Valuation in Other Countries

The acceptable methods of valuing inventory differ considerably around the world. Many countries prohibit the use of LIFO for either tax or financial reporting purposes. Countries in which LIFO is either prohibited or rarely used include the United Kingdom, Canada, New Zealand, Sweden, Denmark, and Brazil. On the other hand, Germany, France, Australia, and Japan allow LIFO for inventory valuation of foreign investments but not for domestic reports.

In Chapter 1 we mentioned the attempts by the International Accounting Standards Committee (IASC) to develop worldwide accounting standards. This group favors the use of either FIFO or weighted average when specific identification is not feasible. The IASC recognizes LIFO as an acceptable alternative if a company discloses information enabling

Exhibit 6-3 Inventory Cost Determination—AICPA Survey

	Number of Companies			
	1998	**1997**	**1996**	**1995**
Methods				
First-in, first-out (FIFO)	409	415	417	411
Last-in, first-out (LIFO)	319	326	332	347
Average cost	176	188	181	185
Other	40	32	37	40
Use of LIFO				
All inventories	30	17	15	14
50% or more of inventories	152	170	178	191
Less than 50% of inventories	95	99	92	88
Not determinable	42	40	47	54
Companies using LIFO	319	326	332	347

SOURCE: *Accounting Trends & Techniques,* 53rd ed. (New York: American Institute of Certified Public Accountants, 1999).

users to reconcile LIFO inventory with either FIFO or weighted average (similar to the idea of a LIFO reserve discussed earlier in this chapter).

Two Inventory Systems: Periodic and Perpetual

In the examples presented so far in this chapter, we have assumed a periodic inventory system to concentrate our attention on the various cost-flow assumptions. Recall from Chapter 5 that with this system, a count of the inventory is necessary at the end of the period to determine the number of units sold and the number on hand. The reason is that the Inventory account is not updated each time a purchase is made and each time a sale is made.

For many years, the simplicity of the periodic system resulted in its widespread use. Because of the need in a perpetual system to record the cost of every individual sale when it occurs, use of the perpetual system was limited to businesses that sold products with a relatively high unit cost and low turnover, such as those of an automobile dealer. The ability to computerize the inventory system has resulted, however, in an increase in the use of the perpetual system in all types of businesses. A company can use any one of the costing methods with either a periodic or a perpetual inventory system. The application of the methods when a company maintains a perpetual inventory system is illustrated in Appendix 6A.

Inventory Errors

LO 5 Analyze the effects of an inventory error on various financial statement items.

Earlier in the chapter we considered the inherent tie between the valuation of assets, such as inventory, and the measurement of income, such as cost of goods sold. The importance of inventory valuation to the measurement of income can be illustrated by considering inventory errors. Many different types of inventory errors exist. Some errors are mathematical; for example, a bookkeeper may incorrectly add a column total. Other errors relate specifically to the physical count of inventory at year-end. For example, the count might inadvertently omit one section of a warehouse. Other errors arise from cutoff problems at year-end.

For example, assume that merchandise in transit at the end of the year is shipped FOB (free on board) shipping point. Under these shipment terms, the inventory belongs to the buyer at the time it is shipped. Because the shipment has not arrived at the end of the year, however, it cannot be included in the physical count. Unless some type of control is in place, the amount in transit may be erroneously omitted from the valuation of inventory at year-end.

To demonstrate the effect of an inventory error on the income statement, consider the following example. Through a scheduling error, two different inventory teams were assigned to count the inventory in the same warehouse on December 31, 2001. The correct amount of ending inventory is $250,000, but because two different teams counted the same inventory in one warehouse, the amount recorded is $300,000. The effect of this error on net income is analyzed in the left half of Exhibit 6-4.

The *overstatement* of *ending inventory* in 2001 leads to an *understatement* of the 2001 cost of goods sold *expense.* Because cost of goods sold is understated, *gross margin* for the year is *overstated.* Operating expenses are unaffected by an inventory error. Thus, *net income* is *overstated* by the same amount of overstatement of gross margin.[2] The most important conclusion from the exhibit is that an overstatement of ending inventory leads to a corresponding overstatement of net income.

Unfortunately, the effect of a misstatement of the year-end inventory is not limited to the net income for that year. As indicated in the right-hand portion of Exhibit 6-4, the error also affects the income statement for the following year. This happens simply because *the ending inventory of one period is the beginning inventory of the following period.* The *overstatement* of the 2002 *beginning inventory* leads to an *overstatement* of *cost of goods available for sale.* Because cost of goods available for sale is overstated, *cost of goods sold* is

[2]An overstatement of gross margin also results in an overstatement of income tax expense. Thus, because tax expense is overstated, the overstatement of net income is not so large as the overstatement of gross margin. For now we will ignore the effect of taxes, however.

EXHIBIT 6-4 Effects of Inventory Error on the Income Statement

	2001			2002		
	Reported	Corrected	Effects of Error	Reported	Corrected	Effects of Error
Sales	$1,000*	$1,000		$1,500	$1,500	
Costs of goods sold:						
Beginning inventory	200	200		**300**	**250**	$50 OS
Add: Purchases	700	700		1,100	1,100	
Cost of goods available for sale	$ 900	$ 900		**$1,400**	**$1,350**	50 OS
Less: Ending inventory	**300**	**250**	$50 OS†	350	350	
Cost of goods sold	**$ 600**	**$ 650**	50 US‡	**$1,050**	**$1,000**	50 OS
Gross margin	**$ 400**	**$ 350**	50 OS	**$ 450**	**$ 500**	50 US
Operating expenses	100	100		120	120	
Net income	**$ 300**	**$ 250**	50 OS	**$ 330**	**$ 380**	50 US

NOTE: Figures that differ as a result of the error are in bold.
*All amounts are in thousands of dollars.
†OS = Overstatement
‡US = Understatement

also *overstated.* The *overstatement* of cost of goods sold *expense* results in an *understatement* of *gross margin* and thus an *understatement* of *net income.*

Exhibit 6-4 illustrates the nature of a *counterbalancing error.* The effect of the overstatement of net income in the first year, 2001, is offset or counterbalanced by the understatement of net income by the same dollar amount in the following year. If the net incomes of two successive years are misstated in the opposite direction by the same amount, what is the effect on retained earnings? Assume that retained earnings at the beginning of 2001 is correctly stated at $300,000. The counterbalancing nature of the error is seen by analyzing retained earnings. For 2001 the analysis would indicate the following (OS = overstated and US = understated):

	2001 Reported	2001 Corrected	Effect of Error
Beginning retained earnings	$300,000	$300,000	Correct
Add: Net income	300,000	250,000	$50,000 OS
Ending retained earnings	$600,000	$550,000	$50,000 OS

An analysis for 2002 would show the following:

	2002 Reported	2002 Corrected	Effect of Error
Beginning retained earnings	$600,000	$550,000	$50,000 OS
Add: Net income	330,000	380,000	$50,000 US
Ending retained earnings	$930,000	$930,000	Correct

Thus, even though retained earnings is overstated at the end of the first year, it is correctly stated at the end of the second year. This is the nature of a counterbalancing error.

The effect of the error on the balance sheet is shown in Exhibit 6-5. The only accounts affected by the error are Inventory and Retained Earnings. The overstatement of the 2001 ending inventory results in an overstatement of total assets at the end of the first year. Similarly, as our earlier analysis indicates, the overstatement of 2001 net income leads to an overstatement of retained earnings by the same amount. Because the error is counterbalancing, the 2002 year-end balance sheet is correct; that is, ending inventory is not affected by the error, and thus the amount for total assets at the end of 2002 is also correct. The effect of the error on retained earnings is limited to the first year because of the counterbalancing nature of the error.

EXHIBIT 6-5 Effects of Inventory Error on the Balance Sheet

	2001		2002	
	Reported	Corrected	Reported	Corrected
Inventory	**$ 300***	**$ 250**	$ 350	$ 350
All other assets	1,700	1,700	2,080	2,080
Total assets	**$2,000**	**$1,950**	$2,430	$2,430
Total liabilities	$ 400	$ 400	$ 500	$ 500
Capital stock	1,000	1,000	1,000	1,000
Retained earnings	**600**	**550**	930	930
Total liabilities and stockholders' equity	**$2,000**	**$1,950**	$2,430	$2,430

NOTE: Figures that differ as a result of the error are in bold.
*All amounts are in thousands of dollars.

The effects of inventory errors on various financial statement items are summarized in Exhibit 6-6. Our analysis focused on the effects of an overstatement of inventory. The effects of an understatement are just the opposite and are summarized in the bottom portion of the exhibit.

Not all errors are counterbalancing. For example, if a section of a warehouse *continues* to be omitted from the physical count every year, both the beginning and the ending inventory will be incorrect each year and the error will not counterbalance.

Part of the auditor's job is to perform the necessary tests to obtain reasonable assurance that inventory has not been overstated or understated. If there is an error and inventory is wrong, however, the balance sheet and the income statement will both be distorted. For example, if ending inventory is overstated, inflating total assets, then cost of goods sold will be understated, boosting profits. Thus, such an error overstates the financial health of the organization in two ways. A lender or an investor must make a decision based on the current year's statement and cannot wait until the next accounting cycle, when this error is reversed. This is one reason that investors and creditors insist on audited financial statements.

EXHIBIT 6-6 Summary of the Effects of Inventory Errors

	Effect of Overstatement of Ending Inventory on	
	Current Year	Following Year
Cost of goods sold	Understated	Overstated
Gross margin	Overstated	Understated
Net income	Overstated	Understated
Retained earnings, end of year	Overstated	Correctly stated
Total assets, end of year	Overstated	Correctly stated

	Effect of Understatement of Ending Inventory on	
	Current Year	Following Year
Cost of goods sold	Overstated	Understated
Gross margin	Understated	Overstated
Net income	Understated	Overstated
Retained earnings, end of year	Understated	Correctly stated
Total assets, end of year	Understated	Correctly stated

Study Tip

Note the logic behind the notion that an overstatement of ending inventory leads to overstatements of both total assets and retained earnings at the end of the year. This is logical because a balance sheet must balance; that is, the left side must equal the right side. If the left side (inventory) is overstated, then the right side (retained earnings) will also be overstated.

Two-Minute Review

Skipper Corp. omits one section of its warehouse in the year-end inventory count.

1. Will the omission understate or overstate cost of goods sold on the income statement in the year the error is made?

2. Will the omission understate or overstate retained earnings on the balance sheet at the end of the year the error is made?

3. Will the omission affect retained earnings on the balance sheet at the end of the following year after the error is made? Explain your answer.

Answers:

1. Cost of goods sold will be overstated because the ending inventory is understated.

2. Retained earnings at the end of the year in which the error is made will be understated because cost of goods sold is overstated, and thus net income, which goes into retained earnings, is understated.

3. Retained earnings at the end of the following year will not be affected because of the counterbalancing nature of this error. Net income in the year of the error is understated, as described above. However, net income of the following year is overstated because cost of goods sold is understated as the result of an understatement of that year's beginning inventory.

VALUING INVENTORY AT LOWER OF COST OR MARKET

LO 6 Apply the lower-of-cost-or-market rule to the valuation of inventory.

LOWER-OF-COST-OR-MARKET (LCM) RULE
A conservative inventory valuation approach that is an attempt to anticipate declines in the value of inventory before its actual sale.

One of the components sold by an electronics firm has become economically obsolete. A particular style of suit sold by a retailer is outdated and can no longer be sold at regular price. In each of these instances, it is likely that the retailer will have to sell the merchandise for less than the normal selling price. In these situations, a departure from the cost basis of accounting may be necessary because the *market value* of the inventory may be less than its *cost* to the company. The departure is called the **lower-of-cost-or-market (LCM) rule.**

At the end of each accounting period, the original cost, as determined using one of the costing methods such as FIFO, is compared with the market price of the inventory. If market is less than cost, the inventory is written down to the lower amount.

For example, if cost is $100,000 and market value is $85,000, the accountant would make the following entry:

Dec. 31	Loss on Decline in Value of Inventory	15,000	
	Inventory		15,000
	To record decline in value of inventory.		

Assets	=	Liabilities	+	Owners' Equity
−15,000				−15,000

Note that the entry reduces both assets, in the form of inventory, and owners' equity. The reduction in owners' equity is the result of reporting the Loss on Decline in Value of Inventory on the income statement as an item of Other Expense.

WHY REPLACEMENT COST IS USED AS A MEASURE OF MARKET

A better name for the lower-of-cost-or-market rule would be the lower-of-cost-or-replacement-cost rule because accountants define *market* as *replacement cost.*[3] To understand why replacement cost is used as a basis to compare with original cost, consider the following

[3]Technically, the use of replacement cost as a measure of market value is subject to two constraints. First, market cannot be more than the net realizable value of the inventory. Second, inventory should not be recorded at less than net realizable value less a normal profit margin. The rationale for these two constraints is covered in intermediate accounting texts. For our purposes, we assume that replacement cost falls between the two constraints.

EXHIBIT 6-7 Gross Margin Percentage before and after Price Change

	Before Price Change	After Price Change
Selling price	$200	$160
Cost	150	120
Gross margin	$ 50	$ 40
Gross margin percentage	25%	25%

example. A clothier pays $150 for a man's double-breasted suit and normally sells it for $200. Thus, the normal markup on selling price is $50/$200, or 25%, as indicated in the column Before Price Change in Exhibit 6-7. Now assume that double-breasted suits fall out of favor with the fashion world. The retailer checks with the distributor and finds that because of the style change, the cost to the retailer to replace a double-breasted suit is now only $120. The retailer realizes that if double-breasted suits are to be sold at all, they will have to be offered at a reduced price. The selling price is dropped from $200 to $160. If the retailer now buys a suit for $120 and sells it for $160, the gross margin will be $40 and the gross margin percentage will be maintained at 25%, as indicated in the right-hand column of Exhibit 6-7.

To compare the results with and without the use of the LCM rule, assume that the facts are the same as before and that the retailer has 10 double-breasted suits in inventory on December 31, 2001. In addition, assume that all 10 suits are sold at a clearance sale in January 2002 at the reduced price of $160 each. If the lower-of-cost-or-market rule is not used, the results for the two years will be as follows:

LCM Rule Not Used	2001	2002	Total
Sales revenue ($160 per unit)	$–0–	$1,600	$1,600
Cost of goods sold			
(original cost of $150 per unit)	–0–	(1,500)	(1,500)
Gross margin	$–0–	$ 100	$ 100

If the LCM rule is not applied, the gross margin is distorted. Instead of the normal 25%, a gross margin percentage of $100/$1,600 or 6.25% is reported in 2002 when the 10 suits are sold. If the LCM rule is applied, however, the results for the two years are as follows:

LCM Rule Used	2001	2002	Total
Sales revenue ($160 per unit)	$–0–	$1,600	$1,600
Cost of goods sold			
(replacement cost of $120 per unit)	–0–	(1,200)	(1,200)
Loss on decline in value of			
inventory: 10 units ×			
($150 – $120)	(300)	–0–	(300)
Gross margin	$(300)	$ 400	$ 100

The use of the LCM rule serves two important functions: (1) to report the loss in value of the inventory, $30 per suit or $300 in total, in the year the loss occurs and (2) to report in the year the suits are actually sold the normal gross margin of $400/$1,600, or 25%, which is not affected by a change in the selling price.

CONSERVATISM IS THE BASIS FOR THE LOWER-OF-COST-OR-MARKET RULE

The departure from the cost basis is normally justified on the basis of *conservatism.* According to the accounting profession, conservatism is "a prudent reaction to uncertainties to try to insure that uncertainties and risks inherent in business situations are

From Concept TO PRACTICE 6.3

READING CIRCUIT CITY'S FOOTNOTES A footnote to Circuit City's financial statements states "Inventory is stated at the lower of cost or market." Why do you think the application of the lower-of-cost-or-market rule would be important to a business like Circuit City?

adequately considered."[4] In our example, the future selling price of a suit is uncertain because of the style changes. The use of the LCM rule serves two purposes. First, the inventory of suits is written down from $150 to $120 each. Second, the decline in value of the inventory is recognized at the time it is first observed rather than waiting until the suits are sold. An investor in a company with deteriorating inventory has good reason to be alarmed. Merchandisers who do not make the proper adjustments to their product lines go out of business as they compete with the lower prices of warehouse clubs and the lower overhead of e-business and home shopping networks.

You should realize that the write-down of the suits violates the historical cost principle, which says that assets should be carried on the balance sheet at their original cost. But the LCM rule is considered a valid exception to the principle because it is a prudent reaction to the uncertainty involved and, thus, an application of conservatism in accounting.

APPLICATION OF THE LCM RULE

We have yet to consider how the LCM rule is applied to the entire inventory of a company. Three different interpretations of the rule are possible:

1. The lower of total cost or total market value for the entire inventory could be reported.
2. The lower of cost or market value for each individual product or item could be reported.
3. The lower of cost or market value for groups of items could be reported. A company is free to choose any one of these approaches in applying the lower-of-cost-or-market rule. Three different answers are possible, depending on the approach selected.

The item-by-item (No. 2 above) approach is the most popular of the three approaches, for two reasons. First, it produces the most conservative result. The reason is that with either a group-by-group or a total approach, increases in the values of some items of inventory will offset declines in the values of other items. The item-by-item approach, however, ignores increases in value and recognizes all declines in value. Second, the item-by-item approach is the method required for tax purposes, although unlike LIFO, it is not required for book purposes merely because it is used for tax computations.

Consistency is important in deciding which of these approaches to use in applying the LCM rule. As is the case with the selection of one of the inventory costing methods discussed earlier in the chapter, the approach chosen to apply the rule should be used consistently from one period to the next.

METHODS FOR ESTIMATING INVENTORY VALUE

LO 7 Explain why and how the cost of inventory is estimated in certain situations.

Situations arise in which it may not be practicable or even possible to measure inventory at cost. At times it may be necessary to *estimate* the amount of inventory. Two similar methods are used for very different purposes to estimate the amount of inventory. They are the gross profit method and the retail inventory method.

GROSS PROFIT METHOD

GROSS PROFIT METHOD A technique used to establish an estimate of the cost of inventory stolen, destroyed, or otherwise damaged or of the amount of inventory on hand at an interim date.

A company that uses a periodic inventory system may experience a problem if inventory is stolen or destroyed by fire, flooding, or some other type of damage. Without a perpetual inventory record, what is the cost of the inventory stolen or destroyed? The **gross profit method** is a useful technique to estimate the cost of inventory lost in these situations. The method relies *entirely* on the ability to reliably estimate the *ratio of gross profit to sales.*[5]

[4] *Statement of Financial Accounting Concepts No. 2,* "Qualitative Characteristics of Accounting Information" (Stamford, Conn.: Financial Accounting Standards Board, May 1980), par. 95.

[5] The terms *gross profit* and *gross margin* are synonymous in this context. Although we have used *gross margin* in referring to the excess of sales over cost of goods sold, the method is typically called the *gross profit method.*

EXHIBIT 6-8 The Gross Profit Method for Estimating Inventory

Income Statement Model	Gross Profit Method Model
Beginning Inventory	Beginning Inventory
+ Purchases	+ Purchases
= Cost of Goods Available for Sale	= Cost of Goods Available for Sale
– Ending Inventory (per count)	– Estimated Cost of Goods Sold
= Cost of Goods Sold	= Estimated Inventory

Exhibit 6-8 illustrates how the normal income statement model that we use to find cost of goods sold can be rearranged to estimate inventory. The model on the left shows the components of cost of goods sold as they appear on the income statement. Assuming a periodic system, the inventory on hand at the end of the period is counted and is subtracted from cost of goods available for sale to determine cost of goods sold. The model is rearranged on the right as a basis for estimating inventory under the gross profit method. The only difference in the two models is in the reversal of the last two components: ending inventory and cost of goods sold. Rather than attempting to estimate *ending* inventory, we are trying to estimate the amount of inventory that should be on hand at a specific date, such as the date of a fire or flood. The estimate of cost of goods sold is found by estimating gross profit and deducting this estimate from sales revenue.

To understand this method, assume that on March 12, 2001, a portion of Hardluck Company's inventory is destroyed in a fire. The company determines, by a physical count, that the cost of the merchandise not destroyed is $200. Hardluck needs to estimate the cost of the inventory lost for purposes of insurance reimbursement. If the insurance company pays Hardluck an amount equivalent to the cost of the inventory destroyed, no loss will be recognized. If the cost of the inventory destroyed exceeds the amount reimbursed by the insurance company, a loss will be recorded for the excess amount.

Assume that the insurance company agrees to pay Hardluck $250 as full settlement for the inventory lost in the fire. From its records, Hardluck is able to determine the following amounts for the period from January 1 to the date of the fire, March 12:

Net sales from January 1 to March 12	$6,000
Beginning inventory—January 1	1,200
Purchases from January 1 to March 12	3,500

Assume that based on recent years' experience, Hardluck estimates its gross profit ratio as 30% of net sales. The steps it will take to estimate the lost inventory follow:

1. Determine gross profit:

Net Sales × Gross Profit Ratio = Gross Profit

$6,000 × 30% = $1,800

2. Determine cost of goods sold:

Net Sales – Gross Profit = Cost of Goods Sold

$6,000 – $1,800 = $4,200

3. Determine cost of goods available for sale at time of fire:

Beginning Inventory + Purchases = Cost of Goods Available for Sale

$1,200 + $3,500 = $4,700

4. Determine inventory at time of the fire:

Cost of Goods Available for Sale – Cost of Goods Sold = Inventory

$4,700 – $4,200 = $500

5. Determine amount of inventory destroyed:

Inventory at Time of Fire	−	Inventory not Destroyed	=	Inventory Destroyed
$500	−	$200	=	$300

Hardluck would record the following journal entry to recognize a loss for the excess of the cost of the lost inventory over the amount of reimbursement from the insurance company:

Mar. 12	Loss on Insurance Settlement	50	
	Cash (from insurance company)	250	
	Inventory		300
	To record the insurance settlement from fire.		

Assets	=	Liabilities	+	Owners' Equity
+250				−50
−300				

Another situation in which the gross profit method is used is for *interim financial statements.* Most companies prepare financial statements at least once every three months. In fact, the Securities and Exchange Commission requires a quarterly report from corporations whose stock is publicly traded. Companies using the periodic inventory system, however, find it cost-prohibitive to count the inventory every three months. The gross profit method is used to estimate the cost of the inventory at these interim dates. A company is allowed to use the method only in interim reports. Inventory reported in the annual report must be based on actual, not estimated, cost.

www.sec.gov

Retail Inventory Method

Retail inventory method A technique used by retailers to convert the retail value of inventory to a cost basis.

The counting of inventory in most retail businesses is an enormous undertaking. Imagine the time involved to count all of the various items stocked in a hardware store. Because of the time and cost involved in counting inventory, most retail businesses take a physical inventory only once a year. The **retail inventory method** is used to estimate inventory for interim statements, typically prepared monthly.

The retail inventory method has another important use. Consider the year-end inventory count in a large supermarket. One employee counts the number of tubes of toothpaste on the shelf and relays the relevant information either to another employee or to a tape-recording device: "16 tubes of 8-ounce ABC brand toothpaste at $1.69." The key is that the price recorded is the *selling price* or *retail price* of the product, not its cost. It is much quicker to count the inventory at retail than it would be to trace the cost of each item to purchase invoices. The retail method can then be used to convert the inventory from retail to cost. The methodology used with the retail inventory method, whether for interim statements or at year-end, is similar to the approach used with the gross profit method and is covered in detail in intermediate accounting text books.

Analyzing the Management of Inventory Turnover

LO 8 Analyze the management of inventory turnover.

Inventory turnover ratio A measure of the number of times inventory is sold during a period.

Managers must strike a balance between maintaining enough inventory to meet customers' needs and incurring the high cost of carrying inventory. The cost of storage and the lost income from the money tied up to own inventory make it very expensive to keep on hand. Investors are also concerned with a company's inventory management. They pay particular attention to a company's **inventory turnover ratio:**

$$\text{Inventory Turnover Ratio} = \frac{\text{Cost of Goods Sold}}{\text{Average Inventory}}$$

EXHIBIT 6-9 Inventory Turnover for Different Types of Companies

Company	Types of Products Sold	Inventory Turnover	Number of Days' Sales in Inventory
Circuit City	Televisions, VCRs, personal computers	5.7 times	63 days
Safeway	Grocery items	10.0 times	36 days

Refer to Circuit City's financial statements as displayed in the chapter opener. From the information presented, we can compute the company's inventory turnover ratio for fiscal year 1999 (amounts are in thousands of dollars):

www.circuitcity.com

$$\text{Inventory Turnover Ratio} = \frac{\text{Cost of Goods Sold}}{\text{Average Inventory}} = \frac{\$8{,}359{,}428}{(\underbrace{\$1{,}517{,}675}_{\text{(2/28/99 balance sheet)}} + \underbrace{\$1{,}410{,}545}_{\text{(2/28/98 balance sheet)}})/2}$$

$$= \frac{\$8{,}359{,}428}{\$1{,}464{,}110}$$

$$= 5.7 \text{ times}$$

This ratio tells us that in fiscal year 1999, Circuit City turned over its inventory 5.7 times. An alternative way to look at a company's efficiency in managing inventory is to calculate the number of days, on average, that inventory is on hand before it is sold. This measure is called the **number of days' sales in inventory** and is calculated as follows (we will assume 360 days in a year):

NUMBER OF DAYS' SALES IN INVENTORY
A measure of how long it takes to sell inventory.

$$\text{Number of Days' Sales in Inventory} = \frac{\text{Number of Days in the Period}}{\text{Inventory Turnover Ratio}}$$

$$= \frac{360}{5.7}$$

$$= 63 \text{ days}$$

How efficient was Circuit City in managing its inventory if it took an average of 63 days, or a little more than two months, to sell an item of inventory in fiscal year 1999? There are no easy answers to this question, but a starting point would be to compare this statistic with the same measure for prior years. Another basis for evaluation is to compare the measure with that for other companies in the same industry or business, in this case consumer electronics. As you can imagine, inventory turnover varies considerably from one industry to the next because of the differences in products. For example, consider Safeway, a large regional grocery chain. Safeway's average inventory turnover ratio in 1998 was approximately 10 times. This means that on average it takes Safeway only about 360/10, or 36 days, to sell its inventory. Given the perishable nature of its products, we would expect Safeway to turn over its inventory more rapidly than a consumer electronics company such as Circuit City. Exhibit 6-9 summarizes the differences in inventory turnover between the two companies.

From Concept **TO PRACTICE 6.4**

READING BEN & JERRY'S FINANCIAL STATEMENTS
Compute Ben & Jerry's inventory turnover ratio for 1998. What is the average length of time it takes to sell its inventory? Does this seem reasonable for the type of business the company is in?

www.safeway.com

HOW INVENTORIES AFFECT THE CASH FLOWS STATEMENT

LO 9 Explain the effects that inventory transactions have on the statement of cash flows.

The effects on the income statement and the statement of cash flows from inventory-related transactions differ significantly. We have focused our attention in the last two chapters on how the purchase and the sale of inventory are reported on the income statement. We found that the cost of the inventory sold during the period is deducted on the income statement as cost of goods sold.

Name: Kim Anne Starke
Education: B.A., DePauw University; M.B.A., University of South Carolina
College Major: Sociology/ Anthropology
Occupation: Senior Manager, Kraft Foods, Inc., Toronto
Age: 31

www.kraftfood.com

Focus on Users

Timing Inventory Buildup to Anticipate Demand

> "... [T]he company is able to meet consumer demand while also containing costs, which are captured as cost of goods sold."
> –Kim Anne Starke

In the consumer packaged-goods industry, the rate at which inventory is produced and the valuation of that inventory in the financial statements are two fundamentals that can have a major impact on a company's financial position. As a senior manager in sales finance at Kraft Foods, Kim Anne Starke explains why, for a company like Kraft, which deals with high inventory volumes, the rate of production is so important to her business: "Demand for our products peaks at certain times during the year—for example, holidays. However, it would not be efficient to produce all of the product just prior to these peak periods. Instead, production is planned more evenly to maximize labor and capacity resources, and inventory is built gradually to meet the peak demand. Under such a paced inventory build, the company is able to meet consumer demand while also containing costs, which are captured as cost of goods sold."

Once goods are produced, their costs have to be measured, and those measurements will affect the company's bottom-line earnings. This is why it is important to choose the method for valuing inventory by evaluating company-specific financial patterns. Kim Anne explains: "The key is the timing of when incremental costs or savings are passed on to the income statement as part of cost of goods sold. Under LIFO, these differences are passed immediately through inventory and into the cost of goods sold. Since the differences are not held as part of inventory, the inventory valuation on the balance sheet is more stable, and this, in turn, facilitates a more predictable future inventory position." It is basic accounting principles like this that can make all the difference to financial managers like Kim Anne and to the ultimate bottom line.

The appropriate reporting on a statement of cash flows for inventory transactions depends on whether the direct or indirect method is used. If the direct method is used to prepare the Operating Activities category of the statement, the amount of cash paid to suppliers of inventory is shown as a deduction in this section of the statement.

If the more popular indirect method is used, it is necessary to make adjustments to net income for the changes in two accounts: Inventories and Accounts Payable. These adjustments are summarized in Exhibit 6-10. An increase in inventory is deducted

EXHIBIT 6-10 Inventories and the Statement of Cash Flows

Item	Cash Flow Statement	
	Operating Activities	
	Net income	xxx
Increase in inventory	→	–
Decrease in inventory	→	+
Increase in accounts payable	→	+
Decrease in accounts payable	→	–
	Investing Activities	
	Financing Activities	

EXHIBIT 6-11 Partial Consolidated Statement of Cash Flows for Circuit City

CONSOLIDATED STATEMENTS OF CASH FLOWS

(Amounts in thousands)	1999	Years Ended February 28 1998	1997
OPERATING ACTIVITIES:			
Net earnings	**$ 142,924**	$ 104,311	$ 136,414
Adjustments to reconcile net earnings to net cash provided by operating activities:			
Depreciation and amortization	**140,293**	116,326	98,977
Loss (gain) on disposition of property and equipment	**3,087**	14,093	(1,540)
Provision for deferred income taxes	**20,632**	15,052	20,973
Changes in operating assets and liabilities, net of effects from business acquisitions:			
Decrease in deferred revenue and other liabilities	**(33,022)**	(23,024)	(47,706)
Decrease (increase) in net accounts receivable	**23,719**	(66,061)	(207,579)
Increase in inventory, prepaid expenses and other current assets	**(97,642)**	(24,526)	(66,594)
Decrease (increase) in other assets	**9,132**	(4,969)	(15,869)
Increase in accounts payable, accrued expenses and other current liabilities	**45,125**	63,379	97,162
NET CASH PROVIDED BY OPERATING ACTIVITIES	**254,248**	194,581	14,238

Increase here is an expenditure of cash to pay for these assets.

Increase here conserves cash and thus adds to net earnings.

because it indicates that the company is building up its stock of inventory and thus expending cash. A decrease in inventory is added to net income. An increase in accounts payable is added because it indicates that during the period, the company has increased the amount it owes suppliers and has therefore conserved its cash. A decrease in accounts payable is deducted because the company actually reduced the amount owed suppliers during the period.

The Operating Activities category of the statement of cash flows for Circuit City is presented in Exhibit 6-11. Note that the company groups inventory, prepaid expenses, and other current assets for purposes of presentation on the statement of cash flows. Similarly, accounts payable, accrued expenses, and other current liabilities are included as one item on the statement.

The increase in inventory, prepaid expenses, and other current assets in 1999 is deducted because the additional investments in these assets required an expenditure of cash by the company. On the other hand, a buildup of accounts payable, accrued expenses, and other current liabilities actually conserves Circuit City's cash. Thus, the increase in these items in 1999 is added to net earnings.

Warmup Exercises

LO 3 **Warmup Exercise 6-1** Inventory Valuation

Busby Corp. began the year with 75 units of inventory that it paid $2 each to acquire. During the year it purchased an additional 100 units for $3 each. Busby sold 150 units during the year.

Required

1. Compute cost of goods sold and ending inventory assuming Busby uses FIFO.
2. Compute cost of goods sold and ending inventory assuming Busby uses LIFO.

Key to the Solution

Review the mechanics of the methods, beginning on page 268.

LO 6 **Warmup Exercise 6-2** Lower of Cost or Market

Glendive reports its inventory on a FIFO basis and has inventory with a cost of $78,000 on December 31. The cost to replace the inventory on this date would be only $71,000.

Required

Prepare the necessary journal entry on Glendive's books on December 31.

Key to the Solution

Recall the need to write down inventory when market is less than cost.

LO 8 **Warmup Exercise 6-3** Inventory Turnover

Sidney began the year with $130,000 in merchandise inventory and ended the year with $190,000. Sales and cost of goods sold for the year were $900,000 and $640,000, respectively.

Required

1. Compute Sidney's inventory turnover ratio.
2. Compute the number of days' sales in inventory.

Key to the Solution

Review how these two statistics are computed on page 283.

Solutions to Warmup Exercises

Warmup Exercise 6-1

1. Cost of goods sold: (75 × $2) + (75 × $3) = $375

   Ending Inventory: 25 × $3 = $ 75

2. Cost of goods sold: (100 × $3) + (50 × $2) = $400

   Ending inventory: 25 × $2 = $ 50

Warmup Exercise 6-2

Dec. 31	Loss on Decline in Value of Inventory	7,000	
	Inventory		7,000
	To record decline in value of inventory.		

Assets	=	Liabilities	+	Owners' Equity
−7,000				−7,000

Warmup Exercise 6-3

1. $$\text{Inventory Turnover Ratio} = \frac{\text{Cost of Goods Sold}}{\text{Average Inventory}}$$

$$= \frac{\$640{,}000}{(\$130{,}000 + \$190{,}000)/2}$$

$$= \frac{\$640{,}000}{\$160{,}000} = 4 \text{ times}$$

2. $$\begin{array}{c}\text{Number of Days'}\\ \text{Sales in Inventory}\end{array} = \frac{\text{Number of Days in the Period}}{\text{Inventory Turnover Ratio}}$$

$$= \frac{360}{4} = 90 \text{ days}$$

REVIEW PROBLEM

Stewart Distributing Company sells a single product for $2 per unit and uses a periodic inventory system. The following data are available for the year:

Date	Transaction	Number of Units	Unit Cost	Total
1/1	Beginning inventory	500	$1.00	$500.00
2/5	Purchase	350	1.10	385.00
4/12	Sale	(550)		
7/17	Sale	(200)		
9/23	Purchase	400	1.30	520.00
11/5	Sale	(300)		

Required

1. Compute cost of goods sold, assuming the use of the weighted average costing method.
2. Compute the dollar amount of ending inventory, assuming the FIFO costing method.
3. Compute gross margin, assuming the LIFO costing method.
4. Assume a 40% tax rate. Compute the amount of taxes saved if Stewart uses the LIFO method rather than the FIFO method.

SOLUTION TO REVIEW PROBLEM

1. Cost of goods sold, weighted average cost method:

Cost of goods available for sale		
$500 + $385 + $520 =	$1,405	
Divided by:		
Units available for sale:		
500 + 350 + 400 =	1,250	units
Weighted average cost	$1.124	per unit
× Number of units sold:		
550 + 200 + 300 =	1,050	units
Cost of goods sold	$1,180.20	

2. Ending inventory, FIFO cost method:

Units available for sale	1,250
− Units sold	1,050
= Units in ending inventory	200
× Most recent purchase price of	$ 1.30
= Ending inventory	$ 260

3. Gross margin, LIFO cost method:			
Sales revenue: 1,050 units × $2 each			$2,100
Cost of goods sold			
400 units × $1.30 =	$520		
350 units × $1.10 =	385		
300 units × $1.00 =	300		1,205
Gross margin			$ 895

4. Taxes saved from using LIFO instead of FIFO:		
LIFO Cost of goods sold		$1,205
– FIFO Cost of goods sold:		
Cost of goods available for sale	$1,405	
Ending inventory from part 2	260	
Cost of goods sold		1,145
Additional expense from use of LIFO		$ 60
× Tax rate		.40
Tax savings from the use of LIFO		$ 24

APPENDIX 6A

ACCOUNTING TOOLS: INVENTORY COSTING METHODS WITH THE USE OF A PERPETUAL INVENTORY SYSTEM

LO 10 Explain the differences between a periodic and a perpetual inventory system.

The illustrations of the inventory costing methods in the chapter assumed the use of a periodic inventory system. In this appendix, we will see how the methods are applied when a company maintains a perpetual inventory system. Before doing so, however, it is useful to look closer at the differences between the two systems.

JOURNAL ENTRIES FOR THE TWO SYSTEMS

To highlight the differences between the two systems, consider the following three transactions:

1. Purchased on account 500 units at $8 each.

2. Returned for credit 100 units damaged in transit.

3. Sold on account 200 units at $10 each.

Exhibit 6-12 shows the journal entries for the three transactions under each of the two inventory systems. Because the inventory account is updated only *periodically* with the periodic system, the purchase of 500 units of merchandise is accumulated in the temporary account Purchases. The cost of the 100 units returned in the second transaction increases the contra-purchases account Purchase Returns and Allowances. The only entry made at the time of a sale records the revenue earned. Because the inventory account has not been updated for purchases and sales during the period, a *physical count* of the merchandise is required at year-end. This establishes the amount to be shown on the balance sheet as the cost of the inventory and helps determine the amount to appear on the income statement for cost of goods sold. Cost of goods sold is in fact a calculated figure determined in the following way:

Beginning inventory	The inventory at the end of the prior period
+ Cost of goods purchased	The balance in the Purchases account, plus any freight-in, less any purchase returns and allowances and any purchase discounts

EXHIBIT 6-12 Comparison of the Periodic and Perpetual Inventory Systems

Periodic System	DR.	CR.	Perpetual System	DR.	CR.
1. Purchases	4,000		Inventory	4,000	
Accounts Payable		4,000	Accounts Payable		4,000
To record purchase of 500 units.			To record purchase of 500 units.		
A = L + OE; L +4,000, OE −4,000			A = L + OE; A +4,000, L +4,000		
2. Accounts Payable	800		Accounts Payable	800	
Purchase Returns and Allowances		800	Inventory		800
To record return of 100 damaged units.			To record return of 100 damaged units.		
A = L + OE; L −800, OE +800			A = L + OE; A −800, L −800		
3. Accounts Receivable	2,000		Accounts Receivable	2,000	
Sales Revenue		2,000	Sales Revenue		2,000
To record sale of 200 units at $10 each.			To record sale of 200 units at $10 each.		
A = L + OE; A +2,000, OE +2,000			A = L + OE; A +2,000, OE +2,000		
			Cost of Goods Sold	1,600	
			Inventory		1,600
			To record 200 units sold at a cost of $8 each.		
			A = L + OE; A −1,600, OE −1,600		

= Cost of goods available for sale
− Ending inventory — Based on a physical count
= Cost of goods sold

As you see in the right-hand side of Exhibit 6-12, in a perpetual system, purchases of merchandise increase the Inventory account directly, and any returns of merchandise reduce it. Unlike the periodic system, the perpetual system requires that *two* entries be made at the time of sale. The first entry is the same as the entry made under the periodic system: to record the sales revenue. Because the inventory account is kept *perpetually* up-to-date, however, a second entry is made to reduce the Inventory account, with a corresponding increase in expense for the cost of the merchandise sold. Finally, because the Inventory account has been updated for each purchase and sale of merchandise, a physical count is not the basis for valuing the inventory at the end of the period in a perpetual system. For control purposes, however, most businesses that use a perpetual system count the inventory once a year. Any differences between the amount on hand per the count and the amount appearing in the Inventory account require an adjusting entry in the records and should be investigated.

INVENTORY COSTING METHODS WITH A PERPETUAL SYSTEM

LO 11 Apply the inventory costing methods using a perpetual system.

It is important to understand the difference between inventory *costing systems* and inventory *methods*. The two inventory systems differ in terms of how often the inventory account is updated: periodically or perpetually. However, when a company sells identical units of product and the cost to purchase each unit is subject to change, it also must choose an inventory costing method, such as FIFO, LIFO, or weighted average.

Earlier in the chapter, we illustrated the various costing methods with a periodic system. We now use the same data to illustrate how the methods differ when a perpetual system is used. Keep in mind that if a company uses specific identification, the results will be the same regardless of whether it uses the periodic or the perpetual system. To compare the periodic and perpetual systems for the other methods, we must add one important piece of information: the date of each of the sales. The original data as well as number of units sold on the various dates are summarized below:

Date	Purchases	Sales	Balance
Beginning inventory			500 units @ $10
January 20	300 units @ $11		800 units
February 18		450 units	350 units
April 8	400 units @ $12		750 units
June 19		300 units	450 units
September 5	200 units @ $13		650 units
October 20		150 units	500 units
December 12	100 units @ $14		600 units

FIFO Costing with a Perpetual System

Exhibit 6-13 illustrates the FIFO method on a perpetual basis. The basic premise of FIFO applies whether a periodic or a perpetual system is used: the first units purchased are assumed to be the first units sold. With a perpetual system, however, this concept is applied *at the time of each sale.* For example, note in the exhibit which 450 units are assumed to be sold on February 18. The 450 units sold are taken from the beginning inventory of 500

Exhibit 6-13 Perpetual System: FIFO Cost-Flow Assumption

	Purchases			Sales			Balance		
Date	Units	Unit Cost	Total Cost	Units	Unit Cost	Total Cost	Units	Unit Cost	Balance
1/1							500	$10	$5,000
1/20	300	$11	$3,300				500	10	
							300	11	8,300
2/18				450	$10	$4,500	50	10	
							300	11	3,800
4/8	400	12	4,800				50	10	
							300	11	
							400	12	8,600
6/19				50	10	500	50	11	
				250	11	2,750	400	12	5,350
9/5	200	13	2,600				50	11	
							400	12	
							200	13	7,950
10/20				50	11	550	300	12	
				100	12	1,200	200	13	6,200
12/12	100	14	1,400				300	12	
							200	13	
							100	14	7,600

units with a unit cost of $10. Thus, the inventory or balance after this sale as shown in the last three columns is 50 units at $10 and 300 units at $11, for a total of $3,800. The purchase on April 8 of 400 units at $12 is added to the running balance. On a FIFO basis, the sale of 300 units on June 19 comes from the remainder of the beginning inventory of 50 units and another 250 units from the first purchase at $11 on January 20. The balance after this sale is 50 units at $11 and 400 units at $12. You should follow through the last three transactions in the exhibit to make sure that you understand the application of FIFO on a perpetual basis. An important point to note about the ending inventory of $7,600 is that it is the same amount that we calculated for FIFO periodic earlier in the chapter:

FIFO periodic (Exhibit 6-2)	$7,600
FIFO perpetual (Exhibit 6-13)	$7,600

Whether the method is applied each time a sale is made or only at the end of the period, the earliest units in are the first units out, and the two systems will yield the same ending inventory under FIFO.

LIFO Costing with a Perpetual System

A LIFO cost flow with the use of a perpetual system is illustrated in Exhibit 6-14. First, note which 450 units are assumed to be sold on February 18. The sale consists of the most recent units acquired, 300 units at $11, and then 150 units from the beginning inventory at $10. Thus, the balance after this sale is simply the remaining 350 units from the beginning inventory priced at $10. The purchase on April 8 results in a balance of 350 units at $10 and 400 units at $12.

Exhibit 6-14 Perpetual System: LIFO Cost-Flow Assumption

	Purchases			Sales			Balance		
Date	Units	Unit Cost	Total Cost	Units	Unit Cost	Total Cost	Units	Unit Cost	Balance
1/1							500	$10	$5,000
1/20	300	$11	$3,300				500	10	
							300	11	8,300
2/18				300	$11	$3,300			
				150	10	1,500	350	10	3,500
4/8	400	12	4,800				350	10	
							400	12	8,300
6/19				300	12	3,600	350	10	
							100	12	4,700
9/5	200	13	2,600				350	10	
							100	12	
							200	13	7,300
10/20				150	13	1,950	350	10	
							100	12	
							50	13	5,350
12/12	100	14	1,400				350	10	
							100	12	
							50	13	
							100	14	6,750

EXHIBIT 6-15 Perpetual System: Moving Average Cost-Flow Assumption

	Purchases			Sales			Balance		
Date	Units	Unit Cost	Total Cost	Units	Unit Cost	Total Cost	Units	Unit Cost	Balance
1/1							500	$10	$5,000
1/20	300	$11	$3,300				800	10.38*	8,304
2/18				450	$10.38	$4,671	350	10.38	3,633
4/8	400	12	4,800				750	11.24†	8,430
6/19				300	11.24	3,372	450	11.24	5,058
9/5	200	13	2,600				650	11.78‡	7,657
10/20				150	11.78	1,767	500	11.78	5,890
12/12	100	14	1,400				600	12.15§	7,290

The moving average prices per unit are calculated as follows:

*($5,000 + $3,300) / 800 units = $10.38 (rounded to nearest cent)

†($3,633 + $4,800) / 750 units = $11.24

‡($5,058 + $2,600) / 650 units = $11.78

§($5,890 + $1,400) / 600 units = $12.15

Note what happens with LIFO when it is applied on a perpetual basis. In essence, a gap is created. Units acquired at the earliest price of $10 and units acquired at the most recent price of $12 are on hand, but none of those at the middle price of $11 remain. This situation arises because LIFO is applied every time a sale is made rather than only at the end of the year. Because of this difference, the amount of ending inventory differs, depending on which system is used:

LIFO periodic (Exhibit 6-2)	$6,100
LIFO perpetual (Exhibit 6-14)	$6,750

MOVING AVERAGE WITH A PERPETUAL SYSTEM

MOVING AVERAGE
The name given to an average cost method when it is used with a perpetual inventory system.

When a weighted average cost assumption is applied with a perpetual system, it is sometimes called a **moving average.** As indicated in Exhibit 6-15, each time a purchase is made, a new weighted average cost must be computed, thus the name *moving average.* For example, the goods available for sale after the January 20 purchase consist of 500 units at $10 and 300 units at $11, which results in an average cost of $10.38. This is the unit cost applied to the 450 units sold on February 18. The 400 units purchased on April 8 require the computation of a new unit cost, as indicated in the second footnote to the exhibit. As you might have suspected, the ending inventory with an average cost flow differs, depending on whether a periodic or a perpetual system is used:

Weighted average periodic (Exhibit 6-2)	$6,840
Moving average perpetual (Exhibit 6-15)	$7,290

CHAPTER HIGHLIGHTS

1. LO 1 A manufacturer's inventory consists of raw materials, work in process, and finished goods. The inventory of a retailer or wholesaler is in a single form called *merchandise inventory.*

2. LO 2 The amount of cost of goods sold reported on the income statement is inherently tied to the value assigned to ending inventory on the balance sheet. All costs necessary to put

inventory into a condition and location for sale should be included in its cost. Freight costs, storage costs, excise and sales taxes, and insurance during the time the merchandise is in transit are all candidates for inclusion in the cost of the asset. As a practical manner, however, some of these costs are very difficult to allocate to individual products and are therefore accounted for as expenses of the period.

3. **LO 3** The purchase of identical units of a product at varying prices necessitates the use of a costing method to assign a dollar amount to ending inventory and cost of goods sold. As alternatives to the use of a specific identification method, which is impractical in many instances as well as subject to manipulation, accountants have devised cost-flow assumptions.
4. **LO 3** The weighted average method assigns the same average unit cost to all units available for sale during the period. It is widely used because of its simplicity.
5. **LO 3** The FIFO method assigns the most recent costs to ending inventory. The older costs are assigned to cost of goods sold. A first-in, first-out approach does tend to parallel the physical flow of products in many businesses, although the actual flow is not our primary concern in choosing a costing method.
6. **LO 3** LIFO assigns the most recent costs to cost of goods sold, and the older costs remain in inventory. In a period of rising prices, this method results in a relatively higher amount assigned to cost of goods sold and, thus, a lower amount of reported net income. Lower net income results in a lower amount of taxes due, and the tax advantages have resulted in the widespread use of the LIFO method.

   A company that chooses to take advantage of the tax break from using LIFO on its tax return must also use the method in preparing the income statement. A concern with the use of LIFO is the possibility of a liquidation. If more units are sold than are bought in any one period, some of the units sold will come from the older, lower-priced units, resulting in a low cost of goods sold and a high gross margin. The high gross margin will necessitate a larger tax amount due.
7. **LO 4** Many accountants favor LIFO because it results in the nearest approximation to the current cost of goods sold. On the other hand, under LIFO, the inventory amount on the balance sheet is, in many cases, very outdated. FIFO gives a much closer approximation to current cost on the balance sheet. It leads, however, to what accountants describe as inventory profit: the portion of the gross margin that is due simply to holding the inventory during an inflationary period.
8. **LO 5** Errors in valuing inventory affect cost of goods sold and thus affect the amount of income reported for the period. An understatement of ending inventory will result in an understatement of net income; an overstatement of ending inventory will result in an overstatement of net income.
9. **LO 6** As used in the lower-of-cost-or-market rule, *market* means *replacement cost.* The purpose of valuing inventory at original cost or replacement cost, whichever is lower, is to anticipate declines in the selling price of goods subject to obsolescence, spoilage, and other types of loss. By being conservative and reducing the carrying value of the inventory at the end of the year, a company is more likely to report its normal gross margin when the units are sold at a reduced price in the next period. The rule can be applied to each item, to a group of items, or to the entire inventory.
10. **LO 7** The gross profit method is used to estimate the cost of inventory lost by theft, fire, flooding, and other types of damage. The method is also useful to estimate the amount of inventory on hand for interim reports, such as quarterly financial statements. It relies on a trustworthy estimate of the gross profit ratio.
11. **LO 7** Retailers use the retail inventory method to estimate the cost of inventory for interim financial statements and to convert the year-end inventory, per a physical count, from retail to cost.
12. **LO 8** Different measures are available to analyze how well a company is managing its inventory levels. The inventory turnover ratio indicates how many times during a period a company sells or turns over its inventory, and the number of days' sales in inventory indicates how long it takes, on average, to sell inventory.
13. **LO 9** The payment of cash to suppliers of inventory represents a cash outflow from operating activities on the statement of cash flows. If a company uses the indirect method, however, adjustments are made to net income for the increase or decrease in the Inventory and Accounts Payable accounts.
14. **LO 10** The periodic system relies on a count of inventory on hand at the end of the year to allocate costs between ending inventory and cost of goods sold. No entry is made in a periodic system to record the cost of inventory sold at the time of sale. Acquisitions of inventory during the period are recorded in the temporary account Purchases. (Appendix 6A)
15. **LO 10** In a perpetual system, the Inventory account is updated at the time of each sale and purchase of merchandise. The computer has made the perpetual system much more feasible for many businesses. (Appendix 6A)
16. **LO 11** Ending inventory costed at FIFO will be the same whether the periodic system or the perpetual system is used. This is not the case when the LIFO method is used: the results under the periodic and the perpetual systems differ. Likewise, ending inventory differs in the periodic system and the perpetual system when a weighted average approach is applied. The average method with a perpetual system is really a moving average approach. (Appendix 6A)

Key Terms Quiz

Read each definition below and then write the number of the definition in the blank beside the appropriate term it defines. The solution appears at the end of the chapter.

4 **Merchandise Inventory**
7 **Raw materials**
2 **Work in process**
12 **Finished goods**

15 **Specific identification method**
3 **Weighted average cost method**
6 **FIFO method**
9 **LIFO method**

17 **LIFO liquidation**
14 **LIFO conformity rule**
18 **LIFO reserve**
16 **Inventory profit**
8 **Replacement cost**
5 **Lower-of-cost-or-market (LCM) rule**
11 **Gross profit method**
13 **Retail inventory method**
19 **Inventory turnover ratio**
10 **Number of days' sales in inventory**
1 **Moving average (Appendix 6A)**

1. The name given to an average cost method when it is used with a perpetual inventory system.
2. The cost of unfinished products in a manufacturing company.
3. An inventory costing method that assigns the same unit cost to all units available for sale during the period.
4. The account that wholesalers and retailers use to report inventory held for sale.
5. A conservative inventory valuation approach that is an attempt to anticipate declines in the value of inventory before its actual sale.
6. An inventory costing method that assigns the most recent costs to ending inventory.
7. The inventory of a manufacturer before the addition of any direct labor or manufacturing overhead.
8. The current cost of a unit of inventory.
9. An inventory costing method that assigns the most recent costs to cost of goods sold.
10. A measure of how long it takes to sell inventory.
11. A technique used to establish an estimate of the cost of inventory stolen, destroyed, or otherwise damaged or of the amount of inventory on hand at an interim date.
12. A manufacturer's inventory that is complete and ready for sale.
13. A technique used by retailers to convert the retail value of inventory to a cost basis.
14. The IRS requirement that if LIFO is used on the tax return, it must also be used in reporting income to stockholders.
15. An inventory costing method that relies on matching unit costs with the actual units sold.
16. The portion of the gross profit that results from holding inventory during a period of rising prices.
17. The result of selling more units than are purchased during the period, which can have negative tax consequences if a company is using LIFO.
18. The excess of the value of a company's inventory stated at FIFO over the value stated at LIFO.
19. A measure of the number of times inventory is sold during a period.

Alternate Terms

Gross margin Gross profit
Interim statements Quarterly or monthly statements
Market (value for inventory) Replacement cost
Raw materials Direct materials
Retail price Selling price
Work in process Work in progress

Questions

1. What are three distinct types of costs that manufacturers incur? Describe each of them.
2. What is the relationship between the valuation of inventory as an asset on the balance sheet and the measurement of income?
3. What is the justification for including freight costs incurred in acquiring incoming goods in the cost of the inventory rather than simply treating the cost as an expense of the period? What is the significance of this decision for accounting purposes?
4. What are the inventory characteristics that would allow a company to use the specific identification method? Give at least two examples of inventory for which the method is appropriate.
5. How can the specific identification method allow management to manipulate income?
6. What is the significance of the adjective *weighted* in the weighted average cost method? Use an example to illustrate your answer.
7. Which inventory method, FIFO or LIFO, more nearly approximates the physical flow of products in most businesses? Explain your answer.
8. York Inc. manufactures notebook computers and has experienced noticeable declines in the purchase price of many of the components it uses, including computer chips. Which inventory costing method should York use if it wants to maximize net income? Explain your answer.
9. Which inventory costing method should a company use if it wants to minimize taxes? Does your response depend on whether prices are rising or falling? Explain your answers.
10. The president of Ace Retail is commenting on the company's new controller: "The woman is brilliant! She has shown us how we can maximize our income and at the same time minimize the amount of taxes we have to pay the government. Because the cost to purchase our inventory constantly goes up, we will use FIFO to calculate cost of goods sold on the income statement to minimize the amount charged to cost of goods sold and thus maximize net income. For tax purposes, however, we will use LIFO because this will minimize taxable income and thus minimize the amount we have to pay in taxes." Should the president be enthralled with the new controller? Explain your answer.

11. What does the term *LIFO liquidation* mean? How can it lead to poor buying habits?

12. Historical-based costing methods are sometimes criticized for leading to inventory profits. In a period of rising prices, which inventory costing method will lead to the most "inventory profit"? Explain your answer.

13. Is it acceptable for a company to disclose, in its annual report, that it is switching from some other inventory costing method to LIFO *to save on taxes?*

14. Delevan Corp. uses a periodic inventory system and is counting its year-end inventory. Due to a lack of communication, two different teams count the same section of the warehouse. What effect will this error have on net income?

15. What is the rationale for valuing inventory at the lower of cost or market?

16. Why is it likely that the result from applying the lower-of-cost-or-market rule using a total approach, that is, by comparing total cost to total market value, and the result from applying the rule on an item-by-item basis will differ?

17. Patterson's controller makes the following suggestion: "I have a brilliant way to save us money. Because we are already using the gross profit method for our quarterly statements, we start using it to estimate the year-end inventory for the annual report and save the money normally spent to have the inventory counted on December 31." What do you think of his suggestion?

18. Why does a company save time and money by using the retail inventory method at the end of the year?

19. Ralston Corp.'s cost of sales has remained steady over the last two years. During this same time period, however, its inventory has increased considerably. What does this information tell you about the company's inventory turnover? Explain your answer.

20. In simple terms, how do the inventory costing methods, such as FIFO and LIFO, and the inventory systems, such as periodic and perpetual, differ? (Appendix 6A)

21. Why is the weighted average cost method called a *moving* average when a company uses a perpetual inventory system? (Appendix 6A)

EXERCISES

LO 1 Exercise 6-1 Classification of Inventory Costs

Put an X in the appropriate column next to the inventory item to indicate its most likely classification on the books of a company that manufactures furniture and then sells it in retail company stores.

	Classification			
Inventory Item	**Raw Material**	**Work in Process**	**Finished Goods**	**Merchandise Inventory**
Fabric				
Lumber				
Unvarnished tables				
Chairs on the showroom floor				
Cushions				
Decorative knobs				
Drawers				
Sofa frames				
Chairs in the plant warehouse				
Chairs in the retail storeroom				

LO 1 Exercise 6-2 Inventoriable Costs

During the first month of operations, ABC Company incurred the following costs in ordering and receiving merchandise for resale. No inventory has been sold.

List price, $100, 200 units purchased
Volume discount, 10% off list price
Paid freight costs, $56
Insurance cost while goods were in transit, $32
Long-distance phone charge to place orders, $4.35
Purchasing department salary, $1,000
Supplies used to label goods at retail price, $9.75
Interest paid to supplier, $46

Required

What amount do you recommend the company record as merchandise inventory on its balance sheet? Explain your answer. For any items not to be included in inventory, indicate their appropriate treatment in the financial statements.

LO 2 Exercise 6-3 Inventory and Income Manipulation

The president of SOS Inc. is concerned that the net income at year-end will not reach the expected figure. When the sales manager receives a large order on the last day of the fiscal year, the president tells the accountant to record the sale but to ignore any inventory adjustment because the physical inventory has already been taken. How will this affect the current year's net income? next year's income? What would you do if you were the accountant? Assume that SOS uses a periodic inventory system.

LO 3 Exercise 6-4 Inventory Costing Methods

VanderMeer Inc. reported the following information for the month of February:

Inventory, February 1	65 units @ \$20
Purchases:	
February 7	50 units @ \$22
February 18	60 units @ \$23
February 27	45 units @ \$24

During February, VanderMeer sold 140 units. The company uses a periodic inventory system.

Required

What is the value of ending inventory and cost of goods sold for February under the following assumptions:

1. Of the 140 units sold, 55 cost \$20, 35 cost \$22, 45 cost \$23, and 5 cost \$24.
2. FIFO
3. LIFO
4. Weighted average

LO 4 Exercise 6-5 Evaluation of Inventory Costing Methods

Write the letter of the method that is most applicable to each statement.

a. Specific identification
b. Average cost
c. First-in, first-out (FIFO)
d. Last-in, first-out (LIFO)

_______ **1.** Is the most realistic ending inventory.
_______ **2.** Results in cost of goods sold being closest to current product costs.
_______ **3.** Results in highest income during periods of inflation.
_______ **4.** Results in highest ending inventory during periods of inflation.
_______ **5.** Smooths out costs during periods of inflation.
_______ **6.** Is not practical for most businesses.
_______ **7.** Puts more weight on the cost of the larger number of units purchased.
_______ **8.** Is an assumption that most closely reflects the physical flow of goods for most businesses.

LO 4 Exercise 6-6 LIFO Liquidation—Sears

www.sears.com

The 1998 annual report of Sears, Roebuck & Co. includes the following in the footnote that describes its accounting policies relating to merchandise inventories:

> Partial liquidation of merchandise inventories valued under the LIFO method resulted in credits of \$2 million in 1997. No layer liquidation occurred in 1998 or 1996.

Required

1. What does Sears mean that the partial liquidation resulted in "credits" in 1997? What was the effect of these credits on cost of sales and on gross margin?
2. Was the LIFO liquidation advantageous to Sears for tax purposes? Explain your answer.

LO 5 Exercise 6-7 Inventory Errors

For each of the following independent situations, fill in the blanks to indicate the effect of the error on each of the various financial statement items. Indicate an understatement (U), an overstatement (O), or no effect (NE). Assume that each of the companies uses a periodic inventory system.

	Balance Sheet		Income Statement	
Error	**Inventory**	**Retained Earnings**	**Cost of Goods Sold**	**Net Income**
1. Goods in transit at year end are not included in the physical count: they were shipped FOB shipping point.	_______	_______	_______	_______
2. One section of a warehouse is counted twice during the year-end count of inventory.	_______	_______	_______	_______
3. During the count at year-end, the inventory sheets for one of the stores of a discount retailer are lost.	_______	_______	_______	_______

LO 5 Exercise 6-8 Transfer of Title to Inventory

For each of the following transactions, indicate which company should include the inventory on its December 31, 2001 balance sheet:

1. Michelson Supplies Inc. shipped merchandise to PJ Sales on December 28, 2001, terms FOB destination. The merchandise arrives at PJ's on January 4, 2002.
2. Quarton Inc. shipped merchandise to Filbrandt on December 25, 2001, FOB destination. Fibrandt received the merchandise on December 31, 2001.
3. James Bros. Inc. shipped merchandise to Randall Company on December 27, 2001, FOB shipping point. Randall Company received the merchandise on January 3, 2002.
4. Hinz Company shipped merchandise to Barner Inc. on December 24, 2001, FOB shipping point. The merchandise arrived at Barner's on December 29, 2001.

LO 7 Exercise 6-9 Gross Profit Method

On February 12, a hurricane destroys the entire inventory of Suncoast Corporation. An estimate of the amount of inventory lost is needed for insurance purposes. The following information is available:

Inventory on January 1	\$ 15,400
Net sales from January 1 to February 12	105,300
Purchases from January 1 to February 12	84,230

Suncoast estimates its gross profit ratio as 25% of net sales. The insurance company has agreed to pay Suncoast \$10,000 as a settlement for the inventory destroyed.

Required

Prepare the journal entry on Suncoast's books to recognize the inventory lost and the insurance reimbursement.

LO 8 Exercise 6-10 Inventory Turnover for Sears

The following amounts are available from the 1998 annual report of Sears, Roebuck & Co. (all amounts are in millions of dollars):

www.sears.com

Cost of sales, buying, and occupancy	\$27,257
Merchandise inventories, January 2, 1999 (the end of fiscal 1998)	4,816
Merchandise inventories, January 3, 1998 (the end of fiscal 1997)	5,044

Required

1. Compute Sears' inventory turnover ratio for 1998.
2. What is the average length of time it takes to sell an item of inventory? Explain your answer.
3. Do you think the average length of time it took Sears to sell inventory in 1998 is reasonable? What other information do you need to fully answer this question?

LO 9 Exercise 6-11 Impact of Transactions Involving Inventories on Statement of Cash Flows
From the following list, identify whether the change in the account balance during the year would be added to (A) or deducted from (D) net income when the indirect method is used to determine cash flows from operating activities.

________ Increase in accounts payable
________ Decrease in accounts payable
________ Increase in inventories
________ Decrease in inventories

LO 9 Exercise 6-12 Effects of Transactions Involving Inventories on the Statement of Cash Flows—Direct Method
Masthead Company's comparative balance sheets included inventory of $180,400 at December 31, 2000, and $241,200 at December 31, 2001. Masthead's comparative balance sheets also included accounts payable of $85,400 at December 31, 2000, and $78,400 at December 31, 2001. Masthead's accounts payable balances are composed solely of amounts due to suppliers for purchases of inventory on account. Cost of goods sold, as reported by Masthead on its 2001 income statement, amounted to $1,200,000.

Required

What is the amount of cash payments for inventory that Masthead will report in the Operating Activities category of its 2001 statement of cash flows assuming that the direct method is used?

LO 9 Exercise 6-13 Effects of Transactions Involving Inventories on the Statement of Cash Flows—Indirect Method
Refer to all of the facts in Exercise 6-12.

Required

Assume instead that Masthead uses the indirect method to prepare its statement of cash flows. Indicate how each item will be reflected as an adjustment to net income in the Operating Activities category of the statement of cash flows.

LO 10 Exercise 6-14 Periodic and Perpetual Journal Entries (Appendix 6A)
Record the journal entries to reflect the following transactions, assuming (a) a periodic system and (b) a perpetual system. Arrange your entries in parallel columns for comparison purposes.

October 1: Purchased 100 units on account for $7 each.
October 3: Returned 5 defective units for full credit.
October 8: Paid $16 freight charges on the October 1 shipment.
October 20: Sold 75 units on account for $10 each.

Multi-Concept Exercises

LO 3, 4 Exercise 6-15 Inventory Costing Methods—Periodic System
The following information is available concerning the inventory of Carter Inc.:

	Units	Unit Cost
Beginning inventory	200	$10
Purchases:		
March 5	300	11
June 12	400	12
August 23	250	13
October 2	150	15

During the year, Carter sold 1,000 units. It uses a periodic inventory system.

Required

1. Calculate ending inventory and cost of goods sold for each of the following three methods:
   a. Weighted average
   b. FIFO
   c. LIFO
2. Assume an estimated tax rate of 30%. How much more or less (indicate which) will Carter pay in taxes by using FIFO instead of LIFO? Explain your answer.

LO 2, 6 **Exercise 6-16** Lower-of-Cost-or-Market Rule

Awards Etc. carries an inventory of trophies and ribbons for local sports teams and school clubs. The cost of trophies has dropped in the past year, which pleases the company except for the fact that it has on hand considerable inventory that was purchased at the higher prices. The president is not pleased with the lower profit margin the company is earning. "The lower profit margin will continue until we sell all of this old inventory," he grumbled to the new staff accountant. "Not really," replied the accountant. "Let's write down the inventory to the replacement cost this year, and then next year our profit margin will be in line with the competition."

Required

Explain why the inventory can be carried at an amount less than its cost. Which accounts will be affected by the write-down? What will be the effect on income in the current year and future years?

LO 4, 11 **Exercise 6-17** Inventory Costing Methods—Perpetual System (Appendix 6A)

The following information is available concerning Oshkosh Inc.:

	Units	Unit Cost
Beginning inventory	200	$10
Purchases:		
March 5	300	11
June 12	400	12
August 23	250	13
October 2	150	15

Oshkosh, which uses a perpetual system, sold 1,000 units for $22 each during the year. Sales occurred on the following dates:

	Units
February 12	150
April 30	200
July 7	200
September 6	300
December 3	150

Required

1. Calculate ending inventory and cost of goods sold for each of the following three methods:
   a. Moving average
   b. FIFO
   c. LIFO
2. For each of the three methods, compare the results with those for Carter in Exercise 6-15. Which of the methods gives a different answer depending on whether a company uses a periodic or a perpetual inventory system?
3. Assume the use of the perpetual system and an estimated tax rate of 30%. How much more or less (indicate which) will Oshkosh pay in taxes by using LIFO instead of FIFO? Explain your answer.

PROBLEMS

LO 1 Problem 6-1 Inventory Costs in Various Businesses

Businesses incur various costs in selling goods and services. Each business must decide which costs are expenses of the period and which should be included in the cost of the inventory. Various types of businesses are listed below, along with certain types of costs they incur:

		Accounting Treatment		
Business	**Types of Costs**	**Expense of the Period**	**Inventory Cost**	**Other Treatment**
Retail shoe store	Shoes for sale			
	Shoe boxes			
	Advertising signs			
Grocery store	Canned goods on the shelves			
	Produce			
	Cleaning supplies			
	Cash registers			
Frame shop	Wooden frame supplies			
	Nails			
	Glass			
Walk-in print shop	Paper			
	Copy machines			
	Toner cartridges			
Restaurant	Frozen food			
	China and silverware			
	Prepared food			
	Spices			

Required

Fill in the table to indicate the correct accounting for each of these types of costs by placing an X in the appropriate column. For any costs that receive other treatment, explain what the appropriate treatment is for accounting purposes.

LO 4 Problem 6-2 Evaluation of Inventory Costing Methods

Users of financial statements rely on the information available to them to decide whether to invest in a company or lend it money. As an investor, you are comparing three companies in the same industry. The cost to purchase inventory is rising in the industry. Assume that all expenses incurred by the three companies are the same except for cost of goods sold. The companies use the following methods to value ending inventory:

Company A—weighted average cost
Company B—first-in, first-out (FIFO)
Company C—last-in, first-out (LIFO)

Required

1. Which of the three companies will report the highest net income? Explain your answer.
2. Which of the three companies will pay the least in income taxes? Explain your answer.
3. Which method of inventory costing do you believe is superior to the others in providing information to potential investors? Explain.
4. Explain how your answers to **1**, **2**, and **3** would change if the costs to purchase inventory had been falling instead of rising.

LO 5 Problem 6-3 Inventory Error

The following highly condensed income statements and balance sheets are available for Budget Stores for a two-year period (all amounts are stated in thousands of dollars):

Income Statements	2001	2000
Revenues	$20,000	$15,000
Cost of goods sold	13,000	10,000
Gross profit	$ 7,000	$ 5,000
Operating expenses	3,000	2,000
Net income	$ 4,000	$ 3,000

Balance Sheets	December 31, 2001	December 31, 2000
Cash	$ 1,700	$ 1,500
Inventory	4,200	3,500
Other current assets	2,500	2,000
Long-term assets	15,000	14,000
Total assets	$23,400	$21,000
Liabilities	$ 8,500	$ 7,000
Capital stock	5,000	5,000
Retained earnings	9,900	9,000
Total liabilities and owners' equity	$23,400	$21,000

Before releasing the 2001 annual report, Budget's controller learns that the inventory of one of the stores (amounting to $600,000) was inadvertently omitted from the count on December 31, 2000. The inventory of the store was correctly included in the December 31, 2001, count.

Required

1. Prepare revised income statements and balance sheets for Budget Stores for each of the two years. Ignore the effect of income taxes.
2. If Budget did not prepare revised statements before releasing the 2001 annual report, what would be the amount of overstatement or understatement of net income for the two-year period? What would be the overstatement or understatement of retained earnings at December 31, 2001, if revised statements were not prepared?
3. Given your answers in part 2, does it matter if Budget bothers to restate the financial statements of the two years to rectify the error? Explain your answer.

LO 7 **Problem 6-4** Gross Profit Method of Estimating Inventory Losses

On August 1, an office supply store was destroyed by an explosion in its basement. A small amount of inventory valued at $4,500 was saved. An estimate of the amount of inventory lost is needed for insurance purposes. The following information is available:

Inventory, January 1	$ 3,200
Purchases, January-July	164,000
Sales, January-July	113,500

The normal gross profit ratio is 40%. The insurance company will pay the store $65,000.

Required

1. Using the gross profit method, estimate the amount of inventory lost in the explosion.
2. Prepare the journal entry to record the inventory loss and the insurance reimbursement.

LO 8 **Problem 6-5** Inventory Turnover for Compaq Computer and Gateway

The following information was summarized from the 1998 annual report of Compaq Computer Corporation:

www.compaq.com

	(in millions)
Product cost of sales for the year ended December 31:	
1998	$21,383
1997	17,500

(Continued)	**(in millions)**
Inventories, December 31:	
1998	$ 2,005
1997	1,570
Product revenue for the year ended December 31:	
1998	27,372
1997	24,122

www.gateway.com The following information was summarized from the 1998 annual report of Gateway:

	(in thousands)
Cost of goods sold for the year ended December 31:	
1998	$5,921,651
1997	5,217,239
Inventory, December 31:	
1998	167,924
1997	249,224
Net sales for the year ended December 31:	
1998	7,467,925
1997	6,293,680

Required

1. Calculate the gross margin (gross profit) ratios for Compaq Computer and Gateway for 1998 and 1997.
2. Calculate the inventory turnover ratios for both companies for 1998.
3. Which company appears to be performing better? What other information should you consider to determine how these companies are performing in this regard?

LO 9 **Problem 6-6** Effects of Changes in Inventory and Accounts Payable Balances on Statement of Cash Flows

Copeland Antiques reported a net loss of $33,200 for the year ended December 31, 2001. The following items were included on Copeland's balance sheets at December 31, 2001 and 2000:

	12/31/01	**12/31/00**
Cash	$ 65,300	$ 46,100
Trade accounts payable	123,900	93,700
Inventories	192,600	214,800

Copeland uses the indirect method to prepare its statement of cash flows. Copeland does not have any other current assets or current liabilities and did not enter into any investing or financing activities during 2001.

Required

1. Prepare Copeland's 2001 statement of cash flows.
2. Draft a brief memo to the president to explain why cash increased during such an unprofitable year.

Multi-Concept Problems

LO 2, 3, 4 **Problem 6-7** Comparison of Inventory Costing Methods—Periodic System

Bitten Company's inventory records show 600 units on hand on October 1 with a unit cost of $5 each. The following transactions occurred during the month of October:

Date		**Unit Purchases**	**Unit Sales**
October	4		500 @ $10.00
	8	800 @ $5.40	
	9		700 @ $10.00
	18	700 @ $5.76	
	20		800 @ $11.00
	29	800 @ $5.90	

All expenses other than cost of goods sold amount to $3,000 for the month. The company uses an estimated tax rate of 30% to accrue monthly income taxes.

Required

1. Prepare a chart comparing cost of goods sold and ending inventory using the periodic system and the following costing methods:

	Cost of Goods Sold	Ending Inventory	Total
Weighted average			
FIFO			
LIFO			

2. What does the Total column represent?
3. Prepare income statements for each of the three methods.
4. Will the company pay more or less tax if it uses FIFO rather than LIFO? How much more or less?

LO 2, 4, 11 Problem 6-8 Comparison of Inventory Costing Methods—Perpetual System (Appendix 6A)

Repeat Problem 6-7 using the perpetual system.

LO 2, 3, 4 Problem 6-9 Inventory Costing Methods—Periodic System

Oxendine Company's inventory records for the month of November reveal the following:

Inventory, November 1	200 units @ $18.00
November 4, purchase	250 units @ $18.50
November 7, sale	300 units @ $42.00
November 13, purchase	220 units @ $18.90
November 18, purchase	150 units @ $19.00
November 22, sale	380 units @ $42.50
November 24, purchase	200 units @ $19.20
November 28, sale	110 units @ $43.00

Selling and administrative expenses for the month were $10,800. Depreciation expense was $4,000. Oxendine's tax rate is 35%.

Required

1. Calculate the cost of goods sold and ending inventory under each of the following three methods (assume a periodic inventory system): (a) FIFO, (b) LIFO, and (c) weighted average.
2. Calculate the gross margin and net income under each costing assumption.
3. Under which costing method will Oxendine pay the least taxes? Explain your answer.

LO 2, 3, 4 Problem 6-10 Inventory Costing Methods—Periodic System

Following is an inventory acquisition schedule for Weaver Corp. for 2001:

	Units	Unit Cost
Beginning inventory	5,000	$10
Purchases:		
February 4	3,000	9
April 12	4,000	8
September 10	2,000	7
December 5	1,000	6

During the year, Weaver sold 12,500 units at $12 each. All expenses except cost of goods sold and taxes amounted to $20,000. The tax rate is 30%.

Required

1. Compute cost of goods sold and ending inventory under each of the following three methods (assume a periodic inventory system): (a) weighted average, (b) FIFO, and (c) LIFO.
2. Prepare income statements under each of the three methods.

3. Which method do you recommend so that Weaver pays the least amount of taxes during 2001? Explain your answer.
4. Weaver anticipates that unit costs for inventory will increase throughout 2002. Will it be able to switch from the method you recommended it use in 2001 to another method to take advantage for tax purposes of the increase in prices? Explain your answer.

LO 1, 4 Problem 6-11 Interpreting Tribune Company's Inventory Accounting Policy

www.tribune.com

The 1998 annual report of Tribune Company and Subsidiaries includes the following in the footnote that summarizes its accounting policies:

> **Inventories** Inventories are stated at the lower of cost or market. Cost is determined on the last-in, first-out ("LIFO") basis for newsprint and on the first-in, first-out ("FIFO") or average basis for all other inventories.

Required

1. What *types* of inventory cost does Tribune Company carry? What about newspapers? Are newspapers considered inventory?
2. Why would the company choose three different methods to value its inventory?

LO 3, 7 Problem 6-12 Interpreting Sears' Inventory Accounting Policy

www.sears.com

The 1998 annual report of Sears, Roebuck and Co. includes the following information in the footnote that describes its accounting policies relating to merchandise inventories:

> Approximately 88% of merchandise inventories are valued at the lower of cost (using the last-in, first-out or "LIFO" method) or market using the retail method. To estimate the effects of inflation on inventories, the Company utilizes internally developed price indices.

The footnote also includes the following information about the company's international operations:

> Merchandise inventories of International operations, operations in Puerto Rico, and certain Sears Tire Group formats, which in total represent approximately 12% of merchandise inventories, are recorded at the lower of cost or market based on the FIFO method.

Your grandfather knows you are studying accounting and asks you what this information means.

Required

1. Sears uses the last-in, first-out method for its domestic merchandise inventories and the first-in, first-out method for its international merchandise inventories. Does this mean it sells its newest merchandise first in the United States and its oldest merchandise first overseas? Explain your answer.
2. Does Sears report merchandise inventories on its balance sheet at their retail value? Explain your answer.

Alternate Problems

LO 1 Problem 6-1A Inventory Costs in Various Businesses

Sound Traxs Inc. sells and rents videos to retail customers. The accountant is aware that at the end of the year she must account for inventory but is unsure what videos are considered inventory and how to value them. Videos purchased by the company are placed on the shelf for rental. Every three weeks the company performs a detailed analysis of the rental income from each video and decides whether to keep it as a rental or to offer it for sale in the resale section of the store. Resale videos sell for $10 each regardless of the price Sound Traxs paid for the tape.

Required

1. How should Sound Traxs account for each of the two types of tapes—rentals and resales—on its balance sheet?
2. How would you suggest Sound Traxs account for the videos as they are transferred from one department to another?

LO 4 **Problem 6-2A** Evaluation of Inventory Costing Methods

Three large mass merchandisers use the following methods to value ending inventory:

Company X—weighted average cost
Company Y—first-in, first-out (FIFO)
Company Z—last-in, first-out (LIFO)

The cost of inventory has steadily increased over the past 10 years of the product life. Recently, however, prices have started to decline slightly due to foreign competition.

Required

1. Will the effect on net income of the decline in cost of goods sold be the same for all three companies? Explain your answer?
2. Company Z would like to change its inventory costing method from LIFO to FIFO. Write an acceptable footnote for its annual report to justify the change.

LO 5 **Problem 6-3A** Inventory Error

The following condensed income statements and balance sheets are available for Planter Stores for a two-year period (all amounts are stated in thousands of dollars):

Income Statements	2001	2000
Revenues	$35,982	$26,890
Cost of goods sold	12,594	9,912
Gross profit	$23,388	$16,978
Operating expenses	13,488	10,578
Net income	$ 9,900	$ 6,400

Balance Sheets	December 31, 2001	December 31, 2000
Cash	$ 9,400	$ 4,100
Inventory	4,500	5,400
Other current assets	1,600	1,250
Long-term assets, net	24,500	24,600
Total assets	$40,000	$35,350
Current liabilities	$ 9,380	$10,600
Capital stock	18,000	18,000
Retained earnings	12,620	6,750
Total liabilities and owners' equity	$40,000	$35,350

Before releasing the 2001 annual report, Planter's controller learns that the inventory of one of the stores (amounting to $500,000) was counted twice in the December 31, 2000, inventory. The inventory was correctly counted in the December 31, 2001, inventory count.

Required

1. Prepare revised income statements and balance sheets for Planter Stores for each of the two years. Ignore the effect of income taxes.
2. Compute the current ratio at December 31, 2000, before the statements are revised, and then compute the current ratio at the same date after the statements are revised. If Planter applied for a loan in early 2001 and the lender required a current ratio of at least 1-to-1, would the error have affected the loan? Explain your answer.
3. If Planter did not prepare revised statements before releasing the 2001 annual report, what would be the amount of overstatement or understatement of net income for the two-year period? What would be the overstatement or understatement of retained earnings at December 31, 2001, if revised statements were not prepared?
4. Given your answers in parts **2** and **3,** does it matter if Planter bothers to restate the financial statements of the two years to correct the error? Explain your answer.

LO 7 **Problem 6-4A** Gross Profit Method of Estimating Inventory Losses

On July 1, an explosion destroyed a fireworks supply company. A small amount of inventory valued at $4,500 was saved. An estimate of the amount of inventory lost is needed for insurance purposes. The following information is available:

Inventory, January 1	$14,200
Purchases, January-June	77,000
Sales, January-June	93,500

The normal gross profit ratio is 70%. The insurance company will pay the supply company $50,000.

Required

1. Using the gross profit method, estimate the amount of inventory lost in the explosion.
2. Prepare the journal entry to record the inventory loss and the insurance reimbursement.

LO 8 **Problem 6-5A** Inventory Turnover for Wal-Mart and Kmart

www.walmart.com

The following information was summarized from the 1999 annual report of Wal-Mart Stores, Inc.:

	(in millions)
Cost of sales for the year ended January 31:	
1999	$108,725
1998	93,438
Inventories, January 31:	
1999	17,076
1998	16,497

www.kmart.com

The following information was summarized from the fiscal year 1998 annual report of Kmart Corporation:

	(in millions)
Cost of sales, buying, and occupancy for the year ended:	
January 27, 1999	$26,319
January 28, 1998	25,152
Merchandise inventories:	
January 27, 1999	6,536
January 28, 1998	6,367

Required

1. Calculate the inventory turnover ratios for Wal-Mart for the year ending January 31, 1999 and Kmart for the year ending January 27, 1999.
2. Which company appears to be performing better? What other information should you consider to determine how these companies are performing in this regard?

LO 9 **Problem 6-6A** Effects of Changes in Inventory and Accounts Payable Balances on Statement of Cash Flows

Carpetland City reported net income of $78,500 for the year ended December 31, 2001. The following items were included on Carpetland's balance sheet at December 31, 2001 and 2000:

	12/31/01	12/31/00
Cash	$ 14,400	$26,300
Trade accounts payable	23,900	93,700
Inventories	105,500	84,900

Carpetland uses the indirect method to prepare its statement of cash flows. Carpetland does not have any other current assets or current liabilities and did not enter into any investing or financing activities during 2001.

Required

1. Prepare Carpetland's 2001 statement of cash flows.
2. Draft a brief memo to the president to explain why cash decreased during a profitable year.

Alternate Multi-Concept Problems

LO 2, 3, 4 Problem 6-7A Comparison of Inventory Costing Methods—Periodic System

Stellar Inc.'s inventory records show 300 units on hand on November 1 with a unit cost of $4 each. The following transactions occurred during the month of November:

Date		Unit Purchases	Unit Sales
November	4		200 @ $9.00
	8	500 @ $4.50	
	9		500 @ $9.00
	18	700 @ $4.75	
	20		400 @ $9.50
	29	600 @ $5.00	

All expenses other than cost of goods sold amount to $2,000 for the month. The company uses an estimated tax rate of 25% to accrue monthly income taxes.

Required

1. Prepare a chart comparing cost of goods sold and ending inventory using the periodic system and the following costing methods:

	Cost of Goods Sold	Ending Inventory	Total
Weighted average			
FIFO			
LIFO			

2. What does the Total column represent?
3. Prepare income statements for each of the three methods.
4. Will the company pay more or less tax if it uses FIFO rather than LIFO? How much more or less?

LO 2, 4, 11 Problem 6-8A Comparison of Inventory Costing Methods—Perpetual System

Repeat Problem 6-7A, using the perpetual system.

LO 2, 3, 4 Problem 6-9A Inventory Costing Methods—Periodic System

SPREADSHEET

Story Company's inventory records for the month of November reveal the following:

Inventory, November 1	300 units @ $27.00
November 4, purchase	375 units @ $26.50
November 7, sale	450 units @ $63.00
November 13, purchase	330 units @ $26.00
November 18, purchase	225 units @ $25.40
November 22, sale	570 units @ $63.75
November 24, purchase	300 units @ $25.00
November 28, sale	165 units @ $64.50

Selling and administrative expenses for the month were $16,200. Depreciation expense was $6,000. Story's tax rate is 35%.

Required

1. Calculate the cost of goods sold and ending inventory under each of the following three methods (assume a periodic inventory system): (a) FIFO, (b) LIFO, and (c) weighted average.
2. Calculate the gross margin and net income under each costing assumption.
3. Under which costing method will Story pay the least taxes? Explain your answer.

LO 2, 3, 4 **Problem 6-10A** Inventory Costing Methods—Periodic System

Following is an inventory acquisition schedule for Fees Corp. for 2001:

	Units	Unit Cost
Beginning inventory	4,000	$20
Purchases:		
February 4	2,000	18
April 12	3,000	16
September 10	1,000	14
December 5	2,500	12

During the year, Fees sold 11,000 units at $30 each. All expenses except cost of goods sold and taxes amounted to $60,000. The tax rate is 30%.

Required

1. Compute cost of goods sold and ending inventory under each of the following three methods (assume a periodic inventory system): (a) weighted average, (b) FIFO, and (c) LIFO.
2. Prepare income statements under each of the three methods.
3. Which method do you recommend so that Fees pays the least amount of taxes during 2001? Explain your answer.
4. Fees anticipates that unit costs for inventory will increase throughout 2002. Will it be able to switch from the method you recommended it use in 2001 to another method to take advantage for tax purposes of the increase in prices? Explain your answer.

LO 1, 4 **Problem 6-11A** Interpreting the New York Times Company's Financial Statements

www.nytimes.com

The 1998 annual report of the New York Times Company includes the following note:

> Inventories. Inventories are stated at the lower of cost or current market value. Inventory cost is generally based on the last-in, first-out ("LIFO") method for newsprint and magazine paper and the first-in, first-out ("FIFO") method for other inventories.

Required

1. What *types* of inventory costs does the New York Times Company have? What about newspapers? Aren't these considered inventory?
2. Why did the company choose two different methods to value its inventory?

LO 3, 7 **Problem 6-12A** Interpreting JCPenney's Financial Statements

www.jcpenney.com

The 1998 annual report for JCPenney includes the following in the footnote that summarizes its accounting policies:

> Merchandise inventory. Substantially all merchandise inventory is valued at the lower of cost (last-in, first-out) or market, determined by the retail method.

A friend knows that you are studying accounting and asks you what this note means.

Required

1. JCPenney uses the last-in, first-out method. Does this mean that it sells its newest merchandise first?
2. Does JCPenney report inventories on its balance sheet at their retail value?

Cases

Reading and Interpreting Financial Statements

LO 1, 3 **Case 6-1** Reading and Interpreting Ben & Jerry's Annual Report

www.benjerry.com

Refer to Ben & Jerry's financial statements included in its annual report.

Required

1. Before you look at Ben & Jerry's annual report, what types of inventory accounts do you expect? What types of inventory accounts does Ben & Jerry's actually report? (refer to the footnote on inventories).

2. What inventory costing method does Ben & Jerry's use? Look in the footnotes to the financial statements.
3. What portion of total assets is represented by inventory at the end of 1997? at the end of 1998? Do these portions seem reasonable for a company in this business? Explain your answer.
4. Look at the statement of cash flows. Under the operating activities, you will find an adjustment for depreciation, yet there is no mention of depreciation on the income statement. Depreciation on equipment and buildings used in the manufacturing process is included in cost of sales. Make a list of other expenses that you would expect to be included in Ben & Jerry's cost of sales rather than listed separately on the income statement.

LO 9 **Case 6-2** Reading Gateway's Statement of Cash Flows

Refer to the statement of cash flows in Gateway's 1998 annual report and answer the following questions: www.gateway.com

1. Did inventories increase or decrease during 1998? Why was the change in the Inventory account added to net income in the Operating Activities category of the statement?
2. Comment on the size of change in inventories over the last three years. Does the level of inventory at the end of 1998 seem appropriate?
3. Did accounts payable increase or decrease during 1998? Why was the change in the account added to net income in the Operating Activities category of the statement?

LO 4 **Case 6-3** Reading and Interpreting JCPenney's Financial Statements

JCPenney reports merchandise inventory in the Current Asset section of the balance sheet in its 1998 annual report as follows (amounts in millions of dollars): www.jcpenney.com

	1998	1997
Merchandise inventory (including LIFO reserves of $227 and $225)	$6,031	$6,162

Required

1. What method does JCPenney use to report the value of its inventory?
2. What is the amount of the LIFO reserve at the end of each of the two years?
3. Explain the meaning of the increase or decrease in the LIFO reserve during 1998. What does this tell you about inventory costs for the company? Are they rising or falling? Explain your answer.

Making Financial Decisions

LO 3, 4 **Case 6-4** Inventory Costing Methods

You are the controller for Georgetown Company. At the end of its first year of operations, the company is experiencing cash flow problems. The following information has been accumulated during the year:

Purchases	
January	1,000 units @ $8
March	1,200 units @ 8
October	1,500 units @ 9

During the year, Georgetown sold 3,000 units at $15 each. The expected tax rate is 35%. The president doesn't understand how to report inventory in the financial statements because no record of the cost of the units sold was kept as each sale was made.

Required

1. What inventory *system* must Georgetown use?
2. Determine the number of units on hand at the end of the year.
3. Explain cost-flow assumptions to the president and the method you recommend. Prepare income statements to justify your position, comparing your recommended method with at least one other method.

LO 5 **Case 6-5** Inventory Errors

You are the controller of a rapidly growing mass merchandiser. The company uses a periodic inventory system. As the company has grown and accounting systems have developed, errors have occurred in both the physical count of inventory and the valuation of inventory on the balance sheet. You have been able to identify the following errors as of December 2000:

- In 1998 one section of the warehouse was counted twice. The error resulted in inventory overstated on December 31, 1998, by approximately $45,600.
- In 1999 the replacement cost of some inventory was less than the FIFO value used on the balance sheet. The inventory would have been $6,000 less on the balance sheet dated December 31, 1999.
- In 2000 the company used the gross profit method to estimate inventory for its quarterly financial statements. At the end of the second quarter, the controller made a math error and understated the inventory by $20,000 on the quarterly report. The error was not discovered until the end of the year.

Required

What, if anything, should you do to correct each of these errors? Explain your answers.

Accounting and Ethics: What Would You Do?

LO 6 Case 6-6 Write-Down of Obsolete Inventory

As a newly hired staff accountant, you are assigned the responsibility of physically counting inventory at the end of the year. The inventory count proceeds in a timely fashion. The inventory is outdated, however. You suggest that the inventory could not be sold for the cost at which it is carried and that the inventory should be written down to a much lower level. The controller replies that experience has taught her how the market changes and she knows that the units in the warehouse will be more marketable again. The company plans to keep the goods until they are back in style.

Required

1. What effect will writing off the inventory have on the current year's income?
2. What effect does not writing off the inventory have on the year-end balance sheet?
3. What factors should you consider in deciding whether to persist in your argument that the inventory should be written down?

LO 4 Case 6-7 Selection of an Inventory Method

As controller of a widely held public company, you are concerned with making the best decisions for the stockholders. At the end of its first year of operations, you are faced with the choice of method to value inventory. Specific identification is out of the question because the company sells a large quantity of diversified products. You are trying to decide between FIFO and LIFO. Inventory costs have increased 33% over the year. The chief executive officer has instructed you to do whatever it takes in all areas to report the highest income possible.

Required

1. Which method will satisfy the CEO?
2. Which method do you believe is in the best interest of the stockholders? Explain your answer.
3. Write a brief memo to the CEO to convince him that reporting the highest income is not always the best approach for the shareholders.

Internet Research Case

www.circuitcity.com

Case 6-8 Circuit City

Circuit City Stores Inc., is a top retailer in the consumer electronics industry (its Circuit City Group), and it is also a significant retailer of autos and trucks (its Carmax Group). The chapter focuses on the Circuit City Group in the chapter opener, in the Business Strategy box, and in the chapter to show how inventory turnover differs by industry.

Read the chapter opening text and the Business Strategy box, research the company and its financial information available on its web site, and answer the following questions.

1. What is the inventory amount shown for the most current year?
2. What is the inventory turnover for the Carmax Group? For the entire company as a whole? Is this information significant for evaluating each of the two groups in the company against competition? Is it significant for evaluating the company as a whole? Why or why not?
3. How would Circuit City's rebate program for new CompuServe customers affect inventories at Circuit City?
4. What inventory system would you expect Circuit City to use, perpetual or periodic? What makes you think so?
5. How could Circuit City reduce its costs for carrying inventory?

Solution to Key Terms Quiz

__4__ Merchandise Inventory (p. 262)
__7__ Raw materials (p. 262)
__2__ Work in process (p. 263)
__12__ Finished goods (p. 263)
__15__ Specific identification method (p. 266)
__3__ Weighted average cost method (p. 267)
__6__ FIFO method (p. 268)
__9__ LIFO method (p. 269)
__17__ LIFO liquidation (p. 271)
__14__ LIFO conformity rule (p. 271)
__18__ LIFO reserve (p. 272)
__16__ Inventory profit (p. 272)
__8__ Replacement cost (p. 278)
__5__ Lower of cost or market (LCM) rule (p. 278)
__11__ Gross profit method (p. 280)
__13__ Retail inventory method (p. 282)
__19__ Inventory turnover ratio (p. 282)
__10__ Number of days' sales in inventory (p. 283)
__1__ Moving average (p. 292)

Chapter 7

Cash, Investments, and Receivables

Study Links

A Look at Previous Chapters

In the two preceding chapters, we discussed the accounting for inventories, a major asset for many companies. The emphasis in Chapter 5 was on merchandise inventory and the accounting for purchases and sales of inventory. In Chapter 6, we considered how inventory is valued in the accounts, using a costing method such as weighted average, FIFO, or LIFO.

A Look at This Chapter

We now turn to those assets, namely cash and receivables, that are increased when a company sells its inventory. We also consider the accounting when a company invests some of its cash in the stocks and bonds of other companies. The last part of the chapter covers various valuation issues relative both to accounts receivable and to notes receivable.

A Look at Upcoming Chapters

Chapter 8 focuses on the long-term operational assets, such as property, plant, and equipment and intangibles, necessary to run a business. In Chapters 9 and 10, we explore the use of liabilities to finance the purchase of assets.

Focus on Financial Results

For the last few years PepsiCo., the world's number-two soft-drink maker, has been in the business of revamping itself. The firm sold off unrelated businesses it held around the world (including KFC, Pizza Hut, and Taco Bell and a baby-food company in Mexico) and invested billions of dollars back into "the heart and soul" of its business—brands. PepsiCo.'s brands include Frito-Lay and the newly acquired Tropicana Products. In 1998, the firm placed more than 190,000 new vending machines and coolers, launched new products like Frappuccino (created with Starbucks), and invested heavily in advertising and marketing. Sales volume grew at its best rate in four years, and market share rose accordingly.

This success is partly reflected in the improved accounts and notes receivable figure shown in PepsiCo.'s 1998 annual report, in the Current Assets section highlighted here. The annual report notes that cash generated by the firm's strengthened position allowed it to spend "aggressively" on boosting sales and to deliver solid growth in earnings per share. Notice, however, that the ending balances in the current assets of cash and cash equivalents and short-term investments are much lower than in 1997. At the same time, inventories are up about 39 percent.

Consolidated Balance Sheet

(in millions)
PepsiCo, Inc. and Subsidiaries
December 26, 1998 and December 27, 1997

	1998	1997
ASSETS		
Current Assets		
Cash and cash equivalents	$ 311	$ 1,928
Short-term investments, at cost	83	955
	394	2,883
Accounts and notes receivable, less allowance: $127 in 1998 and $125 in 1997	2,453	2,150
Inventories	1,016	732
Prepaid expenses, deferred income taxes and other current assets	499	486
Total Current Assets	4,362	6,251
Property, Plant and Equipment, net	7,318	6,261
Intangible Assets, net	8,996	5,855
Investments in Unconsolidated Affiliates	1,396	1,201
Other Assets	588	533
Total Assets	$22,660	$20,101

Lower cash and cash equivalents

Lower short-term investments

Higher accounts and notes receivable

PepsiCo's 1998 Annual Report

PepsiCo. prides itself on its ability to earn profits for its shareholders. If you owned shares in the company, what questions would you ask about the decrease in cash and cash equivalents? Would you be concerned about the rise in inventories or reassured by the increase in receivables? Study the chapter to find out how these variables are related.

www.pepsico.com

Learning Objectives

After studying this chapter, you should be able to:

LO 1 Identify and describe the various forms of cash reported on a balance sheet. (p. 314)

LO 2 Understand various techniques that companies use to control cash. (p. 315)

LO 3 Understand the accounting for various types of investments companies make. (p. 323)

LO 4 Understand how to account for accounts receivable, including bad debts. (p. 334)

LO 5 Understand how to account for interest-bearing notes receivable. (p. 342)

LO 6 Understand how to account for non-interest-bearing notes receivable. (p. 343)

LO 7 Explain various techniques that companies use to accelerate the inflow of cash from sales. (p. 344)

LO 8 Explain the effects of transactions involving liquid assets on the statement of cash flows. (p. 346)

PepsiCo Inc., like all other businesses, relies on *liquid assets* to function smoothly. *Liquidity* is a relative term. It deals with a company's ability to pay its debts as they fall due. Most obligations must be paid in cash, and therefore cash is considered the most liquid of all assets. Accounts and notes receivable are not as liquid as cash. Their collection does result in an inflow of cash, however. Because cash in its purest form does not earn a return, most businesses invest in various types of securities as a way to use idle cash over the short term. The Current Assets section of PepsiCo's balance sheet, as shown in the chapter opener, indicates three highly liquid assets: cash and cash equivalents, short-term investments, and accounts and notes receivable. Inventories are not considered as liquid as these three assets because they depend on a sale to be realized.

We begin the chapter by considering the various forms cash can take and the importance of cash control to a business. Some companies invest cash in various types of financial instruments, as well as in the stocks and bonds of other companies. The chapter illustrates the accounting for these investments. In many instances the cash available to make these investments comes from the collection of receivables. The chapter concludes with a discussion of the accounting both for accounts receivable and for notes receivable.

What Constitutes Cash?

LO 1 Identify and describe the various forms of cash reported on a balance sheet.

Cash takes many different forms. Coin and currency on hand and cash on deposit in the form of checking, savings, and money market accounts are the most obvious forms of cash. Also included in cash are various forms of checks, including undeposited checks from customers, cashier's checks, and certified checks. The proliferation of different types of financial instruments on the market today makes it very difficult to decide on the appropriate classification of these various items. The key to the classification of an amount as cash is that it be *readily available to pay debts.* Technically, a bank has the legal right to demand that a customer notify it before making withdrawals from savings accounts, or time deposits, as they are often called. Because this right is rarely exercised, however, savings accounts are normally classified as cash. In contrast, a certificate of deposit has a specific maturity date and carries a penalty for early withdrawal and is therefore not included in cash.

Cash Equivalents and the Statement of Cash Flows

Cash equivalent An investment that is readily convertible to a known amount of cash and has an original maturity to the investor of three months or less.

Note that the first item on PepsiCo's balance sheet is titled Cash and Cash Equivalents. Examples of items normally classified as cash equivalents are commercial paper issued by corporations, Treasury bills issued by the federal government, and money market funds offered by financial institutions. According to current accounting standards, classification as a **cash equivalent** is limited to those investments that are readily convertible to known amounts of cash and that have an original maturity to the investor of three months or less. Note that according to this definition, a six-month bank certificate of deposit would *not* be classified as a cash equivalent.

The statement of cash flows that accompanies PepsiCo's balance sheet is shown in Exhibit 7-1. Note the direct tie between this statement and the balance sheet (refer to the Current Assets section of PepsiCo's balance sheet as shown in the chapter opener). The cash and cash equivalents of $311 million at the end of 1998, as shown at the bottom of the statement of cash flows, is the same amount that appears as the first line on the balance sheet. The reason for this is that the statement of cash flows traces the flow of cash from the beginning balance of cash for the year—$1,928 million—to the year's ending balance, $311 million. Cash inflow from operating activities, $3,211 million, minus cash outflow from investing activities, $5,019 million, plus cash inflow from financing activities, $190 million, plus the effects of exchange rate changes, $1 million, equals a net decrease in cash of $1,617 million. Deduct $1,617 million from the beginning cash balance to arrive at $311 million.

Note the fifth category listed under Investing Activities on the statement of cash flows. The changes in short-term investments represent the net purchases or sales of short-term investments during the year. Later in the chapter we will consider the accounting for both short-term and long-term investments. For now, note that any purchases or sales of items classified as short-term investments are considered significant and worthy of reporting on the statement of cash flows. Any purchases or sales of items classified as cash equivalents, however, are not considered significant activities. Instead, they are included with cash on the balance sheet and are considered to be its "equivalent."

Control over Cash

In Chapter 5, we discussed the concept of internal control and the critical role it plays for an asset such as cash. Because cash is universally accepted as a medium of exchange, control over it is critical to the smooth functioning of any business, no matter how large or small.

LO 2 Understand various techniques that companies use to control cash.

Cash Management

In addition to the need to guard against theft and other abuses related to the physical custody of cash, management of this asset is also important. Cash management is necessary to ensure that at any point in time, a company has neither too little nor too much cash on hand. The need to have enough cash on hand is obvious: suppliers, employees, taxing agencies, banks, and all other creditors must be paid on time if an entity is to remain in business. It is equally important that a company not maintain cash on hand and on deposit in checking accounts beyond a minimal amount that is necessary to support ongoing operations, since cash is essentially a nonearning asset. Granted, some checking accounts pay a very meager rate of interest. However, the superior return that could be earned by investing idle cash in various forms of marketable securities dictates that companies carefully monitor the amount of cash on hand at all times.

An important tool in the management of cash, the cash flows statement, is discussed in detail in Chapter 12. Cash budgets, which are also critical to the management of cash, are discussed in management accounting and business finance texts. Cash management is just one important aspect of control over cash. Beyond cash management, companies often use two other cash control features: bank reconciliations and petty cash funds. Before we turn to these control devices, we need to review the basic features of a bank statement.

Reading a Bank Statement

Two fundamental principles of internal control discussed in Chapter 5 are worth repeating: all cash receipts should be deposited daily intact, and all cash payments should be made by check. Checking accounts at banks are critical in this regard. These accounts allow a company to carefully monitor and control cash receipts and cash payments. Control is aided

EXHIBIT 7-1 PepsiCo's Statement of Cash Flows

Consolidated Statement of Cash Flows

(in millions)
PepsiCo, Inc. and Subsidiaries
Fiscal years ended December 26, 1998, December 27, 1997 and December 28, 1996

	1998	1997	1996
Operating Activities			
Income from continuing operations	**$ 1,993**	$ 1,491	$ 942
Adjustments to reconcile income from continuing operations to net cash provided by operating activities			
Depreciation and amortization	**1,234**	1,106	1,073
Noncash portion of 1998 tax benefit	**(259)**	–	–
Noncash portion of unusual impairment and other items	**254**	233	366
Deferred income taxes	**150**	51	160
Other noncash charges and credits, net	**237**	342	505
Changes in operating working capital, excluding effects of acquisitions and dispositions			
Accounts and notes receivable	**(104)**	(53)	(67)
Inventories	**29**	79	(97)
Prepaid expenses and other current assets	**(12)**	(56)	84
Accounts payable and other current liabilities	**(195)**	84	297
Income taxes payable	**(116)**	142	(71)
Net change in operating working capital	**(398)**	196	146
Net Cash Provided by Operating Activities	**3,211**	3,419	3,192
Investing Activities			
Capital spending	**(1,405)**	(1,506)	(1,630)
Acquisitions and investments in unconsolidated affiliates	**(4,537)**	(119)	(75)
Sales of businesses	**17**	221	43
Sales of property, plant and equipment	**134**	80	9
Short-term investments, by original maturity			
More than three months – purchases	**(525)**	(92)	(115)
More than three months – maturities	**584**	177	192
Three months or less, net	**839**	(735)	736
Other, net	**(126)**	(96)	(214)
Net Cash Used for Investing Activities	**(5,019)**	(2,070)	(1,054)
Financing Activities			
Proceeds from issuances of long-term debt	**990**	–	1,772
Payments of long-term debt	**(2,277)**	(1,875)	(1,432)
Short-term borrowings, by original maturity			
More than three months – proceeds	**2,713**	146	740
More than three months – payments	**(417)**	(177)	(1,873)
Three months or less, net	**1,753**	(1,269)	89
Cash dividends paid	**(757)**	(736)	(675)
Share repurchases	**(2,230)**	(2,459)	(1,651)
Proceeds from exercises of stock options	**415**	403	323
Other, net	**–**	5	(9)
Net Cash Provided by (Used for) Financing Activities	**190**	(5,962)	(2,716)
Net Cash Provided by Discontinued Operations	**–**	6,236	605
Effect of Exchange Rate Changes on Cash and Cash Equivalents	**1**	(2)	(5)
Net (Decrease) Increase in Cash and Cash Equivalents	**(1,617)**	1,621	22
Cash and Cash Equivalents – Beginning of Year	**1,928**	307	285
Cash and Cash Equivalents – End of Year	**$ 311**	$ 1,928	$ 307
Supplemental Cash Flow Information			
Interest paid	**$ 367**	$ 462	$ 538
Income taxes paid	**$ 521**	$ 696	$ 611
Schedule of Noncash Investing and Financing Activities			
Fair value of assets acquired	**$ 5,359**	$ 160	$ 81
Cash paid and stock issued	**(4,537)**	(134)	(76)
Liabilities assumed	**$ 822**	$ 26	$ 5

This amount appears as first line on the balance sheet

See accompanying Notes to Consolidated Financial Statements.

23

further by the monthly **bank statement.** Most banks mail their customers a monthly bank statement for each account. The statement provides a detailed list of all activity for a particular account during the month. An example of a typical bank statement is shown in Exhibit 7-2. Note that the bank statement indicates the activity in one of the cash accounts maintained by Weber Products Inc. at the Mt. Etna State Bank.

BANK STATEMENT A detailed list, provided by the bank, of all the activity for a particular account during the month.

Before we look at the various items that appear on a bank statement, it is important to understand the route a check takes after it is written. Assume that Weber writes a check on its account at the Mt. Etna State Bank. Weber mails the check to one of its suppliers, Keese Corp., which deposits the check in its account at the Second City Bank. At this point, Second City presents the check to Mt. Etna for payment, and Mt. Etna reduces the balance in Weber's account accordingly. The canceled check has now "cleared" the banking system. Either the canceled check itself or a copy of it is returned with Weber's next bank statement.

The following types of items appear on Weber's bank statement:

Canceled checks—Weber's checks that cleared the bank during the month of June are listed with the corresponding check number and the date paid. Keep in mind that some of these checks may have been written by Weber in a previous month but were not presented for payment to the bank until June. You also should realize

EXHIBIT 7-2 Bank Statement

MT. ETNA STATE BANK
CHICAGO, ILLINOIS
STATEMENT OF ACCOUNT

Weber Products Inc.
502 Dodge St.
Chicago, IL 66606

FOR THE MONTH ENDING June 30, 2001
ACCOUNT 0371-22-514

DATE	DESCRIPTION	SUBTRACTIONS	ADDITIONS	BALANCE
6-01	Previous balance			3,236.41
6-01	Check 497	723.40		2,513.01
6-02	Check 495	125.60		2,387.41
6-06	Check 491	500.00		1,887.41
6-07	Deposit		1,423.16	3,310.57
6-10	Check 494	185.16		3,125.41
6-13	NSF check	245.72		2,879.69
6-15	Deposit		755.50	3,635.19
6-18	Check 499	623.17		3,012.02
6-20	Check 492	125.00		2,887.02
6-22	Deposit		1,875.62	4,762.64
6-23	Service charge	20.00		4,742.64
6-24	Check 493	875.75		3,866.89
6-24	Check 503	402.10		3,464.79
6-26	Customer note, interest		550.00	4,014.79
6-26	Service fee on note	16.50		3,998.29
6-27	Check 500	1,235.40		2,762.89
6-28	Deposit		947.50	3,710.39
6-30	Check 498	417.25		3,293.14
6-30	Interest earned		15.45	3,308.59
6-30	Statement Totals	5,495.05	5,567.23	

that during June, Weber may have written some checks that do not yet appear on the bank statement because they have not been presented for payment. A check written by a company but not yet presented to the bank for payment is called an **outstanding check.**

OUTSTANDING CHECK
A check written by a company but not yet presented to the bank for payment.

Deposits—In keeping with the internal control principle calling for the deposit of all cash receipts intact, most companies deposit all checks, coin, and currency on a daily basis. For the sake of brevity, we have limited to four the number of deposits that Weber made during the month. Keep in mind that Weber also may have made a deposit on the last day or two of the month and that this deposit may not yet be reflected on the bank statement. This type of deposit is called a **deposit in transit.**

DEPOSIT IN TRANSIT
A deposit recorded on the books but not yet reflected on the bank statement.

NSF check—NSF is an abbreviation for *not sufficient funds.* The NSF check listed on the bank statement on June 13 is a customer's check that Weber recorded on its books, deposited, and thus included in its cash account. When Mt. Etna State Bank learned that the check was not good because the customer did not have sufficient funds on hand in its bank account to cover the check, the bank deducted the amount from Weber's account. Weber needs to contact its customer to collect the amount due; ideally, the customer will issue a new check once it has sufficient funds in its account.

Service charge—Banks charge for various services they provide to customers. Among the most common bank service charges are monthly activity fees, fees charged for new checks, for the rental of a lockbox at the bank in which to store valuable company documents, and for the collection of customer notes by the bank.

Customer note and interest—It is often convenient to have customers pay amounts owed to a company directly to that company's bank. The bank simply acts as a collection agency for the company.

Interest earned—Most checking accounts pay interest on the average daily balance in the account. Rates paid on checking accounts are usually significantly less than could be earned on most other forms of investment.

The Bank Reconciliation

BANK RECONCILIATION
A form used by the accountant to reconcile the balance shown on the bank statement for a particular account with the balance shown in the accounting records.

A **bank reconciliation** should be prepared for each individual bank account as soon as the bank statement is received. Ideally, the reconciliation should be performed or, at a minimum, thoroughly reviewed by someone independent of custody, record-keeping, and authorization responsibilities relating to cash. As the name implies, the purpose of a bank reconciliation is to *reconcile* the balance that the bank shows for an account with the balance that appears on the company's books. Differences between the two amounts are investigated, and if necessary, adjustments are made. The following are the steps in preparing a bank reconciliation:

1. Trace deposits listed on the bank statement to the books. Any deposits recorded on the books but not yet shown on the bank statement are deposits in transit. Prepare a list of the deposits in transit.
2. Arrange the canceled checks in numerical order, and trace each of them to the books. Any checks recorded on the books but not yet listed on the bank statement are outstanding. List the outstanding checks.
3. List all items, other than deposits, shown as additions on the bank statement, such as interest paid by the bank for the month and amounts collected by the bank from one of the company's customers. When the bank pays interest or collects an amount owed to a company by one of the company's customers, the bank increases or *credits* its liability to the company on its own books. For this reason, these items are called **credit memoranda.**

CREDIT MEMORANDA
Additions on a bank statement for such items as interest paid on the account and notes collected by the bank for the customer.

4. List all amounts, other than canceled checks, shown as subtractions on the bank statement, such as any NSF checks and the various service charges mentioned earlier. When a company deposits money in a bank, a liability is created on the books of the bank. Therefore, when the bank reduces the amount of its liability for these various

items, it *debits* the liability on its own books. For this reason, these items are called **debit memoranda.**

5. Identify any errors made by the bank or by the company in recording the various cash transactions.
6. Use the information collected in steps 1 through 5 to prepare a bank reconciliation.

DEBIT MEMORANDA
Deductions on a bank statement for such items as NSF checks and various service charges.

Companies use a number of different *formats* in preparing bank reconciliations. For example, some companies take the balance shown on the bank statement and reconcile this amount to the balance shown on the books. Another approach, which we will illustrate for Weber Products, involves reconciling the bank balance and the book balance to an adjusted balance, rather than one to the other. As we will see, the advantage of this approach is that it yields the correct balance and makes it easy for the company to make any necessary adjustments to its books. A bank reconciliation for Weber Products is shown in Exhibit 7-3. The following are explanations for the various items on the reconciliation:

1. The balance per bank statement of $3,308.59 is taken from the June statement as shown in Exhibit 7-2.
2. Weber's records showed a deposit for $642.30 made on June 30 that is not reflected on the bank statement. The deposit in transit is listed as an addition to the bank statement balance.
3. The accounting records indicate three checks written but not yet reflected on the bank statement. The three outstanding checks are as follows:

   496 $ 79.89
   501 $213.20
   502 $424.75

   Outstanding checks are the opposite of deposits in transit and therefore are deducted from the bank statement balance.

Study Tip

Review your own bank statement to see the similarities and differences between it and the one illustrated here. Also, look on the reverse of your statement for the form of a reconciliation the bank provides. It may or may not be the same format as illustrated in Exhibit 7-3.

EXHIBIT 7-3 Bank Reconciliation

WEBER PRODUCTS
BANK RECONCILIATION
JUNE 30, 2001

Balance per bank statement, June 30			$3,308.59
Add:	Deposit in transit		642.30
Deduct:	Outstanding checks:		
	No. 496	$ 79.89	
	No. 501	213.20	
	No. 502	424.75	(717.84)
Adjusted balance, June 30			$3,233.05
Balance per books, June 30			$2,895.82
Add:	Customer note collected	$500.00	
	Interest on customer note	50.00	
	Interest earned during June	15.45	
	Error in recording check 498	54.00	619.45
Deduct:	NSF check	$245.72	
	Collection fee on note	16.50	
	Service charge for lockbox	20.00	(282.22)
Adjusted balance, June 30			$3,233.05

- Do not need to put intrest income in bank statement.
Ledger
DR. Cash 250
CR. Interest Inc. 250
- Do not include Bank Service Charges on Bank Statement
Ledger
DR. Bank Serv. Charges 75
CR. Cash 75

4. The adjusted balance of $3,233.05 is found by adding the deposit in transit and deducting the outstanding checks from the bank statement balance.

5. The $2,895.82 book balance on June 30 is taken from the company's records as of that date.

6. According to the bank statement, $550 was added to the account on June 26 for the collection of a note with interest. We assume that the repayment of the note itself accounted for $500 of this amount and that the other $50 was for interest. The bank statement notifies Weber that the note with interest has been collected. Therefore, Weber must add $550 to the book balance.

7. An entry on June 30 on the bank statement shows an increase of $15.45 for interest earned on the bank account during June. This amount is added to the book balance.

8. A review of the canceled checks returned with the bank statement detected an error made by Weber. The company records indicated that check 498 was recorded incorrectly as $471.25; the check was actually written for $417.25 and reflected as such on the bank statement. This error, referred to as a *transposition error,* resulted from transposing the 7 and the 1 in recording the check in the books. The error is the difference between the amount of $471.25 recorded and the amount of $417.25 that should have been recorded, or $54.00. Because Weber recorded the cash payment at too large an amount, $54.00 must be added back to the book balance.

9. In addition to canceled checks, three other deductions appear on the bank statement. Each of these must be deducted from the book balance:

   a. A customer's NSF check for $245.72 (see June 13 entry on bank statement)

   b. A $16.50 fee charged by the bank to collect the customer's note discussed in item 6 (see June 26 entry on bank statement)

   c. A service fee of $20.00 charged by the bank for rental of a lockbox (see June 23 entry on bank statement)

10. The additions of $619.45 and deductions of $282.22 resulted in an adjusted cash balance of $3,233.05. Note that this adjusted balance agrees with the adjusted bank statement balance on the bank reconciliation (see item 4). Thus, all differences between the two balances have been explained.

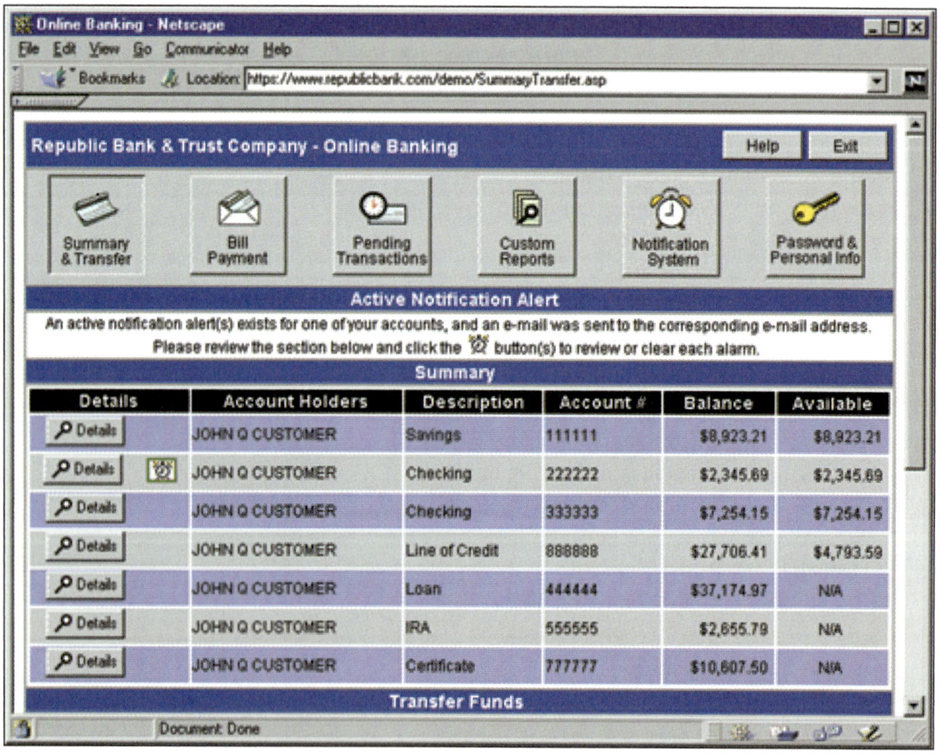

With the popularity of online banking, customers can now access all the account information they need to pay bills and keep their accounts in balance. Some banks offer software that allows the user to pay bills electronically and reconcile their accounts as often as they wish—not once a month as with mailed statements.

The Bank Reconciliation and the Need for Adjustments to the Records

After it completes the bank reconciliation, Weber must prepare a number of adjustments to its records. In fact, all of the information for these adjustments will be from one section of the bank reconciliation. Do you think that the additions and deductions made to the bank balance or the ones made to the book balance are the basis for the adjustments? It is logical that the additions and deductions to the Cash account *on the books* should be the basis for the adjustments because these are items that Weber was unaware of before receiving the bank statement. Conversely, the additions and deductions to the bank's balance, that is, the deposits in transit and the outstanding checks, are items that Weber has already recorded on its books.

The first journal entry recognizes the bank's collection of customer's note, with interest:

June 30	Cash	550.00	
	Notes Receivable		500.00
	Interest Revenue		50.00
	To record the collection of note and interest.		

Assets	=	Liabilities	+	Owners' Equity
+550				+50
−500				

The next entry is needed to record interest earned and paid by the bank on the average daily balance maintained in the checking account during June:

June 30	Cash	15.45	
	Interest Revenue		15.45
	To record interest earned on checking account.		

Assets	=	Liabilities	+	Owners' Equity
+15.45				+15.45

Recall the error in recording check 498: it was actually written for $417.25, the amount paid by the bank. Weber recorded the cash disbursement on its books as $471.25, however. If we assume that the purpose of the cash payment was to buy supplies, the Cash account is understated and the Supplies account is overstated by the amount of the error. The entry needed to correct both accounts is as follows:

June 30	Cash	54.00	
	Supplies		54.00
	To correct for error in recording purchase of supplies.		

Assets	=	Liabilities	+	Owners' Equity
+54				
−54				

The customer's NSF check is handled by reducing the Cash account and reinstating the Account Receivable:

June 30	Accounts Receivable	245.72	
	Cash		245.72
	To record customer's NSF check.		

Assets	=	Liabilities	+	Owners' Equity
+245.72				
−245.72				

Finally, two entries are needed to recognize the expenses incurred in connection with the fees charged by the bank for collecting the customer's note and for renting the lockbox:

June 30	Collection Fee Expense	16.50	
	Cash		16.50
	To record collection fee on note.		

Assets	=	Liabilities	+	Owners' Equity
−16.50				−16.50

June 30	Rent Expense—Lockbox	20.00	
	Cash		20.00
	To record rental charge on lockbox.		

Assets	=	Liabilities	+	Owners' Equity
−20				−20

Note that we made a separate entry to record each of the increases and decreases in the Cash account. Some companies combine all of the increases in Cash in a single journal entry and all of the decreases in a second entry. Finally, we should note that supervisory review and approval should take place before any of these entries are posted.

Establishing a Petty Cash Fund

PETTY CASH FUND
Money kept on hand for making minor disbursements in coin and currency rather than by writing checks.

Recall one of the fundamental rules in controlling cash: all disbursements should be made by check. Most businesses make an exception to this rule in the case of minor expenditures, for which they use a **petty cash fund.** This fund consists of coin and currency kept on hand to make minor disbursements. The necessary steps in setting up and maintaining a petty cash fund follow:

1. A check is written for a lump-sum amount, such as $100 or $500. The check is cashed, and the coin and currency are entrusted to a petty cash custodian.
2. A journal entry is made to record the establishment of the fund.
3. Upon presentation of the necessary documentation, employees receive minor disbursements from the fund. In essence, cash is traded from the fund in exchange for a receipt.
4. Periodically, the fund is replenished by writing and cashing a check in the amount necessary to bring the fund back to its original balance.
5. At the time the fund is replenished, an adjustment is made both to record its replenishment and to recognize the various expenses incurred.

The use of this fund is normally warranted on the basis of cost versus benefits. That is, the benefits in time saved in making minor disbursements from cash are thought to outweigh the cost associated with the risk of loss from decreased control over cash disbursements. The fund also serves a practical purpose for certain expenditures such as taxi fares and messengers which often must be paid in cash.

An Example of a Petty Cash Fund

Assume that on March 1, the treasurer of Keese Corporation cashes a check for $200 and remits the cash to the newly appointed petty cash custodian. On this date, the following journal entry is made:

Mar. 1	Petty Cash Fund	200.00	
	Cash		200.00
	To record establishment of petty cash fund.		

Assets	=	Liabilities	+	Owners' Equity
+200				
−200				

During March the custodian disburses coin and currency to various individuals who present receipts to the custodian for the following:

U.S. Post Office	$ 55.00
Overnight Delivery Service	69.50
Office Supply Express	45.30
Total expenditures	$169.80

Accounting for Your Decisions

You Are the Sorority Treasurer

You are in charge of the sorority's checking account and bank reconciliation. Each month, you are responsible for purchasing supplies, paying for parties, and paying rent and utilities on the sorority house. You also have a card for an automatic teller machine, which you use to draw out cash to pay for miscellaneous activities. Recently, the president of the sorority asked to see you because the sorority's expenses were exceeding revenues by a significant margin. After examining the checkbook and bank reconciliation, she wanted to know why you were spending roughly $200 per month in cash from an ATM. You told her that since there was no cancelled check for these expenditures, you had no record and couldn't answer her question. How could you have avoided this situation?

ANS: First, an important principle of internal control is that the person writing checks on an account should not be the same person who performs the bank reconciliation. Second, an ATM card confers special responsibilities on the user. Because there is no cancelled check, the person receiving cash from an ATM must document all expenses, obtaining receipts whenever possible or documenting the expenditures in a diary.

At the end of March, the custodian counts the coin and currency on hand and determines the balance to be $26.50. Next, the treasurer writes and cashes a check in the amount of $173.50, which is the amount needed to return the balance in the account to $200.00. The treasurer remits the cash to the custodian. The following entry is made:

Mar. 31	Postage Expense	55.00	
	Delivery Expense	69.50	
	Office Expense	45.30	
	Cash Over and Short	3.70	
	Cash		173.50
	To record replenishment of petty cash fund.		

Assets	=	Liabilities	+	Owners' Equity
−173.50				−55.00
				−69.50
				−45.30
				−3.70

The Cash Over and Short account is necessary because the total expenditures for the month were only $169.80 but a check in the amount of $173.50 was necessary to restore the fund balance to $200.00. The discrepancy of $3.70 could be due to any number of factors, such as an error in making change. Any large discrepancies would be investigated, particularly if they recur. Assuming that the discrepancy is immaterial, a debit balance in the Cash Over and Short account is normally closed to Miscellaneous Expense. A credit balance in the account is closed to Other Income.

Accounting for Investments

LO 3 Understand the accounting for various types of investments companies make.

The investments that companies make take a variety of forms and are made for various reasons. Some corporations find themselves with excess cash during certain times of the year and invest this idle cash in various highly liquid financial instruments, such as certificates of deposit and money market funds. Earlier in the chapter it was pointed out that

Name: Barbara Genualdi
Education: A.A.S., Triton College
Major: Nuclear Medicine Technology
Occupation: Owner, The Little Chill, Tucson, Arizona
Age: 39

FOCUS ON USERS

"After a day of work, I deposit the cash I've received. . . ."
–Barbara Genualdi

Cash Is the Lifeblood of This Entrepreneur

Barbara Genualdi runs a small business called The Little Chill, selling frozen beverages directly to consumers from two mobile carts at sporting events and concerts in Tucson. Each of her carts has two granita machines, and each machine has two heads, so Barbara can whip up eight different drink flavors at a time. Because The Little Chill is a coin and currency business, Barbara's cash-management skills are critical to her ability to turn a profit each quarter.

The relationship of cash to inventory is one that Barbara needs to keep very close tabs on. When cash comes in, inventory goes down. When inventory is purchased, cash flows out. Striking a balance between these economic events is what will ensure her a profit. As Barbara explains: "After a day of work, I deposit the cash I've received. Out of that, I will usually need to pay out a percentage to the venue and to payroll, and set tax money aside. Then, I can use a portion of the remaining cash to replenish inventory." With this cycle in mind, Barbara can make certain assumptions that her net cash will continue at a relatively stable level. In fact, this kind of predictability is one of the advantages of operating a cash-only business. As Barbara describes it, "It's a what-you-see, what-you-get situation."

these investments are included with cash and are called cash equivalents if they have an original maturity to the investor of three months or less. Otherwise they are accounted for as short-term investments.

In addition to investments in highly liquid financial instruments, some companies invest in the stocks and bonds of other corporations, as well as bonds issued by various government agencies. Securities issued by corporations as a form of ownership in the business, such as common stock and preferred stock, are called **equity securities.** Because these securities are a form of ownership, they do not have a maturity date. As we will see later, investments in equity securities can be classified as either current or long term, depending on the company's intent. Alternatively, bonds issued by corporations and governmental bodies as a form of borrowing are called **debt securities.** The term of a bond can be relatively short, such as 5 years, or much longer, such as 20 or 30 years. Regardless of the term, classification as a current or noncurrent asset by the investor depends on whether it plans to sell the debt securities within the next year.

EQUITY SECURITIES Securities issued by corporations as a form of ownership in the business.

DEBT SECURITIES Bonds issued by corporations and governmental bodies as a form of borrowing.

INVESTMENTS IN HIGHLY LIQUID FINANCIAL INSTRUMENTS

We now turn our attention to the appropriate accounting for these various types of investments. We begin by considering the accounting for highly liquid financial instruments such as certificates of deposit and then turn to the accounting for investments in the stocks and bonds of other companies.

INVESTING IDLE CASH

The seasonal nature of most businesses leads to the potential for a shortage of cash during certain times of the year and an excess of cash during other times. Companies typically deal with *cash shortages* by borrowing on a short-term basis, either from a bank in the form of notes or from other entities in the form of commercial paper. The maturities of the bank notes or the commercial paper generally range anywhere from 30 days to six months.

To highlight the need to deal with *excess cash* during certain times of the year, consider as an example the seasonal nature of the ice-cream business. Ben & Jerry's 1998 annual report admits the obvious by stating, "The company typically experiences more demand for its products during the summer than during the winter." A footnote from the same report highlights the seasonality of the business (amounts are in thousands of dollars):

www.benjerry.com

	First Quarter	Second Quarter	Third Quarter	Fourth Quarter
Net sales	$41,556	$58,749	$64,566	$44,332

Because sales in the second and third quarters of the year are higher than in the first and fourth quarters, it is natural that Ben & Jerry's had excess cash to invest at the end of the summer selling season. The company uses various financial instruments as a way to invest excess cash during the slower winter months, before using those funds to build up inventory during the busier summer months. We will present the accounting for the most common type of highly liquid financial instrument, a certificate of deposit.

Accounting for an Investment in a Certificate of Deposit (CD)

Assume that on October 2, 2001, Ben & Jerry's invests $100,000 of excess cash in a 120-day certificate of deposit. The CD matures on January 30, 2002, at which time Ben & Jerry's receives the $100,000 invested and interest at an annual rate of 6%. The entry to record the purchase of the CD is as follows:

2001			
Oct. 2	Short-Term Investments—CD	100,000	
	Cash		100,000
	To record purchase of 6%, 120-day CD.		

Assets	=	Liabilities	+	Owners' Equity
+100,000				
−100,000				

Assuming December 31 is the end of Ben & Jerry's fiscal year, an entry is needed on this date to record interest earned during 2001, even though no cash will be received until the CD matures in 2002:

2001			
Dec. 31	Interest Receivable	1,500	
	Interest Revenue		1,500
	To record interest earned: $100,000 × .06 × 90/360.		

Assets	=	Liabilities	+	Owners' Equity
+1,500				+1,500

The basic formula to compute interest is as follows:

$$\text{Interest } (I) = \text{Principal } (P) \times \text{Interest Rate } (R) \times \text{Time } (T)$$

Because interest rates are normally stated on an annual basis, time is interpreted to mean the fraction of a year that the investment is outstanding. The amount of interest is based on the principal or amount invested ($100,000), times the rate of interest (6%), times the fraction of a year the CD was outstanding in 2001 (29 days in October + 30 days in November + 31 days in December = 90 days). To simplify calculations, it is easiest to assume 360 days in a year in computing interest. With the availability of computers to do the work, however, most businesses now use 365 days in a year to calculate interest. Throughout this book, we assume 360 days in a year to allow us to focus on concepts rather than detailed calculations. Thus, in our example, the fraction of a year that the CD is outstanding during 2001 is 90/360.

The entry on January 30 to record the receipt of the principal amount of the CD of $100,000 and interest for 120 days is as follows:

2002			
Jan. 30	Cash	102,000	
	Short-Term Investments—CD		100,000
	Interest Receivable		1,500
	Interest Revenue		500
	To record the maturity of $100,000 CD.		

Assets	=	Liabilities	+	Owners' Equity
+102,000				+500
−100,000				
−1,500				

This combination journal entry results in the removal of both the CD and the interest receivable from the records and the recognition of $500 in interest earned during the first 30 days of 2002: $\$100{,}000 \times .06 \times 30/360 = \$500$.

We now turn to situations in which companies invest in the stocks and bonds of other companies.

Investments in Stocks and Bonds

Corporations frequently invest in the securities of other businesses. These investments take two forms: debt securities and equity securities.

Corporations have varying motivations for investing in the stocks and bonds of other companies. We will refer to the company that invests as the *investor* and the company whose stocks or bonds are purchased as the *investee*. In addition to buying certificates of deposit and other financial instruments, companies invest excess funds in stocks and bonds over the short run. The seasonality of certain businesses may result in otherwise idle cash being available during certain times of the year. In other cases, stocks and bonds are purchased as a way to invest cash over the long run. Often these types of investments are made in anticipation of a need for cash at some distant point in the future. For example, a company may invest today in a combination of stocks and bonds because it will need cash 10 years from today to build a new plant. The investor may be primarily interested in periodic income in the form of interest and dividends, in appreciation in the value of the securities, or in some combination of the two.

Sometimes shares of stock in another company are bought with a different purpose in mind. If a company buys a relatively large percentage of the common stock of the investee, it may be able to secure significant influence over the policies of this company. For example, a company may buy 30% of the common stock of a supplier of its raw materials to ensure a steady source of inventory. When an investor is able to secure influence over the investee, the *equity method* of accounting is used. According to current accounting standards, this method is appropriate when an investor owns at least 20% of the common stock of the investee.

Finally, a corporation may buy stock in another company with the purpose of obtaining control over that other entity. Normally, this requires an investment in excess of 50% of the common stock of the investee. When an investor owns more than half the stock of another company, accountants normally prepare a set of *consolidated financial statements.* This involves combining the financial statements of the individual entities into a single set of statements. An investor with an interest of more than 50% in another company is called the *parent,* and the investee in these situations is called the *subsidiary.*

We will limit our discussion to how companies account for investments that do *not* give them any significant influence over the other company. (Accounting for investments in which there is either significant influence or control is covered in advanced accounting textbooks.) The following chart summarizes the accounting by an investor for investments in the common stock of another company:

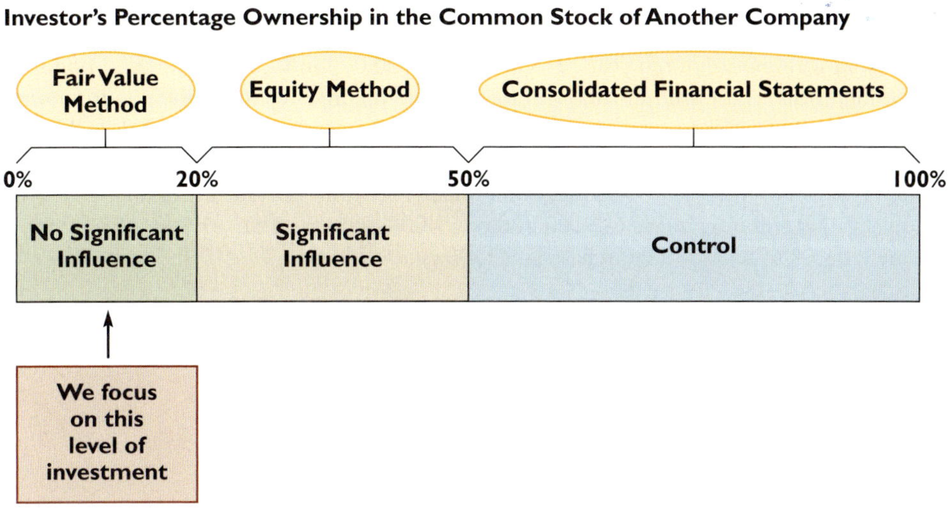

INVESTMENTS WITHOUT SIGNIFICANT INFLUENCE

Companies face a number of major issues in deciding how to account for and report on investments in the stocks and bonds of other companies:

1. What should be the basis for the recognition of periodic income from an investment? That is, what event causes income to be recognized?
2. How should an investment be valued and thus reported at the end of an accounting period? At original cost? At fair value?
3. How should an investment be classified on a balance sheet? As a current asset? As a noncurrent asset?

The answer to each of these questions depends on the type of investment. Accountants classify investments in the securities of other companies into one of three categories.[1]

Held-to-maturity securities are investments in the bonds of other companies when the investor has the positive intent and the ability to hold the securities to maturity. *Note that only bonds can qualify as held-to-maturity securities because shares of stock do not have a maturity date.*

Trading securities are stocks and bonds that are bought and held for the purpose of selling them in the near term. These securities are usually held for only a short period of time with the objective of generating profits on short-term appreciation in the market price of the stocks and bonds.

Available-for-sale securities are stocks and bonds that are not classified as either held-to-maturity or trading securities.

HELD-TO-MATURITY SECURITIES
Investments in bonds of other companies in which the investor has the positive intent and the ability to hold the securities to maturity.

TRADING SECURITIES
Stock and bonds of other companies bought and held for the purpose of selling them in the near term to generate profits on appreciation in their price.

AVAILABLE-FOR-SALE SECURITIES
Stocks and bonds that are not classified as either held-to-maturity or trading securities.

INVESTMENTS IN HELD-TO-MATURITY SECURITIES

By their nature, only bonds, not stock, can qualify as held-to-maturity securities. A bond is categorized as a held-to-maturity security if the investor plans to hold it until it matures. An investor may buy the bonds either on the original issuance date or later. If the investor buys them on the date they are originally issued, the purchase is from the issuer. It is also possible, however, for an investor to buy bonds on the *open market* after they have been outstanding for a period of time.

[1] *Statement of Financial Accounting Standards No. 115,* "Accounting for Certain Investments in Debt and Equity Securities" (Stamford, Conn.: Financial Accounting Standards Board, May 1993), par. 7–12.

Consider the following example. On January 1, 2001, Simpson issues $10,000,000 of bonds that will mature in ten years. Homer buys $100,000 in face value of these bonds at face value, which is the amount that will be repaid to the investor when the bonds mature. In many instances, bonds are purchased at an amount more or less than face value. We will limit our discussion, however, to the simpler case in which bonds are purchased for face value. The bonds pay 10% interest semiannually on June 30 and December 31. This means Homer will receive 5% of $100,000 or $5,000 on each of these dates. The entry on Homer's books to record the purchase is as follows:

2001			
Jan. 1	Investment in Bonds	100,000	
	Cash		100,000
	To record purchase of Simpson bonds.		

Assets	=	Liabilities	+	Owners' Equity
+100,000				
−100,000				

On June 30, Homer must record the receipt of semiannual interest. The entry on this date is as follows:

2001			
June 30	Cash	5,000	
	Interest Income		5,000
	To record interest income on Simpson bonds.		

Assets	=	Liabilities	+	Owners' Equity
+5,000				+5,000

Note that income was recognized when interest was received. If interest is not received at the end of an accounting period, a company should accrue interest earned but not yet received. Also note that an investment in held-to-maturity bonds is normally classified as a *noncurrent asset.* Any held-to-maturity bonds that are one year or less from maturity, however, are classified in the Current Assets section of a balance sheet.

Assume that before the maturity date, Homer needs cash and decides to sell the bonds. Keep in mind that this is a definite change in Homer's plans, since the bonds were initially categorized as held-to-maturity securities. Any difference between the proceeds received from the sale of the bonds and the amount paid for the bonds is recognized as either a gain or a loss.

Assume that on January 1, 2002, Homer sells all its Simpson bonds at 99. This means that the amount of cash received is .99 × $100,000, or $99,000. The entry on January 1, 2002, is as follows:

2002			
Jan. 1	Cash	99,000	
	Loss on Sale of Bonds	1,000	
	Investment in Bonds		100,000
	To record sale of Simpson bonds.		

Assets	=	Liabilities	+	Owners' Equity
+99,000				−1,000
−100,000				

The $1,000 loss on the sale of the bonds is the excess of the amount paid for the purchase of the bonds of $100,000 over the cash proceeds from the sale of $99,000. The loss is reported in the Other Income and Expenses Section on the 2002 income statement.

Investments in Trading Securities

A company invests in trading securities as a way to profit from increases in the market prices of these securities over the short term. Because the intent is to hold them for the short term, trading securities are classified as current assets. All trading securities are recorded initially at cost, including any brokerage fees, commissions, or other fees paid to acquire the shares. Assume that Dexter Corp. invests in the following securities on November 30, 2001:

Security	Cost
Stuart common stock	$50,000
Menlo preferred stock	25,000
Total cost	$75,000

The entry on Dexter's books on the date of purchase is as follows:

2001			
Nov. 30	Investment in Stuart Common Stock	50,000	
	Investment in Menlo Preferred Stock	25,000	
	Cash		75,000
	To record purchase of trading securities for cash.		

Assets	=	Liabilities	+	Owners' Equity
+50,000				
+25,000				
−75,000				

Many companies attempt to pay dividends every year as a signal of overall financial strength and profitability.[2] Assume that on December 10, 2001, Dexter received dividends of $1,000 from Stuart and $600 from Menlo. The dividends received from trading securities are recognized as income as shown in the following entry on Dexter's books:

2001			
Dec. 10	Cash	1,600	
	Dividend Income		1,600
	To record receipt of dividends on trading securities.		

Assets	=	Liabilities	+	Owners' Equity
+1,600				+1,600

Unlike interest on a bond or a note, dividends do not accrue over time. In fact, a company does not have a legal obligation to pay dividends until its board of directors declares them. Up to that point, the investor has no guarantee that dividends will ever be paid.

As noted earlier, trading securities are purchased with the intention of holding them for a short period of time. Assume that Dexter sells the Stuart stock on December 15, 2001, for $53,000. In this case, Dexter recognizes a gain for the excess of the cash proceeds, $53,000, over the amount recorded on the books, $50,000:

2001			
Dec. 15	Cash	53,000	
	Investment in Stuart Common Stock		50,000
	Gain on Sale of Stock		3,000
	To record sale of Stuart common stock.		

Assets	=	Liabilities	+	Owners' Equity
+53,000				+3,000
−50,000				

The gain is considered realized and is classified on the income statement as other income.

Assume that on December 22, 2001, Dexter replaces the Stuart stock in its portfolio by purchasing Canby common stock for $40,000. The entry on this date follows:

[2] IBM's March 2000 dividend of $.24 per share was the computer company's 340th consecutive quarterly dividend, an uninterrupted string of 85 years in which it paid dividends.

2001			
Dec. 22	Investment in Canby Common Stock	40,000	
	Cash		40,000
	To record purchase of trading securities for cash.		

Assets	=	Liabilities	+	Owners' Equity
+40,000				
−40,000				

Now assume that Dexter ends its accounting period on December 31. Should it adjust the carrying value of its investments to reflect their fair values on this date? According to the accounting profession, fair values should be used to report investments in trading securities on a balance sheet. The fair values are thought to be relevant information to the various users of financial statements. Assume the following information for Dexter on December 31, 2001:

Security	Total Cost	Total Fair Value on December 31, 2001	Gain (Loss)
Menlo preferred stock	$25,000	$27,500	$2,500
Canby common stock	40,000	39,000	(1,000)
Totals	$65,000	$66,500	$1,500

The entry on Dexter's books on this date follows:

2001			
Dec. 31	Investment in Menlo Preferred Stock	2,500	
	Investment in Canby Common Stock		1,000
	Unrealized Gain—Trading Securities (Income Statement)		1,500
	To adjust trading securities to fair value.		

Assets	=	Liabilities	+	Owners' Equity
+2,500				+1,500
−1,000				

Note that this entry results in each security being written up or down so that it will appear on the December 31 balance sheet at its market or fair value. This type of fair value accounting for trading securities is often referred to as a *mark-to-market* approach because at the end of each period, the value of each security is adjusted or marked to its current market value. Also, it is important to realize that for trading securities, the changes in value are recognized on the income statement. The difference of $1,500 between the original cost of the two securities, $65,000, and their fair value, $66,500, is recorded in the account Unrealized Gain—Trading Securities to call attention to the fact that the securities have not been sold. Even though the gain or loss is *unrealized,* it is recognized on the income statement as a form of other income or loss.

Assume one final transaction in our Dexter example. On January 20, 2002, Dexter sells the Menlo stock for $27,000. The entry on Dexter's books on this date follows:

2002			
Jan. 20	Loss on Sale of Stock (Income Statement)	500	
	Cash	27,000	
	Investment in Menlo Preferred Stock		27,500
	To record sale of Menlo preferred stock.		

Assets	=	Liabilities	+	Owners' Equity
+27,000				−500
−27,500				

The important point to note about this entry is that the $500 loss represents the difference between the cash proceeds of $27,000 and the *fair value of the stock at the most recent reporting date,* $27,500. Because the Menlo stock was adjusted to a fair value of $27,500 on December 31, the excess of this amount over the cash proceeds of $27,000 results in a loss of $500. Keep in mind that a gain of $2,500 was recognized last year when the stock was adjusted to its fair value at the end of the year.

INVESTMENTS IN AVAILABLE-FOR-SALE SECURITIES

Stocks and bonds that do not qualify as trading securities and bonds that are not intended to be held to maturity are categorized as available-for-sale securities. The accounting for these securities is similar to the accounting for trading securities, with one major exception: *even though fair value accounting is used to report available-for-sale securities at the end of an accounting period, any gains or losses resulting from marking to market are not reported on the income statement but instead are accumulated in a stockholders' equity account.* This inconsistency is justified by the accounting profession on the grounds that the inclusion in income of fluctuations in the value of securities that are available for sale but that are not necessarily being actively traded could lead to volatility in reported earnings. Regardless, reporting gains and losses on the income statement for one class of securities but not for others is a subject of considerable debate. Investments in available-for-sale securities may be classified as either current or noncurrent assets.

To understand the use of fair value accounting for available-for-sale securities, assume that Lenox Corp. purchases two different stocks late in 2001. The costs and fair values at the end of 2001 are as follows:

Security	Total Cost	Fair Value on December 31, 2001	Gain (Loss)
Adair preferred stock	$15,000	$16,000	$ 1,000
Casey common stock	35,000	32,500	(2,500)
Totals	$50,000	$48,500	$(1,500)

The entry on Lenox's books on this date is as follows:

		Debit	Credit
2001			
Dec. 31	Unrealized Gain/Loss—Available-for-Sale Securities (Stockholders' Equity)	1,500	
	Investment in Adair Preferred Stock	1,000	
	Investment in Casey Common Stock		2,500
	To adjust available-for-sale securities to fair value.		

Assets	=	Liabilities	+	Owners' Equity
+1,000				−1,500
−2,500				

Note the similarity between this entry and the one we made at the end of the period in the example for trading securities. In both instances, the individual investments are adjusted to their fair values for purposes of presenting them on the year-end balance sheet. The unrealized loss of $1,500 does not, however, affect income in this case. Instead, the loss is shown as a reduction of stockholders' equity on the balance sheet.

Now assume that Lenox sells its Casey stock for $34,500 on June 30, 2002. The entry on this date is as follows:

		Debit	Credit
2002			
June 30	Cash	34,500	
	Loss on Sale of Stock (Income Statement)	500	
	Investment in Casey Common Stock		32,500
	Unrealized Gain/Loss—Available-for-Sale Securities (Stockholders' Equity)		2,500
	To record sale of Casey common stock.		

Assets	=	Liabilities	+	Owners' Equity
+34,500				− 500
−32,500				+2,500

Lenox recognizes a loss on the income statement of $500, which represents the excess of the cost of the stock of $35,000 over the cash proceeds of $34,500. Note, however, that the Investment in Casey Common Stock is removed from the books at $32,500, the fair value at the end of the prior period. Thus, it is also necessary to adjust the Unrealized Gain/Loss account for $2,500, the difference between the original cost of $35,000 and the fair value at the end of 2001 of $32,500.

Finally, assume that Lenox does not buy any additional securities during the remainder of 2002 and that the fair value of the one investment it holds, the Adair preferred stock, is $19,000 on December 31, 2002. The entry to adjust the Adair stock to fair value on this date is as follows:

2002			
Dec. 31	Investment in Adair Preferred Stock	3,000	
	Unrealized Gain/Loss—Available-for-Sale Securities (Stockholders' Equity)		3,000
	To adjust available-for-sale securities to fair value.		

Assets	=	Liabilities	+	Owners' Equity
+3,000				+3,000

The increase in the Investment in Adair Preferred Stock account results in a balance of $19,000 in this account, the fair value of the stock. The stockholders' equity account now has a *credit* balance of $4,000, as reflected in the following T account:

UNREALIZED GAIN/LOSS—AVAILABLE-FOR-SALE SECURITIES

12/31/01 bal.	1,500		
		2,500	6/30/02 entry
		1,000	6/30/02 bal.
		3,000	12/31/02 entry
		4,000	12/31/02 bal.

From Concept TO PRACTICE 7.1

READING BEN & JERRY'S FOOTNOTES According to Footnote 2 in Ben & Jerry's 1998 annual report, how are its investments classified? In what types of securities does the company invest?

The balance of $4,000 in this account represents the excess of the $19,000 fair value of the one security now held over its original cost of $15,000.

SUMMARY OF ACCOUNTING AND REPORTING REQUIREMENTS

A summary of the accounting and reporting requirements for each of the three categories of investments is shown in Exhibit 7-4. Periodic income from each of these types of investments is recognized in the form of interest and dividends. Held-to-maturity bonds are reported on the balance sheet at *amortized cost* (see second footnote in Exhibit 7-4 below). Both trading securities and available-for-sale securities are reported on the balance sheet at fair value. Unrealized gains and losses from holding trading securities are recognized on the income

EXHIBIT 7-4 Accounting for Investments without Significant Influence

Categories	Types	Asset Classified on Balance Sheet as	Recognize as Income	Report on Balance Sheet at	Report Changes in Fair Value on
Held-to-maturity	Bonds	Noncurrent*	Interest	Cost†	Not applicable
Trading	Bonds, stock	Current	Interest, dividends	Fair value	Income statement
Available-for-sale	Bonds, stock	Current or noncurrent	Interest, dividends	Fair value	Balance sheet (in stockholders' equity)

*Reclassified as current if they mature within one year of the balance sheet date.

†As mentioned earlier, bonds are often purchased at an amount more or less than face value. When this is the case, the bond account must be adjusted periodically and the asset is reported on the balance sheet at amortized cost.

Business Strategy

A big change took place in Pepsi-Cola's market in 1998: its biggest customers, grocery stores, began to merge at an increasing rate. The result was fewer, bigger chains of retail grocers spread out over much larger geographic regions than a few years earlier. Parent company PepsiCo. believed that the change would fundamentally alter Pepsi Cola's bottling business, making size the most important factor in achieving both economies of scale (decreases in cost that result from high volume of production) and the high level of service that the new chains demanded.

So, the company set out to restructure its bottling business, consolidating volume among a few large "anchor bottlers" that are closely aligned with PepsiCo. and that focus solely on manufacturing, selling, and distributing. For its company-owned bottling operations, it created a separate Pepsi Bottling Group, which would handle more than $7 billion in sales—more than half its North American business. And it initiated a plan to form a new and larger bottling company in combination with the largest independent U.S. Pepsi bottler, Whitman Corporation. If its best customers, the retail grocery chains, believe that bigger is better, PepsiCo. wants them to know that *it* does too.

SOURCE: PepsiCo.'s 1998 annual report.

statement, whereas these same gains and losses for available-for-sale securities are accumulated in a stockholders' equity account.

The Controversy over Fair Value Accounting

Only recently have accounting standards changed to require that certain investments be reported at fair value. Before the change, the lower-of-cost-or-market rule was followed when accounting for these investments. The use of market or fair values is clearly an exception to the cost principle as first introduced in Chapter 1. Whether the exception is justified has been, and will continue to be, a matter of debate.

One concern of financial statement users is the hybrid system now used to report assets on a balance sheet. Consider the following types of assets and how we report them on the balance sheet:

Asset	Reported on the Balance Sheet at
Inventories	Lower of cost or market
Investments	Either cost or fair value
Property, plant, and equipment	Original cost, less accumulated depreciation

It is difficult to justify so many different valuation methods to report the assets of a single company. Recall that the lower-of-cost-or-market approach to valuing inventory is based on conservatism. Why should it be used for inventories while fair value is used for investments? Proponents of fair values believe that the information provided to the reader of the statements is more relevant, and they argue that the subjectivity inherent in valuing other types of assets is not an issue when dealing with securities that have a ready market. The controversy surrounding the valuation of assets on a balance sheet is likely to continue.

Two-Minute Review

1. What are the three categories of investments?

2. Two of the three categories of investments can contain either stocks or bonds. Which one of the three can only contain bonds? Explain your answer.

3. What is the one major distinction between the reporting requirements for trading securities and those for available-for-sale securities?

Answers on next page.

Answers:

1. Held-to-maturity, trading, and available-for-sale.

2. Bonds are the only securities that can be held to maturity. Stocks do not have a maturity date.

3. Any changes in fair value of trading securities are reported on the income statement. Changes in fair value of available-for-sale securities are reported in stockholders' equity on the balance sheet.

ACCOUNTS RECEIVABLE

LO 4 Understand how to account for accounts receivable, including bad debts.

www.sears.com

To appreciate the significance of credit sales for many businesses, consider the case of Sears, Roebuck & Co. Sears operates retail outlets throughout the United States and around the world. The balance sheet of Sears reported total assets of approximately $38 billion at the end of 1998. Of this total amount, credit card receivables accounted for almost $19 billion, or 50%, of total assets. Sears or any other company would rather not sell on credit but would prefer to make all sales for cash. Selling on credit causes two problems: it slows down the inflow of cash to the company, and it raises the possibility that the customer may not pay its bill on time or possibly ever. To remain competitive, however, Sears and most other businesses must sell their products and services on credit. Large retailers such as Sears often extend credit through the use of their own credit cards.

www.pepsico.com

The types of receivables reported on a corporate balance sheet depend to some extent on a company's business. The "credit card receivables" on the balance sheet of Sears represent the interest-bearing accounts it carries with its retail customers. Alternatively, consider the case of PepsiCo. The beverage and snack-food businesses usually sell their products to distributors. The asset resulting from a sale by Pepsi on credit, with an oral promise that the customer will pay within a specified period of time, is called an account receivable. This type of account does not bear interest and often gives the customer a discount for early payment. For example, the terms of sale might be 2/10, net 30, which means the customer can deduct 2% from the amount due if the bill is paid within 10 days of the date of sale; otherwise, payment in full is required within 30 days. In some instances, PepsiCo requires from a customer at the time of sale a written promise in the form of a promissory note. The asset resulting from a sale on credit, with a written promise that the customer will pay within a specified period of time, is called a note receivable. This type of account usually bears interest.

Delivering such products as Pepsi's Frappuccino drink to retail stores on account creates large receivables for PepsiCo. Indeed, receivables are a large and important part of the asset side of balance sheets of many companies.

THE USE OF A SUBSIDIARY LEDGER

As mentioned earlier, PepsiCo sells its beverages and snack foods through distributors. Assume that it sells $25,000 of Fritos to ABC Distributors on an open account. The journal entry to record the sale would be as follows:

Accounts Receivable	25,000	
Sales Revenue		25,000
To record sale on open account.		

Assets	=	Liabilities	+	Owners' Equity
+25,000				+25,000

SUBSIDIARY LEDGER The detail for a number of individual items that collectively make up a single general ledger account.

CONTROL ACCOUNT The general ledger account that is supported by a subsidiary ledger.

It is important for control purposes that PepsiCo keeps a record of *whom* the sale was to and includes this amount on a periodic statement or *bill* sent to the customer. What if a company has a hundred or a thousand different customers? Some mechanism is needed to track the balance owed by each of these customers. The mechanism companies use is called a **subsidiary ledger.**

A subsidiary ledger contains the necessary detail on each of a number of items that collectively make up a single general ledger account, called the **control account.** In theory, any one of the accounts in the general ledger could be supported by a subsidiary ledger. In addition to

Accounts Receivable, two other common accounts supported by subsidiary ledgers are Plant and Equipment and Accounts Payable. An accounts payable subsidiary ledger contains a separate account for each of the suppliers or vendors from which a company purchases inventory. A plant and equipment subsidiary ledger consists of individual accounts, along with their balances, for each of the various long-term tangible assets the company owns.

It is important to understand that a subsidiary ledger does *not* take the place of the control account in the general ledger. Instead, at any point in time, the balances of the accounts that make up the subsidiary ledger should total to the single balance in the related control account. In the remainder of this chapter we will illustrate the use of only the control account. Whenever a specific customer's account is increased or decreased we will, however, note the name of the customer next to the control account in the journal entry.

The risk acct. is shown a allowance for doubtful Accts. – (RISK) – you may not be able to collect entire principle.

THE VALUATION OF ACCOUNTS RECEIVABLE – Recorded @ cost

The following presentation of receivables is taken from PepsiCo's 1998 annual report:

	1998	1997
Accounts and notes receivable, less allowance: \$127 in 1998 and \$125 in 1997	\$2,453	\$2,150

– Subsidiary ledger – lists each customer individually

– How do we estimate Allowance for doubtful accts?
- by how the customer has acted with their acct. ie. if they have been paying on time.
- Add up actual credit sales over a period of yrs., then add up actual bad debt over the years. Divide the total credit sales by the bad debt to get a percent. Then the next yr. will record their actual sales, then take the % that we came up w/ of the actual sales + that is that yr's. bad debt amt.
- Aging (see pg. 340)

As you read this excerpt from the balance sheets, keep three points in mind. First, all amounts are stated in millions of dollars. Second, these are the balances at the *end* of each of the two years. Finally, note that PepsiCo combines its accounts receivable and notes receivable on the balance sheet. Apparently, the company sells its products to some customers on an open account while other customers are required to sign a note to repay the amount of products purchased on credit.

PepsiCo does not sell its products to distributors under the assumption that any particular customer will *not* pay its bill. In fact, the credit department of a business is responsible for performing a credit check on all potential customers before they are granted credit. Management of PepsiCo is not naive enough, however, to believe that all customers will be able to pay their accounts when due. This would be the case only if (1) all customers are completely trustworthy and (2) customers never experience unforeseen financial difficulties that make it impossible to pay on time.

The reduction in PepsiCo's receivables for an allowance is the way in which most companies deal with bad debts in their accounting records. Bad debts are unpaid customer accounts that a company gives up trying to collect. Some companies describe the allowance more fully as the allowance for doubtful accounts, and others call it the allowance for

ACCOUNTING FOR YOUR DECISIONS

You Are the Credit Manager

You are the credit manager of USA Department Store, which offers its customers USA Department Store credit cards. An existing customer, Jane Doe, has requested a credit line increase. In processing her request, you must determine the current balance of her account. How would you use the accounting system to find her current balance? What other factors might you consider in granting Jane's request?

ANS: You would find Jane's current balance by looking for her account in the accounts receivable subsidiary ledger. The subsidiary ledger should have a current balance because daily postings are made to each customer's account. Other factors to consider in processing Jane's request can include researching her payment history to see if she paid on time not only for this credit card but for all debts, checking to see if her income is sufficient to cover her existing debt and the new credit line increase, and verifying employment to ensure income stability.

☆ See gateway ex. - pg. 26

uncollectible accounts. Using the end of 1998 as an example, PepsiCo believes that the *net recoverable amount* of its receivables is $2,453 million, even though the *gross* amount of receivables is $127 million higher than this amount. The company has reduced the gross receivables for an amount that it believes is necessary to reflect the asset on the books at the *net recoverable amount* or *net realizable value.* We now take a closer look at how a company accounts for bad debts.

Two Methods to Account for Bad Debts

Assume that Roberts Corp. makes a $500 sale to Dexter Inc. on November 10, 2001, with credit terms of 2/10, net 60. Roberts makes the following entry on its books on this date:

2001			
Nov. 10	Accounts Receivable—Dexter	500	
	Sales Revenue		500
	To record sale on credit, terms of 2/10, net 60.		

Assets	=	Liabilities	+	Owners' Equity
+500				+500

Assume further that Dexter not only misses taking advantage of the discount for early payment but also is unable to pay within 60 days. After pursuing the account for four months into 2002, the credit department of Roberts informs the accounting department that it has given up on collecting the $500 from Dexter and advises that the account should be written off. To do so, the accounting department makes the following entry:

2002			
May 1	Bad Debts Expense	500	
	Accounts Receivable—Dexter		500
	To write off Dexter account.		

Assets	=	Liabilities	+	Owners' Equity
−500				−500

Direct write-off method The recognition of bad debts expense at the point an account is written off as uncollectible.

This approach to accounting for bad debts is called the **direct write-off method.** Do you see any problems with its use? What about Roberts's balance sheet at the end of 2001? By ignoring the possibility that not all of its outstanding accounts receivable will be collected, Roberts is overstating the value of this asset at December 31, 2001. Also, what about the income statement for 2001? By ignoring the possibility of bad debts on sales made during 2001, Roberts has violated the *matching principle.* This principle requires that all costs associated with making sales in a period should be matched with the sales of that period. Roberts has overstated net income for 2001 by ignoring bad debts as an expense. The problem is one of *timing:* even though any one particular account may not prove to be uncollectible until a later period (e.g., the Dexter account), the cost associated with making sales on credit (bad debts) should be recognized in the period of sale.

Allowance method A method of estimating bad debts on the basis of either the net credit sales of the period or the accounts receivable at the end of the period.

Study Tip

Note the similarities between the Allowance for Doubtful Accounts contra account and another contra account, Accumulated Depreciation. Both are used to reduce an asset account to a lower carrying or book value.

Accountants use the **allowance method** to overcome the deficiencies of the direct write-off method. They *estimate* the amount of bad debts before these debts actually occur. For example, assume that Roberts's total sales during 2001 amount to $600,000 and that at the end of the year the outstanding accounts receivable total $250,000. Also assume that Roberts estimates that on the basis of past experience, 1% of the sales of the period, or $6,000, eventually will prove to be uncollectible. Under the allowance method, Roberts makes the following adjusting entry at the end of 2001:

2001			
Dec. 31	Bad Debts Expense	6,000	
	Allowance for Doubtful Accounts		6,000
	To record estimated bad debts for the year.		

Assets	=	Liabilities	+	Owners' Equity
−6,000				−6,000

The debit recognizes the cost associated with the reduction in value of the asset Accounts Receivable. The cost is charged to the income statement, in the form of Bad Debts Expense. A contra-asset account is used to reduce the asset to its net realizable value. This is accomplished by crediting an allowance account, Allowance for Doubtful Accounts. Roberts presents accounts receivable as follows on its December 31, 2001, balance sheet:

Accounts receivable	$250,000
Less: Allowance for doubtful accounts	(6,000)
Net accounts receivable	$244,000

An alternative would be for Roberts to follow the form used by PepsiCo, described earlier in the chapter:

Accounts receivable, less allowance for doubtful accounts of $6,000:	$244,000

From Concept **TO PRACTICE 7.2**

READING PEPSICO'S FINANCIAL STATEMENTS Refer to the chapter opener for the presentation of PepsiCo's accounts and notes receivable on its 1998 and 1997 year-end balance sheets. What was the amount of increase or decrease in the allowance account? What does the change in the account mean?

WRITE-OFFS OF UNCOLLECTIBLE ACCOUNTS WITH THE ALLOWANCE METHOD

Like the direct write-off method, the allowance method reduces Accounts Receivable to write off a specific customer's account. If the account receivable no longer exists, there is no need for the related allowance account and thus this account is reduced as well. For example, assume, as we did earlier, that Dexter's $500 account is written off on May 1, 2002. Under the allowance method, the following entry is recorded:

2002			
May 1	Allowance for Doubtful Accounts	500	
	Accounts Receivable—Dexter		500
	To record the write-off of Dexter account.		

Assets	=	Liabilities	+	Owners' Equity
+500				
−500				

To summarize, whether the direct write-off method or the allowance method is used, the entry to write off a specific customer's account reduces Accounts Receivable. It is the debit that differs between the two methods: under the direct write-off method, an *expense* is increased; under the allowance method, the *allowance* account is reduced.

TWO APPROACHES TO THE ALLOWANCE METHOD OF ACCOUNTING FOR BAD DEBTS

Because the allowance method results in a better *matching,* accounting standards require the use of this method rather than the direct write-off method unless bad debts are immaterial in amount. Accountants use one of two different variations of the allowance method to estimate bad debts. One approach emphasizes matching bad debts expense with revenue on the income statement and bases bad debts on a percentage of the sales of the period. This was the method we illustrated earlier for Roberts Corp. The other approach emphasizes the net realizable amount (value) of accounts receivable on the balance sheet and bases bad debts on a percentage of the accounts receivable balance at the end of the period.

Percentage of Net Credit Sales Approach If a company has been in business for enough years, it may be able to use the past relationship between bad debts and *net* credit sales to predict bad debt amounts. *Net* means that credit sales have been adjusted for sales discounts and returns and allowances. Assume that the accounting records for Bosco Corp. reveal the following:

Year	Net Credit Sales	Bad Debts
1996	$1,250,000	$ 26,400
1997	1,340,000	29,350
1998	1,200,000	23,100
1999	1,650,000	32,150
2000	2,120,000	42,700
	$7,560,000	$153,700

Although the exact percentage varied slightly over the five-year period, the average percentage of bad debts to net credit sales is very close to 2% ($153,700/$7,560,000 = .02033). Bosco needs to determine whether this estimate is realistic for the current period. For example, are current economic conditions considerably different from those in the prior years? Has the company made sales to any new customers with significantly different credit terms? If the answers to these types of questions are yes, Bosco should consider adjusting the 2% experience rate to estimate future bad debts. Otherwise, it should proceed with this estimate. Assuming that it uses the 2% rate and that its net credit sales during 2001 are $2,340,000, Bosco makes the following entry:

2001			
Dec. 31	Bad Debts Expense	46,800	
	Allowance for Doubtful Accounts		46,800
	To record estimated bad debts: .02 × $2,340,000.		

Assets	=	Liabilities	+	Owners' Equity
−46,800				−46,800

Thus, Bosco matches bad debt expense of $46,800 with sales revenue of $2,340,000.

Percentage of Accounts Receivable Approach Some companies believe they can more accurately estimate bad debts by relating them to the balance in the Accounts Receivable account at the end of the period rather than to the sales of the period. The objective with both approaches is the same, however: to use past experience with bad debts to predict future amounts. Assume that the records for Cougar Corp. reveal the following:

Year	Balance in Accounts Receivable December 31	Bad Debts
1996	$ 650,000	$ 5,250
1997	785,000	6,230
1998	854,000	6,950
1999	824,000	6,450
2000	925,000	7,450
	$4,038,000	$32,330

Accounting for Your Decisions

You Are the Owner

Assume you own a retail business that offers credit sales. To estimate bad debts, your business uses the percentage of net credit sales approach. For the new fiscal year, how would you decide what percentage to use to estimate your bad debts?

ANS: To determine the bad debt percentage for the new fiscal year, you can (1) review historical records to see what the actual percentages of bad debts were, (2) check to see if credit policies have substantially changed, (3) consider current and future economic conditions, and (4) consult with your managers and salespeople to see if they are aware of any changes in customers' paying habits.

The ratio of bad debts to the ending balance in Accounts Receivable over the past five years is $32,330/$4,038,000, or approximately .008 (.8%). Assuming balances in Accounts Receivable and the Allowance for Doubtful Accounts on December 31, 2001, of $865,000 (debit) and $2,100, (credit), respectively, Cougar records the following entry:

2001			
Dec. 31	Bad Debts Expense	4,820	
	Allowance for Doubtful Accounts		4,820
	To record estimated bad debts:		

Credit balance required in allowance account after adjustment ($865,000 × 0.8%)	$6,920
Less: Credit balance in allowance account before adjustment	2,100
Amount for bad debt expense entry	$4,820

Assets	=	Liabilities	+	Owners' Equity
−4,820				−4,820

Note the one major difference between this approach and the percentage of sales approach: *under the percentage of net credit sales approach, the balance in the allowance account is ignored, and the bad debts expense is simply a percentage of the sales of the period; under the percentage of accounts receivable approach, however, the balance in the allowance account must be considered.* A T account for Allowance for Doubtful Accounts with the balance before and after adjustment appears as follows:

ALLOWANCE FOR DOUBTFUL ACCOUNTS

Debit	Credit	
	2,100	Bal. before adjustment
	4,820	Adjusting entry
	6,920	Bal. after adjustment

In other words, making an adjustment for $4,820 results in a balance in the account of $6,920, which is .8% of the Accounts Receivable balance of $865,000. The net realizable value of Accounts Receivable is determined as follows:

Accounts receivable	$865,000
Less: Allowance for doubtful accounts	(6,920)
Net realizable value	$858,080

Aging of Accounts Receivable Some companies use a variation of the percentage of accounts receivable approach to estimate bad debts. This variation is actually a refinement of the approach because it considers the length of time that the receivables have been outstanding. It stands to reason that the older an account receivable is, the less likely it is to be collected. An **aging schedule** categorizes the various accounts by length of time outstanding. An example of an aging schedule is shown in Exhibit 7-5. We assume that the company's policy is to allow 30 days for payment of an outstanding account. After that time, the account is past due. An alphabetical list of customers appears in the first column, with the balance in each account shown in the appropriate column to the right. The dotted lines after A. Matt's account indicate that many more accounts appear in the records; we have included just a few to show the format of the schedule. The totals on the aging schedule are used as the basis for estimating bad debts, as shown in Exhibit 7-6.

AGING SCHEDULE
A form used to categorize the various individual accounts receivable according to the length of time each has been outstanding.

Note that the estimated percentage of uncollectibles increases as the period of time the accounts have been outstanding lengthens. If we assume that the Allowance for Doubtful Accounts has a credit balance of $1,230 before adjustment, the adjusting entry is as follows:

EXHIBIT 7-5 Aging Schedule

	Number of Days Past Due				
Customer	**Current**	**1–30**	**31–60**	**61–90**	**Over 90**
L. Ash	$ 4,400				
B. Budd	3,200				
C. Cox		$ 6,500			
E. Fudd					$6,300
G. Hoff			$ 900		
A. Matt	5,500				
......					
......					
......					
T. West				$ 3,100	
M. Young				4,200	
Totals*	$85,600	$31,200	$24,500	$18,000	$9,200

*Only a few of the customer accounts are illustrated; thus the column totals are higher than the amounts for the accounts illustrated.

2001				
Dec. 31	Bad Debts Expense		13,324	
	Allowance for Doubtful Accounts			13,324
	To record estimated bad debts:			
	Credit balance required in allowance account after adjustment	$14,554		
	Less: Credit balance in allowance account before adjustment	1,230		
	Amount for bad debt expense entry	$13,324		

Assets	=	Liabilities	+	Owners' Equity
−13,324				−13,324

The net realizable value of accounts receivable would be determined as follows:

Accounts receivable	$168,500
Less: Allowance for doubtful accounts	14,554
Net realizable value	$153,946

EXHIBIT 7-6 Use of an Aging Schedule to Estimate Bad Debts

Category	Amount	Estimated Percent Uncollectible	Estimated Amount Uncollectible
Current	$ 85,600	1%	$ 856
Past due:			
1–30 days	31,200	4%	1,248
31–60 days	24,500	10%	2,450
61–90 days	18,000	30%	5,400
Over 90 days	9,200	50%	4,600
Totals	$168,500		$14,554

From Concept **TO PRACTICE 7.3**

READING GATEWAY'S FINANCIAL STATEMENTS Does Gateway disclose in its annual report which method it uses to estimate bad debts? In what line item on the income statement would you expect bad debts expense to be included?

Two-Minute Review

1. What is the theoretical justification for recognizing bad debts under the allowance method?

2. What account titles are debited and credited at the end of the period to recognize bad debts?

3. Two approaches are available to recognize bad debts. What are they? Which one of the two takes into account any existing balance in the Allowance for Doubtful Accounts account when the entry is made to recognize bad debts for the period?

Answers:

1. Use of the allowance method is an attempt by accountants to match bad debts as an expense with the revenue of the period in which a sale on credit took place.

2. Bad Debts expense is debited, and Allowance for Doubtful Accounts is credited.

3. The two approaches are the percentage of net credit sales approach and the percentage of accounts receivable approach. Only the latter takes into account the balance in the Allowance for Doubtful Accounts account.

Analyzing the Accounts Receivable Rate of Collection

Managers, investors, and creditors are keenly interested in how well a company manages its accounts receivable. One simple measure is to compare a company's sales to its accounts receivable. The result is the accounts receivable turnover ratio:

$$\text{Accounts Receivable Turnover} = \frac{\text{Net Credit Sales}}{\text{Average Accounts Receivable}}$$

Typically, the faster the turnover is, the better. For example, if a company has sales of \$10 million and an average accounts receivable of \$1 million, it turns over its accounts receivable 10 times per year. If we assume 360 days in a year, that is once every 36 days. An observer would compare that figure with historical figures to see if the company is experiencing slower or faster collections. A comparison could also be made to other companies in the same industry. If receivables are turning over too slowly, that could mean that the company's credit department is not operating effectively and the company therefore is missing opportunities with the cash that isn't available. On the other hand, a turnover rate that is too fast might mean that the company's credit policies are too stringent and that sales are being lost as a result.

From Concept **TO PRACTICE 7.4**

READING BEN & JERRY'S FINANCIAL STATEMENTS Compute Ben & Jerry's accounts receivable turnover for 1998. What is the average length of time it takes to collect a receivable? Does this seem reasonable for the company's type of business?

Notes Receivable

A **promissory note** is a written promise to repay a definite sum of money on demand or at a fixed or determinable date in the future. Promissory notes normally require the payment of interest for the use of someone else's money. The party that agrees to repay money is the **maker** of the note, and the party that receives money in the future is the **payee.** A company that holds a promissory note received from another company has an asset, called a **note receivable;** the company that makes or gives a promissory note to another company has a liability, a **note payable.** Over the life of the note, the maker incurs interest expense on its note payable, and the payee earns interest revenue on its note receivable. The following summarizes this relationship:

Party	Recognizes on Balance Sheet	Recognizes on Income Statement
Maker	Note payable	Interest expense
Payee	Note receivable	Interest revenue

PROMISSORY NOTE
A written promise to repay a definite sum of money on demand or at a fixed or determinable date in the future.

MAKER
The party that agrees to repay the money for a promissory note at some future date.

PAYEE
The party that will receive the money from a promissory note at some future date.

NOTE RECEIVABLE
An asset resulting from the acceptance of a promissory note from another company.

NOTE PAYABLE
A liability resulting from the signing of a promissory note.

Promissory notes are used for a variety of purposes. Banks normally require a company to sign a promissory note to borrow money. They are often used in the sale of consumer durables with relatively high purchase prices, such as appliances and automobiles. At times a promissory note is issued to replace an existing overdue account receivable.

IMPORTANT TERMS CONNECTED WITH PROMISSORY NOTES

KEY TERMS FOR PROMISSORY NOTES
These terms, with their definitions in the text, are important for your understanding.

It is important to understand the following terms when dealing with promissory notes:

Principal—the amount of cash received, or the fair value of the products or services received, by the maker when a promissory note is issued.

Maturity date—the date that the promissory note is due.

Term—the length of time a note is outstanding; that is, the period of time between the date it is issued and the date it matures.

Maturity value—the amount of cash the maker is to pay the payee on the maturity date of the note.

Interest—the difference between the principal amount of the note and its maturity value.

INTEREST-BEARING NOTE
A promissory note in which the interest rate is explicitly stated.

NON-INTEREST-BEARING NOTE
A promissory note in which interest is not explicitly stated but is implicit in the agreement.

In some cases, the interest rate on a promissory note is stated explicitly on the face of the note. Even though the note's term may be less than a year, the interest rate is stated on an annual basis. In other cases, an interest rate does not appear on the face of the note. As we will see, however, there is *implicit* interest, because more is to be repaid at maturity than is owed at the time the note is signed. Notes in which an interest rate is explicitly stated are called **interest-bearing notes.** Notes in which interest is implicit in the agreement are called **non-interest-bearing notes.** We now look at the accounting for each of these types of notes.

INTEREST-BEARING NOTES

LO 5 Understand how to account for interest-bearing notes receivable.

Assume that on December 13, 2001, HighTec sells a computer to Baker Corp. at an invoice price of $15,000. Because Baker is short of cash, it gives HighTec a 90-day, 12% promissory note. The total amount of interest due on the maturity date is determined as follows:

$$\$15{,}000 \times .12 \times 90/360 = \underline{\underline{\$450}}$$

The entry to record receipt of the note by HighTec is as follows:

2001			
Dec. 13	Notes Receivable	15,000	
	Sales Revenue		15,000
	To record sale of computer in exchange for promissory note.		

Assets	=	Liabilities	+	Owners' Equity
+15,000				+15,000

If we assume that December 31 is the end of HighTec's accounting year, an adjustment is needed to recognize interest earned but not yet received. It is required when a company uses the accrual basis of accounting. The question is: how many days of interest have been earned during December? *It is normal practice to count the day a note matures, but not the day it is signed, in computing interest.* Thus, in our example, interest would be earned for 18 days (December 14 to December 31) during 2001 and for 72 days in 2002:

Month	Number of Days Outstanding
December 2001	18 days
January 2002	31 days
February 2002	28 days
March 2002	13 days (matures on March 13, 2002)
Total days	90 days

An adjusting entry is made on December 31 to record interest earned during 2001:

2001			
Dec. 31	Interest Receivable	90	
	Interest Revenue		90
	To record interest earned: $15,000 × .12 × 18/360.		

Assets	=	Liabilities	+	Owners' Equity
+90				+90

On March 13, 2002, HighTec collects the principal amount of the note and interest from Baker and records this entry:

2002			
Mar. 13	Cash	15,450	
	Notes Receivable		15,000
	Interest Revenue		360
	Interest Receivable		90
	To record collection of promissory note.		

Assets	=	Liabilities	+	Owners' Equity
+15,450				+360
−15,000				
−90				

This entry accomplishes a number of purposes. First, it removes the amount of $15,000 originally recorded in the Notes Receivable account. Second, it increases Interest Revenue for the interest earned during the 72 days in 2002 that the note was outstanding. The calculation of interest earned during 2002 is as follows:

$$\$15{,}000 \times .12 \times 72/360 = \underline{\underline{\$360}}$$

Third, the entry decreases Interest Receivable by $90 to remove this account from the records now that the note has been collected. Finally, it increases Cash by $15,450, which represents the principal amount of the note, $15,000, plus interest of $450 for 90 days.

Non-Interest-Bearing Notes

LO 6 Understand how to account for non-interest-bearing notes receivable.

Assume that you walk in to an automobile dealership on November 1, 2001, and find the car of your dreams. After extensive negotiation, the dealer agrees to sell you the car outright for $10,000. Because you are short of cash, you give the dealer $1,000 as a down payment and sign a promissory note to pay $9,900 in six months. Even though interest is never mentioned, it is *implicitly* built into the transaction. You owe the car dealer $10,000 – $1,000, or $9,000, today, and you have agreed to pay $9,900 in six months. The $900 excess of the amount to be paid in six months over the amount owed today is *interest.* The note is called a non-interest-bearing note because no interest is *explicitly* stated. Anytime it is necessary to pay more in the future than is owed today, interest is involved. The *effective interest rate* can be found as follows:

1. The amount of interest implicit in the note: $9,900 – $9,000, or $900
2. The length of the note: 6 months
3. The number of 6-month periods in a year: 12/6 = 2
4. The amount of interest that would apply to a full year: $900 × 2, or $1,800
5. The effective annual interest rate: $1,800/$9,000, or 20%

In essence, the car dealer had you sign a promissory note in the amount of $9,900 but gave you credit equivalent to only $9,000 in cash, that is, the difference between the value of the car today, $10,000, and the amount of your down payment, $1,000. The dealer deducted interest of $900 in advance and gave you the equivalent of a $9,000 loan. Another name for this non-interest-bearing note is a **discounted note.** On the date the note is signed, the car dealer makes this entry:

Discounted note An alternative name for a non-interest-bearing promissory note.

2001			
Nov. 1	Cash	1,000	
	Notes Receivable	9,900	
	Discount on Notes Receivable		900
	Sales Revenue		10,000
	To record sale in exchange for note.		

Assets	=	Liabilities	+	Owners' Equity
+1,000				+10,000
+9,900				
−900				

The debit to Cash represents the down payment. The debit to Notes Receivable is for \$9,900, the maturity amount of the promissory note. The credit to Sales Revenue represents the amount the car could be sold for today. Discount on Notes Receivable is a contra account to the Notes Receivable account and represents the interest that the dealer will earn over the next six months. As interest is earned, this account will be reduced and Interest Revenue will be recognized. For example, at the end of the year, the dealer will make an adjustment to recognize that two months' interest of the total of six months' interest has been earned:

2001			
Dec. 31	Discount on Notes Receivable	300	
	Interest Revenue		300
	To record interest earned for two months: \$900 × 2/6.		

Assets	=	Liabilities	+	Owners' Equity
+300				+300

The Current Assets section of the dealer's balance sheet at December 31, 2001, includes the following:

Notes receivable	\$9,900	
Less: Discount on notes receivable	(600)	\$9,300

The entry on April 30 to record collection of the maturity amount of the note and to recognize the remaining interest earned is as follows:

2002			
Apr. 30	Cash	9,900	
	Discount on Notes Receivable	600	
	Notes Receivable		9,900
	Interest Revenue		600
	To record collection of note.		

Assets	=	Liabilities	+	Owners' Equity
+9,900				+600
+600				
−9,900				

Accelerating the Inflow of Cash from Sales

LO 7 Explain various techniques that companies use to accelerate the inflow of cash from sales.

Earlier in the chapter we pointed out why cash sales are preferable to credit sales: credit sales slow down the inflow of cash to the company and create the potential for bad debts. To remain competitive, most businesses find it necessary to grant credit to customers. That is, if one company won't grant credit to a customer, the customer may find another company willing to do so. Companies have found it possible, however, to circumvent the problems inherent in credit sales. In Chapter 5 we discussed the use of sales discounts to motivate timely repayment of accounts receivable. We now consider other approaches that companies use to speed up the flow of cash from sales.

Credit Card Sales

Most retail establishments, as well as many service businesses, accept one or more major credit cards. Among the most common cards are MasterCard, VISA, American Express, Carte Blanche, Discover Card, and Diners Club. Most merchants believe that they must honor at least one or more of these credit cards to remain competitive. In return for a fee, the merchant passes the responsibility for collection on to the credit card company. Thus, the credit card issuer assumes the risk of nonpayment. The basic relationships among the three parties—the customer, the merchant, and the credit card company—are illustrated in Exhibit 7-7. Assume that Joe Smith entertains clients at Club Cafe and charges $100 in meals to his Diners Club credit card. When Joe is presented with his bill at the end of the evening, he is asked to sign a multiple-copy **credit card draft** or invoice. Joe keeps one copy of the draft and leaves the other two copies at Club Cafe. The restaurant keeps one copy as the basis for recording its sales for the day and sends the other copy to Diners Club for payment. Diners Club uses the copy of the draft it gets for two purposes: to reimburse Club Cafe $95 (keeping $5 or 5% of the original sale as a collection fee) and to include Joe Smith's $100 purchase on the monthly bill it mails him.

Assume that total credit card sales on June 5 amount to $800. The entry on Club Cafe's books on that day is as follows:

June 5	Accounts Receivable—Diners Club	800	
	Sales Revenue		800
	To record daily credit card sales.		

Assets	=	Liabilities	+	Owners' Equity
+800				+800

If credit card sales accelerate the inflow of cash from sales, then credit card scanners such as this one speed up the process even more.

Credit Card Draft
A multiple-copy document used by a company that accepts a credit card for a sale.

Exhibit 7-7 Basic Relationships among Parties with Credit Card Sales

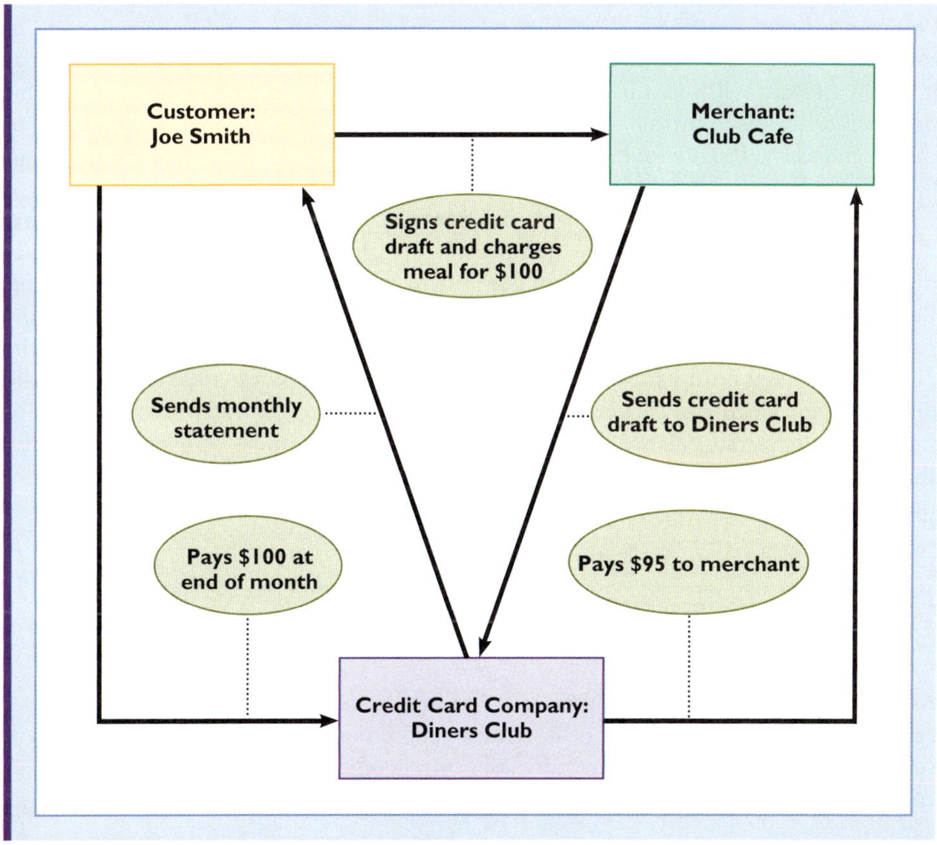

Assume that Club Cafe remits the credit card drafts to Diners Club once a week and that the total sales for the week ending June 11 amount to $5,000. Further assume that on June 13 Diners Club pays the amount due to Club Cafe, after deducting a 5% collection fee. The entry on Club Cafe's books is as follows:

June 13	Cash	4,750	
	Collection Fee Expense	250	
	Accounts Receivable—Diners Club		5,000
	To record weekly receipts from credit card company.		

Assets	=	Liabilities	+	Owners' Equity
+4,750				−250
−5,000				

Some credit cards, such as MasterCard and VISA, allow a merchant to present a credit card draft directly for deposit in a bank account, in much the same way the merchant deposits checks, coins, and currency. Obviously, this type of arrangement is even more advantageous for the merchant because the funds are available as soon as the drafts are credited to the bank account. Assume that on July 9 Club Cafe presents VISA credit card drafts to its bank for payment in the amount of $2,000 and that the collection charge is 4%. The entry on its books on the date of deposit is as follows:

July 9	Cash	1,920	
	Collection Fee Expense	80	
	Sales Revenue		2,000
	To record credit card sales.		

Assets	=	Liabilities	+	Owners' Equity
+1,920				−80
				+2,000

Discounting Notes Receivable

Discounting The process of selling a promissory note.

Promissory notes are negotiable, which means that they can be endorsed and given to someone else for collection. In other words, a company can sign the back of a note, just as it would a check, sell it to a bank, and receive cash before the note's maturity date. This process is called **discounting** and is another way for companies to speed the collection of cash from receivables. A note can be sold immediately to a bank on the date it is issued, or it can be sold after it has been outstanding but before the due date.

When a note is discounted at a bank, it is normally done *with recourse.* This means that if the original customer fails to pay the bank the total amount due on the maturity date of the note, the company that transferred the note to the bank is liable for the full amount. Because there is *uncertainty* as to whether the company will have to make good on any particular note that it discounts at the bank, a *contingent liability* exists from the time the note is discounted until its maturity date. The accounting profession has adopted guidelines to decide whether a particular uncertainty requires that the company record a contingent liability on its balance sheet. Under these guidelines, the contingency created by the discounting of a note with recourse is not recorded as a liability. However, a *footnote* to the financial statements is used to inform the reader of the existing uncertainty.

How Liquid Assets Affect the Cash Flows Statement

LO 8 Explain the effects of transactions involving liquid assets on the statement of cash flows.

As we discussed earlier in the chapter, cash equivalents are combined with cash on the balance sheet. These items are very near maturity and do not present any significant risk of collectibility. Because of this, any purchases or redemptions of cash equivalents are not considered significant activities to be reported on a statement of cash flows.

The purchase and the sale of investments are considered significant activities and are therefore reported on the statement of cash flows. The classification of these activities on the statement depends on the type of investment. Cash flows from purchases, sales, and maturities of held-to-maturity securities and available-for-sale securities are classified as *investing* activities. On the other hand, these same types of cash flows for trading securities are classified as *operating* activities. We present a complete discussion of the statement of cash flows, including the reporting of investments, in Chapter 12.

The collection of either accounts receivable or notes receivable generates cash for a business and affects the Operating Activities section of the statement of cash flows. Most companies use the indirect method of reporting cash flows and begin the statement of cash flows with the net income of the period. Net income includes the sales revenue of the period. Therefore, a decrease in accounts or notes receivable during the period indicates that the company collected more cash than it recorded in sales revenue. Thus, *a decrease in accounts or notes receivable must be added back to net income because more cash was collected than is reflected in the sales revenue number.* Alternatively, an increase in accounts or notes receivable indicates that the company recorded more sales revenue than cash collected during the period. Therefore, *an increase in accounts or notes receivable requires a deduction from the net income of the period to arrive at cash flow from operating activities.* These adjustments, as well as the cash flows from buying and selling investments, are summarized in Exhibit 7-8. Note that any investments are assumed to be in either held-to-maturity or available-for-sale securities.

Refer back to PepsiCo's statement of cash flows in Exhibit 7-1. Note in the Operating Activities section of the statement that accounts and notes receivable are combined. Does the combined change of $104 million in these two accounts during 1998 indicate an increase or a decrease in the receivables for the year? Because the amount is deducted in the Operating Activities section of the statement, we know that the receivables *increased* during 1998. An increase in receivables means that PepsiCo sold more products on open account and on notes than it actually collected in cash from customers. Thus, the increase is deducted from net income to arrive at the actual cash flow from operating activities.

www.pepsico.com

EXHIBIT 7-8 How Investments and Receivables Affect the Statement of Cash Flows

Item	Cash Flow Statement	
	Operating Activities	
	Net income	xxx
Increase in accounts receivable		−
Decrease in accounts receivable		+
Increase in notes receivable		−
Decrease in notes receivable		+
	Investing Activities	
Purchases of held-to-maturity and available-for-sale securities		−
Sales/maturities of held-to-maturity and available-for-sale securities		+
	Financing Activities	

WARMUP EXERCISES

LO 1 Warmup Exercise 7-1 Composition of Cash

For the following items, indicate whether each should be included (I) or excluded (E) from the line item titled Cash and Cash Equivalents on the balance sheet.

_______ **1.** Certificate of deposit maturing in 60 days
_______ **2.** Checking account
_______ **3.** Certificate of deposit maturing in six months
_______ **4.** Savings account
_______ **5.** Shares of GM stock
_______ **6.** Petty cash
_______ **7.** Corporate bonds maturing in 30 days
_______ **8.** Certified check

Key to the Solution

Recall the key to classification as part of cash: the amount must be readily available to pay debts and cash equivalents must have an original maturity to the investor of three months or less.

LO 3 Warmup Exercise 7-2 Investments

Indicate whether each of the following events will result in an increase (I), decrease (D), or no effect (NE) on net income for the period.

_______ **1.** Trading securities are sold for more than their carrying value.
_______ **2.** An interest check is received for held-to-maturity securities.
_______ **3.** Available-for-sale securities increase in value during the period.
_______ **4.** Available-for-sale securities are sold for less than their carrying value.
_______ **5.** Trading securities decrease in value during the period.
_______ **6.** Held-to-maturity securities are redeemed on their maturity date at face value.

Key to the Solution

Recall from earlier in the chapter the differences in accounting for the various types of investments.

LO 4 Warmup Exercise 7-3 Accounting for Bad Debts

Brown Corp. ended the year with balances in Accounts Receivable of $60,000 and in Allowance for Doubtful Accounts of $800 (before adjustment). Net sales for the year amounted to $200,000. Prepare the necessary entry on its books at the end of the year, assuming the following:

1. Estimated percentage of net sales uncollectible is 1%.

2. Estimated percentage of year-end accounts receivable uncollectible is 4%.

Key to the Solution

Recall that the percentage of net sales approach does not take into account any existing balance in the allowance account but the percentage of receivables approach does.

SOLUTIONS TO WARMUP EXERCISES

Warmup Exercise 7-1

1. I **2.** I **3.** E **4.** I **5.** E **6.** I **7.** E **8.** I

Warmup Exercise 7-2

1. I **2.** I **3.** NE **4.** D **5.** D **6.** NE

Warmup Exercise 7-3

1. Bad Debts Expense	2,000	
Allowance for Doubtful Accounts		2,000
To record estimated bad debts.		

Assets	=	Liabilities	+	Owners' Equity
−2,000				−2,000

2. Bad Debts Expense	1,600	
Allowance for Doubtful Accounts		1,600
To record estimated bad debts.		

Assets	=	Liabilities	+	Owners' Equity
−1,600				−1,600

Review Problem

The following items pertain to the Current Assets section of the balance sheet for Jackson Corp. at the end of its accounting year, December 31, 2001. Each item must be considered, and any necessary accounting entry on December 31 must be recorded. Additionally, the accountant for Jackson wants to develop the Current Assets section of the balance sheet as of the end of 2001.

a. Cash in a savings account at the Second State Bank amounts to $13,200.

b. Cash on hand in the petty cash fund amounts to $400.

c. A 9%, 120-day certificate of deposit was purchased on December 1, 2001, for $10,000.

d. The balance on the books for a checking account at the Second State Bank is $4,230. The bank statement indicates that one of Jackson's customers paid a $1,500 promissory note, along with $120 in interest, directly to the bank. The bank deducted a $25 collection fee from the amount it credited to Jackson's account. The statement also indicated that the bank had charged Jackson's account $50 to print new checks.

e. Gross accounts receivable at December 31, 2001, amount to $44,000. Before adjustment, the balance in the Allowance for Doubtful Accounts is $340. Based on past experience, the accountant estimates that 3% of the gross accounts receivable outstanding at December 31, 2001, will prove to be uncollectible.

f. A customer's 12%, 90-day promissory note in the amount of $6,000 is held at the end of the year. (*Note:* This is a different note than the one in item **d.**) The note has been held for 45 days during 2001.

Required

1. Record the accounting entries required in parts **a–f.**
2. Prepare the Current Assets section of Jackson's balance sheet as of December 31, 2001. In addition to items **a–f,** the balances in Inventory and Prepaid Insurance on this date are $65,000 and $4,800, respectively.

Solution to Review Problem

1. The following entries are recorded at December 31, 2001:

   a. & **b.** No entries required.

   c. Jackson needs an adjusting entry to record interest earned on the certificate of deposit at the Second State Bank. The CD has been outstanding for 30 days during 2001, and therefore the amount of interest earned is calculated as follows:

$$\$10{,}000 \times .09 \times 30/360 = \underline{\underline{\$75}}$$

The adjusting entry follows:

2001			
Dec. 31	Interest Receivable	75	
	Interest Revenue		75
	To record interest earned during 2001.		

Assets	=	Liabilities	+	Owners' Equity
+75				+75

d. Entries are needed to record the bank's collection of the promissory note and interest, the collection charge on the note, and the charge for the new checks:

2001			
Dec. 31	Cash	1,620	
	Notes Receivable		1,500
	Interest Revenue		120
	To record collection of note and interest.		

Assets	=	Liabilities	+	Owners' Equity
+1,620				+120
−1,500				

2001			
Dec. 31	Collection Fee Expense	25	
	Cash		25
	To record deduction from account for collection fee on note.		

Assets	=	Liabilities	+	Owners' Equity
−25				−25

2001			
Dec. 31	Miscellaneous Expense	50	
	Cash		50
	To record deduction from account for new checks.		

Assets	=	Liabilities	+	Owners' Equity
−50				−50

e. Based on gross accounts receivable of \$44,000 at year-end and an estimate that 3% of this amount will be uncollectible, the balance in the Allowance for Doubtful Accounts should be \$1,320 (\$44,000 × 3%). Given a current balance of \$340, an adjusting entry for \$980 (\$1,320 – \$340) is needed to bring the balance to the desired amount of \$1,320:

2001			
Dec. 31	Bad Debts Expense	980	
	Allowance for Doubtful Accounts		980
	To record estimated bad debts for the year.		

Assets	=	Liabilities	+	Owners' Equity
−980				−980

f. An adjusting entry is needed to accrue interest on the promissory note (\$6,000 × .12 × 45/360 = \$90):

2001			
Dec. 31	Interest Receivable	90	
	Interest Revenue		90
	To record interest earned on promissory note.		

Assets	=	Liabilities	+	Owners' Equity
+90				+90

2. The Current Assets section of Jackson's balance sheet appears as follows:

JACKSON CORP.
PARTIAL BALANCE SHEET
DECEMBER 31, 2001

Current Assets		
Cash		$ 19,375*
Certificate of deposit		10,000
Accounts receivable	$44,000	
Less: Allowance for doubtful accounts	1,320	42,680
Notes receivable		6,000
Interest receivable		165§
Inventory		65,000
Prepaid insurance		4,800
Total current assets		$148,020

*Savings account	$13,200
Petty cash fund	400
Checking account ($4,230 + $1,620 – $25 – $50)	5,775
Total	$19,375

§$75 from CD and $90 from promissory note

CHAPTER HIGHLIGHTS

1. **LO 1** The amount of cash reported on the balance sheet includes all items that are readily available to satisfy obligations. Items normally included in cash are coin and currency, petty cash funds, customers' undeposited checks, cashier's checks, certified checks, savings accounts, and checking accounts.
2. **LO 1** Cash equivalents include such items as commercial paper, money market funds, certificates of deposit, and Treasury bills. They are included with cash on the balance sheet and are limited to those investments that are readily convertible to known amounts of cash and have original maturities of three months or less.
3. **LO 2** A bank reconciliation is normally prepared monthly for all checking accounts to reconcile the amount of cash recorded on the books with the amount reported on the bank statement. One popular form for the reconciliation, and the one illustrated in the chapter, reconciles the balance on the bank statement and the balance on the books to the correct balance. Adjustments must be made for all items in the balance per books section of the reconciliation.
4. **LO 2** Many companies use a petty cash fund to disburse small amounts of cash that would otherwise require the use of a check and a more lengthy approval process. The fund is established by writing and cashing a check and placing the coin and currency in a secure place controlled by a custodian. At this point, an adjustment is made to record the establishment of the fund. On presentation of a supporting receipt to the custodian, employees receive disbursements from the fund. The fund is replenished periodically, and an adjustment is made to record the replenishment and to recognize the various expenses incurred.
5. **LO 3** At times, companies invest idle cash in highly liquid financial instruments such as certificates of deposit. They also invest in the debt and equity securities of other companies. Some investments are made without the intention of influencing or controlling the other company. Accountants classify these investments as held-to-maturity securities, trading securities, or available-for-sale securities. Other investments are made to exert significant influence over the policies of the other companies. The equity method is used in these instances. Finally, companies may buy enough of the common stock of another company to control it. This situation normally results in the presentation of consolidated financial statements.
6. **LO 3** Held-to-maturity securities are bonds that are purchased with the intention of holding them until they mature. The cost method results in the recognition of periodic interest income and the recognition of a gain or loss if the securities are sold prior to when they mature.
7. **LO 3** Trading securities are stocks and bonds held for the short term with the intention of profiting from appreciation in their trading price. Interest or dividends are recognized as income. Trading securities are adjusted to their fair value at the end of each period, and any increase or decrease in value is reported on the income statement.
8. **LO 3** Available-for-sale securities are investments that are not classified as either held-to-maturity or trading securities. The accounting and reporting requirements for this category are similar to the rules for trading securities. The primary difference is that unrealized gains and losses from holding available-for-sale securities (changes in fair value from one period to the next) are not recognized on the income statement. Instead, these amounts are reported as a separate component of stockholders' equity.
9. **LO 4** The allowance method of accounting for bad debts matches the cost associated with uncollectible accounts to the

revenue of the period in which the sale took place. One of two variations is used to estimate bad debts under the allowance method. Some companies base bad debts on a percentage of net credit sales. Others use an aging schedule as a basis for relating the amount of bad debts to the balance in Accounts Receivable at the end of the period.

10. **LO 5** A promissory note is a written promise to repay a definite sum of money on demand or at a fixed or determinable date in the future. Situations in which a promissory note is used include the purchase of consumer durables, the lending of money to another party, and the replacement of an existing account receivable. Interest earned but not yet collected should be accrued at the end of an accounting period.

11. **LO 6** The interest on certain promissory notes is implicitly included in the agreement instead of stated explicitly as a percentage of the principal amount of the note. Any difference between the cash purchase price of an item or, in the case of a loan, the amount borrowed and the amount to be repaid at maturity is interest. As is the case for interest-bearing notes, any interest earned but not yet collected is recognized as income at the end of an accounting period.

12. **LO 7** Many businesses accept credit cards in lieu of cash. In return for a fee, the credit card company assumes responsibility for collecting the customer charges. A credit card draft or invoice is the basis for recording a credit card sale and an account receivable. When the drafts are presented to the credit card company for payment, the excess of accounts receivable for these sales over the amount of cash received represents the expense associated with accepting credit cards. In some instances, companies do not have to wait to collect from the credit card company but can instead present the drafts for deposit to their bank account.

13. **LO 7** Because a promissory note is negotiable, it can be sold to another party, such as a bank. The sale of a note is called *discounting* and is a way for a company to accelerate the inflow of cash. If the note is sold or discounted with recourse, the company selling it is contingently liable until the maturity date of the loan. A footnote is used to report this contingency to financial statement readers.

14. **LO 8** Cash equivalents are included with cash on the balance sheet, and therefore changes in them do not appear as significant activities on a statement of cash flows. Purchases and sales of investments do appear in the statement of cash flows. Under the indirect method of preparing the Operating Activities category of the statement of cash flows, increases in accounts and notes receivable are deducted from net income; decreases are added back to net income.

KEY TERMS QUIZ

Because of the large number of terms introduced in this chapter, it has two key terms quizzes. Read each definition below and then write the number of the definition in the blank beside the appropriate term it defines. The solution appears at the end of the chapter.

Quiz 1: Cash and Investments

2 **Cash equivalent**
6 **Outstanding check**
9 **Bank reconciliation**
3 **Debit memoranda**
5 **Equity securities**
13 **Held-to-maturity securities**
12 **Available-for-sale securities**
8 **Bank statement**
4 **Deposit in transit**
1 **Credit memoranda**
10 **Petty cash fund**
7 **Debt securities**
11 **Trading securities**

1. Additions on a bank statement for such items as interest paid on the account and notes collected by the bank for the customer.
2. An investment that is readily convertible to a known amount of cash and has an original maturity to the investor of three months or less.
3. Deductions on a bank statement for such items as NSF checks and various service charges.
4. A deposit recorded on the books but not yet reflected on the bank statement.
5. Securities issued by corporations as a form of ownership in the business.
6. A check written by a company but not yet presented to the bank for payment.
7. Bonds issued by corporations and governmental bodies as a form of borrowing.
8. A detailed list, provided by the bank, of all the activity for a particular account during the month.
9. A form used by the accountant to reconcile the balance shown on the bank statement for a particular account with the balance shown in the accounting records.
10. Money kept on hand for making minor disbursements in coin and currency rather than by writing checks.
11. Stocks and bonds of other companies bought and held for the purpose of selling them in the near term to generate profits on appreciation in their price.
12. Stocks and bonds that are not classified as either held-to-maturity or trading securities.
13. Investments in bonds of other companies in which the investor has the positive intent and the ability to hold the securities to maturity.

Quiz 2: Receivables

12 Subsidiary ledger
14 Direct write-off method
10 Aging schedule
8 Maker
6 Note receivable
16 Non-interest-bearing note
18 Credit card draft
20 Control account
13 Allowance method
5 Promissory note
15 Payee
1 Note payable
3 Principal
2 Maturity date
4 Term
17 Maturity value
19 Interest
9 Interest-bearing note
11 Discounted note
7 Discounting

1. A method of estimating bad debts on the basis of either the net credit sales of the period or the amount of accounts receivable at the end of the period.
2. The party that will receive the money from a promissory note at some future date.
3. A written promise to repay a definite sum of money on demand or at a fixed or determinable date in the future.
4. A liability resulting from the signing of a promissory note.
5. A multiple-copy document used by a company that accepts a credit card for a sale.
6. An asset resulting from the acceptance of a promissory note from another company.
7. The process of selling a promissory note.
8. The party that agrees to repay the money for a promissory note at some future date.
9. A promissory note in which the interest rate is explicitly stated.
10. A form used to categorize the various individual accounts receivable according to the length of time each has been outstanding.
11. An alternative name for a non-interest-bearing promissory note.
12. The detail for a number of individual items that collectively make up a single general ledger account.
13. A promissory note in which interest is not explicitly stated but is implicit in the agreement.
14. The recognition of bad debts expense at the point an account is written off as uncollectible.
15. The general ledger account that is supported by a subsidiary ledger.
16. The amount of cash received, or the fair value of the products or services received, by the maker when a promissory note is issued.
17. The date that the promissory note is due.
18. The length of time a note is outstanding; that is, the period of time between the date it is issued and the date it matures.
19. The amount of cash the maker is to pay the payee on the maturity date of the note.
20. The difference between the principal amount of the note and its maturity value.

Alternate Terms

Allowance for doubtful accounts Allowance for uncollectible accounts

Credit card draft Invoice

Debt securities Bonds

Equity securities Stocks

Net realizable value Net recoverable amount

Non-interest-bearing note Discounted note

Short-term investments Marketable securities

Questions

1. What is a cash equivalent? Why is it included with cash on the balance sheet?
2. Why does the purchase of an item classified as a cash equivalent *not* appear on the statement of cash flows as an investing activity?
3. A friend says to you: "I understand why it is important to deposit all receipts intact and not keep coin and currency sitting around the business. Beyond this control feature, however, I believe that a company should strive to keep the maximum amount possible in checking accounts to always be able to pay bills on time." How would you evaluate your friend's statement?
4. A friends says to you: "I'm confused. I have a memo included with my bank statement indicating a $20 service charge for printing new checks. If the bank is deducting this amount from my account, why do they call it a 'debit memorandum'? I thought a decrease in a cash account would be a credit, not a debit." How can you explain this?
5. Different formats for bank reconciliations are possible. What is the format for a bank reconciliation in which a service charge for a lockbox is *added* to the balance per the bank statement? Explain your answer.

6. Stanzel Corp. purchased 1,000 shares of IBM common stock. What will determine whether the shares are classified as trading securities or available-for-sale securities?

7. On December 31, Stockton Inc. invests idle cash in two different certificates of deposit. The first is an 8%, 90-day CD, and the second has an interest rate of 9% and matures in 120 days. How is each of these CDs classified on the December 31 balance sheet?

8. What is the primary difference in the accounting requirements for trading securities and those for available-for-sale securities? How is the primary difference justified?

9. Why are changes in the fair value of trading securities reported in the account *Unrealized* Gains/Losses—Trading Securities even though the gains and losses are reported on the income statement?

10. What is the theoretical justification for the allowance method of accounting for bad debts?

11. In estimating bad debts, why is the balance in Allowance for Doubtful Accounts considered when the percentage of accounts receivable approach is used but not when the percentage of net credit sales approach is used?

12. When estimating bad debts on the basis of a percentage of accounts receivable, what is the advantage to using an aging schedule?

13. What is the distinction between an account receivable and a note receivable?

14. How would you evaluate the following statement? "Given the choice, it would always be better to require an interest-bearing note from a customer as opposed to a non-interest-bearing note. This is because interest on a note receivable is a form of revenue and it is only in the case of an interest-bearing note that interest will be earned."

15. Why does the discounting of a note receivable with recourse result in a contingent liability? Should the liability be reported on the balance sheet?

EXERCISES

LO 2 Exercise 7-1 Items on a Bank Reconciliation

Assume that a company is preparing a bank reconciliation for the month of June. It reconciles the bank balance and the book balance to the correct balance. For each of the following items, indicate whether the item is an addition to the bank balance (A-Bank), an addition to the book balance (A-Book), a deduction from the bank balance (D-Bank), a deduction from the book balance (D-Book), or would not appear on the June reconciliation (NA).

________ 1. Check written in June but not yet returned to the bank for payment

________ 2. Customer's NSF check

________ 3. Customer's check written in the amount of $54 but recorded on the books in the amount of $45*

________ 4. Service charge for new checks

________ 5. Principal and interest on a customer's note collected for the company by the bank

________ 6. Customer's check deposited on June 30 but not reflected on the bank statement

________ 7. Check written on the company's account, paid by the bank, and returned with the bank statement

________ 8. Check written on the company's account for $123 but recorded on the books as $132*

________ 9. Interest on the checking account for the month of June

*Answer in terms of the adjustment needed to correct for the error.

LO 2 Exercise 7-2 Petty Cash Fund

On January 2, 2001, Cleaver Video Stores decided to set up a petty cash fund. The treasurer established the fund by writing and cashing a $300 check and placing the coin and currency in a locked petty cash drawer. Edward Haskell was designated as the custodian for the fund. During January, the following receipts were given to Haskell in exchange for cash from the fund:

U.S. Post Office (stamps)	$76.00
Speedy Delivery Service	45.30
Cake N Cookies (party for retiring employee)	65.40
Office Supply Superstore (paper, pencils)	36.00

A count of the cash in the drawer on January 31 revealed a balance of $74.10. The treasurer wrote and cashed a check on the same day to restore the fund to its original balance of $300. Prepare the necessary journal entries, with explanations, for January. Assume that all stamps and office supplies were used during the month.

LO 3 Exercise 7-3 Certificate of Deposit

On May 31, 2001, Elmer Corp. purchased a 120-day, 9% certificate of deposit for $50,000. The CD was redeemed on September 28, 2001. Prepare the journal entries on Elmer's books to account for the CD, including any entry on June 30, the end of the company's fiscal year. Assume 360 days in a year.

LO 3 Exercise 7-4 Classification of Investments

Red Oak makes the following investments in the stock of other companies during 2001. For each investment, indicate how it would be accounted for and reported on; use the following designations: trading security (T), available-for-sale security (AS), equity investee (E), or a subsidiary included in consolidated statements (S).

_______ **1.** 500 shares of ABC common stock to be held for short-term share appreciation

_______ **2.** 20,000 shares of the 50,000 shares of Ace common stock to be held for the long term

_______ **3.** 100 shares of Creston preferred stock to be held for an indefinite period of time

_______ **4.** 80,000 of the 100,000 shares of Orient common stock

_______ **5.** 10,000 of the 40,000 shares of Omaha preferred stock to be held for the long term

LO 3 Exercise 7-5 Classification of Investments

Fill in the blanks below to indicate whether each of the following investments should be classified as a held-to-maturity security (HM), a trading security (T), or an available-for-sale security (AS):

_______ **1.** Shares of IBM stock to be held indefinitely.

_______ **2.** GM bonds due in 10 years. The intent is to hold them until they mature.

_______ **3.** Shares of Motorola stock. Plans are to hold the stock until the price goes up by 10% and then sell it.

_______ **4.** Ford Motor Company bonds due in 15 years. The bonds are part of a portfolio that turns over on the average of every 60 days.

_______ **5.** Chrysler bonds due in 10 years. Plans are to hold them indefinitely.

LO 3 Exercise 7-6 Purchase and Sale of Bonds

Starship Enterprises enters into the following transactions during 2001 and 2002:

2001	
Jan. 1	Purchased $100,000 face value of Northern Lights Inc. bonds at face value. The newly issued bonds have an interest rate of 8% paid semiannually on June 30 and December 31. The bonds mature in five years.
June 30	Received interest on the Northern Lights bonds.
Dec. 31	Received interest on the Northern Lights bonds.
2002	
Jan. 1	Sold the Northern Lights Inc. bonds for $102,000.

Assume Starship classifies all bonds as held to maturity.

Required

1. Prepare all necessary journal entries on Starship's records to account for its investment in the Northern Lights bonds.
2. Why was Starship able to sell its Northern Lights bonds for $102,000?

LO 3 Exercise 7-7 Investment in Stock

On December 1, 2001, Chicago Corp. purchases 1,000 shares of the preferred stock of Denver Corp. for $40 per share. Chicago expects the price of the stock to increase over the next few months and plans to sell it for a profit. On December 20, 2001, Denver declares a dividend of $1 per share to be paid on January 15, 2002. On December 31, 2001, Chicago's accounting year-end, the Denver stock is trading on the market at $42 per share. Chicago sells the stock on February 12, 2002, at a price of $45 per share.

Required

1. Should Chicago classify its investments as held-to-maturity, trading, or available-for-sale securities? Explain your answer.

2. Prepare all necessary entries on Chicago's books in connection with its investment, beginning with the purchase on December 1, 2001, and ending with the sale on February 12, 2002. Indicate next to each account title in your entries whether the account appears on the balance sheet (BS) or the income statement (IS).
3. In what category of the balance sheet should Chicago classify its investment on its December 31, 2001, balance sheet?

LO 3 **Exercise 7-8** Investment in Stock

On August 15, 2001, Cubs Corp. purchases 5,000 shares of common stock in Sox Inc. at a market price of $15 per share. In addition, Cubs pays brokerage fees of $1,000. Cubs plans to hold the stock indefinitely rather than as a part of its active trading portfolio. The market value of the stock is $13 per share on December 31, 2001, the end of Cubs' accounting year. On July 8, 2002, Cubs sells the Sox stock for $10 per share.

Required

1. Should Cubs classify its investment as held-to-maturity, trading, or available-for-sale securities? Explain your answer.
2. Prepare all necessary entries on Cubs' books in connection with the investment, beginning with the purchase on August 15, 2001, and ending with the sale on July 8, 2002. Indicate next to each account title in your entries whether the account appears on the balance sheet (BS) or the income statement (IS).
3. In what category of the balance sheet should Cubs classify its investment on its December 31, 2001, balance sheet?

LO 4 **Exercise 7-9** Comparison of the Direct Write-Off and Allowance Methods of Accounting for Bad Debts

In its first year of business, Rideaway Bikes has net income of $145,000, exclusive of any adjustment for bad debt expense. The president of the company has asked you to calculate net income under each of two alternatives of accounting for bad debts: the direct write-off method and the allowance method. The president would like to use the method that will result in the higher net income. So far, no entries have been made to write off uncollectible accounts or to estimate bad debts. The relevant data are as follows:

Write-offs of uncollectible accounts during the year	$ 10,500
Net credit sales	$650,000
Estimated percentage of net credit sales that will be uncollectible	2%

Required

Compute net income under each of the two alternatives. Does Rideaway have a choice as to which method to use? Should it base its choice on which method will result in the higher net income? (Ignore income taxes.)

LO 4 **Exercise 7-10** Allowance Method of Accounting for Bad Debts—Comparison of the Two Approaches

Kandel Company had the following data available for 2001 (before making any adjustments):

Accounts receivable, 12/31/01	$320,100 (dr.)
Allowance for doubtful accounts	2,600 (cr.)
Net credit sales, 2001	834,000 (cr.)

Required

1. Prepare the journal entry to recognize bad debts under the following assumptions: (a) bad debt expense is expected to be 2% of net credit sales for the year and (b) Kandel expects it will not be able to collect 6% of the balance in accounts receivable at year-end.
2. Assume instead that the balance in the allowance account is a $2,600 debit. How will this affect your answers to part 1?

LO 4 **Exercise 7-11** Accounts Receivable Turnover for Quaker Oats

The 1998 annual report of Quaker Oats Company reported the following amounts (in millions of dollars).

Net sales	$4,842.5
Trade accounts receivable—net of allowances, December 31, 1998	283.4
Trade accounts receivable—net of allowances, December 31, 1997	305.7

Required

1. Compute Quaker's accounts receivable turnover ratio for 1998. (Assume that all sales are on credit.)
2. What is the average collection period, in days, for an account receivable? Explain your answer.
3. Give some examples of the types of customers you would expect Quaker Oats to have. Do you think the average collection period for sales to these customers is reasonable? What other information do you need to fully answer this question?

LO 5 **Exercise 7-12** Interest-Bearing Notes Receivable

On September 1, 2001, Dougherty Corp. accepted a six-month, 7%, $45,000 interest-bearing note from the Rozelle Company in payment of an accounts receivable. Dougherty's year-end is December 31. Rozelle paid the note and interest on the due date.

Required

1. Who is the maker and who is the payee of the note?
2. What is the maturity date of the note?
3. Prepare all journal entries Dougherty needs to make in connection with this note.

LO 6 **Exercise 7-13** Non-Interest-Bearing Note

On May 1, Radtke's Music Mart sold an electronic keyboard to Mary Reynolds. Reynolds made a $300 down payment and signed a 10-month note for $1,625. The normal selling price of the keyboard is $1,800 in cash. Radtke's fiscal year ends December 31. Reynolds paid Radtke in full on the maturity date.

Required

1. How much total interest did Radtke receive on this note?
2. Prepare the journal entries on Radtke's books on May 1, December 31, and the maturity date.
3. What is the effective interest rate on the note?

LO 7 **Exercise 7-14** Credit Card Sales

Darlene's Diner accepts American Express from its customers. Darlene's is closed on Sundays and on that day records the weekly sales and remits the credit card drafts to American Express. For the week ending on Sunday, June 12, cash sales totaled $2,430, and credit card sales amounted to $3,500. On June 15, Darlene's received $3,360 from American Express as payment for the credit card drafts. Prepare the necessary journal entries on Darlene's books on June 12 and June 15. As a percentage, what collection fee is American Express charging Darlene?

LO 8 **Exercise 7-15** Impact of Transactions Involving Receivables on Statement of Cash Flows

From the following list, identify whether the change in the account balance during the year would be added to or deducted from net income when the indirect method is used to determine cash flows from operating activities.

________ Increase in accounts receivable

________ Decrease in accounts receivable

________ Increase in notes receivable

________ Decrease in notes receivable

LO 8 **Exercise 7-16** Cash Collections—Direct Method

Emily Enterprises' comparative balance sheets included accounts receivable of $224,600 at December 31, 2000, and $205,700 at December 31, 2001. Sales reported on Emily's 2001 income statement amounted to $2,250,000. What is the amount of cash collections that Emily will report in the Operating Activities category of its 2001 statement of cash flows assuming that the direct method is used?

Multi-Concept Exercises

LO 1, 2, 3 Exercise 7-17 Composition of Cash

Using a Y for yes or an N for no, indicate whether each of the following items should be included in cash and cash equivalents on the balance sheet. If an item should not be included in cash and cash equivalents, indicate where it should appear on the balance sheet.

_______ **1.** Checking account at Third County Bank
_______ **2.** Petty cash fund
_______ **3.** Coin and currency
_______ **4.** Postage stamps
_______ **5.** An IOU from an employee
_______ **6.** Savings account at the Ft. Worth Savings & Loan
_______ **7.** A six-month CD
_______ **8.** Undeposited customer checks
_______ **9.** A customer's check returned by the bank and marked NSF
_______ **10.** Sixty-day U.S. Treasury bills
_______ **11.** A cashier's check

LO 1, 3 Exercise 7-18 Classification of Cash Equivalents and Investments on a Balance Sheet

Classify each of the following items as either a cash equivalent (CE), a short-term investment (STI), or a long-term investment (LTI).

_______ **1.** A 120-day certificate of deposit.
_______ **2.** Three hundred shares of GM common stock. The company plans on selling the stock in six months.
_______ **3.** A six-month U.S. Treasury bill.
_______ **4.** A 60-day certificate of deposit.
_______ **5.** Ford Motor Co. bonds maturing in 15 years. The company intends to hold the bonds until maturity.
_______ **6.** Commercial paper issued by ABC Corp., maturing in four months.
_______ **7.** Five hundred shares of Chrysler common stock. The company plans to sell the stock in 60 days to help pay for a note due at that time at the bank.
_______ **8.** Two hundred shares of GE preferred stock. The company intends to hold the stock for 10 years and at that point sell it to help finance construction of a new factory.
_______ **9.** Ten-year U.S. Treasury bonds. The company plans to sell the bonds on the open market in six months.
_______ **10.** A 90-day U.S. Treasury bill.

LO 1, 3, 8 Exercise 7-19 Cash Equivalents

Systematic Enterprises invested its excess cash in the following instruments during December 2001:

Certificate of deposit, due January 31, 2004	$ 75,000
Certificate of deposit, due March 30, 2002	150,000
Commercial paper, original maturity date February 28, 2002	125,000
Deposit into a money market fund	25,000
Investment in stock	65,000
90-day Treasury bills	100,000
Treasury note, due December 1, 2031	500,000

Required

Determine the amount of cash equivalents which should be combined with cash on the company's balance sheet at December 31, 2001, and for purposes of preparing a statement of cash flows for the year ended December 31, 2001.

LO 1, 8 Exercise 7-20 Impact of Transactions Involving Cash and Receivables on Statement of Cash Flows

From the following list, identify each item as operating (O), investing (I), financing (F), or not separately reported on the statement of cash flows (N). Assume that the indirect method is used to determine the cash flows from operating activities.

________ Purchase of cash equivalents

________ Redemption of cash equivalents

________ Purchase of available-for-sale securities

________ Sale of available-for-sale securities

________ Replenishment of the petty cash fund

________ Write-off of customer account (under the allowance method)

PROBLEMS

LO 2 Problem 7-1 Bank Reconciliation and Journal Entries

The following information is available to assist you in preparing a bank reconciliation for Calico Corners on May 31, 2001:

a. The balance on the May 31, 2001, bank statement is $8,432.11.

b. Not included on the bank statement is a $1,250.00 deposit made by Calico Corners late on May 31.

c. A comparison between the canceled checks returned with the bank statement and the company records indicated that the following checks are outstanding at May 31:

No. 123	$ 23.40
No. 127	145.00
No. 128	210.80
No. 130	67.32

d. The Cash account on the company's books shows a balance of $9,965.34.

e. The bank acts as a collection agency for interest earned on some municipal bonds held by Calico Corners. The May bank statement indicates interest of $465.00 earned during the month.

f. Interest earned on the checking account and added to Calico Corners' account during May was $54.60. Miscellaneous bank service charges amounted to $50.00.

g. A customer's NSF check in the amount of $166.00 was returned with the May bank statement.

h. A comparison between the deposits listed on the bank statement and the company's books revealed that a customer's check in the amount of $123.45 was recorded on the books during May but was never added to the company's account. The bank erroneously added the check to the account of Calico Closet, which has an account at the same bank.

i. The comparison of deposits per the bank statement with those per the books revealed that another customer's check in the amount of $101.10 was correctly added to the company's account. In recording the check on the company's books, however, the accountant erroneously increased the Cash account $1,011.00.

Required

1. Prepare a bank reconciliation in good form.
2. Prepare the necessary journal entries on the books of Calico Corners.
3. A friend says to you: "I don't know why companies bother to prepare bank reconciliations—it seems a waste of time. Why don't they just do like I do and adjust the cash account for any difference between what the bank shows as a balance and what shows up in the books?" Explain to your friend *why* a bank reconciliation should be prepared as soon as a bank statement is received.

LO 2 Problem 7-2 The Effect of Petty Cash on Cash and Income

ABC Company established a petty cash fund in the amount of $500. One month later, it replenished the fund based on the following receipts:

a. $40, postage due on computer supplies used in the administrative offices

b. $5.80, postage stamps used by the president when she is on the road and without access to the postage meter

c. $180, advertising fliers to be used by the marketing department and sent COD to the company

d. $95, office supplies purchased at a local store for use in the administrative offices

Required

1. Prepare the journal entry to establish the petty cash fund. Cash on hand at the end of the first month is $174. Do you believe that the $500 amount was an appropriate amount for ABC's petty cash fund? Explain.
2. Prepare the journal entry to replenish the petty cash fund at the end of the month. What is the effect of this entry on the total assets of the company? on income?
3. Explain why a petty cash fund is allowed even though proper accounting control over cash requires that all payments be made by check.

LO 3 Problem 7-3 Investments in Bonds and Stock

Swartz Inc. enters into the following transactions during 2001:

July 1	Paid $10,000 to acquire on the open market $10,000 face value of Gallatin bonds. The bonds have a stated annual interest rate of 6% with interest paid semiannually on June 30 and December 31. The bonds mature in 5½ years.
Oct. 23	Purchased 600 shares of Eagle Rock common stock at $20 per share.
Nov. 21	Purchased 200 shares of Montana preferred stock at $30 per share.
Dec. 10	Received dividends of $1.50 per share on the Eagle Rock stock and $2.00 per share on the Montana stock.
Dec. 28	Sold 400 shares of Eagle Rock common stock at $25 per share.
Dec. 31	Received interest from the Gallatin bonds.
Dec. 31	Noted market price of $29 per share for the Eagle Rock stock and $26 per share for the Montana stock.

Required

1. Prepare all necessary journal entries on Swartz's records to account for its investments during 2001. Swartz classifies the bonds as held-to-maturity securities and all stock investments as trading securities.
2. Prepare a partial balance sheet as of December 31, 2001, to indicate the proper presentation of the investments.
3. Indicate the items, and the amount of each, that will appear on the 2001 income statement relative to the investments.

LO 3 Problem 7-4 Investments in Stock

Atlas Superstores occasionally finds itself with excess cash to invest and consequently entered into the following transactions during 2001:

Jan. 15	Purchased 200 shares of Sears common stock at $50 per share, plus $500 in commissions.
May 23	Received dividends of $2 per share on the Sears stock.
June 1	Purchased 100 shares of Ford Motor Co. stock at $74 per share, plus $300 in commissions.
Oct. 20	Sold all the Sears stock at $42 per share, less commissions of $400.
Dec. 15	Received notification from Ford Motor Co. that a $1.50 per share dividend had been declared. The checks will be mailed to stockholders on January 10, 2002.
Dec. 31	Noted that the Ford Motor Co. stock was quoted on the stock exchange at $85 per share.

Required

1. Prepare journal entries on the books of Atlas Superstores during 2001 to record these transactions, including any necessary entry on December 15, when the dividend was declared, and at the end of the year. Assume that Atlas categorizes all investments as available-for-sale securities.

2. What is the total amount that Atlas should report on its income statement from its investments during 2001?
3. Assume all the same facts except that Atlas categorizes all investments as trading securities. How would your answer to part **2** change? Explain why your answer would change.

LO 4 Problem 7-5 Allowance Method for Accounting for Bad Debts

At the beginning of 2001, EZ Tech Company's Accounts Receivable balance was $140,000, and the balance in the Allowance for Doubtful Accounts was $2,350 (cr.). EZ Tech's sales in 2001 were $1,050,000, 80% of which were on credit. Collections on account during the year were $670,000. The company wrote off $4,000 of uncollectible accounts during the year.

Required

1. Prepare summary journal entries related to the sale, collections, and write-offs of accounts receivable during 2001.
2. Prepare journal entries to recognize bad debts assuming (a) bad debt expense is 3% of credit sales and (b) amounts expected to be uncollectible are 6% of the year-end accounts receivable.
3. What is the net realizable value of accounts receivable on December 31, 2001, under each assumption (**a** and **b**) in part **2?**
4. What effect does the recognition of bad debt expense have on the net realizable value? What effect does the write-off of accounts have on the net realizable value?

LO 4 Problem 7-6 Aging Schedule to Account for Bad Debts

SPREADSHEET

Sparkle Jewels distributes fine stones. It sells on credit to retail jewelry stores and extends terms of 2/10, net 60. For accounts that are not overdue, Sparkle has found that there is a 95% probability of collection. For accounts up to one month past due, the likelihood of collection decreases to 80%. If accounts are between one and two months past due, the probability of collection is 60%, and if an account is more than two months past due, Sparkle Jewels estimates that there is only a 40% chance of collecting the receivable.

On December 31, 2001, the credit balance in Allowance for Doubtful Accounts is $12,300. The amounts of gross receivables, by age, on this date are as follows:

Category	Amount
Current	$200,000
Past due:	
Less than one month	45,000
One to two months	25,000
More than two months	10,000

Required

1. Prepare a schedule to estimate the amount of uncollectible accounts at December 31, 2001.
2. On the basis of the schedule in part 1, prepare the journal entry on December 31, 2001, to estimate bad debts.
3. Show how accounts receivable would be presented on the December 31, 2001, balance sheet.

LO 4 Problem 7-7 Accounts Receivable Turnover for Compaq Computer and Gateway

The following information was summarized from the 1998 annual report of Compaq Computer Corporation: www.compaq.com

	(in millions)
Accounts receivable, net, December 31:	
1998	$ 6,998
1997	2,891
Revenue for the year ended December 31:	
1998	31,169
1997	24,584

www.gateway.com The following information was summarized from the 1998 annual report of Gateway:

	(in thousands)
Accounts receivable, net:	
December 31, 1998	$ 558,851
December 31, 1997	510,679
Net sales for the year ended:	
December 31, 1998	7,467,925
December 31, 1997	6,293,680

Required

1. Calculate the accounts receivable turnover ratios for Compaq Computer and Gateway for 1998.
2. Calculate the average collection period, in days, for both companies for 1998. Comment on the reasonableness of the collection periods considering the types of companies that you would expect to be customers of Compaq Computer and Gateway.
3. Which company appears to be performing better? What other information should you consider to determine how these companies are performing in this regard?

LO 6 **Problem 7-8** Non-Interest-Bearing Note Receivable

Northern Nursery sells a large stock of trees and shrubs to a landscaping business on May 31, 2001. The landscaper makes a down payment of $5,000 and signs a promissory note agreeing to pay $20,000 on August 29, 2001, the end of its busy season. The cash selling price of the nursery stock on May 31 was $24,000.

Required

1. Prepare the appropriate journal entry on Northern's books on each of the following dates:
   a. May 31, 2001, to record the receipt of the down payment and the promissory note
   b. June 30, 2001, the end of Northern's fiscal year
   c. August 29, 2001, to record collection of the note
2. Compute the effective rate of interest earned by Northern on the note. Explain your answer.

LO 7 **Problem 7-9** Credit Card Sales

Gas stations sometimes sell gasoline at a lower price to customers who pay cash than to customers who use a charge card. A local gas station owner pays 2% of the sales price to the credit card company when customers pay with a credit card. He pays $ .75 per gallon of gasoline and must earn at least $ .25 per gallon of gross margin to stay competitive.

Required

1. Determine the price the owner must charge credit card customers to maintain his gross margin.
2. How much discount could the owner offer to cash customers and still maintain the same gross margin?

LO 8 **Problem 7-10** Effects of Changes in Receivable Balances on Statement of Cash Flows

Stegner Inc. reported net income of $130,000 for the year ended December 31, 2001. The following items were included on Stegner's balance sheets at December 31, 2001 and 2000:

	12/31/01	12/31/00
Cash	$105,000	$110,000
Accounts receivable	223,000	83,000
Notes receivable	95,000	100,000

Stegner uses the indirect method to prepare its statement of cash flows. Stegner does not have any other current assets or current liabilities and did not enter into any investing or financing activities during 2001.

Required

1. Prepare Stegner's 2001 statement of cash flows.
2. Draft a brief memo to the owner to explain why cash decreased during a profitable year.

Multi-Concept Problems

LO 1, 3 **Problem 7-11** Cash and Liquid Assets on the Balance Sheet

The following accounts are listed in a company's general ledger. The accountant wants to place the items in order of liquidity on the balance sheet.

Accounts receivable
Certificates of deposit (six months)
Trading securities
Prepaid rent
Money market fund
Cash in drawers

Required

Rank the accounts in terms of liquidity. Identify items to be included in the total of cash, and explain why the items not included in cash on the balance sheet are not as liquid as cash. Explain how these items should be classified.

LO 4, 5 **Problem 7-12** Accounts and Notes Receivable

Linus Corp. sold merchandise for $5,000 to C. Brown on May 15, 2001, with credit terms of net 30. Subsequent to this, Brown experienced cash flow problems and was unable to pay its debt. On August 10, 2001, Linus stopped trying to collect the outstanding receivable from Brown and wrote the account off as uncollectible. On December 1, 2001, Brown sent Linus a check for $1,000 and offered to sign a two-month, 9%, $4,000 promissory note to satisfy the remaining obligation. Brown paid the entire amount due Linus, with interest, on January 31, 2002. Linus ends its accounting year on December 31 each year, and uses the allowance method to account for bad debts.

Required

1. Prepare all of the necessary journal entries on the books of Linus Corp. from May 15, 2001, to January 31, 2002.
2. Why would Brown bother to send Linus a check for $1,000 on December 1 and agree to sign a note for the balance, given that such a long period of time had passed since the original purchase?

Alternate Problems

LO 2 **Problem 7-1A** Bank Reconciliation

The following information is available to assist you in preparing a bank reconciliation for Karen's Catering on March 31, 2001:

a. The balance on the March 31, 2001, bank statement is $6,506.10.

b. Not included on the bank statement is a deposit made by Karen's late on March 31 in the amount of $423.00.

c. A comparison between the canceled checks listed on the bank statement and the company records indicated that the following checks are outstanding at March 31:

No. 112	$ 42.92
No. 117	$307.00
No. 120	$ 10.58
No. 122	$ 75.67

d. The bank acts as a collection agency for checks returned for insufficient funds. The March bank statement indicates that one such check in the amount of $45.00 was collected and deposited and a collection fee of $4.50 was charged.

e. Interest earned on the checking account and credited to Karen's account during March was $4.30. Miscellaneous bank service charges amounted to $22.00.

f. A comparison between the deposits listed on the bank statement and the company's books revealed that a customer's check in the amount of $1,250.00 appears on the bank statement in March but was never credited to the customer's account on the company's books.

g. The comparison of checks cleared per the bank statement with those per the books revealed that the wrong amount was charged to the company's account for a check. The amount of the check was $990.00. The proof machine encoded the check in the amount of $909.00, the amount charged against the company's account.

Required

1. Determine the balance on the books before any adjustments as well as the corrected balance to be reported on the balance sheet.
2. What would you recommend Karen do as a result of the bank error in item **g** above? Why?

LO 2 **Problem 7-2A** The Effect of Petty Cash on Cash and Income

Arlington Inc. established a petty cash fund in the amount of $50. One month later, it replenished the fund based on the following receipts:

a. $4, postage due on computer supplies purchased for the administrative offices

b. $5.80, postage stamps used by the receptionist so that he does not need to leave his desk to use the postage meter

c. $18, a cake for the secretary's birthday

d. $20, materials purchased at a local store for use by the sales staff

Required

1. Prepare the journal entry to establish the petty cash fund. Cash on hand at the end of the month is $1.15. Do you believe that the $50 amount was an appropriate amount for Arlington's petty cash fund? Explain.
2. Prepare the journal entry to replenish the petty cash fund at the end of the month. What is the effect of this entry on the total assets of the company? on income?
3. Who should oversee the petty cash fund? Write a short description of how the process should be handled in the company.

LO 3 **Problem 7-3A** Investments in Bonds and Stock

GENERAL LEDGER

Vermont Corp. enters into the following transactions during 2001:

July 1	Paid $10,000 to acquire on the open market $10,000 face value of Maine bonds. The bonds have a stated annual interest rate of 8% with interest paid semiannually on June 30 and December 31. The remaining life of the bonds on the date of purchase is 3½ years.
Oct. 23	Purchased 1,000 shares of Virginia common stock at $15 per share.
Nov. 21	Purchased 600 shares of Carolina preferred stock at $8 per share.
Dec. 10	Received dividends of $.50 per share on the Virginia stock and $1.00 per share on the Carolina stock.
Dec. 28	Sold 700 shares of Virginia common stock at $19 per share.
Dec. 31	Received interest from the Maine bonds.
Dec. 31	The Virginia Stock and the Carolina stock have market prices of $20 per share and $11 per share, respectively.

Required

1. Prepare all necessary journal entries on Vermont's records to account for its investments during 2001. Vermont classifies the bonds as held-to-maturity securities and all stock investments as trading securities.
2. Prepare a partial balance sheet as of December 31, 2001, to indicate the proper presentation of the investments.
3. Indicate the items, and the amount of each, that will appear on the 2001 income statement relative to the investments.

LO 3 Problem 7-4A Investments in Stock

Trendy Supercenter occasionally finds itself with excess cash to invest and consequently entered into the following transactions during 2001:

Jan. 15	Purchased 100 shares of IBM common stock at $130 per share, plus $250 in commissions.
May 23	Received dividends of $1 per share on the IBM stock.
June 1	Purchased 200 shares of General Motors stock at $60 per share, plus $300 in commissions.
Oct. 20	Sold all of the IBM stock at $140 per share, less commissions of $400.
Dec. 15	Received notification from General Motors that a $.75 per share dividend had been declared. The checks will be mailed to stockholders on January 10, 2002.
Dec. 31	Noted that the General Motors stock was quoted on the stock exchange at $45 per share.

Required

1. Prepare journal entries on the books of Trendy Supercenter during 2001 to record these transactions, including any necessary entry on December 15 when the dividend was declared and at the end of the year. Assume that Trendy categorizes all investments as available-for-sale securities.
2. What is the total amount of income that Trendy should recognize from its investments during 2001?
3. Assume all of the same facts except that Trendy categorizes all investments as trading securities. How would your answer to part **2** change? Explain why your answer would change.

LO 4 Problem 7-5A Allowance Method for Accounting for Bad Debts

At the beginning of 2001, Miyazaki Company's Accounts Receivable balance was $105,000 and the balance in the Allowance for Doubtful Accounts was $1,950 (cr.). Miyazaki's sales in 2001 were $787,500, 80% of which were on credit. Collections on account during the year were $502,500. The company wrote off $3,000 of uncollectible accounts during the year.

Required

1. Prepare summary journal entries related to the sales, collections, and write-offs of accounts receivable during 2001.
2. Prepare journal entries to recognize bad debts assuming (a) bad debt expense is 3% of credit sales or (b) amounts expected to be uncollectible are 6% of the year-end accounts receivable.
3. What is the net realizable value of accounts receivable on December 31, 2001, under each assumption (**a** and **b**) in part **2?**
4. What effect does the recognition of bad debt expense have on the net realizable value? What effect does the write-off of accounts have on the net realizable value?

LO 4 Problem 7-6A Aging Schedule to Account for Bad Debts

Rough Stuff is a distributor of large rocks. It sells on credit to commercial landscaping companies and extends terms of 2/10, net 60. For accounts that are not overdue, Rough has found that there is a 90% probability of collection. For accounts up to one month past due, the likelihood of collection decreases to 75%. If accounts are between one and two months past due, the probability of collection is 65%, and if an account is more than two months past due, Rough estimates that there is only a 25% chance of collecting the receivable.

On December 31, 2001, the credit balance in Allowance for Doubtful Accounts is $34,590. The amounts of gross receivables, by age, on this date are as follows:

Category	**Amount**
Current	$135,000
Past due:	
Less than one month	60,300
One to two months	35,000
More than two months	45,000

Required

1. Prepare a schedule to estimate the amount of uncollectible accounts at December 31, 2001.
2. Rough knows that $40,000 of the $45,000 amount that is more than two months overdue is due from one customer that is in severe financial trouble. It is rumored that the customer will be filing for bankruptcy in the near future. As controller for Rough Stuff, how would you handle this situation?
3. Show how accounts receivable would be presented on the December 31, 2001, balance sheet.

LO 4 Problem 7-7A Accounts Receivable Turnover for Boise Cascade and Georgia-Pacific Corporation

www.boisecascade.com

The following information was summarized from the 1998 annual report of Boise Cascade Corporation and Subsidiaries (receivables are net of allowances):

	(in thousands)
Receivables, December 31:	
1998	$ 526,359
1997	570,424
Sales for the year ended December 31:	
1998	6,162,123
1997	5,493,820

www.gp.com

The following information was summarized from the 1998 annual report of Georgia-Pacific Corporation–Georgia Pacific Group (receivables are net of allowances):

	(in millions)
Receivables, December 31:	
1998	$ 1,231
1997	1,368
Net sales for the year ended December 31:	
1998	13,223
1997	12,979

Required

1. Calculate the accounts receivable turnover ratios for Boise Cascade and Georgia-Pacific for 1998.
2. Calculate the average collection period, in days, for both companies for 1998. Comment on the reasonableness of the collection periods considering the types of companies that you would expect to be customers of Boise Cascade and Georgia-Pacific.
3. Which company appears to be performing better? What other information should you consider to determine how these companies are performing in this regard?

LO 6 Problem 7-8A Non-Interest-Bearing Note Receivable

Midwest Poultry sells a large stock of birds to a processor on May 31, 2001. The processor makes a $12,000 down payment and signs a $36,900 promissory note agreeing to pay the remainder on August 29, 2001, the end of its busy season. The cash selling price of the birds on May 31 was $48,000.

1. Prepare the appropriate journal entry on Midwest's books on August 29, 2001, to record collection of the note. Midwest's accounting year ends on September 30.
2. Compute the effective rate of interest earned by Midwest on the note. Explain your answer.

LO 7 Problem 7-9A Credit Card Sales

A local fast-food store is considering the use of major credit cards in its outlets. Current annual sales are $800,000 per outlet. The company can purchase the equipment needed to handle credit cards and have an additional phone line installed in each outlet for approximately $800 per outlet. The equipment will be an expense in the year it is installed. The employee training time is minimal. The credit card company will charge a fee equal to 1.5% of sales for the use of credit cards.

The company is unable to determine by how much, if any, sales will increase and whether cash customers will use a credit card rather than cash. No other fast-food stores in the local area accept credit cards for sales payment.

Required

1. Assuming only 5% of existing cash customers will use a credit card, what increase in sales is necessary to pay for the credit card equipment in the first year?
2. What other factors might the company consider in addition to an increase in sales dollars?

LO 8 Problem 7-10A Effects of Changes in Receivable Balances on Statement of Cash Flows

St. Charles Antique Market reported a net loss of $6,000 for the year ended December 31, 2001. The following items were included on St. Charles Antique Market's balance sheets at December 31, 2001 and 2000:

	12/31/01	12/31/00
Cash	$ 36,300	$ 3,100
Accounts receivable	79,000	126,000
Notes receivable	112,600	104,800

St. Charles Antique Market uses the indirect method to prepare its statement of cash flows. St. Charles Antique Market does not have any other current assets or current liabilities and did not enter into any investing or financing activities during 2001.

Required

1. Prepare St. Charles Antique Market's 2001 statement of cash flows.
2. Draft a brief memo to the owner to explain why cash increased during such an unprofitable year.

Alternate Multi-Concept Problems

LO 1, 3 Problem 7-11A Cash and Liquid Assets on the Balance Sheet

The following accounts are listed in a company's general ledger:

	December 31, 2001	December 31, 2000
Accounts receivable	$12,300	$10,000
Certificates of deposit (three months)	10,000	10,000
Marketable securities	4,500	4,000
Prepaid rent	1,200	1,500
Money market fund	25,800	28,000
Cash in checking account	6,000	6,000

Required

1. Which items are cash equivalents?
2. Explain where items that are not cash equivalents should be classified on the balance sheet.
3. What are the amount and the direction of change in cash and cash equivalents for 2001? Is the company as liquid at the end of 2001 as it was at the end of 2000? Explain your answer.

LO 4, 5 Problem 7-12A Accounts and Notes Receivable

Tweedy Inc. sold merchandise for $6,000 to P.D. Cat on July 31, 2001, with credit terms of net 30. Subsequent to this, Cat experienced cash flow problems and was unable to pay its debt. On December 24, 2001, Tweedy stopped trying to collect the outstanding receivable from Cat and wrote the account off as uncollectible. On January 15, 2002, Cat sent Tweedy a check for $1,500 and offered to sign a two-month, 8%, $4,500 promissory note to satisfy the remaining obligation. Cat paid the entire amount on the note due Tweedy, with interest, on March 15, 2002. Tweedy ends its accounting year on December 31 each year.

Required

1. Prepare all of the necessary journal entries on the books of Tweedy Inc. from July 31, 2001, to March 15, 2002.
2. Why would Cat bother to send Tweedy a check for $1,500 on January 15 and agree to sign a note for the balance, given that such a long period of time had passed since the original purchase?

CASES

Reading and Interpreting Financial Statements

LO 4 Case 7-1 Reading and Interpreting Ben & Jerry's Financial Statements
Refer to the financial statements for 1998 included in Ben & Jerry's annual report.

Required

1. What is the balance in the Allowance for Doubtful Accounts at the end of each of the two years presented? What is the net realizable value at the end of each year?
2. Calculate the ratio of the Allowance for Doubtful Accounts to Gross Accounts Receivable at the end of each of the two years.
3. Why do you think the balance in the Allowance for Doubtful Accounts was decreased at the end of 1998? Does this mean that the company expects a lesser percentage of bad debts?

LO 3, 8 Case 7-2 Reading Gateway's Statement of Cash Flows
Refer to the financial statements for 1998 included in Gateway's annual report.

Required

1. According to the statement of cash flows, what was the increase or decrease in cash equivalents during 1998? How does this number relate to any of the numbers on Gateway's comparative balance sheets?
2. Gateway's balance sheet does not report any investments but does include under current assets an account titled Marketable Securities. According to the first footnote, how are available-for-sale securities carried on the balance sheet? How are any unrealized gains and losses reported in the financial statements?
3. What was the dollar amount of increase or decrease in accounts receivable for 1998? Why is this number deducted on the statement of cash flows?

Making Financial Decisions

LO 1, 2 Case 7-3 Liquidity
R Montague and J Capulet both distribute films to movie theaters. The following are the current assets for each at the end of the year (all amounts are in millions of dollars):

	R Montague	J Capulet
Cash	$10	$ 5
Six-month certificates of deposit	9	0
Short-term investments in stock	0	6
Accounts receivable	15	23
Allowance for doubtful accounts	(1)	(1)
Total current assets	$33	$33

Required

As a loan officer for the First National Bank of Verona Heights, assume that both companies have come to you asking for a $10 million, six-month loan. If you could lend money to only one of the two, which one would it be? Justify your answer by writing a brief memo to the president of the bank.

LO 5, 6 Case 7-4 Notes Receivable

Warren Land Development is considering two offers for a lot. Builder A has offered to pay $12,000 down and sign a 10%, $80,000 promissory note, with interest and principal due in one year. Builder B would make a down payment of $20,000 and sign a non-interest-bearing, one-year note for $80,000. The president believes that the deal with Builder A is better because it involves interest and the loan to Builder B does not. The vice president of marketing thinks the offer from Builder B is better because it involves more money "up front." The sales manager is indifferent, reasoning that both builders would eventually pay $100,000 in total and that because the lot was recently appraised at $75,000, both would be paying more than fair market value.

Required

1. Regardless of which offer it accepts, how much revenue should Warren recognize from the sale of the lot? Explain your answer.
2. Which offer do you think Warren should accept? Or is the sales manager correct that it doesn't matter which one is accepted? Explain your answer.

Accounting and Ethics: What Would You Do?

LO 3 Case 7-5 Fair Market Values for Investments

Kennedy Corp. operates a chain of discount stores. The company regularly holds stock of various companies in a trading securities portfolio. One of these investments is 10,000 shares of Clean Air Inc. stock purchased for $100 per share during December 2001.

Clean Air manufactures highly specialized equipment used to test automobile emissions. Unfortunately, the market price of Clean Air's stock dropped during December 2001 and closed the year trading at $75 per share. Kennedy expects the Clean Air stock to experience a turn around, however, as states pass legislation to require an emissions test on all automobiles.

As controller for Kennedy, you have followed the fortunes of Clean Air with particular interest. You and the company's treasurer are both concerned by the negative impact that a write-down of the stock to fair value would have on Kennedy's earnings for 2001. You have calculated net income for 2001 to be $400,000, exclusive of the recognition of any loss on the stock.

The treasurer comes to you on January 31, 2002, with the following idea:

> Since you haven't closed the books yet for 2001, and we haven't yet released the 2001 financials, let's think carefully about how Clean Air should be classified. I realize that we normally treat these types of investments as trading securities, but if we categorize the Clean Air stock on the balance sheet as available-for-sale rather than a trading security, we won't need to report the adjustment to fair value on the income statement. I don't see anything wrong with this since we would still report the stock at its fair value on the balance sheet.

Required

1. Compute Kennedy's net income for 2001, under two different assumptions: (a) the stock is classified as a trading security and (b) the stock is classified as an available-for-sale security.
2. Which classification do you believe is appropriate, according to accounting standards? Explain your answer.
3. Would you have any ethical concerns in following the treasurer's advice? Explain your answer.

LO 6 Case 7-6 Notes Receivable

Patterson Company is a large diversified business with a unit that sells commercial real estate. As a company, Patterson has been profitable in recent years with the exception of the real estate business, where economic conditions have resulted in weak sales. The vice president of the real estate division is aware of the poor performance of his group and needs to find ways to "show a profit."

During the current year the division is successful in selling a 100-acre tract of land for a new shopping center. The original cost of the property to Patterson was $4 million. The buyer has agreed to sign a $10 million note with payments of $2 million due at the end of each of the next five years. The property was appraised late last year at a market value of $7.5 million. The vice president has come to you, the controller, and asked that you record the sale as follows:

Notes Receivable	10,000,000	
Sales Revenue		10,000,000
To record sale of 100-acre tract.		

Required

1. Does the entry suggested by the vice president to record the sale violate any accounting principle? If so, explain the principle it violates.
2. What would you do? Write a brief memo to the vice president explaining the proper accounting for the sale.

INTERNET RESEARCH CASE

www.pepsico.com

Case 7-7 PepsiCo

PepsiCo, the number two soft drink maker in the world with major products in snack foods as well, is undergoing changes that it believes will respond to major changes in the grocery business, its biggest customer.

To answer the following questions, examine the chapter-opening text and the financial statements shown in Chapter 7, read the Business Strategy box that details the changes overtaking PepsiCo in 1998, and access its Web site to focus on both the company and its latest financial information.

1. What are the cash and cash equivalents for PepsiCo for the latest year available?
2. What reason does the company give for the change in cash and equivalents for the most recent year available?
3. What are the short-term investments for the latest year available?
4. What reasons does the company give for the change in short-term investments for the latest year available?
5. What are accounts and notes receivable for the latest year available? Can you tell from the notes how much was for accounts receivable and how much for notes receivable?
6. Comparing the latest annual report with the financial information from 1998 in the textbook, what are three most significant changes to the financial statements? What is the most significant change to PepsiCo as a company?

SOLUTIONS TO KEY TERMS QUIZ

Quiz 1: Cash and Investments

2	Cash equivalent (p. 314)	8	Bank statement (p. 317)
6	Outstanding check (p. 318)	4	Deposit in transit (p. 318)
9	Bank reconciliation (p. 318)	1	Credit memoranda (p. 318)
3	Debit memoranda (p. 319)	10	Petty cash fund (p. 322)
5	Equity securities (p. 324)	7	Debt securities (p. 324)
13	Held-to-maturity securities (p. 327)	11	Trading securities (p. 327)
12	Available-for-sale securities (p. 327)		

Quiz 2: Receivables

12	Subsidiary ledger (p. 334)	15	Control account (p. 334)
14	Direct write-off method (p. 336)	1	Allowance method (p. 336)
10	Aging schedule (p. 339)	3	Promissory note (p. 341)
8	Maker (p. 341)	2	Payee (p. 341)
6	Note receivable (p. 341)	4	Note payable (p. 341)
16	Principal (p. 342)	17	Maturity date (p. 342)
18	Term (p. 342)	19	Maturity value (p. 342)
20	Interest (p. 342)	9	Interest-bearing note (p. 342)
13	Non-interest-bearing note (p. 342)	11	Discounted note (p. 343)
5	Credit card draft (p. 345)	7	Discounting (p. 346)

Long term assets

Chapter 8

Operating Assets: Property, Plant, and Equipment, Natural Resources, and Intangibles

Study Links

A Look at Previous Chapters

Chapter 2 introduced long-term assets as an important part of a classified balance sheet. The short-term assets of inventory, cash, and receivables were presented in previous chapters.

A Look at This Chapter

This chapter presents long-term operating assets. The first section of the chapter discusses assets that are generally classified as tangible assets or as property, plant, and equipment. We examine asset acquisition issues concerned with use and depreciation, and the sale or disposition of these assets. The second section of the chapter discusses assets generally classified as intangible assets. The accounting issues involved with the acquisition, use, and disposition of intangible assets are examined. The unique features of certain intangible assets are discussed separately.

A Look at Upcoming Chapters

Later chapters discuss the financing of long-term assets. Chapter 10 presents long-term liabilities as a source of financing. Chapter 11 describes the use of stock as a source of funds for financing long-term assets.

Focus on Financial Results

The media giant Time Warner markets information and entertainment in virtually every medium. The strength of such brands as CNN, TNT, the Cartoon Network, HBO, Time-Life, *People*, *Time*, and *Sports Illustrated*, of recording artists such as Madonna, Eric Clapton, and Alanis Morissette, and of film and TV hits such as *Lethal Weapon 4*, *You've Got Mail*, and *The Sopranos* made 1998 the best year in Time Warner's history. That success was enhanced even more by the 1999 merger of Time Warner and AOL, creating a huge company with more than 20 million subscribers.

For sustainable growth, the firm will leverage its tangible operating assets of plant, property, equipment, and natural resources into new profit opportunities. But intangibles like Time Warner's potent brand names will play as big a part. The company's 1998 annual report acknowledges their power: "The momentum of our business is built in part on Time Warner's mastery of what it takes to originate brands that turn trends into engines of growth."[1]

The merger of AOL and Time Warner represents the first merger between a major Internet company and a conventional media company. AOL has the 20 million subscribers while Time Warner has the programming content, its intangible assets. At the time of the merger AOL's stock market value was more than twice that of Time Warner, even though Time Warner has twice as much profit as AOL. The merged company will allow Time Warner to enhance the value of their assets and, hopefully, it will be reflected in the stock price.

[1] Time Warner's 1998 annual report, p. 19.

Consolidated Balance Sheet

December 31, (millions, except per share amounts)	1998	1997
ASSETS		
Current assets		
Cash and equivalents	$ 442	$ 645
Receivables, less allowances of $1.007 billion and $991 million	2,885	2,447
Inventories	946	830
Prepaid expenses	1,176	1,089
Total current assets	5,449	5,011
Noncurrent inventories	1,900	1,766
Investments in and amounts due to and from Entertainment Group	4,980	5,549
Other investments	794	1,495
Property, plant and equipment, net	1,991	2,089
Music catalogues, contracts and copyrights	876	928
Cable television and sports franchises	2,868	3,982
Goodwill	11,919	12,572
Other assets	863	771
Total assets	$31,640	$34,163

Time Warner's 1998 Annual Report

If you were a Time Warner manager, how would you establish the value of intangibles on the balance sheet? How would you determine the life of such assets? How would you evaluate whether the merged company has effectively utilized the intangibles? As you study this chapter, compare the way organizations report tangible and intangible assets on the balance sheet.

www.timewarner.com

Learning Objectives

After studying this chapter, you should be able to:

- **LO 1** Understand balance sheet disclosures for operating assets. (p. 374)
- **LO 2** Determine the acquisition cost of an operating asset. (p. 375)
- **LO 3** Explain how to calculate the acquisition cost of assets purchased for a lump sum. (p. 376)
- **LO 4** Describe the impact of capitalizing interest as part of the acquisition cost of an asset. (p. 376)
- **LO 5** Compare depreciation methods and understand the factors affecting the choice of method. (p. 377)
- **LO 6** Understand the impact of a change in the estimate of the asset life or residual value. (p. 382)
- **LO 7** Determine which expenditures should be capitalized as asset costs and which should be treated as expenses. (p. 384)
- **LO 8** Analyze the effect of the disposal of an asset at a gain or loss. (p. 385)
- **LO 9** Understand the balance sheet presentation of intangible assets. (p. 389)
- **LO 10** Describe the proper amortization of intangible assets. (p. 392)
- **LO 11** Explain the impact that long-term assets have on the statement of cash flows. (p. 395)

Operating Assets: Property, Plant, and Equipment

Balance Sheet Presentation

LO 1 Understand balance sheet disclosures for operating assets.

Operating assets constitute the major productive assets of many companies. Current assets are important to a company's short-term liquidity; operating assets are absolutely essential to its long-term future. These assets must be used to produce the goods or services the company sells to customers. The dollar amount invested in operating assets may be very large, as is the case with most manufacturing companies. On the other hand, operating assets on the balance sheet may be insignificant to a company's value, as is the case with a computer software firm or many of the so-called Internet firms. Users of financial statements must assess the operating assets to make important decisions. For example, lenders are interested in the value of the operating assets as collateral when making lending decisions. Investors must evaluate whether the operating assets indicate long-term potential and can provide a return to the stockholders.

The terms used to describe the operating assets and the balance sheet presentation of those assets vary somewhat by company. Some firms refer to this category of assets as *fixed* or *plant assets.* Other firms prefer to present operating assets in two categories: *tangible assets* and *intangible assets.* The balance sheet of the toy company Mattel Inc. uses another way to classify operating assets. Mattel presents two classes of operating assets: *property, plant, and equipment* and *other noncurrent assets.* Because the latter term can encompass a variety of items, we will use the more descriptive term *intangible assets* for the second category. We begin by examining the accounting issues concerned with the first category: property, plant, and equipment.

www.mattel.com

The December 31, 1998, balance sheet of Mattel presents property, plant, and equipment as follows (in thousands):

Property, Plant, and Equipment	
Land	$ 35,113
Buildings	271,580
Machinery and equipment	512,225

Capitalized leases	$ 23,271
Leasehold improvements	82,643
	$924,832
Less: Accumulated depreciation	375,724
	549,108
Tools, dies, and molds, net	187,349
Property, plant, and equipment, net	$736,457

You should note that the acquisition costs of the land, buildings, machinery and equipment, capitalized leases, and leasehold improvements are stated and the amount of accumulated depreciation is deducted to determine the net amount. Tools, dies, and molds are stated at the net amount, meaning that the amount of depreciation has been deducted before the number is presented on the balance sheet. Note that Mattel has assets acquired by capital lease arrangements. (Capital leases are discussed in Chapter 10 and will not be addressed in this chapter.) The account Leasehold Improvements indicates that the company has modified or improved leased assets in a manner that enhances their future service potential. The cost of the improvement is shown separately on the balance sheet.

Acquisition of Property, Plant, and Equipment

LO 2 Determine the acquisition cost of an operating asset.

Assets classified as property, plant, and equipment are initially recorded at acquisition cost (also referred to as *historical cost*). As indicated on Mattel's balance sheet, these assets are normally presented on the balance sheet at original acquisition cost minus accumulated depreciation. It is important, however, to define the term *acquisition cost* (also known as original cost) in a more exact manner. What items should be included as part of the original acquisition? **Acquisition cost** should include all of the costs that are normal and necessary to acquire the asset and prepare it for its intended use. Items included in acquisition cost would generally include the following:

Acquisition cost The amount that includes all of the cost normally necessary to acquire an asset and prepare it for its intended use.

Purchase price
Taxes paid at time of purchase (for example, sales tax)
Transportation charges
Installation costs

An accountant must exercise careful judgment to determine which costs are "normal" and "necessary" and should be included in the calculation of the acquisition cost of operating assets. Acquisition cost should not include expenditures unrelated to the acquisition (for example, repair costs if an asset is damaged during installation) or costs incurred after the asset was installed and use begun.

Accounting for Your Decisions

You Are an Attorney

You are a newly licensed attorney who just opened a legal firm. As part of your office operations, you have purchased some "slightly used" computers. Should the cost of repairing the computers be considered as part of the acquisition cost?

ANS: If you were aware that the computers needed to be repaired when purchased, the repair costs are part of the cost of acquisition. If the computers were damaged after they were purchased, the costs should be treated as an expense on the income statement.

LO 3 Explain how to calculate the acquisition cost of assets purchased for a lump sum.

Group Purchase Quite often a firm purchases several assets as a group and pays a lump-sum amount. This is most common when a company purchases land and a building situated on it and pays a lump-sum amount for both. It is important to measure separately the acquisition cost of the land and of the building. Land is not a depreciable asset, but the amount allocated to the building is subject to depreciation. In cases such as this, the purchase price should be allocated between land and building on the basis of the proportion of the *fair market values* of each.

For example, assume that on January 1, Payton Company purchased a building and the land that it is situated on for $100,000. The accountant was able to establish that the fair market values of the two assets on January 1 were as follows:

Land	$ 30,000
Building	90,000
Total	$120,000

On the basis of the estimated market values, the purchase price should be allocated as follows:

To land: $100,000 × $30,000/$120,000 = $25,000
To building: $100,000 × $90,000/$120,000 = $75,000

The journal entry to record the purchase would be as follows:

Jan. 1	Land	25,000	
	Building	75,000	
	Cash		100,000
	To record the purchase of land and building for a lump-sum amount.		

Assets	=	Liabilities	+	Owners' Equity
+25,000				
+75,000				
−100,000				

Market value is best established by an independent appraisal of the property. If such appraisal is not possible, the accountant must rely on the market value of other similar assets, on the value of the assets in tax records, or on other available evidence.

These efforts to allocate dollars between land and buildings will permit the appropriate allocation for depreciation. But when an investor or lender views the balance sheet, he or she is often more interested in the current market value. The best things that can be said about historical cost are that it is a verifiable number and that it is conservative. But it is still up to the lender or the investor to determine the appropriate value for these assets.

LO 4 Describe the impact of capitalizing interest as part of the acquisition cost of an asset.

Capitalization of Interest We have seen that acquisition cost may include several items. But should the acquisition cost of an asset include the interest cost necessary to finance the asset? That is, should interest be treated as an asset, or should it be treated as an expense of the period?

Generally, the interest on borrowed money should be treated as an expense of the period. If a company buys an asset and borrows money to finance the purchase, the interest on the borrowed money is not considered part of the asset's cost. Financial statements generally treat investing and financing as separate decisions. Purchase of an asset, an investing activity, is treated as a business decision that is separate from the decision concerning the financing of the asset. Therefore, interest is treated as a period cost and should appear on the income statement as interest expense in the period incurred.

There is one exception to this general guideline, however. If a company *constructs* an asset over a period of time and borrows money to finance the construction, the amount of interest incurred during the construction period is not treated as interest expense. Instead, the interest must be included as part of the acquisition cost of the asset. This is referred to as **capitalization of interest.** The amount of interest that is capitalized (treated as an asset) is based on the *average accumulated expenditures.* The logic of using the average accumulated

CAPITALIZATION OF INTEREST
Interest on constructed assets is added to the asset account.

expenditure is that this number represents an average amount of money tied up in the project over a year. If it takes $400,000 to construct a building, the interest should not be figured on the full $400,000 because there were times during the year when less than the full amount was being used.

When it costs $400,000 to build an asset and the amount of interest to be capitalized is $10,000, the acquisition cost of the asset is $410,000. The asset should appear on the balance sheet at that amount. Depreciation of the asset should be based on $410,000, less any residual value.

> **Study Tip**
>
> Land improvements represent a depreciable asset with a limited life. Land itself is not depreciable.

Land Improvements It is important to distinguish between land and other costs associated with it. The acquisition cost of land should be kept in a separate account because land has an unlimited life and is not subject to depreciation. Other costs associated with land should be recorded in an account such as Land Improvements. For example, the costs of paving a parking lot or landscaping costs are properly treated as **land improvements,** which have a limited life. Therefore, the acquisition costs of land improvements should be depreciated over their useful lives.

> **LAND IMPROVEMENTS**
> Costs that are related to land but that have a limited life.

USE AND DEPRECIATION OF PROPERTY, PLANT, AND EQUIPMENT

> **LO 5** Compare depreciation methods and understand the factors affecting the choice of method.

All property, plant, and equipment, except land, have a limited life and decline in usefulness over time. The accrual accounting process requires a proper *matching* of expenses and revenue to accurately measure income. Therefore, the accountant must estimate the decline in usefulness of operating assets and allocate the acquisition cost in a manner consistent with the decline in usefulness. This allocation is the process generally referred to as **depreciation.**

> **DEPRECIATION**
> The allocation of the original cost of an asset to the periods benefited by its use.

Unfortunately, proper matching for operating assets is not easy because of the many factors involved. An asset's decline in usefulness is related to *physical deterioration* factors such as wear and tear. In some cases, the physical deterioration results from heavy use of the asset in the production process, but it may also result from the passage of time or exposure to the elements.

The decline in an asset's usefulness is also related to *obsolescence* factors. Some operating assets, such as computers, decline in usefulness simply because they have been surpassed by a newer model or newer technology. Finally, the decline in an asset's usefulness is related to a company's *repair and maintenance* policy. A company with an aggressive and extensive repair and maintenance program will not experience a decline in usefulness of operating assets as rapidly as one without such a policy.

> *From Concept* **TO PRACTICE 8.1**
>
> **READING BEN & JERRY'S ANNUAL REPORT** What amount did Ben & Jerry's report as depreciation in 1998? Where is it disclosed? What depreciation method was used?

Because the decline in an asset's usefulness is related to a variety of factors, several depreciation methods have been developed. In theory, a company should use a depreciation method that allocates the original cost of the asset to the periods benefited and that allows the company to accurately match the expense to the revenue generated by the asset. We will present three methods of depreciation: *straight line, units of production,* and *double declining balance.*

All depreciation methods are based on the asset's original acquisition cost. In addition, all methods require an estimate of two additional factors: the asset's *life* and its *residual value.* The residual value (also referred to as *salvage value*) should represent the amount that could be obtained from selling or disposing of the asset at the end of its useful life. Often this may be a small amount or even zero.

Straight-Line Method The **straight-line method** of depreciation allocates the cost of the asset evenly over time. This method calculates the annual depreciation as follows:

> **STRAIGHT-LINE METHOD**
> A method by which the same dollar amount of depreciation is recorded in each year of asset use.

$$\text{Depreciation} = (\text{Acquisition Cost} - \text{Residual Value})/\text{Life}$$

For example, assume that on January 1, 2001, Kemp Company purchased a machine for $20,000. The company estimated that the machine's life would be five years and its residual value at the end of 2005 would be $2,000. The annual depreciation should be calculated as follows:

$$\text{Depreciation} = (\text{Acquisition Cost} - \text{Residual Value})/\text{Life}$$

$$\text{Depreciation} = (\$20{,}000 - \$2{,}000)/5$$

$$= \$3{,}600$$

Property, plant, and equipment (PP&E) constitute operating assets, which show up in the Assets section of the balance sheet. For example, trucks and satellite equipment are essential for installing, maintaining, and operating cable service to customers and should be reported as property, plant, and equipment.

An asset's **book value** is defined as its acquisition cost minus its total amount of accumulated depreciation. Thus, the book value of the machine in this example is $16,400 at the end of 2001:

$$\text{Book Value} = \text{Acquisition Cost} - \text{Accumulated Depreciation}$$

$$\text{Book Value} = \$20{,}000 - \$3{,}600$$

$$= \$16{,}400$$

The book value at the end of 2002 is $12,800:

$$\text{Book Value} = \text{Acquisition Cost} - \text{Accumulated Depreciation}$$

$$\text{Book Value} = \$20{,}000 - (2 \times \$3{,}600)$$

$$= \$12{,}800$$

The most attractive features of the straight-line method are its ease and its simplicity. It is the most popular method for presenting depreciation in the annual report to stockholders.

BOOK VALUE
The original cost of an asset minus the amount of accumulated depreciation.

UNITS-OF-PRODUCTION METHOD
Depreciation is determined as a function of the number of units the asset produces.

Units-of-Production Method In some cases, the decline in an asset's usefulness is directly related to wear and tear as a result of the number of units it produces. In those cases, depreciation should be calculated by the **units-of-production method.** With this method, the asset's life is expressed in terms of the number of units that the asset can produce. The depreciation *per unit* can be calculated as follows:

$$\text{Depreciation per Unit} = (\text{Acquisition Cost} - \text{Residual Value})/\text{Total Number of Units in Asset's Life}$$

The annual depreciation for a given year can be calculated based on the number of units produced during that year, as follows:

$$\text{Annual Depreciation} = \text{Depreciation per Unit} \times \text{Units Produced in Current Year}$$

For example, assume that Kemp Company in the previous example wanted to use the units-of-production method for 2001. Also assume that Kemp has been able to estimate that the total number of units that will be produced during the asset's five-year life is 18,000. During 2001 Kemp produced 4,000 units. The depreciation per unit for Kemp's machine can be calculated as follows:

$$\text{Depreciation per Unit} = (\text{Acquisition Cost} - \text{Residual Value})/\text{Life in Units}$$

$$\text{Depreciation per Unit} = (\$20{,}000 - \$2{,}000)/18{,}000$$

$$= \$1 \text{ per Unit}$$

The amount of depreciation that should be recorded as an expense for 2001 is $4,000:

$$\text{Annual Depreciation} = \text{Depreciation per Unit} \times \text{Units Produced in 2001}$$

$$\text{Annual Depreciation} = \$1 \text{ per Unit} \times 4{,}000 \text{ Units}$$

$$= \$4{,}000$$

Depreciation will be recorded until the asset produces 18,000 units. The machine cannot be depreciated below its residual value of $2,000.

The units-of-production method is most appropriate when the accountant is able to estimate the total number of units that will be produced over the asset's life. For example, if a factory machine is used to produce a particular item, the life of the asset may be expressed in terms of the number of units produced. Further, the units produced must be related to particular time periods so that depreciation expense can be matched accurately with the related revenue.

Accelerated Depreciation Methods In some cases, more cost should be allocated to the early years of an asset's use and less to the later years. For those assets, an accelerated method of depreciation is appropriate. The term **accelerated depreciation** refers to several depreciation methods by which a higher amount of depreciation is recorded in the early years than in later ones.

One form of accelerated depreciation is the **double declining-balance method.** Under this method, depreciation is calculated at double the straight-line rate but on a declining amount. The first step is to calculate the straight-line rate as a percentage. The straight-line rate for the Kemp asset with a five-year life is

100%/5 Years = 20%.

The second step is to double the straight-line rate:

2 × 20% = 40%

This rate will be applied in all years to the asset's book value at the beginning of each year. As depreciation is recorded, the book value declines. Thus, a constant rate is applied to a declining amount. This constant rate is applied to the full cost or initial book value, not to cost minus residual value as in the other methods. However, the machine cannot be depreciated below its residual value.

The amount of depreciation for 2001 would be calculated as follows:

Depreciation = Beginning Book Value × Rate
Depreciation = $20,000 × 40%
= $8,000

The amount of depreciation for 2002 would be calculated as follows:

Depreciation = Beginning Book Value × Rate
Depreciation = ($20,000 – $8,000) × 40%
= $4,800

The complete depreciation schedule for Kemp Company for all five years of the machine's life would be as follows:

Year	Rate	Book Value At Beginning of Year	Depreciation	Book Value At End of Year
2001	40%	$20,000	$ 8,000	$12,000
2002	40	12,000	4,800	7,200
2003	40	7,200	2,880	4,320
2004	40	4,320	1,728	2,592
2005	40	2,592	592	2,000
Total			$18,000	

In the Kemp Company example, the depreciation for 2005 cannot be calculated as $2,592 × 40% because this would result in an accumulated depreciation amount of more than $18,000. The total amount of depreciation recorded in Years 1 through 4 is $17,408. The accountant should record only $592 depreciation ($18,000 – $17,408) in 2005 so that the remaining value of the machine is $2,000 at the end of 2005.

The double declining-balance method of depreciation results in an accelerated depreciation pattern. It is most appropriate for assets subject to a rapid decline in usefulness as a result of technical or obsolescence factors. Double declining-balance depreciation is not widely used for financial statement purposes but may be appropriate for certain assets. As discussed earlier, most companies use straight-line depreciation for financial statement purposes because it generally produces the highest net income, especially in growing companies that have a stable or expanding base of assets.

ACCELERATED DEPRECIATION
A higher amount of depreciation is recorded in the early years and a lower amount in the later years.

DOUBLE DECLINING-BALANCE METHOD
Depreciation is recorded at twice the straight-line rate, but the balance is reduced each period.

Study Tip

Residual value is deducted for all depreciation methods except for the double declining-balance method.

EXHIBIT 8-1 Comparison of Depreciation and Book Values of Straight-Line and Double Declining-Balance Methods

	Straight Line		Double Declining Balance	
Year	Depreciation	Book Value	Depreciation	Book Value
2001	$ 3,600	$16,400	$ 8,000	$12,000
2002	3,600	12,800	4,800	7,200
2003	3,600	9,200	2,880	4,320
2004	3,600	5,600	1,728	2,592
2005	3,600	2,000	592	2,000
Totals	$18,000		$18,000	

Comparison of Depreciation Methods In this section, you have learned about several methods of depreciating operating assets. Exhibit 8-1 presents a comparison of the depreciation and book values of the Kemp Company asset for 2001–2005 using the straight-line and double declining-balance methods (we have excluded the units-of-production method). Note that both methods result in a depreciation total of $18,000 over the five-year time period. The amount of depreciation per year depends, however, on the method of depreciation chosen.

Nonaccountants often misunderstand the accountant's concept of depreciation. Accountants do not consider depreciation to be a process of *valuing* the asset. That is, depreciation does not describe the increase or decrease in the market value of the asset. Accountants consider depreciation to be a process of *cost allocation.* The purpose is to allocate the original acquisition cost to the periods benefited by the asset. The depreciation method chosen should be based on the decline in the asset's usefulness. A company can choose a different depreciation method for each individual fixed asset or for each class or category of fixed assets.

The choice of depreciation method can have a significant impact on the bottom line. If two companies are essentially identical in every other respect, a different depreciation method for fixed assets can make one company look more profitable than another. Or a company that uses accelerated depreciation for one year can find that its otherwise declining earnings are no longer declining if it switches to straight-line depreciation. Investors should pay some attention to depreciation methods when comparing companies. Statement users must be aware of the different depreciation methods to understand the calculation of income and to compare companies that may not use the same methods.

Some investors ignore depreciation altogether when evaluating a company, not because they do not know that assets depreciate but because they want to focus on cash flow instead of earnings. Depreciation is a "noncash" charge that reduces net income.

Depreciation and Income Taxes Financial accounting involves the presentation of financial statements to external users of accounting information, users such as investors and creditors. When depreciating an asset for financial accounting purposes, the accountant should choose a depreciation method that is consistent with the asset's decline in usefulness and that properly allocates its cost to the periods that benefit from its use.

Depreciation is also deducted for income tax purposes. Sometimes depreciation is referred to as a *tax shield* because it reduces (as do other expenses) the amount of income tax that would otherwise have to be paid. When depreciating an asset for tax purposes, a company should generally choose a depreciation method that reduces the present value of its tax burden to the lowest-possible amount over the life of the asset. Normally, this is best accomplished with an accelerated depreciation method, which allows a company to save more income tax in the early years of the asset. This happens because the higher depreciation charges reduce taxable income more than the straight-line method does. The method allowed for tax purposes is referred to as MACRS, which stands for Modified Accelerated Cost Recovery System. As a form of accelerated depreciation, it results in a larger amount of depreciation in the early years of asset life and a smaller amount in later years.

EXHIBIT 8-2 Management's Choice of Depreciation Method

Factor	Likely Choice
Simplicity →	The straight-line method is easiest to compute and record.
Reporting to stockholders →	Usually firms wish to maximize net income in reporting to stockholders and will use the straight-line method.
Comparability →	Usually firms use the same depreciation method as other firms in the same industry or line of business.
Management bonus plans →	If management is paid a bonus based on net income, they are likely to use the straight-line method.
Technological competitiveness →	If technology is changing rapidly, a firm should consider an accelerated method of depreciation.
Reporting to the Internal Revenue Service →	Firms will usually use an accelerated method of depreciation to minimize taxable income in reporting to the IRS.

Choice of Depreciation Method As we have stated, in theory a company should choose the depreciation method that best allocates the original cost of the asset to the periods benefited by the use of the asset. Theory aside, it is important to examine the other factors that affect a company's decision in choosing a depreciation method or methods. Exhibit 8–2 presents the factors that affect this decision and the likely choice that arises from each factor. Usually, the factors that are the most important are whether depreciation is calculated for presentation on the financial statements to stockholders or is calculated for income tax purposes.

When depreciation is calculated for financial statement purposes, a company generally wants to present the most favorable impression (the highest income) possible. Therefore, most companies choose the straight-line method of depreciation. Exhibit 8–3 indicates the results of a survey in which 600 companies were asked the depreciation method or methods used for their 1998 financial statements. The vast majority (577) used the straight-line method. Twenty-five used the declining-balance method, 9 used the sum-of-the-years' digits method, 43 used accelerated depreciation but did not specify which form of accelerated depreciation, 36 used the units-of-production method, and 9 used other methods of depreciation. The number of companies does not total to 600 because many companies use different methods for different assets.

If the objective of the company's management is to minimize its income tax liability, then the company will generally not choose the straight-line method for tax purposes. As discussed in the preceding section, accelerated depreciation allows the company to save more on income taxes because depreciation is a tax shield. If we could construct an exhibit, similar to Exhibit 8–3, that indicated the methods of depreciation used for tax purposes, it would indicate that the vast majority of companies do, in fact, use accelerated depreciation for tax purposes.

Therefore, it is not unusual for a company to use *two* depreciation methods for the same asset, one for financial reporting purposes and another for tax purposes. This may seem somewhat confusing, but it is the direct result of the differing goals of financial and tax accounting. See Chapter 10 for more about this issue.

EXHIBIT 8-3 Depreciation Methods Used for Financial Reporting Purposes

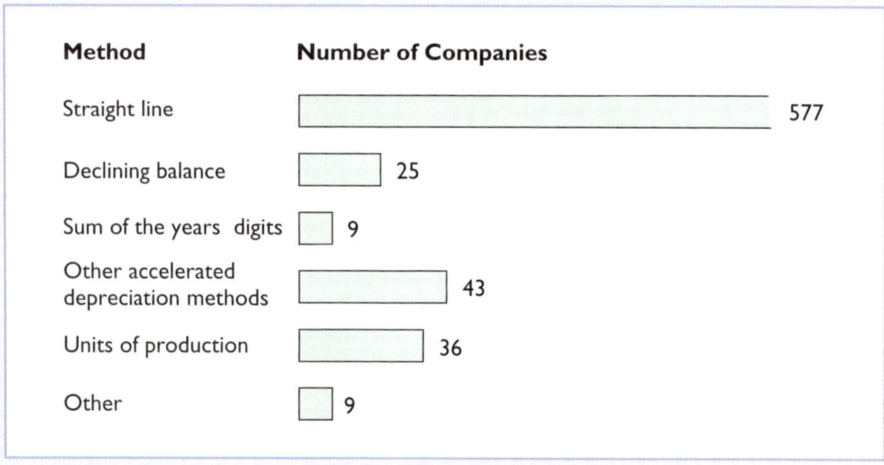

SOURCE: *Accounting Trends & Techniques*, 53rd ed. (New York: American Institute of Certified Public Accountants, 1999).

www.aicpa.org

LO 6 Understand the impact of a change in the estimate of the asset life or residual value.

CHANGE IN ESTIMATE A change in the life of the asset or in its residual value.

Change in Depreciation Estimate An asset's acquisition cost is known at the time it is purchased, but its life and its residual value must be estimated. These estimates are then used as the basis for depreciating it. Occasionally, an estimate of the asset's life or residual value must be altered after the depreciation process has begun. This is an example of an accounting change that is referred to as a **change in estimate.**

Assume the same facts as in the Kemp Company example. The company purchased a machine on January 1, 2001, for $20,000. Kemp estimated that the machine's life would be five years and its residual value at the end of five years would be $2,000. Assume that Kemp has depreciated the machine using the straight-line method for two years. At the beginning of 2003, Kemp believes that the total machine life will be seven years, or another five years beyond the two years the machine has been used. Thus, depreciation must be adjusted to reflect the new estimate of the asset's life.

A change in estimate should be recorded *prospectively,* meaning that the depreciation recorded in prior years is not corrected or restated. Instead, the new estimate should affect the current year and future years. Kemp Company should depreciate the remaining depreciable amount during 2003 through 2007. The amount to be depreciated over that time period should be calculated as follows:

ACCOUNTING FOR YOUR DECISIONS

You Are the Sole Owner

Your accountant has presented you with three sets of financial statements—each with a different depreciation method—and asks you which depreciation method you prefer. You answer that other than for tax purposes, you don't really care. Should you?

ANS: For tax purposes you would prefer to use the accelerated depreciation method, which minimizes your net income so that you can pay the minimum allowable taxes. For financial statement purposes you may use a different method. As a sole owner, you may believe that the depreciation method chosen does not matter because you are more concerned with the cash flow of the firm and depreciation is a noncash item. However, the depreciation method is important if you are going to show your statements to external parties—for example, if you must present your statements to a banker in order to get a loan.

Acquisition Cost, Jan. 1, 2001	$20,000
Less: Accumulated Depreciation	
(2 years at $3,600 per year)	7,200
Book Value, Jan. 1, 2003	$12,800
Less: Residual Value	2,000
Remaining Depreciable Amount	$10,800

The remaining depreciable amount should be recorded as depreciation over the remaining life of the machine. In the Kemp Company case, the depreciation amount for 2003 and the following four years would be $2,160:

Depreciation = Remaining Depreciable Amount/Remaining Life

Depreciation = $10,800 / 5 Years

= $2,160

The journal entry to record depreciation for the year 2003 is as follows:

2003			
Dec. 31	Depreciation Expense	2,160	
	Accumulated Depreciation		2,160
	To record depreciation for 2003 based on remaining life of five years.		

Assets	=	Liabilities	+	Owners' Equity
−2,160				−2,160

If the change in estimate is a material amount, the company should disclose in the footnotes to the 2003 financial statements that depreciation has changed as a result of a change in estimate. The company's auditors have to be very careful that management's decision to change its estimate of the depreciable life of the asset is not simply an attempt to manipulate earnings. Particularly in capital-intensive manufacturing concerns, lengthening the useful life of equipment can have a material impact on earnings.

A change in estimate of an asset's residual value is treated in a manner similar to a change in an asset's life. There should be no attempt to correct or restate the income statements of past periods that were based on the original estimate. Instead, the accountant should use the new estimate of residual value to calculate depreciation for the current and future years.

A change in estimate is not treated the same way as a *change in principle.* If a company changes its *method* of depreciation, for example from accelerated depreciation to the straight-line method, this constitutes a change in accounting principle and must be disclosed separately on the income statement.

Two-Minute Review

1. What items should be included when calculating the acquisition cost of an asset?

2. Which will be higher in the early years of an asset's life—straight-line depreciation or accelerated depreciation? Which will be higher in the later years? Which will be higher in total over the entire life of the asset?

Answers:

1. The general rule for calculating the acquisition cost of an asset is to include all of the costs that were necessary to acquire the asset and prepare it for use. Normally, that would include the purchase price but would also include costs such as freight costs, taxes, and installation costs if they were necessary to prepare the asset for use.

2. Accelerated depreciation will be higher in the early years of the asset, and straight-line will be higher in the later years. Over the life of the asset the total amount of depreciation will be the same under all of the methods, assuming that the same amount of salvage value is estimated for each of the methods.

CAPITAL VERSUS REVENUE EXPENDITURES

LO 7 Determine which expenditures should be capitalized as asset costs and which should be treated as expenses.

CAPITAL EXPENDITURE A cost that improves the asset and is added to the asset account.

REVENUE EXPENDITURE A cost that keeps an asset in its normal operating condition and is treated as an expense.

Accountants must often decide whether certain expenditures related to operating assets should be treated as an addition to the cost of the asset or as an expense. One of the most common examples involving this decision concerns repairs to an asset. Should the repairs constitute capital expenditures or revenue expenditures? A **capital expenditure** is a cost that is added to the acquisition cost of the asset. A **revenue expenditure** is not treated as part of the cost of the asset but as an expense on the income statement. Thus, the company must decide whether to treat an item as an asset (balance sheet) and depreciate its cost over its life or to treat it as an expense (income statement) of a single period.

The distinction between capital and revenue expenditures is a matter of judgment. Generally, the guideline that should be followed is that if an expenditure increases the life of the asset or its productivity, it should be treated as a capital expenditure and added to the asset account. If an expenditure simply maintains an asset in its normal operating condition, however, it should be treated as an expense. The *materiality* of the expenditure must also be considered. Most companies establish a policy of treating an expenditure smaller than a specified amount as a revenue expenditure (an expense on the income statement).

It is very important that a company not improperly capitalize a material expenditure that should have been written off right away. The capitalization policies of companies are closely watched by Wall Street analysts who try to assess the value of these companies. When a company is capitalizing rather than expensing certain items to artificially boost earnings, that revelation can be very damaging to the stock price.

Expenditures related to operating assets may be classified in several categories. For each type of expenditure, its treatment as capital or revenue should be as follows:

Category	Example	Asset or Expense
Normal maintenance	Repainting	Expense
Minor repair	Replace spark plugs	Expense
Major repair	Replace a vehicle's engine	Asset, if life or productivity is enhanced
Addition	Add a wing to a building	Asset

ACCOUNTING FOR YOUR DECISIONS

You Are the Owner

You are a realtor whose business car has just had its transmission rebuilt for $400. Would you classify this "repair" as a capital expenditure or a revenue expenditure? Why is it important to properly classify the $400?

ANS: If the business car's life is not extended, then the repair should be treated as a revenue expenditure, in which the cost is expensed on the income statement. It is important to properly classify capital and revenue expenditures because capitalizing rather than expensing costs can artificially boost earnings. The opposite effect would occur if costs are expensed and not capitalized.

An item treated as a capital expenditure affects the amount of depreciation that should be recorded over the asset's remaining life. We return to the Kemp Company example to illustrate. Assume again that Kemp purchased a machine on January 1, 2001, for $20,000. Kemp estimated that its residual value at the end of five years would be $2,000 and has depreciated the machine using the straight-line method for 2001 and 2002. At the beginning of 2003, Kemp made a $3,000 overhaul to the machine, extending its life by three years. Because the expenditure qualifies as a capital expenditure, the cost of overhauling the machine should be added to the asset account. The journal entry to record the overhaul is as follows:

2003			
Jan. 1	Machine	3,000	
	Cash		3,000
	To record the overhaul of an operating asset.		

Assets	=	Liabilities	+	Owners' Equity
+3,000				
−3,000				

For the years 2001 and 2002, Kemp recorded depreciation of $3,600 per year:

Depreciation = (Acquisition Cost − Residual Value)/Life

Depreciation = ($20,000 − $2,000)/5

= $3,600

Beginning in 2003, Kemp should record depreciation of $2,300 per year, computed as follows:

Original Cost, Jan. 1, 2001	$20,000
Less: Accumulated Depreciation (2 years × $3,600)	7,200
Book Value, Jan. 1, 2003	$12,800
Plus: Major Overhaul	3,000
Less: Residual Value	(2,000)
Remaining Depreciable Amount	$13,800

Depreciation = Remaining Depreciable Amount/Remaining Life

Depreciation per year = $13,800/6 Years

= $2,300

The entry to record depreciation for the year 2003 follows:

2003			
Dec. 31	Depreciation Expense	2,300	
	Accumulated Depreciation—Asset		2,300
	To record annual depreciation on operating asset.		

Assets	=	Liabilities	+	Owners' Equity
−2,300				−2,300

Should the costs of cleaning up a contaminated factory be considered an expense of one period or a capital expenditure added to the cost of the plant asset? To make the best decision, management should gather all the facts about the extent of the proposed cleanup and its environmental impact.

Environmental Aspects of Operating Assets

As the number of the government's environmental regulations has increased, businesses have been required to expend more money complying with them. A common example involves costs to comply with federal requirements to clean up contaminated soil surrounding plant facilities. In some cases the costs are very large and may exceed the value of the property. Should such costs be considered an expense and recorded entirely in one accounting period, or should they be treated as a capital expenditure and added to the cost of the asset? At the present time, there is little accounting guidance on such issues, and management must exercise careful judgment on a case-by-case basis. It is important, however, for companies at least to conduct a thorough investigation to determine the potential environmental considerations that may affect the value of operating assets and to ponder carefully the accounting implications of new environmental regulations.

Disposal of Property, Plant, and Equipment

LO 8 Analyze the effect of the disposal of an asset at a gain or loss.

An asset may be disposed of in any of several different ways. One common method is to sell the asset for cash. Sale of an asset involves two important considerations. First, depreciation must be recorded up to the date of sale. If the sale does not occur at the fiscal year-end, usually December 31, depreciation must be recorded for a partial period from the beginning of the year to the date of sale. Second, the company selling the asset must calculate and record the gain or loss on its sale.

Refer again to the Kemp Company example. Assume that Kemp purchased a machine on January 1, 2001, for $20,000, estimating its life to be five years and the residual value to be $2,000. Kemp used the straight-line method of depreciation. Assume that Kemp sold the machine on July 1, 2003, for $12,400. Depreciation for the six-month time period from January 1 to July 1, 2003, is $1,800 ($3,600 per year × 1/2 year = $1,800) and should be recorded as follows:

2003			
July 1	Depreciation Expense	1,800	
	Accumulated Depreciation—Machine		1,800
	To record depreciation for a six-month time period.		

Assets	=	Liabilities	+	Owners' Equity
−1,800				−1,800

After the July 1 entry, the balance of the Accumulated Depreciation—Machine account is $9,000, which reflects depreciation for the 2½ years from the date of purchase to the date of sale. The entry to record the sale follows:

2003			
July 1	Accumulated Depreciation—Machine	9,000	
	Cash	12,400	
	Machine		20,000
	Gain on Sale of Asset		1,400
	To record the sale of the machine.		

Assets	=	Liabilities	+	Owners' Equity
+9,000				+1,400
+12,400				
−20,000				

GAIN ON SALE OF ASSET
The excess of the selling price over the asset's book value.

When an asset is sold, all accounts related to it must be removed. In the preceding entry the Machine account is reduced (credited) to eliminate the account, and the Accumulated Depreciation—Machine account is reduced (debited) to eliminate it. The **Gain on Sale of Asset** indicates the amount by which the sale price of the machine *exceeds* the book value. Thus, the gain can be calculated as follows:

Asset cost	$20,000
Less: Accumulated depreciation	9,000
Book value	$11,000
Sale price	12,400
Gain on Sale of Asset	$ 1,400

The account Gain on Sale of Asset is an income statement account and should appear in the Other Income/Expense category of the statement. The Gain on Sale of Asset account is not treated as revenue because it does not constitute the company's ongoing or central activity. Instead, it appears as income but in a separate category to denote its incidental nature.

The calculation of a loss on the sale of an asset is similar to that of a gain. Assume in the above example that Kemp had sold the machine on July 1, 2003, for $10,000 cash. As in the previous example, depreciation must be recorded to the date of sale, July 1. The following is the entry to record the sale of the asset:

2003			
July 1	Accumulated Depreciation—Machine	9,000	
	Cash	10,000	
	Loss on Sale of Asset	1,000	
	Machine		20,000
	To record the sale of a machine.		

Assets	=	Liabilities	+	Owners' Equity
+9,000				−1,000
+10,000				
−20,000				

The **Loss on Sale of Asset** indicates the amount by which the asset's sales price *is less than* its book value. Thus, the loss could be calculated as follows:

Loss on sale of asset The amount by which selling price is less than book value.

Asset cost	$20,000
Less: Accumulated depreciation	9,000
Book value	$11,000
Sale price	10,000
Loss on Sale of Asset	$ 1,000

The Loss on Sale of Asset account is an income statement account and should appear in the Other Income/Expense category of the income statement.

Business Strategy

Five of the nation's seven largest media conglomerates boast broadcast television networks among their many assets. Along with book- and magazine-publishing companies, music publishers, theme parks, cable TV stations, professional sports teams, and movie companies, these five giants own the WB Network (Time Warner), ABC (Walt Disney), CBS (Viacom/CBS), Fox (New Corp.), and NBC (GE).

For most of these firms, broadcasting—whether network or cable—provides several billions of dollars of revenue each year, amounting to approximately a quarter to half their annual revenue. The exception is GE, which earns only 5 percent of its $100 billion yearly from NBC and other TV stations it owns. Time Warner's cable programming business includes ownership of HBO, TNT, TBS, Turner Classic Movies, Cinemax, and CNN. Its cable business is particularly profitable, bringing the firm one-quarter of the cable industry's growing advertising budget.

Cable programming is drawing more and more consumers from network television every year, and in 1998 every broadcast network experienced a decline in the number of viewers. Time Warner expects that trend to continue, and from a glance at its cable assets, it appears the firm is well prepared to reap the benefits.

However, *Time* magazine (which is owned by Time Warner) recently reported that Time Warner's vice chairman Ted Turner would be interested in purchasing NBC, perhaps reflecting the recent purchase of CBS by rival Viacom. Will Turner be able to influence the firm's current media strategy and move Time Warner into network broadcasting? How should an asset such as NBC be evaluated, given the continued growth of cable programming at the expense of the networks, and how would its value influence Time Warner's media strategy?

Sources: Time Warner's 1998 annual report; Karl Taro Greenfeld, "A Media Giant," *Time*, Sept. 20, 1999, pp. 48–54.

Operating Assets: Natural Resources

Balance Sheet Presentation

Important operating assets for some companies consists of **natural resources** such as coalfields, oil wells, other mineral deposits, and timberlands. Natural resources share one characteristic: the resource is consumed as it is used. For example, the coal a utility company uses

Natural resources Assets that are consumed during their use.

to make electricity is consumed in the process. Most natural resources cannot be replenished in the foreseeable future. Coal and oil, for example, can be replenished only by nature over millions of years. Timberlands may be replenished in a shorter time period, but even trees must grow for many years to be usable for lumber.

Natural resources should be carried in the Property, Plant, and Equipment category of the balance sheet as an operating asset. Like other assets in the category, natural resources should initially be recorded at *acquisition cost.* Acquisition cost should include the cost of acquiring the natural resource and the costs necessary to prepare the asset for use. The preparation costs for natural resources may often be very large; for example, a utility may spend large sums to remove layers of dirt before the coal can be mined. These preparation costs should be added to the cost of the asset.

Depletion of Natural Resources

When a natural resource is used or consumed, it should be treated as an expense. The process of recording the expense is similar to the depreciation or amortization process but is usually referred to as *depletion.* The amount of depletion expense each period should reflect the portion of the natural resource that was used up during the current year.

Assume, for example, that Local Coal Company purchased a coalfield on January 1, 2001, for $1 million. The company employed a team of engineering experts who estimated the total coal in the field to be 200,000 tons and who determined that the field's residual value after removal of the coal would be zero. Local Coal should calculate the depletion per ton as follows:

Depletion per Ton = (Acquisition Cost − Residual Value)/Total Number of Tons in Asset's Life
= ($1,000,000 − 0)/200,000 tons
= $5 per ton

Depletion expense for each year should be calculated as follows:

Depletion Expense = Depletion per Ton × Tons Mined during Year

Assume that Local Coal Company mined 10,000 tons of coal during 2001. The depletion expense for 2001 for Local Coal follows:

$5 × 10,000 tons = $50,000

Local Coal should record the depletion in an Accumulated Depletion—Coalfield account, which would appear as a contra-asset on the balance sheet. The company should record the following journal entry:

2001			
Dec. 31	Depletion Expense	50,000	
	Accumulated Depletion—Coalfield		50,000
	To record depletion for 2001.		

Assets	=	Liabilities	+	Owners' Equity
−50,000				−50,000

Rather than using an accumulated depletion account, some companies may decrease (credit) the asset account directly.

There is an interesting parallel between depletion of natural resources and depreciation of plant and equipment. That is, depletion is very similar to depreciation using the units-of-production method. Both require an estimate of the useful life of the asset in terms of the total amount that can be produced (for units-of-production method) or consumed (for depletion) over the asset's life.

www.boisecascade.com

Natural resources may be important assets for some companies. For example, Exhibit 8-4 highlights the asset portion of the 1998 balance sheet and the accompanying footnote of Boise Cascade Corporation. Boise Cascade had timber and timberlands, net of

EXHIBIT 8-4 Boise Cascade Corporation and Subsidiaries 1998 Assets Section and Natural Resources Footnote

	December 31	
Property and equipment (in thousands)	1998	1997
Land and land improvements	63,307	57,260
Buildings and improvements	575,509	554,712
Machinery and equipment	4,082,724	4,055,065
	4,721,540	4,667,037
Accumulated depreciation	(2,150,385)	(2,037,352)
	2,571,155	2,629,685
Timber, timberlands, and timber deposits	270,570	273,001
	2,841,725	2,902,686

Cost of company timber harvested and amortization of logging roads are determined on the basis of the annual amount of timber cut in relation to the total amount of recoverable timber. Timber and timberlands are stated at cost, less the accumulated cost of timber previously harvested.

depletion, of $270,570,000 as of December 31, 1998. The footnote indicates that the company records the cost of timber harvested on the basis of annual amount of timber cut in relation to the total amount of recoverable timber.

OPERATING ASSETS: INTANGIBLE ASSETS

Intangible assets are long-term assets with no physical properties. Because one cannot see or touch most intangible assets, it is easy to overlook their importance. Intangibles are recorded as assets, however, because they provide future economic benefits to the company. In fact, an intangible asset may be the most important asset a company owns or controls. For example, a pharmaceutical company may own some property, plant, and equipment, but its most important asset may be its patent for a particular drug or process. Likewise, the company that publishes this textbook may consider the copyrights to textbooks to be among its most important revenue-producing assets.

INTANGIBLE ASSETS Assets with no physical properties.

The balance sheet includes the intangible assets that meet the accounting definition of assets. Patents, copyrights, and brand names are included because they are owned by the company and will produce a future benefit that can be identified and measured. The balance sheet, however, would indicate only the acquisition cost of those assets, not the value of the assets to the company or the sales value of the assets.

From Concept **TO PRACTICE 8.2**

READING TIME WARNER'S BALANCE SHEET Which items on Time-Warner's 1998 balance sheet should be considered intangible assets?

Of course, the balance sheet does not include all of the items that may produce future benefit to the company. A company's employees, its management team, its location, or the intellectual capital of a few key researchers may well provide important future benefits and value. They are not recorded on the balance sheet, however, because they do not meet the accountant's definition of *assets* and cannot be easily identified or measured.

BALANCE SHEET PRESENTATION

LO 9 Understand the balance sheet presentation of intangible assets.

Intangible assets are long-term assets and should be shown separately from property, plant, and equipment. Exhibit 8-5 contains a list of the most common intangible assets. Some companies develop a separate category, Intangible Assets, for the various types of

EXHIBIT 8-5 Most Common Intangible Assets

Intangible Asset	Description
Patent	Right to use, manufacture, or sell a product; granted by the U.S. Patent Office. Patents have a legal life of 20 years.
Copyright	Right to reproduce or sell a published work. Copyrights are granted for 50 years plus the life of the creator.
Trademark	A symbol or name that allows a product or service to be identified; provides legal protection for 20 years plus an indefinite number of renewal periods.
Goodwill	The excess of the purchase price to acquire a business over the value of the individual net assets acquired.

www.quakeroats.com

intangibles. For example, Exhibit 8-6 presents the Assets section and the accompanying footnote of the 1998 balance sheet of Quaker Oats Company. Note that intangibles account for nearly one-tenth of Quaker's total assets. Quaker presents only one line for intangible assets, but the footnote indicates that intangibles consist primarily of goodwill (see below), which is amortized on a straight-line basis. The presentation of intangible assets varies widely, however.

www.alberto-culver.com

Exhibit 8-7 presents the Assets section and the accompanying footnote of the 1998 balance sheet of Alberto-Culver Company. Alberto-Culver presents the intangible assets of goodwill and trade names immediately after the Property, Plant, and Equipment category. Both accounts are presented net of the accumulated amortization. The footnote indicates that amortization was computed on the straight-line basis.

GOODWILL
The excess of the purchase price of a business over the total market value of identifiable assets.

The nature of many intangibles is fairly evident, but goodwill is not so easily understood. **Goodwill** represents the amount of the purchase price paid in excess of the market value of the individual net assets when a business is purchased. Goodwill is recorded only when a business is purchased. It is not recorded when a company engages in activities that do not involve the purchase of another business entity. For example, customer loyalty or a good management team may represent "goodwill," but neither meets the accountants' criteria to be recorded as an asset on a firm's financial statements.

Some investors believe that goodwill is not an asset because it is difficult to determine the factors that caused this asset. They prefer to focus their attention on a company's tangible assets. These investors simply reduce the amount shown on the balance sheet by the amount of goodwill, deducting it from total assets and reducing stockholders' equity by the same amount. That is similar to the goodwill accounting that occurs in many foreign countries. International accounting standards allow firms *either* to present goodwill separately as an asset *or* to deduct it from stockholders' equity at the time of purchase. The result is that the presentation of goodwill on the financial statements of non-U.S. companies can look much different from that for U.S. companies.

ACQUISITION COST OF INTANGIBLE ASSETS

As was the case with property, plant, and equipment, the acquisition cost of an intangible asset includes all of the costs to acquire the asset and prepare it for its intended use. This should include all necessary costs such as legal costs incurred at the time of acquisition. Acquisition cost also should include those costs that are incurred after acquisition and that are necessary to the existence of the asset. For example, if a firm must pay legal fees to protect a patent from infringement, the costs should be considered part of the acquisition cost and should be included in the patent account.

RESEARCH AND DEVELOPMENT COSTS
Costs incurred in the discovery of new knowledge.

You should also be aware of one item that is similar to intangible assets but is *not* on the balance sheet. **Research and development costs** are expenditures incurred in the discovery of new knowledge and the translation of research into a design or plan for a new product or service or in a significant improvement to an existing product or service.

EXHIBIT 8-6 The Quaker Oats Company and Subsidiaries 1998 Assets Section and Intangibles Footnote

Consolidated Balance Sheets

December 31	1998	1997
Assets		
Current Assets		
Cash and cash equivalents	$ 326.6	$ 84.2
Marketable securities	27.5	—
Trade accounts receivable – net of allowances	283.4	305.7
Inventories		
Finished goods	189.1	172.6
Grains and raw materials	48.4	59.0
Packaging materials and supplies	23.9	24.5
Total inventories	261.4	256.1
Other current assets	216.1	487.0
Total Current Assets	1,115.0	1,133.0
Property, Plant and Equipment		
Land	24.1	29.1
Buildings and improvements	390.2	417.2
Machinery and equipment	1,404.5	1,466.8
Property, plant and equipment	1,818.8	1,913.1
Less: accumulated depreciation	748.6	748.4
Property – Net	1,070.2	1,164.7
Intangible Assets – Net of Amortization	245.7	350.5
Other Assets	79.4	48.8
Total Assets	$ 2,510.3	$ 2,697.0

See accompanying notes to the consolidated financial statements.

Intangibles – Intangible assets consist principally of excess purchase price over net tangible assets of businesses acquired (goodwill) and trademarks. Intangible assets are amortized on a straight-line basis over periods ranging from two to 40 years.

Firms that engage in research and development do so because they believe such activities provide future benefit to the company. In fact, many firms have become leaders in an industry by engaging in research and development and the discovery of new products or technology. It is often very difficult, however, to identify the amount of future benefits of research and development and to associate those benefits with specific time periods. Because of the difficulty in predicting future benefits, the FASB has ruled that firms are not allowed to treat research and development costs as assets; all such expenditures must be treated as expenses in the period incurred. Many firms, especially high-technology ones, argue that this accounting rule results in seriously understated balance sheets. In their view, an important "asset" is not portrayed on their balance sheet. They also argue that they are at a competitive disadvantage when compared with foreign companies that are allowed to treat at least a portion of research and development as an asset. Users of financial statements somehow need to be aware of those "hidden assets" when analyzing the balance sheets of companies that must expense research and development costs.

It is important to distinguish between patent costs and research and development costs. Patent costs include legal and filing fees necessary to acquire a patent. Such costs are capitalized as an intangible asset, Patent. However, the Patent account should not include the costs of research and development of a new product. Those costs are not capitalized but are treated as an expense, Research and Development.

EXHIBIT 8-7 Alberto-Culver Company and Subsidiaries 1998 Assets Section and Intangibles Footnote

CONSOLIDATED BALANCE SHEETS

Alberto-Culver Company and Subsidiaries

(In thousands, except per share data)	September 30, 1998	1997
Assets		
Current assets:		
Cash and cash equivalents	$ 72,395	76,040
Short-term investments	910	11,560
Receivables, less allowance for doubtful accounts of $10,868 in 1998 and $9,042 in 1997 (note 3)	129,063	120,774
Inventories:		
Raw materials	37,316	44,175
Work-in-process	6,119	7,252
Finished goods	325,769	292,441
Total inventories	369,204	343,868
Prepaid expenses	19,993	28,017
Total current assets	591,565	580,259
Property, plant and equipment (note 7):		
Land	11,328	10,357
Buildings and leasehold improvements	139,622	124,920
Machinery and equipment	257,458	214,876
Total property, plant and equipment	408,408	350,153
Accumulated depreciation	184,932	159,155
Property, plant and equipment, net	223,476	190,998
Goodwill, net	137,599	114,245
Trade names, net	67,158	70,155
Other assets	48,386	44,402
	$1,068,184	1,000,059

Goodwill and Trade Names The cost of goodwill and trade names is amortized on a straight-line basis over periods ranging from ten to forty years.

ACCOUNTING FOR YOUR DECISIONS

You Are the Student Intern

Your colleagues at the investment house where you are doing a summer internship insist that the intangible assets on the Quaker Oats and Alberto-Culver balance sheets are worthless and should be removed before any analysis can be completed on the two companies. Would you agree or disagree with their position?

ANS: Intangible assets are not worthless. Just because an asset is "intangible" and difficult to quantify doesn't mean it should be removed. Intangible assets such as goodwill and trademarks are frequently listed on balance sheets. They represent assets from an accounting viewpoint and may indeed be some of the most important assets of the company. The patents and trademarks of Quaker Oats and Alberto-Culver are assets because they will provide future benefits in the form of sales of products.

AMORTIZATION OF INTANGIBLES

LO 10 Describe the proper amortization of intangible assets.

Intangibles should be reported on the balance sheet at acquisition cost less accumulated amortization. *Amortization* is very similar to depreciation of property, plant, and equipment. Amortization involves allocating the acquisition cost of the intangible asset to the periods benefited by the use of the asset; and accounting standards state that the period may generally not exceed 20 years. In most cases, companies use the straight-line method of amortization. You may see instances of an accelerated form of amortization, however, if the decline in usefulness of the intangible asset does not occur evenly over time.

Assume that ML Company developed a patent for a new product on January 1, 2001. The costs involved with patent approval were $10,000, and the company wants to record amortization on the straight-line basis over a five-year life with no residual value. The accounting entry to record the amortization for 2001 is as follows:

2001			
Dec. 31	Patent Amortization Expense	2,000	
	Accumulated Amortization—Patent		2,000
	To record amortization of patent for one year		

Assets	=	Liabilities	+	Owners' Equity
−2,000				−2,000

Rather than use an accumulated amortization account, some companies decrease (credit) the intangible asset account directly. In that case, the preceding transaction is recorded as follows:

2001			
Dec. 31	Patent Amortization Expense	2,000	
	Patent		2,000
	To record amortization of patent for one year.		

Assets	=	Liabilities	+	Owners' Equity
−2,000				−2,000

No matter which of the two preceding entries is used, the asset should be reported on the balance sheet at acquisition cost ($10,000) less accumulated amortization ($2,000), or $8,000, as of December 31, 2001.

Some questions exist about the time period over which to amortize intangible assets. The general guideline is that an intangible should be amortized *over its legal life or useful life, whichever is shorter.* For example, a patent has a legal life of 20 years, but many are not useful for that long because new products and technology may surpass them.[2] The patent should be amortized over the number of years in which the firm receives benefits, which may be a period shorter than its legal life.

Certain intangibles have no legal life, and their useful life is very difficult to determine. Goodwill is the primary example. Some accountants argue that goodwill has an unlimited life and should not be amortized. Others argue that the benefits of goodwill are too difficult to determine and this intangible asset should be written off as an expense in its entirety in the year of acquisition. The current accounting guideline takes a compromise approach. Goodwill must be amortized over a time period that cannot exceed 20 years. Thus, goodwill must be amortized in a manner similar to the amortization of other intangible assets: over its estimated useful life. But if it is not possible to determine the useful life, the maximum amortization period is 20 years.[3]

Finally, it is important to monitor the usefulness of intangible assets as time passes. An intangible asset that will not produce future benefit should be written off as an expense.

[2]Patents run for a term of 20 years from the filing date or 17 years from the date they are granted. This text will use 20 years as the time period for amortization.

[3]The accounting rules stated in this section are from the FASB Exposure Draft, "Business Combinations and Intangible Assets," September 7, 1999. There is one exception to the 20-year rule. If an intangible asset has identifiable cash flows that will extend beyond 20 years and meets certain other criteria, then the intangible may be amortized over a longer time period or in some cases may not be amortized at all.

*Amortize is same as deprec.

Assume in the ML example that ML learns on January 1, 2002, when accumulated amortization is $2,000 (or the book value of the patent is $8,000), that a competing company has developed a new product that renders ML's patent worthless. ML has a loss of $8,000 and should record an entry to write off the asset as follows:

2002			
Jan. 1	Loss on Patent	8,000	
	Accumulated Amortization—Patent	2,000	
	Patent		10,000
	To record the write-off of patent.		

Assets	=	Liabilities	+	Owners' Equity
+2,000				−8,000
−10,000				

The treatment of intangibles with diminished value is consistent with the treatment of all assets. Assets existing on the balance sheet date represent future benefits or revenue. If an item does not have future usefulness, it must be removed from the balance sheet and treated as a loss or expense.

Two-Minute Review

1. What are some examples of intangible assets?

2. Over what time period should intangibles be amortized? What method is generally used?

Answers:

1. Intangibles are assets that have no physical properties. Examples are copyrights, trademarks, patents, franchises, and goodwill.

2. Intangibles should be amortized over the legal life of the asset or the useful life, whichever is shorter. The maximum time period for intangibles is generally twenty years, but in some cases a company may be able to justify a longer time period. Most companies use the straight-line method of amortization. Accelerated methods of amortization are allowed but are not often used.

Analyzing Long-Term Assets for Average Life and Asset Turnover

Because long-term assets constitute the major productive assets of most companies, it is important to analyze the age and composition of these assets. We will analyze the assets of Ben & Jerry's in the following section. Analysis of the age of the assets can be accomplished fairly easily for those companies that use the straight-line method of depreciation. A rough measure of the *average life* of the assets can be calculated as follows:

Average Life = Property, Plant, and Equipment/Depreciation Expense

The *average age* of the assets can be calculated as follows:

Average Age = Accumulated Depreciation/Depreciation Expense

www.benjerry.com

At the end of 1998, Ben & Jerry's had property, plant, and equipment of $100,292,000 and accumulated depreciation of $36,841,000. A careful reading of the annual report also indicates depreciation expense of $7,900,000 for 1998. Therefore, the average life of Ben & Jerry's assets is calculated as follows:

Average Life = Property, Plant, and Equipment/Depreciation Expense

Average Life = $100,292,000/$7,900,000

= 12.7 Years

This is a rough estimate because it assumes that the company has purchased assets fairly evenly over time. Because it is an average, it indicates that some assets have a life longer than 12.7 years and others shorter lives.

The average age of Ben & Jerry's assets is calculated as follows:

$$\text{Average Age} = \text{Accumulated Depreciation}/\text{Depreciation Expense}$$

$$\text{Average Age} = \$36{,}841{,}000/\$7{,}900{,}000$$

$$= 4.7 \text{ Years}$$

This indicates that Ben & Jerry's assets are, on average, fairly new and should be productive for several more years.

The asset category of the balance sheet is also important in analyzing the company's *profitability.* The asset turnover ratio is a measure of the productivity of the assets and is measured as follows:

$$\text{Asset Turnover} = \text{Net Sales}/\text{Average Total Assets}$$

This ratio is a measure of how many dollars of assets are necessary for every dollar of sales. If a company is using its assets efficiently, each dollar of assets will create a high amount of sales. Technically, the ratio is based on average *total assets,* but long-term assets often constitute the largest portion of a company's total assets.

How Long-Term Assets Affect the Statement of Cash Flows

LO 11 Explain the impact that long-term assets have on the statement of cash flows.

Determining the impact that acquisition, depreciation, and sale of long-term assets have on the statement of cash flows is important. Each of these business activities influences the statement of cash flows. Exhibit 8-8 illustrates the items discussed in this chapter and their effect on the statement of cash flows.

The acquisition of a long-term asset is an investing activity and should be reflected in the Investing Activities category of the statement of cash flows. The acquisition should appear as a deduction or negative item in that section because it requires the use of cash to purchase the asset. This applies whether the long-term asset is property, plant, and equipment or an intangible asset.

The depreciation or amortization of a long-term asset is *not* a cash item. It was referred to earlier as a noncash charge to earnings. Nevertheless, it must be presented on the statement

Exhibit 8-8 Long-Term Assets and the Statement of Cash Flows

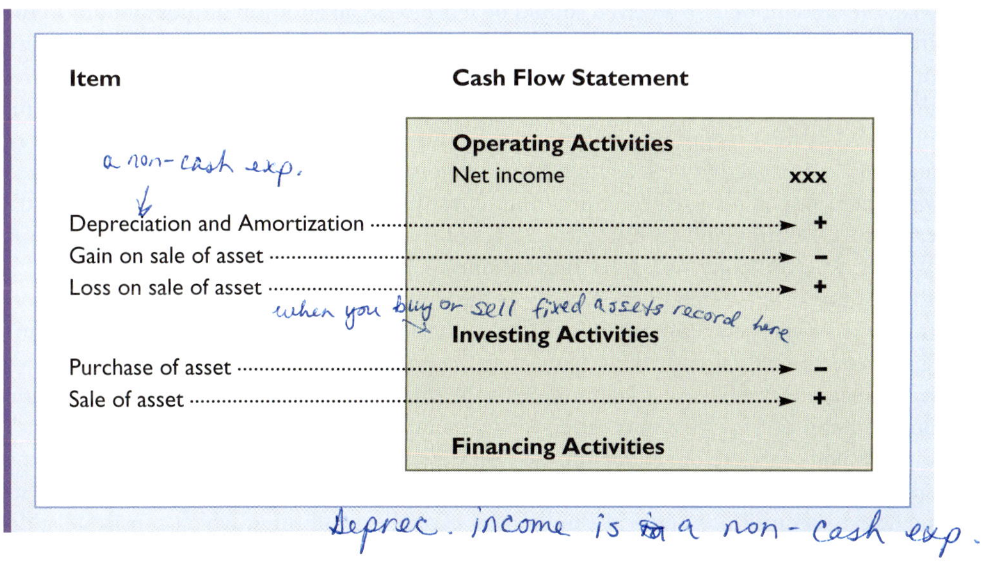

EXHIBIT 8-9 Time Warner Partial Consolidated Statement of Cash Flows

Years Ended December 31, (millions)	1998
Operations	
Net income (loss)	$ 168
Adjustments for noncash and nonoperating items:	
Extraordinary loss on retirement of debt	—
Depreciation and amortization	1,178
Noncash interest expense	30
Excess (deficiency) of distributions over equity in pretax income of Entertainment Group	342
Equity in losses (income) of other investee companies after distributions	147
Changes in operating assets and liabilities:	
Receivables	(597)
Inventories	(312)
Accounts payable and other liabilities	810
Other balance sheet changes	79
Cash provided by operations	1,845
Investing Activities	
Investments and acquisitions	(159)
Capital expenditures	(512)
Investment proceeds	569
Proceeds received from distribution of TWE Senior Capital	455
Cash provided (used) by investing activities	353

Depre. exp., non cash

Trading & held to, available for sale securities

of cash flows (if the indirect method is used for the statement). The reason is that it was deducted from earnings in calculating the net income figure. Therefore, it must be eliminated or "added back" if the net income amount is used to indicate the amount of cash generated from operations. Thus, depreciation and amortization should be presented in the Operating Activities category of the statement of cash flows as an addition to net income.

The sale or disposition of long-term assets is an investing activity. When an asset is sold, the amount of cash received should be reflected as an addition or plus amount in the Investing Activities category of the statement of cash flows. If the asset was sold at a gain or loss, however, one additional aspect should be reflected. Because the gain or loss was reflected on the income statement, it should be eliminated from the net income amount presented in the Operating Activities category (if the indirect method is used). A sale of an asset is not an activity related to normal, ongoing operations, and all amounts involved with the sale should be removed from the Operating Activities category. Exhibit 8-9 indicates the Operating and Investing categories of the 1998 statement of cash flows of Time Warner. The company had a net income during 1998; that income, of $168 million, is the first line of the Operations category of the cash flow statement. Time Warner's performance is an excellent example of the difference between the net income on the income statement and actual cash flow. Note that the company generated a positive cash flow from operations of $1,845 million. One of the primary reasons was that depreciation and amortization of $1,178 million affected the income statement but do not involve a cash outflow and are therefore added on the cash flow statement. Also note that the Investing Activities category indicates major outlays of cash for new assets: $159 million for investments and acquisitions and $512 million for capital expenditures, which constitute additions to property, plant, and equipment.

www.timewarner.com

From Concept **TO PRACTICE 8.3**

REFER TO GATEWAY'S CASH FLOW STATEMENT What amount did the company spend on capital expenditures during 1998?

"When it comes to young companies, I often focus on *intangible* assets such as key personnel, patents on technology, and market share."

–Aishetu Kolo

FOCUS ON USERS

Name: Aishetu Kolo
Education: B.A., Cornell University
College Major: Economics
Occupation: Financial Analyst, Chicago
Age: 23

This Analyst Often Focuses on Intangible Assets

Aishetu Kolo is a financial analyst working in institutional equity sales trading in Chicago. It is her job to sell blocks of stock to institutional clients. As she forms opinions about the variety of stocks she works with every day, the longevity of the companies behind the stocks is a key factor, which Aishetu often gauges by looking at asset holdings.

Operating assets, for instance, can help her predict the long-term viability of a company because they show the sheer strength of its resources. It is possible for traders like Aishetu to make certain assumptions about a company's longevity if it has a solid operating asset base. This is not to say that companies without huge asset holdings do not have the same potential for long-term health. "When it comes to young companies," Aishetu says, "I often focus on *intangible* assets such as key personnel, patents on technology, and market share."

It is important to be aware that intangible assets are not the same as other types of assets, however, and should be viewed accordingly. As Aishetu explains, "They can grossly over- or underestimate the true value of the financial position of a company. The exact value of a patent, for instance, can never be fully determined unless you try to buy or sell shares in the company," thereby assigning a price to the asset. This said, intangible assets can have the same value potential as other types of assets. As Aishetu puts it, "Imagine Microsoft without the vision of Bill Gates!"

WARMUP EXERCISES

LO 5 Warmup Exercise 8-1 Depreciation Methods

Assume that a company purchases a depreciable asset on January 1 for $10,000. The asset has a four-year life and will have zero residual value at the end of the fourth year.

Required

Calculate depreciation expense for each of the four years using the straight-line method and the double declining-balance method.

LO 5 Warmup Exercise 8-2 Depreciation and Cash Flow

Use the information from Exercise 8-1. Assume that the double declining-balance method will be used for tax purposes and the straight-line method will be used for the financial statement to be given to the stockholders. Also assume that the tax rate is 40%.

Required

How much will the tax savings be in the first year as a result of using the accelerated method of depreciation?

Solutions to Warmup Exercises

Warmup Exercise 8-1

	Straight Line	Double Declining Balance	
Year 1	$2,500*	$10,000 × .50** =	$5,000
2	2,500	($10,000 − $5,000) × .50 =	2,500
3	2,500	($10,000 − $7,500) × .50 =	1,250
4	2,500	($10,000 − $8,750) × .50 =	625

*$10,000/4 years
**Straight-line rate as a percentage is 1 year/4 year or 25%. Double the rate is 25% × 2, or 50%.

Warmup Exercise 8-2

The tax savings is equal to the difference in depreciation between the two methods times the tax rate. Therefore the tax savings is ($5,000 – $2,500) × .40 = $1,000.

REVIEW PROBLEM

The accountant for Becker Company wants to develop a balance sheet as of December 31, 2001. A review of the asset records has revealed the following information:

a. Asset A was purchased on July 1, 1999, for $40,000 and has been depreciated on the straight-line basis using an estimated life of six years and a residual value of $4,000.

b. Asset B was purchased on January 1, 2000, for $66,000. The straight-line method has been used for depreciation purposes. Originally, the estimated life of the asset was projected to be six years with a residual value of $6,000; however, at the beginning of 2001, the accountant learned that the remaining life of the asset was only three years with a residual value of $2,000.

c. Asset C was purchased on January 1, 2000, for $50,000. The double declining-balance method has been used for depreciation purposes, with a four-year life and a residual value estimate of $5,000.

Required

1. Assume that these assets represent pieces of equipment. Calculate the acquisition cost, accumulated depreciation, and book value of each asset as of December 31, 2001.
2. How would the assets appear on the balance sheet on December 31, 2001?
3. Assume that Becker Company sold Asset B on January 2, 2002, for $25,000. Calculate the amount of the resulting gain or loss, and prepare the journal entry for the sale. Where would the gain or loss appear on the income statement?

Solution to Review Problem

1.

Asset A

1999	Depreciation	($40,000 – $4,000)/6 × 1/2 Year	=	$ 3,000
2000		($40,000 – $4,000)/6	=	6,000
2001		($40,000 – $4,000)/6	=	6,000
Accumulated Depreciation				$15,000

Asset B

2000	Depreciation	($66,000 – $6,000)/6	=	$10,000
2001		($66,000 – $10,000 – $2,000)/3	=	18,000
Accumulated Depreciation				$28,000

Note the impact of the change in estimate on 2001 depreciation.

Asset C

2000	Depreciation	$50,000 × (25% × 2)	=	$25,000
2001		($50,000 – $25,000) × (25% × 2)	=	12,500
Accumulated Depreciation				$37,500

BECKER COMPANY
SUMMARY OF ASSET COST AND ACCUMULATED DEPRECIATION
AS OF DECEMBER 31, 2001

Asset	Acquisition Cost	Accumulated Depreciation	Book Value
A	$ 40,000	$15,000	$25,000
B	66,000	28,000	38,000
C	50,000	37,500	12,500
Totals	$156,000	$80,500	$75,500

2. The assets would appear in the Long-Term Assets category of the balance sheet as follows:

Equipment	$156,000	
Less: Accumulated depreciation	80,500	
Equipment (net)		$75,500

3.

Asset B Book Value	$38,000
Selling Price	25,000
Loss on Sale of Asset	$13,000

The journal entry to record the sale is as follows:

2002			
Jan. 2	Cash	25,000	
	Accumulated Depreciation	28,000	
	Loss on Sale of Asset	13,000	
	Asset B		66,000
	To record the sale of Asset B.		

Assets	=	Liabilities	+	Owners' Equity
+25,000				−13,000
+28,000				
−66,000				

The Loss on Sale of Asset account should appear in the Other Income/Other Expense category of the income statement. It is similar to an expense but is not the company's major activity.

Chapter Highlights

1. **LO 1** Operating assets are normally presented on the balance sheet in one category for property, plant, and equipment and a second category for intangibles.
2. **LO 1** Operating assets should be presented at original acquisition cost less accumulated depreciation or amortization.
3. **LO 2** Acquisition cost should include all costs necessary to acquire the asset and prepare it for its intended use.
4. **LO 3** When assets are purchased for a lump sum, acquisition cost should be determined as the proportion of the market values of the assets purchased.
5. **LO 4** Interest on assets constructed over time should be capitalized. The amount of interest capitalized should be the average accumulated expenditures times an interest rate.
6. **LO 5** Several depreciation methods are available to describe the decline in usefulness of operating assets. The straight-line method is the most commonly used and assigns the same amount of depreciation to each time period over the asset's life.
7. **LO 5** Accelerated depreciation allocates a greater expense to the earlier years of an asset's life and less to later years. The double declining-balance method is one form of accelerated depreciation.
8. **LO 6** Depreciation is based on an estimate of the life of the asset and the residual value. When it is necessary to change the estimate, the amount of depreciation expense is adjusted for the current year and future years. Past depreciation amounts are not restated.
9. **LO 7** Capital expenditures are costs that increase an asset's life or its productivity. Capital expenditures should be added to the cost of the asset. Revenue expenditures should be treated as an expense in the period in which they are incurred because they benefit only the current period.
10. **LO 8** The gain or loss on the disposal of an asset is the difference between the asset's book value and its selling price.
11. **LO 9** Intangible assets should be presented on the balance sheet at acquisition cost less accumulated amortization. Acquisition cost should include all costs necessary to acquire the asset.
12. **LO 10** Research and development costs are not treated as an intangible asset. Instead, they are treated as an expense in the year they are incurred.
13. **LO 10** Intangibles should be amortized over the shorter of their legal or useful life. All intangibles, including goodwill, should be amortized over a period not exceeding 20 years.
14. **LO 11** The acquisition of long-term assets should be reflected in the Investing Activities category of the statement of cash flows.

Key Terms Quiz

Read each definition below and then write the number of the definition in the blank beside the appropriate term it defines. The solution appears at the end of the chapter.

- 1 Acquisition cost
- 5 Capitalization of interest
- 2 Land improvements
- 7 Depreciation
- 3 Straight-line method
- 9 Book value
- 4 Units-of-production method
- 13 Accelerated depreciation
- 15 Double declining-balance method
- 6 Change in estimate
- 8 Capital expenditure
- 10 Revenue expenditure
- 11 Gain on Sale of Asset
- 12 Loss on Sale of Asset
- 18 Natural resources
- 14 Intangible assets
- 16 Goodwill
- 17 Research and development costs

1. This amount includes all of the costs normally necessary to acquire an asset and prepare it for its intended use.
2. Additions made to a piece of property such as paving or landscaping a parking lot. The costs are treated separately from land for purposes of recording depreciation.
3. A method by which the same dollar amount of depreciation is recorded in each year of asset use.
4. A method by which depreciation is determined as a function of the number of units the asset produces.
5. The process of treating the cost of interest on constructed assets as a part of the asset cost rather than as an expense.
6. A change in the life of an asset or in its expected residual value.
7. The allocation of the original acquisition cost of an asset to the periods benefited by its use.
8. A cost that improves an operating asset and is added to the asset account.
9. The original acquisition cost of an asset minus the amount of accumulated depreciation.
10. A cost that keeps an operating asset in its normal operating condition and is treated as an expense of the period.
11. An account whose amount indicates that the selling price received on an asset's disposal exceeds its book value.
12. An account whose amount indicates that the book value of an asset exceeds the selling price received on its disposal.
13. A term that refers to several methods by which a higher amount of depreciation is recorded in the early years of an asset's life and a lower amount is recorded in the later years.
14. Long-term assets that have no physical properties, for example patents, copyrights, and goodwill.
15. A method by which depreciation is recorded at twice the straight-line rate but the depreciable balance is reduced in each period.
16. The amount indicating that the purchase price of a business exceeded the total fair market value of the identifiable net assets at the time the business was acquired.
17. Expenditures incurred in the discovery of new knowledge and the translation of research into a design or plan for a new product.
18. Assets that are consumed during their use, for example coal or oil.

Alternate Terms

Accumulated depreciation Allowance for depreciation

Acquisition cost Historical cost

Capitalize Treat as asset

Construction in progress Construction in process

Goodwill Purchase price in excess of the market value of assets

Hidden assets Unrecorded or off–balance sheet assets

Property, Plant, and Equipment Fixed assets

Prospective Current and future years

Residual value Salvage value

Revenue expenditure An expense of the period

Questions

1. What are several examples of operating assets? Why are operating assets essential to a company's long-term future?
2. What is the meaning of the term *acquisition cost* of operating assets? Give some examples of costs that should be included in the acquisition cost.
3. When assets are purchased as a group, how should the acquisition cost of the individual assets be determined?
4. Why is it important to account separately for the cost of land and building, even when the two assets are purchased together?

5. Under what circumstances should interest be capitalized as part of the cost of an asset?
6. What factors may contribute to the decline in usefulness of operating assets? Should the choice of depreciation method be related to these factors? Must a company choose just one method of depreciation for all assets?
7. Why do you think that most companies use the straight-line method of depreciation?
8. How should the residual value of an operating asset be treated when using the straight-line method? How should it be treated when using the double declining-balance method?
9. Why do many companies use one method to calculate depreciation for the income statement developed for stockholders and another method for income tax purposes?
10. What should a company do if it finds that the original estimate of the life of an asset or the residual value of the asset must be changed?
11. What are the meanings of the terms *capital expenditures* and *revenue expenditures?* What determines whether an item is a capital or revenue expenditure?
12. How is the gain or loss on the sale of an operating asset calculated? Where would the Gain on Sale of Asset account appear on the financial statements?
13. What are several examples of items that constitute intangible assets? In what category of the balance sheet should intangible assets appear?
14. What is the meaning of the term *goodwill?* Give an example of a transaction that would result in the recording of goodwill on the balance sheet.
15. Do you agree with the FASB's ruling that all research and development costs should be treated as an expense on the income statement? Why or why not?
16. Do you agree with some accountants who argue that intangible assets have an unlimited life and therefore should not be subject to amortization?
17. When an intangible asset is amortized, should the asset's amortization occur over its legal life or over its useful life? Give an example in which the legal life exceeds the useful life.
18. Suppose that an intangible asset is being amortized over a 10-year time period but a competitor has just introduced a new product that will have a serious negative impact on the asset's value. Should the company continue to amortize the intangible asset over the 10-year life?

EXERCISES

LO 2 Exercise 8-1 Acquisition Cost

Ruby Company purchased a piece of equipment with a list price of $60,000 on January 1, 2001. The following amounts were related to the equipment purchase:

- Terms of the purchase were 2/10, net 30. Ruby paid for the purchase on January 8.
- Freight costs of $1,000 were incurred.
- A state agency required that a pollution-control device be installed on the equipment at a cost of $2,500.
- During installation, the equipment was damaged and repair costs of $4,000 were incurred.
- Architect's fees of $6,000 were paid to redesign the work space to accommodate the new equipment.
- Ruby purchased liability insurance to cover possible damage to the asset. The three-year policy cost $8,000.
- Ruby financed the purchase with a bank loan. Interest of $3,000 was paid on the loan during 2001.

Required

Determine the acquisition cost of the equipment.

LO 3 Exercise 8-2 Lump-Sum Purchase

To add to his growing chain of grocery stores, on January 1, 2001, Danny Marks bought a grocery store of a small competitor for $520,000. An appraiser, hired to assess the value of the assets acquired, determined that the land had a market value of $200,000, the building a market value of $150,000, and the equipment a market value of $250,000.

Required

1. What is the acquisition cost of each asset? Prepare a journal entry to record the acquisition.
2. Danny plans to depreciate the operating assets on a straight-line basis for 20 years. Determine the amount of depreciation expense for 2001 on these newly acquired assets.
3. How would the assets appear on the balance sheet as of December 31, 2001?

LO 5 Exercise 8-3 Straight-Line and Units-of-Production Methods

Assume that Sample Company purchased factory equipment on January 1, 2001, for $60,000. The equipment has an estimated life of five years and an estimated residual value of $5,000. Sample's accountant is considering whether to use the straight-line or the units-of-production method to depreciate the asset. Because the company is beginning a new production process, the equipment will be used to produce 10,000 units in 2001, but production subsequent to 2001 will increase by 10,000 units each year.

Required

Calculate the depreciation expense, the accumulated depreciation, and the book value of the equipment under both methods for each of the five years of the asset's life. Do you think that the units-of-production method yields reasonable results in this situation?

LO 5 Exercise 8-4 Accelerated Depreciation

Koffman's Warehouse purchased a forklift on January 1, 2001, for $6,000. It is expected to last for five years and have a residual value of $600. Koffman's uses the double declining-balance method for depreciation.

Required

1. Calculate the depreciation expense, the accumulated depreciation, and the book value for each year of the forklift's life.
2. Prepare the journal entry to record depreciation expense for 2002.
3. Refer to Exhibit 8-2. What factors may have influenced Koffman to use the double declining-balance method?

LO 6 Exercise 8-5 Change in Estimate

Assume that Bloomer Company purchased a new machine on January 1, 2001, for $80,000. The machine has an estimated useful life of nine years and a residual value of $8,000. Bloomer has chosen to use the straight-line method of depreciation. On January 1, 2003, Bloomer discovered that the machine would not be useful beyond December 31, 2006, and estimated its value at that time to be $2,000.

Required

1. Calculate the depreciation expense, the accumulated depreciation, and the book value of the asset for each year, 2001 to 2006.
2. Was the depreciation recorded in 2001 and 2002 wrong? If so, why was it not corrected?

LO 8 Exercise 8-6 Asset Disposal

Assume that Gonzalez Company purchased an asset on January 1, 1999, for $60,000. The asset had an estimated life of six years and an estimated residual value of $6,000. The company used the straight-line method to depreciate the asset. On July 1, 2001, the asset was sold for $40,000 cash.

Required

1. Make the journal entry to record depreciation for 2001. Also record all transactions necessary for the sale of the asset.
2. How should the gain or loss on the sale of the asset be presented on the income statement?

LO 8 Exercise 8-7 Asset Disposal

Refer to Exercise 8-6. Assume that Gonzalez Company sold the asset on July 1, 2001, and received $15,000 cash and a note for an additional $15,000.

Required

1. Make the journal entry to record depreciation for 2001. Also record all transactions necessary for the sale of the asset.
2. How should the gain or loss on the sale of the asset be presented on the income statement?

LO 10 Exercise 8-8 Amortization of Intangibles

For each of the following intangible assets, indicate the amount of amortization expense that should be recorded for the year 2001 and the amount of accumulated amortization on the balance sheet as of December 31, 2001.

	Goodwill	Patent	Trademark
Cost	$40,000	$50,000	$80,000
Date of purchase	1/1/94	1/1/96	1/1/99
Useful life	30 yrs.	10 yrs.	20 yrs.
Legal life	undefined	20 yrs.	20 yrs.
Method	SL*	SL	SL

*Represents the straight-line method.

LO 11 Exercise 8-9 Impact of Transactions Involving Operating Assets on Statement of Cash Flows

From the following list, identify each item as operating (O), investing (I), financing (F), or not separately reported on the statement of cash flows (N).

________ Purchase of land
________ Proceeds from sale of land
________ Gain on sale of land
________ Purchase of equipment
________ Depreciation expense
________ Proceeds from sale of equipment
________ Loss on sale of equipment

LO 11 Exercise 8-10 Impact of Transactions Involving Intangible Assets on Statement of Cash Flows

From the following list, identify each item as operating (O), investing (I), financing (F), or not separately reported on the statement of cash flows (N).

________ Cost incurred to acquire copyright
________ Amortization of organization costs
________ Amortization of copyright
________ Proceeds from sale of patent
________ Gain on sale of patent
________ Research and development costs

Multi-Concept Exercises

LO 1, 7 Exercise 8-11 Capital Versus Revenue Expenditures

On January 1, 1999, Jose Company purchased a building for $200,000 and a delivery truck for $20,000. The following expenditures have been incurred during 2001, related to the building and the truck:

- The building was painted at a cost of $5,000.
- To prevent leaking, new windows were installed in the building at a cost of $10,000.
- To allow an improved flow of production, a new conveyor system was installed at a cost of $40,000.
- The delivery truck was repainted with a new company logo at a cost of $1,000.
- To allow better handling of large loads, a hydraulic lift system was installed on the truck at a cost of $5,000.
- The truck's engine was overhauled at a cost of $4,000.

Required

1. Determine which of these costs should be capitalized. Also record the journal entry for the capitalized costs. Assume that all costs were incurred on January 1, 2001.
2. Determine the amount of depreciation for the year 2001. The company uses the straight-line method and depreciates the building over 25 years and the truck over 6 years. Assume zero residual value for all assets.
3. How would the assets appear on the balance sheet of December 31, 2001?

LO 4, 5 Exercise 8-12 Capitalization of Interest and Depreciation

During 2001, Mercator Company borrowed $80,000 from a local bank and, in addition, used $120,000 of cash to construct a new corporate office building. Based on average accumulated expenditures, the amount of interest capitalized during 2001 was $8,000. Construction was completed and the building was occupied on January 1, 2002.

Required

1. Determine the acquisition cost of the new building.
2. The building has an estimated useful life of 20 years and a $5,000 salvage value. Assuming that Mercator uses the straight-line basis to depreciate its operating assets, determine the amount of depreciation expense for 2001 and 2002.

LO 9, 10 Exercise 8-13 Research and Development and Patents

Erin Company incurred the following costs during 2001.

a. Research and development costs of $20,000 were incurred. The research was conducted to discover a new product to sell to customers in future years. A product was successfully developed and a patent for the new product was granted during 2001. Erin is unsure of the period benefited by the research but believes the product will result in increased sales over the next five years.

b. Legal costs and application fees of $10,000 for the patent were incurred on January 1, 2001. The patent was granted for a life of 20 years.

c. A patent infringement suit was successfully defended at a cost of $8,000. Assume that all costs were incurred on January 1, 2002.

Required

Determine how the costs in parts **a** and **b** should be presented on Erin's financial statements as of December 31, 2001. Also determine the amount of amortization of intangible assets that Erin should record in 2001 and 2002.

PROBLEMS

LO 1 Problem 8-1 Balance Sheet and Footnote Disclosures for Delta Airlines

www.deltaairlines.com

The June 30, 1998, balance sheet of Delta Airlines Inc. revealed the following information in the property and equipment category (in millions):

	1998	1997
Flight equipment	$11,180	$9,619
Less: Accumulated depreciation	3,895	3,510
	$ 7,285	$6,109
Ground property and equipment	$ 3,285	$3,032
Less: Accumulated depreciation	1,854	1,758
	$ 1,431	$1,274

The footnotes that accompany the financial statements revealed the following:

> Depreciation and Amortization—Owned flight equipment is depreciated on a straight-line basis to residual values equal to 5% of cost. Ground property and equipment are depreciated on a straight-line basis over their estimated service lives, which range from 3 years to 30 years.

Required

1. Assume that Delta Airlines did not dispose of any ground property and equipment during the fiscal year 1998. Calculate the amount of depreciation expense for the year.
2. What was the average life of the ground property and equipment as of 1998?
3. What was the average age of the ground property and equipment as of 1998?

LO 3 Problem 8-2 Lump-Sum Purchase of Assets and Subsequent Events

Carter Development Company purchased, for cash, a large tract of land that was immediately platted and deeded into smaller sections:

Section 1, retail development with highway frontage

Section 2, multifamily apartment development

Section 3, single-family homes in the largest section

Based on recent sales of similar property, the fair market values of the three sections are as follows:

Section 1, $630,000

Section 2, $378,000

Section 3, $252,000

Required

1. What value is assigned to each section of land if the tract was purchased for (a) $1,260,000, (b) $1,560,000, or (c) $1,000,000?
2. How does the purchase of the tract affect the balance sheet?
3. Why would Carter be concerned with the value assigned to each section? Would Carter be more concerned with the values assigned if instead of purchasing three sections of land, it purchased land with buildings? Why or why not?

LO 5 **Problem 8-3** Depreciation as a Tax Shield

The term *tax shield* refers to the amount of income tax saved by deducting depreciation for income tax purposes. Assume that Supreme Company is considering the purchase of an asset as of January 1, 2001. The cost of an asset with a five-year life and zero residual value is $100,000. The company will use the straight-line method of depreciation.

Supreme's income for tax purposes before recording depreciation on the asset will be $50,000 per year for the next five years. The corporation is currently in the 35% tax bracket.

Required

Calculate the amount of income tax that Supreme must pay each year if the asset is not purchased. Calculate the amount of income tax that Supreme must pay each year if the asset is purchased. What is the amount of the depreciation tax shield?

LO 5 **Problem 8-4** Book Versus Tax Depreciation

Griffith Delivery Service purchased a delivery truck for $33,600. The truck has an estimated useful life of six years and no salvage value. For the purposes of preparing financial statements, Griffith is planning to use straight-line depreciation. For tax purposes, Griffith follows MACRS. Depreciation expense using MACRS is $6,720 in Year 1, $10,750 in Year 2, $6,450 in Year 3, $3,870 in each of Years 4 and 5, and $1,940 in Year 6.

Required

1. What is the difference between straight-line and MACRS depreciation expense for each of the six years?
2. Griffith's president has asked why you have used one method for the books and another for calculating taxes. "Can you do this? Is it legal? Don't we take the same total depreciation either way?" he asked. Write a brief memo answering his questions and explaining the benefits of using two methods for depreciation.

LO 5 **Problem 8-5** Depreciation and Cash Flow

Ohare Company's only asset as of January 1, 2001, was a limousine. During 2001, only three transactions occurred:

Provided services of $100,000 on account.

Collected all accounts receivable.

Depreciation on the limousine was $15,000.

Required

1. Develop an income statement for Ohare for 2001.
2. Determine the amount of the net cash inflow for Ohare for 2001.
3. Explain in one or more sentences why the amount of the net income on Ohare's income statement does not equal the amount of the net cash inflow.
4. If Ohare developed a cash flow statement for 2001 using the indirect method, what amount would appear in the category titled Cash Flow from Operating Activities?

LO 11 Problem 8-6 Reconstruct Net Book Values Using Statement of Cash Flows

Centralia Stores Inc. had property, plant, and equipment, net of accumulated depreciation of $4,459,000; and intangible assets, net of accumulated amortization, of $673,000 at December 31, 2001. The company's 2001 statement of cash flows, prepared using the indirect method, included the following items.

The Cash Flows from Operating Activities section included three additions to net income: (1) depreciation expense in the amount of $672,000, (2) amortization expense in the amount of $33,000, and (3) the loss on the sale of equipment in the amount of $35,000. The Cash Flows from Operating Activities section also included a subtraction from net income for the gain on the sale of a copyright of $55,000. The Cash Flows from Investing Activities section included outflows for the purchase of a building in the amount of $292,000 and $15,000 for the payment of legal fees to protect a patent from infringement. The Cash Flows from Investing Activities section also included inflows from the sale of equipment in the amount of $315,000 and the sale of a copyright in the amount of $75,000.

Required

1. Determine the book values of the assets that were sold during 2001.
2. Reconstruct the amount of property, plant, and equipment, net of accumulated depreciation, that was reported on the company's balance sheet at December 31, 2000.
3. Reconstruct the amount of intangibles, net of accumulated amortization, that was reported on the company's balance sheet at December 31, 2000.

Multi-Concept Problems

LO 1, 3, 5, 7, 8 Problem 8-7 Cost of Assets, Subsequent Book Values, and Balance Sheet Presentation

The following events took place at Pete's Painting Company during 2001:

a. On January 1, Pete bought a used truck for $14,000. He added a tool chest and side racks for ladders for $4,800. The truck is expected to last four years and then be sold for $800. Pete uses straight-line depreciation.

b. On January 1, he purchased several items at an auction for $2,400. These items had fair market values as follows:

10 cases of paint trays and roller covers	$ 200
Storage cabinets	600
Ladders & scaffolding	2,400

Pete will use all the paint trays and roller covers this year. The storage cabinets are expected to last nine years, and the ladders and scaffolding for four years.

c. On February 1, Pete paid the city $1,500 for a three-year license to operate the business.

d. On September 1, Pete sold an old truck for $4,800. The truck had cost $12,000 when it was purchased on September 1, 1996. It had been expected to last eight years and have a salvage value of $800.

Required

1. For each situation, explain the value assigned to the asset when it is purchased (or for part **d,** the book value when sold).
2. Determine the amount of depreciation or other expense to be recorded for each asset for 2001.
3. How would these assets appear on the balance sheet as of December 31, 2001?

LO 2, 5 Problem 8-8 Cost of Assets and the Effect on Depreciation

Early in its first year of business, Toner Company, a fitness and training center, purchased new workout equipment. The acquisition included the following costs:

Purchase price	$150,000
Tax	15,000
Transportation	4,000
Setup*	25,000
Painting*	3,000

*The equipment was adjusted to Toner's specific needs and painted to match the other equipment in the gym.

The bookkeeper recorded an asset, Equipment, $165,000 (purchase price and tax). The remaining costs were expensed for the year. Toner used straight-line depreciation. The equipment was expected to last 10 years with zero salvage value.

Required

1. How much depreciation did Toner report on its income statement related to this equipment in Year 1? What do you believe is the correct amount of depreciation to report in Year 1 related to this equipment?
2. Income is $100,000, before costs related to the equipment are reported. How much income will Toner report in Year 1? What amount of income should it report? You may ignore income tax.
3. Using the equipment as an example, explain the difference between a cost and an expense.

LO 5, 7, 8 Problem 8-9 Capital Expenditures, Depreciation, and Disposal

Merton Company purchased an office building at a cost of $364,000 on January 1, 2000. Merton estimated that the building's life would be 25 years and the residual value at the end of 25 years would be $14,000.

On January 1, 2001, the company made several expenditures related to the building. The entire building was painted and floors were refinished at a cost of $21,000. A federal agency required Merton to install additional pollution-control devices in the building at a cost of $42,000. With the new devices, Merton believed it was possible to extend the life of the building by an additional six years.

In 2002 Merton altered its corporate strategy dramatically. The company sold the factory building on April 1, 2002, for $392,000 in cash and relocated all operations in another state.

Required

1. Determine the amount of depreciation that should be reflected on the income statement for 2000 and 2001.
2. Explain why the cost of the pollution-control equipment was not expensed in 2001. What conditions would have allowed Merton to expense the equipment? If Merton has a choice, would it prefer to expense or capitalize the equipment?
3. What amount of gain or loss did Merton record when it sold the building? What amount of gain or loss would have been reported if the pollution-control equipment had been expensed in 2001?

LO 6, 10 Problem 8-10 Amortization of Intangible, Revision of Rate

During 1996, Reynosa Inc.'s R&D department developed a new manufacturing process. R&D costs were $85,000. The process was patented on October 1, 1996. Legal costs to acquire the patent were $11,900. Reynosa decided to expense the patent over the maximum period of time allowed for a patent. Reynosa's fiscal year ends on September 30.

On October 1, 2001, Reynosa's competition announced that it had obtained a patent on a new process that would make Reynosa's patent obsolete in two years.

Required

1. How should Reynosa record the $85,000 and $11,900 costs?
2. How much amortization expense should Reynosa report in each year through the year ended September 30, 2001?
3. How much amortization expense should Reynosa report in the year ended September 30, 2002?

LO 8, 11 Problem 8-11 Purchase and Disposal of Operating Asset and Effects on Statement of Cash Flows

On January 1, 2001, Castlewood Company purchased some machinery for its production line for $104,000. Using an estimated useful life of eight years and a residual value of $8,000, the annual straight-line depreciation of the machinery was calculated to be $12,000. Castlewood used the machinery during 2001 and 2002, but then decided to automate its production process. On December 31, 2002, Castlewood sold the machinery at a loss of $5,000 and purchased new, fully automated machinery for $205,000.

Required

1. How would the transactions described above be presented on Castlewood's statements of cash flows for the years ended December 31, 2001 and 2002?
2. Why would Castlewood sell at a loss machinery that had a remaining useful life of six years and purchase new machinery with a cost almost twice that of the old?

LO 9, 10, 11 Problem 8-12 Amortization of Intangibles and Effects on Statement of Cash Flows

Tableleaf Inc. purchased a patent a number of years ago. The patent is being amortized on a straight-line basis over its estimated useful life. The company's comparative balance sheets as of December 31, 2001 and 2000, included the following line item:

	12/31/01	12/31/00
Patent, less accumulated amortization of $119,000 (2001) and $102,000 (2000)	$170,000	$187,000

Required

1. How much amortization expense was recorded during 2001?
2. What was the patent's acquisition cost? When was it acquired? What is its estimated useful life? How was the acquisition of the patent reported on that year's statement of cash flows?
3. Assume that Tableleaf uses the indirect method to prepare its statement of cash flows. How is the amortization of the patent reported annually on the statement of cash flows?
4. How would the sale of the patent on January 1, 2002, for $200,000 be reported on the 2002 statement of cash flows?

Alternate Problems

LO 1 Problem 8-1A Disclosures of Operating Assets for Time Warner

www.timewarner.com

The footnotes to the December 31, 1998, financial statements of Time Warner included the following disclosures for the Property, Plant, and Equipment account:

Property, Plant, and Equipment (in millions):	1998	1997
Land and Buildings	$ 963	$ 962
Cable Television Equipment	1,035	941
Furniture, Fixtures, and other Equipment	1,400	1,337
	$3,398	$3,240
Less Accumulated Depreciation	(1,407)	(1,151)
Total	$1,991	$2,089

Required

Assume that Time Warner disposed of Property, Plant, and Equipment during 1998 with accumulated depreciation of $600 million.

1. Based on the footnote disclosures, what was the amount of depreciation expense for fiscal year 1998 for Property, Plant, and Equipment?
2. What was the average life of the assets in the Property, Plant, and Equipment categories?
3. What was the average age of the assets in the Property, Plant, and Equipment categories?

LO 3 Problem 8-2A Lump-Sum Purchase of Assets and Subsequent Events

Dixon Manufacturing purchased, for cash, three large pieces of equipment. Based on recent sales of similar equipment, the fair market values are as follows:

Piece 1	$200,000
Piece 2	$200,000
Piece 3	$440,000

Required

1. What value is assigned to each piece of equipment if the equipment was purchased for (a) $960,000, (b) $680,000, or (c) $800,000?
2. How does the purchase of the equipment affect total assets?

LO 5 **Problem 8-3A** Depreciation as a Tax Shield

The term *tax shield* refers to the amount of income tax saved by deducting depreciation for income tax purposes. Assume that Rummy Company is considering the purchase of an asset as of January 1, 2001. The cost of the asset with a five-year life and zero residual value is $60,000. The company will use the double declining-balance method of depreciation.

Rummy's income for tax purposes before recording depreciation on the asset will be $62,000 per year for the next five years. The corporation is currently in the 30% tax bracket.

Required

Calculate the amount of income tax that Rummy must pay each year if the asset is not purchased and then the amount of income tax that Rummy must pay each year if the asset is purchased. What is the amount of tax shield over the life of the asset? What is the amount of tax shield for Rummy if it uses the straight-line method over the life of the asset? Why would Rummy choose to use the accelerated method?

LO 5 **Problem 8-4A** Book Versus Tax Depreciation

Payton Delivery Service purchased a delivery truck for $28,200. The truck will have a useful life of six years and zero salvage value. For the purposes of preparing financial statements, Payton is planning to use straight-line depreciation. For tax purposes, Payton follows MACRS. Depreciation expense using MACRS is $5,650 in Year 1, $9,025 in Year 2, $5,400 in Year 3, $3,250 in each of Years 4 and 5, and $1,625 in Year 6.

Required

1. What would be the difference between straight-line and MACRS depreciation expense for each of the six years?
2. Payton's president has asked why you have used one method for the books and another for calculating taxes. "Can you do this? Is it legal? Don't we take the same total depreciation either way?" he asked. Write a brief memo answering his questions and explaining the benefits of using two methods for depreciation.

LO 10 **Problem 8-5A** Amortization and Cash Flow

Book Company's only asset as of January 1, 2001, was a copyright. During 2001, only three transactions occurred:

Royalties earned from copyright use, $500,000 in cash

Cash paid for advertising and clerical services, $62,500

Amortization of copyright, $50,000

Required

1. What amount of income will Book report in 2001?
2. What is the amount of cash on hand at December 31, 2001?
3. Explain how the cash balance increased from zero at the beginning of the year to its end-of-year balance. Why does the increase in cash not equal the income?

LO 11 **Problem 8-6A** Reconstruct Net Book Values Using Statement of Cash Flows

E-Gen Enterprises Inc. had property, plant, and equipment, net of accumulated depreciation, of $1,555,000; and intangible assets, net of accumulated amortization, of $34,000 at December 31, 2001. The company's 2001 statement of cash flows, prepared using the indirect method, included the following items.

The Cash Flows from Operating Activities section included three additions to net income: (1) depreciation expense in the amount of $205,000, (2) amortization expense in the amount of $3,000, and (3) the loss on the sale of land in the amount of $17,000. The Cash Flows from Operating Activities section also included a subtraction from net income for the gain on the sale of a trademark of $7,000. The Cash Flows from Investing Activities section included outflows for the purchase of equipment in the amount of $277,000 and $6,000 for the payment of legal fees to protect a copyright from infringement. The Cash Flows from Investing Activities section also included inflows from the sale of land in the amount of $187,000 and the sale of a trademark in the amount of $121,000.

Required

1. Determine the book values of the assets that were sold during 2001.
2. Reconstruct the amount of property, plant, and equipment, net of accumulated depreciation, that was reported on the company's balance sheet at December 31, 2000.
3. Reconstruct the amount of intangibles, net of accumulated amortization, that was reported on the company's balance sheet at December 31, 2000.

Alternate Multi-Concept Problems

LO 1, 5, 8, 9, 10 Problem 8-7A Cost of Assets, Subsequent Book Values, and Balance Sheet Presentation

The following events took place at Tasty-Toppins Inc., a pizza shop that specializes in home delivery, during 2001:

a. January 1, purchased a truck for $16,000 and added a cab and oven at a cost of $10,900. The truck is expected to last five years and be sold for $300 at the end of that time. The company uses straight-line depreciation for its trucks.

b. January 1, purchased equipment for $2,700 from a competitor who was retiring. The equipment is expected to last three years with zero salvage value. The company uses the double declining-balance method to depreciate its equipment.

c. April 1, sold a truck for $1,500. The truck had been purchased for $8,000 exactly five years earlier, had an expected salvage value of $1,000, and was depreciated over an eight-year life using the straight-line method.

d. July 1, purchased a $14,000 patent for a unique baking process to produce a new product. The patent is valid for 15 more years; however, the company expects to produce and market the product for only four years. The patent's value at the end of the four years is indeterminable.

Required

For each situation, explain the amount of depreciation or amortization recorded for each asset in the current year and the book value of each asset at the end of the year. For part **c,** indicate the accumulated depreciation and book value at the time of sale.

LO 2, 5 Problem 8-8A Cost of Assets and the Effect on Depreciation

Early in its first year of business, Key Inc., a locksmith and security consultant, purchased new equipment. The acquisition included the following costs:

Purchase price	$168,000
Tax	16,500
Transportation	4,400
Setup*	1,100
Operating Cost for First Year	26,400

*The equipment was adjusted to Key's specific needs.

The bookkeeper recorded the asset, Equipment, at $216,400. Key used straight-line depreciation. The equipment was expected to last 10 years with zero residual value.

Required

1. Was $216,400 the proper amount to record for the acquisition cost? If not, explain how each expenditure should be recorded.
2. How much depreciation did Key report on its income statement related to this equipment in Year 1? How much should have been reported?
3. If Key's income before the costs associated with the equipment is $55,000, what amount of income did Key report? What amount should it have reported? You may ignore income tax.
4. Explain how Key should determine the amount to capitalize when recording an asset. What is the effect on the income statement and balance sheet of Key's error?

LO 7, 8 Problem 8-9A Capital Expenditures, Depreciation, and Disposal

Wagner Company purchased a retail shopping center at a cost of $612,000 on January 1, 2000. Wagner estimated that the life of the building would be 25 years and the residual value at the end of 25 years would be $12,000.

On January 1, 2001, the company made several expenditures related to the building. The entire building was painted and floors were refinished at a cost of $115,200. A local zoning agency required Wagner to install additional fire-protection equipment, including sprinklers and built-in alarms, at a cost of $87,600. With the new protection, Wagner believed it was possible to increase the residual value of the building to $30,000.

In 2002 Wagner altered its corporate strategy dramatically. The company sold the retail shopping center on January 1, 2002, for $360,000 of cash.

Required

1. Determine the amount of depreciation that should be reflected on the income statement for 2000 and 2001.
2. Explain why the cost of the fire-protection equipment was not expensed in 2001. What conditions would have allowed Wagner to expense it? If Wagner has a choice, would it prefer to expense or capitalize the improvement?
3. What amount of gain or loss did Wagner record when it sold the building? What amount of gain or loss would have been reported if the fire-protection equipment had been expensed in 2001?

LO 6, 10 Problem 8-10A Amortization of Intangible, Revision of Rate

Dak Inc. purchased Under Company on January 1, 2001, for $500,000. To determine the value of the assets and liabilities purchased, Dak requested an appraisal of Under's assets and liabilities. The appraiser determined that the fair market values of the items purchased as of January 1, 2001, were as follows:

Assets	**Fair Market Value**
Cash	$ 75,000
Receivables	125,000
Building	287,500
Liabilities	
Accounts payable	$125,000

Dak decided to amortize any goodwill in the transaction on a straight-line basis over the maximum possible time period.

On January 1, 2002, Dak's accountants determined that the goodwill should be amortized over a shorter period of time. Accordingly, Dak Inc. agreed to amortize all remaining goodwill for a period of 10 more years.

Required

1. Determine the amount of goodwill that resulted from the January 1, 2001, purchase of Under Company and the amount to be amortized in 2001.
2. Determine the amount of goodwill that should be amortized in 2002.

LO 8, 11 Problem 8-11A Purchase and Disposal of Operating Asset and Effects on Statement of Cash Flows

On January 1, 2001, Mansfield Inc. purchased a medium-sized delivery truck for $45,000. Using an estimated useful life of five years and a residual value of $5,000, the annual straight-line depreciation of the trucks was calculated to be $8,000. Mansfield used the truck during 2001 and 2002, but then decided to purchase a much larger delivery truck. On December 31, 2002, Mansfield sold the delivery truck at a loss of $12,000 and purchased a new, larger delivery truck for $80,000.

Required

1. How would the transactions described above be presented on Mansfield's statements of cash flows for the years ended December 31, 2001 and 2002?
2. Why would Mansfield sell a truck that had a remaining useful life of three years at a loss and purchase a new truck with a cost almost twice that of the old?

LO 9, 10, 11 **Problem 8-12A** Amortization of Intangibles and Effects on Statement of Cash Flows

Quickster Inc. acquired a single trademark a number of years ago. The trademark is being amortized on a straight-line basis over its estimated useful life. The company's comparative balance sheets as of December 31, 2001 and 2000, included the following line item:

	12/31/01	12/31/00
Trademark, less accumulated amortization of $1,661,000 (2001) and $1,510,000 (2000)	$1,357,000	$1,508,000

Required

1. How much amortization expense was recorded during 2001?
2. What was the trademark's acquisition cost? When was it acquired? What is its estimated useful life? How was the acquisition of the trademark reported on that year's statement of cash flows?
3. Assume that Quickster uses the indirect method to prepare its statement of cash flows. How is the amortization of the trademark reported annually on the statement of cash flows?
4. How would the sale of the trademark on January 1, 2002, for $1,700,000 be reported on the 2002 statement of cash flows?

Cases

Reading and Interpreting Financial Statements

LO 1, 9 **Case 8-1** Ben & Jerry's

www.benjerry.com

Refer to the financial statements and footnotes included in the 1998 annual report of Ben & Jerry's.

Required

1. What items does Ben & Jerry's list in the Property, Plant, and Equipment category?
2. What method is used to depreciate the operating assets?
3. What is the estimated useful life of the operating assets?
4. What are the accumulated depreciation and book values of property, plant, and equipment for the most recent fiscal year?
5. Were any assets purchased or sold during the most recent fiscal year?
6. In what category of the balance sheet are intangible assets included?

LO 1, 9 **Case 8-2** Gateway

Refer to the financial statements and footnotes included in the 1998 annual report of Gateway.

Required

1. What items does Gateway list in the Property, Plant, and Equipment category?
2. What method is used to depreciate the assets?
3. What is the estimated life of the assets?
4. What are the accumulated depreciation and book values of property, plant, and equipment for the most recent fiscal year?
5. What is the amount of intangible assets for the most recent year?

LO 11 **Case 8-3** Ben & Jerry's Statement of Cash Flows

www.benjerry.com

Refer to the statement of cash flows in Ben & Jerry's 1998 annual report and answer the following questions:

1. What amount of cash was used to purchase property, plant, and equipment during 1998?
2. Did Ben & Jerry's sell any property, plant, and equipment during 1998?
3. What amount was reported for depreciation and amortization during 1998? Does the fact that depreciation and amortization are listed in the Cash Flow from Operating Activities section mean that Ben & Jerry's created cash by reporting depreciation?

LO 11 Case 8-4 Gateway's Statement of Cash Flows

Refer to the statement of cash flows in Gateway's 1998 annual report and answer the following questions.

1. What amount of cash was used for capital expenditures during 1998?
2. Did Gateway sell any property, plant, and equipment during 1998?
3. What amount was reported for depreciation and amortization during 1998? Does the fact that depreciation and amortization are listed in the cash flow from operating activities section mean that Gateway created cash by reporting depreciation and amortization?

Making Financial Decisions

LO 1, 5 Case 8-5 Comparing Companies

Assume that you are a financial analyst attempting to compare the financial results of two companies. The 2001 income statement of Straight Company is as follows:

Sales		$720,000
Cost of goods sold		360,000
Gross profit		360,000
Administrative costs	$ 96,000	
Depreciation expense	120,000	216,000
Income before tax		144,000
Tax expense (40%)		57,600
Net income		$ 86,400

Straight Company depreciates all operating assets using the straight-line method for tax purposes and for the annual report provided to stockholders. All operating assets were purchased on the same date, and all assets had an estimated life of five years when purchased. Straight Company's balance sheet reveals that on December 31, 2001, the balance of the Accumulated Depreciation account was $240,000.

You want to compare the annual report of Straight Company to that of Accelerated Company. Both companies are in the same industry, and both have exactly the same assets, sales, and expenses except that Accelerated uses the double declining-balance method for depreciation for income tax purposes and for the annual report provided to stockholders.

Required

Develop Accelerated Company's 2001 income statement. As a financial analyst interested in investing in one of the companies, do you find Straight or Accelerated more attractive? Because depreciation is a "noncash" expense, should you be indifferent between the two companies? Explain your answer.

LO 5 Case 8-6 Depreciation Alternatives

Medsupply Inc. produces supplies used in hospitals and nursing homes. Its sales, production, and costs to produce are expected to remain constant over the next five years. The corporate income tax rate is expected to increase over the next three years. The current rate, 15%, is expected to increase to 20% next year and then to 25% and continue at that rate indefinitely.

Medsupply is considering the purchase of new equipment that is expected to last for five years and to cost $150,000 with zero salvage value. As the controller, you are aware that the company can use one method of depreciation for accounting purposes and another method for tax purposes. You are trying to decide between the straight-line and the double declining-balance methods.

Required

Recommend which method to use for accounting purposes and which to use for tax purposes. Be able to justify your answer on both a numerical and a theoretical basis. How does a noncash adjustment to income, such as depreciation, affect cash flow?

Accounting and Ethics: What Would You Do?

LO 3 Case 8-7 Valuing Assets

Denver Company recently hired Terry Davis as an accountant. He was given responsibility for all accounting functions related to fixed asset accounting. Tammy Sharp, Terry's boss, asked him to review all transactions involving the current year's acquisition of fixed assets and to take necessary action to ensure that acquired assets were recorded at proper values. Terry is satisfied that all transactions are proper except for an April 15 purchase of an office building and the land on which it is situated. The purchase price of the acquisition was $200,000. Denver Company has not separately reported the land and building, however.

Terry hired an appraiser to determine the market values of the land and the building. The appraiser reported that his best estimates of the values were $150,000 for the building and $70,000 for the land. When Terry proposed that these values be used to determine the acquisition cost of the assets, Ms. Sharp disagreed. She told Terry to request another appraisal of the property and asked him to stress to the appraiser that the land component of the acquisition could not be depreciated for tax purposes. The second appraiser estimated that the values were $180,000 for the building and $40,000 for the land. Terry and Ms. Sharp agreed that the second appraisal should be used to determine the acquisition cost of the assets.

Required

Did Terry and Ms. Sharp act ethically in this situation? Explain your answer.

LO 5 **Case 8-8** Depreciation Estimates

Langsom's Mfg. is planning for a new project. Usually Langsom's depreciates long-term equipment for 10 years. The equipment for this project is specialized and will have no further use at the end of the project in three years. The manager of the project wants to depreciate the equipment over the usual 10 years and plans on writing off the remaining book value at the end of Year 3 as a loss. You believe that the equipment should be depreciated over the three-year life.

Required

Which method do you think is conceptually better? What should you do if the manager insists on depreciating the equipment over 10 years?

INTERNET RESEARCH CASE

www.timewarner.com
www.AOL.com
www.________ (AOL Time Warner)

Case 8-9 Time Warner (AOL Time Warner)

Time Warner announced a merger with America Online (AOL) in 1999, and that merger became final in 2000. AOL, founded in 1985, is the world's largest online service provider, among other attributes. Theirs is a union driven by Time Warner's huge assets in content and media brands, along with its cable systems, and by the potential audience represented by AOL's over 25 million online members. The resulting company, as the Time Warner 1999 annual report states, will have "multiple revenue streams from branded subscriptions, advertising and commerce, and content." You can explore what effect this merger of titans is having on each company's presence on the Web—including the investor's page(s) of the combined AOL Time Warner. (Fill in the URL for the combined company when available.)

First visit the Student page of Time-Warner's web site to explore the research opportunities within Time Warner. Explore AOL's site and find out more about AOL's core businesses. Then answer the following questions.

1. Of Time Warner's intangible assets, which do you think were the most desirable to AOL? Of its tangible assets, which do you think were the most desirable?
2. Look at Time Warner's multimedia annual report for 1999. What earnings number does Time Warner management focus on to minimize the effect of amortization (depreciation) of intangible assets?
3. Does the 1999 annual report disappear from Time Warner's site at the merger and appear at AOL's?
4. Look at the AOL financial statments from before the merger and after. What are its tangible assets? Its intangible assets? How do these numbers change as a result of the merger?
5. Explain briefly how management saw Time Warner's and AOL's assets as complementary. In what ways do you think this can make for a stronger company?

Solutions to Key Terms Quiz

- 1 Acquisition cost (p. 376)
- 5 Capitalization of interest (p. 376)
- 2 Land improvements (p. 377)
- 7 Depreciation (p. 377)
- 3 Straight-line method (p. 377)
- 9 Book value (p. 378)
- 4 Units-of-production method (p. 378)
- 13 Accelerated depreciation (p. 379)
- 15 Double declining-balance method (p. 379)
- 6 Change in estimate (p. 382)
- 8 Capital expenditure (p. 384)
- 10 Revenue expenditure (p. 384)
- 11 Gain on Sale of Asset (p. 386)
- 12 Loss on Sale of Asset (p. 387)
- 18 Natural resources (p. 387)
- 14 Intangible assets (p. 389)
- 16 Goodwill (p. 390)
- 17 Research and development costs (p. 390)

Part II

Integrative Problem

Correct an income statement and statement of cash flows and assess the impact of a change in inventory method; compute the effect of a bad-debt recognition.

The following income statement, statement of cash flows, and additional information are available for PEK Company:

PEK COMPANY
INCOME STATEMENT
FOR THE YEAR ENDED DECEMBER 31, 2001

Sales revenue		$1,250,000
Cost of goods sold		636,500
Gross profit		$ 613,500
Depreciation on plant equipment	$58,400	
Depreciation on buildings	12,000	
Interest expense	33,800	
Other expenses	83,800	188,000
Income before taxes		$ 425,500
Income tax expense (30% rate)		127,650
Net income		$ 297,850

PEK COMPANY
STATEMENT OF CASH FLOWS
FOR THE YEAR ENDED DECEMBER 31, 2001

Cash flows from operating activities:	
Net income	$297,850
Adjustments to reconcile net income to net cash provided by operating activities (includes depreciation expense)	83,200
Net cash provided by operating activities	$381,050
Cash flows from financing activities:	
Dividends	(35,000)
Net increase in cash	$346,050

Additional information:

a. Beginning inventory and purchases for the one product the company sells are as follows:

	Units	Unit Cost
Beginning inventory	50,000	$2.00
Purchases:		
February 5	25,000	2.10
March 10	30,000	2.20
April 15	40,000	2.50
June 16	75,000	3.00
September 5	60,000	3.10
October 3	40,000	3.25

b. During the year the company sold 250,000 units at $5 each.

c. PEK uses the periodic FIFO method to value its inventory and the straight-line method to depreciate all of its long-term assets.

d. During the year-end audit, it was discovered that a January 3, 2001, transaction for the lump-sum purchase of a mixing machine and a boiler was not recorded. The fair market values of the mixing machine and the boiler were $200,000 and $100,000, respectively. Each asset has an estimated useful life of 10 years with no residual value expected. The purchase of the assets was financed by issuing a $270,000 five-year promissory note directly to the seller. Interest of 8% is paid annually on December 31.

Required

1. Prepare a revised income statement and a revised statement of cash flows to take into account the omission of the entry to record the purchase of the two assets. (*Hint:* You will need to take into account any change in income taxes as a result of changes in any income statement items. Assume that income taxes are paid on December 31 of each year.)

2. Assume the same facts as above, except that the company is considering the use of an accelerated method rather than the straight-line method for the assets purchased on January 3, 2001. All other assets would continue to be depreciated on a straight-line basis. Prepare a revised income statement and a revised statement of cash flows, assuming the company decides to use the accelerated method for these two assets rather than the straight-line method resulting in depreciation of $49,091 for 2001.

Treat the answers in requirements **3** and **4** as independent of the other parts.

3. Assume PEK decides to use the LIFO method rather than the FIFO method to value its inventory and recognize cost of goods sold for 2001. Compute the effect (amount of increase or decrease) this would have on cost of goods sold, income tax expense, and net income.

4. Assume PEK failed to record an estimate of bad debts for 2001 (bad debt expense is normally included in "other expenses"). Before any adjustment, the balance in Allowance for Doubtful Accounts is $8,200. The credit manager estimates that 3% of the $800,000 of sales on account will prove to be uncollectible. Based on this information, compute the effect (amount of increase or decrease) of recognition of the bad debt estimate on other expenses, income tax expense, and net income.

VIDEO CASE II | STRIDE RITE

Stride Rite Corporation is the familiar, well-known designer and marketer of the leading brand of children's footwear in the United States. Many children have taken their first steps in Stride Rite shoes, including dress shoes, play shoes, boots, sandals, and sneakers for consumers aged six months to 12 years. The company, based in Lexington, Massachusetts, also sells athletic and casual footwear for children and adults, as well as marine and outdoor recreational footwear and dress shoes. Its new Baby Collection, introduced in 2000 and designed to mimic barefoot walking and to promote natural development, has stepped out quickly and successfully to take its place among the company's other top brand names like Keds, Sperry Top-Sider, Tommy Hilfiger, Nine West Kids, Grasshoppers, and Street Hot.

Under its new Chairman and CEO, David M. Chamberlain, the company looks forward to a revival of growth and value in the new century. Net sales for the fourth quarter of 1999 were up by the highest percentage since 1993, and net income for the quarter totaled $399,000, a significant turnaround following a $5.7 million loss for the same period in fiscal 1998. Net sales in fiscal 1999 increased 6 percent to $572.7 million, and net income for the year increased 26 percent to $26.4 million. Earnings per share increased 30 percent over fiscal 1998.

New products and new lines boosted sales of many of Stride Rite's brands. Keds had a strong fourth quarter, led by new Keds Stretch and Keds City styles, and the new licensing agreement with fashion leader Tommy Hilfiger began to take off with a 24 percent increase, thanks largely to the new women's line launched the fall before.

Stride Rite showed its renewed marketing savvy early in March 2000, with a combination of new product launch (the Baby Collection), major television and print ad campaigns, and a major tactical switch that turned its information-only Web site into a full-fledged e-commerce site capable of taking orders. Industry experts applauded Stride Rite's strategy for its newly functional Web site, and the company's decision to make it interactive, led it to tap two outside companies to build the site quickly and maintain it. The firm's reliance on information technology experts appears to be paying off. Keds are now selling well online. Stride Rite's internal information technology staff was not idle, however. They were busy perfecting the company's intranet and extranet to allow for smoother internal and business-to-business communications.

Cost-saving moves initiated in recent years have included the gradual transfer of all manufacturing functions overseas. In 1998 Stride Rite closed its last U.S. factory and now buys all its merchandise from foreign makers, mostly in Asia. A new distribution center in Indiana also opened that year.

Questions

1. Characterize Stride Rite's relationship with Tommy Hilfiger. Do you think similar partnerships with other firms could help the company improve its market share or financial position? What firms would you suggest for such partnerships?
2. Do you think Stride Rite made a good decision to outsource the building and maintenance of its updated Web site? What factors do you think led it to choose outsourcing for this critical task?
3. What impact would you expect the closing of domestic manufacturing operations to have on the firm's financial statements? Where will it show up?

Part III

Accounting for Liabilities and Owners' Equity

A Word to Students about Part III

By now it's clear that this book is organized along the lines of a balance sheet. That is, Part II covered assets; Part III will cover liabilities and equity. As we'll see, taking on liabilities to pay for assets is one way to provide financing for the future of the company; the other alternative is to issue stock.

Also, the chapters in Part III continue to discuss how the related transactions affect the statement of cash flows, which is key to understanding how companies' statements—and their activities—are interrelated.

Chapter 9
Current Liabilities, Contingent Liabilities, and the Time Value of Money

Appendix 9A
Accounting Tools: Payroll Accounting

Chapter 10
Long-Term Liabilities

Chapter 11
Stockholders' Equity

Appendix 11A
Accounting Tools: Accounting for Unincorporated Businesses

Chapter 9

Current Liabilities, Contingent Liabilities, and the Time Value of Money

Study Links

A Look at Previous Chapters

Chapter 2 introduced classified balance sheets, which emphasize the distinction between current and noncurrent assets and liabilities. Current liabilities generally represent items to be paid within one year.

A Look at This Chapter

The first part of this chapter more closely examines the items that appear in the current liability category of the balance sheet. The second part examines whether contingent liabilities should be presented on the balance sheet, disclosed in the footnotes, or ignored altogether. The third part of the chapter presents the concept of the time value of money.

A Look at Upcoming Chapters

Chapter 10 presents the accounting for long-term liabilities. The time value of money concept developed in Chapter 9 will be applied to several long-term liability issues in Chapter 10.

Focus on Financial Results

JCPenney wants to be "the customer's first choice for the products and services we offer." Through its 1,148 domestic and international stores, its well-known catalog, and a new Web site, the familiar retailer offers family apparel, jewelry, shoes, accessories, and home furnishings that bear national as well as exclusive and private brand names.

Despite its broad offerings, trusted name, and innovative Web site, JCPenney posted a decline in gross profit for 1998.[1] Improving profitability will thus be a top priority for the next few years. In the 1998 annual report, CEO and Chairman James E. Oesterreicher described a set of short- and long-term strategies that focus on defining target customers, revamping marketing efforts, building a responsive merchandising strategy, and improving execution.

The last two of these objectives have implications for inventory. One goal is to merge department store and catalog inventories—to improve inventory management. Another is to shorten the buying process, improving inventory turnover.

Managing inventory well means managing accounts payable, one of JCPenney's current liabilities. That in turn means having enough current assets on hand to pay current liabilities, such as suppliers' bills, on time. So Penney's realizes that its profitability goals are directly linked to effectively managing inventory and the related current liabilities.

[1] JCPenney's 1998 annual report, p. 2.

J. C. Penney Company, Inc. and Subsidiaries

($ in millions)	1998	1997
Assets		
Current assets		
Cash (including short-term investments of $95 and $208)	$ 96	$ 287
Retained interest in JCP Master Credit Card Trust	415	1,073
Receivables, net (bad debt reserve of $149 and $135)	4,415	3,819
Merchandise inventory (including LIFO reserves of $227 and $225)	6,031	6,162
Prepaid expenses	168	143
Total current assets	11,125	11,484
Property, plant, and equipment		
Land and buildings	3,109	2,993
Furniture and fixtures	4,045	4,089
Leasehold improvements	1,179	1,192
Accumulated depreciation	(2,875)	(2,945)
Property, plant, and equipment, net	5,458	5,329
Investments, principally held by Direct Marketing	1,961	1,774
Deferred policy acquisition costs	847	752
Goodwill and other intangible assets, net (accumulated amortization of $221 and $108)	2,933	2,940
Other assets	1,314	1,214
Total Assets	$ 23,638	$ 23,493

Liabilities and Stockholders' Equity		
Current liabilities		
Accounts payable and accrued expenses	$ 3,465	$ 4,059
Short-term debt	1,924	1,417
Current maturities of long-term debt	438	449
Deferred taxes	143	116
Total current liabilities	5,970	6,041
Long-term debt	7,143	6,986
Deferred taxes	1,517	1,325
Insurance policy and claims reserves	946	872
Other liabilities	893	912
Total Liabilities	16,469	16,136
Stockholders' Equity		
Preferred stock: authorized, 25 million shares; issued and outstanding, 0.8 million and 0.9 million shares Series B ESOP Convertible Preferred	475	526
Guaranteed LESOP obligation	–	(49)
Common stock, par value 50 cents: authorized, 1,250 million shares; issued and outstanding 250 million and 251 million shares	2,850	2,766
Reinvested earnings	3,858	4,066
Accumulated other comprehensive income/(loss)	(14)	48
Total Stockholders' Equity	7,169	7,357
Total Liabilities and Stockholders' Equity	$ 23,638	$ 23,493

JCPenney's 1998 Annual Report

If you were a bank loan officer looking for information about JCPenney's credit rating, what information would you want about current liabilities? While you study this chapter, consider which accounts on JCPenney's balance sheet are current liabilities and how they might influence its financial position.

www.jcpenney.com

Learning Objectives

After studying this chapter, you should be able to:

LO 1 Identify the components of the current liability category of the balance sheet. (p. 422)

LO 2 Examine how accruals affect the current liability category. (p. 427)

LO 3 Understand how changes in current liabilities affect the statement of cash flows. (p. 429)

LO 4 Determine when contingent liabilities should be presented on the balance sheet or disclosed in footnotes and how to calculate their amounts. (p. 430)

LO 5 Explain the difference between simple and compound interest. (p. 436)

LO 6 Calculate amounts using the future value and present value concepts. (p. 437)

LO 7 Apply the compound interest concepts to some common accounting situations. (p. 443)

LO 8 Understand the deductions and expenses for payroll accounting (Appendix 9A). (p. 452)

LO 9 Determine when compensated absences must be accrued as a liability (Appendix 9A). (p. 455)

Current Liabilities

LO 1 Identify the components of the current liability category of the balance sheet.

A classified balance sheet presents financial statement items by category in order to provide more information to financial statement users. The balance sheet generally presents two categories of liabilities, current and long-term.

Current liabilities finance the working capital of the company. At any given time during the year, current liabilities may fluctuate substantially. It is important that the company generates sufficient cash flow to retire these debts as they come due. As long as the company's ratio of current assets to current liabilities stays fairly constant from quarter to quarter or year to year, financial statement users are not going to be too concerned.

www.mcdonalds.com

The current liability portion of the 1998 balance sheet of McDonald's Corporation is highlighted in Exhibit 9-1. Some companies list the accounts in the current liability category in the order of payment due date. That is, the account that requires payment first is listed first, the account requiring payment next is listed second, and so forth. This allows users of the statement to assess the cash flow implications of each account. McDonald's uses a different approach and lists Notes Payable as the first account.

CURRENT LIABILITY Accounts that will be satisfied within one year or the current operating cycle.

Current liabilities were first introduced to you in Chapter 2 of this text. In general, a **current liability** is an obligation that will be satisfied within one year. Although current liabilities are not due immediately, they are still recorded at face value; that is, the time until payment is not taken into account. If it were, current liabilities would be recorded at a slight discount to reflect interest that would be earned between now and the due date. The face value amount is generally used for all current liabilities because the time period involved is short enough that it is not necessary to record or calculate an interest factor. In addition, when interest rates are low, one need not worry about the interest that could be earned in this short period of time. In Chapter 10 we will find that many long-term liabilities must be stated at their present value on the balance sheet.

The current liability classification is important because it is closely tied to the concept of *liquidity.* Management of the firm must be prepared to pay current liabilities within a very short time period. Therefore, management must have access to liquid assets, cash, or other assets that can be converted to cash in amounts sufficient to pay the current liabilities. Firms that do not have sufficient resources to pay their current liabilities are often said to have a liquidity problem.

From Concept **to PRACTICE 9.1**

READING JCPENNEY'S BALANCE SHEET Refer to JCPenney's balance sheet for 1998. What accounts are listed as current liabilities? What was the change in Accounts Payable from 1997 to 1998?

A handy ratio to help creditors or potential creditors determine a company's liquidity is the current ratio. A current ratio of current assets to current liabilities of 2:1 is usually a very comfortable margin. If the firm has a large amount of inventory, it is sometimes useful to exclude inventory when computing the ratio. That provides the "quick" ratio. Usually, one would want a quick ratio of at least 1.5:1 to feel secure that the company could pay its

EXHIBIT 9-1 McDonald's Corporation 1998 Consolidated Balance Sheet

FINANCIAL REVIEW

Consolidated Balance Sheet

(In millions, except per share data)	*December 31,* **1998**	1997
Assets		
Current assets		
Cash and equivalents	**$ 299.2**	$ 341.4
Accounts and notes receivable	**609.4**	483.5
Inventories, at cost, not in excess of market	**77.3**	70.5
Prepaid expenses and other current assets	**323.5**	246.9
Total current assets	**1,309.4**	1,142.3
Other assets		
Notes receivable due after one year	**67.9**	67.0
Investments in and advances to affiliates	**854.1**	634.8
Intangible assets—net	**973.1**	827.5
Miscellaneous	**538.3**	608.5
Total other assets	**2,433.4**	2,137.8
Property and equipment		
Property and equipment, at cost	**21,758.0**	20,088.2
Accumulated depreciation and amortization	**(5,716.4)**	(5,126.8)
Net property and equipment	**16,041.6**	14,961.4
Total assets	**$19,784.4**	$18,241.5
Liabilities and shareholders' equity		
Current liabilities		
Notes payable	**$ 686.8**	$ 1,293.8
Accounts payable	**621.3**	650.6
Income taxes	**94.2**	52.5
Other taxes	**143.5**	148.5
Accrued interest	**132.3**	107.1
Other accrued liabilities	**651.0**	396.4
Current maturities of long-term debt	**168.0**	335.6
Total current liabilities	**2,497.1**	2,984.5
Long-term debt	**6,188.6**	4,834.1
Other long-term liabilities and minority interests	**492.6**	427.5
Deferred income taxes	**1,081.9**	1,063.5
Common equity put options	**59.5**	80.3
Shareholders' equity		
Preferred stock, no par value; authorized—165.0 million shares; issued—none		
Common stock, $.01 par value; authorized—3.5 billion shares; issued—1,660.6 million	**16.6**	16.6
Additional paid-in capital	**989.2**	690.9
Guarantee of ESOP Notes	**(148.7)**	(171.3)
Retained earnings	**13,879.6**	12,569.0
Accumulated other comprehensive income	**(522.5)**	(470.5)
Common stock in treasury, at cost; 304.4 and 289.2 million shares	**(4,749.5)**	(3,783.1)
Total shareholders' equity	**9,464.7**	8,851.6
Total liabilities and shareholders' equity	**$19,784.4**	$18,241.5

Highlighted items will require payments within one year

The accompanying Financial Comments are an integral part of the consolidated financial statements.

bills on time. Of course, the guidelines given for the current ratio, 2:1, and the quick ratio, 1.5:1, are only rules of thumb. The actual current and quick ratios of companies vary widely and depend on the company, the management policies, and the type of industry. Exhibit 9-2 presents the current and quick ratios for the companies that are used as examples in this chapter. The ratios do vary from company to company, yet all are solid companies without liquidity problems.

EXHIBIT 9-2 Current and Quick Ratios of Selected Companies for 1998

Company	Industry	Current Ratio	Quick Ratio
AMD	semiconductor	1.86	1.33
Ben & Jerry's	food	2.43	1.73
Georgia-Pacific	building products/lumber	1.11	.52
JCPenney	retailing	1.86	.83
Johnson Controls	auto	.79	.64
McDonald's	fast food	.52	.52

Accounting for current liabilities is an area in which U.S. accounting standards are very similar to those of most other countries. Nearly all countries encourage firms to provide a breakdown of liabilities into current and long-term in order to allow users to evaluate liquidity.

ACCOUNTING FOR YOUR DECISIONS

You Are a Student

What types of current liabilities could you, as a student, have? What makes them liabilities? What makes them current?

ANS: Your current liabilities might include the current payments due from (1) student loans, (2) car loans, (3) loans from family members, (4) rent or mortgage payments, (5) credit card charges, (6) cafeteria charges, and similar charges. These items are current liabilities because they are obligations that will be satisfied within a year.

ACCOUNTS PAYABLE

ACCOUNTS PAYABLE Amounts owed for inventory, goods, or services acquired in the normal course of business.

Accounts payable represent amounts owed for the purchase of inventory, goods, or services acquired in the normal course of business. Often, Accounts Payable is the first account listed in the current liability category because it requires the payment of cash before other current liabilities. McDonald's is different from most other companies because it lists Notes Payable before Accounts Payable.

Normally, a firm has an established relationship with several suppliers, and formal contractual arrangements with those suppliers are unnecessary. Accounts payable usually do not require the payment of interest, but terms may be given to encourage early payment. For example, terms may be stated as 2/10, n30, which means that a 2% discount is available if payment occurs within the first 10 days and that if payment is not made within 10 days, the full amount must be paid within 30 days.

From Concept **TO PRACTICE 9.2**

READING BEN & JERRY'S FOOTNOTES Refer to Ben & Jerry's foot notes. What items are included in the Accounts Payable and Accrued Expenses line of the balance sheet?

Timely payment of accounts payable is an important aspect of the management of cash flow. Generally, it is to the company's benefit to take advantage of discounts when they are available. After all, if your supplier is going to give you a 2% discount for paying on Day 10 instead of Day 30, that means you are earning 2% on your money over 20/360 of a year. If you took the 2% discount throughout the year, you would be getting a 36% annual return on your money, since there are 18 periods of 20 days each in a year. It is essential, therefore, that the accounts payable system be established in a manner that alerts management to take advantage of offered discounts.

NOTES PAYABLE

NOTES PAYABLE Amounts owed that are represented by a formal contract.

The first current liability on McDonald's balance sheet is notes payable of $686.8 million. How is a note payable different from an account payable? The most important difference is that an account payable is not a formal contractual arrangement, whereas a **note payable** is represented by a formal agreement or note signed by the parties to the transaction. Notes payable may arise from dealing with a supplier or from acquiring a cash loan from a bank or creditor. Those notes that are expected to be paid within one year of the balance sheet date should be classified as current liabilities.

The accounting for notes payable depends on whether the interest is paid on the note's due date or is deducted before the borrower receives the loan proceeds. With the first type of note, the terms stipulate that the borrower receives a short-term loan and agrees to repay the principal and interest at the note's due date. For example, assume that Lamanski Company receives a one-year loan from First National Bank on January 1, 2001. The face amount of the note of $1,000 must be repaid on December 31 along with interest at the rate of 12%. Lamanski would make the following entries to record the loan and its repayment:

Jan. 1	Cash	1,000	
	Notes Payable		1,000
	To record loan of $1,000.		

Assets	=	Liabilities	+	Owners' Equity
+1,000		+1,000		

Dec. 31	Notes Payable	1,000	
	Interest Expense	120	
	Cash		1,120
	To record the repayment of loan with interest.		

Assets	=	Liabilities	+	Owners' Equity
−1,120		−1,000		−120

Banks also use another form of note, one in which the interest is deducted in advance. Suppose that on January 1, 2001, First National Bank granted to Lamanski a $1,000 loan, due on December 31, 2001, but deducted the interest in advance and gave Lamanski the remaining amount of $880 ($1,000 face amount of the note less interest of $120). This is sometimes referred to as *discounting a note* because a Discount on Notes Payable account is established when the loan is recorded. On January 1, Lamanski must make the following entry:

Jan. 1	Cash	880	
	Discount on Notes Payable	120	
	Notes Payable		1,000
	To record loan of $1,000 less interest deducted in advance.		

Assets	=	Liabilities	+	Owners' Equity
+880		−120		
		+1,000		

The **Discount on Notes Payable** account should be treated as a reduction of Notes Payable (and should have a debit balance). If a balance sheet was developed immediately after the January 1 loan, the note would appear in the current liability category as follows:

DISCOUNT ON NOTES PAYABLE
A contra liability that represents interest deducted from a loan in advance.

Notes Payable	$1,000
Less: Discount on Notes Payable	120
Net Liability	$ 880

Study Tip

Discount on Notes Payable is a contra-liability account and will have a debit balance.

The original balance in the Discount on Notes Payable account represents interest that must be transferred to interest expense over the life of the note. Before Lamanski presents its year-end financial statements, it must make an adjustment to transfer the discount to interest expense. The effect of the adjustment on December 31 is as follows:

Dec. 31	Interest Expense	120	
	Discount on Notes Payable		120
	To record interest on note payable.		

Assets	=	Liabilities	+	Owners' Equity
		+120		−120

Thus, the balance of the Discount on Notes Payable account is zero, and $120 has been transferred to interest expense. When the note is repaid on December 31, 2001, Lamanski must repay the full amount of the note as follows:

Dec. 31	Notes Payable	1,000	
	Cash		1,000
	To record payment of the note on its due date.		

Assets	=	Liabilities	+	Owners' Equity
−1,000		−1,000		

It is important to compare the two types of notes payable. In the previous two examples, the stated interest rate on each note was 12%. The dollar amount of interest incurred in each case was $120. However, the interest *rate* on a discounted note, the second example, is always higher than it appears. Lamanski received the use of only $880, yet it was required to repay $1,000. Therefore, the interest rate incurred on the note was actually 120/880, or approximately 13.6%.

Current Maturities of Long-Term Debt

CURRENT MATURITIES OF LONG-TERM DEBT The portion of a long-term liability that will be paid within one year.

Another account that appears in the current liability category of McDonald's balance sheet is **Current Maturities of Long-Term Debt.** On other companies' balance sheets, this item may appear as Long-Term Debt, Current Portion. This account should appear when a firm has a liability and must make periodic payments. For example, assume that on January 1, 2001, your firm obtained a $10,000 loan from the bank. The terms of the loan require you to make payments in the amount of $1,000 per year for 10 years, payable each January 1, beginning January 1, 2002. On December 31, 2001, an entry should be made to classify a portion of the balance as a current liability as follows:

2001			
Dec. 31	Long-Term Liability	1,000	
	Current Portion of Liability		1,000
	To record the current portion of bank loan.		

Assets	=	Liabilities	+	Owners' Equity
		−1,000		
		+1,000		

The December 31, 2001, balance sheet should indicate that the liability for the note payable is classified into two portions: a $1,000 current liability that must be repaid within one year and a $9,000 long-term liability.

On January 1, 2002, the company must pay $1,000, and the entry should be recorded as follows:

2002			
Jan. 1	Current Portion of Liability	1,000	
	Cash		1,000
	To record payment of $1,000 on bank loan.		

Assets	=	Liabilities	+	Owners' Equity
−1,000		−1,000		

On December 31, 2002, the company should again record the current portion of the liability. Therefore, the 2002 year-end balance sheet should indicate that the liability is classified into two portions: a $1,000 current liability and an $8,000 long-term liability. The process should be repeated each year until the bank loan has been fully paid. When an investor or creditor reads a balance sheet, he or she wants to distinguish between debt that is long-term and debt that is short-term. Therefore, it is important to segregate that portion of the debt that becomes due within one year.

The balance sheet category labeled Current Maturities of Long-Term Debt should include only the amount of principal to be paid. The amount of interest that has been incurred but is unpaid should be listed separately in an account such as Interest Payable.

Taxes Payable

LO 2 Examine how accruals affect the current liability category.

Corporations pay a variety of taxes, including federal and state income taxes, property taxes, and other taxes. Usually, the largest dollar amount is incurred for state and federal income taxes. Taxes are an expense of the business and should be accrued in the same manner as any other business expense. A company that ends its accounting year on December 31 is not required to calculate the amount of tax owed to the government until the following March 15 or April 15, depending on the type of business. Therefore, the business must make an accounting entry, usually as one of the year-end adjusting entries, to record the amount of tax that has been incurred but is unpaid. Normally, the entry would be recorded as follows:

Dec. 31	Tax Expense	xxx	
	Tax Payable		xxx
	To accrue income tax for the year.		

Assets	=	Liabilities	+	Owners' Equity
		+xxx		−xxx

From Concept **TO PRACTICE 9.3**

Reading Gateway's Footnotes

One of Gateway's Current Liabilities is Accrued Royalities. How do the footnotes explain that account?

The calculation of the amount of tax a business owes is very complex. For now, the important point is that taxes are an expense when incurred (not when they are paid) and must be recorded as a liability as incurred.

Some analysts prefer to measure a company's profits before it pays taxes for several reasons. For one thing, tax rates change from year to year. A small change in the tax rate may drastically change a firm's profitability. Also, investors should realize that taxes occur in every year but that tax changes are not a recurring element of a business. Additionally, taxes are somewhat beyond the control of a company's management. For these reasons, it is important to consider a firm's operations *before* taxes to better evaluate management's ability to control operations.

Other Accrued Liabilities

McDonald's 1998 balance sheet listed an amount of $651.0 million as current liability under the category of Other Accrued Liabilities. What items might be included in this category?

In previous chapters, especially Chapter 4, we covered many examples of accrued liabilities. **Accrued liabilities** include any amount that has been incurred due to the passage of time but has not been paid as of the balance sheet date. A common example is salary or wages payable. Suppose that your firm has a payroll of $1,000 per day, Monday through Friday, and that employees are paid at the close of work each Friday. Also suppose that December 31 is the end of your accounting year and falls on a Tuesday. Your firm will then have to record the following entry as of December 31:

Accrued Liability
A liability that has been incurred but not yet paid.

Dec. 31	Salary Expense	2,000	
	Salary Payable		2,000
	To record two days' salary as expense.		

Assets	=	Liabilities	+	Owners' Equity
		+2,000		−2,000

The amount of the salary payable would be classified as a current liability and could appear in a category such as Other Accrued Liabilities.

Interest is another item that often must be accrued at year-end. Assume that you received a one-year loan of $10,000 on December 1. The loan carries an interest rate of 12%. On December 31, an accounting entry must be made to record interest, even though the money may not actually be due:

Dec. 31	Interest Expense	100	
	Interest Payable		100
	To record one month's interest as expense.		

Assets	=	Liabilities	+	Owners' Equity
		+100		−100

The Interest Payable account should be classified as a current liability, assuming that it is to be paid within one year of the December 31 date.

Business Strategy

Few department stores today focus on a narrow band of customers. Most savvy retailers realize the value of appealing to as many different market segments as possible while still establishing a distinctive identity for the store to set it apart from its competitors. There are several ways to do this.

JCPenney, mentioned in the chapter opener, uses a wide array of private and national clothing brands to attract customers from many different demographic groups. National brands like Dockers, Vanity Fair, Jockey, Haggar, Adidas, Crazy Horse, and Joneswear all are featured in the stores. Private (store) brands such as Arizona Jeans, Worthington, Stafford, and St. John's Bay have proved successful enough to earn their own store-within-a-store departments, which JCPenney plans to expand in the future. Despite this differentiation by brand, accounting information for all of them is added together for financial reporting purposes.

www.gap.com

Gap, Inc., on the other hand, sells only its own brand of clothes and accessories in Gap stores. When the company decided in 1994 to develop a new brand of trendy, budget-priced clothing, it spun off a whole new line of stores to showcase it, and Old Navy was born. This strategy had already allowed Gap Inc. to open its successful Banana Republic chain of slightly upscale clothing stores, and it looks like the idea is working again. Old Navy will soon exceed Gap's expectations and even Gap's sales. The popular new chain, with its funky decor and mass-market appeal, already boasts 450 stores and has big expansion plans. In fact, Old Navy, essentially a store brand with a home of its own, is already one of the fastest-growing retailers in the country.

Sources: JCPenney's 1998 annual report; Louise Lee, "A Savvy Captain for Old Navy," *Business Week*, Nov. 8, 1999, pp. 132, 134.

Exhibit 9-3 Current Liabilities on the Statement of Cash Flows

Item	Cash Flow Statement	
	Operating Activities	
	Net income	xxxx
Increase in current liability →		+
Decrease in current liability →		−
	Investing Activities	
	Financing Activities	
Increase in notes payable →		+
Decrease in notes payable →		−

EXHIBIT 9-4 McDonald's Corporation 1998 Consolidated Statement of Cash Flows

FINANCIAL REVIEW

Consolidated Statement of Cash Flows

(In millions) Years ended December 31,	**1998**	1997	1996
Operating activities			
Net income	**$ 1,550.1**	$ 1,642.5	$ 1,572.6
Adjustments to reconcile to cash provided by operations			
Depreciation and amortization	**881.1**	793.8	742.9
Deferred income taxes	**35.4**	(1.1)	32.9
Changes in operating working capital items			
Accounts receivable	**(29.9)**	(57.6)	(77.5)
Inventories, prepaid expenses and other current assets	**(18.1)**	(34.5)	(18.7)
Accounts payable	**(12.7)**	52.8	44.5
Taxes and other liabilities	**337.5**	221.9	121.4
Refund of U.S. franchisee security deposits		(109.6)	
Other	**22.9**	(65.9)	42.9
Cash provided by operations	**2,766.3**	2,442.3	2,461.0
Investing activities			
Property and equipment expenditures	**(1,879.3)**	(2,111.2)	(2,375.3)
Purchases of restaurant businesses	**(118.4)**	(113.6)	(137.7)
Sales of restaurant businesses	**149.0**	149.5	198.8
Property sales	**42.5**	26.9	35.5
Other	**(142.0)**	(168.8)	(291.6)
Cash used for investing activities	**(1,948.2)**	(2,217.2)	(2,570.3)
Financing activities			
Net short-term borrowings (repayments)	**(604.2)**	1,097.4	228.8
Long-term financing issuances	**1,461.5**	1,037.9	1,391.8
Long-term financing repayments	**(594.9)**	(1,133.8)	(841.3)
Treasury stock purchases	**(1,089.8)**	(755.1)	(599.9)
Common and preferred stock dividends	**(240.5)**	(247.7)	(232.0)
Series E preferred stock redemption		(358.0)	
Other	**207.6**	145.7	157.0
Cash provided by (used for) financing activities	**(860.3)**	(213.6)	104.4
Cash and equivalents increase (decrease)	**(42.2)**	11.5	(4.9)
Cash and equivalents at beginning of year	**341.4**	329.9	334.8
Cash and equivalents at end of year	**$ 299.2**	$ 341.4	$ 329.9
Supplemental cash flow disclosures			
Interest paid	**$ 406.5**	$ 401.7	$ 369.0
Income taxes paid	**$ 545.9**	$ 650.8	$ 558.1

Note the impact of current liabilities on cash flow

The accompanying Financial Comments are an integral part of the consolidated financial statements.

READING THE STATEMENT OF CASH FLOWS FOR CHANGES IN CURRENT LIABILITIES

LO 3 Understand how changes in current liabilities affect the statement of cash flows.

It is important to understand the impact that current liabilities have on a company's cash flows. Exhibit 9-3 illustrates the placement of current liabilities on the statement of cash flows (using the indirect method) and their effect. Most current liabilities are directly related to a firm's ongoing operations. Therefore, the change in the balance of each current liability account should be reflected in the Operating Activities category of the statement of cash flows. A decrease in a current liability account indicates that cash has been used to pay the liability and should appear as a deduction on the cash flow statement. An increase in a current liability account indicates a recognized expense that has not yet been paid. Look for it as an increase in the Operating Activities category of the cash flow statement.

The cash flow statement of McDonald's Corporation is presented in Exhibit 9-4. Note that one of the items in the Operating Activities category is listed as Taxes and

Other Liabilities of $337.5 million. This means that the balance of those current liabilities increased by $337.5 million, resulting in an increase of cash.

Almost all current liabilities appear in the Operating Activities category of the statement of cash flows, but there are exceptions. If a current liability is not directly related to operating activities, it should not appear in that category. For example, McDonald's uses some notes payable as a means of financing, distinct from operating activities. Therefore, note borrowings and repayments are reflected in the Financing Activities rather than the Operating Activities category (see Exhibit 9-3).

Two-Minute Review

1. What is the definition of current liabilities. Give some examples of items that are typically in the current liability category.

2. How is the current ratio calculated. What is it intended to measure?

3. In which category of the cash flow statement do most current liability items appear?

Answers:

1. Current liabilities are defined as items that will be paid within one year of the balance sheet date. Examples of current liabilities include accounts payable, notes payable if due within one year, taxes payable, and other accrued liabilities. Also, if a portion of a long-term debt will be paid within one year, that portion should be reported as a current liability.

2. The current ratio is calculated as total current assets divided by total current liabilities. It is a measure of the liquidity of the company, or the ability of the company to pay its short-term obligations.

3. Most current liabilities are reported in the operating category of the cash flow statement. You should note that it is the change in the balance of the current liability that is reported.

CONTINGENT LIABILITIES

LO 4 Determine when contingent liabilities should be presented on the balance sheet or disclosed in footnotes and how to calculate their amounts.

CONTINGENT LIABILITY An existing condition for which the outcome is not known but depends on some future event.

We have seen that accountants must exercise a great deal of expertise and judgment in deciding what to record and in determining the amount to record. This is certainly true regarding contingent liabilities. A **contingent liability** is an obligation that involves an existing condition for which the outcome is not known with certainty and depends on some event that will occur in the future. The actual amount of the liability must be estimated because we cannot clearly predict the future. The important accounting issues are whether contingent liabilities should be recorded and, if so, in what amounts.

This is a judgment call that is usually resolved through discussions among the company's management and its outside auditors. Management usually would rather not disclose contingent liabilities until they come due. The reason is that investors' and creditors' judgment of management is based on the company's earnings, and the recording of a contingent liability must be accompanied by a charge to (reduction in) earnings. Auditors, on the other hand, want management to disclose as much as possible because the auditors are essentially representing the interests of investors and creditors, who want to have as much information as possible.

CONTINGENT LIABILITIES THAT ARE RECORDED

Study Tip

Contingent liabilities are recorded only if they are probable and if the amount can be reasonably estimated.

A contingent liability should be accrued and presented on the balance sheet if it is probable and if the amount can be reasonably estimated. But when is an event *probable,* and what does *reasonably estimated* mean? The terms must be defined based on the facts of each situation. A financial statement user would want the company to err on the side of full disclosure. On the other hand, the company should not be required to disclose every remote possibility.

A common contingent liability that must be presented as a liability by firms involves product warranties or guarantees. Many firms sell products for which they provide the customer a warranty against defects that may develop in the products. If a product becomes defective within the warranty period, the selling firm ensures that it will repair or replace the item. This is an example of a contingent liability because the expense of fixing a product depends on some of the products becoming defective—an uncertain, although likely, event.

At the end of each period, the selling firm must estimate how many of the products sold in the current year will become defective in the future and the cost of repair or replacement. This type of contingent liability is often referred to as an **estimated liability** to emphasize that the costs are not known at year-end and must be estimated.

ESTIMATED LIABILITY
A contingent liability that is accrued and reflected on the balance sheet.

As an example, assume that Quickkey Computer sells a computer product for $5,000. When the customer buys the product, Quickkey provides a one-year warranty in case it must be repaired. Assume that in 2001 Quickkey sold 100 computers for a total sales revenue of $500,000. At the end of 2001, Quickkey must record an estimate of the warranty costs that will occur on 2001 sales. Using an analysis of past warranty records, Quickkey estimates that repairs will average 2% of total sales. Therefore, Quickkey should record the following transaction at the end of 2001:

Dec. 31	Warranty Expense	10,000	
	Estimated Liability		10,000
	To record estimated liability at 2% of sales.		

Assets	=	Liabilities	+	Owners' Equity
		+10,000		−10,000

The amount of warranty costs that a company presents as an expense is of interest to investors and potential creditors. If the expense as a percentage of sales begins to rise, one might conclude that the product is becoming less reliable.

Warranties are an excellent example of the matching principle. In our Quickkey example, the warranty costs related to 2001 sales were estimated and recorded in 2001. This was done to match the 2001 sales with the expenses related to those sales. If actual repairs of the computers occurred in 2002, they do not result in an expense. The repair costs incurred in 2002 should be treated as a reduction in the liability that had previously been estimated.

Because items such as warranties involve estimation, you may wonder what happens if the amount estimated is not accurate. The company must analyze past warranty records carefully and incorporate any changes in customer buying habits, usage, technological changes, and other changes. Still, even with careful analysis, the actual amount of the expense is not likely to equal the estimated amount. Generally, firms do not change the amount of the expense recorded in past periods for such differences. They may adjust the amount recorded in future periods, however.

Product warranties represent a *contingent liability* that must be presented on the balance sheet. This is because some amount of warranty work is *probable* and can be *estimated.* As the level of warranty expense rises, often so does investors' skepticism toward these retailers.

Warranties provide an example of a contingent liability that must be estimated and recorded. Another example is premium or coupon offers that accompany many products. Cereal boxes are an everyday example of premium offers. The boxes often allow customers to purchase a toy or game at a reduced price if the purchase is accompanied by cereal box tops or proof of purchase. The offer given to cereal customers represents a contingent liability. At the end of each year, the cereal company must estimate the number of premium offers that will be redeemed and the cost involved and must report a contingent liability for that amount.

Legal claims that have been filed against a firm are also examples of contingent liabilities. In today's business environment, lawsuits and legal claims are a fact of life. They represent a contingent liability because an event has occurred but the outcome of that event, the resolution of the lawsuit, is not known. The defendant in the lawsuit must make a judgment about the outcome of the lawsuit in order to decide whether the item should be recorded on the balance sheet or should be disclosed in the footnotes. If an unfavorable outcome to the legal claim is deemed to be probable, then an amount should be recorded as a contingent liability on the balance sheet. Exhibit 9-5 provides portions of a footnote disclosure that accompanied the 1998 financial statements of Georgia-Pacific

EXHIBIT 9-5 Footnote Disclosure for Contingent Liability from Georgia-Pacific's 1998 Financial Statements

Note 18

The Corporation is involved in environmental remediation activities at approximately 144 sites, both owned by the Corporation and owned by others, where it has been notified that it is or may be a potentially responsible party under the Comprehensive Environmental Response, Compensation and Liability Act or similar state "superfund" laws.

The Corporation has established reserves for environmental remediation costs for these sites in amounts that it believes are probable and reasonably estimable. Based on analysis of currently available information and previous experience with respect to the cleanup of hazardous substances, the Corporation believes that it is reasonably possible that costs associated with these sites may exceed current reserves by amounts that may prove insignificant or that could range, in the aggregate, up to approximately $60 million.

www.gp.com

Corporation. The note concerned litigation over environmental damage that is alleged to have occurred as a result of the company's activities. Environmental remediation claims are very common for companies in many industries. In this case, Georgia-Pacific believed that an unfavorable outcome had become probable and, as a result, recorded a contingent liability of $60 million as an estimate of the amount that will be owed at the eventual outcome of this claim.

As you might imagine, firms are not usually eager to record contingent lawsuits as liabilities because the amount of loss is often difficult to estimate. Also, some may view the accountant's decision as an admission of guilt if a lawsuit is recorded as a liability before the courts have finalized a decision. Accountants must often consult with lawyers or other legal experts to determine the probability of the loss of a lawsuit. In cases involving contingencies, it is especially important that the accountant make an independent judgment based on the facts and not be swayed by the desires of other parties.

CONTINGENT LIABILITIES THAT ARE DISCLOSED

Any contingent liability that both is probable and can be reasonably estimated must be reported as a liability. We now must consider contingent liabilities that do not meet the probable criterion or cannot be reasonably estimated. In either case, a contingent liability must be disclosed in the footnotes but not reported on the balance sheet if the contingent liability is at least reasonably possible.

Although information in the footnotes to the financial statements contains very important data on which investors base decisions, some accountants believe that footnote disclosure does not have the same impact as does recording a contingent liability on the balance sheet. For one thing, footnote disclosure does not affect the important financial ratios that investors use to make decisions.

In the previous section we presented a legal claim involving Georgia-Pacific as an example of a contingent liability that was probable and therefore was recorded on the balance

EXHIBIT 9-6 Footnote Disclosure for Contingencies (Lawsuit and Environmental) from AMD Company's 1998 Annual Report

NOTE 14. CONTINGENCIES

I. Litigation

C. Ellis Investment Co., Ltd v. AMD, et al. This class action complaint was filed against AMD and an individual officer of AMD on March 10, 1999. The complaint alleges that we made misleading statements about the design and production of the AMD-K6 microprocessor in violation of Section 10(b) of the Exchange Act and Rule 10b-5 promulgated thereunder. The plaintiff seeks to represent a class comprised of all persons who purchased our common stock during the period from November 12, 1998 through March 8, 1999. The complaint seeks unspecified damages, cost and fees. Following the filing of this complaint, several law firms published press releases announcing that they had filed, or intend to file, substantially similar class action complaints. As of March 12, 1999, we had not seen or been served with those complaints. Based upon information presently known to management, we do not believe that the ultimate resolution of these lawsuits will have a material adverse effect on our financial condition or results of operations.

II. Environmental Matters

Clean-Up Orders. Since 1981, we have discovered, investigated and begun remediation of three sites where releases from underground chemical tanks at our facilities in Santa Clara County, California adversely affected the ground water. The chemicals released into the ground water were commonly in use in the semiconductor industry in the wafer fabrication process prior to 1979. At least one of the released chemicals (which is no longer used by AMD) has been identified as a probable carcinogen.

In 1991, we received four Final Site Cleanup Requirements Orders from the California Regional Water Quality Control Board, San Francisco Bay Region, relating to the three sites. One of the orders named AMD as well as TRW Microwave, Inc. and Philips Semiconductors Corporation. In January 1999, we entered into a settlement with Philips, whereby Philips will assume costs allocated to AMD under this order, although we would be responsible for these costs in the event that Philips does not fulfill its obligations under the settlement agreement. Another of the orders named AMD as well as National Semiconductor Corporation.

The three sites in Santa Clara County are on the National Priorities List (Superfund). If we fail to satisfy federal compliance requirements or inadequately perform the compliance measures, the government (1) can bring an action to enforce compliance, or (2) can undertake the desired response actions itself and later bring an action to recover its costs, and penalties, which is up to three times the costs of clean-up activities, if appropriate. With regard to certain claims related to this matter, the statute of limitations has been tolled.

We have computed and recorded the estimated environmental liability in accordance with applicable accounting rules and have not recorded any potential insurance recoveries in determining the estimated costs of the clean-up. The amount of environmental charges to earnings has not been material during any of the last three fiscal years. We believe that the potential liability, if any, in excess of amounts already accrued with respect to the foregoing environmental matters, will not have a material adverse effect on our financial condition or results of operations.

sheet as a liability. Most lawsuits, however, are not recorded as liabilities either because the risk of loss is not considered probable or because the amount of the loss cannot be reasonably estimated. If a company does not record a lawsuit as a liability, it must still consider whether the lawsuit should be disclosed in the footnotes. If the risk of loss is at least *reasonably possible,* then the company should provide footnote disclosure. This is the course of action taken for most contingent liabilities involving lawsuits.

Exhibit 9-6 contains two excerpts from the footnotes of the 1998 financial statements of AMD Company, a large company in the semiconductor industry. The first portion of the exhibit indicates the company became a defendant in a lawsuit brought by a group of stockholders who claim to have been damaged by the company's actions. Lawsuits from current or potential investors have become a fairly common occurrence in public companies. The second portion of the exhibit indicates that AMD has been involved in a series of ongoing disputes involving the costs of environmental contamination. In recent years, this has become an area of concern for many companies as society and governmental agencies have become more aware of the need to ensure that firms are responsible for any actions that adversely affect the environment. In AMD's case, the footnote indicates that its clean-up costs relate to activities that occurred many years ago, before 1979.

www.amd.com

You should note that the two excerpts in Exhibit 9-6 are both examples of contingent liabilities that have been disclosed in the footnotes *but have not been recorded as liabilities on the balance sheet.* Readers of the financial statements, and analysts, must carefully read the footnotes to determine the impact of such contingent liabilities.

The amount and the timing of the cash outlays associated with contingent liabilities are especially difficult to determine. Lawsuits, for example, may extend several years into the future, and the dollar amount of possible loss may be subject to great uncertainty.

ACCOUNTING FOR YOUR DECISIONS

You Are the CEO

You run a high-technology company that grows fast some quarters and disappoints investors in other quarters. As a result, your company's stock price fluctuates widely, and you have attracted the unwanted attention of a law firm that filed a lawsuit on behalf of disgruntled shareholders. How do you reflect this lawsuit on your financial statements?

ANS: Your legal counsel should be consulted to determine whether the plaintiff's case has merit. If a loss is probable and the amount can be estimated, the lawsuit should be recorded as a liability. Unfortunately, lawsuits have become very common for many companies. In some cases, the lawsuits are totally without merit and are frivolous. If your attorneys agree that this case will not result in a loss, then no disclosure would be required.

CONTINGENT LIABILITIES VERSUS CONTINGENT ASSETS

CONTINGENT ASSETS An existing condition for which the outcome is not known but by which the company stands to gain.

www.johnsoncontrols.com

Contingent liabilities that are probable and can be reasonably estimated must be presented on the balance sheet before the outcome of the future events is known. This accounting rule applies only to contingent losses or liabilities. It does not apply to contingencies by which the firm may gain. Generally, contingent gains or **contingent assets** are not reported until the gain actually occurs. That is, contingent liabilities may be accrued, but contingent assets are not accrued. Exhibit 9-7 contains a portion of the footnotes from the 1998 financial statements of Johnson Controls, a large company that is a supplier to the auto makers. Like many other companies, Johnson Controls has had to accrue rather large amounts for environmental remediation costs. The footnote indicates that Johnson Controls believes that its insurance policies should cover part of the costs. This is an example of a contingent asset because the company may receive some amounts at a future time. The financial statements reveal that Johnson Controls has recorded liabilities related to the remediation costs but has not recorded any of the potential recoveries from insurance even though it appears quite likely that some amount will be received. This may seem inconsistent—it is. Remember, however, that accounting is a discipline based on a conservative set of principles. It is prudent and conservative to delay the recording of a gain until an asset is actually received but to record contingent liabilities in advance.

Of course, even though the contingent assets are not reported the information may still be important to investors. Wall Street analysts make their living trying to place a value on contingent assets that they believe will result in future benefits. By buying stock of a company that has unrecorded assets, or advising their clients to do so, investment analysts hope to make money when those assets become a reality.

Two-Minute Review

1. Under what circumstances should contingent liabilities be reported in the financial statements?

2. Under what circumstances should contingent liabilities be disclosed in the footnotes and not recorded in the financial statements?

3. Are contingent assets treated the same as contingent liabilities?

EXHIBIT 9-7 Footnote Disclosure for Contingent Asset (Proceeds from Insurance) from Johnson Controls' Financial Statements

NOTE

15 Contingencies

The Company is involved in a number of proceedings and potential proceedings relating to environmental matters. At September 30, 1998, the Company had an accrued liability of approximately $46 million relating to environmental matters. The Company's environmental liabilities are undiscounted and do not take into consideration any possible recoveries of future insurance proceeds. Because of the uncertainties associated with environmental assessment and remediation activities, the Company's future expenses to remediate the currently identified sites could be considerably higher than the accrued liability. Although it is difficult to estimate the liability of the Company related to these environmental matters, the Company believes that these matters will not have a materially adverse effect upon its capital expenditures, earnings or competitive position.

Additionally, the Company is involved in a number of product liability and various other suits incident to the operation of its businesses. Insurance coverages are maintained and estimated costs are recorded for claims and suits of this nature. It is management's opinion that none of these will have a materially adverse effect on the Company's financial position, results of operations or cash flows.

Answers:

1. Contingent liabilities should be reported in the financial statements if they are **probable** *and the amount of the liability can be* **reasonably estimated.**

2. Contingent liabilities should be disclosed in the footnotes if they are **reasonably possible.**

3. Contingent assets are generally not recorded until the amount is received. They are not treated in the same manner as contingent liabilities. This indicates the conservative nature of accounting.

- Contingent Assets are not recorded until amount is received.
- Contingent Liabilities can be recorded before received.

TIME VALUE OF MONEY CONCEPTS

In this section we will study the impact that interest has on decision making because of the time value of money. The **time value of money** concept means that people prefer a payment at the present time rather than in the future because of the interest factor. If an amount is received at the present time, it can be invested, and the resulting accumulation will be larger than if the same amount is received in the future. Thus, there is a *time value* to cash receipts and payments. This time value concept is important to every student for two reasons: it affects your personal financial decisions, and it affects accounting valuation decisions.

TIME VALUE OF MONEY
An immediate amount should be preferred over an amount in the future.

Exhibit 9-8 indicates some of the personal and accounting decisions affected by the time value of money concept. In your personal life, you make decisions based on the time value of money concept nearly every day. When you invest money, you are interested in

EXHIBIT 9-8 Importance of the Time Value of Money

Personal Financial Decision	Action
■ How much money will accumulate if you invest in a CD or money market account? →	Calculate the future value based on compound interest.
■ If you take out an auto loan, what will be the monthly loan payments? →	Calculate the payments based on the present value of the loan.
■ If you invest in the bond market, what should you pay for a bond? →	Calculate the present value of the bond based on compound interest.
■ If you win the lottery, should you take an immediate payment or payment over time? →	Calculate the present value of the alternatives based on compound interest.
Valuation Decisions on the Financial Statements	**Valuation**
■ Long-term assets →	Historical cost, but not higher than present value of the cash flows
■ Notes receivable →	Present value of the cash flows
■ Loan payments →	Based on the present value of the loan
■ Bond issue price →	Present value of the cash flows
■ Leases →	Present value of the cash flows

how much will be accumulated, and you must determine the *future value* based on the amount of interest that will be compounded. When you borrow money, you must determine the amount of the payments on the loan. You may not always realize it, but the amount of the loan payment is based on the *present value* of the loan, another time value of money concept.

Time value of money is also important because of its implications for accounting valuations. We will discover in Chapter 10 that the issue price of a bond is based on the present value of the cash flows that the bond will produce. The valuation of the bond and the recording of the bond on the balance sheet are based on this concept. Further, the amount that is considered interest expense on the financial statements is also based on time value of money concepts. The bottom portion of Exhibit 9-8 indicates that the valuations of many other accounts, including Notes Receivable and Leases, are based on compound interest calculations.

The time value of money concept is used in virtually every advanced business course. Investment courses, marketing courses, and many other business courses will use the time value of money concept. *In fact, it is probably the most important decision-making tool to master in preparation for the business world.* This section of the text begins with an explanation of how simple interest and compound interest differ and then proceeds to the concepts of present values and future values.

SIMPLE INTEREST

LO 5 Explain the difference between simple and compound interest.

Simple interest is interest earned on the principal amount. If the amount of principal is unchanged from year to year, the interest per year will remain the same. Interest can be calculated by the following formula:

$$I = P \times R \times T,$$

where

I = Dollar amount of interest per year

P = Principal

R = Interest rate as a percentage

T = Time in years

SIMPLE INTEREST
Interest is calculated on the principal amount only.

For example, assume that our firm has signed a two-year note payable for $3,000. Interest and principal are to be paid at the due date with simple interest at the rate of 10% per year. The amount of interest on the note would be $600, calculated as $3,000 × .10 × 2. We would be required to pay $3,600 on the due date: $3,000 principal and $600 interest.

COMPOUND INTEREST

COMPOUND INTEREST
Interest calculated on the principal plus previous amounts of interest.

Compound interest means that interest is calculated on the principal plus previous amounts of accumulated interest. Thus, interest is compounded, or we can say that there is interest on interest. For example, assume a $3,000 note payable for which interest and principal are due in two years with interest compounded annually at 10% per year. Interest would be calculated as follows:

Year	Principal Amount at Beginning of Year	Interest at 10%	Accumulated at Year-End
1	$3,000	$300	$3,300
2	3,300	330	3,630

We would be required to pay $3,630 at the end of two years, $3,000 principal and $630 interest. A comparison of the note payable with 10% simple interest in the first example with the note payable with 10% compound interest in the second example clearly indicates that the amount accumulated with compound interest is always a higher amount because of the interest-on-interest feature.

INTEREST COMPOUNDING

LO 6 Calculate amounts using the future value and present value concepts.

For most accounting problems, we will assume that compound interest is compounded annually. In actual business practice, compounding usually occurs over much shorter intervals. This can be confusing because the interest rate is often stated as an annual rate even though it is compounded over a shorter period. If compounding is not done annually, you must adjust the interest rate by dividing the annual rate by the number of compounding periods per year.

For example, assume that the note payable from the previous example carried a 10% interest rate compounded semiannually for two years. The 10% annual rate should be converted to 5% per period for four semiannual periods. The amount of interest would be compounded, as in the previous example, but for four periods instead of two. The compounding process is as follows:

Period	Principal Amount at Beginning of Year	Interest at 5% per Period	Accumulated at End of Period
1	$3,000	$150	$3,150
2	3,150	158	3,308
3	3,308	165	3,473
4	3,473	174	3,647

The example illustrates that compounding more frequently results in a larger amount accumulated. In fact, many banks and financial institutions now compound interest on savings accounts on a daily basis.

Accounting for Your Decisions

You Invest Some Unexpected Cash

You want to invest some extra money you received from a long-lost uncle. You have narrowed your options down to two: (1) invest in a bond that offers 10% interest compounded semi-annually, or (2) invest in a certificate of deposit that offers 10% interest compounded quarterly. Both options cover a one-year time period. Using the time value of money concepts you have learned in this accounting course, would you choose Option 1 or 2? Why?

ANS: You should choose Option 2, offering the same interest rate as the first option but compounding on a quarterly basis instead of a semiannual basis. More frequent compounding results in more interest, thus making Option 2's quarterly compounding more appealing than Option 1's semiannual compounding.

In the remainder of this section, we will assume that compound interest is applicable. Four compound interest calculations must be understood:

1. Future value of a single amount
2. Present value of a single amount
3. Future value of an annuity
4. Present value of an annuity

Future Value of a Single Amount

FUTURE VALUE OF A SINGLE AMOUNT Amount accumulated at a future time from a single payment or investment.

We are often interested in the amount of interest plus principal that will be accumulated at a future time. This is called a *future amount* or *future value.* The future amount is always larger than the principal amount (payment) because of the interest that accumulates. The formula to calculate the **future value of a single amount** is as follows:

$$FV = p(1 + i)^n,$$

where

FV = Future value to be calculated
p = Payment or principal amount
i = Interest rate
n = Number of periods of compounding

Assume you won the lottery and this check is yours. Which payment option would you take—a lump sum or an amount every year for 10 years? Only by understanding time value of money concepts could you make an intelligent choice.

Example 1: Grandpa Phil passed away and left your three-year-old son, Robert, $50,000 in cash and securities. If the funds were left in the bank and in the stock market and received an annual return of 10%, how much would be there in 15 years when Robert starts college?

Solution:

$$FV = \$50,000(1 + .10)^{15}$$
$$= \$50,000(4.177)$$
$$= \$208,850$$

In some cases, we will use time diagrams to illustrate the relationships. A time diagram to illustrate a future value would be of the following form:

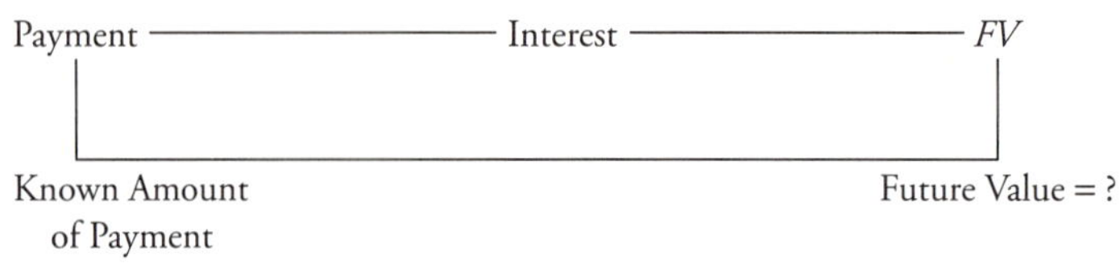

Example 2: Consider a \$2,000 note payable that carries interest at the rate of 10% compounded annually. The note is due in two years, and the principal and interest must be paid at that time. The amount that must be paid in two years is the future value. The future value can be calculated in the manner we have used in the previous examples:

Year	Principal Amount at Beginning of Year	Interest at 10%	Accumulated at Year-End
1	\$2,000	\$200	\$2,200
2	2,200	220	2,420

The future value can also be calculated by using the following formula:

$$FV = \$2{,}000(1 + .10)^2$$
$$= \$2{,}000(1.21)$$
$$= \$2{,}420$$

Many calculators and computer spreadsheets packages are capable of performing compound interest calculations. The future value formula is programmed into the calculator so that you do not see the calculations once you have entered the proper values.

Tables can also be constructed to assist in the calculations. Table 9-1 on page 448 indicates the future value of \$1 at various interest rates and for various time periods. To find the future value of a two-year note at 10% compounded annually, you read across the line for two periods and down the 10% column and see an interest rate factor of 1.210. Because the table has been constructed for future values of \$1, we would determine the future value of \$2,000 as follows:

$$FV = \$2{,}000 \times 1.210$$
$$= \$2{,}420$$

We mentioned that compounding does not always occur annually. How does this affect the calculation of future value amounts?

Example 3: Suppose we want to find the future value of a \$2,000 note payable due in two years. The note payable requires interest to be compounded quarterly at the rate of 12% per year. To calculate the future value, we must adjust the interest rate to a quarterly basis by dividing the 12% rate by the number of compounding periods per year, which in the case of quarterly compounding is four:

$$12\%/4 \text{ Quarters} = 3\% \text{ per Quarter}$$

Also, the number of compounding periods is eight—four per year times two years.

The future value of the note can be found in two ways. First, we can insert the proper values into the future value formula:

$$FV = \$2{,}000(1 + .03)^8$$
$$= \$2{,}000(1.267)$$
$$= \$2{,}534$$

We can arrive at the same future value amount with the use of Table 9-1. Refer to the interest factor in the table indicated for 8 periods and 3%. The future value would be calculated as follows:

$$FV = \$2{,}000(\text{interest factor})$$
$$= \$2{,}000(1.267)$$
$$= \$2{,}534$$

Present Value of a Single Amount

In many situations, we do not want to calculate how much will be accumulated at a future time. Rather, we want to determine the present amount that is equivalent to an amount at a future time. This is the present value concept. The **present value of a single amount**

Present value of a single amount
Amount at a present time that is equivalent to a payment or investment at a future time.

represents the value today of a single amount to be received or paid at a future time. This can be portrayed in a time diagram as follows:

PV ——— Discount ——— Payment

$PV = ?$ ——— Known Amount of Payment

The time diagram portrays discount, rather than interest, because we often speak of "discounting" the future payment back to the present time.

Example 4: Suppose you know that you will receive $2,000 in two years. You also know that if you had the money now, it could be invested at 10% compounded annually. What is the present value of the $2,000? Another way to ask the same question is, What amount must be invested today at 10% compounded annually in order to have $2,000 accumulated in two years?

The formula used to calculate present value is as follows:

$$PV = \text{Payment} \times (1 + i)^{-n}$$

where

PV = Present value amount in dollars

Payment = Amount to be received in the future

i = Interest rate or discount rate

n = Number of periods

We can use the present value formula to solve for the present value of the $2,000 note as follows:

$$PV = \$2{,}000 \times (1 + .10)^{-2}$$
$$= \$2{,}000 \times (.826)$$
$$= \$1{,}652$$

Study Tip

When interest rates *increase*, present values *decrease*. This is called an *inverse relationship*.

Example 5: A recent magazine article projects that it will cost $120,000 to attend a four-year college 10 years from now. If that is true, how much money would you have to put into an account today to fund that education, assuming a 5% rate of return?

Solution:

$$PV = \$120{,}000(1 + .05)^{-10}$$
$$= \$12{,}000(.614)$$
$$= \$73{,}680$$

Tables have also been developed to determine the present value of $1 at various interest rates and number of periods. Table 9-2 on page 449 presents the present value or discount factors for an amount of $1 to be received at a future time. To use the table for our two-year note example, you must read across the line for two periods and down the 10% column to the discount factor of .826. The present value of $2,000 would be calculated as follows:

$$PV = \$2{,}000(\text{discount factor})$$
$$= \$2{,}000(.826)$$
$$= \$1{,}652$$

Two other points are important. First, the example illustrates that the present value amount is always less than the future payment. This happens because of the discount factor. In other words, if we had a smaller amount at the present (the present value), we could invest it and earn interest that would accumulate to an amount equal to the larger amount (the future payment). Second, study of the present value and future value formulas indicates that each is the reciprocal of the other. When we want to calculate a present value amount, we normally use Table 9-2 and multiply a discount factor times the payment. However, we could also use Table 9-1 and divide by the interest factor. Thus, the present value of the $2,000 to be received in the future could also be calculated as follows:

$$PV = \$2{,}000/1.210$$
$$= \$1{,}652$$

FUTURE VALUE OF AN ANNUITY

The present value and future value amounts are useful when a single amount is involved. Many accounting situations involve an annuity, however. **Annuity** means a series of payments of equal amounts. We will now consider the calculation of the future value when a series of payments is involved.

ANNUITY
A series of payments of equal amounts.

Example 6: Suppose that you are to receive $3,000 per year at the end of each of the next four years. Also assume that each payment could be invested at an interest rate of 10% compounded annually. How much would be accumulated in principal and interest by the end of the fourth year? This is an example of an annuity of payments of equal amounts. A time diagram would portray the payments as follows:

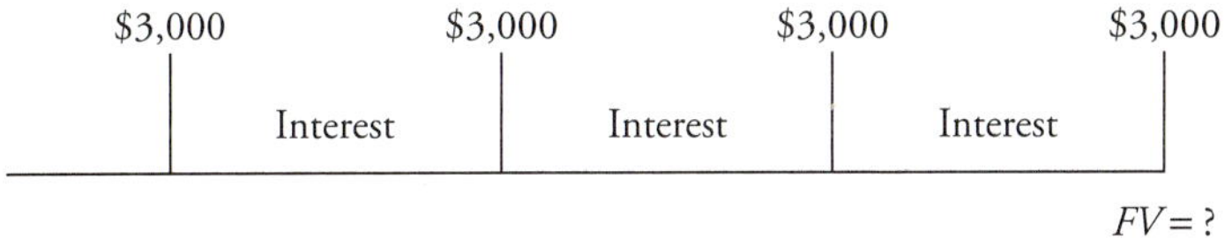

Because we are interested in calculating the future value, we could use the future value of $1 concept and calculate the future value of each $3,000 payment using Table 9-1 as follows:

$3,000 × 1.331 Interest for 3 Periods	$3,993
3,000 × 1.210 Interest for 2 Periods	3,630
3,000 × 1.100 Interest for 1 Period	3,300
3,000 × 1.000 Interest for 0 Periods	3,000
Total Future Value	$13,923

It should be noted that four payments would be received but that only three of them would draw interest because the payments are received at the end of each period.

Fortunately, there is an easier method to calculate the **future value of an annuity.** Table 9-3 on page 450 has been constructed to indicate the future value of a series of payments of $1 per period at various interest rates and number of periods. The table can be used for the previous example by reading across the four-period line and down the 10% column to a table factor of 4.641. The future value of an annuity of $3,000 per year can be calculated as follows:

FUTURE VALUE OF AN ANNUITY
Amount accumulated in the future when a series of payments is invested and accrues interest.

$$FV = \$3{,}000(\text{table factor})$$
$$= \$3{,}000(4.641)$$
$$= \$13{,}923$$

Example 7: You just had a baby girl two weeks ago and are already thinking about college. When she is 15, how much money would be in her college account if you deposit $2,000 into it on each of her 15 birthdays? The interest rate is 10%.

Solution:

$$FV = \$2{,}000(\text{table factor})$$
$$= \$2{,}000(31.772)$$
$$= \$63{,}544$$

When compounding occurs more frequently than annually, adjustments must be made to the interest rate and number of periods, adjustments similar to those discussed previously for single amounts.

Example 8: How would the future value be calculated if the previous example was modified so that we deposited $1,000 semiannually and the interest rate was 10% compounded semiannually (or 5% per period) for 15 years? Table 9-3 could be used by reading across the line for 30 periods and down the column for 5% to obtain a table factor of 66.439. The future value would be calculated as follows:

$$\begin{aligned} FV &= \$1{,}000(\text{table factor}) \\ &= \$1{,}000(66.439) \\ &= \$66{,}439 \end{aligned}$$

Comparing the two examples illustrates once again that more frequent compounding results in larger accumulated amounts.

Present Value of an Annuity

Many accounting applications of the time value of money concept concern situations for which we want to know the present value of a series of payments that will occur in the future. This involves calculating the present value of an annuity. An annuity is a series of payments of equal amounts.

Example 9: Suppose that you will receive an annuity of $4,000 per year for four years, with the first received one year from today. The amounts that are received can be invested at a rate of 10% compounded annually. What amount would you need at the present time to have an amount equivalent to the series of payments and interest in the future? To answer this question, you must calculate the **present value of an annuity.** A time diagram of the series of payments would appear as follows:

Present value of an annuity The amount at a present time that is equivalent to a series of payments and interest in the future.

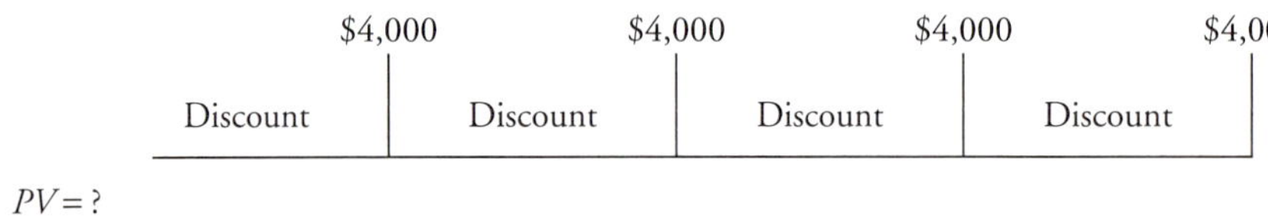

Because you are interested in calculating the present value, you could refer to the present value of $1 concept and discount each of the $4,000 payments individually using table factors from Table 9-2 as follows:

$4,000 × 0.683 Factor for Four Periods	$ 2,732
4,000 × 0.751 Factor for Three Periods	3,004
4,000 × 0.826 Factor for Two Periods	3,304
4,000 × 0.909 Factor for One Period	3,636
Total Present Value	$12,676

For a problem of any size, it is very cumbersome to calculate the present value of each payment individually. Therefore, tables have been constructed to ease the computational burden. Table 9-4 on page 451 provides table factors to calculate the present value of an annuity of $1 per year at various interest rates and number of periods. The previous example can be solved by reading across the four-year line and down the 10% column to obtain a table factor of 3.170. The present value would then be calculated as follows:

$$\begin{aligned} PV &= \$4{,}000(\text{table factor}) \\ &= \$4{,}000(3.170) \\ &= \$12{,}680 \end{aligned}$$

You should note that there is a $4 difference in the present value calculated by the first and second methods. This difference is caused by a small amount of rounding in the table factors that were used.

Example 10: You just won the lottery. You can take your $1 million in a lump sum today, or you can receive $100,000 per year over the next 12 years. Assuming a 5% interest rate, which would you prefer, ignoring tax considerations?

> "If I see accounts receivable going down and accounts payable going up, it could be the early signs of a liquidity crisis."
>
> –Philip Yarrow

Focus on Users

Name: Philip Yarrow
Education: B.S., University of Nottingham (UK); M.M., Kellogg Graduate School of Management
College Majors: Mathematics, Economics
Occupation: Leveraged Finance Transaction Specialist, Banc One Capital Markets Inc., Chicago
Age: 31

Accounts Payables Can Raise Red Flags for This Analyst

Banc One Capital Markets (BOCM) is the investment banking arm of Bank One, which is one of the largest multibank holding companies in the United States. As a BOCM transaction specialist responsible for structuring loans for companies involved in mergers or acquisitions, Philip Yarrow turns to the balance sheet every day to do his job. "I use the balance sheet to evaluate the debt capacity of companies and as a tool to identify potential problems. In the lending business, we consider assets and cash flow to be very important. I use the balance sheet to assess the amount of the assets, focusing on accounts receivable; inventory; and property, plant and equipment. I also consider the amount of equity a company has, as I decide how much to lend," Phil says.

The balance sheet, and the current liabilities section in particular, can also raise all sorts of red flags to professionals who lend cash to corporations. Phil looks for significant changes in any of the current liabilities accounts—for example, dramatic increases that are not accompanied by similar increases in sales. To him, this kind of imbalance is a sign that the company is struggling to pay its creditors. Phil explains: "If I see accounts receivable going down and accounts payable going up, it could be the early signs of a liquidity crisis. The company may be encouraging customers to pay earlier by offering better terms and holding off longer to pay suppliers because of a lack of cash. This position is unsustainable. Eventually, the suppliers will stop supplying the company with the necessary product it needs to continue business effectively. This will impact the company's cash flow and therefore impair the ability of the company to repay its bank loans."

The decision of how to structure a particular financing deal always incorporates analysis of the company's current liabilities position. As Phil says: "By studying the current assets and current liabilities on the company's balance sheets, I can assess the company's need for debt to finance working capital. If the company does have a need for working capital, I would structure a credit arrangement that included a revolving bank loan to allow the company to borrow, repay, and reborrow in a similar manner to a credit card." Liabilities are what enable companies to grow and prosper. However, current liabilities are debts, and they have the potential to impair the solvency of any company. It is Phil's job to figure out whether companies have used debt wisely.

Solution:

$$\begin{aligned} PV &= \$100{,}000(\text{table factor}) \\ &= \$100{,}000(8.863) \\ &= \$886{,}300 \end{aligned}$$

Because the present value of the payments over 12 years is less than the $1 million immediate payment, you should prefer the immediate payment.

Solving for Unknowns

LO 7 Apply the compound interest concepts to some common accounting situations.

In some cases, the present value or future value amounts will be known but the interest rate or the number of payments must be calculated. The formulas that have been presented thus far can be used for such calculations, but you must be careful to analyze each problem to be sure that you have chosen the correct relationship. We will use two examples to illustrate the power of the time value of money concepts.

Assume that you have just purchased a new automobile for $14,420 and must decide how to pay for it. Your local bank has graciously granted you a five-year loan. Because you are a good credit risk, the bank will allow you to make annual payments on the loan at the end of each year. The amount of the loan payments, which include principal and interest, is $4,000 per year. You are concerned that your total payments will be $20,000 ($4,000 per year for five years) and want to calculate the interest rate that is being charged on the loan.

Because the market or present value of the car, as well as the loan, is $14,420, a time diagram of our example would appear as follows:

$4,000	$4,000	$4,000	$4,000	$4,000
Discount	Discount	Discount	Discount	Discount

PV = 14,420

The interest rate that we must solve for represents the discount rate that was applied to the $4,000 payments to result in a present value of $14,420. Therefore, the applicable formula is the following:

$$PV = \$4{,}000(\text{table factor})$$

In this case, PV is known, so the formula can be rearranged as follows:

$$\begin{aligned}\text{Table Factor} &= PV/\$4{,}000\\ &= \$14{,}420/\$4{,}000\\ &= 3.605\end{aligned}$$

The value of 3.605 represents a table factor in Table 9-4. We must read across the five-year line until we find a table factor of 3.605. In this case, that table factor is found in the 12% column. Therefore, the rate of interest being paid on the auto loan is 12%.

The second example involves solving for the number of interest periods. Assume that you want to accumulate $12,000 as a down payment on a home. You believe that you can save $1,000 per semiannual period, and your bank will pay interest of 8% per year, or 4% per semiannual period. How long will it take you to accumulate the desired amount?

The accumulated amount of $12,000 represents the future value of an annuity of $1,000 per semiannual period. Therefore, we can use the interest factors of Table 9-3 to assist in the solution. The applicable formula in this case is the following:

$$FV = \$1{,}000(\text{table factor})$$

The future value is known to be $12,000, and we must solve for the interest factor or table factor. Therefore, we can rearrange the formula as follows:

$$\begin{aligned}\text{Table factor} &= FV/\$1{,}000\\ &= \$12{,}000/\$1{,}000\\ &= 12.00\end{aligned}$$

Using Table 9-3, we must scan down the 4% column until we find a table value that is near 12.00. The closest table value we find is 12.006. That table value corresponds to 10 periods. Therefore, if we deposit $1,000 per semiannual period and invest the money at 4% per semiannual period, it will take 10 semiannual periods (five years) to accumulate $12,000.

Warmup Exercises

LO 1 Warmup Exercise 9-1

A company has the following current assets: Cash, $10,000; Accounts Receivable, $70,000; and Inventory, $20,000. The company also has current liabilities of $40,000. Calculate the company's current ratio and quick ratio.

LO 3 Warmup Exercise 9-2

A company has the following current liabilities at the beginning of the period: Accounts Payable, $30,000; Taxes Payable $10,000. At the end of the period the balances of the account are as follows: Accounts Payable, $20,000; Taxes Payable, $15,000.

What amounts will appear in the cash flow statement, and in what category of the statement will they appear?

LO 6 Warmup Exercise 9-3

A. You invest $1,000 at the beginning of the year. How much will be accumulated in five years if you earn 10% interest compounded annually?

B. You invest $1,000 *per year* at the end of each year for five years. How much will be accumulated in five years if you earn 10% interest compounded annually?

C. You will receive $1,000 in five years. What is the present value of that amount if you can earn 10% interest compounded annually?

D. You will receive $1,000 *per year* at the end of each year for five years. What is the present value of that amount if you can earn 10% interest compounded annually?

Solutions to Warmup Exercises

Warmup Exercise 9-1

Current Ratio: Current Assets/Current Liabilities

Cash ($10,000) + Accounts Receivable ($70,000) + Inventory ($20,000) = $100,000

$100,000/$40,000 = 2.5 Current Ratio

Quick Ratio: Quick Assets/Current Liabilities

Cash ($10,000) + Accounts Receivable ($70,000) = $80,000

$80,000/$40,000 = 2.0 Quick Ratio

Warmup Exercise 9-2

The amounts appearing in the cash flow statement should be in the Operating Activities category of the statement. The amounts shown should be the *changes* in the balances of the accounts.

Accounts Payable decreased by $10,000 and should appear as a decrease in the cash flow statement.

Taxes Payable increased by $5,000 and should appear as an increase in the cash flow statement.

Warmup Exercise 9-3

A. FV = $1,000 (table factor)	using Table 9-1
= $1,000 (1.611)	where i = 10%, n = 5
= $1,611	
B. FV = $1,000 (table factor)	using Table 9-3
= $1,000 (6.105)	where i = 10%, n = 5
= $6,105	
C. PV = $1,000 (table factor)	using Table 9-2
= $1,000 (.621)	where i = 10%, n = 5
= $621	
D. PV = $1,000 (table factor)	using Table 9-4
= $1,000 (3.791)	where i = 10%, n = 5
= $3,791	

Review Problem

Part A

The accountant for Lunn Express wants to develop a balance sheet as of December 31, 2001. The following items pertain to the liability category and must be considered in order to determine the items that should be reported in the Current Liability section of the balance sheet. You may assume that Lunn began business on January 1, 2001, and therefore the beginning balance of all accounts was zero.

a. During 2001 Lunn purchased $100,000 of inventory on account from suppliers. By year-end, $40,000 of the balance has been eliminated as a result of payments. All items were purchased on terms of 2/10, n/30. Lunn uses the gross method of recording payables.

b. On April 1, 2001, Lunn borrowed $10,000 on a one-year note payable from Philips Bank. Terms of the loan indicate that Lunn must repay the principal and 12% interest at the due date of the note.

c. On October 1, 2001, Lunn also borrowed $8,000 from Dove Bank on a one-year note payable. Dove Bank deducted 10% interest in advance and gave to Lunn the net amount. At the due date, Lunn must repay the principal of $8,000.

d. On January 1, 2001, Lunn borrowed $20,000 from Owens Bank by signing a 10-year note payable. Terms of the note indicate that Lunn must make annual payments of principal each January 1 beginning in 2002 and also must pay interest each January 1 in the amount of 8% of the outstanding balance of the loan.

e. The accountant for Lunn has completed an income statement for 2001 that indicates that income before taxes was $10,000. Lunn must pay tax at the rate of 40% and must remit the tax to the Internal Revenue Service by April 15, 2002.

f. As of December 31, 2001, Lunn owes to employees salaries of $3,000 for work performed in 2001. The employees will be paid on the first payday of 2002.

g. During 2001 two lawsuits were filed against Lunn. In the first lawsuit, a customer sued for damages because of an injury that occurred on Lunn's premises. Lunn's legal counsel advised that it is probable that the lawsuit will be settled in 2002 at an amount of $7,000. The second lawsuit involves a patent infringement suit of $14,000 filed against Lunn by a competitor. The legal counsel has advised that there is some possibility that Lunn may be at fault but that a loss does not appear probable at this time.

Part B

a. What amount will be accumulated by January 1, 2005, if $5,000 is invested on January 1, 2001, at 10% interest compounded semiannually?

b. Assume that we are to receive $5,000 on January 1, 2005. What amount at January 1, 2001, is equivalent to the $5,000 that is to be received in 2005? Assume that interest is compounded annually at 10%.

c. What amount will be accumulated by January 1, 2005, if $5,000 is invested each semiannual period for eight periods beginning with June 30, 2001, and ending December 31, 2004? Interest will accumulate at 10% compounded semiannually.

d. Assume that we are to receive $5,000 each semiannual period for eight periods beginning on June 30, 2001. What amount at January 1, 2001, is equivalent to the future series of payments? Assume that interest will accrue at 10% compounded semiannually.

e. Assume that a new bank has begun a promotional campaign to attract savings accounts. The bank advertisement indicates that customers who invest $1,000 will double their money in 10 years. Assuming annual compounding of interest, what rate of interest is the bank offering?

Required

1. Consider all items in part **A.** Develop the Current Liability section of Lunn's balance sheet as of December 31, 2001. To make investment decisions about this company, what additional data would you need? You do not need to consider the footnotes that accompany the balance sheet.
2. Answer the five questions in part **B.**

Solution to Part A

The accountant's decisions for items **a** through **g** of part **A** should be as follows:

a. The balance of the Accounts Payable account should be $60,000. The payables should be reported at the gross amount, and discounts would not be reported until the time of payment.

b. The note payable to Philips Bank of $10,000 should be included as a current liability. Also, interest payable of $900 ($10,000 × 12% × 9/12) should be considered a current liability.

c. The note payable to Dove Bank should be considered a current liability and listed at $8,000 minus the contra account Discount on Note Payable of $600 ($8,000 × 10% × 9/12 remaining).

d. The debt to Owens Bank should be split between current liability and long-term liability with the current portion shown as $2,000. Also, interest payable of $1,600 ($20,000 × 8% × 1 year) should be considered a current liability.

e. Income taxes payable of $4,000 ($10,000 × 40%) is a current liability.

f. Salaries payable of $3,000 represent a current liability.

g. The lawsuit involving the customer must be reported as a current liability of $7,000 because the possibility of loss is probable. The second lawsuit should not be reported but should be disclosed as a footnote to the balance sheet.

LUNN EXPRESS
PARTIAL BALANCE SHEET
AS OF DECEMBER 31, 2001

Current Liabilities		
Accounts payable		$60,000
Interest payable ($900 + $1,600)		2,500
Salaries payable		3,000
Taxes payable		4,000
Note payable to Philips Bank		10,000
Note payable to Dove Bank	$8,000	
Less: Discount on note payable	(600)	7,400
Current maturity of long-term debt		2,000
Contingent liability for pending lawsuit		7,000
Total Current Liabilities		$95,900

Other data necessary to make an investment decision might include current assets, total assets, and current liabilities as of December 31, 2000 and 2001. If current assets are significantly larger than current liabilities, you can be comfortable that the company is capable of paying its short-term debt. The dollar amount of current assets and liabilities must be evaluated with regard to the size of the company. The larger the company, the less significant $95,900 in current liabilities would be. Knowing last year's current liabilities would give you an idea about the trend in current liabilities. If they are rising, you would want to know why.

Solution to Part B

a. $FV = \$5{,}000(\text{table factor})$ using Table 9-1
$= \$5{,}000(1.477)$ where $i = 5\%$, $n = 8$
$= \$7{,}385$

b. $PV = \$5{,}000(\text{table factor})$ using Table 9-2
$= \$5{,}000(.683)$ where $i = 10\%$, $n = 4$
$= \$3{,}415$

c. $FV \text{ annuity} = \$5{,}000(\text{table factor})$ using Table 9-3
$= \$5{,}000(9.549)$ where $i = 5\%$, $n = 8$
$= \$47{,}745$

d. $PV \text{ annuity} = \$5{,}000(\text{table factor})$ using Table 9-4
$= \$5{,}000(6.463)$ where $i = 5\%$, $n = 8$
$= \$32{,}315$

e. $FV = \$1{,}000(\text{table factor})$ using Table 9-1

Because the future value is known to be $2,000, the formula can be written as

$$\$2{,}000 = \$1{,}000(\text{table factor})$$

and rearranged as

$$\text{Table Factor} = \$2{,}000/\$1{,}000 = 2.0.$$

In Table 9-1, the table factor of 2.0 and 10 years correspond with an interest rate of between 7% and 8%.

TABLE 9-1 Future Value of $1

(n) Periods	Rate of Interest in % 2	3	4	5	6	7	8	9	10	11	12	15
1	1.020	1.030	1.040	1.050	1.060	1.070	1.080	1.090	1.100	1.110	1.120	1.150
2	1.040	1.061	1.082	1.103	1.124	1.145	1.166	1.188	1.210	1.232	1.254	1.323
3	1.061	1.093	1.125	1.158	1.191	1.225	1.260	1.295	1.331	1.368	1.405	1.521
4	1.082	1.126	1.170	1.216	1.262	1.311	1.360	1.412	1.464	1.518	1.574	1.749
5	1.104	1.159	1.217	1.276	1.338	1.403	1.469	1.539	1.611	1.685	1.762	2.011
6	1.126	1.194	1.265	1.340	1.419	1.501	1.587	1.677	1.772	1.870	1.974	2.313
7	1.149	1.230	1.316	1.407	1.504	1.606	1.714	1.828	1.949	2.076	2.211	2.660
8	1.172	1.267	1.369	1.477	1.594	1.718	1.851	1.993	2.144	2.305	2.476	3.059
9	1.195	1.305	1.423	1.551	1.689	1.838	1.999	2.172	2.358	2.558	2.773	3.518
10	1.219	1.344	1.480	1.629	1.791	1.967	2.159	2.367	2.594	2.839	3.106	4.046
11	1.243	1.384	1.539	1.710	1.898	2.105	2.332	2.580	2.853	3.152	3.479	4.652
12	1.268	1.426	1.601	1.796	2.012	2.252	2.518	2.813	3.138	3.498	3.896	5.350
13	1.294	1.469	1.665	1.886	2.133	2.410	2.720	3.066	3.452	3.883	4.363	6.153
14	1.319	1.513	1.732	1.980	2.261	2.579	2.937	3.342	3.797	4.310	4.887	7.076
15	1.346	1.558	1.801	2.079	2.397	2.759	3.172	3.642	4.177	4.785	5.474	8.137
16	1.373	1.605	1.873	2.183	2.540	2.952	3.426	3.970	4.595	5.311	6.130	9.358
17	1.400	1.653	1.948	2.292	2.693	3.159	3.700	4.328	5.054	5.895	6.866	10.761
18	1.428	1.702	2.026	2.407	2.854	3.380	3.996	4.717	5.560	6.544	7.690	12.375
19	1.457	1.754	2.107	2.527	3.026	3.617	4.316	5.142	6.116	7.263	8.613	14.232
20	1.486	1.806	2.191	2.653	3.207	3.870	4.661	5.604	6.727	8.062	9.646	16.367
21	1.516	1.860	2.279	2.786	3.400	4.141	5.034	6.109	7.400	8.949	10.804	18.822
22	1.546	1.916	2.370	2.925	3.604	4.430	5.437	6.659	8.140	9.934	12.100	21.645
23	1.577	1.974	2.465	3.072	3.820	4.741	5.871	7.258	8.954	11.026	13.552	24.891
24	1.608	2.033	2.563	3.225	4.049	5.072	6.341	7.911	9.850	12.239	15.179	28.625
25	1.641	2.094	2.666	3.386	4.292	5.427	6.848	8.623	10.835	13.585	17.000	32.919
26	1.673	2.157	2.772	3.556	4.549	5.807	7.396	9.399	11.918	15.080	19.040	37.857
27	1.707	2.221	2.883	3.733	4.822	6.214	7.988	10.245	13.110	16.739	21.325	43.535
28	1.741	2.288	2.999	3.920	5.112	6.649	8.627	11.167	14.421	18.580	23.884	50.066
29	1.776	2.357	3.119	4.116	5.418	7.114	9.317	12.172	15.863	20.624	26.750	57.575
30	1.811	2.427	3.243	4.322	5.743	7.612	10.063	13.268	17.449	22.892	29.960	66.212

TABLE 9-2 Present Value of $1

(n) Periods	Rate of Interest in %											
	2	3	4	5	6	7	8	9	10	11	12	15
1	0.980	0.971	0.962	0.952	0.943	0.935	0.926	0.917	0.909	0.901	0.893	0.870
2	0.961	0.943	0.925	0.907	0.890	0.873	0.857	0.842	0.826	0.812	0.797	0.756
3	0.942	0.915	0.889	0.864	0.840	0.816	0.794	0.772	0.751	0.731	0.712	0.658
4	0.924	0.888	0.855	0.823	0.792	0.763	0.735	0.708	0.683	0.659	0.636	0.572
5	0.906	0.863	0.822	0.784	0.747	0.713	0.681	0.650	0.621	0.593	0.567	0.497
6	0.888	0.837	0.790	0.746	0.705	0.666	0.630	0.596	0.564	0.535	0.507	0.432
7	0.871	0.813	0.760	0.711	0.665	0.623	0.583	0.547	0.513	0.482	0.452	0.376
8	0.853	0.789	0.731	0.677	0.627	0.582	0.540	0.502	0.467	0.434	0.404	0.327
9	0.837	0.766	0.703	0.645	0.592	0.544	0.500	0.460	0.424	0.391	0.361	0.284
10	0.820	0.744	0.676	0.614	0.558	0.508	0.463	0.422	0.386	0.352	0.322	0.247
11	0.804	0.722	0.650	0.585	0.527	0.475	0.429	0.388	0.350	0.317	0.287	0.215
12	0.788	0.701	0.625	0.557	0.497	0.444	0.397	0.356	0.319	0.286	0.257	0.187
13	0.773	0.681	0.601	0.530	0.469	0.415	0.368	0.326	0.290	0.258	0.229	0.163
14	0.758	0.661	0.577	0.505	0.442	0.388	0.340	0.299	0.263	0.232	0.205	0.141
15	0.743	0.642	0.555	0.481	0.417	0.362	0.315	0.275	0.239	0.209	0.183	0.123
16	0.728	0.623	0.534	0.458	0.394	0.339	0.292	0.252	0.218	0.188	0.163	0.107
17	0.714	0.605	0.513	0.436	0.371	0.317	0.270	0.231	0.198	0.170	0.146	0.093
18	0.700	0.587	0.494	0.416	0.350	0.296	0.250	0.212	0.180	0.153	0.130	0.081
19	0.686	0.570	0.475	0.396	0.331	0.277	0.232	0.194	0.164	0.138	0.116	0.070
20	0.673	0.554	0.456	0.377	0.312	0.258	0.215	0.178	0.149	0.124	0.104	0.061
21	0.660	0.538	0.439	0.359	0.294	0.242	0.199	0.164	0.135	0.112	0.093	0.053
22	0.647	0.522	0.422	0.342	0.278	0.226	0.184	0.150	0.123	0.101	0.083	0.046
23	0.634	0.507	0.406	0.326	0.262	0.211	0.170	0.138	0.112	0.091	0.074	0.040
24	0.622	0.492	0.390	0.310	0.247	0.197	0.158	0.126	0.102	0.082	0.066	0.035
25	0.610	0.478	0.375	0.295	0.233	0.184	0.146	0.116	0.092	0.074	0.059	0.030
26	0.598	0.464	0.361	0.281	0.220	0.172	0.135	0.106	0.084	0.066	0.053	0.026
27	0.586	0.450	0.347	0.268	0.207	0.161	0.125	0.098	0.076	0.060	0.047	0.023
28	0.574	0.437	0.333	0.255	0.196	0.150	0.116	0.090	0.069	0.054	0.042	0.020
29	0.563	0.424	0.321	0.243	0.185	0.141	0.107	0.082	0.063	0.048	0.037	0.017
30	0.552	0.412	0.308	0.231	0.174	0.131	0.099	0.075	0.057	0.044	0.033	0.015

TABLE 9-3 Future Value of Annuity of $1

(n) Periods	Rate of Interest in %											
	2	3	4	5	6	7	8	9	10	11	12	15
1	1.000	1.000	1.000	1.000	1.000	1.000	1.000	1.000	1.000	1.000	1.000	1.000
2	2.020	2.030	2.040	2.050	2.060	2.070	2.080	2.090	2.100	2.110	2.120	2.150
3	3.060	3.091	3.122	3.153	3.184	3.215	3.246	3.278	3.310	3.342	3.374	3.473
4	4.122	4.184	4.246	4.310	4.375	4.440	4.506	4.573	4.641	4.710	4.779	4.993
5	5.204	5.309	5.416	5.526	5.637	5.751	5.867	5.985	6.105	6.228	6.353	6.742
6	6.308	6.468	6.633	6.802	6.975	7.153	7.336	7.523	7.716	7.913	8.115	8.754
7	7.434	7.662	7.898	8.142	8.394	8.654	8.923	9.200	9.487	9.783	10.089	11.067
8	8.583	8.892	9.214	9.549	9.897	10.260	10.637	11.028	11.436	11.859	12.300	13.727
9	9.755	10.159	10.583	11.027	11.491	11.978	12.488	13.021	13.579	14.164	14.776	16.786
10	10.950	11.464	12.006	12.578	13.181	13.816	14.487	15.193	15.937	16.722	17.549	20.304
11	12.169	12.808	13.486	14.207	14.972	15.784	16.645	17.560	18.531	19.561	20.655	24.349
12	13.412	14.192	15.026	15.917	16.870	17.888	18.977	20.141	21.384	22.713	24.133	29.002
13	14.680	15.618	16.627	17.713	18.882	20.141	21.495	22.953	24.523	26.212	28.029	34.352
14	15.974	17.086	18.292	19.599	21.015	22.550	24.215	26.019	27.975	30.095	32.393	40.505
15	17.293	18.599	20.024	21.579	23.276	25.129	27.152	29.361	31.772	34.405	37.280	47.580
16	18.639	20.157	21.825	23.657	25.673	27.888	30.324	33.003	35.950	39.190	42.753	55.717
17	20.012	21.762	23.698	25.840	28.213	30.840	33.750	36.974	40.545	44.501	48.884	65.075
18	21.412	23.414	25.645	28.132	30.906	33.999	37.450	41.301	45.599	50.396	55.750	75.836
19	22.841	25.117	27.671	30.539	33.760	37.379	41.446	46.018	51.159	56.939	63.440	88.212
20	24.297	26.870	29.778	33.066	36.786	40.995	45.762	51.160	57.275	64.203	72.052	102.444
21	25.783	28.676	31.969	35.719	39.993	44.865	50.423	56.765	64.002	72.265	81.699	118.810
22	27.299	30.537	34.248	38.505	43.392	49.006	55.457	62.873	71.403	81.214	92.503	137.632
23	28.845	32.453	36.618	41.430	46.996	53.436	60.893	69.532	79.543	91.148	104.603	159.276
24	30.422	34.426	39.083	44.502	50.816	58.177	66.765	76.790	88.497	102.174	118.155	184.168
25	32.030	36.459	41.646	47.727	54.865	63.249	73.106	84.701	98.347	114.413	133.334	212.793
26	33.671	38.553	44.312	51.113	59.156	68.676	79.954	93.324	109.182	127.999	150.334	245.712
27	35.344	40.710	47.084	54.669	63.706	74.484	87.351	102.723	121.100	143.079	169.374	283.569
28	37.051	42.931	49.968	58.403	68.528	80.698	95.339	112.968	134.210	159.817	190.699	327.104
29	38.792	45.219	52.966	62.323	73.640	87.347	103.966	124.135	148.631	178.397	214.583	377.170
30	40.568	47.575	56.085	66.439	79.058	94.461	113.283	136.308	164.494	199.021	241.333	434.745

TABLE 9-4 Present Value of Annuity of $1

(n) Periods	Rate of Interest in %											
	2	3	4	5	6	7	8	9	10	11	12	15
1	0.980	0.971	0.962	0.952	0.943	0.935	0.926	0.917	0.909	0.901	0.893	0.870
2	1.942	1.913	1.886	1.859	1.833	1.808	1.783	1.759	1.736	1.713	1.690	1.626
3	2.884	2.829	2.775	2.723	2.673	2.624	2.577	2.531	2.487	2.444	2.402	2.283
4	3.808	3.717	3.630	3.546	3.465	3.387	3.312	3.240	3.170	3.102	3.037	2.855
5	4.713	4.580	4.452	4.329	4.212	4.100	3.993	3.890	3.791	3.696	3.605	3.352
6	5.601	5.417	5.242	5.076	4.917	4.767	4.623	4.486	4.355	4.231	4.111	3.784
7	6.472	6.230	6.002	5.786	5.582	5.389	5.206	5.033	4.868	4.712	4.564	4.160
8	7.325	7.020	6.733	6.463	6.210	5.971	5.747	5.535	5.335	5.146	4.968	4.487
9	8.162	7.786	7.435	7.108	6.802	6.515	6.247	5.995	5.759	5.537	5.328	4.772
10	8.983	8.530	8.111	7.722	7.360	7.024	6.710	6.418	6.145	5.889	5.650	5.019
11	9.787	9.253	8.760	8.306	7.887	7.499	7.139	6.805	6.495	6.207	5.938	5.234
12	10.575	9.954	9.385	8.863	8.384	7.943	7.536	7.161	6.814	6.492	6.194	5.421
13	11.348	10.635	9.986	9.394	8.853	8.358	7.904	7.487	7.103	6.750	6.424	5.583
14	12.106	11.296	10.563	9.899	9.295	8.745	8.244	7.786	7.367	6.982	6.628	5.724
15	12.849	11.938	11.118	10.380	9.712	9.108	8.559	8.061	7.606	7.191	6.811	5.847
16	13.578	12.561	11.652	10.838	10.106	9.447	8.851	8.313	7.824	7.379	6.974	5.954
17	14.292	13.166	12.166	11.274	10.477	9.763	9.122	8.544	8.022	7.549	7.120	6.047
18	14.992	13.754	12.659	11.690	10.828	10.059	9.372	8.756	8.201	7.702	7.250	6.128
19	15.678	14.324	13.134	12.085	11.158	10.336	9.604	8.950	8.365	7.839	7.366	6.198
20	16.351	14.877	13.590	12.462	11.470	10.594	9.818	9.129	8.514	7.963	7.469	6.259
21	17.011	15.415	14.029	12.821	11.764	10.836	10.017	9.292	8.649	8.075	7.562	6.312
22	17.658	15.937	14.451	13.163	12.042	11.061	10.201	9.442	8.772	8.176	7.645	6.359
23	18.292	16.444	14.857	13.489	12.303	11.272	10.371	9.580	8.883	8.266	7.718	6.399
24	18.914	16.936	15.247	13.799	12.550	11.469	10.529	9.707	8.985	8.348	7.784	6.434
25	19.523	17.413	15.622	14.094	12.783	11.654	10.675	9.823	9.077	8.422	7.843	6.464
26	20.121	17.877	15.983	14.375	13.003	11.826	10.810	9.929	9.161	8.488	7.896	6.491
27	20.707	18.327	16.330	14.643	13.211	11.987	10.935	10.027	9.237	8.548	7.943	6.514
28	21.281	18.764	16.663	14.898	13.406	12.137	11.051	10.116	9.307	8.602	7.984	6.534
29	21.844	19.188	16.984	15.141	13.591	12.278	11.158	10.198	9.370	8.650	8.022	6.551
30	22.396	19.600	17.292	15.372	13.765	12.409	11.258	10.274	9.427	8.694	8.055	6.566

APPENDIX 9A

ACCOUNTING TOOLS: PAYROLL ACCOUNTING

LO 8 Understand the deductions and expenses for payroll accounting.

Salaries payable was one of the current liabilities discussed in Chapter 2. At the end of each accounting period, the accountant must accrue salaries that have been earned by the employees but have not yet been paid. To this point, we have not considered the accounting that must be done for payroll deductions and other payroll expenses.

Payroll deductions and expenses occur not only at year-end but every time, throughout the year, that employees are paid. The amount of cash paid for salaries and wages is the largest cash outflow for many firms. It is imperative that sufficient cash be available not only to meet the weekly or monthly payroll but also to remit the payroll taxes to the appropriate government agencies when required. The purpose of this appendix is to introduce the calculations and the accounting entries that are necessary when payroll is recorded.

The issue of payroll expenses is of great concern to businesses, particularly small entrepreneurial ones. One of the large issues facing companies is how to meet the increasing cost of hiring people. Salary is just one component. How are they going to pay salaries plus benefits such as health insurance, life insurance, disability, unemployment benefits, workers' compensation, and so on? More and more companies are trying to keep their payrolls as small as possible in order to avoid these costs. Unfortunately, this has been a contributing factor in the trends of using more part-time employees and of outsourcing some business functions. Outsourcing, or hiring independent contractors, allows the company to reduce salary expense and the expenses related to fringe benefits. However, it does not necessarily improve the company's profitability. The expenses that are increased as a result of hiring outside contractors must also be considered. A manager must carefully consider all of the costs that are affected before deciding whether to hire more employees or go with an independent contractor.

CALCULATION OF GROSS WAGES

GROSS WAGES
The amount of wages before deductions.

We will cover the payroll process by indicating the basic steps that must be performed. The first step is to calculate the **gross wages** of all employees. The gross wage represents the wage amount before deductions. Companies often have two general classes of employees, hourly and salaried. The gross wage of each hourly employee is calculated by multiplying the number of hours worked times his or her hourly wage rate. Salaried employees are not paid on a per-hour basis but at a flat rate per week, month, or year. For both hourly and salaried employees, the payroll accountant must also consider any overtime, bonus, or other salary supplement that may affect gross wages.

CALCULATION OF NET PAY

NET PAY
The amount of wages after deductions.

The second step in the payroll process is to calculate the deductions from each employee's paycheck to determine **net pay.** Deductions from the employees' checks represent a current liability to the employer because the employer must remit the amounts at a future time to the proper agencies or government offices, for example to the Internal Revenue Service. The deductions that are made depend on the type of company and the employee. The most important deductions are indicated in the following sections.

INCOME TAX

The employer must withhold federal income tax from most employees' paychecks. The amount withheld depends on the employee's earnings and the number of *exemptions* claimed by that employee. An exemption reflects the number of dependents a taxpayer can claim. The more exemptions, the lower is the withholding amount required by the government. Tables are available from the Internal Revenue Service to calculate the proper amount that should be withheld. This amount must be remitted to the Internal Revenue Service periodically; the frequency depends on the company's size and its payroll. Income tax withheld represents a liability to the employer and is normally classified as a current liability.

Many states also have an income tax, and the employer must often withhold additional amounts for the state tax.

FICA—Employees' Share

FICA stands for Federal Insurance Contributions Act; it is commonly called the *social security tax.* The FICA tax is assessed on both the employee and the employer. The employees' portion must be withheld from paychecks at the applicable rate. Currently, the tax is assessed at the rate of 7.65% on the first $72,600 paid to the employee each year. Other rates and special rules apply to certain types of workers and to self-employed individuals. The amounts withheld from the employees' checks must be remitted to the federal government periodically.

FICA taxes withheld from employees' checks represent a liability to the employer until remitted. It is important to remember that the employees' portion of the FICA tax does not represent an expense to the employer.

Voluntary Deductions

If you have ever received a paycheck, you are probably aware that a variety of items was deducted from the amount you earned. Many of these are voluntary deductions chosen by the employee. They may include health insurance, pension or retirement contributions, savings plans, contributions to charities, union dues, and others. Each of these items is deducted from the employees' paychecks, is held by the employer, and is remitted at a future time. Therefore, each represents a current liability to the employer until remitted.

Employer Payroll Taxes

The payroll items discussed thus far do not represent expenses to the employer because they are assessed on the employees and deducted from their paychecks. However, there are taxes that the employer must pay. The two most important are FICA and unemployment taxes.

FICA—Employer's Share

The FICA tax is assessed on both the employee and the employer. The employee amount is withheld from the employees' paychecks and represents a liability but is not an expense to the employer. Normally, an equal amount is assessed on the employer. Therefore, the employer must pay an additional 7.65% of employee wages to the federal government. The employer's portion represents an expense to the employer and should be reflected in a Payroll Tax Expense account or similar type of account. This portion is a liability to the employer until it is remitted.

Unemployment Tax

Most employers must also pay unemployment taxes. The state and federal governments jointly sponsor a program to collect unemployment tax from employers and to pay workers who lose their jobs. The maximum rate of unemployment taxes is 3.4%, of which 2.7%

is the state portion and .7% the federal, on an employee's first $7,000 of wages earned each year. The rate is adjusted according to a company's employment history, however. If a company has been fairly stable and few of its employees have filed for unemployment benefits, the rate is adjusted downward.

Unemployment taxes are levied against the employer, not the employee. Therefore, the tax represents an expense to the employer and should be reflected in a Payroll Tax Expense account or similar type of account. The tax also represents a liability to the employer until it is remitted.

AN EXAMPLE

Assume that Kori Company has calculated the gross wages of all employees for the month of July to be $100,000. Also assume that the following amounts have been withheld from the employees' paychecks:

Income Tax	$20,000
FICA	7,650
United Way Contributions	5,000
Union Dues	3,000

In addition, assume that Kori's unemployment tax rate is 3%, that no employees have reached the $7,000 limit, and that Kori's portion of FICA matches the employees' share. Kori must make the following entries to record the payroll, to pay the employees, and to record the employer's payroll expenses.

July 31	Salary Expense	100,000	
	Salary Payable		64,350
	Income Tax Payable		20,000
	FICA Payable		7,650
	United Way Payable		5,000
	Union Dues Payable		3,000
	To record July salary and deductions.		

Assets	=	Liabilities	+	Owners' Equity
		+64,350		−100,000
		+20,000		
		+7,650		
		+5,000		
		+3,000		

July 31	Salary Payable	64,350	
	Cash		64,350
	To record payment of employee salaries.		

Assets	=	Liabilities	+	Owners' Equity
−64,350		−64,350		

July 31	Payroll Tax Expense	10,650	
	FICA Payable		7,650
	Unemployment Tax Payable		3,000
	To record employer's payroll taxes.		

Assets	=	Liabilities	+	Owners' Equity
		+7,650		−10,650
		+3,000		

Periodically, Kori must remit amounts to the appropriate government body or agency. The accounting entry to record remittance, assuming remittance at the end of July, is as follows:

July 31	Income Tax Expense	20,000	
	FICA Payable	15,300	
	United Way Payable	5,000	
	Union Dues Payable	3,000	
	Unemployment Tax Payable	3,000	
	Cash		46,300
	To record remittance of withheld amounts.		

Assets	=	Liabilities	+	Owners' Equity
−46,300		−20,000		
		−15,300		
		−5,000		
		−3,000		
		−3,000		

Compensated Absences

LO 9 Determine when compensated absences must be accrued as a liability.

Most employers allow employees to accumulate a certain number of sick days and to take a certain number of paid vacation days each year. This causes an accounting question when recording payroll amounts. When should the sick days and vacation days be treated as an expense—in the period they are earned or in the period they are taken by the employee?

The FASB has coined the term **compensated absences.** These are absences from employment, such as vacation, illness, and holidays, for which it is expected that employees will be paid. The FASB has ruled that an expense should be accrued if certain conditions are met: the services have been rendered, the rights (days) accumulate, and payment is probable and can be reasonably estimated. The result of the FASB ruling is that most employers are required to record a liability and expense for vacation days when earned but sick days are not recorded until employees are actually absent.

Compensated absences Employee absences for which the employee will be paid.

Compensated absence is another example of the matching principle at work, and so it is consistent with good accounting theory. Unfortunately, it has also resulted in some complex calculations and additional work for payroll accountants. Part of the complexity is due to unresolved legal issues about compensated absences.

U.S. accounting standards on this issue are much more detailed and extensive than the standards of many foreign countries. As a result, U.S. companies may believe that they are subject to higher record-keeping costs than their foreign competitors.

Chapter Highlights

1. **LO 1** Balance sheets generally have two categories of liability: current liabilities and long-term liabilities. Current liabilities are obligations that will be satisfied within one year or within the next operating cycle.
2. **LO 2** Accruals are expenses that have been incurred, but not paid, by the balance sheet date. They increase current liabilities and should be valued at the face amount or the amount necessary to settle the obligation. They are not reported at the present value because of the short time span until payment.
3. **LO 2** Accounts payable represent amounts owed for the purchase of inventory, goods, or services. Accounts payable usually do not require the payment of interest, but a discount may be available to encourage prompt payment.
4. **LO 2** The accounting for notes payable depends on the terms of the note. Some notes payable require the payment of interest at the due date. If so, accounting entries must be made to accrue interest expense to the proper periods. Interest is an expense when incurred, not when paid. Alternatively, the terms of the note may require interest to be deducted in advance. The interest deducted should initially be recorded in a Discount on Notes Payable account and transferred to Interest Expense over the life of the note.
5. **LO 2** Accrued liabilities include any amount that is owed but not actually due as of the balance sheet date. These liabilities may be grouped together in an account such as Other Accrued Liabilities.
6. **LO 3** The changes in current liabilities affect the cash flow statement and, for most items, are reflected in the Operating Activities category. Decreases in current liabilities indicate a reduction of cash; increases in current liabilities indicate an increase in cash.
7. **LO 4** Contingent liabilities involve an existing condition whose outcome depends on some future event. If a contingent liability

is probable and the amount of loss can be reasonably estimated, it should be reported on the balance sheet. If a contingent liability is reasonably possible, it must be disclosed but not reported.

8. **LO 5** Simple interest is interest earned on the principal amount. It is often calculated by the well-known formula of principal times rate times time. Compound interest is calculated on the principal plus previous amounts of interest accumulated.

9. **LO 6** The future value of a single amount represents the amount of interest plus principal that will be accumulated at a future time. The future value of a single amount can be calculated by formula or by the use of Table 9-1.

10. **LO 6** The present value of a single amount represents the amount at a present time that is equivalent to an amount at a future time. The present value of a single amount can be calculated by formula or by the use of Table 9-2.

11. **LO 6** An annuity is a series of payments of equal amount. The future value of an annuity represents the amount that will be accumulated in principal and interest if a series of payments is invested for a specified time and for a specified rate. The future value of an annuity can be calculated by formula or by the use of Table 9-3.

12. **LO 6** The present value of an annuity represents the amount at a present time that is equivalent to a series of payments in the future that will occur for a specified time and at a specified interest or discount rate. The present value of an annuity can be calculated by formula or by the use of Table 9-4.

13. **LO 7** The compound interest concepts are also useful when solving for unknowns such as the number of interest periods or the interest rate on a series of payments using compound interest techniques.

14. **LO 8** There are two types of payroll deductions and expenses. Deductions from the employee's check are made to determine net pay and represent a current liability to the employer. Employer's payroll taxes are also assessed directly on the employer and represent an expense. (Appendix 9A)

15. **LO 9** Compensated absences such as sick pay and vacation pay are expenses and must be accrued by the employer if certain conditions are met. (Appendix 9A)

Key Terms Quiz

Read each definition below, and then write the number of the definition in the blank beside the appropriate term it defines. The solution appears at the end of the chapter.

1 **Current liability**
3 **Accounts payable**
8 **Notes payable**
4 **Discount on Notes Payable**
6 **Current Maturities of Long-Term Debt**
7 **Accrued liability**
9 **Contingent liability**
11 **Estimated liability**
12 **Contingent asset**
14 **Time value of money**
10 **Simple interest**
13 **Compound interest**
15 **Future value of a single amount**
17 **Present value of a single amount**
5 **Annuity**
16 **Future value of an annuity**
2 **Present value of an annuity**
18 **Gross wages (Appendix 9A)**
20 **Net pay (Appendix 9A)**
19 **Compensated absences (Appendix 9A)**

1. Accounts that will be satisfied within one year or the next operating cycle.

2. The amount needed at the present time to be equivalent to a series of payments and interest in the future.

3. Amounts owed for the purchase of inventory, goods, or services acquired in the normal course of business.

4. A contra-liability account that represents interest deducted from a loan or note in advance.

5. A series of payments of equal amount.

6. The portion of a long-term liability that will be paid within one year of the balance sheet date.

7. A liability that has been incurred but has not been paid as of the balance sheet date.

8. Amounts owed that are represented by a formal contractual agreement. These amounts usually require the payment of interest.

9. A liability that involves an existing condition for which the outcome is not known with certainty and depends on some future event.

10. Interest that is earned or paid on the principal amount only.

11. A contingent liability that is accrued and is reflected on the balance sheet. Common examples are warranties, guarantees, and premium offers.

12. An amount that involves an existing condition dependent on some future event by which the company stands to gain. These amounts are not normally reported.

13. Interest calculated on the principal plus previous amounts of interest accumulated.

14. The concept that indicates that people should prefer to receive an immediate amount at the present time over an equal amount in the future.

15. The amount that will be accumulated in the future when one amount is invested at the present time and accrues interest until the future time.

16. The amount that will be accumulated in the future when a series of payments is invested and accrues interest until the future time.

17. The present amount that is equivalent to an amount at a future time.

18. The amount of an employee's wages before deductions.

19. Employment absences, such as sick days and vacation days, for which it is expected that employees will be paid.

20. The amount of an employee's paycheck after deductions.

Alternate Terms

Accrued Interest Interest payable

Compensated Absences Accrued vacation or sick pay

Compound Interest Interest on interest

Contingent Asset Contingent gain

Contingent Liability Contingent loss

Current Liability Short-term liability

Current Maturities of Long-Term Debt Long-term debt, current portion

Discounting a Note Interest in advance

FICA Social Security

Future Value of an Annuity Amount of an annuity

Gross Wages Gross pay

Income Tax Liability Income tax payable

Warranties Guarantees

Questions

1. What is the definition of *current liabilities?* Why is it important to distinguish between current and long-term liabilities?
2. Most firms attempt to pay their accounts payable within the discount period to take advantage of the discount. Why is that normally a sound financial move?
3. Assume that your local bank gives you a $1,000 loan at 10% per year but deducts the interest in advance. Is 10% the "real" rate of interest that you will pay? How could the true interest rate be calculated?
4. Is the account Discount on Notes Payable an income statement or balance sheet account? Does it have a debit or credit balance?
5. A firm's year ends on December 31. Its tax is computed and submitted to the IRS on March 15 of the following year. When should the taxes be reported as a liability?
6. What is a contingent liability? Why are contingent liabilities accounted for differently than contingent assets?
7. Many firms believe that it is very difficult to estimate the amount of a possible future contingency. Should a contingent liability be reported even if the dollar amount of the loss is not known? Should it be disclosed in the footnotes?
8. Assume that a lawsuit has been filed against your firm. Your legal counsel has assured you that the likelihood of loss is not probable. How should the lawsuit be disclosed on the financial statements?
9. What is the difference between simple interest and compound interest? Would the amount of interest be higher or lower if the interest is simple rather than compound?
10. What is the effect if interest is compounded quarterly versus annually?
11. What is the meaning of the terms *present value* and *future value?* How can you determine whether to calculate the present value of an amount versus the future value?
12. What is the meaning of the word *annuity?* Could the present value of an annuity be calculated as a series of single amounts? If so, how?
13. Assume that you know the total dollar amount of a loan and the amount of the monthly payments on the loan. How could you determine the interest rate as a percentage of the loan?
14. The present value and future value concepts are applied to measure the amount of several accounts commonly encountered in accounting. What are some accounts that are valued in this manner?
15. Your employer withholds federal income tax from your paycheck and remits it to the IRS. How is the federal tax treated on the employer's financial statements? (Appendix 9A)
16. Unemployment tax is a tax on the employer rather than on the employee. How should unemployment taxes be treated on the employer's financial statements? (Appendix 9A)
17. What is the meaning of the term *compensated absences?* Give some examples. (Appendix 9A)
18. Do you agree or disagree with the following statement: "Vacation pay should be reported as an expense when the employee takes the vacation"? (Appendix 9A)

Exercises

LO 1 Exercise 9-1 Current Liabilities

The items listed below are accounts on Smith's balance sheet of December 31, 2001.

Taxes Payable
Accounts Receivable

Notes Payable, 9%, due in 90 days
Investment in Bonds
Capital Stock
Accounts Payable
Estimated Warranty Payable in 2002
Retained Earnings
Trademark
Mortgage Payable ($10,000 due every year until 2018)

Required

Identify which of the above accounts should be classified as a current liability on Smith's balance sheet. For each item that is not a current liability, indicate the category of the balance sheet in which it would be classified.

LO 1 **Exercise 9-2** Current Liabilities

The following items all represent liabilities on a firm's balance sheet.

a. An amount of money owed to a supplier based on the terms 2/20, net 40, for which *no* note was executed

b. An amount of money owed to a creditor on a note due April 30, 2002

c. An amount of money owed to a creditor on a note due August 15, 2003

d. An amount of money owed to employees for work performed during the last week in December

e. An amount of money owed to a bank for the use of borrowed funds due on March 1, 2002

f. An amount of money owed to a creditor as an annual installment payment on a 10-year note

g. An amount of money owed to the federal government, based on the company's annual income

Required

1. For each lettered item, state whether it should be classified as a current liability on the December 31, 2001, balance sheet. Assume that the operating cycle is shorter than one year. If the item should not be classified as a current liability, indicate where on the balance sheet it should be presented.
2. For each item identified as a current liability in part **1,** state the account title that is normally used to report the item on the balance sheet.
3. Why would an investor or creditor be interested in whether an item is a current or a long-term liability?

LO 1 **Exercise 9-3** Current Liabilities Section

Jackie Company had the following accounts and balances on December 31, 2001:

Income Taxes Payable	$61,250
Allowance for Doubtful Accounts	17,800
Accounts Payable	24,400
Interest Receivable	5,000
Unearned Revenue	4,320
Wages Payable	6,000
Notes Payable, 10%, due June 2, 2002	1,000
Accounts Receivable	67,500
Discount on Notes Payable	150
Current Maturities of Long-Term Debt	6,900
Interest Payable	3,010

Required

Prepare the Current Liabilities section of Jackie Company's balance sheet as of December 31, 2001.

LO 2 **Exercise 9-4** Transaction Analysis

Polly's Cards & Gifts Shop had the following transactions during the year:

a. Polly's purchased inventory on account from a supplier for $8,000. Assume that Polly's uses a periodic inventory system.

b. On May 1, land was purchased for $44,500. A 20% down payment was made, and an 18-month, 8% note was signed for the remainder.

c. Polly's returned $450 worth of inventory purchased in item **a,** which was found broken when the inventory was received.

d. Polly's paid the balance due on the purchase of inventory.

e. On June 1, Polly signed a one-year, $15,000 note to 1st State Bank and received $13,800.

f. Polly's sold 200 gift certificates for $25 each for cash. Sales of gift certificates are recorded as a liability. At year-end, 35% of the gift certificates had been redeemed.

g. Sales for the year were $120,000, of which 90% were for cash. State sales tax of 6% applied to all sales and must be remitted to the state by January 31.

Required

1. Record all necessary journal entries relating to these transactions.
2. Assume that Polly's accounting year ends on December 31. Prepare any necessary adjusting journal entries.
3. What is the total of the current liabilities at the end of the year?

LO 2 **Exercise 9-5** Current Liabilities and Ratios

Listed below are several accounts that appeared on Kruse's 2001 balance sheet.

Current Liabilities + Ratios

Accounts Payable	$ 55,000
Marketable Securities	40,000
Accounts Receivable	180,000
Notes Payable, 12%, due in 60 days	20,000
Capital Stock	1,150,000
Salaries Payable	10,000
Cash	15,000
Equipment	950,000
Taxes Payable	15,000
Retained Earnings	250,000
Inventory	85,000
Allowance for Doubtful Accounts	20,000
Land	600,000

Required

1. Prepare the Current Liabilities section of Kruse's 2001 balance sheet.
2. Compute Kruse's working capital.
3. Compute Kruse's current ratio. What does this ratio indicate about Kruse's condition?

LO 2 **Exercise 9-6** Discounts

Each of the following situations involves the use of discounts.

1. How much discount may Seals Inc. take in each of the following transactions? What was the annualized interest rate?
   - **a.** Seals purchases inventory costing $450, 2/10, n/40.
   - **b.** Seals purchases new office furniture costing $1,500, terms 1/10, n/30.
2. Calculate the discount rate Croft Co. received in each of these transactions.
   - **a.** Croft purchased office supplies costing $200 and paid within the discount period with a check for $196.
   - **b.** Croft purchased merchandise for $2,800. It paid within the discount period with a check for $2,674.

LO 2 **Exercise 9-7** Notes Payable and Interest

On July 1, 2001, Jo's Flower Shop borrowed $25,000 from the bank. Jo signed a 10-month, 8% promissory note for the entire amount. Jo's uses a calendar year-end.

Required

1. Prepare the journal entry on July 1 to record the issuance of the promissory note.

2. Prepare any adjusting entries needed at year-end.
3. Prepare the journal entry on May 1 to record the payment of principal and interest.

LO 2 Exercise 9-8 Non-Interest-Bearing Notes Payable

On October 1, 2001, Ratkowski Inc. borrowed $18,000 from 2nd National Bank by issuing a 12-month note. The bank discounted the note at 9%.

Required

1. Prepare the journal entry needed to record the issuance of the note.
2. Prepare the journal entry needed at December 31, 2001, to accrue interest.
3. Prepare the journal entry to record the payment of the note on October 1, 2002.
4. What effective rate of interest did Ratkowski pay?

LO 3 Exercise 9-9 Impact of Transactions Involving Current Liabilities on Statement of Cash Flows

From the following list, identify whether the change in the account balance during the year would be reported as an operating (O), investing (I), or financing (F) activity, or not separately reported on the statement of cash flows (N). Assume that the indirect method is used to determine the cash flows from operating activities.

_______ Accounts payable
_______ Current maturities of long-term debt
_______ Notes payable
_______ Other accrued liabilities
_______ Salaries and wages payable
_______ Taxes payable

LO 3 Exercise 9-10 Impact of Transactions Involving Contingent Liabilities on Statement of Cash Flows

From the following list, identify whether the change in the account balance during the year would be reported as an operating (O), investing (I), or financing (F) activity, or not separately reported on the statement of cash flows (N). Assume that the indirect method is used to determine the cash flows from operating activities.

_______ Estimated liability for warranties
_______ Estimated liability for product premiums
_______ Estimated liability for probable loss relating to litigation

LO 3 Exercise 9-11 Impact of Transactions Involving Payroll Liabilities on Statement of Cash Flows (Appendix 9A)

From the following list, identify whether the change in the account balance during the year would be reported as an operating (O), investing (I), or financing (F) activity, or not separately reported on the statement of cash flows (N). Assume that the indirect method is used to determine the cash flows from operating activities.

_______ Accrued vacation days (compensated absences)
_______ Health insurance premiums payable
_______ FICA payable
_______ Union dues payable
_______ Salary payable
_______ Unemployment taxes payable

LO 4 Exercise 9-12 Warranties

Clean Corporation manufactures and sells dishwashers. Clean provides all customers with a two-year warranty guaranteeing to repair, free of charge, any defects reported during this time period. During the year, it sold 100,000 dishwashers, for $325 each. Analysis of past warranty records indicates that 12% of all sales will be returned for repair within the warranty period. Clean expects to incur expenditures of $14 to repair each dishwasher. The account Estimated Liability for Warranties had a balance of $120,000 on January 1. Clean incurred $150,000 in actual expenditures during the year.

Required

Prepare all journal entries necessary to record the events related to the warranty transactions during the year. Determine the adjusted ending balance in the Estimated Liability for Warranties account.

LO 5 Exercise 9-13 Simple Versus Compound Interest

Part 1. For each of the following notes, calculate the simple interest due at the end of the term.

Note	Face Value (Principal)	Rate	Term
1	$20,000	4%	6 years
2	20,000	6%	4 years
3	20,000	8%	3 years

Part 2. Now assume that the interest on the notes is compounded annually. Calculate the amount of interest due at the end of the term for each note.

Part 3. Now assume that the interest on the notes is compounded semiannually. Calculate the amount of interest due at the end of the term for each note.

What conclusion can you draw from a comparison of your results in parts **1, 2,** and **3?**

LO 6 Exercise 9-14 Present Value, Future Value

Brian Inc. estimates it will need $150,000 in 10 years to expand its manufacturing facilities. A bank has agreed to pay Brian 5% interest, compounded annually, if the company deposits the entire amount now needed to accumulate $150,000 in 10 years. How much money does Brian need to deposit now?

LO 6 Exercise 9-15 Effect of Compounding Period

Kern Company deposited $1,000 in the bank on January 1, 2001, earning 8% interest. Kern Company withdraws the deposit plus accumulated interest on January 1, 2003. Compute the amount of money Kern withdraws from the bank, assuming that interest is compounded (a) annually, (b) semiannually, and (c) quarterly.

LO 6 Exercise 9-16 Present Value, Future Value

The following situations involve time value of money calculations.

1. A deposit of $7,000 is made on January 1, 2001. The deposit will earn interest at a rate of 8%. How much will be accumulated on January 1, 2006, assuming that interest is compounded (a) annually, (b) semiannually, and (c) quarterly?
2. A deposit is made on January 1, 2001, to earn interest at an annual rate of 8%. The deposit will accumulate to $15,000 by January 1, 2006. How much money was originally deposited, assuming that interest is compounded (a) annually, (b) semiannually, and (c) quarterly?

LO 6 Exercise 9-17 Present Value, Future Value

The following are situations requiring the application of the time value of money.

1. On January 1, 2001, $16,000 is deposited. Assuming an 8% interest rate, calculate the amount accumulated on January 1, 2006, if interest is compounded (a) annually, (b) semiannually, and (c) quarterly.
2. Assume that a deposit made on January 1, 2001, earns 8% interest. The deposit plus interest accumulated to $20,000 on January 1, 2006. How much was invested on January 1, 2001, if interest was compounded (a) annually, (b) semiannually, and (c) quarterly?

LO 7 Exercise 9-18 Annuity

Steve Jones has decided to start saving for his son's college education by depositing $2,000 at the end of every year for 15 years. A bank has agreed to pay interest at the rate of 4% compounded annually. How much will Steve have in the bank immediately after his 15th deposit?

LO 7 Exercise 9-19 Calculation of Years

Kelly Seaver has decided to start saving for her daughter's college education. She wants to accumulate $41,000. The bank will pay interest at the rate of 4% compounded annually. If Kelly plans to make payments of $1,600 at the end of each year, how long will it take her to accumulate $41,000?

LO 7 Exercise 9-20 Value of Payments

On graduation from college, Susana Lopez signed an agreement to buy a used car. Her annual payments, due at the end of each year for two years, are $1,480. The car dealer used a 12% rate compounded annually to determine the amount of the payments.

Required

1. What should Susana consider the value of the car to be?
2. If she had wanted to make quarterly payments, what would her payments have been, based on the value of the car as determined in part **1**? How much less interest would she have had to pay if she had been making quarterly payments instead of annual payments? What do you think would have happened to the amount of the payment and the interest if she had asked for monthly payments?

LO 8 Exercise 9-21 Payroll Entries (Appendix 9A)

During the month of January, VanderSalm Company's employees earned $385,000. The following rates apply to VanderSalm's gross payroll:

Federal Income Tax Rate	28%
State Income Tax Rate	5%
FICA Tax Rate	7.65%
Federal Unemployment Tax Rate	.8%
State Unemployment Tax Rate	3.2%

In addition, employee deductions were $7,000 for health insurance and $980 for union dues.

Required

1. Prepare the journal entry the company made to record the January payroll.
2. Prepare the journal entry the company made to record the employer's portion of payroll taxes for January.
3. If the company paid fringe benefits, such as employees' health insurance coverage, how would these contributions affect the payroll entries?

LO 8 Exercise 9-22 Payroll, Employer's Portion (Appendix 9A)

Tasty Bakery Shop has six employees on its payroll. Payroll records include the following information on employee earnings for each employee:

Name	Earnings from 1/1 to 6/30/2001	Earnings for 3rd Quarter, 2001
Dell	$ 23,490	$11,710
Fin	4,240	2,660
Hook	34,100	15,660
Patty	51,000	26,200
Tuss	30,050	19,350
Woo	6,300	3,900
Totals	$149,180	$79,480

FICA taxes are levied at 7.65% on the first $62,700 of each employee's current year's earnings. The unemployment tax rates are .8% for federal and 2.6% for state unemployment. Assume that unemployment taxes are levied on the first $7,000 of each employee's current year's earnings.

Required

1. Calculate the employer's portion of payroll taxes incurred by Tasty Bakery for each employee for the third quarter of 2001. Round your answers to the nearest dollar.
2. Prepare the journal entry that Tasty's should make to record the employer's portion of payroll taxes.

LO 9 Exercise 9-23 Compensated Absences (Appendix 9A)

Wonder Inc. has a monthly payroll of $72,000 for its 24 employees. In addition to their salary, employees earn one day of vacation and one sick day for each month that they work. There are 20 workdays in a month.

Required

1. Prepare the end-of-the-month journal entry, if necessary, to record (a) vacation benefits and (b) sick days.
2. From the owner's perspective, should the company offer the employees vacation and sick pay that accumulates year to year?

Multi-Concept Exercises

LO 6, 7 **Exercise 9-24** Compare Alternatives

Jane Bauer has won the lottery and has four options for receiving her winnings:

1. Receive $100,000 at the beginning of the current year
2. Receive $108,000 at the end of the year
3. Receive $20,000 at the end of each year for 8 years
4. Receive $10,000 at the end of each year for 30 years

Jane can invest her winnings at an interest rate of 8% compounded annually at a major bank. Which of the payment options should Jane choose?

LO 6, 7 **Exercise 9-25** Two Situations

The following situations involve the application of the time value of money concepts.

1. Sampson Company just purchased a piece of equipment with a value of $53,300. Sampson financed this purchase with a loan from the bank and must make annual loan payments of $13,000 at the end of each year for the next five years. Interest is compounded annually on the loan. What is the interest rate on the bank loan?
2. Simon Company needs to accumulate $200,000 to repay bonds due in six years. Simon estimates it can save $13,300 at the end of each semiannual period at a local bank offering an annual interest rate of 8% compounded semiannually. Will Simon have enough money saved at the end of six years to repay the bonds?

Problems

LO 2 **Problem 9-1** Notes and Interest

Glencoe Inc. operates with a June 30 year-end. During 2001, the following transactions occurred:

a. January 1: Signed a one-year, 10% loan for $25,000. Interest and principal are to be paid at maturity.
b. January 10: Signed a line of credit with the Little Local Bank to establish a $400,000 line of credit. Interest of 9% will be charged on all borrowed funds.
c. February 1: Issued a $20,000 non-interest-bearing, six-month note to pay for a new machine. Interest on the note, at 12%, was deducted in advance.
d. March 1: Borrowed $150,000 on the line of credit.
e. June 1: Repaid $100,000 on the line of credit, plus accrued interest.
f. June 30: Made all necessary adjusting entries.
g. August 1: Repaid the non-interest-bearing note.
h. September 1: Borrowed $200,000 on the line of credit.
i. November 1: Issued a three-month, 8%, $12,000 note in payment of an overdue open account.
j. December 31: Repaid the one-year loan (from item **a)**) plus accrued interest.

Required

1. Record all journal entries necessary to report these transactions.
2. As of December 31, which notes are outstanding, and how much interest is due on each?

LO 3 Problem 9-2 Effects of Sara Lee's Current Liabilities on Its Statement of Cash Flows

www.saralee.com

The following items are classified as current liabilities on Sara Lee Corporation's consolidated balance sheet at June 27, 1998 and June 29, 1997 (in millions):

	1998	1997
Notes payable	$ 586	$ 476
Accounts payable	2,003	1,703
Accrued liabilities:		
Payroll and employee benefits	684	701
Advertising and promotions	338	337
Taxes other than payroll and income	223	189
Income taxes	159	119
Other	1,519	1,236
Current maturities of long-term debt	221	255

Required

1. Sara Lee uses the indirect method to prepare its statement of cash flows. Prepare the Operating Activities section of the cash flow statement, which indicates how each item will be reflected as an adjustment to net income. If you did not include any of the items set forth above, explain why not.
2. How would you decide whether Sara Lee has the ability to pay these liabilities as they become due?

LO 3 Problem 9-3 Effects of Tommy Hilfiger's Changes in Current Assets and Liabilities on Statement of Cash Flows

The following items, listed in alphabetical order, are included in the Current Assets and Current Liabilities categories on the consolidated balance sheet of Tommy Hilfiger Corporation at March 31, 1999 and 1998 (in thousands):

www.tommyhilfiger.com

	1999	1998
Accounts payable	$ 27,310	$ 16,201
Accounts receivable	188,640	104,732
Accrued expenses and other liabilities	188,606	76,197
Short-term borrowings	1,234	–0–
Inventories	222,928	150,947
Other current assets	48,638	25,554

Required

1. Tommy Hilfiger uses the indirect method to prepare its statement of cash flows. Prepare the Operating Activities section of the cash flow statement, which indicates how each item will be reflected as an adjustment to net income.
2. If you did not include any of the items set forth above in your answer to part **1**, explain how these items would be reported on the statement of cash flows.

LO 4 Problem 9-4 Warranties

Clearview Company manufactures and sells high-quality television sets. The most popular line sells for $1,000 each and is accompanied by a three-year warranty to repair, free of charge, any defective unit. Average costs to repair each defective unit will be $90 for replacement parts and $60 for labor. Clearview estimates that warranty costs of $12,600 will be incurred during 2001. The company actually sold 600 television sets and incurred replacement part costs of $3,600 and labor costs of $5,400 during the year. The adjusted 2001 ending balance in the Estimated Liability for Warranties account is $10,200.

Required

1. How many defective units from this year's sales does Clearview Company estimate will be returned for repair?
2. What percentage of sales does Clearview Company estimate will be returned for repair?
3. What steps should Clearview take if actual warranty costs incurred during 2002 are significantly higher than the estimated liability recorded at the end of 2001?

LO 4 Problem 9-5 Warranties

Bombeck Company sells a product for $1,500. When the customer buys it, Bombeck provides a one-year warranty. Bombeck sold 120 products during 2001. Based on analysis of past warranty records, Bombeck estimates that repairs will average 3% of total sales.

Required

1. Prepare the journal entry to record the estimated liability.
2. Assume that products under warranty must be repaired during 2001 using repair parts from inventory costing $4,950. Prepare the journal entry to record the repair of products.

LO 5 Problem 9-6 Comparison of Simple and Compound Interest

On June 30, 2001, Rolf Inc. borrowed $25,000 from its bank, signing a 8%, two-year note.

Required

1. Assuming that the bank charges simple interest on the note, prepare the journal entry Rolf will record on each of the following dates:

   December 31, 2001
   December 31, 2002
   June 30, 2003

2. Assume instead that the bank charges 8% on the note, which is compounded semiannually. Prepare the necessary journal entries on the dates in part **1.**
3. How much additional interest expense will Rolf have in part **2** over part **1?**

LO 6 Problem 9-7 Investment with Varying Interest Rate

Investment w/ Varying Interest Rate

Shari Thompson invested $1,000 in a financial institution on January 1, 2001. She leaves her investment in the institution until December 31, 2005. How much money does Shari accumulate if she earned interest, compounded annually, at the following rates?

2001	4%
2002	5%
2003	6%
2004	7%
2005	8%

LO 6 Problem 9-8 Comparison of Alternatives

On January 1, 2001, Chen Yu's Office Supply Store plans to remodel the store and install new display cases. Chen has the following options of payment. Chen's interest rate is 8%.

a. Pay $180,000 on January 1, 2001.
b. Pay $196,200 on January 1, 2002.
c. Pay $220,500 on January 1, 2003.
d. Make four annual payments of $55,000 beginning on December 31, 2001.

Required

Which option should he choose? (*Hint:* Calculate the present value of each option as of January 1, 2001.)

LO 8 Problem 9-9 Payroll Entries (Appendix 9A)

Vivian Company has calculated the gross wages of all employees for the month of August to be $210,000. The following amounts have been withheld from the employees' paychecks:

Income Tax	$42,500
FICA	16,000
Heart Fund Contributions	5,800
Union Dues	3,150

Vivian's unemployment tax rate is 3%, and its portion of FICA matches the employees' share.

Required

1. Prepare the journal entry to record the payroll as an amount payable to employees.
2. Prepare the journal entry that would be recorded to pay the employees.
3. Prepare the journal entry to record the employer's payroll costs.
4. Prepare the journal entry to remit the withholdings.

LO 9 Problem 9-10 Compensated Absences (Appendix 9A)
Hetzel Inc. pays its employees every Friday. For every four weeks that employees work, they earn one vacation day. For every six weeks that they work without calling in sick, they earn one sick day. If employees quit or retire, they can receive a lump-sum payment for their unused vacation days and unused sick days.

Required

Write a short memo to the bookkeeper to explain how and when he should report vacation and sick days. Explain how the matching principle applies and why you believe that the timing you recommend is appropriate.

Multi-Concept Problems

LO 2, 5 Problem 9-11 Interest in Advance Versus Interest Paid When Loan Is Due
On July 1, 2001, Leach Company needs exactly $103,200 in cash to pay an existing obligation. Leach has decided to borrow from State Bank, which charges 14% interest on loans. The loan will be due in one year. Leach is unsure, however, whether to ask the bank for (a) an interest-bearing loan with interest and principal payable at the end of the year or (b) a loan due in one year but with interest deducted in advance.

Required

1. What will be the face value of the note assuming that
   a. interest is paid when the loan is due?
   b. interest is deducted in advance?
2. Calculate the effective interest rate on the note assuming that
   a. interest is paid when the loan is due.
   b. interest is deducted in advance.
3. Assume that Leach negotiates and signs the one-year note with the bank on July 1, 2001. Also assume that Leach's accounting year ends December 31. Prepare all the journal entries necessary to record the issuance of the note and the interest on the note, assuming that
   a. interest is paid when the loan is due.
   b. interest is deducted in advance.
4. Prepare the appropriate balance sheet presentation for July 1, 2001, immediately after the note has been issued, assuming that
   a. interest is paid when the loan is due.
   b. interest is deducted in advance.

LO 1, 4 Problem 9-12 Contingent Liabilities
Listed below are several items for which the outcome of events is unknown at year-end.

a. A company offers a two-year warranty on sales of new computers. It believes that 4% of the computers will require repairs.
b. The company is involved in a trademark infringement suit. The company's legal experts believe an award of $500,000 in the company's favor will be made.
c. A company is involved in an environmental clean-up lawsuit. The company's legal counsel believes it is possible the outcome will be unfavorable but has not been able to estimate the costs of the possible loss.
d. A soap manufacturer has included a coupon offer in the Sunday newspaper supplements. The manufacturer estimates that 25% of the 50-cent coupons will be redeemed.
e. A company has been sued by the federal government for price fixing. The company's legal counsel believes there will be an unfavorable verdict and has made an estimate of the probable loss.

Required

1. Identify which of the items **a** through **e** should be recorded at year-end.
2. Identify which of the items **a** through **e** should not be recorded but should be disclosed in the year-end financial statements.

LO 6, 7 Problem 9-13 Time Value of Money Concepts

The following situations involve the application of the time value of money concept.

1. Janelle Carter deposited $9,750 in the bank on January 1, 1984, at an interest rate of 11% compounded annually. How much has accumulated in the account by January 1, 2001?
2. Mike Smith deposited $21,600 in the bank on January 1, 1991. On January 2, 2001, this deposit has accumulated to $42,487. Interest is compounded annually on the account. What is the rate of interest that Mike earned on the deposit?
3. Lee Spony made a deposit in the bank on January 1, 1994. The bank pays interest at the rate of 8% compounded annually. On January 1, 2001, the deposit has accumulated to $15,000. How much money did Lee originally deposit on January 1, 1994?
4. Nancy Holmes deposited $5,800 in the bank on January 1 a few years ago. The bank pays an interest rate of 10% compounded annually, and the deposit is now worth $15,026. How many years has the deposit been invested?

LO 6, 7 Problem 9-14 Comparison of Alternatives

Brian Imhoff's grandparents want to give him some money when he graduates from high school. They have offered Brian three choices:

a. Receive $15,000 immediately. Assume that interest is compounded annually.

b. Receive $2,250 at the end of each six months for four years. The first check will be received in six months.

c. Receive $4,350 at the end of each year for four years. Assume interest is compounded annually.

Required

Brian wants to have money for a new car when he graduates from college in four years. Assuming an interest rate of 8%, what option should he choose to have the most money in four years?

Alternate Problems

LO 2 Problem 9-1A Notes and Interest

McLaughlin Inc. operates with a June 30 year-end. During 2001, the following transactions occurred:

a. January 1: Signed a one-year, 10% loan for $35,000. Interest and principal are to be paid at maturity.

b. January 10: Signed a line of credit with the Little Local Bank to establish a $560,000 line of credit. Interest of 9% will be charged on all borrowed funds.

c. February 1: Issued a $28,000 non-interest-bearing, six-month note to pay for a new machine. Interest on the note, at 12%, was deducted in advance.

d. March 1: Borrowed $210,000 on the line of credit.

e. June 1: Repaid $140,000 on the line of credit, plus accrued interest.

f. June 30: Made all necessary adjusting entries.

g. August 1: Repaid the non-interest-bearing note.

h. September 1: Borrowed $280,000 on the line of credit.

i. November 1: Issued a three-month, 8%, $16,800 note in payment of an overdue open account.

j. December 31: Repaid the one-year loan (from item **a**) plus accrued interest.

Required

1. Record all journal entries necessary to report these transactions.
2. As of December 31, which notes are outstanding, and how much interest is due on each?

LO 3 Problem 9-2A Effects of Boeing's Current Liabilities on Its Statement of Cash Flows

www.boeing.com

The following items are classified as current liabilities on Boeing Company's consolidated statements of financial condition (or balance sheet) at December 31 (in millions):

	1998	1997
Accounts payable and other liabilities	$10,733	$11,548
Advances in excess of related costs	1,251	1,575
Income taxes payable	569	298
Short-term debt and current portion of long-term debt	869	731

Required

1. Boeing uses the indirect method to prepare its statement of cash flows. Prepare the Operating Activities section of the cash flow statement, which indicates how each item will be reflected as an adjustment to net income. If you did not include any of the items set forth above, explain why not.
2. How would you decide whether Boeing has the ability to pay these liabilities as they become due?

LO 3 Problem 9-3A Effects of Nike's Changes in Current Assets and Liabilities on Its Statement of Cash Flows

The following items, listed in alphabetical order, are included in the Current Assets and Current Liabilities categories on the consolidated balance sheet of Nike Inc. at May 31, 1998 and 1997 (in millions):

www.nike.com

	1998	1997
Accounts payable	$ 584.6	$ 687.1
Accounts receivable	1,674.4	1,754.1
Accrued liabilities	608.5	570.5
Current portion of long-term debt	1.6	2.2
Income taxes payable	28.9	53.9
Inventories	1,396.6	1,338.6
Notes payable	480.2	553.2
Prepaid expenses	196.2	157.1

Required

1. Nike uses the indirect method to prepare its statement of cash flows. Prepare the Operating Activities section of the cash flow statement, which indicates how each item will be reflected as an adjustment to net income.
2. If you did not include any of the items set forth above in your answer to part **1,** explain how these items would be reported on the statement of cash flows.

LO 4 Problem 9-4A Warranties

Sound Company manufactures and sells high-quality stereo sets. The most popular line sells for $2,000 each and is accompanied by a three-year warranty to repair, free of charge, any defective unit. Average costs to repair each defective unit will be $180 for replacement parts and $120 for labor. Sound estimates that warranty costs of $25,200 will be incurred during 2001. The company actually sold 600 sets and incurred replacement part costs of $7,200 and labor costs of $10,800 during the year. The adjusted 2001 ending balance in the Estimated Liability for Warranties account is $20,400.

Required

1. How many defective units from this year's sales does Sound Company estimate will be returned for repair?
2. What percent of sales does Sound Company estimate will be returned for repair?

LO 4 Problem 9-5A Warranties

Beck Company sells a product for $3,200. When the customer buys it, Beck provides a one-year warranty. Beck sold 120 products during 2001. Based on analysis of past warranty records, Beck estimates that repairs will average 4% of total sales.

Required

1. Prepare the journal entry to record the estimated liability.
2. Assume that during 2001, products under warranty must be repaired using repair parts from inventory costing $10,200. Prepare the journal entry to record the repair of products.
3. Assume that the balance of the Estimated Liabilities for Warranties account as of the beginning of 2001 was $1,100. Calculate the balance of the account as of the end of 2001.

LO 5 Problem 9-6A Comparison of Simple and Compound Interest

On June 30, 2001, Rolloff Inc. borrowed $25,000 from its bank, signing a 6% note. Principal and interest are due at the end of two years.

Required

1. Assuming that the note earns simple interest for the bank, calculate the amount of interest accrued on each of the following dates:

   December 31, 2001
   December 31, 2002
   June 30, 2003

2. Assume instead that the note earns 6% for the bank but is compounded semiannually. Calculate the amount of interest accrued on the same dates as in part **1.**
3. How much additional interest expense will Rolloff have to pay with semiannual interest?

LO 6 Problem 9-7A Investment with Varying Interest Rate

Trena Thompson invested $2,000 in a financial institution on January 1, 2001. She leaves her investment in the institution until December 31, 2005. How much money did Trena accumulate if she earned interest, compounded annually, at the following rates?

2001	4%
2002	5%
2003	6%
2004	7%
2005	8%

LO 6 Problem 9-8A Comparison of Alternatives

DECISION MAKING

On January 1, 2001, Li Ping's Office Supply Store plans to remodel the store and install new display cases. Li Ping has the following options of payment. Li's interest rate is 8%.

a. Pay $270,000 on January 1, 2001.
b. Pay $294,300 on January 1, 2002.
c. Pay $334,750 on January 1, 2003.
d. Make four annual payments of $82,500 beginning on December 31, 2001.

Required

Which option should Li choose? (*Hint:* Calculate the present value of each option as of January 1, 2001.)

LO 8 Problem 9-9A Payroll Entries (Appendix 9A)

GENERAL LEDGER

Calvin Company has calculated the gross wages of all employees for the month of August to be $336,000. The following amounts have been withheld from the employees' paychecks:

Income Tax	$68,000
FICA	25,600
Heart Fund Contributions	9,280
Union Dues	5,040

Calvin's unemployment tax rate is 3%, and its portion of FICA matches the employees' share.

Required

1. Prepare the journal entry to record the payroll as an amount payable to employees.
2. Prepare the journal entry that would be recorded to pay the employees.

3. Prepare the journal entry to record the employer's payroll costs.
4. Prepare the journal entry to remit the withholdings, including FICA, and the unemployment tax.

LO 9 **Problem 9-10A** Compensated Absences (Appendix 9A)
Assume that you are the accountant for a large company with several divisions. The manager of Division B has contacted you with a concern. During 2001, several employees retired from Division B. The company's policy is that employees can be paid for days of sick leave accrued at the time they retire. Payment occurs in the year following retirement. The manager has been told by corporate headquarters that she cannot replace the employees in 2002 because the payment of the accrued sick pay will be deducted from Division B's budget in that year.

Required

In a memo to the manager of Division B, explain the proper accounting for accrued sick pay. Do you think that the policies of corporate headquarters should be revised?

Alternate Multi-Concept Problems

LO 2, 5 **Problem 9-11A** Interest in Advance Versus Interest Paid When Loan Is Due
On July 1, 2001, Moton Company needs exactly $206,400 in cash to pay an existing obligation. Moton has decided to borrow from State Bank, which charges 14% interest on loans. The loan will be due in one year. Moton is unsure, however, whether to ask the bank for (a) an interest-bearing loan with interest and principal payable at the end of the year or (b) a non-interest-bearing loan due in one year but with interest deducted in advance.

Required

1. What will be the face value of the note, assuming that
   a. interest is paid when the loan is due?
   b. interest is deducted in advance?
2. Calculate the effective interest rate on the note, assuming that
   a. interest is paid when the loan is due.
   b. interest is deducted in advance.
3. Assume that Moton negotiates and signs the one-year note with the bank on July 1, 2001. Also assume that Moton's accounting year ends December 31. Prepare all the journal entries necessary to record the issuance of the note and the interest on it, assuming that
   a. interest is paid when the loan is due.
   b. interest is deducted in advance.
4. Prepare the appropriate balance sheet presentation for July 1, 2001, immediately after the note has been issued, assuming that
   a. interest is paid when the loan is due.
   b. interest is deducted in advance.

LO 1, 4 **Problem 9-12A** Contingent Liabilities
Listed below are several events for which the outcome is unknown at year-end.

a. A company has been sued by the federal government for price fixing. The company's legal counsel believes there will be an unfavorable verdict and has made an estimate of the probable loss.
b. A company is involved in an environmental clean-up lawsuit. The company's legal counsel believes it is possible the outcome will be unfavorable but has not been able to estimate the costs of the possible loss.
c. The company is involved in a trademark infringement suit. The company's legal experts believe an award of $750,000 in the company's favor will be made.
d. A company offers a three-year warranty on sales of new computers. It believes that 6% of the computers will require repairs.
e. A snack food manufacturer has included a coupon offer in the Sunday newspaper supplements. The manufacturer estimates that 30% of the 40-cent coupons will be redeemed.

Required

1. Identify which of the items **a** through **e** should be recorded at year-end.
2. Identify which of the items **a** through **e** should not be recorded but should be disclosed on the year-end financial statements.

LO 6, 7 **Problem 9-13A** Time Value of Money Concepts

The following situations involve the application of the time value of money concept.

1. Jan Cain deposited $19,500 in the bank on January 1, 1984, at an interest rate of 11% compounded annually. How much has been accumulated in the account by January 1, 2001?
2. Mark Schultz deposited $43,200 in the bank on January 1, 1991. On January 2, 2001, this deposit has accumulated to $84,974. Interest is compounded annually on the account. What is the rate of interest that Mark earned on the deposit?
3. Les Hinckle made a deposit in the bank on January 1, 1994. The bank pays interest at the rate of 8% compounded annually. On January 1, 2001, the deposit has accumulated to $30,000. How much money did Les originally deposit on January 1, 1994?
4. Val Hooper deposited $11,600 in the bank on January 1 a few years ago. The bank pays an interest rate of 10% compounded annually, and the deposit is now worth $30,052. For how many years has the deposit been invested?

LO 6, 7 **Problem 9-14A** Comparison of Alternatives

Darlene Page's grandparents want to give her some money when she graduates from high school. They have offered Darlene three choices.

a. Receive $16,000 immediately. Assume that interest is compounded annually.

b. Receive $2,400 at the end of each six months for four years. The first check will be received in six months.

c. Receive $4,640 at the end of each year for four years. Assume interest is compounded annually.

Required

Darlene wants to have money for a new car when she graduates from college in four years. Assuming an interest rate of 8%, what option should she choose to have the most money in four years?

CASES

Reading and Interpreting Financial Statements

LO 1, 2 **Case 9-1** Analysis of Ben & Jerry's Current Liabilities

Refer to Ben & Jerry's annual report. Using Ben & Jerry's balance sheet, write a response to the following questions: www.benjerry.com

1. Ben & Jerry's total current liabilities increased from $28,668,000 in 1997 to $33,928,000 in 1998. What were the major factors that caused the increase in current liabilities during that time period?
2. Does the increase in Ben & Jerry's current liabilities indicate that the firm was experiencing liquidity problems? What numbers or ratios could be used to determine its liquidity?
3. Refer to footnote number 5. What amounts are included in the category Accounts Payable and Accrued Expenses?
4. The amount listed as Current Portion of Long-Term Debt and Obligations under Capital Lease decreased from $5,402,000 in 1997 to $5,266,000 in 1998. What do those amounts represent?

LO 1, 2 **Case 9-2** Analysis of Gateway's Current Liabilities

Refer to Gateway's annual report. Using Gateway's balance sheet, write a response to the following questions. www.gateway.com

1. Gateway's total current liabilities increased from $1,003,906,000 in 1997 to $1,429,674,000 in 1998. What accounts were the cause of the increase in total current liabilities?

2. Does the increase in Gateway's current liabilities indicate that the firm was experiencing liquidity problems? What numbers or ratios could be used to determine its liquidity?
3. The amount listed as Notes Payable and Current Maturities of Long-Term Obligations decreased from $13,969,000 in 1997 to $11,415,000 in 1998. Does the amount of the decrease indicate the amount of the account that was paid during the year?

LO 3 Case 9-3 Ben & Jerry's Cash Flow Statement

www.benjerry.com

1. Ben & Jerry's balance sheet indicates that accounts payable and accrued expenses increased by $5,396,000. Where is this amount shown on the statement of cash flows? Does it represent an increase or decrease in cash?
2. In 1998, Ben & Jerry's repaid $5,321,000 of long-term debt and capital leases. Which category of the statement of cash flows presents those amounts? For the purposes of the statement of cash flows, what category would include short-term borrowings?
3. Ben & Jerry's December 26, 1998, balance sheet indicated an amount as Deferred Taxes in the liabilities section. Should it be disclosed in the Operating Activities category of the statement of cash flows?

LO 3 Case 9-4 Gateway's Cash Flow Statement

www.gateway.com

1. Gateway's accounts payable account increased from 1997 to 1998. In which category of the cash flow statement is this reported? Why is it listed as a positive amount?
2. Gateway's net cash provided by operating activities increased significantly from 1997 to 1998. What were the primary causes for the increase in cash flow for this time period?
3. What does the account Accrued Royalties mean? Why is it a positive amount in the statement of cash flows?

LO 3, 4 Case 9-5 Microsoft Corporation's Contingent Liabilities

www.microsoft.com

Microsoft Corporation has a fiscal year ending on June 30 and uses the indirect method to prepare its statement of cash flows. The notes to its 1998 financial statements include the following:

> **Contingencies**
> On October 7, 1997, Sun Microsystems, Inc. brought suit against Microsoft in the U.S. District Court for the Northern District of California. Sun's Complaint alleges several claims against Microsoft, all related to the parties' relationship under a March 11, 1996 Technology License and Distribution Agreement (Agreement) concerning certain Java programming language technology. The Complaint seeks: a preliminary and permanent injunction against Microsoft distributing certain products with the Java Compatibility logo, and against distributing Internet Explorer 4.0 unless certain alleged obligations are met; an order compelling Microsoft to perform certain alleged obligations; an accounting; termination of the Agreement; and an award of damages, including compensatory, exemplary and punitive damages, and liquidated damages of $35 million for the alleged source code disclosure.
>
> On March 24, 1998, the court entered an order enjoining Microsoft from using the Java Compatibility logo on Internet Explorer 4.0 and the Microsoft Software Developers Kit for Java 2.0. Microsoft has taken steps to fully comply with the order.

Required

1. Is disclosure of the settlement in the notes to the financial statements all that is required of Microsoft, or is accrual required? If you decide that accrual is required, what amount should be accrued at June 30, 1998, and how would this contingent liability be reported on Microsoft's balance sheet at June 30, 1998?
2. Assume that a settlement was paid to Sun Microsystems sometime during the year ended June 30, 1999. How would the settlement affect Microsoft's statement of cash flows for the years ended June 30, 1998 and 1999?

LO 4 Case 9-6 Sun Microsystems' Contingent Liabilities

The following is an excerpt from Sun Microsystems' 1998 annual report:

> **10. Contingencies**
> In March 1990 Sun received a letter from Texas Instruments Incorporated (TI) alleging that a substantial number of Sun's products infringe certain of TI's patents. Based on discussions with TI, Sun believes that it will be able to negotiate a license agreement with TI and that

the outcome of this matter will not have a material adverse impact on Sun's financial position or its results of operations or cash flows in any given fiscal year. Such a negotiated license may or may not have a material adverse impact on Sun's results of operations or cash flows in a given fiscal quarter depending upon various factors, including but not limited to the structure and amount of royalty payments, offsetting consideration from TI, if any, and allocation of royalties between past and future product shipments, none of which can be forecast with reasonable certainty at this time.

In the normal course of business the Company receives and makes inquiries with regard to other possible patent infringements. Where deemed advisable, the Company may seek or extend licenses or negotiate settlements.

The estimate of the potential impact on the Company's financial position or overall results of operations for the above legal proceedings could change in the future.

Required

After reading this footnote to the financial statements, what accounts would you look for in the balance sheet? income statement? Explain the significance of the words "will not have a material adverse impact on Sun's financial position." How did these words affect the way in which Sun reported its contingent liabilities?

Making Financial Decisions

LO 1, 2 **Case 9-7** Current Ratio Loan Provision

Assume that you are the controller of a small, growing sporting goods company. The prospects for your firm in the future are quite good, but like most other firms, it has been experiencing some cash flow difficulties because all available funds have been used to purchase inventory and finance start-up costs associated with a new business. At the beginning of the current year, your local bank advanced a loan to your company. Included in the loan is the following provision:

> The company is obligated to pay interest payments each month for the next five years. Principal is due and must be paid at the end of Year 5. The company is further obligated to maintain a current assets to current liabilities ratio of 2 to 1 as indicated on quarterly statements to be submitted to the bank. If the company fails to meet any loan provisions, all amounts of interest and principal are due immediately upon notification by the bank.

You, as controller, have just gathered the following information as of the end of the first month of the current quarter:

Current Liabilities:	
Accounts payable	$400,000
Taxes payable	100,000
Accrued expenses	50,000
Total Current Liabilities	$550,000

You are concerned about the loan provision that requires a 2:1 ratio of current assets to current liabilities.

Required

1. Indicate what actions could be taken during the next two months to meet the loan provision. Which of the available actions should be recommended?
2. What is the meaning of the term *window-dressing* financial statements? What are the long-run implications of actions taken to window-dress financial statements?

LO 7 **Case 9-8** Alternative Payment Options

Kathy Clark owns a small company that makes ice machines for restaurants and food-service facilities. Kathy knows a lot about producing ice machines but is less familiar with the best terms to extend to her customers. One customer is opening a new business and has asked Kathy to consider any of the following options to pay for his new $20,000 ice machine.

a. Term 1: 10% down, the remainder paid at the end of the year plus 8% simple interest.
b. Term 2: 10% down, the remainder paid at the end of the year plus 8% interest, compounded quarterly.
c. Term 3: $0 down, but $21,600 due at the end of the year.

Required

Make a recommendation to Kathy. She believes that 8% is a fair return on her money at this time. Should she accept option **a, b,** or **c,** or take the $20,000 cash at the time of the sale? Justify your recommendation with calculations. What factors, other than the actual amount of cash received from the sale, should be considered?

Accounting and Ethics: What Would You Do?

LO 4 Case 9-9 Warranty Cost Estimate

John Walton is an accountant for ABC Auto Dealers, a large auto dealership in a metropolitan area. ABC sells both new and used cars. New cars are sold with a five-year warranty, the cost of which is carried by the manufacturer. For several years, however, ABC has offered a two-year warranty on used cars. The cost of the warranty is an expense to ABC, and John has been asked by his boss, Mr. Sawyer, to review warranty costs and recommend the amount to accrue on the year-end financial statements.

For the past several years, ABC has recorded as warranty expense 5% of used car sales. John has analyzed past repair records and found that repairs, although fluctuating somewhat from year to year, have averaged near the 5% level. John is convinced, however, that 5% is inadequate for the coming year. He bases his judgment on industry reports of increased repair costs and on the fact that several cars that were recently sold on warranty have experienced very high repair costs. John believes that the current-year repair accrual will be at least 10%. He discussed the higher expense amount with Mr. Sawyer, who is the controller of ABC.

Mr. Sawyer was not happy with John's decision concerning warranty expense. He reminded John of the need to control expenses during the recent sales downturn. He also reminded John that ABC is seeking a large loan from the bank and that the bank loan officers may not be happy with recent operating results, especially if ABC begins to accrue larger amounts for future estimated amounts such as warranties. Finally, Mr. Sawyer reminded John that most of the employees of ABC, including Mr. Sawyer, were members of the company's profit-sharing plan and would not be happy with the reduced share of profits. Mr. Sawyer thanked John for his judgment concerning warranty cost but told him that the accrual for the current year would remain at 5%.

John left the meeting with Mr. Sawyer somewhat frustrated. He was convinced that his judgment concerning the warranty costs was correct. He knew that the owner of ABC would be visiting the office next week and wondered whether he should discuss the matter with him personally at that time. John also had met one of the loan officers from the bank several times and considered calling her to discuss his concern about the warranty expense amount on the year-end statements.

Required

Discuss the courses of action available to John. What should John do concerning his judgment of warranty costs?

LO 4 Case 9-10 Retainer Fees As Sales

Bunch o' Balloons markets balloon arrangements to companies who want to thank clients and employees. Bunch o' Balloons has a unique style that has put it in high demand. Consequently, Bunch o' Balloons has asked clients to establish an account. Clients are asked to pay a retainer fee equal to about three months of client purchases. The fee will be used to cover the cost of arrangements delivered and will be reevaluated at the end of each month. At the end of the current month Bunch o' Balloons has $43,900 of retainer fees in its possession. The controller is eager to show this amount as sales because "it represents certain sales for the company."

Required

Do you agree with the controller? When should the sales be reported? Why would the controller be eager to report the cash receipts as sales?

INTERNET RESEARCH CASE

Case 9-11 JCPenney

www.jcpenney.com

JCPenney hopes a network of retail stores, augmented by catalog sales and a burgeoning e-commerce business, will help the company meet its strategic growth goals and respond to intense competition from other retailers. In recent years, JCPenney has established the company as a family of businesses—department stores and catalog, Eckerd drugstores, direct marketing, and international operations. Their mission is to change business processes so as to contain expenses, increase revenue and, especially, raise net income.

JCPenney.com contains a wealth of information about the company. Use this web site to compare the financial numbers presented in this chapter to the latest numbers available; examine management's plans to improve the company's processes; and find news of interest to investors, analysts, and researchers.

1. Based on the latest information available, determine the total current assets and total liabilities for JCPenney Company. How do these compare with the amounts of the previous year?
2. Calculate JCPenney's current ratio based on the latest information available.
3. If you were a supplier of merchandise to JCPenney, how might its current ratio affect your willingness to extend credit to the company?
4. What major changes in JCPenney's operations have been implemented in the latest year available? What do you see as the effect, if any, on the financial statements and notes?

Solution to Key Terms Quiz

__1__ Current liability (p. 422)
__3__ Accounts payable (p. 424)
__8__ Notes payable (p. 424)
__4__ Discount on Notes Payable (p. 425)
__6__ Current Maturities of Long-Term Debt (p. 426)
__7__ Accrued liability (p. 427)
__9__ Contingent liability (p. 430)
__11__ Estimated liability (p. 431)
__12__ Contingent asset (p. 434)
__14__ Time value of money (p. 435)
__10__ Simple interest (p. 437)
__13__ Compound interest (p. 437)
__15__ Future value of a single amount (p. 438)
__17__ Present value of a single amount (p. 439)
__5__ Annuity (p. 441)
__16__ Future value of an annuity (p. 441)
__2__ Present value of an annuity (p. 442)
__18__ Gross wages (p. 452)
__20__ Net pay (p. 452)
__19__ Compensated absences (p. 455)

(warranty, chances of winning or losing)
If probable – we will record
If remote – we will not record
If in middle – not record, but disclose

Chapter 10

Long-Term Liabilities

Study Links

A Look at Previous Chapters

The topic of long-term liabilities was introduced in Chapter 2 as an important aspect of a classified balance sheet, which segregates short-term and long-term assets and liabilities. Chapter 9 introduced compound interest and present value calculations as a method used to value long-term liabilities.

A Look at This Chapter

This chapter examines those items that typically appear in the long-term liability category of the balance sheet. The first section of the chapter will cover bonds, an important source of financing for many companies. The second section covers several other important long-term liabilities: leases, pensions, and deferred taxes. Although these liabilities are based on very complex financial arrangements, our primary purpose is to introduce these topics so that you are aware of their existence when reading financial statements.

A Look at Upcoming Chapters

Chapter 11 will examine the presentation of stockholders' equity, the other major category on the right-hand side of the balance sheet.

Focus on Financial Results

With one of the foremost brands in the world, the Coca-Cola Company reported operating income of nearly $5 billion in 1998, of which a major proportion represents sales in the 200 countries outside the United States where Coca-Cola products are sold. Despite the economic turbulence of 1998 in many of its worldwide markets, the firm maintains its focus on growth. As the 1998 annual report declares: "We know that the global economy is here to stay. Troubled markets will improve. And people will still get thirsty."[1]

In 1998 the company continued to invest heavily in marketing and infrastructure worldwide. Spending in India passed $500 million for the period 1993–98 and exceeded $400 million in the Philippines for 1995–98. Plans to invest nearly $1 billion in Brazil from 1998 to 2001 were announced in the 1998 annual report.

To expand profitably, Coca-Cola requires more money than it generates in profits. Therefore, it uses a common financing tool: long-term debt. As its annual report shows, in the pie graphs highlighted here, the firm's global presence opens doors to financial markets around the world. While most of Coca-Cola's loans in 1998 were in U.S. dollars, management continually adjusts the composition of the debt to accommodate shifting interest rates and currency exchange rates, in order to minimize the overall cost of borrowing.

[1] Coca-Cola's 1998 annual report, p. 5.

December 31,	1998	1997
LIABILITIES AND SHARE-OWNERS' EQUITY		
CURRENT		
Accounts payable and accrued expenses	$ 3,141	$ 3,249
Loans and notes payable	4,459	2,677
Current maturities of long-term debt	3	397
Accrued income taxes	1,037	1,056
TOTAL CURRENT LIABILITIES	8,640	7,379
LONG-TERM DEBT	687	801
OTHER LIABILITIES	991	1,001
DEFERRED INCOME TAXES	424	426
SHARE-OWNERS' EQUITY		
Common stock, $.25 par value		
Authorized: 5,600,000,000 shares		
Issued: 3,460,083,686 shares in 1998; 3,443,441,902 shares in 1997	865	861
Capital surplus	2,195	1,527
Reinvested earnings	19,922	17,869
Accumulated other comprehensive income and unearned compensation on restricted stock	(1,434)	(1,401)
	21,548	18,856
Less treasury stock, at cost (994,566,196 shares in 1998; 972,812,731 shares in 1997)	13,145	11,582
	8,403	7,274
	$ 19,145	$ 16,881

Coca-Cola's long-term debt.

See Notes to Consolidated Financial Statements.

NET OPERATING REVENUES BY OPERATING SEGMENT

The Coca-Cola Company and Subsidiaries

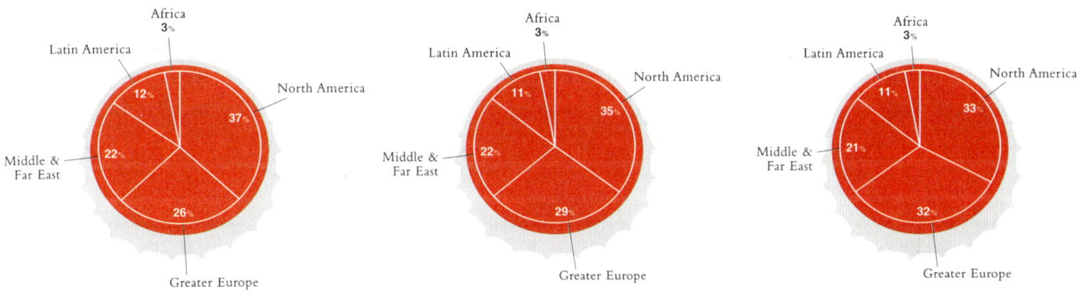

1998 1997 1996

Coca-Cola 1998 annual report

What interest rates does Coca-Cola have to pay on long-term debt? How do accountants record the transactions related to long-term debt? Look for the answers as you study this chapter. Check Coca-Cola's most recent annual report to identify any changes in its long-term liabilities.

www.cocacola.com

Learning Objectives

After studying this chapter, you should be able to:

LO 1 Identify the components of the long-term liability category of the balance sheet. (p. 478)

LO 2 Define the important characteristics of bonds payable. (p. 478)

LO 3 Determine the issue price of a bond using compound interest techniques. (p. 481)

LO 4 Understand the effect on the balance sheet of issuance of bonds. (p. 483)

LO 5 Find the amortization of premium or discount using effective interest amortization. (p. 485)

LO 6 Find the gain or loss on retirement of bonds. (p. 490)

LO 7 Determine whether a lease agreement must be reported as a liability on the balance sheet. (p. 492)

LO 8 Explain the effects that transactions involving long-term liabilities have on the statement of cash flows. (p. 497)

LO 9 Explain deferred taxes and calculate the deferred tax liability. (Appendix 10A) (p. 502)

LO 10 Understand the meaning of a pension obligation and the effect of pensions on the long-term liability category of the balance sheet. (Appendix 10A) (p. 505)

Balance Sheet Presentation

LO 1 Identify the components of the long-term liability category of the balance sheet.

From Concept **to PRACTICE 10.1**

Reading Coca-Cola's Balance Sheet Coca-Cola lists three items as long-term liabilities on its 1998 balance sheet. What are those items? Did they increase or decrease?

In general, **long-term liabilities** are obligations that will not be satisfied within one year. Essentially, all liabilities that are not classified as current liabilities are classified as long-term. We will concentrate on the long-term liabilities of bonds or notes, leases, deferred taxes, and pension obligations. On the balance sheet, the items are listed after current liabilities. For example, the Noncurrent Liabilities section of PepsiCo's balance sheet is highlighted in Exhibit 10-1. PepsiCo has acquired financing through a combination of long-term debt, stock issuance, and internal growth or retained earnings. Exhibit 10-1 indicates that long-term debt is one portion of the long-term liability category of the balance sheet. But the balance sheet also reveals two other items that must be considered part of the long-term liability category: deferred income taxes and other liabilities. We begin by looking at a particular type of long-term debt, bonds payable.

Bonds Payable

Characteristics of Bonds

LO 2 Define the important characteristics of bonds payable.

Long-term liability An obligation that will not be satisfied within one year or the current operating cycle.

Face value The principal amount of the bond as stated on the bond certificate.

A bond is a security or financial instrument that allows firms to borrow money and repay the loan over a long period of time. The bonds are sold, or *issued,* to investors who have amounts to invest and want a return on their investment. The *borrower* (issuing firm) promises to pay interest on specified dates, usually annually or semiannually. The borrower also promises to repay the principal on a specified date, the *due date* or maturity date.

A bond certificate, illustrated in Exhibit 10-2, is issued at the time of purchase and indicates the *terms* of the bond. Generally, bonds are issued in denominations of $1,000. The denomination of the bond is usually referred to as the **face value** or par value. This is the amount that the firm must pay at the maturity date of the bond.

Firms issue bonds in very large amounts, often in millions in a single issue. After bonds are issued, they may be traded on a bond exchange in the same way that stocks are sold on the stock exchanges. Therefore, bonds are not always held until maturity by the initial investor but may change hands several times before their eventual due date.

EXHIBIT 10-1 PepsiCo Balance Sheet

Consolidated Balance Sheet

(in millions)
PepsiCo, Inc. and Subsidiaries
December 26, 1998 and December 27, 1997

	1998	1997
ASSETS		
Current Assets		
Cash and cash equivalents	$ 311	$ 1,928
Short-term investments, at cost	83	955
	394	2,883
Accounts and notes receivable, less allowance: $127 in 1998 and $125 in 1997	2,453	2,150
Inventories	1,016	732
Prepaid expenses, deferred income taxes and other current assets	499	486
Total Current Assets	4,362	6,251
Property, Plant and Equipment, net	7,318	6,261
Intangible Assets, net	8,996	5,855
Investments in Unconsolidated Affiliates	1,396	1,201
Other Assets	588	533
Total Assets	$22,660	$20,101
LIABILITIES AND SHAREHOLDERS' EQUITY		
Current Liabilities		
Short-term borrowings	$ 3,921	$ –
Accounts payable and other current liabilities	3,870	3,617
Income taxes payable	123	640
Total Current Liabilities	7,914	4,257
Long-Term Debt	4,028	4,946
Other Liabilities	2,314	2,265
Deferred Income Taxes	2,003	1,697
Shareholders' Equity		
Capital stock, par value 1 2/3¢ per share: authorized 3,600 shares, issued 1,726 shares	29	29
Capital in excess of par value	1,166	1,314
Retained earnings	12,800	11,567
Accumulated other comprehensive loss	(1,059)	(988)
	12,936	11,922
Less: Treasury stock, at cost: 255 shares and 224 shares in 1998 and 1997, respectively	(6,535)	(4,986)
Total Shareholders' Equity	6,401	6,936
Total Liabilities and Shareholders' Equity	$22,660	$20,101

PepsiCo's long-term debt

See accompanying Notes to Consolidated Financial Statements.

EXHIBIT 10-2 Bond Certificate

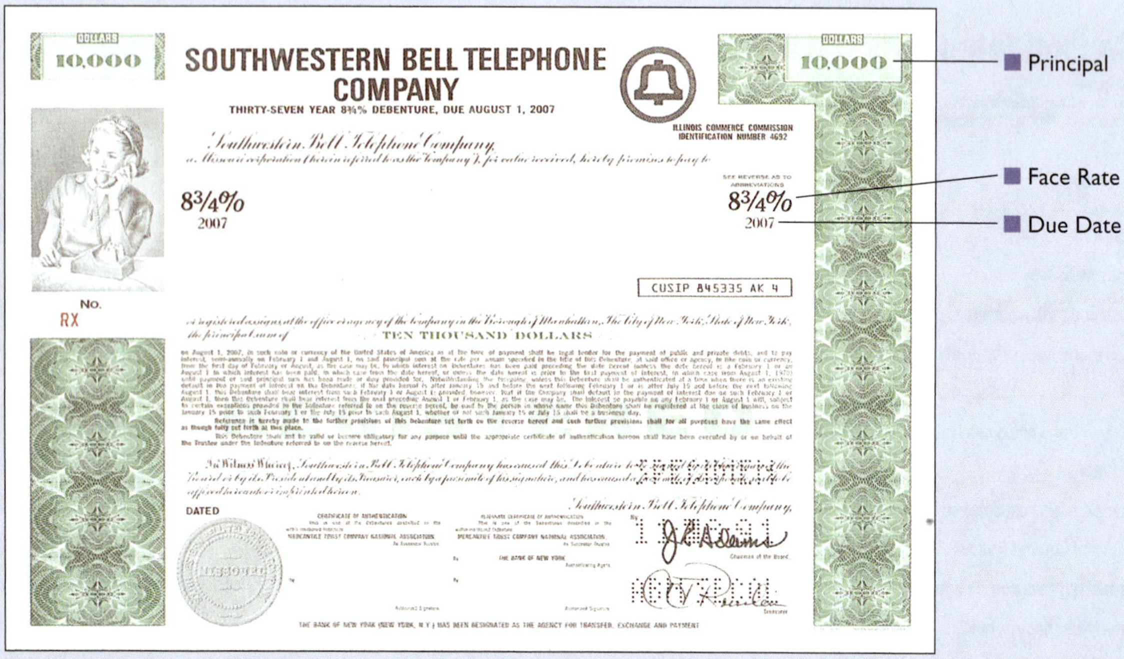

Debenture bonds, like this one from Southwestern Bell Telephone, are backed by the general creditworthiness of the issuing company, not by its assets as collateral. Buyers of such bonds should check the issuer's credit rating, should know how to read the firm's financial statements—and should learn as much as possible about its operations.

Because bond maturities are as long as 30 years, the "secondary" market in bonds—the market for bonds already issued—is a critical factor in a company's ability to raise money. Investors in bonds may want to sell them if interest rates paid by competing investments become more attractive or if the issuer becomes less creditworthy. Buyers of these bonds may be betting that interest rates will reverse course or that the company will get back on its feet. Trading in the secondary market does not affect the financial statements of the issuing company.

We have described the general nature of bonds, but it should not be assumed that all bonds have the same terms and features. Following are some important features that often appear in the bond certificate.

DEBENTURE BONDS Bonds that are not backed by specific collateral.

Collateral The bond certificate should indicate the *collateral* of the loan. Collateral represents the assets that back the bonds in case the issuer cannot make the interest and principal payments and must default on the loan. **Debenture bonds** are not backed by specific collateral of the issuing company. Rather, the investor must examine the general creditworthiness of the issuer. If a bond is a *secured bond,* the certificate indicates specific assets that serve as collateral in case of default.

SERIAL BONDS Bonds that do not all have the same due date; a portion of the bonds comes due each time period.

Due Date The bond certificate specifies the date that the bond principal must be repaid. Normally, bonds are *term bonds,* meaning that the entire principal amount is due on a single date. Alternatively, bonds may be issued as **serial bonds,** meaning that not all of the principal is due on the same date. For example, a firm may issue serial bonds that have a portion of the principal due each year for the next 10 years. Issuing firms may prefer serial bonds because a firm does not need to accumulate the entire amount for principal repayment at one time.

Other Features Some bonds are issued as convertible or callable bonds. *Convertible bonds* can be converted into common stock at a future time. This feature allows the investor to buy a security that pays a fixed interest rate but that can be converted at a future date into an equity security (stock) if the issuing firm is growing and profitable. The conversion feature is also advantageous to the issuing firm because convertible bonds normally carry a lower rate of interest.

Callable bonds may be retired before their specified due date. *Callable* generally refers to the issuer's right to retire the bonds. If the buyer or investor has the right to retire the bonds, they are referred to as *redeemable bonds.* Usually, callable bonds stipulate the price to be paid at redemption; this price is referred to as the *redemption price* or the *reacquisition price.* The callable feature is like an insurance policy for the company. Say a bond pays 10%, but interest rates plummet to 6%. Rather than continuing to pay 10%, the company is willing to offer a slight premium over face value for the right to retire those 10% bonds so that it can borrow at 6%. Of course, the investor is invariably disappointed when the company invokes its call privilege.

CALLABLE BONDS
Bonds that may be redeemed or retired before their specified due date.

As you can see, various terms and features are associated with bonds. Each firm seeks to structure the bond agreement in the manner that best meets its financial needs and will attract investors at the most favorable rates.

Bonds are a popular source of financing because of the tax advantages when compared with the issuance of stock. Interest paid on bonds is deductible for tax purposes, but dividends paid on stock are not. This may explain why the amount of debt on many firms' balance sheets has increased in recent years. Debt became popular in the 1980s to finance mergers and again in the early 1990s when interest rates reached 20-year lows. Still, investors and creditors tend to downgrade a company when the amount of debt it has on the balance sheet is deemed to be excessive.

This bond trader assists investors on the secondary market in buying and selling bonds. On the board behind her, she tallies bond availability information including company name ("Dayton Hudson"), bond rates ("10" for 10%), maturity dates ("1-1-11" for January 1, 2011), and the issue price ("99.479" for 99.479% of face value).

ISSUANCE OF BONDS

When bonds are issued, the issuing firm must recognize the incurrence of a liability in exchange for cash. If bonds are issued at their face amount, the accounting entry is straightforward. For example, assume that on April 1 a firm issues bonds with a face amount of $10,000 and receives $10,000. In this case, the asset Cash and the liability Bonds Payable are both increased by $10,000. The accounting entry is as follows:

Apr. 1	Cash	10,000	
	Bonds Payable		10,000
	To record the issuance of bonds at face value.		

Assets	=	Liabilities	+	Owners' Equity
+10,000		+10,000		

FACTORS AFFECTING BOND PRICE

LO 3 Determine the issue price of a bond using compound interest techniques.

With bonds payable, two interest rates are always involved. The **face rate of interest** (also called the *stated rate, nominal rate, contract rate,* or *coupon rate*) is the rate specified on the bond certificate. It is the amount of interest that will be paid each interest period. For example, if $10,000 worth of bonds is issued with an 8% annual face rate of interest, then interest of $800 ($10,000 × 8% × 1 year) would be paid at the end of each annual period. Alternatively, bonds often require the payment of interest semiannually. If the bonds in our example required the 8% annual face rate to be paid semiannually (at 4%), then interest of $400 ($10,000 × 8% × ½ year) would be paid each semiannual period.

FACE RATE OF INTEREST
The rate of interest on the bond certificate.

MARKET RATE OF INTEREST
The rate that investors could obtain by investing in other bonds that are similar to the issuing firm's bonds.

The second important interest rate is the **market rate of interest** (also called the *effective rate* or *bond yield*). The market rate of interest is the rate that bondholders could obtain by investing in other bonds that are similar to the issuing firm's bonds. The issuing firm does not set the market rate of interest. That rate is determined by the bond market on the basis of many transactions for similar bonds. The market rate incorporates all of the "market's" knowledge about economic conditions and all its expectations about future conditions. Normally, issuing firms try to set a face rate that is equal to the market rate. However, because the market rate changes daily, there are almost always small differences between the face rate and the market rate at the time bonds are issued.

Study Tip

Calculating the issue price of a bond always involves a calculation of the present value of the cash flows.

BOND ISSUE PRICE The present value of the annuity of interest payments plus the present value of the principal.

In addition to the number of interest payments and the maturity length of the bond, the face rate and the market rate of interest must both be known in order to calculate the issue price of a bond. The **bond issue price** equals the *present value* of the cash flows that the bond will produce. Bonds produce two types of cash flows for the investor, interest receipts and repayment of principal (face value). The interest receipts constitute an annuity of payments each interest period over the life of the bonds. The repayment of principal (face value) is a one-time receipt that occurs at the end of the term of the bonds. We must calculate the present value of the interest receipts (using Table 9-4) and the present value of the principal amount (using Table 9-2). The total of the two present-value calculations represents the issue price of the bond.

An Example Suppose that on January 1, 2001, Discount Firm wants to issue bonds with a face value of $10,000. The face or coupon rate of interest has been set at 8%. The bonds will pay interest annually, and the principal amount is due in four years. Also suppose that the market rate of interest for other similar bonds is currently 10%. Because the market rate of interest exceeds the coupon rate, investors will not be willing to pay $10,000 but something less. We want to calculate the amount that will be obtained from the issuance of Discount Firm's bonds.

Discount's bond will produce two sets of cash flows for the investor, an annual interest payment of $800 ($10,000 × 8%) per year for four years and repayment of the principal of $10,000 at the end of the fourth year. To calculate the issue price, we must calculate the present value of the two sets of cash flows. A time diagram portrays the cash flows as follows:

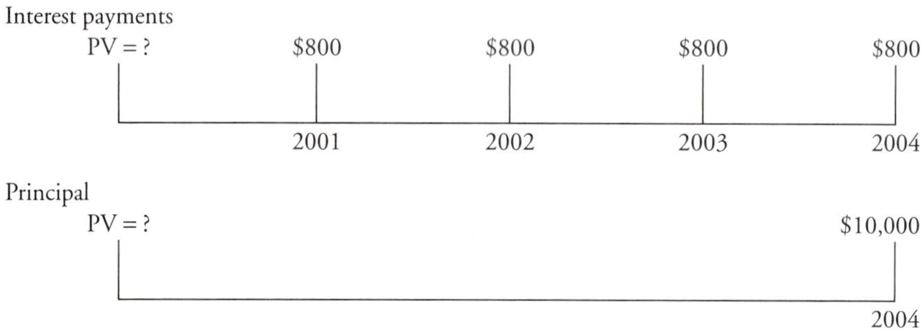

We can calculate the issue price by using the compound-interest tables found in Chapter 9, as follows:

$800 × 3.170 (factor from Table 9-4 for 4 periods, 10%)	$2,536
$10,000 × .683 (factor from Table 9-2 for 4 periods, 10%)	6,830
Issue Price	$9,366

ACCOUNTING FOR YOUR DECISIONS

You Rate the Bonds

One of the factors that determine the rate of interest on a bond is a rating by a rating agency such as Standard & Poor's or Moody's Investor Service. Bonds with a higher rating are considered less risky and can be issued for a lower rate of interest. You have been given an assignment to rate the bonds issued by PepsiCo. What factors would you consider in your rating?

ANS: There are many factors that affect your evaluation of the riskiness of the company's bonds. One factor would be the amount of debt on PepsiCo's books, which can be found by examining the liability section of the balance sheet. It is important to relate the amount of debt to the total equity of the company; this is often done by computing the debt-to-equity ratio. Another important factor is the company's competitive position within its industry. If PepsiCo can operate profitably, it will generate cash that can be used to pay the interest and principal on the bonds.

The table factors used represent four periods and 10% interest. This is a key point. The issue price of a bond is always calculated using the market rate of interest. The face rate of interest determines the amount of the interest payments, but the market rate determines the present value of the payments and the present value of the principal (and therefore the issue price).

Our example of Discount Firm reveals that the bonds with a $10,000 face value amount would be issued for $9,366. The bond markets and the financial press often state the issue price as a percentage of the face amount. The percentage for Discount's bonds can be calculated as ($9,366/$10,000) × 100, or 93.66%.

Exhibit 10-3 illustrates how bonds are actually listed in the reporting of the bond markets. The exhibit lists two types of IBM bonds that were traded on a particular day. The portion immediately after the company name, for example "6⅜ 03," indicates that the face rate of interest is 6⅜% and the due date of the bonds is the year 2003. The next column, for example "6.5," indicates that the bond investor who purchased the bonds on that day will receive a yield of 6.5%. The column labeled "vol" indicates the number of bonds, in thousands, that were bought and sold during the day. The column labeled "close" indicates the market price of the bonds at the end of the day. For example, the first issue of IBM bonds closed at 98¾, which means that the price was 98¾% of the face value of the bonds. These bonds are trading at a discount because the face rate (6⅜%) is less than the market rate of 6.5%. The bonds in the second issue—"7¼ 05"—have a face rate of 7¼%, will become due in the year 2005, and closed at 101½, or at a premium. The net change column indicates the change in the bond price that occurred for the day's trading.

www.ibm.com

Premium or Discount on Bonds

Premium or **discount** represents the difference between the face value and the issue price of a bond. We may state the relationship as follows:

LO 4 Understand the effect on the balance sheet of issuance of bonds.

PREMIUM
The excess of the issue price over the face value of the bonds.

DISCOUNT
The excess of the face value of bonds over the issue price.

Premium = Issue Price − Face Value

Discount = Face Value − Issue Price

In other words, when issue price exceeds face value, the bonds have sold at a premium, and when the face value exceeds the issue price, the bonds have sold at a discount.

We will continue with the Discount Firm example to illustrate the accounting for bonds sold at a discount. Discount Firm's bonds sold at a discount calculated as follows:

Discount = $10,000 − $9,366

Discount = $634

Discount Firm would record both the discount and the issuance of the bonds in the following journal entry:

Jan. 1	Cash	9,366	
	Discount on Bonds Payable	634	
	Bonds Payable		10,000
	To record the issuance of bonds payable.		

Assets	=	Liabilities	+	Owners' Equity
+9,366		−634		
		+10,000		

EXHIBIT 10-3 Listing of Bonds on the Bond Market

Bonds	Cur Yld	Vol	Close	Net Chg
IBM 6⅜03	6.5	280	98¾	−¼
IBM 7¼05	7.1	68	101½	+¼

The Discount on Bonds Payable account is shown as a contra liability on the balance sheet in conjunction with the Bonds Payable account and is a deduction from that account. If Discount Firm prepared a balance sheet immediately after the bond issuance, the following would appear in the Long-Term Liabilities category of the balance sheet:

Long-Term Liabilities:	
Bonds Payable	$10,000
Less: Discount on Bonds Payable	634
	$ 9,366

The Discount Firm example has illustrated a situation in which the market rate of a bond issue is higher than the face rate. Now we will examine the opposite situation, when the face rate exceeds the market rate. Again, we are interested in calculating the issue price of the bonds.

Issuing at a Premium Suppose that on January 1, 2001, Premium Firm wants to issue the same bonds as in the previous example: $10,000 face value bonds, with an 8% face rate of interest and with interest paid annually each year for four years. Assume, however, that the market rate of interest is 6% for similar bonds. The issue price is calculated as the present value of the annuity of interest payments plus the present value of the principal at the market rate of interest. The calculations are as follows:

$800 × 3.465 (factor from Table 9-4 for 4 periods, 6%)	$ 2,772
$10,000 × .792 (factor from Table 9-2 for 4 periods, 6%)	7,920
Issue price	$10,692

We have calculated that the bonds would be issued for $10,692. Because the bonds would be issued at an amount that is higher than the face value amount, they would be issued at a premium. The amount of the premium is calculated as follows:

Premium = $10,692 – $10,000

Premium = $692

The premium is recorded at the time of bond issuance in the following entry:

Jan. 1	Cash	10,692	
	Bonds Payable		10,000
	Premium on Bonds Payable		692
	To record the issuance of bonds payable.		

Assets	=	Liabilities	+	Owners' Equity
+10,692		+10,000		
		+692		

The account Premium on Bonds Payable is an addition to the Bonds Payable account. If Premium Firm presented a balance sheet immediately after the bond issuance, the Long-Term Liabilities category of the balance sheet would appear as follows:

Long-Term Liabilities:	
Bonds Payable	$10,000
Plus: Premium on Bonds Payable	692
	$10,692

Study Tip

When interest rates increase, present values decrease. This is called an *inverse relationship*.

You should learn two important points from the Discount Firm and Premium Firm examples. First, you should be able to determine whether a bond will sell at a premium or discount by the relationship that exists between the face rate and the market rate of interest. *Premium* and *discount* do not mean "good" and "bad." Premium or discount arises solely because of the difference that exists between the face rate and the market rate of interest for a bond issue. The same relationship always exists, so that the following statements hold true:

If Market Rate = Face Rate, THEN bonds are issued at face value amount.

If Market Rate > Face Rate, THEN bonds are issued at a discount.

If Market Rate < Face Rate, THEN bonds are issued at a premium.

Coke's international sales are a major part of its growth strategy. This Malaysian delivery truck reflects what Coke hopes will be good news in its Middle and Fare East Group. In its 1999 annual report, Coke states: "We remain focused on long-term opportunities in these populous markets, and continue to invest in our brands and infrastructure."

The examples also illustrate a second important point. The relationship between interest rates and bond prices is always inverse. To understand the term *inverse relationship,* refer to the Discount Firm and Premium Firm examples. The bonds of the two firms are identical in all respects except for the market rate of interest. When the market rate was 10%, the bond issue price was $9,366 (the Discount Firm example). When the market rate was 6%, the bond issue price increased to $10,692 (the Premium Firm example). The examples illustrate that as interest rates decrease, prices on the bond markets increase and that as interest rates increase, bond prices decrease.

Many investors in the stock market perceive that they are taking a great deal of risk with their capital. In truth, bond investors are taking substantial risk too. The most obvious risk is that the company will fail and not be able to pay its debts. But another risk is that interest rates on comparable investments will rise. Interest rate risk can have a devastating impact on the current-market value of bonds. One way to minimize interest rate risk is to hold the bond to maturity, at which point the company must pay the face amount.

Bond Amortization

LO 5 Find the amortization of premium or discount using effective interest amortization.

Purpose of Amortization The amount of interest expense that should be reflected on a firm's income statement for bonds payable is the true, or effective, interest. The effective interest should reflect the face rate of interest as well as interest that results from issuing the bond at a premium or discount. To reflect that interest component, the amount initially recorded in the Premium on Bonds Payable or the Discount on Bonds Payable account must be amortized or spread over the life of the bond.

Amortization refers to the process of transferring an amount from the discount or premium account to interest expense each time period to adjust interest expense. One commonly used method of amortization is the effective interest method. We will illustrate how to amortize a discount amount and then how to amortize a premium amount.

To illustrate amortization of a discount, we need to return to our Discount Firm example introduced earlier. We have seen that the issue price of the bond could be calculated as $9,366, resulting in a contra-liability (debit) balance of $634 in the Discount on Bonds Payable account (see the entry on page 483). But what does the initial balance of the Discount account really represent? The discount should be thought of as additional interest that Discount Firm must pay over and above the 8% face rate. Remember that Discount received only $9,366 but must repay the full principal of $10,000 at the bond due date. For that reason, the $634 of discount is an additional interest cost that must be reflected as interest expense. It is reflected as interest expense by the process of amortization. In other words, interest expense is made up of two components: cash interest and amortization. We will now consider how to amortize premium or discount.

Effective Interest Method of Amortization
The process of transferring a portion of the premium or discount to interest expense; this method results in a constant effective interest rate.

Effective Interest Method: Impact on Expense The **effective interest method of amortization** amortizes discount or premium in a manner that produces a constant effective interest rate from period to period. The *dollar amount* of interest expense will vary from period to period, but the *rate* of interest will be constant. This interest rate is

CARRYING VALUE The face value of a bond plus the amount of unamortized premium or minus the amount of unamortized discount.

referred to as the *effective interest rate* and is equal to the market rate of interest at the time the bonds are issued.

To illustrate this point, we introduce two new terms. The **carrying value** of bonds is represented by the following:

Carrying Value = Face Value − Unamortized Discount

For example, the carrying value of the bonds for our Discount Firm example, as of the date of issuance of January 1, 2001, could be calculated as follows:

$10,000 − $634 = $9,366

In those situations in which there is a premium instead of a discount, carrying value is represented by the following:

Carrying Value = Face Value + Unamortized Premium

For example, the carrying value of the bonds for our Premium Firm example, as of the date of issuance of January 1, 2001, could be calculated as follows:

$10,000 + $692 = $10,692

The second term has been suggested earlier. The *effective rate of interest* is represented by the following:

Effective Rate = Annual Interest Expense/Carrying Value

Effective Interest Method: An Example The amortization table in Exhibit 10-4 illustrates effective interest amortization of the bond discount for our Discount Firm example.

As illustrated in Exhibit 10-4, the effective interest method of amortization is based on several important concepts. The relationships can be stated in equation form as follows:

Cash Interest (in Column 1) = Bond Face Value × Face Rate

Interest Expense (in Column 2) = Carrying Value × Effective Rate

Discount Amortized (in Column 3) = Interest Expense − Cash Interest

The first column of the exhibit indicates that the cash interest to be paid is $800 ($10,000 × 8%). The second column indicates the annual interest expense at the effective rate of interest (market rate at the time of issuance). This is a constant rate of interest (10% in our example) and is calculated by multiplying the carrying value *as of the beginning of the period* times the market rate of interest. In 2001 the interest expense is $937 ($9,366 × 10%). Note that the amount of interest expense changes each year because the carrying value changes as discount is amortized. The amount of discount amortized each year in Column 3 is the difference between the cash interest in Column 1 and the interest expense in Column 2. Again, note that the amount of discount amortized changes in each of the four years. Finally, the carrying value in Column 4 is the previous year's carrying value plus the discount amortized in

EXHIBIT 10-4 Discount Amortization: Effective Interest Method of Amortization

Date	Column 1 Cash Interest	Column 2 Interest Expense	Column 3 Discount Amortized	Column 4 Carrying Value
	8%	**10%**	**Col. 2 − Col. 1**	
1/1/2001	—	—	—	$ 9,366
12/31/2001	$800	$937	$137	9,503
12/31/2002	800	950	150	9,653
12/31/2003	800	965	165	9,818
12/31/2004	800	982	182	10,000

Column 3. When bonds are issued at a discount, the carrying value starts at an amount less than face value and increases each period until it reaches the face value amount.

The amortization table in Exhibit 10-4 is the basis for the accounting entries that must be recorded. Discount Firm may record two entries for each period. The first entry at the end of 2001 is recorded to reflect the cash interest payment:

Dec. 31	Interest Expense	800	
	Cash		800
	To record annual payment on bonds payable.		

Assets	=	Liabilities	+	Owners' Equity
−800				−800

The second entry is recorded to amortize a portion of the discount and to reflect that amount as an adjustment of interest expense:

Dec. 31	Interest Expense	137	
	Discount on Bonds Payable		137
	To amortize annual portion of discount on bonds payable.		

Assets	=	Liabilities	+	Owners' Equity
		+137		−137

Instead of making two entries, firms often make one entry that combines the two. Thus, the entry for 2001 could also be recorded in the following manner:

Dec. 31	Interest Expense	937	
	Cash		800
	Discount on Bonds Payable		137
	To record annual interest payment and to amortize annual portion of discount on bonds payable.		

Assets	=	Liabilities	+	Owners' Equity
−800		+137		−937

The T accounts of the issuing firm as of December 31, 2001, would appear as follows:

BONDS PAYABLE

		10,000	1/1/01

DISCOUNT ON BONDS PAYABLE

1/1/01	634		
		137	12/31/01
Bal.	497		

INTEREST EXPENSE

12/31/01	800	
12/31/01	137	
Bal.	937	

The balance of the Discount on Bonds Payable account as of December 31, 2001, would be calculated as follows:

Beginning balance, January 1, 2001	$634
Less: Amount amortized	137
Ending balance, December 31, 2001	$497

The December 31, 2001, balance represents the amount *unamortized,* or the amount that will be amortized in future time periods. On the balance sheet presented as of December 31, 2001, the unamortized portion of the discount appears as the balance of the Discount on Bonds Payable account as follows:

Long-term liabilities	
Bonds payable	$10,000
Less: Discount on bonds payable	497
	$ 9,503

The process of amortization would continue for four years, until the balance of the Discount on Bonds Payable account has been reduced to zero. By the end of 2004, all of the balance of the Discount on Bonds Payable account will have been transferred to the Interest Expense account and represents an increase in interest expense each period.

The amortization of a premium has an impact opposite that of the amortization of a discount. We will use our Premium Firm example to illustrate. Recall that on January 1, 2001, Premium Firm issued $10,000 face value bonds with a face rate of interest of 8%. At the time the bonds were issued, the market rate was 6%, resulting in an issue price of $10,692 and a credit balance in the Premium on Bonds Payable account of $692.

The amortization table in Exhibit 10-5 illustrates effective interest amortization of the bond premium for Premium Firm. As the exhibit illustrates, effective interest amortization of a premium is based on the same concepts as amortization of a discount. The following relationships still hold true:

Cash Interest (in Column 1) = Bond Face Value × Face Rate

Interest Expense (in Column 2) = Carrying Value × Effective Rate

Study Tip

Amortization of a discount increases interest expense. Amortization of a premium reduces interest expense.

The first column of the exhibit indicates that the cash interest to be paid is $800 ($10,000 × 8%). The second column indicates the annual interest expense at the effective rate. In 2001 the interest expense is $642 ($10,692 × 6%). Note, however, two differences between Exhibit 10-4 and Exhibit 10-5. In the amortization of a premium, the cash interest in Column 1 exceeds the interest expense in Column 2. Therefore, the premium amortized is defined as follows:

Premium Amortized (in Column 3) = Cash Interest − Interest Expense

Also note that the carrying value in Column 4 starts at an amount higher than the face value of $10,000 ($10,692) and is amortized downward until it reaches face value. Therefore, the carrying value at the end of each year is the carrying value at the beginning of the period minus the premium amortized for that year. For example, the carrying value in Exhibit 10-5 at the end of 2001 ($10,534) was calculated by subtracting the premium amortized for 2001 ($158 in Column 3) from the carrying value at the beginning of 2001 ($10,692).

The amortization table in Exhibit 10-5 again serves as the basis for the accounting entries that must be recorded. Premium Firm may record two entries for each period. The first entry at the end of 2001 is recorded to reflect the cash interest payment:

Dec. 31	Interest Expense	800	
	Cash		800
	To record annual payment on bonds payable.		

Assets	=	Liabilities	+	Owners' Equity
−800				−800

The second entry is recorded to amortize a portion of the premium and to reflect that amount as an adjustment of interest expense:

EXHIBIT 10-5 Premium Amortization: Effective Interest Method of Amortization

Date	Column 1 Cash Interest	Column 2 Interest Expense	Column 3 Premium Amortized	Column 4 Carrying Value
	8%	6%	Col. 1 − Col. 2	
1/1/2001	—	—	—	$10,692
12/31/2001	$800	$642	$158	10,534
12/31/2002	800	632	168	10,366
12/31/2003	800	622	178	10,188
12/31/2004	800	612	188	10,000

Dec. 31	Premium on Bonds Payable	158	
	Interest Expense		158
	To amortize annual portion of premium on bonds payable.		

Assets	=	Liabilities	+	Owners' Equity
		−158		+158

Of course, Premium Firm could combine the preceding two entries into one entry as follows:

Dec. 31	Interest Expense	642	
	Premium on Bonds Payable	158	
	Cash		800
	To record annual interest payment and to amortize annual portion of premium on bonds payable.		

Assets	=	Liabilities	+	Owners' Equity
−800		−158		−642

The balance of the Premium on Bonds payable account as of December 31, 2001, would be calculated as follows:

Beginning balance, January 1, 2001	$692
Less: Amount amortized	158
Ending balance, December 31, 2001	$534

The December 31, 2001, balance represents the amount *unamortized,* or the amount that will be amortized in future time periods. On the balance sheet presented as of December 31, 2001, the unamortized portion of the premium appears as the balance of the Premium on Bonds payable account as follows:

Long-term liabilities	
Bonds payable	$10,000
Plus: Premium on bonds payable	534
	$10,534

The process of amortization would continue for four years, until the balance of the Premium on Bonds Payable account has been reduced to zero. By the end of 2004, all of the balance of the Premium on Bonds Payable account will have been transferred to the Interest Expense account and represents a reduction of interest expense each period.

Two-Minute Review

1. How do you calculate the issue price of a bond?

2. What effect does amortizing a premium have on the amount of interest expense for the bond? What effect does amortizing a discount have?

Answers:

1. To calculate the issue price of a bond, you must calculate the present value of the annuity of interest payments and add to it the present value of the principal to be repaid, using the market rate of interest as the rate in the calculations.

2. When a premium is amortized, it decreases the amount of interest on the bond, and when a discount is amortized, it increases the amount of interest expense on the bond.

REDEMPTION OF BONDS

Redemption at Maturity The term *redemption* refers to retirement of bonds by repayment of the principal. If bonds are retired on their due date, the accounting entry is not difficult. Refer again to the Discount Firm example. If Discount Firm retires its bonds on the due date of December 31, 2004, it must repay the principal of $10,000, and Cash is reduced by $10,000. The following entry is recorded:

Dec. 31	Bonds Payable	10,000	
	Cash		10,000
	To record the retirement of bonds payable.		

Assets	=	Liabilities	+	Owners' Equity
−10,000		−10,000		

This assumes that the interest payment that was paid on December 31, 2004, and the discount amortization on that date have already been recorded. The balance of the Discount on Bonds Payable account is zero, since it has been fully amortized.

Notice that no gain or loss is incurred because the carrying value of the bond at that point is $10,000.

LO 6 Find the gain or loss on retirement of bonds.

Retired Early at a Gain A firm may want to retire bonds before their due date for several reasons. A firm may simply have excess cash and may determine that the best use of those funds is to repay outstanding bond obligations. Bonds may also be retired early because of changing interest rate conditions. If interest rates in the economy decline, firms may find it advantageous to retire bonds that have been issued at higher rates. Of course, what is advantageous to the issuer is not necessarily so for the investor. Early retirement of callable bonds is always a possibility that must be anticipated. Large institutional investors expect such a development and merely reinvest the money elsewhere. Many individual investors are more seriously inconvenienced when a bond issue is called.

Bond terms generally specify that if bonds are retired before their due date, they are not retired at the face value amount but at a call price or redemption price indicated on the bond certificate. Also, the amount of unamortized premium or discount on the bonds must be considered when bonds are retired early. The retirement results in a **gain or loss on redemption** that must be calculated as follows:

GAIN OR LOSS ON REDEMPTION The difference between the carrying value and the redemption price at the time bonds are redeemed.

$$\text{Gain} = \text{Carrying Value} - \text{Redemption Price}$$

$$\text{Loss} = \text{Redemption Price} - \text{Carrying Value}$$

In other words, the issuing firm must calculate the carrying value of the bonds at the time of redemption and compare it with the total redemption price. If the carrying value is higher than the redemption price, the issuing firm must record a gain. If the carrying value is lower than the redemption price, the issuing firm must record a loss.

We will use the Premium Firm example to illustrate the calculation of gain or loss. Assume that on December 31, 2001, Premium Firm wants to retire its bonds due in 2004. Assume, as in the previous section, that the bonds were issued at a premium of $692 at the beginning of 2001. Premium Firm has used the effective interest method of amortization and has recorded the interest and amortization entries for the year (see page 489). This has resulted in a balance of $534 in the Premium on Bonds Payable account as of December 31, 2001. Assume also that Premium Firm's bond certificates indicate that the bonds may be retired early at a call price of 102 (meaning 102% of face value). Thus, the redemption price is 102% of $10,000, or $10,200.

Premium Firm's retirement of bonds would result in a gain. The gain can be calculated using two steps. First, we must calculate the carrying value of the bonds as of the date they are retired. The carrying value of Premium Firm's bonds at that date is calculated as follows:

$$\begin{aligned}\text{Carrying Value} &= \text{Face Value} + \text{Unamortized Premium}\\ &= \$10{,}000 + \$534\\ &= \$10{,}534\end{aligned}$$

Note that the carrying value we have calculated is the same amount indicated for December 31, 2001, in Column 4 of the effective interest amortization table of Exhibit 10-5.

The second step is to calculate the gain:

$$\begin{aligned}\text{Gain} &= \text{Carrying Value} - \text{Redemption Price}\\ &= \$10{,}534 - (\$10{,}000 \times 1.02)\\ &= \$10{,}534 - \$10{,}200\\ &= \$334\end{aligned}$$

It is important to remember that when bonds are retired, the balance of the Bonds Payable account and the remaining balance of the Premium on Bonds Payable account must be eliminated from the balance sheet.

Retired Early at a Loss To illustrate retirement of bonds at a loss, assume that Premium Firm retires bonds at December 31, 2001, as in the previous section. However, assume that the call price for the bonds is 107 (or 107% of face value).

We can again perform the calculations in two steps. The first step is to calculate the carrying value:

$$\begin{aligned}\text{Carrying Value} &= \text{Face Value} + \text{Unamortized Premium}\\ &= \$10{,}000 + \$534\\ &= \$10{,}534\end{aligned}$$

The second step is to compare the carrying value with the redemption price to calculate the amount of the loss:

Business Strategy

It was a marketing nightmare. In June 1999, some teenagers in Belgium became ill from drinking tainted cans of Coke, and the company was soon pulling Coke from store shelves all across Europe. The recall cost an estimated $100 million, and regaining consumer confidence and putting the product back in circulation was another expensive effort for the firm—a cost it won't specify. "This event has humbled us," said Charles S. Frenette, Coca-Cola's chief marketing officer. "But it has proved a tremendous testing ground."

www.cocacola.com

In fact, Coca-Cola realized that new marketing and management strategies were called for in the face of a looming public-relations disaster. When Belgian customers were asked what they wanted from the giant soft-drink firm, they said "a human face." So Coke quickly set out to rethink some of its basic management practices, beginning with streamlined decision-making. In a special "war room" in Brussels, marketing managers, public-relations consultants, distribution experts, and other managers met every morning at nine. Among their solutions to Coca-Cola's problem were a massive door-to-door coupon giveaway, the distribution of free bottles of Coke at 2,000 Belgian supermarkets, and family activities like dances, fairs, and parties staged across Belgium—and in France and Germany as well.

Although Coke is confident of coming out on top, it must still contend with fallout from the incident. Retailers were upset that too little product was shipped in the wake of the coupon giveaway and that the firm may be neglecting its other popular brands like Sprite and Fanta. Meanwhile, Pepsi is ramping up European production, and Virgin Cola, Coke's top competitor in Belgium, quickly doubled its market share during the summer. But Coca-Cola hasn't given up, and it plans to retain many of the new management and marketing strategies that have brought it closer to its customers around the world.

www.pepsico.com

SOURCE: William Echikson, "Have a Coke and a Smile—Please," *Business Week*, Aug. 30, 1999, p. 214A.

$$\text{Loss} = \text{Redemption Price} - \text{Carrying Value}$$
$$= (\$10{,}000 \times 1.07) - \$10{,}534$$
$$= \$10{,}700 - \$10{,}534$$
$$= \$166$$

In this case, a loss of $166 has resulted from the retirement of Premium Firm bonds. A loss means that the company paid more to retire the bonds than the amount at which the bonds were recorded on the balance sheet.

Financial Statement Presentation of Gain or Loss The accounts Gain on Bond Redemption and Loss on Bond Redemption are income statement accounts. A gain on bond redemption increases Premium Firm's income; a loss decreases its income. In that respect, the accounts are similar to gains or losses that occur on the sale of equipment or other assets. There is an important difference, however. The FASB has ruled that gains and losses that occur on bond redemption merit separate recognition on the income statement. Such gains and losses are considered *extraordinary items* and must be shown in a separate section of the income statement.[2] This allows income statement readers to understand that bond redemption is not a part of the firm's "normal operating" activities. That is not to say that investors are not interested in such one-time gains or losses. Although redemptions on bonds are not part of normal operations, a large gain suggests that the company's financial managers are astute enough to take advantage of opportunities in the financial markets.

www.fasb.org

Liability for Leases

Long-term bonds and notes payable are important sources of financing for many large corporations and are quite prominent in the long-term liability category of the balance sheet for many firms. But other important elements of that category of the balance sheet also represent long-term obligations. We will introduce you to leases because they are a major source of financing for many companies. We will introduce two other liabilities, deferred taxes and pensions, in Appendix 10A. In some cases, these liabilities are required to be reported on the financial statements and are important components of the Long-Term Liabilities section of the balance sheet. In other cases, the items are not required to be presented in the financial statements and can be discerned only by a careful reading of the footnotes to the financial statements.

Leases

LO 7 Determine whether a lease agreement must be reported as a liability on the balance sheet.

A *lease,* a contractual arrangement between two parties, allows one party, the *lessee,* the right to use an asset in exchange for making payments to its owner, the *lessor.* A common example of a lease arrangement is the rental of an apartment. The tenant is the lessee and the landlord is the lessor.

Lease agreements are a form of financing. In some cases, it is more advantageous to lease an asset than to borrow money to purchase it. The lessee can conserve cash because a lease does not require a large initial cash outlay. A wide variety of lease arrangements exists, ranging from simple agreements to complex ones that span a long time period. Lease arrangements are popular because of their flexibility. The terms of a lease can be structured in many ways to meet the needs of the lessee and lessor. This results in difficult accounting questions:

1. Should the right to use property be reported as an asset by the lessee?
2. Should the obligation to make payments be reported as a liability by the lessee?
3. Should all leases be accounted for in the same manner regardless of the terms of the lease agreement?

[2] *Statement of Financial Accounting Standards No. 4,* "Reporting Gains and Losses from Extinguishment of Debt" (Stamford, Conn.: FASB, 1975).

Accounting for Your Decisions

Should You Lease or Buy?

You want to acquire a new car and are considering leasing instead of buying. What factors should you consider to determine whether leasing is the better alternative?

ANS: To make this decision, answer the following questions: Do you have the cash to buy the car? If not, what is the cost of borrowing? How long will the car be used? Will another car be needed in the near future? What is the purpose of the car? How will the lease payments compare with the purchase payments? Will you own the car at the end of the lease?

The answers are that some leases should be reported as an asset and a liability by the lessee and some should not. The accountant must examine the terms of the lease agreement and compare those terms with an established set of criteria.

Lease Criteria From the viewpoint of the lessee, there are two types of lease agreements, operating and capital leases. In an **operating lease,** the lessee acquires the right to use an asset for a limited period of time. The lessee is *not* required to record the right to use the property as an asset or to record the obligation for payments as a liability. Therefore, the lessee is able to attain a form of *off-balance-sheet financing.* That is, the lessee has attained the right to use property but has not recorded that right, or the accompanying obligation, on the balance sheet. By escaping the balance sheet, the lease does not add to debt or impair the debt-to-equity ratio that investors usually calculate. Management has a responsibility to make sure that such off-balance-sheet financing is not in fact a long-term obligation. The company's auditors are supposed to analyze the terms of the lease carefully to make sure that management has exercised its responsibility.

Operating lease
A lease that does not meet any of the four criteria and is not recorded as an asset by the lessee.

The second type of lease agreement is a **capital lease.** In this type of lease, the lessee has acquired sufficient rights of ownership and control of the property to be considered its owner. The lease is called a *capital lease* because it is capitalized (recorded) on the balance sheet by the lessee.

Capital lease
A lease that is recorded as an asset by the lessee.

A lease should be considered a capital lease by the lessee if *one or more* of the following criteria are met:[3]

1. The lease transfers ownership of the property to the lessee at the end of the lease term.
2. The lease contains a bargain-purchase option to purchase the asset at an amount lower than its fair market value.
3. The lease term is 75% or more of the property's economic life.
4. The present value of the minimum lease payments is 90% or more of the fair market value of the property at the inception of the lease.

If none of the criteria are met, the lease agreement is accounted for as an operating lease. This is an area in which it is important for the accountant to exercise professional judgment. In some cases, firms may take elaborate measures to evade or manipulate the criteria that would require lease capitalization. The accountant should determine what is full and fair disclosure based on an unbiased evaluation of the substance of the transaction.

Operating Leases You have already accounted for operating leases in previous chapters when recording rent expense and prepaid rent. A rental agreement for a limited time period is also a lease agreement.

Suppose, for example, that Lessee Firm wants to lease a car for a new salesperson. A lease agreement is signed with Lessor Dealer on January 1, 2001, to lease a car for the year for $4,000, payable on December 31, 2001. Typically, a car lease does not transfer title at

[3] *Statement of Financial Accounting Standards No. 13,* "Accounting for Leases" (Stamford, Conn.: FASB, 1976).

EXHIBIT 10-6 Tommy Hilfiger Corporation 1998 Footnote Disclosure of Leases

Operating leases can be used as an important source of financing.

Commitments and Contingencies

(a) Leases

The Company leases office, warehouse and showroom space, retail stores and office equipment under operating leases, which expire not later than 2023. The Company normalizes fixed escalations in rental expense under its operating leases. Minimum annual rentals under non-cancelable operating leases, excluding operating cost escalations and contingent rental amounts based upon retail sales, are payable as follows:

Fiscal Year Ending March 31,	
1999	$10,051,000
2000	11,121,000
2001	10,161,000
2002	9,063,000
2003	8,814,000
Thereafter	46,681,000

Rent expense was $12,551,000, $8,911,000 and $5,768,000 for the years ended March 31, 1998, 1997 and 1996, respectively.

the end of the term, does not include a bargain-purchase price, and does not last for more than 75% of the car's life. In addition, the present value of the lease payments is not 90% of the car's value. Because the lease does not meet any of the specified criteria, it should be presented as an operating lease. Lessee Firm would simply record lease expense, or rent expense, of $4,000 for the year.

Although operating leases are not recorded on the balance sheet by the lessee, they are mentioned in financial statement footnotes. The FASB requires footnote disclosure of the amount of future lease obligations for leases that are considered operating leases. Exhibit 10-6 provides a portion of the footnote from Tommy Hilfiger Corporation's 1998 annual report. The footnote reveals that Tommy Hilfiger has used operating leases as an important source of financing and has significant off-balance-sheet commitments in future periods as a result. An investor might want to add this off-balance-sheet item to the debt on the balance sheet to get a conservative view of the company's obligations.

www.tommy.com

Capital Leases Capital leases are presented as assets and liabilities by the lessee because they meet one or more of the lease criteria. Suppose that Lessee Firm in the previous example wanted to lease a car for a longer period of time. Assume that on January 1, 2001, Lessee signs a lease agreement with Lessor Dealer to lease a car. The terms of the agreement specify that Lessee will make annual lease payments of $4,000 per year for five years, payable each December 31. Assume also that the lease specifies that at the end of the lease agreement, the title to the car is transferred to Lessee Firm. Lessee must decide how to account for the lease agreement.

The contractual arrangement between Lessee Firm and Lessor Dealer is called a lease agreement, but clearly the agreement is much different from a year-to-year lease arrangement. Essentially, Lessee Firm has acquired the right to use the asset for its entire life and does not need to return it to Lessor Dealer. You may call this agreement a lease, but it actually represents a purchase of the asset by Lessee with payments made over time.

Study Tip

It is called a *capital lease* because the lease is capitalized, or put on the books of the lessee as an asset.

The lease should be treated as a capital lease by Lessee because it meets at least one of the four criteria (it meets the first criteria concerning transfer of title). A capital lease must be recorded at its present value by Lessee as an asset and as an obligation. As of January 1, 2001, we must calculate the present value of the annual payments. If we assume an interest rate of 8%, the present value of the payments is $15,972 ($4,000 × an annuity factor of 3.993 from Table 9-4). The first entry is made on the basis of the present value as follows:

Jan. 1	Leased Asset	15,972	
	Lease Obligation		15,972
	To record a capital lease agreement.		

Assets	=	Liabilities	+	Owners' Equity
+15,972		+15,972		

The Leased Asset account is a long-term asset similar to plant and equipment and represents the fact that Lessee has acquired the right to use and retain the asset. Because the leased asset represents depreciable property, depreciation must be reported for each of the five years of asset use. On December 31, 2001, Lessee records depreciation of $3,194 ($15,972/5 years) as follows, assuming that the straight-line method is adopted:

Dec. 31	Depreciation Expense	3,194	
	Accumulated Depreciation—Leased Assets		3,194
	To record depreciation of leased assets.		

Assets	=	Liabilities	+	Owners' Equity
−3,194				−3,194

Depreciation of leased assets is referred to as *amortization* by some firms.

On December 31, Lessee Firm also must make a payment of $4,000 to Lessor Dealer. A portion of each payment represents interest on the obligation (loan), and the remainder represents a reduction of the principal amount. Each payment must be separated into its principal and interest components. Generally, the effective interest method is used for that purpose. An effective interest table can be established using the same concepts as were used to amortize a premium or discount on bonds payable.

Exhibit 10-7 illustrates the effective interest method applied to the Lessee Firm example. Note that the table begins with an obligation amount equal to the present value of the payments of $15,972. Each payment is separated into principal and interest amounts so that the amount of the loan obligation at the end of the lease agreement equals zero. The amortization table is the basis for the amounts that are reflected on the financial statement. Exhibit 10-7 indicates that the $4,000 payment in 2001 should be considered as interest of $1,278 (8% of $15,972) and reduction of principal of $2,722. On December 31, 2001, Lessee Firm records the following entry for the annual payment:

Dec. 31	Interest Expense	1,278	
	Lease Obligation	2,722	
	Cash		4,000
	To record annual lease payment.		

Assets	=	Liabilities	+	Owners' Equity
−4,000		−2,722		−1,278

EXHIBIT 10-7 Lease Amortization: Effective Interest Method of Amortization

Date	Column 1 Lease Payment	Column 2 Interest Expense	Column 3 Reduction of Obligation	Column 4 Lease Obligation
		8%	Col. 1 − Col. 2	
1/1/2001	—	—	—	$15,972
12/31/2001	$4,000	$1,278	$2,722	13,250
12/31/2002	4,000	1,060	2,940	10,310
12/31/2003	4,000	825	3,175	7,135
12/31/2004	4,000	571	3,429	3,706
12/31/2005	4,000	294	3,706	–0–

Therefore, for a capital lease, Lessee Firm must record both an asset and a liability. The asset is reduced by the process of depreciation. The liability is reduced by reductions of principal using the effective interest method. According to Exhibit 10-7, the total lease obligation as of December 31, 2001, is $13,250. This amount must be separated into current and long-term categories. The portion of the liability that will be paid within one year of the balance sheet should be considered a current liability. Reference to Exhibit 10-7 indicates that the liability will be reduced by $2,940 in 2002, and that amount should be considered a current liability. The remaining amount of the liability, $10,310 ($13,250 – $2,940), should be considered long-term. On the balance sheet as of December 31, 2001, Lessee Firm reports the following balances related to the lease obligation:

Assets:		
Leased Assets	$15,972	
Less: Accumulated Depreciation	3,194	
		$12,778
Current Liabilities:		
Lease Obligation		$ 2,940
Long-Term Liabilities:		
Lease Obligation		$10,310

Notice that the depreciated asset does not equal the present value of the lease obligation. That is not unusual. For example, an automobile often may be completely depreciated but still have payments due on it.

The criteria used to determine whether a lease is an operating or a capital lease have provided a standard accounting treatment for all leases. The accounting for leases in foreign countries generally follows guidelines similar to those used in the United States. The criteria used in foreign countries to determine whether a lease is a capital lease are usually less detailed and less specific, however. As a result, capitalization of leases occurs less frequently in foreign countries than in the United States because of the increased use of judgment necessary in applying the accounting rules.

Two-Minute Review

1. When a lease is considered a capital lease to the lessee, what entry is made to initially record the lease agreement?

2. When the lessee makes a lease payment on a capital lease, how is the payment recorded?

Answers:

1. A capital lease is recorded as an asset, in an account such as Leased Asset, and as a liability, in an account such as Lease Obligation. The lease is recorded at the amount of the present value of the lease payments.

2. When a lease payment is made, the portion of the payment that is interest would be recorded to the Interest Expense account, and the portion of the payment that is principal is considered a reduction in the Lease Obligation account.

Analyzing Debt to Assess a Firm's Solvency

Long-term liabilities are a component of the "capital structure" of the company and are included in the calculation of the debt-to-equity ratio:

$$\text{Debt-to-Equity Ratio} = \frac{\text{Total Liabilities}}{\text{Total Stockholders' Equity}}$$

For example, refer to the liability category of PepsiCo's balance sheet given in Exhibit 10-1. PepsiCo's total liabilities are $16,259 million (current liabilities of $7,914, long-term debt of $4,028, other liabilities of $2,314, and deferred income taxes of $2,003). Its total stockholders' equity is $6,401 million. Therefore, the debt-to-equity ratio is $16,259/$6,401 or 2.54, which means that PepsiCo has 2.54 times as much debt as equity, a situation that is not uncommon for companies in the beverage industry.

Most investors would prefer to see equity rather than debt on the balance sheet. Debt, and its interest charges, make up a fixed obligation that must be repaid in a finite period of time. In contrast, equity never has to be repaid, and the dividends that are declared on it are optional. Stock investors view debt as a claim against the company that must be satisfied before they get a return on their money.

Other ratios used to measure the degree of debt obligation include the times interest earned ratio and the debt service coverage ratio:

$$\text{Times Interest Earned Ratio} = \frac{\text{Income before Interest and Tax}}{\text{Interest Expense}}$$

$$\text{Debt Service Coverage Ratio} = \frac{\text{Cash Flow from Operations before Interest and Tax}}{\text{Interest and Principal Payments}}$$

Lenders want to be sure that borrowers can pay the interest and repay the principal on a loan. Both of the preceding ratios, which will be explored in more detail in Chapter 13, reflect the degree to which a company can make its debt payments out of current cash flow.

From Concept **TO PRACTICE 10.2**

READING BEN & JERRY'S BALANCE SHEET Calculate the 1997 and 1998 debt-to-equity ratios for Ben & Jerry's. Did 1998's debt-to-equity ratio go up or down from 1997's?

HOW LONG-TERM LIABILITIES AFFECT THE STATEMENT OF CASH FLOWS

LO 8 Explain the effects that transactions involving long-term liabilities have on the statement of cash flows.

Exhibit 10-8 indicates the impact that long-term liabilities have on a company's cash flow and their placement on the cash flow statement.

Most long-term liabilities are related to a firm's financing activities. Therefore, the change in the balance of each long-term liability account should be reflected in the Financing Activities category of the statement of cash flows. The decrease in a long-term liability account indicates that cash has been used to pay the liability. Therefore, in the cash flow statement, a decrease in a long-term liability account should appear as a subtraction or reduction. The

EXHIBIT 10-8 Long-Term Liabilities on the Statement of Cash Flows

Item	Statement of Cash Flows	
	Operating Activities	
	Net income	xxx
Increase in deferred tax	→	+
Decrease in deferred tax	→	−
	Investing Activities	
	Financing Activities	
Increase in liability	→	+
Decrease in liability	→	−

Name: John Roberts (Rob) Snow
Education: B.A., Middlebury College; M.B.A., Babson College
College Major: Psychology
Occupation: Director of Portfolio Management, FleetBoston Financial Corporation, Providence
Age: 32

Focus on Users

"It is a positive sign when a company is using long-term debt from a stable source to fund assets or activities that support future growth."
–Rob Snow

Long-Term Liabilities Help Reveal the Company's Future

Philip Yarrow, profiled in the previous chapter, talked about how current liabilities affect lending decisions. Rob Snow, a portfolio manager for FleetBoston Financial, here shares his views on how *long-term liabilities* come into play in his own risk-management and lending decisions. Rob says: "The risk management part of the job relates to performing financial and operational analysis of the companies we do business with, as well as analyzing the performance of the assets in the portfolio. In each of these cases, I am concerned with the long-term viability and success of the companies with whom we do business. The amount and composition of the debt on the company's balance sheet is an excellent predictor of future performance. It is a positive sign when a company is using long-term debt from a stable source to fund assets or activities that support future growth."

So, just as current liabilities reveal a company's near-term viability and its ability to pay back loans, long-term liabilities can help analysts forecast how a company will fare well into the future. In fact, Rob sees long-term liabilities as a company's investment in the future, and he offers an analogy to make the point: "Let's say that you need a car to get to work. You need to work to generate cash. If you can't afford to buy a car today, then you borrow the money to work to generate cash. If you can't afford to buy a car today, then you borrow the money even though the interest you pay on the car loan makes the purchase more expensive. Having the car today will dramatically improve your ability to succeed." Of course, not all debt is beneficial. Rob explains: "The amount of debt and whether it is long-term debt or short-term debt needs to be driven by the company's business model. A company with too much debt may eventually become trapped because it is unable to make interest payments and unable to take on new liabilities as a result of the existing leverage." It is the job of financial analysts like Rob, and Philip Yarrow in Chicago, to make judgments about whether the various liabilities that show up on the balance sheets will translate into a company's future growth.

increase in a long-term liability account indicates that the firm has obtained additional cash via a long-term obligation. Therefore, an increase in a long-term liability account should appear in the cash flow statement as an addition.

www.cocacola.com

The cash flow statement of Coca-Cola Company is presented in Exhibit 10-9. Note that the Financing Activities category contains two items related to long-term liabilities. In 1998, long-term debt was issued for $1,818 million and is an addition to cash. This indicates that Coca-Cola increased its cash position by borrowings. Second, the payment of debt is listed as a deduction of $410 million. This indicates that Coca-Cola paid long-term liabilities resulting in a reduction of cash.

From Concept to PRACTICE 10.3

Reading Gateway's Statement of Cash Flows Did Gateway pay off any long-term debt during 1998? Is this a positive or negative amount on the cash flow statement? In which category of the statement do you find the change?

Although most long-term liabilities are reflected in the Financing Activities category of the statement of cash flows, there are exceptions. The most notable exception involves the Deferred Tax account (discussed in Appendix 10A). The change in this account is reflected in the Operating Activities category of the statement of cash flows. This presentation is necessary because the Deferred Tax account is related to an operating item, income tax expense. For example, in Exhibit 10-9, Coca-Cola listed $38 million in the Operating Activities category of the 1998 statement of cash flows. This indicates that $38 million less was recorded as expense than was paid out in cash. Therefore, the amount is a negative amount in, or a subtraction from, the Operating Activities category.

EXHIBIT 10-9 Coca-Cola Company and Subsidiaries 1998 Consolidated Statements of Cash Flows

CONSOLIDATED STATEMENTS OF CASH FLOWS

The Coca-Cola Company and Subsidiaries

Year Ended December 31, (In millions)	1998	1997	1996
OPERATING ACTIVITIES			
Net income	**$ 3,533**	$ 4,129	$ 3,492
Depreciation and amortization	**645**	626	633
Deferred income taxes	**(38)**	380	(145)
Equity income, net of dividends	**31**	(108)	(89)
Foreign currency adjustments	**21**	37	(60)
Gains on issuances of stock by equity investees	**(27)**	(363)	(431)
Gains on sales of assets, including bottling interests	**(306)**	(639)	(135)
Other items	**124**	18	316
Net change in operating assets and liabilities	**(550)**	(47)	(118)
Net cash provided by operating activities	**3,433**	4,033	3,463
INVESTING ACTIVITIES			
Acquisitions and investments, principally bottling companies	**(1,428)**	(1,100)	(645)
Purchases of investments and other assets	**(610)**	(459)	(623)
Proceeds from disposals of investments and other assets	**1,036**	1,999	1,302
Purchases of property, plant and equipment	**(863)**	(1,093)	(990)
Proceeds from disposals of property, plant and equipment	**54**	71	81
Other investing activities	**(350)**	82	(175)
Net cash used in investing activities	**(2,161)**	(500)	(1,050)
Net cash provided by operations after reinvestment	**1,272**	3,533	2,413
FINANCING ACTIVITIES			
Issuances of debt	**1,818**	155	1,122
Payments of debt	**(410)**	(751)	(580)
Issuances of stock	**302**	150	124
Purchases of stock for treasury	**(1,563)**	(1,262)	(1,521)
Dividends	**(1,480)**	(1,387)	(1,247)
Net cash used in financing activities	**(1,333)**	(3,095)	(2,102)
EFFECT OF EXCHANGE RATE CHANGES ON CASH AND CASH EQUIVALENTS	**(28)**	(134)	(45)
CASH AND CASH EQUIVALENTS			
Net increase (decrease) during the year	**(89)**	304	266
Balance at beginning of the year	**1,737**	1,433	1,167
Balance at end of year	**$ 1,648**	$ 1,737	$ 1,433

See Notes to Consolidated Financial Statements.

Changes in long-term debt generally affect the financing activities category.

WARMUP EXERCISES

Warmup Exercise 10-1

A bond, due in 10 years, with face value of $1,000 and face rate of interest of 8%, is issued when the market rate of interest is 6%.

Required

1. What is the issue price of the bond?
2. What is the amount of premium or discount on the bond at the time of issuance?

3. What amount of interest expense will be shown on the income statement for the first year of the bond?
4. What amount of the premium or discount will be amortized during the first year of the bond?

Warmup Exercise 10-2

You have signed an agreement to lease a car for four years and will make annual payments of \$4,000 at the end of each year. (Assume that the lease meets the criteria for a capital lease.)

Required

1. Calculate the present value of the lease payments, assuming an 8% interest rate.
2. What is the journal entry to record the leased asset?
3. When the first lease payment is made, what portion of the payment will be considered interest?

Solution to Warmup Exercises

Warmup Exercise 10-1

1. The issue price of the bond would be calculated as the present value:

\$80 (7.360) =	\$ 588.80	using Table 9-4 where i = 6% and n = 10
plus \$1,000 (.558) =	558.00	using Table 9-2 where i = 6% and n = 10
Issue Price	\$1,146.80	

2. The amount of the premium is the difference between the issue price and the face value:

$$\text{Premium} = \$1{,}146.80 - \$1{,}000$$
$$= \$146.80$$

3. The amount of interest expense can be calculated as follows:

$$\text{Interest Expense} = \$1{,}146.80 \times .06$$
$$= \$68.81$$

4. The amount that will be amortized can be calculated as follows:

$$\text{Amortized} = \text{Cash Interest} - \text{Interest Expense}$$
$$= (\$1{,}000 \times .08) - (\$1{,}146.80 \times .06)$$
$$= \$80.00 - \$68.81$$
$$= \$11.19$$

Warmup Exercise 10-2

1. The present value of the lease payments can be calculated as follows:

$$\text{Present Value} = \$4{,}000\ (3.312) \text{ using Table 9-4 where } i = 8\%,\ n = 4$$
$$= \$13{,}248$$

2. The journal entry to record the lease agreement:

Leased Asset	13,248	
Lease Obligation		13,248

3. The amount of interest can be calculated as follows:

$$\text{Interest} = \$13{,}248 \times .08$$
$$= \$1{,}059.84$$

REVIEW PROBLEM

The following items pertain to the liabilities of Brent Foods. You may assume that Brent Foods began business on January 1, 2001, and therefore the beginning balance of all accounts was zero.

a. On January 1, 2001, Brent Foods issued bonds with a face value of $50,000. The bonds are due in five years and have a face interest rate of 10%. The market rate on January 1 for similar bonds was 12%. The bonds pay interest annually each December 31. Brent has chosen to use the effective interest method of amortization for any premium or discount on the bonds.

b. On December 31, Brent Foods signed a lease agreement with Cordova Leasing. The agreement requires Brent to make annual lease payments of $3,000 per year for four years, with the first payment due on December 31, 2002. The agreement stipulates that ownership of the property is transferred to Brent at the end of the four-year lease. Assume that an 8% interest rate is used for the leasing transaction.

c. On January 1, 2002, Brent redeems its bonds payable at the specified redemption price of 101. Because this item occurs in 2002, it does not affect the balance sheet prepared for year-end 2001.

Required

1. Record the accounting entries necessary on December 31, 2001, to record the interest adjustment in item **a** and the signing of the lease in item **b.**
2. Develop the Long-Term Liabilities section of Brent Foods' balance sheet as of December 31, 2001, based on items **a** and **b.** You do not need to consider the footnotes that accompany the balance sheet.
3. Would the company prefer to treat the lease in item **b** as an operating lease? Why?
4. Calculate the gain or loss on the bond redemption for item **c** and indicate how it should be reported on the 2002 income statement.

Solution to Review Problem

1. a. The issue price of the bonds on January 1 must be calculated as the present value of the interest payments and the present value of the principal, as follows:

$ 5,000 × 3.605	$18,025
$50,000 × 0.567	28,350
Issue price	$46,375

The amount of the discount is calculated as follows:

$50,000 – $46,375 = $3,625

The following is the entry on December 31, 2001, to record interest and to amortize discount:

Dec. 31	Interest Expense	5,565	
	Cash		5,000
	Discount on Bonds Payable		565
	To record interest and amortize discount.		

Assets	=	Liabilities	+	Owners' Equity
–5,000		+565		–5,565

The interest expense is calculated using the effective interest method by multiplying the carrying value of the bonds times the market rate of interest ($46,375 × 12%).

Brent must show two accounts in the Long-Term Liabilities section of the balance sheet: Bonds Payable of $50,000 and Discount on Bonds Payable of $3,060 ($3,625 less $565 amortized).

b. The lease meets the criteria to be a capital lease. Brent must report the lease as an asset and report the obligation for lease payments as a liability. The transaction should be reported at the present value of the lease payments, $9,936 (computed by multiplying $3,000 times the annuity factor of 3.312). The accounting entry should be as follows:

Dec. 31	Leased Asset	9,936	
	Lease Obligation		9,936
	To record lease as a capital lease.		

Assets	=	Liabilities	+	Owners' Equity
+9,936		+9,936		

Because the lease agreement was signed on December 31, 2001, it is not necessary to amortize the Lease Obligation account in 2001. The account should be stated in the Long-Term Liabilities section of Brent's balance sheet at $9,936.

2. The Long-Term Liabilities section of Brent's balance sheet for December 31, 2001, on the basis of items **a** and **b** is as follows:

BRENT FOODS
PARTIAL BALANCE SHEET
AS OF DECEMBER 31, 2001

Long-Term Liabilities:		
Bonds Payable	$50,000	
Less: Unamortized discount on bonds payable	3,060	$46,940
Lease obligation		9,936
Total Long-Term Liabilities		$56,876

3. The company would prefer that the lease be an operating lease because it would not have to report the asset or liability on the balance sheet. This off-balance-sheet financing may give a more favorable impression of the company.
4. Brent must calculate the loss on the bond redemption as the difference between the carrying value of the bonds ($46,940) and the redemption price ($50,000 × 1.01). The amount of the loss is calculated as follows:

$50,500 − $46,940 = $3,560 loss on redemption

The loss should be reported as an extraordinary item on the 2002 income statement.

APPENDIX 10A

ACCOUNTING TOOLS: OTHER LIABILITIES

In this appendix we will discuss two additional items that are found in the long-term liabilities category of many companies: deferred taxes and pensions. Both items are complex financial arrangements, and our primary purpose is to make you aware of their existence when reading financial statements.

DEFERRED TAX

LO 9 Explain deferred taxes and calculate the deferred tax liability.

www.pepsico.com
www.cocacola.com

The financial statements of most major firms include an item titled Deferred Income Tax or Deferred Tax (see PepsiCo's deferred taxes in Exhibit 10-1 and Coca Cola's in the chapter opening). In most cases, the account appears in the Long-Term Liabilities section of the balance sheet, and the dollar amount may be large enough to catch the user's attention. For another example, Exhibit 10-10 illustrates the presentation of deferred tax in the 1998 comparative balance sheets of Tribune Company and Subsidiaries. The Deferred Income Taxes account is listed immediately after Long-Term Debt and for Tribune Company should be considered a long-term liability. At the end of 1998, the firm had more than $701 million of deferred tax. The size of that account relative to the other liabilities should raise questions concerning its exact meaning. In fact, deferred income taxes represent one of the most misunderstood aspects of financial statements. In this section, we will attempt to address some of the questions concerning deferred taxes.

Exhibit 10-10 Tribune Company and Subsidiaries 1998 Liabilities and Shareholders' Equity

liabilities & shareholders' equity		Dec. 27, 1998	Dec. 28, 1997
Current Liabilities	Long-term debt due within one year	**$ 29,905**	$ 33,348
	Accounts payable	**157,708**	138,897
	Employee compensation and benefits	**114,202**	122,007
	Contracts payable for broadcast rights	**260,264**	210,565
	Deferred income	**55,097**	53,065
	Income taxes	**59,607**	6,867
	Accrued liabilities	**151,347**	116,971
	Total current liabilities	**828,130**	681,720
Long-Term Debt	(less portions due within one year)	**1,616,256**	1,521,453
Other Non-Current Liabilities	Deferred income taxes	**701,778**	387,686
	Contracts payable for broadcast rights	**268,099**	230,832
	Compensation and other obligations	**164,690**	129,859
	Total other non-current liabilities	**1,134,567**	748,377
Commitments and Contingent Liabilities (see Notes 8 and 10)		**-**	-
Shareholders' Equity	Series B convertible preferred stock (without par value)		
	Authorized: 1,600,000 shares		
	Issued and outstanding: 1,337,926 shares in 1998 and		
	1,386,572 shares in 1997 (liquidation value $220 per share)	**293,203**	303,864
	Common stock (without par value)		
	Authorized: 400,000,000 shares; 163,543,316 shares issued	**1,018**	1,018
	Additional paid-in capital	**209,474**	201,401
	Retained earnings	**2,819,474**	2,506,292
	Treasury stock (at cost)		
	44,127,511 shares in 1998 and 41,012,883 shares in 1997	**(1,414,661)**	(1,159,832)
	Treasury stock held by Tribune Stock Compensation Fund (at cost)		
	413,774 shares in 1998	**(26,602)**	-
	Unearned compensation related to ESOP	**(156,495)**	(188,380)
	Accumulated other comprehensive income	**631,206**	161,641
	Total shareholders' equity	**2,356,617**	1,826,004
	Total liabilities and shareholders' equity	**$5,935,570**	$4,777,554

Deferred tax is a liability for Tribune Company and Subsidiaries

Deferred tax is an amount that reconciles the differences between the accounting done for purposes of financial reporting to stockholders ("book" purposes) and the accounting done for tax purposes. It may surprise you that U.S. firms are allowed to use accounting methods for financial reporting that differ from those used for tax calculations. The reason is that the Internal Revenue Service defines income and expense differently than does the Financial Accounting Standards Board. As a result, companies tend to use accounting methods that minimize income for tax purposes but maximize income in the annual report to stockholders. This is not true in some foreign countries where financial accounting and tax accounting are more closely aligned. Firms in those countries do not report deferred tax because the difference between methods is not significant.

Deferred Tax
The account used to reconcile the difference between the amount recorded as income tax expense and the amount that is payable as income tax.

www.irs.gov
www.fasb.org

PERMANENT DIFFERENCE A difference that affects the tax records but not the accounting records, or vice versa.

TEMPORARY DIFFERENCE A difference that affects both book and tax records but not in the same time period.

When differences between financial and tax reporting do occur, we can classify them into two types: permanent and temporary. **Permanent differences** occur when an item is included in the tax calculation and is never included for book purposes—or vice versa, when an item is included for book purposes but not for tax purposes.

For example, the tax laws allow taxpayers to exclude interest on certain investments, usually state and municipal bonds, from their income. These are generally called *tax-exempt bonds*. If a corporation buys tax-exempt bonds, it does not have to declare the interest as income for tax purposes. When the corporation develops its income statement for stockholders (book purposes), however, the interest is included and appears in the Interest Income account. Therefore, tax-exempt interest represents a permanent difference between tax and book calculations.

Temporary differences occur when an item affects both the book and the tax calculations but not in the same time period. A difference caused by depreciation methods is the most common type of temporary difference. In previous chapters you have learned that depreciation may be calculated using a straight-line method or an accelerated method such as the double declining-balance method. Most firms do not use the same depreciation method for book and tax purposes, however. Generally, straight-line depreciation is used for book purposes and an accelerated method is used for tax purposes because accelerated depreciation lowers taxable income—at least in early years—and therefore reduces the tax due. The IRS refers to this accelerated method as the *Modified Accelerated Cost Recovery System (MACRS)*. It is similar to other accelerated depreciation methods in that it allows the firm to take larger depreciation deductions for tax purposes in the early years of the asset and smaller deductions in the later years. Over the life of the depreciable asset, the total depreciation using straight-line is equal to that using MACRS. Therefore, this difference is an example of a temporary difference between book and tax reporting.

The Deferred Tax account is used to reconcile the differences between the accounting for book purposes and for tax purposes. It is important to distinguish between permanent and temporary differences because the FASB has ruled that not all differences should affect the Deferred Tax account. The Deferred Tax account should reflect temporary differences but not items that are permanent differences between book accounting and tax reporting.[4]

Example of Deferred Tax Assume that Startup Firm begins business on January 1, 2001. During 2001 the firm has sales of $6,000 and has no expenses other than depreciation and income tax at the rate of 40%. Startup has depreciation on only one asset. That asset was purchased on January 1, 2001, for $10,000 and has a four-year life. Startup has decided to use the straight-line depreciation method for financial reporting purposes. Startup's accountants have chosen to use MACRS for tax purposes, however, resulting in $4,000 depreciation in 2001 and a decline of $1,000 per year thereafter.

The depreciation amounts for each of the four years for Startup's asset are as follows:

Year	Tax Depreciation	Book Depreciation	Difference
2001	$ 4,000	$ 2,500	$1,500
2002	3,000	2,500	500
2003	2,000	2,500	(500)
2004	1,000	2,500	(1,500)
Totals	$10,000	$10,000	$–0–

Startup's tax calculation for 2001 is based on the accelerated depreciation of $4,000, as follows:

Sales	$6,000
Depreciation Expense	4,000
Taxable Income	$2,000
× Tax Rate	40%
Tax Payable to IRS	$ 800

[4]*Statement of Financial Accounting Standards No. 109*, "Accounting for Income Taxes" (Stamford, Conn.: FASB, 1992).

For the year 2001, Startup owes $800 of tax to the Internal Revenue Service. This amount is ordinarily recorded as tax payable until the time it is remitted.

Startup wants also to develop an income statement to send to the stockholders. What amount should be shown as tax expense on the income statement? You may guess that the Tax Expense account on the income statement should reflect $800 because that is the amount to be paid to the IRS. That is not true in this case, however. Remember that the tax payable amount was calculated using the depreciation method that Startup chose for tax purposes. The income statement must be calculated using the straight-line method which Startup uses for book purposes. Therefore, Startup's income statement for 2001 appears as follows:

Sales	$6,000
Depreciation Expense	2,500
Income before Tax	$3,500
Tax Expense (40%)	1,400
Net Income	$2,100

Startup must make the following accounting entry to record the amount of tax expense and tax payable for 2001:

Dec. 31	Tax Expense	1,400	
	Tax Payable		800
	Deferred Tax		600
	To record income tax for the year 2001.		

Assets	=	Liabilities	+	Owners' Equity
		+800		−1,400
		+600		

The Deferred Tax account is a balance sheet account. A balance in it reflects the fact that Startup has received a tax benefit by recording accelerated depreciation, in effect delaying the ultimate obligation to the IRS. To be sure, the amount of deferred tax still represents a liability of Startup. The Deferred Tax account balance of $600 represents the amount of the 2001 temporary difference of $1,500 times the tax rate of 40% ($1,500 × 40% = $600).

What can we learn from the Startup example? First, when you see a firm's income statement, the amount listed as tax expense does not represent the amount of cash paid to the government for taxes. Accrual accounting procedures require that the tax expense amount be calculated using the accounting methods chosen for book purposes.

Second, when you see a firm's balance sheet, the amount in the Deferred Tax account reflects all of the temporary differences between the accounting methods chosen for tax and book purposes. The accounting and financial communities are severely divided on whether the Deferred Tax account represents a "true" liability. For one thing, many investment analysts do not view it as a real liability because they have noticed that it continues to grow year after year. Others look at it as a bookkeeping item that is simply there to balance the books. The FASB has taken the stance that deferred tax is an amount that results in a future obligation and meets the definition of a liability. The controversy concerning deferred taxes is likely to continue for many years.

PENSIONS

LO 10 Understand the meaning of a pension obligation and the effect of pensions on the long-term liability category of the balance sheet.

Many large firms establish pension plans to provide income to employees after their retirement. These pension plans often cover a large number of employees and involve millions of dollars. The large amounts in pension funds have become a major force in our economy, representing billions of dollars in stocks and bonds. In fact, pension funds are among the major "institutional investors" that have an enormous economic impact on our stock and bond exchanges.

PENSION An obligation to pay employees for service rendered while employed.

Pensions are complex financial arrangements that involve difficult estimates and projections developed by specialists and actuaries. Pension plans also involve very difficult accounting issues requiring a wide range of estimates and assumptions about future cash flows.

We will concern ourselves with two accounting questions related to pensions. First, the employer must report the cost of the pension plan as an expense over some time period. How should that expense be reported? Second, the employer's financial statements should reflect a measure of the liability associated with a pension plan. What is the liability for future pension amounts, and how should it be recorded or disclosed? Our discussion will begin with the recording of pension expense.

Pensions on the Income Statement Most pension plans are of the following form:

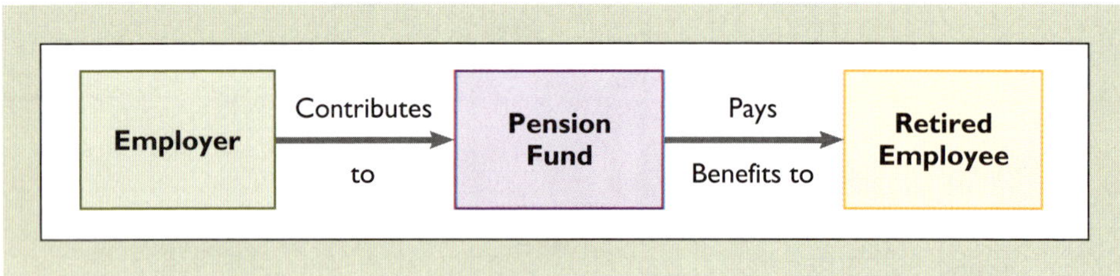

FUNDING PAYMENT
A payment made by the employer to the pension fund or its trustee.

Normally, the employer must make payments to the pension fund at least annually, perhaps more frequently. This is often referred to as *funding the pension* or as the **funding payment.** *Funding* simply means that the employer has contributed cash to the pension fund. The pension fund is usually administered by a trustee, often a bank or other financial institution. The trustee must invest the employer's funds so that they earn interest and dividends sufficient to pay the amounts owed to retired employees.

Our first accounting question concerns the amount that should be shown by the employer as pension expense. This is another example of the difference between cash-basis accounting and accrual accounting. The cash paid as the funding payment is not the same as the expense. When using the accrual basis of accounting, we must consider the amount of pension cost incurred, not the amount paid. Pension expense should be accrued in the period that the employee earns the benefits, regardless of the amount paid to the pension trustee. The amount expensed and the amount paid involve two separate decisions.

The FASB has specified the methods that should be used to calculate the amount of annual pension expense to record on the employer's income statement.[5] The accountant must determine the costs of the separate components of the pension and total them to arrive at the amount of pension expense. The components include the employee's service during the current year, the interest cost, the earnings on pension investments, and other factors. The details of those calculations are beyond our discussion.

To illustrate, suppose that Employer Firm has calculated its annual pension expense to be $80,000 for 2001. Also suppose that Employer has determined that it will make a funding payment of $60,000 to the pension fund. On the basis of those decisions, Employer should make the following accounting entry for the year:

Dec. 31	Pension Expense	80,000	
	Cash		60,000
	Accrued Pension Cost		20,000
	To record annual pension expense and funding payment.		

Assets	=	Liabilities	+	Owners' Equity
−60,000		+20,000		−80,000

The Pension Expense account is an income statement account and is reflected on Employer's 2001 income statement.

ACCRUED PENSION COST
The difference between the amount of pension recorded as an expense and the amount of the funding payment.

Pensions on the Balance Sheet The **Accrued Pension Cost** account in the preceding example is a balance sheet account. The account could represent an asset or a

[5] *Statement of Financial Accounting Standards No. 87,* "Employers' Accounting for Pension Plans" (Stamford, Conn.: FASB, 1985).

EXHIBIT 10-11 PepsiCo Company's Pension Footnote for 1998

Selected information for plans with accumulated benefit obligation in excess of plan assets:

	Pension	
	1998	1997
Projected benefit obligation	**$(1,960)**	$ (161)
Accumulated benefit obligation	**$(1,661)**	$ (83)
Fair value of plan assets	**$ 1,498**	$ 14

liability, depending on whether the amount expensed is more or less than the amount of the funding payment. If the amount expensed is less than the amount paid, it is reported by Employer Firm as an asset and labeled as Prepaid Pension Cost. Normally, the amount expensed is greater than the amount paid, as in the example here. In that case, the Accrued Pension Cost is reported by Employer Firm as a long-term liability.

But what is the meaning of the Accrued Pension Cost account? Is it really a liability? It certainly is not a measure of the amount that is owed to employees at the time of retirement. In fact, the only true meaning that can be given to the account is to say that it is the difference between the amount expensed and the amount funded.[6] In that regard, the Accrued Pension Cost account is inadequate in determining a firm's liability to its employees for future retirement benefits. The FASB requires a great deal of footnote information for pension plans. This footnote section can be used to develop a clearer picture of the status of a firm's pension obligation.

Pension Footnote Information Readers of financial statements are often interested in the *funding status* of pension plans. This indicates whether sufficient assets are available in the pension fund to cover the amounts to be paid to employees as retirement benefits. We will use the footnote disclosures of an actual firm to illustrate the use of pension information.

Exhibit 10-11 presents portions of the 1998 pension footnote for PepsiCo Company. PepsiCo is a large company with thousands of employees who are covered by the company's pension plans. Analysts who follow the industry must assess whether PepsiCo's pension is adequate for its employees. The amounts on the balance sheet give some indication about the status of the plan, but a more complete picture is provided in the company's footnotes. Fortunately, the footnotes can assist us as we determine whether the pension plans could be considered underfunded. Several items in the footnote need to be defined. First, PepsiCo has disclosed the amount of *plan assets* at fair value. This is a measure of the total dollar amount of assets that has been accumulated in the pension fund. The footnote indicates that as of year-end 1998, PepsiCo had assets of $1,498 million. Second, there are two measures of the amount of pension benefits owed to employees at the time of retirement. One measure is referred to as the **accumulated benefit obligation (ABO).** This is a measure of the amount of pension benefits that would be payable to employees if they were to retire at their existing salary levels. The footnote indicates that as of year-end 1998, PepsiCo had an accumulated benefit obligation of $1,661 million.

Another measure provides a higher estimate of that obligation. The **projected benefit obligation (PBO)** is a measure of the amount of pension benefits payable to employees if an assumption is made concerning the future salary increases that will be earned by the employees. This is probably a more realistic view of the amount of the obligation to employees, but it is a less objective number because of the difficulty in estimating future

www.pepsico.com

ACCUMULATED BENEFIT OBLIGATION (ABO)
A measure of the amount owed to employees for pensions if they retire at their existing salary levels.

PROJECTED BENEFIT OBLIGATION (PBO)
A measure of the amount owed to employees for pensions if estimates of future salary increases are considered.

[6] Some pension plans that are underfunded may be required to report an additional amount as a liability. This is referred to as the *minimum liability provision.* Refer to *SFAS No. 87* for more detail.

salary increases for employees. The footnote indicates that as of year-end 1998, PepsiCo had a projected benefit obligation of $1,960 million.

To determine the funding status of the pension plan, we must compare the amount of plan assets with the ABO and PBO. At the end of 1998, PepsiCo had pension plan assets of $1,498 million, which was less than the PBO. When the amount of assets is less than the amount of the obligation, the plan is referred to as *underfunded,* indicating that at this time there are not sufficient assets in the pension fund to cover the amount of liability to employees who will retire. Underfunding is also an example of an "off-balance-sheet" liability that investors use to assess the desirability of a company's stock.

PepsiCo's pension plans may be slightly underfunded but overall their pension plans certainly appear to be quite healthy. Not all firms are as fortunate. There have been many press reports of firms whose pension plans are seriously underfunded and for which it is quite questionable whether sufficient assets are available to pay impending retirement benefits. Such underfunded plans must be considered an off-balance-sheet liability by investors or creditors in assessing the company's health.

Users of the financial statements of U.S. firms are somewhat fortunate because the disclosure of pensions on the balance sheet and in the footnotes is quite extensive. The accounting for pensions by firms outside the United States varies considerably. Many countries do not require firms to accrue pension costs, and the expense is reported only when paid to retirees. Furthermore, within the statements and footnotes, there is much less disclosure, making an assessment of the funding status of pensions much more difficult.

Postretirement Benefits

Pensions represent a benefit paid to employees after their retirement. In addition to pensions, other benefits may be paid to employees after their retirement. For example, many firms promise to pay a portion of retirees' health care costs. The accounting question is whether postretirement benefits should be considered an expense when paid or during the period that the employee worked for the firm.

A few years ago, most firms treated postretirement benefits as an expense when they were paid to the retiree. It was widely believed that costs such as those for health care after retirement were too uncertain to be accrued as an expense and that such costs did not meet the definition of a liability and thus did not merit recording. The result of this expense-as-you-pay accounting was that firms had an obligation that was not recorded as a liability. As health care costs began to escalate, this unrecorded—and often undisclosed—cost became a concern for many firms as well as for stockholders, analysts, and employees.

The FASB has modified the accounting for other postemployment benefits to be consistent with pension costs. Under the matching principle, postretirement costs must now be accrued as an expense during the period that the employee helps the firm generate revenues and thus *earns* the benefits. The accountant must determine the costs of the separate components of postretirement benefits and total them to calculate the amount of the expense. The amount of the expense is reflected on the income statement in the Postretirement Expense account. The balance sheet should normally reflect the Accrued Postretirement Cost account. That account should be classified as a liability in the long-term liability category; it indicates the employer's obligation to present and future retirees.

The dollar amount of the liability represented by postretirement obligations is very large for many companies. For example, in 1998 PepsiCo's obligation to its employees for these retirement costs was $644 million (in addition to its pension plan amounts, disclosed in Exhibit 10-11).

There is still much controversy concerning the accounting for postretirement costs. Many firms object to the accounting requirements because of the uncertainty involved in measuring an obligation that extends far into the future. They also object because the requirements result in reduced profits on the income statement and huge liabilities on the balance sheet. Interestingly, this accounting rule had little impact on the stock market because the investment community already knew the magnitude of the postretirement obligations.

CHAPTER HIGHLIGHTS

1. **LO 1** Balance sheets generally have two categories of liabilities: current liabilities and long-term liabilities. Long-term liabilities are obligations that will not be satisfied within one year.
2. **LO 2** The terms of a bond payable are given in the bond certificate. The denomination of a bond is its face value. The interest rate stated in the bond certificate is referred to as the *face rate* or *stated rate of interest.* Term bonds all have the same due date. Serial bonds are not all due on the same date. Convertible bonds can be converted into common stock by the bondholders. Callable bonds may be redeemed or retired before their due date.
3. **LO 3** The issue price of a bond is the present value of the cash flows that the bond will provide to the investor. To determine the price, you must calculate the present values of the annuity of interest payments and of the principal amount. The present values must be calculated at the market rate of interest.
4. **LO 4** A bond sells at a discount or premium, depending on the relationship of the face rate to the market rate of interest. If the face rate exceeds the market rate, a bond is issued at a premium. If the face rate is less than the market rate, it will be issued at a discount.
5. **LO 5** Premiums or discounts must be amortized by transferring a portion of the premium or the discount each period to interest expense. The effective interest method of amortization reduces the balance of the premium or discount such that the effective interest rate on the bond is constant over its life.
6. **LO 5** The carrying value of the bond equals the face value plus unamortized premium or minus unamortized discount.
7. **LO 6** When bonds are redeemed before their due date, a gain or loss on redemption results. The gain or loss is the difference between the bond carrying value at the date of redemption and the redemption price. The gain or loss is treated as an extraordinary item on the income statement.
8. **LO 7** A lease, a contractual arrangement between two parties, allows the lessee the right to use property in exchange for making payments to the lessor.
9. **LO 7** There are two major categories of lease agreements: operating and capital. The lessee does not report an operating lease as an asset and does not present the obligation to make payments as a liability. Capital leases are reported as assets and liabilities by the lessee. Leases are reported as capital leases if they meet one or more of four criteria.
10. **LO 7** Capital lease assets must be depreciated by the lessee over the life of the lease agreement. Capital lease payments must be separated into interest expense and reduction of principal using the effective interest method.
11. **LO 8** Long-term liabilities represent methods of financing. Therefore, changes in the balances of long-term liability accounts should be reflected in the Financing Activities category of the statement of cash flows.
12. **LO 9** There are many differences between the accounting for tax purposes and the accounting for financial reporting purposes. Permanent differences occur when an item affects one calculation but never affects the other. Temporary differences affect both book and tax calculations but not in the same time period. (Appendix 10A)
13. **LO 9** The amount of tax payable is calculated using the accounting method chosen for tax purposes. The amount of tax expense is calculated using the accounting method chosen for financial reporting purposes. The Deferred Tax account reconciles the differences between tax expense and tax payable. It reflects all of the temporary differences times the tax rate. Deferred taxes is a controversial item on the balance sheet, raising questions as to whether it is a true liability. (Appendix 10A)
14. **LO 10** Pensions represent an obligation to compensate retired employees for service performed while employed. (Appendix 10A)
15. **LO 10** Pension expense is represented on the income statement and is calculated on the basis of several complex components that have been specified by the FASB. (Appendix 10A)
16. **LO 10** Pension expense does not represent the amount of cash paid by the employer to the pension fund. The cash payment is referred to as the *funding payment.* The Accrued Pension account is recorded as the difference between the amount of pension expense and the amount of the funding. (Appendix 10A)
17. **LO 10** The required footnote information on pensions can be used to evaluate the funding status of a firm's pension plan. If the amount of assets in the pension fund exceeds the pension obligation, the fund is considered to be overfunded, generally indicating that it is healthy and well managed. An overfunded plan is an example of an "off-balance-sheet" asset that an investor can count toward the value of the company's stock. (Appendix 10A)

KEY TERMS QUIZ

Read each definition below and then write the number of that definition in the blank beside the appropriate term it defines. The solution appears at the end of the chapter.

5 **Long-term liability**
1 **Face value**
7 **Debenture bonds**
2 **Serial bonds**
9 **Callable bonds**
3 **Face rate of interest**
12 **Market rate of interest**
4 **Bond issue price**
6 **Premium**
8 **Discount**
10 **Effective interest method of amortization**
11 **Carrying value**

13 Gain or loss on redemption
15 Operating lease
17 Capital lease
19 Deferred tax (Appendix 10A)
20 Permanent difference (Appendix 10A)
18 Temporary difference (Appendix 10A)
21 Pension (Appendix 10A)
16 Funding payment (Appendix 10A)
22 Accrued pension cost (Appendix 10A)
23 Accumulated benefit obligation (ABO) (Appendix 10A)
14 Projected benefit obligation (PBO) (Appendix 10A)

1. The principal amount of the bond as stated on the bond certificate.
2. Bonds that do not all have the same due date. A portion of the bonds comes due each time period.
3. The interest rate stated on the bond certificate. It is also called the *nominal* or *coupon rate*.
4. The total of the present value of the cash flows produced by a bond. It is calculated as the present value of the annuity of interest payments plus the present value of the principal.
5. An obligation that will not be satisfied within one year.
6. The excess of the issue price over the face value of bonds. It occurs when the face rate on the bonds exceeds the market rate.
7. Bonds that are backed by the general creditworthiness of the issuer and are not backed by specific collateral.
8. The excess of the face value of bonds over the issue price. It occurs when the market rate on the bonds exceeds the face rate.
9. Bonds that may be redeemed or retired before their specified due date.
10. The process of transferring a portion of premium or discount to interest expense. This method transfers an amount resulting in a constant effective interest rate.
11. The face value of a bond plus the amount of unamortized premium or minus the amount of unamortized discount.
12. The interest rate that bondholders could obtain by investing in other bonds that are similar to the issuing firm's bonds.
13. The difference between the carrying value and the redemption price at the time bonds are redeemed. This amount is presented as an income statement account.
14. A measure of the amount owed to employees for pensions if estimates of future salary increases are incorporated.
15. A lease that does not meet any of four criteria and is not recorded by the lessee.
16. A payment made by the employer to the pension fund or its trustee.
17. A lease that meets one or more of four criteria and is recorded as an asset by the lessee.
18. A difference between the accounting for tax purposes and the accounting for financial reporting purposes. This type of difference affects both book and tax calculations but not in the same time period.
19. The account used to reconcile the difference between the amount recorded as income tax expense and the amount that is payable as income tax.
20. A difference between the accounting for tax purposes and the accounting for financial reporting purposes. This type of difference occurs when an item affects one set of calculations but never affects the other set.
21. An obligation to pay retired employees as compensation for service performed while employed.
22. An account that represents the difference between the amount of pension recorded as an expense and the amount of the funding payment made to the pension fund.
23. A measure of the amount owed to employees for pensions if the employees retire at their existing salary levels.

Alternate Terms

Accumulated Benefit Obligation ABO
Bond Face Value Bond par value
Bonds Payable Notes payable
Bond Retirement Extinguishment of bonds
Carrying Value of Bond Book value of bond
Effective Interest Amortization Interest method of amortization
Face Rate of Interest Stated rate or nominal rate or coupon rate of interest
Long-Term Liabilities Noncurrent liabilities
Market Rate of Interest Yield or effective rate of interest
Postretirement Costs Other postemployment benefits
Projected Benefit Obligation PBO
Redemption Price Reacquisition price
Temporary Difference Timing difference

Questions

1. Which interest rate, the face rate or the market rate, should be used when calculating the issue price of a bond? Why?
2. What is the tax advantage that companies experience when bonds are issued instead of stock?

3. Does the issuance of bonds at a premium indicate that the face rate is higher or lower than the market rate of interest?

4. How does the effective interest method of amortization result in a constant rate of interest?

5. What is the meaning of the following sentence: "Amortization affects the amount of interest expense"? How does amortization of premium affect the amount of interest expense? How does amortization of discount affect the amount of interest expense?

6. Does amortization of a premium increase or decrease the bond carrying value? Does amortization of a discount increase or decrease the bond carrying value?

7. Is there always a gain or loss when bonds are redeemed? How is the gain or loss calculated?

8. Why is it important to show gains or losses on bond redemption separately on the income statement as an extraordinary item?

9. What are the reasons that not all leases are accounted for in the same manner? Do you think it would be possible to develop a new accounting rule that would treat all leases in the same manner?

10. What is the meaning of the term *off-balance-sheet financing?* Why do some firms want to engage in off-balance-sheet transactions?

11. What are the effects on the financial statements if a lease is considered an operating rather than a capital lease?

12. Should depreciation be reported on leased assets? If so, over what period of time should depreciation occur?

13. Why do firms have a Deferred Tax account? Where should that account be shown on the financial statements? (Appendix 10A)

14. How can you determine whether an item should reflect a permanent or a temporary difference when calculating the deferred tax amount? (Appendix 10A)

15. Does the amount of income tax expense presented on the income statement represent the amount of tax actually paid? Why or why not? (Appendix 10A)

16. When an employer has a pension plan for employees, what information is shown on the financial statements concerning the pension plan? (Appendix 10A)

17. How can you determine whether a pension plan is overfunded or underfunded? (Appendix 10A)

18. What is the difference between the two measures of a pension plan's obligation, the projected benefit obligation and the accumulated benefit obligation? (Appendix 10A)

19. Do you agree with this statement: "All liabilities could be legally enforced in a court of law"? (Appendix 10A)

Exercises

LO 2 Exercise 10-1 Relationships

The following components are computed annually when a bond is issued for other than its face value:

- Cash interest payment
- Interest expense
- Amortization of discount/premium
- Carrying value of bond

Required

State whether each component will increase (I), decrease (D), or remain constant (C) as the bond approaches maturity, given the following situations:

1. Issued at a discount.
2. Issued at a premium.

LO 3 Exercise 10-2 Issue Price

Youngblood Inc. plans to issue $500,000 face value bonds with a stated interest rate of 8%. They will mature in 10 years. Interest will be paid semiannually. At the date of issuance, assume the market rate is (a) 8%, (b) 6%, and (c) 10%.

Required

For each market interest rate, answer the following questions:

1. What is the amount due at maturity?
2. How much cash interest will be paid every six months?
3. At what price will the bond be issued?

LO 3 Exercise 10-3 Issue Price

← Issue price

The following terms relate to independent bond issues:

a. 500 bonds; $1,000 face value; 8% stated rate; 5 years; annual interest payments

b. 500 bonds; $1,000 face value; 8% stated rate; 5 years; semiannual interest payments

c. 800 bonds; $1,000 face value; 8% stated rate; 10 years; semiannual interest payments

d. 2,000 bonds; $500 face value; 12% stated rate; 15 years; semiannual interest payments

Required

Assuming the market rate of interest is 10%, calculate the selling price for each bond issue.

LO 4 Exercise 10-4 Impact of Two Bond Alternatives

Yung Chong Company wants to issue 100 bonds, $1,000 face value, in January. The bonds will have a 10-year life and pay interest annually. The market rate of interest on January 1 will be 9%. Yung Chong is considering two alternative bond issues: (a) bonds with a face rate of 8% and (b) bonds with a face rate of 10%.

Required

1. Could the company save money by issuing bonds with an 8% face rate? If it chooses alternative (a), what would be the interest cost as a percentage?
2. Could the company benefit by issuing bonds with a 10% face rate? If it chooses alternative (b), what would be the interest cost as a percentage?

LO 6 Exercise 10-5 Redemption of Bonds

Reynolds Corporation issued $75,000 face value bonds at a discount of $2,500. The bonds contain a call price of 103. Reynolds decides to redeem the bonds early when the unamortized discount is $1,750.

Required

1. Calculate Reynolds Corporation's gain or loss on the early redemption of the bonds.
2. Describe how the gain or loss would be reported on the income statement and in the notes to the financial statements.

LO 6 Exercise 10-6 Redemption of a Bond at Maturity

On March 31, 2001, Sammonds Inc. issued $250,000 face value bonds at a discount of $7,000. The bonds were retired at their maturity date, March 31, 2011.

Required

Assuming the last interest payment and the amortization of discount have already been recorded, calculate the gain or loss on the redemption of the bonds on March 31, 2011. Prepare the journal entry to record the redemption of the bonds.

LO 7 Exercise 10-7 Leased Asset

Hopper Corporation signed a 10-year capital lease on January 1, 2001. The lease requires annual payments of $8,000 every December 31.

Required

1. Assuming an interest rate of 9%, calculate the present value of the minimum lease payments.
2. Explain why the value of the leased asset and the accompanying lease obligation are not initially reported on the balance sheet at $80,000.

LO 7 Exercise 10-8 Financial Statement Impact of a Lease

Benjamin's Warehouse signed a six-year capital lease on January 1, 2001, with payments due every December 31. Interest is calculated annually at 10 percent, and the present value of the minimum lease payments is $13,065.

Required

1. Calculate the amount of the annual payment that Benjamin's must make every December 31.
2. Calculate the amount of the lease obligation that would be presented on the December 31, 2002, balance sheet (after two lease payments have been made).

LO 7 Exercise 10-9 Leased Assets

Koffman and Sons signed a four-year lease for a forklift on January 1, 2001. Annual lease payments of $1,510, based on an interest rate of 8%, are to be made every December 31, beginning with December 31, 2001.

Required

1. Assume the lease is treated as an operating lease.
   - **a.** Will the value of the forklift appear on Koffman's balance sheet?
   - **b.** What account will indicate lease payments have been made?
2. Assume the lease is treated as a capital lease.
   - **a.** Prepare any journal entries needed when the lease is signed. Explain why the value of the leased asset is not recorded at $6,040 ($1,510 × 4).
   - **b.** Prepare the journal entry to record the first lease payment on December 31, 2001.
   - **c.** Prepare the adjusting entry to record depreciation expense on December 31, 2001.
   - **d.** At what amount would the lease obligation be presented on the balance sheet as of December 31, 2001?

LO 8 **Exercise 10-10** Impact of Transactions Involving Bonds on Statement of Cash Flows

From the following list, identify each item as operating (O), investing (I), financing (F), or not separately reported on the statement of cash flows (N).

______ Proceeds from issuance of bonds payable

______ Interest expense

______ Redemption of bonds payable at maturity

LO 8 **Exercise 10-11** Impact of Transactions Involving Capital Leases on Statement of Cash Flows

Assume that Garnett Corporation signs a lease agreement with Duncan Company to lease a piece of equipment and determines that the lease should be treated as a capital lease. Garnett records a leased asset in the amount of $53,400 and a lease obligation in the same amount on its balance sheet.

Required

1. Indicate how this transaction would be reported on Garnett's statement of cash flows.
2. From the following list of transactions relating to this lease, identify each item as operating (O), investing (I), financing (F), or not separately reported on the statement of cash flows (N).

   ______ Reduction of lease obligation (principal portion of lease payment)

   ______ Interest expense

   ______ Depreciation expense—leased assets

LO 8 **Exercise 10-12** Impact of Transactions Involving Tax Liabilities on Statement of Cash Flows

From the following list, identify each item as operating (O), investing (I), financing (F), or not separately reported on the statement of cash flows (N). For items identified as operating, indicate whether the related amount would be added to or deducted from net income in determining the cash flows from operating activities.

______ Decrease in taxes payable

______ Increase in deferred taxes

LO 9 **Exercise 10-13** Temporary and Permanent Differences (Appendix 10A)

Madden Corporation wants to determine the amount of deferred tax that should be reported on its 2001 financial statements. It has compiled a list of differences between the accounting conducted for tax purposes and the accounting used for financial reporting (book) purposes.

Required

For each of the following items, indicate whether the difference should be classified as a permanent or a temporary difference.

1. During 2001, Madden received interest on state bonds purchased as an investment. The interest can be treated as tax-exempt interest for tax purposes.
2. During 2001, Madden paid for a life insurance premium on two key executives. Madden's accountant has indicated that the amount of the premium cannot be deducted for income tax purposes.

3. During December 2001, Madden received money for renting a building to a tenant. Madden must report the rent as income on its 2001 tax form. For book purposes, however, the rent will be considered income on the 2002 income statement.
4. Madden owns several pieces of equipment that it depreciates using the straight-line method for book purposes. An accelerated method of depreciation is used for tax purposes, however.
5. Madden offers a warranty on the product it sells. The corporation records the expense of the warranty repair costs in the year the product is sold (the accrual method) for book purposes. For tax purposes, however, Madden is not allowed to deduct the expense until the period when the product is repaired.
6. During 2001, Madden was assessed a large fine by the federal government for polluting the environment. Madden's accountant has indicated that the fine cannot be deducted as an expense for income tax purposes.

LO 9 **Exercise 10-14** Deferred Tax (Appendix 10A)
On January 1, 2001 Kunkel Corporation purchased an asset for $32,000. Assume this is the only asset owned by the corporation. Kunkel has decided to use the straight-line method to depreciate it. For tax purposes, it will be depreciated over three years. It will be depreciated over five years, however, for the financial statements provided to stockholders. Assume that Kunkel Corporation is subject to a 40% tax rate.

Required

Calculate the balance that should be reflected in the Deferred Tax account for Kunkel Corporation for each year 2001 through 2005.

LO 10 **Exercise 10-15** Pension Analysis (Appendix 10A)
The following information was extracted from a footnote found in the 2001 annual report of a company.

Plan Assets	$2.6 billion
Accumulated Benefit Obligation	$1.7 billion
Projected Benefit Obligation	$2.1 billion

Required

1. Determine whether the pension plan is overfunded or underfunded.
2. Explain what your response to part **1** implies about the ability of the plan to provide benefits to future retirees.

Multi-Concept Exercises

LO 4, 5 **Exercise 10-16** Issuance of a Bond at Face Value
On January 1, 2001, Whitefeather Industries issued 300, $1,000 face value bonds. The bonds have a five-year life and pay interest at the rate of 10%. Interest is paid semiannually on July 1 and January 1. The market rate of interest on January 1 was 10%.

Required

1. Calculate the issue price of the bonds and record the issuance of the bonds on January 1, 2001.
2. Explain how the issue price would have been affected if the market rate of interest had been higher than 10%.
3. Prepare the journal entry to record the payment of interest on July 1, 2001.
4. Prepare the journal to record the accrual of interest on December 31, 2001.

LO 4, 5 **Exercise 10-17** Impact of a Discount
Berol Corporation sold 20-year bonds on January 1, 2001. The face value of the bonds was $100,000, and they carry a 9% stated rate of interest, which is paid on December 31 of every year. Berol received $91,526 in return for the issuance of the bonds when the market rate was 10%. Any premium or discount is amortized using the effective interest method.

Required

1. Prepare the journal entry to record the sale of the bonds on January 1, 2001, and the proper balance sheet presentation on this date.

2. Prepare the journal entry to record interest expense on December 31, 2001, and the proper balance sheet presentation on this date.
3. Explain why it was necessary for Berol to issue the bonds for only $91,526 rather than $100,000.

LO 4, 5 Exercise 10-18 Impact of a Premium

Assume the same set of facts for Berol Corporation as in Exercise 10-17 except that it received $109,862 in return for the issuance of the bonds when the market rate was 8%.

Required

1. Prepare the journal entry to record the sale of the bonds on January 1, 2001, and the proper balance sheet presentation on this date.
2. Prepare the journal entry to record interest expense on December 31, 2001, and the proper balance sheet presentation on this date.
3. Explain why the company was able to issue the bonds for $109,862 rather than for the face amount.

PROBLEMS

LO 3 Problem 10-1 Factors That Affect the Bond Issue Price

Becca Company is considering the issue of $100,000 face value, 10-year term bonds. The bonds will pay 6% interest each December 31. The current market rate is 6%; therefore the bonds will be issued at face value.

Required

1. For each of the following independent situations, indicate whether you believe that the company will receive a premium on the bonds or will issue them at a discount or at face value. Without using numbers, explain your position.
   a. Interest is paid semiannually instead of annually.
   b. Assume instead that the market rate of interest is 7%; the nominal rate is still 6%.
2. For each situation in part **1**, prove your statement by determining the issue price of the bonds given the changes in parts **a** and **b.**

LO 5 Problem 10-2 Amortization of Discount

Stacy Company issued five-year, 10% bonds with face value of $10,000 on January 1, 2001. Interest is paid annually on December 31. The market rate of interest on this date is 12%, and Stacy Company receives proceeds of $9,275 on the bond issuance.

Required

1. Prepare a five-year table (similar to Exhibit 10-4) to amortize the discount using the effective interest method.
2. What is the total interest expense over the life of the bonds? cash interest payment? discount amortization?
3. Prepare the journal entry for the payment of interest and the amortization of discount on December 31, 2003 (the third year), and determine the balance sheet presentation of the bonds on that date.

LO 5 Problem 10-3 Amortization of Premium

Assume the same set of facts for Stacy Company as in Problem 10-2 except that the market rate of interest of January 1, 2001, is 8% and the proceeds from the bond issuance equal $10,803.

Required

1. Prepare a five-year table (similar to Exhibit 10-5) to amortize the premium using the effective interest method.
2. What is the total interest expense over the life of the bonds? cash interest payment? premium amortization?
3. Prepare the journal entry for the payment of interest and the amortization of premium on December 31, 2003 (the third year), and determine the balance sheet presentation of the bonds on that date.

LO 6 Problem 10-4 Redemption of Bonds

McGee Company issued $200,000 face value bonds at a premium of $4,500. The bonds contain a call provision of 101. McGee decides to redeem the bonds, due to a significant decline in interest rates. On that date, McGee had amortized only $1,000 of the premium.

Required

1. Calculate the gain or loss on the early redemption of the bonds.
2. Calculate the gain or loss on the redemption, assuming that the call provision is 103 instead of 101.
3. Indicate where the gain or loss should be presented on the financial statements.
4. Why do you suppose the call price is normally higher than 100?

LO 7 Problem 10-5 Financial Statement Impact of a Lease

On January 1, 2001, Muske Trucking Company leased a semitractor and trailer for five years. Annual payments of $28,300 are to be made every December 31, beginning December 31, 2001. Interest expense is based on a rate of 8%. The present value of the minimum lease payments is $113,000 and has been determined to be greater than 90% of the fair market value of the asset on January 1, 2001. Muske uses straight-line depreciation on all assets.

Required

1. Prepare a table similar to Exhibit 10-7 to show the five-year amortization of the lease obligation.
2. Prepare the journal entry for the lease transaction on January 1, 2001.
3. Prepare all necessary journal entries on December 31, 2002 (the second year of the lease).
4. Prepare the balance sheet presentation as of December 31, 2002, for the leased asset and the lease obligation.

LO 9 Problem 10-6 Deferred Tax (Appendix 10A)

Erinn Corporation has compiled its 2001 financial statements. Included in the Long-Term Liabilities category of the balance sheet are the following amounts:

	2001	2000
Deferred Tax	$180	$100

Included in the income statement are the following amounts related to income taxes:

	2001	2000
Income before Tax	$500	$400
Tax Expense	$200	$160
Net Income	$300	$240

In the footnotes that accompany the 2001 statement are the following amounts:

	2001
Current Provision for Tax	$120
Deferred Portion	80

Required

1. Prepare the journal entry in 2001 for income tax expense, deferred tax, and income tax payable.
2. Assume that a stockholder has inquired about the meaning of the numbers recorded and disclosed about deferred tax. Explain why the Deferred Tax liability account exists. Also, what do the terms *current provision* and *deferred portion* mean? Why is the deferred amount in the footnote $80 when the deferred amount on the 2001 balance sheet is $180?

LO 9 Problem 10-7 Deferred Tax Calculations (Appendix 10A)

Wyhowski Inc. reported income from operations, before taxes, for 1999–2001 as follows:

1999	$210,000
2000	240,000
2001	280,000

When calculating income, Wyhowski deducted depreciation on plant equipment. The equipment was purchased January 1, 1999 at a cost of $88,000. The equipment is expected to last three years and have $8,000 salvage value. Wyhowski uses straight-line depreciation for book purposes. For tax purposes, depreciation on the equipment is $50,000 in 1999, $20,000 in 2000, and $10,000 in 2001. Wyhowski's tax rate is 35%.

Required

1. How much did Wyhowski pay in income tax each year?
2. How much income tax expense did Wyhowski record each year?
3. What is the balance in the Deferred Income Tax account at the end of 1999, 2000, and 2001?

LO 10 Problem 10-8 Financial Statement Impact of a Pension (Appendix 10A)
Smith Financial Corporation prepared the following schedule relating to its pension expense and pension-funding payment for the years 1999 through 2001.

Year	Expense	Payment
1999	$100,000	$ 90,000
2000	85,000	105,000
2001	112,000	100,000

At the beginning of 1999, the Prepaid/Accrued Pension Cost account was reported on the balance sheet as an asset with a balance of $4,000.

Required

1. Prepare the journal entries to record Smith Financial Corporation's pension expense for 1999, 2000, and 2001.
2. Calculate the balance in the Prepaid/Accrued Pension Cost account at the end of 2001. Does this represent an asset or a liability?
3. Explain the effects that pension expense, the funding payment, and the balance in the Prepaid/Accrued Pension Cost account have on the 2001 income statement and balance sheet.

Multi-Concept Problems

LO 4, 6 Problem 10-9 Bond Transactions
Brand Company issued $1,000,000 face value, eight-year, 12% bonds on April 1, 2001, when the market rate of interest was 12%. Interest payments are due every October 1 and April 1. Brand uses a calendar year-end.

Required

1. Prepare the journal entry to record the issuance of the bonds on April 1, 2001.
2. Prepare the journal entry to record the interest payment on October 1, 2001.
3. Explain why additional interest must be recorded on December 31, 2001. What impact does this have on the amounts paid on April 1, 2002?
4. Determine the total cash inflows and outflows that occurred on the bonds over the eight-year life.

LO 1, 9, 10 Problem 10-10 Partial Classified Balance Sheet for Tribune Company
The following items, listed alphabetically, appear on Tribune Company's consolidated balance sheet at December 31, 1998 (in thousands). The information in parentheses was added to aid in your understanding.

www.tribune.com

Accounts payable	$ 115,708
Accrued liabilities	151,347
Compensation and other obligations (due after 1999)	164,690
Contracts payable for broadcast rights (the related payments are due during 1999)	260,264
Contracts payable for broadcast rights (the related payments are due after 1999)	268,099
Deferred income	559,907

Deferred income taxes (Long-term)	$ 701,778
Employee compensation and benefits	114,202
Income taxes	59,607
Long-term debt due within one year	29,905
Long-term debt (less portions due within one year)	1,616,256

Required

1. Prepare the Current Liabilities and Long-Term Liabilities sections of Tribune Company's classified balance sheet at December 31, 1998.
2. Tribune Company had total liabilities of $2,951,550 and total shareholders' equity of $1,826,004 at December 31, 1997. Total stockholders' equity amounted to $2,356,617 at December 31, 1998. (All amounts are in thousands.) Compute the Tribune Company's debt-to-equity ratio at December 31, 1998 and 1997. As an investor, how would you react to the change in this ratio?
3. What other related ratios would the company's lenders use to assess the company? What do these ratios measure?

ALTERNATE PROBLEMS

LO 3 **Problem 10-1A** Factors That Affect the Bond Issue Price

Rivera Inc. is considering the issuance of $500,000 face value, 10-year term bonds. The bonds will pay 5% interest each December 31. The current market rate is 5%; therefore, the bonds will be issued at face value.

Required

1. For each of the following independent situations, indicate whether you believe that the company will receive a premium on the bonds or will issue them at a discount or at face value. Without using numbers, explain your position.
   a. Interest is paid semiannually instead of annually.
   b. Assume instead that the market rate of interest is 4%; the nominal rate is still 5%.
2. For each situation in part **1,** prove your statement by determining the issue price of the bonds given the changes in parts **a** and **b.**

LO 5 **Problem 10-2A** Amortization of Discount

Ortega Company issued five-year, 5% bonds with face value of $50,000 on January 1, 2001. Interest is paid annually on December 31. The market rate of interest on this date is 8%, and Ortega Company receives proceeds of $44,011 on the bond issuance.

Required

1. Prepare a five-year table (similar to Exhibit 10-4) to amortize the discount using the effective interest method.
2. What is the total interest expense over the life of the bonds? cash interest payment? discount amortization?
3. Prepare the journal entry to record interest expense on December 31, 2003 (the third year), and the balance sheet presentation of the bonds on that date.

LO 5 **Problem 10-3A** Amortization of Premium

Assume the same set of facts for Ortega Company as in Problem 10-2A except that the market rate of interest of January 1, 2001, is 4% and the proceeds from the bond issuance equal $52,230.

Required

1. Prepare a five-year table (similar to Exhibit 10-5) to amortize the premium using the effective interest method.
2. What is the total interest expense over the life of the bonds? cash interest payment? premium amortization?

3. Prepare the journal entry to record interest expense on December 31, 2003 (the third year), and the balance sheet presentation of the bonds on that date.

LO 6 Problem 10-4A Redemption of Bonds
Elliot Company issued $100,000 face value bonds at a premium of $5,500. The bonds contain a call provision of 101. Elliot decides to redeem the bonds, due to a significant decline in interest rates. On that date, Elliot has amortized only $2,000 of the premium.

Required

1. Calculate the gain or loss on the early redemption of the bonds.
2. Calculate the gain or loss on the redemption, assuming that the call provision is 104 instead of 101.
3. Indicate how the gain or loss would be reported on the income statement and in the notes to the financial statements.
4. Why do you suppose that the call price of the bonds is normally an amount higher than 100?

LO 7 Problem 10-5A Financial Statement Impact of a Lease
On January 1, 2001, Kiger Manufacturing Company leased a factory machine for six years. Annual payments of $21,980 are to be made every December 31, beginning December 31, 2001. Interest expense is based on a rate of 9%. The present value of the minimum lease payments is $98,600 and has been determined to be greater than 90% of the fair market value of the machine on January 1, 2001. Kiger uses straight-line depreciation on all assets.

Required

1. Prepare a table similar to Exhibit 10-7 to show the six-year amortization of the lease obligation.
2. Prepare the journal entry to record the signing of the lease on January 1, 2001.
3. Prepare all journal entries necessary on December 31, 2002 (the second year of the lease).
4. Prepare the balance sheet presentation as of December 31, 2002, for the leased asset and the lease obligation.

LO 9 Problem 10-6A Deferred Tax (Appendix 10A)
Thad Corporation has compiled its 2001 financial statements. Included in the Long-Term Liabilities category of the balance sheet are the following amounts:

	2001	**2000**
Deferred Tax	$180	$200

Included in the income statement are the following amounts related to income taxes:

	2001	**2000**
Income before Tax	$500	$400
Tax Expense	100	150
Net Income	$400	$250

Required

1. Prepare the journal entry recorded in 2001 for income tax expense, deferred tax, and income tax payable.
2. Assume that a stockholder has inquired about the meaning of the numbers recorded. Explain why the Deferred Tax liability account exists.

LO 9 Problem 10-7A Deferred Tax Calculations (Appendix 10A)
Clemente Inc. has reported income for book purposes as follows for the past three years:

(in Thousands)	**Year 1**	**Year 2**	**Year 3**
Income before Taxes	$120	$120	$120

Clemente has identified two items that are treated differently in the financial records and in the tax records. The first one is interest income on municipal bonds, which is recognized on the financial reports to the extent of $5,000 each year but does not show up as a revenue item on the company's tax return. The other item is equipment that is depreciated using the straight-line method, at the rate of $20,000 each year, for financial accounting but is depreciated for tax purposes at the rate of $30,000 in Year 1, $20,000 in Year 2, and $10,000 in Year 3.

Required

1. Determine the amount of cash paid for income taxes each year by Clemente. Assume that a 40% tax rate applies to all three years.
2. Calculate the balance in the Deferred Tax account at the end of Years 1, 2, and 3. How does this account appear on the balance sheet?

LO 10 Problem 10-8A Financial Statement Impact of a Pension (Appendix 10A)
Premier Consulting Corporation prepared the following schedule relating to its pension expense and pension-funding payment for the years 1999 through 2001:

Year	Expense	Payment
1999	$100,000	$110,000
2000	85,000	80,000
2001	112,000	100,000

At the beginning of 1999, the Prepaid/Accrued Pension Cost account was reported on the balance sheet as an asset with a balance of $5,000.

Required

1. Prepare the journal entries to record Premier Consulting Corporation's pension expense for 1999, 2000, and 2001.
2. Calculate the balance in the Prepaid/Accrued Pension Cost account at the end of 2001.
3. Explain the effects that pension expense, the funding payment, and the balance in the Prepaid/Accrued Pension Cost account have on the 2001 income statement and balance sheet.

Alternate Multi-Concept Problems

LO 4, 6 Problem 10-9A Financial Statement Impact of a Bond
Worthington Company issued $1,000,000 face value, six-year, 10% bonds on July 1, 2001, when the market rate of interest was 12%. Interest payments are due every July 1 and January 1. Worthington uses a calendar year-end.

Required

1. Prepare the journal entry to record the issuance of the bonds on July 1, 2001.
2. Prepare the adjusting journal entry on December 31, 2001, to accrue interest expense.
3. Prepare the journal entry to record the interest payment on January 1, 2002.
4. Prepare the journal entry to record the retirement of the bonds on the maturity date.

LO 1, 9, 10 Problem 10-10A Partial Classified Balance Sheet for Boeing

www.boeing.com

The following items appear on the consolidated balance sheet of Boeing Inc. at December 31, 1998 (in millions). The information in parentheses was added to aid in your understanding.

Accounts payable	$10,733
Accrued healthcare costs	4,813
Advances from customers	1,251
Current portion of long-term debt	869
Income tax payable	569
Long-term debt	6,103

Required

1. Prepare the Current Liabilities and Long-Term Liabilities sections of Boeing's classified balance sheet at December 31, 1998.
2. Boeing had total liabilities of $25,071 and total shareholders' equity of $12,953 at December 31, 1997. Total stockholders' equity amounted to $12,316 at December 31, 1998. (All amounts are in

millions.) Compute Boeing's debt-to-equity ratio at December 31, 1998 and 1997. As an investor, how would you react to the change in this ratio?

3. What other related ratios would the company's lenders use to assess the company? What do these ratios measure?

CASES

Reading and Interpreting Financial Statements

LO 1, 7 Case 10-1 Reading and Interpreting Ben & Jerry's Balance Sheet

Refer to the financial statements included in Ben & Jerry's annual report. www.benjerry.com

Required

1. What is the total amount of long-term liabilities for Ben & Jerry's as of December 31, 1998?
2. Ben & Jerry's has an account titled Long-Term Debt and Capital Lease Obligations. If that account is a long-term item, why is a portion shown in the current liability category?
3. Footnote 6 indicates that there are two notes payable (series A and B) in the long-term debt category. When are the principal and interest payments due, and what is the interest rate of each note? What other types of debt are included as long-term?
4. Assume that you are an analyst who must review Ben & Jerry's financial condition. Assume that Ben & Jerry's has indicated that it plans to issue debt of nearly $10 million. Your boss is concerned that the amount of long-term debt may be excessive and has asked you to review the financial statements. Prepare a memo to your boss with a response to her concerns. Include in the memo a discussion of the factors that you considered to determine whether the amount of long-term debt is too high.
5. Are any assets pledged as collateral for long-term debt? If so, how much has been pledged?

LO 1, 7 Case 10-2 Reading and Interpreting Gateway's Balance Sheet

Refer to the financial statements included in Gateway's annual report. www.gateway.com

Required

1. What is the total amount of long-term liabilities for Gateway as of December 31, 1998?
2. Gateway has an account for Long-Term Obligations, but a portion of the account is shown in the current liability category. Why?
3. Did the account titled Long-term Obligations, Net of Current Maturities, increase or decrease from 1997 to 1998? What effect would the change have on the cash flows of the company?
4. What factors would you consider to determine if Gateway's long-term debt is too high?

LO 7, 8, 9 Case 10-3 Reading Ben & Jerry's Statement of Cash Flows (Appendix 10A)

Refer to the statement of cash flows in Ben & Jerry's 1998 annual report. www.benjerry.com

Required

1. Ben & Jerry's made repayments of its long-term debt. When payments are made, in which category of the cash flow statement are the payments disclosed?
2. Did the amount of the cash balance increase or decrease in 1998? Was the cash used to repay long-term liabilities?
3. Ben & Jerry's has a Deferred Taxes Income account listed in the Assets category of its balance sheet. Would an increase in that account result in an addition or a subtraction on the statement of cash flows? In which category?

Making Financial Decisions

LO 1 Case 10-4 Making a Loan Decision

Assume that you are a loan officer in charge of reviewing loan applications from potential new clients at a major bank. You are considering an application from Molitor Corporation, which is a fairly new company with a limited credit history. It has provided a balance sheet for its most recent fiscal year as follows:

MOLITOR CORPORATION
BALANCE SHEET
DECEMBER 31, 199X

Assets		**Liabilities**	
Cash	$ 10,000	Accounts payable	$100,000
Receivables	50,000	Notes payable	200,000
Inventory	100,000		
Equipment	500,000		
		Stockholders' Equity	
		Common stock	80,000
		Retained earnings	280,000
Total assets	$660,000	Total liabilities and stockholders' equity	$660,000

Your bank has established certain guidelines that must be met before making a favorable loan recommendation. These include minimum levels for several financial ratios. You are particularly concerned about the bank's policy that loan applicants must have a total-assets-to-debt ratio of at least 2-to-1 to be acceptable. Your initial analysis of Molitor's balance sheet has indicated that the firm has met the minimum total-assets-to-debt ratio requirement. On reading the footnotes that accompany the financial statements, however, you discover the following statement:

> Molitor has engaged in a variety of innovative financial techniques resulting in the acquisition of $200,000 of assets at very favorable rates. The company is obligated to make a series of payments over the next five years to fulfill its commitments in conjunction with these financial instruments. Current generally accepted accounting principles do not require the assets acquired or the related obligations to be reflected on the financial statements.

Required

1. How should this footnote affect your evaluation of Molitor's loan application? Calculate a revised total-assets-to-debt ratio for Molitor.
2. Do you believe that the bank's policy concerning a minimum total-assets-to-debt ratio can be modified to consider financing techniques that are not reflected on the financial statements? Write a statement that expresses your position on this issue.

LO 6 **Case 10-5** Bond Redemption Decision

Armstrong Areo Ace, a flight training school, issued $100,000 of 20-year bonds at face value when the market rate was 10%. The bonds have been outstanding for 10 years. The company pays annual interest on January 1. The current rate for similar bonds is 4%. On January 1, the controller would like to purchase the bonds on the open market, retire the bonds, then issue $100,000 of 10-year bonds to pay 4% annual interest.

Required

Draft a memo to the controller advising him to retire the outstanding bonds and issue new debt. Ignore taxes. (*Hint:* find the selling price of bonds that pay 10% when the market rate is 4%.)

Accounting and Ethics: What Would You Do?

LO 7 **Case 10-6** Determination of Asset Life

Jen Latke is an accountant for Hale's Manufacturing Company. Hale's has entered into an agreement to lease a piece of equipment from EZ Leasing. Jen must decide how to report the lease agreement on Hale's financial statements.

Jen has reviewed the lease contract carefully. She has also reviewed the four lease criteria specified in the accounting rules. She has been able to determine that the lease does not meet three of the criteria. However, she is concerned about the criterion that indicates that if the term of the lease is 75% or more of the life of the property, the lease should be classified as a capital lease. Jen is fully aware that Hale's does not want to record the lease agreement as a capital lease but prefers to show it as a type of off-balance-sheet financing.

Jen's reading of the lease contract indicates that the asset has been leased for seven years. She is unsure of the life of such assets, however, and has consulted two sources to determine it. One of them states that equipment similar to that owned by Hale's is depreciated over nine years. The other, a trade publication of the equipment industry, indicates that equipment of this type will usually last for 12 years.

Required

1. How should Jen report the lease agreement in the financial statements?
2. If Jen decides to present the lease as an off-balance-sheet arrangement, has she acted ethically?

LO 10 **Case 10-7** Overfunded Pension Plan (Appendix 10A)

Witty Company has sponsored a pension plan for employees for several years. Each year Witty has paid cash to the pension fund, and the pension trustee has used that cash to invest in stocks and bonds. Because the trustee has invested wisely, the amount of the pension assets exceeds the accumulated benefit obligation as of December 31, 2001.

The president of Witty Company wants to pay a dividend to the stockholders at the end of 2001. The president believes that it is important to maintain a stable dividend pattern. Unfortunately, the company, though profitable, does not have enough cash on hand to pay a dividend and must find a way to raise the necessary cash if the dividend is declared. Several executives of the company have recommended that assets be withdrawn from the pension fund. They have pointed out that the fund is currently "overfunded." Further, they have stated that a withdrawal of assets will not have an impact on the financial statements because the overfunding is an "off-balance-sheet item."

Required

Comment on the proposal to withdraw assets from the pension fund to pay a dividend to stockholders. Do you believe it is unethical?

Internet Research Case

Case 10-8 Coca-Cola

Sold in over 200 countries, Coca-Cola is the most recognized brand name in the world. Sales of Classic Coke, diet Coke, and Sprite provide the company with the cash necessary to pay off debts.

Conduct a search of the World Wide Web, obtain Coca-Cola's most recent annual report, or use library resources to obtain company information to answer the following:

www.cocacola.com

1. Based on the latest information available, what is the amount of Coca-Cola's long-term debt? How does this compare with the long-term debt in the "Focus on Financial Results" in the opening vignette shown at the start of this chapter?
2. What is the face rate on a Coca-Cola bond currently trading on the bond market? How does that rate compare with the current yield for the same bond?
3. During the past three to six months, has the yield for Coca-Cola's bonds increased or decreased?

Optional Research. Obtain information from the company's Web site to determine recent business activities and international expansion that may have affected the amount of long-term debt used by the company.

Solution to Key Terms Quiz

- 5 Long-term liability (p. 478)
- 1 Face value (p. 478)
- 7 Debenture bonds (p. 480)
- 2 Serial bonds (p. 481)
- 9 Callable bonds (p. 481)
- 3 Face rate of interest (p. 481)
- 12 Market rate of interest (p. 481)
- 4 Bond issue price (p. 482)
- 6 Premium (p. 483)
- 8 Discount (p. 483)
- 10 Effective interest method of amortization (p. 485)
- 11 Carrying value (p. 486)
- 13 Gain or loss on redemption (p. 490)
- 15 Operating lease (p. 493)
- 17 Capital lease (p. 493)
- 19 Deferred tax (p. 503)
- 20 Permanent difference (p. 503)
- 18 Temporary difference (p. 504)
- 21 Pension (p. 505)
- 16 Funding payment (p. 506)
- 22 Accrued pension cost (p. 506)
- 23 Accumulated benefit obligation (ABO) (p. 507)
- 14 Projected benefit obligation (PBO) (p. 507)

Chapter 11

Stockholders' Equity

Study Links

A Look at Previous Chapters

Chapters 9 and 10 covered the current and long-term liability portions of the balance sheet. Liabilities are one source of financing of business activities.

A Look at This Chapter

This chapter examines the other major source of financing available to companies: stock and stock transactions. The discussion centers on the corporate form of organization and the stockholders' equity of corporations. The chapter begins with an overview of the stockholders' equity category of Delta Air Lines and American Airlines (AMR) balance sheets. The impact of stock issuance and repurchase is examined along with the declaration and payment of cash and stock dividends.

A Look at Upcoming Chapters

In Chapter 12 we turn our attention to an expanded discussion of the preparation and use of the statement of cash flows.

Focus on Financial Results

The airline industry is volatile. Pricing deregulation and the growth of hub-and-spoke routing have squeezed many airlines out of business, and the surviving carriers face conflicts between heightened customer expectations and the need to cut costs. That makes it all the more remarkable that Delta Air Lines could boast, in its fiscal-year 1999 annual report, that diluted earnings per share had grown over 150 percent from 1995 to 1999, the company's 70th year.[1]

Building shareholder value contributes to the stockholders' equity portion of Delta's balance sheet, shown here. For the world's most-flown airline, that goal is paramount and shares attention only with finding capital resources to reinvest in the business. How is stockholders' equity built?

For Delta, building value means adopting innovative technology to speed check-in and boarding; developing a customer-service initiative to ensure reliable and courteous service; continually refurbishing and renovating its fleet of planes and ground facilities; purchasing Atlantic Southeast Airlines to improve its strategic position in the newest air-travel market, regional jet service; and entering business partnerships with Air France and Priceline.com. Delta also announced a two-for-one common stock split in November 1998, which doubled the number of shares every stockholder owned and halved the price per share.

[1]Delta Air Lines 1999 Annual Report, p. 26.

Delta Air Lines Partial Balance Sheet

	1999	1998
Employee Stock Ownership Plan Preferred Stock:		
Series B ESOP Convertible Preferred Stock, $1.00 par value, $72.00 stated and liquidation value; issued and outstanding 6,547,495 shares at June 30, 1999 and 6,603,429 shares at June 30, 1998	471	475
Unearned compensation under employee stock ownership plan	(276)	(300)
Total Employee Stock Ownership Plan Preferred Stock	195	175
Shareowners' Equity:		
Common stock, $1.50 par value; authorized 450,000,000 shares; issued 179,763,547 shares at June 30, 1999 and 176,566,178 shares at June 30, 1998	270	265
Additional paid-in capital	3,208	3,034
Retained earnings	2,756	1,687
Accumulated other comprehensive income	149	89
Treasury stock at cost, 41,209,828 shares at June 30, 1999 and 26,115,784 shares at June 30, 1998	(1,935)	(1,052)
Total shareowners' equity	4,448	4,023

The accompanying notes are an integral part of these Consolidated Balance Sheets.

Delta Air Lines 1999 annual report

If you were a Delta stockholder, what information about the stock would you want to learn from Delta's balance sheet? What additional information would you want about the company's plans? Use this chapter to help you develop your answers, and look at Delta's most recent annual report to see whether the stock has continued its good performance since the split.

Learning Objectives

After studying this chapter, you should be able to:

LO 1 Identify the components of the Stockholders' Equity category of the balance sheet and the accounts found in each component. (p. 528)

LO 2 Understand the characteristics of common and preferred stock and the differences between the classes of stock. (p. 533)

LO 3 Determine the financial statement impact when stock is issued for cash or for other consideration. (p. 534)

LO 4 Describe the financial statement impact of stock treated as treasury stock. (p. 535)

LO 5 Compute the amount of cash dividends when a firm has issued both preferred and common stock. (p. 538)

LO 6 Understand the difference between cash and stock dividends and the effect of stock dividends. (p. 539)

LO 7 Determine the difference between stock dividends and stock splits. (p. 541)

LO 8 Understand the statement of stockholders' equity and comprehensive income. (p. 543)

LO 9 Understand how investors use ratios to evaluate owners' equity. (p. 545)

LO 10 Explain the effects that transactions involving stockholders' equity have on the statement of cash flows. (p. 548)

LO 11 Describe the important differences between the sole proprietorship and partnership forms of organization versus the corporate form (Appendix 11A). (p. 554)

An Overview of Stockholders' Equity

Equity as a Source of Financing

Whenever a company needs to raise money, it must choose from the alternative financing sources that are available. Financing can be divided into two general categories: debt (borrowing from banks or other creditors) and equity (issuing stock). The company's management must consider the advantages and disadvantages of each alternative. Exhibit 11-1 indicates a few of the factors that must be considered.

Issuing stock is a very popular method of financing because of its flexibility. It provides advantages for the issuing company and the investors (stockholders). Investors are primarily

Accounting for Your Decisions

You Are the Investor

You have the opportunity to buy a company's bonds that pay 8% interest or the same company's stock. The stock has paid an 8% dividend rate for the last few years. The company is a large, reputable firm and has been profitable during recent times. Should you be indifferent between the two alternatives?

ANS: Interest on bonds is a fixed obligation. Unless the company goes out of business, you can count on receiving the 8% interest if you invest in the bonds. Dividends on stock are not fixed. There is no guarantee that the company will continue to pay 8% as the dividend on your investment. If the company is not profitable, it may decrease the size of the dividend. On the other hand, if the company becomes more profitable, it may pay a larger dividend.

EXHIBIT 11-1 Advantages and Disadvantages of Stock versus Debt Financing

Advantages of Financing with Stock

1. Flexibility → Dividends on stock can be increased in profitable years, reduced when the company is less profitable. Debt interest is fixed. (An advantage for issuing company)

2. Exchanges facilitate trading → Large companies have ready markets for stock through the stock exchanges. (An advantage for issuing company and investors) Sometimes debt is not as widely traded.

3. Return on investment → Stock generally provides a higher return in dividends and in growth than interest on debt. (An advantage for investors)

Disadvantages of Financing with Stock

1. Control → Issuing stock involves giving voting rights to new investors, less control of the company for existing stockholders. (A disadvantage for issuing company)

2. Tax consequences → Interest on debt is tax deductible for the issuing company, dividends on stock are not. (A disadvantage for issuing company)

3. Impact on ratios → Issuing stock decreases several important financial ratios, including earnings per share. (A disadvantage for issuing company)

concerned with the return on their investment. With stock, the return may be in the form of dividends paid to the investors but may also be the price appreciation of the stock. Stock is popular because it generally provides a higher rate of return (but also a higher degree of risk) than can be obtained by creditors who receive interest from lending money. Stock is popular with issuing companies because dividends on stock can be adjusted according to the company's profitability; higher dividends can be paid when the firm is profitable and lower dividends when it is not. Interest on debt financing, on the other hand, is generally fixed and is a legal liability that cannot be adjusted when a company experiences lower profitability.

There are several disadvantages in issuing stock. Stock usually has voting rights, and issuing stock allows new investors to vote. Existing investors may not want to share the control of the company with new stockholders. From the issuing company's viewpoint, there is also a serious tax disadvantage to stock versus debt. As indicated in Chapter 10, interest on debt is tax deductible and results in lower taxes. Dividends on stock, on the other hand, are not tax deductible and do not result in tax savings to the issuing company. Finally, the following sections of this chapter indicate the impact that issuing stock has on the company's financial statements. Issuing stock decreases several important financial ratios, such as earnings per share. Issuing debt does not have a similar effect on the earnings per share ratio.

Management should consider many other factors in deciding between debt and equity financing. The company's goal should be financing the company in a manner that results in the lowest overall cost of capital to the firm. Usually, companies attain that goal by having a reasonable balance of both debt and equity financing.

Stockholders' Equity on the Balance Sheet

The basic accounting equation is often stated as follows:

Assets = Liabilities + Owners' Equity

Owners' equity is viewed as a residual amount. That is, the owners of a corporation have a claim to all assets after the claims represented by liabilities to creditors have been satisfied.

In this chapter, we concentrate on the corporate form of organization and refer to the owners' equity as *stockholders' equity*. Therefore, the basic accounting equation for a corporation can be restated as follows:

Assets = Liabilities + Stockholders' Equity

The stockholders are the owners of a corporation. They have a residual interest in its assets after the claims of all creditors have been satisfied.

The stockholders' equity category of all corporations has two major components or subcategories:

Total Stockholders' Equity = Contributed Capital
+
Retained Earnings

Contributed capital represents the amount the corporation has received from the sale of stock to stockholders. Retained earnings is the amount of net income that the corporation has earned but not paid as dividends. Instead, the corporation retains and reinvests the income.

Although all corporations maintain the two primary categories of contributed capital and retained earnings, within these categories they use a variety of accounts that have several alternative titles. The next section examines two important items: income and dividends, and their impact on the Retained Earnings account.

How Income and Dividends Affect Retained Earnings

From Concept **TO PRACTICE 11.1**

Reading Gateway's Annual Report What was the balance of retained earnings for Gateway at the end of 1998? Did the balance increase from the end of 1997?

The Retained Earnings account plays an important role because it serves as a link between the income statement and the balance sheet. The term *articulated statements* refers to the fact that the information on the income statement is related to the information on the balance sheet. The bridge (or link) between the two statements is the Retained Earnings account. Exhibit 11-2 presents this relationship graphically. As the exhibit indicates, the income statement is used to calculate a company's net income for a given period of time. The amount of the net income is transferred to the statement of retained earnings and is added to the beginning balance of retained earnings (with dividends deducted) to calculate the ending balance of retained earnings. The ending balance of retained earnings is the amount that is portrayed on the balance sheet in the stockholders' equity category. That is why you must always prepare the income statement before you prepare the balance sheet, as you have discovered when developing financial statements in previous chapters of the text.

Identifying the Components of the Stockholders' Equity Section of the Balance Sheet

LO 1 Identify the components of the Stockholders' Equity category of the balance sheet and the accounts found in each component.

www.amrcorp.com

The liabilities and stockholders' equity portion of the balance sheet of AMR Corporation (American Airlines) is provided in Exhibit 11-3. We will focus on the Stockholders' (Shareholders') Equity category of the balance sheet. All corporations, including AMR, begin the Stockholders' Equity category with a list of the firm's contributed capital. In some cases, there are two categories of stock: common stock and preferred stock (the latter is discussed later in this chapter). Common stock normally carries voting rights, and the common stockholders elect the officers of the corporation and establish its by-laws and governing rules. It is not unusual for corporations to have more than one

EXHIBIT 11-2 Retained Earnings Connects the Income Statement and the Balance Sheet

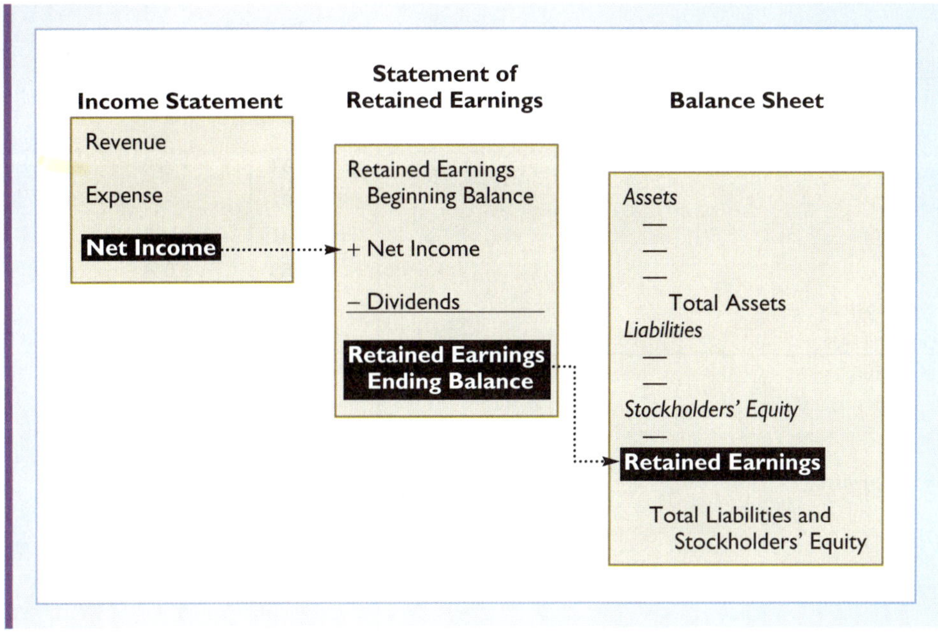

type of common stock, each with different rights or terms. For example, Continental Airlines, one of AMR's competitors, has two classes of common stock listed on its 1998 balance sheet.

www.continental.com

Number of Shares It is important to determine the number of shares of stock for each stock account. Corporate balance sheets report the number of shares in three categories: **authorized, issued,** and **outstanding shares.**

To become incorporated, a business must develop articles of incorporation and apply to the proper state authorities for a corporate charter. The corporation must specify the maximum number of shares that it will be allowed to issue. This maximum number of shares is called the *authorized stock.* A corporation applies for authorization to issue many more shares than it will issue immediately, to allow for future growth and other events that may occur over its long life. For example, AMR Corporation indicates that it has 750,000,000 shares of common stock authorized but that only 182,278,766 shares had been issued as of December 31, 1998.

AUTHORIZED SHARES
The maximum number of shares a corporation may issue as indicated in the corporate charter.

ISSUED SHARES
The number of shares sold or distributed to stockholders.

OUTSTANDING SHARES
The number of shares issued less the number of shares held as treasury stock.

The number of shares *issued* indicates the number of shares that have been sold or transferred to stockholders. The number of shares issued does not necessarily mean, however, that those shares are currently outstanding. The term *outstanding* indicates shares actually in the hands of the stockholders. Shares that have been issued by the corporation and then repurchased are counted as shares issued but not as shares outstanding. Quite often corporations repurchase their own stock as treasury stock (explained in more detail later in this chapter). Treasury stock reduces the number of shares outstanding. The number of AMR's shares of common stock outstanding at December 31, 1998, could be calculated as follows:

Number of shares issued	182,278,766
Less: Treasury stock	20,927,692
Number of shares outstanding	161,351,074

Study Tip

Treasury stock is included in the number of shares issued. It is not part of the number of shares outstanding.

Par Value: The Firm's "Legal Capital" The Stockholders' Equity category of many balance sheets refers to an amount as the *par value* of the stock. For example, AMR's common stock has a par value of $1 per share. **Par value** is an arbitrary amount stated on the face of the stock certificate and represents the legal capital of the corporation.

PAR VALUE
An arbitrary amount that represents the legal capital of the firm.

EXHIBIT 11-3 AMR Corporation's Partial Balance Sheet

(in millions, except shares and par value)	December 31, 1998	1997
Liabilities and Stockholders' Equity		
Current Liabilities		
Accounts payable	**$ 1,152**	$ 1,028
Accrued salaries and wages	**991**	879
Accrued liabilities	**1,131**	1,091
Air traffic liability	**2,163**	2,044
Current maturities of long-term debt	**48**	395
Current obligations under capital leases	**154**	135
Total current liabilities	**5,639**	5,572
Long-Term Debt, Less Current Maturities	**2,436**	2,248
Obligations Under Capital Leases, Less Current Obligations	**1,764**	1,629
Other Liabilities and Credits		
Deferred income taxes	**1,491**	1,112
Deferred gains	**573**	610
Postretirement benefits	**1,649**	1,573
Other liabilities and deferred credits	**2,053**	1,899
	5,766	5,194
Commitments and Contingencies		
Stockholders' Equity		
Common stock - $1 par value; shares authorized: 750,000,000; shares issued: 1998 and 1997 - 182,278,766	**182**	182
Additional paid-in capital	**3,075**	3,104
Treasury shares at cost: 1998 - 20,927,692; 1997 - 9,080,832	**(1,288)**	(485)
Accumulated other comprehensive income	**(4)**	(4)
Retained earnings	**4,733**	3,419
	6,698	6,216
Total Liabilities and Stockholders' Equity	**$ 22,303**	$ 20,859

AMR's contributed capital

Most corporations set the par value of the stock at very low amounts because there are legal difficulties if stock is sold at less than par. Therefore, par value does not indicate the stock's value or the amount that is obtained when it is sold on the stock exchange; it is simply an arbitrary amount that exists to fulfill legal requirements. A company's legal requirement depends on its state of incorporation. Some states do not require corporations to indicate a par value; others require them to designate the *stated value* of the stock. A stated value is accounted for in the same manner as a par value and appears in the Stockholders' Equity category in the same manner as a par value.

The amount of the par value is the amount that is presented in the stock account. That is, the dollar amount in a firm's stock account can be calculated as its par value per share times number of shares issued. For AMR, the dollar amount appearing in the common stock account can be calculated as follows:

$1 Par Value per Share × 182,278,766 Shares Issued =
$182 million (rounded to millions) Balance in the Common Stock Account

Additional Paid-in Capital The dollar amounts of the stock accounts in the Stockholders' Equity category do not indicate the amount that was received when the stock was sold to stockholders. The Common Stock and Preferred Stock accounts indicate only the par value of the stock. When stock is issued for an amount higher than the par value, the excess is reported as **additional paid-in capital.** Several alternative titles are used for this account, including Paid-in Capital in Excess of Par, Capital Surplus (an old term that should no longer be used), and Premium on Stock.

ADDITIONAL PAID-IN CAPITAL The amount received for the issuance of stock in excess of the par value of the stock.

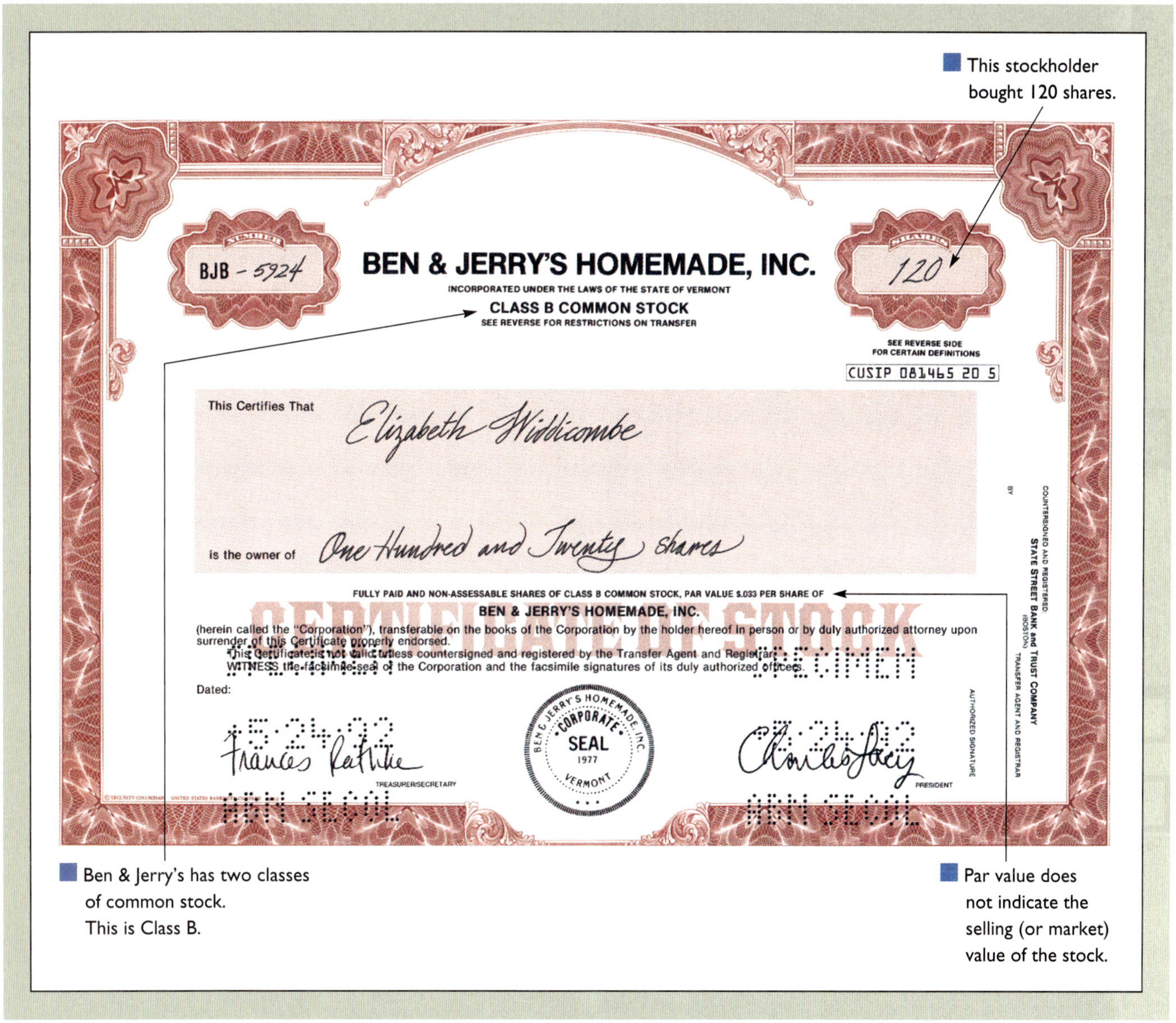

A prospective stockholder may purchase shares and receive certificates, like this one, either directly from the company or through a stockbroker. Usually, a broker purchases shares in its own name for the investor's account—and the investor never sees a certificate.

Regardless of the title, the account represents the amount received in excess of par when stock was issued.

AMR's balance sheet indicates additional paid-in capital of $3,075 million at December 31, 1998. AMR, as well as many other corporations, presents only one amount for additional paid-in capital for all stock transactions. Therefore, we are unable to determine whether the amount resulted from the issuance of common stock or other stock transactions. As a result, it is often impossible to determine the issue price of each category of stock even with a careful analysis of the balance sheet and the accompanying footnotes.

RETAINED EARNINGS Net income that has been made by the corporation but not paid out as dividends.

Retained Earnings: The Amount *Not* Paid as Dividends

Retained earnings represents net income that the firm has earned but has *not* paid as dividends. Remember that retained earnings is an amount that is accumulated over the entire life of the corporation and does not represent the income or dividends for a specific year. For example, the balance of the Retained Earnings account on AMR's balance sheet at December 31, 1998, is $4,733 million. That does not mean that AMR had a net income of this amount in 1998; it simply means that over the life of the corporation, AMR has retained $4,733 million more net income than it paid out as dividends to stockholders.

It is also important to remember that the balance of the Retained Earnings account does not mean that liquid assets of that amount are available to the stockholders. Corporations decide to retain income because they have needs other than paying dividends to stockholders. The needs may include the purchase of assets, the retirement of debt, or other financial needs. Money spent for those needs usually benefits the stockholders in the long run, but liquid assets equal to the balance of the Retained Earnings account are not necessarily available to stockholders. In theory, income should be retained whenever the company can reinvest the money and get a better return within the business than the shareholders can get on their own. In summary, retained earnings is a stockholders' equity account. Although the company's assets have increased, retained earnings does not represent a pool of liquid assets.

www.expedia.com

www.travelocity.com

BUSINESS STRATEGY

Who will control the online travel-booking business? Microsoft hopes to bite off a piece of this huge market with its Web site Expedia, which already receives over 4 million customers a month. "That's a compelling marketplace," says Suzi Levine, an Expedia product manager. Another big player is Travelocity, an online booking service owned by American Airlines.

But these giants face some stiff new competition. Four carriers—Continental, Delta, United, and Northwest—announced late in 1999 that they were joining forces, and pooling a hefty $100 million, to open a new joint Web site in early 2000. Each of the four will continue to maintain its own existing Web site, but the new venture is intended to give them enough clout to capture some of the $29 billion worth of leisure and business travel expected to be booked online annually by 2003.

Part of what fuels the success of online agencies like Expedia and Travelocity are the healthy fees the airlines pay them. United, for instance, paid nearly $250 million in commissions in 1999, and according to industry observers, the airlines "want that money back."

Will their new joint Web site do the job? It's clear the four airlines mean business: they announced their joint venture the day after Expedia's shares went public.

SOURCE: Alex Salkever, "Dogfight in Cyberspace: The Online Travel Biz Heats Up," Business Week Online daily briefing, November 15, 1999, accessed at www.businessweek.com/bwdaily/dnflash/nov1999/nf91115a.htm.

What Is Preferred Stock?

Many companies have a class of stock called *preferred stock.* One of the advantages of preferred stock is the flexibility it provides because its terms and provisions can be tailored to meet the firm's needs. These terms and provisions are detailed in the stock certificate. Generally, preferred stock offers holders a preference to dividends declared by the corporation. That is, if dividends are declared, the preferred stockholders must receive dividends first, before the holders of common stock.

The dividend rate on preferred stock may be stated in two ways. First, it may be stated as a percentage of the stock's par value. For example, if a stock is presented in the balance sheet as $100 par, 7% preferred stock, its dividend rate is $7 per share ($100 times 7%). Second, the dividend may be stated as a per-share amount. For example, a stock may appear in the balance sheet as $100 par, $7 preferred stock, meaning that the dividend rate is $7 per share. Investors in common stock should note the dividend requirements of the preferred shareholder. The greater the obligation to the preferred shareholder, the less desirable the common stock becomes.

Several important provisions of preferred stock relate to the payment of dividends. Some preferred stock issues have a **cumulative feature,** which means that if a dividend is not declared to the preferred stockholders in one year, dividends are considered to be *in arrears.* Before a dividend can be declared to common stockholders in a subsequent period, the preferred stockholders must be paid all dividends in arrears as well as the current year's dividend. The cumulative feature ensures that the preferred stockholders will receive a dividend before one is paid to common stockholders. It does not guarantee a dividend to preferred stockholders, however. There is no legal requirement mandating that a corporation declare a dividend, and preferred stockholders have a legal right to receive a dividend only when it has been declared.

Some preferred stocks have a **participating feature.** Its purpose is to allow the preferred stockholders to receive a dividend in excess of the regular rate when a firm has been particularly profitable and declares an abnormally large dividend. When the participating feature is present and a firm declares a dividend, the preferred stockholders first have a right to the current year's dividend, and then the common stockholders must receive an equal portion (usually based on the par or stated value of the stocks) of the dividend. The participating feature then applies to any dividend declared in excess of the amounts in the first two steps. The preferred stockholders are allowed to share in the excess, normally on the basis of the total par value of the preferred and common stock. The participating feature is explained in more detail in the section of this chapter concerning dividends.

Preferred stock may also be convertible or callable. The **convertible feature** allows the preferred stockholders to convert their stockholdings to common stock. Convertible preferred stock offers stockholders the advantages of the low risk generally associated with preferred stock and the possibility of the higher return that is associated with common stock. The **callable feature** allows the issuing firm to retire the stock after it has been issued. Normally, the call price is specified as a fixed dollar amount. Firms may exercise the call option to eliminate a certain class of preferred stock so that control of the corporation is maintained in the hands of fewer stockholders. The call option also may be exercised when the dividend rate on the preferred stock is too high and other, more cost-effective financing alternatives are available.

Preferred stock is attractive to many investors because it offers a return in the form of a dividend at a level of risk that is lower than that of most common stocks. Usually, the dividend available on preferred stock is more stable from year to year, and as a result, the market price of the stock is also more stable. In fact, if preferred stock carries certain provisions, the stock is very similar to bonds or notes payable. Management must evaluate whether such securities really represent debt and should be presented in the liability category of the balance sheet or whether they represent equity and should be presented in the equity category. Such a decision involves the concept of *substance over form.* That is, a

LO 2 Understand the characteristics of common and preferred stock and the differences between the classes of stock.

From Concept **TO PRACTICE 11.2**

Reading Delta's Annual Report Which financial statements could you look at to identify the different classes of stock issued by Delta? Which classes of stock are issued? How many shares have been issued?

Cumulative feature
The right to dividends in arrears before the current-year dividend is distributed.

Participating feature
Allows preferred stockholders to share on a percentage basis in the distribution of an abnormally large dividend.

Convertible feature
Allows preferred stock to be exchanged for common stock.

Callable feature
Allows the firm to eliminate a class of stock by paying the stockholders a specified amount.

Qwest officials ring the Opening Bell as the first company to be listed on the New York Stock Exchange in the new millenium, on the first day (January 3) of trading in the year 2000.

www.quest.com

company must look not only at the legal form but also at the economic substance of the security to decide whether it is debt or equity.

Issuance of Stock

Stock Issued for Cash

LO 3 Determine the financial statement impact when stock is issued for cash or for other consideration.

Stock may be issued in several different ways. It may be issued for cash or for noncash assets. When stock is issued for cash, the amount of its par value should be reported in the stock account and the amount in excess of par should be reported in an additional paid-in capital account. For example, assume that on July 1 a firm issued 1,000 shares of $10 par common stock for $15 per share. The transaction is recorded as follows:

July 1	Cash	15,000	
	Common Stock		10,000
	Additional Paid-in Capital—Common		5,000
	To record the issuance of 1,000 shares of common stock at $15 per share.		

Assets	=	Liabilities	+	Owners' Equity
+15,000				+10,000
				+5,000

As noted earlier, the Common Stock account and the Additional Paid-in Capital account are both presented in the Stockholders' Equity category of the balance sheet and represent the contributed capital component of the corporation.

If no-par stock is issued, the corporation does not distinguish between common stock and additional paid-in capital. If the firm in the previous example had issued no-par stock on July 1 for $15 per share, the entire amount of $15,000 would be presented in the Common Stock account and would be recorded as follows:

July 1	Cash	15,000	
	Common Stock		15,000
	To record the issuance of 1,000 shares of common stock at $15 per share.		

Assets	=	Liabilities	+	Owners' Equity
+15,000				+15,000

Stock Issued for Noncash Consideration

Occasionally, stock is issued in return for something other than cash. For example, a corporation may issue stock to obtain land or buildings. When such a transaction occurs, the company faces the difficult task of deciding what value to place on the transaction. This is especially difficult when the market values of the elements of the transaction are not known with complete certainty. According to the general guideline, the transaction should be reported at fair market value. Market value may be indicated by the value of the consideration given (stock) or the value of the consideration received (property), whichever can be most readily determined.

Assume that on July 1 a firm issued 500 shares of $10 par preferred stock to acquire a building. The stock is not widely traded, and the current market value of the stock is not evident. The building has recently been appraised by an independent firm as having a market value of $12,000. In this case, the issuance of the stock should be recorded as follows:

July 1	Building	12,000	
	Preferred Stock		5,000
	Additional Paid-in Capital—Preferred		7,000
	To record the issuance of preferred stock for building.		

Assets	=	Liabilities	+	Owners' Equity
+12,000				+5,000
				+7,000

In other situations, the market value of the stock may be more readily determined and should be used as the best measure of the value of the transaction. Market value may be represented by the current stock-market quotation or by a recent cash sale of the stock. The company should attempt to develop the best estimate of the market value of the non-cash transaction and should neither intentionally overstate nor intentionally understate the assets received by the issuance of stock.

What Is Treasury Stock?

LO 4 Describe the financial statement impact of stock treated as treasury stock.

Treasury stock
Stock issued by the firm and then repurchased but not retired.

The Stockholders' Equity category of AMR's balance sheet in Exhibit 11-3 includes **treasury stock** in the amount of $1,288 million. The Treasury Stock account is created when a corporation buys its own stock sometime after issuing it. For an amount to be treated as treasury stock, (1) it must be the corporation's own stock, (2) it must have been issued to the stockholders at some point, (3) it must have been repurchased from the stockholders, and (4) it must not be retired but must be held for some purpose. Treasury stock is not considered outstanding stock and does not have voting rights.

A corporation may repurchase stock as treasury stock for several reasons. The most common is to have stock available to distribute to employees for bonuses or as part of an employee-benefit plan. Firms also may buy treasury stock to maintain a favorable market price for the stock or to improve the appearance of the firm's financial ratios. More recently, firms have purchased their stock to maintain control of the ownership and to prevent unwanted takeover or buyout attempts. Of course, the lower the stock price, the more likely a company is to buy back its own stock and wait for the shares to rise in value before reissuing them.

The two methods to account for treasury stock transactions are the cost method and the par value method. We will present the more commonly used cost method. Assume that the Stockholders' Equity section of Rezin Company's balance sheet on December 31, 2000, appears as follows:

Common stock, $10 par value, 1,000 shares issued and outstanding	$10,000
Additional paid-in capital—Common	12,000
Retained earnings	15,000
Total stockholders' equity	$37,000

Assume that on February 1, 2000, Rezin buys 100 of its shares as treasury stock at $25 per share. Rezin records the following transaction at that time:

Feb. 1	Treasury Stock	2,500	
	Cash		2,500
	To record the purchase of 100 shares of treasury stock.		

Assets	=	Liabilities	+	Owners' Equity
−2,500				−2,500

The purchase of treasury stock does not directly affect the Common Stock account itself. The Treasury Stock account is considered to be a contra account and is subtracted from the total of contributed capital and retained earnings in the Stockholders' Equity section. Treasury Stock is *not* an asset account. When a company buys its own stock, it is contracting its size and reducing the equity of stockholders. Therefore, Treasury Stock is a contra-equity account, not an asset.

The Stockholders' Equity section of Rezin's balance sheet on February 1, 2001, after the purchase of the treasury stock, appears as follows:

Common stock, $10 par value, 1,000 shares issued, 900 outstanding	$10,000
Additional paid-in capital—Common	12,000
Retained earnings	15,000
Total contributed capital and retained earnings	$37,000
Less: Treasury stock, 100 shares at cost	2,500
Total stockholders' equity	$34,500

Corporations may choose to reissue stock to investors after it has been held as treasury stock. When treasury stock is resold for more than it cost, the difference between the sales price and the cost appears in the Additional Paid-in Capital—Treasury Stock account. For example, if Rezin resold 100 shares of treasury stock on May 1, 2001, for $30 per share, the Treasury Stock account would be reduced by $2,500 (100 shares times $25 per share), and the Additional Paid-in Capital—Treasury Stock account would be increased by $500 (100 shares times the difference between the purchase price of $25 and the reissue price of $30).

When treasury stock is resold for an amount less than its cost, the difference between the sales prices and the cost is deducted from the Additional Paid-in Capital—Treasury Stock account. If that account does not exist, the difference should be deducted from the Retained Earnings account. For example, assume that Rezin Company had resold 100 shares of treasury stock on May 1, 2001, for $20 per share, instead of $30 in the previous example. In this example, Rezin has had no other treasury stock transactions, and therefore, no balance existed in the Additional Paid-in Capital—Treasury Stock account. Rezin would then reduce the Treasury Stock account by $2,500 (100 shares times $25 per share) and would reduce Retained Earnings by $500 (100 shares times the difference between the purchase price of $25 and the reissue price of $20 per share). Thus, the Additional Paid-in Capital—Treasury Stock account may have a positive balance, but entries that result in a negative balance in the account should not be made.

Note that *income statement accounts are never involved* in treasury stock transactions. Regardless of whether treasury stock is reissued for more or less than its cost, the effect is reflected in the stockholders' equity accounts. It is simply not possible for a firm to engage in transactions involving its own stock and have the result affect the performance of the firm as reflected on the income statement.

Two-Minute Review

1. Where does the Treasury Stock account appear on the balance sheet?

2. What is the effect on stockholders' equity when stock is purchased as treasury stock?

3. How does treasury stock affect the number of shares issued and outstanding?

Answers:

1. Treasury Stock is a contra-equity account, and the balance should appear as a reduction in the Stockholders' Equity category of the balance sheet.

2. When treasury stock is purchased, it reduces total stockholders' equity.

3. Treasury stock is still stock that has been issued and so does not affect the number of shares issued. But it is stock that is held by the company, rather than the stockholders, and the purchase of treasury stock reduces the number of shares of stock outstanding.

Retirement of Stock

Retirement of stock occurs when a corporation buys back stock after it has been issued to investors and does not intend to reissue the stock. Retirement often occurs because the corporation wants to eliminate a particular class of stock or a particular group of stockholders. When stock is repurchased and retired, the balances of the stock account and the paid-in capital account that were created when the stock was issued must be eliminated. When the original issue price is higher than the repurchase price of the stock, the difference is reflected in the Paid-in Capital from Stock Retirement account. When the repurchase price of the stock is more than the original issue price, the difference reduces the Retained Earnings account. The general principle for retirement of stock is the same as for treasury stock transactions. No income statement accounts are affected by the retirement. The effect is reflected in the Cash account and the stockholders' equity accounts.

Retirement of stock
When the stock is repurchased with no intention to reissue at a later date.

Dividends: Distribution of Income to Shareholders

Cash Dividends

Corporations may declare and issue several different types of dividends, the most common of which is a cash dividend to stockholders. Cash dividends may be declared quarterly, annually, or at other intervals. Normally, cash dividends are declared on one date, referred to as the *date of declaration,* and are paid out on a later date, referred to as the *payment date.* The dividend is paid to the stockholders that own the stock as of a particular date, the *date of record.*

Generally, two requirements must be met before the board of directors can declare a cash dividend. First, sufficient cash must be available by the payment date to pay to the stockholders. Second, the Retained Earnings account must have a sufficient positive balance. Dividends reduce the balance of the account, and therefore Retained Earnings must have a balance before the dividend declaration. Most firms have an established policy concerning the portion of income that will be declared as dividends. The **dividend payout ratio** is calculated as the annual dividend amount divided by the annual net income. The dividend payout ratios of three members of the retail industry are given in Exhibit 11-4. The dividend payout ratio for many firms is 50% or 60% and seldom exceeds 70%. Typically, utilities pay a high proportion of their earnings. In contrast, fast-growing companies in technology often

Dividend payout ratio
The annual dividend amount divided by the annual net income.

Exhibit 11-4 1998 Dividend Payout Ratios to Common Stockholders in the Retail Industry

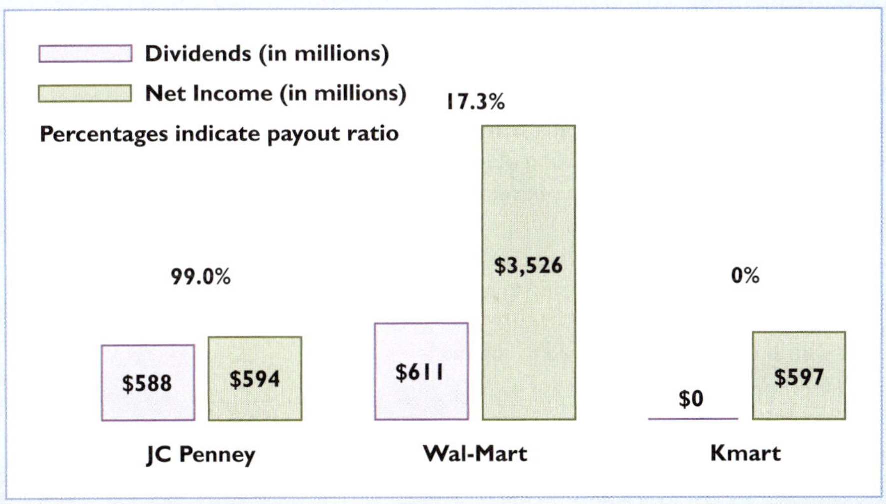

www.jcpenney.com
www.walmart.com
www.bluelight.com

Study Tip

A dividend is not an expense on the income statement. It is a reduction of retained earnings and appears on the retained earnings statement. If it is a cash dividend, it also reduces the cash balance when paid.

pay nothing to shareholders. Some investors want and need the current income of a high-dividend payout, but others would rather not receive dividend income and prefer to gamble that the stock price will appreciate.

Cash dividends become a liability on the date they are declared. An accounting entry should be recorded on that date to acknowledge the liability and reduce the balance of the Retained Earnings account. For example, assume that on July 1 the board of directors of Grant Company declared a cash dividend of $7,000 to be paid on September 1. Grant reflects the declaration as a reduction of Retained Earnings and an increase in Cash Dividend Payable as follows:

July 1	Retained Earnings	7,000	
	Cash Dividend Payable		7,000
	To record the declaration of a cash dividend.		

Assets	=	Liabilities	+	Owners' Equity
		+7,000		−7,000

The Cash Dividend Payable account is a liability and is normally shown in the Current Liabilities section of the balance sheet.

Grant records the following accounting transaction on September 1 when the cash dividend is paid:

Sept. 1	Cash Dividend Payable	7,000	
	Cash		7,000
	To record the payment of a cash dividend.		

Assets	=	Liabilities	+	Owners' Equity
−7,000		−7,000		

The important point to remember is that dividends reduce the amount of retained earnings *when declared.* When dividends are paid, the company reduces the liability to stockholders reflected in the Cash Dividend Payable account.

Cash Dividends for Preferred and Common Stock

LO 5 Compute the amount of cash dividends when a firm has issued both preferred and common stock.

When cash dividends involving more than one class of stock are declared, the corporation must determine the proper amount to allocate to each class of stock. As indicated earlier, the amount of dividends that preferred stockholders have rights to depends on the terms and provisions of the preferred stock. We will illustrate the proper allocation of cash dividends with an example of a firm that has two classes of stock, preferred and common.

Assume that on December 31, 2001, Stricker Company has outstanding 10,000 shares of $10 par, 8% preferred stock and 40,000 shares of $5 par common stock. Stricker was unable to declare a dividend in 1999 or 2000 but wants to declare a $70,000 dividend for 2001. The dividend is to be allocated to preferred and common stockholders in accordance with the terms of the stock agreements.

Noncumulative Preferred Stock If the terms of the stock agreement indicate that the preferred stock is not cumulative, the preferred stockholders do not have a right to dividends in arrears. The dividends that were not declared in 1999 and 2000 are simply lost and do not affect the distribution of the dividend in 2001. Therefore, the cash dividend declared in 2001 is allocated between preferred and common stockholders as follows:

	To Preferred	To Common
Step 1: Distribute current year dividend to preferred		
(10,000 shares × $10 par × 8% × 1 year)	$8,000	
Step 2: Distribute remaining dividend to common		
($70,000 – $8,000)		$62,000
Total allocated	$8,000	$62,000
Dividend per share		
Preferred: $8,000/10,000 shares	$.80	
Common: $62,000/40,000 shares		$1.55

Cumulative Preferred Stock If the terms of the stock agreement indicate that the preferred stock is cumulative, the preferred stockholders have a right to dividends in arrears before the current year's dividend is distributed. Therefore, Stricker performs the following steps:

	To Preferred	To Common
Step 1: Distribute dividends in arrears to preferred		
(10,000 shares × $10 par × 8% × 2 years)	$16,000	
Step 2: Distribute current-year dividend to preferred		
(10,000 shares × $10 par × 8% × 1 year)	8,000	
Step 3: Distribute remainder to common		
($70,000 – $24,000)		$46,000
Total allocated	$24,000	$46,000
Dividend per share		
Preferred: $24,000/10,000 shares	$2.40	
Common: $46,000/40,000 shares		$1.15

Cumulative and Participating Preferred Stock If the terms of the stock agreement indicate that the preferred stock is both cumulative and participating, the preferred stockholders have a right to dividends in arrears (the cumulative feature) and to a portion of the current year's dividend that exceeds a specified amount (the participating feature). Assume that Stricker Company preferred stockholders participate in any dividend in excess of 8% of total par value and that the participation is based on the proportion of the total par value of the preferred and common stock. The 2001 dividend is distributed as follows:

	To Preferred	To Common
Step 1: Distribute dividend in arrears to preferred		
(10,000 shares × $10 par × 8% × 2 years)	$16,000	
Step 2: Distribute current-year dividend to preferred		
(10,000 shares × $10 par × 8% × 1 year)	8,000	
Step 3: Distribute equal percentage to common		
(40,000 shares × $5 par × 8%)		$16,000
Step 4: Remainder to preferred and common on basis of total par value		
Preferred:		
($70,000 – $40,000) × $100,000[a]/$300,000	10,000	
Common:		
($70,000 – $40,000) × $200,000[b]/$300,000		20,000
Total allocated	$34,000	$36,000
Dividend per share		
Preferred: $34,000/10,000 shares	$3.40	
Common: $36,000/40,000 shares		$.90

[a] 10,000 shares × $10 par
[b] 40,000 shares × $5 par

The Stricker Company example illustrates the flexibility available with preferred stock. The provisions and terms of the preferred stock can be established to make the stock attractive to investors and to provide an effective form of financing for the corporation. The cumulative and participating features make the preferred stock more attractive. However, these features may make the *common stock* less attractive because more dividends for the preferred stockholders may mean less dividends for the common stockholders.

Stock Dividends

LO 6 Understand the difference between cash and stock dividends and the effect of stock dividends.

Cash dividends are the most popular and widely used form of dividend, but corporations may at times use stock dividends instead of, or in addition to, cash dividends. A **stock dividend** occurs when a corporation declares and issues additional shares of its own stock

STOCK DIVIDEND The issuance of additional shares of stock to existing stockholders.

to its existing stockholders. Firms use stock dividends for several reasons. First, a corporation may simply not have sufficient cash available to declare a cash dividend. Stock dividends do not require the use of the corporation's resources and allow cash to be retained for other purposes. Second, stock dividends result in additional shares of stock outstanding and may decrease the market price per share of stock if the dividend is large (small stock dividends tend to have little effect on market price). The lower price may make the stock more attractive to a wider range of investors and allow enhanced financing opportunities. Finally, stock dividends normally do not represent taxable income to the recipients and may be attractive to some wealthy stockholders.

Similar to cash dividends, stock dividends are normally declared by the board of directors on a specific date, and the stock is distributed to the stockholders at a later date. The corporation recognizes the stock dividend on the date of declaration. Assume that Shah Company's Stockholders' Equity category of the balance sheet appears as follows as of January 1, 2001:

Common stock, $10 par,	
5,000 shares issued and outstanding	$ 50,000
Additional paid-in capital—Common	30,000
Retained earnings	70,000
Total stockholders' equity	$150,000

Assume that on January 2, 2001, Shah declares a 10% stock dividend to common stockholders to be distributed on April 1, 2001. Small stock dividends (usually those of 20 to 25% or less) normally are recorded at the *market value* of the stock as of the date of declaration. Assume that Shah's common stock is selling at $40 per share on that date. Therefore, the total market value of the stock dividend is $20,000 (10% of 5,000 shares outstanding, or 500 shares, times $40 per share). Shah records the transaction on the date of declaration as follows, with the par value per share recorded in the Common Stock Dividend Distributable account:

Jan. 2	Retained Earnings	20,000	
	Additional Paid-in Capital—Common		15,000
	Common Stock Dividend Distributable		5,000
	To record the declaration of a stock dividend.		

Assets	=	Liabilities	+	Owners' Equity
				−20,000
				+15,000
				+5,000

The Common Stock Dividend Distributable account represents shares of stock to be issued; it is not a liability account because no cash or assets are to be distributed to the stockholders. Thus, it should be treated as an account in the Stockholders' Equity section of the balance sheet and is a part of the contributed capital component of equity.

Note that the declaration of a stock dividend does not affect the total stockholders' equity of the corporation, although the retained earnings are reduced. That is, the Stockholders' Equity section of Shah's balance sheet on January 2, 2001, is as follows after the declaration of the dividend:

Common stock, $10 par,	
5,000 shares issued and outstanding	$ 50,000
Common stock dividend distributable, 500 shares	5,000
Additional paid-in capital—Common	45,000
Retained earnings	50,000
Total stockholders' equity	$150,000

The account balances are different, but total stockholders' equity is $150,000 both before and after the declaration of the stock dividend. In effect, retained earnings has been capitalized (transferred permanently to the contributed capital accounts). When a corporation actually issues a stock dividend, it is necessary to transfer an amount from the Stock Dividend Distributable account to the appropriate stock account.

Our stock dividend example has illustrated the general rule that stock dividends should be reported at fair market value. That is, in the transaction to reflect the stock dividend, retained earnings is decreased in the amount of the fair market value per share of the stock times the number of shares to be distributed. When a large stock dividend is declared, however, accountants do not follow the general rule we have illustrated. A large stock dividend is a stock dividend of more than 20% to 25% of the number of shares of stock outstanding. In that case, the stock dividend is reported at *par value* rather than at fair market value. That is, Retained Earnings is decreased in the amount of the par value per share times the number of shares to be distributed.

Refer again to the Shah Company example. Assume that instead of a 10% dividend, on January 2, 2001, Shah declares and distributes a 100% stock dividend to be distributed on April 1, 2001. The stock dividend results in 5,000 additional shares being issued and certainly meets the definition of a large stock dividend. Shah records the following transaction on January 2, the date of declaration:

Jan. 2	Retained Earnings	50,000	
	Common Stock Dividend Distributable		50,000
	To record the declaration of a large stock dividend.		

Assets	=	Liabilities	+	Owners' Equity
				−50,000
				+50,000

The accounting transaction to be recorded when the stock is actually distributed is as follows:

Apr. 1	Common Stock Dividend Distributable	50,000	
	Common Stock		50,000
	To record the distribution of a stock dividend.		

Assets	=	Liabilities	+	Owners' Equity
				−50,000
				+50,000

The Stockholders' Equity category of Shah's balance sheet as of April 1 after the stock dividend is as follows:

Common stock, $10 par,	
10,000 shares issued and outstanding	$100,000
Additional paid-in capital—Common	30,000
Retained earnings	20,000
Total stockholders' equity	$150,000

Again, you should note that the stock dividend has not affected total stockholders' equity. Shah has $150,000 of stockholders' equity both before and after the stock dividend. The difference between large and small stock dividends is the amount transferred from retained earnings to the contributed capital portion of equity.

Stock Splits

LO 7 Determine the difference between stock dividends and stock splits.

A **stock split** is similar to a stock dividend in that it results in additional shares of stock outstanding and is nontaxable. In fact, firms may use a stock split for nearly the same reasons as a stock dividend: to increase the number of shares, reduce the market price per

EXHIBIT 11-5 Gateway's Stockholders' Equity Section

CONSOLIDATED BALANCE SHEETS
December 31, 1997 and 1998
(in thousands, except per share amounts)

	1997	1998
Stockholders' equity:		
Preferred stock, $.01 par value, 5,000 shares authorized; none issued and outstanding	—	—
Class A common stock, nonvoting, $.01 par value, 1,000 shares authorized; none issued and outstanding	—	—
Common stock, $.01 par value, 220,000 shares authorized; 154,128 shares and 156,569 shares issued and outstanding, respectively	1,541	1,566
Additional paid-in capital	299,483	365,986
Retained earnings	634,509	980,908
Accumulated other comprehensive loss	(5,489)	(4,085)
Total stockholders' equity	930,044	1,344,375
	$ 2,039,271	$ 2,890,380

Shares outstanding before stock split

STOCK SPLIT The creation of additional shares of stock with a reduction of the par value of the stock.

share, and make the stock more accessible to a wider range of investors. There is an important legal difference, however. Stock dividends do not affect the par value per share of the stock, whereas stock splits reduce the par value per share. There also is an important accounting difference. An accounting transaction is *not recorded* when a corporation declares and executes a stock split. None of the stockholders' equity accounts are affected by the split. Rather, the footnote information accompanying the balance sheet must disclose the additional shares and the reduction of the par value per share.

Return to the Shah Company example. Assume that on January 2, 2001, Shah issued a 2-for-1 stock split instead of a stock dividend. The split results in an additional 5,000 shares of stock outstanding but should not be recorded in a formal accounting transaction. Therefore, the Stockholders' Equity section of Shah Company immediately after the stock split on January 2, 2001, is as follows:

Common stock, $5 par, 10,000 shares issued and outstanding	$ 50,000
Additional paid-in capital—Common	30,000
Retained earnings	70,000
Total stockholders' equity	$150,000

You should note that the par value per share has been reduced from $10 to $5 per share of stock as a result of the split. Like a stock dividend, the split does not affect total stockholders' equity because no assets have been transferred. Therefore, the split simply results in more shares of stock with claims to the same net assets of the firm.

www.gateway.com

Exhibit 11-5 presents the stockholders' equity category of Gateway's 1997 and 1998 balance sheets. The exhibit indicates that Gateway had three classes of stock but had issued only the third class, common stock. As of December 31, 1998, the company had 156,569,000 shares of common stock issued and outstanding. In August, 1999 Gateway declared a 2-for-1 stock split for the common stockholders. This split doubled the number of shares over the number indicated on the 1998 balance sheet. Thus, after the stock split, each stockholder had twice as many shares of stock but still had the same proportional

EXHIBIT 11-6 Hewlett-Packard's Statement of Stockholders' Equity, 1998

Consolidated Statement of Shareholders' Equity

		Common stock			
In millions except number of shares in thousands		Number of shares	Par value and capital in excess of par	Retained earnings	Total
	Balance October 31, 1997	1,041,042	1,187	14,968	16,155
1	Shares issued	17,384	868	—	868
2	Shares repurchased	(43,023)	(2,045)	(379)	(2,424)
3	Dividends	—	—	(625)	(625)
4	Net earnings	—	—	2,945	2,945
	Balance October 31, 1998	**1,015,403**	**$ 10**	**$16,909**	**$16,919**

The accompanying notes are an integral part of these financial statements.

ownership of the company. When a company has a stock split, it restates the number of shares for all previous years also. Although a stock split does not increase the wealth of the shareholder, it is usually a good sign. Companies with rising stock prices declare a stock split to make the stock more marketable to the small investor, who would be more likely to buy a stock at $50 per share than at $100.

STATEMENT OF STOCKHOLDERS' EQUITY

LO 8 Understand the statement of stockholders' equity and comprehensive income.

In addition to a balance sheet, an income statement, and a cash flows statement, many annual reports contain a **statement of stockholders' equity.** The purpose of this statement is to explain all the reasons for the difference between the beginning and the ending balance of each of the accounts in the Stockholders' Equity category of the balance sheet. Of course, if the only changes are the result of income and dividends, a statement of retained earnings is sufficient. When other changes have occurred in stockholders' equity accounts, this more complete statement is necessary.

STATEMENT OF STOCKHOLDERS' EQUITY
Reflects the differences between beginning and ending balances for all accounts in the Stockholders' Equity category of the balance sheet.

www.hp.com

The statement of stockholders' equity of Hewlett-Packard Company is presented in Exhibit 11-6 for the year 1998. The statement starts with the beginning balances of each of the accounts as of October 31, 1997. Hewlett-Packard Company stockholders' equity is presented in three categories (the columns on the statement) as of October 31, 1997, as follows (in millions):

Number of shares	1,041,042
Par value and capital in excess of par	$1,187
Retained earnings	14,968

The statement of stockholders' equity indicates the items or events that affected stockholders' equity during 1998. The items or events were as follows:

Item or Event	Effect on Stockholders' Equity
Shares issued →	Increased common stock by $868 million
Shares repurchased →	Decreased common stock by $2,045 and decreased retained earnings by $379 million
Dividends →	Decreased retained earnings by $625 million
Net earnings →	Increased retained earnings by $2,945 million

The last line of the statement of stockholders' equity indicates the ending balances of the stockholders' equity accounts as of the balance sheet date, October 31, 1998. You should note that total stockholders' equity increased during 1998, to $16,919 million at year-end. The statement of stockholders' equity is useful in explaining the reasons for the changes that occurred.

WHAT IS COMPREHENSIVE INCOME?

There has always been some question about which items or transactions should be shown on the income statement and should be included in the calculation of net income. Generally, the accounting rule-making bodies have held that the income statement should reflect an *all-inclusive* approach. That is, all events and transactions that affect income should be shown on the income statement. This approach prevents the manipulation of the income figure by those who would like to show "good news" on the income statement and "bad news" directly on the retained earnings statement or the statement of stockholders' equity. The result of the all-inclusive approach is that the income statement includes items that are not necessarily under management's control, such as losses from natural disasters, and thus the income statement may not be a true reflection of a company's future potential.

The FASB has accepted certain exceptions to the all-inclusive approach and has allowed items to be recorded directly to the stockholders' equity category. This text has discussed one such item: unrealized gains and losses on investment securities. Exhibit 11-7 presents several additional items that are beyond the scope of this text. Items such as these have been excluded from the income statement for various reasons. Quite often, the justification is a concern for the volatility of the net income number. The items we have cited are often large dollar amounts; if included in the income statement, they would cause income to fluctuate widely from period to period. Therefore, the income statement is deemed to be more useful if the items are excluded.

EXHIBIT 11-7 The Relationship of the Income Statement and Statement of Comprehensive Income

Income Statement
For Year Ended December 31, 19XX

Revenues	xxxx
Expenses	xxxx
Other gains and losses	xxxx
Income before tax	xxxx
Income tax expense	xxxx
Net Income	xxxx

All Inclusive Earnings
These items, *excluded* from the income statement, are included on a statement of comprehensive income.

Statement Of Comprehensive Income
For Year Ended December 31, 19XX

Net income	xxxx
Foreign currency translation adjustment	xxxx
Unrealized holding gains/losses	xxxx
Minimum pension liability adjustment	xxxx
Other comprehensive income	xxxx
Comprehensive Income	xxxx

A new term has been coined to incorporate the "income-type" items that escape the income statement. **Comprehensive income** is the net assets increase resulting from all transactions during a time period (except for investments by owners and distributions to owners). Exhibit 11-7 presents the statement of comprehensive income and its relationship to the traditional income statement. It illustrates that comprehensive income encompasses all the revenues and expenses that are presented on the income statement to calculate net income and also includes items that are not presented on the income statement but affect total stockholders' equity.[2] The comprehensive income measure is truly all-inclusive because it includes such transactions as unrealized gains and prior period adjustments that affect stockholders' equity. Firms are required to disclose comprehensive income because it provides a more complete measure of performance.

COMPREHENSIVE INCOME The total change in net assets from all sources except investment or withdrawals by the owners.

WHAT ANALYZING OWNERS' EQUITY REVEALS ABOUT A FIRM'S VALUE

BOOK VALUE PER SHARE

LO 9 Understand how investors use ratios to evaluate owners' equity.

Users of financial statements are often interested in computing the value of a corporation's stock. This is a difficult task because *value* is not a well-defined term and means different things to different users. One measure of value is the book value of the stock. **Book value per share** of common stock represents the rights that each share of common stock has to the net assets of the corporation. The term *net assets* refers to the total assets of the firm minus total liabilities. In other words, net assets equal the total stockholders' equity of the corporation. Therefore, when only common stock is present, book value per share is measured as follows:

BOOK VALUE PER SHARE Total stockholders' equity divided by the number of shares of common stock outstanding.

$$\text{Book Value per Share} = \frac{\text{Total Stockholders' Equity}}{\text{Number of Shares of Stock Outstanding}}$$

www.hp.com

Refer again to the statement of stockholders' equity of Hewlett-Packard that appears in Exhibit 11-6. As of October 31, 1998, the total stockholders' equity is $16,919,000, and the number of outstanding shares of common stock is 1,015,403. Therefore, the book value per share for Hewlett-Packard is $16.66, calculated as follows (shares are in thousands and dollars are in millions):

$$\$16{,}919{,}000/1{,}015{,}403 = \$16.66$$

This means that the company's common stockholders have the right to $16.66 per share of net assets in the corporation.

The book value per share indicates the recorded minimum value per share of the stock. In a sense, it indicates the rights of the common stockholders in the event that the company is liquidated. It does not indicate the market value of the common stock. That is, book value per share does not indicate the price that should be paid by those who want to buy or sell the stock on the stock exchange. Book value is also an incomplete measure of value because the corporation's net assets are normally measured on the balance sheet at the original historical cost, not at the current value of the assets. Thus, book value per share does not provide a very accurate measure of the price that a stockholder would be willing to pay for a share of stock. The book value of a stock is often thought to be the "floor" of a stock price. An investor's decision to pay less than book value for a share of stock suggests that he or she thinks that the company is going to continue to lose money, thus shrinking book value.

From Concept **TO PRACTICE 11.3**

READING BEN & JERRY'S ANNUAL REPORT Refer to Ben & Jerry's 1998 report. What was the book value per share of the common stock? How did that relate to the market value of the stock?

CALCULATING BOOK VALUE WHEN PREFERRED STOCK IS PRESENT

The focus of the computation of book value per share is always on the value per share of the *common* stock. Therefore, the computation must be adjusted for corporations that

[2] The format of Exhibit 11-7 is suggested by the FASB. The FASB also allows other possible formats of the statement of comprehensive income.

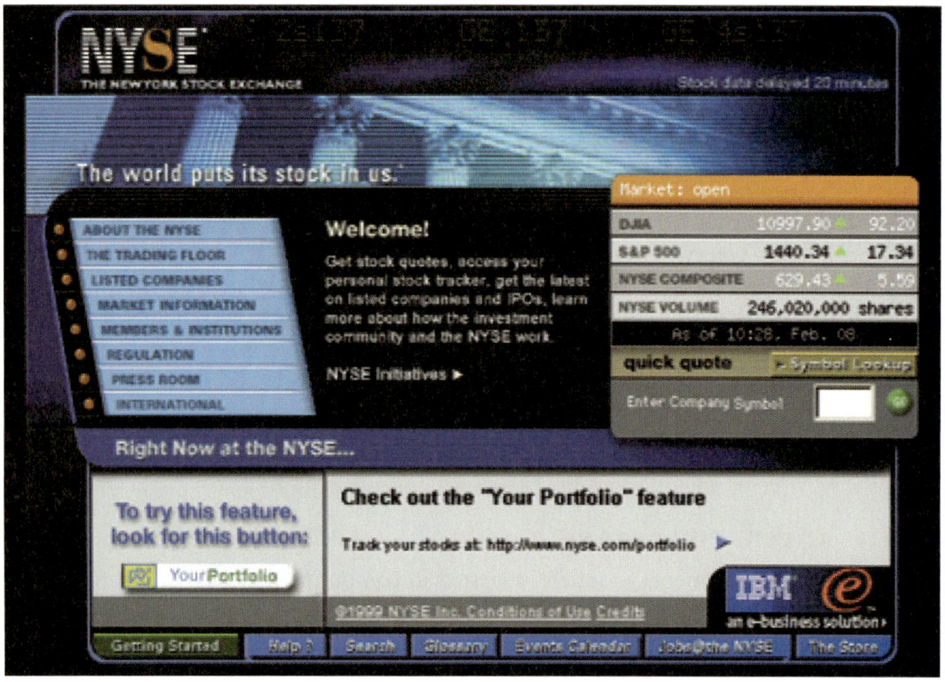

Stockbrokers use screens not only to keep track of the stocks but also to match companies with investors, based on companies' numbers.

have both preferred and common stock. The numerator of the fraction, total stockholders' equity, should be reduced by the rights that preferred stockholders have to the corporation's net assets. Normally, this can be accomplished by deducting the redemption value or liquidation value of the preferred stock along with any dividends in arrears on cumulative preferred stock. The denominator should not include the number of shares of preferred stock.

www.deltaairlines.com

To illustrate the computation of book value per share when both common and preferred stock are present, we will refer to the stockholders' equity category of Delta Air Lines, presented in Exhibit 11-8. When calculating book value per share, we want to consider only the *common* stockholders' equity. Exhibit 11-8 indicates 1 that Delta's total stockholders' equity in 1999 was $4,448 million but also 2 that preferred stockholders had a right to $471 million in the event of liquidation. Therefore, $471 million must be deducted to calculate the rights of the common stockholders:

$4,448 – $471 = $3,977 million common stockholders' equity

The number of shares of common stock *outstanding* can be calculated from Exhibit 11-8 as follows:

179,763,547	shares issued
– 41,209,828	treasury shares
138,553,719	shares outstanding

Therefore, the computation of book value per share is as follows:

$3,977,000,000/138,553,719 = 28.85 Book Value per Share

This indicates that if the company was liquidated and the assets sold at their recorded values, the common stockholders would receive $28.85 per share. Of course, if the company went bankrupt and had to liquidate assets at distressed values, stockholders would receive something less than book value.

EXHIBIT 11-8 Delta Air Lines Stockholders' Equity Section

SHAREOWNERS' EQUITY *(In Millions, Except Share Data)*	1999	1998
Employee Stock Ownership Plan Preferred Stock:		
2 Series B ESOP Convertible Preferred Stock, $1.00 par value, $72.00 stated and liquidation value; issued and outstanding 6,547,495 shares at June 30, 1999 and 6,603,429 shares at June 30, 1998	471	475
Unearned compensation under employee stock ownership plan	(276)	(300)
Total Employee Stock Ownership Plan Preferred Stock	195	175
Shareowners' Equity:		
Common stock, $1.50 par value; authorized 450,000,000 shares; issued 179,763,547 shares at June 30, 1999 and 176,566,178 shares at June 30, 1998	270	265
Additional paid-in capital	3,208	3,034
Retained earnings	2,756	1,687
Accumulated other comprehensive income	149	89
Treasury stock at cost, 41,209,828 shares at June 30, 1999 and 26,115,784 shares at June 30, 1998	(1,935)	(1,052)
1 Total shareowners' equity	4,448	4,023

Deduct preferred stock before calculating book value per share.

Two-Minute Review

1. What effect does a stock dividend have on a firm's stockholders' equity?

2. What effect does a stock split have on a firm's stockholders' equity?

3. How is book value per share calculated?

Answers:

1. A stock dividend does not change a firm's total stockholders' equity but does affect the balances of accounts within that category of the balance sheet. Generally, a stock dividend will reduce the retained earnings account and will increase the capital stock account.

2. A stock split does not affect total stockholders' equity or the accounts within stockholders' equity. No accounting entry is made for a stock split.

3. Book value per share is determined by dividing total stockholders' equity (less an amount representing the rights of preferred shareholders) by the number of shares of common stock.

MARKET VALUE PER SHARE

The market value of the stock is a more meaningful measure of the value of the stock to those financial statement users interested in buying or selling shares of stock. The **market value per share** is the price at which stock is currently selling. When stock is sold on a stock exchange, the price can be determined by its most recent selling price. For example, the listing for General Motors stock on the financial pages of a newspaper may indicate the following:

MARKET VALUE PER SHARE The selling price of the stock as indicated by the most recent transactions.

www.gm.com

52-Week			Daily			
High	**Low**	**Sym**	**High**	**Low**	**Last**	**Change**
59⅜	45¾	GM	57⅝	56½	56½	–⅜

The two left-hand columns indicate the stock price for the last 52-week period. General Motors sold as high as \$59⅜ and as low as \$45¾ during that time period. The right-hand portion indicates the high and low for the previous day's trading and the closing price. General Motors sold as high as \$57⅝ per share and as low as \$56½ per share and closed at \$56½. For the day, the stock decreased by ⅜ or \$0.375 per share.

The market value of the stock depends on many factors. Stockholders must evaluate a corporation's earnings and liquidity as indicated in the financial statements. They must also consider a variety of economic factors and project all of the factors into the future to determine the proper market value per share of the stock. Many investors use sophisticated investment techniques, including large databases, to identify factors that affect a company's stock price.

How Changes in Stockholders' Equity Affect the Statement of Cash Flows

LO 10 Explain the effects that transactions involving stockholders' equity have on the statement of cash flows.

It is important to determine the effect that the issuance of stock, the repurchase of stock, and the payment of dividends have on the statement of cash flows. Each of these business activities' impact on cash must be reflected on the statement. Exhibit 11-9 indicates how these stockholders' equity transactions affect cash flow and where the items should be placed on the statement of cash flows.

The issuance of stock is a method to finance business. Therefore, the cash *inflow* from the sale of stock to stockholders should be reflected as an inflow in the Financing Activities section of the statement of cash flows. Generally, companies do not disclose separately the amount received for the par value of the stock and the amount received in excess of par. Rather, one amount is listed to indicate the total inflow of cash.

Study Tip

Transactions affecting the Stockholders' Equity category of the balance sheet will appear in the Financing Activities category of the cash flow statement. Dividends are included in the cash flow statement when actually paid rather than when they are declared.

The repurchase or retirement of stock also represents a financing activity. Therefore, the cash *outflow* should be reflected as a reduction of cash in the Financing Activities section of the statement of cash flows. Again, companies do not distinguish between the amount paid for the par of the stock and the amount paid in excess of par. One amount is generally listed to indicate the total cash outflow to retire stock.

Dividends paid to stockholders represent a cost of financing the business with stock. Therefore, dividends paid should be reflected as a cash *outflow* in the Financing Activities section of the statement of cash flows. It is important to distinguish between the

Exhibit 11-9 The Effect of Stockholders' Equity Items on the Statement of Cash Flows

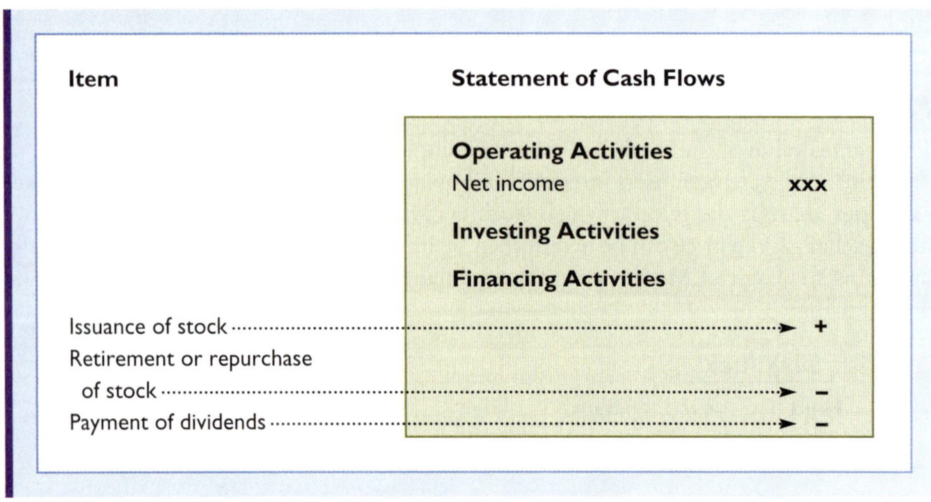

EXHIBIT 11-10 Delta Air Lines 1999 Statement of Cash Flows

CONSOLIDATED STATEMENTS OF CASH FLOWS

FOR THE YEARS ENDED JUNE 30, 1999, 1998 AND 1997

DELTA AIR LINES, INC.

(In Millions)	1999	1998	1997
Cash Flows From Operating Activities:			
Net income	$ 1,101	$ 1,001	$ 854
Adjustments to reconcile net income to cash provided by operating activities:			
Restructuring and other non-recurring charges	–	–	52
Depreciation and amortization	961	860	710
Deferred income taxes	418	294	240
Rental expense in excess of (less than) rent payments	10	(17)	(58)
Pension, postretirement and postemployment expense in excess of payments	34	179	92
Changes in certain current assets and liabilities:			
Decrease in accounts receivable	339	5	25
(Increase) decrease in prepaid expenses and other current assets	(176)	15	(31)
Increase in air traffic liability	152	249	4
Increase in other payables and accrued expenses	12	330	186
Other, net	78	–	(35)
Net cash provided by operating activities	2,929	2,916	2,039
Cash Flows From Investing Activities:			
Property and equipment additions:			
Flight equipment, including advance payments	(2,258)	(1,760)	(1,598)
Ground property and equipment	(561)	(531)	(350)
Decrease (increase) in short-term investments, net	568	(43)	(1)
Proceeds from sale of flight equipment	30	10	8
Acquisition, net of cash acquired	(570)	–	–
Net cash used in investing activities	(2,791)	(2,324)	(1,941)
Cash Flows From Financing Activities:			
Payments on long-term debt and capital lease obligations	(154)	(307)	(196)
Payments on notes payable	(277)	–	–
Cash dividends	(43)	(43)	(44)
Issuance of long-term obligations	324	125	–
Issuance of short-term obligations	779	–	–
Issuance of common stock	131	318	38
Income tax benefit from exercise of stock options	34	84	–
Repurchase of common stock	(885)	(354)	(379)
Net cash used in financing activities	(91)	(177)	(581)
Net Increase (Decrease) In Cash and Cash Equivalents	47	415	(483)
Cash and cash equivalents at beginning of year	1,077	662	1,145
Cash and cash equivalents at end of year	$ 1,124	$ 1,077	$ 662

Changes in stockholders' equity are shown in the Financing Activities category.

declaration of dividends and the payment of dividends. The cash outflow occurs at the time the dividend is paid and should be reflected on the statement of cash flows in that period.

The 1999 statement of cash flows for Delta Air Lines is given in Exhibit 11-10. Note in particular three lines in the Financing Activities category of the cash flow statement. First, the cash dividends line indicates cash payments of $43 million for the payment of dividends. Also, a line for the issuance of stock indicates the company had cash inflows during 1999 of $131 million from such transactions. Finally, Delta repurchased stock during the year, and that line indicates that cash payments of $885 million were made to repurchase the stock.

www.deltaairlines.com

Name: Christopher Morgan
Education: B.A., Dartmouth College
College Major: Psychology
Occupation: Equity Research Analyst (Financial Services), Donaldson, Lufkin & Jenrette Inc., New York
Age: 28

www.dlj.com

FOCUS ON USERS

"[Looking at] stockholder's equity is useful if a company has engaged in any stock transactions and it is not clear where some of the cash flow is coming from."
–Chris Morgan

Financial Statements Are Interrelated, This Analyst Shows

Chris Morgan is an equity research analyst for Donaldson, Lufkin & Jenrette (DLJ), a full-service investment banking firm with headquarters in New York. As an analyst covering the commercial banking industry, Chris researches and generates financial profiles of banking companies for DLJ's clients, who then use his research to make investment decisions. A company's income statement is paramount to his initial research as he judges a company's earnings potential and its ability to consistently turn a profit. Chris says: "First, I look at the net interest margin, the pretax margin before and after loan loss provisioning, the efficiency ratio (expenses divided by net revenues), the return on assets, and then return on equity."

In addition to looking at earnings, Chris considers the *composition* of earnings to determine the growth potential of a particular company because where earnings *come from* is often as important as their *amount.* Also, the statement of cash flows is an important source of information concerning a company's growth potential. But, the statement often reveals that cash was generated from sources other than earnings and one possible source involves the company's stock. To determine whether stock was involved, Chris might turn from the statement of cash flows to the Stockholder's Equity section of the consolidated balance sheet. He says: "[Looking at] stockholder's equity is useful if a company has engaged in any stock transactions and it is not clear where some of the cash flow is coming from. I also periodically scan the proxy [a statement that is prepared for a company's annual shareholders' meeting] in conjunction with the Shareholders' Equity section to determine the impact of stock options on the share base." Chris's example shows how the financial statements are interrelated and how an analyst moves from statement to statement to develop a precise picture of a company's earnings potential.

WARMUP EXERCISES

Warmup Exercise 11-1

A company has a retained earnings account with a January 1 balance of $500,000. The accountant has reviewed the following information for the current year:

Increase in cash balance	$50,000
Net income	80,000
Dividends declared	30,000
Dividends paid	20,000
Decrease in accounts receivable balance	10,000

Required

Calculate the ending balance of the Retained Earnings account.

Key to the Solution

Cash and accounts receivable do not affect retained earnings. Also note that dividends are deducted from retained earnings at the time they are declared rather than when they are paid.

Warmup Exercise 11-2

A company begins business on January 1 and issues 100,000 shares of common stock. On July 1, the company declares and issues a 2-for-1 stock split. On October 15, the company purchases 20,000 shares of stock as treasury stock and reissues 5,000 shares by the end of the month.

Required

Calculate the number of shares issued and the number of shares outstanding as of the end of the first year of operations.

Warmup Exercise 11-3

A. Company A has total stockholders' equity at year-end of $500,000 and has 10,000 shares of stock.

B. Company B has total stockholders' equity at year-end of $500,000 and has 10,000 shares of stock. The company also has 50,000 shares of preferred stock, which has a $1 par value and a liquidation value of $3 per share.

Required

Calculate the book value per share for Company A and Company B.

Key to the Solution

Book value per share is calculated for the common stockholder. If preferred stock is present, an amount must be deducted that represents the amount the preferred stockholder would receive at liquidation.

Solution to Warmup Exercises

Warmup Exercise 11-1

The ending balance of the Retained Earnings account should be calculated as follows:

Beginning balance	$500,000
Plus: Net income	80,000
Less: Dividends declared	(30,000)
Ending balance	$550,000

Warmup Exercise 11-2

The number of shares of stock issued is 200,000, or 100,000 times 2 because of the stock split. The number of shares outstanding is 185,000, calculated as follows:

Number of shares after split	100,000 × 2 = 200,000
Less purchase of treasury stock	(20,000)
Plus stock reissued	5,000
Total outstanding	185,000 shares

Warmup Exercise 11-3

A. Book value per share is $50, or $500,000/10,000.

B. Book value per share is $45 or ($500,000 – $50,000)/10,000.

Review Problem

Andrew Company was incorporated on January 1, 2001, under a corporate charter that authorized the issuance of 50,000 shares of $5 par common stock and 20,000 shares of $100 par, 8% preferred stock. The following events occurred during 2001. Andrew wants to record the events and develop financial statements on December 31, 2001.

a. Issued for cash 10,000 shares of common stock at $25 per share and 1,000 shares of preferred stock at $110 per share on January 15, 2001.

b. Acquired a patent on April 1 in exchange for 2,000 shares of common stock. At the time of the exchange, the common stock was selling on the local stock exchange for $30 per share.

c. Repurchased 500 shares of common stock on May 1 at $20 per share. The corporation is holding the stock to be used for an employee bonus plan.

d. Declared a cash dividend of $1 per share to common stockholders and an 8% dividend to preferred stockholders on July 1. The preferred stock is noncumulative, nonparticipating. The dividend will be distributed on August 1.

e. Distributed the cash dividend on August 1.

f. Declared and distributed to preferred stockholders a 10% stock dividend on September 1. At the time of the dividend declaration, preferred stock was valued at $130 per share.

g. On December 31, calculated the annual net income for the year to be $200,000.

Required

1. Record the accounting entries for items **a** through **g.**
2. Develop the Stockholders' Equity section of Andrew Company's balance sheet at December 31, 2001. You do not need to consider the footnotes that accompany the balance sheet.
3. Determine the book value per share of the common stock. Assume that the preferred stock can be redeemed at par.

Solution to Review Problem

1. The following entries should be recorded:

   a. The entry to record the issuance of stock:

Jan. 15	Cash	360,000	
	Common Stock		50,000
	Additional Paid-in Capital—Common		200,000
	Preferred Stock		100,000
	Additional Paid-in Capital—Preferred		10,000
	To record the issuance of stock for cash.		

Assets	=	Liabilities	+	Owners' Equity
+360,000				+50,000
				+200,000
				+100,000
				+10,000

   b. The patent received for stock should be recorded at the value of the stock:

Apr. 1	Patent	60,000	
	Common Stock		10,000
	Additional Paid-in Capital—Common		50,000
	To record the issuance of stock for patent.		

Assets	=	Liabilities	+	Owners' Equity
+60,000				+10,000
				+50,000

   c. Stock reacquired constitutes treasury stock and should be recorded as follows:

May 1	Treasury Stock	10,000	
	Cash		10,000
	To record the purchase of treasury stock.		

Assets	=	Liabilities	+	Owners' Equity
−10,000				−10,000

   d. A cash dividend should be declared on the number of shares of stock outstanding as of July 1. The dividend is recorded as follows:

July 1	Retained Earnings	19,500	
	Dividends Payable—Common		11,500
	Dividends Payable—Preferred		8,000
	To record the declaration of a cash dividend.		

Assets	=	Liabilities	+	Owners' Equity
		+11,500		−19,500
		+8,000		

The number of shares of common stock outstanding should be calculated as the number of shares issued (12,000) less the number of shares of treasury stock (500). The preferred stock dividend should be calculated as 1,000 shares times $100 par times 8%.

e. The entry to record the distribution of a cash dividend is as follows:

Aug. 1	Dividends Payable—Common	11,500	
	Dividends Payable—Preferred	8,000	
	Cash		19,500
	To record the payment of cash dividend.		

Assets	=	Liabilities	+	Owners' Equity
−19,500		−11,500		
		−8,000		

f. A stock dividend should be based on the number of shares of stock outstanding and should be declared and recorded at the market value of the stock as follows:

Sept. 1	Retained Earnings	13,000	
	Preferred Stock		10,000
	Additional Paid-in Capital—Preferred		3,000
	To record the declaration of a stock dividend.		

Assets	=	Liabilities	+	Owners' Equity
				−13,000
				+10,000
				+3,000

The amount of the debit to retained earnings should be calculated as the number of shares outstanding (1,000) times 10% times $130 per share.

g. The entry to close the Income Summary account to stockholders' equity should be recorded as follows:

Dec. 31	Income Summary	200,000	
	Retained Earnings		200,000
	To record the annual net income.		

Assets	=	Liabilities	+	Owners' Equity
				−200,000
				+200,000

2. The Stockholders' Equity for Andrew Company after completing these transactions appears as follows:

Preferred stock, $100 par, 8%, 20,000 shares authorized, 1,100 issued	$110,000
Common stock, $5 par, 50,000 shares authorized, 12,000 issued	60,000
Additional paid-in capital—Preferred	13,000
Additional paid-in capital—Common	250,000
Retained earnings	167,500*
Total contributed capital and retained earnings	$600,500
Less: Treasury stock, 500 shares, common	(10,000)
Total stockholders' equity	$590,500

*$200,000 − $19,500 − $13,000 = $167,500

3. The book value per share of the common stock is calculated as follows:

($590,500 − $110,000)/11,500 shares = $41.78

APPENDIX 11A

ACCOUNTING TOOLS: UNINCORPORATED BUSINESSES

LO 11 Describe the important differences between the sole proprietorship and partnership forms of organization versus the corporate form.

The focus of Chapter 11 has been on the corporate form of organization. Most of the large, influential companies in the United States are organized as corporations. They have a legal and economic existence that is separate from that of the owners of the business, the stockholders. Yet many other companies in the economy are organized as sole proprietorships or partnerships. The purpose of this appendix is to show briefly how the characteristics of such organizations affect the accounting, particularly the accounting for the Owners' Equity category of the balance sheet.

SOLE PROPRIETORSHIPS

SOLE PROPRIETORSHIP A business with a single owner.

A **sole proprietorship** is a business owned by one person. Most sole proprietorships are small in size, with the owner serving as the operator or manager of the company. The primary advantage of the sole proprietorship form of organization is its simplicity. The Owners' Equity category of the balance sheet consists of one account, the owner's capital account. The owner answers to no one but himself or herself. A disadvantage of the sole proprietorship is that all the responsibility for the success or failure of the venture attaches to the owner, who often has limited resources.

There are three important points to remember about this form of organization. First, a sole proprietorship is not a separate entity for legal purposes. This means that the law does not distinguish between the assets of the business and those of its owner. If an owner loses a lawsuit, for example, the law does not limit an owner's liability to the amount of assets of the business but extends liability to the owner's personal assets. Thus, the owner is said to have *unlimited liability.*

Second, accountants adhere to the *entity principle* and maintain a distinction between the owner's personal assets and the assets of the sole proprietorship. The balance sheet of a sole proprietorship should reflect only the "business" assets and liabilities, with the difference reflected as owner's capital.

Third, a sole proprietorship is not treated as a separate entity for federal income tax purposes. That is, the sole proprietorship does not pay tax on its income. Rather, the business income must be declared as income on the owner's personal tax return, and income tax is assessed at the personal tax rate rather than the rate that applies to companies organized as corporations. This may or may not be advantageous, depending on the amount of income involved and the owner's tax situation.

Typical Transactions When the owners of a corporation, the stockholders, invest in the corporation, they normally do so by purchasing stock. When investing in a sole proprietorship, the owner simply contributes cash, or other assets, into the business. For example, assume that on January 1, 2001, Peter Tom began a new business by investing $10,000 cash. Peter Tom Company records the transaction as follows:

Jan. 1	Cash	10,000	
	Peter Tom, Capital		10,000
	To record the investment of cash in the business.		

Assets	=	Liabilities	+	Owners' Equity
+10,000				+10,000

The Peter Tom, Capital account is an owners' equity account and reflects the rights of the owner to the business assets.

An owner's withdrawal of assets from the business is recorded as a reduction of owners' equity. Assume that on July 1, 2001, Peter Tom took an auto valued at $6,000 from the business to use as his personal auto. The transaction is recorded as follows:

July 1	Peter Tom, Drawing	6,000	
	Equipment		6,000
	To record the withdrawal of an auto from the business.		

Assets	=	Liabilities	+	Owners' Equity
−6,000				−6,000

The Peter Tom, Drawing account is a contra-equity account. Sometimes a drawing account is referred to as a *withdrawals account,* as in Peter Tom, Withdrawal. An increase (debit) in the account reduces the owners' equity. At the end of the fiscal year, the drawing account should be closed to the capital account as follows:

Dec. 31	Peter Tom, Capital	6,000	
	Peter Tom, Drawing		6,000
	To close the drawing account to capital.		

Assets	=	Liabilities	+	Owners' Equity
				−6,000
				+6,000

The amount of the net income of the business should also be reflected in the capital account. Assume that all revenue and expense accounts of Peter Tom Company have been closed to the Income Summary account, resulting in a credit balance of $4,000, the net income for the year. The Income Summary account is closed to capital as follows:

Dec. 31	Income Summary	4,000	
	Peter Tom, Capital		4,000
	To close income summary to the capital account.		

Assets	=	Liabilities	+	Owners' Equity
				−4,000
				+4,000

The Owners' Equity section of the balance sheet for Peter Tom Company consists of one account, the capital account, calculated as follows:

Beginning balance, Jan. 1, 2001	$ –0–
Plus: Investments	10,000
Net income	4,000
Less: Withdrawals	(6,000)
Ending balance, Dec. 31, 2001	$ 8,000

PARTNERSHIPS

A **partnership** is a company owned by two or more persons. Like sole proprietorships, most partnerships are fairly small businesses formed when individuals combine their capital and managerial talents for a common business purpose. Other partnerships are large, national organizations. For example, the major public accounting firms are very large, national companies but are organized in most states as partnerships.

PARTNERSHIP
A business owned by two or more individuals and with the characteristic of unlimited liability.

Partnerships have characteristics similar to those of sole proprietorships. The following are the most important characteristics of partnerships:

1. *Unlimited liability.* Legally, the assets of the business are not separate from the partners' personal assets. Each partner is personally liable for the debts of the partnership. Creditors have a legal claim first to the assets of the partnership and then to the assets of the individual partners.
2. *Limited life.* Corporations have a separate legal existence and an unlimited life, but partnerships do not. The life of a partnership is limited; it exists as long as the contract between the partners is valid. The partnership ends when a partner withdraws or a new partner is added. A new partnership must be created for the business to continue.

3. *Not taxed as a separate entity.* Partnerships are subject to the same tax features as sole proprietorships. The partnership itself does not pay federal income tax. Rather, the income of the partnership is treated as personal income on each of the partners' individual tax returns and is taxed as personal income. All partnership income is subject to federal income tax on the individual partners' returns even if it is not distributed to the partners. A variety of other factors affects the tax consequences of partnerships versus the corporate form of organization. These aspects are quite complex and beyond the scope of this text.

PARTNERSHIP AGREEMENT Specifies how much the owners will invest, their salaries, and how profits will be shared.

A partnership is based on a **partnership agreement.** It is very important that the partners agree, in writing, about all aspects of the partnership. The agreement should detail items such as how much capital each partner is to invest, the time each is expected to devote to the business, the salary of each, and how income of the partnership is to be divided. If a partnership agreement is not present, the courts may be forced to settle disputes among partners. Therefore, the partners should develop a partnership agreement when the firm is first established and should review the agreement periodically to determine whether changes are necessary.

Investments and Withdrawals In a partnership, it is important to account separately for the capital of each of the partners. A capital account should be established in the Owners' Equity section of the balance sheet for each partner of the company. Investments into the company should be credited to the partner making the investment. For example, assume that on January 1, 2001, Page Thoms and Amy Rebec begin a partnership named AP Company. Page contributes $10,000 cash, and Amy contributes equipment valued at $5,000. The accounting transaction that should be recorded by AP Company follows:

Jan. 1	Cash	10,000	
	Equipment	5,000	
	Page Thoms, Capital		10,000
	Amy Rebec, Capital		5,000
	To record the contribution of assets to the business.		

Assets	=	Liabilities	+	Owners' Equity
+10,000				+10,000
+5,000				+5,000

A drawing account also should be established for each owner of the company to account for withdrawals of assets. Assume that on April 1, 2001, each owner withdraws $2,000 of cash from AP Company. The accounting entry is recorded:

Apr. 1	Page Thoms, Drawing	2,000	
	Amy Rebec, Drawing	2,000	
	Cash		4,000
	To record the withdrawal of assets from the business.		

Assets	=	Liabilities	+	Owners' Equity
−4,000				−2,000
				−2,000

Distribution of Income The partnership agreement governs the manner in which income should be allocated to partners. The distribution may recognize the partners' relative investment in the business, their time and effort, their expertise and talents, or other factors. We will illustrate three methods of income allocation, but you should be aware that partnerships use many other allocation methods. Although these allocation methods are straightforward, partnerships dissolve often because one or more of the partners believes that the allocation is unfair. It is very difficult to devise a method that will make all partners happy.

One way to allocate income is to divide it evenly between or among the partners. In fact, when a partnership agreement is not present, the courts specify that an equal allocation must be applied, regardless of the relative contributions or efforts of the partners. For example, assume that AP Company has $30,000 net income for the period and has established an agreement that income should be allocated evenly between the two partners,

Page and Amy. The accounting entry that AP Company records during the closing entry process is as follows:

Dec. 31	Income Summary	30,000	
	Page Thoms, Capital		15,000
	Amy Rebec, Capital		15,000
	To record the allocation of income between partners.		

Assets	=	Liabilities	+	Owners' Equity
				−30,000
				+15,000
				+15,000

An equal distribution of income to all partners is easy to apply but is not fair to those partners who have contributed more in money or time to the partnership.

Another way to allocate income is to specify in the partnership agreement that income be allocated according to a *stated ratio.* For example, Page and Amy may specify that all income of AP Company should be allocated on a 2-to-1 ratio, with Page receiving the larger portion. If that allocation method is applied to the preceding example, AP Company records the following transaction at year-end:

Dec. 31	Income Summary	30,000	
	Page Thoms, Capital		20,000
	Amy Rebec, Capital		10,000
	To record the allocation of income between partners.		

Assets	=	Liabilities	+	Owners' Equity
				−30,000
				+20,000
				+10,000

Finally, we illustrate an allocation method that more accurately reflects the partners' input. It is based on salaries, interest on invested capital, and a stated ratio. Assume that the partnership agreement of AP Company specifies that Page and Amy be allowed a salary of $6,000 and $4,000 respectively, that each partner receive 10% on her capital balance, and that any remaining income be allocated equally. Assume that AP Company has been in operation for several years and the capital balances of the owners at the end of 2001, before the income distribution, are as follows:

Page Thoms, Capital	$40,000
Amy Rebec, Capital	50,000

If AP Company calculated that its 2001 net income (before partner salaries) was $30,000, income would be allocated between the partners as follows:

	Page	Amy
Distributed for salaries:	$ 6,000	$ 4,000
Distributed for interest:		
Page: ($40,000 × 10%)	4,000	
Amy: ($50,000 × 10%)		5,000
Remainder = $30,000 − $10,000 − $9,000 = $11,000		
Remainder distributed equally:		
Page: ($11,000/2)	5,500	
Amy: ($11,000/2)		5,500
Total distributed	$15,500	$14,500

The accounting transaction to transfer the income to the capital accounts is as follows:

Dec. 31	Income Summary	30,000	
	Page Thoms, Capital		15,500
	Amy Rebec, Capital		14,500
	To record the allocation of income to partners.		

Assets	=	Liabilities	+	Owners' Equity
				−30,000
				+15,500
				+14,500

This indicates that the amounts of $15,500 and $14,500 were allocated to Page and Amy respectively. It does not indicate the amount actually paid to (or withdrawn by) the partners. However, for tax purposes, the income of the partnership is treated as personal income on the partners' individual tax returns regardless of whether the income is actually paid in cash to the partners. This aspect often encourages partners to withdraw income from the business and makes it difficult to retain sufficient capital for the business to operate profitably.

CHAPTER HIGHLIGHTS

1. **LO 1** The Stockholders' Equity category is composed of two parts. Contributed capital is the amount derived from stockholders and other external parties. Retained earnings is the amount of net income not paid as dividends.
2. **LO 1** The Stockholders' Equity category reveals the number of shares authorized, issued, and outstanding. Treasury stock is stock that the firm has issued and repurchased but not retired.
3. **LO 2** *Preferred stock* refers to a stock that has preference to dividends declared. If a dividend is declared, the preferred stockholders must receive a dividend before the common stockholders.
4. **LO 3** When stock is issued for cash, the par value of the stock should be reported in the stock account and the amount in excess of par should be reported in an additional paid-in capital account.
5. **LO 3** When stock is issued for a noncash asset, the transaction should reflect the value of the stock given or the value of the property received, whichever is more evident.
6. **LO 4** Treasury stock is accounted for as a reduction of stockholders' equity. When treasury stock is reissued and the cost is less than reissue price, the difference is added to additional paid-in capital. When cost exceeds reissue price, additional paid-in capital or retained earnings is reduced for the difference.
7. **LO 5** The amount of cash dividends to be paid to common and preferred stockholders depends on the terms of the preferred stock. If the stock is cumulative, preferred stockholders have the right to dividends in arrears before current-year dividends are paid. Participating preferred stock indicates that preferred stockholders can share in the dividend amount that exceeds a specified amount.
8. **LO 6** Stock dividends involve the issuance of additional shares of stock. The dividend should normally reflect the fair market value of the additional shares.
9. **LO 7** Stock splits are similar to stock dividends except that splits reduce the par value per share of the stock. No accounting transaction is necessary for splits.
10. **LO 8** The statement of stockholders' equity reflects the changes in the balances of all stockholder equity accounts.
11. **LO 9** Book value per share is calculated as net assets divided by the number of shares of common stock outstanding. It indicates the rights that stockholders have, based on recorded values, to the net assets in the event of liquidation and is therefore not a measure of the market value of the stock.
12. **LO 9** When a corporation has both common and preferred stock, the net assets attributed to the rights of the preferred stockholders must be deducted from the amount of net assets to determine the book value per share of the common stock.
13. **LO 10** Transactions involving stockholders' equity accounts should be reflected in the Financing Activities category of the statement of cash flows.
14. **LO 11** A sole proprietorship is a business owned by one person. It is not a separate entity for legal purposes and does not pay taxes on its income. However, a balance sheet should present the assets and liabilities of the business separate from those of the owner. (Appendix 11A)
15. **LO 11** A partnership is a company owned by two or more persons. Like sole proprietorships, partnerships are not a separate legal or tax entity. The balance sheet of the partnership should present the assets and liabilities of the business separate from those of the owners. (Appendix 11A)

KEY TERMS QUIZ

Read each definition below and then write the number of the definition in the blank beside the appropriate term it defines. The solution appears at the end of the chapter.

13 **Authorized shares**
1 **Issued shares**
14 **Outstanding shares**
2 **Par value**
15 **Additional paid-in capital**
3 **Retained earnings**
4 **Cumulative feature**
16 **Participating feature**

5 Convertible feature
17 Callable feature
6 Treasury stock
18 Retirement of stock
7 Dividend payout ratio
19 Stock dividend
9 Stock split
8 Statement of stockholders' equity
11 Comprehensive income
10 Book value per share
12 Market value per share
22 Sole proprietorship (Appendix 11A)
20 Partnership (Appendix 11A)
21 Partnership agreement (Appendix 11A)

1. The number of shares sold or distributed to stockholders.
2. An arbitrary amount that is stated on the face of the stock certificate and that represents the legal capital of the firm.
3. Net income that has been made by the corporation but not paid out as dividends.
4. Stock for which holders have a right to dividends in arrears before the current-year dividend is distributed.
5. Allows preferred stock to be returned to the corporation in exchange for common stock.
6. Stock issued by the firm and then repurchased but not retired.
7. The annual dividend amount divided by the annual net income.
8. A statement that reflects the differences between beginning and ending balances for all accounts in the Stockholders' Equity category.
9. Creation of additional shares of stock and reduction of the par value of the stock.
10. Total stockholders' equity divided by the number of shares of common stock outstanding.
11. The amount that reflects the total change in net assets from all sources except investment or withdrawals by the owners of the company.
12. The selling price of the stock as indicated by the most recent stock transactions on, for example, the stock exchange.
13. The maximum number of shares a corporation may issue as indicated in the corporate charter.
14. The number of shares issued less the number of shares held as treasury stock.
15. The amount received for the issuance of stock in excess of the par value of the stock.
16. A provision allowing the preferred stockholders to share, on a percentage basis, in the distribution of an abnormally large dividend.
17. Allows the issuing firm to eliminate a class of stock by paying the stockholders a fixed amount.
18. When the stock of a corporation is repurchased with no intention to reissue at a later date.
19. A corporation's declaration and issuance of additional shares of its own stock to existing stockholders.
20. A business owned by two or more individuals and with the characteristic of unlimited liability.
21. A document that specifies how much each owner should invest, the salary of each owner, and how profits are to be shared.
22. A business with a single owner.

Alternate Terms

Additional paid-in capital Paid-in capital in excess of par value

Additional paid-in capital—treasury stock Paid-in capital from treasury stock transactions

Callable Redeemable

Capital account Owners' equity account

Contributed capital Paid-in capital

Retained earnings Retained income

Small stock dividend Stock dividend less than 20%

Stockholders' equity Owners' equity

Questions

1. What are the two major components of stockholders' equity? Which accounts generally appear in each component?
2. Corporations disclose the number of shares authorized, issued, and outstanding. What is the meaning of these terms? What causes a difference between the number of shares issued and the number outstanding?
3. Why do firms designate an amount as the par value of stock? Does par value indicate the selling price or market value of the stock?
4. If a firm has a net income for the year, will the balance in the Retained Earnings account equal the net income? What is the meaning of the balance of the account?
5. What is the meaning of the statement that preferred stock has a preference to dividends declared by the corporation? Do preferred stockholders have the right to dividends in arrears on preferred stock?
6. Why might some stockholders be inclined to buy preferred stock rather than common stock? What are the advantages of investing in preferred stock?
7. Why are common shareholders sometimes called *residual owners* when a company has both common and preferred stock outstanding?

8. When stock is issued in exchange for an asset, at what amount should the asset be reported? How could the fair market value be determined?

9. What is treasury stock? Why do firms use it? Where does it appear on a corporation's financial statements?

10. When treasury stock is bought and sold, the transactions do not result in gains or losses reported on the income statement. What account or accounts are used instead? Why are no income statement amounts recorded?

11. Many firms operate at a dividend payout ratio of less than 50%. Why do firms not pay a larger percentage of income as dividends?

12. What is a *stock dividend*? How should it be recorded?

13. Would you rather receive a cash dividend or a stock dividend from a company? Explain.

14. What is the difference between stock dividends and stock splits? How should stock splits be recorded?

15. How is the book value per share calculated? Does the amount calculated as book value per share mean that stockholders will receive a dividend equal to the book value?

16. Can the market value per share of stock be determined by the information on the income statement?

17. What is the difference between a statement of stockholders' equity and a retained earnings statement?

18. What is an advantage of organizing a company as a corporation rather than a partnership? Why don't all companies incorporate? (Appendix 11A)

19. What are some ways that partnerships could share income among the partners? (Appendix 11A)

EXERCISES

LO 1 Exercise 11-1 Stockholders' Equity Accounts

MJ Company has identified the following items. Indicate whether each item is included in an account in the Stockholders' Equity category of the balance sheet. Also indicate whether the item would increase or decrease stockholders' equity.

1. Preferred stock issued by MJ
2. Amount received by MJ in excess of par value when preferred stock was issued
3. Dividends in arrears on MJ preferred stock
4. Cash dividend declared but unpaid on MJ stock
5. Stock dividend declared but unissued by MJ
6. Treasury stock
7. Amount received in excess of cost when treasury stock is reissued by MJ
8. Retained earnings

LO 1 Exercise 11-2 Solve for Unknowns

The Stockholders' Equity category of Zache Company's balance sheet appears below.

Common stock, $10 par, 10,000 shares issued, 9,200 outstanding	$??
Additional paid-in capital	??
Total contributed capital	$350,000
Retained earnings	100,000
Treasury stock, ?? shares at cost	10,000
Total stockholders' equity	??

Required

1. Determine the missing values that are indicated by question marks.
2. What was the cost per share of the treasury stock?

LO 3 Exercise 11-3 Stock Issuance

Horace Company had the following transactions during 2001, its first year of business.

a. Issued 5,000 shares of $5 par common stock for cash at $15 per share.

b. Issued 7,000 shares of common stock on May 1 to acquire a factory building from Barkley Company. Barkley had acquired the building in 1997 at a price of $150,000. Horace estimated that the building was worth $175,000 on May 1, 2001.

c. Issued 2,000 shares of stock on June 1 to acquire a patent. The accountant has been unable to estimate the value of the patent but has determined that Horace's common stock was selling at $25 per share on June 1.

Required

1. Record an entry for each of the transactions.
2. Determine the balance sheet amounts for common stock and additional paid-in capital.

LO 3 **Exercise 11-4** Stock Issuances

The following transactions are for Weber Corporation in 2001:

a. On March 1, the corporation was organized and received authorization to issue 5,000 shares of 8%, $100 par value preferred stock and 2,000,000 shares of $10 par value common stock.

b. On March 10, Weber issued 5,000 shares of common stock at $35 per share.

c. On March 18, Weber issued 100 shares of preferred stock at $120 per share.

d. On April 12, Weber issued another 10,000 shares of common stock at $45 per share.

Required

1. Determine the effect on the accounting equation of each of the events.
2. Prepare the Stockholders' Equity section of the balance sheet as of December 31, 2001.
3. Does the balance sheet indicate the market value of the stock at year-end? Explain.

LO 4 **Exercise 11-5** Treasury Stock

The Stockholders' Equity category of Bradford Company's balance sheet on January 1, 2001, appeared as follows:

Common stock, $10 par, 10,000 shares issued and outstanding	$100,000
Additional paid-in capital	50,000
Retained earnings	80,000
Total stockholders' equity	$230,000

The following transactions occurred during 2001:

a. Reacquired 2,000 shares of common stock at $20 per share on July 1.

b. Reacquired 400 shares of common stock at $18 per share on August 1.

Required

1. Record the entries in journal form.
2. Assume the company resold the shares of treasury stock at $28 per share on October 1. Did the company benefit from the treasury stock transaction? If so, where is the "gain" presented on the balance sheet?

LO 4 **Exercise 11-6** Treasury Stock Transactions

The stockholders' equity category of Little Joe's balance sheet on January 1, 2001, appeared as follows:

Common stock, $5 par, 40,000 shares issued and outstanding	$200,000
Additional paid-in capital	90,000
Retained earnings	100,000
Total stockholders' equity	$390,000

The following transactions occurred during 2001:

a. Reacquired 5,000 shares of common stock at $20 per share on February 1.

b. Reacquired 1,200 shares of common stock at $13 per share on March 1.

Required

1. Record the entries in journal form.
2. Assume that the treasury stock was reissued on October 1 at $12 per share. Did the company benefit from the treasury stock reissuance? Where is the "gain" or "loss" presented on the financial statements?
3. What effect did the two transactions to purchase treasury stock and the later reissuance of that stock have on the Stockholders' Equity section of the balance sheet?

LO 5 Exercise 11-7 Cash Dividends

Kerry Company has 1,000 shares of $100 par value, 9% preferred stock and 10,000 shares of $10 par value common stock outstanding. The preferred stock is cumulative and nonparticipating. Dividends were paid in 1997. Since 1997, Kerry has declared and paid dividends as follows:

1998	$ 0
1999	10,000
2000	20,000
2001	25,000

Required

1. Determine the amount of the dividends to be allocated to preferred and common stockholders for each year, 1999 to 2001.
2. If the preferred stock had been noncumulative, how much would have been allocated to the preferred and common stockholders each year?

LO 5 Exercise 11-8 Cash Dividends

The Stockholders' Equity category of Jackson Company's balance sheet as of January 1, 2001, appeared as follows:

Preferred stock, $100 par, 8%, 2,000 shares issued and outstanding	$200,000
Common stock, $10 par, 5,000 shares issued and outstanding	50,000
Additional paid-in capital	300,000
Total contributed capital	$550,000
Retained earnings	400,000
Total stockholders' equity	$950,000

The footnotes that accompany the financial statements indicate that Jackson has not paid dividends for the two years prior to 2001. On July 1, 2001, Jackson declares a dividend of $100,000 to be paid to preferred and common stockholders on August 1.

Required

1. Determine the amounts of the dividend to be allocated to preferred and common stockholders, assuming that the preferred stock is noncumulative, nonparticipating stock.
2. Record the appropriate journal entries on July 1 and August 1, 2001.
3. Determine the amounts of the dividend to be allocated to preferred and common stockholders, assuming instead that the preferred stock is cumulative, nonparticipating stock.

Cash Dividends

LO 5 Exercise 11-9 Cash Dividends—Participating Feature

Refer to Jackson Company's Stockholders' Equity category in Exercise 11-8. Assume that the footnotes to the financial statements indicate that Jackson has not paid dividends for the two years prior to 2001. On July 1, 2001, Jackson declares a dividend of $100,000 to be paid to preferred and common stockholders on August 1.

Required

1. Determine the amounts of the dividend to be allocated to preferred and common stock, assuming that the preferred stock is cumulative and participates in dividends in proportion to the total par value of preferred and common stock.
2. Record the appropriate journal entries on July 1 and August 1, 2001.

LO 6 Exercise 11-10 Stock Dividends

The Stockholders' Equity category of Worthy Company's balance sheet as of January 1, 2001, appeared as follows:

Common stock, $10 par, 40,000 shares issued and outstanding	$400,000
Additional paid-in capital	100,000
Retained earnings	400,000
Total stockholders' equity	$900,000

The following transactions occurred during 2001:

a. Declared a 10% stock dividend to common stockholders on January 15. At the time of the dividend, the common stock was selling for $30 per share. The stock dividend was to be issued to stockholders on January 30, 2001.

b. Distributed the stock dividend to the stockholders on January 30, 2001.

Required

1. Record the 2001 transactions in journal form.
2. Develop the Stockholders' Equity category of Worthy Company's balance sheet as of January 31, 2001, after the stock dividend was issued. What effect did these transactions have on total stockholders' equity?

LO 7 **Exercise 11-11** Stock Dividends versus Stock Splits

Campbell Company wants to increase the number of shares of its common stock outstanding and is considering a stock dividend versus a stock split. The Stockholders' Equity of the firm on its most recent balance sheet appeared as follows:

Common stock, $10 par,	
50,000 shares issued and outstanding	$ 500,000
Additional paid-in capital	750,000
Retained earnings	880,000
Total stockholders' equity	$2,130,000

If a stock dividend is chosen, the firm wants to declare a 100% stock dividend. Because the stock dividend qualifies as a "large stock dividend," it must be recorded at par value. If a stock split is chosen, Campbell will declare a 2-for-1 split.

Required

1. Compare the effects of the stock dividends and stock splits on the accounting equation.
2. Develop the Stockholders' Equity category of Campbell's balance sheet (a) after the stock dividend and (b) after the stock split.

LO 7 **Exercise 11-12** Stock Dividends and Stock Splits

Whitacre Company's Stockholders' Equity section of the balance sheet on December 31, 2000, was as follows:

Common stock, $10 par value,	
60,000 shares issued and outstanding	$ 600,000
Additional paid-in capital	480,000
Retained earnings	1,240,000
Total stockholders' equity	$2,320,000

On May 1, 2001, Whitacre declared and issued a 15% stock dividend, when the stock was selling for $20 per share. Then on November 1, it declared and issued a 2-for-1 stock split.

Required

1. How many shares of stock are outstanding at year-end?
2. What is the par value per share of these shares?
3. Develop the Stockholders' Equity category of Whitacre's balance sheet as of December 31, 2001.

LO 8 **Exercise 11-13** Reporting Changes in Stockholders' Equity Items

On May 1, 2000, Ryde Inc. had common stock of $345,000, additional paid-in capital of $1,298,000 and retained earnings of $3,013,000. Ryde did not purchase or sell any common stock during the year. The company reported net income of $556,000 and declared dividends in the amount of $78,000 during the year ended April 30, 2001.

Required

Prepare a financial statement that explains all the reasons for the differences between the beginning and ending balances for the accounts in the Stockholders' Equity category of the balance sheet.

LO 8 Exercise 11-14 Comprehensive Income

Assume that you are the accountant for Ellis Corporation, which has issued its 2001 annual report. You have received an inquiry from a stockholder who has questions about several items in the annual report, including why Ellis has not shown certain transactions on the income statement. In particular, Ellis's 2001 balance sheet revealed two accounts in Stockholders' Equity (Unrealized Gain/Loss—Available-for-Sale Securities and Loss on Foreign Currency Translation Adjustments) for which the dollar amounts involved were not reported on the income statement.

Required

Draft a written response to the stockholder's inquiry that explains the nature of the two accounts and the reason that the amounts involved were not recorded on the 2001 income statement. Do you think the concept of comprehensive income would be useful to explain the impact of all events for Ellis Corporation?

LO 9 Exercise 11-15 Payout Ratio and Book Value per Share

Divac Company has developed a statement of stockholders' equity for the year 2001 as follows:

	Preferred Stock	Paid-in Capital—Preferred	Common Stock	Paid-in Capital—Common	Retained Earnings
Balance Jan. 1	$100,000	$50,000	$400,000	$40,000	$200,000
Stock issued			100,000	10,000	
Net income					80,000
Cash dividend					– 45,000
Stock dividend	10,000	5,000			– 15,000
Balance Dec. 31	$110,000	$55,000	$500,000	$50,000	$220,000

Divac's preferred stock is $100 par, 8% stock. If the stock is liquidated or redeemed, stockholders are entitled to $120 per share. There are no dividends in arrears on the stock. The common stock has a par value of $5 per share.

Required

1. Determine the dividend payout ratio for the common stock.
2. Determine the book value per share of Divac's common stock.

LO 10 Exercise 11-16 Impact of Transactions Involving Issuance of Stock on Statement of Cash Flows

From the following list, identify each item as operating (O), investing (I), financing (F), or not separately reported on the statement of cash flows (N).

_______ Issuance of common stock for cash
_______ Issuance of preferred stock for cash
_______ Issuance of common stock for equipment
_______ Issuance of preferred stock for land and building
_______ Conversion of preferred stock into common stock

LO 10 Exercise 11-17 Impact of Transactions Involving Treasury Stock on Statement of Cash Flows

From the following list, identify each item as operating (O), investing (I), financing (F), or not separately reported on the statement of cash flows (N).

_______ Repurchase common stock as treasury stock
_______ Reissuance of common stock (held as treasury stock)
_______ Retirement of treasury stock

LO 10 Exercise 11-18 Impact of Transactions Involving Dividends on Statement of Cash Flows

From the following list, identify each item as operating (O), investing (I), financing (F), or not separately reported on the statement of cash flows (N).

________ Payment of cash dividend on common stock
________ Payment of cash dividend on preferred stock
________ Distribution of stock dividend
________ Declaration of stock split

LO 10 Exercise 11-19 Determining Dividends Paid on Statement of Cash Flows
Clifford Company's comparative balance sheet included dividends payable of $80,000 at December 31, 2000, and $100,000 at December 31, 2001. Dividends declared by Clifford during 2001 amounted to $400,000.

Required

1. Calculate the amount of dividends actually paid to stockholders during 2001.
2. How will Clifford report the dividend payments on its 2001 statement of cash flows?

LO 11 Exercise 11-20 Sole Proprietorship (Appendix 11A)
Terry Woods opened Par Golf as a sole proprietor by investing $50,000 cash on January 1, 2001. Because the business was new, it operated at a net loss of $10,000 for 2001. During the year, Terry withdrew $20,000 from the business for living expenses. Terry also had $4,000 of interest income from sources unrelated to the business.

Required

1. Record all the necessary entries for 2001 on the books of Par Golf.
2. Present the Owner's Equity category of Par Golf's balance sheet as of December 31, 2001.

LO 11 Exercise 11-21 Partnerships (Appendix 11A)
Sports Central is a sporting goods store owned by Lewis, Jamal, and Lapin in partnership. On January 1, 2001, their capital balances were as follows:

Lewis, Capital	$20,000
Jamal, Capital	50,000
Lapin, Capital	30,000

During 2001, Lewis withdrew $5,000; Jamal, $12,000; and Lapin, $9,000. Income for the partnership for 2001 was $50,000.

Required

If the partners agreed to allocate income equally, what was the ending balance in each of their capital accounts on December 31, 2001?

PROBLEMS

LO 1 Problem 11-1 Stockholders' Equity Category
Peeler Company was incorporated as a new business on January 1, 2001. The corporate charter approved on that date authorized the issuance of 1,000 shares of $100 par, 7% cumulative, nonparticipating preferred stock and 10,000 shares of $5 par common stock. On January 10, Peeler issued for cash 500 shares of preferred stock at $120 per share and 4,000 shares of common at $80 per share. On January 20, it issued 1,000 shares of common stock to acquire a building site, at a time when the stock was selling for $70 per share.

During 2001, Peeler established an employee benefit plan and acquired 500 shares of common stock at $60 per share as treasury stock for that purpose. Later in 2001, it resold 100 shares of the stock at $65 per share.

On December 31, 2001, Peeler determined its net income for the year to be $40,000. The firm declared the annual cash dividend to preferred stockholders and a cash dividend of $5 per share to the common stockholders. The dividends will be paid in 2002.

Required

Develop the Stockholders' Equity category of Peeler's balance sheet as of December 31, 2001. Indicate on the statement the number of shares authorized, issued, and outstanding for both preferred and common stock.

LO 2 Problem 11-2 Evaluating Alternative Investments

Ellen Hays received a windfall from one of her investments. She would like to invest $100,000 of the money in Linwood Inc., which is offering common stock, preferred stock, and bonds on the open market. The common stock has paid $8 per share in dividends for the past three years and the company expects to be able to perform as well in the current year. The current market price of the common stock is $100 per share. The preferred stock has an 8% dividend rate, cumulative and nonparticipating. The bonds are selling at par with an 8% stated rate.

1. What are the advantages and disadvantages of each type of investment?
2. Recommend one type of investment over the others to Ellen, and justify your reason.

LO 5 Problem 11-3 Dividends for Preferred and Common Stock

The Stockholders' Equity category of Greenbaum Company's balance sheet as of December 31, 2001, appeared as follows:

Preferred stock, $100 par, 8%, 1,000 shares issued and outstanding	$ 100,000
Common stock, $10 par, 20,000 shares issued and outstanding	200,000
Additional paid-in capital	250,000
Total contributed capital	$ 550,000
Retained earnings	450,000
Total stockholders' equity	$1,000,000

The footnotes to the financial statements indicate that dividends were not declared or paid for 1999 or 2000. Greenbaum wants to declare a dividend of $59,000 for 2001.

Required

Determine the total and the per-share amounts that should be declared to the preferred and common stockholders under the following assumptions:

1. The preferred stock is noncumulative, nonparticipating.
2. The preferred stock is cumulative, nonparticipating.
3. The preferred stock is cumulative and participating on the basis of the proportion of the total par values of the preferred and common stock.

LO 6 Problem 11-4 Effect of Stock Dividend

Favre Company has a history of paying cash dividends on its common stock. The firm did not have a particularly profitable year, however, in 2001. At the end of the year, Favre found itself without the necessary cash for a dividend and therefore declared a stock dividend to its common stockholders. A 50% stock dividend was declared to stockholders on December 31, 2001. The board of directors is unclear about a stock dividend's effect on Favre's balance sheet and has requested your assistance.

Required

1. Write a statement to indicate the effect that the stock dividend has on the financial statements of Favre Company.
2. A group of common stockholders has contacted the firm to express its concern about the effect of the stock dividend and to question the effect the stock dividend may have on the market price of the stock. Write a statement to address the stockholders' concerns.

LO 7 Problem 11-5 Dividends and Stock Splits

On January 1, 2001, Frederiksen's Inc.'s Stockholders' Equity category appeared as follows:

Preferred stock, $80 par value, 7%, 3,000 shares issued and outstanding	$240,000
Common stock, $10 par value, 15,000 shares issued and outstanding	150,000
Additional paid-in capital—Preferred	60,000
Additional paid-in capital—Common	225,000

Total contributed capital	$ 675,000
Retained earnings	2,100,000
Total stockholders' equity	$2,775,000

The preferred stock is noncumulative and nonparticipating. During 2001, the following transactions occurred:

a. On March 1, declared a cash dividend of $16,800 on preferred stock. Paid the dividend on April 1.

b. On June 1, declared a 5% stock dividend on common stock. The current market price of the common stock was $18. The stock was issued on July 1.

c. On September 1, declared a cash dividend of $.50 per share on the common stock; paid the dividend on October 1.

d. On December 1, issued a 2-for-1 stock split of common stock, when the stock was selling for $50 per share.

Required

1. Explain each transaction's effect on the stockholders' equity accounts and the total stockholders' equity.

2. Develop the Stockholders' Equity category of the December 31, 2001, balance sheet. Assume the net income for the year was $650,000.

3. Write a paragraph that explains the difference between a stock dividend and a stock split.

LO 8 **Problem 11-6** Statement of Stockholders' Equity
Refer to all the facts in Problem 11-1.

Required

Develop a statement of stockholders' equity for Peeler Company for 2001. The statement should start with the beginning balance of each stockholders' equity account and explain the changes that occurred in each account to arrive at the 2001 ending balances.

LO 8 **Problem 11-7** Wrigley's Comprehensive Income
The consolidated statement of common stockholders' equity of Wm. Wrigley Jr. Company for the year ended December 31, 1998, appears below:

www.wrigley.com

Consolidated Statement of Stockholders' Equity Including Comprehensive Income

	Common Shares Outstanding	Common Stock	Class B Common Stock	Additional Paid-in Capital	Retained Earnings	Common Stock In Treasury	Other Compre-hensive Income	Total Stock-Holders' Equity
BALANCE DECEMBER 31, 1997	92,293	$12,339	3,157	226	1,032,139	(13,363)	(49,119)	985,379
Net earnings					304,501			304,501
Other comprehensive income:								
Currency translation							3,695	3,695
Unrealized holding gain on marketable equity securities, net of $4,729 tax							8,783	8,783
Total comprehensive income								316,979
Dividends to shareholders					(152,023)			(152,023)
Treasury share sales, net of purchases	104					4,078		4,078
Options exercised and stock awards granted	37			46		2,573		2,619
Conversion from Class B Common to Common	462	62	(62)	—				
BALANCE DECEMBER 31, 1998	92,896	$12,401	3,095	272	1,184,617	(6,712)	(36,641)	1,157,032

Required

1. Which items were included in comprehensive income? If these items had been included on the income statement as part of net income, what would have been the effect?
2. Do you think that the concept of comprehensive income would be useful to explain the impact of all the events that took place during 1998 to the stockholders of Wrigley?

LO 10 **Problem 11-8** Effects of Stockholders' Equity Transactions on Statement of Cash Flows

Refer to all the facts in Problem 11-1.

Required

Indicate how each of the transactions affects the cash flows of Peeler Company, by preparing the Financing Activities section of the 2001 statement of cash flows. Provide an explanation for the exclusion of any of these transactions from the Financing Activities section of the statement.

LO 11 **Problem 11-9** Income Distribution of a Partnership (Appendix 11A)

Louise Abbott and Buddie Costello are partners in a comedy club business. The partnership agreement specifies the manner in which income of the business is to be distributed. Louise is to receive a salary of $20,000 for managing the club, and Buddie is to receive interest at the rate of 10% on her capital balance of $300,000. Remaining income is to be distributed on a 2-to-1 ratio.

Required

Determine the amount that should be distributed to each partner, assuming the following business net incomes:

1. $15,000
2. $50,000
3. $80,000

LO 11 **Problem 11-10** Sole Proprietorships (Appendix 11A)

On May 1, Chong Yu deposited $120,000 of his own savings in a separate bank account to start a printing business. He purchased copy machines for $42,000. Expenses for the year, including depreciation on the copy machines, were $84,000. Sales for the year, all in cash, were $108,000. Chong withdrew $12,000 during the year.

Required

1. Prepare the journal entries for the following transactions: the May 1 initial investment, Chong's withdrawal of cash, and the December 31 closing entries. Chong closes revenues and expenses to an Income Summary account.
2. What is the balance in Chong's capital account at the end of the year?
3. Explain why the balance in Chong's capital account is different from the amount of cash on hand.

LO 11 **Problem 11-11** Partnerships (Appendix 11A)

Kirin Nerise and Milt O'Brien agreed to form a partnership to operate a sandwich shop. Kirin contributed $25,000 cash and will manage the store. Milt contributed computer equipment worth $8,000 and $92,000 cash. Milt will keep the financial records. During the year, sales were $90,000 and expenses were $76,000. Kirin withdrew $500 per month. Milt withdrew $4,000 (total). Their partnership agreement specified that Kirin would receive a salary of $7,200 for the year. Milt would receive 6% interest on his initial capital investment. All remaining income or loss would be equally divided.

Required

Calculate the ending balance in the equity account of each of the partners.

Multi-Concept Problems

LO 1, 4 **Problem 11-12** Analysis of Stockholders' Equity

The Stockholders' Equity section of the December 31, 2001, balance sheet of Eldon Company appeared as follows:

Preferred stock, $30 par value, 5,000 shares authorized, ? shares issued	$120,000
Common stock, ? par, 10,000 shares authorized, 7,000 shares issued	70,000
Additional paid-in capital—Preferred	6,000
Additional paid-in capital—Common	560,000
Additional paid-in capital—Treasury stock	1,000
Total contributed capital	$757,000
Retained earnings	40,000
Less: Treasury stock, preferred, 100 shares	(3,200)
Total stockholders' equity	??

Required

Determine the following items, based on Eldon's balance sheet:

1. The number of shares of preferred stock issued
2. The number of shares of preferred stock outstanding
3. The average per-share sales price of the preferred stock when issued
4. The par value of the common stock
5. The average per-share sales price of the common stock when issued
6. The cost of the treasury stock per share
7. The total stockholders' equity
8. The per-share book value of the common stock, assuming that there are no dividends in arrears and that the preferred stock can be redeemed at its par value

LO 3, 4, 7 **Problem 11-13** Effects of Stockholders' Equity Transactions on the Balance Sheet

The following transactions occurred at Horton Inc. during its first year of operation:

a. Issued 100,000 shares of common stock at $5 each; 1,000,000 shares are authorized at $1 par value.

b. Issued 10,000 shares of common stock for a building and land. The building was appraised for $20,000, but the value of the land is undeterminable. The stock is selling for $10 on the open market.

c. Purchased 1,000 shares of its own common stock on the open market for $16 per share.

d. Declared a dividend of $.10 per share on outstanding common stock. The dividend is to be paid after the end of the first year of operations. Market value of the stock is $26.

e. Declared a 2-for-1 stock split. The market value of the stock was $37 before the stock split.

f. Reported $180,000 of income for the year.

Required

1. Indicate each transaction's effect on the assets, liabilities, and owners' equity of Horton Inc.
2. Prepare the Owners' Equity section of the balance sheet.
3. Write a paragraph that explains the number of shares of stock issued and outstanding at the end of the year.

LO 2, 4 **Problem 11-14** Owner's Equity Section of the Balance Sheet

The newly hired accountant at Ives Inc. prepared the following balance sheet:

Assets	
Cash	$ 3,500
Accounts receivable	5,000
Treasury stock	500
Plant, property, and equipment	108,000
Retained earnings	1,000
Total assets	$118,000

Liabilities	
Accounts payable	$ 5,500
Dividends payable	1,500
Owners' Equity	
Common stock, $1 par,	
100,000 shares issued	100,000
Additional paid-in capital	11,000
Total liabilities and owners' equity	$118,000

Required

1. Prepare a corrected balance sheet. Write a short explanation for each correction.
2. Why does the Retained Earnings account have a negative balance?

ALTERNATE PROBLEMS

LO 1 Problem 11-1A Stockholders' Equity Category

Kebler Company was incorporated as a new business on January 1, 2001. The corporate charter approved on that date authorized the issuance of 2,000 shares of $100 par 7% cumulative, nonparticipating preferred stock and 20,000 shares of $5 par common stock. On January 10, Kebler issued for cash 1,000 shares of preferred stock at $120 per share and 8,000 shares of common at $80 per share. On January 20, it issued 2,000 shares of common stock to acquire a building site, at a time when the stock was selling for $70 per share.

During 2001 Kebler established an employee benefit plan and acquired 1,000 shares of common stock at $60 per share as treasury stock for that purpose. Later in 2001, it resold 100 shares of the stock at $65 per share.

On December 31, 2001, Kebler determined its net income for the year to be $80,000. The firm declared the annual cash dividend to preferred stockholders and a cash dividend of $5 per share to the common stockholders. The dividend will be paid in 2002.

Required

Develop the Stockholders' Equity category of Kebler's balance sheet as of December 31, 2001. Indicate on the statement the number of shares authorized, issued, and outstanding for both preferred and common stock.

LO 2 Problem 11-2A Evaluating Alternative Investments

Rob Lowe would like to invest $100,000 in Franklin Inc., which is offering common stock, preferred stock, and bonds on the open market. The common stock has paid $1 per share in dividends for the past three years, and the company expects to be able to double the dividend in the current year. The current market price of the common stock is $10 per share. The preferred stock has an 8% dividend rate. The bonds are selling at par with a 5% stated rate.

Required

1. Explain Franklin's obligation to pay dividends or interest on each instrument.
2. Recommend one type of investment over the others to Rob, and justify your reason.

LO 5 Problem 11-3A Dividends for Preferred and Common Stock

The Stockholders' Equity category of Rausch Company's balance sheet as of December 31, 2001, appeared as follows:

Preferred stock, $100 par, 8%,	
2,000 shares issued and outstanding	$ 200,000
Common stock, $10 par,	
40,000 shares issued and outstanding	400,000
Additional paid-in capital	500,000
Total contributed capital	$1,100,000
Retained earnings	900,000
Total stockholders' equity	$2,000,000

The footnotes to the financial statements indicate that dividends were not declared or paid for 1999 or 2000. Rausch wants to declare a dividend of $118,000 for 2001.

Required

Determine the total and the per-share amounts that should be declared to the preferred and common stockholders under the following assumptions:

1. The preferred stock is noncumulative, nonparticipating.
2. The preferred stock is cumulative, nonparticipating.
3. The preferred stock is cumulative and participating on the basis of the proportion of the total par values of the preferred and common stock.

LO 6 **Problem 11-4A** Effect of Stock Dividend

Travanti Company has a history of paying cash dividends on its common stock. Although the firm has been profitable this year, the board of directors has been planning construction of a second manufacturing plant. To reduce the amount that they must borrow to finance the expansion, the directors are contemplating replacing their usual cash dividend with a 40% stock dividend. The board is unsure what the effect of a stock dividend will be on the company's balance sheet and has requested your assistance.

Required

1. Write a statement to indicate the effect that the stock dividend has on the financial statements of Travanti Company.
2. A group of common stockholders has contacted the firm to express its concern about the effect of the stock dividend and to question the effect that the stock dividend may have on the market price of the stock. Write a statement to address the stockholders' concerns.

LO 7 **Problem 11-5A** Dividends and Stock Splits

On January 1, 2001, Svenberg Inc.'s Stockholders' Equity category appeared as follows:

Preferred stock, $80 par value, 8%,	
1,000 shares issued and outstanding	$ 80,000
Common stock, $10 par value,	
10,000 shares issued and outstanding	100,000
Additional paid-in capital—	
Preferred	60,000
Additional paid-in capital—	
Common	225,000
Total contributed capital	465,000
Retained earnings	1,980,000
Total stockholders' equity	$2,445,000

The preferred stock is noncumulative and nonparticipating. During 2001, the following transactions occurred:

a. On March 1, declared a cash dividend of $6,400 on preferred stock. Paid the dividend on April 1.

b. On June 1, declared an 8% stock dividend on common stock. The current market price of the common stock was $26. The stock was issued on July 1.

c. On September 1, declared a cash dividend of $.70 per share on the common stock; paid the dividend on October 1.

d. On December 1, issued a 3-for-1 stock split of common stock, when the stock was selling for $30 per share.

Required

1. Explain each transaction's effect on the stockholders' equity accounts and the total stockholders' equity.
2. Develop the Stockholders' Equity category of the balance sheet. Assume the net income for the year was $720,000.
3. Write a paragraph that explains the difference between a stock dividend and a stock split.

LO 8 Problem 11-6A Statement of Stockholders' Equity
Refer to all the facts in Problem 11-1A.

Required

Develop a statement of stockholders' equity for Kebler Company for 2001. The statement should start with the beginning balance of each stockholders' equity account and explain the changes that occurred in each account to arrive at the 2001 ending balances.

LO 8 Problem 11-7A Intel's Comprehensive Income

www.intel.com The consolidated statement of stockholders' equity of Intel Corporation for the year ended December 26, 1998, appears below:

Consolidated Statements of Stockholders' Equity

(in millions—except per share amounts)	Common Stock and Capital in Excess of Par Value: Number of Shares	Common Stock and Capital in Excess of Par Value: Amount	Retained Earnings	Accumulated Other Comprehensive Income	Total
Balance at December 27, 1997	**3,256**	**3,311**	**15,926**	**58**	**19,295**
Components of comprehensive income:					
Net income	—	—	6,068	—	6,068
Change in unrealized gain on available-for-sale investments	—	—	—	545	545
Total comprehensive income					6,613
Proceeds from sales of shares through employee stock plans, tax benefit of $415 and other	66	922	—	—	922
Proceeds from exercise of 1998 Step-Up Warrants	155	1,620	—	—	1,620
Proceeds from sales of put warrants	—	40	—	—	40
Reclassification of put warrant obligation, net	—	53	588	—	641
Repurchase and retirement of Common Stock	(162)	(1,124)	(4,462)	—	(5,586)
Cash dividends declared ($.050 per share)	—	—	(168)	—	(168)
Balance at December 26, 1998	**3,315**	**$ 4,822**	**$17,952**	**$ 603**	**$23,377**

Required

1. Explain the item that caused Intel's net income to be different from its comprehensive income. What does the term *unrealized gain* mean? What does a positive amount of $545 for unrealized gain mean?
2. Do you think that Intel's stockholders would find the concept of comprehensive income useful to evaluate the performance of the company?

LO 10 Problem 11-8A Effects of Stockholders' Equity Transactions on the Statement of Cash Flows
Refer to all the facts in Problem 11-1A.

Required

Indicate how each of the transactions affects the cash flows of Kebler Company, by preparing the Financing Activities section of the 2001 statement of cash flows. Provide an explanation for the exclusion of any of these transactions from the Financing Activities section of the statement.

LO 11 Problem 11-9A Income Distribution of a Partnership (Appendix 11A)
Kay Katz and Doris Kan are partners in a dry-cleaning business. The partnership agreement specifies the manner in which income of the business is to be distributed. Kay is to receive a salary of $40,000 for managing the business. Doris is to receive interest at the rate of 10% on her capital balance of $600,000. Remaining income is to be distributed on a 2-to-1 ratio.

Required

Determine the amount that should be distributed to each partner, assuming the following business net incomes:

1. $30,000
2. $100,000
3. $160,000

LO 11 **Problem 11-10A** Sole Proprietorships (Appendix 11A)

On May 1, Chen Chien Lao deposited $150,000 of her own savings in a separate bank account to start a printing business. She purchased copy machines for $52,500. Expenses for the year, including depreciation on the copy machines, were $105,000. Sales for the year, all in cash, were $135,000. Chen withdrew $15,000 during the year.

Required

1. Prepare the journal entries for the following transactions: the May 1 initial investment, Chen's withdrawal of cash, and the December 31 closing entries. Chen closes revenues and expenses to an Income Summary account.
2. What is the balance in Chen's capital account at the end of the year?
3. Explain why the balance in Chen's capital account is different from the amount of cash on hand.

LO 11 **Problem 11-11A** Partnerships (Appendix 11A)

Karen Locke and Gina Keyes agreed to form a partnership to operate a sandwich shop. Karen contributed $35,000 cash and will manage the store. Gina contributed computer equipment worth $11,200 and $128,800 cash. Gina will keep the financial records. During the year, sales were $126,000 and expenses were $106,400. Karen withdrew $700 per month. Gina withdrew $5,600 (total). Their partnership agreement specified that Karen would receive a salary of $10,800 for the year. Gina would receive 6% interest on her initial capital investment. All remaining income or loss would be equally divided.

Required

Calculate the ending balance in the equity account of each of the partners.

Alternate Multi-Concept Problems

LO 1, 4 **Problem 11-12A** Analysis of Stockholders' Equity

The Stockholders' Equity section of the December 31, 2001, balance sheet of Carter Company appeared as follows:

Preferred stock, $50 par value,	
10,000 shares authorized, ? shares issued	$ 400,000
Common stock, ? par value,	
20,000 shares authorized, 14,000 shares issued	280,000
Additional paid-in capital—Preferred	12,000
Additional paid-in capital—Common	980,000
Additional paid-in capital—Treasury stock	2,000
Total contributed capital	$1,674,000
Retained earnings	80,000
Less: Treasury stock, preferred, 200 shares	(12,800)
Total stockholders' equity	$?

Determine the following items, based on Carter's balance sheet.

1. The number of shares of preferred stock issued
2. The number of shares of preferred stock outstanding
3. The average per-share sales price of the preferred stock when issued
4. The par value of the common stock
5. The average per-share sales price of the common stock when issued
6. The cost of the treasury stock per share
7. The total stockholders' equity
8. The per-share book value of the common stock, assuming that there are no dividends in arrears and that the preferred stock can be redeemed at its par value

LO 3, 4, 7 **Problem 11-13A** Effects of Stockholders' Equity Transactions on Balance Sheet
The following transactions occurred at Hilton Inc. during its first year of operation:

a. Issued 10,000 shares of common stock at $10 each; 100,000 shares are authorized at $1 par value.

b. Issued 10,000 shares of common stock for a patent, which is expected to be effective for the next 15 years. The value of the patent is undeterminable. The stock is selling for $10 on the open market.

c. Purchased 1,000 shares of its own common stock on the open market for $10 per share.

d. Declared a dividend of $.50 per share of outstanding common stock. The dividend is to be paid after the end of the first year of operations. Market value of the stock is $10.

e. Income for the year is reported as $340,000.

Required

1. Indicate each transaction's effect on the assets, liabilities, and owners' equity of Hilton Inc.
2. Hilton's president has asked you to explain the difference between contributed capital and retained earnings. Discuss these terms as they relate to Hilton.
3. Determine the book value per share of the stock at the end of the year.

LO 2, 4 **Problem 11-14A** Equity Section of the Balance Sheet
The newly hired accountant at Grainfield Inc. is considering the following list of accounts as he prepares the balance sheet. All of the accounts have positive balances. The company is authorized to issue 1,000,000 shares of common stock and 10,000 shares of preferred stock. The treasury stock was purchased at $5 per share.

Treasury stock (common)	$ 15,000
Retained earnings	54,900
Dividends payable	1,500
Common stock, $1 par	100,000
Additional paid-in capital	68,400
Preferred stock, $10 par, 5%	50,000

Required

1. Prepare the Owners' Equity section of the balance sheet for Grainfield.
2. Explain why some of the listed accounts are not shown in the Owners' Equity section.

CASES

Reading and Interpreting Financial Statements

LO 1, 2 **Case 11-1** Ben & Jerry's Stockholders' Equity Category

www.benjerry.com

Refer to Ben & Jerry's 1998 annual report.

Required

1. What are the numbers of shares of preferred stock authorized, issued, and outstanding as of the balance sheet date?
2. The preferred stock indicates an "aggregate preference on liquidation." What does that provision of the preferred stock mean?
3. Calculate the book value per share of the common stock.
4. The balance of the Retained Earnings account increased during the year. What are the possible factors that affect its balance?
5. The total stockholders' equity as of December 26, 1998, is $90,908,000. Does that mean that stockholders will receive that amount if the company is liquidated?

LO 1, 2 **Case 11-2** Gateway's Stockholders' Equity Category

www.gateway.com

Refer to Gateway's 1998 annual report.

Required

1. What are the numbers of shares of common stock authorized, issued, and outstanding as of the balance sheet date?

2. Calculate the book value per share of the common stock.
3. The balance of the Retained Earnings account increased during the year. What are the possible factors that affect the balance of this account?
4. The total stockholders' equity as of December 31, 1998, is $1,344,375,000. Does that mean that the stockholders will receive that amount if the company is liquidated?

LO 10 Case 11-3 Reading The Gap's Statement of Cash Flows

A portion of the cash flow statement of The Gap for the year ended January 30, 1999, is as follows:

	52 Weeks Ended		
Consolidated Statements of Cash Flows	**Jan. 30, 1999**	**Jan. 31, 1998**	**Feb. 1, 1997**
Cash Flows from Financing Activities			
Net increase in notes payable	1,357	44,462	18,445
Net issuance of long-term debt	—	495,890	—
Issuance of common stock	49,421	30,653	37,053
Net purchase of treasury stock	(892,149)	(593,142)	(466,741)
Cash dividends paid	(76,888)	(79,503)	(83,854)
Net cash used for financing activities	(918,259)	(101,640)	(495,097)

Required

1. Explain how each of the items in the Financing Activities category affected the amount of the company's cash. www.gap.com
2. The Gap used a large amount of cash to purchase treasury stock during the year. What are possible reasons for buying stock as treasury stock? What will happen to the treasury stock in future time periods?
3. The cash flow statement indicates a use of cash for dividends paid. How do dividends affect the Stockholders' Equity category of the balance sheet?

Making Financial Decisions

LO 1, 2 Case 11-4 Debt versus Preferred Stock

Assume that you are an analyst attempting to compare the financial structures of two companies. In particular, you must analyze the debt and equity categories of the two firms and calculate a debt-to-equity ratio for each firm. The liability and equity categories of First Company at year-end appeared as follows:

Liabilities	
Accounts payable	$ 500,000
Loan payable	800,000
Stockholders' Equity	
Common stock	300,000
Retained earnings	600,000
Total debt and equity	$2,200,000

First Company's loan payable bears interest at 8%, which is paid annually. The principal is due in five years.

The liability and equity categories of Second Company at year-end appeared as follows:

Liabilities	
Accounts payable	$ 500,000
Stockholders' Equity	
Common stock	300,000
Preferred stock	800,000
Retained earnings	600,000
Total debt and equity	$2,200,000

Second Company's preferred stock is 8%, cumulative stock. A provision of the stock agreement specifies that the stock must be redeemed at face value in five years.

Required

1. It appears that the loan payable of First Company and the preferred stock of Second Company are very similar. What are the differences between the two securities?
2. When calculating the debt-to-equity ratio, do you believe that the Second Company preferred stock should be treated as debt or as stockholders' equity? Write a statement expressing your position on this issue.

LO 2 Case 11-5 Preferred versus Common Stock

Rohnan Inc. needs to raise $500,000. It is considering two options:

a. Issue preferred stock, $100 par, 8%, cumulative, nonparticipating, callable at $110. The stock could be issued at par.

b. Issue common stock, $1 par, market $10. Currently, the company has 400,000 shares outstanding equally in the hands of five owners. The company has never paid a dividend.

Required

Rohnan has asked you to consider both options and make a recommendation. It is equally concerned with cash flow and company control. Write your recommendations.

Accounting and Ethics: What Would You Do?

LO 9 Case 11-6 Inside Information

Jim Brock was an accountant with Hubbard Inc., a large corporation with stock that was publicly traded on the New York Stock Exchange. One of Jim's duties was to manage the corporate reporting department, which was responsible for developing and issuing Hubbard's annual report. At the end of 2001, Hubbard closed its accounting records, and initial calculations indicated a very profitable year. In fact, the net income exceeded the amount that had been projected during the year by the financial analysts who followed Hubbard's stock.

Jim was very pleased with the company's financial performance. In January 2002, he suggested that his father buy Hubbard's stock because he was sure the stock price would increase when the company announced its 2001 results. Jim's father followed the advice and bought a block of stock at $25 per share.

On February 15, 2002, Hubbard announced its 2001 results and issued the annual report. The company received favorable press coverage about its performance, and the stock price on the stock exchange increased to $32 per share.

Required

What was Jim's professional responsibility to Hubbard Inc. concerning the issuance of the 2001 annual report? Did Jim act ethically in this situation?

LO 5 Case 11-7 Dividend Policy

Hancock Inc. is owned by nearly 100 shareholders. Judith Stitch owns 48% of the stock. She needs cash to fulfill her commitment to donate the funds to construct a new art gallery. Some of her friends have agreed to vote for Hancock to pay a larger-than-normal dividend to shareholders. Judith has asked you to vote for the large dividend because she knows that you also support the arts. When informed that the dividend may create a working capital hardship on Hancock, Judith responded: "There is plenty of money in Retained Earnings. The dividend will not affect the cash of the company." Respond to her comment. What ethical questions do you and Judith face? How would you vote?

Internet Research Case

www.deltaairlines.com

Case 11-8 Delta Air Lines

Delta Air Lines operates in the highly volatile airline industry. It must respond to competition and to innovative technology, and it must do so in ways that continue to build shareholder value.

Conduct a search of the World Wide Web, obtain Delta's most recent annual report, or use library resources to obtain company information to answer the following:

1. Based on the latest information available, what is Delta's (a) authorized number of common stock shares, (b) issued number of shares, (c) outstanding number of shares, and (d) the average issue price for those shares?

2. For the most recent year available, what dividend per common share did Delta pay its stockholders?
3. Locate the past 52-week high and low and the most current market price for Delta Air Lines common stock. What financial factors may have affected the company's stock price over the past three to six months? Would you buy Delta stock at this time? Explain your response.

Optional Research. Use an online reservation system to investigate how the prices of Delta Air Lines plane tickets compare with those of the other airlines. Are they higher or lower? Are there some routes where Delta has a competitive advantage?

www.travelocity.com
www.expedia.com

SOLUTION TO KEY TERMS QUIZ

13 Authorized shares (p. 529)	18 Retirement of stock (p. 537)
1 Issued shares (p. 529)	7 Dividend payout ratio (p. 537)
14 Outstanding shares (p. 529)	19 Stock dividend (p. 540)
2 Par value (p. 529)	9 Stock split (p. 542)
15 Additional paid-in capital (p. 531)	8 Statement of stockholders' equity (p. 543)
3 Retained earnings (p. 532)	11 Comprehensive Income (p. 545)
4 Cumulative feature (p. 533)	10 Book value per share (p. 545)
16 Participating feature (p. 533)	12 Market value per share (p. 547)
5 Convertible feature (p. 533)	22 Sole proprietorship (p. 554)
17 Callable feature (p. 533)	20 Partnership (p. 555)
6 Treasury stock (p. 535)	21 Partnership agreement (p. 556)

Part III
INTEGRATIVE PROBLEM

Evaluating financing options for asset acquisition and their impact on financial statements

Following are the financial statements for Griffin Inc. for the year 2001.

GRIFFIN INC.
BALANCE SHEET
AS OF DECEMBER 31, 2001
(IN MILLIONS)

Assets		Liabilities	
Cash	$ 1.6	Current portion of lease obligation	$ 1.0
Other current assets	6.4	Other current liabilities	3.0
Leased assets (net of accumulated depreciation)	7.0	Lease obligation—Long-term	6.0
Other long-term assets	45.0	Other long-term liabilities	6.0
		Total liabilities	$16.0

		Stockholders' Equity	
		Preferred stock	$ 1.0
		Additional paid-in capital on preferred stock	2.0
		Common stock	4.0
		Additional paid-in capital on common stock	16.0
		Retained earnings	21.0
		Total stockholders' equity	$44.0
Total assets	$60.0	Total liabilities and stockholders' equity	$60.0

GRIFFIN INC.
INCOME STATEMENT
FOR THE YEAR ENDED DECEMBER 31, 2001
(IN MILLIONS)

Revenues		$50.0
Expenses:		
Depreciation of leased asset	$ 1.0	
Depreciation—Other assets	3.2	
Interest on leased asset	.5	
Other expenses	27.4	
Income tax (30% rate)	5.4	
Total expenses		(37.5)
Income before extraordinary loss		$12.5
Extraordinary loss (net of $.9 taxes)		(2.1)
Net income		$10.4
EPS before extraordinary loss		$3.10
EPS extraordinary loss		(.53)
EPS—Net income		$2.57

Additional Information:

Griffin Inc. has authorized 500,000 shares of 10%, $10 par value cumulative preferred stock. There were 100,000 shares issued and outstanding at all times during 2001. The firm has also authorized 5 million shares of $1 par common stock, with 4 million shares issued and outstanding.

On January 1, 2001, Griffin Inc. acquired an asset, a piece of specialized heavy equipment, for $8 million with a capital lease. The lease contract indicates that the term of the lease is eight years. Payments of $1.5 million are to be made each December 31. The first lease payment was made December 31, 2001 and consisted of $1 million principal and $.5 million of interest expense. The capital lease is depreciated using the straight-line method over eight years with zero salvage value.

Required

1. Assuming the acquisition of the equipment using a capital lease, provide the entries for the acquisition, depreciation, and lease payment.
2. The management of Griffin Inc. is considering the financial statement impact of methods of financing, other than the capital lease, that could have been used to acquire the equipment. For each alternative **a**, **b**, and **c**, provide all necessary entries, each entry's impact on the accounting equation, and revised 2001 financial statements and calculate, as revised, the following amounts or ratios:

   Current ratio
   Debt-to-equity ratio
   Net income
   EPS—Net income

Assume that the following alternative actions would have taken place on January 1, 2001.

a. Instead of acquiring the equipment with a capital lease, the company negotiated an operating lease to use the asset. The lease requires annual year-end payments of $1.5 million and results in "off-balance sheet" financing. (*Hint:* The $1.5 million should be treated as rental expense.)

b. Instead of acquiring the equipment with a capital lease, Griffin Inc. issued bonds for $8 million and purchased the equipment with the proceeds of the bond issue. Assume the bond interest of $.5 million was accrued and paid on December 31, 2001. A portion of the principal also is paid each year for eight years. On December 31, 2001, the company paid $1 million of principal and anticipated another $1 million of principal to be paid in 2002. Assume the equipment would have an eight-year life and would be depreciated on a straight-line basis with zero salvage value.

c. Instead of acquiring the equipment with a capital lease, Griffin Inc. issued 200,000 additional shares of 10% preferred stock to raise $8 million and purchased the equipment for $8 million with the proceeds from the stock issue. Dividends on the stock are declared and paid annually. Assume that a dividend payment was made on December 31, 2001. Assume the equipment would have an eight-year life and would be depreciated on a straight-line basis with zero salvage value.

UNO RESTAURANT CORPORATION — VIDEO CASE III

Founded in Chicago in 1943, Pizzeria Uno . . . Chicago Bar & Grill, now under the corporate umbrella of **Uno Restaurant Corporation (www.pizzeriauno.com),** has been growing steadily in the competitive $20 billion casual dining industry. With its unique Uno's Original Chicago Deep Dish Pizza and other entrées, appetizers, salads, beverages, and desserts, the retail chain has expanded to include more than 150 restaurants in 29 states, the District of Columbia, Puerto Rico, and Seoul, South Korea. The company's consumer products division supplies Pizzeria Uno-brand food products to theaters, hotels, supermarkets, and American Airlines.

In 1999, the company received two prestigious food industry awards that recognized and highlighted the popularity of the Uno's brand: first place winner in the "Choice of Chains" customer survey conducted annually by Restaurants & Institutions magazine and the Platinum Award, the survey's highest honor for overall customer satisfaction scores. Also, that year for the first time Uno's was listed among the nation's top 25 restaurant chains in sales per unit in an annual study conducted by Nation's Restaurant News. In fact, 1999 was a record year for revenue, net income, and earnings per share, all of which hit historical highs. These successes not only exceeded the company's financial goals but helped to bring its long-term operational goals nearer to completion. In fact, net income increased 63 percent over 1998, to $9.8 million, and diluted per share earnings were up 68 percent, to $.84.

Aside from attracting widespread industry attention, the company's steady progress toward its operational goals also gratified the firm's managers and shareholders. Uno's has improved menus, remodeled some restaurants, and continued its ongoing repositioning strategy, broadening its appeal to the mainstream casual dining market. The company's heightened brand recognition and solid increases in customer satisfaction combined with outstanding financial results to make the company's managers very optimistic about its future. They are targeting ambitious 15 to 20 percent growth rates over the next several years.

Plans for the near term include the addition of about 25 new restaurants. The strong performance of Uno's existing franchise operations, which currently account for about a third of its restaurants, led the company to project that about half the new outlets would be franchised.

Toward the end of 1999, Uno's planned its second public stock offering, to increase trading volume and increase liquidity. However, due to the high volatility in the market and generally weak stock values among the leading restaurant companies, the offering was withdrawn. It remains a possible option for the future, when the company finds market conditions more favorable.

In the spring of 2000, the company also approved an additional repurchase of up to 500,000 shares of its common stock, extending a 1.1 million-share stock repurchase program it first announced in 1998 and extended in 1999. As of the publication of its 1999 annual report, the firm had repurchased over 700,000 of its shares. The company carries about $666,000 in capital lease obligations and a $4.6 million mortgage debt. It also relies on a revolving line of credit that it anticipates will help finance the development of additional restaurants as well as providing working capital. Other sources of financing include existing cash balances and cash generated from operations.

Questions

1. Why do you think Uno's might be looking to increase the proportion of franchise restaurants it operates? What makes Uno's attractive to a franchisee?
2. Current liabilities increased in 1999 as well as revenue. Can you suggest why?
3. What is the purpose of the stock repurchase plan, and why has it been extended?

Part IV

Additional Topics in Financial Reporting

A Word to Students about Part IV

Part IV will be fascinating and even fun—as long as you *keep practicing the concepts and reading the links from chapter to chapter.* **How does the corporation report cash flows?** See Chapter 12 to learn how to evaluate a company based on its cash flows. **Can you find the trends in a company's performance?** Use any set of financial statements you can find to practice the analysis concepts and skills presented in Chapter 13.

Chapter 12
The Statement of Cash Flows

Appendix 12A
Accounting Tools: A Work Sheet Approach to the Statement of Cash Flows

Chapter 13
Financial Statement Analysis

e-business

e-business

Study Links

A Look at Previous Chapters

In previous chapters we have seen that assets and liabilities involve important cash flows to a business at one time or another. In Chapter 2, we introduced the statement of cash flows along with the other financial statements.

Chapter 11 completed our examination of the accounting and reporting issues for a company's various assets, liabilities, and equities. Specifically, in that chapter, we considered how companies account for stockholders' equity.

A Look at This Chapter

Now that we have a fuller appreciation of how to account for the various assets and liabilities of a business, we turn our attention in this chapter to an in-depth examination of the statement of cash flows.

A Look at the Upcoming Chapter

Stockholders, creditors, and other groups use financial statements, including the statement of cash flows, to analyze a company. We called attention in earlier chapters to various ratios often used to aid in these analyses. In the final chapter, we discuss the use of ratios and other types of analysis to better understand the financial strength and health of companies.

Chapter 12

The Statement of Cash Flows

Focus on Financial Results

International Business Machines (IBM), the world's top provider of computer hardware, also makes and sells enough software to rank second only to industry powerhouse Microsoft. IBM's service operation is the largest in the world and brings in 35 percent of the company's sales. IBM also owns Lotus Development, the pioneering maker of Lotus Notes, and Tivoli Systems, whose products help manage corporate computer networks. And, as it expands its international business, IBM bends its focus increasingly to the Internet.

According to CEO Louis Gerstner Jr., IBM plans to capture "a good chunk" of the exploding e-business segment of the information technology marketplace. In coming years, that might help replace some of the cash inflow the firm has been losing in its unsuccessful entry into the retail PC market, from which it withdrew at the end of 1999.

In 1998, however, the firm earned record revenue for the fourth straight year. As you can see from the consolidated statement of cash flows, after using $4.2 billion to buy marketable securities and other investments, and another $6.5 billion for capital expenditures, IBM still had substantial cash available to pay dividends to stockholders, to purchase various securities, and to invest in its ongoing stock buyback program.

CONSOLIDATED STATEMENT OF CASH FLOWS International Business Machines Corporation and Subsidiary Companies

(Dollars in millions)

For the year ended December 31:	1998	1997	1996*
Cash flow from operating activities:			
Net income	**$ 6,328**	$ 6,093	$ 5,429
Adjustments to reconcile net income to cash provided from operating activities:			
Depreciation	**4,475**	4,018	3,676
Amortization of software	**517**	983	1,336
Effect of restructuring charges	**(355)**	(445)	(1,491)
Deferred income taxes	**(606)**	358	11
Gain on disposition of fixed and other assets	**(261)**	(273)	(300)
Other changes that (used) provided cash:			
Receivables	**(2,736)**	(3,727)	(650)
Inventories	**73**	432	196
Other assets	**880**	(1,087)	(545)
Accounts payable	**362**	699	319
Other liabilities	**596**	1,814	2,294
Net cash provided from operating activities	**9,273**	8,865	10,275
Cash flow from investing activities:			
Payments for plant, rental machines and other property	**(6,520)**	(6,793)	(5,883)
Proceeds from disposition of plant, rental machines and other property	**905**	1,130	1,314
Acquisition of Tivoli Systems, Inc.	**—**	—	(716)
Investment in software	**(250)**	(314)	(295)
Purchases of marketable securities and other investments	**(4,211)**	(1,617)	(1,613)
Proceeds from marketable securities and other investments	**3,945**	1,439	1,470
Net cash used in investing activities	**(6,131)**	(6,155)	(5,723)
Cash flow from financing activities:			
Proceeds from new debt	**7,567**	9,142	7,670
Short-term borrowings less than 90 days—net	**499**	(668)	(919)
Payments to settle debt	**(5,942)**	(4,530)	(4,992)
Preferred stock transactions—net	**(5)**	(1)	—
Common stock transactions—net	**(6,278)**	(6,250)	(5,005)
Cash dividends paid	**(834)**	(783)	(706)
Net cash used in financing activities	**(4,993)**	(3,090)	(3,952)
Effect of exchange rate changes on cash and cash equivalents	**120**	(201)	(172)
Net change in cash and cash equivalents	**(1,731)**	(581)	428
Cash and cash equivalents at January 1	**7,106**	7,687	7,259
Cash and cash equivalents at December 31	**$ 5,375**	$ 7,106	$ 7,687
Supplemental data:			
Cash paid during the year for:			
Income taxes	**$ 1,929**	$ 2,472	$ 2,229
Interest	**$ 1,605**	$ 1,475	$ 1,563

* Reclassified to conform to 1998 presentation.
The notes on pages 69 through 89 of the 1998 IBM Annual Report are an integral part of this statement.

IBM's 1998 Annual Report

If you were an IBM stockholder, what evidence from the statement of cash flows would help you determine whether IBM's stock repurchase and its investments in marketable securities will generate long-term benefits? What additional information would you want? Look up IBM's most recent annual report; do you understand how the company has generated and used cash since 1998?

www.ibm.com

Learning Objectives

After studying this chapter, you should be able to:

LO 1 Explain the purpose of a statement of cash flows. (p. 585)

LO 2 Explain what cash equivalents are and how they are treated on the statement of cash flows. (p. 587)

LO 3 Describe operating, investing, and financing activities, and give examples of each. (p. 588)

LO 4 Describe the difference between the direct and the indirect methods of computing cash flow from operating activities. (p. 592)

LO 5 Use T accounts to prepare a statement of cash flows, using the direct method to determine cash flow from operating activities. (p. 597)

LO 6 Use T accounts to prepare a statement of cash flows, using the indirect method to determine cash flow from operating activities. (p. 612)

LO 7 Use a work sheet to prepare a statement of cash flows, using the indirect method to determine cash flow from operating activities (Appendix 12A). (p. 621)

Cash Flows and Accrual Accounting

The *bottom line* is a phrase used in many different ways in today's society. "I wish politicians would cut out all of the rhetoric and get to the bottom line." "The bottom line is that the manager was fired because the team wasn't winning." "Our company's bottom line is twice what it was last year." This last use of the phrase, in reference to a company's net income, is probably the way in which *bottom line* was first used. In recent years, managers, stockholders, creditors, analysts, and other users of financial statements have become more and more wary of focusing on any one number as an indicator of a company's overall performance. Most experts now agree that there has been a tendency to rely far too heavily on net income and its companion, earnings per share, and in many cases to ignore a company's cash flows. As you know by now from your study of accounting, you can't pay bills with net income; you need cash!

www.ibm.com

To understand the difference between a company's bottom line and its cash flow, consider the case of IBM Corporation in 1998. IBM reported net earnings (income) of over $6 billion in 1998. However, as shown in the chapter opener, during this same time period its cash actually decreased by $1,731 million. How is this possible? First, net income is computed on an accrual basis, not a cash basis. Second, the income statement primarily reflects events related to the operating activities of a business, that is, selling products or providing services.

If you think about it, any one of four combinations is possible. That is, a company's cash position can increase or decrease during a period, and it can report a net profit or a net

Exhibit 12-1 Cash Flows and Net Income for Four Computer Companies in 1998 (all amounts in millions of dollars)

Company	Beginning Balance in Cash	Ending Balance in Cash	Increase (Decrease) in Cash	Net Income (Loss)
Dell Computer (fiscal year ended January 29, 1999)	$ 320	$ 520	$ 200	$1,460
IBM	7,106	5,375	(1,731)	6,328
Compaq	6,418	4,091	(2,327)	(2,743)
Western Digital (fiscal year ended June 27, 1998)	208	460	252	(290)

loss. Exhibit 12-1 illustrates this point by showing the performance of four well-known computer companies, including IBM, during 1998. Dell Computer Corporation is the only one of the four companies that both improved its cash position in 1998 and reported a net profit. As discussed in the chapter opener, IBM reported a net profit; nevertheless, it experienced a net decrease in cash during 1998. Compaq reported a net loss in 1998 and also saw its cash decline. Finally, Western Digital experienced a net loss in 1998, but improved its cash position. To summarize, a company with a profitable year does not necessarily increase its cash position, nor does a company with an unprofitable year always experience a decrease in cash.

Purpose of the Statement of Cash Flows

LO 1 Explain the purpose of a statement of cash flows.

The **statement of cash flows** is an important complement to the other major financial statements. It summarizes the operating, investing, and financing activities of a business over a period of time. The balance sheet summarizes the cash on hand and the balances in other assets, liabilities, and owners' equity accounts, providing a snapshot at a specific point in time. The statement of cash flows reports the changes in cash over a period of time and, most important, *explains these changes.*

STATEMENT OF CASH FLOWS The financial statement that summarizes an entity's cash receipts and cash payments during the period from operating, investing, and financing activities.

The income statement summarizes performance on an accrual basis. As you have learned in your study of accrual accounting, income on this basis is considered a better indicator of *future* cash inflows and outflows than is a statement limited to current cash flows. The statement of cash flows complements the accrual-based income statement by allowing users to assess a company's performance on a cash basis. As we will see in the following simple example, however, it also goes beyond presenting data related to operating performance and looks at other activities that affect a company's cash position.

An Example

Consider the following discussion between the owner of Fox River Realty and the company accountant. After a successful first year in business in 2000, in which it earned a profit of $100,000, the owner reviews the income statement for the second year, as presented in Exhibit 12-2.

The owner is pleased with the results and asks to see the balance sheet. Comparative balance sheets for the first two years are presented in Exhibit 12-3.

Where Did the Cash Go? At first glance, the owner is surprised to see the significant decline in the Cash account. She immediately presses the accountant for answers. With such a profitable year, where has the cash gone? Specifically, why has cash decreased from $150,000 to $50,000, even though income rose from $100,000 in the first year to $250,000 in the second year?

EXHIBIT 12-2 Income Statement for Fox River Realty

FOX RIVER REALTY
INCOME STATEMENT
FOR THE YEAR ENDED DECEMBER 31, 2001

Revenues	$400,000
Depreciation expense	$ 50,000
All other expenses	100,000
Total expenses	$150,000
Net income	$250,000

EXHIBIT 12-3 Balance Sheets for Fox River Realty

FOX RIVER REALTY COMPARATIVE BALANCE SHEETS DECEMBER 31	December 31	
	2001	2000
Cash	$ 50,000	$150,000
Plant and equipment	600,000	350,000
Accumulated depreciation	(150,000)	(100,000)
Total assets	$500,000	$400,000
Notes payable	$100,000	$150,000
Common stock	250,000	200,000
Retained earnings	150,000	50,000
Total equities	$500,000	$400,000

The accountant begins his explanation to the owner by pointing out that income on a cash basis is even *higher* than the reported $250,000. Because depreciation expense is an expense that does not use cash (cash is used when the plant and equipment are purchased, not when they are depreciated), cash provided from operating activities is calculated as follows:

Net income	$250,000
Add back: Depreciation expense	50,000
Cash provided by operating activities	$300,000

Further, the accountant reminds the owner of the additional $50,000 that she invested in the business during the year. Now the owner is even more bewildered: with cash from operations of $300,000 and her own infusion of $50,000, why did cash *decrease* by $100,000? The accountant refreshes the owner's memory on three major outflows of cash during the year. First, even though the business earned $250,000, she withdrew $150,000 in dividends during the year. Second, the comparative balance sheets indicate that notes payable with the bank were reduced from $150,000 to $100,000, requiring the use of $50,000 in cash. Finally, the comparative balance sheets show an increase in plant and equipment for the year from $350,000 to $600,000—a sizable investment of $250,000 in new long-term assets.

Statement of Cash Flows To summarize what happened to the cash, the accountant prepares a statement of cash flows as shown in Exhibit 12-4. Although the owner is not particularly happy with the decrease in cash for the year, she is at least satisfied with the statement as an explanation of where the cash came from and how it was used. The statement summarizes the important cash activities for the year and fills a void created with the presentation of just an income statement and a balance sheet.

REPORTING REQUIREMENTS FOR A STATEMENT OF CASH FLOWS

Accounting standards specify both the basis for preparing the statement of cash flows and the classification of items on the statement.[1] First, the statement must be prepared on a cash basis. Second, the cash flows must be classified into three categories:

[1] *Statement of Financial Accounting Standards No. 95,* "Statement of Cash Flows" (Stamford, Conn.: Financial Accounting Standards Board, November 1987).

EXHIBIT 12-4 Statement of Cash Flows for Fox River Realty

FOX RIVER REALTY
STATEMENT OF CASH FLOWS
FOR THE YEAR ENDED DECEMBER 31, 2001

Cash provided (used) by operating activities:	
Net income	$ 250,000
Add back: Depreciation expense	50,000
Net cash provided (used) by operating activities	$ 300,000
Cash provided (used) by investing activities:	
Purchase of new plant and equipment	$(250,000)
Cash provided (used) by financing activities:	
Additional investment by owner	$ 50,000
Cash dividends paid to owner	(150,000)
Repayment of notes payable to bank	(50,000)
Net cash provided (used) by financing activities	$(150,000)
Net increase (decrease) in cash	$(100,000)
Cash balance at beginning of year	150,000
Cash balance at end of year	$ 50,000

- Operating activities
- Investing activities
- Financing activities

We now take a closer look at each of these important requirements in preparing a statement of cash flows.

THE DEFINITION OF CASH: CASH AND CASH EQUIVALENTS

LO 2 Explain what cash equivalents are and how they are treated on the statement of cash flows.

The purpose of the statement of cash flows is to provide information about a company's cash inflows and outflows. Thus, it is essential to have a clear understanding of what the definition of *cash* includes. According to accounting standards, certain items are recognized as being equivalent to cash and are combined with cash on the balance sheet and the statement of cash flows.

Commercial paper (short-term notes issued by corporations), money market funds, and Treasury bills are examples of cash equivalents. To be classified as a **cash equivalent,** an item must be readily convertible to a known amount of cash and have a maturity *to the investor* of three months or less. For example, a three-year Treasury note purchased two months before its maturity is classified as a cash equivalent. The same note purchased two years before maturity is not classified as a cash equivalent but as an investment.

CASH EQUIVALENT
An item readily convertible to a known amount of cash and with a maturity to the investor of three months or less.

To understand why cash equivalents are combined with cash when preparing a statement of cash flows, assume that a company has a cash balance of $10,000 and no assets that qualify as cash equivalents. Further assume that the $10,000 is used to purchase 90-day Treasury bills and is recorded by the following entry:

Investment in Treasury Bills	10,000	
Cash		10,000
To record the purchase of 90-day Treasury bills.		

Assets	=	Liabilities	+	Owners' Equity
+10,000				
−10,000				

For record-keeping purposes, it is important to recognize this transaction as a transfer between cash in the bank and an investment in a government security. In the strictest sense, the investment represents an outflow of cash. The purchase of a security with such a short maturity does not, however, involve any significant degree of risk in terms of price changes and thus is not reported on the statement of cash flows as an outflow. Instead, for purposes of classification on the balance sheet and the statement of cash flows, this is merely a transfer *within* the cash and cash equivalents category. The important point is that before the purchase of the Treasury bills the company had $10,000 in cash and cash equivalents and that after the purchase it still had $10,000 in cash and cash equivalents. *Because nothing changed, the transaction is not reported on the statement of cash flows.*

Consider a different transaction involving the $10,000 and the following entry:

Investment in GM Common Stock	10,000	
Cash		10,000
To record the purchase of GM common stock.		

Assets	=	Liabilities	+	Owners' Equity
+10,000				
−10,000				

This purchase involves a certain amount of risk for the company making the investment. The GM stock is not convertible to a known amount of cash because its market value is subject to change. Thus, for balance sheet purposes, the investment is not considered a cash equivalent and is not therefore combined with cash but is classified as either a trading security or an available-for-sale security, depending on the company's intent in holding the stock (the distinction between these two types was discussed in Chapter 7). In the preparation of a statement of cash flows, the *investment in stock of another company is considered a significant activity and thus is reported on the statement of cash flows.*

CLASSIFICATION OF CASH FLOWS

LO 3 Describe operating, investing, and financing activities, and give examples of each.

For the statement of cash flows, companies are required to classify activities into three categories: operating, investing, or financing. These categories represent the major functions of an entity, and classifying activities in this way allows users to look at important relationships. For example, one important financing activity for many businesses is borrowing money. Grouping the cash inflows from borrowing money during the period with the cash outflows from repayments of loans during the period makes it easier for analysts and other users of the statements to evaluate the company.

Each of the three types of activities can result both in cash inflows and in cash outflows to the company. Thus, the general format for the statement is as shown in Exhibit 12-5. Note the direct tie between the bottom portion of this statement and the balance sheet. The beginning and ending balances in cash and cash equivalents, shown as the last two lines on the statement of cash flows, are taken directly from the comparative balance sheets. Some companies end their statement of cash flows with the figure for the net increase or decrease in cash and cash equivalents and do not report the beginning and ending balances in cash and cash equivalents directly on the statement of cash flows. Instead, the reader must turn to the balance sheet for these amounts. We now take a closer look at the types of activities that appear in each of the three categories on the statement of cash flows.

OPERATING ACTIVITIES
Activities concerned with the acquisition and sale of products and services.

Operating Activities

Operating activities involve acquiring and selling products and services. The specific activities of a business depend on its type. For example, the purchase of raw materials is an important operating activity for a manufacturer. For a retailer, the purchase of inventory from a distributor constitutes an operating activity. For a realty company, the payment of a commission to a salesperson is an operating activity. All three types of businesses sell either products or services, and their sales are important operating activities.

A statement of cash flows reflects the cash effects, either inflows or outflows, associated with each of these activities. For example, the manufacturer's payment for purchases of raw materials results in a cash outflow. The receipt of cash from collecting an account receivable results in a cash inflow. The income statement reports operating activities on an accrual basis. The statement of cash flows reflects a company's operating activities on a cash basis.

EXHIBIT 12-5 Format for the Statement of Cash Flows

THE SMITH CORPORATION
STATEMENT OF CASH FLOWS
FOR THE YEAR ENDED DECEMBER 31, 2001

Cash flows from operating activities:		
Inflows	$ xxx	
Outflows	(xxx)	
Net cash provided (used) by operating activities		$xxx
Cash flows from investing activities:		
Inflows	xxx	
Outflows	(xxx)	
Net cash provided (used) by investing activities		xxx
Cash flows from financing activities:		
Inflows	xxx	
Outflows	(xxx)	
Net cash provided (used) by financing activities		xxx
Net increase (decrease) in cash and cash equivalents		$xxx
Cash and cash equivalents at beginning of year		xxx
Cash and cash equivalents at end of year		$xxx

INVESTING ACTIVITIES Activities concerned with the acquisition and disposal of long-term assets.

Investing Activities

Investing activities involve acquiring and disposing of long-term assets. Replacing worn-out plant and equipment and expanding the existing base of long-term assets are essential to all businesses. In fact, cash paid for these acquisitions, often called *capital expenditures,* is usually the largest single item in the Investing Activities section of the statement. The following excerpt from IBM's 1998 statement of cash flows (also shown in the chapter opener) indicates 1 that the company spent over $6,520 million for plant, rental machines, and other property during 1998 (all amounts are in millions of dollars):

	Cash flow from investing activities:	
1	Payments for plant, rental machines and other property	(6,520)
2	Proceeds from disposition of plant, rental machines and other property	905
	Investment in software	(250)
3	Purchases of marketable securities and other investments	(4,211)
	Proceeds from marketable securities and other investments	3,945
	Net cash used in investing activities	(6,131)

Sales of long-term assets, such as plant and equipment, are not generally a significant source of cash. These assets are acquired to be used in producing goods and services, or to support this function, rather than to be resold, as is true for inventory. Occasionally, however, plant and equipment may wear out or no longer be needed and are offered for sale. In fact, the excerpt from IBM's report indicates that it generated $905 million of cash in 1998 from 2 disposals of plant, rental machines, and other property.

In Chapter 7 we explained why companies sometimes invest in the stocks and bonds of other companies. The classification of these investments on the statement of cash flows depends on the type of investment. The acquisition of one company by another, whether in the form of a merger or a stock acquisition, is an important *investing* activity to bring to the attention of statement readers. Although IBM did not acquire any other companies during 1998, its statements of cash flows in the chapter opener reveal that it spent $716 million in 1996 to acquire Tivoli Systems. Note that in 1998 IBM spent $4,211 million to buy 3 marketable securities and other investments and generated $3,945 million from

From Concept
TO PRACTICE 12.1

READING GATEWAY'S STATEMENT OF CASH FLOWS According to Gateway's Investing Activities section of its statement of cash flows, what does the company spend a significant amount of cash for every year? What types of expenditures would you expect to find in this category?

FINANCING ACTIVITIES
Activities concerned with the raising and repayment of funds in the form of debt and equity.

selling these investments. According to a footnote to IBM's statements, the company classifies marketable securities as available for sale.

Cash flows from purchases, sales, and maturities of held-to-maturity securities (bonds) and available-for-sale securities (stocks and bonds) are classified as *investing* activities. On the other hand, these same types of cash flows for trading securities are classified as *operating* activities. This apparent inconsistency in the accounting rules is based on the idea that trading securities are held for the express purpose of generating short-term profits and thus are operating in nature.

Financing Activities All businesses rely on internal financing, external financing, or a combination of the two in meeting their needs for cash. Initially, a new business must have a certain amount of investment by the owners to begin operations. After this, many companies use notes, bonds, and other forms of debt to provide financing.[2] Issuing stock and various forms of debt results in cash inflows that appear as **financing activities** on the statement of cash flows. On the other side, the repurchase of a company's own stock and the repayment of borrowings are important cash outflows to be reported in the Financing Activities section of the statement. Another important activity listed in the Financing Activities section of the statement is the payment of dividends to stockholders. IBM's 1998 statement of cash flows lists most of the common cash inflows and outflows from financing activities (amounts in millions of dollars):

	Cash flow from financing activities:	
1	Proceeds from new debt	7,567
	Short-term borrowings less than 90 days—net	499
2	Payments to settle debt	(5,942)
	Preferred stock transactions—net	(5)
	Common stock transactions—net	(6,278)
	Cash dividends paid	(834)
	Net cash used in financing activities	(4,993)

In 1998 IBM 1 received $7,567 million from issuing new debt and 2 paid over $5.9 billion to retire old debt. In analyzing IBM, you would probably next read the long-term debt footnote to see whether the company essentially refinanced the old debt with new debt at a lower interest rate and, if it did, what the interest saving is, because this will continue to be a benefit for many years.

Summary of the Three Types of Activities To summarize the categorization of the activities of a business as operating, investing, and financing, refer to Exhibit 12-6. The exhibit lists examples of each of the three activities along with the related accounts on the balance sheet and the account classifications on the balance sheet.

Study Tip

Later in the chapter, you will learn a technique to use in preparing the statement of cash flows. Recall the observations made here regarding what types of accounts affect each of the three activities when you get to that section of the chapter.

In the exhibit, operating activities center on the acquisition and sale of products and services and related costs, such as wages and taxes. Two important observations can be made about the cash flow effects from the operating activities of a business. *First, the cash flows from these activities are the cash effects of transactions that enter into the determination of net income.* For example, the sale of a product enters into the calculation of net income. The cash effect of this transaction—that is, the collection of the account receivable—results in a cash inflow from operating activities. *Second, cash flows from operating activities usually relate to an increase or decrease in either a current asset or a current liability.* For example, the payment of taxes to the government results in a decrease in taxes payable, which is a current liability on the balance sheet.

Note that investing activities normally relate to long-term assets on the balance sheet. For example, the purchase of new plant and equipment increases long-term assets, and the sale of these same assets reduces long-term assets on the balance sheet.

[2]Wm. Wrigley Jr. Company is unusual in this regard in that it relies almost solely on funds generated from stockholders, in the form of common stock, for financing. The company had no short-term notes payable at December 31, 1998, and total long-term liabilities accounted for less than 10% of the total liabilities and stockholders' equity on the balance sheet on that date.

EXHIBIT 12-6 Classification of Items on the Statement of Cash Flows

Activity	Examples	Effect on Cash	Related Balance Sheet Account	Classification on Balance Sheet
Operating	Collection of customer accounts	Inflow	Accounts receivable	Current asset
	Payment to suppliers for inventory	Outflow	Accounts payable Inventory	Current liability Current asset
	Payment of wages	Outflow	Wages payable	Current liability
	Payment of taxes	Outflow	Taxes payable	Current liability
Investing	Capital expenditures	Outflow	Plant and equipment	Long-term asset
	Purchase of another company	Outflow	Long-term investment	Long-term asset
	Sale of plant and equipment	Inflow	Plant and equipment	Long-term asset
	Sale of another company	Inflow	Long-term investment	Long-term asset
Financing	Issuance of capital stock	Inflow	Capital stock	Stockholders' equity
	Issuance of bonds	Inflow	Bonds payable	Long-term liability
	Issuance of bank note	Inflow	Notes payable	Long-term liability
	Repurchase of stock	Outflow	Treasury stock	Stockholders' equity
	Retirement of bonds	Outflow	Bonds payable	Long-term liability
	Repayment of notes	Outflow	Notes payable	Long-term liability
	Payment of dividends	Outflow	Retained earnings	Stockholders' equity

Finally, *note that financing activities usually relate to either long-term liabilities or stockholders' equity accounts.* There are exceptions to these observations about the type of balance sheet account involved with each of the three types of activities, but these rules of thumb are useful as we begin to analyze transactions and attempt to determine their classification on the statement of cash flows.

BUSINESS STRATEGY

Whether lower profit margins are the result of falling hardware prices, the increasing ability of smaller computers to do the work of mainframes, or the failure of its retail personal-computer operation doesn't really matter to IBM. The company has announced it is changing tack. Rather than promoting the continuity the company promised its shareholders in the 1990s, IBM is now positioning itself to take advantage of what CEO Louis Gerstner Jr. terms "a historic shift" in the way we work, learn, govern, shop, and entertain ourselves.

That shift is powered by the Internet, which Gerstner and many other observers call a new mass medium that will fundamentally change the way we use technology in our lives. IBM sees this change as an opportunity not merely to join a global information network but to build entirely new ways of doing business. Technology alone is no longer the point—something faster or cheaper is always being invented. But by helping its business customers find new ways to *use* technology, to transform such critical business processes as supply chain management, customer service and support, and product distribution, IBM hopes also to reinvent itself as the premier provider of information technology services. The strategy is to lead the way into what Gerstner calls "a truly rare opportunity . . . to start something totally new."

Whether the promised new era comes to pass, and whether IBM's strategy will prove a winner for the firm and its shareholders, time will tell.

SOURCE: IBM's 1998 annual report.

One of IBM's many software products is WebSphere, a development platform allowing teams to organize and manage web development projects. Success of new versions of products like WebSphere will help keep IBM's future bright.
www-4.ibm.com/software/webservers/studio/

EXHIBIT 12-7 Boulder Company Income Statement

BOULDER COMPANY
INCOME STATEMENT
FOR THE YEAR ENDED DECEMBER 31, 2001

Revenues	$80,000
Operating expenses	(64,000)
Income before tax	$16,000
Income tax expense	(4,000)
Net income	$12,000

TWO METHODS OF REPORTING CASH FLOW FROM OPERATING ACTIVITIES

LO 4 Describe the difference between the direct and the indirect methods of computing cash flow from operating activities.

DIRECT METHOD
For preparing the Operating Activities section of the statement of cash flows, the approach in which cash receipts and cash payments are reported.

INDIRECT METHOD
For preparing the Operating Activities section of the statement of cash flows, the approach in which net income is reconciled to net cash flow from operations.

Companies use one of two different methods to report the amount of cash flow from operating activities. The first approach, called the **direct method,** involves reporting major classes of gross cash receipts and cash payments. For example, cash collected from customers is reported separately from any interest and dividends received. Each of the major types of cash payments related to the company's operations follows, such as cash paid for inventory, for salaries and wages, for interest, and for taxes. An acceptable alternative to this approach is the **indirect method.** Under the indirect method, net cash flow from operating activities is computed by adjusting net income to remove the effect of all deferrals of past operating cash receipts and payments and all accruals of future operating cash receipts and payments.

Although the direct method is preferred by the Financial Accounting Standards Board, it is used much less frequently than the indirect method in practice. In fact, an annual survey of 600 companies reported that 593 companies used the indirect method and only 7 companies used the direct method.[3]

To compare and contrast the two methods, assume that Boulder Company begins operations as a corporation on January 1, 2001, with the owners' investment of $10,000 in cash. An income statement for 2001 and a balance sheet as of December 31, 2001, are presented in Exhibits 12-7 and 12-8, respectively.

Direct Method To report cash flow from operating activities under the direct method, we look at each of the items on the income statement and determine how much

EXHIBIT 12-8 Boulder Company Balance Sheet

BOULDER COMPANY
BALANCE SHEET
AS OF DECEMBER 31, 2001

Assets		**Liabilities and Stockholders' Equity**	
Cash	$15,000	Accounts payable	$ 6,000
Accounts receivable	13,000	Capital stock	10,000
		Retained earnings	12,000
Total	$28,000	Total	$28,000

[3] *Accounting Trends & Techniques,* 53rd ed. (New York: American Institute of Certified Public Accountants, 1999).

EXHIBIT 12-9 Statement of Cash Flows Using the Direct Method

BOULDER COMPANY
STATEMENT OF CASH FLOWS
FOR THE YEAR ENDED DECEMBER 31, 2001

Cash flows from operating activities	
Cash collected from customers	$ 67,000
Cash payments for operating purposes	(58,000)
Cash payments for taxes	(4,000)
Net cash inflow from operating activities	$ 5,000
Cash flows from financing activities	
Issuance of capital stock	$ 10,000
Net increase in cash	$ 15,000
Cash balance, beginning of period	–0–
Cash balance, end of period	$ 15,000

cash each of these activities either generated or used. For example, revenues for the period were $80,000. Since the balance sheet at the end of the period shows a balance in Accounts Receivable of $13,000, however, Boulder collected only $80,000 – $13,000, or $67,000, from its sales of the period. Thus, the first line on the statement of cash flows in Exhibit 12-9 reports $67,000 in cash collected from customers. Remember that the *net increase* in Accounts Receivable must be deducted from sales to find cash collected. For a new company, this is the same as the ending balance because the company starts the year without a balance in Accounts Receivable.

The same logic can be applied to determine the amount of cash expended for operating purposes. Operating expenses on the income statement are reported at $64,000. According to the balance sheet, however, $6,000 of the expense is unpaid at the end of the period as evidenced by the balance in Accounts Payable. Thus, the amount of cash expended for operating purposes as reported on the statement of cash flows in Exhibit 12-9 is $64,000 – $6,000, or $58,000. The other cash payment in the Operating Activities section of the statement is $4,000 for income taxes. Because no liability for income taxes is reported on the balance sheet, we know that $4,000 represents both the income tax expense of the period and the amount paid to the government. The only other item on the statement of cash flows in Exhibit 12-9 is the cash inflow from financing activities for the amount of cash invested by the owner in return for capital stock.

Indirect Method When the indirect method is used, the first line in the Operating Activities section of the statement of cash flows as shown in Exhibit 12-10 is the net income of the period. Net income is then *adjusted* to reconcile it to the amount of cash provided by operating activities. As reported on the income statement, this net income figure includes the sales of $80,000 for the period. As we know, however, the amount of cash collected was $13,000 less than this because not all customers paid Boulder the amount due. *The increase in Accounts Receivable for the period is deducted from net income on the statement because the increase indicates that the company sold more during the period than it collected in cash.*

The logic for the addition of the increase in Accounts Payable is similar, although the effect is the opposite. The amount of operating expenses deducted on the income statement was $64,000. We know, however, that the amount of cash paid was $6,000 less than this, as the balance in Accounts Payable indicates. *The increase in Accounts Payable for the period is added back to net income on the statement because the increase indicates that the company paid less during the period than it recognized in expense on the income statement.* One observation can be noted about this example. Because this is the first year of operations for Boulder, we wouldn't be too concerned that accounts receivable is increasing

EXHIBIT 12-10 Statement of Cash Flows Using the Indirect Method

BOULDER COMPANY
STATEMENT OF CASH FLOWS
FOR THE YEAR ENDED DECEMBER 31, 2001

Cash flows from operating activities	
Net income	$ 12,000
Adjustments to reconcile net income to net cash from operating activities:	
Increase in accounts receivable	(13,000)
Increase in accounts payable	6,000
Net cash inflow from operating activities	$ 5,000
Cash flows from financing activities	
Issuance of capital stock	$ 10,000
Net increase in cash	$ 15,000
Cash balance, beginning of period	–0–
Cash balance, end of period	$ 15,000

From Concept **TO PRACTICE 12.2**

READING IBM'S STATEMENT OF CASH FLOWS Does IBM use the direct or the indirect method in the Operating Activities section of its statement of cash flows? How can you tell which it is?

faster than accounts payable. If this becomes a trend, however, we would try to improve the accounts receivable collections process.

Two important observations should be made in comparing the two methods illustrated in Exhibits 12-9 and 12-10. First, the amount of cash provided by operating activities is the same under the two methods: $5,000; the two methods are simply different computational approaches to arrive at the cash generated from operations. Second, the remainder of the statement of cash flows is the same, regardless of which method is used. The only difference between the two methods is in the Operating Activities section of the statement.

NONCASH INVESTING AND FINANCING ACTIVITIES

Occasionally, companies engage in important investing and financing activities that do not affect cash. For example, assume that at the end of the year Wolk Corp. issues capital stock to an inventor in return for the exclusive rights to a patent. Although the patent has no ready market value, the stock could have been sold on the open market for $25,000. Thus, the following entry is made on Wolk's books:

Patent	25,000	
Capital Stock		25,000
To record issuance of stock in exchange for patent.		

Assets	=	Liabilities	+	Owners' Equity
+25,000				+25,000

This transaction does not involve cash and is therefore not reported on the statement of cash flows. However, what if we changed the scenario slightly? Assume that Wolk wants the patent but the inventor is not willing to accept stock in return for it. So instead Wolk sells stock on the open market for $25,000 and then pays this amount in cash to the inventor for the rights to the patent. Now Wolk records two journal entries. The first is as follows:

Cash	25,000	
Capital Stock		25,000
To record issuance of capital stock for cash.		

Assets	=	Liabilities	+	Owners' Equity
+25,000				+25,000

It next records this entry:

Patent	25,000	
Cash		25,000
To record acquisition of patent for cash.		

Assets	=	Liabilities	+	Owners' Equity
+25,000				
−25,000				

How would each of these two transactions be reported on a statement of cash flows? The first transaction appears as a cash inflow in the Financing Activities section of the statement; the second is reported as a cash outflow in the Investing Activities section. The point is that even though the *form* of this arrangement (with stock sold for cash and then the cash paid to the inventor) differs from the form of the first arrangement (with stock exchanged directly for the patent), the *substance* of the two arrangements is the same. That is, both involve a significant financing activity, the issuance of stock, and an important investing activity, the acquisition of a patent. Because the substance is what matters, accounting standards require that any significant noncash transactions be reported either in a separate schedule or in a footnote to the financial statements. For our transaction in which stock was issued directly to the inventor, presentation in a schedule is as follows:

Supplemental schedule of noncash investing and financing activities	
Acquisition of patent in exchange for capital stock	$25,000

To this point, we have concentrated on the purpose of a statement of cash flows and the major reporting requirements related to it. We turn our attention next to a methodology to use in actually preparing the statement.

Two-Minute Review

1. What are cash equivalents, and why are any increases or decreases in them not reported on a statement of cash flows?

2. What are the three types of activities reported on a statement of cash flows?

3. What are the two methods of reporting cash flow from operating activities, and how do they differ?

Answers:

1. A cash equivalent is an item readily convertible to a known amount of cash and with an original maturity to the investor of three months or less. Because the maturity date of these items, such as a 60-day certificate of deposit, is so near, they are not considered to carry any significant risks in terms of price changes. Thus, any changes in cash equivalents are not reported on the statement of cash flows.

2. Operating, investing, and financing activities.

3. Direct and indirect methods. The direct method involves reporting major classes of gross cash receipts and cash payments. Under the indirect method, net cash flow from operating activities is computed by adjusting net income to remove the effect of all deferrals of past operating cash receipts and payments and all accruals of future operating cash receipts and payments.

How the Statement of Cash Flows Is Put Together

Two interesting observations can be made about the statement of cash flows. First, the "answer" to a statement of cash flows is known before we start to prepare it. That is, the change in cash for the period is known by comparing two successive balance sheets. Thus, it is not the change in cash itself that is emphasized on the statement of cash flows but the *explanations* for the change in cash. That is, each item on a statement of cash flows helps to explain why cash changed by the amount it did during the period. The second important observation about the statement of cash flows relates even more specifically to how we prepare it. Both an income statement and a balance sheet are prepared simply by taking the balances in each of the various accounts in the general ledger and putting them in the right place on the right statement. This is not true for the statement of cash flows, however. Instead, it is necessary to analyze the transactions during the period and attempt to (1) determine which of these affected cash and (2) classify each of the cash effects into one of the three categories.

In the simple examples presented so far in the chapter, we prepared the statement of cash flows without the use of any special tools. In more complex situations, however, some type of methodology is needed. We first will review the basic accounting equation and then illustrate a T-account approach for preparing the statement. Appendix 12A presents a work-sheet approach to the preparation of the statement of cash flows.

The Accounting Equation and the Statement of Cash Flows

The basic accounting equation is as follows:

Assets = Liabilities + Owners' Equity

Next, consider this refinement of the equation:

Assets	=	**Liabilities and Owner's Equity**
Cash + Noncash current assets + Long-term assets	=	Current liabilities + Long-term liabilities + Capital stock + Retained earnings

The equation can be rearranged so that only cash is on the left side and all other items are on the right side:

Cash	=	Current liabilities + Long-term liabilities + Capital stock + Retained earnings – **Non-cash current assets** – **Long-term assets**

Therefore, any changes in cash must be accompanied by a corresponding change in the right side of the equation. For example, an increase or inflow of cash could result from an *increase* in long-term liabilities in the form of issuing bonds payable, an important financing activity for many companies. Or an increase in cash could come from a *decrease* in long-term assets in the form of a sale of fixed assets. The various possibilities for inflows (+) and outflows (–) of cash can be summarized by activity as follows:

Activity	Left Side	Right Side	Example
Operating			
	+ Cash	– Noncash current assets	Collect accounts receivable
	– Cash	+ Noncash current assets	Prepay insurance
	+ Cash	+ Current liabilities	Collect customer's deposit
	– Cash	– Current liabilities	Pay suppliers
	+ Cash	+ Retained earnings	Make a cash sale
Investing			
	+ Cash	– Long-term assets	Sell equipment
	– Cash	+ Long-term assets	Buy equipment
Financing			
	+ Cash	+ Long-term liabilities	Issue bonds
	– Cash	– Long-term liabilities	Retire bonds
	+ Cash	+ Capital stock	Issue capital stock
	– Cash	– Capital stock	Buy capital stock
	– Cash	– Retained earnings	Pay dividends

By considering these examples we see that inflows and outflows of cash relate to increases and decreases in the various balance sheet accounts. We now turn to analyzing these accounts as a way to assemble a statement of cash flows.

A Master T-Account Approach to Preparing the Statement of Cash Flows: Direct Method

LO 5 Use T accounts to prepare a statement of cash flows, using the direct method to determine cash flow from operating activities.

The following steps can be used to prepare a statement of cash flows:

1. Set up three master T accounts with the following headings:

a. Cash Flows from Operating Activities

b. Cash Flows from Investing Activities

c. Cash Flows from Financing Activities

These master T accounts take the place of the Cash account. As we analyze the transactions that affect each of the noncash balance sheet accounts, any cash effects are entered on the appropriate master account. When completed, the three master accounts contain all of the information needed to prepare a statement of cash flows.

2. Determine the cash flows from operating activities. Generally, this requires analyzing each item on the *income statement* and the *current asset* and *current liability* accounts. Draft journal entries for each transaction, using a lettering system for identification purposes, and post them to the appropriate balance sheet accounts. In many instances, these will be summary entries for the entire period. For example, we make one entry for all credit sales for the period, one entry for all collections on account, and so forth. Enter any increases in cash on the left side of the Cash Flow from Operating Activities master T account and any decreases on the right side.

3. Determine the cash flows from investing activities. Generally, this requires analyzing the *long-term asset* accounts and any additional information provided. Draft journal entries for each transaction, and post them to the appropriate balance sheet accounts. Enter any increases in cash on the left side of the Cash Flow from Investing Activities master T account and any decreases on the right side. Enter any significant noncash activities on a supplemental schedule.

4. Determine the cash flows from financing activities. Generally, this requires analyzing the *long-term liability* and *stockholders' equity* accounts and any additional information provided. Draft journal entries for each transaction. Enter any increases in cash on the left side of the Cash Flow from Financing Activities master T account and any decreases on the right side of the T account. Enter any significant noncash activities on a supplemental schedule.

Remember that these are general rules that the cash effects of changes in current accounts are reported in the operating section, those relating to long-term asset accounts in the investing section, and those relating to long-term liabilities and stockholders' equity in the financing section. The general rules for classification of activities have a few exceptions, but we will not concern ourselves with them.

To illustrate this approach, we will refer to the income statement in Exhibit 12-11 and to the comparative balance sheets and the additional information provided for Julian Corp. in Exhibit 12-12.

Determine the Cash Flows from Operating Activities To do this, we need to consider each of the items on the income statement and any related current assets or liabilities from the balance sheet.

Sales Revenue and Accounts Receivable Sales as reported on the income statement in Exhibit 12-11 amounted to $670,000. The journal entry was as follows:

(a)	Accounts Receivable	670,000	
	Sales Revenue		670,000
	To record sales on account.		

Assets	=	Liabilities	+	Owners' Equity
+670,000				+670,000

Based on the beginning and ending balances in Exhibit 12-12, a T account for Accounts Receivable appears as follows after posting the debit for the sales of the period:

ACCOUNTS RECEIVABLE

Bal. Jan. 1	57,000		
(a) Sales on account	670,000	?	Cash collections (b)
Bal. Dec. 31	63,000		

EXHIBIT 12-11 Julian Corp. Income Statement

JULIAN CORP.
INCOME STATEMENT
FOR THE YEAR ENDED DECEMBER 31, 2001

Revenues and gains:		
Sales revenue	$670,000	
Interest revenue	15,000	
Gain on sale of machine	5,000	
Total revenues and gains		$690,000
Expenses and losses:		
Cost of goods sold	$390,000	
Salaries and wages	60,000	
Depreciation	40,000	
Insurance	12,000	
Interest	15,000	
Income taxes	50,000	
Loss on retirement of bonds	3,000	
Total expenses and losses		570,000
Net income		$120,000

EXHIBIT 12-12 Julian Corp. Comparative Balance Sheets

JULIAN CORP.
COMPARATIVE BALANCE SHEETS

	December 31 2001	December 31 2000
Cash	$ 35,000	$ 46,000
Accounts receivable	63,000	57,000
Inventory	84,000	92,000
Prepaid insurance	12,000	18,000
Total current assets	$194,000	$213,000
Long-term investments	$120,000	$ 90,000
Land	150,000	100,000
Property and equipment	320,000	280,000
Accumulated depreciation	(100,000)	(75,000)
Total long-term assets	$490,000	$395,000
Total assets	$684,000	$608,000
Accounts payable	$ 38,000	$ 31,000
Salaries and wages payable	7,000	9,000
Income taxes payable	8,000	5,000
Total current liabilities	$ 53,000	$ 45,000
Notes payable	$ 85,000	$ 35,000
Bonds payable	200,000	260,000
Total long-term liabilities	$285,000	$295,000
Capital stock	$100,000	$ 75,000
Retained earnings	246,000	193,000
Total stockholders' equity	$346,000	$268,000
Total liabilities and stockholders' equity	$684,000	$608,000

Additional Information

1. Long-term investments were purchased for $30,000. The securities are classified as available for sale.
2. Land was purchased by issuing a $50,000 note payable.
3. Equipment was purchased for $75,000.
4. A machine with an original cost of $35,000 and a book value of $20,000 was sold for $25,000.
5. Bonds with a face value of $60,000 were retired by paying $63,000 in cash.
6. Capital stock was issued in exchange for $25,000 in cash.
7. Dividends of $67,000 were paid.

Accounts Receivable increased by $6,000 for the period. *This indicates that Julian had $6,000 more in sales to its customers than it collected in cash from them* (assuming that all sales are on credit). Thus, cash collections must have been $670,000 – $6,000, or $664,000. Another way to look at this is as follows:

Beginning accounts receivable	$ 57,000
+ Sales revenue	670,000
– Cash collections	(*X*)
= Ending accounts receivable	$ 63,000

Solving for X, we can find cash collections:

$$57{,}000 + 670{,}000 - X = 63{,}000$$
$$X = \underline{\underline{664{,}000}}$$

The journal entry to record cash collections was as follows:

(b)	Cash	664,000	
	Accounts Receivable		664,000
	To record cash collected on account.		

Assets	=	Liabilities	+	Owners' Equity
+664,000				
−664,000				

At this point, note the debit to Cash for $664,000 as shown in the master T account Cash Flows from Operating Activities, in Exhibit 12-13.

Interest Revenue Julian reported interest revenue on the income statement of $15,000. Did the company actually receive this amount of cash, or was it merely an accrual of revenue earned but not yet received? The answer can be found by examining the Current Assets section of the balance sheet. *Because there is no Interest Receivable account, the amount of interest earned was the amount of cash received:*

(c)	Cash	15,000	
	Interest Revenue		15,000
	To record interest earned and received.		

Assets	=	Liabilities	+	Owners' Equity
+15,000				+15,000

The debit should be entered in the master T account Cash Flows from Operating Activities, as shown in Exhibit 12-13.

Gain on Sale of Machine A gain on the sale of machine of $5,000 is reported as the next line on the income statement. Any cash received from the sale of a long-term asset is reported in the Investing Activities section of the statement of cash flows. Thus, we ignore the gain when reporting cash flows from operating activities under the direct method.

Cost of Goods Sold, Inventory, and Accounts Payable Cost of goods sold, as reported on the income statement, amounts to $390,000 and was recorded with this entry:

(d)	Cost of Goods Sold	390,000	
	Inventory		390,000
	To record cost of goods sold.		

Assets	=	Liabilities	+	Owners' Equity
−390,000				−390,000

EXHIBIT 12-13 Master T Account for Cash Flows from Operating Activities

CASH FLOWS FROM OPERATING ACTIVITIES

Cash receipts from:		Cash payments for:	
(b) Sales on account	664,000	(f) Inventory purchases	375,000
(c) Interest	15,000	(h) Salaries and wages	62,000
		(k) Insurance	6,000
		(l) Interest	15,000
		(n) Taxes	47,000

We see that $390,000 is not the amount of cash expended to pay suppliers of inventory. First, cost of goods sold represents the cost of the inventory sold during the period, not the amount purchased. Thus, we must analyze the Inventory account to determine the purchases of the period. Second, the amount of purchases is not the same as the cash paid to suppliers, because purchases are normally on account. Thus, we must analyze the Accounts Payable account to determine the cash payments.

Based on the beginning and ending balances from Exhibit 12-12, a T account for Inventory appears as follows after posting the reduction in the account for cost of goods sold:

INVENTORY

Bal. Jan. 1	92,000		
(e) Purchases on account	?	390,000	Cost of goods sold (d)
Bal. Dec. 31	84,000		

Note the $8,000 net decrease in Inventory. *This means that the cost of inventory sold was $8,000 more than the purchases of the period.* Thus, purchases must have been $390,000 – $8,000, or $382,000. Another way to look at this is as follows:

Beginning inventory	$ 92,000
+ Purchases	*X*
– Cost of goods sold	(390,000)
= Ending inventory	$ 84,000

Solving for *X*, we can find purchases:

$$92{,}000 + X - 390{,}000 = 84{,}000$$
$$X = \underline{\underline{382{,}000}}$$

The journal entry to record purchases was as follows:

(e)	Inventory	382,000	
	Accounts Payable		382,000
	To record purchases on account.		

Assets	=	Liabilities	+	Owners' Equity
+382,000		+382,000		

From Exhibit 12-12, a T account for Accounts Payable, after posting the credit for purchases of the period, is as follows:

ACCOUNTS PAYABLE

		31,000	Bal. Jan. 1
(f) Cash payments	?	382,000	Purchases (e)
		38,000	Bal. Dec. 31

Note the $7,000 net increase in Accounts Payable. *This means that Julian's purchases were $7,000 more during the period than its cash payments.* Thus, cash payments must have been $382,000 – $7,000, or $375,000. Another way to look at this is as follows:

Beginning accounts payable	$ 31,000
+ Purchases	382,000
– Cash payments	(*X*)
= Ending accounts payable	$ 38,000

Solving for *X*, we can find cash payments:

$$31{,}000 + 382{,}000 - X = 38{,}000$$
$$X = \underline{\underline{375{,}000}}$$

The journal entry to record payments on account was as follows:

(f)	Accounts Payable	375,000	
	Cash		375,000
	To record cash payments on account.		

Assets	=	Liabilities	+	Owners' Equity
−375,000		−375,000		

At this point, the credit to cash should be entered in the master T account Cash Flows from Operating Activities, as shown in Exhibit 12-13.

Salaries and Wages Expense and Salaries and Wages Payable The entry to record salaries and wages expense was as follows:

(g)	Salaries and Wages Expense	60,000	
	Salaries and Wages Payable		60,000
	To record salaries and wages.		

Assets	=	Liabilities	+	Owners' Equity
		+60,000		−60,000

After this entry is posted to Salaries and Wages Payable, note the $2,000 net decrease in the account for the period:

SALARIES AND WAGES PAYABLE

		9,000	Bal. Jan. 1
(h) Cash payments	?	60,000	Expense (g)
		7,000	Bal. Dec. 31

This means that the amount of cash paid to employees was $2,000 more than the amount of expense accrued. Another way to look at the cash payments of $60,000 + $2,000, or $62,000, is as follows:

Beginning salaries and wages payable	$ 9,000
+ Salaries and wages expense	60,000
− Cash payments to employees	(*X*)
= Ending accounts payable	$ 7,000

Solving for *X*, we can find cash payments:

$$9{,}000 + 60{,}000 - X = 7{,}000$$
$$X = \underline{\underline{62{,}000}}$$

The journal entry to record the cash paid was as follows:

(h)	Salaries and Wages Payable	62,000	
	Cash		62,000
	To record cash paid to employees.		

Assets	=	Liabilities	+	Owners' Equity
−62,000		−62,000		

As you see in Exhibit 12-13, the credit of $62,000 in this entry appears in the T account for Cash Flows from Operating Activities.

Depreciation Expense The next item on the income statement is depreciation of $40,000. The entry to record depreciation was as follows:

(i)	Depreciation Expense	40,000	
	Accumulated Depreciation		40,000
	To record depreciation.		

Assets	=	Liabilities	+	Owners' Equity
−40,000				−40,000

ACCOUNTING FOR YOUR DECISIONS

You Are an Entrepreneur

You operate a coffee cart in the lobby of an office building. You started the business this year by investing \$5,000 of your own money to buy the coffee cart. Even though you think the cart will last for five years, a friend who has studied accounting has advised you to recognize the entire cost of the cart as an expense the first year. He reasons that "the first year is very crucial to any business and since depreciation is added back in the Operating Activities section of the statement of cash flows, why not add back the maximum amount so that you will maximize the cash flow from operations?" Is your friend's reasoning sound?

ANS: Your friend is correct in stating that depreciation is added back in the Operating Activities section, assuming use of the indirect method. The only reason that depreciation is added back, however, is because it was deducted as an expense on the income statement but does not use any cash. Depreciation is not a cash flow, and any manipulation of the amount of depreciation expensed in any one year will not affect the amount of cash generated from operations.

Depreciation of tangible long-term assets, amortization of intangible assets, and depletion of natural resources are different from most other expenses in that they have no effect on cash flow. The only related cash flows are from the purchase and the sale of these long-term assets, and these are reported in the Investing Activities section of the statement of cash flows.

Insurance Expense and Prepaid Insurance According to the income statement in Exhibit 12-11, Julian recorded Insurance Expense of \$12,000 during 2001. This amount is not the cash payments for insurance, however, because Julian has a Prepaid Insurance account on the balance sheet. The entry to record expense involves a reduction in the Prepaid Insurance account as follows:

(j)	Insurance Expense	12,000	
	Prepaid Insurance		12,000
	To record expiration of insurance.		

Assets	=	Liabilities	+	Owners' Equity
−12,000				−12,000

When the credit to Prepaid Insurance is posted, note the \$6,000 net decrease in the account for the period:

PREPAID INSURANCE

	Debit	Credit	
Bal. Jan. 1	18,000		
(k) Cash payments	?	12,000	Expense (j)
Bal. Dec. 31	12,000		

This means that the amount of cash paid for insurance was \$6,000 less than the amount of expense recognized. Thus, the cash payments must have been \$12,000 – \$6,000, or \$6,000. Another way to look at the cash payments is as follows:

Beginning prepaid insurance	\$18,000
+ Cash payments for insurance	*X*
− Insurance expense	(12,000)
= Ending prepaid insurance	\$12,000

Solving for *X*, we can find the amount of cash paid:

$$18{,}000 + X - 12{,}000 = 12{,}000$$

$$X = \underline{\underline{6{,}000}}$$

The journal entry to record the cash paid was as follows:

(k)	Prepaid Insurance	6,000	
	Cash		6,000
	To record cash paid to employees.		

Assets	=	Liabilities	+	Owners' Equity
+6,000				
−6,000				

Note that the credit to Cash is entered in Exhibit 12-13 in the T account for Cash Flows from Operating Activities.

Interest Expense The amount of interest expense reported on the income statement is $15,000. Because the balance sheet does not report an accrual of interest owed but not yet paid (an Interest Payable account), we know that $15,000 is also the amount of cash paid:

(l)	Interest Expense	15,000	
	Cash		15,000
	To record interest expense.		

Assets	=	Liabilities	+	Owners' Equity
−15,000				−15,000

The entry is recorded as as cash outflow in Exhibit 12-13. Whether interest paid is properly classified as an operating activity is subject to considerable debate. The Financial Accounting Standards Board decided in favor of classification of *interest* as an *operating* activity because, unlike dividends, it appears on the income statement. This, it was argued, provides a direct link between the statement of cash flows and the income statement. Many argue, however, that it is inconsistent to classify dividends paid as a financing activity but interest paid as an operating activity. After all, both represent returns paid to providers of capital: interest to creditors and dividends to stockholders.

Income Tax Expense and Income Taxes Payable The entry to record Income Tax Expense was as follows:

(m)	Income Taxes Expense	50,000	
	Income Taxes Payable		50,000
	To record income taxes.		

Assets	=	Liabilities	+	Owners' Equity
		+50,000		−50,000

When the credit to Income Taxes Payable is posted, note the $3,000 net increase in the account for the period:

INCOME TAXES PAYABLE

		5,000	Bal. Jan. 1
(n) Cash payments	?	50,000	Expense (m)
		8,000	Bal. Dec. 31

This means that the amount of cash paid to the government in taxes was $3,000 less than the amount of expense accrued. Another way to look at the cash payments of $50,000 – $3,000, or $47,000, is as follows:

Beginning income taxes payable	$ 5,000
+ Income tax expense	50,000
− Cash payments for taxes	(*X*)
= Ending income taxes payable	$ 8,000

Solving for X, we can find the amount of cash paid:

$$5{,}000 + 50{,}000 - X = 8{,}000$$
$$X = \underline{\underline{47{,}000}}$$

The journal entry to record cash paid was as follows:

(n)	Income Taxes Payable	47,000	
	Cash		47,000
	To record cash paid in taxes.		

Assets	=	Liabilities	+	Owners' Equity
−47,000		−47,000		

As you see by examining Exhibit 12-13, the cash payments for taxes is the last item in the T account for Cash Flows from Operating Activities.

Loss on Retirement of Bonds A $3,000 loss on the retirement of bonds is reported as the last item under expenses and losses on the income statement in Exhibit 12-11. Any cash paid to retire a long-term liability is reported in the Financing Activities section of the statement of cash flows. Thus, we ignore the loss when reporting cash flows from operating activities under the direct method.

Compare Net Income with Net Cash Flow from Operating Activities. At this point, all of the items on the income statement have been analyzed, as have all of the current asset and current liability accounts. All of the information needed to prepare the Operating Activities section of your statement of cash flows has been gathered.

To summarize, the preparation of the Operating Activities section of the statement of cash flows requires the conversion of each item on the income statement to a cash basis. The current asset and current liability accounts are analyzed to discover the cash effects of each item on the income statement. Exhibit 12-14 summarizes this conversion process.

Note in the exhibit the various adjustments made to put each income statement item on a cash basis. For example, the $6,000 increase in accounts receivable for the period is deducted from sales revenue of $670,000 to arrive at cash collected from customers. Similar adjustments are made to each of the other income statement items with the exception of depreciation, the gain, and the loss. Depreciation is ignored because it does not have an effect on cash flow. The gain relates to the sale of a long-term asset, and any cash effect is reflected in the Investing Activities section of the statement of cash flows. Similarly, the loss resulted from the retirement of bonds, and any cash flow effect is reported in the Financing Activities section. The bottom of the exhibit highlights an important point: Julian reported net income of $120,000 but actually generated $174,000 in cash from operations.

Determine the Cash Flows from Investing Activities At this point, we turn our attention to the long-term asset accounts and any additional information available about these accounts. Julian has three long-term assets on its balance sheet: Long-Term Investments, Land, and Property and Equipment.

Long-Term Investments Item 1 in the additional information in Exhibit 12-12 indicates that Julian purchased $30,000 of investments during the year. The $30,000 net increase in the Long-Term Investments account confirms this (no mention is made of the sale of any investments during 2001):

LONG-TERM INVESTMENTS

Bal. Jan. 1	90,000	
(o) Purchases	?	
Bal. Dec. 31	120,000	

Exhibit 12-14 Conversion of Income Statement Items to Cash Basis

Income Statement	Amount	Adjustments	Cash Flows
Sales revenue	$670,000		$670,000
		+ Decreases in accounts receivable	–0–
		– Increases in accounts receivable	(6,000)
		Cash collected from customers	$664,000
Interest revenue	15,000		$ 15,000
		+ Decreases in interest receivable	–0–
		– Increases in interest receivable	–0–
		Cash collected in interest	$ 15,000
Gain on sale of machine	5,000	*Not an operating activity*	$ –0–
Cost of goods sold	390,000		$390,000
		+ Increases in inventory	–0–
		– Decreases in inventory	(8,000)
		+ Decreases in accounts payable	–0–
		– Increases in accounts payable	(7,000)
		Cash paid to suppliers	$375,000
Salaries and wages	60,000		$ 60,000
		+ Decreases in salaries/wages payable	2,000
		– Increases in salaries/wages payable	–0–
		Cash paid to employees	$ 62,000
Depreciation	40,000	*No cash flow effect*	$ –0–
Insurance	12,000		$ 12,000
		+ Increases in prepaid insurance	–0–
		– Decreases in prepaid insurance	(6,000)
		Cash paid for insurance	$ 6,000
Interest	15,000		$ 15,000
		+ Decreases in interest payable	–0–
		– Increases in interest payable	–0–
		Cash paid for interest	$ 15,000
Income taxes	50,000		$ 50,000
		+ Decreases in income taxes payable	–0–
		– Increases in income taxes payable	(3,000)
		Cash paid for taxes	$ 47,000
Loss on retirement of bonds	3,000	*Not an operating activity*	$ –0–
Net income	$120,000	Net cash flow from operating activities	$174,000

The entry to record the purchase was as follows:

(o)	Long-Term Investments	30,000	
	Cash		30,000
	To record purchase of investments.		

Assets	=	Liabilities	+	Owners' Equity
+30,000				
−30,000				

The credit in this entry is the first cash outflow in the master T account Cash Flows from Investing Activities, as shown in Exhibit 12-15.

EXHIBIT 12-15 Master T Account for Cash Flows from Investing Activities

CASH FLOWS FROM INVESTING ACTIVITIES

Cash inflows from:		Cash outflows for:	
(r) Sale of machine	25,000	(o) Purchase of investments	30,000
		(q) Purchase of plant and equipment	75,000

Land Note the $50,000 net increase in land:

LAND

Bal. Jan. 1	100,000	
(p) Acquisitions	?	
Bal. Dec. 31	150,000	

Item 2 in the additional information indicates that Julian purchased land by issuing a $50,000 note payable. The entry to record the purchase was as follows:

(p) Land	50,000	
Notes Payable		50,000
To record acquisition of land in exchange for note.		

Assets	=	Liabilities	+	Owners' Equity
+50,000		+50,000		

This entry obviously does not involve cash. The transaction has both an important financing element and an investing component, however. The issuance of the note is a financing activity, and the acquisition of land is an investing activity. Because no cash was involved, the transaction is reported in a separate schedule instead of directly on the statement of cash flows:

Supplemental schedule of noncash investing and financing activities

Acquisition of land in exchange for note payable	$50,000

Property and Equipment Property and equipment increased by $40,000 during 2001. However, Julian both acquired equipment and sold a machine (items 3 and 4 in the additional information). The acquisition of the equipment for $75,000 resulted in this journal entry:

(q) Property and Equipment	75,000	
Cash		75,000
To record acquisition of equipment for cash.		

Assets	=	Liabilities	+	Owners' Equity
+75,000				
−75,000				

As we discussed earlier in the chapter, acquisitions of new plant and equipment are important investing activities for most businesses. Thus, the credit to Cash appears in the master T account Cash Flows from Investing Activities in Exhibit 12-15.

After this entry is posted to the Property and Equipment account, it appears as follows:

PROPERTY AND EQUIPMENT

Bal. Jan. 1	280,000		
(q) Acquisitions	75,000	?	Disposals (r)
Bal. Dec. 31	320,000		

Julian obviously disposed of fixed assets during the period. In fact, item 4 in the additional information in Exhibit 12-12 reports the sale of a machine with an original cost of \$35,000. An analysis of the Property and Equipment account at this point confirms this amount:

Beginning property and equipment	\$280,000
+ Acquisitions	75,000
− Disposals	(*X*)
= Ending property and equipment	\$320,000

Solving for *X*, we can find the *cost* of the fixed assets sold during the year:

$$280{,}000 + 75{,}000 - X = 320{,}000$$
$$X = \$35{,}000$$

A T account for Accumulated Depreciation appears as follows after posting Depreciation Expense in entry (i):

ACCUMULATED DEPRECIATION

		75,000	Bal. Jan. 1
(r) Disposals	?	40,000	Depreciation expense (i)
		100,000	Bal. Dec. 31

The additional information also indicates that the book value of the machine sold was \$20,000. This means that if the original cost was \$35,000 and the book value was \$20,000, the Accumulated Depreciation on the machine sold must have been \$35,000 − \$20,000, or \$15,000. An analysis similar to the one we just looked at for Property and Equipment confirms this amount:

Beginning accumulated depreciation	\$ 75,000
+ Depreciation expense (entry i)	40,000
− Accumulated depreciation on assets sold	(*X*)
= Ending accumulated depreciation	\$100,000

Solving for *X*, we can find the accumulated depreciation on the assets disposed of during the year:

$$75{,}000 + 40{,}000 - X = 100{,}000$$
$$X = \$15{,}000$$

Finally, we are told in the additional information that the machine was sold for \$25,000. *If the selling price was \$25,000 and the book value was \$20,000, Julian reports a gain on sale of \$5,000, an amount that is confirmed on the income statement in Exhibit 12-11.* The journal entry to record the sale of the machine was as follows:

(r)	Cash	25,000	
	Accumulated Depreciation	15,000	
	Property and Equipment		35,000
	Gain on Sale of Machine (Retained Earnings)		5,000
	To record sale of machine.		

Assets	=	Liabilities	+	Owners' Equity
+25,000				+5,000
+15,000				
−35,000				

To summarize, the machine was sold for \$25,000, an amount that exceeded its book value of \$20,000, thus generating a gain of \$5,000. The debit to Cash is entered in the master T account for Cash Flows from Investing Activities in Exhibit 12-15.

Determine the Cash Flows from Financing Activities These activities generally involve long-term liabilities and stockholders' equity. We first consider Julian's two long-term liabilities, Notes Payable and Bonds Payable, and then the two stockholders' equity accounts: Capital Stock and Retained Earnings.

Notes Payable Recall that item 2 in the additional information reported that Julian purchased land in exchange for a $50,000 note payable. The T account for Notes Payable confirms this amount:

NOTES PAYABLE

		35,000	Bal. Jan. 1
		?	Additional issuances (p)
		85,000	Bal. Dec. 31

In our discussion of investing activities, we recorded entry (p) to account for this exchange and entered the transaction on a supplemental schedule of noncash activities because it was a significant financing activity but did not involve cash.

Bonds Payable A T account for Bonds Payable appears as follows:

BONDS PAYABLE

		260,000	Bal. Jan. 1
(s) Retirement	?		
		200,000	Bal. Dec. 31

Item 5 in the additional information in Exhibit 12-12 indicates that bonds with a face value of $60,000 were retired by paying $63,000 in cash. The book value of the bonds retired is the same as the face value of $60,000 because there is no unamortized discount or premium on the records. *When a company has to pay more in cash ($63,000) to settle a debt than the book value of the debt ($60,000), it reports a loss.* Recall the $3,000 loss reported on the income statement in Exhibit 12-11. The entry to record the retirement of the bonds was as follows:

(s)	Loss on Retirement of Bonds (Retained Earnings)	3,000	
	Bonds Payable	60,000	
	Cash		63,000
	To record retirement of bonds.		

Assets	=	Liabilities	+	Owners' Equity
−63,000		−60,000		−3,000

The credit to Cash in this entry is presented in the master T account Cash Flows from Financing Activities, as shown in Exhibit 12-16.

Capital Stock The Capital Stock account indicates a $25,000 net increase during 2001:

CAPITAL STOCK

		75,000	Bal. Jan. 1
		?	Stock issued (t)
		100,000	Bal. Dec. 31

Julian issued capital stock in exchange for $25,000 in cash, according to item 6 in the additional information in Exhibit 12-12. Some companies issue additional stock after the initial formation of a corporation to raise needed capital. The entry was as follows:

(t)	Cash	25,000	
	Capital Stock		25,000
	To record issuance of stock in exchange for cash.		

Assets	=	Liabilities	+	Owners' Equity
+25,000				+25,000

The debit to Cash in this entry is presented as a cash inflow in the master T account Cash Flows from Financing Activities, as shown in Exhibit 12-16.

EXHIBIT 12-16 Master T Account for Cash Flows from Financing Activities

CASH FLOWS FROM FINANCING ACTIVITIES

Cash inflows from:		Cash outflows for:	
(t) Issuance of stock	25,000	(s) Retirement of bonds	63,000
		(u) Payment of cash dividends	67,000

ACCOUNTING FOR YOUR DECISIONS

You Decide for Your Investment Club

You are a member of an investment club and have been given the assignment of analyzing the statements of cash flows for the Norfolk Corp. for the last three years. The company has neither issued nor retired any stock during this time period. You notice that the company's cash balance has increased steadily during this period but that a majority of the increase is due to a large net inflow of cash from financing activities in each of the three years. Should you be concerned?

ANS: The net inflow of cash from financing activities indicates that the company is borrowing more than it is repaying. Certainly borrowing can be an attractive means of financing the purchase of new plant and equipment. At some point, however, the debt, along with interest, will need to be repaid. The company must be able to generate sufficient cash from its operations to make these payments.

Retained Earnings An analysis of the Retained Earnings account indicates the following:

RETAINED EARNINGS

		193,000	Bal. Jan. 1
(u) Cash dividends	?	120,000	Net income for 2001
		246,000	Bal. Dec. 31

We can determine the amount of cash dividends for 2001 in the following manner:

Beginning retained earnings	$193,000
+ Net income	120,000
− Cash dividends	(*X*)
= Ending retained earnings	$246,000

Solving for *X*, we can find the amount of cash dividends paid during the year:[4]

$$193{,}000 + 120{,}000 - X = 246{,}000$$

$$X = \$67{,}000$$

Item 7 in the additional information confirms that this was in fact the amount of dividends paid during the year. The final entry was as follows:

[4]Any decrease in Retained Earnings represents the dividends *declared* during the period rather than the amount paid. If there had been a Dividends Payable account, we would analyze it to find the amount of dividends paid. The lack of a balance in such an account at either the beginning or the end of the period tells us that Julian paid the same amount of dividends that it declared during the period.

(u) Retained Earnings 67,000
Cash 67,000
To record cash dividends paid.

Assets	=	Liabilities	+	Owners' Equity
−67,000				−67,000

The credit to Cash in this entry appears in the master T account Cash Flows from Financing Activities, as presented in Exhibit 12-16.

Using the Master T Accounts to Prepare a Statement of Cash Flows All of the information needed to prepare a statement of cash flows is now available in the three master T accounts, along with the supplemental schedule prepared earlier. From the information gathered in Exhibits 12-13, 12-15, and 12-16, a completed statement of cash flows appears in Exhibit 12-17.

EXHIBIT 12-17 Completed Statement of Cash Flows for Julian Corp.

JULIAN CORP.
STATEMENT OF CASH FLOWS
FOR THE YEAR ENDED DECEMBER 31, 2001

Cash flows from operating activities	
Cash receipts from:	
Sales on account	$ 664,000
Interest	15,000
Total cash receipts	$ 679,000
Cash payments for:	
Inventory purchases	$(375,000)
Salaries and wages	(62,000)
Insurance	(6,000)
Interest	(15,000)
Taxes	(47,000)
Total cash payments	$(505,000)
Net cash provided by operating activities	$ 174,000
Cash flows from investing activities	
Purchase of investments	$ (30,000)
Purchase of plant and equipment	(75,000)
Sale of machine	25,000
Net cash used by investing activities	$ (80,000)
Cash flows from financing activities	
Retirement of bonds	$ (63,000)
Issuance of stock	25,000
Payment of cash dividends	(67,000)
Net cash used by financing activities	$(105,000)
Net decrease in cash	$ (11,000)
Cash balance, December 31, 2000	$ 46,000
Cash balance, December 31, 2001	$ 35,000
Supplemental schedule of noncash investing and financing activities	
Acquisition of land in exchange for note payable	$ 50,000

EXHIBIT 12-18 Indirect Method for Reporting Cash Flows from Operating Activities

JULIAN CORP.
PARTIAL STATEMENT OF CASH FLOWS
FOR THE YEAR ENDED DECEMBER 31, 2001

Net cash flows from operating activities	
Net income	$120,000
Adjustments to reconcile net income to net cash provided by operating activities:	
Increase in accounts receivable	(6,000)
Gain on sale of machine	(5,000)
Decrease in inventory	8,000
Increase in accounts payable	7,000
Decrease in salaries and wages payable	(2,000)
Depreciation expense	40,000
Decrease in prepaid insurance	6,000
Increase in income taxes payable	3,000
Loss on retirement of bonds	3,000
Net cash provided by operating activities	$174,000

What does Julian's statement of cash flows tell us? Cash flow from operations totaled $174,000. Cash used to acquire investments and equipment amounted to $80,000, after receiving $25,000 from the sale of a machine. A net amount of $105,000 was used for financing activities. Thus, Julian used more cash than it generated, and that's why the cash balance declined. That's okay for a year or two, but if this continues, the company won't be able to pay its bills.

A Master T-Account Approach to Preparing the Statement of Cash Flows: Indirect Method

LO 6 Use T accounts to prepare a statement of cash flows, using the indirect method to determine cash flow from operating activities.

The purpose of the Operating Activities section of the statement changes when we use the indirect method. Instead of reporting cash receipts and cash payments, *the objective is to reconcile net income to net cash flow from operating activities.* The other two sections of the completed statement in Exhibit 12-17, the investing and financing sections, are unchanged. The use of the indirect or the direct method for presenting cash flow from operating activities does not affect these two sections.

A T-account methodology, similar to that used for the direct method can be used to prepare the Operating Activities section of the statement of cash flows under the indirect method.

Net Income Recall that the first line in the Operating Activities section of the statement under the indirect method is net income. That is, we start with the assumptions that all revenues and gains reported on the income statement increase cash flow and that all expenses and losses decrease cash flow. Julian's net income of $120,000, as reported on its income statement in Exhibit 12-11, is reported as the first item in the Operating Activities section of the statement of cash flows as shown in Exhibit 12-18.

Accounts Receivable The net increase in Accounts Receivable, as shown below in T-account form, indicates that Julian recorded more sales than cash collections during the period:

ACCOUNTS RECEIVABLE

Bal. Jan. 1	57,000		
Net increase	6,000		
Bal. Dec. 31	63,000		

Because net income includes sales, as opposed to cash collections, the $6,000 *net increase* must be *deducted* to adjust net income to cash from operations. To help remember to deduct the net increase in accounts receivable in the Operating Activities section of the statement, consider the following. The $6,000 net increase appears in the preceding T account as a *debit.* Think of the deduction on the statement of cash flows as the equivalent of a *credit.* That is, the debit is to Accounts Receivable, and the credit is recorded as a bracketed amount (i.e., as a deduction) on the statement of cash flows.

From Concept TO PRACTICE 12.3

READING BEN & JERRY'S STATEMENT OF CASH FLOWS

Did Accounts Receivable increase or decrease during 1998? Why is the change in this account deducted on the statement of cash flows?

Gain on Sale of Machine The gain itself did not generate any cash, but the *sale* of the machine did. And as we found earlier, the cash generated by selling the machine was reported in the Investing Activities section of the statement. The cash proceeds included the gain. Because the gain is included in the net income figure, it must be *deducted* to determine cash from operations. Also note that the gain is included twice in cash inflows if it is not deducted from the net income figure in the Operating Activities section. Note the deduction of $5,000 in Exhibit 12-18.

Inventory As the $8,000 net decrease in the Inventory account indicates, Julian liquidated a portion of its stock of inventory during the year:

INVENTORY

Bal. Jan. 1	92,000		
		8,000	Net decrease
Bal. Dec. 31	84,000		

A net decrease in this account indicates that the company sold more products than it purchased during the year. As shown in Exhibit 12-18, the *net decrease* of $8,000 is *added back* to net income. As discussed for Accounts Receivable, note the debit and credit logic for this adjustment. Because Inventory is credited in the T account for the decrease, the statement of cash flows shows an increase, which is equivalent to a debit to Cash.

Accounts Payable Julian owed suppliers $31,000 at the start of the year. By the end of the year, the balance had grown to $38,000. A T account for Accounts Payable follows:

ACCOUNTS PAYABLE

		31,000	Bal. Jan. 1
		7,000	Net increase
		38,000	Bal. Dec. 31

Effectively, the company saved cash by delaying the payment of some of its outstanding accounts payable. The *net increase* of $7,000 in this account is *added back* to net income, as shown in Exhibit 12-18.

Salaries and Wages Payable A T account for Salaries and Wages Payable indicates a net decrease of $2,000:

SALARIES AND WAGES PAYABLE

		9,000	Bal. Jan. 1
Net decrease	2,000		
		7,000	Bal. Dec. 31

The rationale for *deducting* the $2,000 *net decrease* in this liability in Exhibit 12-18 follows from what we just said about an increase in Accounts Payable. The payment to employees of $2,000 more than the amount included in expense on the income statement requires an additional deduction under the indirect method.

Depreciation Expense Depreciation is a noncash expense. Because it was deducted to arrive at net income, we must *add back* $40,000, the amount of depreciation, to find cash from operations. The same holds true for amortization of intangible assets and depletion of natural resources.

Prepaid Insurance This account decreased by $6,000, according to the T account:

PREPAID INSURANCE

Bal. Jan. 1	18,000		
		6,000	Net decrease
Bal. Dec. 31	12,000		

A decrease in this account indicates that Julian deducted more on the income statement for the insurance expense of the period than it paid in cash for new policies. That is, the cash outlay for insurance protection was not as large as the amount of expense reported on the income statement. Thus, the *net decrease* in the account is *added back* to net income in Exhibit 12-18.

Income Taxes Payable A T account for Income Taxes Payable indicates a net increase of $3,000:

INCOME TAXES PAYABLE

		5,000	Bal. Jan. 1
		3,000	Net increase
		8,000	Bal. Dec. 31

The *net increase* of $3,000 in this liability is *added back* to net income in Exhibit 12-18 because the payments to the government were $3,000 less than the amount included on the income statement.

Loss on Retirement of Bonds The $3,000 loss from retiring bonds was reported on the income statement as a deduction. There are two parts to the explanation for *adding back* the loss to net income to eliminate its effect in the Operating Activities section of the statement. First, any cash outflow from retiring bonds is properly classified as a financing activity, not an operating activity. The entire cash outflow should be reported in one classification rather than being allocated between two classifications. Second, the amount of the cash outflow is $63,000, not $3,000. To summarize, to convert net income to a cash basis, we add the loss back in the Operating Activities section to eliminate its effect. The actual use of cash to retire the bonds is shown in the financing section of the statement.

Study Tip

Note from this list how changes in current assets and current liabilities are treated on the statement. For example, because accounts receivable and accounts payable are on opposite sides of the balance sheet, increases in each of them are handled in opposite ways. But an increase in one and a decrease in the other are treated in the same way.

Summary of Adjustments to Net Income under the Indirect Method The following is a list of the most common adjustments to net income when the indirect method is used to prepare the Operating Activities section of the statement of cash flows:

Additions to Net Income	Deductions from Net Income
Decrease in accounts receivable	Increase in accounts receivable
Decrease in inventory	Increase in inventory
Decrease in prepayments	Increase in prepayments
Increase in accounts payable	Decrease in accounts payable
Increase in accrued liabilities	Decrease in accrued liabilities
Losses on sales of long-term assets	Gains on sales of long-term assets
Losses on retirements of bonds	Gains on retirements of bonds
Depreciation, amortization, and depletion	

Comparison of the Indirect and Direct Methods

Earlier in the chapter we pointed out that the amount of cash provided by operating activities is the same under the direct and the indirect methods. The relative merits of the two methods, however, have stirred considerable debate in the accounting profession. The Financial Accounting Standards Board has expressed a strong preference for the direct method but allows companies to use the indirect method.

If a company uses the indirect method, it must separately disclose two important cash payments: income taxes paid and interest paid. Thus, if Julian uses the indirect method, it reports the following either at the bottom of the statement of cash flows or in a footnote:[5]

Income taxes paid	\$47,000
Interest paid	\$15,000

Advocates of the direct method believe that the information provided with this approach is valuable in evaluating a company's operating efficiency. For example, the use of the direct method allows the analyst to follow any trends in cash receipts from customers and compare them with cash payments to suppliers. The information presented in the Operating Activities section of the statement under the direct method is certainly user-friendly. Someone without a technical background in accounting can easily tell where cash came from and where it went during the period.

Advocates of the indirect method argue two major points. Many companies believe that the use of the direct method reveals too much about their business by telling readers exactly the amount of cash receipts and cash payments from operations. Whether the use of the direct method tells the competition too much about a company is subject to debate. The other argument made for the indirect method is that it focuses attention on the differences between income on an accrual basis and a cash basis. In fact, this reconciliation of net income and cash provided by operating activities is considered to be important enough that *if a company uses the direct method, it must present a separate schedule to reconcile net income to net cash from operating activities.* This schedule, in effect, is the same as the Operating Activities section for the indirect method.

The Use of Cash Flow Information

The statement of cash flows is a critical disclosure to a company's investors and creditors. Many investors focus on cash flow from operations, rather than net income, as their key statistic. Similarly, many bankers are as concerned with cash flow from operations as they are with net income because they care about a company's ability to pay its bills. There is the concern that accrual accounting can mask cash flow problems. For example, a company with smooth earnings could be building up accounts receivable and inventory. This may not become evident until the company is in deep trouble.

The statement of cash flows provides investors, analysts, bankers, and other users with a valuable starting point as they attempt to evaluate a company's financial health. From this point, these groups must decide *how* to use the information presented on the statement. They pay particular attention to the *relationships* among various items on the statement, as well as to other financial statement items. In fact, many large banks have their own cash flow models, which typically involve a rearrangement of the items on the statement of cash flows to suit their needs. We now turn our attention to two examples of how various groups use cash flow information.

[5]The same *Accounting Trends & Techniques* survey referred to earlier in the chapter (see footnote 3) indicated that of those companies using the indirect method, approximately 55% disclose interest and taxes paid in notes to the financial statements and approximately 45% report these amounts either within or at the bottom of the statement of cash flows.

Managers, investors, and brokers gauge the relative strengths of retailers by observing which stores are the most popular. But they also study the financial statements, particularly the statement of cash flows and its indicators of cash flow adequacy, as the most fundamental way to measure a firm's strength.

www.sec.gov
www.ibm.com

CREDITORS AND CASH FLOW ADEQUACY

Bankers and other creditors are especially concerned with a company's ability to meet its principal and interest obligations. *Cash flow adequacy* is a measure intended to help in this regard.[6] It gauges the cash available to meet future debt obligations after paying taxes and interest costs and making capital expenditures. Because capital expenditures on new plant and equipment are a necessity for most companies, analysts are concerned with the cash available to repay debt *after* the company has replaced and updated its existing base of long-term assets.

Cash flow adequacy can be computed as follows:

$$\text{Cash Flow Adequacy} = \frac{\text{Cash Flow from Operating Activities} - \text{Capital Expenditures}}{\text{Average Amount of Debt Maturing over Next Five Years}}$$

How could you use the information in an annual report to measure a company's cash flow adequacy? First, whether a company uses the direct or indirect method to report cash flow from operating activities, this number represents cash flow *after* paying interest and taxes. The numerator of the ratio is determined by deducting capital expenditures, as they appear in the Investing Activities section of the statement, from cash flow from operating activities. A disclosure required by the Securities and Exchange Commission provides the information needed to calculate the denominator of the ratio. This regulatory body requires companies to report the annual amount of long-term debt maturing over each of the next five years.

IBM's Cash Flow Adequacy As an example of the calculation of this ratio, consider the following amounts from IBM's statement of cash flows for the year ended December 31, 1998 (amounts in millions of dollars):

Net cash provided from operating activities	\$9,273
Payments for plant, rental machines, and other property	\$6,520

Note K in IBM's 1998 annual report provides the following information:

> Annual maturities in millions of dollars on long-term debt outstanding at December 31, 1998, are as follows: 1999, \$2,650; 2000, \$5,120; 2001, \$1,491; 2002, \$1,676; 2003, \$1,116; 2004 and beyond, \$6,136.

We can now compute IBM's cash flow adequacy for the year ended December 31, 1998, as follows:

$$\text{Cash Flow Adequacy} = \frac{\$9{,}273 - \$6{,}520}{(\$2{,}650 + \$5{,}120 + \$1{,}491 + \$1{,}676 + \$1{,}116)/5} = \frac{\$2{,}753}{\$2{,}410.6} = 1.14$$

Would you feel comfortable lending to IBM if you knew that its ratio of cash flow from operations, after making necessary capital expenditures, to average maturities of debt over the next five years was slightly over 1 to 1? Before answering this question, you would want to compare the ratio with the ratios for prior years as well as with the ratio for companies of similar size and in lines of business similar to those of IBM. As a starting point, however, IBM's ratio of 1 to 1 indicates that its 1998 cash flow was sufficient to repay its average annual debt over the next five years.

STOCKHOLDERS AND CASH FLOW PER SHARE

As we will see in Chapter 13, one measure of the relative worth of an investment in a company is the ratio of the stock's market price per share to the company's earnings per share (that is, the price/earnings ratio). But many stockholders and Wall Street analysts are even more interested in the price of the stock in relation to the company's cash flow per share. Cash flow for purposes of this ratio is normally limited to cash flow from operating activities. This ratio has been used by these groups to evaluate investments—even

[6]An article appearing in the January 10, 1994, edition of the *Wall Street Journal* reported that Fitch Investors Service Inc. has published a rating system to compare the cash flow adequacy of companies that it rates single-A in its credit ratings. The rating system is intended to help corporate bond investors assess the ability of these companies to meet their maturing debt obligations. Lee Berton, "Investors Have a New Tool for Judging Issuers' Health: 'Cash-Flow Adequacy,'" p. C1.

"[O]ur primary business activity is to invest in ownership of other companies on behalf of investors. Purchases and sales of these companies are called *investing activities*, . . ."

–Sara Luedtke

FOCUS ON USERS

Name: Sara Luedtke
Education: B.S., Georgetown University (School of Business)
College Major: Accounting
Occupation: Senior Accountant, The Carlyle Group, Washington, D.C.
Age: 26

Understanding the Relevance of the Cash Flow Statement to Decision Making

Sara Luedtke is an accountant for The Carlyle Group, a private merchant bank based in Washington, D.C., so she is very familiar with financial statements and the flow of data from one statement to the next. In preparing the statements, accountants like Sara draw relationships among the various line items so that analysts, like the ones discussed in previous chapters, can better evaluate the performance of investments. To illustrate this principle of how the decisions of analysts are affected by the work of accountants, Sara points to the statement of cash flows: "As a private merchant bank, our primary business activity is to invest in ownership of other companies on behalf of investors. Purchases and sales of these companies are called *investing activities,* and our investors review cash flows from these activities to compare how much cash flowed out of the firm into new investments to how much cash flowed into the firm from either sales of, or distributions received from, our investments."

As Sara helps prepare financial statements for the dozens of companies she is responsible for at The Carlyle Group, she is constantly aware that analysts and other external users will interpret her data and base investment decisions on it. Additionally, because The Carlyle Group is itself in the business of buying and selling (i.e., investing in) companies, Sara knows that the financial statements she prepares will be used *internally* for decision making by upper management. If the statements show that investment purchases exceed their sales during the year, for example, The Carlyle Group would need additional cash from investors to fund new investments. Conversely, if The Carlyle Group is selling off more investments than it is buying during a particular period, it would be able to pass some of the excess cash on to investors.

though the accounting profession has expressly forbidden the reporting of cash flow per share information in the financial statements. The accounting profession's belief is that this type of information is not an acceptable alternative to earnings per share as an indicator of company performance.

ACCOUNTING FOR YOUR DECISIONS

You Are the Banker

You and your old college roommate are having an argument. You say that cash flow is all that matters when looking at a company's prospects. Your roommate says that the most important number is earnings per share. Who's right?

ANS: You're both wrong. True, bankers are interested in cash flow to make sure that a company can pay back its loans. But earnings per share is important also because it is less easily manipulated. After all, companies can decide when they want to finance expansion, pay down debt, or invest in new businesses. A company with strong earnings can appear weak from a cash flow perspective if it invests too much in new operating assets or other businesses. On the other hand, a company that wants to appear cash-rich can avoid making all of the investments that it ought to be making. Although companies can manipulate earnings to some extent, the matching principle ensures that revenues and expenses relating to those revenues take place during the same period.

WARMUP EXERCISES

LO 1 Warmup Exercise 12-1 Purpose of the Statement of Cash Flows

Most companies begin the statement of cash flows by indicating the amount of net income and ending it with the beginning and ending cash balances. Why is the statement necessary if net income already appears on the income statement and the cash balances can be found on the balance sheet?

Key to the Solution

Recall the *purpose* of the statement of cash flows as described in the beginning of the chapter.

LO 3 Warmup Exercise 12-2 Classification of Activities

For each of the following activities, indicate whether it should appear on the statement of cash flows as an operating (O), investing (I), or financing (F) activity. Assume the company uses the direct method of reporting in the Operating Activities section.

_______ **1.** New equipment is acquired for cash.
_______ **2.** Thirty-year bonds are issued.
_______ **3.** Cash receipts from the cash register are recorded.
_______ **4.** The bi-weekly payroll is paid.
_______ **5.** Common stock is issued for cash.
_______ **6.** Land that was being held for future expansion is sold at book value.

Key to the Solution

Recall the general rules for each of the categories: operating activities involve acquiring and selling products and services; investing activities deal with acquiring and disposing of long-term assets; and financing activities are concerned with the raising and repayment of funds in the form of debt and equity.

LO 6 Warmup Exercise 12-3 Adjustments to Net Income with the Indirect Method

Assume that a company uses the indirect method to prepare the Operating Activities section of the statement of cash flows. For each of the following items, indicate whether it would be added to net income (A), deducted from net income (D), or not reported in this section of the statement under the indirect method (NR).

_______ **1.** Decrease in accounts payable
_______ **2.** Increase in accounts receivable
_______ **3.** Decrease in prepaid insurance
_______ **4.** Purchase of new factory equipment
_______ **5.** Depreciation expense
_______ **6.** Gain on retirement of bonds

Key to the Solution

Refer to the summary of adjustments to net income under the indirect method on page 614.

SOLUTIONS TO WARMUP EXERCISES

Warmup Exercise 12-1

The statement of cash flows is a complement to the other statements in that it summarizes the operating, investing, and financing activities over a period of time. Even though the net income and cash balances are available on other statements, the statement of cash flows explains to the reader *why* net income is different than cash flow from operations and *why* cash changed by the amount it did during the period.

Warmup Exercise 12-2

1. I **2.** F **3.** O **4.** O **5.** F **6.** I

Warmup Exercise 12-3

1. D **2.** D **3.** A **4.** NR **5.** A **6.** D

REVIEW PROBLEM

An income statement and comparative balance sheets for Dexter Company are shown below:

DEXTER COMPANY
INCOME STATEMENT
FOR THE YEAR ENDED DECEMBER 31, 2001

Sales revenue	$89,000
Cost of goods sold	57,000
Gross margin	$32,000
Depreciation expense	6,500
Advertising expense	3,200
Salaries expense	12,000
Total operating expenses	$21,700
Operating income	$10,300
Loss on sale of land	2,500
Income before tax	$ 7,800
Income tax expense	2,600
Net income	$ 5,200

DEXTER COMPANY
COMPARATIVE BALANCE SHEETS

	December 31	
	2001	**2000**
Cash	$ 12,000	$ 9,500
Accounts receivable	22,000	18,400
Inventory	25,400	20,500
Prepaid advertising	10,000	8,600
Total current assets	$ 69,400	$ 57,000
Land	120,000	80,000
Equipment	190,000	130,000
Accumulated depreciation	(70,000)	(63,500)
Total long-term assets	$240,000	$146,500
Total assets	$309,400	$203,500
Accounts payable	$ 15,300	$ 12,100
Salaries payable	14,000	16,400
Income taxes payable	1,200	700
Total current liabilities	$ 30,500	$ 29,200
Capital stock	$200,000	$100,000
Retained earnings	78,900	74,300
Total stockholders' equity	$278,900	$174,300
Total liabilities and stockholders' equity	$309,400	$203,500

Additional Information

1. Land was acquired during the year for $70,000.
2. An unimproved parcel of land was sold during the year for $27,500. Its original cost to Dexter was $30,000.

3. A specialized piece of equipment was acquired in exchange for capital stock in the company. The value of the capital stock was $60,000.
4. In addition to the capital stock issued in item 3, stock was sold for $40,000.
5. Dividends of $600 were paid.

Required

Prepare a statement of cash flows for 2001 using the direct method in the Operating Activities section of the statement. Include supplemental schedules to report any noncash investing and financing activities and to reconcile net income to net cash provided by operating activities.

Solution to Review Problem

DEXTER COMPANY
STATEMENT OF CASH FLOWS
FOR THE YEAR ENDED DECEMBER 31, 2001

Cash flows from operating activities	
Cash collections from customers	$ 85,400
Cash payments:	
To suppliers	$(58,700)
For advertising	(4,600)
To employees	(14,400)
For income taxes	(2,100)
Total cash payments	$(79,800)
Net cash provided by operating activities	$ 5,600
Cash flows from investing activities	
Purchase of land	$(70,000)
Sale of land	27,500
Net cash used by investing activities	$(42,500)
Cash flows from financing activities	
Issuance of capital stock	$ 40,000
Payment of cash dividends	(600)
Net cash provided by financing activities	$ 39,400
Net increase in cash	$ 2,500
Cash balance, December 31, 2000	9,500
Cash balance, December 31, 2001	$ 12,000
Supplemental schedule of noncash investing and financing activities	
Acquisition of specialized equipment in exchange for capital stock	$ 60,000
Reconciliation of net income to net cash provided by operating activities	
Net income	$ 5,200
Adjustments to reconcile net income to net cash provided by operating activities:	
Increase in accounts receivable	(3,600)
Increase in inventory	(4,900)
Increase in prepaid advertising	(1,400)
Increase in accounts payable	3,200
Decrease in salaries payable	(2,400)
Increase in income taxes payable	500
Depreciation expense	6,500
Loss on sale of land	2,500
Net cash provided by operating activities	$ 5,600

APPENDIX 12A

ACCOUNTING TOOLS: A WORK-SHEET APPROACH TO THE STATEMENT OF CASH FLOWS

LO 7 Use a work sheet to prepare a statement of cash flows, using the indirect method to determine cash flow from operating activities.

In the chapter, we illustrated the use of T accounts to aid in the preparation of a statement of cash flows. We pointed out that T accounts are simply tools to help in analyzing the transactions of the period. We now consider the use of a work sheet as an alternative tool to organize the information needed to prepare the statement. We will use the information given in the chapter for Julian Corp. (refer to Exhibits 12-11 and 12-12 for the income statements and comparative balance sheets). Although it is possible to use a work sheet to prepare the statement when the Operating Activities section is prepared under the direct method, we illustrate the use of a work sheet using the more popular *indirect* method.

A work sheet for Julian Corp. is presented in Exhibit 12-19. The following steps were followed in preparing the work sheet:

Step 1: The balances in each account at the end and at the beginning of the period are entered in the first two columns of the work sheet. For Julian, these balances can be found in its comparative balance sheets in Exhibit 12-12. Note that credit balances are bracketed on the work sheet. Because the work sheet lists all balance sheet accounts, the total of the debit balances must equal the total of the credit balances, and thus, the totals at the bottom for these first two columns equal $0.

Step 2: The additional information listed at the bottom of Exhibit 12-12 is used to record the various investing and financing activities on the work sheet (the item numbers discussed below correspond to the superscript numbers on the work sheet in Exhibit 12-19):

1. Long-term investments were purchased for $30,000. Because this transaction required the use of cash, it is entered as a bracketed amount in the Investing column and as an addition to the Long-term Investments account in the Changes column.
2. Land was acquired by issuing a $50,000 note payable. This transaction is entered on two lines on the work sheet. First, $50,000 is added to the Changes column for Land and as a corresponding deduction in the Noncash column (the last column on the work sheet). Likewise, $50,000 is added for Notes Payable to the Changes column and to the Noncash column.
3. Item 3 in the additional information indicates the acquisition of equipment for $75,000. This amount appears on the work sheet as an addition to Property and Equipment in the Changes column and as a deduction (cash outflow) in the Investing column.
4. A machine with an original cost of $35,000 and a book value of $20,000 was sold for $25,000, resulting in four entries on the work sheet. First, the amount of cash received, $25,000, is entered as an addition in the Investing column on the line for property and equipment. On the same line, the cost of the machine, $35,000, is entered as a deduction in the Changes column. The difference between the cost of the machine, $35,000, and its book value, $20,000, is its accumulated depreciation of $15,000. This amount is shown as a deduction from this account in the Changes column. Because the gain of $5,000 is included in net income, it is deducted in the Operating column (on the Retained Earnings line).
5. Bonds with a face value of $60,000 were retired by paying $63,000 in cash, resulting in the entry of three amounts on the work sheet. The face value of the bonds, $60,000, is entered as a reduction of Bonds Payable in the Changes column. The amount paid to retire the bonds, $63,000, is entered on the same line in the Financing column. The loss of $3,000 is added in the Operating column because it was a deduction to arrive at net income.

EXHIBIT 12-19 Julian Corp. Statement of Cash Flows Work Sheet

JULIAN CORP.
STATEMENT OF CASH FLOWS WORK SHEET (INDIRECT METHOD)
(ALL AMOUNTS IN THOUSANDS OF DOLLARS)

	Balances			Cash Inflows (Outflows)			
Accounts	**12/31/01**	**12/31/00**	**Changes**	**Operating**	**Investing**	**Financing**	**Noncash Activities**
Cash	35	46	(11)[16]				
Accounts receivable	63	57	6[10]	(6)[10]			
Inventory	84	92	(8)[11]	8[11]			
Prepaid Insurance	12	18	(6)[12]	6[12]			
Long-term investments	120	90	30[1]		(30)[1]		
Land	150	100	50[2]				(50)[2]
Property and equipment	320	280	75[3]		(75)[3]		
			(35)[4]		25[4]		
Accumulated depreciation	(100)	(75)	15[4]				
			(40)[9]	40[9]			
Accounts payable	(38)	(31)	(7)[13]	7[13]			
Salaries and wages payable	(7)	(9)	2[14]	(2)[14]			
Income taxes payable	(8)	(5)	(3)[15]	3[15]			
Notes payable	(85)	(35)	(50)[2]				50[2]
Bonds payable	(200)	(260)	60[5]			(63)[5]	
Capital stock	(100)	(75)	(25)[6]			25[6]	
Retained earnings	(246)	(193)	67[7]	(5)[4]		(67)[7]	
				3[5]			
			(120)[8]	120[8]			
Totals	–0–	–0–	–0–	174	(80)	(105)	–0–
Net decrease in cash				(11)[16]			

SOURCE: The authors are grateful to Jeannie Folk for the development of this work sheet.

6. Capital stock was issued for $25,000. This amount is entered on the Capital Stock line under the Changes column (as an increase in the account) and under the Financing column as an inflow.
7. Dividends of $67,000 were paid. This amount is entered as a reduction in Retained Earnings in the Changes column and as a cash outflow in the Financing Activities column.

Step 3: Because the indirect method is being used, net income of $120,000 for the period is entered as an addition to Retained Earnings in the Operating column of the work sheet (entry 8). The amount is also entered as an increase (bracketed) in the Changes column.

Step 4: Any noncash revenues or expenses are entered on the work sheet on the appropriate lines. For Julian, depreciation expense of $40,000 is added (bracketed) to Accumulated Depreciation in the Changes column and in the Operating column. This entry is identified on the work sheet as entry 9.

Step 5: Each of the changes in the noncash current asset and current liability accounts is entered in the Changes column and in the Operating column. These entries are identified on the work sheet as entries 10 through 15.

Step 6: Totals are determined for the Operating, Investing, and Financing columns and entered at the bottom of the work sheet. The total for the final column, Noncash Activities, of $0, is also entered.

Step 7: The net cash inflow (outflow) for the period is determined by adding the totals of the operating, investing, and financing columns. For Julian, the net cash *outflow* is $11,000, shown as entry 16 at the bottom of the statement. This same amount is then transferred to the line for Cash in the Changes column. Finally, the total of the Changes column at this point should net to $0.

Chapter Highlights

1. **LO 1** The purpose of a statement of cash flows is to summarize the cash flows of an entity during a period of time. The cash inflows and outflows are categorized into three activities: operating, investing, and financing.
2. **LO 2** Cash equivalents are convertible to a known amount of cash and are therefore included with cash on the balance sheet. Because such items as commercial paper, money market funds, and Treasury bills do not involve any significant risk, neither their purchase nor their sale is shown as an investing activity on the statement of cash flows.
3. **LO 3** Operating activities are generally the effects of items that enter into the determination of net income, such as the effects of buying and selling products and services. Other operating activities include payments of compensation to employees, taxes to the government, and interest to creditors. Preparation of the Operating Activities section of the statement of cash flows requires an analysis of the current assets and current liabilities.
4. **LO 3** Investing activities are critical to the success of a business because they involve the replacement of existing productive assets and the addition of new ones. Capital expenditures are normally the single largest cash outflow for most businesses. Occasionally, companies generate cash from the sale of existing plant and equipment. The information needed to prepare the Investing Activities section of the statement of cash flows is found by analyzing the long-term asset accounts.
5. **LO 3** All businesses rely on financing in one form or another. At least initially, all corporations sell stock to raise funds. Many turn to external sources as well, generating cash from the issuance of promissory notes and bonds. The repayment of debt and the reacquisition of capital stock are important uses of cash for some companies. Given the nature of financing activities, long-term liability and stockholders' equity accounts must be examined in preparing this section of the statement of cash flows.
6. **LO 4** Two different methods are acceptable to report cash flow from operating activities. Under the direct method, cash receipts and cash payments related to operations are reported. Under the indirect method, net income is reconciled to net cash flow from operating activities. Regardless of which method is used, the amount of cash generated from operations is the same.
7. **LO 5** Preparation of the Operating Activities section under the direct method requires the conversion of income statement items from an accrual basis to a cash basis. Certain items, such as depreciation, do not have a cash effect and are not included on the statement. Gains and losses typically relate to either investing or financing activities and are not included in the Operating Activities section of the statement. When the direct method is used to present cash flow from operating activities, a separate schedule is required to reconcile net income to net cash flow from operating activities. This schedule is the same as the Operating Activities section under the indirect method. Some type of methodology, such as a T-account approach, can be helpful in preparing the statement for more complex situations.
8. **LO 6** When the indirect method is used, the reconciliation of net income to net cash flow from operating activities appears on the face of the statement. Adjustments are made for the changes in each of the operating-related current asset and current liability accounts, as well as adjustments for noncash items, such as depreciation. The effects of gains and losses on net income must also be removed to convert to a cash basis. If the indirect method is used, a company must separately disclose the amount of cash paid for taxes and for interest.
9. **LO 7** A work sheet is sometimes used in preparing a statement of cash flows. Similar to T accounts, the work sheet acts as a tool to aid in the preparation of the statement. (Appendix 12A)

Key Terms Quiz

Read each definition below and then write the number of that definition in the blank beside the appropriate term it defines. The solution appears at the end of the chapter.

3 **Statement of cash flows** 585

4 **Cash equivalent** 587

1 **Operating activities** 588

5 **Investing activities** 589

7 **Financing activities** 590

6 **Direct method** 592

2 **Indirect method** 592

1. Activities concerned with the acquisition and sale of products and services.
2. For preparing the Operating Activities section of the statement of cash flows, the approach in which net income is reconciled to net cash flow from operations.
3. The financial statement that summarizes an entity's cash receipts and cash payments during the period from operating, investing, and financing activities.
4. An item readily convertible to a known amount of cash and with a maturity to the investor of three months or less.
5. Activities concerned with the acquisition and disposal of long-term assets.
6. For preparing the Operating Activities section of the statement of cash flows, the approach in which cash receipts and cash payments are reported.
7. Activities concerned with the raising and repayment of funds in the form of debt and equity.

ALTERNATE TERMS

Bottom line Net income

Cash flow from operating activities Cash flow from operations

Statement of cash flows Cash flows statement

QUESTIONS

1. What is the purpose of the statement of cash flows? As a flows statement, explain how it differs from the income statement.
2. What is a cash equivalent? Why is it included with cash for purposes of preparing a statement of cash flows?
3. Preston Corp. acquires a piece of land by signing a $60,000 promissory note and making a down payment of $20,000. How should this transaction be reported on the statement of cash flows?
4. Hansen Inc. made two purchases during December. One was a $10,000 Treasury bill that matures in 60 days from the date of purchase. The other was a $20,000 investment in Motorola common stock that will be held indefinitely. How should each of these be treated for purposes of preparing a statement of cash flows?
5. Companies are required to classify cash flows as operating, investing, or financing. Which of these three categories do you think will most likely have a net cash *outflow* over a number of years? Explain your answer.
6. A fellow student says to you: "The statement of cash flows is the easiest of the basic financial statements to prepare because you know the answer before you start. You compare the beginning and ending balances in cash on the balance sheet and compute the net inflow or outflow of cash. What could be easier?" Do you agree? Explain your answer.
7. What is your evaluation of the following statement? "Depreciation is responsible for providing some of the highest amounts of cash for capital-intensive businesses. This is obvious by examining the Operating Activities section of the statement of cash flows. Other than the net income of the period, depreciation is often the largest amount reported in this section of the statement."
8. Which method for preparing the Operating Activities section of the statement of cash flows, the direct or the indirect method, do you believe provides more information to users of the statement? Explain your answer.
9. Assume that a company uses the indirect method to prepare the Operating Activities section of the statement of cash flows. Why would a decrease in accounts receivable during the period be added back to net income?
10. Why is it necessary to analyze both inventory and accounts payable in trying to determine cash payments to suppliers when the direct method is used?
11. A company has a very profitable year. What explanations might there be for a decrease in cash?
12. A company reports a net loss for the year. Is it possible that cash could increase during the year? Explain your answer.
13. What effect does a decrease in income taxes payable for the period have on cash generated from operating activities? Does it matter whether the direct or the indirect method is used?
14. Why do accounting standards require a company to separately disclose income taxes paid and interest paid if it uses the indirect method?
15. Is it logical that interest paid is classified as a cash outflow in the *Operating* Activities section of the statement of cash flows but that dividends paid are included in the *Financing* Activities section? Explain your answer.
16. Jackson Company prepays the rent on various office facilities. The beginning balance in Prepaid Rent was $9,600, and the

ending balance was $7,300. The income statement reports Rent Expense of $45,900. Under the direct method, what amount would appear for cash paid in rent in the Operating Activities section of the statement of cash flows?

17. Baxter Inc. buys 2,000 shares of its own common stock at $20 per share as treasury stock. How is this transaction reported on the statement of cash flows?

18. Duke Corp. sold a delivery truck for $9,000. Its original cost was $25,000, and the book value at the time of the sale was $11,000. How does the transaction to record the sale appear on a statement of cash flows prepared under the indirect method?

19. Billings Company has a patent on its books with a balance at the beginning of the year of $24,000. The ending balance for the asset was $20,000. The company neither bought nor sold any patents during the year, nor does it use an Accumulated Amortization account. Assuming that the company uses the indirect method in preparing a statement of cash flows, how is the decrease in the Patents account reported on the statement?

20. Ace Inc. declared and distributed a 10% stock dividend during the year. Explain how, if at all, you think this transaction should be reported on a statement of cash flows.

EXERCISES

LO 2 Exercise 12-1 Cash Equivalents

Metropolis Industries invested its excess cash in the following instruments during December 2001:

Certificate of deposit, due January 31, 2002	$ 35,000
Certificate of deposit, due June 30, 2002	95,000
Investment in City of Elgin bonds, due May 1, 2003	15,000
Investment in Quantum Data stock	66,000
Money Market Fund	105,000
90-day Treasury bills	75,000
Treasury note, due December 1, 2002	200,000

Required

Determine the amount of cash equivalents that should be combined with cash on the company's balance sheet at December 31, 2001, and for purposes of preparing a statement of cash flows for the year ended December 31, 2001.

LO 3 Exercise 12-2 Classification of Activities

For each of the following transactions reported on a statement of cash flows, fill in the blank to indicate if it would appear in the Operating Activities section (O), in the Investing Activities section (I), or in the Financing Activities section (F). Put an *S* in the blank if the transaction does not affect cash but is reported in a supplemental schedule of noncash activities. Assume the company uses the direct method in the Operating Activities section.

______ 1. A company purchases its own common stock in the open market and immediately retires it.

______ 2. A company issues preferred stock in exchange for land.

______ 3. A six-month bank loan is obtained.

______ 4. Twenty-year bonds are issued.

______ 5. A customer's open account is collected.

______ 6. Income taxes are paid.

______ 7. Cash sales for the day are recorded.

______ 8. Cash dividends are declared and paid.

______ 9. A creditor is given shares of common stock in the company in return for cancellation of a long-term loan.

______ 10. A new piece of machinery is acquired for cash.

______ 11. Stock of another company is acquired as an investment.

______ 12. Interest is paid on a bank loan.

______ 13. Factory workers are paid.

Retirement of Bonds Payable

LO 3 Exercise 12-3 Retirement of Bonds Payable on the Statement of Cash Flows—Indirect Method

Redstone Inc. has the following debt outstanding on December 31, 2001:

10% bonds payable, due 12/31/05	$500,000	
Discount on bonds payable	(40,000)	$460,000

On this date, Redstone retired the entire bond issue by paying cash of $510,000.

Required

1. Prepare the journal entry to record the bond retirement.
2. Describe how the bond retirement would be reported on the statement of cash flows, assuming that Redstone uses the indirect method.

LO 5 Exercise 12-4 Cash Collections—Direct Method

Stanley Company's comparative balance sheets included accounts receivable of $80,800 at December 31, 2000, and $101,100 at December 31, 2001. Sales reported by Stanley on its 2001 income statement amounted to $1,450,000. What is the amount of cash collections that Stanley will report in the Operating Activities section of its 2001 statement of cash flows assuming that the direct method is used?

LO 5 Exercise 12-5 Cash Payments—Direct Method

Lester Enterprises' comparative balance sheets included inventory of $90,200 at December 31, 2000, and $70,600 at December 31, 2001. Lester's comparative balance sheets also included accounts payable of $57,700 at December 31, 2000, and $39,200 at December 31, 2001. Lester's accounts payable balances are composed solely of amounts due to suppliers for purchases of inventory on account. Cost of goods sold, as reported by Lester on its 2001 income statement, amounted to $770,900. What is the amount of cash payments for inventory that Lester will report in the Operating Activities section of its 2001 statement of cash flows assuming that the direct method is used?

LO 5 Exercise 12-6 Operating Activities Section—Direct Method

The following account balances for the noncash current assets and current liabilities of Labrador Company are available:

	December 31	
	2001	**2000**
Accounts receivable	$ 4,000	$ 6,000
Inventory	32,000	25,000
Office supplies	7,000	10,000
Accounts payable	7,500	4,500
Salaries and wages payable	1,500	2,500
Interest payable	500	1,000
Income taxes payable	4,500	3,000

In addition, the income statement for 2001 is as follows:

	2001
Sales revenue	$100,000
Cost of goods sold	75,000
Gross profit	$ 25,000
General and administrative expense	$ 8,000
Depreciation expense	3,000
Total operating expenses	$ 11,000
Income before interest and taxes	$ 14,000
Interest expense	3,000
Income before tax	$ 11,000
Income tax expense	5,000
Net income	$ 6,000

Required

1. Prepare the Operating Activities section of the statement of cash flows using the direct method.
2. What does the use of the direct method reveal about a company that the indirect method does not?

LO 5 Exercise 12-7 Determination of Missing Amounts—Cash Flow from Operating Activities

The computation of cash provided by operating activities requires analysis of the noncash current asset and current liability accounts. Using T accounts, determine the missing amounts for each of the following independent cases:

Case 1	
Accounts receivable, beginning of year	$150,000
Accounts receivable, end of year	100,000
Credit sales for the year	175,000
Cash sales for the year	60,000
Write-offs of uncollectible accounts	35,000
Total cash collections for the year (from cash sales and collections on account)	?
Case 2	
Inventory, beginning of year	$ 80,000
Inventory, end of year	55,000
Accounts payable, beginning of year	25,000
Accounts payable, end of year	15,000
Cost of goods sold	175,000
Cash payments for inventory (assume all purchases of inventory are on account)	?
Case 3	
Prepaid insurance, beginning of year	$ 17,000
Prepaid insurance, end of year	20,000
Insurance expense	15,000
Cash paid for new insurance policies	?
Case 4	
Income taxes payable, beginning of year	$ 95,000
Income taxes payable, end of year	115,000
Income tax expense	300,000
Cash payments for taxes	?

LO 5 Exercise 12-8 Dividends on the Statement of Cash Flows

The following selected account balances are available from the records of Lewistown Company:

	December 31	
	2001	**2000**
Dividends payable	$ 30,000	$ 20,000
Retained earnings	375,000	250,000

Other information available for 2001 follows:

a. Lewistown reported $285,000 net income for the year.

b. It declared and distributed a stock dividend of $50,000 during the year.

c. It declared cash dividends at the end of each quarter and paid them within the next 30 days of the following quarter.

Required

1. With the use of T accounts, determine the amount of cash dividends *paid* during the year for presentation in the Financing Activities section of the statement of cash flows.
2. Should the stock dividend described in part **b** appear on a statement of cash flows? Explain your answer.

LO 6 Exercise 12-9 Adjustments to Net Income with the Indirect Method

Assume that a company uses the indirect method to prepare the Operating Activities section of the statement of cash flows. For each of the following items, fill in the blank to indicate whether it would be added to net income (A), deducted from net income (D), or not reported in this section of the statement under the indirect method (NR).

_______ 1. Depreciation expense
_______ 2. Gain on sale of used delivery truck
_______ 3. Bad debts expense
_______ 4. Increase in accounts payable
_______ 5. Purchase of new delivery truck
_______ 6. Loss on retirement of bonds
_______ 7. Increase in prepaid rent
_______ 8. Decrease in inventory
_______ 9. Increase in short-term investments (classified as available-for-sale securities)
_______ 10. Amortization of patents

Indirect method—Operating Activities

LO 6 Exercise 12-10 Operating Activities Section—Indirect Method

The following account balances for the noncash current assets and current liabilities of Suffolk Company are available:

	December 31	
	2001	**2000**
Accounts receivable	$43,000	$35,000
Inventory	30,000	40,000
Prepaid rent	17,000	15,000
Totals	$90,000	$90,000
Accounts payable	$26,000	$19,000
Income taxes payable	6,000	10,000
Interest payable	15,000	12,000
Totals	$47,000	$41,000

Net income for 2001 is $40,000. Depreciation expense is $20,000. Assume that all sales and all purchases are on account.

Required

1. Prepare the Operating Activities section of the statement of cash flows using the indirect method.
2. Provide a brief explanation as to why cash flow from operating activities is more or less than the net income of the period.

Multi-Concept Exercises

LO 2, 3 Exercise 12-11 Classification of Activities

Use the following legend to indicate how each of the following transactions would be reported on the statement of cash flows (assume that the stocks and bonds of other companies are classified as available-for-sale securities):

II = Inflow from investing activities
OI = Outflow from investing activities
IF = Inflow from financing activities
OF = Outflow from financing activities
CE = Classified as a cash equivalent and included with cash for purposes of preparing the statement of cash flows

_______ 1. Purchased a six-month certificate of deposit.
_______ 2. Purchased a 60-day Treasury bill.
_______ 3. Issued 1,000 shares of common stock.
_______ 4. Purchased 1,000 shares of stock in another company.

________ **5.** Purchased 1,000 shares of its own stock to be held in the treasury.
________ **6.** Invested $1,000 in a money market fund.
________ **7.** Sold 500 shares of stock of another company.
________ **8.** Purchased 20-year bonds of another company.
________ **9.** Issued 30-year bonds.
________ **10.** Repaid a six-month bank loan.

LO 3, 5 Exercise 12-12 Classification of Activities

Use the following legend to indicate how each of the following transactions would be reported on the statement of cash flows (assume that the company uses the direct method in the Operating Activities section):

IO = Inflow from operating activities
OO = Outflow from operating activities
II = Inflow from investing activities
OI = Outflow from investing activities
IF = Inflow from financing activities
OF = Outflow from financing activities
NR = Not reported in the body of the statement of cash flows but included in a supplemental schedule

________ **1.** Collected $10,000 in cash from customers' open accounts for the period.
________ **2.** Paid one of the company's inventory suppliers $500 in settlement of an open account.
________ **3.** Purchased a new copier for $6,000; signed a 90-day note payable.
________ **4.** Issued bonds at face value of $100,000.
________ **5.** Made $23,200 in cash sales for the week.
________ **6.** Purchased an empty lot adjacent to the factory for $50,000. The seller of the land agrees to accept a five-year promissory note as consideration.
________ **7.** Renewed the property insurance policy for another six months. Cash of $1,000 is paid for the renewal.
________ **8.** Purchased a machine for $10,000.
________ **9.** Paid cash dividends of $2,500.
________ **10.** Reclassified as short-term a long-term note payable of $5,000 that is due within the next year.
________ **11.** Purchased 500 shares of the company's own stock on the open market for $4,000.
________ **12.** Sold 500 shares of Nike stock for book value of $10,000 (they had been classified as available-for-sale securities).

LO 3, 6 Exercise 12-13 Long-Term Assets on the Statement of Cash Flows—Indirect Method

The following account balances are taken from the records of Martin Corp. for the past two years (credit balances are in parentheses):

	December 31	
	2001	**2000**
Plant and equipment	$750,000	$500,000
Accumulated depreciation	(160,000)	(200,000)
Patents	92,000	80,000
Retained earnings	(825,000)	(675,000)

Other information available for 2001 follows:

a. Net income for the year was $200,000.
b. Depreciation expense on plant and equipment was $50,000.
c. Plant and equipment with an original cost of $150,000 were sold for $64,000 (you will need to determine the book value of the assets sold).
d. Amortization expense on patents was $8,000.
e. Both new plant and equipment and patents were purchased for cash during the year.

Required

Indicate, with amounts, how all items related to these long-term assets would be reported in the 2001 statement of cash flows, including any adjustments in the Operating Activities section of the statement. Assume that Martin uses the indirect method.

LO 1, 5 **Exercise 12-14** Income Statement, Statement of Cash Flows (Direct Method), and Balance Sheet

The following events occurred at Handsome Hounds Grooming Company during its first year of business:

a. To establish the company, the two owners contributed a total of $50,000 in exchange for common stock.

b. Grooming service revenue for the first year amounted to $150,000, of which $40,000 was on account.

c. Customers owe $10,000 at the end of the year from the services provided on account.

d. At the beginning of the year a storage building was rented. The company was required to sign a three-year lease for $12,000 per year and make a $2,000 refundable security deposit. The first year's lease payment and the security deposit were paid at the beginning of the year.

e. At the beginning of the year the company purchased a patent at a cost of $100,000 for a revolutionary system to be used for dog grooming. The patent is expected to be useful for 10 years. The company paid 20% down in cash and signed a four-year note at the bank for the remainder.

f. Operating expenses, including amortization of the patent and rent on the storage building, totaled $80,000 for the first year. No expenses were accrued or unpaid at the end of the year.

g. The company declared and paid a $20,000 cash dividend at the end of the first year.

Required

1. Prepare an income statement for the first year.
2. Prepare a statement of cash flows for the first year, using the direct method in the Operating Activities section.
3. Did the company generate more or less cash flow from operations than it earned in net income? Explain why there is a difference.
4. Prepare a balance sheet as of the end of the first year.

PROBLEMS

LO 6 **Problem 12-1** Statement of Cash Flows—Indirect Method

The following balances are available for Chrisman Company:

	December 31	
	2001	**2000**
Cash	$ 8,000	$ 10,000
Accounts receivable	20,000	15,000
Inventory	15,000	25,000
Prepaid rent	9,000	6,000
Land	75,000	75,000
Plant and equipment	400,000	300,000
Accumulated depreciation	(65,000)	(30,000)
Totals	$462,000	$401,000
Accounts payable	$ 12,000	$ 10,000
Income taxes payable	3,000	5,000
Short-term notes payable	35,000	25,000
Bonds payable	75,000	100,000
Common stock	200,000	150,000
Retained earnings	137,000	111,000
Totals	$462,000	$401,000

Bonds were retired during 2001 at face value, plant and equipment were acquired for cash, and common stock was issued for cash. Depreciation expense for the year was $35,000. Net income was reported at $26,000.

Required

1. Prepare a statement of cash flows for 2001, using the indirect method in the Operating Activities section.
2. Did Chrisman generate sufficient cash from operations to pay for its investing activities? How did it generate cash other than from operations? Explain your answers.

LO 7 **Problem 12-2** Statement of Cash Flows Using a Work Sheet—Indirect Method (Appendix 14A)

Refer to all of the facts in Problem 12-1.

Required

1. Using the format in Appendix 12A, prepare a statement of cash flows work sheet.
2. Prepare a statement of cash flows for 2001, using the indirect method in the Operating Activities section.
3. Did Chrisman generate sufficient cash from operations to pay for its investing activities? How did it generate cash other than from operations? Explain your answers.

LO 5 **Problem 12-3** Statement of Cash Flows—Direct Method

DECISION MAKING

Peoria Corp. has just completed another very successful year, as indicated by the following income statement:

	For the year ended December 31, 2001
Sales revenue	$1,250,000
Cost of goods sold	700,000
Gross profit	$ 550,000
Operating expenses	150,000
Income before interest and taxes	$ 400,000
Interest expense	25,000
Income before taxes	$ 375,000
Income tax expense	150,000
Net income	$ 225,000

Presented below are comparative balance sheets:

	December 31	
	2001	2000
Cash	$ 52,000	$ 90,000
Accounts receivable	180,000	130,000
Inventory	230,000	200,000
Prepayments	15,000	25,000
Total current assets	$ 477,000	$ 445,000
Land	$ 750,000	$ 600,000
Plant and equipment	700,000	500,000
Accumulated depreciation	(250,000)	(200,000)
Total long-term assets	$1,200,000	$ 900,000
Total assets	$1,677,000	$1,345,000
Accounts payable	$ 130,000	$ 148,000
Other accrued liabilities	68,000	63,000
Income taxes payable	90,000	110,000
Total current liabilities	$ 288,000	$ 321,000
Long-term bank loan payable	$ 350,000	$ 300,000
Common stock	$ 550,000	$ 400,000

Retained earnings	489,000	324,000
Total stockholders' equity	$1,039,000	$ 724,000
Total liabilities and stockholders' equity	$1,677,000	$1,345,000

Other information follows:

a. Dividends of $60,000 were declared and paid during the year.

b. Operating expenses include $50,000 of depreciation.

c. Land and plant and equipment were acquired for cash, and additional stock was issued for cash. Cash was also received from additional bank loans.

The president has asked you some questions about the year's results. She is very impressed with the profit margin of 18% (net income divided by sales revenue). She is bothered, however, by the decline in the cash balance during the year. One of the conditions of the existing bank loan is that the company maintain a minimum cash balance of $50,000.

Required

1. Prepare a statement of cash flows for 2001, using the direct method in the Operating Activities section.
2. On the basis of your statement in requirement **1,** draft a brief memo to the president to explain why cash decreased during such a profitable year. Include in your explanation any recommendations for improving the company's cash flow in future years.

LO 6 **Problem 12-4** Statement of Cash Flows—Indirect Method
Refer to all of the facts in Problem 12-3.

Required

1. Prepare a statement of cash flows for 2001, using the indirect method in the Operating Activities section.
2. On the basis of your statement in requirement **1,** draft a brief memo to the president to explain why cash decreased during such a profitable year. Include in your explanation any recommendations for improving the company's cash flow in future years.

LO 7 **Problem 12-5** Statement of Cash Flows Using a Work Sheet—Indirect Method (Appendix 12A)
Refer to all of the facts in Problem 12-3.

Required

1. Using the format in Appendix 12A, prepare a statement of cash flows work sheet.
2. Prepare a statement of cash flows for 2001, using the indirect method in the Operating Activities section.
3. On the basis of your statement in requirement **2,** draft a brief memo to the president to explain why cash decreased during such a profitable year. Include in your explanation any recommendations for improving the company's cash flow in future years.

LO 5 **Problem 12-6** Statement of Cash Flows—Direct Method
The income statement for Astro Inc. for 2001 follows:

	For the year ended December 31, 2001
Sales revenue	$ 500,000
Cost of goods sold	400,000
Gross profit	$ 100,000
Operating expenses	180,000
Loss before interest and taxes	$ (80,000)
Interest expense	20,000
Net loss	$(100,000)

Presented below are comparative balance sheets:

	December 31	
	2001	2000
Cash	$ 95,000	$ 80,000
Accounts receivable	50,000	75,000
Inventory	100,000	150,000
Prepayments	55,000	45,000
Total current assets	$ 300,000	$ 350,000
Land	$ 475,000	$ 400,000
Plant and equipment	870,000	800,000
Accumulated depreciation	(370,000)	(300,000)
Total long-term assets	$ 975,000	$ 900,000
Total assets	$1,275,000	$1,250,000
Accounts payable	$ 125,000	$ 100,000
Other accrued liabilities	35,000	45,000
Interest payable	15,000	10,000
Total current liabilities	$ 175,000	$ 155,000
Long-term bank loan payable	$ 340,000	$ 250,000
Common stock	$ 450,000	$ 400,000
Retained earnings	310,000	445,000
Total stockholders' equity	$ 760,000	$ 845,000
Total liabilities and stockholders' equity	$1,275,000	$1,250,000

Other information follows:

a. Dividends of $35,000 were declared and paid during the year.

b. Operating expenses include $70,000 of depreciation.

c. Land and plant and equipment were acquired for cash, and additional stock was issued for cash. Cash was also received from additional bank loans.

The president has asked you some questions about the year's results. He is disturbed with the $100,000 net loss for the year. He notes, however, that the cash position at the end of the year is improved. He is confused about what appear to be conflicting signals: "How could we have possibly added to our bank accounts during such a terrible year of operations?"

Required

1. Prepare a statement of cash flows for 2001, using the direct method in the Operating Activities section.
2. On the basis of your statement in requirement **1,** draft a brief memo to the president to explain why cash increased during such an unprofitable year. Include in your memo your recommendations for improving the company's bottom line.

LO 6 **Problem 12-7** Statement of Cash Flows—Indirect Method
Refer to all of the facts in Problem 12-6.

Required

1. Prepare a statement of cash flows for 2001, using the indirect method in the Operating Activities section.
2. On the basis of your statement in requirement **1,** draft a brief memo to the president to explain why cash increased during such an unprofitable year. Include in your memo your recommendations for improving the company's bottom line.

LO 7 **Problem 12-8** Statement of Cash Flows Using a Work Sheet—Indirect Method (Appendix 12A)
Refer to all of the facts in Problem 12-6.

Required

1. Using the format in Appendix 12A, prepare a statement of cash flows work sheet.
2. Prepare a statement of cash flows for 2001, using the indirect method in the Operating Activities section.
3. On the basis of your statement in requirement **2,** draft a brief memo to the president to explain why cash increased during such an unprofitable year. Include in your memo your recommendations for improving the company's bottom line.

LO 6 Problem 12-9 Year-end Balance Sheet and Statement of Cash Flows—Indirect Method
The balance sheet of Terrier Company at the end of 2000 is presented below, along with certain other information for 2001:

	December 31, 2000
Cash	$ 140,000
Accounts receivable	155,000
Total current assets	$ 295,000
Land	$ 300,000
Plant and equipment	500,000
Accumulated depreciation	(150,000)
Investments	100,000
Total long-term assets	$ 750,000
Total assets	$1,045,000
Current liabilities	$ 205,000
Bonds payable	$ 300,000
Common stock	400,000
Retained earnings	140,000
Total stockholders' equity	$ 540,000
Total liabilities and stockholders' equity	$1,045,000

Other information follows:

a. Net income for 2001 was $70,000.
b. Included in operating expenses was $20,000 in depreciation.
c. Cash dividends of $25,000 were declared and paid.
d. An additional $150,000 of bonds was issued for cash.
e. Common stock of $50,000 was purchased for cash and retired.
f. Cash purchases of plant and equipment during the year were $200,000.
g. An additional $100,000 of bonds was issued in exchange for land.
h. Sales exceeded cash collections on account during the year by $10,000. All sales are on account.
i. The amount of current liabilities remained unchanged during the year.

Required

1. Prepare a statement of cash flows for 2001, using the indirect method in the Operating Activities section. Include a supplemental schedule for noncash activities.
2. Prepare a balance sheet at December 31, 2001.
3. Provide a possible explanation as to why Terrier decided to issue additional bonds for cash during 2001.

LO 7 Problem 12-10 Statement of Cash Flows Using a Work Sheet—Indirect Method (Appendix 12A)
Refer to all of the facts in Problem 12-9.

Required

1. Prepare a balance sheet at December 31, 2001.
2. Using the format in Appendix 12A, prepare a statement of cash flows work sheet.

3. Prepare a statement of cash flows for 2001, using the indirect method in the Operating Activities section.
4. Provide a possible explanation as to why Terrier decided to issue additional bonds for cash during 2001.

Multi-Concept Problems

LO 4, 5 Problem 12-11 Statement of Cash Flows—Direct Method

SPREADSHEET

Glendive Corp. is in the process of preparing its statement of cash flows for the year ended June 30, 2001. An income statement for the year and comparative balance sheets follow:

	For the year ended June 30, 2001
Sales revenue	$550,000
Cost of goods sold	350,000
Gross profit	$200,000
General and administrative expenses	$ 55,000
Depreciation expense	75,000
Loss on sale of plant assets	5,000
Total expenses and losses	$135,000
Income before interest and taxes	$ 65,000
Interest expense	15,000
Income before taxes	$ 50,000
Income tax expense	17,000
Net income	$ 33,000

	June 30	
	2001	2000
Cash	$ 31,000	$ 40,000
Accounts receivable	90,000	75,000
Inventory	80,000	95,000
Prepaid rent	12,000	16,000
Total current assets	$213,000	$226,000
Land	$250,000	$170,000
Plant and equipment	750,000	600,000
Accumulated depreciation	(310,000)	(250,000)
Total long-term assets	$690,000	$520,000
Total assets	$903,000	$746,000
Accounts payable	$155,000	$148,000
Other accrued liabilities	32,000	26,000
Income taxes payable	8,000	10,000
Total current liabilities	$195,000	$184,000
Long-term bank loan payable	$100,000	$130,000
Common stock	$350,000	$200,000
Retained earnings	258,000	232,000
Total stockholders' equity	$608,000	$432,000
Total liabilities and stockholders' equity	$903,000	$746,000

Dividends of $7,000 were declared and paid during the year. New plant assets were purchased for $195,000 in cash during the year. Also, land was purchased for cash. Plant assets were sold during 2001 for $25,000 in cash. The original cost of the assets sold was $45,000, and their book value was $30,000. Additional stock was issued for cash, and a portion of the bank loan was repaid.

Required

1. Prepare a statement of cash flows, using the direct method in the Operating Activities section.
2. Evaluate the following statement: "Whether a company uses the direct or the indirect method to report cash flows from operations is irrelevant because the amount of cash flow from operating activities is the same regardless of which method is used."

LO 4, 6 Problem 12-12 Statement of Cash Flows—Indirect Method
Refer to all of the facts in Problem 12-11.

Required

1. Prepare a statement of cash flows for 2001, using the indirect method in the Operating Activities section.
2. Evaluate the following statement: "Whether a company uses the direct or indirect method to report cash flows from operations is irrelevant because the amount of cash flow from operating activities is the same regardless of which method is used."

LO 2, 5 Problem 12-13 Statement of Cash Flows—Direct Method
Lang Company has not yet prepared a formal statement of cash flows for 2001. Comparative balance sheets as of December 31, 2001 and 2000, and a statement of income and retained earnings for the year ended December 31, 2001, follow:

LANG COMPANY
BALANCE SHEET
DECEMBER 31
(THOUSANDS OMITTED)

Assets	**2001**	**2000**
Current assets:		
Cash	$ 60	$ 100
U.S. Treasury bills (six-month)	–0–	50
Accounts receivable	610	500
Inventory	720	600
Total current assets	$1,390	$1,250
Long-term assets:		
Land	$ 80	$ 70
Buildings and equipment	710	600
Accumulated depreciation	(180)	(120)
Patents (less amortization)	105	130
Total long-term assets	$ 715	$ 680
Total assets	$2,105	$1,930
Liabilities and Owners' Equity		
Current liabilities:		
Accounts payable	$ 360	$ 300
Taxes payable	25	20
Notes payable	400	400
Total current liabilities	$ 785	$ 720
Term notes payable—due 2005	200	200
Total liabilities	$ 985	$ 920
Owners' equity:		
Common stock outstanding	$ 830	$ 700
Retained earnings	290	310
Total owners' equity	$1,120	$1,010
Total liabilities and owners' equity	$2,105	$1,930

LANG COMPANY
STATEMENT OF INCOME AND RETAINED EARNINGS
FOR THE YEAR ENDED DECEMBER 31, 2001
(THOUSANDS OMITTED)

Sales		$2,408
Less expenses and interest:		
Cost of goods sold	$1,100	
Salaries and benefits	850	
Heat, light, and power	75	
Depreciation	60	
Property taxes	18	
Patent amortization	25	
Miscellaneous expense	10	
Interest	55	2,193
Net income before income taxes		$ 215
Income taxes		105
Net income		$ 110
Retained earnings—January 1, 2001		310
		$ 420
Stock dividend distributed		130
Retained earnings—December 31, 2001		$ 290

Required

1. For purposes of a statement of cash flows, are the U.S. Treasury bills cash equivalents? If not, how should they be classified? Explain your answers.
2. Prepare a statement of cash flows for 2001, using the direct method in the Operating Activities section. (CMA adapted)

ALTERNATE PROBLEMS

LO 6 **Problem 12-1A** Statement of Cash Flows—Indirect Method

The following balances are available for Madison Company:

	December 31	
	2001	**2000**
Cash	$ 12,000	$ 10,000
Accounts receivable	10,000	12,000
Inventory	8,000	7,000
Prepaid rent	1,200	1,000
Land	75,000	75,000
Plant and equipment	200,000	150,000
Accumulated depreciation	(75,000)	(25,000)
Totals	$231,200	$230,000
Accounts payable	$ 15,000	$ 15,000
Income taxes payable	2,500	2,000
Short-term notes payable	20,000	22,500
Bonds payable	75,000	50,000
Common stock	100,000	100,000
Retained earnings	18,700	40,500
Totals	$231,200	$230,000

Bonds were issued during 2001 at face value, and plant and equipment were acquired for cash. Depreciation expense for the year was $50,000. A net loss of $21,800 was reported.

Required

1. Prepare a statement of cash flows for 2001, using the indirect method in the Operating Activities section.
2. Explain briefly how Madison was able to increase its cash balance during a year in which it incurred a net loss.

LO 7 **Problem 12-2A** Statement of Cash Flows Using a Work Sheet—Indirect Method (Appendix 12A)

Refer to all of the facts in Problem 12-1A.

Required

1. Using the format in Appendix 12A, prepare a statement of cash flows work sheet.
2. Prepare a statement of cash flows for 2001, using the indirect method in the Operating Activities section.
3. Explain briefly how Madison was able to increase its cash balance during a year in which it incurred a net loss.

LO 5 **Problem 12-3A** Statement of Cash Flows—Direct Method

Wabash Corp. has just completed another very successful year, as indicated by the following income statement:

	For the year ended December 31, 2001
Sales revenue	$2,460,000
Cost of goods sold	1,400,000
Gross profit	$1,060,000
Operating expenses	460,000
Income before interest and taxes	$ 600,000
Interest expense	100,000
Income before taxes	$ 500,000
Income tax expense	150,000
Net income	$ 350,000

The following are comparative balance sheets:

	December 31	
	2001	**2000**
Cash	$ 140,000	$ 210,000
Accounts receivable	60,000	145,000
Inventory	200,000	180,000
Prepayments	15,000	25,000
Total current assets	$ 415,000	$ 560,000
Land	$ 600,000	$ 700,000
Plant and equipment	850,000	600,000
Accumulated depreciation	(225,000)	(200,000)
Total long-term assets	$1,225,000	$1,100,000
Total assets	$1,640,000	$1,660,000
Accounts payable	$ 140,000	$ 120,000
Other accrued liabilities	50,000	55,000
Income taxes payable	80,000	115,000
Total current liabilities	$ 270,000	$ 290,000
Long-term bank loan payable	$ 200,000	$ 250,000
Common stock	$ 450,000	$ 400,000
Retained earnings	720,000	720,000
Total stockholders' equity	$1,170,000	$1,120,000
Total liabilities and stockholders' equity	$1,640,000	$1,660,000

Other information follows:

a. Dividends of $350,000 were declared and paid during the year.

b. Operating expenses include $25,000 of depreciation.

c. Land was sold for its book value, and new plant and equipment was acquired for cash.

d. Part of the bank loan was repaid, and additional common stock was issued for cash.

The president has asked you some questions about the year's results. She is very impressed with the profit margin of 14% (net income divided by sales revenue). She is bothered, however, by the decline in the company's cash balance during the year. One of the conditions of the existing bank loan is that the company maintain a minimum cash balance of $100,000.

Required

1. Prepare a statement of cash flows for 2001, using the direct method in the Operating Activities section.
2. On the basis of your statement in requirement **1,** draft a brief memo to the president to explain why cash decreased during such a profitable year. Include in your explanation any recommendations for improving the company's cash flow in future years.

LO 6 **Problem 12-4A** Statement of Cash Flows—Indirect Method

Refer to all of the facts in Problem 12-3A.

Required

1. Prepare a statement of cash flows for 2001, using the indirect method in the Operating Activities section.
2. On the basis of your statement in requirement **1,** draft a brief memo to the president to explain why cash decreased during such a profitable year. Include in your explanation any recommendations for improving the company's cash flow in future years.

LO 7 **Problem 12-5A** Statement of Cash Flows Using a Work Sheet—Indirect Method (Appendix 12A)

Refer to all of the facts in Problem 12-3A.

Required

1. Using the format in Appendix 12A, prepare a statement of cash flows work sheet.
2. Prepare a statement of cash flows for 2001, using the indirect method in the Operating Activities section.
3. On the basis of your statement in requirement **2,** draft a brief memo to the president to explain why cash decreased during such a profitable year. Include in your explanation any recommendations for improving the company's cash flow in future years.

LO 5 **Problem 12-6A** Statement of Cash Flows—Direct Method

The income statement for Pluto Inc. for 2001 follows:

	For the year ended December 31, 2001
Sales revenue	$350,000
Cost of goods sold	150,000
Gross profit	$200,000
Operating expenses	250,000
Loss before interest and taxes	$ (50,000)
Interest expense	10,000
Net loss	$ (60,000)

Presented below are comparative balance sheets:

	December 31	
	2001	2000
Cash	$ 25,000	$ 10,000
Accounts receivable	30,000	80,000
Inventory	100,000	100,000
Prepayments	36,000	35,000
Total current assets	$191,000	$225,000
Land	$300,000	$200,000
Plant and equipment	500,000	250,000
Accumulated depreciation	(90,000)	(50,000)
Total long-term assets	$710,000	$400,000
Total assets	$901,000	$625,000
Accounts payable	$ 50,000	$ 10,000
Other accrued liabilities	40,000	20,000
Interest payable	22,000	12,000
Total current liabilities	$112,000	$ 42,000
Long-term bank loan payable	$450,000	$100,000
Common stock	$300,000	$300,000
Retained earnings	39,000	183,000
Total stockholders' equity	$339,000	$483,000
Total liabilities and stockholders' equity	$901,000	$625,000

Other information follows:

a. Dividends of $84,000 were declared and paid during the year.

b. Operating expenses include $40,000 of depreciation.

c. Land and plant and equipment were acquired for cash. Cash was received from additional bank loans.

The president has asked you some questions about the year's results. He is disturbed with the net loss of $60,000 for the year. He notes, however, that the cash position at the end of the year is improved. He is confused about what appear to be conflicting signals: "How could we have possibly added to our bank accounts during such a terrible year of operations?"

Required

1. Prepare a statement of cash flows for 2001, using the direct method in the Operating Activities section.
2. On the basis of your statement in requirement **1**, draft a brief memo to the president to explain why cash increased during such an unprofitable year. Include in your memo your recommendations for improving the company's bottom line.

LO 6 **Problem 12-7A** Statement of Cash Flows—Indirect Method

Refer to all of the facts in Problem 12-6A.

Required

1. Prepare a statement of cash flows for 2001, using the indirect method in the Operating Activities section.
2. On the basis of your statement in requirement **1**, draft a brief memo to the president to explain why cash increased during such an unprofitable year. Include in your memo your recommendations for improving the company's bottom line.

LO 7 **Problem 12-8A** Statement of Cash Flows Using a Work Sheet—Indirect Method (Appendix 12A)

Refer to all of the facts in Problem 12-6A.

Required

1. Using the format in Appendix 12A, prepare a statement of cash flows work sheet.
2. Prepare a statement of cash flows for 2001, using the indirect method in the Operating Activities section.
3. On the basis of your statement in requirement **2,** draft a brief memo to the president to explain why cash increased during such an unprofitable year. Include in your memo your recommendations for improving the company's bottom line.

LO 6 Problem 12-9A Year-end Balance Sheet and Statement of Cash Flows—Indirect Method

The balance sheet of Poodle Company at the end of 2000 is presented below along with certain other information for 2001:

	December 31, 2000
Cash	$ 155,000
Accounts receivable	140,000
Total current assets	$ 295,000
Land	$ 100,000
Plant and equipment	700,000
Accumulated depreciation	(175,000)
Investments	125,000
Total long-term assets	$ 750,000
Total assets	$1,045,000
Current liabilities	$ 325,000
Bonds payable	$ 100,000
Common stock	500,000
Retained earnings	120,000
Total stockholders' equity	$ 620,000
Total liabilities and stockholders' equity	$1,045,000

Other information follows:

a. Net income for 2001 was $50,000.
b. Included in operating expenses was $25,000 in depreciation.
c. Cash dividends of $40,000 were declared and paid.
d. An additional $50,000 of common stock was issued for cash.
e. Bonds payable of $100,000 were purchased for cash and retired at no gain or loss.
f. Cash purchases of plant and equipment during the year were $60,000.
g. An additional $200,000 of land was acquired in exchange for a long-term note payable.
h. Sales exceeded cash collections on account during the year by $15,000. All sales are on account.
i. The amount of current liabilities decreased by $20,000 during the year.

Required

1. Prepare a statement of cash flows for 2001, using the indirect method in the Operating Activities section. Include a supplemental schedule for noncash activities.
2. Prepare a balance sheet at December 31, 2001.
3. What primary uses did Poodle make of the cash it generated from operating activities?

LO 7 Problem 12-10A Statement of Cash Flows Using a Work Sheet—Indirect Method (Appendix 12A)

Refer to all of the facts in Problem 12-9A.

Required

1. Prepare a balance sheet at December 31, 2001.
2. Using the format in Appendix 12A, prepare a statement of cash flows work sheet.

3. Prepare a statement of cash flows for 2001, using the indirect method in the Operating Activities section.
4. Provide a possible explanation as to why Poodle decided to purchase and retire bonds during 2001.

Alternate Multi-Concept Problems

LO 4, 5 Problem 12-11A Statement of Cash Flows—Direct Method

Bannack Corp. is in the process of preparing its statement of cash flows for the year ended June 30, 2001. An income statement for the year and comparative balance sheets follow:

	For the year ended June 30, 2001
Sales revenue	$400,000
Cost of goods sold	240,000
Gross profit	$160,000
General and administrative expenses	$ 40,000
Depreciation expense	80,000
Loss on sale of plant assets	10,000
Total expenses and losses	$130,000
Income before interest and taxes	$ 30,000
Interest expense	15,000
Income before taxes	$ 15,000
Income tax expense	5,000
Net income	$ 10,000

	June 30	
	2001	2000
Cash	$ 25,000	$ 40,000
Accounts receivable	80,000	69,000
Inventory	75,000	50,000
Prepaid rent	2,000	18,000
Total current assets	$182,000	$177,000
Land	$ 60,000	$150,000
Plant and equipment	575,000	500,000
Accumulated depreciation	(310,000)	(250,000)
Total long-term assets	$325,000	$400,000
Total assets	$507,000	$577,000
Accounts payable	$145,000	$140,000
Other accrued liabilities	50,000	45,000
Income taxes payable	5,000	15,000
Total current liabilities	$200,000	$200,000
Long-term bank loan payable	$ 75,000	$150,000
Common stock	$100,000	$100,000
Retained earnings	132,000	127,000
Total stockholders' equity	$232,000	$227,000
Total liabilities and stockholders' equity	$507,000	$577,000

Dividends of $5,000 were declared and paid during the year. New plant assets were purchased for $125,000 in cash during the year. Also, land was sold for cash at its book value. Plant assets were sold during 2001 for $20,000 in cash. The original cost of the assets sold was $50,000, and their book value was $30,000. A portion of the bank loan was repaid.

Required

1. Prepare a statement of cash flows for 2001, using the direct method in the Operating Activities section.
2. Evaluate the following statement: "Whether a company uses the direct or the indirect method to report cash flows from operations is irrelevant because the amount of cash flow from operating activities is the same regardless of which method is used."

LO 4, 6 Problem 12-12A Statement of Cash Flows—Indirect Method
Refer to all of the facts in Problem 12-11A

Required

1. Prepare a statement of cash flows for 2001, using the indirect method in the Operating Activities section.
2. Evaluate the following statement: "Whether a company uses the direct or the indirect method to report cash flows from operations is irrelevant because the amount of cash flow from operating activities is the same regardless of which method is used."

LO 2, 5 Problem 12-13A Statement of Cash Flows—Direct Method
Shepard Company has not yet prepared a formal statement of cash flows for 2001. Comparative balance sheets as of December 31, 2001 and 2000, and a statement of income and retained earnings for the year ended December 31, 2001, follow:

SHEPARD COMPANY
BALANCE SHEET
DECEMBER 31
(THOUSANDS OMITTED)

Assets	**2001**	**2000**
Current assets:		
Cash	$ 50	$ 75
U.S. Treasury bills (six-month)	25	–0–
Accounts receivable	125	200
Inventory	525	500
Total current assets	$ 725	$ 775
Long-term assets:		
Land	$ 100	$ 80
Buildings and equipment	510	450
Accumulated depreciation	(190)	(150)
Patents (less amortization)	90	110
Total long-term assets	$ 510	$ 490
Total assets	$1,235	$1,265
Liabilities and Owners' Equity		
Current liabilities:		
Accounts payable	$ 370	$ 330
Taxes payable	10	20
Notes payable	300	400
Total current liabilities	$ 680	$ 750
Term notes payable—due 2005	200	200
Total liabilities	$ 880	$ 950
Owners' equity:		
Common stock outstanding	$ 220	$ 200
Retained earnings	135	115
Total owners' equity	$ 355	$ 315
Total liabilities and owners' equity	$1,235	$1,265

SHEPARD COMPANY
STATEMENT OF INCOME AND RETAINED EARNINGS
YEAR ENDED DECEMBER 31, 2001
(THOUSANDS OMITTED)

Sales		\$1,416
Less expenses and interest:		
Cost of goods sold	\$990	
Salaries and benefits	195	
Heat, light, and power	70	
Depreciation	40	
Property taxes	2	
Patent amortization	20	
Miscellaneous expense	2	
Interest	45	1,364
Net income before income taxes		\$ 52
Income taxes		12
Net income		\$ 40
Retained earnings—January 1, 2001		115
		\$ 155
Stock dividend distributed		20
Retained earnings—December 31, 2001		\$ 135

Required

1. For purposes of a statement of cash flows, are the U.S. Treasury bills cash equivalents? If not, how should they be classified? Explain your answers.
2. Prepare a statement of cash flows for 2001, using the direct method in the Operating Activities section.

(CMA adapted)

CASES

Reading and Interpreting Financial Statements

LO 2, 3 **Case 12-1** Reading and Interpreting Ben & Jerry's Statement of Cash Flows

www.benjerry.com

Refer to Ben & Jerry's statement of cash flows for 1998 and any other pertinent information in its annual report.

Required

1. According to a footnote in the annual report, how does the company define cash equivalents?
2. According to the statement of cash flows, did inventories increase or decrease during the most recent year? Explain your answer.
3. What are the major reasons for the difference between net income and net cash provided by operating activities?
4. Excluding operations, what was Ben & Jerry's largest source of cash during the most recent year? the largest use of cash?
5. What common type of cash outflow from financing activities is missing from Ben & Jerry's statement?

LO 2, 3 **Case 12-2** Reading and Interpreting Gateway's Statement of Cash Flows

www.gateway.com

Refer to Gateway's statement of cash flows for 1998 and any other pertinent information in its annual report.

Required

1. According to a footnote in the annual report, how does the company define cash equivalents?
2. According to the statement of cash flows, did accounts receivable increase or decrease during 1998? Explain your answer.
3. What are the major reasons net cash provided by operating activities is nearly double net income?
4. What activity has generated $10,000,000 of cash for Gateway in each of the last two years?
5. What common type of cash outflow from financing activities is missing from Gateway's statement?

LO 4 Case 12-3 Reading and Interpreting Sara Lee's Statement of Cash Flows

Presented below is the Operating Activities section of Sara Lee's 1998 statement of cash flows, along with an excerpt from the Financial Review section of the 1998 annual report (in millions of dollars):

www.saralee.com

Operating Activities	
Net loss	$ (523)
Adjustments for noncash charges included in net (loss) income:	
Depreciation	427
Amortization of intangibles	191
Restructuring charge	2,040
(Decrease) increase in deferred taxes	(405)
Other noncash credits, net	(5)
Changes in current assets and liabilities, net of businesses acquired and sold	
Decrease in trade accounts receivable	6
(Increase) in inventories	(27)
Decrease in other current assets	34
Increase in accounts payable	20
Increase in accrued liabilities	177
Net cash from operating activities	$1,935

1998 Restructuring In the second quarter of fiscal 1998, the corporation provided for the cost of restructuring its worldwide operations. The planned restructuring activities include the disposition of 116 manufacturing and distribution facilities—86 facilities are owned and 30 are leased. This restructuring provision reduced income before income taxes, net income and basic earnings per share in 1998 by $2,040 million, $1,625 million and $3.46 per share, respectively.

Required

1. Which method, direct or indirect, does Sara Lee use in preparing the Operating Activities section of its statement of cash flows? Explain.
2. Based on your review of this section of Sara Lee's 1998 statement of cash flows, what is the primary reason the company reported a net loss but was able to generate significant cash from operations?
3. Refer to the excerpt from the Financial Review. What was the dollar effect of the 1998 restructuring on income before income taxes? What was the dollar effect of the 1998 restructuring on cash flow during 1998? Relate your answer to the answer you provided in **2.** above.

Making Financial Decisions

LO 1, 5 Case 12-4 Dividend Decision and the Statement of Cash Flows—Direct Method

Bailey Corp. just completed the most profitable year in its 25-year history. Reported earnings of $1,020,000 on sales of $8,000,000 resulted in a very healthy profit margin of 12.75%. Each year before releasing the financial statements, the board of directors meets to decide on the amount of dividends to declare for the year. For each of the past nine years, the company has declared a dividend of $1 per share of common stock, which has been paid on January 15 of the following year.

Presented below are the income statement for the year and comparative balance sheets as of the end of the last two years.

	For the year ended December 31, 2001
Sales revenue	$8,000,000
Cost of goods sold	4,500,000
Gross profit	$3,500,000
Operating expenses	1,450,000
Income before interest and taxes	$2,050,000
Interest expense	350,000
Income before taxes	$1,700,000
Income tax expense 40%	680,000
Net income	$1,020,000

	December 31	
	2001	2000
Cash	$ 480,000	$ 450,000
Accounts receivable	250,000	200,000
Inventory	750,000	600,000
Prepayments	60,000	75,000
Total current assets	$1,540,000	$1,325,000
Land	$3,255,000	$2,200,000
Plant and equipment	4,200,000	2,500,000
Accumulated depreciation	(1,250,000)	(1,000,000)
Long-term investments	500,000	900,000
Patents	650,000	750,000
Total long-term assets	$7,355,000	$5,350,000
Total assets	$8,895,000	$6,675,000
Accounts payable	$ 350,000	$ 280,000
Other accrued liabilities	285,000	225,000
Income taxes payable	170,000	100,000
Dividends payable	–0–	200,000
Notes payable due within next year	200,000	–0–
Total current liabilities	$1,005,000	$ 805,000
Long-term notes payable	$ 300,000	$ 500,000
Bonds payable	2,200,000	1,500,000
Total long-term liabilities	$2,500,000	$2,000,000
Common stock, $10 par	$2,500,000	$2,000,000
Retained earnings	2,890,000	1,870,000
Total stockholders' equity	$5,390,000	$3,870,000
Total liabilities and stockholders' equity	$8,895,000	$6,675,000

Additional information follows:

a. All sales are on account, as are all purchases.

b. Land was purchased through the issuance of bonds. Additional land (beyond the amount purchased through the issuance of bonds) was purchased for cash.

c. New plant and equipment were acquired during the year for cash. No plant assets were retired during the year. Depreciation expense is included in operating expenses.

d. Long-term investments were sold for cash during the year.

e. No new patents were acquired, and none were disposed of during the year. Amortization expense is included in operating expenses.

f. Notes payable due within next year represents the amount reclassified from long-term to short-term.

g. Fifty thousand shares of common stock were issued during the year at par value.

As Bailey's controller, you have been asked to recommend to the board whether to declare a dividend this year and, if so, whether the precedent of paying a $1 per share dividend can be maintained. The president is eager to keep the dividend at $1 in view of the successful year just completed. He is also concerned, however, about the effect of a dividend on the company's cash position. He is particularly concerned about the large amount of notes payable that comes due next year. He further notes the aggressive growth pattern in recent years, as evidenced this year by large increases in land and plant and equipment.

Required

1. Using the format in Exhibit 12-14, convert the income statement from an accrual basis to a cash basis.
2. Prepare a statement of cash flows, using the direct method in the Operating Activities section.
3. What do you recommend to the board of directors concerning the declaration of a cash dividend? Should the $1 per share dividend be declared? Should a smaller amount be declared? Should no dividend be declared? Support your answer with any necessary computations. Include in your response your concerns, from a cash flow perspective, about the following year.

LO 1, 6 Case 12-5 Equipment Replacement Decision and Cash Flows from Operations

Conrad Company has been in operation for four years. The company is pleased with the continued improvement in net income but is concerned about a lack of cash available to replace existing equipment. Land, buildings, and equipment were purchased at the beginning of Year 1. No subsequent fixed asset purchases have been made, but the president believes that equipment will need to be replaced in the near future. The following information is available (all amounts are in millions of dollars):

	Year of Operation			
	Year 1	**Year 2**	**Year 3**	**Year 4**
Net income (loss)	$(10)	$ (2)	$15	$20
Depreciation expense	30	25	15	14
Increase (decrease) in:				
Accounts receivable	32	5	12	20
Inventories	26	8	5	9
Prepayments	0	0	10	5
Accounts payable	15	3	(5)	(4)

Required

1. Compute the cash flow from operations for each of Conrad's first four years of operation.
2. Write a memo to the president explaining why the company is not generating sufficient cash from operations to pay for the replacement of equipment.

Accounting and Ethics: What Would You Do?

LO 1, 6 Case 12-6 Loan Decision and the Statement of Cash Flows—Indirect Method

Mega Enterprises is in the process of negotiating an extension of its existing loan agreements with a major bank. The bank is particularly concerned with Mega's ability to generate sufficient cash flow from operating activities to meet the periodic principal and interest payments. In conjunction with the negotiations, the controller prepared the following statement of cash flows to present to the bank:

MEGA ENTERPRISES
STATEMENT OF CASH FLOWS
FOR THE YEAR ENDED DECEMBER 31, 2001
(ALL AMOUNTS IN MILLIONS OF DOLLARS)

Cash flows from operating activities	
Net income	$ 65
Adjustments to reconcile net income to net cash provided by operating activities:	
Depreciation and amortization	56
Increase in accounts receivable	(19)

Decrease in inventory	27
Decrease in accounts payable	(42)
Increase in other accrued liabilities	18
Net cash provided by operating activities	$ 105
Cash flows from investing activities	
Acquisitions of other businesses	$(234)
Acquisitions of plant and equipment	(125)
Sale of other businesses	300
Net cash used by investing activities	$ (59)
Cash flows from financing activities	
Additional borrowings	$ 150
Repayments of borrowings	(180)
Cash dividends paid	(50)
Net cash used by financing activities	$ (80)
Net decrease in cash	$ (34)
Cash balance, January 1, 2001	42
Cash balance, December 31, 2001	$ 8

During 2001 Mega sold one of its businesses in California. A gain of $150 million was included in 2001 income as the difference between the proceeds from the sale of $450 million and the book value of the business of $300 million. The entry to record the sale is as follows:

Cash	450	
California Properties		300
Gain on Sale of Business		150
To record sale of a business.		

Required

1. Comment on the presentation of the sale of the California business on the statement of cash flows. Does the way in which the sale was reported violate generally accepted accounting principles? Regardless of whether it violates GAAP, does the way in which the transaction was reported on the statement result in a misstatement of the net decrease in cash for the period? Explain your answers.
2. Prepare a revised statement of cash flows for 2001, with the proper presentation of the sale of the California business.
3. Has the controller acted in an unethical manner in the way the sale was reported on the statement of cash flows? Explain your answer.

LO 2, 3 Case 12-7 Cash Equivalents and the Statement of Cash Flows

In December 2001, Rangers Inc. invested $100,000 of idle cash in U.S. Treasury notes. The notes mature on October 1, 2002, at which time Rangers expects to redeem them at face value of $100,000. The treasurer believes that the notes should be classified as cash equivalents because of the plans to hold them to maturity and receive face value. He would also like to avoid presentation of the purchase as an investing activity because the company has made sizable capital expenditures during the year. The treasurer realizes that the decision about classification of the Treasury notes rests with you, as controller.

Required

1. According to generally accepted accounting principles, how should the investment in U.S. Treasury notes be classified for purposes of preparing a statement of cash flows for the year ended December 31, 2001? Explain your answer.
2. As controller for Rangers, what would you do in this situation? What would you tell the treasurer?

INTERNET RESEARCH CASE

Case 12-8 IBM

www.ibm.com

IBM is firmly in e-business, its annual reports proclaim. Its 1999 annual report, for example, indicates that revenues from e-business services (one of IBM's operations) increased 60 percent to more than $3 billion. While that's still small in comparison to its total revenues of over $87 billion for 1999, the annual report clearly projects e-business affecting many parts of the company, its revenues and expenses, and its operations.

IBM is so large that you can spend hours exploring the Web presence of IBM's various groups in its annual report pages alone. Turn to IBM's Web site to get an overview of the company in the "About IBM" section, review the financial statements and notes for the latest year available, and answer the following questions.

1. What are the groups in which IBM reports its operations on the income statement?
2. Try to determine how pervasive e-business is in the operations and financial contributions IBM touts for each group. (You probably won't find that information directly in the financial statements. For the 1999 annual report, start with the highlights pages, the transformation pages, and the letter to shareholders.)
3. From what you can learn, is IBM truly transforming itself into an e-business powerhouse?
4. Based on the latest financial information, what is the amount of IBM's (a) cash flows from operating activities; (b) cash flows from investing activities; and (c) cash flows from financing activities? How do these compare to the corresponding numbers from 1998 in the "Focus on Financial Results" vignette at the start of the chapter? What is the trend?
5. What are three major changes in line items you see in the latest year's statement of cash flows? Using information available in the annual report, and in business news services, what changes do they represent within the company?

SOLUTION TO KEY TERMS QUIZ

__3__ Statement of cash flows (p. 585)
__4__ Cash equivalent (p. 587)
__1__ Operating activities (p. 588)
__5__ Investing activities (p. 589)
__7__ Financing activities (p. 590)
__6__ Direct method (p. 592)
__2__ Indirect method (p. 592)

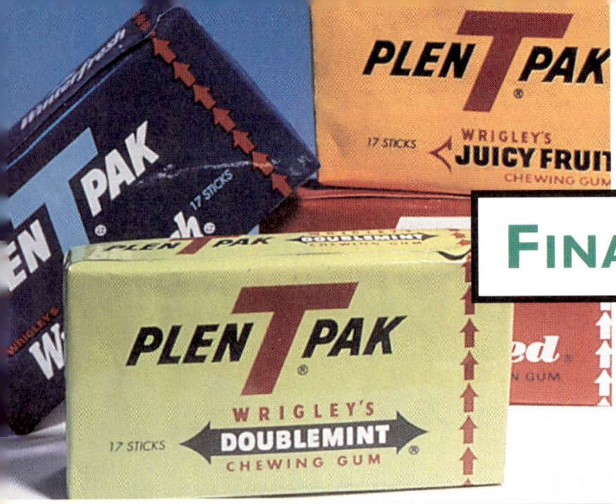

Chapter 13

Financial Statement Analysis

Study Links

A Look at Previous Chapters

In Chapter 2, we introduced a few key financial ratios and saw the way that investors and creditors use them to better understand a company's financial statements. In many of the subsequent chapters, we introduced ratios relevant to the particular topic being discussed.

A Look at This Chapter

Ratio analysis is one important type of analysis used to interpret financial statements. In this chapter, we expand our discussion of ratio analysis and introduce other valuable techniques used by investors, creditors, and analysts in reaching informed decisions. We will find that ratios and other forms of analyses can provide additional insight beyond that available from merely reading the financial statements.

Focus on Financial Results

Although its products are variations on a single theme of chewing gum, the 109-year-old Wm. Wrigley Jr. Company has enjoyed a long and highly successful run. In the best year of its first decade, the firm had sales of about $40,000 each month. Now sales reach that number every 10 minutes, with customers in over 140 countries around the world. What accounts for this success?

Basic data for assessing the results of Wrigley's steady investments in marketing and new product innovations appear in the Highlights of Operations section of the company's annual report, pictured here. Net earnings increased over 12 percent from 1997 to 1998 and reached a record level of $304 million. About half those earnings ($150 million) were paid out in dividends to shareholders. However, the company has to make some trade-offs. The more of its earnings it pays in dividends, the less it has available to invest in future growth in such markets as China and Russia, where it has made inroads that it plans to continue. Most companies would be envious of the robust return on average equity of over 28 percent in each of the last two years.

highlights of operations

	1998	1997
	In thousands of U.S. dollars except for per share amounts	
Net Sales	**$2,004,719**	1,937,021
Earnings before factory closure and sale	**$ 297,738**	273,771
—Per Share of Common Stock (basic and diluted)	**$ 2.57**	2.36
Net Earnings	**$ 304,501**	271,626
—Per Share of Common Stock (basic and diluted)	**$ 2.63**	2.34
Dividends Paid	**$ 150,835**	135,680
—Per Share of Common Stock	**$ 1.30**	1.17
Additions to Property, Plant and Equipment	**$ 148,027**	126,509
Stockholders' Equity	**$1,157,032**	985,379
Return on Average Equity	**28.4%**	28.9%
Stockholders at Close of Year	**38,052**	36,587
Average Shares Outstanding (000)	**115,964**	115,964

Net earnings increased 12%

About half of earnings paid out as dividends

Wrigley's 1998 Annual Report

If you were considering buying shares of Wrigley stock, you would want to compare Wrigley with alternative investments and assess its ability to generate income and pay dividends. What measures of financial performance would therefore be most important to you? Find the company's most recent annual report and determine whether those measures have improved since 1998.

www.wrigley.com

Learning Objectives

After studying this chapter, you should be able to:

LO 1 Explain the various limitations and considerations in financial statement analysis. (p. 652)

LO 2 Use comparative financial statements to analyze a company over time (horizontal analysis). (p. 655)

LO 3 Use common-size financial statements to compare various financial statement items (vertical analysis). (p. 658)

LO 4 Compute and use various ratios to assess liquidity. (p. 662)

LO 5 Compute and use various ratios to assess solvency. (p. 667)

LO 6 Compute and use various ratios to assess profitability. (p. 670)

Precautions in Statement Analysis

Various groups have different purposes for analyzing a company's financial statements. For example, a banker is primarily interested in the likelihood that a loan will be repaid. Certain ratios, as we will see, indicate the ability to repay principal and interest. A stockholder, on the other hand, is concerned with a fair return on the amount invested in the company. Again, certain ratios are helpful in assessing the return to the stockholder. The managers of a business is also interested in the tools of financial statement analysis because various outside groups judge managers by using certain key ratios. Fortunately, most financial statements provide information about financial performance. Publicly held corporations are required to include in their annual reports a section that reviews the past year, with management's comments on its performance as measured by selected ratios and other forms of analysis.

Before we turn to various techniques commonly used in the financial analysis of a company, it is important to understand some of the limitations and other considerations in statement analysis.

Watch for Alternative Accounting Principles

LO 1 Explain the various limitations and considerations in financial statement analysis.

Every set of financial statements is based on various assumptions. For example, a cost-flow method must be assumed in valuing inventory and recognizing cost of goods sold. The accountant chooses FIFO, LIFO, or one of the other acceptable methods. The analyst or other user finds this type of information in the footnotes to the financial statements. The selection of a particular inventory valuation method has a significant effect on certain key ratios. Recognition of the acceptable alternatives is especially important in comparing two or more companies. *Changes* in accounting methods, such as a change in the depreciation method, also make comparing results for a given company over time more difficult. Again, the reader must turn to the footnotes for information regarding these changes.

Take Care When Making Comparisons

Users of financial statements often place too much emphasis on summary indicators and key ratios, such as the current ratio and the earnings per share amount. No single ratio is capable of telling the user everything there is to know about a particular company. The calculation of various ratios for a company is only a starting point. One technique we discuss is the comparison of ratios for different periods of time. Has the ratio gone up or down from last year? What is the percentage of increase or decrease in the ratio over the last five years? Recognizing trends in ratios is important in analyzing any company.

The potential investor must also recognize the need to compare one company with others in the same industry. For example, a particular measure of performance may cause an investor to conclude that the company is not operating efficiently. Comparison with an industry standard, however, might indicate that the ratio is normal for companies in that industry. Various organizations publish summaries of selected ratios for a sample of companies in the United States. The ratios are usually organized by industry. Dun & Bradstreet's *Industry Norms and Key Business Ratios,* for example, is an annual review that organizes companies into five major industries and approximately 800 specific lines of business.

Although industry comparisons are useful, caution is necessary in interpreting the results of such analyses. Few companies in today's economy operate in a single industry. Exceptions exist (Wrigley is almost exclusively in the business of making and selling chewing gum), but most companies cross the boundaries of a single industry. *Conglomerates,* companies operating in more than one industry, present a special challenge to the analyst. Keep in mind also the point made earlier about alternative accounting methods. It is not unusual to find companies in the same industry using different inventory valuation techniques or depreciation methods.

Finally, many corporate income statements contain nonoperating items, such as extraordinary items, cumulative effects from accounting changes, and gains and losses from discontinued operations. When these items exist, the reader must exercise extra caution in making comparisons. To assess the future prospects of a group of companies, you may want to compare income statements *before* taking into account the effects these items have on income.

Understand the Possible Effects of Inflation

Inflation, or an increase in the level of prices, is another important consideration in analyzing financial statements. The statements, to be used by outsiders, are based on historical costs and are not adjusted for the effects of increasing prices. For example, consider the following trend in a company's sales for the past three years:

	2001	2000	1999
Net sales	$121,000	$110,000	$100,000

Business Strategy

Wrigley Co. faces the same difficulties in Asia today as do many other marketers of consumer products. Asian currencies have declined dramatically, and local economies have been unstable. Retail sales are generally down. Although these markets are large and therefore attractive to many U.S. firms, success there will be hard-won.

Yet Wrigley, a traditional family-run firm, perseveres. Sometimes the company selectively raises prices to compensate for currency devaluations, but then it faces declines in sales volume. Then the firm might try a new-product introduction or a bigger ad campaign.

In the case of Hong Kong in 1998, Wrigley adopted a three-part strategy to increase volume at a time when retail sales in general had dropped 15 percent due to economic difficulties. First, Extra for Kids, a new product that had been successful in Europe, was introduced in Hong Kong in June. Next, an aggressive distribution campaign and the use of front-end displays for Wrigley products earned the firm prime display space at all Wellcome stores, the biggest supermarket chain in Hong Kong. Small stores and nontraditional outlets made up an important distribution component for Wrigley too. Finally, Wrigley turned a poor economic environment into a marketing asset. With advertising spending down in Hong Kong, the company was able to trade additional discounts and bonus TV spots for an increase in its advertising presence in the media, just when it was needed.

The techniques suited this conservative but steadily growing firm. They weren't flashy or innovative, but they were well executed. The strategy of "leave no stone unturned" allowed Wrigley to post a 14 percent gain in volume in an otherwise depressed economy.

SOURCE: "All Around Wrigley: Country Update," accessed at www.wrigley.com/aaw/country1998.htm, December 22, 1999.

www.wrigley.com

As measured by the actual dollars of sales, sales have increased by 10% each year. Caution is necessary in concluding that the company is better off in each succeeding year because of the increase in sales *dollars.* Assume, for example, that 1999 sales of $100,000 are the result of selling 100,000 units at $1 each. Are 2000 sales of $110,000 the result of selling 110,000 units at $1 each or of selling 100,000 units at $1.10 each? Although on the surface it may seem unimportant which result accounts for the sales increase, the answer can have significant ramifications. If the company found it necessary to increase selling price to $1.10 in the face of increasing *costs,* it may be no better off than it was in 1999 in terms of gross profit. On the other hand, if the company is able to increase sales revenue by 10% primarily based on growth in unit sales, then its performance would be considered stronger than if the increase is merely due to a price increase. The point to be made is one of caution: published financial statements are stated in historical costs and therefore have not been adjusted for the effects of inflation.

Fortunately, inflation has been relatively subdued in the past several years. During the late 1970s, the FASB actually required a separate footnote in the financial statements to calculate the effects of inflation. The requirement was abandoned in the mid-1980s when inflation had subsided and the profession decided that the cost of providing inflation-adjusted information exceeded the benefits to the users.

EXHIBIT 13-1 Comparative Balance Sheets—Horizontal Analysis

Read from earlier year to later year. Usually this is from right to left.

HENDERSON COMPANY
COMPARATIVE BALANCE SHEETS
DECEMBER 31, 2001 AND 2000
(ALL AMOUNTS IN THOUSANDS OF DOLLARS)

	December 31		Increase (Decrease)		
	2001	2000	Dollars		Percent
Cash	**$ 320**	**$ 1,350**	**$(1,030)**	1	**(76)%**
Accounts receivable	5,500	4,500	1,000		22
Inventory	**4,750**	**2,750**	**2,000**	2	**73**
Prepaid insurance	150	200	(50)		(25)
Total current assets	$10,720	$ 8,800	$ 1,920		22
Land	2,000	2,000	–0–		–0–
Buildings and equipment	6,000	4,500	1,500		33
Accumulated depreciation	(1,850)	(1,500)	(350)		(23)
Total long-term assets	$ 6,150	$ 5,000	$ 1,150		23
Total assets	$16,870	$13,800	$ 3,070		22
Accounts payable	**$ 4,250**	**$ 2,500**	**$ 1,750**	3	**70**
Taxes payable	2,300	2,100	200		10
Notes payable	600	800	(200)		(25)
Current portion of bonds	100	100	–0–		–0–
Total current liabilities	$ 7,250	$ 5,500	$ 1,750		32
Bonds payable	700	800	(100)		(13)
Total liabilities	$ 7,950	$ 6,300	$ 1,650		26
Preferred stock, $5 par	500	500	–0–		–0–
Common stock, $1 par	1,000	1,000	–0–		–0–
Retained earnings	7,420	6,000	1,420		24
Total stockholders' equity	$ 8,920	$ 7,500	$ 1,420		19
Total liabilities and stockholders' equity	$16,870	$13,800	$ 3,070		22

NOTE: Referenced amounts boldfaced for convenience.

The base year is normally on the right.

Dollar change from year to year.

Percentage change from one year to the next year.

In **horizontal analysis,** read right to left to compare one year's results with the next as a dollar amount of change and as a percentage of change from year to year.

Analysis of Comparative and Common-Size Statements

We are now ready to analyze a set of financial statements. We will begin by looking at the comparative statements of a company for a two-year period. The analysis of the statements over a series of years is often called **horizontal analysis.** We will then see how the statements can be recast in what are referred to as *common-size statements.* The analysis of common-size statements is called **vertical analysis.** Finally, we will consider the use of a variety of ratios to analyze a company.

Horizontal analysis
A comparison of financial statement items over a period of time.

Vertical analysis
A comparison of various financial statement items within a single period with the use of common-size statements.

Horizontal Analysis

LO 2 Use comparative financial statements to analyze a company over time (horizontal analysis).

Comparative balance sheets for a hypothetical entity, Henderson Company, are presented in Exhibit 13-1. The increase or decrease in each of the major accounts on the balance sheet is shown in both absolute dollars and as a percentage. The base year for computing the percentage increase or decrease in each account is the first year, 2000, and is normally shown on the right side. By reading across from right to left (thus the term *horizontal analysis*), the analyst can quickly spot any unusual changes in accounts from the previous year. Three accounts stand out: 1 Cash decreased by 76%, 2 Inventory increased by 73%, and 3 Accounts Payable increased by 70%. (These lines are also boldfaced for convenience.) Individually, each of these large changes is a red flag. Taken together, these changes send the financial statement user the warning that the business may be deteriorating. Each of these large changes should be investigated further.

Exhibit 13-2 shows comparative statements of income and retained earnings for Henderson for 2001 and 2000. At first glance, 1 the 20% increase in sales to $24 million appears promising, but management was not able to limit the increase in either 2 cost of goods sold

Exhibit 13-2 Comparative Statements of Income and Retained Earnings—Horizontal Analysis

HENDERSON COMPANY
COMPARATIVE STATEMENTS OF INCOME AND RETAINED EARNINGS
FOR THE YEARS ENDED DECEMBER 31, 2001 AND 2000
(ALL AMOUNTS IN THOUSANDS OF DOLLARS)

	December 31		Increase (Decrease)		
	2001	2000	Dollars		Percent
Net sales	**$24,000**	**$20,000**	**$ 4,000**	1	**20%**
Cost of goods sold	**18,000**	**14,000**	**4,000**	2	**29**
Gross profit	$ 6,000	$ 6,000	$ –0–		–0–
Selling, general, and administrative expense	**3,000**	**2,000**	**1,000**	3	**50**
Operating income	**$ 3,000**	**$ 4,000**	**$(1,000)**	4	**(25)**
Interest expense	140	160	(20)		(13)
Income before tax	$ 2,860	$ 3,840	$ (980)		(26)
Income tax expense	1,140	1,540	(400)		(26)
Net income	$ 1,720	$ 2,300	$ (580)		(25)
Preferred dividends	50	50			
Income available to common	$ 1,670	$ 2,250			
Common dividends	250	250			
To retained earnings	$ 1,420	$ 2,000			
Retained earnings, 1/1	6,000	4,000			
Retained earnings, 12/31	$ 7,420	$ 6,000			

These three increases in revenue and expenses resulted in an operating income *decrease* of 25%.

NOTE: Referenced amounts boldfaced for convenience.

EXHIBIT 13-3 Wrigley Financial Summary

selected financial data

	1998	1997	1996	1995
OPERATING DATA				
Net Sales	**$2,004,719**	1,937,021	1,835,987	1,754,931
Cost of Sales	**848,363**	847,366	814,483	778,019
Income Taxes	**136,378**	122,614	128,840	126,492
Earnings before factory closure and sale in 1998-96, nonrecurring gain on sale of Singapore property in 1994, and cumulative effect of accounting changes in 1992	**297,738**	273,771	243,262	223,739
—Per Share of Common Stock (basic and diluted)	**2.57**	2.36	2.10	1.93
Net Earnings	**304,501**	271,626	230,272	223,739
—Per Share of Common Stock (basic and diluted)	**2.63**	2.34	1.99	1.93
Dividends Paid	**150,835**	135,680	118,308	111,401
—Per Share of Common Stock	**1.30**	1.17	1.02	.96
—As a Percent of Net Earnings	**50%**	50%	51%	50%
Dividends Declared				
—Per Share of Common Stock	**1.31**	1.19	1.02	.99
Average Shares Outstanding	**115,964**	115,964	115,983	116,066
OTHER FINANCIAL DATA				
Net Property, Plant and Equipment	**$ 520,090**	430,474	388,149	347,491
Total Assets	**$1,520,855**	1,343,126	1,233,543	1,099,219
Working Capital	**$ 624,546**	571,857	511,272	458,683
Stockholders' Equity	**$1,157,032**	985,379	897,431	796,852
Return on Average Equity	**28.4%**	28.9%	27.2%	30.1%
Stockholders at Close of Year	**38,052**	36,587	34,951	28,959
Employees at Close of Year	**9,200**	8,200	7,800	7,300
Market Price of Stock—High	**$ 104.313**	82.063	62.875	54.000
—Low	**$ 70.938**	54.563	48.375	42.875

Net sales has increased every year in the 11-year period.

EXHIBIT 13-3 Wrigley Financial Summary (continued)

In thousands of U.S. dollars and shares except for per share amounts

1994	1993	1992	1991	1990	1989	1988
1,596,551	1,428,504	1,286,921	1,148,875	1,110,639	992,853	891,392
697,442	617,156	572,468	507,795	508,957	451,773	392,460
122,746	103,944	83,730	79,362	70,897	64,277	53,491
205,767	174,891	148,573	128,652	117,362	106,149	87,236
1.77	1.50	1.27	1.09	1.00	.90	.73
230,533	174,891	141,295	128,652	117,362	106,149	87,236
1.98	1.50	1.21	1.09	1.00	.90	.73
104,694	87,344	72,511	64,609	58,060	53,506	43,591
.90	.75	.62	.55	.49	.45	.36
45%	50%	51%	50%	49%	50%	50%
.94	.75	.63	.55	.51	.47	.37
116,358	116,511	117,055	117,517	117,743	118,035	120,308
289,420	239,868	222,137	201,386	188,959	171,951	155,260
978,834	815,324	711,372	625,074	563,665	498,624	440,400
413,414	343,132	299,149	276,047	229,735	186,588	165,430
688,470	575,182	498,935	463,399	401,386	342,994	308,538
36.5%	32.6%	29.4%	29.8%	31.5%	32.6%	29.2%
24,078	18,567	14,546	11,086	10,497	10,218	9,440
7,000	6,700	6,400	6,250	5,850	5,750	5,500
53.875	46.125	39.875	27.000	19.750	17.917	13.750
38.125	29.500	22.125	16.375	14.583	11.833	10.667

or **3** selling, general, and administrative expense to 20%. The analysis indicates that cost of goods sold increased by 29% and selling, general, and administrative expense increased by 50%. The increases in these two expenses more than offset the increase in sales and resulted in a **4** decrease in operating income of 25%.

Companies that experience sales growth often become lax about controlling expenses. Their managements sometimes forget that it is the bottom line that counts, not the top line. Perhaps the salespeople are given incentives to increase sales without considering the costs of the sales. Maybe management is spending too much on overhead, including its own salaries. The owners of the business will have to address these concerns if they want to get a reasonable return on their investment.

Horizontal analysis can be extended to include more than two years of results. At a minimum, publicly held companies are required to include income statements and statements of cash flows for the three most recent years and balance sheets as of the end of the two most recent years. Many annual reports include, as supplementary information, financial summaries of operations for extended periods of time. As illustrated in Exhibit 13-3, for example, Wrigley includes an 11-year summary of selected financial data, such as net sales, dividends paid, return on average equity, and total assets. Note the increase in net sales in every year over the 11-year period. Also note, however, that Wrigley does not include in the summary the gross profit ratio (gross profit divided by net sales). A comparison of the trend in this ratio would help to determine whether the company has effectively controlled the cost to manufacture its products. The summary does show that Wrigley has reported an increase in net earnings before any nonrecurring gains and accounting changes for 10 consecutive years, an enviable record for any company.

From Concept **TO PRACTICE 13.1**

READING BEN & JERRY'S ANNUAL REPORT Where does Ben & Jerry's annual report provide a financial summary? How many years does it include? In terms of a trend over time, which item on the summary do you think is the most significant?

Tracking items over a series of years, a practice called *trend analysis,* can be a very powerful tool for the analyst. Advanced statistical techniques are available for analyzing trends in financial data and, most important, for projecting those trends to future periods. Some of the techniques, such as time series analysis, have been used extensively in forecasting sales trends.

Historically, attention has focused on the balance sheet and income statement in analyzing a company's position and results of operation. Only recently have analysts and other users begun to appreciate the value in incorporating the statement of cash flows into their analyses.

From Concept **TO PRACTICE 13.2**

READING WRIGLEY'S ANNUAL REPORT Refer to Wrigley's financial highlights in Exhibit 13-3. Compute the company's gross profit ratio for each of the 11 years. Is there a noticeable upward or downward trend in the ratio over this time period?

Comparative statements of cash flows for Henderson appear in Exhibit 13-4. Henderson's financing activities remained constant over the two-year period, as indicated in that section of the statements. Each year the company paid $200,000 on notes, another $100,000 to retire bonds, and $300,000 to stockholders in dividends. Cash outflow from investing activities slowed down somewhat in 2001, with the purchase of $1,500,000 in new buildings, compared with $2,000,000 the year before.

The most noticeable difference between Henderson's statements of cash flows for the two years is in the Operating Activities section. Operations **1** generated almost $2 million less in cash in 2001 than in 2000 ($1.07 million in 2001 versus $2.95 million in 2000). The decrease in net income **2** was partially responsible for this reduction in cash from operations. However, the increases in **3** accounts receivable and **4** inventories in 2001 had a significant impact on the decrease in cash generated from operating activities.

VERTICAL ANALYSIS

LO 3 Use common-size financial statements to compare various financial statement items (vertical analysis).

Often it is easier to examine comparative financial statements if they have been standardized. *Common-size statements* recast all items on the statement as a percentage of a selected item on the statement. This excludes size as a relevant variable in the analysis. One could use this type of analysis to compare Wal-Mart with the smaller KMart or to compare IBM with the much smaller Apple Computer. It is also a convenient way to compare the same company from year to year.

Vertical analysis involves looking at the relative size and composition of various items on a particular financial statement. Common-size comparative balance sheets for Henderson Company are presented in Exhibit 13-5. Note that all asset accounts are stated as

EXHIBIT 13-4 Comparative Statements of Cash Flow—Horizontal Analysis

HENDERSON COMPANY
COMPARATIVE STATEMENTS OF CASH FLOW
FOR THE YEARS ENDED DECEMBER 31, 2001 AND 2000
(ALL AMOUNTS IN THOUSANDS OF DOLLARS)

			Increase (Decrease)	
	2001	**2000**	**Dollars**	**Percent**
Net Cash Flows from Operating Activities				
2 Net income	**$1,720**	**$2,300**	**$ (580)**	**(25)%**
Adjustments:				
Depreciation expense	350	300		
Changes in:				
3 Accounts receivable	**(1,000)**	**500**		
4 Inventory	**(2,000)**	**(300)**		
Prepaid insurance	50	50		
Accounts payable	1,750	(200)		
Taxes payable	200	300		
Net cash provided by operating activities 1 Unfavorable	**$1,070** ◄	**$2,950**	**$(1,880)**	**(64)%**
Net Cash Flows from Investing Activities				
Purchase of buildings	**$(1,500)**	**$(2,000)**	**$ (500)**	**(25)%**
Net Cash Flows from Financing Activities				
Repayment of notes	**$ (200)**	**$ (200)**	–0–	–0–
Retirement of bonds	**(100)**	**(100)**	–0–	–0–
Cash dividends—preferred	**(50)**	**(50)**	–0–	–0–
Cash dividends—common	**(250)**	**(250)**	–0–	–0–
Net cash used by financing activities	$ (600)	$ (600)	–0–	–0–
Net increase (decrease) in cash	$ (1,030)	$ 350		
Beginning cash balance	1,350	1,000		
Ending cash balance	$ 320	$ 1,350		
Supplemental Information				
Interest paid	$ 140	$ 160		
Income taxes paid	$ 940	$ 1,440		

NOTE: Referenced amounts boldfaced for convenience.

a percentage of total assets. Similarly, all liability and stockholders' equity accounts are stated as a percentage of total liabilities and stockholders' equity. The combination of the comparative balance sheets for the two years and the common-size feature allows the analyst to spot critical changes in the composition of the assets. We noted in Exhibit 13-1 that cash had decreased by 76% over the two years. The decrease of cash from 9.8% of total assets to only 1.9% 1 is highlighted in Exhibit 13-5.

One can also observe in the exhibit that 2 total current assets have continued to represent just under two-thirds (63.5%) of total assets. If cash has decreased significantly in terms of the percentage of total assets, what accounts have increased to maintain current assets at two-thirds of total assets? We can quickly determine from the data in Exhibit 13-5 that 3 although inventory represented 19.9% of total assets at the end of 2000, the percentage is up to 28.1% at the end of 2001. This change in the relative composition of current assets between cash and inventory may have important implications. The change, for instance, may signal that the company is having trouble selling inventory.

EXHIBIT 13-5 Common-Size Comparative Balance Sheets—Vertical Analysis

HENDERSON COMPANY
COMMON-SIZE COMPARATIVE BALANCE SHEETS
DECEMBER 31, 2001 AND 2000
(ALL AMOUNTS IN THOUSANDS OF DOLLARS)

	December 31, 2001		December 31, 2000	
	Dollars	Percent	Dollars	Percent
Cash	$ 320	1.9%	$ 1,350 [1]	9.8%
Accounts receivable	5,500	32.6	4,500	32.6
Inventory	4,750	28.1	2,750 [3]	19.9
Prepaid insurance	150	0.9	200	1.5
Total current assets	$10,720	[2] 63.5%	$ 8,800	63.8%
Land	2,000	11.9	2,000	14.5
Buildings and equipment, net	4,150	24.6	3,000	21.7
Total long-term assets	$ 6,150	36.5	$ 5,000	36.2
Total assets	$ 16,870	100.0%	$13,800	100.0
Accounts payable	$ 4,250	25.2%	$ 2,500	18.1%
Taxes payable	2,300	13.6	2,100	15.2
Notes payable	600	3.6	800	5.8
Current portion of bonds	100	0.6	100	0.7
Total current liabilities	$ 7,250	[4] 43.0%	$ 5,500	39.8%
Bonds payable	700	[5] 4.1	800	5.8
Total liabilities	$ 7,950	47.1%	$ 6,300	45.6%
Preferred stock, $5 par	500	3.0	500	3.6
Common stock, $1 par	1,000	5.9	1,000	7.3
Retained earnings	7,420	44.0	6,000	43.5
Total stockholders' equity	$ 8,920	[6] 52.9%	$ 7,500	54.4%
Total liabilities and stockholders' equity	$ 16,870	100.0%	$13,800	100.0%

NOTE: Referenced amounts boldfaced for convenience.

Compare percentages across years to spot year-to-year trends.

In **vertical analysis**, compare each line item as a percent of total (100%) to highlight a company's overall condition.

Total current liabilities [4] represent a slightly higher percentage of total liabilities and stockholders' equity at the end of 2001 than at the end of 2000. The increase is balanced by a slight decrease in the relative percentages of [5] long-term debt (the bonds) and of [6] stockholders' equity. We will return later to further analysis of the composition of both the current and the noncurrent accounts.

Common-size comparative income statements for Henderson are presented in Exhibit 13-6. The *base,* or benchmark, on which all other items in the income statement are compared is [1] net sales. Again, observations from the comparative statements alone are further confirmed by examining the common-size statements. Although the **gross profit ratio**—*gross profit as a percentage of net sales*—was 30% in 2000, the same ratio for 2001 is only 25% [2]. Recall the earlier observation that although sales increased by 20% from one year to the next, [3] cost of goods sold increased by 29%.

GROSS PROFIT RATIO
Gross profit to net sales.

In addition to the gross profit ratio, an important relationship from Exhibit 13-6 is the *ratio of net income to net sales,* or **profit margin ratio.** The ratio, an overall indicator of management's ability to control expenses, reflects the amount of income for each dollar of sales. Some analysts prefer to look at income before tax, rather than final net

PROFIT MARGIN RATIO
Net income to net sales.

EXHIBIT 13-6 Common-Size Comparative Income Statements—Vertical Analysis

HENDERSON COMPANY
COMMON-SIZE COMPARATIVE INCOME STATEMENTS
FOR THE YEARS ENDED DECEMBER 31, 2001 AND 2000
(ALL AMOUNTS IN THOUSANDS OF DOLLARS)

	2001		2000	
	Dollars	**Percent**	**Dollars**	**Percent**
Net sales	**$24,000**	1 **100.0%**	**$20,000**	**100.0%**
Cost of goods sold	3 18,000	75.0	14,000	70.0
Gross profit	**$ 6,000**	2 **25.0%**	**$ 6,000**	**30.0%**
Selling, general, and administrative expense	3,000	12.5	2,000	10.0
Operating income	$ 3,000	12.5%	$ 4,000	20.0%
Interest expense	140	0.6	160	0.8
Income before tax	**$ 2,860**	**11.9%**	**$ 3,840**	**19.2%**
Income tax expense	1,140	4.8	1,540	7.7
Net income	**$ 1,720**	4 **7.1%**	**$ 2,300**	**11.5%**

NOTE: Referenced amounts boldfaced for convenience.

Gross profit as a percentage of sales is the **gross profit ratio.**

The ratio of net income to net sales is the **profit margin ratio.**

income, because taxes are not typically an expense that can be controlled. Further, if the company does not earn a profit before tax, it will incur no tax expense. Note 4 the decrease in Henderson's profit margin: from 11.5% in 2000 to 7.1% in 2001 (or from 19.2% to 11.9% on a before-tax basis).

Two-Minute Review

1. Explain the basic difference between horizontal and vertical analysis.

2. Assume that you are concerned about whether accounts receivable has been increasing over the last few years. Which type of analysis, horizontal or vertical, would you perform to help address your concern?

3. Assume that you are concerned about whether selling and administrative expenses were unreasonable this past year given the level of sales. Which type of analysis, horizontal or vertical, would you perform to help address your concern?

Answers:

1. Horizontal analysis is used to compare a particular financial statement item over a period of time, whereas vertical analysis allows someone to compare various financial statement items within a single period. With vertical analysis, all of the items are stated as a percentage of a specific item on that statement, such as sales on the income statement or total assets on the balance sheet.

2. Horizontal analysis could be used to examine the trend in accounts receivable over recent years.

3. Vertical analysis could be used to examine the relationship between selling and administrative expenses and sales. However, you may also want to compare this percentage with the ratio in prior years (thus, you would be performing horizontal analysis as well).

LIQUIDITY ANALYSIS AND THE MANAGEMENT OF WORKING CAPITAL

LO 4 Compute and use various ratios to assess liquidity.

Two ratios were discussed in the last section: the *gross profit ratio* and the *profit margin ratio.* A ratio is simply the relationship, normally stated as a percentage, between two financial statement amounts. In this section, we consider a wide range of ratios used by management, analysts, and others for a variety of purposes. We classify the ratios in three main categories according to their use in performing (1) liquidity analysis, (2) solvency analysis, and (3) profitability analysis.

LIQUIDITY The nearness to cash of the assets and liabilities.

Liquidity is a relative measure of the nearness to cash of the assets and liabilities of a company. Nearness to cash deals with the length of time before cash is realized. Various ratios are used to measure liquidity, and they basically concern the company's ability to pay its debts as they come due. Recall the distinction between the current and long-term classifications on the balance sheet. Current assets are assets that will be either converted into cash or consumed within one year or the operating cycle, if the cycle is longer than one year. The operating cycle for a manufacturing company is the length of time between the purchase of raw materials and the eventual collection of any outstanding account receivable from the sale of the product. Current liabilities are a company's obligations that require the use of current assets or the creation of other current liabilities to satisfy them.

The nearness to cash of the current assets is indicated by their placement on the balance sheet. Current assets are listed on the balance sheet in descending order of their nearness to cash. Liquidity is, of course, a matter of degree, with cash being the most liquid of all assets. With few exceptions, such as prepaid insurance, most current assets are convertible into cash. However, accounts receivable is closer to being converted into cash than is inventory. An account receivable need only be collected to be converted to cash. An item of inventory must first be sold, and then, assuming that sales of inventory are on account, the account must be collected before cash is realized.

WORKING CAPITAL

WORKING CAPITAL Current assets minus current liabilities.

Working capital is the excess of current assets over current liabilities at a point in time:

Working Capital = Current Assets – Current Liabilities

Reference to Henderson's comparative balance sheets in Exhibit 13-1 indicates the following:

	December 31	
	2001	**2000**
Current assets	$10,720,000	$8,800,000
Current liabilities	7,250,000	5,500,000
Working capital	$ 3,470,000	$3,300,000

The management of working capital is an extremely important task for any business. A comparison of Henderson's working capital at the end of each of the two years indicates a slight increase in the degree of protection for short-term creditors of the company. Management must always strive for the ideal balance of current assets and current liabilities. The amount of working capital is limited in its informational value, however. For example, it tells us nothing about the composition of the current accounts. Also, the dollar amount of working capital may not be useful for comparison with other companies of different sizes in the same industry. Working capital of $3,470,000 may be adequate for Henderson Company, but it might signal impending bankruptcy for a company much larger than Henderson.

CURRENT RATIO

CURRENT RATIO The ratio of current assets to current liabilities.

The **current ratio** is one of the most widely used of all financial statement ratios and is calculated as follows:

$$\text{Current Ratio} = \frac{\text{Current Assets}}{\text{Current Liabilities}}$$

For Henderson Company, the ratio at each year-end is as follows:

December 31	
2001	**2000**
$\frac{\$10,720,000}{\$7,250,000} = 1.48 \text{ to } 1$	$\frac{\$8,800,000}{\$5,500,000} = 1.60 \text{ to } 1$

At the end of 2001, Henderson had $1.48 of current assets for every $1 of current liabilities. Is this current ratio adequate? Or is it a sign of impending financial difficulties? There is no definitive answer to either of these questions. Some analysts use a general rule of thumb of 2:1 for the current ratio as a sign of short-term financial health. The answer depends first on the industry. Companies in certain industries have historically operated with current ratios much less than 2:1.

A second concern in interpreting the current ratio involves the composition of the current assets. Cash is usually the only acceptable means of payment for most liabilities. Therefore, it is important to consider the makeup, or *composition,* of the current assets. Refer to Exhibit 13-5 and Henderson's common-size balance sheets. Not only did the current ratio decline during 2001 but also the proportion of the total current assets made up by inventory increased whereas the proportion made up by accounts receivable remained the same. Recall that accounts receivable is only one step removed from cash, whereas inventory requires both sale and collection of the subsequent account.

Study Tip

Some of the ratios discussed in this chapter, such as the current ratio, were introduced in earlier chapters. Use the information here as a review of those earlier introductions.

Acid-Test Ratio

The **acid-test** or **quick ratio** is a stricter test of a company's ability to pay its current debts as they are due. Specifically, it is intended to deal with the composition problem because it *excludes* inventories and prepaid assets from the numerator of the fraction:

Acid-test or quick ratio
A stricter test of liquidity than the current ratio; excludes inventory and prepayments from the numerator.

$$\text{Acid-Test or Quick Ratio} = \frac{\text{Quick Assets}}{\text{Current Liabilities}}$$

where

$$\text{Quick Assets} = \text{Cash} + \text{Marketable Securities} + \text{Current Receivables}$$

Henderson's quick assets consist of only cash and accounts receivable, and its quick ratios are as follows:

December 31	
2001	**2000**
$\frac{\$320,000 + \$5,500,000}{\$7,250,000} = 0.80 \text{ to } 1$	$\frac{\$1,350,000 + \$4,500,000}{\$5,500,000} = 1.06 \text{ to } 1$

Does the quick ratio of less than 1:1 at the end of 2001 mean that Henderson will be unable to pay creditors on time? *For many companies, an acid-test ratio below 1 is not desirable because it may signal the need to liquidate marketable securities to pay bills, regardless of the current trading price of the securities.* Although the quick ratio is a better indication of short-term debt-paying ability than the current ratio, it is still not perfect. For example, we would want to know the normal credit terms that Henderson extends to its customers, as well as the credit terms that the company receives from its suppliers.

Assume that Henderson requires its customers to pay their accounts within 30 days and that the normal credit terms extended by Henderson's suppliers allow payment anytime within 60 days. The relatively longer credit terms extended by Henderson's suppliers give it some cushion in meeting its obligations. The due date of the $2,300,000 in taxes payable could also have a significant effect on the company's ability to remain in business.

Cash Flow from Operations to Current Liabilities

Two limitations exist with either the current ratio or the quick ratio as a measure of liquidity. First, almost all debts require the payment of cash. Thus, a ratio that focuses on cash is more useful. Second, both ratios focus on liquid assets at a *point in time.* Cash flow from operating activities, as reported on the statement of cash flows, can be used to indicate the flow of cash during the year to cover the debts due.[1] The **cash flow from operations to current liabilities ratio** is computed as follows:

Cash flow from operations to current liabilities ratio
A measure of the ability to pay current debts from operating cash flows.

$$\text{Cash Flow from Operations to Current Liabilities Ratio} = \frac{\text{Net Cash Provided by Operating Activities}}{\text{Average Current Liabilities}}$$

Note the use of *average* current liabilities in the denominator. This results in a denominator that is consistent with the numerator, which reports the cash flow over a period of time. Because we need to calculate the *average* current liabilities for both years, it is necessary to add the ending balance sheet for 1999 for use in the analysis. The balance sheet for Henderson on December 31, 1999, is given in Exhibit 13-7. The ratio for Henderson for each year is as follows:

2001	2000
$\frac{\$1,070,000}{(\$7,250,000 + \$5,500,000)/2} = 16.8\%$	$\frac{\$2,950,000}{(\$5,500,000 + \$5,600,000)/2} = 53.2\%$

Two factors are responsible for the large decrease in this ratio from 2000 to 2001. First, cash generated from operations during 2001 was less than half what it was during 2000 (the numerator). Second, average current liabilities were smaller in 2000 than in 2001 (the denominator). In examining the health of the company in terms of its liquidity, an analyst would concentrate on the reason for these decreases.

Accounts Receivable Analysis

The analysis of accounts receivable is an important component in the management of working capital. A company must be willing to extend credit terms that are liberal enough to attract and maintain customers, but at the same time, management must continually monitor the accounts to ensure collection on a timely basis. One measure of the efficiency of the collection process is the **accounts receivable turnover ratio:**

Accounts receivable turnover ratio
A measure of the number of times accounts receivable are collected in a period.

$$\text{Accounts Receivable Turnover Ratio} = \frac{\text{Net Credit Sales}}{\text{Average Accounts Receivable}}$$

Note an important distinction between this ratio and either the current or the quick ratio. Although both of those ratios measure liquidity at a point in time and all numbers come from the balance sheet, a turnover ratio is an *activity* ratio and consists of an activity (sales, in this case) divided by a base to which it is naturally related (accounts receivable). Because an activity such as sales is for a period of time (a year, in this case), the base should be stated as an average for that same period of time.

The accounts receivable turnover ratios for both years can now be calculated (we assume that all sales are on account):

2001	2000
$\frac{\$24,000,000}{(\$5,500,000 + \$4,500,000)/2} = 4.8 \text{ times}$	$\frac{\$20,000,000}{(\$4,500,000 + \$5,000,000)/2} = 4.2 \text{ times}$

Accounts turned over, on average, 4.2 times in 2000, compared with 4.8 times in 2001. This means that the average number of times accounts were collected during each year was

[1] For a detailed discussion on the use of information contained in the statement of cash flows in performing ratio analysis, see Charles A. Carslaw and John R. Mills, "Developing Ratios for Effective Cash Flow Statement Analysis," *Journal of Accountancy* (November 1991), pp. 63–70.

EXHIBIT 13-7 Henderson's Balance Sheet, End of 1999

HENDERSON COMPANY
BALANCE SHEET
DECEMBER 31, 1999
(ALL AMOUNTS IN THOUSANDS OF DOLLARS)

Cash	$ 1,000
Accounts receivable	5,000
Inventory	2,450
Prepaid insurance	250
Total current assets	$ 8,700
Land	2,000
Buildings and equipment, net	1,300
Total long-term assets	$ 3,300
Total assets	$12,000
Accounts payable	$ 2,700
Taxes payable	1,800
Notes payable	1,000
Current portion of bonds	100
Total current liabilities	$ 5,600
Bonds payable	900
Total liabilities	$ 6,500
Preferred stock, $5 par	500
Common stock, $1 par	1,000
Retained earnings	4,000
Total stockholders' equity	$ 5,500
Total liabilities and stockholders' equity	$12,000

between four and five times. What does this mean about the average length of time that an account was outstanding? Another way to measure efficiency in the collection process is to calculate the **number of days' sales in receivables:**

NUMBER OF DAYS' SALES IN RECEIVABLES
A measure of the average age of accounts receivable.

$$\text{Number of Days' Sales in Receivables} = \frac{\text{Number of Days in the Period}}{\text{Accounts Receivable Turnover}}$$

For simplicity, we assume 360 days in a year:

2001	**2000**
$\frac{360\text{ Days}}{4.8\text{ Times}} = 75\text{ Days}$	$\frac{360\text{ Days}}{4.2\text{ Times}} = 86\text{ Days}$

The average number of days an account is outstanding, or the average collection period, is 75 days in 2001, down from 86 days in 2000. Is this acceptable? The answer depends on the company's credit policy. If Henderson's normal credit terms require payment within 60 days, further investigation is needed, even though the number of days outstanding has decreased from the previous year.

Management needs to be concerned with both the collectibility of an account as it ages and the cost of funds tied up in receivables. For example, a $1 million average receivable balance that requires an additional month to collect suggests that the company is forgoing $10,000 in lost profits if we assume that the money could be reinvested in the business to earn 1% per month, or 12% per year.

ACCOUNTING FOR YOUR DECISIONS

You Examine Your Business's Trends

You are a small business owner and have noticed that over the past two years, sales have increased but the accounts receivable turnover ratio has decreased. Should you be concerned?

ANS: You should certainly be pleased with an increase in sales, but a decrease in accounts receivable turnover should concern you. A decline in this ratio indicates that the average time to collect an open account is increasing. Regardless of the specific reason for this change (e.g., more liberal credit terms, change in creditworthiness of customers, lack of follow-up on overdue accounts), the increase in the time to collect may result in cash flow problems for you.

INVENTORY ANALYSIS

INVENTORY TURNOVER RATIO A measure of the number of times inventory is sold during a period.

A similar set of ratios can be calculated to analyze the efficiency in managing inventory. The **inventory turnover ratio** is as follows:

$$\text{Inventory Turnover Ratio} = \frac{\text{Cost of Goods Sold}}{\text{Average Inventory}}$$

The ratio for each of the two years follows:

2001	2000
$\frac{\$18{,}000{,}000}{(\$4{,}750{,}000 + \$2{,}750{,}000)/2} = 4.8$ times	$\frac{\$14{,}000{,}000}{(\$2{,}750{,}000 + \$2{,}450{,}000)/2} = 5.4$ times

Henderson was slightly more efficient in 2000 in moving its inventory. The number of "turns" each year varies widely for different industries. For example, a wholesaler of perishable fruits and vegetables may turn over inventory at least 50 times per year. An airplane manufacturer, however, may turn over its inventory once or twice a year. What does the number of turns per year tell us about the average length of time it takes to sell an item of inventory? The **number of days' sales in inventory** is an alternative measure of the company's efficiency in managing inventory. It is the number of days between the date an item of inventory is purchased and the date it is sold:

NUMBER OF DAYS' SALES IN INVENTORY A measure of how long it takes to sell inventory.

$$\text{Number of Days' Sales in Inventory} = \frac{\text{Number of Days in the Period}}{\text{Inventory Turnover}}$$

ACCOUNTING FOR YOUR DECISIONS

You Are the Analyst

You have been presented with two companies—Boeing and Safeway. Boeing, a commercial aircraft company, has a very slow inventory turnover, while Safeway, a grocery chain, has a very fast inventory turnover. Would it be correct to conclude that Safeway is a better investment because its inventory turns over faster?

www.boeing.com
www.safeway.com
www.albertsons.com

ANS: Not at all. These industries are completely different and not comparable. On the contrary, comparing Safeway's inventory turnover with Albertson's, another grocery chain, might be useful, just as comparing Boeing with Lockheed Martin Marietta might make sense. Ratios can be used when comparing companies in the same industry, but not companies in different industries.

The number of days' sales in inventory for Henderson is as follows:

2001	2000
$\frac{360 \text{ Days}}{4.8 \text{ Times}} = 75 \text{ Days}$	$\frac{360 \text{ Days}}{5.4 \text{ Times}} = 67 \text{ Days}$

This measure can reveal a great deal about inventory management. For example, an unusually low turnover (and, of course, high number of days in inventory) may signal a large amount of obsolete inventory or problems in the sales department. Or, it may indicate that the company is pricing its products too high and the market is reacting by reducing demand for the company's products.

Due to the perishable nature of their products, grocery chains have high inventory turnovers and short cash to cash operating cycles. Firms in other segments have relatively longer cycles.

Cash Operating Cycle

The **cash to cash operating cycle** is the length of time between the purchase of merchandise for sale, assuming a retailer or wholesaler, and the eventual collection of the cash from the sale. One method to approximate the number of days in a company's operating cycle involves combining two measures:

Cash to Cash Operating Cycle The length of time from the purchase of inventory to the collection of any receivable from the sale.

$$\text{Cash to Cash Operating Cycle} = \text{Number of Days' Sales in Inventory} + \text{Number of Days' Sales in Receivables}$$

Henderson's operating cycles for 2001 and 2000 are as follows:

2001	2000
75 Days + 75 Days = 150 Days	67 Days + 86 Days = 153 Days

The average length of time between the purchase of inventory and the collection of cash from sale of the inventory was 150 days in 2001. Note that although the length of the operating cycle did not change significantly from 2000 to 2001, the composition did change: the increase in the average number of days in inventory was offset by the decrease in the average number of days in receivables.

Solvency Analysis

LO 5 Compute and use various ratios to assess solvency.

Solvency refers to a company's ability to remain in business over the long term. It is related to liquidity but differs in time. Although liquidity relates to the firm's ability to pay next year's debts as they come due, solvency concerns the ability of the firm to stay financially healthy over the period of time that existing debt (short- and long-term) will be outstanding.

Solvency The ability of a company to remain in business over the long term.

Debt-to-Equity Ratio

Capital structure is the focal point in solvency analysis. This refers to the composition of the right side of the balance sheet and the mix between debt and stockholders' equity. The composition of debt and equity in the capital structure is an important determinant of the cost of capital to a company. We will have more to say later about the effects that the mix of debt and equity has on profitability. For now, consider the **debt-to-equity ratio:**

Debt-to-Equity Ratio The ratio of total liabilities to total stockholders' equity.

$$\text{Debt-to-Equity Ratio} = \frac{\text{Total Liabilities}}{\text{Total Stockholders' Equity}}$$

Henderson's debt-to-equity ratio at each year-end is as follows:

December 31	
2001	2000
$\frac{\$7{,}950{,}000}{\$8{,}920{,}000} = 0.89 \text{ to } 1$	$\frac{\$6{,}300{,}000}{\$7{,}500{,}000} = 0.84 \text{ to } 1$

The 2001 ratio indicates that for every $1 of capital that stockholders provided, creditors provided $.89. Variations of the debt-to-equity ratio are sometimes used to assess solvency. For example, an analyst might calculate the ratio of total liabilities to the sum of total liabilities and stockholders' equity. This results in a ratio that differs from the debt-to-equity ratio, but the objective of the measure is the same—to determine the degree to which the company relies on outsiders for funds.

What is an *acceptable* ratio of debt to equity? As with all ratios, the answer depends on the company, the industry, and many other factors. You should not assume that a lower debt-to-equity ratio is better. Certainly taking on additional debt is risky. Many companies are able to benefit from borrowing money, however, by putting the cash raised to good uses in their businesses. Later in the chapter we discuss the concept of leverage: using borrowed money to benefit the company and its stockholders.

Study Tip

The elements in many ratios are intuitive and should not require memorization to remember. For example, it is logical that the debt-to-equity ratio is computed by dividing total liabilities by total stockholders' equity.

In the 1980s, investors and creditors tolerated a much higher debt-to-equity ratio than is considered prudent today. The savings and loan crisis in the 1980s prompted the federal government to enact regulations requiring financial institutions to have a lower proportion of debt-to-equity. By the mid-1990s, investors and creditors were demanding that all types of companies display lower debt-to-equity ratios.

Times Interest Earned

TIMES INTEREST EARNED RATIO An income statement measure of the ability of a company to meet its interest payments.

The debt-to-equity ratio is a measure of the company's overall long-term financial health. Management must also be aware of its ability to meet current interest payments to creditors. The **times interest earned ratio** indicates the company's ability to meet current-year interest payments out of current-year earnings:

$$\text{Times Interest Earned Ratio} = \frac{\text{Net Income} + \text{Interest Expense} + \text{Income Tax Expense}}{\text{Interest Expense}}$$

Both interest expense and income tax expense are added back to net income in the numerator because interest is a deduction in arriving at the amount of income subject to tax. Stated slightly differently, if a company had just enough income to cover the payment of interest, tax expense would be zero. The greater the interest coverage is, the better, as far as lenders are concerned. Bankers often place more importance on the times interest earned ratio than even on earnings per share. The ratio for Henderson for each of the two years indicates a great deal of protection in this regard:

2001	2000
$\frac{\$1{,}720{,}000 + \$140{,}000 + \$1{,}140{,}000}{\$140{,}000}$	$\frac{\$2{,}300{,}000 + \$160{,}000 + \$1{,}540{,}000}{\$160{,}000}$
= 21.4 to 1	= 25 to 1

Debt Service Coverage

Two problems exist with the times interest earned ratio as a measure of the ability to pay creditors. First, the denominator of the fraction considers only *interest.* Management must also be concerned with the *principal* amount of loans maturing in the next year. The second problem deals with the difference between the cash and the accrual bases of accounting. The numerator of the times interest earned ratio is not a measure of the *cash* available to repay loans. Keep in mind the various noncash adjustments, such as depreciation, that enter into the determination of net income. Also, recall that the denominator of the times interest earned ratio is a measure of interest expense, not interest payments. The **debt service coverage ratio** is a measure of the amount of cash that is generated from operating activities during the year and that is available to repay interest due and any maturing principal amounts (that is, the amount available to "service" the debt):

DEBT SERVICE COVERAGE RATIO A statement of cash flows measure of the ability of a company to meet its interest and principal payments.

$$\text{Debt Service Coverage Ratio} = \frac{\text{Cash Flow from Operations before Interest and Tax Payments}}{\text{Interest and Principal Payments}}$$

Some analysts use an alternative measure in the numerator of this ratio, as well as for other purposes. The alternative is referred to as EBITDA, which stands for earnings before interest, taxes, depreciation, and amortization. Whether EBITDA is a good substitute for cash flow from operations before interest and tax payments depends on whether there were significant changes in current assets and current liabilities during the period. If significant changes in these accounts occurred during the period, cash flow from operations before interest and tax payments is a better measure of a company's ability to cover interest and debt payments.

Cash flow from operations is available on the comparative statement of cash flows in Exhibit 13-4. As was the case with the times interest earned ratio, the net cash provided by operating activities is adjusted to reflect the amount available *before* paying interest and taxes.

Keep in mind that the income statement in Exhibit 13-2 reflects the *expense* for interest and taxes each year. The amounts of interest and taxes *paid* each year are shown as supplemental information at the bottom of the statement of cash flows in Exhibit 13-4 and are relevant in computing the debt service coverage ratio.

We must include any principal payments with interest paid in the denominator of the debt service coverage ratio. According to the Financing Activities section of the statements of cash flows in Exhibit 13-4, Henderson repaid $200,000 each year on the notes payable and $100,000 each year on the bonds. The debt service coverage ratios for the two years are calculated as follows:

2001

$$\frac{\$1{,}070{,}000 + \$140{,}000 + \$940{,}000}{\$140{,}000 + \$200{,}000 + \$100{,}000} = 4.89 \text{ times}$$

2000

$$\frac{\$2{,}950{,}000 + \$160{,}000 + \$1{,}440{,}000}{\$160{,}000 + \$200{,}000 + \$100{,}000} = 9.89 \text{ times}$$

Like Henderson's times interest earned ratio, its debt service coverage ratio decreased during 2001. According to the calculations, however, Henderson still generated almost $5 of cash from operations during 2001 to "cover" every $1 of required interest and principal payments.

Skip

Cash Flow from Operations to Capital Expenditures Ratio

One final measure is useful in assessing the solvency of a business. The **cash flow from operations to capital expenditures ratio** measures a company's ability to use operations to finance its acquisitions of productive assets. To the extent that a company is able to do this, it should rely less on external financing or additional contributions by the owners to replace and add to the existing capital base. The ratio is computed as follows:

Cash Flow from Operations to Capital Expenditures Ratio
A measure of the ability of a company to finance long-term asset acquisitions with cash from operations.

$$\text{Cash Flow from Operations to Capital Expenditures Ratio} = \frac{\text{Cash Flow from Operations} - \text{Total Dividends Paid}}{\text{Cash Paid for Acquisitions}}$$

Note that the numerator of the ratio measures the cash flow *after* meeting all dividend payments.[2] The calculation of the ratios for Henderson follows:

2001

$$\frac{\$1{,}070{,}000 - \$300{,}000}{\$1{,}500{,}000} = 51.3\%$$

2000

$$\frac{\$2{,}950{,}000 - \$300{,}000}{\$2{,}000{,}000} = 132.5\%$$

[2]Dividends paid are reported on the statement of cash flows in the Financing Activities section. The amount *paid* should be used for this calculation rather than the amount declared, which appears on the statement of retained earnings.

Although the amount of capital expenditures was less in 2001 than in 2000, the company generated considerably less cash from operations in 2001 to cover these acquisitions. In fact, the ratio of less than 100% in 2001 indicates that Henderson was not able to finance all of its capital expenditures from operations *and* cover its dividend payments.

Two-Minute Review

1. Explain the difference between liquidity and solvency as it relates to a company's financial position.

2. Assume that you are a supplier and are considering whether to sell to a company on account. Which of the two, liquidity or solvency, are you more concerned with?

Answers:

1. Liquidity is a relative measure of the nearness to cash of the assets and liabilities of a company. Measures of liquidity are intended to determine the company's ability to pay its debts as they come due. Solvency refers to a company's ability to remain in business over the long term. Liquidity and solvency are certainly related, but the latter takes a much more long-term view of the financial health of the company.

2. Because you need to assess the ability of the company to pay its account on a timely basis, you would be more concerned with the liquidity of the company over the short term.

PROFITABILITY ANALYSIS

LO 6 Compute and use various ratios to assess profitability.

PROFITABILITY
How well management is using company resources to earn a return on the funds invested by various groups.

Liquidity analysis and solvency analysis deal with management's ability to repay short- and long-term creditors. Creditors are concerned with a company's profitability because a profitable company is more likely to be able to make principal and interest payments. Of course, stockholders care about a company's profitability because it affects the market price of the stock and the ability of the company to pay dividends. Various measures of **profitability** indicate how well management is using the resources at its disposal to earn a return on the funds invested by various groups. Two frequently used profitability measures, the gross profit ratio and the profit margin ratio, were discussed earlier in the chapter. We now turn to other measures of profitability.

RATE OF RETURN ON ASSETS

RETURN ON ASSETS RATIO
A measure of a company's success in earning a return for all providers of capital.

Before computing the rate of return, we must answer an important question: *return to whom? Every return ratio is a measure of the relationship between the income earned by the company and the investment made in the company by various groups.* The broadest rate of return ratio is the **return on assets ratio** because it considers the investment made by *all* providers of capital, from short-term creditors to bondholders to stockholders. Therefore, the denominator, or base, for the return on assets ratio is average total liabilities and stockholders' equity—which of course is the same as average total assets.

The numerator of a return ratio will be some measure of the company's income for the period. The income selected for the numerator must match the investment or base in the denominator. For example, if average total assets is the base in the denominator, it is necessary to use an income number that is applicable to all providers of capital. Therefore, the income number used in the rate of return on assets is income *after* adding back interest expense. This adjustment considers creditors as one of the groups that have provided funds to the company. In other words, we want the amount of income before either creditors or stockholders have been given any distributions (that is, interest to creditors or dividends to stockholders). Interest expense must be added back on a net-of-tax basis. Because net income is on an after-tax basis, for consistency purposes interest must also be placed on a net, or after-tax, basis.

The return on assets ratio is as follows:

$$\text{Return on Assets Ratio} = \frac{\text{Net Income + Interest Expense, Net of Tax}}{\text{Average Total Assets}}$$

If we assume a 40% tax rate (which *is* the actual ratio of income tax expense to income before tax for Henderson), its return on assets ratios are as follows:

		2001		**2000**
Net income		$ 1,720,000		$ 2,300,000
Add back:				
Interest expense	$140,000		$160,000	
× (1 − tax rate)	0.6	84,000	0.6	96,000
Numerator		$ 1,804,000		$ 2,396,000
Assets, beginning of year		$13,800,000		$12,000,000
Assets, end of year		16,870,000		13,800,000
Total		$30,670,000		$25,800,000
Denominator:				
Average total assets (total above divided by 2)		$15,335,000		$12,900,000
		$ 1,804,000 / $15,335,000		$ 2,396,000 / $12,900,000
Return on assets ratio		= 11.76%		= 18.57%

Components of Return on Assets

What caused Henderson's return on assets to decrease so dramatically from the previous year? The answer can be found by considering the two individual components that make up the return on assets ratio. The first of these components is the **return on sales ratio** and is calculated as follows:

RETUN ON SALES RATIO A variation of the profit margin ratio; measures earnings before payments to creditors.

$$\text{Return on Sales Ratio} = \frac{\text{Net Income + Interest Expense, Net of Tax}}{\text{Net Sales}}$$

The return on sales ratios for Henderson for the two years follow:

2001	**2000**
$\frac{\$1{,}720{,}000 + \$84{,}000}{\$24{,}000{,}000} = 7.52\%$	$\frac{\$2{,}300{,}000 + \$96{,}000}{\$20{,}000{,}000} = 11.98\%$

The ratio for 2001 indicates that for every $1 of sales, the company was able to earn a profit, before the payment of interest, of between 7 and 8 cents, as compared with a return of almost 12 cents on the dollar in 2000.

The other component of the rate of return on assets is the **asset turnover ratio.** The ratio is similar to both the inventory turnover and the accounts receivable turnover ratios because it is a measure of the relationship between some activity (net sales, in this case) and some investment base (average total assets):

ASSET TURNOVER RATIO The relationship between net sales and average total assets.

$$\text{Asset Turnover Ratio} = \frac{\text{Net Sales}}{\text{Average Total Assets}}$$

For Henderson, the ratio for each of the two years follows:

2001	**2000**
$\frac{\$24{,}000{,}000}{\$15{,}335{,}000} = 1.57$ times	$\frac{\$20{,}000{,}000}{\$12{,}900{,}000} = 1.55$ times

It now becomes evident that the explanation for the decrease in Henderson's return on assets lies in the drop in the return on sales, since the asset turnover ratio was almost the same. To summarize, note the relationship among the three ratios:

$$\text{Return on Assets} = \text{Return on Sales} \times \text{Asset Turnover}$$

For 2001, Henderson's return on assets consists of the following:

$$\frac{\$1{,}804{,}000}{\$24{,}000{,}000} \times \frac{\$24{,}000{,}000}{\$15{,}335{,}000} = 7.52\% \times 1.57 = 11.8\%$$

Finally, notice that net sales cancels out of both ratios, leaving the net income adjusted for interest divided by average assets as the return on assets ratio.

Return on Common Stockholders' Equity

Reasoning similar to that used to calculate return on assets can be used to calculate the return on capital provided by the common stockholder. Because we are interested in the return to the common stockholder, our base is no longer average total assets but average common stockholders' equity. Similarly, the appropriate income figure for the numerator is net income less preferred dividends because we are interested in the return to the common stockholder after all claims have been settled. Income taxes and interest expense have already been deducted in arriving at net income, but preferred dividends have not been because dividends are a distribution of profits, not an expense.

RETURN ON COMMON STOCKHOLDERS' EQUITY RATIO A measure of a company's success in earning a return for the common stockholders.

The **return on common stockholders' equity ratio** is computed as follows:

$$\text{Return on Common Stockholders' Equity Ratio} = \frac{\text{Net Income} - \text{Preferred Dividends}}{\text{Average Common Stockholders' Equity}}$$

The average common stockholders' equity for Henderson is calculated using information from Exhibits 13-1 and 13-7:

	Account Balances at December 31 2001	2000	1999
Common stock, $1 par	$1,000,000	$1,000,000	$1,000,000
Retained earnings	7,420,000	6,000,000	4,000,000
Total common equity	$8,420,000	$7,000,000	$5,000,000

Average common equity:
2000: ($7,000,000 + $5,000,000)/2 = $6,000,000
2001: ($8,420,000 + $7,000,000)/2 = $7,710,000

Net income less preferred dividends—or "income available to common," as it is called—can be found by referring to net income on the income statement and to preferred dividends on the statement of retained earnings. The combined statement of income and retained earnings in Exhibit 13-2 gives the relevant amounts for the numerator. Henderson's return on equity for the two years is as follows:

2001	2000
$\frac{\$1{,}720{,}000 - \$50{,}000}{\$7{,}710{,}000} = 21.66\%$	$\frac{\$2{,}300{,}000 - \$50{,}000}{\$6{,}000{,}000} = 37.50\%$

Even though Henderson's return on stockholders' equity ratio decreased significantly from one year to the next, most stockholders would be very happy to achieve these returns on their money. Very few investments offer much more than 10% return unless substantial risk is involved.

Return on Assets, Return on Equity, and Leverage

The return on assets for 2001 was 11.8%. But the return to the common stockholders was much higher: 21.7%. How do you explain this phenomenon? Why are the stockholders receiving a higher return on their money than all of the providers of money combined are getting? A partial answer to these questions can be found by reviewing the cost to Henderson of the various sources of capital.

Exhibit 13-1 indicates that notes, bonds, and preferred stock are the primary sources of capital other than common stock (accounts payable and taxes payable are *not* included because they represent interest-free loans to the company from suppliers and the government). These sources and the average amount of each outstanding during 2001 follow:

	Account Balances at December 31		
	2001	**2000**	**Average**
Notes payable	$ 600,000	$ 800,000	$ 700,000
Current portion of bonds	100,000	100,000	100,000
Bonds payable—Long-term	700,000	800,000	750,000
Total liabilities	$1,400,000	$1,700,000	$1,550,000
Preferred stock	$ 500,000	$ 500,000	$ 500,000

What was the cost to Henderson of each of these sources? The cost of the money provided by the preferred stockholders is clearly the amount of dividends of $50,000. The cost as a percentage is $50,000/$500,000, or 10%. The average cost of the borrowed money can be approximated by dividing the 2001 interest expense of $140,000 by the average of the notes payable and bonds payable of $1,550,000. The result is an average cost of these two sources of $140,000/$1,550,000, or approximately 9%.

The concept of **leverage** refers to the practice of using borrowed funds and amounts received from preferred stockholders in an attempt to earn an overall return that is higher than the cost of these funds. Recall the rate of return on assets for 2001: 11.8%. Because this return is on an after-tax basis, it is necessary, for comparative purposes, to convert the average cost of borrowed funds to an after-tax basis. Although we computed an average cost for borrowed money of 9%, the actual cost of the borrowed money is 5.4% [9% × (100% − 40%)] after taxes. Because dividends are *not* tax-deductible, the cost of the money provided by preferred stockholders is 10%, as calculated earlier.

Leverage
The use of borrowed funds and amounts contributed by preferred stockholders to earn an overall return higher than the cost of these funds.

Has Henderson successfully employed favorable leverage? That is, has it been able to earn an overall rate of return on assets that is higher than the amounts that it must pay creditors and preferred stockholders? Henderson has been successful in using outside money: neither of the sources must be paid a rate in excess of the 11.8% overall rate on assets used. Also keep in mind that Henderson has been able to borrow some amounts on an interest-free basis. As mentioned earlier, the accounts payable and taxes payable represent interest-free loans from suppliers and the government, although the loans are typically for a short period of time, such as 30 days.

In summary, the excess of the 21.7% return on equity over the 11.8% return on assets indicates that the Henderson management has been successful in employing leverage; that is, there is favorable leverage. Is it possible to be unsuccessful in this pursuit; that is, can there be unfavorable leverage? If the company must pay more for the amounts provided by creditors and preferred stockholders than it can earn overall, as indicated by the return on assets, there will, in fact, be unfavorable leverage. This may occur when interest requirements are high and net income is low. A company would likely have a high debt-to-equity ratio as well when there is unfavorable leverage.

Earnings per Share

Earnings per share is one of the most quoted statistics for publicly traded companies. Stockholders and potential investors want to know what their share of profits is, not just

Earnings per share
A company's bottom line stated on a per-share basis.

the total dollar amount. Presentation of profits on a per-share basis also allows the stockholder to relate earnings to what he or she paid for a share of stock or to the current trading price of a share of stock.

In simple situations, such as our Henderson Company example, earnings per share (EPS) is calculated as follows:

$$\text{Earnings per Share} = \frac{\text{Net Income} - \text{Preferred Dividends}}{\text{Weighted Average Number of Common Shares Outstanding}}$$

Because Henderson had 1,000,000 shares of common stock outstanding throughout both 2000 and 2001, its EPS for each of the two years is as follows:

2001	2000
$\frac{\$1{,}720{,}000 - \$50{,}000}{1{,}000{,}000 \text{ shares}} = \$1.67$ per share	$\frac{\$2{,}300{,}000 - \$50{,}000}{1{,}000{,}000 \text{ shares}} = \$2.25$ per share

A number of complications can arise in the computation of EPS, and the calculations can become exceedingly complex for a company with many different types of securities in its capital structure. These complications are beyond the scope of this book and are discussed in more advanced accounting courses.

PRICE/EARNINGS RATIO

Earnings per share is an important ratio for an investor because of its relationship to dividends and market price. Stockholders hope to earn a return by receiving periodic dividends or eventually selling the stock for more than they paid for it, or both. Although earnings are related to dividends and market price, the latter two are of primary interest to the stockholder.

PRICE/EARNINGS (P/E) RATIO The relationship between a company's performance according to the income statement and its performance in the stock market.

We mentioned earlier the desire of investors to relate the earnings of the company to the market price of the stock. Now that we have stated Henderson's earnings on a per-share basis, we can calculate the **price/earnings (P/E) ratio.** What market price is relevant? Should we use the market price that the investor paid for a share of stock, or should we use the current market price? Because earnings are based on the most recent evaluation of the company for accounting purposes, it seems logical to use current market price, which is based on the stock market's current assessment of the company. Therefore, the ratio is computed as follows:

$$\text{Price/Earnings Ratio} = \frac{\text{Current Market Price}}{\text{Earnings per Share}}$$

Assume that the current market price for Henderson's common stock is \$15 per share at the end of 2001 and \$18 per share at the end of 2000. The price/earnings ratio for each of the two years is as follows:

2001	2000
$\frac{\$15 \text{ per Share}}{\$1.67 \text{ per Share}} = 9$ to 1	$\frac{\$18 \text{ per Share}}{\$2.25 \text{ per Share}} = 8$ to 1

Making financial decisions requires having the right tools at hand, including the annual reports of companies under consideration and recent stock market quotations, printed in most large newspapers.

What is normal for a P/E ratio? As is the case for all other ratios, it is difficult to generalize as to what is good or bad. The P/E ratio compares the stock market's assessment of a company's performance with its success as reflected on the income statement. A relatively high P/E ratio may indicate that a stock is overpriced by the market; one that is relatively low could indicate that it is underpriced.

The P/E ratio is often thought to indicate the "quality" of a company's earnings. For example, assume that two companies have identical EPS ratios of \$2 per share. Why should investors be willing to pay \$20 per share (or 10 times earnings) for the stock of one company but only \$14 per share (or 7 times earnings) for the stock of the other company? First, we must realize that many factors in addition to the reported earnings of the company affect market prices. General economic conditions, the outlook for the particular industry, and pending lawsuits are just three examples of the various factors that can affect the trading price of a company's stock. The difference in P/E ratios for the two companies may reflect the market's assessment of the accounting practices of the companies, however. Assume that the company with a market price of $20 per share uses LIFO in valuing inventory and that the company trading at $14 per share uses FIFO. The difference in prices may indicate that investors believe that even though the companies have the same EPS, the LIFO company is "better off" because it will have a lower amount of taxes to pay. (Recall that in a period of inflation, the use of LIFO results in more cost of goods sold, less income, and therefore less income taxes.) Finally, aside from the way investors view the accounting practices of different companies, they also consider the fact that, to a large extent, earnings reflect the use of historical costs, as opposed to fair market values, in assigning values to assets. Investors must consider the extent to which a company's assets are worth more than what was paid for them.

ACCOUNTING FOR YOUR DECISIONS

You Are the CEO

You have just been promoted to the chief executive officer position at Orange Computer, a company that has recently fallen on hard times. Sales and earnings have been sluggish. Part of the reason that the prior CEO was dismissed by the board was the lagging stock price. Although the typical computer company stock price is roughly 25 times earnings, Orange Computer is languishing at just 8 times earnings. What can you do to restore the company's stock price?

ANS: The best way to boost your company's stock price is to restore earnings to levels comparable to that of other companies in the industry. If investors see that you are cutting costs, boosting sales, and restoring earnings, they may see a future earnings and dividends stream from Orange Computer that matches other competing investments. Consider the case of Lou Gerstner, IBM's CEO. Since Gerstner joined the company, IBM's earnings have experienced a dramatic turnaround, from a loss of $5 billion in 1992, to a profit of $6 billion in 1998. By the fourth quarter of 1998, IBM's common stock was trading at an all-time high.

DIVIDEND RATIOS

Two ratios are used to evaluate a company's dividend policies: the **dividend payout ratio** and the **dividend yield ratio.** The dividend payout ratio is the ratio of the common dividends per share to the earnings per share:

$$\text{Dividend Payout Ratio} = \frac{\text{Common Dividends per Share}}{\text{Earnings per Share}}$$

Exhibit 13-2 indicates that Henderson paid $250,000 in common dividends each year, or with 1 million shares outstanding, $.25 per share. The two payout ratios are as follows:

2001	2000
$\frac{\$.25}{\$1.67} = 15.0\%$	$\frac{\$.25}{\$2.25} = 11.1\%$

Henderson management was faced with an important financial policy decision in 2001. Should the company maintain the same dividend of $.25 per share, even though EPS dropped significantly? Many companies prefer to maintain a level dividend pattern, hoping that a drop in earnings is only temporary.

DIVIDEND PAYOUT RATIO
The percentage of earnings paid out as dividends.

DIVIDEND YIELD RATIO
The relationship between dividends and the market price of a company's stock.

From Concept **TO PRACTICE 13.3**

READING GATEWAY'S ANNUAL REPORT Refer to Gateway's statement of cash flows. Why is it not possible to compute Gateway's dividend payout ratio for 1998? Why do you think Gateway has adopted the policy it has concerning the payment of dividends?

Name: Stephen Carmichael
Education: B.A., Vanderbilt University; M.B.A., University of Michigan
College Major: English
Occupation: Senior Associate, Deloitte Consulting/Braxton Associates, London
Age: 28

FOCUS ON USERS

> "We read the financial statements of our clients and their competitors to ... help [clients] improve their competitiveness."
> –Stephen Carmichael

Keys to Competitiveness: Knowing Industry, Company, and Financial Statements

"In the consulting business, one of our main sources of information is corporate financial statements," says Steve Carmichael, a consultant for Deloitte Consulting/Braxton Associates, the strategy arm of the international business advisory firm Deloitte Touche Tohmatsu. Steve's job is to help upper management of large corporations determine how they can increase profits by growing their business and shrinking costs. The consulting process—that is, learning everything possible about a company and then advising it accordingly—always involves intense scrutiny of the financial statements. A good consultant examines every number on every statement and is able to advise which of those numbers need to change in order to take a company to the next level. As Steve says, "we read the financial statements of our clients and their competitors to develop a deep understanding of industry issues and gain insights we can take back to clients to help them improve their competitiveness."

Trend analysis, or looking at the financial statements for a period of years, can make it easy to spot a particular weakness or "red flag." An example of such a red flag might be a fluctuation in a company's cash balance. Steve explains: "Significant changes in a company's cash position could indicate a number of things: The company has made significant acquisitions using cash, has changed its payables/receivables policy, or has made investments in equipment which require significant cash outlays. The important thing that we do as consultants is ensure that we have found the reason for the red flag and establish how it affects the client's strategy."

In-depth analysis of the statements from year to year is often just a starting point when plotting strategy for a company. To illustrate how the statements might fit into a multistep analysis process, Steve uses the example of consulting a CEO of a large bank: "We would first analyze the markets of the bank and its competitors, using financial statements. Then, we would look at internal and external market analysis and form a picture of the landscape. We might then conclude that e-business solutions, for example, would help the company reach more customers, give them competitive advantage over others in the industry, and let them communicate more effectively."

In this case, Steve recommended e-business as a way to grow and reduce costs, but each company will have a different set of problems and needs. To target solutions to a specific company in a specific industry, he might rely on some kind of ratio analysis to further substantiate his opinion. "For instance," Steve says, "for a company with large inventories, inventory turnover and return on assets would be important. Service-related companies, on the other hand, rely less on these types of ratios and more on margin analysis. It is crucial to find the business drivers for a particular client and focus on those. Clients tend to be convinced that the most flattering ratio is usually the best. The fun part, though, is helping the client realize what the best drivers are."

The second dividend ratio of interest to stockholders is the dividend yield ratio:

$$\text{Dividend Yield Ratio} = \frac{\text{Common Dividends per Share}}{\text{Market Price per Share}}$$

The yield to Henderson's stockholders would be calculated as follows:

2001	2000
$\frac{\$.25}{\$15} = 1.7\%$	$\frac{\$.25}{\$18} = 1.4\%$

As we see, Henderson common stock does not provide a high yield to its investors. The relationship between the dividends and the market price indicates that investors buy the stock for reasons other than the periodic dividend return.

The dividend yield is very important to investors who depend on dividend checks to pay their living expenses. Utility stocks are popular among retirees because these shares have dividend yields as high as 5%. That is considered a good investment with relatively low risk and some opportunity for gains in the stock price. On the other hand, investors who want to put money into growing companies are willing to forgo dividends if it means the potential for greater price appreciation.

Quote Quotes sponsored by Salomon Smith Barney

WWY Wrigley (Wm Jr) Co — **Last:** 73 15/16

News | Charts | Profile | Financials | Analysis | Insiders | SEC

Last:	73 15/16	**Market:**	NYSE
Change:	-15/16 (-1.3%)	**Market Capitalization:**	8,559.52 (mil)
Volume:	224,700	**Average Volume:**	270,000
Bid:	N/A	**Dividend/Share:**	0.350
Ask:	N/A	**Yield:**	1.800
Open:	74 5/8	**P/E:**	27.000
Previous Close:	74 7/8	**Ex-Dividend:**	01/12
Day's Range:	73 3/4 - 74 3/4	**52 Week Range:**	66 1/2 - 100.62

Most major newspapers provide summaries of company stock performance on the leading stock exchanges. Immediate tracking of this information is available online, however, such as this stock quote for Wrigley found at Netscape.com, with data from Salomon Smith Barney. The price/earnings ratio (P/E) and the dividend yield ("yield") are two of the statistics included.

Summary of Selected Financial Ratios

We have now completed our review of the various ratios used to assess a company's liquidity, solvency, and profitability. For ease of reference, Exhibit 13-8 summarizes the ratios discussed in this chapter. Keep in mind that this list is not all-inclusive and that certain ratios used by analysts and others may be specific to a particular industry or type of business.

Accounting for Your Decisions

You Decide on a Stock Purchase

You are starting college and your parents have agreed to help pay your tuition. They will put money into a stock fund for four years and allow you to use the dividends from the fund to pay your quarterly tuition. Should you advise your parents to find a stock with a relatively low dividend yield ratio if it has an above-average return on stockholders' equity?

ANS: Regardless of how attractive a company's return on equity ratio might be, you need cash on a regular basis to pay tuition. You should advise your parents to find a stock with a relatively high dividend yield ratio.

Warmup Exercises

LO 4, 5, 6 Warmup Exercise 13-1 Types of Ratios

Fill in the blanks on the following page to indicate whether each of the following ratios is concerned with a company's liquidity (L), its solvency (S), or its profitability (P).

EXHIBIT 13-8 Summary of Selected Financial Ratios

Liquidity Analysis	
Working capital	Current Assets − Current Liabilities
Current ratio	$\frac{\text{Current Assets}}{\text{Current Liabilities}}$
Acid-test ratio (quick ratio)	$\frac{\text{Cash + Marketable Securities + Current Receivables}}{\text{Current Liabilities}}$
Cash flow from operations to current liabilities ratio	$\frac{\text{Net Cash Provided by Operating Activities}}{\text{Average Current Liabilities}}$
Accounts receivable turnover ratio	$\frac{\text{Net Credit Sales}}{\text{Average Accounts Receivable}}$
Number of days' sales in receivables	$\frac{\text{Number of Days in the Period}}{\text{Accounts Receivable Turnover}}$
Inventory turnover ratio	$\frac{\text{Cost of Goods Sold}}{\text{Average Inventory}}$
Number of days' sales in inventory	$\frac{\text{Number of Days in the Period}}{\text{Inventory Turnover}}$
Cash to cash operating cycle	Number of Days' Sales in Inventory + Number of Days' Sales in Receivables
Solvency Analysis	
Debt-to-equity ratio	$\frac{\text{Total Liabilities}}{\text{Total Stockholders' Equity}}$
Times interest earned ratio	$\frac{\text{Net Income + Income Expense + Income Tax Expense}}{\text{Interest Expense}}$
Debt service coverage ratio	$\frac{\text{Cash Flow from Operations before Interest and Tax Payments}}{\text{Interest and Principal Payments}}$

_______ **1.** Return on assets ratio
_______ **2.** Current ratio
_______ **3.** Debt-to-equity ratio
_______ **4.** Earnings per share
_______ **5.** Inventory turnover ratio
_______ **6.** Gross profit ratio

Key to the Solution
Review the summary of selected ratios in Exhibit 13-8.

LO 4 Warmup Exercise 13-2 Accounts Receivable Turnover
Company A reported sales during the year of $1,000,000. Its average accounts receivable balance during the year was $250,000. Company B reported sales during the same year of $400,000 and had an average accounts receivable balance of $40,000.

Required

1. Compute the accounts receivable turnover for both companies.
2. What is the average length of time each company takes to collect its receivables?

Key to the Solution
Review the summary of selected ratios in Exhibit 13-8.

Cash flow from operations to capital expenditures ratio	$\frac{\text{Cash Flow from Operations} - \text{Total Dividends Paid}}{\text{Cash Paid for Acquisitions}}$
Profitability Analysis	
Gross profit ratio	$\frac{\text{Gross Profit}}{\text{Net Sales}}$
Profit margin ratio	$\frac{\text{Net Income}}{\text{Net Sales}}$
Return on assets ratio	$\frac{\text{Net Income} + \text{Interest Expense, Net of Tax}}{\text{Average Total Assets}}$
Return on sales ratio	$\frac{\text{Net Income} + \text{Interest Expense, Net of Tax}}{\text{Net Sales}}$
Asset turnover ratio	$\frac{\text{Net Sales}}{\text{Average Total Assets}}$
Return on common stockholders' equity ratio	$\frac{\text{Net Income} - \text{Preferred Dividends}}{\text{Average Common Stockholders' Equity}}$
Earnings per share	$\frac{\text{Net Income} - \text{Preferred Dividends}}{\text{Weighted Average Number of Common Shares Outstanding}}$
Price/earnings ratio	$\frac{\text{Current Market Price}}{\text{Earnings per Share}}$
Dividend payout ratio	$\frac{\text{Common Dividends per Share}}{\text{Earnings per Share}}$
Dividend yield ratio	$\frac{\text{Common Dividends per Share}}{\text{Market Price per Share}}$

LO 6 Warmup Exercise 13-3 Earnings Per Share

A company reported net income during the year of $90,000 and paid dividends of $15,000 to its common stockholders and $10,000 to its preferred stockholders. During the year, 20,000 shares of common stock were outstanding and 10,000 shares of preferred stock were outstanding.

Required

Compute earnings per share for the year.

Key to the Solution

Recall that earnings per share only has relevance to the common stockholders and therefore it is a measure of the earnings per common share outstanding, after taking into account any claims of preferred stockholders.

SOLUTIONS TO WARMUP EXERCISES

Warmup Exercise 13-1

1. P **2.** L **3.** S **4.** P **5.** L **6.** P

Warmup Exercise 13-2

1. Company A turns over its accounts receivable, on the average, 4 times during the year ($1,000,000/$250,000) and Company B 10 times during the year ($400,000/$40,000).
2. Assuming 360 days in a year, Company A takes, on the average, 90 days to collect its accounts receivable, and Company B takes, on the average, 36 days.

Warmup Exercise 13-3

Earnings per share: ($90,000 – $10,000)/20,000 shares = $4 per share.

REVIEW PROBLEM

On the following pages are the comparative financial statements for Wm. Wrigley Jr. Company, the chewing gum manufacturer, as shown in its 1998 annual report.

Required

1. Compute the following ratios for the two years 1998 and 1997, either for each year or as of the end of each of the years, as appropriate. Beginning balances for 1997 are not available; that is, you do not have a balance sheet as of the end of 1996. Therefore, to be consistent, use year-end balances for both years where you would normally use average amounts for the year. To compute the return on assets ratio, you will need to find the tax rate. Use the relationship between income taxes and earnings before taxes to find the rate for each year.
   - **a.** Current ratio
   - **b.** Quick ratio
   - **c.** Cash flow from operations to current liabilities ratio
   - **d.** Number of days' sales in receivables
   - **e.** Number of days' sales in inventory
   - **f.** Debt-to-equity ratio
   - **g.** Debt service coverage ratio
   - **h.** Cash flow from operations to capital expenditures ratio
   - **i.** Return on assets ratio
   - **j.** Return on common stockholders' equity ratio
2. Comment on Wrigley's liquidity. Has it improved or declined over the two-year period?
3. Does Wrigley appear to be solvent to you? Does there appear to be anything unusual about its capital structure?
4. Comment on Wrigley's profitability. Would you buy stock in the company?

Solution to Review Problem

1. Ratios:

a. 1998: $843,172/$218,626 = 3.86

1997: $797,673/$225,816 = 3.53

b. 1998: ($214,572 + $137,112 + $194,977)/$218,626 = 2.50

1997: ($206,627 + $120,728 + $175,967)/$225,816 = 2.23

c. 1998: $323,847/$218,626 = 1.48

1997: $294,478/$225,816 = 1.30

d. 1998: 360 days/[($2,004,719/$194,977)] = 360/10.28 = 35 days

1997: 360 days/[($1,937,021/$175,967)] = 360/11.01 = 33 days

e. 1998: 360 days/[($848,363/$256,108)] = 360/3.31 = 109 days

1997: 360 days/[($847,366/$247,392)] = 360/3.43 = 105 days

f. 1998: ($218,626 + $40,312 + $104,885)/$1,157,032 = 0.31

1997: ($225,816 + $30,874 + $101,057)/$985,379 = 0.36

g. 1998: ($323,847 + $133,530 + $1,164)/$1,164 = 394

1997: ($294,478 + $126,925 + $900)/$900 = 469

consolidated statement of earnings

	1998	1997	1996
	In thousands of U.S. dollars except for per share amounts		
EARNINGS			
Revenues:			
Net sales	**$2,004,719**	1,937,021	1,835,987
Investment and other income	**18,636**	17,153	14,614
Total revenues	**2,023,355**	1,954,174	1,850,601
Costs and expenses:			
Cost of sales	**848,363**	847,366	814,483
Costs (Gains) related to factory closure and sale	**(10,404)**	3,300	19,436
Selling, distribution and general administrative	**743,902**	708,310	656,473
Interest	**615**	958	1,097
Total costs and expenses	**1,582,476**	1,559,934	1,491,489
Earnings before income taxes	**440,879**	394,240	359,112
Income taxes	**136,378**	122,614	128,840
Net earnings	**$ 304,501**	271,626	230,272
PER SHARE AMOUNTS			
Net earnings per share of Common Stock (basic and diluted)	**$ 2.63**	2.34	1.99
Dividends paid per share of Common Stock	**$ 1.30**	1.17	1.02

See accompanying accounting policies and notes.

h. 1998: ($323,847 – $150,835)/$148,027 = 1.17

1997: ($294,478 – $135,680)/$126,509 = 1.26

i. 1998: $304,501 + [$615(1 – .31*)]/$1,520,855 = 20.0%

1997: $271,626 + [$958(1 – .31*)]/$1,343,126 = 20.3%

j. 1998: $304,501/$1,157,032† = 26.3%

1997: $271,626/$985,379† = 27.6%

---

*Tax rate for each of the two years:
1998: $136,378/$440,879 = .31
1997: $122,614/$394,240 = .31

†In addition to its common stock, Wrigley has outstanding Class B common stock. Because this is a second class of stock (similar in many respects to preferred stock), the contributed capital attributable to it should be deducted from total stockholders' equity in the denominator. Similarly, any dividends paid on the Class B common stock should be deducted from net income in the numerator to find the return to the regular common stockholders. We have ignored the difficulties involved in determining these adjustments in our calculations of return on equity.

consolidated statement of cash flows

	1998	1997	1996
		In thousands of U.S. dollars	
OPERATING ACTIVITIES			
Net earnings	**$ 304,501**	271,626	230,272
Adjustments to reconcile net earnings to net cash provided by operating activities:			
Depreciation	**55,774**	50,439	47,288
(Gain) Loss on sales of property, plant and equipment	**168**	(1,141)	(1,771)
Gain related to factory sale	**(10,404)**	—	—
(Increase) Decrease in:			
Accounts receivable	**(16,319)**	(26,318)	2,154
Inventories	**(6,299)**	(26,916)	973
Other current assets	**5,332**	(12,712)	3,777
Other assets and deferred charges	**(17,350)**	11,123	(24,075)
Increase (Decrease) in:			
Accounts payable	**4,499**	1,549	474
Accrued expenses	**(3,869)**	16,182	3
Income and other taxes payable	**(4,445)**	1,779	6,095
Deferred income taxes	**9,826**	(2,608)	(4,496)
Other noncurrent liabilities	**2,433**	11,475	25,149
Net cash provided by operating activities	**323,847**	294,478	285,843
INVESTING ACTIVITIES			
Additions to property, plant and equipment	**(148,027)**	(126,509)	(101,977)
Proceeds from property retirements	**10,662**	6,888	10,785
Purchases of short-term investments	**(109,292)**	(156,553)	(78,549)
Maturities of short-term investments	**92,676**	153,550	61,157
Net cash used in investing activities	**(153,981)**	(122,624)	(108,584)
FINANCING ACTIVITIES			
Dividends paid	**(150,835)**	(135,680)	(118,308)
Common Stock purchased	**(7,679)**	(3,676)	(6,779)
Net cash used in financing activities	**(158,514)**	(139,356)	(125,087)
Effect of exchange rate changes on cash and cash equivalents	**(3,407)**	(7,104)	3,336
Net increase in cash and cash equivalents	**7,945**	25,394	55,508
Cash and cash equivalents at beginning of year	**206,627**	181,233	125,725
Cash and cash equivalents at end of year	**$ 214,572**	206,627	181,233
SUPPLEMENTAL CASH FLOW INFORMATION			
Income taxes paid	**$ 133,530**	126,925	130,499
Interest paid	**$ 1,164**	900	631
Interest and dividends received	**$ 19,458**	16,598	14,477

See accompanying accounting policies and notes.

consolidated balance sheet

	1998	1997
	In thousands of U.S. dollars	
ASSETS		
Current assets:		
Cash and cash equivalents	**$ 214,572**	206,627
Short-term investments, at amortized cost	**137,112**	120,728
Accounts receivable		
(less allowance for doubtful accounts: **1998—$7,564;** 1997—$7,524)	**194,977**	175,967
Inventories—		
Finished goods	**64,934**	63,912
Raw materials and supplies	**191,174**	183,480
	256,108	247,392
Other current assets	**25,376**	30,538
Deferred income taxes—current	**15,027**	16,421
Total current assets	**843,172**	797,673
Marketable equity securities, at fair value	**39,888**	26,375
Deferred charges and other assets	**92,183**	59,566
Deferred income taxes—noncurrent	**25,522**	29,038
Property, plant and equipment, at cost:		
Land	**36,013**	26,298
Buildings and building equipment	**310,212**	277,808
Machinery and equipment	**642,556**	566,766
	988,781	870,872
Less accumulated depreciation	**468,691**	440,398
Net property, plant and equipment	**520,090**	430,474
TOTAL ASSETS	**$1,520,855**	1,343,126

2. Both the current ratio and the quick ratio improved during 1998. In addition, the amount of cash flow from operations was up in 1998, as was the ratio of cash flow from operations to current liabilities. Wrigley appears to be quite liquid and should have no problems meeting its short-term obligations.

3. Wrigley is extremely solvent. Its capital structure reveals that it does not rely in any significant way on long-term debt to finance its business. The amount of noncurrent liabilities is less than 10% of total liabilities and stockholders' equity at the end of each year. In fact, a majority of Wrigley's debt is in the form of interest-free current liabilities. Most revealing is the debt service coverage ratio of 394 times in 1998 and 469 times in 1997. The total interest expense each year is insignificant.

(consolidated balance sheet continued)

	1998	1997
	In thousands of U.S. dollars and shares	
LIABILITIES AND STOCKHOLDERS' EQUITY		
Current liabilities:		
Accounts payable	**$ 76,691**	71,001
Accrued expenses	**67,848**	78,378
Dividends payable	**23,222**	22,034
Income and other taxes payable	**49,491**	53,460
Deferred income taxes—current	**1,374**	943
Total current liabilities	**218,626**	225,816
Deferred income taxes—noncurrent	**40,312**	30,874
Other noncurrent liabilities	**104,885**	101,057
Stockholders' equity:		
Preferred Stock—no par value Authorized: 20,000 shares Issued: None		
Common Stock—no par value		
Common Stock Authorized: 400,000 shares Issued: **1998—93,007 shares;** 1997—92,545 shares	**12,401**	12,339
Class B Common Stock—convertible Authorized: 80,000 shares Issued and outstanding: **1998—23,214 shares;** 1997—23,676 shares	**3,095**	3,157
Additional paid-in capital	**272**	226
Retained earnings	**1,184,617**	1,032,139
Common Stock in treasury, at cost (**1998—111 shares;** 1997—252 shares)	**(6,712)**	(13,363)
Other comprehensive income—		
Foreign currency translation adjustment	**(61,339)**	(65,034)
Unrealized holding gains on marketable equity securities	**24,698**	15,915
	(36,641)	(49,119)
Total stockholders' equity	**1,157,032**	985,379
TOTAL LIABILITIES AND STOCKHOLDERS' EQUITY	**$1,520,855**	1,343,126

See accompanying accounting policies and notes.

4. The return on assets for 1998 is 20%, and the return on common stockholders' equity is 26.3%. Although these return ratios are down slightly from the prior year, they indicate a very profitable company. It should be noted that the company paid nearly half of its 1998 earnings in dividends. Wrigley appears to be a very sound investment, but many other factors, including information on the current market price of the stock, should be considered before making a decision.

Chapter Highlights

1. **LO 1** Various parties, including management, creditors, stockholders, and others, perform financial statement analysis. Care must be exercised, however, in all types of financial analysis. For example, the existence of alternative accounting principles can make comparing different companies difficult. Published financial statements are not adjusted for the effects of inflation, and thus comparisons over time must be made with caution.
2. **LO 2** Horizontal analysis uses comparative financial statements to examine the increases and decreases in items from one period to the next. The analysis can look at the change in items over an extended period of time. Many companies present a summary of selected financial items for a 5- or 10-year period.
3. **LO 3** Vertical analysis involves stating all items on a particular financial statement as a percentage of one item on the statement. For example, all expenses on a common-size income statement are stated as a percentage of net sales. This technique, along with horizontal analysis, can be useful in spotting problem areas within a company.
4. **LO 4** Ratios can be categorized according to their primary purpose. Liquidity ratios indicate the company's ability to pay its debts as they are due. The focus of liquidity analysis is on a company's current assets and current liabilities.
5. **LO 5** Solvency ratios deal with a company's long-term financial health, that is, its ability to repay long-term creditors. The right side of the balance sheet is informative in this respect because it reports on the various sources of capital to the business.
6. **LO 6** Profitability ratios measure how well management has used the assets at its disposal to earn a return for the various providers of capital. Return on assets indicates the return to all providers; return on common stockholders' equity measures the return to the residual owners of the business. Certain other ratios are used to relate a company's performance according to the financial statements with its performance in the stock market.

Key Terms Quiz

Because of the number of terms introduced in this chapter, there are two key term quizzes. For each quiz, read each definition below and then write the number of that definition in the blank beside the appropriate term it defines. The solution appears at the end of the chapter.

Quiz 1:

___ **Horizontal analysis**
___ **Vertical analysis**
___ **Gross profit ratio**
___ **Profit margin ratio**
___ **Liquidity**
___ **Working capital**
___ **Current ratio**
___ **Acid-test or quick ratio**
___ **Cash flow from operations to current liabilities ratio**
___ **Accounts receivable turnover ratio**
___ **Number of days' sales in receivables**
___ **Inventory turnover ratio**
___ **Number of days' sales in inventory**
___ **Cash to cash operating cycle**

1. A stricter test of liquidity than the current ratio; excludes inventory and prepayments from the numerator.
2. Current assets minus current liabilities.
3. The ratio of current assets to current liabilities.
4. A measure of the average age of accounts receivable.
5. A measure of the ability to pay current debts from operating cash flows.
6. A measure of the number of times accounts receivable are collected in a period.
7. A measure of how long it takes to sell inventory.
8. The length of time from the purchase of inventory to the collection of any receivable from the sale.
9. A measure of the number of times inventory is sold during a period.
10. Gross profit to net sales.
11. A comparison of various financial statement items within a single period with the use of common-size statements.
12. Net income to net sales.
13. The nearness to cash of the assets and liabilities.
14. A comparison of financial statement items over a period of time.

Quiz 2:

___ **Solvency**
___ **Debt-to-equity ratio**
___ **Times interest earned ratio**
___ **Debt service coverage ratio**
___ **Cash flow from operations to capital expenditures ratio**
___ **Profitability**
___ **Return on assets ratio**
___ **Return on sales ratio**

___ Asset turnover ratio
___ Return on common stockholders' equity ratio
___ Leverage
673 _5_ Earnings per share
674 _2_ Price/earnings (P/E) ratio
___ Dividend payout ratio
___ Dividend yield ratio

1. A measure of a company's success in earning a return for the common stockholders.
2. The relationship between a company's performance according to the income statement and its performance in the stock market.
3. The ability of a company to remain in business over the long term.
4. A variation of the profit margin ratio; measures earnings before payments to creditors.
5. A company's bottom line stated on a per-share basis.
6. The percentage of earnings paid out as dividends.
7. The ratio of total liabilities to total stockholders' equity.
8. A measure of the ability of a company to finance long-term asset acquisitions with cash from operations.
9. A measure of a company's success in earning a return for all providers of capital.
10. The relationship between net sales and total assets.
11. The relationship between dividends and the market price of a company's stock.
12. The use of borrowed funds and amounts contributed by preferred stockholders to earn an overall return higher than the cost of these funds.
13. An income statement measure of the ability of a company to meet its interest payments.
14. A statement of cash flows measure of the ability of a company to meet its interest and principal payments.
15. How well management is using company resources to earn a return on the funds invested by various groups.

ALTERNATE TERMS

Acid-test ratio Quick ratio

Horizontal analysis Trend analysis

Number of days' sales in receivables Average collection period

Price/earnings ratio P/E ratio

QUESTIONS

1. Two companies are in the same industry. Company A uses the LIFO method of inventory valuation, and Company B uses FIFO. What difficulties does this present when comparing the two companies?
2. You are told to compare the company's results for the year, as measured by various ratios, with one of the published surveys that arranges information by industry classification. What are some of the difficulties you may encounter when making comparisons using industry standards?
3. What types of problems does inflation cause in analyzing financial statements?
4. Distinguish between horizontal and vertical analysis. Why is the analysis of common-size statements called *vertical* analysis? Why is horizontal analysis sometimes called *trend* analysis?
5. A company experiences a 15% increase in sales over the previous year. However, gross profit actually decreased by 5% from the previous year. What are some of the possible causes for an increase in sales but a decline in gross profit?
6. A company's total current assets have increased by 5% over the prior year. Management is concerned, however, about the composition of the current assets. Why is the composition of current assets important?
7. Ratios were categorized in the chapter according to their use in performing three different types of analysis. What are the three types of ratios?
8. Describe the operating cycle for a manufacturing company. How would the cycle differ for a retailer?
9. What accounts for the order in which current assets are presented on a balance sheet?
10. A company has a current ratio of 1.25 but an acid-test or quick ratio of only 0.65. How can this difference in the two ratios be explained? What are some concerns that you would have about this company?
11. Explain the basic concept underlying all turnover ratios. Why is it advisable in computing a turnover ratio to use an average in the denominator (for example, average inventory)?
12. Sanders Company's accounts receivable turned over nine times during the year. The credit department extends terms of 2/10, net 30. Does the turnover ratio indicate any problems that management should investigate?
13. The turnover of inventory for Ace Company has slowed from 6.0 times per year to 4.5 times. What are some of the possible explanations for this decrease?
14. How does the operating cycle for a manufacturer differ from the operating cycle for a service company, for example, an airline?
15. What is the difference between liquidity analysis and solvency analysis?
16. Why is the debt service coverage ratio a better measure of solvency than the times interest earned ratio?

17. A friend tells you that the best way to assess solvency is by comparing total debt to total assets. Another friend says that solvency is measured by comparing total debt to total stockholders' equity. Which one is right?

18. A company is in the process of negotiating with a bank for an additional loan. Why will the bank be very interested in the company's debt service coverage ratio?

19. What is the rationale for deducting dividends when computing the ratio of cash flow from operations to capital expenditures?

20. The rate of return on assets ratio is computed by dividing net income and interest expense, net of tax, by average total assets. Why is the numerator net income and interest expense, net of tax, rather than just net income?

21. A company has a return on assets of 14% and a return on common stockholders' equity of 11%. The president of the company has asked you to explain the reason for this difference. What causes the difference? How is the concept of financial leverage involved?

22. What is meant by the "quality" of a company's earnings? Explain why the price/earnings ratio for a company may indicate the quality of earnings.

23. Some ratios are more useful for management, whereas others are better suited to the needs of outsiders, such as stockholders and bankers. What is an example of a ratio that is primarily suited to management use? What is one that is more suited to use by outsiders?

24. The needs of service-oriented companies in analyzing financial statements differ from those of product-oriented companies. Why is this true? Give an example of a ratio that is meaningless to a service business.

EXERCISES

LO 4 Exercise 13-1 Accounts Receivable Analysis

The following account balances are taken from the records of the Faraway Travel Agency:

	December 31		
	2001	2000	1999
Accounts receivable	$150,000	$100,000	$80,000
	2001	2000	
Net credit sales	$600,000	$540,000	

Faraway extends credit terms requiring full payment in 60 days, with no discount for early payment.

Required

1. Compute Faraway's accounts receivable turnover ratio for 2001 and 2000.
2. Compute the number of days' sales in receivables for 2001 and 2000. Assume 360 days in a year.
3. Comment on the efficiency of Faraway's collection efforts over the two-year period.

LO 4 Exercise 13-2 Inventory Analysis

The following account balances are taken from the records of Lewis Inc., a wholesaler of fresh fruits and vegetables:

	December 31		
	2001	2000	1999
Merchandise inventory	$ 200,000	$ 150,000	$120,000
	2001	2000	
Cost of goods sold	$7,100,000	$8,100,000	

Required

1. Compute Lewis's inventory turnover ratio for 2001 and 2000.
2. Compute the number of days' sales in inventory for 2001 and 2000. Assume 360 days in a year.
3. Comment on your answers in parts **1** and **2** relative to the company's management of inventory over the two years. What problems do you see in its inventory management?

LO 4 Exercise 13-3 Accounts Receivable and Inventory Analyses for Coca-Cola and Pepsi

The following information was obtained from the 1998 and 1997 financial statements of Coca-Cola Company and Subsidiaries and PepsiCo Inc. and Subsidiaries:

www.cocacola.com
www.pepsico.com

(in millions)		Coca-Cola	PepsiCo
Accounts and notes receivable*	12/31/98	$ 1,666	$ 2,453
	12/31/97	1,639	2,150
Inventories	12/31/98	890	1,016
	12/31/97	959	732
Net sales**	1998	18,813	22,348
	1997	18,868	20,917
Cost of goods sold or	1998	5,562	9,330
Cost of sales	1997	6,015	8,525

*Described as "trade accounts" receivable by Coca-Cola.

**Described as "net operating revenues" by Coca-Cola.

Required

1. Using the information provided above, compute the following for each company for 1998:
   a. Accounts receivable turnover ratio
   b. Number of days' sales in receivables
   c. Inventory turnover ratio
   d. Number of days' sales in inventory
   e. Cash to cash operating cycle
2. Comment briefly on the liquidity of each of these two companies.

LO 4 Exercise 13-4 Liquidity Analyses for Coca-Cola and Pepsi

www.cocacola.com
www.pepsico.com

The following information was summarized from the balance sheets of the Coca-Cola Company and Subsidiaries and PepsiCo Inc. and Subsidiaries at December 31, 1998:

(in millions)	Coca-Cola	Pepsi
Cash and cash equivalents	$1,648	$ 311
Short-term investments/marketable securities	159	83
Accounts, notes, and other receivables, net	1,666	2,453
Inventories	890	1,016
Other current assets	2,017	499
Total current assets	$6,380	$4,362
Current liabilities	$8,640	$7,914
Other liabilities	2,102	8,345
Stockholders' equity	8,403	6,401

Required

1. Using the information provided above, compute the following for each company at December 31, 1998:
   a. Current ratio
   b. Quick ratio
2. Comment briefly on the liquidity of each of these two companies. Which appears to be more liquid?
3. What other ratios would help you to more fully assess the liquidity of these companies?

LO 4 Exercise 13-5 Liquidity Analyses for McDonald's and Wendy's

www.mcdonalds.com
www.wendy.com

The following information was summarized from the balance sheets of McDonald's Corporation and Wendy's International Inc. at December 31, 1998 and January 3, 1999, respectively:

	McDonald's (in millions)	Wendy's (in thousands)
Current Assets:		
Cash and cash equivalents	$ 299.2	$ 160,743
Accounts receivable, net*	609.4	74,737
Notes receivable, net	–	19,952

Inventories	$ 77.3	$ 35,085
Other current assets	323.5	23,177
Total current assets	$1,309.4	$ 313,694
Current liabilities	$2,497.1	$ 249,412
Other liabilities	$7,822.6	$ 520,468
Stockholders' equity	$9,464.7	$1,068,067

*McDonald's combines accounts and notes receivable.

Required

1. Using the information provided above, compute the following for each company at year end:
   a. Working capital
   b. Current ratio
   c. Quick ratio
2. Comment briefly on the liquidity of each of these two companies. Which appears to be more liquid?
3. McDonald's reported cash flows from operations of $2,766.3 million during 1998. Wendy's reported cash flows from operations of $233,836 thousand. Current liabilities reported by McDonald's at December 31, 1997, and Wendy's at December 28, 1997, were $2984.5 million and $212,614 thousand, respectively. Calculate the cash flow from operations to current liabilities ratio for each company. Does the information provided by this ratio change your opinion as to the relative liquidity of each of these two companies?
4. What steps might be taken by McDonald's to cover its short-term cash requirements?

LO 5 **Exercise 13-6** Solvency Analyses for Tommy Hilfiger

The following information was obtained from the comparative financial statements included in Tommy Hilfiger Corporation's 1999 annual report (all amounts are in thousands of dollars):

www.hilfiger.com

	March 31, 1999	March 31, 1998
Total liabilities	$1,114,371	$ 98,948
Total shareholders' equity	1,092,249	519,062

	For the Fiscal Years Ended March 31	
	1999	1998
Interest expense	$ 39,525	$ 1,258
Provision for income taxes	72,654	55,590
Net income	173,717	113,180
Net cash provided by operating activities	259,985	110,782
Total dividends paid	—	—
Cash used to purchase property and equipment	79,422	67,814
Payments on long-term debt	10,000	1,510

Required

1. Using the information provided above, compute the following for 1999 and 1998:
   a. Debt-to-equity ratio (at each year-end)
   b. Times interest earned ratio
   c. Debt service coverage ratio
   d. Cash flow from operations to capital expenditures ratio
2. Comment briefly on the company's solvency.

LO 5 **Exercise 13-7** Solvency Analysis

The following information is available from the balance sheets at the ends of the two most recent years and the income statement for the most recent year of Impact Company:

	December 31	
	2001	2000
Accounts payable	$ 65,000	$ 50,000
Accrued liabilities	25,000	35,000
Taxes payable	60,000	45,000
Short-term notes payable	–0–	75,000
Bonds payable due within next year	200,000	200,000
Total current liabilities	$ 350,000	$ 405,000
Bonds payable	$ 600,000	$ 800,000
Common stock, $10 par	$1,000,000	$1,000,000
Retained earnings	650,000	500,000
Total stockholders' equity	$1,650,000	$1,500,000
Total liabilities and stockholders' equity	$2,600,000	$2,705,000

	2001
Sales revenue	$1,600,000
Cost of goods sold	950,000
Gross profit	$ 650,000
Selling and administrative expense	300,000
Operating income	$ 350,000
Interest expense	89,000
Income before tax	$ 261,000
Income tax expense	111,000
Net income	$ 150,000

Other Information

a. Short-term notes payable represents a 12-month loan that matured in November 2001. Interest of 12% was paid at maturity.

b. One million dollars of serial bonds had been issued 10 years earlier. The first series of $200,000 matured at the end of 2001, with interest of 8% payable annually.

c. Cash flow from operations was $185,000 in 2001. The amounts of interest and taxes paid during 2001 were $89,000 and $96,000, respectively.

Required

1. Compute the following for Impact Company:
   a. The debt-to-equity ratio at December 31, 2001, and December 31, 2000
   b. The times interest earned ratio for 2001
   c. The debt service coverage ratio for 2001
2. Comment on Impact's solvency at the end of 2001. Do the times interest earned ratio and the debt service coverage ratio differ in terms of their indication of Impact's ability to pay its debts?

LO 6 **Exercise 13-8** Return Ratios and Leverage

The following selected data are taken from the financial statements of Evergreen Company:

Sales revenue	$ 650,000
Cost of goods sold	400,000
Gross profit	$ 250,000
Selling and administrative expense	100,000
Operating income	$ 150,000
Interest expense	50,000
Income before tax	$ 100,000
Income tax expense (40%)	40,000
Net income	$ 60,000

Accounts payable	$ 45,000
Accrued liabilities	70,000
Income taxes payable	10,000
Interest payable	25,000
Short-term loans payable	150,000
Total current liabilities	$ 300,000
Long-term bonds payable	$ 500,000
Preferred stock, 10%, $100 par	$ 250,000
Common stock, no par	600,000
Retained earnings	350,000
Total stockholders' equity	$1,200,000
Total liabilities and stockholders' equity	$2,000,000

Required

1. Compute the following ratios for Evergreen Company:
   a. Return on sales
   b. Asset turnover (assume that total assets at the beginning of the year were $1,600,000)
   c. Return on assets
   d. Return on common stockholders' equity (assume that the only changes in stockholders' equity during the year were from the net income for the year and dividends on the preferred stock)
2. Comment on Evergreen's use of leverage. Has it successfully employed leverage? Explain your answer.

LO 6 **Exercise 13-9** Relationships among Return on Assets, Return on Sales, and Asset Turnover

A company's return on assets is a function of its ability to turn over its investment (asset turnover) and earn a profit on each dollar of sales (return on sales). For each of the *independent* cases below, determine the missing amounts. (*Note:* Assume in each case that the company has no interest expense; that is, net income is used as the definition of income in all calculations.)

Case 1	
Net income	$ 10,000
Net sales	$ 80,000
Average total assets	$ 60,000
Return on assets	?
Case 2	
Net income	$ 25,000
Average total assets	$250,000
Return on sales	2%
Net sales	?
Case 3	
Average total assets	$ 80,000
Asset turnover	1.5 times
Return on sales	6%
Return on assets	?
Case 4	
Return on assets	10%
Net sales	$ 50,000
Asset turnover	1.25 times
Net income	?
Case 5	
Return on assets	15%
Net income	$ 20,000
Return on sales	5%
Average total assets	?

DECISION MAKING

LO 6 Exercise 13-10 EPS, P/E Ratio, and Dividend Ratios

The stockholders' equity section of the balance sheet for Cooperstown Corp. at the end of 2001 appears as follows:

8%, $100 par, cumulative preferred stock, 200,000 shares authorized, 50,000 shares issued and outstanding	$ 5,000,000
Additional paid-in capital on preferred	2,500,000
Common stock, $5 par, 500,000 shares authorized, 400,000 shares issued and outstanding	2,000,000
Additional paid-in capital on common	18,000,000
Retained earnings	37,500,000
Total stockholders' equity	$65,000,000

Net income for the year was $1,300,000. Dividends were declared and paid on the preferred shares during the year, and a quarterly dividend of $.40 per share was declared and paid each quarter on the common shares. The closing market price for the common shares on December 31, 2001, was $24.75 per share.

Required

1. Compute the following ratios for the common stock:
   a. Earnings per share
   b. Price/earnings ratio
   c. Dividend payout ratio
   d. Dividend yield ratio
2. Assume that you are an investment adviser. What other information would you want to have before advising a client regarding the purchase of Cooperstown stock?

LO 6 Exercise 13-11 Earnings Per Share and Extraordinary Items

The stockholders' equity section of the balance sheet for Lahey Construction Company at the end of 2001 follows:

9%, $10 par, cumulative preferred stock, 500,000 shares authorized, 200,000 shares issued and outstanding	$ 2,000,000
Additional paid-in capital on preferred	7,500,000
Common stock, $1 par, 2,500,000 shares authorized, 1,500,000 shares issued and outstanding	1,500,000
Additional paid-in capital on common	21,000,000
Retained earnings	25,500,000
Total stockholders' equity	$57,500,000

The lower portion of the 2001 income statement indicates the following:

Net income before tax		$9,750,000
Income tax expense (40%)		(3,900,000)
Income before extraordinary items		$5,850,000
Extraordinary loss from flood	$(6,200,000)	
Less: related tax effect (40%)	2,480,000	(3,720,000)
Net income		$2,130,000

Assume the number of shares outstanding did not change during the year.

Required

1. Compute earnings per share *before* extraordinary items.
2. Compute earnings per share *after* the extraordinary loss.

3. Which of the two EPS ratios is more useful to management? Explain your answer. Would your answer be different if the ratios were to be used by an outsider, for example, by a potential stockholder? Why?

Multi-Concept Exercises

LO 2, 3 Exercise 13-12 Common-Size Balance Sheets and Horizontal Analysis
Comparative balance sheets for Farinet Company for the past two years are as follows:

	December 31	
	2001	**2000**
Cash	$ 16,000	$ 20,000
Accounts receivable	40,000	30,000
Inventory	30,000	50,000
Prepaid rent	18,000	12,000
Total current assets	$104,000	$112,000
Land	$150,000	$150,000
Plant and equipment	800,000	600,000
Accumulated depreciation	(130,000)	(60,000)
Total long-term assets	$820,000	$690,000
Total assets	$924,000	$802,000
Accounts payable	$ 24,000	$ 20,000
Income taxes payable	6,000	10,000
Short-term notes payable	70,000	50,000
Total current liabilities	$100,000	$ 80,000
Bonds payable	$150,000	$200,000
Common stock	$400,000	$300,000
Retained earnings	274,000	222,000
Total stockholders' equity	$674,000	$522,000
Total liabilities and stockholders' equity	$924,000	$802,000

Required

1. Using the format in Exhibit 13-5, prepare common-size comparative balance sheets for the two years for Farinet Company.
2. What observations can you make about the changes in the relative composition of Farinet's accounts from the common-size balance sheets? List at least five observations.
3. Using the format in Exhibit 13-1, prepare comparative balance sheets for Farinet Company, including columns both for the dollars and for the percentage increase or decrease in each item on the statement.
4. Identify the four items on the balance sheet that experienced the largest change from one year to the next. For each of these, explain where you would look to find additional information about the change.

LO 2, 3 Exercise 13-13 Common-Size Income Statements and Horizontal Analysis
Income statements for Mariners Corp. for the past two years follow:

	(Amounts in Thousands of Dollars)	
	2001	**2000**
Sales revenue	$60,000	$50,000
Cost of goods sold	42,000	30,000
Gross profit	$18,000	$20,000
Selling and administrative expense	9,000	5,000
Operating income	$ 9,000	$15,000
Interest expense	2,000	2,000
Income before tax	$ 7,000	$13,000
Income tax expense	2,000	4,000
Net income	$ 5,000	$ 9,000

Required

1. Using the format in Exhibit 13-6, prepare common-size comparative income statements for the two years for Mariners Corp.
2. What observations can you make about the common-size statements? List at least four observations.
3. Using the format in Exhibit 13-2, prepare comparative income statements for Mariners Corp., including columns both for the dollars and for the percentage increase or decrease in each item on the statement.
4. Identify the two items on the income statement that experienced the largest change from one year to the next. For each of these, explain where you would look to find additional information about the change.

PROBLEMS

LO 4 **Problem 13-1** Effect of Transactions on Working Capital, Current Ratio, and Quick Ratio

(*Note:* Consider completing Problem 13-2 after this problem to ensure that you obtain a clear understanding of the effect of various transactions on these measures of liquidity.)

The following account balances are taken from the records of Liquiform Inc.:

Cash	$ 70,000
Trading securities (short-term)	60,000
Accounts receivable	80,000
Inventory	100,000
Prepaid insurance	10,000
Accounts payable	75,000
Taxes payable	25,000
Salaries and wages payable	40,000
Short-term loans payable	60,000

Required

1. Use the information provided above to compute the amount of working capital and Liquiform's current and quick ratios (round to three decimal points).
2. Determine the effect that each of the following transactions will have on Liquiform's working capital, current ratio, and quick ratio by recalculating each and then indicating whether the measure is increased, decreased, or not affected by the transaction. (For the ratios, round to three decimal points.) Consider each transaction independently; that is, assume that it is the *only* transaction that takes place.

	Effect of Transaction On:		
Transaction	**Working Capital**	**Current Ratio**	**Quick Ratio**
a. Purchased inventory on account for $20,000.			
b. Purchased inventory for cash, $15,000.			
c. Paid suppliers on account, $30,000.			
d. Received cash on account, $40,000.			
e. Paid insurance for next year, $20,000.			
f. Made sales on account, $60,000.			
g. Repaid short-term loans at bank, $25,000.			
h. Borrowed $40,000 at bank for 90 days.			
i. Declared and paid $45,000 cash dividend.			
j. Purchased $20,000 of trading securities (classified as current assets).			
k. Paid $30,000 in salaries.			
l. Accrued additional $15,000 in taxes.			

LO 4 **Problem 13-2** Effect of Transactions on Working Capital, Current Ratio, and Quick Ratio

(*Note:* Consider completing this problem after Problem 13-1 to ensure that you obtain a clear understanding of the effect of various transactions on these measures of liquidity.)

The following account balances are taken from the records of Veriform Inc.:

Cash	$ 70,000
Trading securities (short-term)	60,000
Accounts receivable	80,000
Inventory	100,000
Prepaid insurance	10,000
Accounts payable	75,000
Taxes payable	25,000
Salaries and wages payable	40,000
Short-term loans payable	210,000

Required

1. Use the information provided above to compute the amount of working capital and Veriform's current and quick ratios (round to three decimal points).
2. Determine the effect that each of the following transactions will have on Veriform's working capital, current ratio, and quick ratio by recalculating each and then indicating whether the measure is increased, decreased, or not affected by the transaction. (For the ratios, round to three decimal points.) Consider each transaction independently; that is, assume that it is the *only* transaction that takes place.

	Effect of Transaction On:		
Transaction	**Working Capital**	**Current Ratio**	**Quick Ratio**
a. Purchased inventory on account for $20,000.			
b. Purchased inventory for cash, $15,000.			
c. Paid suppliers on account, $30,000.			
d. Received cash on account, $40,000.			
e. Paid insurance for next year, $20,000.			
f. Made sales on account, $60,000.			
g. Repaid short-term loans at bank, $25,000.			
h. Borrowed $40,000 at bank for 90 days.			
i. Declared and paid $45,000 cash dividend.			
j. Purchased $20,000 of trading securities (classified as current assets).			
k. Paid $30,000 in salaries.			
l. Accrued additional $15,000 in taxes.			

LO 6 **Problem 13-3** Goals for Sales and Return on Assets

The president of Blue Skies Corp. is reviewing with his vice presidents the operating results of the year just completed. Sales increased by 15% from the previous year to $60,000,000. Average total assets for the year were $40,000,000. Net income, after adding back interest expense, net of tax, was $5,000,000.

The president is happy with the performance over the past year but is never satisfied with the status quo. He has set two specific goals for next year: (1) a 20% growth in sales and (2) a return on assets of 15%.

To achieve the second goal, the president has stated his intention to increase the total asset base by 12.5% over the base for the year just completed.

Required

1. For the year just completed, compute the following ratios:
   a. Return on sales
   b. Asset turnover
   c. Return on assets

2. Compute the necessary asset turnover for next year to achieve the president's goal of a 20% increase in sales.

3. Calculate the income needed next year to achieve the goal of a 15% return on total assets. (*Note:* Assume that *income* is defined as net income plus interest, net of tax.)

4. Based on your answers to parts **2** and **3**, comment on the reasonableness of the president's goals. What must the company focus on to attain these goals?

LO 6 Problem 13-4 Goals for Sales and Income Growth

Sunrise Corp. is a major regional retailer. The chief executive officer (CEO) is concerned with the slow growth both of sales and of net income and the subsequent effect on the trading price of the common stock. Selected financial data for the past three years follow.

SUNRISE CORP.
(IN MILLIONS)

	2001	2000	1999
1. Sales	$200.0	$192.5	$187.0
2. Net income	6.0	5.8	5.6
3. Dividends declared and paid	2.5	2.5	2.5
December 31 balances:			
4. Owners' equity	70.0	66.5	63.2
5. Debt	30.0	29.8	30.3
Selected year-end financial ratios			
Net income to sales	3.0%	3.0%	3.0%
Asset turnover	2 times	2 times	2 times
6. Return on owners' equity*	8.6%	8.7%	8.9%
7. Debt to total assets	30.0%	30.9%	32.4%

*Based on year-end balances in owners' equity.

The CEO believes that the price of the stock has been adversely affected by the downward trend of the return on equity, the relatively low dividend payout ratio, and the lack of dividend increases. To improve the price of the stock, she wants to improve the return on equity and dividends. She believes that the company should be able to meet these objectives by (1) increasing sales and net income at an annual rate of 10% a year and (2) establishing a new dividend policy that calls for a dividend payout of 50% of earnings or $3,000,000, whichever is larger.

The 10% annual sales increase will be accomplished through a new promotional program. The president believes that the present net income to sales ratio of 3% will be unchanged by the cost of this new program and any interest paid on new debt. She expects that the company can accomplish this sales and income growth while maintaining the current relationship of total assets to sales. Any capital that is needed to maintain this relationship and that is not generated internally would be acquired through long-term debt financing. The CEO hopes that debt would not exceed 35% of total liabilities and owners' equity.

Required

1. Using the CEO's program, prepare a schedule that shows the appropriate data for the years 2002, 2003, and 2004 for the items numbered 1 through 7 on the preceding schedule.

2. Can the CEO meet all of her requirements if a 10% per year growth in income and sales is achieved? Explain your answer.

3. What alternative actions should the CEO consider to improve the return on equity and to support increased dividend payments?

2. Explain the reasons that the CEO might have for wanting to limit debt to 35% of total liabilities and owners' equity. (CMA adapted)

Multi-Concept Problems

LO 4, 5, 6 Problem 13-5 Basic Financial Ratios

The accounting staff of CCB Enterprises has completed the financial statements for the 2001 calendar year. The statement of income for the current year and the comparative statements of financial position for 2001 and 2000 follow.

CCB ENTERPRISES
STATEMENT OF INCOME
FOR THE YEAR ENDED DECEMBER 31, 2001
(THOUSANDS OMITTED)

Revenue:	
Net sales	$800,000
Other	60,000
Total revenue	$860,000
Expenses:	
Cost of goods sold	$540,000
Research and development	25,000
Selling and administrative	155,000
Interest	20,000
Total expenses	$740,000
Income before income taxes	$120,000
Income taxes	48,000
Net income	$ 72,000

CCB ENTERPRISES
COMPARATIVE STATEMENTS OF FINANCIAL POSITION
DECEMBER 31, 2001 AND 2000
(THOUSANDS OMITTED)

	2001	2000
Assets		
Current assets:		
Cash and short-term investments	$ 26,000	$ 21,000
Receivables, less allowance for doubtful accounts ($1,100 in 2001 and $1,400 in 2000)	48,000	50,000
Inventories, at lower of FIFO cost or market	65,000	62,000
Prepaid items and other current assets	5,000	3,000
Total current assets	$144,000	$136,000
Other assets:		
Investments, at cost	$106,000	$106,000
Deposits	10,000	8,000
Total other assets	$116,000	$114,000
Property, plant, and equipment:		
Land	$ 12,000	$ 12,000
Buildings and equipment, less accumulated depreciation ($126,000 in 2001 and $122,000 in 2000)	268,000	248,000
Total property, plant, and equipment	$280,000	$260,000
Total assets	$540,000	$510,000
Liabilities and Stockholders' Equity		
Current liabilities:		
Short-term loans	$ 22,000	$ 24,000
Accounts payable	72,000	71,000
Salaries, wages, and other	26,000	27,000
Total current liabilities	$120,000	$122,000
Long-term debt	$160,000	$171,000
Total liabilities	$280,000	$293,000
Stockholders' equity:		
Common stock, at par	$ 44,000	$ 42,000
Paid-in capital in excess of par	64,000	61,000
Total paid-in capital	$108,000	$103,000
Retained earnings	152,000	114,000
Total stockholders' equity	$260,000	$217,000
Total liabilities and stockholders' equity	$540,000	$510,000

Required:

1. Calculate the following financial ratios for 2001 for CCB Enterprises:
   - **a.** Times interest earned
   - **b.** Return on total assets
   - **c.** Return on common stockholders' equity
   - **d.** Debt-equity ratio (at December 31, 2001)
   - **e.** Current ratio (at December 31, 2001)
   - **f.** Quick (acid-test) ratio (at December 31, 2001)
   - **g.** Accounts receivable turnover ratio (assume that all sales are on credit)
   - **h.** Number of days' sales in receivables
   - **i.** Inventory turnover ratio (assume that all purchases are on credit)
   - **j.** Number of days' sales in inventory
   - **k.** Number of days in cash operating cycle
2. Prepare a few brief comments on the overall financial health of CCB Enterprises. For each comment, indicate any information that is not provided in the problem and that you would need to fully evaluate the company's financial health. (CMA adapted)

LO 5, 6 **Problem 13-6** Projected Results to Meet Corporate Objectives

Tablon Inc. is a wholly owned subsidiary of Marbel Co. The philosophy of Marbel's management is to allow the subsidiaries to operate as independent units. Corporate control is exercised through the establishment of minimum objectives for each subsidiary, accompanied by substantial rewards for success and penalties for failure. The time period for performance review is long enough for competent managers to display their abilities.

Each quarter the subsidiary is required to submit financial statements. The statements are accompanied by a letter from the subsidiary president explaining the results to date, a forecast for the remainder of the year, and the actions to be taken to achieve the objectives if the forecast indicates that the objectives will not be met.

Marbel management, in conjunction with Tablon management, had set the objectives listed below for the year ending May 31, 2002. These objectives are similar to those set in previous years.

- Sales growth of 20%
- Return on stockholders' equity of 15%
- A long-term debt-to-equity ratio of not more than 1.0
- Payment of a cash dividend of 50% of net income, with a minimum payment of at least $400,000

Tablon's controller has just completed the financial statements for the six months ended November 30, 2001, and the forecast for the year ending May 31, 2002. The statements are presented below.

After a cursory glance at the financial statements, Tablon's president concluded that not all objectives would be met. At a staff meeting of the Tablon management, the president asked the controller to review the projected results and recommend possible actions that could be taken during the remainder of the year so that Tablon would be more likely to meet the objectives.

TABLON INC.
INCOME STATEMENT
(THOUSANDS OMITTED)

	Year Ended May 31, 2001	Six Months Ended November 30, 2001	Forecast for Year Ending May 31, 2002
Sales	$25,000	$15,000	$30,000
Cost of goods sold	$13,000	$ 8,000	$16,000
Selling expenses	5,000	3,500	7,000
Administrative expenses and interest	4,000	2,500	5,000
Income taxes (40%)	1,200	400	800
Total expenses and taxes	$23,200	$14,400	$28,800
Net income	$ 1,800	$ 600	$ 1,200
Dividends declared and paid	600	0	600
Income retained	$ 1,200	$ 600	$ 600

TABLON INC.
STATEMENT OF FINANCIAL POSITION
THOUSANDS OMITTED)

	May 31, 2001	November 30, 2001	Forecast for May 31, 2002
Assets			
Cash	$ 400	$ 500	$ 500
Accounts receivable (net)	4,100	6,500	7,100
Inventory	7,000	8,500	8,600
Plant and equipment (net)	6,500	7,000	7,300
Total assets	$18,000	$22,500	$23,500
Liabilities and Equities			
Accounts payable	$ 3,000	$ 4,000	$ 4,000
Accrued taxes	300	200	200
Long-term borrowing	6,000	9,000	10,000
Common stock	5,000	5,000	5,000
Retained earnings	3,700	4,300	4,300
Total liabilities and equities	$18,000	$22,500	$23,500

Required

1. Calculate the projected results for each of the four objectives established for Tablon Inc. State which results will not meet the objectives by year-end.
2. From the data presented, identify the factors that seem to contribute to the failure of Tablon Inc. to meet all of its objectives.
3. Explain the possible actions that the controller could recommend in response to the president's request.

(CMA adapted)

LO 4, 5, 6 **Problem 13-7** Comparison with Industry Averages

Heartland Inc. is a medium-size company that has been in business for 20 years. The industry has become very competitive in the last few years, and Heartland has decided that it must grow if it is going to survive. It has approached the bank for a sizable five-year loan, and the bank has requested its most recent financial statements as part of the loan package.

The industry in which Heartland operates consists of approximately 20 companies relatively equal in size. The trade association to which all of the competitors belong publishes an annual survey of the industry, including industry averages for selected ratios for the competitors. All companies voluntarily submit their statements to the association for this purpose.

Heartland's controller is aware that the bank has access to this survey and is very concerned about how the company fared this past year compared with the rest of the industry. The ratios included in the publication, and the averages for the past year, are as follows:

Ratio	Industry Average
Current ratio	1.23
Acid-test (quick) ratio	0.75
Accounts receivable turnover	33 times
Inventory turnover	29 times
Debt-to-equity ratio	0.53
Times interest earned	8.65 times
Return on sales	6.57%
Asset turnover	1.95 times
Return on assets	12.81%
Return on common stockholders' equity	17.67%

The financial statements to be submitted to the bank in connection with the loan follow:

HEARTLAND INC.
STATEMENT OF INCOME AND RETAINED EARNINGS
FOR THE YEAR ENDED DECEMBER 31, 2001
(THOUSANDS OMITTED)

Sales revenue	$542,750
Cost of goods sold	(435,650)
Gross margin	$107,100
Selling, general, and administrative expenses	(65,780)
Loss on sales of securities	(220)
Income before interest and taxes	$ 41,100
Interest expense	(9,275)
Income before taxes	$ 31,825
Income tax expense	(12,730)
Net income	$ 19,095
Retained earnings, January 1, 2001	58,485
	$ 77,580
Dividends paid on common stock	(12,000)
Retained earnings, December 31, 2001	$ 65,580

HEARTLAND INC.
COMPARATIVE STATEMENTS OF FINANCIAL POSITION
(THOUSANDS OMITTED)

	December 31, 2001	December 31, 2000
Assets		
Current assets:		
Cash	$ 1,135	$ 750
Marketable securities	1,250	2,250
Accounts receivable, net of allowances	15,650	12,380
Inventories	12,680	15,870
Prepaid items	385	420
Total current assets	$ 31,100	$ 31,670
Long-term investments	$ 425	$ 425
Property, plant, and equipment:		
Land	$ 32,000	$ 32,000
Buildings and equipment, net of accumulated depreciation	216,000	206,000
Total property, plant, and equipment	$248,000	$238,000
Total assets	$279,525	$270,095
Liabilities and Stockholders' Equity		
Current liabilities:		
Short-term notes	$ 8,750	$ 12,750
Accounts payable	20,090	14,380
Salaries and wages payable	1,975	2,430
Income taxes payable	3,130	2,050
Total current liabilities	$ 33,945	$ 31,610
Long-term bonds payable	$ 80,000	$ 80,000
Stockholders' equity:		
Common stock, no par	$100,000	$100,000
Retained earnings	65,580	58,485
Total stockholders' equity	$165,580	$158,485
Total liabilities and stockholders' equity	$279,525	$270,095

Required

1. Prepare a columnar report for the controller of Heartland Inc., comparing the industry averages for the ratios published by the trade association with the comparable ratios for Heartland. For Heartland, compute the ratios as of December 31, 2001, or for the year ending December 31, 2001, whichever is appropriate.
2. Briefly evaluate Heartland's ratios relative to the industry averages.
3. Do you think that the bank will approve the loan? Explain your answer.

ALTERNATE PROBLEMS

LO 5 Problem 13-1A Effect of Transactions on Debt-To-Equity Ratio
(*Note:* Consider completing Problem 13-2A after this problem to ensure that you obtain a clear understanding of the effect of various transactions on this measure of solvency.)

The following account balances are taken from the records of Monet's Garden Inc.:

Current liabilities	$150,000
Long-term liabilities	375,000
Stockholders' equity	400,000

Required

1. Use the information provided above to compute Monet's debt-to-equity ratio (round to three decimal points).
2. Determine the effect that each of the following transactions will have on Monet's debt-to-equity ratio by recalculating the ratio and then indicating whether the ratio is increased, decreased, or not affected by the transaction. (Round to three decimal points.) Consider each transaction independently; that is, assume that it is the *only* transaction that takes place.

Transaction	Effect of Transaction on Debt-To-Equity Ratio
a. Purchased inventory on account for $20,000.	
b. Purchased inventory for cash, $15,000.	
c. Paid suppliers on account, $30,000.	
d. Received cash on account, $40,000.	
e. Paid insurance for next year, $20,000.	
f. Made sales on account, $60,000.	
g. Repaid short-term loans at bank, $25,000.	
h. Borrowed $40,000 at bank for 90 days.	
i. Declared and paid $45,000 cash dividend.	
j. Purchased $20,000 of trading securities (classified as current assets).	
k. Paid $30,000 in salaries.	
l. Accrued additional $15,000 in taxes.	

LO 5 Problem 13-2A Effect of Transactions on Debt-To-Equity Ratio
(*Note:* Consider completing this problem after Problem 13-1A to ensure that you obtain a clear understanding of the effect of various transactions on this measure of solvency.)

The following account balances are taken from the records of Degas Inc.:

Current liabilities	$ 25,000
Long-term liabilities	125,000
Stockholders' equity	400,000

Required

1. Use the information provided above to compute Degas' debt-to-equity ratio (round to three decimal points).

2. Determine the effect that each of the following transactions will have on Degas's debt-to-equity ratio by recalculating the ratio and then indicating whether the ratio is increased, decreased, or not affected by the transaction. (Round to three decimal points.) Consider each transaction independently; that is, assume that it is the *only* transaction that takes place.

Transaction	**Effect of Transaction on Debt-To-Equity Ratio**
a. Purchased inventory on account for $20,000.	
b. Purchased inventory for cash, $15,000.	
c. Paid suppliers on account, $30,000.	
d. Received cash on account, $40,000.	
e. Paid insurance for next year, $20,000.	
f. Made sales on account, $60,000.	
g. Repaid short-term loans at bank, $25,000.	
h. Borrowed $40,000 at bank for 90 days.	
i. Declared and paid $45,000 cash dividend.	
j. Purchased $20,000 of trading securities (classified as current assets).	
k. Paid $30,000 in salaries.	
l. Accrued additional $15,000 in taxes.	

DECISION MAKING

LO 6 **Problem 13-3A** Goals for Sales and Return on Assets

The president of Blue Moon Corp. is reviewing with her department managers the operating results of the year just completed. Sales increased by 12% from the previous year to $750,000. Average total assets for the year were $400,000. Net income, after adding back interest expense, net of tax, was $60,000.

The president is happy with the performance over the past year but is never satisfied with the status quo. She has set two specific goals for next year: (1) a 15% growth in sales and (2) a return on assets of 20%.

To achieve the second goal, the president has stated her intention to increase the total asset base by 10% over the base for the year just completed.

Required

1. For the year just completed, compute the following ratios:
   - **a.** Return on sales
   - **b.** Asset turnover
   - **c.** Return on assets
2. Compute the necessary asset turnover for next year to achieve the president's goal of a 15% increase in sales.
3. Calculate the income needed next year to achieve the goal of a 20% return on total assets. (*Note:* Assume that *income* is defined as net income plus interest, net of tax.)
4. Based on your answers to parts 2 and 3, comment on the reasonableness of the president's goals. What must the company focus on to attain these goals?

DECISION MAKING

SPREADSHEET

LO 6 **Problem 13-4A** Goals for Sales and Income Growth

Sunset Corp. is a major regional retailer. The chief executive officer (CEO) is concerned with the slow growth both of sales and of net income and the subsequent effect on the trading price of the common stock. Selected financial data for the past three years follow.

SUNSET CORP.
(IN MILLIONS)

	2001	**2000**	**1999**
1. Sales	$100.0	$96.7	$93.3
2. Net income	3.0	2.9	2.8
3. Dividends declared and paid	1.2	1.2	1.2

December 31 balances:			
4. Owners' equity	$ 40.0	$38.2	$36.5
5. Debt	10.0	10.2	10.2
Selected year-end financial ratios			
Net income to sales	3.0%	3.0%	3.0%
Asset turnover	2 times	2 times	2 times
6. Return on owners' equity*	7.5%	7.6%	7.7%
7. Debt to total assets	20.0%	21.1%	21.8%

*Based on year-end balances in owners' equity.

The CEO believes that the price of the stock has been adversely affected by the downward trend of the return on equity, the relatively low dividend payout ratio, and the lack of dividend increases. To improve the price of the stock, he wants to improve the return on equity and dividends.

He believes that the company should be able to meet these objectives by (1) increasing sales and net income at an annual rate of 10% a year and (2) establishing a new dividend policy that calls for a dividend payout of 60% of earnings or $2,000,000, whichever is larger.

The 10% annual sales increase will be accomplished through a product enhancement program. The president believes that the present net income to sales ratio of 3% will be unchanged by the cost of this new program and any interest paid on new debt. He expects that the company can accomplish this sales and income growth while maintaining the current relationship of total assets to sales. Any capital that is needed to maintain this relationship and that is not generated internally would be acquired through long-term debt financing. The CEO hopes that debt would not exceed 25% of total liabilities and owners' equity.

Required

1. Using the CEO's program, prepare a schedule that shows the appropriate data for the years 2002, 2003, and 2004 for the items numbered 1 through 7 on the preceding schedule.
2. Can the CEO meet all of his requirements if a 10% per-year growth in income and sales is achieved? Explain your answers.
3. What alternative actions should the CEO consider to improve the return on equity and to support increased dividend payments? (CMA adapted)

Alternate Multi-Concept Problems

LO 4, 5, 6 **Problem 13-5A** Basic Financial Ratios

The accounting staff of SST Enterprises has completed the financial statements for the 2001 calendar year. The statement of income for the current year and the comparative statements of financial position for 2001 and 2000 follow.

SST ENTERPRISES
STATEMENT OF INCOME
YEAR ENDED DECEMBER 31, 2001
(THOUSANDS OMITTED)

Revenue:	
Net sales	$600,000
Other	45,000
Total revenue	$645,000
Expenses:	
Cost of goods sold	$405,000
Research and development	18,000
Selling and administrative	120,000
Interest	15,000
Total expenses	$558,000
Income before income taxes	$ 87,000
Income taxes	27,000
Net income	$ 60,000

SST ENTERPRISES
COMPARATIVE STATEMENTS OF FINANCIAL POSITION
DECEMBER 31, 2001 AND 2000
(THOUSANDS OMITTED)

	2001	2000
Assets		
Current assets:		
Cash and short-term investments	$ 27,000	$ 20,000
Receivables, less allowance for doubtful accounts ($1,100 in 2001 and $1,400 in 2000)	36,000	37,000
Inventories, at lower of FIFO cost or market	35,000	42,000
Prepaid items and other current assets	2,000	1,000
Total current assets	$100,000	$100,000
Property, plant, and equipment:		
Land	$ 9,000	$ 9,000
Buildings and equipment, less accumulated depreciation ($74,000 in 2001 and $62,000 in 2000)	191,000	186,000
Total property, plant, and equipment	$200,000	$195,000
Total assets	$300,000	$295,000
Liabilities and Stockholders' Equity		
Current liabilities:		
Short-term loans	$ 20,000	$ 15,000
Accounts payable	80,000	68,000
Salaries, wages, and other	5,000	7,000
Total current liabilities	$105,000	$ 90,000
Long-term debt	15,000	40,000
Total liabilities	$120,000	$130,000
Stockholders' equity:		
Common stock, at par	$ 50,000	$ 50,000
Paid-in capital in excess of par	25,000	25,000
Total paid-in capital	$ 75,000	$ 75,000
Retained earnings	105,000	90,000
Total stockholders' equity	$180,000	$165,000
Total liabilities and stockholders' equity	$300,000	$295,000

Required

1. Calculate the following financial ratios for 2001 for SST Enterprises:
   a. Times interest earned
   b. Return on total assets
   c. Return on common stockholders' equity
   d. Debt-equity ratio (at December 31, 2001)
   e. Current ratio (at December 31, 2001)
   f. Quick (acid-test) ratio (at December 31, 2001)
   g. Accounts receivable turnover ratio (assume that all sales are on credit)
   h. Number of days' sales in receivables
   i. Inventory turnover ratio (assume that all purchases are on credit)
   j. Number of days' sales in inventory
   k. Number of days in cash operating cycle
2. Prepare a few brief comments on the overall financial health of SST Enterprises. For each comment, indicate any information that is not provided in the problem and that you would need to fully evaluate the company's financial health.

(CMA adapted)

LO 5, 6 Problem 13-6A Projected Results to Meet Corporate Objectives

Grout Inc. is a wholly owned subsidiary of Slait Co. The philosophy of Slait's management is to allow the subsidiaries to operate as independent units. Corporate control is exercised through the establishment of minimum objectives for each subsidiary, accompanied by substantial rewards for success and penalties for failure. The time period for performance review is long enough for competent managers to display their abilities.

Each quarter the subsidiary is required to submit financial statements. The statements are accompanied by a letter from the subsidiary president explaining the results to date, a forecast for the remainder of the year, and the actions to be taken to achieve the objectives if the forecast indicates that the objectives will not be met.

Slait management, in conjunction with Grout management, had set the objectives listed below for the year ending September 30, 2002. These objectives are similar to those set in previous years.

- Sales growth of 10%
- Return on stockholders' equity of 20%
- A long-term debt-to-equity ratio of not more than 1.0
- Payment of a cash dividend of 50% of net income, with a minimum payment of at least $500,000

Grout's controller has just completed preparing the financial statements for the six months ended March 31, 2002, and the forecast for the year ending September 30, 2002. The statements are presented below.

After a cursory glance at the financial statements, Grout's president concluded that not all objectives would be met. At a staff meeting of the Grout management, the president asked the controller to review the projected results and recommend possible actions that could be taken during the remainder of the year so that Grout would be more likely to meet the objectives.

GROUT INC.
INCOME STATEMENT
(THOUSANDS OMITTED)

	Year Ended September 30, 2001	Six Months Ended March 31, 2002	Forecast for Year Ending September 30, 2002
Sales	$10,000	$6,000	$12,000
Cost of goods sold	$ 6,000	$4,000	$ 8,000
Selling expenses	1,500	900	1,800
Administrative expenses and interest	1,000	600	1,200
Income taxes	500	300	600
Total expenses and taxes	$ 9,000	$5,800	$11,600
Net income	$ 1,000	$ 200	$ 400
Dividends declared and paid	500	0	400
Income retained	$ 500	$ 200	$ 0

GROUT INC.
STATEMENT OF FINANCIAL POSITION
(THOUSANDS OMITTED)

	September 30, 2001	March 31, 2002	Forecast for September 30, 2002
Assets			
Cash	$ 400	$ 500	$ 500
Accounts receivable (net)	2,100	3,400	2,600
Inventory	7,000	8,500	8,400
Plant and equipment (net)	2,800	2,500	3,200
Total assets	$12,300	$14,900	$14,700

Liabilities and Equities			
Accounts payable	$ 3,000	$ 4,000	$ 4,000
Accrued taxes	300	200	200
Long-term borrowing	4,000	5,500	5,500
Common stock	4,000	4,000	4,000
Retained earnings	1,000	1,200	1,000
Total liabilities and equities	$12,300	$14,900	$14,700

Required

1. Calculate the projected results for each of the four objectives established for Grout Inc. State which results will not meet the objectives by year-end.
2. From the data presented, identify the factors that seem to contribute to the failure of Grout Inc. to meet all of its objectives.
3. Explain the possible actions that the controller could recommend in response to the president's request. (CMA adapted)

LO 4, 5, 6 Problem 13-7A A Comparison with Industry Averages

Midwest Inc. is a medium-size company that has been in business for 20 years. The industry has become very competitive in the last few years, and Midwest has decided that it must grow if it is going to survive. It has approached the bank for a sizable five-year loan, and the bank has requested its most recent financial statements as part of the loan package.

The industry in which Midwest operates consists of approximately 20 companies relatively equal in size. The trade association to which all of the competitors belong publishes an annual survey of the industry, including industry averages for selected ratios for the competitors. All companies voluntarily submit their statements to the association for this purpose.

Midwest's controller is aware that the bank has access to this survey and is very concerned about how the company fared this past year compared with the rest of the industry. The ratios included in the publication, and the averages for the past year, are as follows:

Ratio	Industry Average
Current ratio	1.20
Acid-test (quick) ratio	0.50
Inventory turnover	35 times
Debt-to-equity ratio	0.50
Times interest earned	25 times
Return on sales	3%
Asset turnover	3.5 times
Return on common stockholders' equity	20%

The financial statements to be submitted to the bank in connection with the loan follow:

MIDWEST INC.
STATEMENT OF INCOME AND RETAINED EARNINGS
FOR THE YEAR ENDED DECEMBER 31, 2001
(THOUSANDS OMITTED)

Sales revenue	$420,500
Cost of goods sold	(300,000)
Gross margin	$120,500
Selling, general, and administrative expenses	(85,000)
Income before interest and taxes	$ 35,500
Interest expense	(8,600)
Income before taxes	$ 26,900
Income tax expense	(12,000)
Net income	$ 14,900
Retained earnings, January 1, 2001	12,400
	$ 27,300
Dividends paid on common stock	(11,200)
Retained earnings, December 31, 2001	$ 16,100

MIDWEST INC.
COMPARATIVE STATEMENTS OF FINANCIAL POSITION
(THOUSANDS OMITTED)

	December 31, 2001	December 31, 2000
Assets		
Current assets:		
Cash	$ 1,790	$ 2,600
Marketable securities	1,200	1,700
Accounts receivable, net of allowances	400	600
Inventories	8,700	7,400
Prepaid items	350	400
Total current assets	$ 12,440	$ 12,700
Long-term investments	$ 560	$ 400
Property, plant, and equipment:		
Land	$ 12,000	$ 12,000
Buildings and equipment, net of accumulated depreciation	87,000	82,900
Total property, plant, and equipment	$ 99,000	$ 94,900
Total assets	$112,000	$108,000
Liabilities and Stockholders' Equity		
Current liabilities:		
Short-term notes	$ 800	$ 600
Accounts payable	6,040	6,775
Salaries and wages payable	1,500	1,200
Income taxes payable	1,560	1,025
Total current liabilities	$ 9,900	$ 9,600
Long-term bonds payable	$ 36,000	$ 36,000
Stockholders' equity:		
Common stock, no par	$ 50,000	$ 50,000
Retained earnings	16,100	12,400
Total stockholders' equity	$ 66,100	$ 62,400
Total liabilities and stockholders' equity	$112,000	$108,000

Required

1. Prepare a columnar report for the controller of Midwest Inc., comparing the industry averages for the ratios published by the trade association with the comparable ratios for Midwest. For Midwest, compute the ratios as of December 31, 2001, or for the year ending December 31, 2001, whichever is appropriate.
2. Briefly evaluate Midwest's ratios relative to the industry.
3. Do you think that the bank will approve the loan? Explain your answer.

CASES

Reading and Interpreting Financial Statements

LO 2 **Case 13-1** Horizontal Analysis for Ben & Jerry's

Refer to Ben & Jerry's comparative income statements included in its annual report.

Required

1. Prepare a work sheet with the following headings:

	Increase (Decrease) From			
	1997 to 1998		1996 to 1997	
Income Statement Accounts	**Dollars**	**Percent**	**Dollars**	**Percent**

2. Complete the work sheet using each of the account titles on Ben & Jerry's income statement. Round dollar amounts to the nearest one-tenth of $1 million and percentages to the nearest one-tenth of a percent.
3. What observations can you make from this horizontal analysis? What is your overall analysis of operations? Has the company's operations improved over the three-year period?

LO 2 Case 13-2 Horizontal Analysis for Gateway

Refer to Gateway's comparative income statements included in its annual report.

Required

Refer to the requirements in Case 13-1 and respond to each of them for Gateway rather than for Ben & Jerry's.

LO 3 Case 13-3 Vertical Analysis for Ben & Jerry's

Refer to Ben & Jerry's financial statements included in its annual report.

Required

1. Using the format in Exhibit 13-6, prepare common-size comparative income statements for 1998 and 1997. Round dollar amounts to the nearest one-tenth of $1 million and percentages to the nearest one-tenth of a percent.
2. What changes do you detect in the income statement relationships from 1997 to 1998?
3. Using the format in Exhibit 13-5, prepare common-size comparative balance sheets at the end of 1998 and 1997. Round dollar amounts to the nearest one-tenth of $1 million and percentages to the nearest one-tenth of a percent.
4. What observations can you make about the relative composition of Ben & Jerry's assets from the common-size statements? What observations can be made about the changes in the relative composition of liabilities and owners' equity accounts?

LO 3 Case 13-4 Vertical Analysis for Gateway

Refer to Gateway's financial statements in its annual report.

Required

Refer to the requirements in Case 13-3 and respond to each of them for Gateway rather than for Ben & Jerry's.

LO 4, 5, 6 Case 13-5 Ratio Analysis for Ben & Jerry's

Refer to Ben & Jerry's financial statements included in its annual report.

Required

1. Compute the following ratios and other amounts for each of the two years, 1998 and 1997. Because only two years of data are given on the balance sheets, to be consistent you should use year-end balances for each year in lieu of average balances. Assume a 40% tax rate and 360 days to a year. State any other necessary assumptions in making the calculations. Round all ratios to the nearest one-tenth of a percent.
   a. Working capital
   b. Current ratio
   c. Acid-test ratio
   d. Cash flow from operations to current liabilities
   e. Number of days' sales in receivables
   f. Number of days' sales in inventory
   g. Debt-to-equity ratio
   h. Times interest earned
   i. Debt service coverage

j. Cash flow from operations to capital expenditures

k. Asset turnover

l. Return on sales

m. Return on assets

n. Return on common stockholders' equity

2. What is your overall analysis of the financial health of Ben & Jerry's? What do you believe are the company's strengths and weaknesses?

LO 4, 5, 6 Case 13-6 Ratio Analysis for Gateway

Refer to Gateway's financial statements included in its annual report.

Required

Refer to the requirements in Case 13-5 and respond to each of them for Gateway rather than Ben & Jerry's.

Making Financial Decisions

LO 4, 5, 6 Case 13-7 Acquisition Decision

Diversified Industries is a large conglomerate and is continually in the market for new acquisitions. The company has grown rapidly over the last 10 years through buyouts of medium-size companies. Diversified does not limit itself to companies in any one industry but looks for firms with a sound financial base and the ability to stand on their own financially.

The president of Diversified recently told a meeting of the company's officers: "I want to impress two points on all of you. First, we are not in the business of looking for bargains. Diversified has achieved success in the past by acquiring companies with the ability to be a permanent member of the corporate family. We don't want companies that may appear to be a bargain on paper but can't survive in the long run. Second, a new member of our family must be able to come in and make it on its own—the parent is not organized to be a funding agency for struggling subsidiaries."

Ron Dixon is the vice president of acquisitions for Diversified, a position he has held for five years. He is responsible for making recommendations to the board of directors on potential acquisitions. Because you are one of his assistants, he recently brought you a set of financials for a manufacturer, Heavy Duty Tractors. Dixon believes that Heavy Duty is a "can't-miss" opportunity for Diversified and asks you to confirm his hunch by performing basic financial statement analysis on the company. The most recent income statement and comparative balance sheets for the company follow:

HEAVY DUTY TRACTORS INC.
STATEMENT OF INCOME AND RETAINED EARNINGS
FOR THE YEAR ENDED DECEMBER 31, 2001
(THOUSANDS OMITTED)

Sales Revenue	$875,250
Cost of goods sold	542,750
Gross margin	$332,500
Selling, general, and administrative expenses	264,360
Operating income	$ 68,140
Interest expense	45,000
Net income before taxes and extraordinary items	$ 23,140
Income tax expense	9,250
Income before extraordinary items	$ 13,890
Extraordinary gain, less taxes of $6,000	9,000
Net income	$ 22,890
Retained earnings, January 1, 2001	169,820
	$192,710
Dividends paid on common stock	10,000
Retained earnings, December 31, 2001	$182,710

HEAVY DUTY TRACTORS INC.
COMPARATIVE STATEMENTS OF FINANCIAL POSITION
(THOUSANDS OMITTED)

	December 31, 2001	December 31, 2000
Assets		
Current assets:		
Cash	$ 48,500	$ 24,980
Marketable securities	3,750	–0–
Accounts receivable, net of allowances	128,420	84,120
Inventories	135,850	96,780
Prepaid items	7,600	9,300
Total current assets	$324,120	$215,180
Long-term investments	$ 55,890	$ 55,890
Property, plant, and equipment:		
Land	$ 45,000	$ 45,000
Buildings and equipment, less accumulated depreciation of $385,000 in 2001 and $325,000 in 2000	545,000	605,000
Total property, plant, and equipment	$590,000	$650,000
Total assets	$970,010	$921,070
Liabilities and Stockholders' Equity		
Current liabilities:		
Short-term notes	$ 80,000	$ 60,000
Accounts payable	65,350	48,760
Salaries and wages payable	14,360	13,840
Income taxes payable	2,590	3,650
Total current liabilities	$162,300	$126,250
Long-term bonds payable, due 2008	$275,000	$275,000
Stockholders' equity:		
Common stock, no par	$350,000	$350,000
Retained earnings	182,710	169,820
Total stockholders' equity	$532,710	$519,820
Total liabilities and stockholders' equity	$970,010	$921,070

Required

1. How liquid is Heavy Duty Tractors? Support your answer with any ratios that you believe are necessary to justify your conclusion. Also indicate any other information that you would want to have in making a final determination on its liquidity.
2. In light of the president's comments, should you be concerned about the solvency of Heavy Duty Tractors? Support your answer with the necessary ratios. How does the maturity date of the outstanding debt affect your answer?
3. Has Heavy Duty demonstrated the ability to be a profitable member of the Diversified family? Support your answer with the necessary ratios.
4. What will you tell your boss? Should he recommend to the board of directors that Diversified put in a bid for Heavy Duty Tractors?

LO 3 **Case 13-8** Pricing Decision

BPO's management believes that the company has been successful at increasing sales because it has not increased the selling price of the products, even though its competition has increased prices and costs have increased. Price and cost relationships in Year 1 were established because they represented industry averages. The following income statements are available for BPO's first three years of operation:

	Year 3	Year 2	Year 1
Sales	$125,000	$110,000	$100,000
Cost of goods sold	62,000	49,000	40,000
Gross profit	$ 63,000	$ 61,000	$ 60,000
Operating expenses	53,000	49,000	45,000
Net income	$ 10,000	$ 12,000	$ 15,000

Required

1. Using the format in Exhibit 13-6, prepare common-size comparative income statements for the three years.
2. Explain why net income has decreased while sales have increased.
3. Prepare an income statement for Year 4. Sales volume in units is expected to increase by 10%, and costs are expected to increase by 8%.
4. Do you think BPO should raise its prices or maintain the same selling prices? Explain your answer.

Accounting and Ethics: What Would You Do?

LO 4, 5 Case 13-9 Provisions in a Loan Agreement

As controller of Midwest Construction Company, you are reviewing with your assistant, Dave Jackson, the financial statements for the year just ended. During the review, Jackson reminds you of an existing loan agreement with Southern National Bank. Midwest has agreed to the following conditions:

- The current ratio will be maintained at a minimum level of 1.5 to 1.0 at all times.
- The debt-to-equity ratio will not exceed .5 to 1.0 at any time.

Jackson has drawn up the following preliminary, condensed balance sheet for the year just ended:

MIDWEST CONSTRUCTION COMPANY
BALANCE SHEET
DECEMBER 31
(IN MILLIONS OF DOLLARS)

Current assets	$16	Current liabilities	$10
Long-term assets	64	Long-term debt	15
		Stockholders' equity	55
Total	$80	Total	$80

Jackson wants to discuss two items with you. First, long-term debt currently includes a $5 million note payable, to Eastern State Bank, that is due in six months. The plan is to go to Eastern before the note is due and ask it to extend the maturity date of the note for five years. Jackson doesn't believe that Midwest needs to include the $5 million in current liabilities because the plan is to roll over the note.

Second, in December of this year, Midwest received a $2 million deposit from the state for a major road project. The contract calls for the work to be performed over the next 18 months. Jackson recorded the $2 million as revenue this year because the contract is with the state; there shouldn't be any question about being able to collect.

Required

1. Based on the balance sheet Jackson prepared, is Midwest in compliance with its loan agreement with Southern? Support your answer with any necessary computations.
2. What would you do with the two items in question? Do you see anything wrong with the way Jackson has handled each of them? Explain your answer.
3. Prepare a revised balance sheet based on your answer to part **2.** Also, compute a revised current ratio and debt-to-equity ratio. Based on the revised ratios, is Midwest in compliance with its loan agreement?

LO 4 Case 13-10 Inventory Turnover

Garden Fresh Inc. is a wholesaler of fresh fruits and vegetables. Each year it submits a set of financial ratios to a trade association. Even though the association doesn't publish the individual ratios for each company, the president of Garden Fresh thinks it is important for public relations that his company look as good as possible. Due to the nature of the fresh fruits and vegetables business, one of the major ratios tracked by the association is inventory turnover. Garden Fresh's inventory stated at FIFO cost was as follows:

	Year Ending December 31	
	2001	**2000**
Fruits	$10,000	$ 9,000
Vegetables	30,000	33,000
Totals	$40,000	$42,000

Sales revenue for the year ending December 31, 2001, is $3,690,000. The company's gross profit ratio is normally 40%.

Based on these data, the president thinks the company should report an inventory turnover ratio of 90 times per year.

Required

1. Explain, using the necessary calculations, how the president came up with an inventory turnover ratio of 90 times.
2. Do you think the company should report a turnover ratio of 90 times? If not, explain why you disagree and explain, with calculations, what you think the ratio should be.
3. Assume you are the controller for Garden Fresh. What will you tell the president?

INTERNET RESEARCH CASE

INTERNET

www.wrigley.com

Case 13-11 Wrigley

Wrigley chewing gum is one of the most recognizable in the U.S. and most of its sales are from its international segments. In total, it is the number one maker of chewing gum in the world. After what it terms a year of transition in 1999, Wrigley believes 2000 will be a new era of growth.

By reading Wrigley's financial statement and notes, and using them to calculate selected financial ratios, as in the review problem, you can develop a current picture of Wrigley's performance that can help you interpret how Wrigley proposes to make 2000 and beyond a new era.

1. Based on the financial information for the last two years available, compute the 20 ratios required in the Review Problem on page 680.
2. Comment on Writley's liquidity. Has it improved or declined over the two-year period?
3. Comment on Wrigley's solvency and Wrigley's capital structure.
4. Comment on Wrigley's profitability.
5. By looking at various sources such as the financial news and Wrigley's Financial Data pages, what management plans and initiatives, such as announced increases in building of plants or increases in hiring, are likely to change your analysis of Wrigley's performance the most in future years?

SOLUTIONS TO KEY TERMS QUIZ

Quiz 1:

14 Horizontal analysis (p. 655)
11 Vertical analysis (p. 655)
10 Gross profit ratio (p. 660)
12 Profit margin ratio (p. 660)
13 Liquidity (p. 662)
2 Working capital (p. 662)
3 Current ratio (p. 662)
1 Acid-test or quick ratio (p. 663)
5 Cash flow from operations to current liabilities ratio (p. 664)
6 Accounts receivable turnover ratio (p. 664)
4 Number of days' sales in receivables (p. 665)
9 Inventory turnover ratio (p. 666)
7 Number of days' sales in inventory (p. 666)
8 Cash to cash operating cycle (p. 667)

Quiz 2:

- 3 Solvency (p. 667)
- 7 Debt-to-equity ratio (p. 667)
- 13 Times interest earned ratio (p. 668)
- 14 Debt service coverage ratio (p. 668)
- 8 Cash flow from operations to capital expenditures ratio (p. 669)
- 15 Profitability (p. 670)
- 9 Return on assets ratio (p. 670)
- 4 Return on sales ratio (p. 671)
- 10 Asset turnover ratio (p. 671)
- 1 Return on common stockholders' equity ratio (p. 672)
- 12 Leverage (p. 673)
- 5 Earnings per share (p. 673)
- 2 Price/earnings (P/E) ratio (p. 674)
- 6 Dividend payout ratio (p. 675)
- 11 Dividend yield ratio (p. 675)

Part IV

INTEGRATIVE PROBLEM

Presented below are comparative balance sheets and a statement of income and retained earnings for Gallagher, Inc., which operates a national chain of sporting goods stores:

GALLAGHER, INC.
COMPARATIVE BALANCE SHEETS
DECEMBER 31, 2001 AND 2000
(ALL AMOUNTS IN THOUSANDS OF DOLLARS)

	December 31	
	2001	**2000**
Cash	$ 840	$ 2,700
Accounts receivable	12,500	9,000
Inventory	8,000	5,500
Prepaid insurance	100	400
Total current assets	$21,440	$17,600
Land	$ 4,000	$ 4,000
Buildings and equipment	12,000	9,000
Accumulated depreciation	(3,700)	(3,000)
Total long-term assets	$12,300	$10,000
Total assets	$33,740	$27,600
Accounts payable	$ 7,300	$ 5,000
Taxes payable	4,600	4,200
Notes payable	2,400	1,600
Current portion of bonds	200	200
Total current liabilities	$14,500	$11,000
Bonds payable	1,400	1,600
Total liabilities	$15,900	$12,600
Preferred stock, $5 par	$ 1,000	$ 1,000
Common stock, $1 par	2,000	2,000
Retained earnings	14,840	12,000
Total stockholders' equity	$17,840	$15,000
Total liabilities and stockholders' equity	$33,740	$27,600

GALLAGHER, INC.
STATEMENT OF INCOME AND RETAINED EARNINGS
FOR THE YEAR ENDED DECEMBER 31, 2001
(ALL AMOUNTS IN THOUSANDS OF DOLLARS)

Net sales	$48,000
Cost of goods sold	36,000
Gross profit	$12,000
Selling, general and administrative expense	6,000
Operating income	$ 6,000
Interest expense	280
Income before tax	$ 5,720
Income tax expense	2,280
Net income	$ 3,440
Preferred dividends	100
Income available to common	$ 3,340
Common dividends	500
To retained earnings	$ 2,840
Retained earnings, 1/1	12,000
Retained earnings, 12/31	$14,840

Required

1. Prepare a statement of cash flows for Gallagher, Inc. for the year ended December 31, 2001, using the **indirect** method in the Operating Activities section of the statement.
2. Gallagher's management is concerned with both its short-term liquidity and its solvency over the long run. To help it evaluate these, compute the following ratios, rounding all answers to the nearest one-tenth of a percent:
   - **a.** Current ratio
   - **b.** Acid-test ratio
   - **c.** Cash flow from operations to current liabilities ratio
   - **d.** Accounts receivable turnover ratio
   - **e.** Number of days' sales in receivables
   - **f.** Inventory turnover ratio
   - **g.** Number of days' sales in inventory
   - **h.** Debt-to-equity ratio
   - **i.** Debt service coverage ratio
   - **j.** Cash flow from operations to capital expenditures ratio
3. Comment on Gallagher's liquidity and its solvency. What additional information do you need to fully evaluate the company?

VIDEO CASE IV — LYCOS INC.

Founded in 1995, **Lycos (www.lycos.com)** is a rapidly growing Internet service company that in its short history has already reinvented itself. It began as a search engine that guided users to individual Web sites with its patented search technology. With the addition of ever-more-powerful navigation technology and tools, the purchase of several other Internet service companies, and an attractive array of free user services including e-mail, chat rooms, shopping, and personal home pages, Lycos soon became an Internet destination in its own right. The youngest company in NASDAQ's history to go public, Lycos now considers its comprehensive network of sites not as a portal but as a "hub," the place at the center of users' experience on the Web.

The Lycos philosophy is that communities are at the core of the hub, personalizing the Web and allowing people with common interests to act as participants rather than observers in a global medium. Its goal? Nothing short of being the world's number one destination on the Web.

Users have responded to Lycos' growing network of services with enthusiasm. Visitors to the hub currently number over 30 million a month, making Lycos one of the most-visited sites on the Internet, reaching one of every two Web users. The Lycos Network includes Lycos.com, Tripod, Angelfire, WhoWhere, MailCity, Hotbot, HotWired, Wired News, Webmonkey, Quote.com, and others. These top-rated destinations are integrated to allow each user in the Lycos community to locate, retrieve, and manage information tailored to his or her unique interests.

Because Lycos provides services free to users, it must get most of its revenues from the advertising it carries on its sites and from electronic commerce agreements. Many of Lycos' recent acquisitions were strategic—the company gained access not only to powerful new technology, highly talented employees, and depth and breadth on the Web but also to new members. Members join communities, and communities attract advertisers. Tripod and Angelfire in particular have generated significant advertising revenues. Through its recent addition of the Lycoshop service, Lycos offers business-to-consumer e-commerce. The company can build a store for its corporate clients or can link to an existing electronic storefront. In addition, the company can add a company's products to its existing database. All of these shopping alternatives draw approximately 12 million buyers monthly for its clients.

In September 1999, Lycos acquired Quote.com, a comprehensive financial information site numbered among the top five in the market. With this purchase, the Lycos Network entered the online financial information industry, a critical growth area it hopes will draw customers and advertisers alike.

Lycos is growing internationally as well, with offices in Brazil, Germany, Italy, France, Japan, Korea, Mexico, the United Kingdom, Spain, and the Netherlands and localized services in countries around the world. A recent agreement with Bell Canada created a new company, Sympatico-Lycos, to offer Canadians expanded Internet resources in the retailer consumer marketplace.

With its impressive internal growth and savvy acquisitions, Lycos has earned revenues that totaled $56 million in late 1999, reflecting the firm's growing appeal for advertisers and the addition of countless new e-commerce customers. But the net loss under which it operates also continued to grow, reaching $27.5 million for the same period. The loss reflects higher amortization from developed technology and goodwill.

Questions

1. What steps has Lycos taken to reach its operational goal? What additional strategies do you think it might follow in the future?
2. What do you think are Lycos' financial goals? How can it be sure of meeting them?
3. From watching the video, researching the "About Lycos" page on their website, and checking the current financial news, what are some of Lycos' strategic, operational, competitive, and financial goals? How are they related?

Index for "From Concept to Practice" Assignments

"From Concept to Practice" assignments, printed in the margins throughout the book, are based on annual reports from Ben & Jerry's, Gateway, and other companies profiled in the opening vignette of each chapter. This Index is a convenient list of these financial statement assignments, which can be used in conjunction with the chapter or as cumulative problems at key points in the course.

Chapter 1

1.1 Reading Gateway's **Income Statement** p. 11
Now that you've seen Ben & Jerry's income statement, turn to the end of the book to Gateway's income statement. Note the large amount of Cost of Sales—$5,921,651—on Gateway's 1998 income statement (consolidated income statement). What types of costs would fall into the Cost of Sales category for Gateway?

1.2 Reading Ben & Jerry's **Auditor's Report** p. 18
Note the date at the bottom of the report. Why do you think it takes one month after the end of the year to issue this report?

Chapter 2

2.1 Reading Ben & Jerry's **Income Statement** p. 62
Which income statement format does Ben & Jerry's use: single-step or multiple-step? Calculate Ben & Jerry's 1998 and 1997 gross profit ratio. Explain what happened from 1997 to 1998.

2.2 Reading Gateway's **Income Statement** p. 67
Compute Gateway's profit margin for the past two years. Did it go up or down from the prior year to the current year?

Chapter 3

3.1 Reading K2's **Financial Statements** p. 94
K2 Inc. purchases materials to use in making snowboards. Is this an internal or an external event? The company subsequently uses the materials in the production process. Is this an internal or an external event?

3.2 Reading Ben & Jerry's **Balance Sheet and Footnotes** p. 101
How many liability accounts does the company report on its balance sheet? How are these liability accounts broken down in the accompanying notes?

3.3 Reading Gateway's **Financial Statements** p. 109
Refer to Gateway's income statement and its balance sheet. Using the appropriate accounts from these statements, prepare the journal entry Gateway would record if it sold a computer for $2,000 and gave the customer 30 days to pay.

Chapter 4

4.1 Reading McDonald's **Income Statement** p. 147
Refer to McDonald's comparative income statements for 1998, 1997, and 1996 in the chapter opener. What percentage of total revenues were derived from franchised restaurants? Has this percentage changed over the three year period?

4.2 Reading Ben & Jerry's **Balance Sheet** p. 151
Refer to the balance sheet in Ben & Jerry's annual report. How does Ben & Jerry's classify prepaid expenses? What types of prepaid expenses would you expect the company to have?

4.3 Reading Gateway's **Balance Sheet** p. 157
Refer to the balance sheet in Gateway's annual report. How does Gateway classify accrued liabilities? By how much did they go up or down from 1997 to 1998? What types of accrued liabilities would you expect the company to have?

CHAPTER 5

5.1 Reading Ben & Jerry's **Annual Report** p. 212
Is Ben & Jerry's a merchandiser? What items in the annual report can you cite to support your answer?

5.2 Understanding Gateway's **Inventory System** p. 219
Given the nature of its products, would you expect that Gateway uses a perpetual or a periodic inventory system? Explain your answer.

5.3 Reading The Gap's **Management Report** p. 227
Refer to the management's report for The Gap in Exhibit 5-8. What is the composition of its Audit and Finance Committee? Why do you think it is comprised the way it is?

CHAPTER 6

6.1 Reading Gateway's **Footnotes** p. 263
Footnote 10 in Gateway's 1998 annual report includes information about the composition of its inventory. How does Gateway categorize these elements of its inventory? What percentage of its total inventory at the end of 1998 is made up of finished goods?

6.2 Reading Ben & Jerry's **Annual Report** p. 274
Which inventory method does Ben & Jerry's use? Where did you find this information? Do you think the company is justified in using the method it does?

6.3 Reading Circuit City's **Footnotes** p. 280
A footnote to Circuit City's financial statements indicates that "Inventory is stated at the lower of cost or market." Why do you think the application of the lower-of-cost-or-market rule would be important to a business like Circuit City?

6.4 Reading Ben & Jerry's **Financial Statements** p. 283
Compute Ben & Jerry's inventory turnover ratio for 1998. What is the average length of time it takes to sell its inventory? Does this seem reasonable for the type of business the company is in?

CHAPTER 7

7.1 Reading Ben & Jerry's **Footnotes** p. 332
According to Footnote 2 in Ben & Jerry's 1998 annual report, how are its investments classified? In what types of securities does the company invest?

7.2 Reading PepsiCo's **Financial Statements** p. 337
Refer to the chapter opener for the presentation of PepsiCo's accounts and notes receivable on its 1998 and 1997 year-end balance sheets. What was the amount of increase or decrease in the allowance account? What does the change in the account mean?

7.3 Reading Gateway's **Financial Statements** p. 340
Does Gateway disclose in its annual report which method it uses to estimate bad debts? In what line item on the income statement would you expect bad debts expense to be included?

7.4 Reading Ben & Jerry's **Financial Statements** p. 341
Compute Ben & Jerry's accounts receivable turnover for 1998. What is the average length of time it takes to collect a receivable? Does this seem reasonable for the company's type of business?

CHAPTER 8

8.1 Reading Ben & Jerry's **Annual Report** p. 377
What amount did Ben & Jerry's report as depreciation in 1998? Where is it disclosed? What depreciation method was used?

8.2 Reading Time Warner's **Balance Sheet** p. 389
Which items on Time-Warner's 1998 balance sheet should be considered intangible assets?

8.3 Refer to Gateway's **Cash Flow Statement** p. 396
What amount did the company spend on capital expenditures during 1998?

CHAPTER 9

9.1 Reading JCPenney's **Balance Sheet** p. 422
Refer to JCPenney's balance sheet for 1998. What accounts are listed as current liabilities? What was the change in Accounts Payable from 1997 to 1998?

9.2 Reading Ben & Jerry's **Annual Report** p. 424
Refer to Ben & Jerry's foot notes. What items are included in the Accounts Payable and Accrued Expenses line of the balance sheet?

9.3 Reading Gateway's **Footnotes** p. 427
One of Gateway's Current Liabilities is Accrued Royalities. How do the footnotes explain that account?

CHAPTER 10

10.1 Reading Coca-Cola's **Balance Sheet** p. 478
Coca-Cola lists three items as long-term liabilities on its 1998 balance sheet. What are those items? Did they increase or decrease?

10.2 Reading Ben & Jerry's **Balance Sheet** p. 497
Calculate the 1997 and 1998 debt-to-equity ratios for Ben & Jerry's. Did 1998's debt-to-equity ratio go up or down from 1997?

10.3 Reading Gateway's **Statement of Cash Flows** p. 498
Did Gateway's Accounts Payable account increase or decrease from 1997 to 1998? Is this a positive or negative amount on the cash flow statement? In which category of the statement do you find the change?

CHAPTER 11

11.1 Reading Gateway's **Annual Report** p. 528
What was the balance of retained earnings for Gateway at the end of 1998? Did the balance increase from the end of 1997?

11.2 Reading Delta's **Annual Report** p. 533
Which financial statements could you look at to identify the different classes of stock issued by Delta? Which classes of stock are issued? How many shares have been issued?

11.3 Reading Ben & Jerry's **Annual Report** p. 545
Refer to Ben & Jerry's 1998 report. What was the book value per share of the common stock? How did that relate to the market value of the stock?

CHAPTER 12

12.1 Reading Gateway's **Statement of Cash Flows** p. 590
According to Gateway's Investing Activities section of its statement of cash flows, what does the company spend a significant amount of cash for every year? What types of expenditures would you expect to find in this category?

12.2 Reading IBM's **Statement of Cash Flows** p. 594
Does IBM use the direct or indirect method in the Operating Activities section of its statement of cash flows? How can you tell which it is?

12.3 Reading Ben & Jerry's **Statement of Cash Flows** p. 613
Did Accounts Receivable increase or decrease during 1998? Why is the change in this account deducted on the statement of cash flows?

CHAPTER 13

13.1 Reading Ben & Jerry's **Annual Report** p. 658
Where does Ben & Jerry's annual report provide a financial summary? How many years does it include? In terms of a trend over time, which item on the summary do you think is the most significant?

13.2 Reading Wrigley's **Annual Report** p. 658
Refer to Wrigley's Financial Highlights in Exhibit 13-3. Compute the company's gross profit ratio for each of the 11 years. Is there a noticeable upward or downward trend in the ratio over this time period?

13.3 Reading Gateway's **Annual Report** p. 675
Refer to Gateway's statement of cash flows. Why is it not possible to compute Gateway's dividend payout ratio for 1998? Why do you think Gateway has adopted the policy it has concerning the payment of dividends?

Glossary

Accelerated depreciation A higher amount of depreciation is recorded in the early years and a lower amount in the later years. (p. 379)

Account Record used to accumulate amounts for each individual asset, liability, revenue, expense, and component of owners' equity. (p. 101)

Accounting The process of identifying, measuring, and communicating economic information to various users. (p. 6)

Accounting controls Procedures concerned with safeguarding the assets or the reliability of the financial statements. (p. 228)

Accounting cycle A series of steps performed each period and culminating with the preparation of a set of financial statements. (p. 163)

Accounting system Methods and records used to accurately report an entity's transactions and to maintain accountability for its assets and liabilities. (p. 227)

Accounts payable Amounts owed for inventory, goods, or services acquired in the normal course of business. (p. 424)

Accounts receivable turnover ratio A measure of the number of times accounts receivable are collected in a period. (p. 664)

Accrual Cash has not yet been paid or received, but expense has been incurred or revenue earned. (p. 158)

Accrual basis A system of accounting in which revenues are recognized when earned and expenses when incurred. (p. 143)

Accrued asset An asset resulting from the recognition of a revenue before the receipt of cash. (p. 158)

Accrued liability A liability resulting from the recognition of an expense before the payment of cash. (p. 158, 427)

Accrued pension cost The difference between the amount of pension recorded as an expense and the amount of the funding payment. (p. 506)

Accumulated benefit obligation (ABO) A measure of the amount owed to employees for pensions if they retire at their existing salary levels. (p. 507)

Acid-test or quick ratio A stricter test of liquidity than the current ratio; excludes inventory and prepayments from the numerator. (p. 663)

Acquisition cost The amount that includes all of the cost normally necessary to acquire an asset and prepare it for its intended use. (p. 375)

Additional paid-in capital The amount received for the issuance of stock in excess of the par value of the stock. (p. 531)

Adjusting entries Journal entries made at the end of a period by a company using the accrual basis of accounting. (p. 150)

Administrative controls Procedures concerned with efficient operation of the business and adherence to managerial policies. (p. 228)

Aging schedule A form used to categorize the various individual accounts receivable according to the length of time each has been outstanding. (p. 339)

Allowance method A method of estimating bad debts on the basis of either the net credit sales of the period or the accounts receivable at the end of the period. (p. 336)

American Accounting Association The professional organization for accounting educators. (p. 20)

American Institute of Certified Public Accountants (AICPA) The professional organization for certified public accountants. (p. 16)

Annuity A series of payments of equal amounts. (p. 441)

Asset turnover ratio The relationship between net sales and average total assets. (p. 671)

Audit committee Board of directors subset that acts as a direct contact between stockholders and the independent accounting firm. (p. 227)

Auditing The process of examining the financial statements and the underlying records of a company in order to render an opinion as to whether the statements are fairly represented. (p. 18)

Auditors' report The opinion rendered by a public accounting firm concerning the fairness of the presentation of the financial statements. (p. 18)

Authorized shares The maximum number of shares a corporation may issue as indicated in the corporate charter. (p. 529)

Available-for-sale securities Stocks and bonds that are not classified as either held-to-maturity or trading securities. (p. 327)

Balance sheet The financial statement that summarizes the assets, liabilities, and owners' equity at a specific point in time. (p. 9)

Bank reconciliation A form used by the accountant to reconcile the balance shown on the bank statement for a particular account with the balance shown in the accounting records. (p. 318)

Bank statement A detailed list, provided by the bank, of all the activity for a particular account during the month. (p. 317)

Blind receiving report Form used by the receiving department to account for the quantity and condition of merchandise received from a supplier. (p. 239)

Board of directors Group composed of key officers of a corporation and outside members responsible for general oversight of the affairs of the entity. (p. 227)

Bond issue price The present value of the annuity of interest payments plus the present value of the principal. (p. 482)

Book value The original cost of an asset minus the amount of accumulated depreciation. (p. 378)

Book value per share Total stockholders equity divided by the number of shares of common stock outstanding. (p. 545)

Callable bonds Bonds that may be redeemed or retired before their specified due date. (p. 481)

Callable feature Allows the firm to eliminate a class of stock by paying the stockholders a specified amount. (p. 533)

Capital expenditure A cost that improves the asset and is added to the asset account. (p. 384)

Capital lease A lease that is recorded as an asset by the lessee. (p. 493)

Capitalization of interest Interest on constructed assets is added to the asset account. (p. 376)

Carrying value The face value of a bond plus the amount of unamortized premium or minus the amount of unamortized discount. (p. 486)

Cash basis A system of accounting in which revenues are recognized when cash is received and expenses when cash is paid. (p. 143)

Cash equivalent An investment that is readily convertible to a known amount of cash and a maturity to the investor of three months or less. (p. 314, 587)

Cash flow from operations to capital expenditures ratio A measure of the ability of a company to finance long-term asset acquisitions with cash from operations. (p. 669)

Cash flow from operations to current liabilities ratio A measure of the ability to pay current debts from operating cash flows. (p. 664)

Cash to cash operating cycle The length of time from the purchase of inventory to the collection of any receivable from the sale. (p. 667)

Change in estimate A change in the life of the asset or in its residual value. (p. 382)

Chart of accounts A numerical list of all the accounts used by a company. (p. 101)

Closing entries Journal entries made at the end of the period to return the balance in all nominal accounts to zero and transfer the net income or loss and the dividends to Retained Earnings. (p. 165)

Comparability For accounting information, the quality that allows a user to analyze two or more companies and look for similarities and differences. (p. 50)

Compensated absences Employee absences for which the employee will be paid. (p. 455)

Compound interest Interest calculated on the principal plus previous amounts of interest. (p. 437)

Comprehensive income The total change in net assets from all sources except investment or withdrawals by the owners. (p. 545)

Conservatism The practice of using the least optimistic estimate when two estimates of amounts are about equally likely. (p. 51)

Consistency For accounting information, the quality that allows a user to compare two or more accounting periods for a single company. (p. 50)

Contingent assets An existing condition for which the outcome is not known but by which the company stands to gain. (p. 434)

Contingent liability An existing condition for which the outcome is not known but depends on some future event. (p. 430)

Contra account An account with a balance that is opposite that of a related account. (p. 152)

Control account The general ledger account that is supported by a subsidiary ledger. (p. 334)

Controller The chief accounting officer for a company. (p. 16)

Convertible feature Allows preferred stock to be exchanged for common stock. (p. 533)

Cost of goods available for sale Beginning inventory plus cost of goods purchased. (p. 217)

Cost of goods sold Cost of goods available for sale minus ending inventory. (p. 217)

Cost principle Assets recorded at the cost to acquire them. (p. 14)

Credit An entry on the right side of an account. (p. 103)

Credit card draft A multiple-copy document used by a company that accepts a credit card for a sale. (p. 345)

Credit memoranda Additions on a bank statement for such items as interest paid on the account and notes collected by the bank for the customer. (p. 318)

Cumulative feature The right to dividends in arrears before the current-year dividend is distributed. (p. 533)

Current asset An asset that is expected to be realized in cash or sold or consumed during the operating cycle or within one year if the cycle is shorter than one year. (p. 54)

Current liability An obligation that will be satisfied within the next operating cycle or within one year if the cycle is shorter than one year. (p. 57, 422)

Current maturities of long-term debt The portion of a long-term liability that will be paid within one year. (p. 426)

Current ratio Current assets divided by current liabilities. (p. 58, 662)

Current value The amount of cash, or its equivalent, that could be received by selling an asset currently. (p. 141)

Debenture bonds Bonds that are not backed by specific collateral. (p. 480)

Debit An entry on the left side of an account. (p. 103)

Debit memoranda Deductions on a bank statement for such items as NSF checks and various service charges. (p. 319)

Debt securities Bonds issued by corporations and governmental bodies as a form of borrowing. (p. 324)

Debt service coverage ratio A statement of cash flow measure of the ability of a company to meet its interest and principal payments. (p. 668)

Debt-to-equity ratio The ratio of total liabilities to total stockholders' equity. (p. 667)

Deferral Cash has either been paid or received, but expense or revenue has not yet been recognized. (p. 157)

Deferred expense An asset resulting from the payment of cash before the incurrence of expense. (p. 157)

Deferred revenue A liability resulting from the receipt of cash before the recognition of revenue. (p. 157)

Deferred tax The account used to reconcile the difference between the amount recorded as income tax expense and the amount that is payable as income tax. (p. 503)

Deposit in transit A deposit recorded on the books but not yet reflected on the bank statement. (p. 318)

Depreciation The process of allocating the cost of a long-term tangible asset over its useful life. (p. 50, 377)

Direct method For preparing the Operating Activities section of the statement of cash flows, the approach in which cash receipts and cash payments are reported. (p. 592)

Direct write-off method The recognition of bad debts expense at the point an account is written off as uncollectible. (p. 336)

Discount The excess of the face value of bonds over the issue price. (p. 483)

Discount on notes payable A contra liability that represents interest deducted from a loan in advance. (p. 425)

Discounted note An alternative name for a non-interest-bearing promissory note. (p. 343)

Discounting The process of selling a promissory note. (p. 346)

Dividend payout ratio The annual dividend amount divided by the annual net income. (p. 537, 675)

Dividend yield ratio The relationship between dividends and the market price of a company's stock. (p. 675)

Dividends A distribution of the net income of a business to its owners. (p. 11)

Double declining-balance method Depreciation is recorded at twice the straight-line rate, but the balance is reduced each period. (p. 379)

Double-entry system A system of accounting in which every transaction is recorded with equal debits and credits and the accounting equation is kept in balance. (p. 106)

Earnings per share A company's bottom line stated on a per-share basis. (p. 673)

Effective interest method of amortization The process of transferring a portion of the premium or discount to interest expense; this method results in a constant effective interest rate. (p. 485)

Equity securities Securities issued by corporations as a form of ownership in the business. (p. 324)

Estimated liability A contingent liability that is accrued and reflected on the balance sheet. (p. 431)

Event A happening of consequence to an entity. (p. 94)

Expenses Outflows of assets or incurrences of liabilities resulting from delivering goods, rendering services, or carrying out other activities. (p. 149)

External event An event involving interaction between an entity and its environment. (p. 94)

Face rate of interest The rate of interest on the bond certificate. (p. 481)

Face value The principal amount of the bond as stated on the bond certificate. (p. 478)

FIFO method An inventory costing method that assigns the most recent costs to ending inventory. (p. 268)

Financial Accounting Standards Board (FASB) The group in the private sector with authority to set accounting standards. (p. 16)

Financial accounting The branch of accounting concerned with the preparation of financial statements for outsider use. (p. 7)

Financing activities Activities concerned with the raising and repayment of funds in the form of debt and equity. (p. 590)

Finished goods A manufacturer's inventory that is complete and ready for sale. (p. 263)

FOB destination point Terms that require the seller to pay for the cost of shipping the merchandise to the buyer. (p. 222)

FOB shipping point Terms that require the buyer to pay for the shipping costs. (p. 222)

Foreign Corrupt Practices Act Legislation intended to increase the accountability of management for accurate records and reliable financial statements. (p. 227)

Funding payment A payment made by the employer to the pension fund or its trustee. (p. 506)

Future value of a single amount Amount accumulated at a future time from a single payment or investment. (p. 438)

Future value of an annuity Amount accumulated in the future when a series of payments is invested and accrues interest. (p. 441)

Gain on sale of asset The excess of the selling price over the asset's book value. (p. 386)

Gain or loss on redemption The difference between the carrying value and the redemption price at the time bonds are redeemed. (p. 490)

General journal The journal used in place of a specialized journal. (p. 109)

General ledger A book, file, hard drive, or other device containing all the accounts. (p. 102)

Generally accepted accounting principles (GAAP) The various methods, rules, practices, and other procedures that have evolved over time in response to the need to regulate the preparation of financial statements. (p. 15)

Going concern The assumption that an entity is not in the process of liquidation and that it will continue indefinitely. (p. 14)

Goodwill The excess of the purchase price of a business over the total market value of identifiable assets. (p. 390)

Gross profit Sales less cost of goods sold. (p. 60)

Gross profit method A technique used to establish an estimate of the cost of inventory stolen, destroyed, or otherwise damaged or of the amount of inventory on hand at an interim date. (p. 280)

Gross profit ratio Gross profit to net sales. (p. 62, 660)

Gross wages The amount of wages before deductions. (p. 452)

Held-to-maturity securities Investments in bonds of other companies in which the investor has the positive intent and the ability to hold the securities to maturity. (p. 327)

Historical cost The amount paid for an asset and used as a basis for recognizing it on the balance sheet and carrying it on later balance sheets. (p. 141)

Horizontal analysis A comparison of financial statement items over a period of time. (p. 655)

Income statement A statement that summarizes revenues and expenses. (p. 9)

Indirect method For preparing the Operating Activities section of the statement of cash flows, the approach in which net income is reconciled to net cash flow from operations. (p. 592)

Installment method The method in which revenue is recognized at the time cash is collected. (p. 148)

Intangible assets Assets with no physical properties. (p. 389)

Interest The difference between the principal amount of the note and its maturity value. (p. 342)

Interest-bearing note A promissory note in which the interest rate is explicitly stated. (p. 342)

Interim statements Financial statements prepared monthly, quarterly, or at other intervals less than a year in duration. (p. 166)

Internal audit staff Department responsible for monitoring and evaluating the internal control system. (p. 226)

Internal auditing The department responsible in a company for the review and appraisal of its accounting and administrative controls. (p. 17)

Internal control system Policies and procedures necessary to ensure the safeguarding of an entity's assets, the reliability of its accounting records, and the accomplishment of overall company objectives. (p. 225)

Internal event An event occurring entirely within an entity. (p. 94)

International Accounting Standards Committee (IASC) The organization formed to develop worldwide accounting standards. (p. 16)

Inventory profit The portion of the gross profit that results from holding inventory during a period of rising prices. (p. 272)

Inventory turnover ratio A measure of the number of times inventory is sold during a period. (p. 282, 666)

Investing activities Activities concerned with the acquisition and disposal of long-term assets. (p. 589)

Invoice Form sent by the seller to the buyer as evidence of a sale. (p. 239)

Invoice approval form Form the accounting department uses before making payment to document the accuracy of all the information about a purchase. (p. 240)

Issued shares The number of shares sold or distributed to stockholders. (p. 529)

Journal A chronological record of transactions, also known as the book of original entry. (p. 108)

Journalizing The act of recording journal entries. (p. 109)

Land improvements Costs that are related to land but that have a limited life. (p. 377)

Leverage The use of borrowed funds and amounts contributed by preferred stockholders to earn an overall return higher than the cost of these funds. (p. 673)

LIFO conformity rule The IRS requirement that if LIFO is used on the tax return, it must also be used in reporting income to stockholders. (p. 271)

LIFO liquidation The result of selling more units than are purchased during the period, which can have negative tax consequences if a company is using LIFO. (p. 271)

LIFO method An inventory method that assigns the most recent costs to cost of goods sold. (p. 269)

LIFO reserve The excess of the value of a company's inventory stated at FIFO over the value stated at LIFO. (p. 272)

Liquidity The nearness to cash of the assets and liabilities. (p. 58, 662)

Long-term liability An obligation that will be settled within one year or the current operating cycle. (p. 478)

Loss on sale of asset The amount by which selling price is less than book value. (p. 387)

Lower-of-cost-or-market (LCM) rule A conservative inventory valuation approach that is an attempt to anticipate declines in the value of inventory before its actual sale. (p. 278)

Maker The party that agrees to repay the money for a promissory note at some future date. (p. 341)

Management accounting The branch of accounting concerned with providing management with information to facilitate planning and control. (p. 6)

Market rate of interest The rate that investors could obtain by investing in other bonds that are similar to the issuing firm's bonds. (p. 481)

Market value per share The selling price of the stock as indicated by the most recent transactions. (p. 547)

Matching principle The association of revenue of a period with all of the costs necessary to generate that revenue. (p. 148)

Materiality The magnitude of an accounting information omission or misstatement that will affect the judgment of someone relying on the information. (p. 51)

Maturity date The date that the promissory note is due. (p. 342)

Maturity value The amount of cash the maker is to pay the payee on the maturity date of the note. (p. 342)

Merchandise inventory The account wholesalers and retailers use to report inventory held for resale. (p. 262)

Monetary unit The yardstick used to measure amounts in financial statements; the dollar in the United States. (p. 14)

Moving average The name given to an average cost method when it is used with a perpetual inventory system. (p. 292)

Multiple-step income statement An income statement that shows classifications of revenues and expenses as well as important subtotals. (p. 60)

Natural resources Assets that are consumed during their use. (p. 387)

Net pay The amount of wages after deductions. (p. 452)

Net sales Sales revenue less sales returns and allowances and sales discounts. (p. 213)

Nominal accounts The name given to revenue, expense, and dividend accounts because they are temporary and are closed at the end of the period. (p. 165)

Non-interest-bearing note A promissory note in which interest is not explicitly stated but is implicit in the agreement. (p. 342)

Note payable A liability resulting from the signing of a promissory note. (p. 341)

Note receivable An asset resulting from the acceptance of a promissory note from another company. (p. 341, 424)

Number of days' sales in inventory A measure of how long it takes to sell inventory. (p. 283, 666)

Number of days' sales in receivables A measure of the average age of accounts receivable. (p. 665)

Operating activities Activities concerned with the acquisition and sale of products and services. (p. 588)

Operating cycle The period of time between the purchase of inventory and the collection of any receivable from the sale of the inventory. (p. 53)

Operating lease A lease that does not meet any of the four criteria and is not recorded as an asset by the lessee. (p. 493)

Outstanding check A check written by a company but not yet presented to the bank for payment. (p. 318)

Outstanding shares The number of shares issued less the number of shares held as treasury stock. (p. 529)

Owners' equity The owners' claim on the assets of an entity. (p. 9)

Par value An arbitrary amount that represents the legal capital of the firm. (p. 529)

Participating feature Allows preferred stockholders to share on a percentage basis in the distribution of an abnormally large dividend. (p. 533)

Partnership A business owned by two or more individuals and with the characteristic of unlimited liability. (p. 555)

Partnership agreement Specifies how much the owners will invest, their salaries, and how profits will be shared. (p. 556)

Payee The party that will receive the money from a promissory note at some future date. (p. 341)

Pension An obligation to pay employees for service rendered while employed. (p. 505)

Percentage-of-completion method The method used by contractors to recognize revenue before the completion of a long-term contract. (p. 146)

Periodic system System in which the Inventory account is updated only at the end of the period. (p. 218)

Permanent difference A difference that affects the tax records but not the accounting records, or vice versa. (p. 503)

Perpetual system System in which the inventory account is increased at the time of each purchase and decreased at the time of each sale. (p. 218)

Petty cash fund Money kept on hand for making minor disbursements in coin and currency rather than by writing checks. (p. 322)

Posting The process of transferring amounts from a journal to the ledger accounts. (p. 108)

Premium The excess of the issue price over the face value of the bonds. (p. 483)

Present value of a single amount Amount at a present time that is equivalent to a payment or investment at a future time. (p. 439)

Present value of an annuity The amount at a present time that is equivalent to a series of payments and interest in the future. (p. 442)

Price/earnings (P/E) ratio The relationship between a company's performance according to the income statement and its performance in the stock market. (p. 674)

Principal The amount of cash received, or the fair value of the products or services received, by the maker when a promissory note is issued. (p. 342)

Production method The method in which revenue is recognized when a commodity is produced rather than when it is sold. (p. 148)

Profit margin Net income divided by sales. (p. 62)

Profitability How well management is using company resources to earn a return on the funds invested by various groups. (p. 670)

Projected benefit obligation (PBO) A measure of the amount owed to employees for pensions if estimates of future salary increases are considered. (p. 507)

Promissory note A written promise to repay a definite sum of money on demand or at a fixed or determinable date in the future. (p. 341)

Purchase Discounts Contra-purchases account used to record reductions in purchase price for early payment to a supplier. (p. 222)

Purchase order Form sent by the purchasing department to the supplier. (p. 237)

Purchase requisition form Form a department uses to initiate a request to order merchandise. (p. 237)

Purchase Returns and Allowances Contra-purchases account used in a periodic inventory system when a refund is received from a supplier or a reduction given in the balance owed to a supplier. (p. 221)

Purchases Account used in a periodic inventory system to record acquisitions of merchandise. (p. 221)

Quantity discount Reduction in selling price for buying a large number of units of a product. (p. 215)

Raw materials The inventory of a manufacturer before the addition of any direct labor or manufacturing overhead. (p. 262)

Real accounts The name given to balance sheet accounts because they are permanent and are not closed at the end of the period. (p. 164)

Recognition The process of recording an item in the financial statements as an asset, liability, revenue, expense, or the like. (p. 140)

Relevance The capacity of information to make a difference in a decision. (p. 48)

Reliability The quality that makes accounting information dependable in representing the events that it purports to represent. (p. 49)

Replacement cost The current cost of a unit of inventory. (p. 272)

Report of management Written statement in the annual report indicating the responsibility of management for the financial statements. (p. 226)

Research and development costs Costs incurred in the discovery of new knowledge. (p. 390)

Retail inventory method A technique used by retailers to convert the retail value of inventory to a cost basis. (p. 282)

Retained earnings The part of owners' equity that represents the income earned less dividends paid over the life of an entity. (p. 9, 532)

Retirement of stock When the stock is repurchased with no intention to reissue at a later date. (p. 537)

Retun on sales ratio A variation of the profit margin ratio; measures earnings before payments to creditors. (p. 671)

Return on assets ratio A measure of a company's success in earning a return for all providers of capital. (p. 670)

Return on common stockholders' equity ratio A measure of a company's success in earning a return for the common stockholders. (p. 672)

Revenue expenditure A cost that keeps an asset in its normal operating condition and is treated as an expense. (p. 384)

Revenue recognition principle Revenues are recognized in the income statement when they are realized, or realizable, and earned. (p. 146)

Revenues Inflows of assets or settlements of liabilities from delivering or producing goods, rendering services, or conducting other activities. (p. 146)

Sales Discounts Contra-revenue account used to record discounts given customers for early payment of their accounts. (p. 216)

Sales Returns and Allowances Contra-revenue account used to record both refunds to customers and reductions of their accounts. (p. 214)

Securities and Exchange Commission (SEC) The federal agency with ultimate authority to determine the rules in preparing statements for companies whose stock is sold to the public. (p. 16)

Serial bonds Bonds that do not all have the same due date; a portion of the bonds comes due each time period. (p. 481)

Simple interest Interest is calculated on the principal amount only. (p. 437)

Single-step income statement An income statement in which all expenses are added together and subtracted from all revenues. (p. 60)

Sole proprietorship A business with a single owner. (p. 554)

Solvency The ability of a company to remain in business over the long term. (p. 667)

Source document A piece of paper that is used as evidence to record a transaction. (p. 94)

Specific identification method An inventory costing method that relies on matching unit costs with the actual units sold. (p. 266)

Statement of cash flows The financial statement that summarizes an entity's cash receipts and cash payments during the period from operating, investing, and financing activities. (p. 585)

Statement of retained earnings The statement that summarizes the income earned and dividends paid over the life of a business. (p. 11)

Statement of stockholders' equity Reflects the differences between beginning and ending balances for all accounts in the Stockholders' Equity category of the balance sheet. (p. 543)

Stock dividend The issuance of additional shares of stock to existing stockholders. (p. 540)

Stock split The creation of additional shares of stock with a reduction of the par value of the stock. (p. 542)

Stockholders' equity The owners' equity in a corporation. (p. 9)

Straight-line method A method by which the same dollar amount of depreciation is recorded in each year of asset use. (p. 152, 377)

Subsidiary ledger The detail for a number of individual items that collectively make up a single general ledger account. (p. 334)

Temporary difference A difference that affects both book and tax records but not in the same time period. (p. 504)

Term The length of time a note is outstanding; that is, the period of time between the date it is issued and the date it matures. (p. 342)

Time period Artificial segment on the calendar, used as the basis for preparing financial statements. (p. 15)

Time value of money An immediate amount should be preferred over an amount in the future. (p. 435)

Times interest earned ratio An income statement measure of the ability of a company to meet its interest payments. (p. 668)

Trade discount Selling price reduction offered to a special class of customers. (p. 214)

Trading securities Stock and bonds of other companies bought and held for the purpose of selling them in the near term to generate profits on appreciation in their price. (p. 327)

Transaction Any event that is recognized in a set of financial statements. (p. 94)

Transportation-in Adjunct account used to record freight costs paid by the buyer. (p. 220)

Treasurer The officer responsible in an organization for the safeguarding and efficient use of a company's liquid assets. (p. 16)

Treasury stock Stock issued by the firm and then repurchased but not retired. (p. 535)

Trial balance A list of each account and its balance; used to prove equality of debits and credits. (p. 111)

Understandability The quality of accounting information that makes it comprehensible to those willing to spend the necessary time. (p. 48)

Units-of-production method Depreciation is determined as a function of the number of units the asset produces. (p. 378)

Vertical analysis A comparison of various financial statement items within a single period with the use of common-size statements. (p. 655)

Weighted average cost method An inventory costing method that assigns the same unit cost to all units available for sale during the period. (p. 267)

Work in process The cost of unfinished products in a manufacturing company. (p. 263)

Work sheet A device used at the end of the period to gather the information needed to prepare financial statements without actually recording and posting adjusting entries. (p. 163)

Working capital Current assets minus current liabilities. (p. 58, 662)

CREDITS

Chapter 1: page 2, Photo courtesy of Ben & Jerry's Homemade Holdings, Inc. © Ben & Jerry's Homemade Holdings, Inc.; page 9, http://lib.benjerry.com/fin/index.html Used by permission. ©Ben & Jerry's Homemade Holdings, Inc.; page 15, © Photopia; page 21, © Stuart Weiss. **Chapter 2:** page 49, Lawrence M. Fisher, "Inside Dell Computer Corporation: Managing Working Capital," *Strategy and Business*, First Quarter 1998, Issue 10, pp. 68–75. Used with permission; page 56, © Corel; page 69, Courtesy of Matthew Butler. **Chapter 3:** page 92, Reprinted by permission from K2 Corporation. www.k2sports.com; page 95, © PhotoDisc; page 98, © PhotoDisc; page 111, Photo courtesy of Mark Gleason. **Chapter 4:** page 138, © Photopia; page 142, © PhotoDisc; page 167, Courtesy of Michael Clarke. **Chapter 5:** page 210, © Photopia; page 216, Carol Emert, "Old Navy's Model Plan: Reasonable Prices, Lively Stores, Offbeat Ads Fuel the Gap's Powerhouse Division," San Francisco Chronicle, October 20, 1999, p. C1. © *San Francisco Chronicle*. Reprinted by permission; page 230, Courtesy of Julie Weston; page 214, © PhotoDisc; page 227, © PhotoDisc. **Chapter 6:** page 260, © Photopia; page 263, Digital Stock; page 284, Courtesy of Kim Anne Starke. **Chapter 7:** page 312, © 2000 Don Couch Photography; page 324, Courtesy of Barbara Genualdi; page 334, © 2000 Don Couch Photography; page 345, © PhotoDisc. **Chapter 8:** page 372, © 1997 Don Couch Photography; page 378, © 1997 Don Couch Photography; page 385, © Christian Bassu-Picca/Tony Stone Images; page 397, Courtesy of Aishetu Kolo. **Chapter 9:** page 420, © 2000 Don Couch Photography; page 431, Courtesy of Tandy Corporation; page 438, Texas Lottery Commission; page 443, Courtesy of Philip Yarrow. **Chapter 10:** page 476, © Audrey Gibson/Corbis; page 480, © Bill Varie/Image Bank; page 485, © Sergio Dorantes/CORBIS; page 498, Courtesy of John Roberts Snow. **Chapter 11:** page 524, AP/Wide World Photos; page 531, Used with permission from Ben & Jerry's Homemade Holdings, Inc. © Ben & Jerry's Homemade Holdings, Inc.; page 532, Alex Salkever, "Dogfight in Cyberspace: The Online Travel Biz Heats Up," *BusinessWeek Online* daily briefing, November 15, 1999, accessed at www.businessweek.com/bwdaily/dnflash/nov1999/nf91115a.htm ; page 533, Ami Schrager MPG, Inc./Photo courtesy of New York Stock Exchange; page 546, Screen capture courtesy of New York Stock Exchange; page 550, Courtesy of Christopher Morgan. **Chapter 12:** page 581, Courtesy of International Business Machines Corporation. Unauthorized use not permitted; page 616, © PhotoDisc. **Chapter 13:** page 650, © Photopia; page 667, © PhotoDisc; page 674, © StockYard; page 676, Courtesy of Stephen Carmichael.

To the Student: page xxiii, © PhotoDisc. **Getting Started:** page GS2, © Richard T. Nowitz/CORBIS; page GS8, © PhotoDisc

Cover Image Credits: Ben & Jerry's, Logo used with permission from BEN & JERRY'S HOMEMADE INC. **Time Warner,** Used by permission from Time Warner. **Walgreen's,** Cover logo used by permission of Walgreen Company. **Circuit City,** © Zaruba Photography for Circuit City. **IBM,** Courtesy of International Business Machines Corporation. Unauthorized use not permitted.

Gateway 1998 annual report courtesy Gateway, Inc.

Video Case I: Tweeter Home Entertainment Group's 1999 Annual Report; "Company Profile," Tweeter Web site, accessed March 7, 2000, www.tweeter.com; "Tweeter Home Entertainment Group Completes Public Offering of 2,550,000 Shares of Common Stock," company press release, February 8, 2000; "Tweeter Home Entertainment Group Reports Record Earnings for Its First Quarter Ending December 31, 1999," company press release, January 20, 2000; Chet Dembeck, "Cyberian Outpost and Tweeter Join Forces: Execs Talk about Venture," E-commerce Times, August 3, 1999, www.ecomercetimes.com. **Video Case II:** Stride Rite Corporation Web site, www.strideritecorp.com, accessed March 10, 2000, Antone Gonsalves, "Stride Rite Gets E-com Footing," *PC Week Online,* September 27, 1999; company press releases "Stride Rite's Operating Earnings Up 33% for 1999 Fiscal Year," January 6, 2000, and "Stride Rite's Baby Collection a Hit at Retail," February 23, 2000; Stride Rite 1998 Annual Report. **Video Case III:** Uno Restaurant Corporation 1999 Annual Report; Pizzeria Uno . . . Chicago Bar & Grill Web site, www.pizzeriauno.com, accessed April 2000; "Uno's Restaurant Corporation," company capsule accessed March 31, 2000, at www.hoovers.com; and "Uno Increases Stock Repurchase Authorization," PR Newswire, February 28, 2000. **Video Case IV:** The Lycos Network Web site, www.lycos.com, accessed April 2000; Lycos 1998 Annual Report; Lycos, Inc., company capsule, Hoover's Online, March 15, 2000, www.hoovers.com; Katherine Bull, "Ron Sege: Lycos' Executive VP Outlines the Company's New Corporate/Vertical Strategy," Infoworld.com, January 14, 2000.

Company Index

Bold indicates key terms and the page on which the definition can be found.

All Natural
BEN&JERRY'S
VERMONT'S FINEST

1998 Annual Report

“Let there be no purpose in giving save reciprocity. For a people whose spirituality lies within life’s wholeness, who share the gifts of the sky and the mountains and the seas and the forests, who exchange abundance in the circle of animal brethren, giving is not a matter of pure altruism and benevolence but a mutual responsibility to make the world a better place.”

Rebecca Adamson
First Nations Development Institute

Table of Contents

Social Spotlight

Putting together our annual social assessment is always a great look back at our partnerships with outside organizations. But it's also a look forward, for these are groups working to make our world a healthier and more humane place to live, now and in the future. Compiling our 1998 report made us think about the importance of their efforts and the importance of sharing them with you.

In some instances, as with the Greyston Foundation Bakery, makers of the brownies we use in our ice cream, or with Common Ground, a nonprofit housing agency operating a Ben & Jerry's PartnerShop® in Times Square, these have been partnerships in which our business itself helps provide solutions. In other cases, as with the Children's Defense Fund, we've had a special advocacy relationship in which we helped raise awareness about children and poverty. Similarly, we've begun working with Greenpeace to draw attention to the issues of toxins in our environment.

There are organizations like the Environmental Working Group and Rural Vermont who have been invaluable resources for us as we reconceive our business as a force for preserving family farms and creating agricultural sustainability. And there are groups like Business for Social Responsibility, an organization we helped establish with over 1400 members. BSR has become a vital resource for information about socially and environmentally responsible business practices. Another guiding light is the Coalition for Environmentally Responsible Economies. Established in the wake of Alaska's disastrous Exxon Valdez oil spill, CERES advocates ten principles for corporate environmental management and monitors companies for compliance. As the first public company to sign these principles, we continue to strongly support the ideas they embrace.

Through the 7.5% of pretax profits we commit to philanthropy, we've also been involved with hundreds of grassroots organizations working for progressive social change. Regrettably, we cannot mention all of them. But in the pages that follow, we're featuring as many as we can along with some of our other partnerships. We urge you to contact these groups and learn more about their efforts. It's work done on behalf of our children, ourselves and our future, and work for which we continue to be grateful.

GREENPEACE

Greenpeace

An independent campaigning organization using nonviolent creative confrontation to expose global environmental problems, and forcing the solutions which are essential to a green and peaceful future. Greenpeace's campaigns arise out of a few simple global imperatives: saving ancient forests, protecting the oceans, ending nuclear threats, stopping global warming, stopping toxic pollutions and ending threats posed by genetic engineering.

1436 U Street, NW
Washington, DC 20009
(800) 893-8526

www.greenpeaceusa.org

Greenpeace raised our awareness about the issue of dioxin in paper manufacturing, inspiring us to rethink our packaging.

Ben & Jerry's
Statement of Mission

Ben & Jerry's is dedicated to the creation & demonstration of a new corporate concept of linked prosperity. Our mission consists of three interrelated parts: Product, Economic and Social.

Product Mission

To make, distribute & sell the finest quality, all natural ice cream and related products in a wide variety of innovative flavors made from Vermont dairy products.

Economic Mission

To operate the Company on a sound financial basis of profitable growth, increasing value for our shareholders & creating career opportunities & financial rewards for our employees.

Social Mission

To operate the Company in a way that actively recognizes the central role that business plays in the structure of society by initiating innovative ways to improve the quality of life of a broad community: local, national & international.

Underlying the mission of Ben & Jerry's is the determination to seek new & creative ways of addressing all three parts, while holding a deep respect for individuals inside and outside the Company and for the communities of which they are a part.

CEO's Letter

On the threshold of our third decade in business, Ben & Jerry's is on track and gaining the forward momentum that will ensure continuous improvements and breakthrough innovations well into the new millennium.

With aggressive new product development and an increased focus on brand equity, net sales for 1998 were $209,203,000—a 20.1% increase over 1997's net sales of $174,206,000. All quarters displayed double-digit net sales increases, with a particularly strong 29.2% increase in the third quarter of 1998. The Company's 1998 net income of $6,242,000 represents a 60.2% increase over 1997's net income of $3,896,000.

I am pleased to note that we were able to increase our 1998 earnings in spite of substantial increases in dairy commodity costs. Our annual costs for cream alone increased by more than $7 million over 1997. Offsetting the increased dairy commodity costs were savings at the manufacturing level, resulting from better plant utilization and higher volumes. Current projections on dairy pricing are encouraging, suggesting that we will not experience as substantial an increase in dairy costs in 1999 as compared to 1998.

Gains in our sales and market share growth can largely be attributed to the strategic reinvigoration of the Ben & Jerry's brand. Of significant impact was our package redesign, a fresh new look that has proven to be popular among Ben & Jerry's loyalists and new consumers alike.

As awareness of the Ben & Jerry's brand has increased, so has household penetration–up 24% over last year, from 4.5% of U.S. households in 1997 to 5.6% in 1998. In round numbers, that means we've added an impressive one million households as our customers.

Reaching customers, both existing and new, was a high priority in 1998. During the summer, we supported the brand with our second successful foray into national radio advertising, targeting 16 key markets with the popular "phone fan" campaign. The advertisement dovetailed with trade promotion and key retailer marketing programs, bolstering domestic performance while leveraging our high brand awareness.

We continue to build awareness in less traditional ways—generating visibility for the brand in newspapers, magazines, radio and television. Ben & Jerry's products are frequently seen on top-rated sitcoms and movies—a frequent source of irritation to competitors who outspend us in advertising by more than 6:1.

All told, Ben & Jerry's enjoyed 450 million media impressions in 1998, a 50% increase over 1997. That may be one reason why a 1998 Harris Poll that asked adults to name "major companies that you think are really good companies" found Ben & Jerry's in the top 20. This score placed Ben & Jerry's ahead of such household names as Johnson & Johnson, DuPont and Apple Computer.

In 1998, we delivered on our goal of aggressive new product development, introducing 19 new products into the marketplace. Among the most successful of these introductions were three new Ben & Jerry's Low Fat Ice Cream flavors. Led by S'Mores™, the popular line was a significant factor in the growth of our business.

Another highlight of our 1998 introductions was Dilbert's World™—Totally Nuts™, an original ice cream flavor that exemplified a successful co-branding effort. We got a lot of mileage out of the launch event—an April Fools' Day promotion targeting airline business commuters. Our novelty line enjoyed a boost from Dilbert's World™—Totally Nuts™ bars and Phish Sticks™, which were reintroduced in a decidedly upscale, totally chlorine-free package, more consistent with the brand image.

Ben & Jerry's franchised scoop shop network saw continued expansion in 1998 with the opening of 38 additional shops, including three in Paris, France. That trend promises to continue in 1999, with 60 new shops slated to join our existing 195 shops in the U.S. and abroad.

Ben & Jerry's international presence took a marked upturn in 1998, primarily in the United Kingdom, where we opened 34 UCI Cinema locations, and in the Benelux region, where we've established a growing presence in Holland's popular Jamin chain of candy shops. Japan has also proven to be a significant market for Ben & Jerry's, where the introduction of a single-serve container exceeded our sales projections. Closer to home, our Canadian licensee, Delicious Alternative

B S R

Business for Social Responsibility

An organization of over 1,400 businesses, BSR's mission is to be the leading global resource providing members with innovative products and services that help companies be commercially successful in ways that demonstrate respect for ethical values, people, communities and the environment. BSR member companies also work closely with the BSR education fund, a nonprofit organization serving the broader business community and the general public through research and educational programs about responsible business practices.

609 Mission Street
2nd Floor
San Francisco, CA
94105-3506
(415) 537-0888
fax (415) 537-0889

www.bsr.org

Ben & Jerry's is a founding member of BSR.

Children's Defense Fund

Children's Defense Fund

An advocacy organization for the nation's children, the Children's Defense Fund is a strong and effective voice for those who haven't the power to speak for themselves. Assisting children and their parents in a wide variety of ways, the CDF seeks to ensure that every child receives the health care, education, respect and support they need to realize their full potential and successfully complete their passage from childhood to maturity.

25 E Street, NW
Washington, DC 20001
(202) 628-8787

www.childrensdefense.org

We have a long-standing relationship with the Children's Defense Fund. We particularly like CDF's Child Watch Program that brings business, political and social service leaders directly in contact with children in their communities.

Desserts Ltd., began distribution of a number of Ben & Jerry's ice cream and frozen yogurt flavors.

Essential to our reputation both at home and abroad is a renewed commitment to our social mission as an integral part of every Ben & Jerry's corporate decision. A major accomplishment for the Company was the November 1998 debut of unbleached packaging for our World's Best™ Vanilla. Our new "ECO Pint" carton is made from unbleached brown kraft paper with a non-toxic, printable clay coating on the outside. Standard paper-making uses chlorine compounds as a bleaching agent–a process that discharges millions of gallons of organochlorine-laced wastewater daily, according to Greenpeace. Some of these chemicals are considered human health hazards, and EPA has identified a few, such as dioxins, as carcinogens and highly toxic. As the first ice cream company to use this new packaging, we know we're doing our part for the environment, and we encourage other manufacturers to follow suit.

We plan to further this initiative by converting a significant percentage of our product line to unbleached packaging in 1999. And by working in partnership with the nonprofit organization Greenpeace, we plan to heighten consumer awareness about dioxins while enhancing Ben & Jerry's brand equity.

Our concern for the safety of the food chain continues to be reflected in our commitment to using only milk and cream from cows that have not been treated with recombinant Bovine Growth Hormone (rBGH), a genetically-engineered copy of a naturally-occurring hormone. Our 1997 legal victory cleared the way for our Company and other dairy processors nationwide to label products with an anti-rBGH message, giving consumers the right to make an informed choice about rBGH and the dairy products they buy. In 1999, we'll continue to bring greater consumer awareness to the rBGH issue.

Along with a renewed emphasis on social mission initiatives, our key objectives for 1999 include strengthening the Company's overall economics through brand extensions and the implementation of strategies for further growth.

As part of our initiative to improve the Company's economics, we will be instituting a number of changes in our distribution, including the adoption in 1999 of new, non-exclusive distribution agreements. Recognizing the potential pitfalls posed by previous arrangements which concentrated almost 60% of distribution through a single company, we have reapportioned our distribution to ensure that no one distributor accounts for any more than 40% of our business. We've created an internal sales force that now has responsibility for direct selling into the trade. Given our growth, we have also been able to negotiate better terms with distributors, changes that will enable Ben & Jerry's to gain additional control over retail sales while helping to streamline our delivery process.

Expansion is on our horizon, with significant opportunities for the Ben & Jerry's brand name in, for example, novelties and confectionery items. We've also identified and are investigating potential opportunities to expand through licensing arrangements, partnerships and acquisitions. As we pursue these opportunities, however, we remain committed to supporting our core business without cannibalizing the assets and brand loyalty upon which we've built our success.

The successes we achieved in 1998 would not have been possible without the talents and hard work of our dedicated Ben & Jerry's employees and the loyal support of our shareholders. Together, we approach our 21st year in business conscious that it will bring both opportunities and challenges.

While our marketing and communication challenges have never been bigger–our expectations have never been higher. I remain committed to building on the forward momentum we've achieved to produce steady, sustained growth for our shareholders, with a conscientious eye toward our economic, product and social missions.

Perry D. Odak
President & Chief Executive Officer

Chairman's Letter

Okay, where'd he go? Oh good, he's right there. I mean Ben, of course. We've had a little switch here, and apparently I am now Chair and Ben is Vice-Chair. Somebody told me it would be a good career move. I guess that means there won't be any chanting at our Annual Meeting. Sure, I'm disappointed too, but I think there's only one guy who could pull that off.

Prior to writing this I looked over the letters in the Annual Reports from the last few years. They were either from Ben as Chair or from both of us as Founders, but even then the words were mostly Ben's. It is no accident.

From the very beginning Ben has been the creative driving force in the Company. It was Ben's tastes that led us first to invent incredibly rich, intensely-flavored concoctions. Those were then followed by smooth, creamy ice cream with humongous chunks of chewy, crunchy cookies, nuts and candies. And let us not forget the swirls, not the wispy ones but the thick veins of fudge, caramel, peanut butter and marshmallow. His fanatical devotion to high quality took those concepts to products which are unparalleled. But Ben's real creation is the vision for a company which seeks to proactively integrate addressing social concerns into the day-to-day operations. The words we used last year were "a company which creates profit-making activities which at the same time help to bring about a more just and equitable society." It is an incredibly powerful concept for both its business and larger societal impacts.

Over the years we have made strides toward that vision, finding actual ways to implement it. We have also stumbled and at times gone backwards. Fulfilling our mission and creating those integrations can be difficult and we often struggle with it. I'm not sure we fully appreciate how fortunate we are to have a mission which is so meaningful—something which allows us to bring not only our skills, but also our hearts and souls to work with us.

We have had and continue to have extraordinarily talented and dedicated people working at Ben & Jerry's. I can't express my appreciation enough. We are getting better at accomplishing things; our level of competence continues to improve. My hope is that we can bring even greater creativity and initiative in order to continue realizing our vision.

Jerry

Jerry Greenfield
Chairman of the Board

BLSP

Business Leaders for Sensible Priorities

Founded by Ben Cohen, BLSP is a diverse group of 450 senior business executives and military leaders working to increase federal government investment in essential human needs like education and healthcare. BLSP believes that by trimming the enormous budget of the Pentagon, enough financial resources can be freed to substantially improve the quality of life for all Americans.

1350 Broadway
Suite 2210
New York, NY
10018-7802

www.businessleaders.org

Ben & Jerry's is a member of BLSP.

Ice Cream

NEW!

Triple Caramel Chunk
Caramel ice cream with a swirl of caramel and fudge covered caramel chunks

Bovinity Divinity™
Milk chocolate ice cream and white chocolate cows swirled with white chocolate ice cream and dark fudge cows

Pistachio Pistachio™
Pistachio ice cream with lightly roasted whole pistachios

Special Batch!™

(Limited Editions)

Southern Pecan Pie™
Brown sugar ice cream with golden roasted pecans, chunks of pecan pie pieces and a pecan caramel swirl

Marble Mint Chunk™
Peppermint ice cream with marbled dark and white fudge chunks

Candy Bar Crunch™
Vanilla malt ice cream with fudge covered vanilla cookies and a caramel swirl

Frozen Yogurt

Chunky Monkey®
Banana frozen yogurt with fudge flakes and walnuts

Chocolate HEATH® Bar Crunch
Chocolate frozen yogurt with HEATH® Bar Crunch

NEW!

Low Fat Ice Cream

Chocolate Comfort™
Chocolate truffle low fat ice cream with swirls of white chocolate low fat ice cream

Mocha Latte™
Sweet coffee low fat ice cream with a hint of cinnamon and swirls of chocolate low fat ice cream

Frozen Smoothie™

Strawberry Banana Manna™
A soothing mix of strawberries, bananas, yogurt & chamomile

Raspberry Renewal™
An energizing blend of raspberries, yogurt and ginseng

Tropic of Mango™
A tropical paradise of mangos, guava, yogurt & echinacea

Chai Tea Latte™
A comforting blend of Chai tea, sweet cream and five spices

NEW!

Novelties

S'mores™
A chocolate ice cream bar with gooey marshmallow on a crunchy graham cracker, all covered in milk chocolate.

New 1999 Flavors

All Natural
BEN & JERRY'S®
VERMONT'S FINEST

Frozen Smoothie

A New Kind of Cool...

In 1999, Ben & Jerry's will introduce a totally new kind of cool to freezers everywhere with Frozen Smoothies.

Retailers are looking for the innovative new product that will drive sales in the "non-ice cream" frozen dessert category. Anticipating that industry trend and noting the growth of the premium beverage category where Smoothies have taken off, Ben & Jerry's developed Frozen Smoothies. Frozen Smoothies will build on beverage smoothie growth and supplement our strong frozen yogurt and low fat ice cream lines in the "better for you" category.

"Our Frozen Smoothies take smoothies from your local juice bar into your freezer! Filled with the light refreshing taste of naturally sweet real fruit, they're the nutritious treat that's good for you. Eat them right out of the container for a fast healthy snack or blend them for a delicious frozen drink. Enjoy!

For the best flavor, soften at room temperature to desired consistency (15–30 min.) or microwave on high for 40-50 seconds, stir and enjoy! Or blend with skim milk or apple juice to create a delicious smoothie."

1999 Flavor List

Domestic Ice Cream
Bovinity Divinity™
Butter Pecan
Cherry Garcia®
Chocolate Chip Cookie Dough
Chocolate Fudge Brownie
Chubby Hubby®
Chunky Monkey®
Coffee HEATH® Bar Crunch
Coconut Almond Fudge Chip
• Coffee, Coffee BuzzBuzzBuzz!™
• Coffee Olé™
• Deep Dark Chocolate
Dilbert's World™-Totally Nuts™
• Maple Walnut
• Mint Chocolate Chunk
Mint Chocolate Cookie
New York Super Fudge Chunk®
Peanut Butter Cup
Phish Food™
Pistachio Pistachio™
• Strawberry
• Sweet Cream Cookie
Triple Caramel Chunk
Vanilla Caramel Fudge
• Vanilla Chocolate Chunk
Vanilla HEATH® Bar Crunch
• Wavy Gravy
• White Russian
World's Best™ Vanilla

Special Batch!™
(Limited Editions)
• Candy Bar Crunch™
Marble Mint Chunk™
Southern Pecan Pie™

Low Fat Ice Cream
Blackberry Cobbler™
Chocolate Comfort™
Coconut Cream Pie
Mocha Latte™
• Rockin' Road™
S'mores™
Vanilla & Chocolate Mint Patty

Frozen Yogurt
• Black Raspberry Swirl – no fat
Cherry Garcia®
• Chocolate Cherry Garcia®
• Chocolate Chip Cookie Dough
Chocolate Fudge Brownie
Chocolate HEATH® Bar Crunch
Chunky Monkey®
• Coffee Almond Fudge
• Coffee Fudge Swirl – no fat
• Vanilla – no fat
• Vanilla Fudge Swirl – no fat

Frozen Smoothie™
Chai Tea Latté™
Raspberry Renewal™
Strawberry Banana Manna™
Tropic of Mango™

Sorbet
• Devil's Food Chocolate™
Doonesberry™
Lemon Swirl™
Purple Passion Fruit™
• Strawberry Kiwi

• flavors available in scoop shops only
• flavors available in pints only

Novelties
Cherry Garcia®
Cookie Dough
Dilbert's World Totally Nuts™
Phish Stick™
S'Mores™
Vanilla HEATH® Bar Crunch
Vanilla

Canada Ice Cream
Cherry Garcia®
Chocolate Chip Cookie Dough
Chocolate Fudge Brownie
Chunky Monkey™/MC
Coffee, Coffee BuzzBuzzBuzz!™/MC
New York Super Fudge Chunk™/MC
Vanilla Toffee Crunch
World's Best™/MC Vanilla

Frozen Yogurt
Cherry Garcia®
Chocolate Fudge Brownie

Sorbet
Forest Berry™
Lemon Swirl™

Europe Ice Cream
Butter Almond Toffee
Caramel Chew Chew™
• Cherry Garcia™
• Chocolate
Chocolate Chip Cookie Dough
Chocolate Fudge Brownie
• Chunky Monkey™
• Dilbert's World Totally Nuts™
Double Trouble™
• New York Super Fudge Chunk™
Phish Food™
Vanilla Caramel Fudge
• Vanilla Like It Oughta Be™

Novelties
Cherry Garcia™
Dilbert's World Totally Nuts™
Phish Stick™

Israel Ice Cream
Butter Almond Toffee
• Cherry Garcia™
• Chocolate
Chocolate Chip Cookie Dough
Chocolate Fudge Brownie
• Chunky Monkey™
Cookies & Cream
• Dilbert's World Totally Nuts™
Double Trouble™
• New York Super Fudge Chunk™
Sweet 50
• Vanilla Like It Oughta Be™

Novelties
Cookies & Cream Cone

Japan Ice Cream
Banana Chocolate Walnut
Chocolate Brownie Walnut
Chocolate Nut Chunk
Coconut Cream Pie
Coffee Chocolate Chunk
Green Tea & White Chocolate
Orange Chocolate Chunk
Strawberry Cookie Crunch

• flavors available in single-serve size

Domestic Scoop Shops

Arizona

Phoenix
- Bank One Ballpark
- America West Arena*

Scottsdale
- The Boulders, 34505 North Scottsdale Rd.

Tempe
- 411 South Mill Ave.

Tucson
- Foothills Mall, 704 N. La Cholla Blvd.

California

Berkeley
- Oxford Center, 2128 Oxford St.

Brentwood
- 11740 San Vincente Blvd.

Burbank
- 164 E. Palm Ave.

Burlingame
- 290 Primrose Rd.

Century City
- 10250 Santa Monica Blvd.

Concord
- Brenden Theatre Complex, 1985 Willow Pass Rd.

Costa Mesa
- Mesa Verde Center, 2701 Harbor Blvd.

Davis
- 500 First St.

Fullerton
- 1343 East Chapman Ave.

Glendale
- 119 N. Maryland St.

Irvine
- Alton Square, 5365 Alton Pkwy.
- Irvine Spectrum, 31 Fortune Dr.

Long Beach
- 245 Pine Ave.
- 605 & Carson*

Malibu
- 3824 Crosscreek Rd.

Napa
- 1299 Napa Town Center

Northridge
- Northridge Fashion Center*

Orange
- 20 City Blvd.

Redondo Beach
- 234 S. Pacific Coast Hwy.

Riverside
- 1201 University Ave.

Roseville
- 2050 Douglas Blvd.

Sacramento
- Arden Square Mall, 1735 Arden Way

San Diego
- 1254 University Ave., Hillcrest
- 471 Horton Plaza
- 16761 Bernardo Center Dr., Rancho Bernardo
- Seaport Village, 859 A West Harbor Dr.

San Dimas
- Raging Waters Water Park

San Francisco
- 2146 Chestnut St.
- 1480 Haight St., Haight Ashbury
- 79 Jefferson St.
- 543 Columbus Ave., North Beach
- 451 Castro St.
- 102 Powell St.
- Fisherman's Wharf, Pier 41
- Macy's Union Square, 170 O'Farrell St.*

San Jose
- 115 E. San Carlos

San Luis Obispo
- 892 Marsh St.

Santa Clara
- 3155 Mission College Blvd.

Santa Clarita
- Creekside Plaza, 23630 Valencia Blvd.
- Valencia Town Center Dr.*

Santa Monica
- 2441 Main St.

Sherman Oaks
- 14318 Ventura Blvd.

Simi Valley
- Iapo Canyon Rd. & Alamo*

Temecula
- Tower Plaza Shopping Center, 27531 Ynez Rd.

Torrance
- 3550 Carson St.

Ventura
- NW Corner of Main & Chestnut St.*

Colorado

Boulder
- 1203 Pearl St.

Denver
- 1404 Larimer Square

Fort Collins
- 1 Old Town Square

Connecticut

Danbury
- 61 Newton Rd.

Delaware

Dewey Beach
- 1905 Highway 1**

Rehoboth Beach
- 52 Rehoboth Ave.**

District of Columbia

Washington
- 3135 M Street, NW, Georgetown
- Dupont Circle, 1339 19th St. NW*
- Eastern Market, 327 7th Avenue
- Pavilion at the Old Post Office, 1100 Pennsylvania Ave.

Florida

Aventura
- 19575 Biscayne Blvd.

Bonita Springs
- The Shop on the Promenade, 26841 South Bay Dr.

Fort Myers
- 12995 So. Cleveland Ave.

Key West
- 425 Front St.

Miami
- 760 Ocean Dr., South Beach

Naples
- The Village, 4320 Gulfshore Blvd.

Oviedo
- Oviedo Crossing, 1270 Oviedo Marketplace Blvd.

Sarasota
- 372A St. Armand Circle
- 5129 Ocean Blvd.**

Georgia

Atlanta
- Hartsfield Atlanta International Airport, Concourses A & C
- 800 Highland Ave.
- Zoo Atlanta, 800 Cherokee Ave. SE***

Duluth
- Medlock Bridge Rd.*

Illinois

Chicago
- 338 W. Armitage Ave.
- Lawson House, 30 W. Chicago Ave.*

Elmhurst
- 535 Spring Rd.

Normal
- Illinois State University, 202 Watterson Food Court***

Palatine
- 807 N. Quentin Rd. at NW Highway

Schaumburg
- 1562 East Golf Rd.

Vernon Hills
- 701 N. Milwaukee Ave.

Indiana

Bloomington
- 413 E. Kirkwood St.

Indianapolis
- 6336 Guilford Ave.
- 3956 East 82nd St.
- 1516 West 86th St.
- Circle Center Mall, 49 W. Maryland Ave.**

Noblesville
- 12880 East 146th St.**

West Lafayette
- 300 West State St.

Louisiana

New Orleans
- Jackson Square, 537 Saint Ann St.
- Louisiana Audubon Zoo, 6500 Magazine St.***
- New Orleans Airport***
- The Superdome, 1501 Girod St.***

Maine

Freeport
- 83 Main St.

Kennebunkport
- Coneport, Union St. and Ocean Ave.***

Kittery
- Bob's Clam Hut, 315 Rt. 1***

Ogunquit
- Udder Delights at the Ogunquit Pharmacy, 16 Main St.***

Portland
- 97 Exchange St.

Maryland

Annapolis
- 139 Main St.

Baltimore
- Harborplace, 201 East Pratt St.
- The Gallery, Pratt St. Pavilion

Bethesda
- 4901-B Fairmont Ave.

Rockville
- Rockville Center, 250 Hungerford Dr.*

Massachusetts

Arlington
- 451 Massachusetts Ave.

Boston
- 174 Newbury St.
- 20 Park Plaza

Dennisport
- 193 Shad Hole Rd.**

Hingham
- 191 Lincoln St.

Hyannis
- 352 Main St.**

Natick
- 1265 Worcester Rd. (Rt. 9)

New Seabury
- Popponesset Marketplace, Rocklanding Rd.**

North Eastham
- Rt. 6**

Pittsfield
- 179 South St.

Provincetown
- 258 Commercial St.**

Michigan

Auburn Hills
- Great Lakes Crossings, 4308 Baldwin Rd.

Nevada

Henderson
- Sunset Station, 1301 West Sunset Rd.

Las Vegas
- Santa Fe Hotel & Casino, 4949 N. Rancho Dr.
- Rio Hotel & Casino, 3700 W. Flamingo Rd.

New Hampshire

Hampton Beach
- Screams, 367 Ocean Blvd.***

Hanover
- 11 Lebanon St.

Meredith
- Mills Falls Marketplace***

North Conway
- 29 Norcross Circle

Weirs Beach
- Across from the Boardwalk***

New Jersey

Beach Haven
- Pier 18 Mall, 3rd & Bay Ave.**

Manasquan
- 223 Beach Front Stand**

Normandy Beach
- 549 Rt. 35 North**

Princeton
- Princeton Forrestal Village, 10 Market Hall

New York

Albany
- 250 Lark St.

Bolton Landing
- Rt. 9 N**

Ithaca
- 104 N. Cayuga St.

Lake George
- 170 Canada St.**

Lake Placid
- 83 Main St.

Montauk
- Checkers Ice Cream & Cafe, Flamingo Rd.***

Mt. Kisco
- 639 E. Main St.

New Rochelle
- New Roc City, Huguenot & Harrison*

New York City
- 41 Third Ave.
- 680 8th Ave., Times Square
- 222 East 86th St.
- 109 World Trade Center, Concourse Level

Niagara Falls
- Niagara International Factory Outlet, 1994 Military Rd.

Scoop Shop Locations

Saratoga Springs
- 34 Phila St.
- Saratoga Raceway**

Troy
- RPI Student Union, Sage and 15th St.

Westhampton
- 121 Main St.***

Woodstock
- 65 Tinker Street**

North Carolina

Chapel Hill
- 102 West Franklin St.

Charlotte
- Arboretum, 8200 Providence Rd.
- 507 Providence Rd.
- Foxcroft East Shopping Center, 7800 Fairview Rd.

Davidson
- 202 South Main St.

Durham
- 609 Broad St.

Ohio

Dayton
- 1934 Brown St.

Oregon

Portland
- 1428 SE 36th St.
- Uptown Center, Burnside & NW 23rd Pl.

Pennsylvania

Hershey
- Hershey Park, 100 W. Hersheypark Dr.***

Philadelphia
- Coming Soon*

State College
- 124 S. Allen St.

Rhode Island

Block Island
- Sweet Inspirations at the Old Harbor Inn, Block Island***

Cranston
- 48 Hillside Rd.

Narragansett
- South County Ice Cream, 855 Pt. Judith Rd.***

Newport
- 33 Bannister's Wharf**
- 359 Thames St.**

Providence
- 237 Meeting St.

South Carolina

Charleston
- 96 N. Market St.

Myrtle Beach
- 2 locations at Broadway at the Beach, 1303 Celebrity Circle

Vermont

Burlington
- 36 Church St.

Essex Junction
- 159 Pearl St.

Manchester Center
- Historic Main St.

Middlebury
- Star Mill, 5 Park St.

Montpelier
- City Center, 89 Main St.

Rutland
- 170 South Main St.

Shelburne
- The Commons, 2031 Shelburne Rd.

Waterbury
- Rt. 100

Virginia

Alexandria
- 103 South Union St.

Chantilly
- Dulles Airport, Concourse B

Norfolk
- 33 Waterside Dr.

Richmond
- 3008-A West Cary St.*

Virginia Beach
- 2865-41 Lynn Haven Dr.
- 2502 Atlantic Ave.**
- Beach Mall, 1400 Atlantic Ave.*

Williamsburg
- Patriot Plaza, 3044 Richmond Rd.
- 7097 Pocahontas Trail
- Berkley Common Outlet Center, Rt. 60, Richmond Rd.

Washington

Bellevue
- Bellevue Galleria, 550 106th Ave., NE*

Seattle
- 428 Broadway Ave.
- University Village, 4500 25th Ave., NE

International Scoop Shops

Canada

Quebec

Knowlton
- 255 E. Knowlton Rd.

Montreal
- 1316 De Maisonneuve St., West
- 5582 Monkland Ave.
- 433 Place Jacques Cartier**

France

Paris
- 18 boulevard Montmartre
- 22 rue de la Roquette
- 4 rue Pierre Lescot

Israel

Eilat
- King's Wharf/Lagoona Hotel
- Canion Mall Hayam

Jerusalem
- 5 Hillel St.

Rechovot
- Canion Rechovot

Rishon Lezion
- Canion Hazahav

Tel Aviv
- 1 Allenby St./Opera Tower
- 284 Dizengoff St.
- Ramada Hotel/Gordon Beach

Yavne
- 1 Hameisav St.

Holland

Amsterdam
- Centraal Station
- Leidsestraat 90

Delft
- Brabantse Turfmarkt 59

The Hague
- Passage 53

Jamin Shops

Almere
- Stationsstraat 64****

Amersfoort
- Langestraat 39****

Amsterdam
- Kalverstraat 39****

Den Haag
- Spuistraat 19****

Enschede
- Raadhuisstraat 1-5****

Goes
- Lange Kerkstraat 12****

Katwijk
- Voorstraat 18****

Leiden
- Haarlemmerstraat 114****

Leidschendam
- Berkenhove 17****

Maastricht
- Grote Staat 1****

Nijmegen
- Broerstraat 13****

Rotterdam
- Lijnbaan 57****

Utrecht
- Radboudtraverse 14****

Venlo
- Vleesstraat 3-5****

Lebanon

Beirut
- Bliss St.*

Peru

Lima
- LarcoMar Entertainment Center

UK

England

Tyneside
- Metrocentre, Gateshead*****

Hull
- St. Andrews Quay, Clive Sullivan Way*****

Huddersfield
- Alfred MacAlpine Stadium, Bradley Mills Rd.*****

Warrington
- 100 Westbrook Centre, Cromwell Ave.*****

Preston
- Riversway, Ashton on Ribbie*****

Manchester
- 201, The Dome, The Trafford Centre*****

Derby
- Meteor Centre, Mansfield Rd.*****

Sheffield
- Crystal Peaks Shopping Centre*****

Telford
- Forgegate, Telford Town Centre*****

Hatfield
- The Galleria, Comet Way*****

Milton Keynas
- The Point, 602 Midsummer Blvd.*****

High Wycombe
- Great Rd.*****

London
- Whiteleys of Bayswater, Queensway*****
- The Mast Leisure Dev., Surrey Quays, Southwark*****
- Lee Valley, Picketts Lock Ln., Edmonton*****

Poole
- Tower Park, Mannings Heath*****

Surrey
- St. Nicholas Centre, St. Nicholas Way, Sutton*****

Essex
- Lakeside Retail Pk., Graus, West Thurrock*****
- Festival Leisure Pk., Basildon*****

Ireland

Coolock
- 84 Malahide Rd., Dublin 8*****

Blanchardstown
- Blanchardstown Rd. South, Dublin 15*****

Tallaght
- The Square, Old Blessington Rd.*****

Wales

Solihull
- 120 Highlands Rd.*****

Dudley
- Merry Hill Centre, Brioriey Hill*****

Cardiff
- Atlantic Wharf Leisure Pk., Hemingsway Rd., Butstown*****

Scotland

Edinburgh
- Kinnaird Park, Neweraignall Rd.*****

Clydebank
- Clydebank Regional Centre, 23 Brittania Way*****

** projected locations for 1999   ** indicates a seasonal Ben & Jerry's Scoop Shop   *** indicates a seasonal location featuring Ben & Jerry's*
***** indicates Jamin Candy Shop locations featuring Ben & Jerry's   ***** indicates UCI Cinema locations featuring Ben & Jerry's*

Social Performance

Social Auditor's Letter to the Board of Directors & Stakeholders

From many perspectives 1998 was a good year for Ben & Jerry's. Financially it was an outstanding year, as the Company recorded impressive growth in sales and earnings. The Company introduced new products and entered new markets. It continued to strengthen its management, positioning the business for steady growth in years to come. There is little doubt that the Company is a stronger business organization, more focused on key economic objectives, and more capable of achieving those objectives than at any other time in its recent history.

The focus here is on the Company's social mission objectives, and particularly on its record in meeting those objectives in 1998. As a result of its financial successes and stronger management, Ben & Jerry's is in a much better position to achieve social mission objectives than in the past. Employees have a better understanding of their responsibilities. Social mission objectives have been established throughout the Company, and the incentive compensation of the CEO and other senior managers depends in part on achievement of those objectives.

The actual results in 1998, however, were mixed. As described elsewhere in this report and in my analysis, Ben & Jerry's made significant progress on a number of fronts. It continued to fall short on others. If one were grading for achievement in 1998, Ben & Jerry's probably deserves a "B." Given the resources and management talent now available, the Company is fully capable of scoring an "A." The challenge for Ben & Jerry's now is to bring the same level of energy to bear on achieving social mission objectives that the Company has devoted to its economic objectives.

What follows is my independent evaluation of Ben & Jerry's social mission performance in 1998. The emphasis is on performance relative to objectives that the Company set for itself in 1998. In preparing this evaluation, I have reviewed a significant amount of written material, interviewed the founders and senior managers at the Company's South Burlington, VT headquarters, and have met with managers and employees at the St. Albans, Springfield and Waterbury plants and at the Vermont Distribution Center. I have also reviewed and commented on the management's Social Performance Report, which follows this letter. The Social Mission and Work Culture Committee of the Board, whose members bring independent judgment and commitment to the social mission, have reviewed my evaluation. In the final analysis, however, the conclusions here represent my own findings.

Workplace

The 1998 Work Life Survey results present a very positive picture. On the whole, employees have a favorable view of the Company and its social mission. Employee benefits continue to improve, and by all indications, employees are very happy with the benefits that Ben & Jerry's provides. The Company is directing more resources to training, and it is making progress in redesigning job levels and linking pay to job skill requirements, responding to employee concerns for more opportunities for personal growth and advancement. At the senior management level and also at the board level, the Company has done well with respect to diversity, though the workforce as a whole, like the Vermont population from which it is largely drawn, remains overwhelmingly white.

There are, however, a number of areas of concern. Among senior non-executive managers (approximately 45 men and women directly below the CEO and those who report directly to him) there appears to be a pay equity issue between men and women, with women earning approximately 12 percent less than men. Though wages and benefits levels are excellent, the Company has yet to realize its stated vision of creating "linked prosperity" between the Company and its employees to ensure that future prosperity is shared widely throughout the Company. In fact, the income disparity between the highest and

LIVING DEMOCRACY

Center for Living Democracy

We can all do democracy—this is the mission of the Center for Living Democracy. Working to create a unique "multiplier effect," the Center spreads and publicizes stories of citizen-based problem solving. CLD's American News Service has appeared in 300 newspapers nationwide and its Tool Box catalog offers invaluable resources for increasing the practice of local democracy in our towns and cities.

289 Fox Farm Road
PO Box 8187
Brattleboro, VT
05304-8187
(802) 254-1234
fax (802) 254-1227

www.americannews.com
www.livingdemocracy.org

Ben & Jerry's subscribes to the CLD American News Service where we learn about positive social change happening at the local level.

lowest paid employees is near its historical high at 16-1 (the ratio would be even higher if the present value of unexercised stock options were included), and stock option benefits to date have gone largely to senior management, many of whom are fairly new to Ben & Jerry's. The decision at the end of the year to allocate stock to each employee's 401(k) plan and to award 316 stock options to each employee (excluding officers and directors) regardless of position, were important steps toward realizing the goal of linked prosperity.

Closing the Waterbury daycare center was inevitable, given its high costs and the small number of employees served. The decision to close this facility, however, only brings into focus a larger question: how committed is Ben & Jerry's to helping employees balance family and work obligations? The issues go beyond child care; they include flexible work hours, job sharing and telecommuting. The Company has a good record and an excellent reputation on family and work issues; to maintain its leadership position it should address these issues in a focused way.

At this juncture, it is hard to know what to make of the partial unionization of employees at the St. Albans plant. Ben & Jerry's has never had a union before, and it likes to think of itself as a company where employees do not need a collective bargaining agent to be treated fairly. But in a drive that began in 1998 and ended with a favorable vote in early 1999, 19 hourly employees at the St. Albans plant narrowly voted to be represented by the International Brotherhood of Electrical Workers. Notwithstanding the small number of employees in the bargaining unit (the 19 employees represent less than 3 percent of the Company's full-time workforce) the voting outcome raises questions about the quality of employer-employee relations.

Operations

Ben & Jerry's made progress in 1998 in extending the scope of its vendor certification program. It also created a database of potential suppliers from among women- and minority-owned firms. It continued to purchase a significant amount of product ingredients from socially-aligned vendors, the most important of which remains the St. Albans Co-op, whose members receive above-market premiums to produce rBGH-free milk and cream. However, the Company got only halfway to its modest purchasing goal for minority- and female-owned businesses.

The Company revisited the question of whether to produce an organic line and once again, as it did in 1997, decided not to proceed in that direction. It has now shifted focus to how it might support sustainable agriculture. This is an area of enormous potential for Ben & Jerry's to demonstrate leadership if it can determine ways in which, working with its own suppliers, it can encourage agricultural practices that are both economically beneficial to providers and environmentally benign.

Safety remains a problematic issue for Ben & Jerry's. Safety can be measured in a number of ways, and depending on which measure is used, Ben & Jerry's record can look like it is improving or getting worse. However measured, though, the injury rate remains higher than the food industry average. Ben & Jerry's plant safety managers, interviewed during the course of this audit, acknowledged that the Company's safety record is unsatisfactory. Improving safety will require that top management make safety a priority. New safety education programs at the plant level will help. So will reengineering production methods in ways designed to promote safety.

Environment

Ben & Jerry's major environmental achievement in 1998 was the introduction of unbleached packaging for its products. The production of unbleached paper virtually eliminates reliance on chlorine in the production process, which in turn reduces the amount of dioxin, a known carcinogen, in the environment. When it decided several years ago that it wanted to use unbleached containers, Ben & Jerry's discovered that no one made them. Not only that, no paper manufacturer made unbleached paper that could be used to make unbleached ice cream containers. The Company persuaded manufacturers of both paper and containers to provide it with unbleached products—no mean feat given the relatively small amount of production involved. At some cost, Ben & Jerry's in late 1998 became the first frozen food company to offer its products in unbleached containers. Should other companies decide to follow its example, the cost of unbleached paper and containers will drop, making unbleached containers

ENVIRONMENTAL WORKING GROUP

Environmental Working Group

The Environmental Working Group is an environmental think tank whose innovative environmental testing and research, detailed analysis of government environmental data, and award-winning internet sites provide crucial information to the public. In addition to a variety of collaborations with state and local environmental groups, the EWG's work has uncovered important evidence of pesticides in baby food, tap water and schoolyard air, and revealed the dangers of using toxic industrial waste "recycled" as fertilizer.

1718 Connecticut Ave., NW,
Suite 600
Washington, DC 20009
(202) 667-6982

www.ewg.org

EWG has been a terrific resource in thinking about sustainability across our business.

an even more attractive alternative to other food companies, and Ben & Jerry's will have pioneered a manufacturing and packaging change with significant environmental benefits to society.

Levels of solid waste and dairy waste declined in 1998 for the third consecutive year. However, the Company did not meet its waste reduction goals in 1998. The Company seems to have hit a point of diminishing returns in its ongoing efforts to reduce waste. Switching the packaging of incoming ingredients to large containers known as totes (as recommended in 1998 by an employee group created to study how packaging affects solid waste) should make it possible to achieve further reductions in solid waste. In the future, achieving significant reductions in levels of dairy waste is likely to require reengineering manufacturing processes. Dairy waste levels are also affected by production decisions that can be hard to anticipate. For example, the Company's decision to gear up for rapid production to serve the Japanese market, where ice cream is sold primarily in individual serving-size containers, resulted in higher than anticipated dairy waste levels in 1998.

Franchise and Retail Operations

Retail Operations did not achieve its goal of opening five new PartnerShops in 1998. The Company appears to have badly under-estimated the amount of time and effort required to get PartnerShops up and running. Realizing that it was not properly staffed, the Company decided late in 1998 to hire a full-time PartnerShop coordinator. Several of the PartnerShops originally slated to be opened in 1998 are scheduled to open in 1999. The Company developed the concept of the "Entrepreneurial Shop" in 1998 and entered into a contract with one licensee who is scheduled to open in 1999; this is an effort to adapt the nonprofit PartnerShop concept to the for-profit sector.

The number of scoop shops owned by women and people of color increased slightly in 1998. This is an area where the Company could have a much bigger impact than it has had in the past. For the third consecutive year, Ben & Jerry's faced no franchise-related litigation. By any measure, this is an outstanding achievement.

Sales/Marketing/International

As noted in last year's audit, Ben & Jerry's entered 1998 in a position "to consider carefully the strategic significance of values-led marketing to the Company's future." Domestically, the introduction of unbleached paper containers in 1998 was not only an important environmental but also an exemplary values-led marketing initiative.

However, the Company has yet to come fully to grips with how to pursue the social mission in general, and values-led marketing in particular in the international arena. Partly this was due to management's decision in 1998 to concentrate its international efforts on boosting sales and improving earnings in existing markets and on opening new markets abroad, and partly it was due to the fact that international activities pose special challenges.

Cultural and political norms regarding the proper role of business in society vary considerably around the world. It would be foolhardy to assume that what is acceptable in the United States and what works here will be acceptable and will work elsewhere. Among the issues that need to be addressed are how the Company should use philanthropy abroad; whether political activism outside the U.S. is appropriate; and whether the Company should use human rights criteria to decide whether it even wishes to do business in countries like Peru, which has a long history of human rights abuses.

Defining the social mission globally; setting country-specific objectives that are consistent with Ben & Jerry's values and the values of each country in which the Company does business; and dedicating sufficient

Institute for Sustainable Communities

The Institute for Sustainable Communities seeks to protect the earth's ecosystems and simultaneously enhance the quality of human life in countries around the world. By developing and supporting creative solutions to pressing local problems, the Institute's international projects emphasize active participation in civic life, the development of strong democratic institutions, the engagement of diverse interests in decision-making, and the protection of local natural resources.

56 College Street
Montpelier, VT 05602
(802) 229-2900

www.iscvt.org

Ben & Jerry's sponsored ISC's ecological poster contest for Russian children. An exhibit of their art helped promote greater public awareness of local environmental issues in their country.

human and financial resources to achieving those objectives all require that top management make the social mission a higher priority in its international business activities.

Philanthropy

In 1998 Ben & Jerry's continued its well-established practice of using philanthropy to advance social mission objectives. The program is noteworthy for the relatively high percentage of profits the Company contributes to the Foundation, for the involvement of employees in grant-making decisions, and for the emphasis placed on support of grassroots organizations. In addition, the presence of Community Action Teams (CATs) at each location provides opportunities for all employees to perform community service. For many employees CAT team activities are an important expression of the Company's social mission.

Finance and Shareholders

Financial returns to shareholders continued to improve in 1998, reflecting the impressive growth in sales and earnings. Long-term investors in Ben & Jerry's can now take satisfaction knowing that the Company is capable of accomplishing both social and financial objectives. However, the price of the Company's common stock at year-end ($22.50 a share) was still significantly lower than the price ($30.50 a share) at which the Company sold additional shares to the public in 1992. These investors may still have cause to wonder whether returns to shareholders are adequate.

The Company's decision in late 1998 to add stock to all employees' 401(k) accounts and award stock options was a positive development, aligning the interests of shareholders and employees. This should be accompanied by a companywide educational campaign stressing the benefits of retaining shares for the long-term.

Conclusion

Ben & Jerry's did some things well in 1998. The introduction of unbleached containers probably ranks as the single most important social mission achievement, serving as a model of how the Company can lead with its values. But the Company also fell short in a number of areas. The absence of new strategic values-led initiatives in the international arena is perhaps the most notable shortfall.

Looking ahead, Ben & Jerry's is in a better position to achieve its social mission objectives than ever before. The management team installed in 1997 is strong. Economically, the Company is charging ahead. The human, financial and organizational resources needed to raise the level of social mission performance are available.

How well the Company does in meeting its social mission objectives will depend importantly on how hard top management, particularly the CEO, pushes to achieve social mission objectives. The leadership and management skills that have so impressively guided the Company's economic turnaround now need to be applied with equal determination to the social mission.

It will also be important for the Company's board of directors to work constructively with management. Board members, especially the founders, are passionate advocates of the social mission. Some tension is to be expected between a board that champions the social mission and management that must make practical judgments. This can, however, be a constructive process, and one that produces beneficial results for everyone with a stake in the Company's future.

James E. Heard
March 1999

National Association of Child Advocates

NACA is the only organization in the United States dedicated solely to creating and maintaining state and local child advocacy groups across the country. Working at the increasingly vital level of U.S. statehouses, county commissions and city councils, NACA represents and supports a national network of multi-issue child advocacy organizations; helping its members provide critical leadership on children's issues.

1522 K Street NW
Suite 600
Washington, DC 20005
(202) 824-0777

www.childadvocacy.org

A number of Ben & Jerry's franchise store owners have partnered with children's organizations in their states that are members of the NACA.

Social Performance Report

Association for Enterprise Opportunity

The AEO is a national association of organizations committed to the development of microenterprises (the smallest and most disadvantaged of small businesses). AEO provides a forum, information and a voice to expand enterprise opportunities and financial choices for people and communities with limited access to economic resources. AEO believes that all individuals have a right and the capacity to participate in the economy according to their values and beliefs.

70 East Lake Street
Suite 1102
Chicago, IL 60601-5907
(703) 357-0177

www.wva.com\~aeo

AEO keeps us in touch with micro-economic development projects.

Our social performance assessment is constructed around goals which management set for 1998, as well as around key findings from last year's social performance assessment. This audit is divided into eight sections: Workplace, Manufacturing Operations, Environment, Franchise Operations, Marketing and Sales, International Operations, Social Mission and Philanthropy, and Finance and Shareholders. Each section begins with goals set for 1998 and a description of issues raised in the prior year, followed by a discussion of the outcomes.

Workplace

Issues & Goals Summary

The primary workplace goals for 1998 were: to improve the quality of work life at Ben & Jerry's; to complete the compensation redesign project; to recruit and retain people of color; and to advance the concept of linked prosperity, whereby opportunities are created for staff members at all levels to build financial assets as the Company prospers. Key issues raised in the prior audit were attention to racial diversity across the business, career development opportunities for staff at all levels, and lack of management structures to support the social mission. Following is a discussion of activities and progress in these areas in 1998.

Work Life Survey Results

Since 1990 we have administered a biennial Work Life Survey. In 1998 we undertook a survey to assess whether, under new leadership, progress had been made in the areas of management, the work environment, the Social Mission, and staff confidence in the future of Ben & Jerry's.

In June 1998, surveys were completed by 82% of the 645 full- and part-time employees. Seven benchmark questions were asked in both 1997 and 1998. Scores on six of the seven questions rose significantly between 1997 and 1998. Major findings were:

- Staff's confidence in the Company's future rose by 47% (from 3.53 to 4.22 on a scale of 0-5).
- The perception that management at each of our sites cares about what staff members think and feel increased by 29% (from 2.82 to 3.46 on a scale of 0-5). Belief that senior management had improved its openness and caring increased by 18%.
- The percentage of staff members who view our social mission as critical to success increased by 26% (from 3.60 to 3.96 on a scale of 0-5).
- Although satisfaction with the level of communication of important information increased (from 3.47 to 3.74 on a scale of 0-5), communication between work groups, shifts and departments continues to be an area of concern. Despite improved perceptions about senior management, many staff members still state that senior management does not appear to be adequately open to staff issues and concerns.
- Staff members expressed some concerns about lack of opportunities for advancement; perceived poor performance of some supervisors and managers; increased bureaucracy and a fear that the Company is becoming too corporate.

Union Organizing/Vote

During 1998 a union organizing effort took place at Ben & Jerry's. In November we received notification from the National Labor Relations Board (NLRB) that the International Brotherhood of Electrical Workers (IBEW) had petitioned to represent maintenance employees at our St. Albans plant. This petition defined the bargaining unit as being 19 maintenance employees. We took the position that since the plant is managed and operated as an integrated team, the bargaining unit should consist of all employees at the St. Albans plant. A hearing was conducted at the regional NLRB office to resolve this issue. The NLRB's final decision was that the election/bargaining unit would consist of 19 maintenance department employees. Early in 1999 the vote was held, resulting in an 11-8 vote to be represented by the IBEW for the purpose of collective bargaining. We are currently in contract negotiations with the union.

Compensation Redesign

In 1998, the process underway over the last two years of evaluating and regrading all positions was completed. Enhancements to the job levels were implemented as part of the redesign, to recognize and reward cross-training experience, and to provide an additional promotional level within manufacturing. This has resulted in a higher earning potential—up to one third more—for manufacturing workers, particularly those who have held similar positions for many years.

Livable Wage Calculation & Comparison

In 1995 we made a commitment to pay a livable wage. While no consensus exists on the precise meaning of the term, we include housing, utilities, out-of-pocket health care, transportation, nutrition, recreation, savings, taxes and miscellaneous expenses for a single person in this calculation. We have consulted with other organizations, such as the Peace and Justice Center in Burlington, Vermont, and the California, Washington and Maryland Livable Wage Coalitions

TOP-TO-BOTTOM COMPENSATION RATIO

	1997	1998
Entry-level salary including benefits	$25,911	$28,719
Highest salary including benefits & stock options	$433,231*	$465,248*
Effective salary ratio	17-to-1	16-to-1

** Does not include unrealized gains on stock options.*

that have endeavored to define a basic livable wage. Again, while there is no agreement on a set number, we determined this figure to be $9.25 per hour, or $19,240 annually. This is considerably higher than calculations done by other organizations we contacted, whose figures averaged approximately $8.50/hour. In our calculation we used the same criteria as the Peace and Justice Center but added retirement, savings and recreation allowances. In 1998 with Board leadership, we established a policy setting a floor of $9.25 per hour for all full-time employees. This figure includes salary and profit sharing.

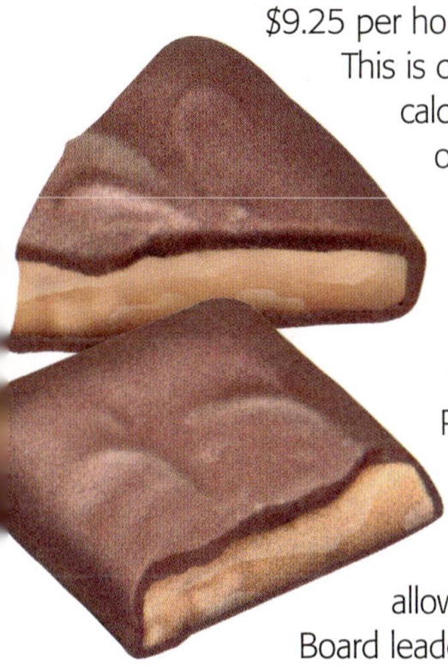

Positions Filled Internally vs. Externally

In 1998 54% of open positions (outside of Office of the Chief Executive Officer-OCEO) were filled internally.

POSITIONS FILLED
Internally vs. Externally - 1998

Position Level	External	Internal
Senior ($74,885-$168,491) (not including OCEO)	2	0
Mid-level ($47,186-$93,608) (One promotion)	4	2
All other ($17,680-$61,548) (23 Lateral Moves; 55 Promotions)	63	78
Total positions filled - 149	69	80

Benefits & Salary Enhancements

Our manufacturing wages remained in the 75th percentile for our region of the country. In 1998 we added 1% of salary as an automatic contribution to every eligible employee's 401(k) account, bringing the total company contribution to 3%. Also in 1998 we approved another 1% match to the 401(k), effective January 1, 1999. This additional match brings the Company's total 401(k) contribution to 4%. We voted in a one-time stock bonus award amounting to $250,000 to be awarded to each eligible employee's 401(k) account. Total shares awarded to each employee were based on a combination of tenure and headcount. A grant of 200,000 stock options was approved that will result in an award of 316 options per employee for all full-time employees hired as of December 31, 1998. Profit sharing resulted in an average 50% increase in distributions to all employees. Profit sharing is calculated on a combination of total employee numbers and length of service. A COLA (cost of living adjustment) adjustment of 5% was applied to all current pay grades at the beginning of 1999, covering cost-of-living increases for 1997 of 2.9% and 1998 of 2.1%.

Tuition reimbursement was increased from $2,000 to $5,000 annually. Additional benefits enhancements included offering eyewear coverage; increasing paid holidays by 2 days to 10 per year; increasing maximum vacation time to 4 weeks from the previous 18 day maximum; increasing short-term disability coverage by 4 weeks; offering free financial management seminars for staff; adding a Preferred Provider Option to our health care options; adding insurance coverage for orthodontics; and adding accelerated benefit payments and survivor support programs for employee life insurance.

In 1998 the Board of Directors initiated a dialogue with management about linked prosperity, as the company prospers how do we build

CEP
COUNCIL ON ECONOMIC PRIORITIES

Council on Economic Priorities

Celebrating its 30th anniversary in 1999, the Council on Economic Priorities is a public service research organization committed to the accurate and impartial analysis of the social and environmental records of the world's corporations. Through detailed research and reporting, CEP helps consumers, investors, corporate managers, employers and activists make informed decisions everyday and empowers them to use their purchasing power to promote human rights, fair labor standards, environmental health and responsible corporate policies.

30 Irving Place
New York, NY 10003-2386
(212) 420-1133

www.cepnyc.org

CEP has developed a very helpful and useful set of Social Accountability Standards (SA8000) for international business.

income and assets for staff at all levels? Although there were a number of initiatives in this regard, such as strengthening our 401(k) and an across-the-board award of stock options to all staff regardless of position, we have yet to define a long-term strategy to accomplish this objective.

Training

In 1998 we offered various ongoing and discrete training opportunities for staff including: Tuition reimbursement for approved courses at colleges, universities, vocational schools and other accredited learning centers; internal training in such areas as interpersonal skills and creating work-team missions and standards; contracted training in subjects such as business writing, presentation skills, specialized computer training, career exploration, resume writing and interview skills; manufacturing process training; conferences and seminars in such fields as dairy accounting and maintenance skills; and training courses offered by equipment vendors. Virtually all employees participated in *Understanding and Appreciating Individual Style Differences*. The purpose of this training was to sensitize staff to the diversity inherent in our work force–from gender and ethnic diversity to more individual differences in work styles, motivations and skills.

Virtually every employee in the Company received some form of both interpersonal skills and job development training in 1998. We have not yet developed the systems to track this training. Career development was a concern our staff raised in our last audit and in the Work Life Survey. Our focus on training is in response to those concerns.

Closing of Child Care Center

In 1998 we closed our subsidized child care center located at the Waterbury production facility. The center had been noted in previous Social Performance Reports because of the organizational inequity inherent in a center available at only one of five sites. The center opened in 1989 and never served more than 20 Ben & Jerry's families in a given year. In 1998, 14 of Ben & Jerry's 700 employees sent children to the center, even with a sliding scale fee based on income for staff families. The Company subsidy totaled $162,608 in 1997 and $120,841 in 1998. An additional 13 slots at the center were open to non-employee families.

We retained an independent consultant, Work Family Directions of Boston, MA to evaluate the center's operations. Its report addressed high operating costs and low utilization by Ben & Jerry's employees. Insurance concerns also arose related to the center's proximity to the manufacturing plant, a highway and a running brook. In closing the facility, we provided assistance to both employee and non-employee families in finding alternative child care arrangements; offered severance packages with six months of free benefits to employees terminated by the closing; and gave center employees preference for other jobs at Ben & Jerry's.

We offer family-friendly benefits such as an Employee Assistance Program, flexible spending for child care, personal financial planning and home buying counseling. In addition, since 1997 we have contracted with Work Family Directions for their *LifeWorks* program that provides counselors, practical advice, information and referrals on a range of family issues, including day care for all staff.

Even though the Center closed, with the range of family friendly benefits we offer, we were again recognized by the Child Care Fund of Vermont on their *Child Care Counts Honor Roll.* We have made a commitment to support the work of the Child Care Fund with a $25,000 contribution in 1999 and 2000 from the tour revenue at our Waterbury site.

Gender Equity

The Company's gender balance in 1998 was 57% men and 43% women, compared to 56% men and 44% women in 1997. Whereas pay equity is for the most part in balance, there is a gap emerging at the senior levels that requires analysis and attention.

Workplace Diversity

In 1998 approximately 3% of our work force were people of color, slightly more than the proportion in the state of Vermont. Among the eight senior managers that comprise the Office of the CEO, there were two African Americans

C·A·M·P TA·KUM·TA

Camp Ta-Kum-Ta

Camp Ta-Kum-Ta is a free, week-long resident camp on the shores of Lake Champlain that provides challenging and rewarding experiences to children who have or have had cancer. Combining the fun of a traditional summer camp and the special needs its participants require, the program creates a safe and nurturing environment that gives kids with cancer the opportunity to develop friendships with other children who are having similar experiences.

PO Box 576
Waterbury, VT 05676
(802) 244-8701

www.pwshift.com/takumta

Camp Ta-Kum-Ta was founded by one of our staff members, Debby Kessler, and her husband Ted. Every year a group of Ben & Jerry's participate in camp activities.

GENDER PAY EQUITY

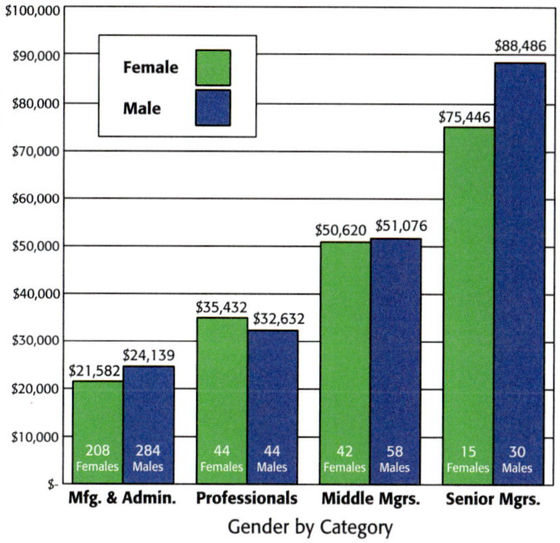

and two women. Despite the loss in 1997 of four people of color in management jobs, we maintained a 3% proportion of people of color on staff in 1998.

On our nine-member Board of Directors there are two African Americans (one of whom is a woman) and one white woman, as of the end of 1998, the same as in 1997.

PEOPLE OF COLOR	1997	1998
Total employed	19	23
Asian-American/Pacific Islander	4	5
African-American	4	9
Hispanic	3	2
Abenaki	8	7
Percentage of B&J's Total	3%	3%
VT minority population (1990 census)	1.8%	1.8%
People of color among managers, professionals & technicians	2 (2%)	3(1.3%)

Temporary Workers

At the beginning of 1998, there were 177 temporary workers on staff. At the end of the year there were 105. Ninety-two of the temporary positions were part-time or seasonal slots in our tour and company scoop shops. During 1998, 30 temporary manufacturing positions were converted to full- or part-time permanent jobs. There are 13 temporary positions in manufacturing. These positions include medical benefits.

Regulatory Actions/Litigation

There were no workplace-related regulatory actions or litigation against the Company in 1998.

Manufacturing Operations

Issues & Goals Summary

Social mission goals in 1998 were to increase the ethnic diversity of our supplier base; continue to work with socially aligned suppliers; and to introduce a values screen process into our Vendor Certification Program. Issues raised in our prior audit were diversity of our supplier base, safety and commodity purchasing. What follows is a summary of work and progress in these and other areas.

Vendor Certification; Values Alignment Screen

In 1996 we started a Vendor Certification Program. This effort grew out of a business need to increase efficiency, reliability and profitability in manufacturing while maintaining quality. Thirteen vendors representing 75% of purchases were in this program as of the end of 1998.

In 1998 we added a values alignment survey to this program. Twelve of the 13 major vendors in this program responded. This values alignment screen raises with vendors such issues as diversity in management, environmental practices, entry-level wages and workplace safety. Our aim in this process is to do business whenever possible with companies which share our social values, and to learn from such companies when their practices in these areas could inform our own efforts. We do not feel that to date we are putting the data we have collected to the best use. Our next step is to convene a meeting with our major suppliers to explore how we can share and benefit from best practices and how we might work together as a supplier chain to reduce environmental impacts.

Supplier Diversity

In 1998, we created a Supplier Diversity Program and established a database of 109 potential minority- and/or women-owned businesses. Our intent in this effort is to have readily available options to match our supply needs with the most ethnic- and gender-diverse array of possible suppliers.

Actual payments to minority/women-owned businesses totaled $838,291 in 1998, or .73% of purchases.

Concerned Citizens of Franklin County

Concerned Citizens of Franklin County was formed in response to plans to build the first livestock factory farm in the state of Vermont. While the group's initial efforts focused solely on opposing Vermont Egg Farms, they have since grown to become one of the most effective statewide voices for sustainable agriculture. CCFC's public education efforts, citizen and family farmer organizing, and legislative lobbying have successfully protected Vermont's small farms and communities from giant corporate farms and their consequences.

RR 1, Box 101B
Highgate, VT 05459
(802) 868-4968

This group was a Ben & Jerry's Foundation Grant Recipient.

Greyston Foundation

In its bakery in inner-city Yonkers, NY, the Foundation employs 55 previously hard-to-employ people and bakes the brownies used in Ben & Jerry's products. In addition to offering income and opportunity for under-served members of the community, the Foundation also provides permanent housing and social services to formerly homeless and very-low income families, operates a child care center and a nationally-recognized housing and healthcare center for people living with HIV/AIDS. They also coordinate five community gardens.

21 Park Avenue
Yonkers, NY
10703-3401
(914) 376-3900

www.greystonfoundation.org

Since 1988 the Greyston Bakery has been making brownies for our Chocolate Fudge Brownie Ice Cream and Frozen Yogurt.

SOCIALLY ALIGNED SUPPLIERS

Supplier & Location	Product	PURCHASES 1996	1997	1998
St. Albans Cooperative St. Albans, Vermont	Milk and Cream	$25,830,000	$22,624,000	$34,899,000
Premium payments for rBGH-free supply pledge.		350,000*	350,000*	460,000*
Greyston Bakery Yonkers, New York Owned by Greyston Foundation which provides employment, training, child care and other services to this low-income community.	Brownies	$2,363,000	$2,705,000	$2,828,000
Community Products Montpelier, Vermont Purchases sustainably harvested nuts from cooperatives in Amazon Rainforest. CPI was sold to the Rainforest Company of St. Louis, MO in 1998. Ben & Jerry's has since discontinued the Rainforest Crunch ice cream flavor which used the original CPI product.	Nut brittle	$1,040,000	$774,000	0
Coffee Enterprises Burlington, Vermont Sources coffee from Aztec Harvests Cooperative, which works to raise income for growers and promote economic development in Oaxaca, Mexico. Ben & Jerry's pays floor price to protect growers from commodity pricing swings.	Coffee extract	$1,059,000	$745,000	$918,000
Cia. Agricola La Gavilana Savegre River, Costa Rica Agricultural and cultural practices certified by two nonprofit organizations, The Rainforest Alliance and Earth College, to be better than norm.	Vanilla	$248,000	$254,000	$214,000
TOTAL		**$30,540,000**	**$27,102,000**	**$38,859,000**
TOTAL PERCENTAGE OF PURCHASES		**N/A**	**35.5%**	**38.6%**

**Premium payments to St. Albans Cooperative are reflected in milk & cream total purchases.*

This was short of our goal of 1.5% of purchases but greater than our minority/women-owned source purchases of .10% in 1997. Progress in this area was impeded in 1998 by staffing issues in our purchasing function; two key staff members for this effort were on leave and one position was open as of the end of 1998. Staffing issues have been addressed.

In 1998 we improved our efforts to recruit minority consultants. Their work included assisting in the writing of our strategic plan, conducting marketing research, assisting us in writing a diversity plan and working on organizational development. Payments in 1998 amounted to $215,000.

Socially Aligned Suppliers

Approximately one-third of our ingredient and supply purchases in 1998 were from companies which we view as being especially aligned with Ben & Jerry's values.

St. Albans Cooperative Creamery is owned by the Vermont farmers who produce its milk supply. The Co-op has supplied all of Ben & Jerry's milk and cream since 1985. In addition to market prices for these ingredients which were at an all-time high in 1998, we paid a premium to those farmer-members who provided rBGH-free milk to the Co-op to meet our requirement for an rBGH-free dairy supply. In 1998, this premium amounted to $460,000 or 1.4% of total dairy purchases from the Co-op. In 1998 the Co-op elected to allow a small number of member farmers to use rBGH instead of asking them to leave the Co-op. The Co-op segregates its supply of rBGH-free milk and the premium paid by Ben & Jerry's is not paid to those members using rBGH. Ben & Jerry's recognizes that it is not in the best long-term interests of the St. Albans Cooperative to lose membership and thereby risk its financial viability. We are confident the Co-op will continue to meet our desire for rBGH-free milk.

Greyston Bakery of Yonkers, NY has been a supplier of brownies to Ben & Jerry's since 1988. This ingredient is used in our Chocolate Fudge Brownie ice cream and frozen yogurt. The Greyston Bakery is owned by the Greyston Foundation, a nonprofit social service network which operates its bakery to train homeless and low-income people for self-sufficiency. In 1998 we began a three-year phase-out of the premium we have paid to Greyston, having mutually agreed that the Bakery should orient itself to charging market prices for its products if it is to be economically viable over time. We continued in 1998 to provide technical assistance to Greyston to help the bakery redesign and renovate its plant to facilitate

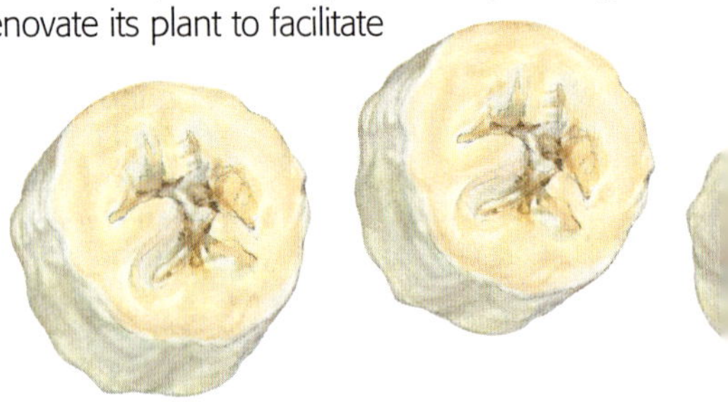

diversification of its product line and customer base. Greyston has decided to relocate its production facilities in order to increase the efficiency and flexibility of its operation. Ben & Jerry's will provide technical support to their effort to select and equip the new facility.

During 1998 we discontinued purchasing blond brownies from Greyston due to declining sales of Blond Brownie Sundae Low Fat Ice Cream; Greyston reports no adverse impact on its operations from the discontinuation of this product.

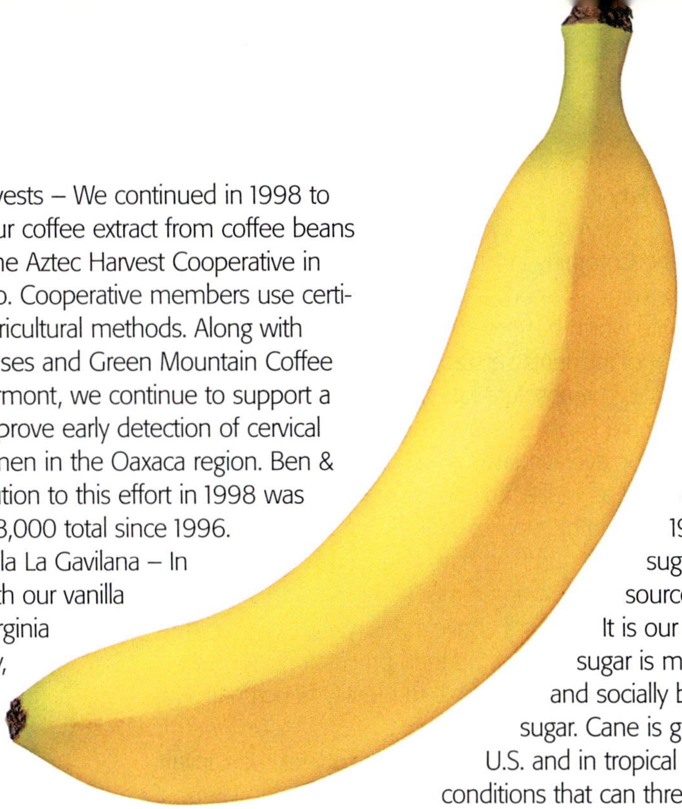

Aztec Harvests – We continued in 1998 to source all of our coffee extract from coffee beans produced by the Aztec Harvest Cooperative in Oaxaca, Mexico. Cooperative members use certified organic agricultural methods. Along with Coffee Enterprises and Green Mountain Coffee Roasters of Vermont, we continue to support a program to improve early detection of cervical cancer for women in the Oaxaca region. Ben & Jerry's contribution to this effort in 1998 was $3,200, and $8,000 total since 1996.

Cia. Agricola La Gavilana – In conjunction with our vanilla supplier, the Virginia Dare Company, we use a blended vanilla extract that contains vanilla beans from the Savegre River region of Costa Rica. Our supplier purchases about 10,000 pounds of vanilla beans–all that this organization is capable of producing. One result of this relationship is that over 3,000 acres of Costa Rican rainforest have been reforested or reclaimed for sustainable production. This trading relationship helps to reduce pressure to clear-cut additional forest in this area. These purchases have also facilitated community development projects, including a regional health center, acquisition of supplies for schools and infrastructure improvements. The region also recently received a $3.3 million grant from the Spanish government to implement and manage a five-year conservation project in the Savegre

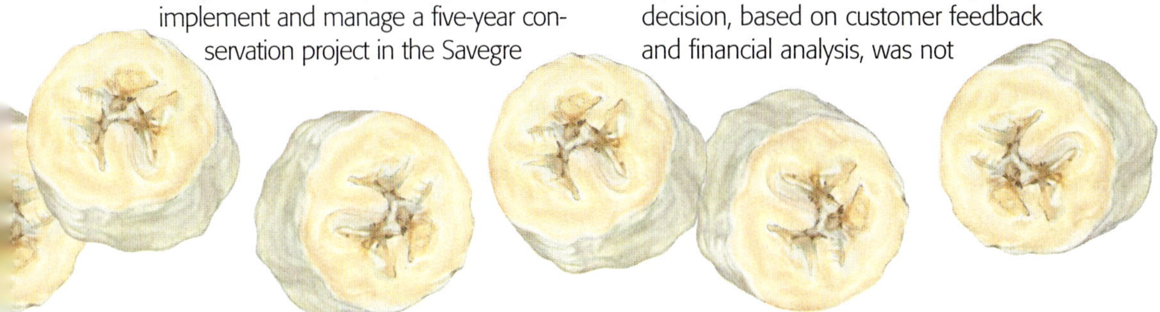

watershed; this grant, according to its recipients, would not have been made without the model provided by its relationship with Ben & Jerry's.

Our purchase of vanilla from Cia. Agricola La Gavilana declined 13.8% from 1997 because we did not repeat a vanilla quart promotion that occurred in 1997. However, pint sales of vanilla were up in 1998.

Social Impacts of Ingredients

SUGAR–During 1998 Ben & Jerry's asked its sugar supplier to convert its sugar source from cane sugar to beet sugar. Our contract allows for exceptions if the supply of beet sugar is insufficient to meet our needs. Since making this change in June 1998, 93% of our sugar purchases were sourced from beet sugar. It is our belief that beet sugar is more environmentally and socially benign than cane sugar. Cane is grown in both the U.S. and in tropical countries, under conditions that can threaten watersheds and local ecologies, and its harvest can involve dangerous conditions for laborers.

COCOA–A significant ingredient in our production needs, cocoa is often cited as a product that is not sustainably produced. We have investigated sources of fair-traded cocoa, but have not found sources that meet our specifications at affordable prices. We continue to source cocoa from conventional suppliers.

A Word About Sustainable Agriculture

We continue to be concerned about how food is produced. In last year's audit we reported on our research on organic, and our decision, based on customer feedback and financial analysis, was not to move in that direction at this time. In considering this issue we were struck by the polar nature of the debate–either you use chemically-reliant, outmoded methods of the past 50 years or you transition to organic.

Inherent in the definition of agricultural sustainability are three principles: reducing environmental degradation; maintaining agricultural productivity over time; and promoting the economic viability for both farms and rural communities. We sought information from

WRI

World Resources Institute

The World Resources Institute is an independent center for policy research and technical assistance on global environmental and developmental issues. Believing that people are inspired by ideas and moved by greater understanding to create positive change, WRI offers objective information and practical proposals that help policymakers, governments and other institutions around the world promote environmentally sound and socially equitable development.

10 G Street, NE
Suite 800
Washington, DC 20002
(202) 729-7600
fax (202) 729-7616

www.wri.org

We look to WRI as a resource to help define the relationship between business and sustainability and to develop winning solutions for both industry and society.

the University of Vermont, Cornell and University of California at Davis to inform our thinking and strategies around sustainable agriculture.

We concluded that although organic may not be a viable option for all farmers, making gains in sustainable methods of food production is. The leading environmental impact of dairy farming is potential adverse impacts on ground water. These impacts come not just from pesticides and herbicides used to grow corn, but also from inadequate manure management and field practices. Although Vermont does not have the dire water quality problems experienced in many other agricultural areas of the country, there is always room for improvement. Our goal is to work with the St. Albans Co-op and others to develop a farm level environmental audit process, including software and data collection tools, that will, we feel, lead to better environmental management and improved profitability for individual farmers.

Quality Assurance

There were no significant occurrences during 1998 in our manufacturing and distribution chains that caused concern over our product quality.

Tamper-evident packaging is a concern raised in earlier audits. We continue to have the goal of packaging our products in tamper-evident containers. If possible, we would like to do this without increasing the net amount of material used in our packaging. We experimented with technologies that did not function adequately. In addition, our major paper supplier was sold during this time, which raised questions about the availability of both the technologies and supplier commitments necessary to invest in new packaging equipment. Also, applicable tamper-evident technologies will need to be reevaluated with the type of paper we have sourced for our new unbleached containers described in the environmental section of this report.

Safety

No regulatory actions were brought against the Company in 1998. In 1997 we began tracking a rolling 12-month average of the injury incidence rate which has proven to be a better trend indicator of incidents versus the absolute Injury Incident Rate. The absolute rate is somewhat biased toward larger employee groups than ours. The rolling average rate decreased by 11% during 1998 as well as the absolute Injury Incident Rate. It should be noted that the 1996 and 1997 incident rate numbers have been restated to correct previous reporting errors. While our trend is downward, we are still above industry averages for the broad category of the food processing industry. We have not been able to identify benchmarks for ice cream manufacturing.

A substantial number of safety-related capital improvement projects were completed in 1998. In Waterbury we completed the production area upgrade project that significantly reduced conges-

INJURY INCIDENT RATES

Number of illnesses/injuries per 100 full-time workers

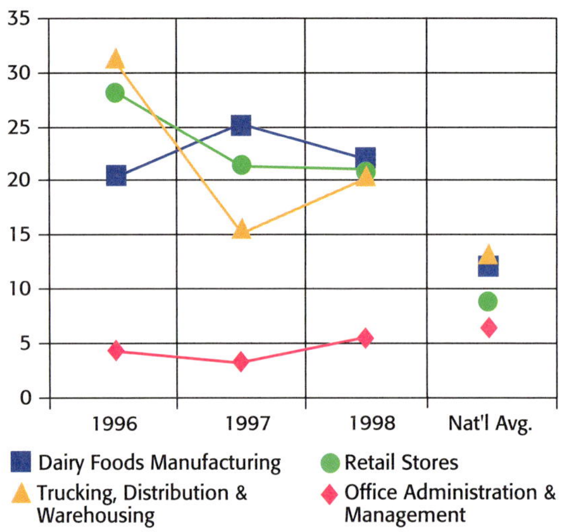

National Average figures from U.S. Dept. of Labor Office of Safety, Health & Working Conditions.

tion, improved equipment access and reduced the amount of overhead piping disassembly required for cleaning. In addition, several material-handling projects such as lift tables and powered barrel movers were completed. New cherry handling equipment was installed in St. Albans, which will reduce manual lifting and handling. The stacking platform was also upgraded to improve ergonomics. Our Springfield facility incorporated a bucket dumper to reduce manual lifting of buckets, and

The Learning Web
Learning by Doing

The Learning Web

A networking initiative that connects young people with unique educational opportunities, the Learning Web offers apprenticeships, guided career explorations, paid employment, and small business management training to its participants. By creating links between schools, regional agencies and businesses, the organization has established an impressive base of adults who volunteer about 20,000 hours annually to share their time, expertise and workplaces with youth.

515 West Seneca Street
Ithaca, NY 14850
(607) 275-0122
fax (607) 275-0312

This nonprofit organization is part of the Ben & Jerry's PartnerShop program.

Common Ground Community

Common Ground Community specializes in innovative solutions to homelessness through the creation and maintenance of supportive housing, the development of alternatives to the shelter system and through a large scale economic development and job training department that specializes in incorporating paid training opportunities for the formerly homeless.

255 W. 43rd Street
New York, NY 10036
(212) 768-8989
ext. 1607

www.commonground.org

This nonprofit organization is part of the Ben & Jerry's PartnerShop program.

ROLLING AVERAGE OSHA INCIDENCE RATE 1998

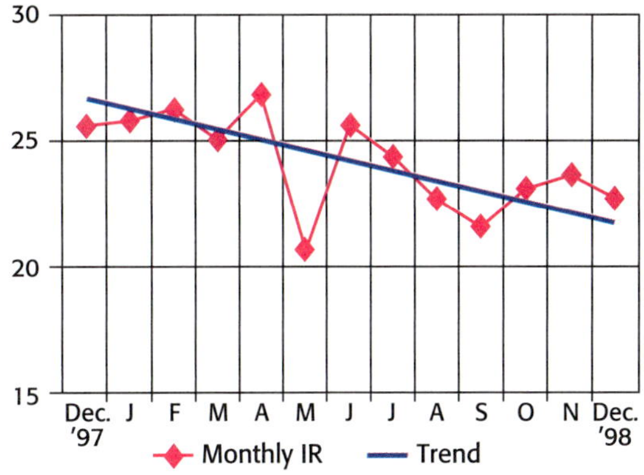

added a new cartoner and conveyors that will reduce the risk of cumulative trauma injuries. The Distribution Center began behavior-based safety training and made forklift enhancements to eliminate manual loading of product made for Japan.

EXPERIENCE MODIFICATION RATE

Compares Ben & Jerry's compensation losses due to injury to average for similar companies; 1.00 represents industry average.

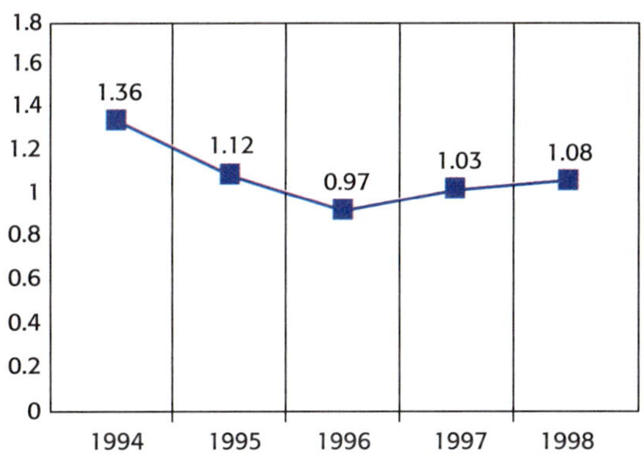

In addition, we began conversion to bulk totes versus barrels and smaller quantity packages, which will reduce lifting injury risk as well as solid waste. In 1999 we will complete this project, continue the focus on material handling improvements and move into behavior-based safety training.

Environment

Issues & Goals Summary

Continuing work done in 1997 and reported in our Social Report for that year, high priority was given in 1998 to the introduction of unbleached paperboard for our ice cream, frozen yogurt and sorbet pint packages. Additionally, we set further goals to reduce production of dairy and solid waste. Following is a discussion of work done in 1998 toward these and other goals.

Unbleached Packaging

During 1998, we completed the development work on unbleached paperboard for our pint packaging and introduced this packaging on a limited scale in the fourth quarter of 1998. This was the culmination of 24 months of effort, which began with a sustainability analysis of our packaging and the goal of producing a compostable pint. The first part of this process focused on the paper used to form the actual container. Our concern in this area related to the traditional methods used to whiten the paper used to make ice cream containers. The bleaching of paper with chlorine is one of the leading sources of dioxins, which are among the most deadly chemicals known to humans.

The conversion of our product packaging to unbleached paperboard is ongoing. We plan to convert one-third of the line in 1999.

Non-Packaging Paper Use

All office paper and marketing support material have been converted to totally chlorine-free. Our Franchise department is pursuing the change of all paper products to chlorine-free or unbleached by year 2000. At this time the scoop shops use unbleached napkins and cake boxes.

Waste Reduction

In 1998, in order to achieve greater gains in solid waste reduction, we focused on supplier issues. We created a Packaging Improvement Group (PIG) to assess the impact of incoming ingredients on our waste streams. We began testing reusable, returnable bulk containers, known as totes, for ingredients such as caramel, marshmallow and fruit. We expect in 1999 to begin more comprehensive use of these containers, and thus reduce significantly our generation of solid wastes.

We are reaching a point at which further reductions in our dairy and solid waste stream will be difficult to achieve without a major technological redesign of the way we manufacture our

SOLID WASTE

Pounds per 10,000 gallons first quality product produced

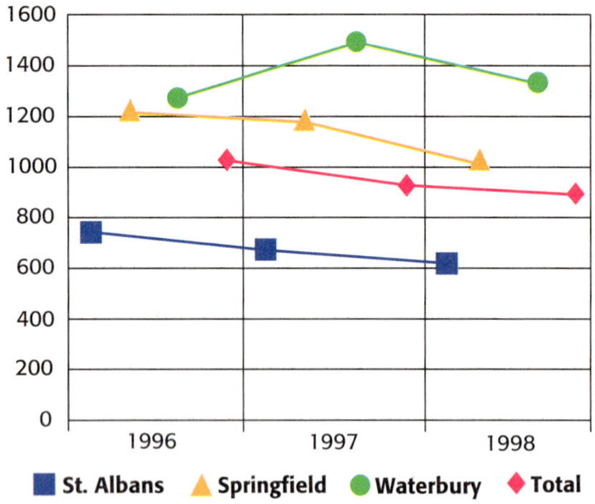

**Total for all plants per 10,000 gallons first quality product produced: 1996 - 1,014 pounds 1997 - 962 pounds 1998 - 915 pounds*

ENERGY CONSUMPTION

BTUs per gallon produced

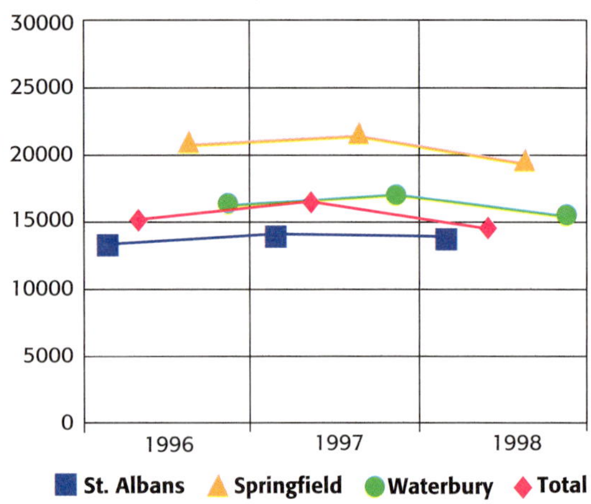

ice cream products. Work in the area of reusable containers for incoming ingredients represents the beginning of this redesign process.

Our targets for 1998 were an overall reduction in dairy waste of 10% from 1997 levels, and a 25% reduction in solid waste. We did not meet these goals. We achieved a 7% reduction in dairy waste and a 14% reduction in solid waste.

We achieved a 14% reduction in dairy waste in Springfield, exceeding our goal of 10%. At our Waterbury plant our gains were delayed by the reformatting of the production floor. The reformatting of the production floor requires extensive flushing of piping as a necessary part of start up. Because of that our dairy waste gains were not achieved until late in the year. We would note, however, that by year's end the plant was back on

WASTE REDUCTION GOALS

Site	1998 Goal	1998 Result
St. Albans		
Dairy Waste	10% reduction	4% reduction
Solid Waste	10% reduction	3% reduction
Waterbury		
Dairy Waste	15% reduction	6% reduction
Solid Waste	10% reduction	12% increase
Springfield		
Dairy Waste	10% reduction	14% reduction
Solid Waste	10% reduction	10% reduction

Overall company solid waste consumption - 14% reduction
Overall company dairy waste consumption - 7% reduction

track to meeting dairy waste reduction goals. Dairy waste in St. Albans decreased 4% as compared to a goal of 10%. A new process line was installed on an accelerated schedule to produce product for our entry into the Japanese market, which negatively impacted dairy waste. Line modifications were made to correct this issue.

Our goal for 25% solid waste reduction proved to be overly ambitious as it depended upon activities we could not fully control such as our incoming ingredient packaging. As already noted we established a Packaging Improvement Group to address those issues. Changes in incoming packaging will be achieved through the PIG group. Implementing totes will dramatically reduce solid waste as well as reduce injuries and improve variances.

Despite a 23% increase in volume, we reduced by 10.25% our energy consumption as measured by BTUs per gallon produced.

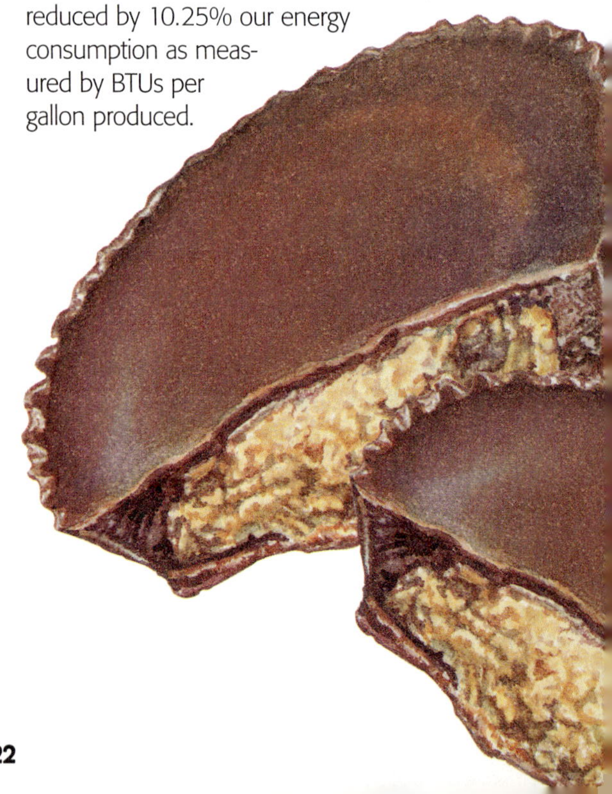

ceres

Coalition for Environmentally Responsible Economies

CERES is a coalition of investors, environmentalists and other public interest groups committed to corporate environmental responsibility and full environmental reporting. As part of its work toward a sustainable economy, CERES is continually creating new collaborations between environmental groups and the investment community and has become a recognized leader in corporate accountability, shareholder activism and multi-stakeholder dialogue.

11 Arlington Street
6th Floor
Boston, MA 02116-3411
(617) 247-0700
fax (617) 267-5400

www.ceres.org

We are proud to have been the first public company to sign onto the CERES principles.

HIGH STRENGTH DAIRY WASTE

(Waste ice cream managed primarily through permitted compost facilities & manure pits)

Gallons of dairy waste per 10,000 gallons first quality product produced

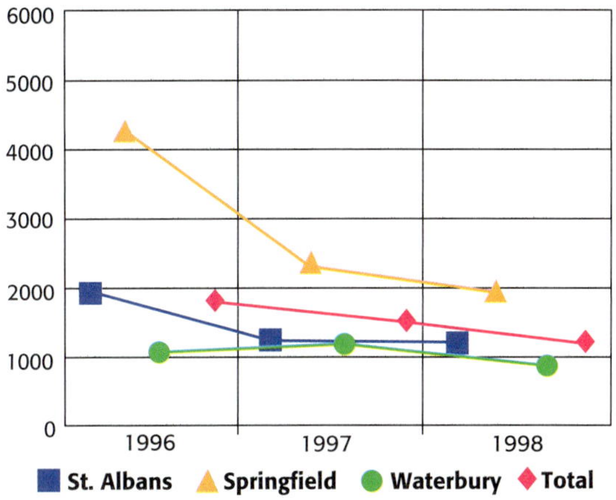

**Total for all plants per 10,000 gallons first quality product produced: 1996 - 1,992 gallons 1997 - 1,509 gallons 1998 - 1,289 gallons*

In 1992 we became the first public company to sign and endorse the CERES Principles (Coalition for Environmentally Responsible Economies). These ten principles which guide our environmental management efforts are: protection of the biosphere, sustainable use of natural resources, reduction and disposal of wastes, energy conservation, risk reduction, safe products and services, environmental restoration, informing the public, management commitment, and audits and reports. As part of our commitment to CERES we annually complete an environmental audit. That audit, the CERES Report, is available through CERES or by contacting us directly.

Hazardous Materials

Our primary source of hazardous material is waste oil. The Company had no hazardous material spills in 1998. All used waste oils were recycled. This re-refining of waste oil is the soundest environmental method of managing waste oil. The amount of hazardous materials in need of reporting dramatically dropped in 1998 due to the oil recycling. Ben & Jerry's recycled 1,040 gallons of waste oil in 1998.

Regulatory Issues/Litigation

No environmental regulatory actions or litigations occurred in 1998.

Green Teams

Each site has a Green Team composed of employees who voluntarily seek out conservation opportunities for their coworkers. During 1998 Green Teams sponsored compost giveaways, plant exchanges, clothing drives and published EcoNotes, a company environmental awareness newsletter. A 1998 company-wide project was Environmental Awareness Week, involving outside speakers and environmental games.

Franchise Operations

Issues & Goals Summary

As an outgrowth of our 1997 Social Report, we set a goal of increasing the number of PartnerShops from 5 to 10 in 1998. Our prior audit highlighted the need for attention to this program. Also, we committed to an increase in women and people of color ownership of franchise shops. Following are descriptions of actions toward meeting these goals and other social mission activities.

PartnerShops®

During 1998 we investigated several potential PartnerShop opportunities, but did not meet our goal of opening 5 new shops. There were as many as 15 prospective PartnerShops under review at any given time. The selection process takes longer than we originally anticipated. One satellite PartnerShop was opened with Common Ground. By the end of 1998, four applications were approved and were in the site selection process: Southend Community Services, Hartford, CT; West Philadelphia Enterprise Center and Lawson House YMCA, Chicago, IL; and Crispus Attucks Community Development, York, PA. We concluded in 1998 that in order to advance our long-term goal of increasing PartnerShop numbers, we needed to hire a full-time PartnerShop coordinator. As of the time of this report's publication, this position had been filled.

FRANCHISE PROFILE	1996	1997	1998
Stores Open			
Regular, Satellite & Featuring	128	145	165
Company-owned	3	3	3
PartnerShops®	5	5	6
International	15	16	21
Total # of Stores Open	**151**	**169**	**195**

Our existing PartnerShops include: Youth Scoops, Ithaca, NY; Common Ground, New York City; Postgraduate Center for Mental Health, New York City; and two PartnerShops owned by Juma Ventures, both in San Francisco, CA.

Entrepreneurial Shops

In 1998 we introduced a new concept known as an Entrepreneurial Shop. We work with

Juma Ventures

Juma Ventures is a social-entrepreneurial nonprofit whose mission is to help youth from low-income backgrounds reach their highest potential. Juma provides youth with quality jobs and training in five small businesses it owns and operates. Four of these are Ben & Jerry's ventures, including a thriving stadium concession selling ice cream at both San Francisco Giants and 49ers games, two PartnerShops®, and a catering operation.

116 New Montgomery St.
Suite 600
San Francisco, CA
94105-3607
(415) 247-6580

www.jumaventures.org

This nonprofit organization is part of the Ben & Jerry's PartnerShop® program.

community development organizations to identify potential storeowners from traditionally disenfranchised groups. The first shop in this model in Richmond, VA was due to open as this report was being published.

People of Color Ownership

In 1998, 31 new franchise shops were opened, adding four Asian owners to our franchise system.

At the end of the year, nine percent of our franchise shops were owned by minorities, an increase of 1% over 1997.

Franchisee Social Initiatives

In 1998 the 4% franchise marketing obligation was changed to direct two of the 4% back to the Company for system-wide brand and franchise marketing. Although franchisees continued to spend over 4% on marketing, the amount available for community-based efforts was reduced. This was reflected in a change in community spending from $442,320 in 1997 to $356,080 in 1998. This shift in spending is prompting us to look at ways we can encourage more support for our scoop shops' community activities. For example, the franchise marketing budget for 1999 includes new funding for shop materials such as position papers and dioxin/Greenpeace information, which would have previously been purchased by franchises.

Litigation

There was no franchise-related litigation against the Company in 1998.

NUTRITION CONTENT

	Ice Cream	Low Fat Ice Cream	Frozen Yogurt	Sorbet	Novelties
Calories	307	176	190	140	343
Cal. from Fat	169	25	32	0*	206
Total fat (g)	19	3	4	0	23
Saturated Fat (g)	11	1.5	2	0	13
Cholesterol (mg)	59	16	11	0	44
Sodium (mg)	106	82	99	23	87
Carbohydrate (g)	30	33	34	31	33
Protein (g)	5	4	5	3	5
Vitamin A**	14	6	1	2	8
Calcium**	11.5	2.5	2	2	4
Iron**	5.5	2.5	2	2	4

** Devil's Food Chocolate™ contains fat, all other sorbet flavors are fat-free.*
*** % daily value*

Marketing and Sales

Issues & Goals Summary

Goals for 1998 included a major initiative of the introduction of unbleached packaging, continued support for rBGH-free labeling and continued use of product donations to support progressive social change work. The 1997 audit noted the absence of specific marketing initiatives with a social mission focus.

Recombinant Bovine Growth Hormone (rBGH)

We continue to maintain our pledge to purchase milk and cream only from farms which do not use rBGH. Following the successful court case in the State of Illinois in 1997, we provide a message about this commitment on our pint containers which states:

"We oppose recombinant Bovine Growth Hormone. The family farmers who supply our milk and cream pledge not to treat their cows with rBGH. The FDA has said no significant difference has been shown and no test can now distinguish between milk from rBGH treated and untreated cows."

Customer Comments

In 1998 the Consumer Affairs department began a process of revising the systems used to log and respond to consumer's contacts. Our existing system had not kept up with recording and categorizing the increasing amount of e-mail we receive from consumers. For these reasons it is difficult to report actual consumer contacts by category for 1998. We do, however, estimate the overall volume of comments in 1998 is similar to 1997, about 20,000 over the course of the year. These comments fell into three basic categories: Complaints, albeit from generally satisfied customers (68%), praise (13%), and other miscellaneous questions and comments (19%). Nonetheless the data shows that the top six product quality complaint categories showed a decrease of 23% in 1998 when compared to 1997.

In 1998 we revised our packaging graphics. Our objectives were to enhance the quality image of the product and make it easier to shop in the stores. On the package we asked for consumers to e-mail their response. In rough numbers, 41% of consumers liked the new packaging better, 30% liked it as much as the

Rural Vermont

Founded by farmers in 1985, Rural Vermont believes that the safety of our food, the health of our environment, and the economic viability of our small farms and rural communities are inseparable. This vision of a sustainable world is a key part of the organization's current work to end factory farm development, ban the use of toxic sludge as fertilizer, achieve fair prices for family farmers, and keep genetically engineered foods out of our nation's food supply.

15 Barre Street
Montpelier, VT
05602-3504
(802) 223-7222
fax (802) 223-0269
ruralvt@sover.net

Ben & Jerry's was glad to work with Rural Vermont in their successful effort to secure a rBGH labeling law in Vermont.

THE WHITE HOUSE PROJECT

The White House Project

From Jane Addams, the first U.S. woman to win the Nobel Peace Prize, to Rosa Parks, whose simple act of courage ignited the civil rights movement, U.S. history is full of women who changed the nation's political landscape. The men and women of The White House Project are dedicated to changing the climate of American politics, so that in the future women will launch successful campaigns for the U.S. presidency. We are working toward the day when our country celebrates its first woman president and women participate fully in leading the nation.

110 Wall St., 2nd Floor
New York, NY 10005
(212) 785-6001
fax (212) 785-6007

www.thewhitehouseproject.org

Our franchise stores were one of the main outlets for the White House Project ballots.

old packaging, and 28% liked it less. Our market research studies indicate that the number of households purchasing our products increased and we retained more users than in the prior year.

Marketing Initiatives

In 1998 the White House Project was launched. This was a bipartisan effort to encourage women candidates to run for President through the dissemination of 8 million ballots, listing the names of 20 potential women candidates from many walks of life. We lent our name to the ballot and assisted in distributing it through our retail stores.

In 1998 we participated in a major music festival in Philadelphia with Green Mountain Energy Resources to promote green power.

Product Royalties

Several of our royalty agreements generate funds for nonprofit organizations independent of our 7.5% commitment of pre-tax profits to philanthropy.

- Phish Food™ ice cream produces royalties for the WaterWheel Foundation, created in 1998 by the Vermont-based band Phish. The Foundation supports "the protection and preservation of the Lake Champlain region of Vermont." Royalties donated in 1998 totaled $200,482. In January of 1999 the WaterWheel Foundation made its first grants which totaled $78,000.
- Doonesberry™ Sorbet produced royalties totaling $40,150 compared to $55,000 in 1997 for the Pauley Trudeau Foundation, which supports a variety of nonprofits working in the areas of education, AIDS treatment and prevention, reducing poverty, human rights and other progressive causes.
- Wavy Gravy ice cream produced royalties totaling $20,445 compared to $21,000 in 1997 for Camp Win-A-Rainbow, which was founded by Wavy Gravy to offer summer camp experiences to low income children.

Licensees

In 1998 the Board of Directors adopted a policy on Licensing that calls for working with values-aligned companies and using licensing opportunities that fully

express our social mission such as the Greyston relationship. We did not accomplish such an initiative in 1998.

We completed four licensing agreements in 1998: Cronies–a t-shirt manufacturer in Chatsworth, CA; Fresh Caps–a minority-owned business in Hopkins, MN; Mattel/Tyco–a one-time agreement which produced 50,000-100,000 Ben & Jerry's Super Rig trucks and an equal number of Ben & Jerry's Barbie pints for use in Barbie's kitchen; and Douglas Cuddle Toy of Keene, NH which produced 1,700 Peace Bears for Ben & Jerry's 20th birthday. The bear included information about Results, a grassroots advocacy organization dedicated to ending hunger. In 1998 these agreements combined totaled $10,000 in revenue.

All prospective licensees are required to complete a social performance questionnaire and licensees with offshore manufacturing operations are reviewed under the Council on Economic Priorities SA8000 (Social Accountability) standards.

Product Donations

Donations of first quality product in 1998 amounted to $70,000 (our cost; not retail value) the same as in 1997. $70,000 represented a 40% increase from 1996. Examples of donation recipients include: The Children's Defense Fund's Child Watch Program which brings business, political and social service leaders directly into contact with children to encourage these community decision-makers to take action on children's issues; and Youth Service America's National Youth Service Day. In Vermont we gave away 24,502 gallons of second quality product in support of a wide range of nonprofits and community activities.

International Operations

Issues & Goals Summary

Our goal for 1998 in the area of international operations was to develop a strategy to include a social mission component in all International agreements. This was a key finding in last year's audit. We did not fully meet this goal in 1998. Following is a description of our international activities and a discussion of social mission-related projects.

BENELUX – A Business Development Agreement exists between Ben & Jerry's

POSTGRADUATE CENTER FOR MENTAL HEALTH

Postgraduate Center For Mental Health

One of the largest nonprofit mental health treatment and training centers in the country, the Postgraduate Center for Mental Health is strongly committed to helping people in need and maximizing the potential of each individual it treats. Serving an ethically and culturally diverse population, the center offers a network of services that include individual and group therapy for children, adolescents and adults; psychiatric rehabilitation; and residential and vocational services for those with persistent mental health difficulties.

124 East 28th Street
New York, NY 10016
(212) 689-7700
fax (212) 576-4198

This nonprofit organization is part of the Ben & Jerry's PartnerShop® program.

Homemade, Inc. and PYMWYMIC (Put Your Money Where Your Mouth Is Co.) Holdings, B.V. and Sfeerbeheer, B.V. This Agreement allows for wholesale distribution throughout The Netherlands, Luxembourg and Belgium of Ben & Jerry's products and the establishment of retail scoop shops. Currently there are four scoop shops in operation. During 1998 PYMWYMIC and Sfeerbeheer, along with one of their largest accounts, Jamin, focused their social mission efforts on two primary endeavors—de Wolkenboom, an organization that builds group homes for abandoned children; and War Child, a nonprofit organization dedicated to helping children who live in the world's war zones. Through a combination of financial contributions and product donations, support for these organizations amounted to approximately $7,500. Other product donations included scooping at the Gay Olympics, which amounted to approximately $6,000.

FRANCE—We opened three retail scoop shops in France which supported the Marie-Claire-Parene Project with a grant of $26,000 to assist low income women in creating their own businesses. We also sponsored a team of youth volunteers under the Unis-Cite program. Working with two like-minded companies, Putumayo and The Body Shop, we organized a Woman's Day concert. Disadvantaged youth were hired to scoop our products during the concert. We employed several disadvantaged youth as our scooping ambassadors during all of the major events where our product was available, including the Soccer World Cup and Urban and Winter Sports Exhibition.

UNITED KINGDOM—We operate approximately 25 shop-within-a-shop retail units as well as a substantial wholesale distribution network. Several local charities, including organizations that support terminally ill, underprivileged and abused children, were supported throughout the year by product donations and financial support totaling approximately $32,000. In 1998 we developed a PartnerBus program with ChildLine, a national help line for children in trouble or danger. The PartnerBus will be used to raise money for ChildLine and to increase awareness of children's issues.

CANADA – A Licensing Agreement was signed with Delicious Alternative Desserts, Ltd. (DADs), allowing us to manufacture and distribute products in Canada. As part of the opening day celebration of the new manufacturing facility, DADs donated $5,000 to the Children's Aid Foundation of Ontario. DADs shares our opposition to rBGH and encouraged customers at their grand opening to send postcards to the Canadian government urging that the ban on rBGH continue. The Canadian government has acted to continue the ban.

JAPAN—In 1998 our business in Japan was through a distribution agreement. We are in the process of establishing a company-owned business in Japan and have not yet designed the social mission component.

ISRAEL—Our Licensee in Israel continues to support the work of the ELI organization whose focus is abused children. All pints are stickered with the ELI logo and toll-free telephone number. Product is routinely donated to several camps for underprivileged, handicapped and chronically ill children.

PERU and LEBANON – In 1998 we signed Development and License Agreements with companies in Peru and Lebanon. We also signed an Amended and Restated License Agreement with our existing partner in Israel. Each of these agreements contains a provision which obligates Licensees to include a reasonable number of social mission-related activities in their annual business plans.

We note that our decision to sell our products in Peru did not include a discussion about Human Rights issues in that country, and it should have. According to the latest U.S. Department of State's Human Rights Report, although egregious abuses of human rights continue to decline, serious concerns exist in several areas. These include a lack of an independent judiciary, a lack of press freedom, and an infringement of citizens' privacy rights. We will look for appropriate ways to encourage the government of Peru to fully establish the rule of law and freedom of expression, the hallmarks of a democracy.

Social Mission and Philanthropy

Since 1988 we have donated 7.5% of our pre-tax profits through employee-led philanthropy to nonprofit organizations committed to positive social change. In 1998 7.5% of our pre-tax profits was $792,595. Of that amount, at year's end we had given away $479,289. We have no way of knowing how much money there will be in the 7.5% pool until year's end, so much of it accrues to the next year. The remaining funds will be included in 1999 grant making. For the past five years we have divided these monies among three separate funds: The Ben & Jerry's Foundation (grants are made by an all-employee advisory board), Community Action Teams at each site, and Corporate Giving which is managed by the Social Mission department.

Although we have been making some grants through our international business relationships, most of these ventures have not reached a stage of profitability to warrant a formal program of philanthropy at this time. In 1999 we intend to return the equivalent of 7.5% of profits generated internationally to NGOs (Non-Government Organizations) in the foreign countries in which we do business.

FOUNDATION – About half of our philanthropic dollars go to the Ben & Jerry's Foundation. Its mission is to support progressive social change in the United States by contributing to grassroots groups that focus on the underlying conditions that create social problems such as racism, sexism, poverty and environmental destruction.

Since 1994 a nine-member Foundation grant-making committee (composed of employees representing each site) has researched the applications and made funding decisions subject to approval or ratification by the Foundation's Board of Trustees.

COMMUNITY ACTION TEAMS – Each of our five manufacturing, distribution and administrative sites has a Community Action Team (CAT) that is made up of employees elected by their coworkers. These teams make small grants to local community organizations. The CATs also organize service projects which involve our employees in local community building.

Site Projects: In 1998 the Springfield staff worked with the Visiting Nurses Association and identified seniors who needed assistance with projects in or around their homes. Waterbury staff worked to restore stream banks along the Lord's Creek on Route 14 in Irasburg, VT by planting trees and making revetments along the stream. Central Support worked on a similar project with the Winooski Valley Park District (WVPD) and planted 150 trees along the Winooski River at the Ethan Allen Homestead. This project, the first phase of three, has enabled the WVPD to secure a grant for future restoration work along the river. Staff from St. Albans undertook a major clean-up

FUNDS DISBURSED	1996	1997	1998
Foundation	$323,143	$287,010	$280,954
# of recipients	**64**	**50**	**42**
Community Action Teams	$114,145	$154,709	$155,763
# of recipients	**188**	**20**	**19**
Corporate Giving	$ 55,000	$ 42,720	$42,572
# of recipients	**54**	**48**	**48**
Totals	**$493,288**	**$484,439**	**$479,289**

erf

Environmental Research Foundation

ERF provides understandable scientific information about the influence of toxic substances on human health and the environment. The main goal of ERF is to strengthen democracy by helping people find the information they need to fight for environmental justice in their own communities. ERF specializes in information on hazardous substances and hazardous technologies, including landfills, incinerators, pesticides, organochlorine compounds, risk assessments, and their effects on human and environmental health.

PO Box 5036
Annapolis, MD 21403-7036
(410) 263-1584
fax (410) 263-8944
www.rachel.org

We refer to ERF's newsletter, Rachel's Environmental & Health Weekly, as a resource on rBGH and dioxin issues.

project at Camps Abnaki and Hochelaga in North Hero, VT. And employees at the Distribution Center refurbished the fence and gates surrounding the Meeting House in Rockingham, VT, and due to vandalism, reset some headstones.

CORPORATE GIVING – Corporate Giving supports social mission issues of interest to us such as rBGH and sustainable agriculture. We also support nonprofit organizations such as Business for Social Responsibility, The Social Venture Network, The Council on Economic Priorities and Vermont Businesses for Social Responsibility.

In 1998 Corporate Giving introduced a Matching Gift Program to encourage and support our staff's commitment to their communities. We match dollar-for-dollar, up to $1,000 per employee, to nonprofit 501(c)(3) organizations.

SUPPORT FOR POLITICAL POSITIONS – During 1998 we took the following positions:

- In 1998 we sought an amendment to the Vermont Business Corporation Act that would allow Directors to take stakeholder concerns into account in determining what is in the best interest of the corporation. The amendment, which became law, included employees, suppliers and customers, as well as the economy of the region and societal considerations. This provision was enacted into law.
- We testified in support of Vermont bill S.73 to reauthorize and improve Vermont's expiring voluntary rBGH labeling law. This bill was enacted into law.
- We submitted testimony in support of Vermont bill H.749 that would enable the State of Vermont to recover Medicaid expenses for the treatment of tobacco-caused health problems. This bill was enacted into law.
- We signed a letter to President Clinton regarding the budget surplus initiated by the OMB Watch. The letter asked Congress to make investments in education, basic human needs, infrastructure, environmental protection, and research and development.

SHAREHOLDER INFORMATION

Shares Outstanding	**12/27/97**	**12/26/98**
Class A Common	6,370,303	6,301,360
Class B Common	865,143	823,388
Estimated Institutional Ownership	2,024,893-28%	3,003,458-47.9%
Stock Held by Staff		
Officers & Directors -		
Class A Common	685,980-11%	633,986-10%
Class B Common	608,786-70%	608,786-74%
Stock Options held by staff		
Officers & Directors	723,155	753,155
Other Staff	187,656	157,146
	12/28/97	**12/27/98**
Stock Price	$16.13	$22.50

Finance and Shareholders

Screened Investments

We maintain cash balances to sustain operations, finance growth, and to serve as a contingency fund for unforeseen spending needs. Investment of these funds is guided by our policy requiring preservation of capital, maintenance of liquidity, furtherance of social responsibility, and maximum after-tax yield. The resulting investment options include bank deposits, money market funds, and state, municipal and corporate bonds. Negative screens are used to avoid investing in socially harmful industries (e.g. tobacco, military weapons and nuclear power), and positive screens are used to identify beneficial programs such as low-income housing, education financing and community development.

PUEBLO

People United for a Better Oakland

PUEBLO is dedicated to building the capacity of Oakland's citizens to participate in the economic, social and civic decisions that affect their lives. The group's Safe Health Project is a three-year organizing and reform initiative that seeks to reduce community members' exposure to environmental toxins. By developing a comprehensive toxins database and accompanying maps, the project is educating residents about their specific risks and mobilizing them to create a healthier urban environment.

132 East 12th Street
Oakland, CA 94606
(510) 452-2010
fax (510) 452-2017

www.peopleunited.org

This group was a Ben & Jerry's Foundation Grant Recipient.

TOTAL SHAREHOLDER RETURNS

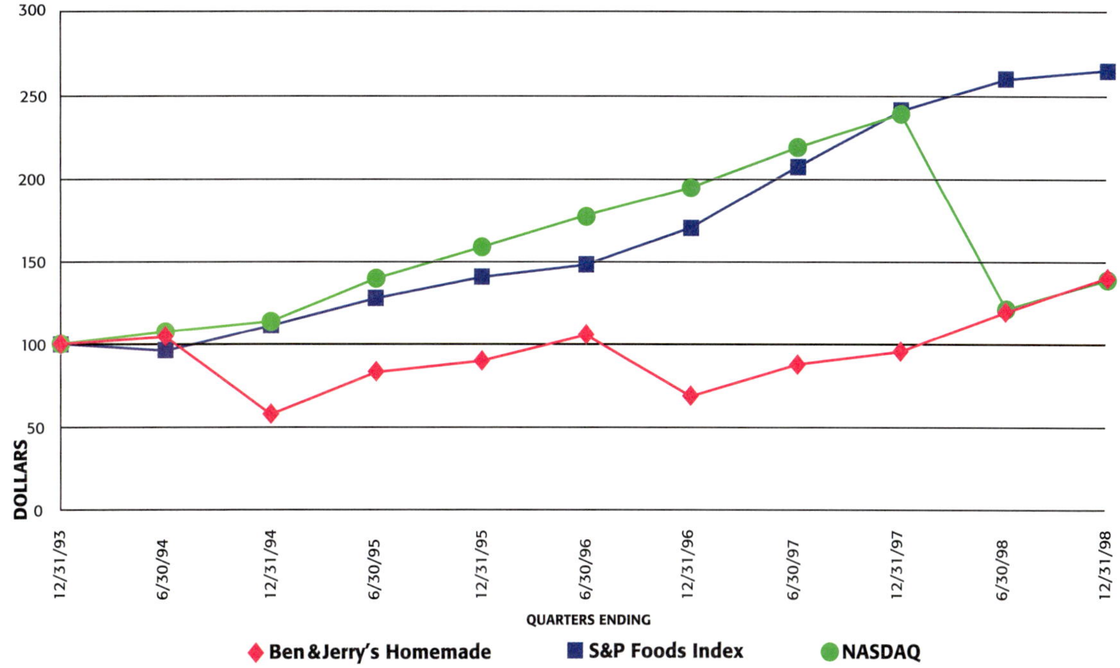

Prepared by Standard & Poor's Compustat Custom Products Division

In 1998 we had $44,521,480 in socially screened investments, or 94% of our total cash under management, down from 95% in 1997.

Company Credit Card

Our corporate credit card is issued through the Vermont National Bank, which donates 1% of all purchases to organizations that help kids including: Camp Ta-Kum-Ta, David's House, Foster Grandparents, Lund Family Center, Make-A-Wish Foundation, Vermont Arts Exchange, Vermont Campaign to End Childhood Hunger and Vermont Youth Conservation Corps.

Litigation

There was no shareholder-related litigation against the Company in 1998.

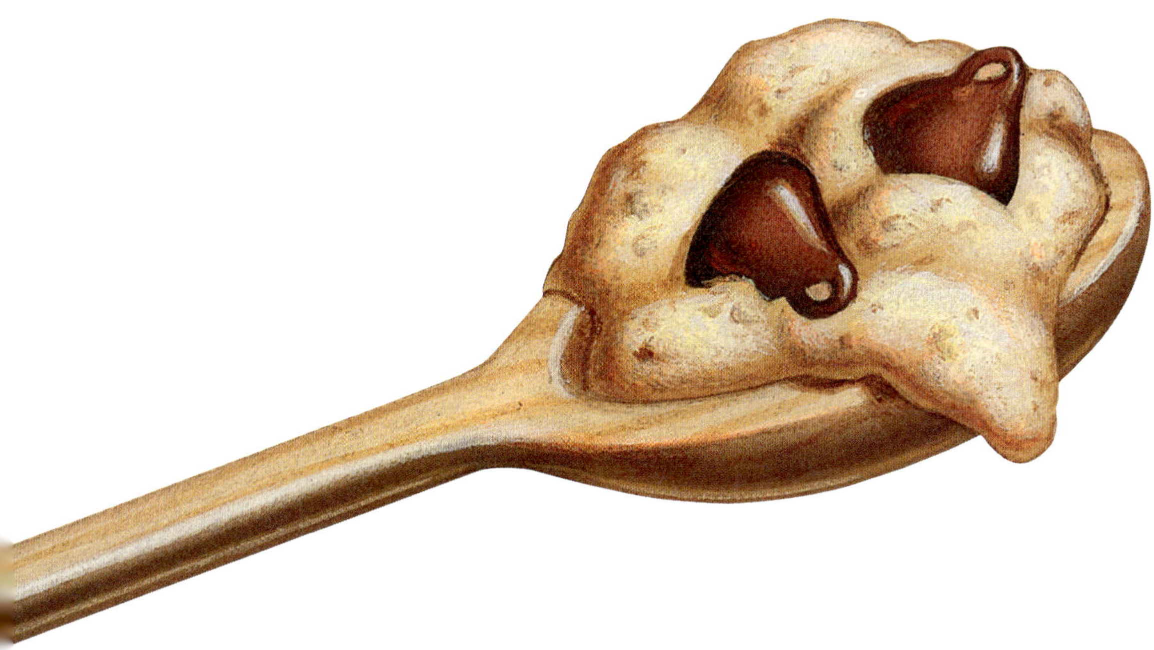

Alternatives for Community & Environment

Working together with low-income residents throughout the metropolitan Boston region, ACE provides the crucial legal and technical support, educational programs and community organizing assistance that helps people achieve environmental justice in their often forgotten neighborhoods. ACE's Clear the Air project is teaching young people and others to advocate for cleaner and higher quality mass transit alternatives in Boston's Roxbury section, a neighborhood suffering from the highest rate of asthma hospitalization in the state of Massachusetts.

2343 Washington Street
Roxbury, MA 02119
(617) 442-3343

www.netcom.com\~psloh

This group was a Ben & Jerry's Foundation Grant Recipient.

Centro Independiente de Trabajadores Agricolas

Encouraging and empowering farmworkers and former farmworkers to bring their own firsthand perspectives to the current debates on food safety and pesticide-intensive agriculture, CITA is a unique voice in the sustainable agriculture movement. In addition to special programs that train farmworkers to be policy advocates and future trainers themselves, CITA's Project ACCESS has created the first-of-its-kind farmworker developed and accessed database documenting cases of pesticide abuse and illegal use.

PO Box 78
Florida, NY 10921
(914) 651-5570

This group was a Ben & Jerry's Foundation Grant Recipient.

Market for Registrant's Common Equity & Related Stockholder Matters

The Company's Class A Common Stock is traded on the NASDAQ National Market System under the symbol BJICA. The following table sets forth for the period December 29, 1996 through March 5, 1999, the high and low closing sales prices of the Company's Class A Common Stock for the periods indicated.

1997	**High**	**Low**
First Quarter	$ 14 3/8	$ 10 7/8
Second Quarter	14 1/2	11
Third Quarter	14 1/2	12
Fourth Quarter	18 3/4	12 1/4

1998	**High**	**Low**
First Quarter	$ 19	$ 14
Second Quarter	21 1/8	17
Third Quarter	19 7/8	13 1/16
Fourth Quarter	23 7/8	14 7/8

1999	**High**	**Low**
First Quarter *(through March 5, 1999)*	$ 24 5/16	$ 21 3/8

The Class B Common Stock is generally non-transferable and there is no trading market for this stock. However, the Class B Common Stock is freely convertible into Class A Common Stock on a share-for-share basis, and transferable thereafter. A stockholder who does not wish to complete the prior conversion process may effect a sale by simply delivering the certificate for such shares of Class B Stock to a broker, properly endorsed. The broker may then present the certificate to the Company's transfer agent which, if the transfer is otherwise in good order, will issue to the purchaser a certificate for the number of shares of Class A Common Stock thereby sold.

As of March 5, 1999 there were 10,202 holders of record of the Company's Class A Common Stock and 2,025 holders of record of the Company's Class B Common Stock.

Selected Financial Data

The following table contains selected financial information for the Company's fiscal years 1994 through 1998.

(In thousands except per share data)			Fiscal Year		
Summary of Operations	**1998**	**1997**	**1996**	**1995**	**1994**
Net sales	$ 209,203	$ 174,206	$ 167,155	$ 155,333	$ 148,802
Cost of sales	136,225	114,284	115,212	109,125	109,760
Gross profit	72,978	59,922	51,943	46,208	39,042
Selling, general & administrative expenses	63,895	53,520	45,531	36,362	36,253
Asset write-down[1]					6,779
Other income (expense) – net	693	(118)	(77)	(441)	228
Income (loss) before income taxes	9,776	6,284	6,335	9,405	(3,762)
Income taxes	3,534	2,388	2,409	3,457	(1,893)
Net income (loss)	6,242	3,896	3,926	5,948	(1,869)
Net income (loss) per share – diluted	$ 0.84	$ 0.53	$ 0.54	$ 0.82	$ (0.26)
Shares outstanding – diluted	7,463	7,334	7,230	7,222	7,148

			Fiscal Year		
Balance Sheet Data	**1998**	**1997**	**1996**	**1995**	**1994**
Working capital	$ 48,381	$ 51,412	$ 50,055	$ 51,023	$ 37,456
Total assets	149,501	146,471	136,665	131,074	120,296
Long-term debt and capital lease obligations	20,491	25,676	31,087	31,977	32,419
Stockholders' equity[2]	90,908	86,919	82,685	78,531	72,502

[1] Write-down of assets – In 1994, the Company replaced certain of the software and equipment installed at the plant in St. Albans, Vermont. The loss from the write-down of the related assets included a portion of the previously capitalized interest and project management costs.

[2] No cash dividends have been declared or paid by the Company on its capital stock since the Company's organization. The Company intends to reinvest earnings for use in its business and to finance future growth. Accordingly, the Board of Directors does not anticipate declaring any cash dividends in the foreseeable future.

Management's Discussion & Analysis of Financial Condition & Results of Operations

Results of Operations

The following table shows certain items as a percentage of net sales, which are included in the Company's Statement of Operations.

	Percentage of Net Sales			Annual Increase (Decrease)		
		Fiscal Year		1998	1997	1996
	1998	1997	1996	Compared To 1997	Compared To 1996	Compared To 1995
Net sales	100.0%	100.0%	100.0%	20.1%	4.2%	7.6%
Cost of sales	65.1	65.6	68.9	19.2	(0.8)	5.6
Gross profit	34.9	34.4	31.1	21.8	15.4	12.4
Selling, general and administrative expenses	30.5	30.7	27.2	19.4	17.5	25.2
Other income (expense)	0.3	(0.1)	0.1	687.3	53.2	(82.5)
Income before income taxes	4.7	3.6	3.8	55.6	(0.8)	(32.6)
Income taxes	1.7	1.4	1.5	48.0	(0.9)	(30.3)
Net income	3.0%	2.2%	2.3%	60.2%	(0.8)%	(34.0)%

Net Sales

Net sales in 1998 increased 20.1% to $209 million from $174 million in 1997. Domestic pint volume increased 10% compared to 1997, which was primarily attributable to the Company's original line of products. This volume increase was combined with a price increase of 3% on pints sold to distributors that went into effect in July 1998. Unit volume of 2.5 gallon bulk container products increased 17% compared to the same period in 1997. Also contributing to the increase in sales for 1998 was the launch of the Company's new single-serve products in Japan and the introduction of a new line of premium plus ice cream, Newman's Own™ All Natural Ice Cream, manufactured and sold under a license agreement with Paul Newman and Newman's Own™.

Packaged sales (primarily pints) represented approximately 81% of total net sales in 1998, 84% of total net sales in 1997, and 85% of total net sales in 1996. Net sales of 2.5 gallon bulk containers represented approximately 8% of total net sales in 1998 and 1997 and 7% of total net sales in 1996. Net sales of novelties accounted for approximately 9% of total net sales in 1998 and 6% of total net sales in 1997 and 1996. Net sales from the Company's retail stores represented 2% of total net sales in 1998, 1997 and 1996.

International sales were $17.4, $7.6 and $6.9 million in 1998, 1997 and 1996, respectively, which represents 8% of net sales in 1998, 4% in 1997 and 4% in 1996. The increase in 1998 was primarily due to the introduction of single-serve products in Japan and higher sales to Canada.

Net sales in 1997 increased 4% to $174 million from $167 million in 1996 primarily due to price increases of approximately 3% for pints that went into effect in August 1996 and April 1997. Pint volume increased 0.7% compared to 1996. Net sales of 2.5 gallon bulk containers had a modest increase in 1997.

Cost of Sales

Cost of sales in 1998 increased approximately $22 million or 19% over the same period in 1997 and overall gross profit as a percentage of net sales increased from 34.4% in 1997 to 34.9% in 1998. The slightly higher gross profit margin primarily resulted from increases in selling prices effective in January 1998 and July 1998, better plant utilization due to higher production volumes and a decrease in reserves for potential product obsolescence, partially offset by substantial increases in dairy commodity costs.

The Company experienced significant increases in dairy prices in 1998 compared to 1997 levels. In response to higher dairy costs, the Company instituted a 3% price increase effective in July 1998 for its packaged pint products and a combined 10% price increase for its 2.5 gallon bulk containers effective in January 1998 and July 1998 to offset these increased costs. If dairy commodity prices begin to rise again to higher levels, there is the possibility that these costs will not be passed on to customers, which will negatively impact future gross profit margins. See Risk Factors on page 34.

In 1997, cost of sales decreased approximately $900,000 or 0.8% over 1996 and overall gross profit as a percentage of net sales increased from 31.1% in 1996 to 34.4% in 1997. The higher gross profit as a percentage of net sales in 1997 was a result of higher selling prices instituted in August 1996 and April 1997, improved operating efficiencies and decreases in certain raw material commodity prices. The Company experienced a modest decrease in dairy commodity prices during 1997 compared to 1996. Dairy costs started to increase in the summer and fall of 1996 and continued into the first half of 1997. In response to higher dairy commodity costs, the Company instituted a price increase of approximately 3% for its packaged pint products effective April 1997. Though dairy commodity prices were lower in the third quarter of 1997 as compared to the comparable quarter in the prior year, they began to escalate in the latter half of the fourth quarter.

Bay Area Nuclear (BAN) Waste Coalition

BAN is working with concerned citizens to stop construction of a dangerous shallow trench nuclear waste dump in the Mojave Desert's Ward Valley wilderness. In this and other efforts to create a healthier world, BAN provides the grassroots organizing, technical research, legal help, outreach and education that's helping others actively seek source reduction and responsible containment of nuclear wastes, protect priceless ecosystems and endangered species, and promote Native American human rights and environmental justice.

2760 Golden Gate
San Francisco, CA 94118
(415) 752-8678

www.banwaste.envirolink.org

This group was a Ben & Jerry's Foundation Grant Recipient.

Selling, General and Administrative Expenses

Selling, general and administrative expenses increased 19% to $64 million in 1998 from $54 million in 1997 and decreased slightly as a percentage of net sales to 30.5% in 1998 from 30.7% in 1997. The $10 million increase in expenses is attributable to increased sales and marketing expenses to support the launch of a new line of premium plus ice cream under the name of Newman's Own™ All Natural Ice Cream, increased international costs, increases in radio advertising, in-store programs to drive product trial and brand awareness, scoop truck marketing and the rollout of the new pint package design.

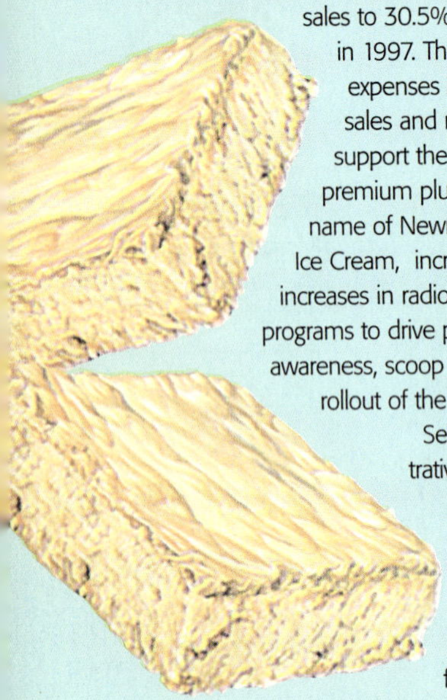

Selling, general and administrative expenses increased 17% to $54 million in 1997 from $46 million in 1996 and increased as a percentage of net sales to 30.7% in 1997 from 27.2% in 1996. This increase primarily reflects increased marketing and sales expenses and includes national radio advertising and increased trade promotions to support the Company's brand both domestically and in Europe.

Other Income (Expense)

Interest income increased from $1.9 million in 1997 to $2.2 million in 1998. The increase in interest income was due to higher average invested balance throughout 1998. Interest expense in 1998 decreased $104,000 in 1998 as compared to 1997 due to the $5 million Senior Notes principal installment payment. Other income (expense) increased in 1998 from other expense of $118,000 in 1997 to other income of $693,000 in 1998. This is primarily due to increased losses associated with foreign currency exchange in comparison to 1997, combined with income received from the Company's cost basis investment.

Interest income increased from $1.7 million in 1996 to $1.9 million in 1997. The increase in interest income was due to a higher average invested balance throughout 1997. Interest expense in 1997 remained level with 1996. Other income (expense) decreased in 1997 from other income of $243,000 in the prior year to other expense of $64,000 in 1997. This is primarily due to the receipt of insurance settlement proceeds.

Income Taxes

The Company's effective income tax rate in 1998 decreased to 36% from 38% in 1997 and 1996. The decrease was a result of lower state income taxes, more tax-exempt interest income, and the overall geographic mix of earnings. Management expects 1999's effective income tax rate to decrease to approximately 35%, based upon the expected geographic mix of earnings.

Net Income

Net income for 1998 increased to $6.2 million compared to $3.9 million in 1997. Net income as a percentage of net sales was 2.9% in 1998 as compared to 2.2% in 1997 and 2.3% in 1996.

Seasonality

The Company typically experiences more demand for its products during the summer than during the winter.

Inflation

Inflation has not had a material effect on the Company's business to date, with the exception of dairy raw material commodity costs. See the Risk Factors below. Management believes that the effects of inflation and changing prices were successfully managed in 1998, with both margins and earnings being protected through a combination of pricing adjustments, cost control programs and productivity gains.

Liquidity and Capital Resources

As of December 26, 1998, the Company had $47.2 million of cash, cash equivalents and marketable securities ($25.1 million of cash and cash equivalents and $22.1 million of marketable securities), a $570,000 decrease since December 27, 1997. Net cash provided by operations in 1998 was $16.1 million of which approximately $8.8 million was used for net additions to property, plant and equipment, primarily for improvements at the Company's manufacturing facilities, the build out of three Company-owned scoop shops in France and fit-up costs for a chain of cinemas in the United Kingdom. In addition, $3.1 million cash was used to repurchase shares of the Company's Class A Common Stock and $5.3 million was used to pay down debt and capital leases.

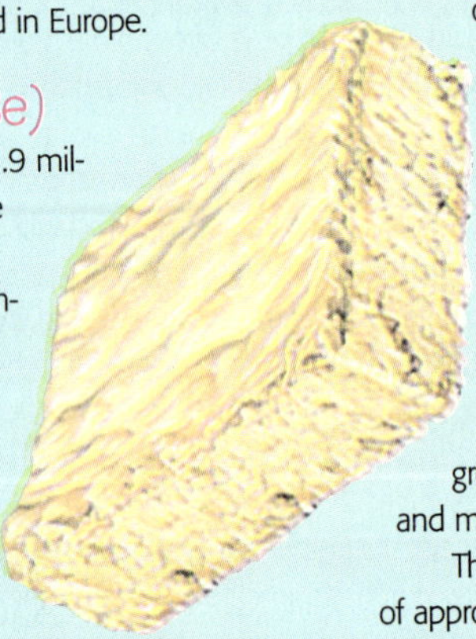

From December 27, 1997 to December 26, 1998 inventories and the sum of accounts payable and accrued expenses have increased $2 million and $5 million, respectively. These increases reflect the growth in the Company's business and increased sales and marketing expenses.

The Company anticipates capital expenditures in 1999 of approximately $9 million plus $1 million for its acquisition of 60% of its licensee in Israel during 1999. Most of these projected capital expenditures relate to equipment upgrades and enhancements at the Company's manufacturing facilities, research and development equipment, computer-related expenditures and corporate space expansion.

During the year ended December 26, 1998, the Company repurchased a total of 166,500 shares of the Company's Class A Common Stock for approximately $3.1 million. Pursuant to the repurchase program announced May 8, 1997, 122,500 shares were purchased for use in connection with stock option awards under the 1995 Equity Incentive Plan. These transactions, together with earlier repurchases of 77,500 shares in 1997, complete the repurchase of the 200,000 shares authorized under this program. An additional 44,000 shares were purchased through December 26, 1998 for approximately $733,000 under a repurchase program announced in September 1998, authorizing the Company to purchase shares of the Company's Class A Common Stock up to an aggregate cost of $5 million for use for general corporate purposes. Subsequent to December 26, 1998 and through

WASHINGTON TOXICS COALITION

Washington Toxics Coalition

The Washington Toxics Coalition works to reduce children's exposure to hazardous pesticides and educate parents, children's organizations, the health care community and farmers about the impact of these pollutants on the children in our lives. In addition to persuading schools to halt pesticide use, the Coalition encourages community support for local organic farms, advocates for strong pesticide control policies, and has been instrumental in attempts to end the dangerous practice of using industrial waste as food crop fertilizer.

4649 Sunnyside Ave. N
Suite 540-East
Seattle, WA 98103
(206) 632-1545
fax (206) 632-8661

www.accessone.com/~watoxics

This group was a Ben & Jerry's Foundation Grant Recipient.

C-Beyond

An organization of young people in the suburbs of California's Contra Costa County, C-Beyond is working to create innovative new solutions that reverse troubling trends of racism and hate in the region's predominantly white communities. Using a unique combination of neighborhood action, education and community service, C-Beyond unites youth of different racial and ethnic backgrounds around common interests and concerns, and helps move their communities beyond the vicious downward spiral of scapegoating and hatred.

3629 Clayton Road
Concord, CA 94521
(925) 676-6556

This group was a Ben & Jerry's Foundation Grant Recipient.

March 5, 1999 the Company repurchased an additional 68,000 shares under this program for approximately $1.5 million.

The Company's short- and long-term debt at December 26, 1998 includes $25 million aggregate principal amount of Senior Notes issued in 1993 and 1994. The first principal payment of $5 million was paid in September 1998 and the remainder of principal is payable in annual installments through 2003.

The Company has available two $10,000,000 unsecured working capital line of credit agreements with two banks. Interest on borrowings under the agreements is set at the banks' base rate or at LIBOR plus a margin based on a predetermined formula. No amounts were borrowed under these or any bank agreements during 1998. The working capital line of credit agreements expire December 23, 2001.

Management believes that internally generated funds, cash, cash equivalents and marketable securities and equipment lease financing and/or borrowings under the Company's two unsecured bank lines of credit will be adequate to meet anticipated operating and capital requirements.

Year 2000 Readiness Disclosure

Background of Year 2000 Issues. The "Year 2000" issue is the result of computer systems and software programs using two rather than four digits to define a year. As a result, computer systems that have date sensitive software may recognize a date using "00" as the year 1900 rather than the year 2000. Unless remedied, the Year 2000 issue could result in system failures, miscalculations, and the inability to process necessary transactions or engage in similar normal business activities. In addition to computer systems and software, equipment using embedded chips, such as manufacturing and telephone equipment, could also be at risk.

State of Readiness. The Company has developed and is implementing a Year 2000 plan to address Year 2000 issues. The plan focuses on the following three broad categories: (a) information technology systems; (b) manufacturing facilities including embedded technology; and (c) external noncompliance by customers, distributors, suppliers and other business partners.

The Company has substantially completed the inventory and assessment of the core software applications and hardware infrastructure. The Company has identified and is in various stages of remediating software and hardware deficiencies caused by the Year 2000 issue. The financial, human resources, manufacturing and distribution systems are currently being repaired; testing and validation of these systems are scheduled during the second quarter of 1999. The Company's networking equipment is not compliant and is scheduled to undergo renovation and testing during the second quarter of 1999 as well.

While the Company is continuing detailed assessment of its manufacturing facilities and embedded chip technology, it has not identified any problems thus far that would have a material impact upon operations. The assessment phase for the manufacturing facilities is expected to be completed in April 1999. At the same time, the Company is testing and remediating certain equipment and software systems known to have possible Year 2000 issues and is expected to complete this phase during the second quarter of 1999.

A critical step in this project is the coordination of Year 2000 readiness with third parties. The Company is communicating with its significant suppliers, distributors and customers to determine the extent to which the Company is vulnerable if the third parties fail to resolve their Year 2000 issues. The Company will continue to assess and work with all of its major partners to understand the associated risks and plan for contingencies.

Risks Related to Year 2000 Issues. The Company presently believes that the Year 2000 issue will not pose significant operational problems and that the internal Year 2000 issues will be resolved in a timely manner. However, the future compliance of Year 2000 processing within the Company is dependent upon key personnel, vendor software, vendor equipment and components. In the unlikely event that no further progress is made on the Company's Year 2000 project, the Company may be unable to manufacture or ship product, invoice customers or collect payments. As a result, Year 2000 issues could have a material adverse impact on the Company's operations and its financial results. In addition, if systems operated by third parties (including municipalities or utilities) are not Year 2000 compliant, this could also have a material adverse affect on the Company.

Costs to Address Year 2000 Issues. The Company does not separately track the internal costs incurred for the Year 2000 project, which are primarily the related payroll costs for its information systems ("IS") group. There have been no incremental payroll costs related to the Year 2000 project, however non-critical IS projects have been deferred due to concentration on Year 2000 efforts. The delay of these projects is not expected to have a material impact on the operations of the Company.

The external costs for software, hardware, equipment and services related to the Year 2000 project are expected to be approximately $1.2 million. The Company will expense the costs of modifying existing systems and capitalize the replacement cost of software or equipment that is not Year 2000 compliant. There can be no guarantee, however, that the systems of other entities which the Company relies upon will be converted on a timely basis or that any failure to convert by another entity would not have an adverse effect on the Company's systems and operations.

Contingency Plans. Due to the general uncertainty inherent in the Year 2000 problem, including uncertainty regarding the Year 2000 readiness of suppliers, distributors and other manufacturers, the Company is developing contingency plans. This process includes, among others, developing backup procedures in case of systems failures, identifying alternative production plans and developing alternative plans to engage in business activities with customers, distributors and suppliers that are not experiencing Year 2000 problems.

The above forward-looking statements with regard to the timing and overall cost estimates of the Company's efforts to address the Year 2000 problem are based upon the

Western Shoshone Defense Project

The Western Shoshone Defense Project is dedicated to affirming and promoting its people's jurisdiction of their historic homeland, a region of the Nevada desert which has been claimed by the federal government amid great controversy. Until their lands are returned to their control, the Project's Mining Action Program is protecting the region's natural resources from devastating mining operations with a working combination of public protest, regulatory process, legal intervention, public education and shareholder activism.

PO Box 211106
Crescent Valley, NV 89821
(702) 468-0230
fax (702) 468-0237

www.alphacdc.com/wsdp

This group was a Ben & Jerry's Foundation Grant Recipient.

Company's experience thus far in this effort. Should the Company encounter unforeseen difficulties either in the continuing review of its internal systems, the ultimate remediation, or the responses of its business partners, the actual results could vary significantly from the estimates in these forward-looking statements.

Forward-Looking Statements

This section, as well as other portions of this document, includes certain forward-looking statements about the Company's business, new products, sales, dairy prices, other expenditures and cost savings, Year 2000 program costs, effective tax rate, operating and capital requirements and refinancing. Any such statements are subject to risks that could cause the actual results or needs to vary materially. These risks are discussed below.

Risk Factors

Dependence on Independent Ice Cream Distributors. Historically, the Company has been dependent on maintaining satisfactory relationships with Dreyer's Grand Ice Cream, Inc. ("Dreyer's") and the other independent ice cream distributors that have acted as the Company's exclusive or master distributor in their assigned territories. In 1998, Dreyer's distributed significantly more than a majority of the sales of Ben & Jerry's products. While the Company believes its relationships with Dreyer's and its other distributors generally have been satisfactory and have been instrumental in the Company's growth, the Company has at times experienced difficulty in maintaining such relationships to its satisfaction. In addition, in early 1998 Dreyer's made overtures to Ben Cohen and Jerry Greenfield, the Company's co-founders, to obtain their support for an offer that Dreyer's would make to acquire the Company. The co-founders rejected these overtures.

In August 1998 – January 1999, the Company redesigned its distribution network, entering into a distribution agreement with The Pillsbury Company ("Pillsbury") and a new agreement with Dreyer's. These arrangements take effect September 1, 1999, except for certain territories, which are effective, in April – May 1999. The Company believes the terms of the new arrangements will, on balance, be more favorable to its Company and expects that under the distribution network redesign, no one distributor will account for more than 40% of the Company's net sales. However, both Pillsbury, through its Häagen-Daz unit, and Dreyer's are competitors of the Company.

Since available distribution alternatives are limited, there can be no assurance that difficulties in maintaining satisfactory relationships with Pillsbury, Dreyer's and its other distributors, some of which are also competitors of the Company, will not have a material adverse effect on the Company's business.

Growth in Sales and Earnings. In 1998, net sales of the Company increased 20.1% to $209 million from $174 million in 1997. Pint volume increased 10.2% compared to 1997. The super premium ice cream, frozen yogurt and sorbet industry category sales increased 4% in 1998 as compared to 1997. Given these overall domestic super premium industry trends, the successful introduction of innovative flavors on a periodic basis has become increasingly important to sales growth by the Company. Accordingly, the future degree of market acceptance of any of the Company's new products, which will be accompanied by significant promotional expenditures, is likely to have an important impact on the Company's 1999 and future financial results.

Competitive Environment. The super premium frozen dessert market is highly competitive with the distinctions between the super premium category, and the "adjoining" premium and premium plus categories less marked than in the past. As noted above, the ability to successfully introduce innovative flavors on a periodic basis that are accepted by the marketplace is a significant competitive factor. In addition, the Company's principal competitors are large, diversified companies with resources significantly greater than the Company's, two of which are distributors for the Company. The Company expects strong competition to continue, including competition for adequate distribution and competition for the limited shelf space for the frozen dessert category in supermarkets and other retail food outlets.

Increased Cost of Raw Materials. Management believes that the general trend of increased dairy ingredient commodity costs may continue, and it is possible that at some future date both gross margins and earnings may not be adequately protected by pricing adjustments, cost control programs and productivity gains.

Reliance on a Limited Number of Key Personnel. The success of the Company is significantly dependent on the services of Perry Odak, the Chief Executive Officer, and a limited number of executive managers working under Mr. Odak, as well as certain continued services of Jerry Greenfield, the Chairperson of the Board and co-founder of the Company; and Ben Cohen, Vice Chairperson and co-founder of the Company. Loss of the services of any of these persons could have a material adverse effect on the Company's business.

The Company's Social Mission. The Company's basic business philosophy is embodied in a three-part "mission statement," which includes a "social mission" to "operate the Company in a way that actively recognizes the central role that business plays in the structure of society by initiating innovative ways to improve the quality of life of a broad community: local, national and international. Underlying the mission of Ben & Jerry's is the determination to seek new and creative ways of addressing all three parts, while holding a deep respect for individuals inside and outside the Company and for the communities of which they are a part." The Company believes that implementation of its social mission, which is being more integrated into the Company's business, has been beneficial to the Company's overall financial performance. However, it is possible that at some future date the amount of the Company's energies and resources devoted to its social mission could have some material adverse financial effect.

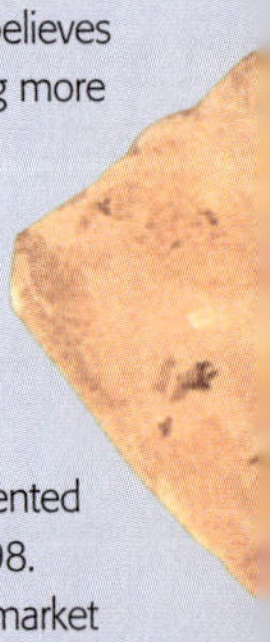

International. Total international net sales represented approximately 8% of total consolidated net sales in 1998. The Company's principal competitors have substantial market shares in various countries outside the United States, principally Europe and Japan. The Company sells product in Japan,

Canada, the United Kingdom, Ireland, France, the Netherlands, Belgium and will start selling in Peru and Lebanon in 1999. In 1987, the Company granted an exclusive license to manufacture and sell Ben & Jerry's products in Israel. In February 1999, the Company made an investment commitment in the Israeli licensee, which gave the Company a 60% ownership interest. In May 1998, the Company signed a Licensing Agreement with Delicious Alternative Desserts, Ltd. to manufacture, sell and distribute Ben & Jerry's products through the wholesale distribution channels in Canada. The Company is investigating the possibility of further international expansion. However, there can be no assurance that the Company will be successful in entering (directly or indirectly through licensing), on a long-term profitable basis, such international markets as it selects.

Control of the Company. The Company has two classes of common stock - the Class A Common Stock, entitled to one vote per share, and the Class B Common Stock (authorized in 1987), entitled, except to the extent otherwise provided by law, to ten votes per share. Ben Cohen, Jerry Greenfield and Jeffrey Furman (collectively the "Principal Stockholders") hold shares representing 46% of the aggregate voting power in elections for directors, permitting them as a practical matter to elect all members of the Board of Directors and thereby effectively control the business, policies and management of the Company. Because of their significant holdings of Class B Common Stock, the Principal Stockholders may continue to exercise this control even if they sell substantial portions of their Class A Common Stock.

In addition, the Company issued all of the authorized Class A Preferred Stock to the Foundation in 1985. All current directors of the Foundation are directors of the Company. The Class A Preferred Stock gives the Foundation a class voting right to act with respect to certain Business Combinations (as defined in the Company's charter) and significantly limits the voting rights that holders of the Class A Common Stock and Class B Common Stock, the owners of virtually all of the equity in the Company, would otherwise have with respect to such Business Combinations.

Also, in April 1998 the Legislature of the State of Vermont amended a provision of the Vermont Business Corporation Act to provide that the directors of a Vermont corporation may also consider, in determining whether an acquisition offer or other matter is in the best interests of the corporation, the interests of the corporation's employees, suppliers, creditors and customers, the economy of the state in which the corporation is located, and including the possibility that the best interests of the corporation may be served by the continued independence of the corporation.

Also in August 1998, following approval by its Board of Directors, the Company put in place two Shareholder Rights Plans, one pertaining to the Class A Common Stock and one pertaining to the Class B Common Stock. These Plans are intended to protect stockholders by compelling someone seeking to acquire the Company to negotiate with the Company's Board of Directors in order to protect stockholders from unfair takeover tactics and to assist in the maximization of stockholder value. These Rights Plans, which are common for public companies in the United States, may also be deemed to be "anti-takeover" provisions in that the Board of Directors believes that these Plans will make it difficult for a third party to acquire control of the Company on terms which are unfair or unfavorable to the stockholders.

While the Board of Directors believes that the Class B Common Stock and the Class A Preferred Stock are important elements in keeping Ben & Jerry's an independent, Vermont-based business focused on its three-part corporate mission, the Class B Common Stock and the Class A Preferred Stock may be deemed to be "anti-takeover" provisions in that the Board of Directors believes the existence of these securities will make it difficult for a third party to acquire control of the Company on terms opposed by the holders of the Class B Common Stock, including primarily the Principal Stockholders, or The Foundation, or for incumbent management and the Board of Directors to be removed. In addition, the 1997 amendments to the Company's Articles of Association to classify the Board of Directors and to add certain other related provisions, the April 1998 Vermont Legislative Amendment of the Vermont Business Corporation Act and the Shareholder Rights Plans put in place in August 1998 may be deemed to be "anti-takeover" provisions in that the Board of Directors believes that these amendments and legislation will make it difficult for a third party to acquire control of the Company on terms opposed by the holders of the Class B Common Stock, including primarily the Principal Stockholders and the Foundation, or for incumbent management and the Board of Directors to be removed.

Market Risk

The Company is exposed to a variety of market risks, including changes in interest rates affecting the return on its investments and foreign currency fluctuations. The Company's exposure to market risk for a change in interest rates relates primarily to the Company's investment portfolio. The Company has classified all of its short-term and long-term investments as "available for sale" except for certificates of deposits which are held to maturity. The majority of these investments are municipal bonds and fixed income preferred stock in which the market value approximates its cost at December 26, 1998. The Company does not intend to hold such investments to maturity if there is an underlying change in interest rates or the Company's cash flow requirements. Certificates of deposits do not expose the consolidated statement of operations or balance sheets to fluctuations in interest rates. The Company's exposure to market risk for fluctuations in foreign currency relate primarily to the amounts due from subsidiaries. Exchange gains and losses related to amounts due from subsidiaries have not been material for each of the years presented.

Black Workers for Justice

Black Workers for Justice is a workplace-based community organization helping African-American workers in the southeast confront the destructive forces of globalization. Through education and conference sponsorship, BWJ teaches participating workers about the ever-increasing impacts of globalization and the social costs they exact both at home and abroad. More importantly, BWJ organizes and empowers its participants to work for positive change, thereby creating a vital link between knowledge and subsequent action.

PO Box 491317
College Park, GA 30349
(404) 768-8801

This group was a Ben & Jerry's Foundation Grant Recipient.

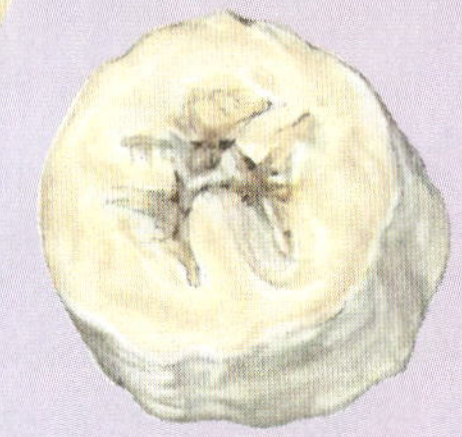

Consolidated Balance Sheets

(In thousands except share amounts)

Assets	December 26, 1998	December 27, 1997
Current assets:		
Cash and cash equivalents	$ 25,111	$ 47,318
Short-term investments	22,118	481
Trade accounts receivable (less allowance of $979 in 1998 and $1,066 in 1997 for doubtful accounts)	11,338	12,710
Inventories	13,090	11,122
Deferred income taxes	7,547	6,071
Prepaid expenses and other current assets	3,105	2,378
Total current assets	82,309	80,080
Property, plant and equipment, net	63,451	62,724
Investments	303	1,061
Other assets	3,438	2,606
	$ 149,501	$ 146,471
Liabilities and Stockholders' Equity		
Current liabilities:		
Accounts payable and accrued expenses	$ 28,662	$ 23,266
Current portion of long-term debt and obligations under capital leases	5,266	5,402
Total current liabilities	33,928	28,668
Long-term debt and obligations under capital leases	20,491	25,676
Deferred income taxes	4,174	5,208
Stockholders' equity:		
$1.20 noncumulative Class A preferred stock – par value $1.00 per share, redeemable at $12.00 per share; 900 shares authorized, issued and outstanding; aggregated preference on liquidation – $9,000	1	1
Class A common stock – $.033 par value; authorized 20,000,000 shares; issued: 6,592,392 at December 26, 1998 and 6,494,835 at December 27, 1997	218	214
Class B common stock – $.033 par value; authorized 3,000,000 shares; issued: 824,480 at December 26, 1998 and 866,235 at December 27, 1997	27	29
Additional paid-in-capital	50,556	49,681
Retained earnings	45,328	39,086
Accumulated other comprehensive loss	(151)	(129)
Treasury stock, at cost: 291,032 Class A and 1,092 Class B shares at December 26, 1998 and 124,532 Class A and 1,092 Class B shares at December 27, 1997	(5,071)	(1,963)
Total stockholders' equity	90,908	86,919
	$ 149,501	$ 146,471

See notes to consolidated financial statements.

SENIOR ACTION NETWORK

Senior Action Network

A coalition of 122 member groups representing more than 27,000 senior citizens from all walks of San Franciscan life, SAN founded the city's unique Senior University. This volunteer-led leadership training program teaches seniors how to organize themselves in order to better advocate for improved health care, crime prevention, pedestrian safety, transportation and housing. Currently offered in English and Spanish, the program is being expanded to aid the underserved Chinese and Russian-speaking senior communities as well.

1370 Mission Street
San Francisco, CA 94103
(415) 863-2033

This group was a Ben & Jerry's Foundation Grant Recipient.

Consolidated Statements of Operations

(In thousands except share amounts)

	Fiscal Year Ended December 26, 1998	December 27, 1997	December 28, 1996
Net sales	$ 209,203	$ 174,206	$ 167,155
Cost of sales	136,225	114,284	115,212
Gross profit	72,978	59,922	51,943
Selling, general and administrative expenses	63,895	53,520	45,531
Other income (expense):			
Interest income	2,248	1,938	1,676
Interest expense	(1,888)	(1,992)	(1,996)
Other income (expense), net	333	(64)	243
	693	(118)	(77)
Income before income taxes	9,776	6,284	6,335
Income taxes	3,534	2,388	2,409
Net income	$ 6,242	$ 3,896	$ 3,926
Shares used to compute net income per common share			
Basic	7,197	7,247	7,189
Diluted	7,463	7,334	7,230
Net income per common share			
Basic	$ 0.87	$ 0.54	$ 0.55
Diluted	$ 0.84	$ 0.53	$ 0.54

See notes to consolidated financial statements.

Klamath Siskiyou Wildlands Center

The Klamath Siskiyou Wildlands Center monitors federal stewardship of publicly-owned lands in Oregon's ecologically unique Klamath Siskiyou bioregion. Through scrutiny of land management decisions and the use of strong legal and administrative action whenever necessary, the Center's Public Lands Oversight Campaign is successfully reducing forest destruction by making sure that federal land managers adhere to the letter and spirit of all applicable environmental laws and procedures.

PO Box 332
Williams, OR 97544
(541) 846-9273

This group was a Ben & Jerry's Foundation Grant Recipient.

Consolidated Statement of Stockholders' Equity

(In thousands except per share data)

	Preferred Stock Par Value	Common Stock Class A Par Value	Common Stock Class B Par Value	Additional Paid-in Capital
Balance at December 30, 1995	$ 1	$ 209	$ 30	$ 48,521
Net income				
Common stock issued under stock purchase plan (15,674 Class A shares)				205
Conversion of Class B shares to Class A shares (16,661 shares)		1	(1)	
Common stock issued under restricted stock plan (2,096 Class A shares)				27
Foreign currency translation adjustment				
Net comprehensive income				
Balance at December 28, 1996	1	210	29	48,753
Net income				
Common stock issued under stock purchase plan (15,406 Class A shares)		1		148
Conversion of Class B shares to Class A shares (31,451 shares)		1		
Common stock issued under stock and option plans (83,267 Class A shares)		2		907
Repurchase of common stock (77,500 Class A shares)				
Issuance of treasury stock for compensation (20,000 Class A shares)				(127)
Foreign currency translation adjustment				
Net comprehensive income				
Balance at December 27, 1997	1	214	29	49,681
Net income				
Common stock issued under stock purchase plan (14,277 Class A shares)		-		179
Conversion of Class B shares to Class A shares (41,755 shares)		2	(2)	
Common stock issued under stock and option plans (41,525 Class A shares)		2		696
Repurchase of common stock (166,500 Class A shares)				
Foreign currency translation adjustment				
Net comprehensive income				
Balance at December 26, 1998	$ 1	$ 218	$ 27	$ 50,556

See notes to consolidated financial statements.

Farmworker Institute for Education and Leadership Training

FIELD provides leadership training to farmworkers seeking justice and self-determination, and promotes public support for the farm-worker movement. Their Alliance for Safety project is working to change the policies and practices of California's strawberry industry, a heavy user of agricultural chemicals. The project's three separate components — Farmworker, Community and Coalition Mobilization — are working together to improve farmworker safety, local water quality and the safety of California strawberries themselves.

PO Box 62, La Paz
Keene, CA 93531
(520) 319-1646

This group was a Ben & Jerry's Foundation Grant Recipient.

Retained Earnings	Accumulated Other Comprehensive Loss	Treasury Stock Class A Cost	Treasury Stock Class B Cost	Total Stockholders' Equity	Comprehensive Income
$ 31,264	$ (114)	$ (1,375)	$ (5)	$ 78,531	
3,926				3,926	$ 3,926
				205	
				27	
	(4)			(4)	(4)
					$ 3,922
35,190	(118)	(1,375)	(5)	82,685	
3,896				3,896	$ 3,896
				149	
				1	
				909	
		(988)		(988)	
		405		278	
	(11)			(11)	(11)
					$ 3,885
39,086	(129)	(1,958)	(5)	86,919	
6,242				6,242	$ 6,242
				179	
				698	
		(3,108)		(3,108)	
	(22)			(22)	(22)
					$ 6,220
$ 45,328	$ (151)	$ (5,066)	$ (5)	$ 90,908	

Center for Young Women's Development

Organized and operated by young people themselves, the Center for Young Women's Development is working to address the unfortunate lack of youth-oriented services, leadership opportunities and self-advocacy training for young women living on their own in the city of San Francisco. Their successful Girls In Charge project helps its participants achieve self-determination by training them to be social advocates, community organizers and active members of local boards and commissions whose decisions affect their lives.

1095 Market Street
San Francisco, CA 94103
(415) 487-8662

This group was a Ben & Jerry's Foundation Grant Recipient.

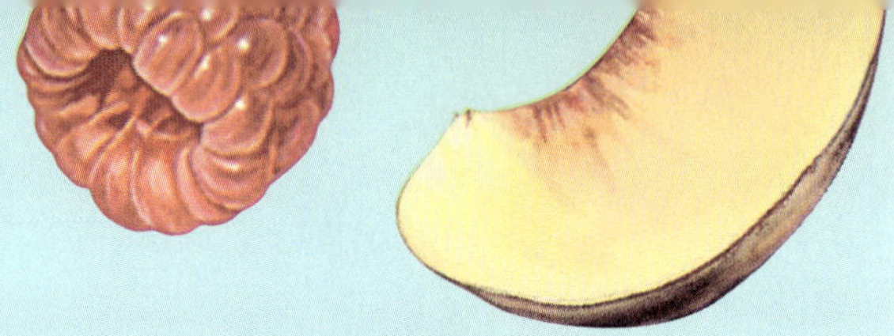

Consolidated Statements of Cash Flow

(In thousands)

		Fiscal Year Ended	
	December 26, 1998	**December 27, 1997**	**December 28, 1996**
Cash flows from operating activities:			
Net income	$ 6,242	$ 3,896	$ 3,926
Adjustments to reconcile net income to net cash provided by operating activities:			
Depreciation and amortization	8,181	7,711	7,091
Provision for bad debts	50	630	408
Deferred income taxes	(2,510)	(1,599)	809
Stock compensation		405	10
Loss on disposition of assets	112	124	
Changes in operating assets and liabilities:			
Accounts receivable	1,460	(5,318)	3,146
Inventories	(1,968)	4,243	(89)
Prepaid expenses	(501)	(64)	(2,749)
Accounts payable and accrued expenses	5,385	5,868	897
Income taxes payable/receivable	(364)	1,743	806
Net cash provided by operating activities	16,087	17,639	14,255
Cash flows from investing activities:			
Additions to property, plant and equipment	(8,770)	(5,236)	(12,333)
Proceeds from sale of assets	0	48	168
Changes in other assets	(1,082)	(425)	(466)
Increase in investments	(20,879)	(76)	(320)
Net cash used for investing activities	(30,731)	(5,689)	(12,951)
Cash flows from financing activities:			
Repayments of long-term debt and capital leases	(5,321)	(669)	(678)
Repurchase of common stock	(3,108)	(988)	
Proceeds from issuance of common stock	877	932	232
Net cash used for financing activities	(7,552)	(725)	(446)
Effect of exchange rate changes on cash	(11)	(11)	(160)
(Decrease) increase in cash and cash equivalents	(22,207)	11,214	698
Cash and cash equivalents at beginning of year	47,318	36,104	35,406
Cash and cash equivalents at end of year	$25,111	$ 47,318	$36,104

See notes to consolidated financial statements.

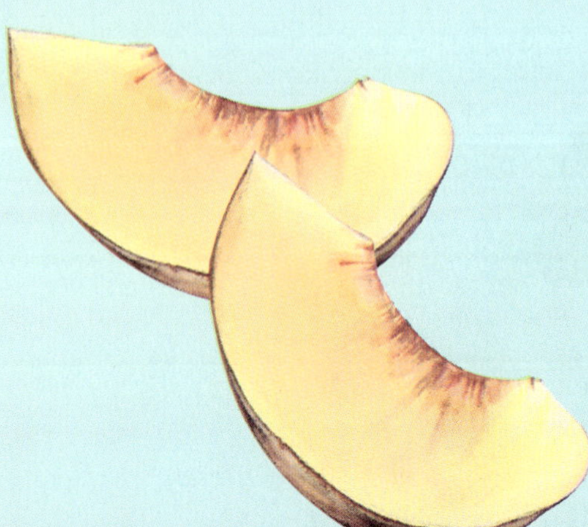

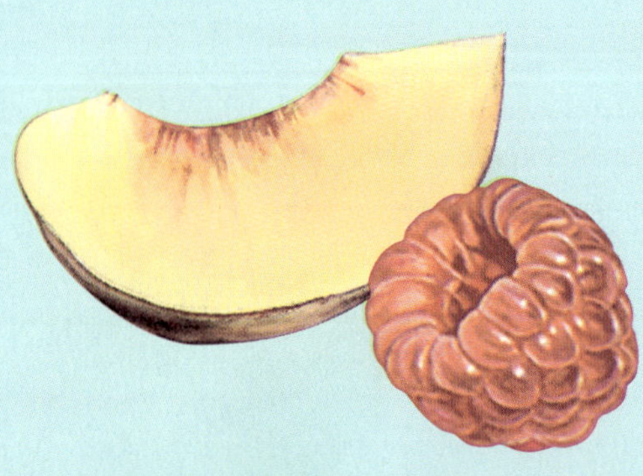

Coalition of Montanans Concerned with Disabilities

The Coalition is dedicated to ensuring the equal participation of all Montana residents in all aspects of the state's civic and cultural life. As part of its work to encourage people with disabilities to remain active and fully involved in state and local affairs, CMCD offers disabled Montanans the organizing skills, education and resources they need to engage in direct action and other efforts that create long-term positive change in their lives.

PO Box 5679
Missoula, MT 59806
(406) 243-6535

www.angelfire.com/mt/cmcd

This group was a Ben & Jerry's Foundation Grant Recipient.

ORANGE
THE TOWN WITH APPEAL

Orange Revitalization Partnership

A self-reliant, resident-operated community development organization, the Orange Revitalization Partnership sponsors the Youth Entrepreneur Society, an innovative program providing hope to local youth. Conceived and designed by the young people involved, YES established an Odd Job Co-op, and provided business skills training and wage subsidies for the Co-op's teenaged participants. A concurrent local currency project enables low-income residents and small businesses to hire Co-op workers and ensures that the money earned remains in the community.

20 South Main Street
Orange, MA 01364
(978) 544-2845

This group was a Ben & Jerry's Foundation Grant Recipient.

Notes to Consolidated Financial Statements

Dollars in tables in thousands except share data.

1. Significant Accounting Policies

Business

Ben & Jerry's Homemade, Inc. (the "Company") makes and sells super premium ice cream and other frozen dessert products through distributors and directly to retail outlets primarily located in the United States and selected foreign countries, including Company-owned and franchised ice cream parlors.

Principles of Consolidation

The consolidated financial statements include the accounts of the Company and all its wholly-owned subsidiaries. Inter-company accounts and transactions have been eliminated.

Fiscal Year

The Company's fiscal year is the 52 or 53 weeks ending on the last Saturday in December. Fiscal years 1998, 1997 and 1996 consisted of the 52 weeks ended December 26, 1998, December 27, 1997 and December 28, 1996, respectively.

Use of Estimates

The preparation of the financial statements in accordance with generally accepted accounting principles requires management to make estimates and assumptions that affect the amounts reported in the financial statements and accompanying notes. Actual results could differ from those estimates.

Inventories

Inventories are stated at the lower of cost or market. Cost is determined by the first-in, first-out method.

Cash Equivalents

Cash equivalents represent highly liquid investments with maturities of three months or less at date of purchase.

Investments

Management determines the appropriate classification of investments at the time of purchase and reevaluates such designation as of each balance sheet date. At December 26, 1998 the Company considers all its investments, except for certificates of deposit, as available-for-sale. Available-for-sale securities are carried at cost, which approximates fair value for the years ended December 26, 1998 and December 27, 1997. The amortized cost of debt securities in this category is adjusted for amortization of premiums and accretion of discounts to maturity. Such amortization is included in interest income. Held-to-maturity securities and available-for-sale securities are stated at amortized cost, adjusted for amortization of premium and accretion of discounts to maturity. Such amortization is included in interest income. Realized gains and losses and declines in value judged to be other-than-temporary on available-for-sale securities are included in income. The cost of securities sold is based on the specific identification method. Interest and dividends on securities classified as available-for-sale are included in interest income.

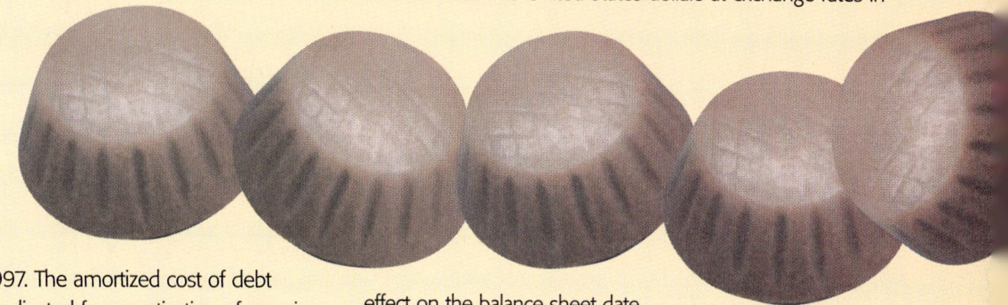

Concentration of Credit Risk

Financial instruments, which potentially subject the Company to significant concentration of credit risk, consist of cash and cash equivalents, investments and trade accounts receivable. The Company places its investments in highly rated financial institutions, obligations of the United States Government and investment grade short-term instruments. No more than 20% of the total investment portfolio is invested in any one issuer or guarantor other than United States Government instruments which limits the amount of credit exposure.

The Company sells its products primarily to well-established frozen dessert distribution or retailing companies throughout the United States and in certain countries outside the United States. The Company performs ongoing credit evaluations of its customers and maintains reserves for potential credit losses. Historically, the Company has not experienced significant losses related to investments or trade receivables.

Property, Plant and Equipment

Property, plant and equipment are carried at cost. Depreciation, including amortization of leasehold improvements, is computed using the straight-line method over the estimated useful lives of the related assets. Amortization of assets under capital leases is computed on the straight-line method over the lease term and is included in depreciation expense.

Other Assets

Other assets include intangible and other noncurrent assets. Intangible assets are reviewed for impairment based on an assessment of future operations to ensure that they are appropriately valued. Intangible assets are amortized on a straight-line basis over their estimated economic lives.

Translation of Foreign Currencies

Assets and liabilities of the Company's foreign operations are translated into United States dollars at exchange rates in effect on the balance sheet date. Income and expense items are translated at average exchange rates prevailing during the year. Translation adjustments are included in accumulated other comprehensive loss. Transaction gains or losses are recognized as other income or expense in the period incurred. Translation and transaction gains or losses have been immaterial for all periods presented.

Foreign Currency Hedging

The Company hedges foreign currency risk by entering into future options based on projected forecasts of a portion of the Company's International Business. In addition, from time to

time, the Company enters into forward contracts to hedge foreign currency denominated sales. Realized and unrealized gains or losses on contracts or options that hedge anticipated cash flows are determined by comparison of contract or option value upon execution (realized) and at each balance sheet for open contracts or options (unrealized). Realized gains and losses are recognized at the balance sheet date as other income or expense for the period. In the case of options entered into based on projected forecasts, unrealized gains and losses are recognized upon the determination that circumstances have changed which cause the hedged instrument to be speculative in nature.

Transaction gains or losses have been immaterial for all periods presented.

Revenue Recognition

The Company recognizes revenue and the related costs when product is shipped. The Company recognizes franchise fees as income for individual stores when services required by the franchise agreement have been substantially performed and the store opens for business. Franchise fees relating to area franchise agreements are recognized in proportion to the number of stores for which the required services have been substantially performed. Franchise fees recognized as income and included in net sales were approximately $708,000, $553,000 and $301,000 in 1998, 1997 and 1996, respectively.

Advertising

Advertising costs are expensed as incurred. Advertising expense (excluding cooperative advertising with distribution companies) amounted to approximately $10.6 million, $6.7 million and $3.4 million in 1998, 1997 and 1996, respectively.

Income Taxes

The Company accounts for income taxes under the liability method in accordance with Statement of Financial Accounting Standards No. 109, *Accounting for Income Taxes.* Under the liability method, deferred tax liabilities and assets are recognized for the tax consequences of temporary differences between the financial reporting and tax bases of assets and liabilities.

Stock-Based Compensation

The Company has adopted Statement of Financial Accounting Standards No. 123, *Accounting for Stock-Based Compensation* (FAS 123). As permitted by FAS 123, the Company continues to account for its stock-based plans under Accounting Principles Board Opinion No. 25, *Accounting for Stock Issued to Employees*, and provides pro forma disclosures of the compensation expense determined under the fair value provisions of FAS 123.

Earnings Per Share

In 1997, the Financial Accounting Standards Board issued Statement No. 128, *Earnings per Share* (FAS 128). FAS 128 replaced the calculation of primary and fully diluted earnings per share with basic and diluted earnings per share. Unlike primary earnings per share, basic earnings per share excludes any dilutive effects of options, warrants or convertible securities. Diluted earnings per share is very similar to the previously reported fully diluted earnings per share.

Comprehensive Income

As of December 28, 1997 the Company adopted Statement No. 130, *Reporting Comprehensive Income* (FAS 130). FAS 130 establishes new rules for the reporting and display of comprehensive income and its components; however, the adoption of this statement had no impact on the Company's net income or shareholders' equity. Statement 130 requires unrealized gains or losses on the Company's available-for-sale securities and foreign currency translation adjustments to be included in other comprehensive income.

Total comprehensive income amounted to $6.2 million for the year ended December 26,, 1998 and $3.9 million for each of the years ended December 27, 1997 and December 28,, 1996. Other comprehensive loss consisted of adjustments for net foreign currency translation losses in the amounts of $22,000, $11,000 and $4,000 for, 1998, 1997 and 1996, respectively.

Segment Information

As of December 28, 1997 the Company adopted the Financial Accounting Standards Board's Statement of Financial Accounting Standards No. 131, *Disclosures about Segments of an Enterprise and Related Information* (Statement 131). Statement 131 superseded FASB Statement No. 14, *Financial Reporting for Segments of a Business Enterprise*. Statement 131 establishes standards for the way that public business enterprises report information about operating segments in annual financial statements and requires that those enterprises report selected information about operating segments in interim financial reports. Statement 131 also establishes standards for related disclosures about products and services, geographic areas, and major customers. The adoption of Statement 131 did not affect results of operations or financial position, but did affect the disclosure of segment information. See Note 15.

Impact of Recently Issued Accounting Standards

In June 1998, the Financial Accounting Standards Board issued Statement No. 133, *Accounting for Derivative Instruments and Hedging Activities* (FAS 133). FAS 133 establishes standards for public companies regarding the recognition and measurement of derivatives and hedging activities. The statement is effective for the Company in fiscal year 2000. The Company does not believe the adoption of this statement will have a material impact on the Company's financial statements based on the nature and extent of the Company's use of derivative instruments at the present time.

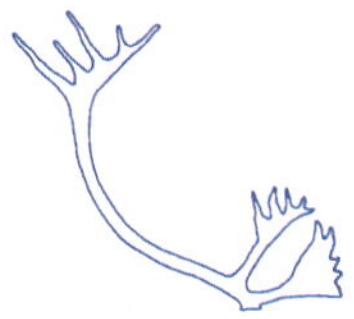

Gwich'in Steering Committee

Formed by members of Alaska's indigenous Gwich'in community, the Gwich'in Steering Committee is helping its people defend their native homeland and the Arctic National Wildlife Refuge it encompasses. A 19.6 million acre wilderness, the fragile Refuge contains some of the most spectacular wildlife and terrain in the world. It's preservation is vital to Gwich'in survival, and ongoing Committee efforts are helping to protect it from oil exploration and other permanently damaging development.

PO Box 202768
Anchorage, AK 99520
(907) 258-6814

This group was a Ben & Jerry's Foundation Grant Recipient.

2. Cash and Investments

The following is a summary of cash, cash equivalents and investments as of December 26, 1998 and December 27, 1997:

1998	Cash and Cash Equivalents	Short-Term Investments	Investments
Cash	$ 7,834		
Commercial paper	3,277		
Tax exempt floating rate notes	800		
Municipal bonds	13,200	$ 14,926	
Convertible bonds		955	
Preferred stock		5,649	
	25,111	21,530	
Certificates of deposit		588	$ 303
	$ 25,111	$ 22,118	$ 303

1997	Cash and Cash Equivalents	Short-Term Investments	Investments
Cash	$ 1,750		
Municipal bonds	45,568		
	47,318		
Certificates of deposit		$ 481	$ 1,061
	$ 47,318	$ 481	$ 1,061

The Company considers all of its investments, except for certificates of deposit, as available-for-sale. Certificates of deposit are held to maturity. Municipal bonds included in cash and cash equivalents mature at par in 30 to 45 days, at which time the interest rate is reset to the then market rate, and the Company may convert the investment to cash. Municipal bonds and convertible bonds recorded as short-term investments have varying maturities in 1999 and beyond; however, the Company does not intend to hold such investments to maturity. During 1998, the Company also invested in fixed income preferred stock of primarily financial institutions.

The costs of all short-term investments approximated the estimated fair value of such investments. Gross unrealized gains and losses were not significant for all short-term investments held at December 26, 1998 or December 27, 1997.

Gross purchases and maturities aggregated $221.6 million and $228.4 million in 1998, $43.1 million and $25.4 million in 1997, and $61.1 million and $63.9 million in 1996. Realized gains and losses were not material for all periods presented.

3. Inventories

	1998	1997
Ice cream and ingredients	$ 12,025	$ 10,294
Paper goods	524	536
Food, beverages & gift items	541	292
	$ 13,090	$ 11,122

The Company purchased certain ingredients from a company owned by the Company's Vice Chairperson and a member of the Board of Directors, which amounted to approximately $800,000 in 1997. No such purchases were made in 1998 or 1996.

Food Project

The Food Project is bridging the gap between people and their food supply. Working in Greater Boston, organizers bring together people from diverse backgrounds to grow and distribute food. With an emphasis on engaging young people, the Project teaches care for the land and community, and continually fosters new opportunities in a local food system. Their Common Ground Initiative connects children and teenagers, urban gardeners and local farmers in a field-to-table network that feeds those in need.

PO Box 705
Lincoln, MA 01773
(781) 259-8621

www.thefoodproject.org

This group was a Ben & Jerry's Foundation Grant Recipient.

4. Property, Plant and Equipment

	1998	1997	Estimated Useful Lives/ Lease Term
Land and improvements	$ 4,520	$ 4,520	15-25 yrs
Buildings	37,940	37,650	25 yrs
Equipment and furniture	52,047	44,609	3-20 yrs
Leasehold improvements	3,727	3,221	3-10 yrs
Construction in progress	2,058	2,676	
	100,292	92,676	
Less accumulated depreciation	36,841	29,952	
	$63,451	$62,724	

Depreciation expense for the years ended December 26, 1998, December 27, 1997 and December 28, 1996 was $7.9 million, $7.4 million and $6.7 million respectively.

5. Accounts Payable and Accrued Expenses

	1998	1997
Trade accounts payable	$ 4,623	$ 3,832
Accrued expenses	12,552	10,313
Accrued payroll and related costs	3,272	2,076
Accrued promotional costs	4,297	3,581
Accrued marketing costs	2,837	2,230
Accrued insurance expense	1,081	1,234
	$28,662	$23,266

6. Long-Term Debt and Capital Lease Obligations

	1998	1997
Senior Notes – Series A payable in annual installments beginning in 1998 through 2003 with interest payable semiannually at 5.9%	$16,680	$20,000
Senior Notes – Series B payable in annual installments beginning in 1998 through 2003 with interest payable semiannually at 5.73%	8,333	10,000
Other long-term obligations	744	1,078
	25,757	31,078
Less current portion	5,266	5,402
	$20,491	$25,676

Property, plant and equipment having a net book value of approximately $19.5 million at December 26, 1998 are pledged as collateral under certain long-term debt arrangements.

Long-term debt and capital lease obligations at December 26, 1998 maturing in each of the next five years and thereafter are as follows:

	Capital Lease Obligations	Long-Term Debt
1999	$ 78	$ 5,219
2000	78	5,076
2001	57	5,039
2002	15	5,033
2003	15	5,098
Thereafter	199	-
Total minimum payments	442	25,465
Less amounts representing interest	150	-
	$ 292	$ 25,465

The Company capitalized no interest in 1998, 1997 or 1996. Interest paid amounted to $1,832,000, $1,975,000 and $1,973,000 for 1998, 1997 and 1996, respectively.

The Company has available two $10,000,000 unsecured working capital line of credit agreements with two banks. Interest on borrowings under the agreements is set at the banks' base rate or at LIBOR plus a margin based on a pre-determined formula. No amounts were borrowed under these or any bank agreements during 1998. The working capital line of credit agreements expire December 23, 2001.

Certain of the debt agreements contain restrictive covenants requiring maintenance of minimum levels of working capital, net worth and debt to capitalization ratios. As of December 26, 1998, the Company was in compliance with the provisions of these agreements. Under the most restrictive of these covenants, distributions are limited to an amount of $5 million plus 75% of earnings and 100% of net losses since June 30, 1993; approximately $20.6 million of retained earnings at December 26, 1998 was available for payment of dividends.

As of December 26, 1998, the carrying amount and fair value of the Company's long-term debt were $25.8 million and $24.4 million, respectively, and as of December 27, 1997, they were $31.1 million and $29.7 million, respectively.

EQUALITY COLORADO

Equality Colorado

Equality Colorado is a grassroots organization fighting homophobia, hatred and sexual discrimination throughout the state of Colorado. In the face of anti-gay initiatives promoted by the state's radical right and other hate-motivated activities, EC has tirelessly worked to organize community resistance and conducted much needed public education on critical issues of lesbian, gay, bisexual and transgender equality and justice.

PO Box 300476
Denver, CO 80203
(303) 839-5540

members.tde.com/equality

This group was a Ben & Jerry's Foundation Grant Recipient.

7. Stockholders' Equity

The Class A Preferred Stock has one vote per share on all matters on which it is entitled to vote, and is entitled to vote as a separate class in certain business combinations, such that approval of two-thirds of the class is required for such business combinations. The Class A Preferred Stock is redeemable by the Company, by vote of the Continuing Directors (as defined in the Articles of Association). The Class A Common Stock has one vote per share on all matters on which it is entitled to vote. In June 1987 the Company's shareholders adopted an amendment to the Company's Articles of Association that authorized 3 million shares of a new Class B Common Stock and redesignated the Company's existing Common Stock as Class A Common Stock. The Class B Common Stock has ten votes per share on all matters on which it is entitled to vote, except as may be otherwise provided by law, is generally non-transferable as such and is convertible into Class A Common Stock on a one-for-one basis. A stockholder who does not wish to complete the prior conversion process may effect a sale by simply delivering the certificate for such shares of Class B Stock to a broker, properly endorsed. The broker may then present the certificate to the Company's Transfer Agent, which, if the transfer is otherwise in good order, will issue to the purchaser a certificate for the number of shares of Class A Common Stock thereby sold.

8. Shareholder Rights Plan

In early August, 1998 following approval by its Board of Directors, the Company put in place two Shareholder Rights Plans, one pertaining to the Class A Common Stock and one pertaining to the Class B Common Stock. These Plans are intended to protect stockholders by compelling someone seeking to acquire the Company to negotiate with the Company's Board of Directors in order to protect stockholders from unfair takeover tactics and to assist in the maximization of stockholder value. These Rights Plans, which are common for public companies in the United States, may also be deemed to be "anti-takeover" provisions in that the Board of Directors believes that these Plans will make it difficult for a third party to acquire control of the Company on terms which are unfair or unfavorable to the stockholders. Also, in April 1998 the Legislature of the State of Vermont amended a provision of the Vermont Business Corporation Act to provide that the directors of a Vermont corporation may also consider, in determining whether an acquisition offer or other matter is in the best interests of the corporation, the interests of the corporation's employees, suppliers, creditors and customers, the economy of the state in which the corporation is located, and including the possibility that the best interests of the corporation may be served by the continued independence of the corporation.

9. Stock Based Compensation Plans

The Company has two stock option plans:

The 1985 Option Plan provides for the grant of incentive and non-incentive stock options to employees or consultants. The 1985 Option Plan provides that options are granted with an exercise price equal to the market price of the Company's common stock on the date of grant. The 1985 Option Plan expired in August 1995, however, some options granted under this plan are outstanding as of December 26, 1998. While the Company grants options which may become exercisable at different times or within different periods, the Company has generally granted options to employees which vest over a period of four, five or eight years, and in some cases with provisions for acceleration of vesting upon the occurrence of certain events. The exercise period cannot exceed ten years from the date of grant.

Support Committee for Maquiladora Workers

Working on both sides of the U.S./Mexican border, SCMW seeks to advance the rights of workers in Mexico's U.S.-owned assembly plants. Guided directly by needs and requests voiced by the workers themselves, the Committee is achieving much-needed improvements in living and working conditions through a highly effective mix of corporate pressure, public awareness, and worker organizing that allows those most affected by rights abuses to claim a better future for themselves.

3909 Centre Street #210
San Diego, CA 92103
(619) 283-7705
fax (619) 283-7713

This group was a Ben & Jerry's Foundation Grant Recipient.

A summary of the 1985 Option Plan activity is as follows:

	Number of Options	Weighted Average Exercise Price Per Share	Option Price Per Share
Outstanding at December 30, 1995	357,437	$13.40	$10.63 - $16.75
Granted	-	-	- - -
Exercised	-	-	- - -
Forfeited	(109,819)	11.34	10.81 - 16.75
Outstanding at December 28, 1996	247,618	14.31	10.63 - 16.75
Granted	-	-	- - -
Exercised	(80,000)	10.81	10.81 - 10.81
Forfeited	(10,807)	16.75	16.75 - 16.75
Outstanding at December 27, 1997	156,811	15.92	10.63 - 16.75
Granted	-	-	- - -
Exercised	(34,859)	16.75	16.75 - 16.75
Forfeited	(6,381)	16.75	16.75 - 16.75
Outstanding at December 26, 1998	115,571	$15.63	10.63 - 16.75
Options vested at December 26, 1998	100,571	$15.87	10.63 - 16.75

The 1995 Equity Incentive Plan provides for the grant to employees and other key persons or entities, including non-employee directors who are in the position, in the opinion of the Compensation Committee, to make a significant contribution to the success of the Company, of incentive and non-incentive stock options, stock appreciation rights, restricted stock, unrestricted stock awards, deferred stock awards, cash or stock performance awards, loans or supplemental grants, or combinations thereof. While the Company grants options which may become exercisable at different times or within different periods, the Company has generally granted options to employees which vest over a period of four, five or six years, and in some cases subject to acceleration of vesting upon specified events. All options vest upon a change in control as defined. The exercise period cannot exceed ten years from the date of grant. At December 26, 1998, 103,500 shares of Class A Common Stock were available under the 1995 Equity Incentive Plan.

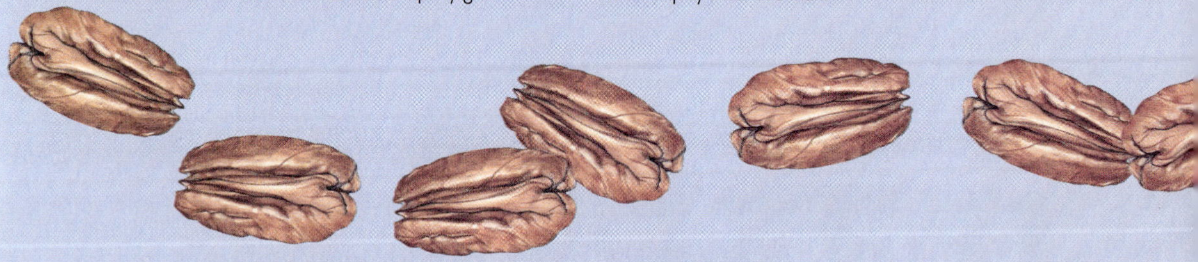

A summary of the 1995 Equity Incentive Plan activity is as follows:

	Number of Options	Weighted Average Exercise Price Per Share	Option Price Per Share
Outstanding at December 30, 1995	25,000	$19.00	$19.00 - $19.00
Granted	62,500	13.97	12.38 - 16.00
Exercised	-	-	- - -
Forfeited	-	- -	
Outstanding at December 28, 1996	87,500	15.41	12.38 - 19.00
Granted	694,000	12.04	10.88 - 13.89
Exercised	-	-	- - -
Forfeited	(27,500)	16.00	16.00 - 16.00
Outstanding at December 27, 1997	754,000	12.28	10.88 - 19.00
Granted	42,500	18.19	14.75 - 19.25
Exercised	(1,770)	12.63	12.63 - 12.63
Forfeited	-	-	- - -
Outstanding at December 26, 1998	794,730	$ 12.60	10.88 - 19.25
Options vested at December 26, 1998	281,450	$ 12.37	10.88 - 19.25

Youth In Action, Inc.

YIA is a new organization founded and led entirely by young people. Its mission is to support local youth to become community leaders. Experienced youth leaders train their peers to identify community problems (like poverty, teenage pregnancy, substance abuse and violence) and to create projects to help combat them. Youth are trained in community-organizing and work on projects lik ArtPark, designed to bring local youth and adults together to create a safe and fun gathering place.

115 Empire Street
Providence, RI 02903
(401) 751-3086

This group was a Ben & Jerry's Foundation Grant Recipient.

The Company maintains an Employee Stock Purchase Plan, which authorizes the issuance of up to 300,000 shares of common stock. All employees with six months of continuous service are eligible to participate in this plan. Participants in the plan are entitled to purchase Class A Common Stock during specified semi-annual periods through the accumulation of payroll, at the lower of 85% of market value of the stock at the beginning or end of the offering period. At December 26, 1998 142,021 shares had been issued under the plan and 157,979 were available for future issuance.

The Company has a Restricted Stock Plan (the 1992 Plan) which provides that non-employee directors, on becoming eligible, may be awarded shares of Class A Common Stock by the compensation Committee of the Board of Directors. Shares issued under the plan become vested over periods of up to five years. The Company has also adopted the 1995 Plan, which provides that non-employee directors can elect to receive stock in lieu of a Director's annual cash retainer. In 1998, 4,896 shares were issued to non-employee directors. These shares vest immediately. At December 26, 1998 a total of 12,259 shares had been awarded under these plans, all of which were fully vested, and 22,741 shares were available for future awards. Unearned compensation on unvested shares is recorded as of the award date and is amortized over the vesting period.

Exercise prices for options outstanding at December 26, 1998 under all of the Company's stock plans ranged from $10.63 - $19.25. The weighted average remaining contractual life of those options is 8.0 years.

As of December 26, 1998 a total of 284,220 shares are reserved for future grant or issue under all of the Company's stock plans.

The Company's stock option plans provide for the grant of options to purchase shares of the Company's common stock to both employees and consultants. The Company has elected to follow Accounting Principles Board Opinion No. 25, Accounting for Stock Issued to Employees (APB 25) and related interpretations. In accounting for its employee stock options under APB 25, when the exercise price of the Company's employee stock options equals the market price of the underlying stock on the date of grant, no compensation expense is recognized. The Company has followed FAS 123 for stock options granted to non-employees as required.

Pro forma information regarding net income and earnings per share is required by FAS 123, which also requires that the information be determined as if the Company has accounted for its employee stock options granted subsequent to December 31, 1994 under the fair value method of that Statement. The fair value for these options was estimated at the date of grant using a Black-Scholes option-pricing model with the following weighted-average assumptions:

	1998	1997	1996
Risk-free interest rates	5.10%	5.53%	6.15%
Dividend yield	0.00%	0.00%	0.00%
Volatility factor	0.32	0.34	0.39
Weighted average expected lives (in years)	2.4	3.6	3.3

For purposes of pro forma disclosures, the estimated fair value of the options is amortized to expense over the options' vesting period. The impact on pro forma net income may not be representative of compensation expense in future years when the effect of the amortization of multiple awards would be reflected in the pro forma disclosures. The Company's pro forma information follows:

	1998	1997	1996
Pro forma net income	$5,935	$3,600	$3,796
Pro forma earnings per share – diluted	$ 0.80	$ 0.49	$ 0.53
Weighted average fair value of options at the date of grant	$ 4.22	$ 4.16	$ 4.26

10. Income Taxes

The provision for income taxes consists of the following:

Federal	1998	1997	1996
Current	$5,041	$3,300	$1,348
Deferred	(2,093)	(1,388)	681
	2,948	1,912	2,029
State			
Current	1,003	686	252
Deferred	(417)	(210)	128
	586	476	380
	$3,534	$2,388	$2,409

Income taxes computed at the federal statutory rate differ from amounts provided as follows:

	1998	1997	1996
Tax at statutory rate	34.0%	34.0%	34.0%
State tax, less federal tax effect	4.0	5.0	6.0
Income tax credits	(1.0)	(1.0)	(1.0)
Tax exempt interest	(3.0)	(2.9)	(2.4)
Other, net	2.1	2.9	1.4
Provision for income taxes	36.1%	38.0%	38.0%

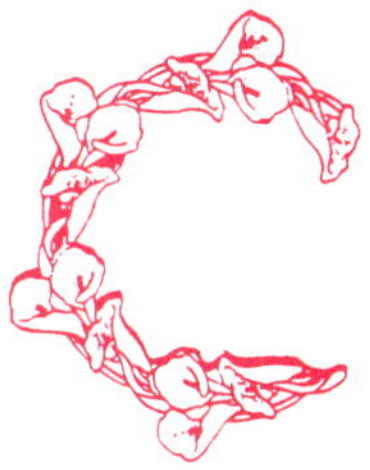

Newtown Florist Club, Inc.

Established in 1950 by African-American women seeking to provide support and assistance to neighborhood families in times of bereavement, the Newtown Florist Club was in a unique position to observe odd clusters of fatal disease in its minority community, a place built upon an old dump and surrounded by polluting industrial plants. The unusually high local incidence of cancer and lupus first noted by club members led to their current focus on community organizing for environmental justice.

PO Box 908403
1067 Desota Street
Gainesville, GA 30501
(770) 718-1343

members.aol.com
/newtown193/politics
/index.htm

This group was a Ben & Jerry's Foundation Grant Recipient.

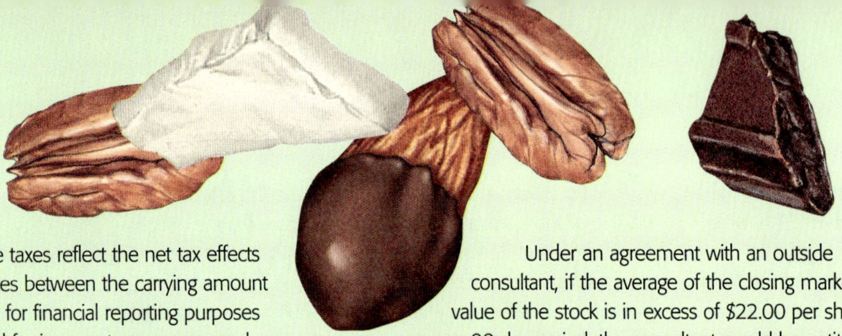

Deferred income taxes reflect the net tax effects of temporary differences between the carrying amount of assets and liabilities for financial reporting purposes and the amounts used for income tax purposes and are attributable to the following:

	1998	1997
Deferred tax assets:		
Accrued liabilities	$6,425	$ 3,872
Inventories	1,413	1,503
Accounts receivable	430	475
Other	475	221
Total deferred tax assets	8,743	6,071
Deferred tax liabilities:		
Depreciation	5,231	5,193
Other	139	15
Total deferred tax liabilities	5,370	5,208
Net deferred tax assets	$3,373	$ 863

Income taxes paid amounted to $6.2 million, $2.2 million and $1.7 million during 1998, 1997 and 1996, respectively.

11. Earnings Per Share

The following table sets forth the computation of basic and diluted earnings per share:

	1998	1997	1996
Numerator:			
Net income	$6,242	$3,896	$3,926
Denominator:			
Denominator for basic earnings per share – weighted-average shares	7,197	7,247	7,189
Dilutive employee stock options	266	87	41
Denominator for diluted earnings per share – adjusted weighted-average shares and assumed conversions	7,463	7,334	7,230
Net income per common share			
Basic	$ 0.87	$ 0.54	$ 0.55
Diluted	$ 0.84	$ 0.53	$ 0.54

Options to purchase 32,500 shares of common stock at $19.25 were outstanding during 1998 but were not included in the computation of diluted earnings per share because the options' exercise price was greater than the average market price of the common shares and, therefore, the effect would be antidilutive. Options to purchase 146,811 shares of common stock at prices ranging from $16.75 - $19.00 and 194,033 shares of common stock at prices ranging from $12.38 - $16.75 were outstanding in 1997 and 1996, respectively, but were not included in the computation of diluted earnings per share because the options' exercise price was greater than the average market price of the common shares and, therefore, the effect would be antidilutive.

Under an agreement with an outside consultant, if the average of the closing market value of the stock is in excess of $22.00 per share over a 90-day period, the consultant would be entitled to purchase 125,000 shares of common stock at $14.00 per share. These 125,000 additional warrants, which expire on July 1, 2004, are not included in the computation of diluted earnings per share because the stock did not exceed $22.00 for the specified period during 1998.

12. The Ben & Jerry's Foundation, Inc.

In October 1985, the Company issued 900 shares of Class A Preferred Stock to the Ben & Jerry's Foundation, Inc. (the Foundation), a not-for-profit corporation qualified under Section 501(c)(3) of the Internal Revenue Code. The primary purpose of the Foundation is to be the principal recipient of cash contributions from the Company which are then donated to various community organizations and other charitable institutions. Contributions to the Foundation and directly to other charitable organizations, at the rate of approximately 7.5% of income before income taxes, amounted to approximately $793,000, $510,000 and $514,000 for 1998, 1997 and 1996, respectively.

The Class A Preferred Stock is entitled to vote as a separate class in certain business combinations, such that approval of two-thirds of the class is required for such business combination. The three directors of the Foundation, including one of the founders of the Company, are members of the Board of Directors of the Company.

13. Employee Benefit Plans

The Company maintains profit sharing and savings plans for all eligible employees. The Company has also implemented a management incentive program, which provides for discretionary bonuses for management. Contributions to the profit sharing plan are allocated among all current full-time and regular part-time employees (other than the co-founders, Chief Executive Officer and Officers that are Senior Directors of functions) and are allocated 50 percent based upon length of service and 50 percent split evenly among all employees. The profit sharing plan and the management incentive plan are informal and discretionary. Recipients who participate in the management incentive program are not eligible to participate in the profit sharing plan. The savings plan is maintained in accordance with the provisions of Section 401(k) of the Internal Revenue Code and allows all employees with at least 12 months of service to make annual tax-deferred voluntary contributions up to 15 percent of their salary. The Company contributes one percent of eligible employees' gross annual salary and may match the contribution up to an additional three percent of the employee's gross annual salary. Effective January 1, 1998 the Company amended its employees' retirement plan to permit contributions of shares of its stock to the plan from time to time. For 1998 the Board of Directors approved the contribution of $250,000 worth of Class A Common Stock to be allocated among all eligible employees' accounts. Total contributions by the Company to the profit sharing, management incentive program and savings plans were approximately $2.7 million, $1.2 million and $670,000 for 1998, 1997 and 1996, respectively.

Gateway Green Alliance

The Gateway Green Alliance organized and hosted the First Grassroots Gathering on Biodevastation: Genetic Engineering. This groundbreaking event brought together over 25 leading critics of biotechnology and hundreds of environmentally concerned citizens, family farmers and food activists for three days of valuable discussions, networking and planning. One of the many important conference outcomes was the Fall 1998 Global Days of Action Against Genetic Engineering, an event that helped bring biotechnology issues into mainstream debate.

PO Box 8094
St. Louis, MO 63156
(314) 727-8554

This group was a Ben & Jerry's Foundation Grant Recipient.

Death Valley Land Restoration Project

The DVLRP was created by the Timbisha Shoshone to restore ancestral homelands encompassed by this vast desert to their people. The Project is holding the National Park Service accountable for provisions of the 1994 California Desert Protection Act that mandates stewardship of the region be returned to their nation. It also protects the area's irreplaceable cultural and natural resources by drawing attention to damaging cyanide heap-leaching mines and working to provide meaningful environmental oversight of those operations.

PO Box 206
Death Valley, CA
92328-0206
(760) 786-2374

This group was a Ben & Jerry's Foundation Grant Recipient.

14. Commitments

The Company leases certain property and equipment under operating leases. Minimum payments for operating leases having initial or remaining noncancellable terms in excess of one year are as follows:

1999	$ 1,093	**2002**	$ 598
2000	889	**2003**	553
2001	767	**Thereafter**	1,442

Rent expense for operating leases amounted to approximately $1.5 million, $1.2 million and $1.1 million in 1998, 1997 and 1996, respectively.

15. Segment Information

Ben & Jerry's Homemade, Inc. has one reportable segment: ice cream manufacturing and distribution. The Company manufactures super premium ice cream, frozen yogurt, sorbet and various ice cream novelty products. These products are distributed throughout the United States primarily through independent distributors and in certain countries outside the United States.

During 1998, 1997 and 1996 the Company's most significant customer, Dreyer's Grand Ice Cream, Inc., accounted for 57%, 57% and 55% of net sales, respectively. Sales and cash receipts are recorded and received primarily in U.S. dollars. Foreign exchange variations have little or no effect on the Company at this time.

Information concerning operations by geographic area are as follows:

	Fiscal Year Ended		
	1998	**1997**	**1996**
Sales to Unaffiliated Customers			
United States	$ 191,777	$ 6,592	$ 160,263
Foreign	17,426	7,614	6,892
	$ 209,203	$ 174,206	$ 167,155
Profit or Loss			
United States	$ 6,444	$ 4,136	$ 3,662
Foreign	(202)	(240)	264
	$ 6,242	$ 3,896	$ 3,926
Assets			
United States	$ 143,308	$ 12,051	$ 132,481
Foreign	6,193	4,420	4,184
	$ 149,501	$ 146,471	$ 136,665

All intersegment sales are made from the United States to the Company's foreign locations and amounted to $14.6 million, $13.2 million and $12.3 million for 1998, 1997 and 1996, respectively.

Note: Foreign operations include the United Kingdom, France, Canada, The Netherlands, Belgium and Japan.

16. Selected Quarterly Financial Information (Unaudited)

	1998			
	1st Quarter[1]	**2nd Quarter[1]**	**3rd Quarter[1]**	**4th Quarter[1]**
Net sales	$ 41,556	$ 58,749	$ 64,566	$ 44,332
Gross profit	13,964	21,153	24,227	13,634
Net income	380	2,130	2,892	840
Net income per common share				
Basic	.05	.29	40	.12
Diluted	.05	.28	.39	.11

	1997			
	1st Quarter[1]	**2nd Quarter[1]**	**3rd Quarter[1]**	**4th Quarter[1]**
Net sales	$ 36,148	$ 50,701	$ 49,956	$ 37,401
Gross profit	10,003	19,150	19,118	11,651
Net (loss) income	(1,059)	1,741	2,528	686
Net (loss) income per common share				
Basic	(.15)	.24	.35	.09
Diluted	(.15)	.24	.34	.09

[1] *Each quarter represents a 13-week period for all periods presented.*

17. Subsequent Event

Effective February 26, 1999 the Company made an investment commitment of $1 million in its Israeli Licensee, which gave the Company a 60% ownership interest. The Company will consolidate this majority-owned subsidiary beginning March 1999.

Report of Ernst & Young LLP, Independent Auditors

The Board of Directors and Stockholders Ben & Jerry's Homemade, Inc.

We have audited the accompanying consolidated balance sheets of Ben & Jerry's Homemade, Inc. as of December 26, 1998 and December 27, 1997, and the related consolidated statements of operations, stockholders' equity, and cash flows for each of the three years in the period ended December 26, 1998. These financial statements are the responsibility of the Company's management. Our responsibility is to express an opinion on these financial statements based on our audits.

We conducted our audits in accordance with generally accepted auditing standards. Those standards require that we plan and perform the audit to obtain reasonable assurance about whether the financial statements are free of material misstatement. An audit includes examining, on a test basis, evidence supporting the amounts and disclosures in the financial statements. An audit also includes assessing the accounting principles used and significant estimates made by management, as well as evaluating the overall financial statement presentation. We believe that our audits provide a reasonable basis for our opinion.

In our opinion, the consolidated financial statements referred to above present fairly, in all material respects, the consolidated financial position of Ben & Jerry's Homemade, Inc. at December 26, 1998 and December 27, 1997 and the consolidated results of its operations and its cash flows for each of the three years in the period ended December 26, 1998, in conformity with generally accepted accounting principles.

Ernst & Young LLP

Boston, Massachusetts
January 22, 1999, except for Note 17,
as to which the date is February 26, 1999

Northwest Connections

Northwest Connections

Northwest Connections is dedicated to conserving and restoring critical wildlife corridors that link together larger habitats in northwest Montana. Using a variety of community-based strategies, group members are overcoming the social fragmentation that has undermined previous conservation efforts in the region. Their Ecological Monitoring Project is just one part of this successful work. It provides volunteer opportunities and employment to local residents after training them to monitor the health of the region's wildlife and migration corridors.

PO Box 1340
Swan Valley, MT 59826
(406) 754-3185

This group was a Ben & Jerry's Foundation Grant Recipient.

Corporate Profile

Ben & Jerry's Homemade, Inc., a Vermont corporation, manufactures and markets Ben & Jerry's super premium ice cream, low fat ice cream, nonfat frozen yogurt, ice cream novelties and sorbets. The Company's products are distributed nationwide and in selected international markets in supermarkets, grocery stores, convenience stores, scoop shops, restaurants and other venues.

Company Headquarters

30 Community Drive
South Burlington, Vermont
05403-6828
Phone: (802) 846-1500
Fax: (802) 846-1555

Our Form 10-K Annual Report, filed with the Securities & Exchange Commission, is available to shareholders at no charge upon written request to: Ben & Jerry's Homemade, Inc., *Attn:* Shareholder Relations, 30 Community Drive, So. Burlington, VT 05403-6828. Or, please visit our website at www.benjerry.com.

Board of Directors

Elizabeth Bankowski
Director & Senior Director of Social Mission Development

Ben Cohen
Director & Vice Chairperson

Pierre Ferrari
Director

Jeffrey Furman
Director

Jerry Greenfield
Director & Chairperson

Jennifer Henderson
Director

Frederick A. Miller
Director

Henry Morgan
Director

Perry Odak
Director, Chief Executive Officer & President

Senior Directors & Officers

Lawrence E. Benders
Chief Marketing Officer

Bruce Bowman
Senior Director of Operations

Richard Doran
Senior Director of Human Resources

Charles Green
Senior Director of Sales & Distribution

Angelo Pezzani
Senior Director of Business Development

Frances Rathke
Chief Financial Officer & Secretary

Corporate Counsel

Ropes & Gray
One International Place
Boston, MA 02110

Auditors

Ernst & Young LLP
200 Clarendon Street
Boston, MA
02116-5072

Transfer Agent

American Stock
Transfer & Trust Co.
40 Wall Street
New York, NY 10005
Phone: (800) 937-5449

Credits

Writing:
Liz Bankowski
Geoff Davis
Rebecca Golden
James Heard
Chrystie Heimert
Alan Parker
Lisa Pendolino
Lynn Ronci
Leslie Wells

Financials:
Alison Godard
Mickey Wiles

Design:
Sue Hudson

Page Layout:
Gail Cummings
Lori Myers

Illustration:
Robert Evans
Edgar Stewart

Creative Direction:
Sarah Forbes

Production Coordination:
Ben Nooney

Printing:
TDS Printers
Nashua, NH

Paper:
Fox River
Confetti Cover,
100% Recycled,
50% Post-Consumer
Mohawk Options -
Totally Chlorine Free
Text & Postcards

Our Annual Meeting &...

The Ben & Jerry's Annual Shareholders' Meeting will be held on:

Saturday, June 26, 1999 10:00 am

At Lincoln Peak, Sugarbush Resort in Warren, Vermont, followed by the annual Ben & Jerry's One World One Heart Festival at Mt. Ellen, Sugarbush Resort in Fayston, Vermont.

...One World One Heart® Festival

11:00 am – 7:00 pm

For more information about Festival events and performers call ***1-800-BJ-FESTS.***

For lodging information in the Sugarbush area for the Annual Meeting and Festival weekend, please call ***1-800-53-SUGAR.***

Moving beyond the box • 1998 Gateway Annual Report

Gateway broke virtually every performance record in 1998

Ted Waitt, Chairman and CEO

while laying the groundwork for explosive growth in 1999.

"Only by exceeding our clients' expectations can we exceed our own dreams."

— Ted Waitt, Chairman and CEO

Dear Fellow Stockholders:

Gateway had a record year in 1998. We set company records for sales, market share, number of units shipped, margins and earnings and finished the fourth quarter with a record cash position. Our sales improved 19% to $7.47 billion. We were number one in U.S. home desktop PCs for the fourth quarter,[1] and our total brand awareness increased from 87% to 95% during 1998. During the year Gateway shipped 3.541 million systems. Net income for the year was $346.4 million or $2.18 earnings per diluted share. That's better than 200% more than the earnings per share we posted in 1997.

While putting up all those great numbers, Gateway also set the stage for an explosive 1999 by building a world-class leadership team and improving our tools and infrastructure.

Also in 1998, we started work on the four sides of our future in 1999 and beyond:

- Understanding our clients
- Understanding technology
- Building the world's most efficient engine
- Fortifying our rock solid financial base

You'll hear more about our 1998 results and 1999 plans in the pages to come. The enthusiasm and focus throughout Gateway remind me of our early days back in the late '80s. I'm more excited about Gateway's potential than ever.

I hope you, too, catch the excitement and join our quest to be number one.

Sincerely,

Ted Waitt
Gateway Chairman and CEO
March 4, 1999

1. According to GartnerGroup/Dataquest US PC Quarterly Statistics.

Whether you think the CD-ROM tray is a cup holder or know how to edit your

Jeff Weitzen, President and COO

registry without fear, Gateway speaks your language and can deliver the right technology.

"Knowing our clients and serving their needs is absolutely everything at Gateway."

— Jeff Weitzen, President and COO

It all begins, continues and ends with clients. In 1998, we stopped saying "customer" and started saying "clients." Semantics? Maybe, but to us "customer" sounded too transitory. A "customer" completes a transaction with a business and then leaves. We don't want anyone to leave. A "client," on the other hand, establishes a long-lasting relationship with a business that includes the familiarity of a common history and the interdependence of a joined future.

So long as Gateway tends to that relationship, we'll continue our success. Our clients responded to this approach by making Gateway number one in brand loyalty.[2] Gateway nurtures client relationships by living a set of values as powerful as they are simple — caring, aggressiveness, common sense, teamwork, respect, efficiency, honesty and fun. But that's just the start.

We also mix in lots of honest, two-way communications. Gateway has always talked directly to clients. Every day we talk to 50,000 people on the phone or at our Gateway Country® stores. Some 200,000 more land on our Web site every day. In 1999, we'll accelerate plans to expand communications with our clients.

We want our clients to get what they want, when they want it, at a fair price and with peace of mind that Gateway will stand behind our products and services. Our company makes profits that help us grow and deliver returns on our shareholders' investments today. More importantly, we earn clients' respect, loyalty and referrals. That all helps us grow even faster tomorrow. That's Gateway's version of the win-win situation.

2. According to the 1997 Technology User Profile from ZD Market Intelligence announced in the spring of 1998, 75% of Gateway clients who bought a new computer in 1997 repurchased a Gateway™ system.

Our Your:)Ware program helps technology evolve along with your computer skills.

The Renaissance of Client Focus

Gateway's success rests on serving clients better than anyone. But in order to serve clients, we need to know what they want.

They want great products and great services. That's the easy part. But just knowing that and selling hardware alone won't cut it in this industry. You have to focus on client needs to survive. For them to have a great computing experience, we had to offer more. More what? We asked our clients.

Your Trusted Guide

They told us they're looking for a trusted guide. Especially in a time when they're accosted daily by all manner of technology claiming to help them work less, play more and generally enhance the quality of their existence. Gateway thinks the key to navigating this digital journey is asking people what they want and then finding a way to deliver. People want help getting through the edgy, tangled technology maze. They want products and services that bring the power of computers to bear on life's challenges. They want help connecting to and getting more out of the World Wide Web.

Gateway Country stores bring technology to you.

Humanize the Digital Revolution

Here's some Gateway bedrock: technology must mold itself to human need, never the other way around. That's why we first determine what clients want and then go find technology to meet that desire.

The Your:)Ware℠ Program

A lot of clients told us they want their technology to evolve as their skills evolve. So, in May 1998, Gateway introduced the Your:)Ware program that connects people with the right customized hardware and software, offers them Internet access and then lets them trade that computer toward the purchase of a new system in as few as two years. The Your:)Ware program makes it easier for your computer to keep pace with your skills.

Welcome to Gateway Country Stores

Part of knowing your clients is knowing the ways they want to do business. It's not always on the phone. Some people want to buy face to face. So, rather than change people, we changed Gateway. We started building Gateway Country® stores in 1996. We kept it up in 1998, building 107 new Gateway Country locations around the U.S., bringing our total at the end of 1998 to 144.

At each Gateway Country store, clients can try our products and get answers from highly trained sales reps. Our reps answer all the questions and then ask for the client's business. Orders from each store are built fresh and shipped to the clients' doors.

Many Gateway Country locations also offer service centers and training on popular software, as well as Gateway Business Solution℠ Centers to help small firms grow and prosper.

Our Gateway Country locations also give us a local presence, increasing brand awareness and complementing our Web and phone sales. In fact, our research has shown that about 50% of people who visit our stores have also contacted Gateway online or on the phone.

gateway.com has been part of Gateway since 1995.

Click Over to www.gateway.com

Nothing matches the Web for convenience, selection and comparison. And as more and more people go online, companies offer more information on the Web and ease-of-use steadily improves. Gateway's goal is to be number one on the Web, not because we're the biggest, but because we're the best.

About 200,000 visitors land on www.gateway.com and order millions of dollars worth of products every day. In 1998, we focused on developing our Web site as a place where clients can purchase our products and get help with their systems.

That emphasis will accelerate dramatically in 1999, and we'll take better advantage of the unique ways our site lets us interact with clients. Why? Because that's what our clients want. And that's more than enough reason for Gateway.

By combining the greatest people with the best tools,

David Robino, Executive VP and CAO

Gateway will build an organization that builds lifelong relationships.

"Every company, even those with the greatest technology, absolutely depends on quality people."

– David Robino, Executive Vice President and CAO

Delivering quality goods and services to clients, better, faster and for less. It's the goal of free enterprise. Striving for the goal weeds out weak businesses and helps the strong survive. Because if you don't serve your clients better, faster and for less, your competition will gladly do it for you.

It starts with quality people who care about the company's goals. We help our employees build the right skills and then give them the best tools. The best people with the best tools can serve our clients better and better. That's the key to Gateway's survival as the fittest. In 1998 we invested heavily in "infrastructure," a four-syllable word that includes employees, systems and everything from huge manufacturing buildings to ethereal digital networks.

Our employees drive Gateway. Our Information Technologies systems supply the right tools. In 1998 we started our quest to add talent to the team and efficiency to the machine. It's going to hit a higher gear in 1999. We know that powering Gateway requires a high-octane mixture of great talent and efficient technology. Look for our machine to crank it up a notch in 1999.

It Starts with People

In many ways, Gateway retooled in 1998. We added people, facilities and technology, and we did it in a big way.

A big part of that effort came in April when Gateway announced an expansion to San Diego and Irvine, California. We moved administrative headquarters to San Diego and based Gateway Business in Irvine. The moves took some people inside and outside Gateway by surprise. After all, we had always been the Midwestern company that zigged when the industry zagged. While everyone else flocked to the Silicon Valley in 1985, our founders chose to plant roots in a Midwestern cornfield.

Even in a high-tech company, you're only as good as your people.

Staying in the Midwest was the right move in 1985. Thirteen years later, branching West toward the largest technology and marketing talent pool in the U.S. was the right move. We had already built a great team in the Midwest and expanded operations centers on the East Coast and across the ocean. When it came time to look for people to add to our leadership team, all signs pointed west.

And it's working. Early in 1998, Gateway hired Jeff Weitzen as president and chief operating officer and David Robino as executive vice president and chief administrative officer. Along with Jeff and CEO Ted Waitt, David led an exhaustive search for the right senior executives to take Gateway to the next level. In 1998, that search yielded 10 of Gateway's top 15 senior-level leaders. They've all had immediate, positive impacts on Gateway.

Our trip to the next level led Gateway administrative headquarters to San Diego .

Values and Passion

No matter whether they work in North Sioux City, South Dakota; Hampton, Virginia; Colorado Springs, Colorado; or Dublin, Ireland, Gateway employees share a common set of values: caring, honesty, teamwork, respect, aggressiveness, efficiency, fun and common sense. The values form the foundation of all Gateway does. We look to hire employees at all levels who embrace and practice these values, who are passionate about the potential of Gateway and who know achieving that potential depends on living by the values and serving clients.

The best people plus the best tools equals the best company.

Building The Rock

Giving great employees great tools unlocks their talents. So, in 1998, Gateway launched a new initiative aimed at assessing our technology systems from top to bottom. Led by new senior vice president and CIO Maynard Webb, we started improving what worked, scrapping what didn't and revamping everything from a client perspective. Maynard named the top few IT projects "The Rock" as a symbol that those priorities would become the foundation for our efficient machine.

Adding to our Address

Gateway also added sites in 1998 aimed at improving efficiency and serving clients better. Our 271,600-square-foot manufacturing center in Salt Lake City, Utah, started production in 1998, ramping quickly to meet our intense fourth quarter demand. Besides administrative headquarters in San Diego, we also added Information Technology headquarters in Lakewood, Colorado, and phone centers in Colorado Springs and Rio Rancho, New Mexico.

Investment, not Expense

All these additions cost money. But, we look at them as investments in our future. Climbing to the next level means spending wisely on talent and tools. We did a lot of that in 1998, and we'll do some more in 1999. But, most importantly, we're starting to see results.

If it's new and cool, we should always sell it, right? Wrong.

Peter Ashkin, Sr. VP Gateway Products

Does it meet client need now or in the future? That's the main question.

"Molding technology to fit human need requires intimate knowledge of both."

– Peter Ashkin, Senior Vice President, Gateway Products

When Gateway was founded in 1985, the 286 processor was the hot chip, CDs were only for stereos, "DVD" sounded like a brand of underwear and color monitors seemed lavish. Today's computers steadily shrink in size while increasing in power. Moore's Law, which says processing power will double every 18 months while cost will stay the same, has held up since the 1960s. Tomorrow's computers will become more and more woven into everyday life in ways that make the familiar monitor and keyboard seem quaint.

Gateway's job is to sort through the crush of products and come up with the best answers for client needs. To do that, we maintain an expertise in technology that hacks through the hype on behalf of the clients we guide. Our rule is simple: if it doesn't hold current or future benefits for our clients, it's not for us.

In 1998 Gateway improved the broadest product line in company history, introducing new hardware, software and services that our clients told us they wanted. There's more of everything on the way in 1999. In our industry, the days of "build it and they will come," — if they ever were truly here — are long gone. Instead, the challenge is "build what they want, and they will come."

The Solo 3100, code name "FireAnt," hatched in October 1998.

1998 Products

In 1998, Gateway again introduced new products aimed at satisfying specific client needs. Shipments of our Solo® portables line grew by 62%. Client input helped us develop the broadest line of portable PCs in Gateway history, each model aimed at satisfying the needs of a client group. That effort led to the Solo 3100, code named "FireAnt." The ant was hatched only after we asked clients what they wanted in a very thin portable.

In desktops, Gateway diversified offerings to put the power of Intel® Pentium® II processor-based systems within reach of more clients. We also recognized the great value of the Intel Celeron™ processor in the second half of 1998. The Celeron chip helped us offer a budget line of PCs without sacrificing a lot of power and versatility.

Helping Businesses do More

For our business, government and education clients, the Gateway™ E-Series desktops continued to evolve. We designed the E-Series with all the functions our clients want plus new levels of flexibility. For qualifying purchases, our Custom Integration Services can build in virtually anything our business clients need right at our factory. That includes client-specific hardware and software, hard drive image loading, asset tagging and more.

The ALR® Series servers crown Gateway's business offerings. We acquired the server company, ALR, in 1997 and moved Gateway Business headquarters to the ALR center in Irvine, California, in April 1998. The ALR designs, now under Gateway's name, continue to be among the industry leaders by exceeding client expectations in function, durability, quality and value.

The Irvine center also hosts Gateway Partners, another division launched in 1998. It's Gateway's response to business clients who said they want our products and services in combination with other services value-added reseller partners can provide.

Gateway's Destination XTV is becoming a common sight in American classrooms.

At the Head of the Class

Teachers love the way the PC and TV combination Destination® XTV's 35.5-inch or 27-inch screen can include everyone in computer-assisted learning. The Destination XTV has also found success as a business presentation system and as a home entertainment center. And, as home video and television turn digital, the XTV has turned more heads.

At Your Service

Knowing technology goes beyond just offering great products. It also means helping clients when their PCs don't run smoothly. Gateway expanded and diversified the ways we can help clients in 1998.

We start with prevention. Gateway's exclusive HelpSpot™ client assistance software monitors the performance of Gateway G- and GP-Series desktops, heading off many problems before they turn serious. Our online, interactive troubleshooting tool, Technical Assistant, (www.gateway.com/support) puts some of the same tools Gateway phone technicians use within reach of clients through the World Wide Web.

We also started a conference call program that matches one technician with a small group of clients who are having similar PC difficulties. Plus we still offer traditional one-on-one phone technical support. No matter how you get support, Gateway's goal is to resolve the problem on the first contact, every time.

On top of all these basic services, in 1998 Gateway continued to develop an array of specialized free and fee-based technical support offerings for business.

Whether for home or business, Gateway masters the fine nuances of technology and monitors the computer evolution so you don't have to. After all, you have better things to do.

Gateway's troubleshooting array includes preloaded help programs, Web-based support and the best technicians in the business.

• Jan. 22
Jeff Weitzen hired as President and COO.

David Robino hired as Executive VP and Chief Administrative Officer.

Y2k SUMMIT

Feb. 18
Gateway Sponsors Year 2000 Summit.

TRUTH WELL TOLD

McCANN-ERICKSON

March 31
McCann-Erickson becomes Gateway's global ad agency.

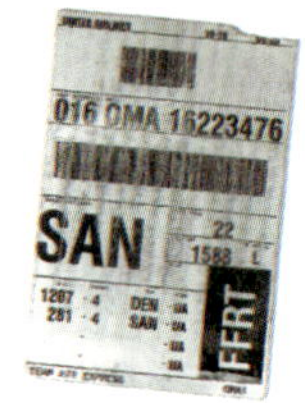

April 7
Announced plans for administrative headquarters in San Diego, CA.

• April 20
Gateway Partners formed.

April 23
Gateway drops the "2000," unveils new logo.

May 27
Introduced revolutionary Your:)Ware℠ program, Ted finally sells a system to his dad.

• June 1
Anil Arora, Sr. VP and Chief Marketing Officer hired.

June 2
Gateway ships its exclusive HelpSpot™ client assistance software standard with every G- and GP- Series desktop PC.

June
Gateway is number o
brand loyalty according t
1997 Technology User Pr
from ZD Market Intellige

1998 Time Line/ Milestones

A Year of Milestones

In 1998 Gateway expanded the leadership team, focused more on clients and built relationships that move us beyond the box.

In January Gateway set the tone for the year by hiring President and COO Jeff Weitzen, and Executive Vice President and CAO David Robino.

Jeff, David and Chairman and CEO Ted Waitt immediately launched an exhaustive executive talent search.

While building a world-class executive team, we further developed our brand and improved the tools and infrastructure we need to build the best client relationships in the business.

Along the way we introduced new products, found new ways to deliver technical support to our clients, hosted a prime minister and a president, and won rave reviews in the trade press.

Changing our Look

With the year 2000 less than two years off, the time was right to drop the "2000" from our name. So we introduced the new name and new company logo in April. In conjunction with the name and new look, Gateway launched the industry-first Your:)Ware℠ program, a revolutionary way to buy a computer and build a relationship.

Your:)Ware Program Mind-Set

The Your:)Ware program symbolized our commitment to complete personalization and being a trusted guide for our clients. The same spirit accelerated the evolution of our business model.

In 1998, we moved away from focusing on how our goods and services were marketed, sold and delivered to the client. Instead we spent more and more time understanding individual client needs and building business units specifically focused on those clients. And we'll continue to transform our company to become far more client-centered.

July 21
Gateway's Salt Lake City manufacturing plant readies for a Q4 start-up.

- **July 23**
Maynard Webb hired as Chief Information Officer.

- **August 6**
Lakewood, Colorado announced as site for Gateway's global IT center.

- **August 21**
Peter Ashkin joined Gateway Products.

Sept. 4
U.S. President Bill Clinton and Ireland Prime Minister Bertie Ahern meet with Ted before digitally signing a joint communique at Gateway European Headquarters in Dublin, Ireland.

- **Sept. 14**
Hampton center expanded.

- **Sept. 18**
R. Todd Bradley hired as Sr. VP and Regional Managing Director of Europe, Middle East and Africa Operations.

- **Sept. 25**
Van Andrews became Sr. VP of Gateway Business.

- **October 6**
John Todd becomes Gateway's Sr. VP, Chief Financial Officer and Treasurer.

- **October 15**
Frank Smilovic hired as Sr. VP, Regional Managing Director of Asia Pacific Operations.

- **Nov. 11**
Daniel Pittard named Sr. VP of Strategy and New Ventures.

In doing that, Gateway started viewing our three main connections with clients — the phones, World Wide Web and Gateway Country retail outlets — as complementing each other.

Also in the spirit of the Your:)Ware program, Gateway offered clients increased financing options, putting more products within their reach. Gateway clients qualified for $1 billion in commercial loans in 1998.

Gateway's own gateway.net℠ Internet service added clients at a record pace in 1998, connecting about 200,000 clients to the Web by the end of the year.

Awareness Grows

Gateway did more television advertising than ever and backed it by an increasing volume of direct mail and online communications efforts. The approach, along with excellent client satisfaction and loyalty, boosted Gateway™ U.S. consumer desktop brand awareness from 78% in Q4 1997 to 92% in Q4 1998.[4] Gateway exited the fourth quarter of 1998 with approximately 17% consumer market share and the number-one ranking in home desktops. Our loyal clients continued to support Gateway through referrals, which remain the number-one source of new business for our company.

Accelerating in 1999

In 1999 Gateway will move outside the box and focus on all the relationships and needs that go on behind, beyond and beneath the box.

Those relationships, along with knowing clients, knowing technology, having the best people with the best tools and keeping finances sound are the keys to 1999 and beyond.

3. 75% of Gateway clients who bought a new computer in 1997 repurchased a Gateway system.
4. According to Intelliquest.

Company finances can show its health, and they can show how well the company

John Todd, Sr. VP and CFO

can support its initiatives. Gateway is sound by both measures.

"A company has three kinds of resources — human, technology and financial."

– John Todd, Senior Vice President and Chief Financial Officer

It takes people, tools and money to run a company. No one element is more important than the others. In 1998, Gateway improved all three elements, including our financial performance.

Great financial results remain key, but so does consistency. We're striving to be consistent in our financial performance, especially as measured by earnings per share, by using all our resources efficiently to support company goals.

Underlying all our financial plans are expectations that Gateway will move toward more consistent, solid financial results every quarter. It's our responsibility to shareholders — many of whom are also employees — to maximize the value of their holdings over the long term. Gateway realizes successful financial performance requires the same thing as any other kind of performance — planning and execution.

Gateway's financial planners have a big role in our overall company plans. That lets Gateway use its financial resources wisely, plan for future needs and insure that our financial health supports our initiatives.

Gateway's time line of accomplishments in 1998 includes improved, more consistent financial results. We're working to extend that time line through 1999, 2000 and beyond.

Management's Discussion and Analysis of Financial Condition and Results of Operations

This Report includes forward-looking statements made based on current management expectations pursuant to the safe harbor provisions of the Private Securities Litigation Reform Act of 1995. These statements are not guarantees of future performance and actual outcomes may differ materially from what is expressed or forecasted. Factors that could cause future results to differ from the Company's expectations include the following: competitive market conditions; infrastructure requirements; financial instruments; suppliers; short product cycles; access to technology; international operations; credit risk; e-commerce issues; risks of acquisition; inventory risks; customer or geographic sales mix; loss of key managers; and the Year 2000 transition. For a discussion of these factors, see "Item 1 Business - Factors that May Affect Gateway's Business and Future Results" in the Company's Annual Report on Form 10-K.

Results of Operations

The following table sets forth, for the periods indicated, certain data derived from the Company's consolidated income statements:

	1996	Increase (Decrease)	1997	Increase	1998
			(dollars in thousands)		
Net sales	$ 5,035,228	25%	$ 6,293,680	19%	$ 7,467,925
Gross profit	$ 936,155	15%	$ 1,076,441	44%	$ 1,546,274
Percentage of net sales	18.6%		17.1%		20.7%
Selling, general and administrative expenses	$ 580,061	36%	$ 786,168	34%	$ 1,052,047
Percentage of net sales	11.5%		12.5%		14.1%
Nonrecurring expenses	—		$ 113,842		—
Percentage of net sales	—		1.8%		—
Operating income	$ 356,094	(50%)	$ 176,431	180%	$ 494,227
Percentage of net sales	7.1%		2.8%		6.6%
Net income	$ 250,679	(56%)	$ 109,797	215%	$ 346,399

Sales. Gateway added over $1.1 billion in sales in 1998 compared to 1997, achieving annual sales of $7.47 billion. This represents an increase of 19% over 1997. Sales to the consumer segment represented 53% of total sales while business segment sales were 47% of total sales. Sales were driven by continued strong unit growth of 37% in 1998 compared to unit growth of 35% in 1997. The Company's unit growth outpaced the worldwide market in 1998 by approximately three times the market growth rate, leading to continued gains in market share. Based on shipments in the fourth quarter, Gateway improved its ranking to number 3 in the U.S. PC market and was number 6 worldwide. These market share gains were driven by several top line initiatives including the development and execution of a new advertising strategy; the Your:)Ware℠ marketing program; and significant expansion of Gateway Country Stores. The new marketing strategy focuses on reaching an expanded customer base through a new branding campaign and the use of broader advertising media such as television and newspapers. The Your:)Ware℠ program offers customers internet access, financing options, software bundles, and provides for trade-in options. As a result of these initiatives, Gateway was able to reach a broader cross section of customers in 1998. Partially offsetting strong unit growth, the Company's average unit prices (AUPs) were approximately 14% lower in 1998 compared to an 8% decline in 1997. AUPs continued to decline in 1998 due to component cost decreases and significant growth in the sub $1,000 PC market. The Company expects the industry trend of declining AUPs to continue and intends to mitigate this by diversifying its revenue stream with software bundles, internet service, financing and other service offerings.

The following table summarizes the Company's net sales, for the periods indicated, by geographic region:

	1996	Increase	1997	Increase (Decrease)	1998
			(dollars in thousands)		
Net sales:					
United States	$ 4,246,047	25%	$ 5,303,828	21%	$ 6,412,405
Europe	552,671	15%	634,616	(10%)	570,191
Asia Pacific	236,510	50%	355,236	37%	485,329
Consolidated	$ 5,035,228	25%	$ 6,293,680	19%	$ 7,467,925

In the United States unit shipments rose 39% in 1998 and 35% in 1997 due to the factors discussed above. The Asia Pacific region ("APAC") continued to achieve significant increases in unit shipments with growth of 63% in 1998 and 84% in 1997. Unit shipments in the European region ("EMEA") increased 5% in 1998 down from 20% in 1997. The Company has put new management in place in EMEA and is focusing on the top line initiatives previously discussed to address the declining unit shipment growth.

Gross Profit. Gross profit in 1998 rose to $1.55 billion, an increase of approximately 44% from 1997. Gross profit for the consumer and business segments for 1998 was $760.8 million and $783.3 million, respectively. Approximately 40% of the gross profit increase was the result of sales growth, while approximately 60% resulted from margin productivity. Margin productivity was driven by the diversified revenue stream with Your:)Ware℠ bundles, effective pricing initiatives, aggressive supplier management and decreasing component costs. As a percentage of sales, gross profit for 1998 increased to 20.7% from 17.1% in 1997, improving sequentially every quarter during 1998. For additional quarterly financial information, see Note 13 of the notes to the consolidated financial statements. The increase over 1997 is partially attributable to the adverse effects of excess inventories experienced in the third quarter of 1997.

Selling, General and Administrative Expenses. To support its significant growth during 1998, the Company made investments in infrastructure, personnel, marketing and internet development which contributed to an increase of 34% in selling, general and administrative expenses over 1997. Gateway opened a new manufacturing and sales facility in Salt Lake City, an administrative headquarters in San Diego and a new Information Technology and Support facility in Lakewood, Colorado. In addition, the Company made a significant investment in new employees, including the expansion of its executive management team. As a result, personnel costs increased 35% in 1998 compared to 1997. The Company expects selling, general and administrative expenses to continue to increase in support of its anticipated growth, but at a rate below that of anticipated revenue growth.

Operating Income. Strong unit growth and gross margin efficiencies contributed to a 180% increase in operating income for 1998. In addition, the increase is attributable to the nonrecurring pre-tax charges recorded in the third quarter of 1997. Operating income improved to 6.6% in 1998 from 2.8% in 1997. Operating income in 1998 for the consumer and business segments were $461.4 million and $600.8 million, respectively, while operating expenses in 1998 not allocated to a segment were $568.0 million. Operating income for the consumer and business segments includes selling, general and administrative expenses and other overhead charges directly attributable to the segment and excludes certain expenses managed outside the reportable segments. Costs excluded from the consumer and business segments primarily consist of corporate marketing costs and other general and administrative expenses that are separately managed.

Other Income. Other income, net includes other income net of expenses, such as interest income and expense and foreign exchange transaction gains and losses. Other income, net increased to $47.0 million in 1998 from $27.2 million in 1997, primarily due to the additional interest income generated by increases in cash balances and marketable securities.

Income Taxes. The Company's annualized effective tax rate decreased to 36% for 1998 from the 46.1% recorded in 1997. The effective tax rate for 1997 was impacted unfavorably by the nonrecurring expenses relating to the write-off of in-process research and development arising in connection with the acquisitions of ALR and certain assets of Amiga Technologies which were nondeductible for income taxes.

Liquidity and Capital Resources

The following table presents selected financial statistics and information for the periods indicated:

	1996	1997	1998
		(dollars in thousands)	
Cash and marketable securities	$ 516,360	$ 632,249	$ 1,328,467
Days of sales in accounts receivable	26	23	22
Inventory turnover	21	21	40
Days in accounts payable	29	27	36

At December 31, 1998, the Company had cash and cash equivalents of $1.17 billion, marketable securities of $158.7 million and an unsecured committed credit facility with certain banks aggregating $225 million, consisting of a revolving line of credit facility and a sub-facility for letters of credit. At December 31, 1998, no amounts were outstanding under the revolving line of credit. Approximately $2.0 million was committed to support outstanding standby letters of credit. Management believes the Company's current sources of working capital, including amounts available under existing credit facilities, will provide adequate flexibility for the Company's financial needs for at least the next 12 months.

The Company generated $907.7 million in cash from operations during the year, including $398.3 million of net income adjusted for non-cash items. Other significant factors increasing available cash include a decrease in inventory levels of $81.3 million and an increase in accounts payable and other accrued liabilities of $479.8 million, partially offset by an increase in accounts receivable. The decrease in inventory levels, decrease in days sales in accounts receivable and increase in days purchases in accounts payable is attributable to the Company's increased focus on working capital management. The Company used approximately $235.4 million for the construction of new facilities, information systems and equipment and $120.0 million to purchase investments in marketable securities, net of proceeds of securities sold. As discussed previously, the Company continued to expand the retail Gateway Country stores with 107 new stores added in 1998, bringing the total number of stores to 144 as of December 31, 1998.

At December 31, 1998, the Company had long-term indebtedness and capital lease obligations of approximately $14.8 million. These obligations relate to the Company's investments in equipment and facilities. The Company anticipates that it will retain all earnings in the foreseeable future for development of its business and will not distribute earnings to its stockholders as dividends.

As of February 28, 1999, the Company has made a commitment to purchase approximately $290 million of consumer finance receivables used to purchase the Company's products which were originated by a financial institution on behalf of Gateway.

New Accounting Pronouncements

In June of 1998, the Financial Accounting Standards Board issued SFAS No. 133, "Accounting for Derivative Instruments and Hedging Activities" which is effective for fiscal years beginning after June 15, 1999. The objective of the statement is to establish accounting and reporting standards for derivative instruments and hedging activities. The Company uses foreign currency forward contracts, a derivative instrument, to hedge foreign currency transactions and anticipated foreign currency transactions. The adoption of this new accounting pronouncement is not expected to be material to the Company's consolidated financial position or results of operations.

In 1998, the Accounting Standards Executive Committee (AcSEC) issued Statement of Accounting Position ("SOP") No. 98-1, "Accounting for the Costs of Computer Software Developed or Obtained for Internal Use," which is effective for fiscal years beginning after December 15, 1998. The SOP provides guidance on when costs incurred for internal-use computer software are and are not to be capitalized, and on the accounting for such software that is marketed to customers. The adoption of this SOP is not expected to have a material impact on the Company's consolidated financial position or results of operations.

Year 2000

The "Year 2000" issue has arisen because many existing computer programs and chip-based embedded technology systems use only the last two digits to refer to a year, and therefore, do not properly recognize a year that begins with "20" instead of the familiar "19." If not corrected, many computer applications could fail or create erroneous results.

State of Readiness: The Company has adopted a seven-step process toward Year 2000 readiness consisting of the following: (i) awareness: fostering an understanding of and commitment to the problem and its potential risks; (ii) inventory: identifying and locating systems and technology components that may be affected; (iii) assessment: reviewing these components for Year 2000 compliance and assessing the scope of potential Year 2000 issues; (iv) planning: defining the technical solutions, labor and work plans necessary for each affected system; (v) remediation/replacement: completing the programming to upgrade or replace the problem software or hardware; (vi) testing and compliance validation: conducting testing followed by independent validation by a separate internal verification team; and (vii) implementation: placing the corrected systems and technology back into the business environment with a management monitoring system to ensure ongoing compliance.

The Company has grouped its internal systems and technology into the following three categories for purposes of Year 2000 compliance: (i) information resource applications and technology consisting of enterprise-wide systems supported by the Company's centralized information technology organization (IT); (ii) business processes consisting of hardware, software, and associated computer chips as well as external vendors used in the operation of the Company's core business functions; and (iii) building systems consisting of non-IT equipment that use embedded computer chips such as elevators, automated room key systems and HVAC equipment. The Company is prioritizing its efforts based on the severity with which non compliance would affect service, core business processes or revenues, and whether there are viable, non-automated fallback procedures (Mission Criticality).

As of the end of the fourth quarter, the Company believes the Awareness and Inventory phases are complete for both IT systems and building systems and 50% complete for business processes. For IT systems, the Company believes the assessment, planning and remediation/replacement phases are over 65% complete with testing and compliance validation complete for 20% of the inventory. For business processes and building systems, the Company believes the assessment and planning phases are over 40% complete with a substantial amount of work in process. The progress level for remediation/replacement and testing and compliance validation is currently at 20%. The Company plans to complete the remediation/replacement and testing phases for its mission critical IT systems by the end of the second quarter of 1999 with the remaining half of 1999 reserved for unplanned contingencies and compliance validation and quality assurance. For mission critical business processes and building systems, the same level of completion is targeted for October 1999.

The Company has also initiated Year 2000 compliance communications with its significant third party suppliers, vendors and business partners. The Company is focusing its efforts on the business interfaces most critical to its customer service, core business processes and revenues, including those third parties that support the most critical enterprise-wide IT systems, the Company's primary suppliers of non-IT products, or provide the most critical payment processing functions. Responses have been received from a majority of the third parties that comprise this group.

Costs: During 1998, the Company expensed incremental costs of approximately $3.3 million related to the Year 2000 remediation efforts, and has expensed $3.6 million on a life-to-date basis. The current total estimated cost to complete the Year 2000 remediation efforts is from $14 to $16 million, exclusive of upgrades to existing applications and implementation of new systems. Internal and external costs specifically associated with modifying internal-use software for the Year 2000 will be charged to expense as incurred. All of these costs are being funded through operating cash flows.

Year 2000 Contingency Plans: The Company is reviewing its existing contingency plans for potential modification to address specific Year 2000 issues as they arise and expects to continue this process during the next four fiscal quarters.

Company Products: With respect to PC products sold to customers, for all the Company hardware based on the Intel(r) family of Pentium processors (Pentium(r), Pentium(r) Pro, Pentium II(r), Pentium(r)II Xeon(tm) and Celeron(tm) processors) and using an operating system provided by the Company, the Company warrants to customers that such systems sold after January 1, 1997, will process dates correctly before, during and after January 1, 2000. This warranty applies to desktop, portable, Destination(r), and server products, and it is governed by the terms and conditions outlined in the original system warranty. It does not include application software, or non-Company branded external hardware peripherals such as printers, scanners and joysticks. Because the Company does not control the design of these products, it cannot ensure how they access or calculate date information in the computer. Certain hardware sold before January 1, 1997 will require remediation or replacement to become Year 2000 compliant. The Company may experience increased customer claims for Year 2000 failures for these products and for failures resulting from software or non-Company branded external hardware peripherals. Additional information concerning the Year 2000 issue and the Company's compliance program is available on the Company's website at www.gateway.com/.

Risks of the Company's Year 2000 Issues: Based on current information, the Company believes that the Year 2000 problem will not have a material adverse effect on the Company, its consolidated financial position, results of operations or cash flows. However, there are no assurances that Year 2000 remediation by the Company or third parties will be properly and timely completed, and failure to do so could have a material adverse effect on the Company, its business and its financial condition. The Company cannot predict the effects that Year 2000 non-compliance would have on it, which would ultimately depend on numerous uncertainties such as: (i) whether significant third parties properly and timely address the Year 2000 issue; (ii) whether broad-based or systemic economic failures may occur, and the severity and duration of such failures, including loss of utility and/or telecommunications services, and errors or failures in financial transactions or payment processing systems such as credit cards; and (iii) whether the Company becomes the subject of litigation or other proceedings regarding any Year 2000-related events and the outcome of any such litigation or proceedings.

Quantitative and Qualitative Disclosures About Market Risk

The results of the Company's foreign operations are affected by changes in exchange rates between certain foreign currencies and the United States dollar. The functional currency for most of the Company's foreign operations is the U.S. dollar. The functional currency for the remaining operations is the local currency in which the subsidiaries operate. Sales made in foreign currencies translate into higher or lower sales in U.S. dollars as the U.S. dollar strengthens or weakens against other currencies. Therefore, changes in exchange rates may negatively affect the Company's consolidated net sales (as expressed in U.S. dollars) and gross margins from foreign operations. The majority of the Company's component purchases are denominated in U.S. dollars.

The Company uses foreign currency forward contracts to hedge foreign currency transactions and probable anticipated foreign currency transactions. These forward contracts are designated as a hedge of international sales by U.S. dollar functional currency entities and intercompany purchases by certain foreign subsidiaries. The principal currencies hedged are the British Pound, Japanese Yen, French Franc, Australian Dollar, Singapore Dollar, and the Deutsche Mark over periods ranging from one to six months. Forward contracts are accounted for on a mark-to-market basis, with realized and unrealized gains or losses recognized currently. Gains or losses arising from forward contracts that are effective as a hedge are included in the basis of the designated transactions. Fluctuations in U.S. dollar currency exchange rates did not have a significant impact on the Company's consolidated financial position, results of operations or cash flows in any given reporting period. Forward contracts designated to hedge foreign currency transaction exposure of $257,051,000 and $266,471,000 were outstanding at December 31, 1997 and 1998, respectively. The estimated fair value of these forward contracts at December 31, 1997 and 1998 was $253,519,000 and $271,573,000, respectively, based on quoted market prices.

Foreign currency exchange contracts are sensitive to changes in foreign currency exchange rates. At December 31, 1998, a hypothetical 10% adverse change in foreign currency exchange rates underlying the Company's open forward contracts would result in an unrealized loss of approximately $29.1 million. Unrealized gains/losses in foreign currency exchange contracts represent the difference between the hypothetical rates and the current market exchange rates. Consistent with the nature of an economic hedge any unrealized gains or losses would be offset by corresponding decreases or increases, respectively, of the underlying transaction being hedged.

The Company is not subject to material market risk with respect to its investment in marketable securities.

Report of Independent Accountants

To the Stockholders and Board of Directors of Gateway 2000, Inc.

In our opinion, the accompanying consolidated balance sheets and the related consolidated statements of income, cash flows and changes in stockholders' equity and comprehensive income presents fairly, in all material respects, the consolidated financial position of Gateway 2000, Inc. at December 31, 1997 and 1998, and the consolidated results of its operations and its cash flows for each of the three years in the period ended December 31, 1998, in conformity with generally accepted accounting principles. These financial statements are the responsibility of the Company's management; our responsibility is to express an opinion on these financial statements based on our audits. We conducted our audits of these statements in accordance with generally accepted auditing standards which require that we plan and perform the audit to obtain reasonable assurance about whether the financial statements are free of material misstatement. An audit includes examining, on a test basis, evidence supporting amounts and disclosures in the financial statements, assessing the accounting principles used and significant estimates made by management, and evaluating the overall financial statement presentation. We believe that our audits provide a reasonable basis for the opinion expressed above.

PricewaterhouseCoopers LLP

San Diego, California
January 21, 1999

CONSOLIDATED INCOME STATEMENTS
For the years ended December 31, 1996, 1997 and 1998
(in thousands, except per share amounts)

	1996	1997	1998
Net sales	$ 5,035,228	$ 6,293,680	$ 7,467,925
Cost of goods sold	4,099,073	5,217,239	5,921,651
Gross profit	936,155	1,076,441	1,546,274
Selling, general and administrative expenses	580,061	786,168	1,052,047
Nonrecurring expenses	–	113,842	–
Operating income	356,094	176,431	494,227
Other income, net	26,622	27,189	47,021
Income before income taxes	382,716	203,620	541,248
Provision for income taxes	132,037	93,823	194,849
Net income	$ 250,679	$ 109,797	$ 346,399
Net income per share:			
Basic	$ 1.64	$ .71	$ 2.23
Diluted	$ 1.60	$ .70	$ 2.18
Weighted average shares outstanding:			
Basic	152,745	153,840	155,542
Diluted	156,237	156,201	158,929

The accompanying notes are an integral part of the consolidated financial statements.

CONSOLIDATED BALANCE SHEETS

December 31, 1997 and 1998

(in thousands, except per share amounts)

	1997	1998
ASSETS		
Current assets:		
Cash and cash equivalents	$ 593,601	$ 1,169,810
Marketable securities	38,648	158,657
Accounts receivable, net	510,679	558,851
Inventory	249,224	167,924
Other	152,531	172,944
Total current assets	1,544,683	2,228,186
Property, plant and equipment, net	376,467	530,988
Intangibles, net	82,590	65,944
Other assets	35,531	65,262
	$ 2,039,271	$ 2,890,380
LIABILITIES AND STOCKHOLDERS' EQUITY		
Current liabilities:		
Notes payable and current maturities of long-term obligations	$ 13,969	$ 11,415
Accounts payable	488,717	718,071
Accrued liabilities	271,250	415,265
Accrued royalties	159,418	167,873
Other current liabilities	70,552	117,050
Total current liabilities	1,003,906	1,429,674
Long-term obligations, net of current maturities	7,240	3,360
Warranty and other liabilities	98,081	112,971
Total liabilities	1,109,227	1,546,005
Commitments and Contingencies (Notes 3 and 4)		
Stockholders' equity:		
Preferred stock, $.01 par value, 5,000 shares authorized; none issued and outstanding	—	—
Class A common stock, nonvoting, $.01 par value, 1,000 shares authorized; none issued and outstanding	—	—
Common stock, $.01 par value, 220,000 shares authorized; 154,128 shares and 156,569 shares issued and outstanding, respectively	1,541	1,566
Additional paid-in capital	299,483	365,986
Retained earnings	634,509	980,908
Accumulated other comprehensive loss	(5,489)	(4,085)
Total stockholders' equity	930,044	1,344,375
	$ 2,039,271	$ 2,890,380

The accompanying notes are an integral part of the consolidated financial statements.

CONSOLIDATED STATEMENTS OF CASH FLOWS
For the years ended December 31, 1996, 1997 and 1998
(in thousands)

	1996	1997	1998
Cash flows from operating activities:			
Net income	$ 250,679	$ 109,797	$ 346,399
Adjustments to reconcile net income to net cash provided by operating activities:			
Depreciation and amortization	61,763	86,774	105,524
Provision for uncollectible accounts receivable	20,832	5,688	3,991
Deferred income taxes	(13,395)	(63,247)	(58,425)
Other, net	1,986	42	770
Nonrecurring expenses	—	113,842	—
Changes in operating assets and liabilities:			
Accounts receivable	(66,052)	(41,950)	(52,164)
Inventory	(54,261)	59,486	81,300
Other assets	(13,311)	(54,513)	451
Accounts payable	176,724	66,253	228,921
Accrued liabilities	51,390	48,405	144,899
Accrued royalties	1,885	34,148	8,455
Other current liabilities	43,057	35,816	76,278
Warranty and other liabilities	22,699	42,256	21,252
Net cash provided by operating activities	483,996	442,797	907,651
Cash flows from investing activities:			
Capital expenditures	(143,746)	(175,656)	(235,377)
Purchases of available-for-sale securities	—	(49,619)	(168,965)
Proceeds from maturities or sales of available-for-sale securities	3,030	10,985	48,924
Acquisitions, net of cash acquired	—	(142,320)	—
Other, net	2,667	(4,055)	(992)
Net cash used in investing activities	(138,049)	(360,665)	(356,410)
Cash flows from financing activities:			
Proceeds from issuances of notes payable	10,000	10,000	—
Principal payments on long-term obligations and notes payable	(14,047)	(15,588)	(13,173)
Stock options exercised	9,520	5,741	36,159
Net cash provided by financing activities	5,473	153	22,986
Foreign exchange effect on cash and cash equivalents	(1,457)	(5,044)	1,982
Net increase in cash and cash equivalents	349,963	77,241	576,209
Cash and cash equivalents, beginning of year	166,397	516,360	593,601
Cash and cash equivalents, end of year	$ 516,360	$ 593,601	$ 1,169,810

The accompanying notes are an integral part of the consolidated financial statements.

CONSOLIDATED STATEMENTS OF CHANGES IN STOCKHOLDERS' EQUITY AND COMPREHENSIVE INCOME

For the years ended December 31, 1996, 1997 and 1998

(in thousands)

	Common Stock Shares	Common Stock Amount	Additional Paid-in Capital	Retained Earnings	Accumulated Other Comprehensive Income (Loss)	Total
Balances at December 31, 1995	149,106	$ 1,492	$ 279,701	$ 274,033	$ 293	$ 555,519
Comprehensive income:						
Net income	—	—	—	250,679	—	250,679
Other comprehensive income:						
Foreign currency translation	—	—	—	—	225	225
Unrealized gain on available-for-sale securities	—	—	—	—	31	31
Comprehensive income						250,935
Stock issuances under employee plans, including tax benefit of $30,451	6,545	66	39,905	—	—	39,971
Stock retirement	(2,139)	(22)	(30,862)	—	—	(30,884)
Balances at December 31, 1996	153,512	1,536	288,744	524,712	549	815,541
Comprehensive income:						
Net income	—	—	—	109,797	—	109,797
Other comprehensive income:						
Foreign currency translation	—	—	—	—	(6,053)	(6,053)
Unrealized gain on available-for-sale securities	—	—	—	—	15	15
Comprehensive income						103,759
Stock issuances under employee plans, including tax benefit of $5,003	616	5	10,739	—	—	10,744
Balances at December 31, 1997	154,128	1,541	299,483	634,509	(5,489)	930,044
Comprehensive income:						
Net income	—	—	—	346,399	—	346,399
Other comprehensive income:						
Foreign currency translation	—	—	—	—	1,549	1,549
Unrealized loss on available-for-sale securities	—	—	—	—	(145)	(145)
Comprehensive income						347,803
Stock issuances under employee plans, including tax benefit of $29,769	2,423	24	65,904	—	—	65,928
Stock issued to officer	18	1	599	—	—	600
Balances at December 31, 1998	156,569	$ 1,566	$ 365,986	$ 980,908	$ (4,085)	$ 1,344,375

 The accompanying notes are an integral part of the consolidated financial statements.

1. Summary of Significant Accounting Policies:

Gateway 2000, Inc. (the "Company") is a direct marketer of personal computers ("PCs") and PC-related products. The Company develops, manufactures, markets and supports a broad line of desktop and portable PCs, digital media (convergence) PCs, servers, workstations and PC-related products used by individuals, families, businesses, government agencies and educational institutions.

The significant accounting policies used in the preparation of the consolidated financial statements of the Company are as follows:

(a) Principles of Consolidation:

The consolidated financial statements include the accounts of the Company and its wholly-owned subsidiaries. All significant intercompany accounts and transactions have been eliminated.

(b) Use of Estimates and Certain Concentrations:

The preparation of financial statements in conformity with generally accepted accounting principles requires management to make estimates and assumptions that affect the reported amounts of assets and liabilities and disclosure of contingent assets and liabilities at the date of the financial statements and the reported amounts of revenues and expenses during the reporting period. Actual results could differ from those estimates.

Certain components used by the Company in manufacturing of PC systems are purchased from a limited number of suppliers. An industry shortage or other constraints of any key component could result in delayed shipments and a possible loss of sales, which could affect operating results adversely.

(c) Cash and Cash Equivalents:

The Company considers all highly liquid debt instruments and money market funds with an original maturity of three months or less to be cash equivalents. The carrying amount approximates fair value because of the short maturities of these instruments.

(d) Marketable Securities:

The carrying amounts of marketable securities used in computing unrealized and realized gains and losses are determined by specific identification. Fair values are determined using quoted market prices. For available-for-sale securities, which are carried at fair value at the balance sheet dates, net unrealized holding gains and losses are reported in accumulated other comprehensive income (loss). Held-to-maturity securities are recorded at amortized cost. Amortization of related discounts or premiums is included in the determination of net income.

Marketable securities at December 31, 1998 consisted of available-for-sale mutual funds, commercial paper and debt securities, with a market value of $158,657,000 and an amortized cost of $158,788,000, with variable maturities through 1999. Realized and unrealized gains and losses are not material for any of the periods presented.

(e) Inventory:

Inventory, which is comprised of component parts, subassemblies and finished goods, is valued at the lower of first-in, first-out (FIFO) cost or market. On a quarterly basis, the Company compares on a part by part basis, the amount of the inventory on hand and under commitment with its latest forecasted requirements to determine whether write-downs for excess or obsolete inventory are required.

(f) Property, Plant and Equipment:

Property, plant and equipment are stated at cost. Depreciation is provided using straight-line and accelerated methods over the assets' estimated useful lives, ranging from four to forty years. Amortization of leasehold improvements is computed using the shorter of the lease term or the estimated useful life of the underlying asset. Upon sale or retirement of property, plant and equipment, the related costs and accumulated depreciation or amortization are removed from the accounts and any gain or loss is included in the determination of net income.

The Company capitalizes costs of purchased software and, once technological feasibility has been established, costs incurred in developing software for internal use. Amortization of software costs begins when the software is placed in service and is computed on a straight-line basis over the estimated useful life of the software, generally from three to five years.

(g) Intangible Assets:

Intangible assets principally consist of technology, a customer base and distribution network, an assembled work force and trade name obtained through acquisition. The cost of intangible assets is amortized on a straight-line basis over the estimated periods benefited, ranging from three to ten years.

(h) Long-lived Assets:

The Company reviews for the impairment of long-lived assets whenever events or changes in circumstances indicate that the carrying amount of an asset may not be recoverable. An impairment loss would be recognized when the sum of the expected undiscounted future net cash flows expected to result from the use of the asset and its eventual disposition is less than its carrying amount.

(i) Royalties:

The Company has royalty-bearing license agreements that allow the Company to sell certain hardware and software which is protected by patent, copyright or license. Royalty costs are accrued and included in cost of goods sold when products are shipped or amortized over the period of benefit when the license terms are not specifically related to the units shipped.

(j) Warranty and Other Post-sales Support Programs:

The Company provides currently for the estimated costs that may be incurred under its warranty and other post-sales support programs.

(k) Comprehensive Income:

Effective January 1, 1998, the Company adopted Statement of Financial Accounting Standards (SFAS) No. 130, "Reporting Comprehensive Income." SFAS 130 establishes new rules for the reporting of comprehensive income and its components; however the adoption of this statement had no impact on the Company's current or previously reported net income or stockholders' equity. SFAS 130 requires the display and reporting of comprehensive income, which includes all changes in stockholders' equity with the exception of additional investments by stockholders or distributions to stockholders. Comprehensive income for the Company includes net income, foreign currency translation effects and unrealized gains or losses on available-for-sale securities which are charged or credited to the accumulated other comprehensive income (loss) account within stockholders' equity.

(l) Revenue Recognition:

Sales are recorded when products are shipped. A provision for estimated sales returns is recorded in the period in which related sales are recognized. Revenue from separately priced extended warranty programs is deferred and recognized over the extended warranty period on a straight-line basis.

(m) Income Taxes:

The provision for income taxes is computed using the liability method, under which deferred tax assets and liabilities are recognized for the expected future tax consequences of temporary differences between the financial reporting and tax bases of assets and liabilities. Deferred tax assets are reduced by a valuation allowance when it is more likely than not that some portion or all of the deferred tax assets will not be realized.

(n) Net Income Per Share:

Basic earnings per common share is computed using the weighted average number of common shares outstanding during the period. Diluted earnings per common share is computed using the combination of dilutive common stock equivalents and the weighted average number of common shares outstanding during the period.

The following table sets forth a reconciliation of shares used in the computation of basic and diluted earnings per share.

	1996	1997	1998
		(in thousands)	
Net income for basic and diluted earnings per share	$ 250,679	$ 109,797	$ 346,399
Weighted average shares for basic earnings per share	152,745	153,840	155,542
Dilutive effect of stock options	3,492	2,361	3,387
Weighted average shares for diluted earnings per share	156,237	156,201	158,929

All references in the financial statements to number of common shares and per share amounts have been retroactively restated to reflect a two-for-one common stock split effective in June 1997.

(o) Stock-based Compensation:

The Company measures compensation expense for its employee stock-based compensation using the intrinsic value method. Compensation charges related to non-employee stock-based compensation are measured using fair value methods.

(p) Foreign Currency:

The Company uses the U.S. dollar as its functional currency for the majority of its international operations. For subsidiaries where the local currency is the functional currency, the assets and liabilities are translated into U.S. dollars at exchange rates in effect at the balance sheet date. Income and expense items are translated at the average exchange rates prevailing during the period. Gains and losses from translation are included in accumulated other comprehensive income (loss). Gains and losses resulting from remeasuring monetary asset and liability accounts that are denominated in currencies other than a subsidiary's functional currency are included in "Other income, net".

The Company uses foreign currency forward contracts to hedge foreign currency transactions and probable anticipated foreign currency transactions. These forward contracts are designated as a hedge of international sales by U.S. dollar functional currency entities and intercompany purchases by certain foreign subsidiaries. The principal currencies hedged are the British Pound, Japanese Yen, French Franc, Australian Dollar, Singapore Dollar and the Deutsche Mark over periods ranging from one to six months. Forward contracts are accounted for on a mark-to-market basis, with realized and unrealized gains or losses recognized currently. Gains or losses arising from forward contracts which are effective as a hedge are included in the basis of the designated transactions. The related receivable or liability with counterparties to the forward contracts is recorded in the consolidated balance sheet. Cash flows from settlements of forward contracts are included in operating activities in the consolidated statements of cash flows. Aggregate transaction gains and losses included in the determination of net income are not material for any period presented. Forward contracts designated to hedge foreign currency transaction exposure of $257,051,000 and $266,471,000 were outstanding at December 31, 1997 and 1998, respectively. The estimated fair value of these forward contracts at December 31, 1997 and 1998 was $253,519,000 and $271,573,000, respectively, based on quoted market prices.

The Company continually monitors its positions with, and the credit quality of, the major international financial institutions which are counterparties to its foreign currency forward contracts, and does not anticipate nonperformance by any of these counterparties.

(q) Segment Data:

During 1998, the Company adopted SFAS No. 131, "Disclosures about Segments of an Enterprise and Related Information." SFAS No. 131 supercedes SFAS No. 14, "Financial Reporting for Segments of a Business Enterprise", replacing the "industry segment" approach with the "management" approach. The management approach designates the internal reporting that is used by management for making operating decisions and assessing performance as the source of the Company's reportable segments. SFAS 131 also requires disclosures about products and services, geographic areas and major customers. The adoption of SFAS 131 did not affect the consolidated financial position or results of operations of the Company but did affect its disclosure of segment information (Note 12).

(r) New Accounting Pronouncements:

In June of 1998, the Financial Accounting Standards Board issued SFAS No. 133, "Accounting for Derivative Instruments and Hedging Activities" which is effective for fiscal years beginning after June 15, 1999. The objective of the statement is to establish accounting and reporting standards for derivative instruments and hedging activities. The Company uses foreign currency forward contracts, a derivative instrument, to hedge foreign currency transactions and anticipated foreign currency transactions. The adoption of this new accounting pronouncement is not expected to be material to the Company's consolidated financial position or results of operations.

In 1998, the Accounting Standards Executive Committee (AcSEC) issued Statement of Accounting Position ("SOP") No. 98-1, "Accounting for the Costs of Computer Software Developed or Obtained for Internal Use," which is effective for fiscal years beginning after December 15, 1998. The SOP provides guidance on when costs incurred for internal-use computer software are and are not to be capitalized, and on the accounting for such software that is marketed to customers. The adoption of this SOP is not expected to have a material impact on the Company's consolidated financial position or results of operations.

2. Financing Arrangements:

(a) Credit Agreement:

The Company is party to an unsecured bank credit agreement (the "Agreement"), totaling $225 million. The Agreement consists of (1) a revolving line of credit facility for committed loans and bid loans; and (2) a sub-facility for letters of credit. Borrowings under the agreement bear interest at the banks' base rate or, at the Company's option, borrowing rates based on a fixed spread over the London Interbank Offered Rate (LIBOR). The Agreement requires the Company to maintain a minimum tangible net worth and maximum debt leverage ratio, as well as minimum fixed charge coverage. There were no borrowings outstanding at the end of 1997 and 1998.

At December 31, 1997 and 1998, approximately $3,515,000 and $2,000,000, respectively, was committed to support outstanding standby letters of credit.

(b) Long-term Obligations:

The carrying amount of the Company's long-term obligations approximates fair value, which is estimated based on current rates offered to the Company for obligations of the same remaining maturities. Long-term obligations consist of the following:

	December 31, 1997	December 31, 1998
	(in thousands)	
Notes payable through 2001 with interest rates ranging from zero to 7.03%	$ 20,568	$ 14,408
Obligations under capital leases, payable in monthly installments at fixed rates ranging from 3.28% to 15.33% through 2002 (Note 3)	641	367
	21,209	14,775
Less current maturities	13,969	11,415
	$ 7,240	$ 3,360

The long-term obligations, excluding obligations under capital leases, have the following maturities as of December 31, 1998:

	(in thousands)
1999	$ 11,085
2000	2,841
2001	482
2002	—
2003	—
	$ 14,408

3. Commitments:

The Company leases certain operating facilities and equipment under noncancelable operating leases expiring at various dates through 2013. Rent expense was approximately $11,873,000, $16,105,000, and $25,713,000 for 1996, 1997 and 1998, respectively.

Future minimum lease payments under terms of these leases as of December 31, 1998 are as follows:

	Capital Leases	Operating Leases
	(in thousands)	
1999	$ 330	$ 39,400
2000	38	39,695
2001	12	38,794
2002	1	36,256
2003	—	26,523
Thereafter	—	25,910
Total minimum lease payments	$ 381	$ 206,578
Less amount representing interest	14	
Present value of net minimum lease payments	$ 367	

The Company has entered into licensing and royalty agreements which allow it to use certain hardware and software intellectual properties in its products. Minimum royalty payments due under these agreements for the period 1999 through 2002 total approximately $350,000,000. Total royalty expense is expected to be greater than this minimum amount for these periods.

4. Contingencies:

The Company is a party to various lawsuits and administrative proceedings arising in the ordinary course of its business. The Company evaluates such lawsuits and proceedings on a case-by-case basis, and its policy is to vigorously contest any such claims which it believes are without merit. The Company's management believes that the ultimate resolution of such pending matters will not materially adversely affect the Company's business, financial position, results of operations or cash flows.

5. Income Taxes:

The components of the provision for income taxes are as follows:

	For the year ended December 31,		
	1996	1997	1998
		(in thousands)	
Current:			
United States	$ 140,451	$ 154,049	$ 244,076
Foreign	4,981	3,021	9,198
Deferred:			
United States	(1,727)	(49,564)	(40,055)
Foreign	(11,668)	(13,683)	(18,370)
	$ 132,037	$ 93,823	$ 194,849

Income before income taxes included approximately $2,400,000, ($24,000,000) and ($13,100,000) related to foreign operations for the years ended December 31, 1996, 1997 and 1998, respectively.

A reconciliation of the provision for income taxes and the amount computed by applying the federal statutory income tax rate to income before income taxes is as follows:

	1996	1997	1998
		(in thousands)	
Federal income tax at statutory rate	$ 133,951	$ 71,267	$ 189,437
Nondeductible purchased research and development costs	—	20,704	—
Other, net	(1,914)	1,852	5,412
Provision for income taxes	$ 132,037	$ 93,823	$ 194,849

Deferred tax assets and deferred tax liabilities result from temporary differences in the following accounts:

	December 31,	
	1997	1998
	(in thousands)	
U.S. deferred tax assets:		
Inventory	$ 20,572	$ 17,721
Accounts receivable	6,775	5,206
Accrued liabilities	35,793	52,143
Other liabilities	36,912	60,539
Other	3,612	8,048
Total U.S.	103,664	143,657
Foreign deferred tax assets:		
Operating loss carryforwards	17,832	33,454
Other	2,459	5,207
Total foreign	20,291	38,661
Total deferred tax assets	123,955	182,318
U.S. deferred tax liabilities:		
Intangible assets	34,006	29,440
Property, plant & equipment	2,668	4,104
Other	3,439	6,507
Total deferred tax liabilities	40,113	40,051
Net deferred tax assets	$ 83,842	$ 142,267

The Company has foreign net operating loss carryforwards of $67,600,000. Of this amount, $10,500,000 expires in the year 2000, $27,400,000 in the year 2002, $14,300,000 in the year 2006 and $7,100,000 in the year 2008. The remaining $8,300,000 can be carried forward indefinitely. The Company has assessed its forecast of future taxable income and the expiration of carryforwards and has determined that is it more likely than not that the deferred tax asset relating to foreign net operating loss carryforwards will be realized.

6. Stock Option Plans:

The Company maintains various stock option plans for its employees. Employee options are generally granted at the fair market value of the related common stock at the date of grant. These options generally vest over a four-year period from the date of grant or the employee's initial date of employment. In addition, these options expire, if not exercised, ten years from the date of grant. The Company also maintains option plans for non-employee directors. Option grants to non-employee directors generally have an exercise price equal to the fair market value of the related common stock on the date of grant. These options generally vest over one to three-year periods and expire, if not exercised, ten years from the date of grant.

For all of the Company's stock option plans, options for 1,283,000, 2,582,000 and 2,728,000 shares of common stock were exercisable at December 31, 1996, 1997 and 1998 with a weighted average exercise price of $4.28, $9.86 and $17.42, respectively. In addition, options for 672,000, 556,000 and 280,000 shares of Class A common stock were exercisable at December 31, 1996, 1997 and 1998 with a weighted average exercise price of $2.06, $2.01 and $1.93, respectively. Class A common stock may be converted into an equal number of shares of common stock at any time. There were 12,309,000, 8,328,000 and 11,265,000 shares of common stock available for grant under the plans at December 31, 1996, 1997 and 1998, respectively.

The following table summarizes activity under the stock option plans for 1996, 1997 and 1998 (in thousands, except per share amounts):

	Common Stock	Weighted-Average Price	Class A Common Stock	Weighted-Average Price
Outstanding, December 31, 1995	8,739	$ 3.16	962	$ 2.14
Granted	3,260	15.75	—	—
Exercised	(6,305)	1.43	(241)	2.13
Forfeited	(254)	14.15	(8)	3.25
Outstanding, December 31, 1996	5,440	12.20	713	2.12
Granted	5,253	36.08	—	—
Exercised	(463)	11.56	(153)	2.50
Forfeited	(775)	23.69	—	—
Outstanding, December 31, 1997	9,455	22.98	560	2.02
Granted	6,118	45.17	—	—
Exercised	(2,143)	16.59	(280)	2.10
Forfeited	(1,103)	32.76	—	—
Outstanding, December 31, 1998	12,327	$ 34.19	280	$ 1.93

The following table summarizes information about the Company's Common Stock options outstanding at December 31, 1998 (in thousands, except per share amounts):

	Options Outstanding			Options Exercisable	
Range of Exercise Prices	Number Outstanding at 12/31/98	Weighted-Average Remaining Contractual Life	Weighted-Average Price	Number Exercisable at 12/31/98	Weighted-Average Price
$ 1.19 -13.38	1,928	5.57	$ 9.01	1,259	$ 6.76
13.44 -29.07	2,287	7.65	22.93	939	20.01
29.31 -33.75	2,405	8.87	33.06	267	32.35
34.00 -44.75	2,811	8.94	39.55	262	43.88
45.06 -62.50	2,896	9.68	55.56	1	61.75

The weighted average fair value per share of options granted during 1996, 1997 and 1998 was $9.65, $21.61 and $27.33, respectively. The fair value of these options was estimated on the date of grant using the Black-Scholes option pricing model with the following weighted-average assumptions used for all grants in 1996, 1997 and 1998: dividend yield of zero percent; expected volatility of 60 percent; risk-free interest rates ranging from 4.7 to 7.2 percent; and expected lives of the options of three and one-half years from the date of vesting.

Since all stock options have been granted with exercise prices equal to the fair market value of the related common stock at the date of grant, no compensation expense has been recognized under the Company's stock option plans. Had compensation cost under the plans been determined based on the estimated fair value of the stock options granted in 1996, 1997 and 1998, net income and net income per share would have been reduced to the pro forma amounts indicated below:

	1996	1997	1998
	(in thousands, except per share amounts)		
Net income - as reported	$ 250,679	$ 109,797	$ 346,399
Net income - pro forma	$ 241,729	$ 85,804	$ 297,470
Net income per share - as reported			
Basic	$ 1.64	$ .71	$ 2.23
Diluted	$ 1.60	$ .70	$ 2.18
Net income per share - pro forma			
Basic	$ 1.58	$ .56	$ 1.91
Diluted	$ 1.55	$ .55	$ 1.87

The pro forma effect on net income for 1996, 1997 and 1998 is not fully representative of the pro forma effect on net income in future years because it does not take into consideration pro forma compensation expense related to the vesting of grants made prior to 1995.

7. Retirement Savings Plan:

The Company has a 401(k) defined contribution plan which covers employees who have attained 18 years of age and have been employed by the Company for at least six months. Participants may contribute up to 20% of their compensation in any plan year and receive a 50% matching employer contribution of up to 6% of their annual eligible compensation. The Company contributed $871,000, $2,068,000, and $4,730,000 to the Plan during 1996, 1997 and 1998, respectively.

8. Acquisition:

During the third quarter of 1997, the Company acquired substantially all of the outstanding shares of common stock of Advanced Logic Research, Inc. (ALR), a manufacturer of network servers and personal computers, for a cash purchase price of approximately $196,400,000. The operating results of ALR were not material for all periods presented.

9. Nonrecurring Expenses:

The Company recorded several nonrecurring pretax charges during the third quarter of 1997 totaling approximately $113,800,000. Of the nonrecurring charges, approximately $59,700,000 was for the write-off of in-process research and development acquired in the purchase of ALR and certain assets of Amiga Technologies. Also included in the nonrecurring charges was a non-cash write-off of approximately $45,200,000 resulting from the abandonment of a capitalized internal use software project and certain computer equipment. In addition, approximately $8,600,000 was recorded for severance of employees and the closing of a foreign office.

10. Selected Balance Sheet Information:

	December 31, 1997	December 31, 1998
	(in thousands)	
Accounts receivable, net:		
Accounts receivable	$ 530,743	$ 573,799
Allowance for uncollectible accounts	(20,064)	(14,948)
	$ 510,679	$ 558,851
Inventory:		
Components and subassemblies	$ 215,318	$ 155,746
Finished goods	33,906	12,178
	$ 249,224	$ 167,924
Property, plant and equipment, net:		
Land	$ 21,431	$ 21,784
Leasehold improvements	21,666	57,118
Buildings	162,318	186,361
Construction in progress	15,448	74,105
Internal use software	81,412	94,306
Office and production equipment	186,281	249,924
Furniture and fixtures	42,055	66,578
Vehicles	4,105	15,402
	534,716	765,578
Accumulated depreciation and amortization	(158,249)	(234,590)
	$ 376,467	$ 530,988

11. Supplemental Statements of Cash Flows Information:

	Year ended December 31, 1996	1997 (in thousands)	1998
Supplemental disclosure of cash flow information:			
Cash paid during the year for interest	$ 665	$ 716	$ 930
Cash paid during the year for income taxes	$ 101,774	$ 163,710	$ 200,839
Supplemental schedule of noncash investing and financing activities:			
Capital lease obligations incurred for the purchase of new equipment	$ 3,126	$ 4,593	$ 6,741
Acquisitions			
Fair value of assets acquired		$ 271,189	
Less: Liabilities assumed		70,773	
Cash acquired		58,096	
Acquisitions, net of cash acquired		$ 142,320	

12. Segment Data:

Prior to 1998, the Company managed its business segments principally on a geographic basis. The reportable segments were comprised of the United States; Europe, Middle East and Africa ("EMEA"); and Asia Pacific ("APAC"). During 1998, the Company began to manage its business activities primarily in two customer focused segments: consumer and business. The accounting policies of the various segments are the same as those described in the "Summary of Significant Accounting Policies" in Note 1. The Company evaluates the performance of its consumer and business segments based on segment sales, gross profit and operating income and does not include segment assets or other income and expense items for management reporting purposes. Operating income for these segments includes selling, general, and administrative expenses and other overhead charges directly attributable to the segment and excludes certain expenses managed outside the reportable segments. Costs excluded from the consumer and business segments primarily consist of corporate marketing costs and other general and administrative expenses that are separately managed. Prior periods' segment information has not been restated to reflect the consumer and business segments as it is impractical to do so.

The following table sets forth summary information by segment:

	Consumer	Business	Non-segment (in thousands)	Consolidated
1998:				
Net sales	$ 3,945,071	$ 3,522,854	$ —	$ 7,467,925
Gross profit	760,816	783,262	2,196	1,546,274
Operating income (loss)	$ 461,351	$ 600,844	$ (567,968)	$ 494,227

The following table sets forth information about the Company's operations by geographic area:

	United States	EMEA	APAC *(in thousands)*	Inter-segment Eliminations	Consolidated
1998:					
Net sales to external customers	$ 6,412,405	$ 570,191	$ 485,329	$ —	$ 7,467,925
Net sales between geographic segments	53,073	22,298	11,358	(86,729)	—
Operating income (loss)	500,881	(6,685)	1,233	(1,202)	494,227
Segment assets	2,473,627	209,820	206,933	—	2,890,380
Long-lived assets	522,972	57,548	30,184	—	610,704
Other income, net	44,524	1,380	2,041	(924)	47,021
Income taxes	205,129	(3,048)	(7,232)	—	194,849
Depreciation and amortization	84,378	9,820	12,318	(992)	105,524
1997:					
Net sales to external customers	$ 5,303,828	$ 634,616	$ 355,236	$ —	$ 6,293,680
Net sales between geographic segments	56,922	16,163	21,071	(94,156)	—
Operating income (loss)	198,638	(11,566)	(9,733)	(908)	176,431
Non-recurring expenses	111,394	1,100	1,348	—	113,842
Segment assets	1,701,654	187,215	150,402	—	2,039,271
Long-lived assets	380,757	59,261	34,278	—	474,296
Other income, net	25,223	2,946	(798)	(182)	27,189
Income taxes	104,552	568	(11,297)	—	93,823
Depreciation and amortization	67,895	6,695	12,292	(108)	86,774
1996:					
Net sales to external customers	$ 4,246,047	$ 552,671	$ 236,510	$ —	$ 5,035,228
Net sales between geographic segments	30,208	23,538	4,087	(57,833)	—
Operating income (loss)	347,348	19,930	(9,946)	(1,238)	356,094
Segment assets	1,349,781	178,988	144,642	—	1,673,411
Long-lived assets	248,272	48,025	44,815	—	341,112
Other income, net	24,533	2,108	(19)	—	26,622
Income taxes	138,724	1,572	(8,259)	—	132,037
Depreciation and amortization	46,688	4,236	10,839	—	61,763

Net sales between geographic segments are recorded using internal transfer prices set by the Company. The United Sates operating income is net of corporate expenses. Export sales from the United States to unaffiliated customers are not material for any period presented.

13. Selected Quarterly Financial Data (Unaudited):

The following tables contain selected unaudited consolidated quarterly financial data for the Company:

	1st Quarter	2nd Quarter	3rd Quarter	4th Quarter
		(in thousands, except per share amounts)		
1998:				
Net sales	$1,727,927	$1,618,909	$1,815,516	$ 2,305,573
Gross profit	336,494	333,688	377,807	498,285
Operating income	109,201	83,989	113,355	187,682
Net income	75,871	60,740	80,645	129,143
Net income per share:				
Basic	$.49	$.39	$.52	$.83
Diluted	$.48	$.38	$.51	$.81
Weighted average shares outstanding:				
Basic	154,548	155,427	155,849	156,324
Diluted	157,575	158,887	159,518	159,567
Stock sales price per share:				
High	$48.25	$58.81	$67.13	$61.63
Low	$32.50	$42.56	$46.44	$41.50
1997:				
Net sales	$1,419,336	$1,392,658	$1,504,851	$ 1,976,835
Gross profit	265,793	260,358	195,250	355,040
Nonrecurring expenses	—	—	113,842	—
Operating income (loss)	94,878	79,851	(137,850)	139,551
Net income (loss)	67,516	56,483	(107,113)	92,910
Net income (loss) per share:				
Basic	$ .44	$ .37	$ (.70)	$ .60
Diluted	$ .43	$ .36	$ (.68)	$ .59
Weighted average shares outstanding:				
Basic	153,557	153,740	153,980	153,840
Diluted	157,291	156,231	156,875	156,526
Stock sales price per share:				
High	$ 32.63	$ 37.38	$ 44.75	$ 36.13
Low	$ 23.81	$ 26.19	$ 31.50	$ 25.13

14. Subsequent Event (Unaudited):

As of February 28, 1999, the Company has made a commitment to purchase approximately $290 million of consumer finance receivables used to purchase the Company's products which were originated by a financial institution on behalf of Gateway. These receivables have terms of two to four years and earn interest at rates ranging from 14.9% to 26.99%.

Common Stock

The Company's Common Stock is traded on the New York Stock Exchange under the symbol GTW. For information on market prices of Gateway's Common Stock, please refer to note 13 above. There were 4,226 stockholders of record as of March 25, 1999.

Gateway (NYSE: GTW), a *Fortune* 500 company founded in 1985, provides complete computing solutions for clients worldwide. The company employs more than 19,000 people around the globe.

Gateway shipped 3,541,000 PCs to customers throughout the world in 1998, generating total revenue of $7.47 billion.

Our administrative headquarters is in San Diego, California. Manufacturing headquarters is located in North Sioux City, South Dakota, along with sales and client support operations. Gateway Business headquarters is in Irvine, California.

Gateway also has a manufacturing and phone center in Hampton, Virginia, and a manufacturing center in Salt Lake City, Utah. Additional U.S. sales and customer support facilities are located in Sioux Falls, South Dakota, and Kansas City, Missouri, with customer support phone centers in Vermillion, South Dakota, Colorado Springs, Colorado, and Rio Rancho, New Mexico. Our Information Technology headquarters is in Lakewood, Colorado.

European operations are based in Dublin, Ireland. Active European markets now include the United Kingdom, Ireland, France, Germany, Belgium, Luxembourg, Switzerland, Austria, Sweden and the Netherlands. Along the Pacific Rim, the company has sales and support operations in Japan, Australia, Hong Kong and Malaysia, manufacturing facilities in Malaysia and operations in Cyprus.

The Gateway 1998 Annual Report is printed on recycled paper with soy inks in keeping with the Company's commitment to protect the environment.

Corporate Headquarters
Gateway
4545 Towne Centre Court
San Diego, CA 92121
Telephone: 619-799-3401
Fax: 619-799-3459

European Headquarters
Gateway Ireland Limited
Clonshaugh Industrial Estate
Dublin 17, Ireland
Telephone: 353-1-797-2000
Fax: 353-1-797-2022

Asia Pacific Headquarters
Gateway Hong Kong Limited
Suite 2015-16 City Plaza One
1111 King's Road
Hong Kong
Telephone: 852-2886-3395
Fax: 852-2886-2588

Company Information
Copies of the Gateway Annual Report and Form 10-K for the fiscal year 1998 are available to shareholders without charge. If you wish to receive these reports or other company information, please contact:

Investor Relations
Gateway 2000, Inc.
610 Gateway Drive
North Sioux City,
South Dakota 57049-2000
Telephone: 800-846-4503
Fax: 605-232-2757

Annual Meeting
The Annual Meeting of Stockholders of Gateway 2000, Inc. will be held at 9:00 a.m. on Thursday, May 20, 1999, at the Sioux City Convention Center, 801 Fourth Street, Sioux City, Iowa 51101.

Transfer Agent
If you have questions about stock certificates, change of address, consolidation of accounts, transfer of ownership or other stock matters, please contact Gateway's transfer agent:
UMB Bank, n.a.
Securities Transfer Division
P.O. Box 410064
Kansas City, MO 64141-0064
Telephone: 800-884-4225
Fax: 816-221-0438
E-mail: sec_xfer@umb.com

Independent Accountants
PricewaterhouseCoopers LLP
San Diego, California

Gateway Board of Directors
Theodore W. Waitt
Chairman of the Board and
Chief Executive Officer
Gateway

Jeffrey Weitzen
President and
Chief Operating Officer
Gateway

Chase Carey
Chairman of the Board and
Chief Executive Officer
Fox Television Division
Fox, Inc.
Los Angeles, California

George H. Krauss
Of Counsel
Kutak Rock Law Firm
Omaha, Nebraska

Douglas L. Lacey
Partner
Nichols, Rise & Company,
Certified Public Accountants
Sioux City, Iowa

James F. McCann
President and Chief Executive Officer
1-800-FLOWERS
Westbury, New York

Richard D. Snyder
President
Avalon Investments, Inc.
Ann Arbor, Michigan

Executive Officers
Theodore W. Waitt
Chairman of the Board and
Chief Executive Officer

Jeffrey Weitzen
President and Chief Operating Officer

David J. Robino
Executive Vice President,
Chief Administrative Officer

Van M. Andrews
Senior Vice President,
Gateway Business

Anil Arora
Senior Vice President,
Chief Marketing Officer

Peter B. Ashkin
Senior Vice President,
Gateway Products

R. Todd Bradley
Senior Vice President,
Regional Managing Director of
Europe, Middle East and Africa Operations

Joseph J. Burke
Senior Vice President,
Global Business Development

William M. Elliott
Senior Vice President, General Counsel
and Secretary

Michael D. Hammond
Senior Vice President,
Global Manufacturing

Daniel E. Pittard
Senior Vice President,
Strategy and New Ventures

Frank Smilovic
Senior Vice President,
Regional Managing Director of
Asia Pacific Operations

John J. Todd
Senior Vice President, Chief Financial Officer,
and Treasurer

Maynard G. Webb
Senior Vice President,
Chief Information Officer

Gateway™

1998 Annual Report

Gateway™

1998 Annual Report